The Real World

FOURTH EDITION

The Real World

An Introduction to Sociology

FOURTH EDITION

Kerry Ferris | Jill Stein

W.W. NORTON
NEW YORK · LONDON

W. W. Norton & Company has been independent since its founding in 1923, when William Warder Norton and Mary D. Herter Norton first published lectures delivered at the People's Institute, the adult education division of New York City's Cooper Union. The firm soon expanded its program beyond the Institute, publishing books by celebrated academics from America and abroad. By midcentury, the two major pillars of Norton's publishing program—trade books and college texts—were firmly established. In the 1950s, the Norton family transferred control of the company to its employees, and today—with a staff of four hundred and a comparable number of trade, college, and professional titles published each year—W. W. Norton & Company stands as the largest and oldest publishing house owned wholly by its employees.

Editor: Karl Bakeman
Associate Editor: Nicole Sawa
Assistant Editor: Lindsey Thomas
Marketing Manager: Julia Hall
Managing Editor, College: Marian Johnson
Project Editor: Melissa Atkin
Copyeditor: Ellen Lohman
Digital Media Editor: Eileen Connell
Associate Digital Media Editor: Laura Musich
Digital Media Assistants: Cara Folkman and Kathryn Young
Photo Editor: Trish Marx
Permissions Manager: Megan Jackson
Permissions Associate: Bethany Salminen
Art Director: Hope Miller Goodell
Designer: Faceout Studio
Illustrator: Alex Eben Meyer
Production Manager: Jane Searle
Composition: Jouve
Manufacturing: Transcontinental Printing

Library of Congress Cataloging-in-Publication Data

Ferris, Kerry.
The real world : an introduction to sociology / Kerry Ferris and Jill Stein. —Fourth edition.
    pages cm
Includes bibliographical references and index.
 ISBN 978-0-393-92258-5 (pbk.)
 1. Sociology.   2. United States—Social conditions—21st century.   3. Popular culture—United States.   I. Stein, Jill.
II. Title.
   HM586.F48 2014
   301—dc23

                    2013033139

W. W. Norton & Company, Inc., 500 Fifth Avenue, New York, NY 10110
www.wwnorton.com
W. W. Norton & Company, Ltd., Castle House, 75/76 Wells Street, London W1T 3QT

1 2 3 4 5 6 7 8 9 0

About the Authors

KERRY FERRIS is Associate Professor of Sociology at Northern Illinois University. She uses ethnographic methods and a symbolic interactionist approach to study celebrity as a system of social power. Her past studies have included analyses of fan-celebrity relations, celebrity sightings, celebrity stalking, red-carpet celebrity interviews, and the work lives of professional celebrity impersonators. Her current project examines small-market television newscasters in the American Midwest and their experiences of celebrity on a local level. Her work has been published in *Symbolic Interaction, Journal of Contemporary Ethnography, The Journal of Popular Culture,* and *Text & Performance Quarterly.* She is the co-author, with Scott R. Harris, of *Stargazing: Celebrity, Fame, and Social Interaction.*

JILL STEIN is Professor of Sociology and Chair of the Sociology and Anthropology Department at Santa Barbara City College, which was recently named the top community college in the United States by the Aspen Institute. In addition to teaching Introduction to Sociology every semester, she is involved in many student-success initiatives at the local and state levels. Her research examines narrative processes in twelve-step programs, the role of popular culture in higher learning, and group culture among professional rock musicians.

Contents

CHAPTER 2: Studying Social Life: Sociological Research Methods 40

PART III: Understanding Inequality 177

CHAPTER 7: Social Class: The Structure of Inequality 180

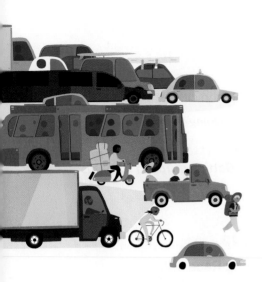

CHAPTER 8: Race and Ethnicity as Lived Experience 214

CHAPTER 9: Constructing Gender and Sexuality 240

CHAPTER 12: Life at Home: Families and Relationships 350

PART V: Envisioning the Future and Creating Social Change 429

CHAPTER 15: Populations, Cities, and Environments 432

CHAPTER 16: Social Change: Looking Toward Tomorrow 466

Preface

Welcome to the new fourth edition of *The Real World: An Introduction to Sociology*. We hope you will appreciate what is new not only in the textbook's fresh look and updated materials, but also what is new in the innovative ways it goes about teaching sociology. That's exactly what we set out to do when we first embarked on the original project of writing this textbook, and it's what we continue to do here in the fourth edition.

At the beginning, we'd had years of experience in college and university classrooms, teaching Introductory Sociology to thousands of students from all backgrounds and walks of life; we had discovered a lot about what works and what doesn't when it comes to making sociology exciting and effective. As seasoned instructors, we had developed an approach to teaching and learning that reflected our passion for the subject and our concern with best practices in pedagogy. But we were having trouble finding a textbook that encompassed all the elements we had identified and that made such a difference in our own experience. We were tired of seeing the same old formulas found in almost every textbook. And we figured we were not alone. Other students and instructors were probably equally frustrated with repetitive formats, stodgy styles, and seemingly irrelevant or overly predictable materials. That is a great misfortune, for sociology, at its best, is a discipline that holds great value and is both intellectually stimulating and personally resonant. While the impetus to write this textbook began as a way of answering our own needs, our goal became to create a textbook of even greater benefit to others who might also be looking for something new.

We are gratified by the response *The Real World* has received from instructors and students alike, so we are preserving many of the features that have made the textbook a success. At the same time, we have done more than just simply revise the textbook. In this edition, you will find significant new content and added features that will further enhance the teaching and learning process, and keep us as close to the cutting-edge as possible. Many of the original elements we developed for students and instructors appear again in these pages. As a foundation, we have maintained a writing style that we hope is accessible and interesting as well as scholarly. One of the core pedagogical strengths of this textbook is its focus on everyday life, the mass media, technology, and popular culture. We know that the combination of these themes is inherently appealing to students, and that it relates to their lives. And since both new generation and more experienced sociology instructors might also be looking for something different, another of this book's strengths is an integrated emphasis on critical thinking and analytic skills. Rather than merely presenting or reviewing major concepts in sociology, which can often seem dry and remote, we seek to make the abstract more concrete through real-world examples and hands-on applications.

In this text we take a fresh and accessible theoretical approach appropriate to our contemporary world. While we emphasize the interactionist perspective, we cover a range of theoretical thought, including postmodernism. We also build innovative methodological exercises into each chapter, giving students the opportunity to put into practice what they are learning. We present material that is familiar and relevant to students in a way that allows them to make profound analytic connections between their individual lives and the structure of their society. We provide instructors with ways to reenergize their teaching, and we give even General Education students a reason to be fascinated by and engrossed in their sociology courses. We do this by staying in touch with our students and the rapidly changing real world, and by bringing our insight, experience, and intellectual rigor to bear on a new way of teaching introductory sociology.

Whether you are a student or an instructor, you have probably seen a lot of textbooks. As authors, we have thought very carefully about how to write this textbook so as to make it more meaningful and effective for you. We think it is important to point out some newly added and unique features of this textbook and to tell you why they are included and what we hope you will get out of them.

Part Introductions

The 16 chapters in this text are grouped into five Parts, and each Part opens with its own introductory essay. Each Part Introduction highlights a piece of original sociological research that encompasses the major themes that group the chapters together. The in-depth discussion of the featured book shows what the real work of academic sociologists consists of and reveals how sociological research frequently unites topics covered in separate chapters in introductory textbooks.

Opening Vignettes

Each chapter begins with an opening vignette which gives students an idea about the topics or themes they will encounter in the chapter. The vignettes are drawn from current events and everyday life, the media, arts, and popular culture. They are designed to grab your attention and stimulate your curiosity to learn more by reading the chapter that follows.

How to Read This Chapter

After the vignette, you will find a section that provides you with some goals and strategies that we believe will be useful in reading that particular chapter. We know from our experience in teaching Introductory Sociology that it is often worthwhile to let students know what to expect in advance so that they can better make their way through the material. Not all chapters require the same approach; we want to bring to your attention what we think is the best approach to each one, so you can keep that in mind while reading.

Theory in Everyday Life

Although we provide thorough coverage in Chapter 1, we find that students often benefit from additional help with understanding the mechanics of social theory and how to apply it to various real-world phenomena. These boxes in every chapter break down the major theoretical approaches and illustrate how each perspective might be used to analyze a particular real-world case study. This serves as a simple, practical model for students to then make their own applications and analyses.

Bolded In-Text Terms

As a student of sociology, you will be learning many new concepts and terms. Throughout each chapter, you will see a number of words or phrases in bold type. You may already recognize some of these from their more common vernacular use. But it is important to pay special attention to the way that they are used sociologically. For this reason you will find definitions in the margins of each page, where you can refer to them as you read. You should consider these bolded words and phrases your conceptual "tools" for doing sociology. As you progress through the chapters in this textbook, you will be collecting the contents of a toolkit that you can use to better understand yourself and the world around you. The bolded terms can also be found in the Glossary at the back of the book and in the coursepack.

Relevance Boxes

In each chapter you will find Relevance Boxes with three different themes: "On the Job," "In Relationships," and " In the Future." Relevance Boxes allow students to see the practical implications and personal value of sociology in their lives. "On the Job" explores the ways different people use sociological training or insights in a variety of work settings. "In Relationships" looks at how sociology can help us to better understand our friendships, intimate partnerships, and family relations. "In the Future" provides a glimpse into emerging trends in a rapidly changing society, and what students might expect to encounter on the horizon. We include these boxes to show how taking this course could bear fruit in your life (and in the lives of others) beyond just fulfilling your college requirements.

Data Workshops

Data Workshops are designed to give students the opportunity to gain hands-on experience in the practice of sociology while they are learning. We think this is one of the most fun parts of being a sociologist. Each chapter features two Data Workshops, one on "Analyzing Everyday Life" and one on "Analyzing Mass Media and Popular Culture." Students will use one of the research methods covered in Chapter 2 to deal with actual data from the real world—whether they are data they collect themselves or raw data provided from another source. The Data Workshops lead students through the process of analyzing data using the related conceptual tools they have just acquired in the chapter. There are two options for completion from which instructors can choose. The Data Workshops can serve as a homework assignment, small-group activity, or in-class discussion, or as the basis for a formal essay or research project. Each Data Workshop is also included in the Interactive Instructor's Guide (IIG), so they're easy to assign whether an instructor teaches online or in the classroom.

Global Perspective Boxes

While this textbook focuses primarily on contemporary American society, we believe that in this time of increasing globalization, it is also important to look at other societies around the world. Each chapter includes a "Global Perspective" box that highlights some of the differences and similarities between the United States and other cultures. This feature will help students develop the ability to see comparative and analogous patterns across cultures, which is one of the key functions of a sociological perspective.

Images and Graphics

We think that it is crucial to include not only written information but also images and graphics in the textbook. This kind of presentation is increasingly common and students are likely to encounter complex information in graphical form in many of their textbooks. We want to help students gain in visual literacy as they are exposed to a variety of materials and learn in different ways. We also know that students share our interest in media, technology, and popular culture, and we want to show the connections between real life and sociological thinking. For these reasons, you will find many kinds of images and graphics in each chapter. These are not just decorations; they are an integral part of the text, so please study these as carefully as you would the rest of the printed page.

Closing Comments

Each chapter ends with closing comments that wrap up the discussion and give some final thoughts about the important themes that have been covered. This gives us a chance not so much to summarize or reiterate but to reflect, in a slightly different way, on what we have discussed, as well as to point to the future. We hope that the closing comments will give you something to think about, or even talk about with others, long after you've finished reading the chapter.

End-of-Chapter Materials

The end of each chapter contains additional materials that will enhance the learning process. The fourth edition features new "Everything You Need to Know About ____" review apparatus at the end of each chapter, which includees checklists, review questions, prompts about the Everyday Sociology Blog, and infographics. They are designed to be easy to read and understand quickly, condensing the most important information from the chapter into two pages.

In our experience, the most important thing for students to take away from an introductory sociology class is a sociological perspective—not just a storehouse of facts, which will inevitably fade over time. Sociology promises a new way of looking at and thinking about the social world, which can serve students in good stead no matter what they find

themselves doing in the future. We hope that this textbook delivers on that promise, making introductory sociology an intellectually stimulating and personally relevant enterprise for professors and students, in the classroom as well as outside it.

Resources

The Real World ebook
Available at NortonEbooks.com
"Same great book, a fraction of the price"

The Real World is also available in the Norton ebook format. An affordable and convenient alternative, the ebook retains the content of the print book and allows students to highlight and take notes with ease.

Everyday Sociology Blog
www.everydaysociologyblog.com

Designed for a general audience, this exciting and unique online forum encourages visitors to actively explore sociology's relevance to popular culture, mass media, and everyday life. Moderated by Karen Sternheimer (University of Southern California), the blog features postings on topical subjects, video interviews with well-known sociologists, as well as contributions from special guests during the academic year.

Contributors include Sally Raskoff (Los Angeles Valley College), Peter Kaufman (SUNY New Paltz), and Jon Wynn (University of Massachusettes, Amherst).

Sociology DVDs: 3 DVDs including the new *Sociology in Practice: Family* DVD

These 3 DVDs contain over nine hours of video clips drawn from documentaries by independent filmmakers. The "Sociology in Practice" DVD series has been expanded to include a new DVD of documentary clips on family. The DVDs are ideal for initiating classroom discussion and encouraging students to apply sociological concepts to popular and real-world issues. The clips are also offered in streaming versions in the Coursepack. Each streamed clip is accompanied by a quiz, exercise, or activity.

Instructor's Website
wwnorton.com/instructors

The Instructor's website features instructional content for use in lecture and distance education, including coursepacks, test banks, PowerPoint lecture slides, images, figures, and more.

The Instructor's Website features:

* FREE, customizable Blackboard, WebCT, Angel, and D2L coursepacks

* Lecture PowerPoints with Clicker Questions

* Art from book in PowerPoint and JPEG formats

* Test Bank in ExamView, WebCT, Blackboard, and RTF formats

Coursepack (available for free download at /instructors; BlackBoard/WebCT, Angel, Desire2Learn, Moodle)

The Real World's new Coursepack offers a variety of activities, and assessment and review materials for instructors who use BlackBoard and other learning management systems. In addition to chapter-based assignments, test banks, and quizzes, this Coursepack includes the kind of interactive learning tools many of our most expert LMS users have requested. Designed by an instructional technologist who understands how to make each LMS as user-friendly and attractive as possible, the Coursepack includees an optional ebook and many exclusive features, including:

* All of the interactive, concept-based activities and assessments included in the very popular 3e Coursepack

* One new practice or assessment activity per chapter

* Exercises that allow students to work with 2010 Census and Community Survey Data

* A short pre-reading quiz for every chapter

* A writing about sociology section that includes practice activities and assessments

* Revised & improved chapter review quizzes that use a variety of LMS question types

* New Sociology in Practice DVD activities that include multiple-choice assessments that connect each clip to key sociological concepts (select clips only)

* New, gradable activities based on the Society Pages podcasts, "graphic sociology" posts, and other media-rich content.

Coursepack authors include Christina Partin and Danielle Schwied of the University of South Florida. Stephen Ostertag of Tulane University wrote the writing about sociology section.

Interactive Instructor's Guide

Written by Natasha Chen Christensen of Monroe Community College. The Interactive Instructor's Guide makes it easy for instructors to seamlessly integrate the "Real World Approach" into their Introduction to Sociology courses. This online database of hundreds of free resources places Norton's extensive collection of teaching resources at instructors' fingertips—from veteran professors looking for something to enliven tried and true lectures to first time instructors building lesson plans from scratch, Norton offers hundreds of activities, lecture ideas, and media for use in the classroom. With its search tools, the Interactive Instructor Guide will help instructor's search for exactly the resources they need by topic and resource type. The website will alert subscribing instructors as new resources are made available, so that instructors have fresh material to incorporate into their course each semester.

Materials include:

* Service Learning Projects

* Everyday Sociology Blog exercises

* Handouts for Data Workshops with estimated completion times

* Suggested documentary clips from the *Sociology in Practice* DVD (divided by chapter) including a description of how to incorporate them in the classroom

* Article on teaching in the online classroom by Christina Partin of University of South Florida and Pasco-Hernandez Community College

* YouTube video suggestions with exercises designed to be deployed in the classroom as well as in an online learning environment

* Expanded materials include longer recommended film, reading, and web reference lists

Updated Test Bank

Written by Dina Giovanelli of Monroe Community College, Stephen Lippmann of Miami University of Ohio, Deric Shannon of Oxford College of Emory University, Christopher Oliver of University of Kentucky, Claire Whitlinger of University of Michigan, and Madison Van Oort of University of Minnesota. The Test Bank for *The Real World,* Fourth Edition is designed to help instructors prepare exams. Newly revised and updated to conform to Bloom's taxonomy, the test bank includes approximately 100 questions per chapter. In addition to Bloom's each question is tagged with metadata that places it in the context of the chapter, as well as difficulty level, making it easy to construct tests that are meaningful and diagnostic. Available in print, CD-ROM, Word, PDF, and ExamView formats.

Instructor's Resource Disc

Prepared by Christina Partin of the University of South Florida, this helpful classroom presentation tool includes visually dynamic lecture PowerPoint slides that feature a suggested classroom lecture script in the notes field that will be particularly helpful to first-time teachers. A separate set of art from the book in PowerPoint and JPEG formats is also included on the disc.

Norton Sociology, Your Way

With the *Norton Mix: Sociology* (www.wwnorton.com/web /socmix), instructors can create the perfect book for their course by mixing and matching chapters from *The Real World* and Norton's other introductory sociology texts and adding their own collection of readings from a database of more than 200 selections. Also, as with previous editions, these paperbacks can be packaged for free with *The Real World*: Elijah Anderson's *The Cosmopolitan Canopy*, *More than Just Race* by William Julius Wilson, and any volume from *The Society Pages* series edited by Douglas Hartmann and Chris Uggen. For only $10 more, instructors can choose to package *The Contexts Reader*, 2e; *The Everyday Sociology Reader*; or Garth Massey's *Readings for Sociology*, 7e with *The Real World*.

Acknowledgments

The authors would like to thank the many people who helped make this textbook possible. To everyone at W. W. Norton, we believe you are absolutely the best publishers in the business and that we are fortunate to get to work with you. Thank you, Roby Harrington, for signing us. Our deep appreciation goes out to Steve Dunn for believing in us and playing such a critical role in shaping the original vision of this project. Thank you for showing us we could do this and for your substantial support throughout. We would like to acknowledge Melea Seward for her efforts during the early drafts of the book. Her innovative approach and enthusiasm were much appreciated. We owe much gratitude to Karl Bakeman for his tremendous talent, work, and dedication as our editor. His vision and leadership has been an inspiration, and a central reason for the success of this book. Thanks for your continued faith, boundless energy, and great ideas, which make this new edition all the better. We feel so lucky to be a part of your team.

We have many others to thank as well. We are especially grateful to our project editor Melissa Atkin; production director Jane Searle; associate editor Nicole Sawa, and editorial assistant Lindsey Thomas for managing the countless details involved in creating this book. Copyeditor Ellen Lohman and proofreader Kate Feighery did a marvelous job suggesting improvements to the manuscript that have contributed in important ways to the book's final form. Danielle Nilva and Trish Marx showed wonderful creativity in the photo research that they did for *The Real World*. Digital media editor Eileen Connell, associate digital media editor Laura Musich, and digital media assistants Cara Folkman and Kathryn Young developed the best textbook support materials in sociology. Associate Design Director Hope Miller Goodell, illustrator

Alex Eben Meyer, and the designers at Faceout Studio deserve special thanks for creating the beautiful design and art for the book. And we are very appreciative of the exceptional Norton "travelers"; it is through their efforts that this book has gotten out into the world.

In the course of our creating the fourth edition, many instructors offered advice and comments on particular chapters, or in some cases, large sections of the text. We are deeply indebted to them.

Brooke Bain, California State University-Fullerton
Chris Baker, Walters State Community College
Leslie Baker-Kimmons, Chicago State University
Marissa Bañuelos, California State University-Fullerton
Mike Bossick, Central Piedmont Community College
Sergio Bouda, California State University-Fullerton
Jeneve Brooks, Troy University
Laura Colmenero-Chilberg, Black Hills State University
Molly Cueto, Lone Star College-Kingwood
Sophia Demasi, Montgomery County Community College
Gianna Durso-Finley, Mercer County Community College
Marilyn Espitia, San Diego Miramar College
Janie Filoteo, Lone Star College-Tomball
John Gannon, College of Southern Nevada-Charleston
Tiffany Gause, Saddleback College
Jan Gordon, Surry Community College
Edward Gott, Northeast Wisconsin Technical College
Matt Gregory, University of Massachusetts Boston
Tara Hefferan, Central Michigan University
Anthony Hickey, Western Carolina University
David Hilton, Mississippi Gulf Coast Community College
Christopher Huggins, University of Kentucky
Andrew Lash, Valencia College
Jon Loessin, Wharton County Junior College
Crystal Lupo, Auburn University
Lori Maida, Westchester County Community College
Kenneth Mentor, University of North Carolina-Pembroke
Barret Michalec, University of Delaware
Susan Miller, Palomar College
Ken Muir, Appalachian State University
Layana Navarre-Jackson, University of Iowa
Christina Partin, University of South Florida
Michael Perez, California State University-Fullerton
Robert Pullen, Troy University
Carter Rakovski, California State University-Fullerton
Julie Reid, University of Southern Mississippi
Tamatha Renae Esguerra, California State University-Fullerton
Emery Smith, Umpqua Community College
Mindy Stombler, Georgia State University
Linda Vang, Fresno City College
Terri Winnick, Ohio State University-Mansfield
Amy Wong, San Diego State University
Susan Wurtzburg, University of Hawaii-Manoa

Sharon Wiederstein, Blinn College
Matt Wray, Temple University

We would also like to thank the research assistants who worked with us on this project: Nathaniel Burke, Whitney Bush, Neil Dryden, Kate Grimaldi, Mary Ingram, Ja'Nean Palacios, and Karl Thulin. Very special thanks, also, to Natasha Chen Christensen, whose thoughtful contributions to each edition of the text have proven invaluable.

We wish to especially thank Al Ferris for his wise and generous counsel in helping us to establish our corporate identity and at every juncture along the way. Thanks to Kevin Ebenhoch for his friendly and efficient services. We would like to thank our families and friends whose encouragement and support helped to sustain us through the length of this project and beyond. It is also with great pleasure that we thank our spouses Greg Wennerdahl and David Unger, respectively—you appeared in our lives just as we were completing the first edition, and your continued presence through this process has been a source of strength and joy. We are happy to share this (and future editions) with you. To Marissa Unger, thanks for being such a positive model of your generation for us. And we welcome our newest (future) reader, Eliot Julian Ferris-Wennerdahl (E.J.): may you always approach life's challenges with wonder, hope and a sense of endless possibility.

We are grateful to colleagues who have served as mentors in our intellectual development and as inspiration to a life of writing. And finally, we offer our thanks to all of the students we have had the privilege to work with over the years. Getting to share the sociological imagination with you makes it all worthwhile.

Kerry Ferris
Jill Stein

Changes in the 4th Edition

Updated Data Workshops:

* "Theories of Celebrity Gossip" Data Workshop has been revised with the phenomenally popular livejournal community Oh No They Didn't, which features up-to-the-minute celebrity news, one of several celebrity gossip websites that arguably emphasize speed over accuracy. (Chapter 1)

* "Seeing Culture in Popular Magazines" Data Workshop has been extensively revised to focus on how culture shapes our views of clothes and car brands. (Chapter 3)

* "Television as an Agent of Socialization" includes more current television shows as examples. (Chapter 4)

* The new "Who's in Your Feed?" Data Workshop explores how Facebook influences group ties and social identity. (Chapter 5)

* The television shows in "Norm Breaking on Television" Data Workshop have been updated. (Chapter 6)

* The new "Mega-Hits (and Flops) and the Movie *Business*" Data Workshop asks students to analyze the movie industry, thus becoming more aware of how much money and effort goes into marketing films. Using the Walt Disney Company's acquisitions of Marvel and Lucasfilm in recent years, this workshop explains how companies promote products across media and protect themselves against potential failures. (Chapter 13)

* Data Workshop "The 'Unplug' Experiment" has been significantly revised based on Jill Stein's observations when doing the experiment with her class. (Chapter 16)

All new sports examples:

* Caster Semenya's story now includes her silver medal at the 2012 London Olympics. (Chapter 9)

* The opening vignette examines the death of Florida A&M University drum major Robert Champion through the lens of hazing as a method of group initiation. (Chapter 5)

* Rapper M.I.A.'s display of the middle finger during the 2011 Super Bowl illustrates the tension between the Super Bowl as family entertainment and a lucrative spectacle of physical prowess and provocative commercials. (Chapter 13)

New examples from the media and popular culture:

* We include Michelle Haimoff's 2012 analysis of how the top-rated 2012 sitcoms don't reflect the reality that unemployment for men is higher than for women. (Chapter 2)

* Numbers for Burning Man festival participants have been updated. (Chapter 4)

* The opening discussion now analyses the different reactions to Osama bin Laden's death. (Chapter 6)

* Characters from *The Dark Knight* are included as examples of conformists, innovators, ritualists, retreatists, and rebels. (Chapter 6)

* Mother Teresa is shown as an example of someone who has little personal wealth but significant prestige. (Chapter 7)

* The 2012 strike that shut down the Los Angeles and Long Beach ports and cost billions of dollars a day shows that strikes can still be very successful even though union power has waned. (Chapter 11)

* The section on corporate America points out that the financial giants who went to extraordinarily lengths to help Sandler O'Neill and Partners after the latter was nearly wiped out after 9/11 were some of the same companies that precipitated the Great Recession. (Chapter 11)

* The section on sweatshops details recent fires in countries like Bangladesh and Pakistan, where factories that violated fire codes were making clothes for American companies. (Chapter 11)

* The Aurora, Colorado, shooting during a midnight showing of *The Dark Knight Rises* is mentioned as a tragic event that raises concerns about the effect violent media has on real life. (Chapter 13)

* Malala Yousafzai is discussed in the section on the ways free speech protections affect the mobilization of resources for social movements. (Chapter 16)

* Recent strikes by workers in the fast food, airport, retail, and car washing industries in New York City have been added to the section on the participants of social movements. (Chapter 16)

* Gluten-free products are mentioned as a recent health fad. (Chapter 16)

New research and expanded coverage:

* Jody Miller and Joshua Gamson are new examples of American sociologists. (Part Opener I)

* Information on heavily gendered occupations of auto mechanics, secretaries, and administrative assistants has been updated. (Chapter 1)

* There is a new discussion about Earl Babbie's 2002 work on research bias, which argues that William Graham Sumner's research stating that morality cannot be legislated affected the Supreme Court's decision on *Plessy v. Ferguson*. (Chapter 2)

* Statistics on drunk driving by gender have been updated. (Chapter 2)

* Statistics on militia groups in the United States have been updated. (Chapter 3)

* Data for homicide rates and other crime rates by gender, age, and race have been updated. (Chapter 6)

* We have expanded the social class section to include the concept of intersectionality. Karyn R. Lacy's work shows that black middle-class suburbanites must negotiate society's conflicting assumptions about their race and affluence. (Chapter 7)

* Statistics on how education and income affects health have been updated. (Chapter 7)

* Data for educational levels, people receiving Temporary Assistance for Needy Families, childhood malnutrition, poverty, and credit card debt have been updated. (Chapter 7)

* We have included a PEW study showing that Americans' opinions of poor people and what the government should do to help them have declined in the past decade. (Chapter 7)

* There is a new poll asking Millennials if they believe in the American Dream. (Chapter 7)

* A Gallup poll asking Americans if race relations have changed since President Obama's election has been added. (Chapter 8)

* Howard Winant and Michael Omi's research on the unreliability of biological traits like skin color and hair to identify race has been added to enhance students' understanding of race as a social construction. (Chapter 8)

* We have updated data for marriage and birth rates, health care access, workforce numbers, education, and crime by race. (Chapter 8)

* In the new Intersectionality section, France Winddance Twine explores the experience of white women who marry and have children with black men. Twine finds that these women become "honorary blacks" and less white to their white friends and family. They must also have or get racial literacy to raise their biracial children. (Chapter 8)

* Data on marriage and divorce rates, custody of children, household work, college graduation, income, workforce participation, occupations, and crime rates by gender have been updated. (Chapter 9)

* In the new Intersectionality section, Miliann Kang explains that Asian immigrant women working in nail salons demonstrates the intersection of gender with race and immigrant status. (Chapter 9)

* The authoritarianism section includes updates on Liberian president Charles Taylor's conviction for crimes against humanity and on Kim Jong Un's accession after Kim Jong Il's death. (Chapter 10)

* Statistics for the 2012 election turnout, average lifetime earnings for various educational levels, high school dropout rates, Americans claiming no religious affiliation, and source of campaign news by age group have been updated. (Chapter 10)

* The recent rise of Super PACs, in which groups can give staggering amounts of money to influence elections, is a trend that has and will continue to affect elections. (Chapter 10)

* The new Intersectionality section looks at how women create agency for themselves when they belong to a conservative religion. One example is Orit Avishai's research of Orthodox Jewish women. (Chapter 10)

* In the section on Religion in the White House, the efforts of Mitt Romney's advisors to minimize his Mormon background and the persistent rumor that President Obama is a Muslim point out how much religion matters to American voters, even if a candidate does not technically need to be religious, and specifically Christian. (Chapter 10)

* We have updated information on American unions; the rise of Chinese firms in the group of top transnational firms; and alternate types of work, which includes outsourcing, temping, and volunteering. (Chapter 11)

* France Winddance Twine researches American women paying Indian women to be surrogates as one of the surprising frontiers of outsourcing outside of manufacturing and computer programming. (Chapter 11)

* New developments in the Affordable Care Act of 2010 have been added. (Chapter 11)

* There are updated statistics for marriage and divorce and people who live alone. (Chapter 12)

* We have updated the data for how much Americans spend on entertainment per year, how many televisions are in American households, and workers and profits in the travel and tourism industries. (Chapter 13)

* The new section on the changing meaning of mental illness describes the various methods for treating mental illness. Today we consider previous methods like bleeding, induced vomiting, and lobotomies inhumane, but future generations may look back at our methods and say the same thing. (Chapter 14)

* End of life care is an example of medical technology affecting society, as patients, families, and doctors grapple with length of life versus quality of life. (Chapter 14)

* Data has been updated for health markers by race and current events regarding the new health care law. (Chapter 14)

* Many statistics have been updated, including world statistics for fertility, life expectancy, mortality, net migration rates and the population growth rate; the population of U.S. megacities; growth in world agriculture; food insecurity in the United States; the types of energy we rely on; and U.S. waste production and recycling. (Chapter 15)

* The discussion on ecological disasters includes the 2011 Tohoku earthquake and the resulting nuclear meltdown in Fukushima, Japan. (Chapter 15)

* We have updated the statistics on blood donors and the top-rated television shows. (Chapter 16)

Revised relevance boxes:

* The In Relationships box has been revised to reflect changes in social networking trends and recent research about social networking. (Chapter 2)

* The new Global Perspectives box examines social media's effects on social change, in particular countries in the Middle East. (Chapter 3)

* The In Relationships box is now about Sister Pauline Quinn and training dogs in prison. (Chapter 4)

* The On the Job box has been revised in light of the doping scandal surrounding Lance Armstrong and other medal-winning cyclists. (Chapter 5)

* Data on employee fraud in the On the Job box have been updated. (Chapter 6)

* The On the Job box has been updated with data on internet usage by race, age, and other factors. (Chapter 7)

* Data in the Global Perspective box about Irish Americans have been updated. (Chapter 8)

* The new On the Job box highlights the opposite ways the Great Recession has affected traditionally male and female occupations. More service and less manufacturing jobs meant that men were more affected by the recession, leading some to label the trend the "mancession." (Chapter 9)

* We have included Shane Sharp's research on people speaking with God for emotional support in the In Relationships box. (Chapter 10)

* The In Relationships box is now called "With Virtual Colleagues," and reframes the emphasis on virtual communication, which requires more deliberate thought and can be more difficult to establish mutually satisfying relationships than in-person relationships. (Chapter 11)

* The On the Job box examines foster care and adoption as methods of creating and maintaining families. Social workers help the family through the adoption process and even after, when the parents and adopted children are working to establish their family. (Chapter 12)

* The new On the Job box features John Peterson and his farm, Angelic Organics Learning Center, near Chicago. His operation emphasizes sustainable architecture, such as community supported architecture, classes on backyard gardening and composting, and teaching local youth to grow their own produce in city plots. (Chapter 15)

* The In Relationships box includes reasons that people might violate civil inattention. A dog is a good example of Erving Goffman's "bridging device," since the dog can be a conversation starter or even get the attention of someone attractive. (Chapter 15)

* The new In Relationships box examines the timeline of Occupy Wall Street and the role of social media in OWS's rise to prominence. (Chapter 16)

NEW! In the Future boxes

* The In the Future box features C. Wright Mills and the sociological imagination. (Chapter 1)

* The In the Future box is about the growing use of action research, such as the Community Organizing and Family Issues group in Chicago. (Chapter 2)

* The In the Future box highlights *otaku*, or devoted fans of geek culture like manga or video games. Thanks to the Internet, *otaku* can now connect with others around the world with similar interests. (Chapter 3)

* The In the Future box examines Edward O. Wilson and sociobiology in the context of nature versus nurture. Examples of the debate include Richard Hernstein and

Charles Murray's *The Bell Curve,* which argues that intelligence differs by race, and former Harvard president Larry Summers' speech in which he suggests that fewer women in the science and engineering disciplines were a result of genetic differences between men and women. (Chapter 4)

* The In the Future box asks students to consider the tension between friendship "IRL" or "in real life" versus only through social networking. Are people more or less connected to each other because of social media? Do we prioritize technologies over relationships, or does technology enhance relationships? (Chapter 5)

* The In the Future box features Dr. Chauntelle Tibbals, who studies pornography in relation to several under-studied topics like cybersex, women's consumption of porn, and how porn elements have been incorporated into other forms of media. (Chapter 6)

* The In the Future box explores what Joel Kotkin calls "Generation Screwed," or Millennials struggling with student loans, minimal job prospects, and extreme inequality. (Chapter 7)

* The In the Future box highlights the U.S. Census' prediction that the United States will become a "majority-minority" country by the mid-21st century. (Chapter 8)

* The In the Future box points to the lightning-rod issue of human trafficking and slavery, particularly of girls and women for the sex industry around the world but also shockingly in the United States. (Chapter 9)

* The In the Future box explains the growing phenomenon of "flipping the classroom," in which organizations like the Khan Academy have students watch lectures as much as they need to grasp a concept, and then use classroom time to solve problems with other students and with help from the teacher. (Chapter 10)

* The In the Future box delves into the question on every student's mind: whether having a college degree affects job prospects, especially in light of increasing numbers of students with high college debt and being unemployed or underemployed. (Chapter 11)

* The In the Future box explains which states allow same sex marriages, civil unions, and other protections for same sex couples. The patchwork legal rights of same sex couples result in difficulties living in another state or later divorcing in another state. Other questions arise, such as taxes and the death of a partner. (Chapter 12)

* The In the Future box considers changes in the media industry, from ebook readers and tablets, to the combination of traditional and new media. For example,

during NRA head Wayne LaPierre's speech on the Newtown, Connecticut, shooting, cable TV pundit Rachel Maddow posted on Twitter about the speech. However, changes in media can still reflect old patterns of racial divides: sociologist danah boyd argues that white people tend to use Facebook more over MySpace. (Chapter 13)

* The In the Future box focuses on the way society views autism. Types of autism, like Asperger Syndrome, may be categorized one way, then in another way years later. Parents of autistic children may learn how to live with autism through other families' examples. (Chapter 14)

* The In the Future box raises the issue of much longer life spans due to better health and medical advances. The phenomenon, if it ever happens, will significantly affect major elements of society, including work and retirement, religion, marriage, and procreation. (Chapter 15)

* The In the Future box is a discussion starter: What's next? Students now have a sociological toolbox to reflect upon that question. (Chapter 16)

PART I
Thinking Sociologically and Doing Sociology

Pepper went to Yale when the school had just begun to admit female students, and some campus buildings didn't even have women's restrooms. She wrote the sex advice column for *Glamour* magazine for nine years.

Andrew is an outspoken Roman Catholic priest and the author of more than fifty best-selling mystery novels. Jody was a cheerleader and a beauty queen in her small midwestern town; she married a man from Sri Lanka and founded a philanthropic organization there. Josh was a "good boy" — he did well in school and played by the rules. He didn't have much to rebel against, and so he wasn't much of a rebel. That is, until he went into the "family business."

Jessie was a "corsetless coed," a term for young women in the 1920s who rejected the restrictive undergarments of their mothers' era and instead rolled their stockings down below their knees.

What do these people have in common? They are all prominent American sociology professors. You may not have heard of them (yet), but they have each made an exceptional impact on their profession:

Pepper Schwartz, sociology professor at the University of Washington, is a leading researcher on sex and intimate relationships. Father Andrew Greeley, an expert in the sociology of religion, taught at the University of Arizona and ran the National Opinion Research Center at the University of Chicago for many years. Jody Miller's work on gender and violence led her to South Asia to study the commercial sex trade; she runs her Sri Lankan charitable organization from her office at Rutgers University. Joshua Gamson, the son of two sociology Ph.D.'s, studies culture, media, and sexuality and is a professor at the University of San Francisco. And Jessie Bernard, the "grande dame" of American sociology, was a professor at Pennsylvania State University for most of her career, studying women, marriage, and the family. The American Sociological Association gives an annual award in her name to a scholar whose career in the study of gender is as distinguished as Bernard's.

Their stories can be found in two compilations: Bennett Berger's *Authors of Their Own Lives: Intellectual Autobiographies of Twenty American Sociologists,* and *Our Studies, Ourselves: Sociologists' Lives and Work,* by Barry Glassner and Rosanna Hertz. Both are collections of autobiographical essays by well-known contemporary sociologists in a variety of fields. Each sociologist has his or her own story of entering the discipline and navigating a career path in academia — the obstacles she encountered, the triumphs he experienced, and the relationships between her personal life and her professional career.

Their paths to sociology were very different, and they each taught and researched different topics. Despite these differences, they share a way of looking at the world. Sociologists have a unique perspective called the "sociological imagination." In fact, we hope that you will acquire your own version of the sociological imagination over the course of this term. Then you will share something in common with these and other sociology professors, including your own.

Jody Miller, Andrew Greeley, Pepper Schwartz, and the others also hold in common their commitment to sociological

Andrew Greeley

Pepper Schwartz

Jody Miller

theories and concepts. This means that their ideas, and the questions they ask and answer, are guided by the established traditions of sociological thought. They may build on those traditions or criticize them, but every sociologist engages in a theoretical dialogue that links centuries and generations. You will become part of this dialogue as you learn more about sociological theory.

Finally, Schwartz, Greeley, Miller, and the rest conduct their research using specific sociological methods. Whether quantitative or qualitative, these means of gathering and analyzing data are distinctive to sociology, and every sociologist develops research projects using the methods best suited to the questions she wants to answer.

Each sociologist's personal journey affects his professional legacy, and knowing something about an author's life helps students understand his work. A person's values, experiences, and family context all shape her interests and objectives — and this is as true of eminent sociologists like Jessie Bernard as it will be for you.

In the following section, we will introduce you to the discipline of sociology and its theoretical traditions (Chapter 1) and to the work of sociology and its research methodologies (Chapter 2). This section is your opportunity to get to know sociology — its perspectives, theories, and research practices.

Perhaps someday your intellectual autobiography will be added to those of Miller, Greeley, Schwartz, and the rest — and your story will start by opening this book.

CHAPTER 1

Sociology and the Real World

A group of four "little people" led by Shorty Rossi — a former gang member who spent ten years in Folsom State Prison on attempted murder charges — rescue and place pit bulls while pursuing acting and entertainment jobs. Ronald and Sebastian, two of Shorty's employees, frequently find themselves in dangerous situations rescuing abused and abandoned pit bulls while also suffering the humilities of making money playing Oompa Loompas and Munchkins at Hollywood birthday parties. Ashley, Shorty's receptionist, books entertainment gigs and works as a stand-up comic while dealing with Shorty's volatile

temper and dog-related demands. The humans average about forty-eight inches in height, so most of the pit bulls they rescue are taller than they are.

Television and movie stars from decades ago compete in ballroom dancing every week. Jaleel White (aka Urkel from *Family Matters*), Shannen Doherty from *Beverly Hills 90210*, and Ralph Macchio (the original "Karate Kid") find themselves doing the fox-trot and cha-cha with a professional dance partner to the critiques of a panel of dance-expert judges (including a hula specialist). After their grueling performances, America votes on whom to eliminate from the show. Although the "stardom" of the contestants is frequently questioned, millions vote every week after watching the contestants struggle through the *paso doble* or the hustle.

A blond Brit rants and raves, haranguing aspiring chefs until they break down in tears. Fear of Gordon Ramsey's famous temper causes brawls and accusations among the cooks. The winner of the competition has the opportunity to be head chef in a high-end restaurant; yet to win the competition, the chefs are put through a rigorous hazing process where losing teams have to clean kitchens, hand-wash the winning team's laundry, or prep all of the ingredients for the next competition. Ramsey is given full discretion over who leaves the contest, and he often changes the rules as he goes along. The competitors are allowed to vent in a confession booth, but this does not seem to give pause to Ramsey, who bullies, humiliates, and even physically abuses the contestants on a regular basis.

Is any of this real? Yes—kind of. It's "reality television." Specifically Animal Planet's *Pit Boss*, ABC's *Dancing with the Stars*, and Fox's *Hell's Kitchen*. And there's a lot more where that came from. In the spring 2012 lineup, there were literally hundreds of reality shows on the major networks and cable stations, with an unknown number of programs undoubtedly in the works. *So You Think You Can Dance*, *Hillbilly Hand Fishing*, *Pawn Stars*, *16 and Pregnant*, *Undercover Boss*, and *Dance Moms* were just a few of the more popular shows, as well as the show that started it all, MTV's *The Real World*, now in its twentieth year and twenty-seventh season.

Some of the shows claim to follow real people through their everyday lives or on the job, while others impose bizarre conditions on participants, subject them to stylized competitions and gross-out stunts, or make their dreams come true. Millions tune in every week to see real people eat bugs, get fired, suffer romantic rejection, reveal their poor parenting, get branded as fat or ugly, cry over their misfortunes, or get voted out of the house or off the island—mortifying themselves on camera for the possibility of success, money, or fame.

Why are we so interested in these people? Because people are interesting! Because we are people too—no matter how different we are from the folks on reality TV, we are part of the same society, and for that reason we are curious about how they live. We compare their lives with ours, wonder how common or unusual they or we are, and marvel that we are all part of the same, real world. We too may want to win competitions, date an attractive guy or girl, find a high-profile job, feel pretty or handsome, be part of an exclusive group, or have a lovely home and family. We may even want to get on a reality show ourselves.

HOW TO READ THIS CHAPTER

You are embarking on a fascinating journey as you learn to see, think, and analyze yourself and the world around you from a sociological perspective. The tools presented here will help you build a foundation for new knowledge and insights into social life.

We will also share the story of the historical and intellectual development of the discipline of sociology. We want to show you how the ideas that shape sociology are linked, and to introduce you to the interesting men and women who came up with those ideas. Too often, theorists seem to be talking heads, icons of social analysis who experience neither life-altering calamities nor shifting professional fortunes. We want to overcome that perception. We believe that individual experiences and historical contexts shape our thoughts and the professional worlds we choose to join. This is as true for Karl Marx as it is for Kerry Ferris, as true for Jane Addams as it is for Jill Stein — it's true for all of us; your own experiences and cultural and historical contexts will shape your ideas and work. In fact, someday, someone may write a chapter about you!

As authors and teachers, we encourage you to develop some basic study techniques that will assist you in your success as a new student to sociology (and perhaps beyond). You may want to highlight portions of the text or take notes while you are reading. Mark passages you don't understand, or keep a list of questions about any aspect of the chapter. Don't hesitate to discuss those questions with your instructor or fellow students; those dialogues can be one of the most gratifying parts of the learning process. Finally, we recommend that you attend class regularly — whether you're in a face-to-face classroom or online — as there is really no substitute for the shared experience of learning sociology with others.

We are excited to join you on this journey of discovery. Though you may know a lot about social life already, we hope to introduce you to even more — about yourself and the world around you — and to provide valuable tools for the future. We wouldn't want you to miss a thing. So here is where we start.

Practical vs. Scientific Knowledge

You already possess many of the skills of an astute analyst of social life, but you take your knowledge for granted because you gained it as an everyday actor. In this course, you will build a new identity: social analyst. These are two very different ways of experiencing the same social world.

The everyday actor approaches his social world with what is referred to as "reciped," or practical, knowledge (Schutz 1962), which allows him to get along in his everyday life. However, practical knowledge is not necessarily as coherent, clear, and consistent as it could be. For example, you are probably very skilled at using a cell phone. It brings you into daily contact with friends and family, puts you in touch with the pizza delivery guy, and allows you to register for classes and pick up your grades at the end of the term. But you probably can't explain how it works in a technical way; you know only how it works for you in a practical, everyday way. This is the important feature of the everyday actor's knowledge: it is practical, not scientific.

To acquire knowledge about the social world that is systematic, comprehensive, coherent, clear, and consistent, you'll need to take a different approach. The social analyst has to "place in question everything that seems unquestionable" to the everyday actor (Schutz 1962, p. 96). In other words, the social analyst takes the perspective of a stranger in the social world; she tries to verify what the everyday actor might just accept as truth. For instance, people tend to believe that women are more talkative than men. This might seem so evident, in fact, as not to be worth investigating. The social analyst, however, *would* investigate, and deliver a more complex conclusion than you might think.

There are strengths and weaknesses in both approaches: the analyst sees with clarity what the actor glosses over, but the actor understands implicitly what the analyst labors to grasp. Once you've learned more about the theories and methods that come next, you'll be able to combine the virtues of both analyst and actor. The result will be a more profound and comprehensive understanding of the social world in which we all live.

What Is Sociology?

Even among those working in the field, there is some debate about defining **sociology**. A look at the term's Latin and Greek roots, *socius* and *logos*, suggests that sociology means the study of **society**, which is a good place to start. A slightly more elaborate definition might be the systematic or scientific study of human society and social behavior. This could include almost any level within the structure of society, from large-scale institutions and mass culture to small groups and relationships between individuals.

SOCIOLOGY the systematic or scientific study of human society and social behavior, from large-scale institutions and mass culture to small groups and individual interactions

SOCIETY a group of people who shape their lives in aggregated and patterned ways that distinguish their group from other groups

Another definition comes from Howard Becker, who suggests that sociology can best be understood as the study of people "doing things together" (1986). This version reminds us that neither society nor the individual exists in isolation and that humans are essentially social beings. Not only is our survival contingent upon the fact that we live in various groups (families, neighborhoods, dorms), but our sense of self derives from our membership in society. In turn, the accumulated activities that people do together create the patterns and structures we call society. So sociologists want to understand how humans affect society, as well as how society affects humans.

One way to better understand sociology is to contrast it with other **social sciences** (disciplines that examine the human or social world, much as the natural sciences examine the natural or physical world) — anthropology, psychology, economics, political science, and sometimes history, geography, and communication studies. Each has its own particular focus on the social world. In some ways, sociology's territory overlaps with other social sciences, even while maintaining its own approach.

Like history, sociology compares the past and the present in order to understand both; unlike history, sociology is more likely to focus on contemporary society. Sociology is interested in societies at all levels of development, while anthropology is more likely to concentrate on traditional or primitive cultures. Sociology looks at a range of social institutions, unlike economics or political science, which each focus on a single institution. Like geography, sociology considers the relationship of people to places, though geography is more concerned with the places themselves. And like communication studies, sociology examines human communication — at both the social and the interpersonal levels, rather than one or the other. Finally, sociology looks at the individual in relationship to external social forces, whereas psychology specializes in internal states of mind. As you can begin to see, sociology covers a huge intellectual territory, making it exceptional among the social sciences in taking a comprehensive, integrative approach to understanding human life (Figure 1.1).

SOCIAL SCIENCES the disciplines that use the scientific method to examine the social world, in contrast to the natural sciences, which examine the physical world

SOCIOLOGICAL PERSPECTIVE a way of looking at the world through a sociological lens

BEGINNER'S MIND approaching the world without preconceptions in order to see things in a new way

Figure 1.1 **Sociology and the Social Sciences**

Sociology overlaps with other social sciences, but much of the territory it covers is unique.

The Sociological Perspective

How do sociologists go about understanding human life in society? The first step is to develop what we call the **sociological perspective**, which is also referred to as taking a sociological approach or thinking sociologically. In any case, it means looking at the world in a unique way and seeing it in a whole new light. You may be naturally inclined to think sociologically, but, for many, the following practices are helpful.

Beginner's Mind

One technique for gaining a sociological perspective comes from Bernard McGrane, who promotes a shift in thinking that's borrowed from the Zen Buddhist tradition. McGrane suggests that we practice what is called **beginner's mind** — the opposite of expert's mind, which is so filled with facts, projections, assumptions, opinions, and explanations that it can't learn anything new (McGrane 1994). If we would like to better understand the world around us, then we must unlearn what we already know. Beginner's mind approaches the world without knowing in advance what it will find; it is open and receptive to experience.

Perhaps our greatest obstacle to making new discoveries is our habitual ways of thinking. "Discovery," McGrane says, "is not the seeing of a new thing — but rather a new way of seeing things" (1994, p. 3). One way to achieve this kind of awareness is to practice being present in the moment. We are all too often preoccupied with thoughts and feelings that prevent us from fully participating in reality. If we can find some inner stillness and stop our normal mental chatter, then McGrane says there is a possibility for true learning to occur. It is in this quiet space that a personal "paradigm shift" (a new model for understanding self and society) can take place.

DATA WORKSHOP
Analyzing Everyday Life

Doing Nothing

Bernard McGrane suggests that we actually "do" sociology, rather than just study it. His book *The Un-TV and the 10 MPH Car* (1994) features exercises designed to help students experience the mundane, routine, and everyday level of society in a new way. This Data Workshop is an adaptation of one of his experiments.

Step 1: Conducting the Experiment
This exercise requires that you go to a relatively busy public space (a mall, street corner, park, or campus quad) and literally do nothing for ten minutes. That means just stand there and be unoccupied. Don't wait for someone, take a break, sightsee, or otherwise engage in a normal kind of activity. Also don't daydream or think about the past or the future; don't entertain yourself with plans or internal dialogues. Don't whistle, hum, fidget, look in your purse, play with your phone, take notes, or do anything else that might distract you from just being there and doing nothing. Do, however, observe the reactions of others to you, and pay attention to your own thoughts and feelings during these ten minutes.

Step 2: Thinking and Writing about the Experience
After conducting the experiment, write a journal entry (casual in tone and written in the first person) describing the experience and its meaning to you. Describe other people's reactions and your own thoughts in as much detail as possible.

The purpose of this exercise is to get you to see that changing your perspective (from "doing something" to "doing nothing") makes everything different. It helps turn the ordinary world into a strange place. It makes you more aware of your own sense (or lack) of self and how identity is constructed in society. You can't take for granted that you "just know" what other people are doing or thinking, or how the meaning of a situation is being defined or interpreted. Divested of your perspective as an everyday actor, you'll learn how the most mundane activities (like just standing around) can become major objects of critical inquiry.

There are two options for completing this Data Workshop.

Option 1 (informal): Complete the exercise and bring your journal entry to class. Discuss your findings with other students in small groups.

Doing Nothing How does standing in a crowded place and doing nothing change how you experience the ordinary world?

Option 2 (formal): Complete the exercise and write a two- to three-page essay describing your findings. You may want to include snippets of your journal entry to illustrate your points.

Culture Shock

Peter Berger describes what kind of person becomes a sociologist: someone with a passionate interest in the world of human affairs, someone who is intense, curious, and daring in the pursuit of knowledge. "People who like to avoid shocking discoveries . . . should stay away from sociology," he warns (Berger 1963, p. 24). The sociologist will care about the issues of ultimate importance to humanity, as well as the most mundane occurrences of everyday existence.

Another way to gain a sociological perspective is to attempt to create in ourselves a sense of **culture shock**. Anthropologists use the term to describe the experience of visiting an exotic foreign culture. The first encounters with the local natives and their way of life can seem so strange to us that they produce a kind of disorientation and doubt about our ability to make sense of things. Putting all judgment aside for the moment, this state of mind can be very useful. For it is at this point, when we so completely lack an understanding of

CULTURE SHOCK a sense of disorientation that occurs when you enter a radically new social or cultural environment

IN RELATIONSHIPS

It's Official: Men Talk More than Women

The practice of sociology may look pretty simple or natural at the outset. It doesn't seem to require much special training to figure out other people and to know something about how the world works. All it takes is membership in society and some life experience to count yourself an expert on the topic. Look at how successful you are already just to have arrived at the point of being a college student. So what more can sociology deliver? The practice of sociology may also seem to be about just a bunch of common sense. But this is true only part of the time. Some of what you learn may indeed seem familiar from what you already know about people and the world around you, and may confirm some of the conclusions you've made about it. Drawing upon the personal knowledge we have accumulated in life will be a valuable asset as a starting place, but it can also be a stumbling block to deeper understanding. There are times that the things that "everyone knows" turn out not to be true, or at least not as sure and simple as we might have thought.

Take for instance the widely held belief that women talk more than men. Experience seems to confirm that this is true, obviously! Women are chatty; you can't get them to stop talking. And a lot of men, if not the strong silent type, definitely have trouble getting a word in edgewise if they're having a conversation with a woman. And women have a hard time getting men to talk when they want them to; sometimes, to get a man to tell you what he's thinking, you have to drag it out of him. These statements make pretty good sense to anyone who's ever had a relationship with the opposite sex. While you may recognize this description of the different genders, and may be able to relate with your own anecdote of such an encounter (or perhaps many such encounters), your casual assumptions about who talks most may need some revising. Numerous sociological studies that analyze conversational dynamics show that, despite stereotypes to the contrary, it's actually the men who are slightly more talkative (Leaper and Ayres 2007). How could that be?

Actually, there are some nuances. It's true that researchers have found that men are more talkative overall, but especially in certain contexts. Men are more talkative with their wives and with strangers. Women are more talkative with their children and with college classmates. With close friends and families, men and women are equally talkative. Studies also showed other, perhaps more easily predictable, gender differences, that men use more assertive speech (they want to persuade others), while women use speech that is more affiliative (they are more focused on connecting with others). These findings even seem to defy what had been considered a biological fact, that the female brain is wired to be more verbal. But because who talks more varies

our surroundings, that we are truly able to perceive what is right in front of our eyes.

As sociologists, we try to create this effect without necessarily displacing ourselves geographically: we become curious and eager visitors to our own lives. We often find that what is familiar to us, if seen as if from an outsider's perspective, is just as exotic as some foreign culture, only we've forgotten this is true because it's our own and we know it so well. To better understand this state of mind, you might imagine what it would be like to return home from a desert island.

Consider the real-life case of Roger Lextrait, who worked for eight years as the caretaker of Palmyra, a small, remote island in the South Pacific. During that time, Lextrait had limited radio contact with Honolulu and Tahiti, and lived mostly in the company of his three dogs. He arrived with a boat full of canned food, 500 pounds of flour, thirty gallons of olive oil, and plenty of red wine. His provisions lasted for two years; after that, he managed to live off the land. He fished, hunted, sang, and played guitar to try to keep loneliness and boredom at bay. In 1992, when Lextrait moved to Palmyra, the internet only transmitted text, no images, and was used only by people in technology and higher education. By 2000, technology had changed exponentially, and more than 350 million people were using the World Wide Web (users now number in the billions). When Lextrait finally reentered civilization, he experienced immense culture shock. "I had no idea that the cellular phone existed, I was so lost," he said. "I came back with different eyes — I was a different person" (Maslin 2010). You don't have to live on a deserted island to

SOCIOLOGICAL IMAGINATION a quality of the mind that allows us to understand the relationship between our individual circumstances and larger social forces by situation, the evidence seems to point to language and conversational differences as influenced more by social than biological forces. So despite how it might feel from your own personal experience, sociology has debunked a very common myth about women and men, requiring that we rethink simplistic gender stereotypes.

Think about that the next time you converse with a member of the opposite sex. If it's your spouse, your child, a classmate, or a complete stranger, you may see an example emerge right before your eyes of what sociologists have already known about who talks more in what kinds of social settings. And, if so, it just might challenge some of your beliefs about the world that you could have sworn were true.

This is why doing sociology is in some regards a radical undertaking. It requires of us a willingness to suspend our own preconceptions, assumptions, and beliefs about the way things are. As sociologists, we need to learn to question everything, especially our own taken-for-granted notions about others and ourselves. Once these have been set aside, even temporarily, we gain a fresh perspective with which to uncover and discover aspects of social life we hadn't noticed before. We are then able to reinterpret our previous understanding of the world, perhaps challenging, or possibly confirming, what we thought we already knew.

Kanye West takes the microphone from Taylor Swift to make a speech at the MTV Video Music Awards.

experience culture shock. Perhaps it's something you've also experienced, but didn't know what to call, if you've traveled or moved away to attend college.

The Sociological Imagination

One of the classic statements about the sociological perspective comes from C. Wright Mills (1916–62), who describes a quality of mind that all great social analysts seem to possess: the **sociological imagination**. By this, he means the ability to understand "the intersection between biography and history," or the interplay of self and the world; this is sociology's task and its "promise" (Mills 1959).

We normally think of our own problems as being a private matter of character, chance, or circumstance, and we overlook the fact that these may be caused in part by, or are at least occurring within, a specific cultural and historical context. For example, if you can't find a job, you may feel that this is because you don't have the right skills, educational background, or experience. But it may also be the result of problems in the larger economy like outsourcing, downsizing, restrictive policies, changing technologies, or migration patterns. In other words, your individual unemployment may be part of a larger social and historical phenomenon.

Most of the time, we use psychological rather than sociological arguments to explain the way things are. For instance, if someone is carrying a lot of credit card

C. Wright Mills

Sociology continues to be a popular major at colleges and universities in the United States and in countries such as Canada, the United Kingdom, and Australia. According to the American Sociological Association (ASA), over a half million Bachelor of Arts degrees in sociology were awarded in the United States between 1990 and 2010 (ASA 2012). Clearly, there are many reasons why students are enthusiastic about the subject. What may be less clear is how to turn this passion into a paycheck. Students considering majoring in the subject often ask, "What can I do with a degree in sociology?" Their parents may be asking the same question. Students interested in academic careers can pursue graduate degrees and become professors and researchers—real, practicing sociologists. But the vast majority of sociology majors will not necessarily become sociologists with a capital S. Their studies have prepared them to be valuable, accomplished participants in a variety of different fields, including law and government, business administration, social welfare, public health, education, counseling and human resources, advertising and marketing, public relations and the media, and work in nonprofit organizations.

A major in sociology, in other words, can lead almost anywhere. And while the roster of former sociology majors contains names both well known and unsung, from president Ronald Reagan and civil rights leader Martin Luther King Jr. to the public defender giving legal aid to low-income clients and the health-care professional bringing wellness programs into large corporations, we will focus here on three important Americans you may not have associated with sociology.

The first individual may be the least likely to be identified as a sociology major, since his career was centered in the arts. Saul Bellow (1915–2005) was one of the most acclaimed American novelists of the twentieth century; his books include *Seize the Day, Herzog,* and *Humboldt's Gift*. His numerous literary awards included the National Book Award (three times), the Pulitzer Prize, and the Nobel Prize for Literature. He was also a successful playwright and journalist, and taught at several universities. Bellow was born in Montreal to Jewish parents, Russian émigrés who later settled in the slums of Chicago while he was still a child.

He began his undergraduate studies in English at the University of Chicago, but left within two years after being told by the department chair that no Jew could really grasp English literature. He then enrolled at Northwestern University, graduating in 1937 with honors in sociology. Literary critics have noted that Bellow's background in sociology, as well as his own personal history, may have influenced both the style and subject of his work. Many of the

Saul Bellow

Michelle Obama   **Kal Penn**

debt, psychological reasoning might focus on his lack of self-control or inability to delay gratification. Sociological reasoning, however, might focus on the impact of cultural norms that promote a lifestyle beyond most people's means, or on economic changes that require more Americans to rely on credit cards because their wages have not kept up with inflation.

The sociological imagination searches for the link between micro and macro levels of analysis. We must look for how larger social forces, such as race, class, gender, religion, economics, or politics, are involved in creating the context of a person's life. Mills's characterization of sociology as the intersection between biography and history reminds us that the process works in both directions: while larger social forces influence individual lives, individual lives can affect society as well.

One of the most important benefits of using the sociological imagination is access to a world beyond our own immediate sphere, where we can discover radically different ways of experiencing life and interpreting reality. It can help us appreciate great themes of American social life appear in his novels: culture, power, wealth and poverty, war, religion, urban life, gender relations, and, above all, the social contract that keeps us together in the face of forces that threaten to tear us apart.

Our next profile is of Michelle Robinson Obama (b. 1964), the first African American first lady of the United States. Michelle Obama has quickly become one of the most recognizable and widely admired sociology majors in the world, using her role as first lady to fight against childhood obesity, help working mothers and military families, and encourage public service. Born and raised in working-class Chicago, she can trace her ancestry to slaves on both sides of her family tree. Her father worked for the city's water department, but saw both of his children graduate from Princeton University and go on to successful professional careers. After obtaining her bachelor's in sociology — her senior thesis dealt with alienation experienced by African American students in an Ivy League institution — she earned her law degree at Harvard, worked at a prestigious law firm in Chicago, and then served in the mayor's office. In addition to law and politics, her choice of majors was a critical stepping stone on the way to her success.

Our last sociology major is Kalpen Modi (b. 1977), who served as an associate director with the White House Office of Public Engagement (OPE) beginning in 2009. This may have come as a surprise to those who know him as the actor Kal Penn, most famous for his role as the wisecracking, easy-going stoner Kumar in the *Harold and Kumar* film series, and perhaps as Dr. Lawrence Kutner on the television show *House*. Joining the OPE meant that Penn had to temporarily leave acting (some would say at the peak of his career) to become the liaison to young Americans, the arts, and Asian American and Pacific Islander communities. As much as Penn wanted success as an actor, he also has been critical of the racial and ethnic stereotypes often associated with playing a person of South Asian descent. At one point, he nearly turned down a recurring role as a terrorist on the TV drama *24* because he didn't want to reinforce the negative "connection between media images and people's thought processes" (Yuan 2007). While it might be easy to make similar claims against *Harold and Kumar Go to White Castle*, one of his costars defended the film, arguing that it "approached the level of sociology, albeit scatological, sexually obsessed sociology," as "it probed questions of ethnic identity, conformism and family expectations vs. personal satisfaction" (Garvin 2008, p. M1). Penn's career change reflects his deep commitment to sociological ideals and a desire to use his influence to help build more positive media portrayals of minorities. In addition to his activities on behalf of the White House, Penn has taught courses in Asian American studies at the University of Pennsylvania and is currently pursuing a graduate certificate in international security at Stanford. He has intermittently returned to acting, in 2010 to reprise his role as Kumar in another movie sequel, and in 2013 to host the Discovery Channel's "Big Brain Theory: Pure Genius." Some fans might also find it ironic that in real life Penn is a vegetarian who says that smoking pot is not for him.

Regardless of whether you go any further in this discipline, or if you end up working in politics, the arts, or public service, the most important thing to take away from an introductory sociology class is a sociological perspective. Sociology promises a new way of looking at, thinking about, and taking action in the world around us, all of which can serve you in good stead no matter where you find yourself in the future.

alternative viewpoints and understand how they may have come about. This, in turn, helps us to understand better how we developed our own values, beliefs, and attitudes.

Sociology asks us to see our familiar world in a new way, and doing so means we may need to abandon, or at least reevaluate, our opinions about that world and our place in it. It is tempting to believe that our opinions are widely held, that our worldview is the best or, at least, most common. Taking a sociological perspective forces us to see fallacies in our way of thinking. Because other individuals are different from us — belonging to different social groups, participating in different social institutions, living in different cities or countries, listening to different songs, watching different TV programs, engaging in different religious practices — they may look at the world very differently than we do. But a sociological perspective also allows us to see the other side of this equation: in cases where we assume that others are different from us, we may be surprised to find that their approach to their everyday world is quite similar to ours.

The Sociological Perspective **15**

Levels of Analysis: Micro- and Macrosociology

Consider a photographer with state-of-the-art equipment. She could view her subject through either a zoom lens or a wide-angle lens. Through the zoom lens, she sees intricate details about the subject's appearance; through the wide-angle lens, she gets the "big picture" and a sense of the broader context in which the subject is located. Both views are valuable in understanding the subject, and both result in photographs of the same thing.

Sociological perspectives are like the photographer's lenses, allowing us different ways of looking at a common subject (Newman 2000). Sociologists can take a microsociological (zoom lens) perspective, a macrosociological (wide-angle lens) perspective, or any number of perspectives located on the continuum between the two (Figure 1.2).

Microsociology concentrates on the interactions between individuals and the ways in which those interactions construct the larger patterns, processes, and institutions of society. As the word indicates ("micro" means small), microsociology looks at the smallest building blocks of society in order to understand its large-scale structure. A classic example of research that takes a micro approach is Pam Fishman's article "Interaction: The Work Women Do" (1978). Like many scholars who had observed the feminist movements of the 1960s and 70s, Fishman was concerned with issues of power and domination in male-female relationships: Are men more powerful than women in our society? If so, how is this power created and maintained in everyday interactions? In her research, Fishman recorded and analyzed heterosexual couples' everyday conversations in their homes. She found some real differences in the conversational strategies of men and women, as the transcript in Figure 1.3 illustrates.

As you can see, the woman is having a difficult time getting her partner to join her in a discussion about the history of education. He frequently interrupts, changes the subject, fails to respond for long stretches, and even flips on the garbage disposal while she is speaking. She perseveres, trying to gain control of the conversation. Fishman recorded many such conversations and found a variety of patterns. One of her findings was that women ask nearly three times as many questions as men do. While other researchers have proposed that women's psychological insecurities are the reason for this finding, Fishman noted that women are in fact following a firmly held rule of conversational structure: when the speaker cannot guarantee that she or he will get a response, she or he is more likely to ask a question. Questions provoke answers, which makes them a useful conversational tool for those who may have less power in interpersonal relationships and in society at large. And women are more likely to be in this position than men. Thus, in her micro-level analysis of conversation, Fishman was able to see how macro-level ("macro" means large) phenomena like gender and power are manifested in everyday interactions.

Macrosociology approaches the study of society from the opposite direction, by looking at large-scale social structure in order to determine how it affects the lives of groups and individuals. If we want to stick to the same topic of gender inequality, we can find plenty of examples of research

MICROSOCIOLOGY the level of analysis that studies face-to-face and small-group interactions in order to understand how they affect the larger patterns and institutions of society

MACROSOCIOLOGY the level of analysis that studies large-scale social structures in order to determine how they affect the lives of groups and individuals

Microsociology and Macrosociology Two views of the New York Public Library. Sociologists bring different levels of analysis to the study of people and groups. Microsociology zooms in to focus on individuals and their interactions in order to understand larger social structures. In contrast, macrosociology pulls back to study large-scale social processes and their effects on individuals and groups.

IN THE FUTURE

C. Wright Mills and the Sociological Imagination

The "sociological imagination" is a term that seemingly every sociology student encounters. It was first introduced by C. Wright Mills in his 1959 book by the same name, and over time has become an enduring cornerstone of the discipline. It captures the spirit of inquiry, the quality of mind, and the guiding principles that all sociologists should embrace. Mills was sometimes critical of sociology as a discipline, so he offered himself as a "public intellectual," one who could speak beyond the confines of academia and address some of the most pressing social issues of the time. Mills was convinced that sociology had something to offer everyone, not just academics. He would have wanted you to develop your sociological imagination not just to help you read this textbook, but because it is useful far beyond the classroom.

Mills highlighted the distinction between "personal troubles" and "public issues" as "an essential tool of the sociological imagination and a feature of all classic work in social science" (Mills 1959, p. 8). He explained that almost any feature of an individual's daily life can be better understood if this distinction is applied to it. Unemployment, war, marriage, and housing are all experienced as personal troubles, but to be fully understood they must also be seen as manifestations of long-standing institutions and larger social structures. As Mills pointed out, "in so far as an economy is so arranged that slumps occur, the problem of unemployment becomes incapable of personal solution" (Mills 1959, p. 10). This lesson was driven home again in what is often called the "great recession" that began in 2007. A series of major banks had created securities that bundled together a large number of mortgages made to so-called subprime borrowers. When many of these mortgages went into default, it led to an economic chain reaction that culminated in unemployment levels higher than any seen since the Great Depression of the 1930s. For the many millions of people thrown out of work, unemployment was experienced as a personal trouble, but one that could be understood only as a public issue.

In even more fundamental ways, Mills believed that people were shaped by the connections between "the patterns of their own lives and the course of world history" (Mills 1959, p. 4). This could influence the most personal features of someone's life, shaping the very kind of people

"they are becoming" (Mills 1959, p. 4). In her book *Unbearable Weight*, Susan Bordo describes the appearance of anorexia as a mental health problem. Anorexia and bulimia are experienced in intensely personal ways, and eating disorders are usually explained in purely psychological terms. But Bordo, thinking about them sociologically, points out that while in 1973, psychiatrists described anorexia as quite rare it has become increasingly common since then. Some of this might simply result from improved awareness of the problem, but Bordo argues that cultural factors help create eating disorders. Contemporary culture's obsession with bodies that are "slim, tight, and young" (1995, p. 140) shapes our individual psychologies. Eating disorders, then, are symptoms of a troubled culture as well as a troubled individual. This is not to deny that personal and psychological factors aren't important, but it is a reminder that social and cultural factors create the environment that makes it possible to experience problems like eating disorders in the first place.

Today you may be a student in an introductory sociology class; this year, more than 25,000 students will receive bachelor's degrees in sociology. Whether you end up majoring in sociology or not, C. Wright Mills wanted everyone to develop and sharpen a sociological imagination. In fact, that is the goal we share in writing this textbook. How might the sociological imagination be useful to you in the future?

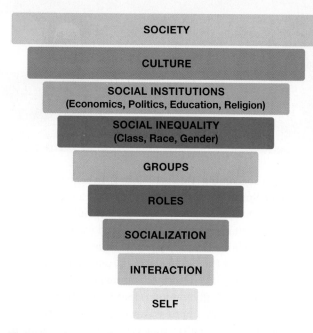

| SOCIETY |
| CULTURE |
| SOCIAL INSTITUTIONS (Economics, Politics, Education, Religion) |
| SOCIAL INEQUALITY (Class, Race, Gender) |
| GROUPS |
| ROLES |
| SOCIALIZATION |
| INTERACTION |
| SELF |

Figure 1.2   The Macro-Micro Continuum

Sociology covers a wide range of topics at different levels of analysis.

Glass Escalators Christine Williams's study of the occupational status of men in a female-dominated industry, such as teaching, is a good example of macrosociology.

projects that take a macro approach; many deal with the workplace. Despite the gains made in recent years, the U.S. labor market is still predominantly sex segregated—that is, men and women are concentrated in different occupations. For example, in 2012, 98.8 percent of auto mechanics were male, whereas 95.3 percent of secretaries and administrative assistants were female (U.S. Bureau of Labor Statistics 2013). This feature of social structure, some argue, has a direct effect on the experiences of individual workers, male and female.

A related example comes from the work of Christine Williams. She found that while women in male-dominated fields experience limits on their advancement, dubbed the "glass ceiling" effect, men in female-dominated occupations experience unusually rapid rates of upward mobility, the "glass escalator" (C. Williams 1995). Here, then, we see a macro approach to the topic of gender and power: large-scale features of social structure (patterns of occupational sex segregation) create the constraints within which individuals and groups (women and men in the workplace) experience successes or failures in their everyday lives.

As you can see, these two perspectives make different assumptions about how society works: the micro perspective assumes that society's larger structures are shaped through individual interactions, while the macro perspective assumes that society's larger structures

THEORIES in sociology, abstract propositions that explain the social world and make predictions about the future

PARADIGMS a set of assumptions, theories, and perspectives that make up a way of understanding social reality

shape those individual interactions. It is useful to think of these perspectives as being on a continuum with each other; while some sociologists adhere to radically micro or exclusively macro perspectives, most are somewhere in between. The next part of this chapter explores some specific theoretical traditions within sociology, and shows you where each falls along this continuum.

Sociology's Family Tree

Great thinkers have been trying to understand the world and our place in it since the beginning of time. Some have done this by developing **theories**: abstract propositions about how things are as well as how they should be. Sometimes we also refer to theories as "approaches," "schools of thought," "**paradigms**," or "perspectives." Social theories, then, are guiding principles or abstract models that attempt to explain and predict the social world.

As we embark on the discussion of theory, it may be useful to think of sociology as having a "family tree" made up of real people who were living in a particular time and place, and who were related along various intertwining lines to other members of the same larger family tree. First, we will examine sociology's early historical roots. Then, as we follow the growth of the discipline, we will identify its major branches and trace the relationships between their offshoots and the other "limbs" that make up the entire family tree. Finally, we will examine some of the newest theoretical approaches and members of the family tree (page 21), and consider the possible future of sociological theory.

Sociology's Roots

The earliest Western social theorists focused on establishing society as an appropriate object of scientific scrutiny, which was itself a revolutionary concept. None of these

TRANSCRIPT

1	F: I didn't know that. (=) Um you know that ((garbage disposal on)) that organizational	
	M: Hmmm? (=)	
2	F: stuff about Frederick Taylor and Bishopsgate and all that stuff? (=) ⌐ in the early	
	M: UmHm ((yes)) ⌐	
3	F: 1900's people were trying to fight favoritism to the schools (4)	
	M: That's what we needed. (18) |	
4	F:	
	M: never did get my smoked oysters, I'm going to look for ((inaudible)) (14) Should we try the	
5	F: OK. That's a change. (72) Hmm. That's very interesting. Did	
	M: Riviera French Dressing? (=)	
6	F: you know that teachers used to be men until about the 1840's when it became a female occupa-	
	M:	
7	F: tion? (2) Because they needed more teachers because of the increased enroll-	
	M: Nhhmm ((no)) (=)	
8	F: ment. (5) Yeah relatively and the status (7)	
	M: And the the salaries started going down probably. (=)	
9	F: ⌐ There's two bottles I think ⌐	
	M: Um, it's weird. We're out of oil again. ⌐ Now we have to buy that. ⌐ ((whistling)) (8) Dressing	
10	F: It does yeah. (76) That's really interesting. They didn't start	
	M: looks good. See? (2) See babe? (1)	
11	F: using the test to measure and find the you know categorize and track people in American	
	M:	
12	F: schools until like the early 1900's after the army y'know introduced their array alpha things	
	M:	
13	F: to the draftees (?) And then it caught on with the schools and there was a lot of opposition right	
	M:	
14	F: at the beginning to that, which was as sophisticated as today's arguments. The same argu-	
	M:	
15	F: ments y'know (=) But it didn't work and they came (4) ⌐ heh	
	M: Yeah (=) Leslie White is probably right. ⌐	

Figure 1.3 Gender and Conversational Patterns

Conversation analysis allows us to see patterns like who interrupts more (men) and who asks more questions (women).

Auguste Comte

Harriet Martineau

early theorists were themselves sociologists (since the discipline didn't yet exist) but rather people from a variety of backgrounds — philosophers, theologians, economists, historians, or journalists — who were trying to look at society in a new way. In doing so, they laid the groundwork not only for the discipline as a whole but also for the different schools of thought that are still shaping sociology today.

AUGUSTE COMTE (1798–1857)

was the first to provide a program for the scientific study of society, or a "social physics," as he labeled it. Comte, a French scientist, developed a theory of the progress of human thinking from its early theological and metaphysical stages toward a final "positive," or scientific, stage. **Positivism** seeks to identify laws that describe the behavior of a particular reality, like the laws of mathematics and physics, where you can gain knowledge of the world directly through your senses. Having grown up in the aftermath of the French Revolution and its lingering political instability, Comte felt that society needed positivist guidance toward both social progress and social order. After studying at an elite science and technology college, where he was introduced to the newly discovered **scientific method** (see Chapter 2), he began to imagine a way of applying the methodology to social affairs. His ideas, featured in *Introduction to Positive Philosophy* (1842), became the foundation of a scientific

Herbert Spencer

discipline that would describe the laws of social phenomena and help control social life: he called it "sociology."

Although Comte is remembered today mainly for coining the term, he played a significant role in the development of sociology as a discipline. His efforts to distinguish appropriate methods and topics for sociologists provided the kernel of a discipline. Other social thinkers advanced his work: Harriet Martineau and Herbert Spencer in England and Émile Durkheim in France.

HARRIET MARTINEAU (1802–76)

was born in England to progressive parents who made sure their daughter was well educated. She became a journalist and political economist, proclaiming views that were radical for her time: endorsing labor unions, the abolition of slavery, and women's suffrage. Though Martineau never married, she preferred to be addressed as "Mrs." — not because she wished for a husband (indeed, she strongly rejected marriage, seeing it as a tool for the subjugation of women) but because she recognized that the title conveyed respect and status in her culture. She felt that respect was denied to her as a single woman.

In 1835, "Mrs." Martineau traveled to the United States to judge the new democracy on its own terms rather than by European standards. But she was disappointed: by condoning slavery and denying full citizenship rights to women and blacks, the American experiment was, in her eyes, flawed and hypocritical. She wrote two books describing her observations, *Society in America* (1837) and *Retrospect of Western Travel* (1838), both critical of American leadership and culture. By holding the United States to its own publicly stated democratic standards, rather than seeing the country from an ethnocentric British perspective, she was a precursor to the naturalistic sociologists who would establish the discipline in America. In 1853, Martineau made perhaps her most important contribution to sociology: she translated Comte's *Introduction to Positive Philosophy* into English, thus making his ideas accessible in England and America.

HERBERT SPENCER (1820–1903)

was primarily responsible for the establishment of sociology in Britain and America. Although Spencer did not receive academic training, he grew up in a highly individualistic family and was encouraged to think and learn on his own. His interests leaned heavily toward physical science, and, instead of attending college, Spencer chose to become a railway engineer. When railway work dried up, he turned to journalism and eventually worked for a major periodical in London. There Spencer became acquainted with leading English academics and began to publish his own thoughts in book form.

In 1862, Spencer drew up a list of what he called "first principles" (in a book by that name), and near the top of the list was the notion of evolution driven by natural selection. (Charles Darwin is the best-known proponent of the theory,

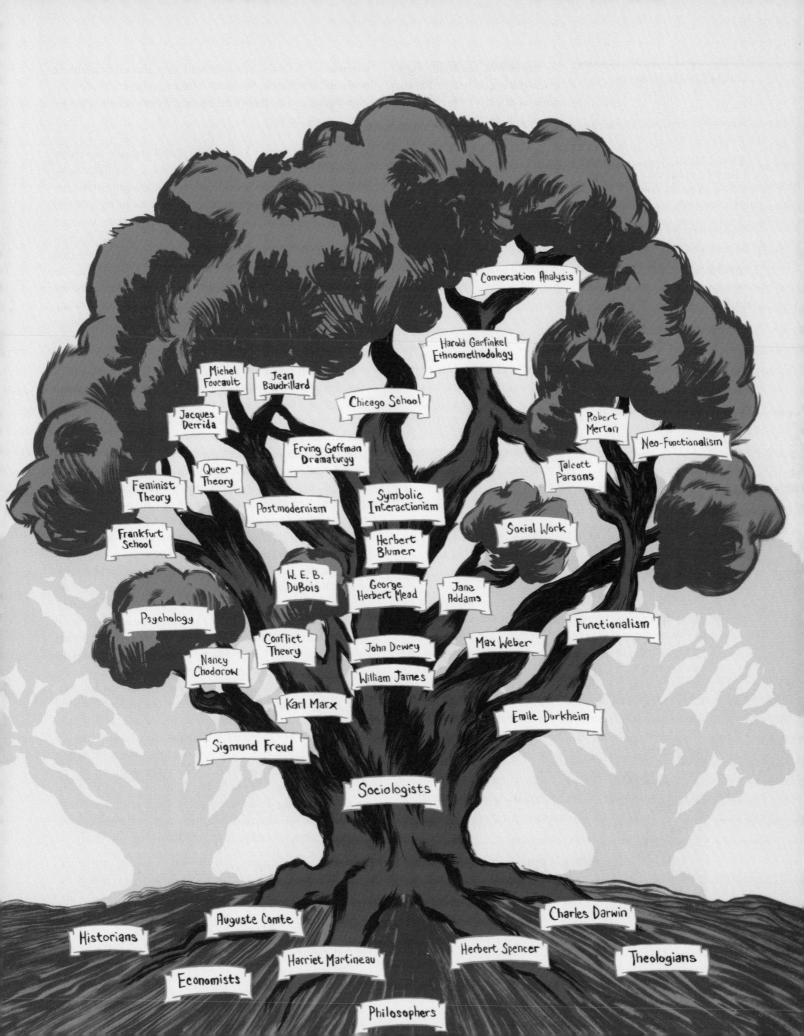

SOCIAL DARWINISM the application of the theory of evolution and the notion of "survival of the fittest" to the study of society

STRUCTURAL FUNCTIONALISM a paradigm based on the assumption that society is a unified whole that functions because of the contributions of its separate structures

MECHANICAL SOLIDARITY term developed by Émile Durkheim to describe the type of social bonds present in premodern, agrarian societies, in which shared traditions and beliefs created a sense of social cohesion

ORGANIC SOLIDARITY term developed by Émile Durkheim to describe the type of social bonds present in modern societies, based on difference, interdependence, and individual rights

but the idea of evolution was in wide circulation before Darwin made it famous.) Spencer proposed that societies, like biological organisms, evolve through time by adapting to changing conditions, with less successful adaptations falling by the wayside. He coined the phrase "survival of the fittest," and his social philosophy is sometimes known as **social Darwinism**. In the late 1800s, Spencer's work, including *The Study of Sociology* (1873) and *The Principles of Sociology* (1897), was virtually synonymous with sociology in the English-speaking world. The scope and volume of his writing served to announce sociology as a serious discipline and laid the groundwork for the next generation of theorists, whose observations of large-scale social change would bring a new viewpoint to social theory.

Macrosociological Theory

Theorists in late-nineteenth-century Europe were living during extraordinary times. They were attempting to explain social order, social change, and social inequality — especially as they watched their world changing around them in the rapid transformation of the Industrial Revolution and witnessed the changes wrought by the French and American Revolutions, each of which had overthrown monarchist rule to establish a democracy in its place. These were changes on the grandest of scale in the macro order of society. Frequently referred to as classical sociology, the theories that arose during this period reflect the broad subject matter of a sweeping era.

Émile Durkheim

Structural Functionalism

Structural functionalism, or functionalist theory, was the dominant theoretical perspective within sociology well into the mid-twentieth century. New (or neo-) functionalists continue to apply their own vision of the theory to study a wide variety of social phenomena today.

FOUNDER AND KEY CONTRIBUTIONS Émile Durkheim (1858–1917) is the central figure in functionalist theory. He was born into a close-knit and deeply religious Jewish family who instilled in him a strong sense of morality (not just as an abstract concept but as a concrete influence on social relations) and a strong work ethic. After witnessing the ravages of the Franco-Prussian War (1870–71), he hoped that applied science could stabilize and revitalize France in the aftermath of its devastating defeat. He did not believe that traditional, abstract moral philosophy was effective in increasing understanding and bringing about social change, so he turned instead to the concrete science of sociology as represented in Comte's work.

In his first major study, *The Division of Labor in Society* (1893), Durkheim stated that social bonds were present in all types of societies but that different types of societies created different types of bonds. He suggested that the **mechanical solidarity** experienced by people in a simple, agricultural society bound them together on the basis of shared traditions, beliefs, and experiences. In industrial societies, where factory work was becoming increasingly specialized, **organic solidarity** prevailed: people's bonds were based on the tasks they performed, interdependence, and individual rights. Both types of solidarity have interpersonal bonds — just with different qualities.

Durkheim believed that even the most individualistic actions had sociological explanations and set out to establish a scientific methodology for studying these actions. He chose for his case study the most individualistic of actions, suicide, and used statistical data to show that suicides were related to social factors such as religious affiliation, marital status, and employment. Explaining a particular suicide by focusing exclusively on the victim's psychological makeup neglected the impact of social bonds. According to Durkheim in his now-classic study *Suicide* (1897), even the darkest depression has its roots in an individual's connections to the social world, or rather his lack of connection. He theorized that suicide was one result of **anomie**, a sense of disconnection brought about by the changing conditions of modern life. The more firmly anchored a person was to family, religion, and the workplace, the less anomie he was likely to experience.

In his final major study, *The Elementary Forms of Religious Life* (1912), Durkheim suggested that religion was a powerful source of social **solidarity**, or unity, because it reinforced collective bonds and shared moral values. He believed that society could be understood through examining the most basic forms of religion. Durkheim's study of the indigenous peoples of Australia led him to a universal definition of religion: though religious traditions might differ, any form of religion was unified in its definition of what is considered to be **sacred** and **profane**. Every person who follows a particular set of beliefs and practices will "unite into one single moral community" (Durkheim 1912/1995, p. 44).

Durkheim also noted that rituals or ceremonies that brought people together into communities were created and practiced to enhance the feeling of emotional unity that reaffirmed solidarity and social order. When people gathered for religious events, their individual acts, taken together, created a feeling of being swept up in something larger than themselves. It made them feel as if they had entered a "special world inhabited by exceptionally intense forces that invade and transform" them (Durkheim 1912/1995, p. 220). Durkheim referred to this as **collective effervescence**. This sense of participants being transported by a shared wave of energy can happen during a Catholic mass, for instance, as much as it can by attending a live concert or sporting event at a sold-out arena.

A distinction between the sacred and the profane, and the creation and participation in shared ritual activity creates a **collective conscience** (or collective consciousness) that contains the morality, the cosmology, and the beliefs "common to the group" (Durkheim 1912/1995, p. 379). The shared beliefs and values that make up the collective conscience of the group are what make social solidarity possible, but they must be frequently renewed through the ritual, through which a group "revitalizes the sense it has of itself and its unity" (Durkheim 1912/1995, p. 379). Durkheim believed that this process happens in all societies, whether those united through a common religious tradition or through shared secular beliefs and practices.

Durkheim's attempt to establish sociology as an important, independent academic discipline was enormously successful. He not only made significant contributions to the existing literature but also demonstrated the effectiveness of using scientific, **empirical** methods to study "social reality," essentially validating Comte's proposal from half a century earlier. Durkheim became the first professor of social science in France at the University of Bordeaux in 1887 and later won a similar appointment at the Sorbonne in Paris, the very heart of French academic life. Today, Durkheim's eminence in the social sciences is as strong as ever, and his ideas are still applied and extended by contemporary theorists.

ORIGINAL PRINCIPLES The origins of structural functionalism can be traced back to the roots of sociology. Auguste Comte proposed that society itself could and should be studied. Herbert Spencer added the idea that societies are living organisms that grow and evolve, just like other species on the planet. As the discipline of biology might study the physical organism of the human body, the discipline of sociology could study social organisms in the world of human development. Durkheim integrated and advanced these insights into a comprehensive theory for understanding the nature of society.

There are two main principles of functionalism. First, society is conceived as a stable, ordered system made up of interrelated parts, or **structures**. Second, each structure has a function that contributes to the continued stability or equilibrium of the unified whole. Structures are identified as social institutions like the family, the educational system, politics, the economy, and religion. They meet society's needs by performing different functions, and every function is necessary to maintain social order and stability. Any disorganization or **dysfunction** in a structure leads to change and a new equilibrium—if one structure is transformed, the others must also adjust. For example, if families fail to discipline children, schools, churches, and the courts must take up the slack.

It may seem contradictory that a theory concerned with order and stability would emerge in a discipline that arose in a period of rapid social change. But it is important to remember that change had previously occurred much more slowly, and that one response to rapid social change is to try to understand what had come before — stability, order, and equilibrium.

OFFSHOOTS Structural functionalism was the dominant theoretical perspective in Europe for much of the early twentieth century. It was exported and updated by American functionalists, who increased its popularity and helped spread its reach well into the 1960s. Talcott Parsons (1902–79), for example, elaborated on the theory and applied it to modern society, specifying some of the functions that social structures might fulfill in contemporary life. A healthy society must provide a means for people to adapt to their environment, for example, families, schools, and religious institutions working together to socialize children. A functional society includes opportunities for success; for example, promoting education

ANOMIE "normlessness"; term used to describe the alienation and loss of purpose that result from weaker social bonds and an increased pace of change

SOLIDARITY the degree of integration or unity within a particular society; the extent to which individuals feel connected to other members of their group

SACRED the holy, divine, or supernatural

PROFANE the ordinary, mundane, or everyday

COLLECTIVE EFFERVESCENCE an intense energy in shared events where people feel swept up in something larger than themselves

COLLECTIVE CONSCIENCE the shared morals and beliefs that are common to a group and which foster social solidarity

EMPIRICAL based on scientific experimentation or observation

STRUCTURE a social institution that is relatively stable over time and that meets the needs of society by performing functions necessary to maintain social order and stability

DYSFUNCTION a disturbance to or undesirable consequence of some aspect of the social system

Talcott Parsons   **Robert Merton**

to help its members pursue and realize their goals. For society to survive, there must be social cohesion; for example, shared religious and moral values.

Another modern American functionalist, Robert Merton (1910–2003), delineated the theory even further, identifying manifest and latent functions for different social structures. **Manifest functions** are the obvious, intended functions of a social structure, while **latent functions** are the less obvious, perhaps unintended functions. For example, the manifest functions of education are to prepare future members of society by teaching them how to read and write and by instructing them on society's system of norms, values, and laws. However, education has a latent function as well, which is to keep kids busy and out of trouble eight hours a day, five days a week, for twelve years (or longer). Do not doubt that this is also an important contribution to social order!

Functionalism's influence waned in the late twentieth century, but did not die out. A "neofunctionalist" movement, begun in the 1980s and 90s, attempts to reconstruct functionalist theories so that they remain relevant in a rapidly changing world. Theorists such as Neil Smelser and Jeffrey Alexander have attempted to modify functionalist theory to better incorporate problems like racial and ethnic identity in a diverse society (Alexander 1988; Alexander and Smelser 1998; Smelser 1985).

MANIFEST FUNCTIONS the obvious, intended functions of a social structure for the social system

LATENT FUNCTIONS the less obvious, perhaps unintended functions of a social structure

CONFLICT THEORY a paradigm that sees social conflict as the basis of society and social change, and emphasizes a materialist view of society, a critical view of the status quo, and a dynamic model of historical change

SOCIAL INEQUALITY the unequal distribution of wealth, power, or prestige among members of a society

COMMUNISM a political system based on the collective ownership of the means of production; opposed to capitalism

CONFLICT generated by the competition among different class groups for scarce resources and the source of all social change, according to Karl Marx

ADVANTAGES AND CRITIQUES One of the great advantages of functionalism is its inclusion of all social institutions. Functionalism attempts to provide a universal social theory, a way of explaining society in one comprehensive model. Part of functionalism's appeal may also lie in its ability to bring order to a potentially disorderly world. Were it not for some of the volcanic social upheavals of recent history—the Civil Rights, antiwar, and women's liberation movements are not easily explained using this model—functionalist theory might still reign supreme in American sociology. Functionalism, generally preoccupied with stability, takes the position that only dysfunction can create social change. This conservative bias is part of a larger problem with the theory: functionalism provides little insight into social processes because its model of society is static rather than dynamic. Its focus on the macro level also means that functionalism has less interest in explaining independent human action; there is no apparent approach to the lives of individuals except as part of social institutions.

Functionalism's explanations of social inequality are especially unsatisfying: if poverty, racism, and sexism exist, they must serve a function for society; they must be necessary and inevitable. This view is problematic for many. Sociologist Herbert Gans, in a critical essay (1971), reviews the functions of poverty for society. The poor, for example, do our "dirty work," filling the menial, low-wage jobs that are necessary to keep society running smoothly but that others refuse to do. The poor provide a market for used and off-price goods, and keep thrift stores and social welfare agencies in business. They have symbolic value as well, allowing those higher in the social hierarchy to feel compassion toward the "deserving" poor as well as feeling threatened by the "undeserving" poor, who are often seen as dangerous social deviants. Ultimately, the circular reasoning that characterizes functionalist thought turns out to be its biggest problem: the mere persistence of an institution should not be seen as an adequate explanation for its existence.

Conflict Theory

Conflict theory is the second major school of thought in sociology. Like structural functionalism, it's a macro-level approach to understanding social life that dates to mid-nineteenth-century Europe. As conflict theory developed, however, its emphasis on **social inequality** as the basic characteristic of society helped to answer some of the critiques of structural functionalism.

FOUNDER AND KEY CONTRIBUTIONS The work of Karl Marx (1818–83), a German social philosopher, cultural commentator, and political activist, was the inspiration for conflict theory, so sometimes the terms "conflict theory" and "Marxism" are used interchangeably in the social sciences. Marx's ideas have become more well known to the world as the basis for **communism**, the political system adopted by numerous countries (such as China, North Korea, and Cuba) that have often been viewed as enemies of democracy and the United States. This association has led many to a narrow belief that Marx was nothing more than a misguided agitator who helped cause more than a century of political turmoil. It is important to separate Marx himself from the current, political application of communism, and to consider the possibility that he might not have supported the ways political leaders used his ideas decades later. Sociologists have found that Marx's theory continues to provide a powerful tool for understanding social phenomena. The idea that **conflict** between social groups is central to the workings of society and serves as the engine of social change is one of the most vital perspectives in sociology today.

Marx grew up in a modernizing, industrializing yet politically and religiously conservative monarchy; this, plus the fact that his was a restless, argumentative personality, accounts in great part for his social theory. Marx studied law and philosophy in Bonn and Berlin, receiving a Ph.D. in 1841. His personal ties with radicals effectively barred him from entering academia, so he turned to journalism, writing stories that often antagonized government censors and officials.

For most of his life, Marx led an economically fragile existence. He managed to maintain a tenuous middle-class lifestyle, but only with financial support from his close friend and chief intellectual collaborator Friedrich Engels, who studied the conditions of the English working class. Marx's own circumstances may have sparked his interest in social inequality, or the uneven and often unfair distribution of resources (in this case, wealth) in society, but he never experienced firsthand the particular burdens and difficulties of the working class.

The Industrial Revolution was a time of rapid social change, when large numbers of people were moving from an agricultural life in rural areas to manufacturing jobs in urban areas. Technological advances and a wage-based economy promised an age of prosperity and abundance, but they created new kinds of poverty, crime, and disease. Marx believed that most of those problems were a result of **capitalism**, the emerging economic system based on the private for-profit operation of industry. He proposed a radical alternative to the inherent inequalities of this system in the *Manifesto of the Communist Party* (1848), perhaps his most famous book.

In industrial society, the forces of capitalism were creating distinct social and economic classes, exacerbating the disparities between the wealthy and the poor. Marx felt that this would inevitably lead to class struggle between those who owned the **means of production** (anything that could create more wealth: money, property, factories, other types of businesses) and those who worked for them. He argued that the most important factor in social life was a person's relationship to the means of production; in other words, whether someone was a worker, and thus a member of the **proletariat**, or an owner, and thus a member of the **bourgeoisie**.

Everything of value in society resulted from human labor, which was the proletariat's most valuable asset. Yet, they suffered from what Marx called **alienation** because they were unable to directly benefit from the fruits of their own labor. Workers were paid wages, but it was the factory owners who grew rich as a result of their toil.

Karl Marx

The powerful few in the bourgeoisie not only were wealthy but also enjoyed social privilege and power. They were able to protect their interests, preserve their positions, and pass along their advantages to their heirs. The proletariat were often so absorbed in making a living that they were less apt to protest the conditions that led to their oppression. But eventually, Marx believed, the oppression would become unbearable, and the proletariat would rise up against the bourgeoisie, abolishing capitalism for good. He envisioned in its place a classless society — **socialism** — in which each person contributed to and benefited from the public good. Freed from oppressive conditions, individuals would then be able to pursue higher interests such as art and education and eventually live in a more egalitarian, utopian society. But in order to achieve such a state, the oppressed must first recognize how the current system worked against them.

In 1849, Marx withdrew from political activity in order to concentrate on writing *Das Kapital* (edited by Engels and published in 1890). The multivolume book provided a thorough exposition of his program for social change, which later became the foundation of political systems such as communism and socialism. Marx intended it to be his main contribution to sociology, but developments in the social sciences

CAPITALISM an economic system based on private ownership of the means of production and characterized by competition, the profit motive, and wage labor

MEANS OF PRODUCTION anything that can create wealth: money, property, factories, and other types of businesses, and the infrastructure necessary to run them

PROLETARIAT workers; those who have no means of production of their own and so are reduced to selling their labor power in order to live

BOURGEOISIE owners; the class of modern capitalists who own the means of production and employ wage laborers

ALIENATION the sense of dissatisfaction the modern worker feels as a result of producing goods that are owned and controlled by someone else, according to Karl Marx

SOCIALISM a political system based on state ownership or control of principal elements of the economy in order to reduce levels of social inequality have placed more emphasis on his earlier writings. Because Marx held such radical ideas, his thought was not immediately embraced by sociologists in general. It was not until the 1960s when conflict theory became a dominant perspective that Marx was truly received as a giant of sociology.

ORIGINAL PRINCIPLES Conflict theory proposes that conflict and tension are basic facts of social life, and suggests that people have disagreements over goals and values and are involved in struggles over both resources and power. The theory thus focuses on the processes of dominance, competition, upheaval, and social change.

Conflict theory takes a materialist view of society (focused on labor practices and economic reality) and extends it to other social inequalities. Marx maintained that economic productivity was related to other processes in society, including political and intellectual life. The wealthy and powerful bourgeoisie controlled major social institutions, reinforcing the class structure so that the state, education, religion, and even the family were organized to represent their interests. Conflict theory takes a critical stance toward existing social arrangements and attempts to expose their inner workings.

Because the **ideology**, or belief system, that permeated society arose from the values of the ruling class, beliefs that seemed to be widely held were actually a kind of justification that helped to rationalize and explain the status quo. Most people readily accepted the prevailing ideology, despite its failure to represent the reality of their lives. Marx referred to this acceptance as **false consciousness**, a denial of the truth that allowed for the perpetuation of the inequalities inherent in the class structure. For example, he is often quoted as saying, "Religion is the opiate of the masses." This is not a criticism of religion as much as it is a criticism of the use of religion to create false consciousness in the working class. Encouraged in their piety, the proletariat focus on the happiness promised in the afterlife rather than on deprivations

suffered in this world. Indeed, heaven is seen as a reward for patiently suffering those deprivations. How does this serve the interests of the ruling class? By keeping the working class from demanding better conditions in this life.

Conflict theory sees the transformation of society over time as inevitable. Marx argued that the only way to change the status quo was for the masses to attain **class consciousness**, or revolutionary consciousness. This can happen only when people recognize how society works and challenge those in power. He believed that social change would occur when there was enough tension and conflict. Marx proposed a **dialectical model** of historical or social change, whereby two extreme positions would eventually necessitate some kind of compromise between them: the resulting "middle ground" would mean that society had actually moved forward. Any existing social arrangement, called the **thesis**, would inevitably generate its opposite, or **antithesis**, and the contradictions and conflicts between the two would lead to an altogether new social arrangement, or **synthesis**.

OFFSHOOTS Marx's work has been reinterpreted and applied in various ways, and conflict theory has evolved within the greater intellectual community. Despite Marx's single-minded focus on economic exploitation and transformation, his ideas have helped inspire theorists interested in all forms of power and inequality.

One of the most widely adopted forms of modern Marxism is called **critical theory** (also sometimes referred to as the Frankfurt School or neo-Marxism). From the 1930s to the 1960s, critical theory was arguably at the cutting edge of social theory. Critical theorists were among the first to see the importance of mass communications and popular culture as powerful ideological tools in capitalist societies. They coined the term "culture industries" to refer to these increasingly important social institutions, which came to dominate and permeate social life (Adorno and Horkheimer 1979). They also criticized the growing consumerism associated with the spread of capitalism, believing that this could ultimately lead to a decline in personal freedom and the decay of democracy (Marcuse 1964/1991). Critical theory influenced several generations of radical thinkers throughout Europe and the United States, inspiring the cultural studies movement and the postmodernists, who were considered the cutting edge of social theory in the 1980s and 90s (Habermas 1984, 1987).

Other modern perspectives have taken conflict theory's insights on economic inequality and adapted them to the study of contemporary inequalities of race, gender, and sexuality (Crenshaw et al. 1996; Matsuda et al. 1993). Beginning with the pioneering work of W.E.B. DuBois, sociology started to focus on inequalities of race and ethnicity, inspiring important studies about the causes and consequences of prejudice and discrimination, and helping to propel momentous social changes resulting from the Civil Rights Movement of the 1960s.

IDEOLOGY a system of beliefs, attitudes, and values that directs a society and reproduces the status quo of the bourgeoisie

FALSE CONSCIOUSNESS a denial of the truth on the part of the oppressed when they fail to recognize the interests of the ruling class in their ideology

CLASS CONSCIOUSNESS the recognition of social inequality on the part of the oppressed, leading to revolutionary action

DIALECTICAL MODEL Karl Marx's model of historical change, whereby two extreme positions come into conflict and create some new third thing between them

THESIS the existing social arrangements in a dialectical model

ANTITHESIS the opposition to the existing arrangements in a dialectical model

SYNTHESIS the new social system created out of the conflict between thesis and antithesis in a dialectical model

CRITICAL THEORY a contemporary form of conflict theory that criticizes many different systems and ideologies of domination and oppression

The Frankfurt School Critical theorist Theodore Adorno with his colleagues in Frankfurt.

Feminist theory developed alongside the twentieth-century women's rights movement. By applying assumptions about gender inequality to various social institutions — the family, education, the economy, or mass media — feminist theory allows for a new way of understanding those institutions and the changing role of gender in contemporary society. Theorists such as Judith Butler (1999), bell hooks (2003), and Catharine MacKinnon (2005) link gender with inequality in other social hierarchies — race and ethnicity, class, and sexual orientation — and argue that gender and power are inextricably intertwined in our society.

The gay and lesbian rights movement that gained momentum in the 1970s and 80s inspired a new set of theoretical and conceptual tools for social scientists: **queer theory**. Queer theory proposes that categories of sexuality — homo,

hetero, bi, trans — should be viewed as "social constructs" (Seidman 2003). It asserts that no sexual category is fundamentally deviant or normal; we create such definitions, so we can change them as well. Indeed, some theorists, such as Marjorie Garber (1997), argue that strict categories themselves are no longer relevant and that more fluid notions of identity should replace conventional dichotomies like gay / straight. In this way, queer theory is related to another theoretical perspective we'll be examining later: postmodernism.

ADVANTAGES AND CRITIQUES One of Karl Marx's great contributions to the social sciences is the principle of **praxis**, or practical action: intellectuals should act on what they believe. Marx wished not only to describe the world but also to change it. Indeed, Marxist ideas have been important in achieving change through many twentieth-century social movements, including civil rights, antiwar, women's rights, gay rights, animal rights, environmentalism, and multiculturalism. If these groups had not protested the status quo, we might never have addressed some of the century's social problems. Conflict theory is useful in understanding not only macro-level social issues (like systematic discrimination against minority groups) but also micro-level personal interactions (like those between bosses and employees).

> **FEMINIST THEORY** a theoretical approach that looks at gender inequities in society and the way that gender structures the social world
>
> **QUEER THEORY** a paradigm that proposes that categories of sexual identity are social constructs and that no sexual category is fundamentally either deviant or normal
>
> **PRAXIS** practical action that is taken on the basis of intellectual or theoretical understanding

Conflict theory stands in sharp contrast to structural functionalism. Conflict theory argues that a social arrangement's existence does not mean that it's beneficial; it may merely represent the interests of those in power. The theory

bell hooks

RATIONALIZATION the application of economic logic to human activity; the use of formal rules and regulations in order to maximize efficiency without consideration of subjective or individual concerns

BUREAUCRACIES secondary groups designed to perform tasks efficiently, characterized by specialization, technical competence, hierarchy, written rules, impersonality, and formal written communication

IRON CAGE Max Weber's pessimistic description of modern life, in which we are caught in bureaucratic structures that control our lives through rigid rules and rationalization

DISENCHANTMENT the rationalization of modern society

challenges the status quo and emphasizes the need for social upheaval. In focusing on tension and conflict, however, conflict theory can often ignore those parts of society that are truly orderly, stable, and enduring. Although society certainly has its share of disagreements, there are also shared values and common beliefs that hold it together. Conflict theory can be criticized for overlooking these less-controversial dimensions of social reality.

Weberian Theory

Max Weber (1864–1920) was another important European macrosociological theorist during the Industrial Revolution. His work forms another large branch of sociology's family tree, and his ideas continue to inspire in their current application, yet he is not always included among the three *major* branches of the discipline. Weberian theory is not a minor branch of sociology, nor is it considered merely an offshoot of one or the other major branches of the tree. It draws from a background shared by the other macro theorists but forms its own independent limb.

Weber grew up in the German city of Berlin. His father was a successful entrepreneur and member of a traditional and authoritarian aristocracy. Both his parents were Protestants and descendants of victims of religious persecution. Weber, though not religious himself, exhibited the relentless work ethic held in high regard by devout Protestants. Although he was sickly and withdrawn as a young

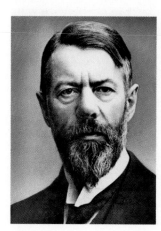

Max Weber

man, work served as a way for him to rebel against his father and the leisure classes in general. He studied law and history and worked as a lawyer while establishing his credentials for a university teaching position.

While pursuing his studies, Weber remained at home and financially dependent on his father, a situation he came to resent. Eventually he broke away, marrying his second cousin in 1893 and

beginning a career teaching economics at the University of Freiburg and later the University of Heidelberg. Weber rapidly established himself as a prominent member of the German intellectual scene. He might have continued in this manner had it not been for a disastrous visit from his parents in 1897, during which Weber fought bitterly with his father and threw him out of the house. When his father died a month later, Weber suffered a nervous breakdown that left him unable to work for several years. The strain of these events and years of incessant labor had apparently caught up with him. He eventually recovered and resumed his intense scholarship, but the breakdown left Weber disillusioned with the strict academic regimen.

Weber subsequently expressed a pessimistic view of social forces, such as the work ethic, that shaped modern life. Like other social theorists of his time, Weber was interested in the shift from a more traditional society to a modern industrial one. Perhaps his most overriding concern was with the process of **rationalization**, or the application of economic logic to all spheres of human activity. In *Economy and Society* (1921), Weber proposed that modern industrialized societies were characterized by efficient, goal-oriented, rule-governed **bureaucracies**. He believed that individual behavior was increasingly driven by such bureaucratic goals, which had become more important motivational factors than traditions, values, or emotions. Weber's classic sociological discussion of the origins of the capitalist system, *The Protestant Ethic and the Spirit of Capitalism* (1904), concluded with the image of people trapped by their industrious way of life in what he called an **iron cage** of bureaucratic rules. He believed that contemporary life was filled with **disenchantment** (similar to Durkheim's concept of anomie and Marx's of alienation) as the inevitable result of the dehumanizing features of the bureaucracies that dominated the modern social landscape.

Weber provided invaluable insights into the nature of society that continue to inspire sociologists today. The key concepts we have touched on here will be expanded as we apply Weberian theory to a variety of topics in upcoming chapters of the text. In addition to making some of the most important contributions to theory within the discipline, Weber was also influential in improving research methods by suggesting that researchers should avoid imposing their own opinions on their scientific analysis; we'll examine these ideas more closely in Chapter 2.

Weber's work served as a bridge between early social theory, which focused primarily on the macro level of society, and subsequent theories that focused more intently on the micro level. He was interested in how individual motivation led to certain social actions, and how those actions helped shape society as a whole. Unlike Marx and Durkheim, Weber was cautious about attributing any reality to social institutions or forces independent of individual action and meaningful thought. He invoked the German term *verstehen* ("empathic understanding") to describe how a social scientist should study human action: with a kind of scientific empathy for actors' experiences, intentions, and actions. In this way, Weber helped lay the groundwork for the third major school of thought.

Microsociological Theory

As the twentieth century dawned and the careers of the macro theorists like Durkheim, Marx, and Weber matured, political, cultural, and academic power began to shift from Europe. As manifested by the waves of emigrants leaving the Old World for the New, America was seen as the land of opportunity, both material and intellectual. So it was in the twentieth century, and increasingly in the United States, that the discipline of sociology continued to develop and the ideas of its third major school of thought began to coalesce.

Symbolic Interactionism

Sociology's third major school of thought, **symbolic interactionism** (or interactionist theory), proved its greatest influence through much of the 1900s. It is America's unique contribution to the discipline and an answer to many of the criticisms of other paradigms. Symbolic interactionism helps us explain both our individual personalities and the ways in which we are all linked together; it allows us to understand the processes by which social order and social change are constructed. As a theoretical perspective, it is vital, versatile, and still evolving.

FOUNDER AND KEY CONTRIBUTIONS Symbolic interactionism is derived largely from the teachings of George Herbert Mead (1863–1931). But there were many others involved in the development of this particular school of thought, and it is worthwhile to examine the social context in which they lived and worked.

At the start of the twentieth century, sociology was still something of an import from the European intellectual scene, and American practitioners had just begun developing their own ideas regarding the nature and workings of society. The University of Chicago of the 1920s provided a stimulating intellectual setting for a handful of academics who built on each other's work and advanced what became known as the first new major branch within the discipline. Since there were so few social theorists in the country, the head of the department, Albion Small, a philosopher by training, recruited professors from various eastern colleges who had often studied other disciplines such as theology and psychology as well. The fledgling sociology department grew to include such influential members as Robert Park, W. I. Thomas, Charles Horton Cooley, and later Mead and Herbert Blumer. This group, the theories they developed together, and the way they went about studying the social world are frequently referred to (either individually or collectively) as **the Chicago School** of sociology.

Chicago was in many ways a frontier city in the early twentieth century. Rapidly transformed by industrialization, immigration, and ethnic diversity, Chicago became a unique laboratory in which to practice a new type of sociology that differed both theoretically and methodologically from the European models. Instead of doing comparative and historical work as had the macro theorists before them, the members of the Chicago School went out and into the city to conduct interviews and collect observational data. Their studies were particularly inspired by Max Weber's concept of *verstehen* as the proper attitude to adopt in the field. Their focus was on the micro level of everyday interactions (such as race relations in urban neighborhoods) as the building blocks of larger social phenomena (such as racial inequality).

The new school of thought was strongly influenced by a philosophical perspective called **pragmatism**, developed largely by William James and John Dewey, which was gaining acceptance among American social theorists in the early 1900s. James was a Harvard professor whose interests spanned art, medicine, law, education, theology, philosophy, and psychology; he also traveled extensively and was acquainted with some of the most important scholars of the time. To James, pragmatism meant seeking the truth of an idea by evaluating its usefulness in everyday life; in other words, if it works, it's true! He thought that living in the world involved making practical adaptations to whatever we encountered; if those adaptations made our lives run more smoothly, then the ideas behind them must be both useful and true. James's ideas inspired educational psychologist and philosopher John Dewey, who also grappled with pragmatism's main questions: How do we adapt to our environments? How do

George Herbert Mead

GLOBAL PERSPECTIVE

Eurocentrism and Sociological Theory

You might get the impression from this chapter that the major sociological theorists were all either European or American. In fact, some ideas central to sociological theory were proposed in Asia, Africa, and the Middle East centuries before Marx, Weber, and Durkheim were even born, but we give these Western thinkers all the credit. Why?

Both the social world and social theory are often **Eurocentric**: they tend to privilege Europe and the West over other cultures. This means that hierarchies of global power, in which superpowers like the United States and former colonial rulers like Britain and France dominate, are replicated in academic disciplines like sociology. Scholars who work against inequality and exploitation should note this distressing irony.

One influential non-Western thinker was Ibn Khaldun (1332–1406), an Arab Muslim philosopher and politician who lived in fourteenth-century North Africa. His coining of the term *as sabiyah,* or "social cohesion," precedes

Ibn Khaldun

Durkheim's work on the same subject by more than 500 years, and his argument that larger social and historical forces shape individual lives predates Mills's insight about sociology as "the intersection of biography and history" by almost 600 years! Yet Khaldun is rarely credited for proposing sociology as a discipline — *ilm alumran,* he called it, or "the science

of civilization." This honor is reserved for French scholar Auguste Comte, working centuries later in the West.

Also overlooked in conventional histories of sociology are Indian scholar Benoy Sarkar (1887–1949), Filipino activist and poet José Rizal (1861–96), and Japanese folklorist Kunio Yanagita (1875–1962) — all of whom applied sociological insights to the problems of their nations. Sarkar explored India's religious divisions, Rizal analyzed the Philippines' fight for independence from Spain, and Yanagita used qualitative methods to explore Japan's culture and its long-standing isolationism. They have received virtually no notice for their achievements outside their own countries (Alatas and Sinha 2001).

Filipino sociologist Clarence Batan (2004) argues

> **EUROCENTRIC** the tendency to favor European or Western histories, cultures, and values over other non-Western societies

that Western theorists like Marx, Weber, and Durkheim may inspire non-Western scholars but that their theories arose in response to specific social problems that were particular to Western societies. Non-Western societies face different issues, including the legacy of colonialism imposed by the Western countries from which those classical sociological theories sprang. Batan calls for sociologists in non-Western countries to respond to the needs of their societies by developing new theoretical frameworks that take postcolonial realities into account. Batan himself, along with other contemporary non-Western sociologists, works toward this goal every day in his research and teaching. Shouldn't your sociology professors do the same?

we acquire the knowledge that allows us to act in our everyday lives? Unlike the social Darwinists, pragmatists implied that the process of adaptation was essentially immediate and that it involved conscious thought. George Herbert Mead would be the one who eventually pulled these ideas (and others, too) together into a theory meant to address questions about the relationship between thought and action, the individual and society.

Mead came from a progressive family and grew up in the Midwest and Northeast during the late 1800s, where his father, a professor of theology at Oberlin College, died

when he was a teenager, and his widowed mother eventually became president of Mount Holyoke College. Mead attended college at Oberlin and Harvard, and did his graduate studies in psychology at the universities of Leipzig and Berlin in Germany. Before he became a full-time professor of psychology at the University of Michigan and later the University of Chicago, Mead waited tables and did railroad surveying and construction work. He was also a tutor to William James's family in Cambridge, Massachusetts; since his later theories were influenced by James, we can only wonder exactly who was tutoring whom in this arrangement! Mead's background and training uniquely positioned him to bridge the gap between sociology and psychology, and to address the links between the individual and society.

Mead proposed that both human development and the meanings we assign to everyday objects and events are fundamentally social processes—they require the interaction of multiple individuals. And what is crucial to the development of self and society is language, the means by which we communicate with one another. For Mead, there is no mind without language, and language itself is a product of social interactions (1934, pp. 191–92). According to Mead, the most important human behaviors consist of linguistic "gestures," such as words and facial expressions. People develop the ability to engage in conversation using these gestures; further, both society and individual selves are constructed through this kind of symbolic communication. Mead argued that we use language to "name ourselves, think about ourselves, talk to ourselves, and feel proud or ashamed of ourselves" and that "we can act toward ourselves in all the ways we can act toward others" (Hewitt 2000, p. 10). He was curious about how the mind developed but did not believe that it developed separately from its social environment. For Mead, then, society and self were created through communicative acts like speech and gestures; the individual personality was shaped by society, and vice versa.

Herbert Blumer, a graduate student and later a professor at the University of Chicago, was closely associated with Mead and was largely credited with continuing his life's work. While completing his master's degree, Blumer played football for the University of Missouri Tigers, and during the 1920s and 30s he maintained dual careers as a sociology professor and a professional football player for the former Chicago Cardinals. On Mondays, he would often come to class wrapped in bandages after a tough Sunday game. What he did off the gridiron, however, was of critical importance to the discipline. Blumer appealed for researchers to get "down and dirty" with the dynamics of social life. He also published a clear and compelling series of works based on Mead's fundamental ideas. After Mead's death in 1931, Blumer gave Mead's theory the name it now goes by: symbolic interactionism. Thus, Mead and Blumer became the somewhat-unwitting founders of a much larger theoretical perspective. Blumer's long career at the University of Chicago and later at University of California, Berkeley ensured the training of many future scholars and secured the inclusion of symbolic interactionism as one of the major schools of thought within the discipline.

Despite its geographical location in a city full of real-world inequality (or perhaps because of it), the Chicago School of sociology had very few women or people of color among its membership. Take W.E.B. DuBois and Jane Addams, for examples: these two scholars, were neither students nor faculty members at the University of Chicago, though both are often associated with Chicago School perspectives, values, and methods. Both led the way for other

Herbert Blumer

W.E.B. DuBois (1868–1963)

minorities and women to become influential scholars in the discipline of sociology.

William Edward Burghardt (W.E.B.) DuBois was a notable pioneer in the study of race relations as a professor of sociology at Atlanta University and one of the most influential African American leaders of his time. After becoming the first African American to earn a Ph.D. from Harvard University, DuBois did groundbreaking research on the history of the slave trade, post–Civil War reconstruction, the problems of urban ghetto life, and the nature of black American society. DuBois was so brilliant and prolific that it is often said that all subsequent studies of race and racial inequality in America depend to some degree on his work. Throughout his life, DuBois was involved in various forms of social activism. He was an indispensible forerunner in the Civil Rights Movement; among his many civic and political achievements, DuBois was a founding member, in 1909, of the National Association for the Advancement of Colored People (NAACP), an organization committed to the cause of ending racism and injustice. Because of his anti-racist, anti-poverty, and anti-war activism, DuBois was targeted by FBI Director J. Edgar Hoover and Senator Joseph McCarthy as a communist. However, he did not become a member of the Communist Party until he was 93 years old, and then only did so as a form of political protest against the persecution of its members by the U.S. government. Eventually, DuBois became disillusioned by the persistent injustices of American society, and emigrated to Ghana, where he died at 95, one year before the historic Civil Rights Act of 1964 was signed into law.

Jane Addams was another pioneer in the field of sociology whose numerous accomplishments range from the halls of academia to the forefront of social activism. Though she never officially joined the faculty because she feared it would curtail her political activism, Addams did teach extension courses at the University of Chicago and was among a small handful of women teaching in American universities at the time. Though not a mother herself, Addams believed that women had a special kind of responsibility toward solving social problems because

Jane Addams (1860–1935)

Erving Goffman

they were trained to care for others. She was one of the first proponents of applied sociology—addressing the most pressing problems of her day through hands-on work with the people and places that were the subject of her research. This practical approach is perhaps best demonstrated by Hull House, the Chicago community center she established in 1889 to offer shelter, medical care, legal advice, training, and education to new immigrants, single mothers, and the poor. As a result of her commitment to delivering support and services where they were most needed, Addams is often considered the founder of what is now a separate field outside the discipline: social work. Addams also helped found two important organizations that continue to fight for freedom and equality today: the American Civil Liberties Union (ACLU) and, along with W.E.B. DuBois, the NAACP. She served as the president of the Women's International League for Peace and Freedom and in 1931, became the first American woman to receive the Nobel Peace Prize.

ORIGINAL PRINCIPLES For symbolic interactionists, society is produced and reproduced through our interactions with each other by means of language and our interpretations of that language. Symbolic interactionism sees face-to-face interaction as the building block of everything else in society, because it is through interaction that we create a meaningful social reality.

Here are the three basic tenets of symbolic interactionism, as laid out by Blumer (1969, p. 2). First, *we act toward things on the basis of their meanings.* For example, a tree can provide a shady place to rest, or it can be an obstacle to building a road or home; each of these meanings suggests a different set of actions. This is as true for physical objects like trees as it is for

DRAMATURGY a theoretical paradigm that uses the metaphor of the theater to understand how individuals present themselves to others

ETHNOMETHODOLOGY the study of "folk methods" and background knowledge that sustains a shared sense of reality in everyday interactions

people (like mothers or cops), institutions (church or school), beliefs (honesty or equality), or any social activity. Second, *meanings are not inherent; rather, they are negotiated through interaction with others.* That is, whether the tree is an obstacle or an oasis is not an intrinsic quality of the tree itself but rather something that people must figure out among themselves. The same tree can mean one thing to one person and something else to another. And third, *meanings can change or be modified through interaction.* For example, the contractor who sees the tree as an obstacle might be persuaded to spare it by the neighbor who appreciates its shade. Now the tree means the same thing to both of them: it is something to protect and build around rather than to condemn and bulldoze.

Symbolic interactionism proposes that social facts exist only because we create and re-create them through our interactions; this gives the theory wide explanatory power and a versatility that allows it to address any sociological issue. Although symbolic interactionism is focused on how self and society develop through interaction with others, it is useful in explaining and analyzing a wide variety of specific social issues, from inequalities of race and gender to the group dynamics of families or co-workers.

OFFSHOOTS Symbolic interactionism opened the door for innovative sociologists who focused on social acts (like face-to-face interaction) rather than social facts (like vast bureaucratic institutions). They were able to extend the field in a variety of ways, allowing new perspectives to come under the umbrella of symbolic interactionism.

Erving Goffman (1922–82) furthered symbolic interactionist conceptions of the self in a seemingly radical way, indicating that the self is essentially "on loan" to us from society; it is created through interaction with others and hence ever-changing within various social contexts. For example, you may want to make a different kind of impression on a first date than you do on a job interview or when you face an opponent in a game of poker. Goffman used the theatrical metaphor of **dramaturgy** to describe the ways in which we engage in a strategic presentation of ourselves to others. In this way, he elaborated on Mead's ideas in a specific fashion, utilizing a wide range of data to help support his arguments.

Harold Garfinkel, the founder of **ethnomethodology** (the study of "folk methods," or everyday analysis of interaction), maintains that as members of society we must acquire the necessary knowledge and skills to act practically in our everyday lives. He argues that much of this knowledge remains in the background, "seen but unnoticed," and that we assume that others have the same knowledge we do when we interact with them. These assumptions allow us to make meaning out of even seemingly troublesome or ambiguous events; but such shared understandings can also be quite precarious, and there is a good deal of work required to sustain them, even as we are unaware that we are doing so.

Conversation analysis, pioneered by sociologists at University of California, Los Angeles, is also related to symbolic interactionism. It is based on the ethnomethodological idea that as everyday actors we are constantly analyzing and giving meaning to our social world (Schegloff 1986, 1999; Clayman 2002). Conversation analysts are convinced that the best place to look for the social processes of meaning-production is in naturally occurring conversation, and that the best way to get at the meanings an everyday actor gives to the things others say and do is to look closely at how he responds. Conversation analysts therefore use highly technical methods to scrutinize each conversational turn closely, operating on the assumption that any larger social phenomenon is constructed step-by-step through interaction.

ADVANTAGES AND CRITIQUES As society changes, so must the discipline that studies it, and symbolic interactionism has invigorated sociology in ways that are linked to the past and looking toward the future. The founding of symbolic interactionism provided a new and different way of looking at the world. It is "the only perspective that assumes an active, expressive model of the human actor and that treats the individual and the social at the same level of analysis" (O'Brien and Kollock 1997, p. 39). Therein lies much of its power and its appeal.

As a new school of thought focusing on the micro level of society, symbolic interactionism was not always met with immediate approval by the academy. Over time, symbolic interactionism has been integrated relatively seamlessly into sociology, and its fundamental precepts have become widely accepted. During the second half of the twentieth century, the scope of symbolic interactionism has widened, its topics multiplied, and its theoretical linkages became more varied. In fact, there was some concern that symbolic interactionism was expanding so much that it may risk erupting into something else entirely (Fine 1993). One of symbolic interactionism's most enduring contributions is in the area of research methods. Practices such as ethnography and conversation analysis are data-rich, technically complex, and empirically well grounded (Schegloff 1999; J. Katz 1997), giving us new insights into perennial questions about social life.

As a relative newcomer to the field of social theory, symbolic interactionism was dubbed "the loyal opposition" (Mullins 1973) by those who saw it solely as a reaction or as merely a supplement to the more dominant macrosociological theories that preceded it. Gary Fine sums up the critiques in this way: symbolic interactionism is "apolitical (and hence, supportive of the status quo), unscientific (hence, little more than tenured journalism), hostile to the classical questions of macrosociology (hence, limited to social psychology), and astructural (hence, fundamentally nonsociological)" (1993, p. 65). These critiques argue that the scope of symbolic interactionism is limited, that it cannot properly address the most important sociological issues, and that its authority is restricted to the study of face-to-face interaction.

Each of these critiques has been answered over the years. Ultimately, some critics have seen the usefulness of an interactionist perspective and have even begun incorporating it into more macro work. Even in the hotly contested micro-versus-macro debate, a kind of détente has been established, recognizing that all levels of analysis are necessary for sociological understanding and that interactionist theories and methods are critical for a full picture of social life.

DATA WORKSHOP
Analyzing Mass Media and Popular Culture

Theories of Celebrity Gossip

Oh No They Didn't! (ohnotheydidnt.livejournal.com) is one of the most popular celebrity gossip sites in the world. In operation since 2004, the site won Best Gossip Blog at the 2008 "Bloggie" Awards, and is the largest community on LiveJournal, its host site. ONTD relies on internet sources as well as its own users for up-to-the-minute pop culture news, and publishes hundreds of posts each day exposing the real and rumored doings of celebrities. These entries are accompanied by paparazzi photos and typically snide commentary by the throngs of readers who post their own observations and criticisms, humorous and serious. The enthusiasm of ONTD's users famously crashed LiveJournal's servers on June 25, 2009, following the death of Michael Jackson.

ONTD is part of a new breed of celebrity gossip outlets, including Perezhilton.com, Gawker.com, TMZ.com, and What Would Tyler Durden Do? (WWTDD.com), among others. These sites can almost instantly consolidate and present information that used to take at least a week to appear in printed gossip magazines like *People*, *In Touch*, or

Oh No They Didn't often features news about tabloid celebrities like Lindsey Lohan.

Us. They can also provide more explicit editorial commentary than the print magazines or mainstream television programs like *Entertainment Tonight* or *E! News* can. For example, consider the coverage of Kim Kardashian in early 2011. *People* showed a picture of her leaving a restaurant, with the headline "Kim: She's So Hip" and copy that said "Kardashian flaunts her curves." WWTDD.com showed a picture of her at a gas station with the headline "Kim Kardashian Has Ass for Days" and continued with the comments "Kim Kardashian normally does a pretty good job at hiding how big her ass is, but she's fashion savvy, not magic, so she can't hide it all the time. Like this weekend. From the waist down it looks like a horse."

It gets worse. Sometimes the commentary is so racy we wouldn't want to include it in a "family" textbook! Finally, these sites allow for almost immediate feedback from and discussion among far-flung readers, something not possible in the pre-internet gossip magazine days.

Other staples of celebrity gossip sites are photos of celebrities with evaluative commentary about their bodies, outfits, mates, children, and other aspects of their beings and behaviors. While many criticize such information as mean, stupid, and shallow, you don't have to enjoy celebrity gossip to see its sociological relevance. And sometimes, items from celebrity gossip blogs can end up in the mainstream news: in 2007, Perezhilton.com's Mario Lavandeira "broke a story" on the death of Cuban president Fidel Castro that was picked up by the conventional media and broadcast widely. The story turned out to be untrue, but the incident speaks to the influence of such blogs on our understanding of what constitutes news.

For this Data Workshop, we'd like you to immerse yourself in the celebrity gossip site of your choice. Pick five entries—scrutinize the pictures, read the headlines and text carefully, and review the reader comments. Now ask yourself the following questions based on each of sociology's three major schools of thought:

1. Structural Functionalism
What is the function (or functions) of celebrity gossip blogs for society? What purpose(s) do they serve, and how do they help society maintain stability and order? Discuss how notions of the sacred and profane are characterized. Are there manifest and latent functions of celebrity gossip blogs? And are there any dysfunctions built into such publications?

2. Conflict Theory
What forms of inequality are revealed in celebrity gossip blogs? In particular, what do these blogs have to say about class, race, gender, or sexuality inequalities? Whose interests are being served and who gets exploited? Who suffers and who benefits from the publication of celebrity gossip blogs?

3. Symbolic Interactionism
What do celebrity gossip blogs mean to society as a whole? What do they mean to individual members of society? Can they have different meanings for different individuals or groups of individuals? How do those meanings get constructed in interaction? And how do these blogs shape and influence our everyday lives?

Make sure you can explain your answers to each of these questions, and complete one of the following two options, as directed by your instructor.

Option 1 (informal): Answer each of the three sets of questions above, and prepare some notes that you can refer to in class. Discuss your answers with other students in small groups.

Option 2 (formal): Answer each of the three sets of questions above in a three-page essay explaining your positions. You may want to include snippets from your chosen blog to illustrate your points.

New Theoretical Approaches

Because the three major schools of thought and their offshoots all have weaknesses as well as strengths, they will probably never fully explain the totality of social phenomena, even when taken together. And because society itself is always changing, there are always new phenomena to explain. So new perspectives will, and indeed must, continue to arise. In this

Jacques Derrida, Michel Foucault, and Jean Baudrillard While many commentators and critics identify these French intellectuals as "postmodernists," each one distanced himself from the label.

section, we will consider two more contemporary approaches: postmodernism and midrange theory. Both grew out of the deep groundwork established by the other major schools of thought within sociology, and by looking beyond the confines of the discipline for inspiration. Each is a response to conditions both in the fast-changing social world around us and within the ongoing intellectual dialogues taking place among those continuing to study our times and selves.

Postmodern Theory

In the late twentieth century, some social thinkers looked at the proliferation of theories and data and began to question whether we could ever know society or ourselves with any certainty. What is truth, and who has the right to claim it? Or, for that matter, what is reality, and how can it be known? In an era of increasing doubt and cynicism, has meaning become meaningless? **Postmodernism**, a theory that encompasses a wide range of areas — from art and architecture, music and film, to communications and technology — addresses these and other questions.

The postmodern perspective developed primarily out of the French intellectual scene in the second half of the twentieth century and is still associated with three of its most important proponents. It's probably worth noting that postmodernists themselves don't really like that label, but nonetheless Jacques Derrida (1930–2004), Jean Baudrillard (1929–2007), and Michel Foucault (1926–84) are the major figures most often included in the group.

In order to understand postmodernism, we first need to juxtapose it with **modernism**, the movement against which it reacted. Modernism is both a historical period and an ideological stance that began with the eighteenth-century Enlightenment, or Age of Reason. Modernist thought values scientific knowledge, a linear (or timeline-like) view of history, and a belief in the universality of human nature. In postmodernism, on the other hand, there are no absolutes — no claims to truth, reason, right, order, or stability. Everything is therefore relative — fragmented, temporary, and contingent. Postmodernists believe that certainty is illusory and prefer to play with the possibilities created by

fluidity, complexity, multidimensionality, and even nonsense. They propose that there are no universal human truths from which we can interpret the meaning of existence. On one hand, postmodernism can be celebrated as a liberating influence that rescues us from the stifling effects of rationality and tradition. On the other, it can be condemned as a detrimental influence that imprisons us in a world of relativity, nihilism, and chaos.

Postmodernists are also critical of what they call "grand narratives," overarching stories and theories that justify dominant beliefs and give a (false) sense of order and coherence to the world. Postmodernists are interested in **deconstruction**, or taking apart and examining these stories and theories. For example, they claim that "factual" accounts of history are no more accurate than those that might be found in fiction. They prefer the notion of mini-narratives, or small-scale stories, which describe individual or group practices rather than narratives that attempt to be universal or global. These mini-narratives can then be combined in a variety of ways, creating a collage of meaning.

One way of understanding what postmodernism looks like is to examine how it has crept into our popular culture. Hip-hop is an example of a postmodern art form. It is a hybrid that borrows from other established genres, from rhythm and blues to rock and reggae. Hip-hop also takes samples from existing songs, mixes these with new musical tracks, and overlays it all with rap lyrics, resulting in a unique new sound. Mash-ups are another postmodern twist in music. Take for instance the *Grey Album* by DJ Danger Mouse, which uses tracks from the Beatles' classic rock album called the *White Album* and combines them with Jay-Z's *Black Album* to create something wholly new yet borrowed.

Many resist the postmodern position against essential meaning or truth; the rise in religious fundamentalism may

POSTMODERNISM a paradigm that suggests that social reality is diverse, pluralistic, and constantly in flux

MODERNISM a paradigm that places trust in the power of science and technology to create progress, solve problems, and improve life

DECONSTRUCTION a type of critical postmodern analysis that involves taking apart or disassembling old ways of thinking be a reaction to the postmodern view, an expression of the desire to return to absolute truths and steadfast traditions. Sociologists are quick to criticize postmodernism for discarding the scientific method and the knowledge they believe it has generated. Social leaders with a conservative agenda have been suspicious of the postmodern impulse to dismiss moral standards. While it is clear that many people criticize postmodernism, a much larger number are probably oblivious to it, which in itself may be more damning than any other response.

Although it is not a widely practiced perspective, postmodernism *has* nevertheless gained supporters. Those who challenge the status quo, whether in the arts, politics, or the academy, find attractive postmodernism's ability to embrace a multiplicity of powerful and promising alternatives. At the very least, postmodernism allows us to question scientific ideals about clarity and coherence, revealing inherent shortcomings and weaknesses in our current arguments, and providing a way toward a deeper, more nuanced understanding of social life. As one of the most contemporary of the theoretical perspectives, postmodernism corresponds to the Information Age and feels natural and intuitive for many students whose lives are immersed in this world. By focusing on individuals and small-scale activities in which change happens on a local, limited basis, postmodernism offers an alternative to such cultural trends as consumerism and globalization. However unwelcome the theory might be to some critics, it is likely that the postmodern shifts we have seen in society (in music and films, for example) will continue.

MIDRANGE THEORY an approach that integrates empiricism and grand theory

Midrange Theory

The second new theoretical approach is **midrange theory**. It shares some views with postmodernism, especially in its preference for mini-narratives over sweeping statements or "grand theories" made by the classical social theorists—a period dominated by what Robert Merton calls "total sociological systems" (1996, p. 46), which provided an overarching, comprehensive explanation of society as a whole.

Merton feared that an uncritical reverence for classical theory and an excessive attachment to tradition could impede the flow of new ideas, and was just as likely to hold sociology back as to advance it. Because classical theories sought to develop large-scale theoretical systems that applied to the most macro level of society, they were often extremely difficult to test or research in any practical way. As one critic lamented, too "many sociological products can—effectively and unfortunately—be considered both bad science and bad literature" (Boudon 1991, p. 522).

To counter this tendency, Merton proposed sociologists focus more on "theories of the middle range." Midrange (or

middle range) theory is not a theory of something in particular, but rather a *style* of theorizing. It is an attempt not so much to make the elusive macro-micro link, but to strike a balance somewhere between those polarities, shifting both the sights and the process of doing sociology. Work in this vein concentrates on incorporating research questions and empirical data into smaller-scale theories that eventually build into a more comprehensive body of sociological theory. Midrange theories are those "that lie between the minor but necessary working hypotheses that evolve in abundance during day-to-day research and the all-inclusive systematic efforts to develop a unified theory that will explain" the whole social world (Merton 1996, p. 41).

Since the 1990s and 2000s, a host of sociologists have taken up the call to midrange theory, from Sharon Hays's study of the contradictions within modern motherhood (1996) to Dalton Conley's work on racial identity (2000) or our shifting notions of the workplace and what constitutes leisure in the digital age (2009). Midrange theory connects specific research projects that generate empirical data with larger-scale theories about social structure. It aims to build knowledge cumulatively while offering a way to make sociology more effective as a science rather than just a way of thinking. With more sociologists appreciating such a stance, midrange theory is helping to push the discipline forward into the sociology of the future.

CLOSING COMMENTS

We hope that this chapter has given you a thorough and compelling introduction to the study of sociology, and perhaps you too will find it an appealing pursuit. Many of you will have already started a sociological journey, although likely a casual or personal one . . . until now. The popularity of reality TV speaks to our fascination with the everyday lives of other people, whether *Hoarders* or *Ice Road Truckers* or *The Real Housewives of* _____ (fill in the blank). As students of sociology, we are interested in everyday life because we are excited to understand more about how its patterns and processes create our larger social reality. As we become better social analysts, using strategies to set aside any blinding preconceptions or distracting conclusions, we can become better acquainted with some of the fundamental tools that can turn our natural curiosity into scientific inquiry. A sociological perspective allows us to grasp the connection between our individual experiences and the forces and structures of society. As Bernard McGrane says, "Sociology is both dangerous and liberating" (1994, p. 10), as much because of what we can learn about ourselves as because of what we can learn about the world around us.

As a discipline, sociology possesses some of the qualities of the society it seeks to understand: it is broad, complex,

Table 1.1 Theory in Everyday Life

Perspective	Approach to Society	Case Study: College Admissions in the United States
Structural Functionalism	Assumes that society is a unified whole that functions because of the contributions of its separate structures.	Those who are admitted are worthy and well-qualified, while those who are not admitted do not deserve to be. There are other places in society for them besides the university.
Conflict Theory	Sees social conflict as the basis of society and social change and emphasizes a materialist view of society, a critical view of the status quo, and a dynamic model of historical change.	Admissions decisions may be made on the basis of criteria other than grades and scores. For example, some applicants may get in because their fathers are major university donors, while others may get in because of their talents in sports or music. Some may be denied admission based on criteria like race, gender, or sexuality.
Symbolic Interactionism	Asserts that interaction and meaning are central to society and assumes that meanings are not inherent but are created through interaction.	University admissions processes are all about self-presentation and meaning-making in interaction. How does an applicant present himself or herself to impress the admissions committee? How does the admissions committee develop an understanding of the kind of applicant it's looking for? How do applicants interpret their acceptances and rejections?
Postmodernism	Suggests that social reality is diverse, pluralistic, and constantly in flux.	An acceptance doesn't mean you're smart, and a rejection doesn't mean you're stupid; be careful of any "facts" you may be presented with, as they are illusory and contingent.

and ever-changing. This can make mastering sociology a rather unwieldy business, as much for the students and teachers who grapple with it in the classroom as for the experts out working in the field. We want you to become familiar with the members of sociology's family tree from its varied historical roots to the tips of its offshoots that might one day become important future branches. Because we have no single acknowledged universal sociological theory that satisfactorily explains all social phenomena (despite claims otherwise by some theorists), new theories can be developed all the time. Social theory tries to explain what is happening in, to, and around us. For any and every

possible new, different, or important phenomenon — from the most mundane personal experience to questions of ultimate global significance — sociologists will attempt to explain it, understand it, analyze it, and predict its future. By looking at the development of the discipline, we can remember that the contemporary grows out of the classical, and that older theories inspire and provoke newer ones. Theorists past and present remain engaged in a continual and evolving dialogue through their ideas and their work, and until such time as society is completely explained, the branches of sociology's family tree will continue to grow in remarkable ways.

Everything You Need to Know about Sociology

> ❝ Sociology is the systematic or scientific study of human society and social behavior, from large-scale institutions and mass culture to small groups and individual interactions. ❞

THEORIES OF SOCIOLOGY

* **Structural functionalism:** the assumption that society is a unified whole that functions because of the contributions of its separate structures

* **Conflict theory:** the belief that social conflict is the basis of society and social change that emphasizes a materialist view of society, a critical view of the status quo, and a dynamic model of historical change

* **Weberian theory:** the application of economic logic to human activity that uses formal rules and regulations in order to maximize efficiency without consideration of subjective or individual concerns

* **Symbolic interactionism:** sees interaction and meaning as central to society and assumes that meanings are not inherent but are created through interaction

* **Postmodern theory:** suggests that social reality is diverse, pluralistic, and constantly in flux

* **Midrange theory:** an approach that integrates empiricism and grand theory

REVIEW

1. What does it mean to possess a sociological imagination? Think of your favorite food. What historical events had to happen and what institutions have to function in order for this food to be available? What sort of meanings does it have?

2. How does the level of analysis you adopt affect your assumptions about how society works? Could Pam Fishman have done her research on gender and power in conversations from a macro perspective? Perhaps with a survey? Could Christine Williams have done her research on gender and power in occupations from a micro perspective? Perhaps with interviews? How might this change their conclusions?

3. Symbolic interactionism argues that meanings are not inherent in things themselves but are socially derived and negotiated through interaction with others. Think of some recent fashion trend. Can you describe this trend in terms of what it means to those who embrace it? What sorts of interactions produce and maintain this meaning?

Key Works in Sociology

1837	Harriet Martineau, *Society in America*
1838	Auguste Comte, *Cours de Philosophie Positive*
1848	Karl Marx & Friedrich Engels, *Communist Manifesto*
1867	Karl Marx, *Das Kapital*
1893	Emile Durkheim, *The Division of Labor in Society*
1897	Emile Durkheim, *Suicide*
1902	Charles Cooley, *Human Nature and the Social Order*
1903	W. E. B. Du Bois, *The Souls of Black Folk*
1904	Max Weber, *The Protestant Ethic and the Spirit of Capitalism*
1912	Emile Durkheim, *The Elementary Forms of the Religious Life*
1921	Max Weber, *Economy and Society*
1934	George Herbert Mead, *Mind, Self, and Society*
1937	Talcott Parsons, *The Structure of Social Action*
1949	Robert Merton, *Social Theory and Social Structure*
1956	C. Wright Mills, *The Power Elite*
1959	C. Wright Mills, *The Sociological Imagination*
1959	Erving Goffman, *The Presentation of Self in Everyday Life*
1966	Peter Berger & Thomas Luckmann, *The Social Construction of Reality*
1981	bell hooks, *Ain't I a Woman?*
1984	Pierre Bourdieu, *Distinction*
1989	Catharine MacKinnon, *Toward a Feminist Theory of the State*

EXPLORE

The Rationality of Irrationality

George Ritzer applied Max Weber's theories of bureaucracy and rationality to the fast food industry. Visit the Everyday Sociology Blog to learn how Weber's theories adapt to everyday life.

http://wwnPag.es/trw401

CHAPTER 2

Studying Social Life: Sociological Research Methods

Humorist Dave Barry, the Pulitzer Prize–winning columnist and author, has written many entertaining articles as a reporter and social commentator. Some of his thoughts on college, however, seem particularly appropriate for this chapter. In one of his most popular essays, Barry advises students not to choose a major that involves "known facts" and "right answers" but rather a subject in which "nobody really understands what anybody else is talking about, and which involves virtually no actual facts" (Barry 1987, p. 203). For example, sociology:

For sheer lack of intelligibility, sociology is far and away the number-one subject. I sat through hundreds of hours of sociology courses, and read gobs of sociology writing, and I never once heard or read a coherent statement. This is because sociologists want to be considered scientists, so they spend most of their time translating simple, obvious observations into scientific-sounding code. If you plan to major in sociology, you'll have to learn to do the same thing. For example, suppose you have observed that children cry when they fall down. You should write: "Methodological observation of the sociometrical behavior tendencies of prematurated isolates indicates that a causal relationship exists between groundward tropism and lachrimatory, or 'crying' behavior forms." If you can keep this up for fifty or sixty pages, you will get a large government grant.

Although Barry exaggerates a bit, if there weren't some truth to what he is saying, his joke would be meaningless. While sociologists draw much of their inspiration from the natural (or "hard") sciences (such as chemistry and biology) and try to study society in a scientific way, many people still think of sociology as "unscientific" or a "soft" science. In response, some sociologists may try too hard to sound scientific and incorporate complicated terminology in their writing.

It is possible, of course, to conduct research and write about it in a clear, straightforward, and even elegant way, as the best sociologists have demonstrated. Contrary to Barry's humorous claims, sociology can be both scientific and comprehensible. So let's turn now to a discussion of how sociologists conduct their research, which includes the methods of gathering information and conveying that information to others. For the record, Dave Barry went to Haverford College near Philadelphia, where he majored in English.

HOW TO READ THIS CHAPTER

In Chapter 1 we introduced you to a set of tools that will help you develop a sociological imagination and apply particular theoretical perspectives to the social world. In this chapter you will acquire methodological tools that will help you to further understand social life. The tools will also help you in the Data Workshops throughout the book, which are designed to give you the experience of conducting the same type of research that professional sociologists do. For this reason, we recommend that you look at this chapter as a sort of "how-to" guide: read through all the "directions" first, recognizing that you will soon be putting each method into practice. Then remember that you have this chapter as a resource for future reference. These methods are your tools for real-world research — it's important that you understand them, but even more important that you get a chance to use them.

An Overview of Research Methods

While theories make hypothetical claims, methods produce data that will support, disprove, or modify those claims. Sociologists who do **quantitative research** work with numerical data; that is, they translate the social world into numbers that can then be manipulated mathematically. Any type of social statistic is an example of quantitative data: you may have read in the newspaper, for instance, that in 2010 some 37 percent of male drivers involved in fatal motor vehicle crashes had a blood alcohol content at or above 0.08 percent, compared with 22 percent of female drivers (Insurance Institute for Highway Safety 2010). Quantitative methodologies distill large amounts of information into numbers that are more easily communicated to others, often in the form of rates and percentages or charts and graphs.

Sociologists who do **qualitative research** work with nonnumerical data such as texts, written fieldnotes, interview transcripts, photographs, and tape recordings. Rather than condensing lived experience into numbers, qualitative researchers try to describe the cases they study in great detail. They may engage in participant observation, in which they enter the social world they wish to study, they may do in-depth interviews, analyze transcripts of conversations, glean data from historical books, letters, or diaries, or even use photos or videos in their investigations. Sociologist Gary Fine, for example, has observed a variety of different social worlds, including those of professional restaurant chefs (1996), people who harvest wild mushrooms in the woods (1998), and members of high school debate teams (2001)! He is currently working on a study of competitive chess players. Fine was able to discover important sociological insights through immersion in each of the social worlds he studied. Qualitative researchers like Fine find patterns in their data by using interpretive rather than statistical analysis.

The Scientific Approach

The **scientific method** is the standard procedure for acquiring and verifying empirical (concrete, scientific) knowledge. The scientific method provides researchers with a series of basic steps to follow; over the years, sociologists have updated and modified this model so that it better fits the study of human behaviors. While not every sociologist adheres to each of the steps in order, the scientific method provides a general plan for conducting research in a systematic way (see Figure 2.1 for a graphic representation).

1. In the first step, the researcher identifies a problem or asks a general question, like "Does violent TV lead

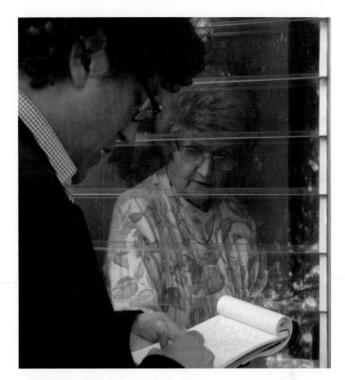

Sociological Methods Take Many Forms. They can be quantitative, but they can also include interviews, surveys, and participant observation.

QUANTITATIVE RESEARCH research that translates the social world into numbers that can be treated mathematically; this type of research often tries to find cause-and-effect relationships

QUALITATIVE RESEARCH research that works with nonnumerical data such as texts, fieldnotes, interview transcripts, photographs, and tape recordings; this type of research more often tries to understand how people make sense of their world

SCIENTIFIC METHOD a procedure for acquiring knowledge that emphasizes collecting concrete data through observation and experiment

Does Watching Violence on Television Cause Children to Behave Violently? In his famous 1965 study, Albert Bandura supported his hypothesis by observing children who had watched a video of an adult beating a doll behaving similarly toward the doll afterward.

LITERATURE REVIEW
a thorough search through previously published studies relevant to a particular topic

HYPOTHESIS a theoretical statement explaining the relationship between two or more phenomena

VARIABLE one of two or more phenomena that a researcher believes are related and hopes to prove are related through research

OPERATIONAL DEFINITION a clear and precise definition of a variable that facilitates its measurement

CORRELATION a relationship between variables in which they change together, and may or may not be causal

CAUSATION a relationship between variables in which a change in one directly produces a change in the other

INTERVENING VARIABLE a third variable, sometimes overlooked, that explains the relationship between two other variables

to violent behavior?" and begins to think about a specific research plan designed to answer that question.

2. Before proceeding, however, a researcher usually does a **literature review** to become thoroughly familiar with all other research done previously on a given topic. This will prevent a researcher from duplicating work that has already been done and may also provide the background upon which to conduct new research.

3. Next, the researcher forms a **hypothesis**, a theoretical statement that she thinks will explain the relationship between two phenomena, which are known as **variables**. In the hypothesis "Watching violence on TV causes children to act violently in real life," the two variables are "watching violence on TV" and "acting violently." In short, the researcher is saying one variable causes the

other. The researcher can use the hypothesis to predict possible outcomes: "If watching violence on TV causes children to act violently in real life, then exposing five-year-olds to violent TV shows will make them more likely to hit the inflatable clown doll placed in the room with them." The researcher must clearly give an **operational definition** to the variables so that she can observe and measure them accurately. For example, there is a wide range of violence on television and in real life. Does "violence" include words as well as actions, a slap as well as murder?

4. In this step, the researcher chooses a research design or method. A classic example is to perform an experiment meant to isolate the variables in order to best examine their relationship to one another. Other methods are also available and will be discussed later in the chapter.

5. The researcher then collects the data. In this case, the researcher would conduct the experiment by first exposing kids to TV violence, then observing their behavior toward the clown doll. Data might be collected by using video equipment as well as by taking notes.

6. Next, the researcher must analyze the data, evaluating the accuracy or inaccuracy of the hypothesis in predicting the outcome. In the real-life experiment this example is based on, the children were more likely to hit the clown doll themselves if they saw the TV actors being rewarded for their violent behavior; if the actors were punished for their behavior, the children were less likely to hit the doll (Bandura 1965).

7. Finally, the researcher then disseminates the findings of the experiment in the scientific community (often through presentations at professional meetings, through publications, or in the classroom) as well as among the general public, thus completing the last step in the research process.

One limit of the scientific method is that it can't always distinguish between **correlation** and **causation**. If two variables change in conjunction with each other, or if a change in one seems to lead to a change in the other, they are correlated. Even if they are correlated, though, the change in one variable may not be caused by the change in the other variable. Instead, there may be some **intervening variable** that causes the changes in both. The classic example of this is the correlation between ice cream sales and rates of violent crime. As ice cream sales increase, so do rates of violent crime like murder and rape. Does ice cream consumption cause people to act violently? Or do violent actions cause people to buy ice cream? Turns out, it's neither — this is what

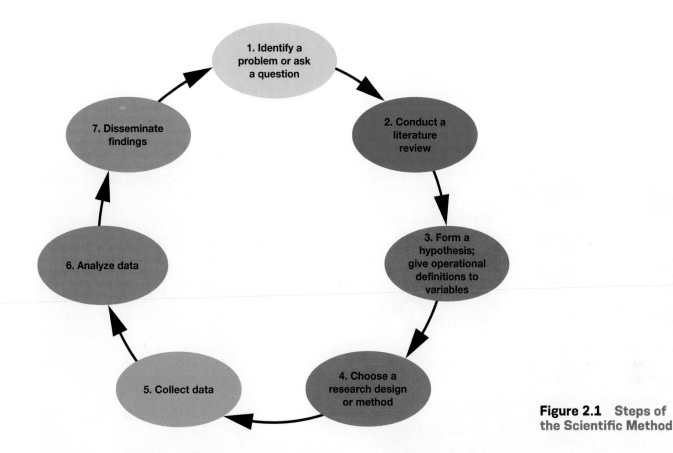

Figure 2.1 Steps of the Scientific Method

is known as a **spurious correlation**. Both ice cream sales and violent crime rates are influenced by a third variable: weather. As the temperature climbs, so do people's rates of ice cream purchase and the likelihood that they'll be involved in a violent crime (probably because they are outside for more hours of the day and hence available to each other in a way that makes violent crime possible). Knowing that correlation does not equal causation is important, as it can help us all be more critical consumers of scientific findings.

We are constantly gathering data in order to understand what is true. Philosopher of science Thomas Kuhn, in fact, argues that truth is relative and dependent on the paradigm through which one sees the world (1962/1970). Paradigms are broad theoretical models about how things work in the social and natural worlds. For example, humans believed for centuries that the universe revolved around the earth. It's easy to understand why. The available data, after all, seemed to support such a theory: we don't feel the earth moving beneath us, and it appears from our vantage point that the stars, sun, and moon rise and set on our horizon. This earth-centered, or geocentric, view of the universe was the basis for all scientific theory until 1543, when the Polish astrono-mer Nicolaus Copernicus proposed that the earth revolved around the sun (Armitage 1951). Using mathematical meth-ods, Copernicus arrived at a new theory, heliocentrism, in which the earth rotates around the sun and on its own axis—thereby accounting for the twenty-four-hour days as well as the four seasons of the year. This caused what Kuhn calls a **paradigm shift**, a major break from the assumptions made by the previous model. Paradigm shifts occur when new data force new ways of looking at the world. And meth-ods are what generate data.

Which Method to Use?

Since each sociological method has specific benefits and limitations, each is more appropriate for certain types of research. Thus, when a researcher begins a project, one of her most important decisions is which methods to use. Suppose, for example, a sociologist is interested in studying Wood-stock, one of the major musical and cultural milestones of the 1960s. Although there are many ways to approach this event, our sociologist wants to study the attendees' experi-ences. What was it really like to be at Woodstock? What did it mean to those who were there? What are their interpreta-tions of this iconic moment in hippie culture?

During the event itself, the ideal method for studying the festival-goers at Woodstock might have been to assemble a team of researchers trained in participant observation; that is, they would actually be in the thick of things, observing and participating at the same time.

SPURIOUS CORRELATION the appearance of causation produced by an intervening variable

PARADIGM SHIFT the term used to describe a change in basic assumptions of a particular scientific discipline

What Was It Really Like at Woodstock? You could use many different methodologies to investigate this question, including ethnography, interviews, surveys, existing sources, or experiments.

They could gather firsthand data on the music, clothes, dancing, drugs, "free love," and so forth. However, the opportunity to conduct an ethnography (written record) of that particular cultural phenomenon has long since passed. What are some other options?

Interviews are a possibility. The researcher could ask Woodstock attendees to recount their experiences. But how would she recruit them? Woodstock-goers live all over the world now, and it might be difficult (and expensive) to track down enough of them to make an interview study feasible. Another problem with interviewing this group: the three-day concert happened more than forty years ago. How did the drugs that were so widely used at the time affect their memories, and how much detail could they remember about the experience after so long?

How about a survey? The researcher could certainly send a questionnaire through the mail or by e-mail, and this method would be much less expensive than face-to-face interviews. But here she runs into the same problem as with an interview study: how does she find all these folks? A standard tactic for recruiting survey participants

involves placing an ad in a local newspaper. But an ad in the *New York Times*, for example, or even a community web site like Craigslist would draw only a limited number of Woodstock alumni. Also, some attendees might want to put that part of their lives behind them; others who received the questionnaire in the mail might send it straight into the trash. Finally, the researcher might encounter the problem of impostors — people who say they were at Woodstock but were really nowhere near it.

What about using existing sources? Plenty has been written about Woodstock over the years. Many firsthand accounts have been published, and there is an abundance of film and photography as well. Our researcher could use these articles to analyze the concert from the perspectives of the participants. These accounts would necessarily be selective, focusing only on particular aspects of the Woodstock experience.

Is it possible to conduct an experiment that replicates the original Woodstock? Some would say that Woodstock '99 was such an experiment and that it failed miserably, with fires, violence, arrests, and acres of mud. However, systematic scientific experiments are different from blatant attempts to cash in on the Woodstock mystique. While the unique conditions of the 1969 gathering cannot be recreated in a lab setting, it is possible to identify some of the defining features of the Woodstock experience and to explore those experimentally. Over a three-day period, tens of thousands of strangers came together in a mass gathering, mostly devoid of any official presence (no cops, fences, roads, ticket booths, or porta-potties) and had an almost entirely peaceful experience. How did this happen? Altruism, cooperation, and trust between strangers are some of the measurable group qualities that seem to have been present. An experimenter might be able to create laboratory environments in which subjects participate in activities that highlight one or more of these qualities — even without the mud, music, and drugs that were part of the original Woodstock experience.

No matter what methodological choice our researcher makes, she will sacrifice some types of information in order to acquire others, and she will trade in one set of advantages and disadvantages for another. Her choices will be guided not only by what she wants to accomplish sociologically but also by the methods she is a competent practitioner of, the time in which she wants to complete the project, the resources available from any funding agencies, and her access to cooperative, qualified people, both as respondents and as research assistants. The rest of this chapter will discuss five methods in detail: ethnography, interviews, surveys, existing sources, and experiments. We will see how various sociologists have used these methods to conduct research on the general topic of "family dynamics."

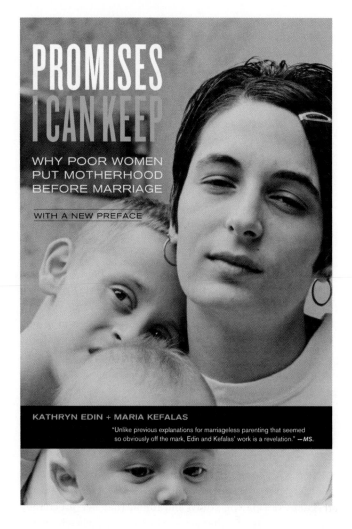

PROMISES I CAN KEEP

WHY POOR WOMEN PUT MOTHERHOOD BEFORE MARRIAGE

WITH A NEW PREFACE

KATHRYN EDIN + MARIA KEFALAS

"Unlike previous explanations for marriageless parenting that seemed so obviously off the mark, Edin and Kefalas' work is a revelation." —*MS.*

Ethnographic Methods

Ethnography means "writing [from the Greek *graphos*] culture [*ethnos*]." Ethnographers collect data by producing written records of their observations, with the goal of not only describing the activities they observe and participate in but also understanding what those activities mean to the members of the group they are studying.

One example of ethnography is Kathryn Edin and Maria Kefalas's study of poor moms, in their work, *Promises I Can Keep: Why Poor Women Put Motherhood before Marriage* (2005). Edin and Kefalas wanted to examine a group that faces harsh judgments from the mainstream — urban single moms. For years, policymakers and mainstream Americans have focused on single motherhood as a source of a variety of social problems. Edin and Kefalas wanted to see the issue from the perspective and lives of the women being stigmatized in order to uncover the realities of single motherhood from the perspective of the mothers themselves. Their goal was to give poor single mothers the ability to personally answer the question that wealthier Americans ask of them:

why don't they get married? And why have babies if they have to struggle so hard to support them?

Because Edin and Kefalas knew they needed to access a group that was notorious for being hard to study, their **participant observation** required full immersion in the community. Edin moved her entire family into an apartment that she rented in East Camden, New Jersey. They lived there for a total of two and a half years while she did her research. In order to become more integrated into the community, she joined the local church, volunteered at after-school and summer programs, ate at local restaurants, shopped at local stores, taught Sunday school, and went to community events. She made herself part of the community in order to help the young women she was interested in understanding become more comfortable with her presence. Kefalas volunteered at the local GED tutoring program for teen

ETHNOGRAPHY a naturalistic method based on studying people in their own environment in order to understand the meanings they attribute to their activities; also the written work that results from the study

PARTICIPANT OBSERVATION a methodology associated with ethnography whereby the researcher both observes and becomes a member in a social setting mothers. Once she gained the confidence of a small group of mothers, she was invited into their homes to hang out with them.

Edin and Kefalas were able to interview 162 mothers with an even distribution between black, white, and Puerto Rican. All of them were single parents who earned less than $16,000 a year. The women's ages ranged from fifteen to fifty-six with the average age being twenty-five years old. What Edin and Kefalas discovered was that motherhood, from the perspective of many of the women they interviewed, was a stabilizing agent in their lives. Rather than the middle-class expectations that single motherhood would disrupt a path to success, many of the moms they interviewed viewed their babies as the only positive factor in their lives. Numerous stories detailed the troubled directions the women's lives were heading before they had their children. The conclusions Edin and Kefalas were able to draw from their ethnographic research were contrary to widespread opinion about the consequences of single motherhood: for many women in poverty, the (perceived) low cost of early child-rearing and the high value and worth of mothering are enough to combat the difficulties of single motherhood.

The fact that the researchers were women and mothers themselves played a role in their ability to create **rapport** and gain **access** as they lived and worked in East Camden. The fact that Edin had children who accompanied her everywhere she went in the community helped to secure her position as a trustworthy fellow member. Kefalas became pregnant during the study, and found that her pregnancy allowed her even further access; in fact, the girls whom she tutored were eager to talk to her about pregnancy and child-rearing since she now shared those experiences with them. Ethnographic researchers must pay attention to how their own social statuses — including gender, age, race, and parenthood — shape the kind of access they can have, and hence the kind of knowledge they can obtain as part of their research.

Once access is negotiated, research can begin in earnest. Like Kathryn Edin and Maria Kefalas, most ethnographers are "overt" about their research roles; that is, they are open about their sociological intentions. Overt research is generally preferred, because it eliminates the potential ethical problems of deceit. Sometimes, however,

circumstances dictate that researchers take a "covert" role and observe members without letting them know that they are doing research. One researcher who kept his identity secret is Richard Mitchell, who studied militant survivalist groups for many years (2001). In order to be a participant-observer in such groups, Mitchell sometimes had to present himself as an eager apostle, a true believer in the survivalists' paranoid, racist ideologies. Often, this meant being surrounded by men who were heavily armed and deeply suspicious of outsiders (Mitchell and Charmaz 1996). However, he also felt that the value of the research was worth the risk, that it was more important than his own personal peril and the ethical objections of those who disapprove of covert research because it provided insight into a secretive group whose actions could pose a danger to the larger society.

Participant-observers collect data by writing detailed **fieldnotes** every day. These notes describe the activities and interactions of the researcher and the members in as much detail as possible; they become the basis of the data analysis the researcher does later on. Sometimes, ethnographers take brief, sketchy notes in the field, writing key words or short quotations in small notebooks, on cocktail napkins, or in text messages. These jottings can help jog their memories when they sit down at a computer at the end of the day to elaborate on the details. Sometimes, however, ethnographers must rely on "head notes" — memory alone.

Anthropologist Clifford Geertz, well known for his work on Indonesian culture and society, coined the term **thick description** to convey the qualities of well-written fieldnotes (Geertz 1973). It takes more than mere photographic detail to make fieldnotes "thick"; sensitivity to the context and to interactional details such as facial expressions and tone of voice enrich what might otherwise be just a list of events. Thick description involves exploring all the possible meanings of a phenomenon (for example, a blinking eye) within a particular cultural setting. In order to truly understand members' meanings, one has to be fully immersed in their world, usually for a sustained period of time (some ethnographers spend years in the field).

Another issue that participant-observers must consider is that their own presence probably affects the interactions and relationships in the group they are observing, an idea known as **reflexivity**. For example, the gender of the researcher may be important in particular settings, as it was for Edin in negotiating access. A researcher's personal feelings about the members of a group also come into play. Ethnographers may feel respect, contempt, curiosity, boredom, and other emotions during their time in the field, and these feelings may influence their observations. It is true that other kinds of researchers also have to take their feelings into account. But because ethnographers have such close personal ties to the people they study, the issue of reflexivity is especially important to them.

RAPPORT a positive relationship often characterized by mutual trust or sympathy

ACCESS the process by which an ethnographer gains entry to a field setting

FIELDNOTES detailed notes taken by an ethnographer describing her activities and interactions, which later become the basis of the ethnographic analysis

THICK DESCRIPTION the presentation of detailed data on interactions and meaning within a cultural context, from the perspective of its members

REFLEXIVITY how the identity and activities of the researcher influence what is going on in the field setting

Richard Mitchell's *Dancing at Armageddon* In order to learn about militant groups' ideologies, Richard Mitchell had to conceal his identity and use covert methods.

Analyzing the Data

Ethnographers look for patterns and processes that are revealed in their fieldnotes. In other words, they use an inductive approach: they start by immersing themselves in their fieldnote data and fitting the data into categories, such as "episodes of conflict" or "common vocabulary shared by members." Identifying relationships between these categories then allows ethnographers to build theoretical propositions, a form of analysis known as **grounded theory**.

Advantages and Disadvantages

ADVANTAGES

1. Ethnographies offer a means of studying groups that are often overlooked by other methods (J. Katz 1997). These include deviant groups such as fight clubs (Jackson-Jacobs 2004) and exceptional groups such as elite college athletes (Adler and Adler 1991). Ethnographic methods excel at telling stories that otherwise might not have been told.

2. Ethnographies can challenge our taken-for-granted notions about groups we thought we knew. For instance, from Edin and Kefalas's work on single mothers, we learn that these women aren't the irresponsible, unstable individuals we may have thought they were. They desire and seek out the best for their children, just like mothers in other groups and communities.

3. The detailed nature of ethnographies can help to reshape the stereotypes we hold about others and on which social policy is often based. A study like Edin and Kefalas's can have policy consequences because it sheds light on the motivations and needs of single urban mothers, as well as giving us a clear picture of the resources available to them.

4. Much of the pioneering methodological innovation of the last half-century has come from within the field of ethnography, especially on the issue of reflexivity and researcher roles in the field.

DISADVANTAGES

1. Ethnographies suffer from a lack of **replicability**, the ability of another researcher to repeat or replicate the study. Repeating a study in order to test the validity of its results is an important element of the scientific method, but because of the unique combinations of people, timing, setting, and researcher role, no one can ever undertake the same study twice.

GROUNDED THEORY an inductive method of generating theory from data by creating categories in which to place data and then looking for relationships among categories

REPLICABILITY research that can be repeated, and thus verified, by other researchers later

2. A major critique has to do with ethnographies' degree of **representativeness**, whether they apply to anything larger than themselves. What is the value of studying relatively small groups of people if one cannot then say that these groups represent parts of the society at large? Though Edin and Kefalas's work focused on East Camden, their conclusions are supposed to apply to single mothers in other cities as well.

3. Ethnographers must also be wary of **bias**. There is always a possibility that prejudice or favor can slip into the research process. Not all researchers are transparent about their own agendas. We need to keep in mind how a researcher's own values and opinions might affect his research and analysis.

DATA WORKSHOP
Analyzing Everyday Life

Observing and Describing Verbal and Nonverbal Communication

While producing fieldnotes may sound fairly easy (don't we all know how to describe the things we've observed?), it turns out to be one of the most grueling forms of data collection in the social sciences. Why? Because thick description is a much more demanding accomplishment than the description you're used to providing in everyday conversation. It requires a rigorous consciousness of what is going on around you while it is happening and a strenuous effort to recall those goings-on after leaving the field and returning to your computer.

This Data Workshop is a practicum in thick description. To make things a little easier for you, we have separated the verbal and the visual so that you can concentrate on one kind of description at a time. But in your future ethnographic work, you'll be writing fieldnotes that describe both verbal and nonverbal behavior at once.

REPRESENTATIVENESS the degree to which a particular studied group is similar to, or represents, any part of the larger society

BIAS an opinion held by the researcher that might affect the research or analysis

INTERVIEW face-to-face, information-seeking conversations, sometimes defined as a conversation with a purpose

RESPONDENT someone from whom a researcher solicits information

* *Observation*: First, for ten to fifteen minutes, listen to (eavesdrop on) a conversation whose participants you can't see. They might be sitting behind you on a bus or in a restaurant—you're close enough to hear them but positioned so that you can't see them. Then, for ten to fifteen minutes, observe a conversation you can't hear—one taking place, for example, on the other side of the campus quad. Even though you can't hear what's being said, you can see the interaction as it takes place.

* *Written Description*: Write an extremely detailed description of each conversation. Describe the participants and the setting, and include your ideas about what you think is going on and what you think you know about the participants. Try to describe everything you heard or saw to support any conclusions you draw. For each ten- to fifteen-minute observation period, your written description should be two to three typed pages.

There are two options for completing this Data Workshop.

Option 1 (informal): Choose a partner from your class and exchange your written descriptions with your partner. As you read through your partner's descriptions, mark with a star (*) the passages where you can see and hear clearly the things your partner describes. Circle the passages that contain evaluative words (like "angry" or "sweet") or summaries of action or conversation rather than detailed description (like "They argued about who would pay the bill"). And place a question mark next to the passages where you are left feeling like you would like to know more. Your partner will do this with your description as well, and you can discuss your responses to each other's work. Finally, as a class, use your discussions to develop a group consensus about what constitutes good descriptive detail. This is the kind of detail ethnographers strive to produce in their fieldnotes every day.

Option 2 (formal): Turn in your written descriptions to your instructor for individual feedback.

Interviews

Sociologists use **interviews**—face-to-face, information-seeking conversations—to gather information directly from research subjects, or **respondents**. When researchers conduct interviews, they try to do so systematically and with a more scientific approach than is typically seen in some familiar kinds of journalism (more casual TV or news interviews).

Sometimes, interviews are the only method used in a research project, but sociologists may also combine interviews with other methods, such as participant observation or analysis of existing sources. Closely related to interviews are surveys, which we will consider in the next section. Interviews, however, are always conducted by the researcher, whereas surveys may be taken independently by the respondent.

When using interviews to collect data about a particular question or project, sociologists must identify a **target population**, the larger group they wish to generalize about, and then select a **sample**, or smaller group who are representative of the larger group. The number of possible respondents depends on the type of study, the nature of the questions, and the amount of time and staff available. In most research studies, interviews can be administered to a limited number of people, so the scope of such projects is usually smaller than for other methods, such as surveys. The researcher must get **informed consent** from those participating; in other words, respondents must know what they are getting into and explicitly agree to participate. This is particularly important because most interviews are recorded, audio or video.

Arlie Hochschild (Hochschild and Machung 1989) used interviews to conduct her landmark study on parents in two-career families, *The Second Shift*. In this book, Hochschild looks at how couples handle the pressures of working at a job and then coming home to what she calls "the second shift" — doing housework and taking care of children. Hochschild, who was herself in a two-career family, wanted to find out how couples were dealing with changing family roles in

light of the fact that more women had entered the workforce. Were women able to juggle all their responsibilities, and to what extent were men helping their wives in running the household? Hochschild and her assistants interviewed fifty couples in two-career marriages (many were interviewed more than once) and forty-five other people who were also a part of the respondents' social arrangements, such as babysitters, day-care providers, and teachers.

When conducting an interview, how do you know what to ask? Composing good questions is one of the most difficult parts of interviewing. Most interviewers use many different questions, covering a range of issues related to the project. Questions may be closed- or open-ended. A **closed-ended question** imposes a limit on the possible response: for example, "Are you for or against couples living together before they are married?" An **open-ended question**, on the other hand, allows for a wide variety of responses: "What do you think about couples living together before they are married?"

Researchers must be careful to avoid biased or **leading questions**, those that predispose a respondent to answer in a certain way. Overly complex questions are a problem, as are **double-barreled questions**, those that involve too many different issues at one time. It is also important to be aware of any ambiguous or emotional language that might confuse or spark an emotional reaction on the part of the respondent. Asking a single parent how difficult her life is will elicit data about the difficulties, but not about the joys, of parenthood. More neutral language ("Tell me about the pluses and minuses of single parenthood") is preferable.

The Second Shift In her groundbreaking book, Arlie Hochschild interviewed working women and their partners to learn about the time-binds that they face as they balance work, family, and running a household.

TARGET POPULATION the entire group about which a researcher would like to be able to generalize

SAMPLE the part of the population that will actually be studied

INFORMED CONSENT a safeguard through which the researcher makes sure that respondents are freely participating and understand the nature of the research

CLOSED-ENDED QUESTION a question asked of a respondent that imposes a limit on the possible responses

OPEN-ENDED QUESTION a question asked of a respondent that allows the answer to take whatever form the respondent chooses

LEADING QUESTIONS questions that predispose a respondent to answer in a certain way

DOUBLE-BARRELED QUESTIONS questions that attempt to get at multiple issues at once, and so tend to receive incomplete or confusing answers

Analyzing the Data

Once the interviews have been conducted, they are usually transcribed so that researchers can analyze them in textual form; they can sort through the material looking for patterns of similarities and differences among the answers. Some researchers may use computer programs designed to help analyze such data; others do it "by hand." For her analysis,

IN THE FUTURE

Action Research

In addition to the other methods discussed in this chapter, **action research** is a growing trend in social science methodology. Action research combines social science research with community problem-solving and social change, in a way that calls into question some of sociology's closely held beliefs about ethics, bias, and the role of the researcher.

While action research is not exactly new, it has been gaining popularity recently, across the social sciences as well as in practice-oriented disciplines such as nursing, public health, education, urban planning, and management. Pioneers in action research tended to come from the areas of inequality studies such as feminist research, critical race studies, and poverty and community development research, and there is a clear historical link to the ethnographers of the Chicago School, with their community and reform-oriented approaches (Emerson 2002; Marullo 1999).

Action researchers are more likely than traditional researchers to be invested in social change and community improvement goals. They see their research skills as problem-solving tools, and they view those whom others might call "research subjects" as active, collaborative, equal participants in the project. In other words, action researchers do research *with* people, not *on* people, and see their work as part of a "scholarship of engagement" (Rajaram 2007, p. 139), rather than one of erudite distance.

An award-winning example of action research is the work of Chicago's Community Organizing and Family Issues group (COFI). Their project, "Why Isn't Johnny in Preschool?", sought the answer to this question, in particular among families in low-income, racially diverse neighborhoods, where kids are less likely to be enrolled in early childhood education programs. They sent community members, trained in sociological interview methods, out into their Chicago neighborhoods to talk with more than 5,000 other parents about the barriers to preschool enrollment. Their findings included family concerns about cost, transportation, and confusing paperwork and bureaucracies, among other obstacles. These findings were used to design outreach and public awareness campaigns that promoted the importance of preschool attendance and provided information packets that helped families find solutions to some of the problems identified in the research. Preschool attendance increased in the targeted neighborhoods as a result (COFI 2009), and COFI received the Leo P. Chall Award for its work, "successfully link[ing] research with social action, thereby strengthening community

ACTION RESEARCH the presentation of detailed data on interactions and meaning within a cultural context, from the perspective of its members

---

Hochschild categorized the types of household chores done by men and women and quantified the amount of time spent daily and weekly on those chores. She then categorized couples as "traditional," "transitional," or "egalitarian," depending on how their household labor was divided.

Advantages and Disadvantages

ADVANTAGES

1. Interviews allow respondents to speak in their own words; they can reveal their own thoughts, feelings, and beliefs, internal states that would not necessarily be accessible by any other means. In so many other instances, it is the researcher who tells the story. A book like *The Second Shift*, which features direct quotations from interview transcripts, provides the reader with an authentic and intimate portrait of the lives of married couples. Hochschild was able to get at the different subjective experiences of the women and men in her study and to see how each of them perceived the reality of his or her situation.

2. Interviews may help the researcher dispel certain preconceptions and discover issues that might have otherwise been overlooked. For example, before Hochschild began her project, many other studies had already been conducted on families with two work-

organizations and influencing public policy" (Sociological Initiatives Foundation 2010).

As citizens become research collaborators and sociologists become research activists, there will inevitably be some tension between research goals and practical

Head Start A teacher works with the children of migrant and seasonal workers in Illinois.

goals. Addressing real-world problems means that methodologies must be tailored to the constraints of the actual situation, rather than adhering to the ideal-type models required by the discipline. All participants must be allowed to be part of the decision-making process, and all must be provided equal access to information, data, and findings (which even the most open-minded traditional researchers may balk at). Ethical considerations differ from those of traditional research, as well: action research is designed to bring about change and is "aligned with values" (Riel 2010), so claims of objectivity are out of the question.

These differences make action research controversial among more traditional social scientists but are gaining popularity among students. Action research provides both graduate and undergraduate students with the opportunity to be of service in their communities, while also fulfilling academic requirements, and many students prefer this active approach to social change over a research project that takes place entirely in a library or lab. More high schools and colleges are requiring community service projects as part of their graduation requirements, and even more will likely do so in the near future. Action research itself is fundamentally future oriented due to its focus on social change and community improvement, and it provides a way to make a positive impact while also advancing social science research. Does it get any better than that?

ing parents, but few seemed to examine in depth the real-life dilemma of the two-career family that Hochschild herself was experiencing.

DISADVANTAGES

1. Respondents are not always forthcoming or truthful. They may be selective about what they say in order to present themselves in the most favorable light. Sometimes they are difficult to talk to, and at other times they may try too hard to be helpful. Although an adept interviewer will be able to encourage meaningful responses, she can never take at face value what any respondent might say. To counteract this problem, Hochschild observed a

few of the families she had interviewed. She saw that what these couples said about themselves in interviews was sometimes at odds with how they acted at home.

2. Another problem is representativeness: whether the conclusions of interview research can be applied to larger groups. Because face-to-face interviewing is time consuming, interviews are rarely used with large numbers of people. Can findings from a small sample be generalized to a larger population? In regard to Hochschild's research, can we say that interviews with fifty couples, although carefully selected by the researcher, give a true picture of the lives of all two-career families? Hochschild answered this

question by comparing selected information about her couples with data from a huge national survey.

Surveys

How many times have you filled out a survey? Probably more times than you realize. If you responded to the last U.S. government census, if you have ever been solicited by a polling agency to give your opinion about a public issue, or if you have ever been asked to evaluate your college classes and instructors at the end of a semester, you were part of somebody's survey research.

Surveys are questionnaires that are administered to a sample of respondents selected from a target population. One of the earliest sociologists to use informal surveys was Karl Marx. In the 1880s, Marx sent questionnaires to more than 25,000 French workers in an effort to determine the extent to which they were exploited by employers. Although we don't know how many surveys were returned to him or what the individual responses were, the project clearly influenced his writing, which focused heavily on workers' rights.

Today, many universities have research centers devoted to conducting survey research. One such center is the National Marriage Project at Rutgers University in New Jersey, where sociologists have been engaged in ongoing studies on the health of marriage and family in America, and issuing a series of reports on what they call "The State of Our Unions" over the past several years. Researchers have surveyed young adults in their twenties about a range of topics including their attitudes toward dating, cohabitation, marriage, and parenthood.

Survey research tends to be macro and quantitative in nature: it looks at large-scale social patterns and employs statistics and other mathematical means of analysis. Social scientists who use surveys must follow specific procedures in order to produce valid results. They

need a good questionnaire and wise sample selection. Most surveys are composed of closed-ended questions, or those for which all possible answers are provided. Answers may be as simple as a "yes" or "no," or more complex. A common type of questionnaire is based on the **Likert scale**, a format in which respondents can choose along a continuum — from "strongly agree" to "strongly disagree," for example. Some questionnaires also offer such options as "don't know" or "doesn't apply." Surveys may include open-ended questions, or those to which the respondents provide their own answers. These are often formatted as write-in questions and can provide researchers with more qualitative data.

Both questions and possible (given) answers on a survey must be written in such a way as to avoid confusion or ambiguity. While this is also true for interviews, it is even more important for surveys because the researcher is not generally present to clarify any misunderstandings. Common pitfalls are leading questions; **negative questions**, which ask respondents what they don't think instead of what they do; and double-barreled questions. Bias can also be a problem if questions or answers are worded in a slanted fashion.

The format of a questionnaire is also important. Something as simple as the order in which the different items are presented can influence responses. Mentioning an issue like divorce or infidelity in earlier questions can mean that respondents are thinking about it when they answer later questions, and as a result, their answers might be different than they would otherwise have been. Questionnaires should be clear and easy to follow. Once a questionnaire is constructed, it is a good idea to have a small group pretest it to help eliminate flaws and make sure it is clear and comprehensible.

Another important element in survey research is sampling techniques. As with interviews, the researcher must identify the specific population she wishes to study: for example, "all married couples with children living at home" or "all young adults between the ages of twenty and twenty-nine." By using correct sampling techniques, researchers can survey a smaller number of respondents and then make accurate inferences about the larger population. For example, in the National Marriage Project study, researchers surveyed a statistically **representative sample** of 1,003 young adults. In quantitative research, social scientists use **probability sampling**, in which the sample group mathematically represents the larger population. Researchers might generate a **simple random sample**, where each member of the larger target population has an equal chance of being included in the sample. Or they might use more sophisticated manipulating or **weighting** techniques, in which the proportion of certain variables such as race, class, gender, or age in the sample group is more closely representative of the larger population.

SURVEY a research method based on questionnaires that are administered to a sample of respondents selected from a target population

LIKERT SCALE a way of organizing categories on a survey question so that the respondent can choose an answer along a continuum

NEGATIVE QUESTIONS survey questions that ask respondents what they don't think instead of what they do

REPRESENTATIVE SAMPLE a sample taken so that findings from members of the sample group can be generalized to the whole population

PROBABILITY SAMPLING any sampling scheme in which any given unit has the same probability of being chosen

SIMPLE RANDOM SAMPLE a particular type of probability sample in which every member of the population has an equal chance of being selected

WEIGHTING techniques for manipulating the sampling procedure so that the sample more closely resembles the larger population

An increasing number of survey researchers have turned to utilizing the internet rather than conducting research person-to-person or by mail (Best and Krueger 2004; Sue and Ritter 2007). The internet has opened up new possibilities for reaching respondents as more and more people have online access. While online surveys promise a certain amount of ease and cost effectiveness, they also present researchers with significant challenges, especially in terms of scientific sampling.

Analyzing the Data

In order for a survey to be considered valid, there must be a sufficiently high **response rate**. It is sometimes difficult to get enough individuals to participate in a survey. Even if only half of a sample group actually returned the completed surveys, that would be considered a very good result. General claims can be made about a larger population from a lower response rate of 20 or 30 percent. Once the surveys are returned, the researchers begin the process of tabulating and analyzing the data. Responses are usually coded or turned into numerical figures so that they can be more easily analyzed on a computer. Researchers often want to understand the relationship between certain variables; for instance, what is the effect of "infidelity" on "divorce"? There are many computer programs, such as SPSS (Statistical Package for the Social Sciences), that can help researchers perform complicated calculations and reach conclusions about relationships. This is where advanced statistical skills become an important part of social analysis.

Advantages and Disadvantages

ADVANTAGES

1. Survey research is one of the best methods to use for gathering original data on a population that is too large to study by other means, such as by direct observation or interviewing. Surveys can be widely distributed, reaching a large number of people. Researchers can then generalize their findings to an even larger population.

2. Survey research is also relatively quick and economical and can provide a vast amount of data. Online surveys now promise a way to gain access to even greater numbers of people at even lower cost.

3. In general, survey research is comparatively strong on **reliability**. This means that we can be sure that the same kind of data is collected each time the same question is asked.

4. In survey research, there is less concern about interviewer or observer bias entering into the research process. Respondents may feel more comfortable giving candid answers to sensitive questions because they answer the questions in private and are usually assured of the **confidentiality** of their responses.

DISADVANTAGES

1. Survey research generally lacks qualitative data that might better capture the social reality the researcher wishes to examine. Because most survey questions don't allow the respondent to qualify his answer, they don't allow for a full range of expression and may not accurately reflect the true meaning of the respondent's thoughts. For example, asking a respondent to choose one reason from a list of reasons for divorce might not provide a full explanation for the failure of that person's marriage. The reasons may have been both financial and emotional, but the survey may not provide the respondent with the ability to convey this. Adding write-in questions is one way to minimize this disadvantage.

2. In general, since not all respondents are honest in self-reports, survey research is comparatively weak on **validity**. For example, a respondent may be ashamed about his divorce and may not want to reveal the true reasons behind it to a stranger on a questionnaire.

3. Often, there are problems with the sampling process, especially when respondents self-select to participate, that make generalizability more difficult. Gathering data online only exacerbates this problem. If a survey seeking to know the true incidence of domestic violence in the population is administered only to the members of a domestic violence support group, then the incidence of domestic violence will be 100 percent — misrepresenting the incidence in the larger population.

4. It's possible that survey research will be used to support a point of view rather than for pure scientific discovery; for example, a manufacturer of SUVs may report that 90 percent of all American families wish they had a larger car. We will consider this limitation later, in the section on nonacademic uses of research methods.

RESPONSE RATE the number or percentage of surveys completed by respondents and returned to researchers

RELIABILITY the consistency of a question or measurement tool; the degree to which the same questions will produce similar answers

CONFIDENTIALITY the assurance that no one other than the researcher will know the identity of a respondent

VALIDITY the accuracy of a question or measurement tool; the degree to which a researcher is measuring what he thinks he is measuring

DATA WORKSHOP

Analyzing Mass Media and Popular Culture

Comparative Media Usage Patterns

Recent studies have shown that the average American spends around eight and a half hours a day using some type of media—computers, TV, radio, and so on (Council for Research Excellence 2009). That's more than half of our waking hours each day. With the media playing such an increasingly important role in society, researchers continue to study their impact across a wide range of issues. In this Data Workshop, you will be conducting your own research about media usage in everyday life. Your task is twofold. First, you will get some practice constructing and administering surveys as a method of data collection. Second, you will do a preliminary analysis of your data and discover something for yourself about the patterns of media usage among those who participate in your **pilot study**.

There is much more to the picture than just the number of hours Americans spend using media; we want to understand more about the role the media play in these people's lives. What do you consider an interesting or important aspect of media usage to study? Here are some suggestions.

What kind of media are people using—books, television, radio, iPods, CDs, DVDs, computers, video games, smart phones, or other handheld devices? Do different groups prefer different types of media? How many different kinds of devices do people have access to or own? How much do they multitask, using more than one device at a time? How much money do individuals spend on media-related activities? How does age, education, gender, ethnicity, or religion influence media usage? What else do people do while using media—do they work, eat, clean, drive, exercise, study, or even sleep?

Now come up with more of your own questions!

Because there are a variety of ways of doing such a project, you should choose just how you would like to customize your research. Since this is only a preliminary effort at survey research, the project will have to be somewhat limited. Nonetheless, try to follow the necessary steps in the research process in order to be as scientific as possible.

1. Decide what aspects of media use you want to study.

2. Select a sample of the target population you wish to study (teenagers, minority groups, people with a college degree, and so on).

3. Write and format your survey questionnaire.

4. Administer the questionnaire to the individuals in your sample.

5. Analyze the data collected in the survey.

6. Present your findings.

There are two options for completing this Data Workshop.

Option 1 (informal): Working in small groups of three to four students, begin designing a survey project by discussing steps 1 and 2 above. Members of the group can then collaborate on step 3. If time allows, they can play the role of a pilot group and test the questionnaire by taking the survey themselves as in step 4. Finally, the group should discuss what needs to be changed or what else needs to be accomplished to complete an actual survey.

Option 2 (formal): Design your own survey research project, completing all of the above steps. Choose at least five to eight people to be included in your sample. After administering the questionnaire, write a three- to four-page essay discussing the research process and your preliminary findings.

Existing Sources

Nearly all sociologists use **existing sources** when they approach a particular research question. For instance, social demography uses statistical data to study the size, composition, growth, and distribution of human populations (J. Fox 1997). The original data used in such research are often collected by social scientists other than the researcher and by government agencies, such as census bureaus and public health departments. In fact, the U.S. Census Bureau makes some of its data available to the public on its web site, census.gov, to help you analyze family size, income levels, or other relevant questions.

Other sociologists use what are called **comparative and historical methods**, which seek to understand relationships between elements of society in various regions and time periods. These sociologists often analyze cultural artifacts, such as literature, paintings, newspapers, and photography

PILOT STUDY a small study carried out to test the feasibility of a larger one

EXISTING SOURCES materials that have been produced for some other reason, but that can be used as data for social research

COMPARATIVE AND HISTORICAL METHODS methods that use existing sources to study relationships among elements of society in various regions and time periods

(Bauer and Gaskell 2000). As an example, Alice Miller consulted child-rearing manuals and family records for her book *For Your Own Good: Hidden Cruelty in Child-Rearing and the Roots of Violence* (1990) in order to investigate the childhood experiences of several notorious German historical figures, including Adolf Hitler. Miller found that Hitler was the product of a fairly traditional child-rearing, with traditional gender-role socialization and disciplinary practices. Her findings force us to acknowledge that seemingly "normal" child-rearing practices have the potential to create someone like Hitler — that it is not always the exceptions but the rules themselves that can make a monster. Miller's use of existing records allowed her to gain insight into not only the development of an individual personality but also the structure of an entire society and the role that society played in creating one of the twentieth century's most malevolent individuals.

Consulting existing data can be somewhat less involved than collecting original data (and it can be especially helpful to students, who usually don't have the resources to collect original data themselves). Researchers can generally find survey, census, or other historical information on the internet or obtain it from the social scientists or government bureaus that conducted the original studies. New technology is also making more material more readily available to researchers. We now have unprecedented access to a variety of media in digital form (books, magazines, articles, e-mail, web pages, music, photos, TV programs, videos, and films) that are regularly retrievable through the internet. While all of these materials may have been created for another purpose, they can constitute valuable data to be used in social research.

Analyzing the Data

After obtaining their data, researchers must decide which analytic tools will be best suited to their research questions. For instance, a researcher might want to look at the relationship between a woman's age and her likely marital status. In 2006, *Newsweek* magazine revisited a controversial article written twenty years earlier, "The Marriage Crunch," that reported that college-educated women over the age of forty had less than a 3 percent chance of getting married. After reviewing new census data, *Newsweek* had to revise that number to more than 40 percent (McGinn 2006).

Content analysis is a method in which researchers count the number of times specific variables — such as particular words — appear in a text, image, or media message. They then analyze the variables and relationships between them. For example, content analysis shows that the roles women play on television are of lower status than men's, with women more likely to be portrayed as housewives, mothers, secretaries, and nurses, while men are doctors, judges, celebrities, and athletes in addition to being husbands and fathers (Kolbe and Langefeld 1993). If we look at the top-rated network sitcoms of 2012 (*The Big Bang Theory, Modern Family, Two Broke Girls, Two and a Half Men,* and *How I Met Your Mother*) we see that the majority of men were highly accomplished professionals while the women were unemployed or struggling; this contradicts reality in that the U.S. rate of unemployment for men at 9.3 percent is actually higher than for women at 8.3 percent (Haimoff 2012).

> **CONTENT ANALYSIS** a method in which researchers identify and study specific variables — such as words — in a text, image, or media message

Alice Miller's *For Your Own Good* By analyzing historical sources and child-rearing guides, Miller argued that some of the methods we use to raise children, which we accept as normal and ordinary, can create seriously aberrant individuals as well as regular folks.

Advantages and Disadvantages

ADVANTAGES

1. Researchers are able to work with information they could not possibly obtain for themselves. Census bureaus, for example, collect information about entire national populations (family size, income, occupational and residential patterns), something an individual researcher has neither the time nor funds to do. In addition, existing data analysis can be a convenient way for sociologists to pool their resources; one researcher can take data collected

EXPERIMENTS formal tests of specific variables and effects, performed in a controlled setting where all aspects of the situation can be controlled

CONTROL in an experiment, the process of regulating all factors except for the independent variable

EXPERIMENTAL GROUP the part of a test group that receives the experimental treatment

CONTROL GROUP the part of a test group that is allowed to continue without intervention so that it can be compared with the experimental group

INDEPENDENT VARIABLE factor that is predicted to cause change

DEPENDENT VARIABLE factor that is changed (or not) by the independent variable

by another for his own project, increasing what we can learn from those data.

2. Using sources such as newspapers, political speeches, and cultural artifacts, sociologists are able to learn about many social worlds, in different time periods, that they would never be able to enter themselves; for example, preserved letters and diaries from the early 1800s have allowed researchers to analyze the experiences of wives and mothers on the American frontier (Peavy and Smith 1998).

3. Researchers can use the same data to replicate projects that have been conducted before, which is a good way to test findings for reliability or to see changes across time.

DISADVANTAGES

1. Researchers drawing on existing sources often seek to answer questions that the original authors did not have in mind. If you were interested in the sex lives of those frontier women in the early 1800s, for example, you would be unlikely to find any clear references in their letters or diaries.

2. Similarly, content analysis, although it can describe the messages inherent in the media, does not illuminate how such messages are interpreted. So we can say that women's roles on television have lower status than men's, but additional research would be required to identify the effects of these images on viewers.

Experimental Methods

Unlike ethnographies, interviews, surveys, or existing sources, **experiments** actually closely resemble the scientific method with which we began this chapter. You might associate experiments with laboratory scientists in white coats, but experimental research methods are also used by social scientists, especially those who are interested in such issues as group power dynamics, racial discrimination, and gender socialization. Experiments take place not only in laboratories but also in corporate boardrooms and even on street corners.

When sociologists conduct experiments, they start with two basic goals. First, they strive to develop precise tools with which to observe, record, and measure their data. Second, they attempt to **control** for all possible variables except the one under investigation: they regulate everything except the variable they're interested in so that they can draw clearer conclusions about what caused that variable to change (if it did).

For instance, a researcher interested in divorce may want to investigate whether marriage counseling actually helps couples stay together. He would recruit couples for the experiment and divide them into two groups, making sure that members of each group were similar in terms of age, income, education, and religion as well as length of time married. One group, the **experimental group**, would receive marriage counseling, while the other, the **control group**, would not. The **independent variable** (factor that is predicted to cause change) is marriage counseling. The **dependent variable** (factor that is changed by the independent variable) is the chance of staying married or getting divorced. In such an experiment, the researcher could compare the two groups and then make conclusions about whether marriage counseling leads to more couples staying together, or leads to more couples getting divorced, or has no impact at all.

Another area in which sociological experiments have been conducted is gender-role socialization in families. Research has shown that a child's earliest exposure to what it means to be a boy or girl comes from parents and other caregivers. Boy and girl infants are treated differently by adults—from the way they're dressed to the toys they're given to play with—and are expected to act differently (Thorne 1993). In one experiment, adult subjects were asked to play with a small baby, who was dressed in either pink or blue. The subjects assumed the gender of the infant by the color of its clothes and acted accordingly. When they thought it was a boy (blue), they handled the baby less gently and talked in a louder voice, saying things like, "Aren't you a big, strong boy?" When they thought it was a girl (pink), they held the baby closer to themselves and spoke more softly: "What a sweet little girl!" In both cases, the baby was the same; only the color of the clothing was changed. From this experiment, we can see how gender influences the way that we perceive and interact with others from a very early age.

Sociologists sometimes also use quasi-experimental methods when they study ethnic and gender discrimination in housing, employment, or policing (McIntyre et al. 1980; Brief et al. 1995; Charles 2001). In such studies, individuals who were similar in all respects except for ethnicity or gender were asked to interview for the same jobs, apply for the same mortgage loans, or engage in some other activity. As in the pink-and-blue baby experiment, people who had exactly the same qualifications were treated differently based on their race and gender, with whites and men given better jobs

IN RELATIONSHIPS

Social Networking Sites as Sources of Data

While sociologists interested in studying interpersonal relationships use a wide variety of archival materials, the internet has created whole new ways of conducting research. Letters, journals, and diaries have always been a rich source of data, but ones that have usually been unavailable until many years after they were produced. On the other hand, social networking sites like Twitter, YouTube, or Facebook create a treasure-trove of data that can be accessed unobtrusively in real time. Given that Facebook is one of the most-visited sites on the internet, and is full of sociologically fascinating phenomena, it's not surprising to find that numerous researchers are using Facebook as a source of data to study such issues as relationships, identity, self-esteem, and popularity.

One of the earliest and most ambitious projects using social networking sites was conducted by Nicholas Christakis and Jason Kaufman of Harvard and Andreas Wimmer of UCLA. Their data consisted of all the publicly available Facebook profiles of an entire class at an anonymous East Coast university from their freshman to senior years. The researchers were interested in examining the relationship "between patterns of social affiliation and aesthetic proclivities" (Kaufman 2008). In other words, they were looking at the relationship between the number and type of friends someone has and the kind of books, music, and movies they like.

The researchers found that online social networks looked a lot like social networks established through traditional, real-life, face-to-face contact. People's networks on Facebook tended to exhibit "homophily"; that is, people tend to be Facebook friends with other people like them, especially in terms of race and gender. In some ways, this isn't surprising. Increasingly, an individual's online profile is an extension of her everyday life. What might be more surprising, however, is the way in which social networks can spread influence. Researchers now have the data to show how such seemingly individual things as a person's taste in clothes, their level of happiness, and even their body size are influenced by social networks (Christakis and Fowler 2009). For researchers, Facebook is

Mining social media As more people of varying ages, races, and backgrounds use social media, researchers can analyze these networks as a major part of real life.

especially exciting because it offers a data set rich enough to test ideas that up to now have only been theorized about. As Harvard sociologist Christakis points out, concepts about how social networks function were "first described by Simmel 100 years ago.... He just theorize[d] about it 100 years ago, but he didn't have the data. Now we can engage that data" (Rosenbloom 2007).

But social networking web sites do more than just provide researchers with new data to answer old questions; they also connect friends and family in new ways. Young people use the "relationship status" feature of Facebook as the new standard for evaluating dating; they aren't really a couple until they change their status to "in a relationship." And Facebook has also changed the ways that families interact. The extended family, which is often now separated geographically, is more easily reunited online. Facebook was originally created for college students, but it now attracts their parents, and even their grandparents, all logging on to stay in touch. And be aware that with our interconnected web of relationships, if your friend's friend's friend on Facebook has quit smoking or gained weight, it can impact the likelihood that you will do the same.

What Does It Mean to Be a Boy or a Girl? In Barrie Thorne's experiment, she asked adults to play with babies dressed in either blue or pink. Thorne found that people treated the baby differently depending on whether they thought it was a girl or a boy.

or mortgage rates, and women and minorities given inferior jobs or rates, or none at all. Through such studies, researchers are able to observe behaviors that may indicate discrimination or unequal treatment.

Analyzing the Data

On the whole, data analysis for experimental sociology tends to be quantitative rather than qualitative because the main goal of an experiment is to isolate a variable and explore the degree to which this variable affects a particular social situation (H. Smith 1990). The quantitative techniques for analyzing data range from straightforward statistical analyses to complex mathematical modeling.

Advantages and Disadvantages

ADVANTAGES

1. Experiments give sociologists a way to manipulate and control the social environment they seek to understand. They can be designed so that there is a minimal amount of outside interference. Researchers can also select participants who have exactly the characteristics they want to explore, such as the babies and adults in the gender-socialization experiment.

2. Experimental methods are especially appropriate for researchers who are developing theories about the way the social world operates: a researcher can construct a model of the social situation she is interested in and watch as it unfolds before her, without any of the unpredictable intrusions of the real world. For instance, if she wants to study what makes bystanders want to intervene, this might be easier to measure in a laboratory setting than among strangers on a busy public street.

3. Much like physics experiments, highly controlled sociological experiments can theoretically be repeated — they have replicability — so that findings can be tested more than once. An experiment such as the pink-and-blue baby study could easily be performed again and again to gauge historical and cultural changes in gender socialization. Ethnographies and surveys, on the other hand, are almost impossible to repeat in any reliable way.

DISADVANTAGES

1. Experiments are applicable only to certain types of research that can be constructed and measured in a controlled setting. Laboratories are by design artificial environments. We take a leap in claiming that the same results found in the lab will also occur in the real world.

2. Achieving distance from the messy realities of the social world is also the major weakness with sociological experiments. Although experiments can be useful for the development of theory and for explaining the impact of isolated variables, they are generally not very effective for describing more complex processes and interactions. By definition, experiments seek to eliminate elements that will have an unforeseen effect, and that's just not the way the real world works.

Issues in Sociological Research

As sociologists, we don't conduct our research in a cultural vacuum. In our professional as well as personal lives, all our actions have consequences, and we must be aware of how the things we do affect others. For this reason, any introduction to sociological methods is incomplete without a discussion of three topics: the nonacademic uses of sociological research; values, objectivity, and reactivity in the research process; and the importance of ethics in conducting social research.

Nonacademic Uses of Research Methods

The research methods discussed in this chapter are frequently applied outside the field of sociology. The U.S. Census Bureau, for example, has been taking a survey of the total population once every ten years since 1790. The census attempts to reach every person residing in the country and makes reports available on a wide range of social, demographic, and economic features. Many government decisions, from where to build a new school or hospital to where to install a new stoplight, are made using demographic data from the census and other major surveys.

Sociological research methods are also used by private organizations, such as political campaign offices and news agencies. You are probably familiar with polls (another form of survey research) conducted by organizations like Gallup, Zogby, and Roper. And you have certainly seen the results of election polls, which indicate the candidates or issues voters are likely to support. Polls, however, do not just reflect public opinion; they can also be used to shape it. Not all of them are conducted under strict scientific protocols. Whenever you hear poll results, try to learn who commissioned the poll and determine whether they are promoting (or opposing) any particular agenda.

Businesses and corporations have turned to sociological research in order to better understand the human dynamics within their companies. Some ethnographers, for instance, have studied organizational culture and reported their findings to executives. Edgar Schein (1997, 2010) is often referred to as an industrial ethnographer because he conducts fieldwork in business settings in order to help management identify and deal with dilemmas in the workplace, such as how to motivate workers. Many of the experimental "games" developed by sociological researchers can be put to use in the business world to build teams, train employees, or even conduct job interviews. During a corporate retreat, for example, employees might be asked to participate in an obstacle or ropes course, in which they have to work together in order to succeed. By observing the strategies participants use, an employer might learn how task-oriented networks are formed, how leaders are chosen, or how cooperation emerges under pressure. Similarly, experimental games that require subjects to budget imaginary money or communicate an idea in a round of charades may offer insight into how social groups operate or may identify the most effective communicators from a pool of applicants. These experiments clearly benefit the corporation; do they help workers as well?

Market research is perhaps the most common of all non-academic uses of sociological methods. In order to be successful, most companies will engage in some sort of study of the marketplace, either through their own internal sales and marketing departments or by hiring an outside consultant. The efforts of all these companies to understand the buying public have created a multibillion-dollar marketing and advertising industry. If you've ever filled out a product warranty card after making a purchase, clicked "yes" on a pop-up dialog box from a web site, or cast a vote for your favorite contestants on *Dancing with the Stars*, then someone has gathered data about your tastes and habits. It is important to note, however, that not all market studies, in fact probably very few, meet the rigorous standards that are otherwise applied to "scientific" research. Remember, too, that the bottom line for any company that uses market research is the desire to sell you their products or services. Just how well do these marketers know you already?

Values, Objectivity, and Reactivity

It's important to recognize that scientific research is done by human beings, not robots. Humans have flaws, prejudices, and blind spots, and all of these things can affect the way we conduct research.

VALUES Like biological or physical scientists, most sociologists believe that they should not allow their personal beliefs to influence their research. The classic sociological statement on neutrality comes from Max Weber (1925/1946), who, in his essay "Science as a Vocation," coined the phrase **value-free sociology** to convey the idea that in doing research sociologists need to separate facts from their own individual values. Although most sociologists have agreed with this ideal, some have challenged the notion of value-free sociology. For instance, some Marxist researchers believe it is appropriate to combine social research and social action or praxis. For them, the study of society is intimately linked to a commitment to actively solve social problems. On the other hand, some symbolic interactionists, like David Matza (1969), believe that the very intention of changing the world prohibits a researcher from understanding that world. The question of whether sociologists should engage only in **basic research**, which is justified as the search for knowledge for its own sake, or rather engage in **applied research**, which

VALUE-FREE SOCIOLOGY an ideal whereby researchers identify facts without allowing their own personal beliefs or biases to interfere

BASIC RESEARCH the search for knowledge without any agenda or desire to use that knowledge to effect change

APPLIED RESEARCH research designed to gather knowledge that can be used to create some sort of change

ON THE JOB

Commercial Ethnography

Recently, advertisers have become interested in the complex relationships between people and products and are looking to ethnographic methods to help them understand these relationships. Companies are hiring commercial ethnographers to learn how ordinary citizens bathe, dress, make breakfast, drive to work, do laundry, or flip hamburgers on their backyard grill — all in order to understand how consumers relate to various products. While Nissan Motors was developing the Infiniti line, for example, the company used ethnographic market research to help them understand the differences between Japanese and American perceptions of luxury. That's right — they drove around with people and talked to them about their cars! Nissan found that to Americans, high-end goods are more valuable if their lavish features are visible. This is in contrast to the Japanese concept of luxury, which values simplicity and hidden charm. Understanding these differences allowed Nissan to successfully redesign the Infiniti line to be more attractive to American buyers; other automakers realized the benefits of ethnographic market research and followed in Nissan's footsteps (Osborne 2002).

Some commercial ethnographers, known as "cool hunters," search for the newest, hippest trends in popular culture. Look-Look, a Hollywood trend-forecasting firm, recruited "youth correspondents" and amateur photographers in cities around the world as part of its "living research" strategy. Founded by Dee Dee Gordon and Sharon Lee, Look-Look counted on these correspondents to provide information on the latest trends in music, fashion, technology, and hip activities and hangouts. Says Gordon, "We look for kids who are ahead of the pack, because they'll influence what all the other kids do" (PBS 2001). Look-Look is somewhat secretive about its client list, which includes Universal Pictures, Disney Films, and Skyy Vodka. Other market research firms report that companies such as Xerox, Colgate-Palmolive, Kraft Foods, Duracell, Playtex, Honda, Pioneer Stereo, and Anheuser-Busch have all utilized qualitative market research to direct their production, distribution, and marketing strategies. Sociology students who become proficient in ethnographic methods may well be the hottest new hires in the field of commercial ethnography.

Cool Hunter Loic Bizel, a French "cool hunter" in Japan, picks up a pair of hand-painted sneakers in Tokyo's Harajuku shopping district. His job is to observe and report on the fast-changing street fads of Japan.

requires putting into action what is learned, continues to be debated within the discipline.

Despite the safeguards built into research methodologies, there are still opportunities for bias, or personal preferences, to subtly influence how the work is done. Bias can infiltrate every part of the research process—from identifying a project to selecting a sample, from the wording of questions to the analysis and write-up of the data. Earl Babbie (2002) claims that research biases have come into play in the area of U.S. racial relations and documents several historical cases to illustrate the point. In 1896, the Supreme Court established the doctrine of "separate but equal" as a means of "guaranteeing equal protection" for African Americans while still allowing racial segregation. Although no research was directly cited, it is widely believed that the ruling was influenced by the work of William Graham Sumner (1906), a leading social scientist at the time. Sumner believed that the customs of a society were relatively impervious to outside influence and that therefore the legal system should not be used to enforce social change. The saying "You can't legislate morality" is a reflection of such thinking. So instead of allowing blacks the same rights and access to resources, the Court continued to uphold segregation.

The doctrine of "separate but equal" persisted until it was finally overturned in 1954 in the landmark civil rights case *Brown vs. Board of Education of Topeka, Kansas*, which outlawed racial segregation in schools. This time, the Supreme Court justices based their unanimous decision on several other, more contemporary sociological and psychological studies (Blaunstein and Zangrando 1970). Apparently, the Court was now of the belief that morality *could* be legislated. A decade later, controversy erupted again when in 1966 a noted sociologist, James Coleman, published his findings about a national study on race and education. Coleman claimed that the academic performance of African American students attending integrated schools was no better than that of those attending segregated schools; that such things as libraries, laboratories, or expenditures per student had less influence on academic performance than neighborhoods or family. While some criticized Coleman on methodological grounds, others were more concerned that his findings might be used to support a return to segregation. This has not happened, but neither has complete integration. We still need to work toward creating an educational system that serves all students, and social research will continue to be part of that process. Most social scientists, and the American public in general, support civil rights and racial equality. These beliefs inspire research at the same time that research inspires continued social change. Even though we aim for value-free sociology, there are some topics on which it is hard to remain neutral.

Little Rock Nine A mob tries to prevent Elizabeth Eckford from getting to Little Rock's Central High School after a federal court ordered the school to desegregate.

OBJECTIVITY The notion of **objectivity**, or impartiality, plays a fundamental role in scientific practice. As far back as Auguste Comte, sociologists have maintained that they could study society rationally and objectively. If a researcher is rational and objective, then he should be able to observe reality, distinguish actual facts from mental concepts, and separate truth from feeling or opinion. This ideal may be desirable and reasonable, but can "facts" really speak for themselves? And if so, can we discover those facts without somehow involving ourselves in them?

Some "facts" that sociologists once took to be objective reality have since been invalidated. Racist, sexist, and ethnocentric perspectives long dominated the field and passed for "truth." For many years, scientific reality consisted only of the experience of white European males, and the realities of women, ethnic minorities, and others outside the mainstream were categorically ignored or dismissed.

For example, until recently, heart problems in women were likely to go undiagnosed, which meant that women were more likely than men to die from heart attacks. Why? Because medical research on heart attacks used mostly male subjects and so had not discovered that women's symptoms are different from men's (Rabin 2008). It is easy now, through hindsight, to see that our "knowledge" was severely distorted. We must, therefore, be willing to recognize that what presently passes for fact may some day be challenged.

Another obstacle to achieving objectivity is our subjective nature as human beings. Our own experience of the world, and therefore sense of reality, is inevitably personal and idiosyncratic. Although we recognize our innate subjectivity, we still long for and actively pursue what we call absolute truth. But some social scientists question this ideal; they propose that subjectivity is not only unavoidable, it may be preferable when it comes to the study of human beings. This is especially true of sociologists who do "autoethnography," research in which they themselves—and their own thoughts, feelings, and experiences—are the focus of their study (Ellis 1997). On the other hand, some postmodern thinkers have gone so far as to reject the notion that there is any objective reality out there in the first place. Their arguments parallel certain trends in the physical sciences as well, where developments such as chaos theory and fuzzy logic suggest the need to reconsider the assumption of an orderly universe.

OBJECTIVITY impartiality, the ability to allow the facts to speak for themselves

REACTIVITY the tendency of people and events to react to the process of being studied

HAWTHORNE EFFECT a specific example of reactivity, in which the desired effect is the result not of the independent variable but of the research itself

REACTIVITY In addition to maintaining their objectivity, social scientists must also be concerned with **reactivity**, the ways that people and events respond to being studied. One classic example of reactivity comes from studies that were conducted from 1927 to 1932 at the Hawthorne plant of Western Electric in Chicago. Elton Mayo (1949), a Harvard business school professor, sought to examine the effect of varying work conditions on motivation and productivity in the factory. When he changed certain conditions—such as lighting levels, rest breaks, and even rates of pay—he found that each change resulted in a rise in productivity both in the individual worker and in the group. What was more surprising, however, was that returning to the original conditions also resulted in a rise in productivity. Mayo concluded, then, that the variables he had manipulated were not the causes of productivity; rather, *it was the effect of being studied*, or what is now referred to as the **Hawthorne effect**. In other words, the workers had responded to the researchers' taking interest in their performance, and it was this attention that had caused the improvement.

Researchers must always be aware that their subjects, whether in an experiment or in a natural observation, are active and intelligent participants. The subjects may be able to sense what the researchers are trying to understand or prove and in effect "give them what they want" by responding to even the unspoken goals of the research. Our presence as researchers always has some effect on those we study, whether noticeable to us or not.

Research Ethics

Doing research that involves other human beings means that we must address moral issues (questions about right and wrong conduct) as we make decisions that will affect them. For this reason, various academic disciplines have developed ethical guidelines—professional standards for honest and honorable dealings with others—meant to help direct the decision making of such researchers. When we use other people as means to an end, we must protect them as ends in themselves.

It's easy to understand the risks of participating in, say, a pharmaceutical drug trial or a study of the effects of radiation treatment on certain types of cancers. The risks of participating in social research are different and more subtle. It is often the case, for example, that social researchers don't fully explain the details of their research project to the participating subjects. Sometimes this is necessary: survey respondents, for example, must be able to answer questions without interference from the researcher and the potential for bias. Also, ethnographic fieldworkers operate on various levels of secrecy

GLOBAL PERSPECTIVE

The Nuremberg Code and Research Ethics

The origins of contemporary research ethics can be traced back to the Nuremberg military tribunals of the late 1940s, in which a group of Nazi doctors were tried for the horrific "experiments" they had performed during World War II. These experiments involved the torture and death of thousands of concentration camp inmates. Of the twenty-three Nazi doctors tried at Nuremberg, sixteen were convicted of war crimes. Besides a kind of justice for the deaths of so many, the other enduring result of the trials was the Nuremberg Code, a set of moral and ethical guidelines for performing research on human beings. According to these guidelines, developed by two doctors, Andrew Ivy and Leo Alexander, scientists must accept certain responsibilities: to perform only research that can "yield fruitful results for the good of society, unprocurable by other methods"; to protect their human subjects from "all unnecessary physical and mental suffering and injury"; and to perform research only on subjects who give their informed, noncoerced consent.

In America, there was strong support for the Nuremberg Code. But at the same time that the code was being developed, the U.S. government was involved in its own medical atrocity, though it would not be revealed to the public until decades later: the Tuskegee Syphilis Study. In 1932, the U.S. Public Health Service began a forty-year-long study of "untreated syphilis in the male negro": 399 African American men from Tuskegee, an impoverished region of Alabama, who were infected with syphilis were left untreated so that doctors could observe the natural progression of the disease. The symptoms include painful sores, hair loss, sterility, blindness, paralysis, and insanity, and almost always lead to death. The disease can be transmitted by men to their sexual partners, and infected women can pass it on to their infants. By 1947, penicillin was widely accepted as the preferred treatment for syphilis, but government doctors decided to leave the Tuskegee men untreated to avoid interfering with the study's results.

While these doctors had not intentionally inflicted the disease upon subjects, neither had they offered a cure when it became available. The full story of the Tuskegee experiment was not revealed until 1972, and it was not until 1997 that President Bill Clinton issued an official apology from the U.S. government to the victims and their families. Clearly, Americans were as guilty of violating moral and ethical codes as Germans had been at a similar time in history.

What is important to take away from this lesson is the need for all scientific research to adhere to ethical standards—this includes the social as well as medical sciences. In either case, researchers must consider the potential harm that they can cause to human subjects. You may not think of sociologists as dealing with life-and-death issues; yet, as researchers, we often find ourselves in positions where certain kinds of studies can't be undertaken because of concerns for the well-being of the potential subjects.

The Nuremberg Code In the wake of the Nuremberg Military Tribunals after World War II, science organizations adopted a set of guidelines to regulate researchers' ethical conduct. Whether studying biology, psychiatry, or sociology, researchers must consider the potential harm they could cause to research participants.

or **deception**: even when an ethnographer has openly declared herself a researcher, it is often impossible for her to remind every person she speaks with that she is a scientific observer as well as a participant. And if she engages in "covert" research and deliberately presents an inauthentic self to the group, then that makes all her interactions inauthentic as well. This can affect the fieldworker's ability to discover the members' real, grounded meanings. What, then, has she really been able to learn about the setting and its members?

Codes of ethics in the social sciences do not provide strict rules for researchers to abide by in these cases; rather, they set out principles to guide the researcher's decision making. Secrecy and deceit are thus never strictly prohibited; instead, researchers are cautioned to acquire the informed consent of their subjects and to conduct themselves in a way that protects the subjects from harm.

DECEPTION the extent to which the participants in a research project are unaware of the project or its goals

What other kinds of harm can come to participants? They're not likely to get diseases, and there is usually little physical risk in sitting down to complete a survey questionnaire! But harm *can* result, mostly as a result of the breaching of confidentiality. Research subjects are entitled to "rights of biographical anonymity": researchers are required to protect their privacy. This protection is essential to gathering valid data, especially when dealing with controversial topics or vulnerable populations. Respondents must be guaranteed that no one will be able to identify them from reading the research findings. But while most researchers take steps to disguise the identities of individuals and locations, it is sometimes difficult to keep others from uncovering them. For example, a classic sociological pseudonym, "Middletown" (Lynd and Lynd 1929/1959, 1937), was long ago revealed to be Muncie, Indiana—and since the Middletown studies were seen as an example of the shallowness and triviality of American culture, this was not such a good thing for Muncie's reputation!

Sometimes worse than having others recognize a place or person is having subjects themselves find out what was written about them. Carolyn Ellis (1995) had an unsettling experience when she returned to the small mid-Atlantic fishing village in which she had spent years living and doing fieldwork. In the time she had been gone, she had published a book about the village, and excerpts had made their way

"Middletown" Although Robert S. Lynd and Helen Merrell Lynd used the pseudonym "Middletown" in their classic studies of the shallowness and triviality of American culture, it was long ago revealed that Middletown is Muncie, Indiana.

back to the villagers, who were upset at the way that Ellis had depicted them. These villagers, who had considered Ellis to be their friend, felt deeply betrayed; they felt that she had abused their hospitality and misrepresented them as uncouth, uneducated hicks. Despite her protests that she was simply doing her job as a sociologist, many villagers refused to speak with her again, and she was shut out of a social world of which she had once been an integral part.

Researchers may undertake other kinds of risks as well. Particularly in ethnographic research, and especially if researching a dangerous subculture, researchers may be at risk of life and limb. Sociologist Martin Sanchez-Jankowski (1991) became a member of a street gang in order to conduct his research. Ethnographer John Van Maanen (1973, 1983, 1988) found himself at risk of a prison term and in what he called a "moral fix" when he witnessed a controversial beating during the course of his fieldwork at an urban police department. A subpoena was issued requiring him to testify in the case. If he did, it would incriminate the police officers whose trust he had gained over months of fieldwork; if he didn't, it would doom the beating victim, a drifter whose only crime was being in the wrong place at the wrong time. Van Maanen felt a strong moral obligation to protect the confidentiality of his subjects and was ultimately successful in keeping his fieldnotes out of court (Adler and Adler 2000).

In order to encourage the protection of research subjects, each academic discipline has adopted its own **code of ethics** to provide guidelines for researchers. The American Sociological Association Code of Ethics, for example, sets out recommendations for how to avoid bias, adhere to professional standards, and protect respondents from harm. In addition, universities where research is conducted have a body known as an **institutional review board**, or IRB, a group of scholars who meet regularly to review the research proposals of their colleagues. If an IRB has reservations about the safety of the subjects in a given research project, it may require changes to the protocol or even stop the project from going forward. In extreme cases, funding may be revoked if the subjects are being put at undue risk; entire university power structures have been undermined as a result of pervasive research ethics problems.

The power invested in IRBs is seen as controversial by some. The boards are often made up entirely of scholars in medicine, biology, chemistry, and physics; social scientists have questioned their ability to make judgments about social research. Because IRBs have the power to shut down research projects, perhaps they should be discipline specific, with biologists judging biologists, psychologists judging psychologists, and sociologists judging sociologists.

CLOSING COMMENTS

In this chapter, you have learned the different methods used by sociologists to investigate the social world. Each method has its strengths and limitations, and each can be fruitfully applied to a variety of research questions. In fact, this is exactly what you will be doing in future chapters.

Each chapter from this point on will feature two Data Workshops in which you will be asked to apply one of the methods from this chapter to an actual sociological research project. You will get a chance to practice doing the work of sociological research, and analyzing (and sometimes gathering) your own data. You may find yourself referring back to this chapter to remind yourself of the specifics of each methodology. This is exactly what you should be doing; it's okay if two months from now you don't remember the details. Just because you're moving on to Chapter 3, don't forget that Chapter 2 can continue to be useful to you throughout the term—and maybe even beyond that.

CODE OF ETHICS ethical guidelines for researchers to consult as they design a project

INSTITUTIONAL REVIEW BOARD a group of scholars within a university who meet regularly to review and approve the research proposals of their colleagues and make recommendations for how to protect human subjects

Everything You Need to Know about
Sociological Research Methods

> **"** Research methods are strategies that produce data to support, disprove, or modify theoretical claims. **"**

THE SCIENTIFIC METHOD

1. Identify a problem or ask a question

2. Conduct a literature review

3. Form a hypothesis; give operational definitions to variables

4. Choose research design or method

5. Collect data

6. Analyze data

7. Disseminate findings

REVIEW

1. Try to write a survey or interview question that asks about a respondent's political affiliation without being biased or using language that might spark an emotional response.

2. Imagine that your teacher asks you to do a simple random sample of your class. How would you select your sample so that you could be sure each member had an equal chance of being included?

3. Researchers are now using social networking web sites like Facebook and Twitter to gather a wide variety of data. If researchers read your profile (or those of your friends or family), do you think they would have a valid understanding of who you (or they) are? Is there a weakness of research that relies on existing sources?

Sociological Research Methods

Method	Disadvantages	Advantages
Ethnography	Study groups that are often overlooked by other methods Challenge our taken-for-granted notions about groups we thought we knew Reshape the stereotypes we hold about others	Lack of replicability Lack of representativeness Respondents are not always forthcoming or truthful
Interviews	Allow respondents to speak in their own words Dispel certain preconceptions Discover issues that might have otherwise been overlooked	Lack of representativeness
Surveys	Gather original data on a population that is too large to study by other means Relatively quick and economical and can provide a vast amount of data Comparatively strong on reliability Less concern about research bias	Lacks qualitative data that might better capture the social reality Not all respondents are honest in self-reports Problems with the sampling process can make generalizability difficult
Existing Sources	Work with information researchers could not possibly obtain for themselves.	Answers to questions that the original authors did not have in mind are not available Does not illuminate how original sources were interpreted
Experiments	Manipulate and control the social environment researchers to minimize outside interference High replicability	Applicable only to certain types of research that can be constructed and measured in a controlled setting Not very effective for describing more complex processes and interactions

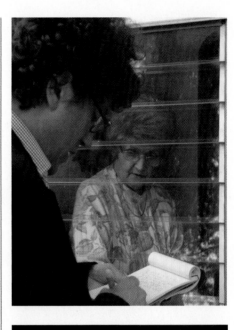

EXPLORE

A Random Invitation: The American Community Survey

The ACS is a survey conducted by the U.S. Census Bureau each year to learn more about the American population. The survey not only provides data on population changes but also provides us with data annually on marital status, housing, education, and income. Visit the Everyday Sociology Blog to find out if the American Community Survey really paints an accurate picture of the American population.

http://wwnPag.es/trw402

PART II
Framing Social Life

How does culture shape our social worlds? How are our personal identities produced by our cultural contexts and social interactions? How does participation in group life shape both individual experience and social structure? How are what is normal and what is deviant defined, and what are the consequences for people who are labeled accordingly? Part II of this text addresses these questions in the next four chapters on culture (Chapter 3), the self and interaction (Chapter 4), groups (Chapter 5), and deviance (Chapter 6). The ability to examine, describe, analyze, and explain the points of intersection between the individual world and the social world is sociology's special contribution to the larger scholarly endeavor. Within the next four chapters, you will encounter many works by sociologists that illustrate the links between the individual and society. Leila Rupp and Verta Taylor's book *Drag Queens at the 801 Cabaret* (2003) is perfect for highlighting these themes.

Drag Queens at the 801 Cabaret is an ethnographic portrait of a Key West drag club, where gay male performers don sexy dresses, lavish wigs, and theatrical makeup and sing and dance for a diverse audience: tourists and locals, men and women, gays and straights. Rupp and Taylor get to know the "801 Girls" and their friends, family, and audience members, and the authors even try out their own sort of drag. (That's right—women dressed as men dressed as women!)

Rupp and Taylor recognize that the particular culture of the 801 Cabaret is nestled within multiple contemporary American subcultures. For example, Key West is an island subculture that offers a year-round, touristy, carnivalesque atmosphere as part of its charm. It "remains a flamboyant mix of cultures. . . . [I]t shelters not only vibrant Cuban and Bahamian enclaves, but also artistic, hippie, and gay communities. . . . The city, [says journalist Charles Kuralt,] is 'full of dreamers, drifters, and dropouts, spongers and idlers and barflies, writers and fishermen, islanders from the Caribbean and gays from the big cities, painters and pensioners, treasure hunters, real estate speculators, smugglers, runaways, old Conchs and young lovers . . . all elaborately tolerant of one another'" (Rupp and Taylor 2003, pp. 50–51). For the 801 girls, this means that the subcultures associated with both gay masculinity and drag performance are supported and sustained on the island in ways they might not be on the mainland. Because of the island's unique mix of subcultures, one of the performers asserts that "Key West is the true home of accepted diversity" (p. 55).

In Key West's culture, many kinds of people feel free to be themselves. But what does that really mean? For the drag queens at the 801 Cabaret, their performances are about putting on a different identity than the one they present in their everyday lives. These are men with flashy female alter-egos—Kevin becomes "Kylie"; Roger becomes "Inga"; Dean becomes "Milla." And their process of becoming is elaborate and grueling:

Sociologists Verta Taylor and Leila Rupp The authors getting into drag themselves.

Some of the girls shave all over their bodies, some their faces, chests, legs, and arms, some just their faces. . . . They powder their faces, necks, and chests, using a thick base to hide their beards. . . . Eyeliner, eye shadow, mascara, false eyelashes, lip liner, and lipstick are painstakingly applied. (pp. 12–13)

So far, this doesn't sound all that different than the rituals many women perform every morning in front of the mirror. After the makeup, however, things get a little more intricate, as the "girls" tuck their penises and testicles between their legs, using a gaff [a special panty], or several, to make sure everything stays out of sight . . . panty hose, sometimes several layers . . . corsets and waist cinchers . . . they all, of course, wear bras . . . [filled with] water balloons (the tied end makes an amazingly realistic nipple), half a Nerf football, lentil beans in a pair of nylons, foam or silicone prostheses. (pp. 20–21)

All this work to look like women — and that's not taking into account the exhausting work of acting the part, onstage and off. While drag queens do not seek to convince their audiences that they are "real" women, they do move, speak, sing, and dance in stereotypically feminine style as part of their performances. And that's the insight that drag queens provide about our own identities: it's *all* performance! Our male and female selves are the products of interactional accomplishments, and "real" women do many of the same things that drag queens do in order to express femininity.

Because the drag queens perform different identities onstage and off, the 801 Cabaret calls into question some of our most important and taken-for-granted boundaries between social groups: males and females, and gays and straights. In fact, drag queens are living examples of the intersections between these groups. One of the performers says:

Last night — though this happens almost every night — [this woman] goes, "I'm straight, I'm a woman, I'm not a lesbian, but you're so beautiful, I find you so attractive" . . . [and] a straight guy, has been straight for like fifty years or something like that . . . goes, "You know, I've been straight all my life, and I know you're a man, but you're so beautiful . . . I can't keep my eyes off you." (p. 201)

Drag queens and drag shows allow others to cross between groups, to see what life might be like in a world in which gender boundaries are fluid and homosexuality is normal:

As one of the few ways that straight people encounter gay culture — where, in fact, straight people live for an hour or two in an environment where gay is normal and straight is other — drag shows . . . play an important role for the gay/lesbian movement. Precisely because drag shows are entertaining, they attract people who might never otherwise be exposed to gay politics. As one female audience member put it, they "take something difficult and make it light." (pp. 207–8)

Finally, drag shows also challenge our notions about what is normal and what is deviant, when performers embrace what would otherwise be considered a stigmatized identity and turn it into something to be proud of. Drag queens can be seen as voluntary outsiders, unconcerned about fitting into mainstream society. Rupp and Taylor make the argument that

Performing Gender Drag queens and "real" women perform femininity in similar ways.

drag is a form of social protest — against a society in which gender and sexual orientation are crammed into limiting, two-category systems; against a society in which identities are seen as immutable; and against a society in which certain forms of cultural expression are marginalized. Their analysis of the social world of one Key West drag club offers sociological insights into the lives of the individual performers who work against social stigma and limitations to provide new ways of looking at culture, self, and society.

Drag Queens on Stage How do drag queens use entertainment and performance to undermine gender stereotypes?

CHAPTER 3

Culture

Heavy metal music has long been associated with young, white, alienated, angry, blue collar men in America. With extremely loud, pounding music accompanied by lyrics dealing with the themes of death, sex, and alienation, heavy metal has many critics among mainstream conservative Americans. Acrassicauda (the word is Arabic for "black scorpion") is an Iraqi heavy metal band that represents both a clash and a connection between American and Iraqi culture. Heavy metal music became popular in Iraq in the early 1990s, as middle-class Iraqi teenagers discovered bands like Metallica, Slayer, and

the Scorpions through black market CDs. The themes of anger, death, rebellion, and violence were all too familiar for Iraqi teens.

In 2001, four Iraqi nationals formed the band Acrassicauda, which gained fame through the 2007 documentary *Heavy Metal in Baghdad* (VBS.tv 2007). During Saddam Hussein's regime, the band was able to perform but was forced to write a song glorifying Hussein with lyrics like "Following our leader Saddam Hussein, we'll make them fall, we'll drive them insane!" They were also subject to restrictions on the heavy metal custom of headbanging because of the dance's similarity to a Jewish prayer ritual called *davening*. After Hussein was overthrown, the group's lyrics became increasingly political and reflected on the horrors of a country torn apart by war. In *Vice*, a youth culture magazine, writer Gideon Yago asserts that Acrassicauda's version of metal was intensified through the terror and violence that Iraqis had to encounter on a daily basis.

Because any gathering of people in Iraq becomes a target for terrorists, Acrassicauda was only able to play six live concerts in a span of five years. Islamic militants equated heavy metal music with Satan-worshipping, much like Christian conservatives in the United States did. However, in the United States, opponents attempted to use legislation to rid the culture of heavy metal. In Iraq, the perception of heavy metal as Satan-worshipping was exacerbated by the American origins of the music. Acrassicauda received death threats that read, "You are Americanized, playing Western music. You either quit or you will be dead." These death threats escalated to the point where the members of Acrassicauda feared for their lives.

Acrassicauda did not quit playing, but instead used strategies like having random band practices rather than playing at regular times. They would hold concerts while mortar shells dropped around the venues. At the same time, they realized the danger of continuing to live in Iraq while spreading their message through heavy metal.

After watching the band's story in *Heavy Metal in Baghdad*, Alex Skolnick, from the metal band Testament, met the band and helped them record an EP, *Only the Dead See the End of the War*. The EP gathered more publicity for the group, and *Vice* magazine set up a PayPal account for donations to help members of Acrassicauda emigrate to the United States. Metal fans throughout the world donated a total of $40,000, the United States granted the band refugee status, and now Acrassicauda is living and performing in the United States.

It's interesting how an alienated U.S. subculture like heavy metal can come to represent mainstream Western culture to militant Islamic fundamentalists. It's also enlightening to see how music enjoyed by disenfranchised, rebellious American youth can be fascinating to those living in the real-life horrors of a war-torn nation. The study of culture provides an endless number of fascinating possibilities for understanding ourselves and others.

HOW TO READ THIS CHAPTER

Culture is one of the fundamental elements of social life and thus a very important topic in sociology. Many of the concepts presented here will come up again in almost every subsequent chapter. You will need to keep these concepts in mind as you learn about other substantive areas. You will also want to think about how culture is relevant to the things you already know from your own life experience. Try to come up with some of your own examples as you read along. The subject of culture is probably inherently interesting to most people. But although culture is familiar to all of us, you should be seeing it in a new and different way by the time you finish this chapter.

What Is Culture?

Culture encompasses practically all of human civilization and touches on almost every aspect of social life. It is so much a part of the world around us that we may not recognize the extent to which it shapes and defines who we are. In the broadest sense, we can say that **culture** is the entire way of life of a group of people. It can include everything from language and gestures to style of dress and standards of beauty, from customs and rituals to tools and artifacts, from music and child-rearing practices to the proper way for customers to line up in a grocery store. It forms basic beliefs and assumptions about the world and the way things work, and defines the moral parameters of what is right and wrong, good and bad.

Although culture varies from group to group, all societies develop some form of culture. It is the human equivalent of instinct in animals: although we humans do have some basic instincts, culture actually accounts for our great success as a species. We are totally dependent on it to deal with the demands of life in society. As culture develops, it is shared among members of a group, handed down from generation to generation, and passed along from one group or individual to another.

Although culture may seem to us to be "second nature," it is actually something that is learned, rather than innate. Because we learn it so slowly and incrementally, we are often unaware of the process. For instance, few of us would be conscious of having *learned* all the slang words we currently use or the distance we typically maintain from someone while talking with him. We may not remember exactly when we first felt patriotic or how we formed our opinions about people from the upper class. We all carry culture inside ourselves; it becomes ingrained and internalized into our way of thinking and acting. Culture guides the way we make sense of the world around us and the way we make decisions about what to do and how to do it. We can talk about the culture of a given country, state, or community, of people belonging to an ethnic or religious group, or of those working in the same profession. We can even say that sports enthusiasts, schoolmates, or a clique of friends share in a common culture. We'll discuss some of these cultural variations later in the chapter.

How Has Culture Been Studied?

People study culture in a variety of ways. Theologians and philosophers, for example, might debate the morals and values of an ideal culture. Anthropologists often investigate smaller societies outside the United States. They travel around the world and engage in empirical fieldwork, collecting stories and artifacts that document the realities of the cultures they study (Margaret Mead and Gregory Bateson are two of the most well known). In many cases, though, these cultures are often seen as "other"—interesting because of their distinctive differences from the anthropologist's home culture, which often goes unexamined.

In contrast, sociologists mainly focus on culture closer to home, usually the same societies to which they belong. They do this by using the different theories discussed in Chapter 1—functionalism, conflict theory, symbolic interactionism, and postmodernism—as well as the research methods discussed in Chapter 2. At the same time, however, sociologists may also engage in the process of "othering" by studying the unusual, extraordinary, or deviant in cultural groups. In so doing, they may fail to consider some aspects of the culture that is right in front of them. This is where the sociology of everyday life offers certain benefits. By studying the mundane as well as the exceptional, we can learn about culture in all of its interesting permutations. We can learn not only about the differences between cultural groups—"us" and "them"—but also the similarities.

> **CULTURE** the entire way of life of a group of people (including both material and symbolic elements) that acts as a lens through which one views the world and is passed from one generation to the next

Ethnocentrism and Cultural Relativism

Culture acts as a lens through which we view the world. That lens, however, can either elucidate or obscure what we are looking at. Often, we can't clearly see our own culture, precisely because we are so familiar with it. Yet, when exposed to another culture, through travel, television, or other means, we can readily see what is different or exotic. Rarely does our perspective allow us to recognize the strangeness in our own culture.

One of the best examples of the challenges in observing culture is presented in a famous article by Horace Miner called "Body Ritual among the Nacirema" (1956). The article focuses on the beliefs and practices of this North American people concerning the care of their bodies. Miner observes that their fundamental belief appears to be that the human body is ugly and is susceptible to decay and disease, and the only way to counter these conditions is to engage in elaborate ceremonies and rituals. All members of the Nacirema culture conform to a greater or lesser degree to these practices and then pass them along to their children. One passage describes the household shrine where many of the body rituals take place:

> While each family has at least one shrine, the rituals associated with it are not family ceremonies but are private and secret. . . . The focal point of the shrine is a box or chest which is built into a wall. In this chest are kept the many charms and magical potions without which no native believes he could live. . . . Beneath the charm-box is a small font. Each day every member of the family, in succession, enters the shrine room, bows his head before the charm-box, mingles different sorts of holy water in the font, and proceeds with a brief rite of ablution (p. 504).

The Nacirema regularly visit medicine men, "holy-mouth men," and other specialized practitioners from whom they procure magical potions.

> The Nacirema have an almost pathological horror of and fascination with the mouth, the condition of which is believed to have a supernatural influence on all social relationships. Were it not for the rituals of the mouth, they believe that their teeth would fall out, their gums bleed, their jaws shrink, their friends desert them, and their lovers reject them. The daily body ritual performed by everyone includes a mouth-rite. It was reported to me that the ritual consists of inserting a small bundle of hog hairs into the mouth, along with certain magical powders, and then moving the bundle in a highly formalized series of gestures.

"Body Ritual among the Nacirema" Horace Miner reminds us how easy it is to overlook aspects of our own culture, precisely because it seems so normal to us.

embellish or make up anything; he merely approaches the topic as if he knew nothing about its meaning. So the "charm-box" is the standard medicine cabinet, the "holy water" font is a sink, the medicine men and "holy-mouth men" are doctors and dentists, and the exotic "mouth-rite" is the practice of brushing teeth.

One of the reasons that Miner's article has become so popular is that it demonstrates how easy it is to fail to see our own culture, precisely because we take it for granted. The article reminds students who are becoming social analysts how useful culture shock is in helping to see even what is most familiar to us as bizarre or strange. Throughout this chapter, keep in mind that your powers of observation must be applied to looking at both "them" and "us."

Another, related problem arises when trying to understand cultures other than our own. Generally, we think of our own culture as being the "normal" one, a belief known as **ethnocentrism**. We don't realize that culture is something learned and that there is nothing inherently better about ours. Ethnocentrism means that we use our own culture as a kind of measuring stick with which to judge other individuals or societies; anyone outside our group seems "off-center" or abnormal.

As sociologists, we want to have as clear a view of any society as possible; this requires that we suspend, at least temporarily, our ethnocentrism. There are several ways to do this. In Chapter 1, we learned about the sociological imagination, culture shock, and beginner's mind—all ways to see the world anew. We can add to that list **cultural relativism**, which means seeing each different culture as simply that—different. Not better or worse, not right or wrong, but on its own terms. This helps us place different values, beliefs, norms, and practices within their own cultural context. By

ETHNOCENTRISM the principle of using one's own culture as a means or standard by which to evaluate another group or individual, leading to the view that cultures other than one's own are abnormal or inferior

CULTURAL RELATIVISM the principle of understanding other cultures on their own terms, rather than judging or evaluating according to one's own culture

Do the Nacirema seem like a strange group of people, or are they somehow familiar? Miner writes as though he were an anthropologist studying some exotic tribe of primitive people. In actuality, the passages above describe the bathroom and personal health-care habits of the average American. (Note that "Nacirema" is "American" spelled backward.) He doesn't practicing cultural relativism, or being culturally sensitive, we begin to see others more clearly, and without judgment, and therefore to appreciate their way of life. We can discover viewpoints and interpretations of reality different from our own. Cultural relativism becomes all the more important in our increasingly diverse society. The Data Workshop below will help you see how.

DATA WORKSHOP
Analyzing Everyday Life

Seeing Culture in Religious Services

Some people argue that religions are cultures within themselves. This is easiest to see in the case of groups such as the FLDS (a fundamentalist Mormon sect whose members practice polygamy and tend to live in isolated rural compounds) and the white-supremacist World Church of the Creator (whose leader, Matt Hale, is currently in prison for conspiring to kill a federal judge), but even your friendly neighborhood congregation has a specific set of norms and beliefs that are particular to itself.

This Data Workshop will challenge you to suspend ethnocentrism and practice cultural relativism as you uncover aspects of the material and symbolic culture of a particular religious group. You will be doing participant observation at a service and writing fieldnotes which will become the basis for an ethnography. (Refer back to Chapter 2 if you need a refresher on ethnographic methods.)

Step 1: Observing Services
Select a house of worship — church, synagogue, temple, mosque, or other place of worship — and attend a service there. It may be of a faith you belong to already, or one that is unfamiliar. Sometimes it can be more difficult to "see" culture in a familiar setting than in one that is very different for you. Any choice is fine as long as it is open to the public. You may want to call their offices first, to find out if there are any dress codes or other requirements you should know about before attending. Remember, when you visit your chosen house of worship, you must behave in a respectful manner. If you suspect that you can't maintain a quiet and respectful demeanor (if that's what is called for), then choose a different service to attend. You will need to closely observe all that takes place around you. Since it is probably not appropri-

ate for you to jot down notes during a religious service, you should write your fieldnotes as soon as you can afterward.

Describe all the material culture you see such as the architecture, any decorations, clothing worn by different participants, and the other physical objects — books, scrolls, musical instruments, statues, paintings, vessels, collection plates — that are part of the service.

Record in as much detail as possible the symbolic culture — what was said, done, or sung during your period of observation. Pay as much attention as possible to the interactions that are a central part of the ritual, as well as those that occur on the margins (either just before or just after the ceremony).

* How are the services structured?

* When do participants stand, sit or kneel, speak, read, pray, sing, meditate, or take part in other activities?

* When do people act in unison, or when do they act individually?

* Are there both adults and children present? Do men and women participate in the same ways? What types of different roles do people take on in the ceremony — leaders, helpers, participants?

* Is everybody deeply involved at all times? How do participants behave toward each other?

Step 2: Identifying Culture
Read through your fieldnotes and reflect on your experience. Then answer the following questions.

* What aspects of material culture did you notice at the house of worship? How were things arranged in the space? Was there furniture, statues, or other objects that were part of the service?

* What about the "text" and "script"; the types of words that were uttered (and by whom, and when); their sources (sacred books, hymnals, photocopied programs); the music that was played or sung; the periods of prayer or meditation; the ways in which participants were invited to speak (or to remain silent) or otherwise take part? What similarities and differences did you notice in the behavior of the participants? Did all participants engage in similar actions and interactions? Or were there differences among the individuals?

* Can you identify any of the religious beliefs as a result of your observations? For example, according to Émile Durkheim (1912/1995), most religions feature beliefs about what happens after we die, and also beliefs about the relationship between the sacred (holy, godlike, supernatural) and the profane (the ordinary, of this world).

In addition, every religion has a set of practices that are designed to connect the holy and the worldly in some

Comparing Religious Cultures Every religion has a culture — its own set of norms, values, beliefs, and practices that differ from those of other congregations, even within the same denomination. As an ethnographic exercise, visit a house of worship and describe your experience.

way. Think about the different rituals you observed: taking communion, for example, or simply praying or singing in a specially designated space. These rituals each create a sense of collective effervescence and serve to connect the sacred and profane.

＊ What did you observe in the service that seemed especially unfamiliar to you? What did you observe that seemed the most familiar, even if it was in an unfamiliar setting?

There are two options for completing this Data Workshop.

Option 1 (informal): Consider the bulleted questions above, and prepare some written notes that you can refer to during in-class discussions. Compare your notes and experiences with other students in small-group discussions. Take this opportunity to learn more about culture and different religious traditions.

Option 2 (formal): Write a three- to four-page essay analyzing your field experiences and taking into consideration the bulleted questions above. Make sure to refer to your fieldnotes in the essay, and include them as an attachment to your paper.

Components of Culture

Since culture is such a broad concept, it is more easily grasped if we break it down into its constituent parts. Sociologists conceive of culture as consisting of two major categories: material culture and symbolic culture.

Material Culture

Material culture is any physical object to which we give social meaning: art and artifacts, tools and utensils, machines and weapons, clothing and furniture, buildings and toys — the list is immense. Any physical thing that people create, use, or appreciate might be considered material culture.

Examining material culture can tell us a great deal about a particular group or society. Just look around you, whether in your dorm room, a library, a coffee house, or a park — there should be many items that you can identify as belonging to material culture. Start with your own clothes and accessories and then extend your observations to your surroundings — the room, building, landscaping, street, neighborhood, community, and further outward. For instance, the designer label on a woman's purse might convey that she follows the current fashion trends, or the athletic logo on a man's T-shirt might tell us that he is into skateboarding. Likewise, the carpeting, light fixtures, furniture, and artwork in a building can tell us something about the people who live or work there. And the sports arenas, modes of transportation, historical monuments, and city dumps reveal the characteristics of a community. Perhaps the proliferation of drive-thru fast-food restaurants in practically every corner of the United States says something about American tastes and lifestyle: we spend more time on the road, cook fewer meals at home, and prefer the ease and predictability of knowing what we'll get each time we pull up to our favorite chain. If you were visiting another country, then you might see some very different items of material culture.

Studying the significance of material culture is like going on an archeological dig, but learning about the present rather than the distant past. Let's take as an example a sociological "dig" in Santa Barbara, California, where one of the authors of this book lives. Local leaders there have been active in preserving the image of the city, particularly in its downtown historical area. The original mission, *presidio* (military post), courthouse, and other landmarks built by early Spanish settlers are all still intact. Although the town has grown up around these buildings, zoning regulations require that new construction fit with the distinctive Mediterranean architecture of the "red tile roof" district. The size and design are restricted as are the use of signs, lighting, paint, and landscaping. Thus, the newly built grocery store with its textured stucco walls, tile murals, and arched porticos may be difficult to distinguish from the century-old post office a few blocks away. By studying its material culture, we can see how Santa Barbara manages to preserve its history and heritage and successfully resist the pressures of encroaching urban development. The distinctive "old California" look and feel of the city is perhaps its greatest charm, something that appeals to locals and a steady flock of tourists alike.

Symbolic Culture

Nonmaterial or **symbolic culture** reflects the ideas and beliefs of a group of people. It can be something as specific as a certain rule or custom, like driving on the right side of the road in the United States and on the left side in the United Kingdom. It can also be a broad social system, such as democracy, or a large-scale social pattern, such as marriage. Because symbolic culture is so important to social life, let's look further at some of its main aspects.

FORMS OF COMMUNICATION: SIGNS, GESTURES, AND LANGUAGE One of the most important functions of symbolic culture is to allow us to communicate—through signs, gestures, and language. These form the basis of social interaction, a subject so central to sociology that the entire next chapter is devoted to it.

Signs (or symbols) such as a traffic signal, price tag, sheet of music, or product logo are something designed to meaningfully represent something else. They all convey information. Numbers and letters are the most common signs, but you are probably familiar with other graphic symbols indicating, for instance, which is the men's or women's bathroom, where the elevator is going, how to eject a DVD from the disk drive, or in what lane you should be driving.

While we can easily take for granted the meaning of most symbols, others we may have to learn—like emoticons, those cute (or devious) little expressions that we can now create on our computers. Some symbols may be nearly universal, while others may be particular to a given culture. It may take some interpretive work to understand what a sign means if you are unfamiliar with the context in which it is displayed.

MATERIAL CULTURE the objects associated with a cultural group, such as tools, machines, utensils, buildings, and artwork; any physical object to which we give social meaning

SYMBOLIC CULTURE the ideas associated with a cultural group, including ways of thinking (beliefs, values, and assumptions) and ways of behaving (norms, interactions, and communication)

SIGN a symbol that stands for or conveys an idea

How Is the Architecture of Santa Barbara an Example of Material Culture? Local leaders in Santa Barbara have preserved the city's history and resisted the pressures of encroaching urban development by insisting on maintaining the look of "old California."

Gestures are signs that we make with our body—clapping our hands, nodding our head, or smiling. Sometimes, these acts are referred to as "body language" or "nonverbal communication," since they don't require any words. Gestures can be as subtle as a knowing glance or as obvious as a raised fist.

Most of the time, we can assume that other people will get what we are trying to say with our gestures. But, while gestures might seem natural and universal, just a matter of common sense, few of them besides those that represent basic emotions are innate; most have to be learned. For instance, the "thumbs up" sign, which is associated with praise or approval in the United States, might be interpreted as an obscene or insulting gesture in parts of Asia or South America. Every culture has its own way of expressing praise and insulting others. So before leaving for a country whose culture is unfamiliar, it might be worth finding out whether shaking hands and waving good-bye are appropriate ways to communicate.

Language, probably the most significant component of culture, is what has allowed us to fully develop and express ourselves as human beings, and is what distinguishes us from all other species on the planet. Although language varies from culture to culture, it is a human universal and present in all societies. It is one of the most complex, fluid, and creative symbol systems: letters or pictograms are combined to form words, and words combined to form sentences, in an almost infinite number of possible ways.

Language is the basis of symbolic culture and the primary means through which we communicate with one another. It allows us to convey complicated abstract concepts and to pass along a culture from one generation to the next. Language helps us to conceive of the past and to plan for the future; to categorize the people, places, and things around us; and to share our perspectives on reality. In this way, the cumulative experience of a group of people—their culture—can be contained in and presented through language.

Language is so important that many have argued that it shapes not only our communication but our perception—the way that we see things—as well. In the 1930s, two anthro-

GESTURES the ways in which people use their bodies to communicate without words; actions that have symbolic meaning

LANGUAGE a system of communication using vocal sounds, gestures, or written symbols; the basis of symbolic culture and the primary means through which we communicate with one another and perpetuate our culture

Gestures and Body Language If you travel to a foreign culture, pay special attention to how others interpret your body language. Common friendly gestures in one culture can be offensive or confusing in another.

pologists, Edward Sapir and Benjamin Lee Whorf, conducted research on the impact of language on the mind. In working with the Hopi in the American Southwest, the anthropologists claimed to have discovered that the Hopi had no words to distinguish the past, present, or future and that, therefore, they did not "see" or experience time in the same way as those whose language provided such words. The result of this research was what is known as the **Sapir-Whorf hypothesis** (sometimes referred to as the principle of linguistic relativity), which, breaking with traditional understandings about language, asserts that language actually structures thought, that perception not only suggests the need for words with which to express what is perceived but also that the words themselves help create those same perceptions (Sapir 1949; Whorf 1956).

The studies by Sapir and Whorf were not published until the 1950s, when they were met with competing linguistic theories. In particular, the idea that Eskimos (or Inuits, as they are now called) had many more words for snow than people of Western cultures was sharply challenged, as was the notion that the Hopi had no words for future or past tense (Martin 1986; Pullum 1991). Although there is still some disagreement about how strongly language influences thought (Edgerton 1992), the ideas behind the Sapir-Whorf hypothesis continue to influence numerous social thinkers. Language does play a significant role in how people construct a sense of reality and how they categorize the people, places, and things around them. For instance, the work of sociologist Eviatar Zerubavel (2003) looks at how different groups (like Jews and Arabs, or Serbs and Croats) use language to construct an understanding of their heritage — through what he calls "social memory." In a country like the United States, where there are approximately 50 million foreign-born people who speak well over 100 different languages, there are

bound to be differences in perceptual realities as a result.

Does the Sapir-Whorf hypothesis hold true for your world? Let's take an example closer to home. Perhaps you have seen the 2004 movie *Mean Girls*, loosely based on a pop sociology book by Rosalind Wiseman, *Queen Bees and Wannabes*, about the culture of high school girls (2002). Both book and film present a social map of the cafeteria and school grounds, identifying where different groups of students — the "jocks," "cheerleaders," "goths," "preppies," "skaters," "nerds," "hacky-sack kids," "easy girls," and "partiers" — hang out. The book also includes the "populars" (referred to in the movie as the "plastics") and the popular "wannabes."

You were probably aware of similar categories for distinguishing groups at your school. Do such classification systems influence the way you see other people? Do they lead you to identify people by type and place them into those categories? If no such labels existed (or if your school had different labels), would you still perceive your former classmates the same way? Probably not. These kinds of questions highlight how important language is to the meanings we give to our everyday world.

SAPIR-WHORF HYPOTHESIS
the idea that language structures thought and that ways of looking at the world are embedded in language

Values, Norms, and Sanctions

Values and norms are symbolic culture in action. When we know the values and norms of a group (and see how they are controlled by sanctions), then we can understand their beliefs and ideals and see the evidence of these throughout their everyday lives.

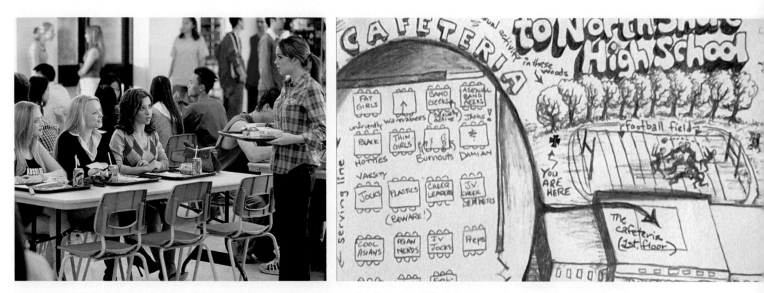

Mean Girls and the Cafeteria Classification System This map from the film *Mean Girls* is an example of how we use different classification schemes to identify and categorize the world around us. Do these classification systems influence the way that you see other people?

VALUES **Values** are the set of shared beliefs that a group of people consider to be worthwhile or desirable in life—what is good or bad, right or wrong, beautiful or ugly. They articulate the essence of everything that a cultural group cherishes in its society. For instance, most Americans value the equality and individual freedoms of democracy. Structural functionalists, like Durkheim, stress the strength of shared values and their role in regulating the behavior of society's members. However, there is not always widespread agreement about which values should represent a society, and values may change or new values may emerge over time. For example, workers' loyalty to their company was once much more important than it is currently. In today's economy, workers realize that they may be "downsized" in times of financial trouble or that they may change careers over the course of their lifetime and hence feel less obligation to an employer.

NORMS **Norms** are the rules and guidelines regarding what kinds of behavior are acceptable; they develop directly out of a culture's value system. Whether legal regulations or just social expectations, norms are largely agreed upon by most members of a group. Some norms are *formal*, or officially codified. These include **laws** (such as those making it illegal to speed in a school zone or drink before you turn age twenty-one), rules for playing basketball or for membership at your local gym, the Amendments to the U.S. Constitution, and the behavioral prescriptions conveyed in the Ten Commandments. Despite the relative authority of formal norms, they are not *always* followed.

Other norms are *informal*, meaning that they are implicit and unspoken. For instance, when we wait in line to buy tickets for a movie, we expect that no one will cut in front of us. Informal norms are so much a part of our assumptions about life that they are embedded in our consciousness; they cover almost every aspect of our social lives, from what we say and do to even how we think and feel. Though we might have difficulty listing all the norms that are a part of everyday life, most of us have learned them quite well. They are simply "the way things are done." Often, it is only when norms are broken (as when someone cuts in line) that we recognize they exist.

Norms can be broken down further in three ways. **Folkways** are the ordinary conventions of everyday life and are not strictly enforced. Examples are standards of dress and rules of etiquette: in most places, wearing flip-flops with a tuxedo is just not done! When people do not conform to folkways, they are thought of as peculiar or eccentric but not really dangerous. **Mores** are norms that carry a greater moral significance and are more closely related to the core values of a cultural group. Unlike folkways, mores are norms to which we all are expected to conform. Breaches are treated seriously and often bring severe repercussions. Such mores as the prohibition of theft, rape, and murder are also formalized, so that there is not only public condemnation for such acts but also strict laws against them. **Taboos**, a type of more, are the most powerful of all norms. We sometimes use the word in a casual way to indicate, say, a forbidden sub-

VALUES ideas about what is desirable or contemptible and right or wrong in a particular group; they articulate the essence of everything that a cultural group cherishes and honors

NORM a rule or guideline regarding what kinds of behavior are acceptable and appropriate within a culture

LAW a common type of formally defined norm providing an explicit statement about what is permissible and what is illegal in a given society

FOLKWAY a loosely enforced norm involving common customs, practices, or procedures that ensure smooth social interaction and acceptance

MORE a norm that carries great moral significance, is closely related to the core values of a cultural group, and often involves severe repercussions for violators

TABOO a norm ingrained so deeply that even thinking about violating it evokes strong feelings of disgust, horror, or revulsion

Norms Are Specific to a Situation, Culture, and Time Period For example, at Mardi Gras or during spring break trips, mild norm violations are tolerated.

ject. But as a sociological term it holds even greater meaning. Taboos are extremely serious. Sociologists say that our sense of what is taboo is so deeply ingrained that the very thought of committing a taboo act, such as cannibalism or incest, evokes strong feelings of disgust or horror.

Norms are specific to a culture, time period, and situation. What would be a folkway to one group might be a more to another. For instance, public nudity is acceptable in many cultures, whereas it is not only frowned upon in American culture but also illegal in most instances. At the same time, Americans do permit nudity in such situations as strip clubs and nudist resorts, allowing for a kind of moral holiday from the strictures of imposed norms. At certain times like Mardi Gras and spring break, mild norm violations are tolerated. Certain places may also lend themselves to the suspension of norms — think Las Vegas (and the slogan "What happens in Vegas, stays in Vegas").

Similarly, what would be considered murder on the city streets might be regarded as valor on the battlefield. And we are probably all aware of how the folkways around proper etiquette and attire can vary greatly from one generation to the next; fifty years ago, girls would never wear jeans to school, for example.

SANCTIONS **Sanctions** are a means of enforcing norms. They include rewards for conformity and punishments for violations. *Positive sanctions* express approval and may come in the form of a handshake or a smile, praise, or perhaps an award. *Negative sanctions* express disapproval and may come in the form of a frown, harsh words, or perhaps a fine or incarceration.

From a functionalist perspective, we can see how sanctions help to establish **social control**, ensuring that people behave to some degree in acceptable ways and thus promoting social cohesion. There are many forms of authority in our culture — from the government and police to school administrators, work supervisors, and even parents. Each has a certain amount of power that they can exercise to get others to follow their rules. So when someone is caught violating a norm, there is usually some prescribed sanction that will then be administered, serving as a deterrent to that behavior.

But equally important in maintaining social order is the process of socialization by which people internalize norms. For instance, in 1983, the U.S. Department of Transportation pioneered the slogan "Friends Don't Let Friends Drive Drunk"; over the years, the slogan has helped change the way we think about our personal responsibility for others, with nearly 80 percent of Americans now claiming that they have taken action to prevent someone from driving while intoxicated. What began as an external statement of a social more quickly became our own personal sense of morality. We are often unaware of the extent to which our own conscience keeps us from violating social norms in

the first place. If we have internalized norms, then outside sanctions are no longer needed to make us do the right thing. Social control, then, frequently looks like self control.

Variations in Culture

We know there are differences between cultures, but there can also be variations within cultures. For instance, sociologists who have tried to identify the core values that make up American society (Robin Williams 1965; Bellah et al. 1985) have found that while there do seem to be certain beliefs that most Americans share, such as freedom and democracy, there are also inconsistencies between such beliefs as individualism (in which we do what is best for ourselves) and humanitarianism (in which we do what is best for others), and between equality and group superiority. New values such as self-fulfillment and environmentalism could also be added to the list, having gained popularity in recent years.

It is even difficult to speak of an "American culture." "Cultural diversity" and "multiculturalism" have both become buzzwords in the past few decades, precisely because people are aware of the increasing variety of cultural groups within American society. **Multiculturalism** generally describes a policy that involves honoring the diverse racial, ethnic, national, and linguistic backgrounds of various individuals and groups. In the following chapters, we will explore some of these differences in greater depth.

Dominant Culture

Although "culture" is a term we usually apply to an entire group of people, what we find in reality is that there are often many subgroups within a larger culture, each with its own particular makeup. These subgroups, however, are not all equal. Some, by virtue of size, wealth, or historical happenstance, are able to lay claim to greater power and influence in society than others. The values, norms, and practices of the most powerful groups are referred to as the mainstream or **dominant culture**, while others are seen as "alternative" or minority views. The power of the dominant culture may mean that other ways of seeing and doing things are relegated to second-class status — in this way, dominant culture

SANCTION positive or negative reactions to the ways that people follow or disobey norms, including rewards for conformity and punishments for violations

SOCIAL CONTROL the formal and informal mechanisms used to elicit conformity to values and norms and thus increase social cohesion

MULTICULTURALISM a policy that values diverse racial, ethnic, national, and linguistic backgrounds and so encourages the retention of cultural differences within society rather than assimilation

DOMINANT CULTURE the values, norms, and practices of the group within society that is most powerful (in terms of wealth, prestige, status, influence, etc.)

As a college student, you may live on campus or make use of the student health services. In doing either of these things, you are in a situation in which someone else's values (in this case, those of the college) can influence your individual choices. For example, even if you get to choose your own roommate, the university has adopted a set of values that narrows your choice for you before you even make it. And if your student health service is operated by an outside contractor (for example, the local Catholic hospital), there may be constraints placed on the type of reproductive health services you can receive there.

Rules like these come from a tradition in which the university acts *in loco parentis* — in place of the parents — to protect and provide moral guidance for its students. The Bradley University Student Handbook for 1952–53, for example, forbids women from entering men's residences at any time and places severe constraints on when and under what conditions men may enter women's residences. This same handbook lists a complicated procedure for female students to follow in order to attend off-campus events in the evenings, and there are even lists of appropriate attire for the classroom, athletic events, and other university functions.

While most universities have abandoned the strict behavior codes that were once widespread, they still act *in loco parentis* in a variety of ways. One of them is the restrictions they place on different-sex roommates, even in coed dorms. The university has taken on the job of protecting students from the apparently undesirable consequences of living with a romantic partner. And if the student health service limits your access to certain means of birth control, then choices about whom to live with, how to conduct your sex life, and how to include your romantic partner in your domestic life have already been made for you by the university. If you want to live in university housing and use student health services, you must accept the constraints imposed by university values, even if you do not share those values. If you want to live without those constraints, then you must choose to live in a private, off-campus setting.

---

can produce cultural **hegemony**, or dominance (Gramsci 1985, 1988).

Let's take popular music as an example. Commercial radio stations often have very limited playlists. No matter what the genre (country, pop, hip-hop, metal), the songs played are determined by station and record company business interests, not your artistic preferences. Truly new artists and alternative sounds can be heard only on public, college, or pirate radio stations or online — and these outlets may have significantly fewer financial resources and reach far fewer listeners. The dominant status of commercial radio and the corporate interests of the music industry dictate that musicians outside the mainstream like Lower Dens, Warpaint, or The Divine Comedy will never be as big as Lady Gaga or Justin Bieber.

HEGEMONY term developed by Antonio Gramsci to describe the cultural aspects of social control, whereby the ideas of the dominant social group are accepted by all of society

SUBCULTURE a group within society that is differentiated by its distinctive values, norms, and lifestyle

COUNTERCULTURE a group within society that openly rejects and/or actively opposes society's values and norms

Subcultures

If sociologists focus only on the dominant culture in American society, we risk overlooking the inequalities that structure our society — as well as the influences that even nondominant cultural groups can exert. The United States is filled with thousands of nondominant groups, any of which could be called a **subculture** — a culture within a culture. A subculture is a particular social world that has a distinctive way of life, including its own set of values and norms, practices, and beliefs, but that exists harmoniously within the larger mainstream culture. A subculture can be based on ethnicity, age, interests, or anything else that draws individuals together. Any of the following groups could be considered subcultures within American society: Korean Americans, senior citizens, snowboarders, White Sox fans, greyhound owners, firefighters, Trekkers.

Countercultures

A **counterculture**, another kind of subgroup, differs from a subculture in that its norms and values are often incompatible with or in direct opposition to the mainstream (Zellner

1995). Some countercultures are political or activist groups attempting to bring about social change; others resist mainstream values by living outside society or practicing an alternative lifestyle. In the 1960s, hippies, antiwar protesters, feminists, and others in the so-called political left were collectively known as "the counterculture." But radicals come in many stripes. Any group that opposes the dominant culture, whether they are eco-terrorists, computer hackers, or modern-day polygamists, can be considered a counterculture.

In the mid-1990s, American countercultures of the far right gained prominence with the revelation that the main perpetrator of the April 1995 bombing of the Alfred R. Murrah Federal Building in Oklahoma City, Timothy McVeigh, had ties to "militia" or "patriot" groups. And he wasn't the only American with such ties. In 1996, the Southern Poverty Law Center counted 858 active groups in the United States belonging to the "militia movement" (the number was at 1,360 in 2012 (Southern Poverty Law Center 2013)). Members of this movement, who trace their heritage to the Minutemen of the American Revolution (an elite fighting force, the first to arrive at a battle), see themselves as the last line of defense for the liberties provided in the U.S. Constitution. They believe, moreover, that the federal government has become the enemy of those liberties. They hold that gun control, environmental protection laws, and other legislation violates individual and states' rights and that events like the FBI's 1993 siege of the Branch Davidian compound in Waco, Texas (resulting in eighty-two deaths), call for armed grassroots organization.

Since the Oklahoma City bombing, some militia groups have courted recognition as legitimate American institutions rather than radical organizations. Others have remained openly countercultural. While members of such groups consider themselves "patriots" and "true Americans," they believe that the institutions and values of contemporary American society need drastic revision.

At the furthest extreme are militia groups who hold that the present American government is entirely illegitimate and that they are not its subjects but rather "sovereign citizens," "common-law citizens," or "freemen." Members refuse to carry such documents as driver's licenses and social security cards, and refuse to pay taxes or observe any government restrictions on their property. They have gone so far as to establish "common-law courts" that oppose local and federal government regulations and seek to prosecute government officials (Diamond 1995). In May 2010, West Memphis, Arkansas, police officers Brandon Paudert and Bill Evans were gunned down during a traffic stop by Jerry and Joe Kane, a father and son on their way from Las Vegas to Florida. The Kanes, who were later killed as they attempted to escape, were "sovereign citizens." Their complicated conspiracy theories framed all official authority figures (such as law enforcement officers) as enemies in their attempt to access secret Treasury Department accounts that they believed were set up by the federal government to control their identities. Unfortunately, Officers Paudert and Evans were not the first murdered by sovereign citizens—police in Alabama, New Hampshire, and Idaho have been killed at what should have been routine traffic stops when the "sovereigns" they pulled over began arguing about their rights.

As bizarre as their beliefs seem, and as tragic as their consequences have been, some of their claims have gained traction in more mainstream circles. For example, sovereign citizens' refusal to pay taxes seems to have caught on: in a 2008 criminal tax evasion trial, actor Wesley Snipes claimed to be a sovereign tax protester in his attempt to avoid paying federal taxes. Despite the roots of the movement in extreme, violent, racist ideologies, this influential African American celebrity used sovereign citizen arguments to defend himself. He was ultimately sentenced to three years in prison, but it remains to be seen whether his sentence will have a chilling effect on the activities of the estimated 300,000 sovereigns around the country.

Culture Wars

Although a countercultural group can pose a threat to the larger society, conflict does not always come from the extreme margins of society; it can also emerge from within the mainstream. Culture in any diverse society is characterized by points of tension and division. There is not always uniform agreement about which values and norms ought to be upheld. The term **culture wars** is often used to describe the clashes that arise as a result (Bloom 1987; Garber 1998). The clashes are frequently played out in the media, where social commentators and pundits debate the issues. Culture wars are mainly waged over values and morality and the solutions to social problems, with liberals and conservatives fighting to define culture in America. One notable example of a battle in the culture wars was the scuffle over media and morality that surrounded singer Janet Jackson's breast-baring during the 2004 Super Bowl telecast; another was the rise of the ultraconservative "Tea Party" movement during 2010. Tea Partyers favor anti-gay rhetoric and call for drastic cuts in taxes and social welfare funding. Other questions of family values, changing gender roles, frontiers in bioethics, violence in the media, and school prayer have all been recent topics for discussion. Culture wars are bound to continue as we confront the difficult realities that are a part of living in a democratic society.

> **CULTURE WARS** clashes within mainstream society over the values and norms that should be upheld

IN THE FUTURE

Otaku Culture and the Globalization of Niche Interests

If you are not an *otaku*, you probably don't know what *otaku* is. If you are an *otaku*, you may not want others to know what *otaku* is, since *otaku* culture has often been misunderstood by those on the outside. So, what is *otaku*?

Otaku is a Japanese word used to describe devoted fans, usually of manga, anime, or video games. *Otaku* are extremely knowledgeable about whatever it is they are fans of—and while that kind of obsessive interest is sometimes looked down upon by others who don't share it, *otaku* themselves see this intense knowledge as a badge of honor. They view themselves as dedicated rather than obsessed, connoisseurs rather than fanatics, and superior to other hobbyists who aren't as erudite about the object of their enthusiasm. In fact, *otaku* may now be certified as experts in Japan by taking a rigorous, nationally recognized exam (McNicol 2006).

Organizing and displaying their belongings is a central part of *otaku* culture—many *otaku* have special rooms in their homes for their museum-like collections of action figures, paintings, or comic books. Photographs of *otaku* in their "*otaku* spaces" (Galbraith 2012) illuminate the connection between fantasy worlds, material commodities, and virtual communities that *otaku* culture uniquely embodies.

Once confined entirely to Japan (and to small neighborhood clubs even there), the internet has made *otaku* culture accessible to people all over the world. Indeed, fans of just about everything now depend on social media to connect them with each other, and to allow them to share their fascinations with others who understand and appreciate what it means to be truly dedicated. *Otaku* who in the past might have been viewed with suspicion because of their intense involvement in what others considered a fringe pastime can now validate their commitments by interacting with others who share them, whether they are a mile down the street or a world away.

Closely related to its reliance on social media, *otaku* culture is also characterized by its global reach. Indeed, what is distinctive about *otaku* culture is the uncommon direction in which it has traveled. Instead of the U.S. or another Western culture spreading eastward, *otaku* culture is an example of the East influencing the West: *otaku* represents the global-

ization and transnationalization of what had previously been Japan-specific.

This is one of the ways that *otaku*, to quote the science fiction writer William Gibson, "live in the future" (Gibson 2001). "There is something post-national about it, extrageographic," Gibson goes on to say, meaning that in *otaku* culture, citizenship matters less than shared interests, nationality less than knowledge, and location less than expertise. Your identity is defined by what you're into, by where your passions lie, and by what "geeks you out."

And here lies the paradox of *otaku* culture: *otaku* are both extraordinarily detached and extraordinarily connected (LaMarre 2004). Detached from the local, connected to the global; detached from broad knowledge, connected to hyperfocused data; detached from conventional interactions, connected via mediated relationships. Is this paradox of detachment and connection a "harbinger for the future" (Hayase 2010)? Will we all be *otaku* someday?

East to West The internet helped spread *otaku* culture from Japan to the rest of the world.

Ideal vs. Real Culture

Some norms and values are more aspired to than actually practiced. It is useful to draw a distinction between **ideal culture**, the norms and values that members of a society believe should be observed in principle, and **real culture**, the patterns of behavior that actually exist. Whether it is an organization that falls short of its own mission statement or a person who says one thing and does another (a devout Catholic, for example, who finds himself seeking a divorce), what we believe in and what we do may be two different things.

Let's take, as another example, corporate culture in America. The ideal culture of the workplace usually dictates that raises and promotions be given to employees who have demonstrated exemplary performance or productiveness through skill, dedication, or innovative thinking. In practice, these rewards are also given to less-deserving employees who are appreciated for other qualities, such as obedience, charisma, or their special relationship with the boss. While most people believe that hard work or initiative should be what determines success, they know that in reality it is not always these qualities that are rewarded and that, indeed, sometimes employees climb the ladder for more dubious reasons (Hagberg and Heifetz 2002).

Another example of how real and ideal culture may clash in the workplace comes from a management book called *Weird Ideas That Work* (2001), by Stanford professor Robert Sutton, who observes that while corporate executives often claim they value innovation, they usually reward conformity instead. Sutton recommends that instead of hiring comfortable, familiar types of people who know the rules and submit without argument to the authority of their superiors, corporations should hire eccentrics who ignore the rules, enjoy a good fight, and defy authority. For those who claim they value creativity, Sutton argues this is the only way to really achieve their ideals.

DATA WORKSHOP
Analyzing Mass Media and Popular Culture

Seeing Culture in Popular Magazines and Web Sites

Clothes and cars do not fulfill instinctual drives for survival, but for most people, they are necessary for modern living. Cultural norms dictate that we cover our bodies. And, in most areas of the United States, you need a car in order to get to work, school, or the grocery store.

For young women, the clothing brands Apple Bottom, House of Dereon, and Baby Phat conjure up a markedly separate image than the clothing brands Abercrombie and Fitch, Hollister, and American Eagle. For young men, the shoe brands Adidas and Air Jordan call up a distinct lifestyle when compared to the shoe brands Birkenstock and Teva. In the same way, an energy-efficient Toyota Prius seems diametrically opposed to a gas-guzzling Cadillac Escalade. These images seem very different, but they have one thing in common: culture shapes each of them.

IDEAL CULTURE the norms, values, and patterns of behavior that members of a society believe should be observed in principle

REAL CULTURE the norms, values, and patterns of behavior that actually exist within a society (which may or may not correspond to the society's ideals)

Culture Wars Often Play Out on Early-Morning or Late-Night Television George Stephanopoulos (second from left) spends every Sunday morning interviewing politicians on *This Week with George Stephanopoulos*. On Saturday nights, comic actors on *Saturday Night Live* satirize politicians, media pundits, and other participants in the latest cultural clash.

In this Data Workshop, you will use existing sources — in this case, popular magazines and web sites — to discover how culture gives meaning to items considered necessary for modern living. You will use content analysis to study the magazines and web sites and arrive at some conclusions. You may want to refer back to Chapter 2 to reread the section on existing sources, just for a quick review.

Pick your necessity — clothes or cars. Now go to your local bookstore or newsstand and identify magazines that are dedicated to that necessity. For example, *Lucky, Glamour, Essence, Ebony*, and *GQ* (for clothes); *Car and Driver, Road and Track*, and *Motor Trend* (for cars) cover these territories. You may also look at relevant web sites such as Pinterest (www.pinterest.com), fashion blogs, and car web sites. Immerse yourself in the content of the magazine and web site and answer the following questions. Support your answers with data (like clippings of photos or articles) from the magazines or web sites.

> **TECHNOLOGY** material artifacts and the knowledge and techniques required to use them

* How much of what is contained in these magazines or web sites deal with the bare minimum of clothing or transportation (plain white t-shirts; basic three-cylinder cars; $10 shoes)? How are these topics presented in the magazines?

* What types of subcultural or regional differences in clothes or cars are revealed?

* What types of products and services are advertised?

* What elements of material and symbolic culture are visible?

* What types of values and beliefs are embedded in the fashion layouts, beauty tips, ads, car detailing, car accessories, or car models?

Popular Magazines What kinds of lifestyles are these magazines trying to sell to consumers?

* How does the content of the magazine or web site reflect the specific cultural context in which they are produced?

* How does the content affect you and your desires? Do you find yourself craving the clothes or cars pictured?

* Who benefits when you act out these desires by purchasing the goods and services presented (spa services, clothes, car detailing, auto parts)?

Finally, which force is more important in shaping human behavior when it comes to modern necessities — basic needs or culture?

There are two options for completing this Data Workshop.

Option 1 (informal): Jot down notes based on your answers to the Data Workshop questions, and bring pictures or articles that support your observation. Then get together into small groups to share your findings.

Option 2 (formal): Translate those jotted notes into a three- or four-page essay, supplemented with clippings that support your points. Make sure you address the Data Workshop questions in your essay.

Cultural Change

Cultures usually change slowly and incrementally, although change can also happen in rapid and dramatic ways. We saw rapid change as a result of the social movements of the 1960s, and we may be seeing it again, albeit for different reasons, as we move through the early part of the 2000s. Change is usually thought of as "progress" — we move from what seem to be outmoded ways of doing things to more innovative practices. Earlier in the chapter, we saw how variations in culture, whether they resulted from multiculturalism, countercultures, or culture wars, could all lead to growth and change in the larger society. Now we look at several other important processes that can also contribute to cultural change.

Technological Change

One of the most significant influences on any society is its material culture. And most changes in material culture tend to be technological. We usually equate **technology** with new "hi-tech" electronic or digital devices. But technology can be anything from a hammer to the space shuttle, from graffiti to a search engine algorithm hypertext markup language (HTML), as well as the "know-how" it takes to use it.

New technology often provides the basis and structure through which culture is disseminated to members of a social group. For instance, we are currently living in the digital age or Information Age, a revolutionary time in history spurred by the invention of the microchip. This technology has already produced radical changes in society, much as the steam engine did during the Industrial Revolution of the eighteenth and nineteenth centuries.

One of the most prominent features of this Information Age is the spread of mass media. It was not until the 1950s that television became a regular part of daily life in America, and only in the 1990s that the internet became commonplace. Most of us now would have trouble remembering life before these technological advancements; that's how much we rely on them and take them for granted. This digital revolution is shaping our culture — and the rest of the world's — at an increasingly rapid pace.

Some postmodern theorists argue that the rapid proliferation of new technologies creates a disconnect between old social values (like hard work and thrift) and new cultural ideals like consumerism (Bell 1976). In fact, many social thinkers believe that technology is the single greatest influence on society today, a concept known as **technological determinism** (Veblen 1921/2004). This would mean that computers, cell phones, and other forms of mass communication are defining who we become — how we think, feel, and act in the world. Educator Marshall McLuhan, who studied the impact of media technology on human perception, is famous for his assertion that "the medium is the message" (1964). What he meant is that it is not so much the content (for instance, the advertisement, sitcom, or song) with which we should be concerned, but rather the medium itself (radio, television, or the internet), through which the content is delivered. The medium is what actually has the greater power to change our cultural framework.

This is an important proposition to consider in our increasingly connected world. We can now be in almost constant contact with each other and with sources of information and entertainment. But media and information technology also have the potential to distort our sense of time and space, identity and reality. The Information Age has not arrived without great cultural consequence.

Cultural Diffusion and Cultural Leveling

Cultural change can also occur when different groups share their material and nonmaterial culture with each other, a process called **cultural diffusion**. Since each culture has its own tools, beliefs, and practices, exposure to another culture may mean that certain aspects of it will then be appropriated. For example, as McDonald's-style restaurants set up shop in cultures where fast food had previously been unknown, it wasn't only hamburgers that got relocated: other aspects of fast-food culture came along as well. According to Eric Schlosser (2002), Japanese diners during the 1980s doubled their consumption of fast-food

meals — and their rates of obesity. Heart disease and stroke risks also have increased. While there is no direct proof of cause and effect here, it is clear that a single cultural product cannot be exported without carrying a raft of cultural consequences with it.

Cultural diffusion usually occurs in the direction from more developed to less developed nations. In particular, "Western" culture has spread rapidly to the rest of the world — driven by capitalism and globalization and aided by new forms of transportation and communication that allow for ever-faster exchanges.

Cultural leveling occurs when cultures that were once distinct become increasingly similar to one another. If you travel, you may have already seen this phenomenon in towns across the United States and countries around the world. The Wal-Marts on the interstates, for instance, have driven independent mom-and-pop stores from town squares all over the country. Many people bemoan this development and the consequent loss of uniqueness and diversity it represents. As cultures begin to blend, new mixes emerge. This can result in an interesting hybrid, for example, of East and West, but can also mean a blander, more diluted culture of sameness. While Western culture is a dominant force in this process, cultural diffusion and cultural leveling do not have to occur in a one-way direction. Other societies have also had an influence on culture in the United States. For instance, Japanese anime was for many years a fringe interest in America, usually associated with computer geeks and other outsiders; now Hayao Miyazaki, Japan's leading anime filmmaker, has teamed up with Disney to sell his movies (like *Spirited Away, Howl's Moving Castle*, and *Ponyo*) to a mainstream American audience. Still, America, the dominant producer of global media, remains the primary exporter of cultural content throughout the world.

Cultural Imperialism

Other countries around the world are becoming inundated with America's television programs, movies, CDs, satellite radio broadcasts, magazines, and web content. You can watch MTV in India and *Jackass 3D* in Uzbekistan, surf the internet in Vietnam, or listen to Rihanna in Morocco. Many see this as good news for the spread of freedom and democracy, for others to have the kind of access to information and entertainment that Americans regularly enjoy. But the media are necessarily a reflection of the culture in which they are produced. So not only are we selling entertainment, we are also implicitly promoting

TECHNOLOGICAL DETERMINISM the notion that developments in technology provide the primary driving force behind social change

CULTURAL DIFFUSION the dissemination of material and symbolic culture (tools and technology, beliefs and behavior) from one group to another

CULTURAL LEVELING the process by which cultures that were once unique and distinct become increasingly similar

ON THE JOB

U.S. Military: Cultural Emissaries

An e-mail from Afghanistan, sent May 30, 2003, reads as follows:

A couple of hours after we landed, we had a convoy to Kabul. It took about two hours, but I will never forget the trip. The scenery was incredible. I knew that there were mountains in Afghanistan, but there are so many that it is an unbelievable sight. . . . The native people are also a sight to see. These people are incredibly resourceful making shelter from clay and mud and using the minimal resources they have to work with. (Carroll 2006, p. 67)

Like most Americans, the writer of this e-mail, Army Sergeant Andrew Simkiewicz, had never been to Afghanistan before. His deployment there was part of Operation Enduring Freedom, America's post–September 11 effort to hunt Al Qaeda terrorists, depose Taliban leaders, and find Osama bin Laden. You might not think a soldier would notice the beauty of the Afghan landscape, but soldiers aren't one-dimensional warriors, and their missions aren't solely combat oriented. Wherever they serve, American military personnel have the opportunity to learn about other cultures and to act as representatives of American culture to the people they encounter.

When "in country," soldiers notice the effects of war on the citizens of places like Iraq. They also notice the differences between the foreign citizens' experiences and those of ordinary Americans at home. Here Army Captain James R. Sosnicky describes an Iraqi woman he knew who sold cigarettes in the Baghdad Green Zone:

When she was a young girl, Iranian missiles pounded the street. The Americans have bombed her three times since, in 1991, 1998, and 2003. Mariam . . . knows things women her age in the United States do not. A couple of weeks ago, I was in Baghdad visiting with Mariam. There was an explosion in the distance. "What do you think," I asked, "car bomb or mortar round?" "Definitely a mortar round," she replied. Most girls in the U.S. have a tin ear for such things. (Carroll 2006, p. 130)

Soldiers also come to recognize the deep connections and similarities between the people whose territory they occupy and their friends and family members back in the United States, as does Army First Sergeant August C. Hohl Jr., writing from Afghanistan:

[T]heir personal and religious beliefs are not unlike ours in that everyone understands the importance of reaching out to and being charitable towards one another. . . . [W]hile we all might live differently due to environmental, geographical, and educational conditions, people are basically the same inside. Learning some of the history, social habits, and religion of this country has left me with a profound sense of hope that we can assist the people here. But we're not so smart that we can't learn from them, too. (Carroll 2006, p. 68)

U.S. service personnel represent U.S. culture anywhere they are posted — often in war zones where they may or may not be welcome. So they engage in humanitarian work in addition to their combat assignments — here, Sergeant Simkiewicz tells of breaking Army rules to help Afghan children:

We were told not to give any of our food or water to the natives. However, I find it hard to see these cute children starving on the side of the road while I have a case of bottled water next to me in the cab. Needless to say, a half dozen of my waters were hurled from my window along the way. (Carroll 2006, p. 67)

Elsewhere in Afghanistan, soldiers like Army Chief Warrant Officer II Jared S. Jones distribute humanitarian aid, "ranging from personal hygiene to school supplies, shoes, and soccer balls. It is always a pleasure to see the difference we are making for these people, even if it is only one small village" (Carroll 2006, p. 70). As Jones reminds us, "combat is only one facet of the military, a necessary evil" (Carroll 2006, p. 71). Their other roles will include "cultural emissary" and "cultural observer" as well, roles that are just as important — and perhaps even more important — than the role of warrior.

Of the countries that consider the messages in Western media dangerous, some forbid or restrict the flow of information, others impose various kinds of censorship, and still others try to promote their own cultural productions. Iran, for example, officially censors all non-Islamic media content on television, radio, film, and the internet (though many Iranians use hidden satellite dishes to plug into illegal Western programming). In the long run, it may be very difficult to prevent cultural imperialism from spreading.

American Culture in Perspective

Because American culture is highly visible worldwide, the country's moral and political values have equally high visibility. That means when reruns of *Friends* or *Grey's Anatomy* air in places like Egypt or Malaysia or Lebanon, American values on the topics of sex, gender, work, and family are being transmitted as well. When such military ventures as Operation Enduring Freedom (in Afghanistan) or Operation Iraqi Freedom are undertaken, part of their mission involves exporting the political values associated with democracy, capitalism, and even Christianity. Well, you may say, *Friends* is funny, and *Grey's* is a great way to kill time, and democracy is a good thing — so what's the problem here?

In some parts of the world, the premise of these shows would be unthinkable in real life: in many traditional cultures, both women and men live with their parents until they marry, sometimes to partners chosen for them by their families. A show in which young men and women live on their own, with almost no family involvement, dating and sleeping with people to whom they are not married, presents values that are distasteful in these cultures. American values, or at least the perceptions of them shaped by Hollywood and pop-culture exports, can breed negative feelings toward the United States. The value placed on individualism, sexual freedom, and material satisfaction in American life can antagonize cultures that place a higher value on familial involvement and moral and social restraint, and may result in anti-American sentiment.

CULTURAL IMPERIALISM the imposition of one culture's beliefs and practices on another culture through mass media and consumer products rather than by military force

Politics can generate the same anti-American feeling. For example, the United States has recently been involved in attempts to stem the development of nuclear weapons in developing countries like Iran and Pakistan while still maintaining our own nuclear arsenal at home. Other nations may question why American politicians think they should be able to withhold from other countries privileges the United States itself enjoys, such as developing a nuclear weapons program. Much of the resentment against America abroad

Shoppers at a Gap Store in Downtown Tokyo, Japan As global capitalism and large multinational corporations become more dominant, we increasingly see the same companies, brands, and products around the world. Is this cultural leveling good or bad?

certain Western ideas. And it can become a problem when the images and ideas found in the media conflict with the traditional norms and values of other countries.

The proliferation of Western media amounts to what some social critics call **cultural imperialism** (Schiller 1995). These critics conceive of media as a kind of invading force that enters a country and takes it over — much like an army, but with film, television, music, soft drinks, and running shoes instead of guns. Historically, imperialism involved the conquering of other nations by monarchies for their own glory and enrichment. The British Empire, for example, was once able to use its military might to occupy and control a third of the world's total land area. But now it is possible to cross a border and to occupy a territory culturally, without setting foot on foreign soil. Because they command so many economic resources, Western media companies are powerful enough to create a form of cultural domination wherever their products go.

GLOBAL PERSPECTIVE

New Social Media and Social Change

On June 20, 2009, while attending a protest over the disputed presidential election in Iran, Nedā Āghā-Soltān was shot and killed. While this sort of tragedy is all too common at political protests around the world, this death was different because it was caught on video. Within minutes of her death, the heartbreaking video had been uploaded to Facebook and YouTube, where it quickly went viral. Although the protests were ultimately unsuccessful in their attempt to challenge the election results, Nedā Āghā-Soltān's death has remained a powerful rallying point for the Iranian opposition — in Iran and around the world.

The use of social media during the protests in Iran, as well as similar unrest in Moldova, led some commentators to call it the "Twitter revolution," in recognition of the growing role that social media played in the protests (Musgrove 2009). The next few years saw even more prominent revolutions and protests in Tunisia, Egypt, Libya, Yemen, Bahrain, and Syria that seemed to be facilitated by social media use. Although they were originally used exclusively for entertainment, social media web sites like Twitter, Facebook, YouTube, and Flickr were playing an increasingly prominent role in social protests all around the world, both as an organizing tool and a way to document events as they happened. In many countries where the government exercised control over traditional mass media outlets, social media provided protesters with a way to coordinate their activities and let the rest of the world know what was happening.

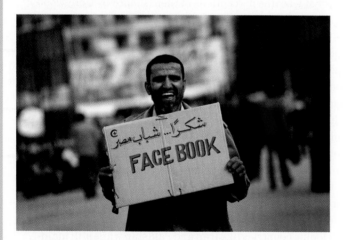

Social Media for Social Change A protestor during an anti-government protest in Cairo.

Philip Howard, a sociologist and director of the Project on Information Technology and Political Islam, studied the effect that social media like Twitter had on the revolutions in Tunisia and Egypt. He concluded that "social media played a central role in shaping political debates" during the so-called Arab Spring. Although this conclusion is hotly contested by some, Howard and his fellow researchers looked at patterns of activity on Twitter, concluding that not only did the volume of tweets from Egypt increase almost tenfold during their protests, but that "spike(s) in online revolutionary conversations often preceded major events on the ground." The report went on to conclude that the relatively young and tech-savvy populations in Tunisia and Egypt, combined with the justified distrust many had for mass media, made social media a powerful tool for protesters. They also found that more than 30 percent of the tweets with hash tags connected to the protests were from female tweeters, suggesting that social media sites may enable much greater female participation in social movements than might have otherwise been possible.

Not everyone believes that social media were instrumental in these protests. Some argue that widely connected social networks spread confusion as much as they coordinate action. Others believe that the sort of weak social ties created online are incapable of supporting anything as difficult as a revolution. Despite these objections, social media have their defenders, who point out that although "the Arab world has long had democratic activists," before the social media–rich Arab Spring they had never "toppled a dictator" (Howard 2011). As Howard pointed out, revolutionaries "were not inspired by Facebook; they were inspired by the real tragedies documented on Facebook." However, almost everyone agrees that there is a dark side to the use of social media as well. In the days following the failed protests in Iran (a non-Arab country), the government showed it could also use social media to rally its own supporters and as a source of incriminating evidence when arresting protesters. Some reports have even suggested that Iranian officials monitor the social media activity of Iranians abroad, and use the information to crack down on their families.

From the start, the internet has been used in unexpected and unintended ways, toward both harmful and helpful ends. How will the internet be used in the future? Keep your eye on the global news to find out.

Table 3.1 Theory in Everyday Life

Perspective	Approach to Culture	Case Study: Religion
Structural Functionalism	Values and norms are widely shared and agreed upon; they contribute to social stability by reinforcing common bonds and constraining individual behavior.	Religion is an important social institution that functions as the basis for the morals and ethics that followers embrace, and that are applied to both society and the individual, thus promoting social order.
Conflict Theory	Values and norms are part of the dominant culture and tend to represent and protect the interests of the most powerful groups in society.	Religion serves to control the masses by creating rules for behavior; sanctions against violators may not be equally or fairly applied. Culture wars reflect tensions among groups over which values and norms will dominate.
Symbolic Interactionism	Values and norms are social constructions; meaning is created, maintained, and changed through ongoing social interaction.	Religion consists of beliefs and rituals that are part of the interaction among followers. Reciting the Lord's Prayer, bowing toward Mecca, or keeping a kosher home are meaningful displays of different religious values and norms. Leaders may play a role in creating social change.

emerges as a result of this type of phenomenon — our perceived failure to live up to our own political values and ideals, or to apply them fairly to others.

Putting American culture in perspective means recognizing that because it is pervasive, it may also be viewed with suspicion and even contempt when the values it expresses clash with those of other cultures. But the nature of anti-Americanism is complex — it's not merely a failure by other nations to understand "good" television shows or accept "superior" political systems. There are meaningful cultural differences between Americans and others, and we should keep those differences in mind as we read about or travel to other cultures. Indeed, there are cultural differences of similar magnitude within the United States as well. The question of the meaning of American culture in a larger global context is a complicated one.

CLOSING COMMENTS

In this chapter, we have seen how seemingly simple elements of material culture (cars and comic books) and symbolic culture (norms and values) create complex links between the individual and her society, as well as between different societies around the globe. American culture in particular, sociologists often argue, is hegemonic (dominant), in that certain interests (such as creating a global market for American products) prevail, while others (such as encouraging local development and self-determination) are subordinated. Within the United States, this can mean that the cultural norms, values, beliefs, and practices of certain subcultures — such as minority ethnic or religious groups — are devalued. Elsewhere, it can mean that America is accused of cultural imperialism by nations whose values and practices are different from ours.

Whose cultural values and practices are "better" or "right"? The sociological perspective avoids these evaluative terms when examining culture, choosing instead to take a relativistic approach. In other words, different cultures should (in most cases) be evaluated not according to outside standards but according to their own sets of values and norms. But we should always recognize that this commitment to cultural relativism is a value in itself — which makes cultural relativism neither right nor wrong but rather a proper subject for intellectual examination.

Everything You Need to Know about Culture

> " Culture is the entire way of life of a group of people, including both material and symbolic elements, that acts as a lens through which one views the world and is passed from one generation to the next. "

COMPONENTS OF CULTURE

* **Material culture:** any physical object to which we give social meaning

* **Signs:** a symbol that stands for or conveys an idea

* **Gestures:** the ways people use their bodies to communicate without words

* **Language:** a system of communication using vocal sounds, gestures, or written symbols; the primary means through which we communicate with each other and perpetuate our culture

* **Values:** shared beliefs that a group of people consider to be worthwhile or desirable; they articulate everything that a cultural group cherishes and honors

* **Norms:** rules or guidelines regarding what kinds of behavior are acceptable and appropriate

* **Sanctions:** positive or negative reactions to the ways people follow or disobey norms

REVIEW

1. List five pieces of material culture you have with you right now, and explain what these pieces indicate about the tastes, habits, and lifestyles supported by your cultural group.

2. When was the last time you violated a folkway? How were you sanctioned? What sorts of sanctions do we impose on those who go against our accepted mores?

3. Make a list of ways in which the media—including advertisements—reach you each day. How many of these media messages represent mainstream Western ideals? What kinds of media messages do not conform to these norms?

Seeing Red

What does the color red mean in different cultures?

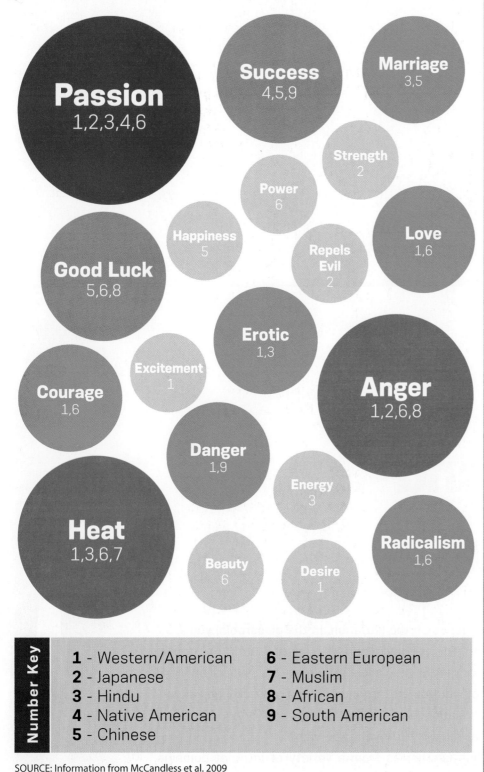

Passion
1,2,3,4,6

Success
4,5,9

Marriage
3,5

Strength
2

Power
6

Happiness
5

Repels Evil
2

Love
1,6

Good Luck
5,6,8

Erotic
1,3

Excitement
1

Anger
1,2,6,8

Courage
1,6

Danger
1,9

Energy
3

Heat
1,3,6,7

Radicalism
1,6

Beauty
6

Desire
1

Number Key

1 - Western/American
2 - Japanese
3 - Hindu
4 - Native American
5 - Chinese
6 - Eastern European
7 - Muslim
8 - African
9 - South American

SOURCE: Information from McCandless et al. 2009

EXPLORE

Breaching Age Norms on Television

Norm breaching tells us a lot about the unwritten rules of social life. When everyday norms are violated, people often get very uncomfortable. Visit the Everyday Sociology Blog to find out what a hidden camera show can tell us about how society deals with people who break norms.

http://wwnPag.es/trw403

CHAPTER 4

The Self and Interaction

Who are you? Well, it really depends on the situation. In the classroom, you are a student; at home, you are a child, a sibling, a parent, a spouse, and/or a partner. In your office, you are the boss or the employee; in your studio, you are an artist or a woodworker. These are all facets of who you are, grounded in the real activities of your everyday life—school, work, hobbies, relationships. Online, though, reality need not limit you to such mundane identities. Online, you can be anyone you want!

Below is a sampling of actual online usernames from a variety of internet domains. Since people generally choose their own usernames, we can assume that they are meant

to express something about the user's personality — sort of like a personalized license plate. Some names might cause us to modify our opening question a bit: who do these people *think* they are? Or, perhaps, *wish* they *were*?

angelbabee3	mostwanted
bluechihuahua	motherwitch
crazyaboutjesus	nerd87
heartbreakah	rebelcutie
intensejello	superman22
laker4life	viciousvixen
luvsexxy	yummmiest
mauiwowee	zendoc

Choosing a username is one of many ways we express ourselves in social interaction. Because our online identities are often disembodied and may be removed from the context of our everyday lives, we can say anything we want about who we are (or think we are, or wish to be). Whether or not these folks are actually heartbreakers, rebel cuties, or superheroes in real life, they can be those things online. What's your username?

HOW TO READ THIS CHAPTER

In this chapter, you will learn how the self is connected to all social phenomena (such as gender and race, and the effects of mass media) and how interaction constructs them all. You will be acquiring some new analytic tools, including the concepts of socialization and impression management, which will be referenced again in the chapters to come. In addition, you will be introduced to a new way of looking at the self — indeed, a new way of looking at *your* self — that emphasizes the role of the social in creating the individual. And you will be reminded of the reverse: as your society makes you who you are, you have a role (in fact, many roles) to play in shaping your society.

What Is Human Nature?

"That's just human nature" is a phrase we often use to explain everything from violence and jealousy to love and altruism. But what is human nature, really? What is the thing about us that is unique and irreducible, that we all have in common and that separates us from other creatures? From a sociologist's perspective, it is culture and society that make us human. These things that we have created also make us who we are. We have to learn the meanings we give to food, housing, sex, and everything else, and society is the teacher.

You would be a very different person had you been born in fourteenth-century Japan, in an Aztec peasant family, or in the Norwegian royal court. You would have learned a different language, a different set of everyday skills, and a different set of meanings about how the world works. Also, your sense of who you are would be radically different in each case because of the particular social structures and interactions you would encounter. If you were a member of an Aztec peasant family, for example, you would expect to be married to someone of your parents' choosing in your early teens (McCaa 1994). Girls would be considered old maids if they were still single at age fifteen and might end up as prostitutes or concubines if they did not find a husband by this tender age.

The Nature vs. Nurture Debate

If it is culture and society that make us human, what role does our genetic makeup play? Aren't we *born* with certain instincts? These are questions posed in what is often called the **nature vs. nurture debate**. Those taking the nature side, often sociobiologists, some psychologists, and others in the natural sciences, argue that behavioral traits can be explained by genetics. Those taking the nurture side, soci-

ologists and others in the social sciences, argue that human behavior is learned and shaped through social interaction. Which of these arguments is right?

Both are right. You don't have to look far to see that genetics, or nature, plays a role in who we are. For example, research shows that high levels of testosterone contribute to stereotypically masculine traits such as aggressiveness and competitiveness (Van Goozen et al. 1994). However, it is also true that facing a competitive challenge (such as a baseball game) causes testosterone levels to rise (Booth et al. 1989). So is it the hormone that makes us competitive, or is it competition that stimulates hormone production? An additional example involves a study of moral and social development in people with brain injuries. Stephen W. Anderson and colleagues (1999) studied patients whose prefrontal cortex had been damaged. Those who had received the injury as infants struggled with moral and social reasoning, finding it difficult or impossible to puzzle out questions like "Is it acceptable for a man to steal the drug needed to save his wife's life if he can't afford to pay for it?" People who received the same injury as adults, however, were able to deal with such issues. Anderson and his research team hypothesized that there is a crucial period in brain development when people acquire the capacity for moral reasoning. In other words, nature provides a biological window through which social and moral development occurs.

The point is, there is a complex relationship between nature and nurture. Either one alone is insufficient to explain what makes us human. Certainly, heredity gives us a basic potential, but it is primarily our social environment that determines whether we will realize or fall short of that potential or develop new ones. We are subject to social influences from the moment we are born (and even before), and these influences only increase over the years. In part because the influence of social contact happens so gradually and to some extent unconsciously, we don't really notice what or how we are learning.

NATURE VS. NURTURE DEBATE the ongoing discussion of the respective roles of genetics and socialization in determining individual behaviors and traits

SOCIALIZATION the process of learning and internalizing the values, beliefs, and norms of our social group, by which we become functioning members of society

The Process of Socialization

We often speak of "socializing" with our friends, yet the idea of "socializing" is only part of what sociologists mean by **socialization**. Socialization is a twofold process. It includes the process by which a society, culture, or group teaches individuals to become functioning members, and the process by which individuals learn and internalize the values

IN THE FUTURE

Genetics and Sociology

Sociologists have long been interested in resolving the nature vs. nurture debate and just how much each side contributes to human behavior, or even determines it. In the 1990s, dramatic new possibilities for gathering scientific data were available as a result of new discoveries in the emerging field of genetics. In 2003, the Human Genome Project was completed, which identified all the human genes constituting our DNA. At the same time that geneticists had hoped that knowledge of the genes would reveal all the answers to human behavior, they were finding that the social environment could actually change genes. Thus geneticists became interested in some of the same questions that a small but influential offshoot of sociologists had also been studying.

Although the term dates back to the middle of the twentieth century, **sociobiology** became a controversial topic within sociology in 1975 with the publication of Edward O. Wilson's *Sociobiology: The New Synthesis*. Many sociologists criticized the book, seeing it as an example of genetic determinism, as Wilson came down squarely on the nature side of the debate when he proposed that genes play a far greater role in human behavior than social or cultural factors. Wilson continued to develop these ideas in his 1978 work *On Human Nature*, where he argued "that the evidence is strong that a substantial fraction of human behavioral variation is based on genetic difference" (Wilson 1978, p. 43).

Other sociologists who followed Wilson's argument that genes play a larger role in human behavior caused further controversy as they stood in opposition to long-held and widely embraced sociological models of the self. In 1994, Richard Herrnstein and Charles Murray published *The Bell Curve: Intelligence and Class Structure in American Life*, which argued, among other things, that there were measurable differences in intelligence between races. In 2005, Larry Summers, then president of Harvard University, gave a speech in which he suggested that one of the reasons there were so few women teaching science and engineering at elite universities was because of genetic differences between the sexes. Despite widespread criticism, psychologist Steven Pinker publicly defended Summers's remarks. Pinker argued that if there was greater innate variability in men's mathematical

> **SOCIOBIOLOGY** a branch of science that uses biological and evolutionary explanations for social behavior

abilities, then "there would be a slightly higher proportion of men at the high end of the scale," which would lead to an overrepresentation of men in elite positions, and that there is certainly enough evidence for the hypothesis to be taken seriously" (Pinker 2005). Needless to say, many sociologists were less than convinced.

For other sociologists, these debates made any discussion of genes and behavior frustrating. For example, there was an enormous amount of evidence that intelligence was not simply inheritable, and that it certainly didn't vary by race. Likewise, the "evidence" that Pinker cited, showing that men and women have natural differences in their mathematical ability, is suspect. While studies in the United States, and

and norms of the group. Socialization thus works on both an individual and a social level: we learn our society's way of life and make it our own. Socialization accomplishes two main goals. First, it teaches members the skills necessary to satisfy basic human needs and to defend themselves against danger, thus ensuring that society itself will continue to exist. Second, socialization teaches individuals the norms, values, and beliefs associated with their culture and provides ways to ensure that members adhere to their shared way of life.

> **FERAL CHILDREN** in myths and rare real-world cases, children who have had little human contact and may have lived in social isolation from a young age

Social Isolation

We can appreciate how important socialization is when we see what happens to people who are deprived of social contact. When infants are born, they exhibit almost none of the learned behaviors that characterize human beings. Even their instincts for food or shelter or self-preservation are barely recognizable and almost impossible for them to act on alone. Babies do have innate capacities but can fully develop as human beings only through contact with others. There are several startling cases that demonstrate this (Newton 2004).

Perhaps you have heard myths about **feral children**, or children who have grown up in the wild. Supposedly, there "gay" gene to the "promiscuity" gene, the mass media rushed to report, often in oversimplified ways, new research on the relationship between genetics and behavior.

A new generation of sociologists is trying to unite genetics and sociology in more interesting ways, beyond a simple opposition between nature and nurture. The term "sociobiology" is even falling out of favor, as researchers like University of North Carolina sociologist Guang Go have taken to calling their work "genetically informed sociology" instead. These trailblazers caution us to remember that genetics are conditioned by social experience, and that there may be no simple cause-and-effect equation between genes and behavior. With the human genome containing 25,000 individual genes, it should not be surprising that behaviors do not spring from a single gene. Instead, "genes 'hunt in packs,' meaning that behaviors likely reflect networks of genes that work together" (Shanahan, Bauldry, and Freeman 2010, p. 36). Moreover, these genes do not work instead of social or cultural factors; rather, they work with them. Today there is increasing evidence "pointing to the importance of social factors in regulating genetic action" (Shanahan, Bauldry, and Freeman 2010, p. 37). For example, some researchers now suggest that social or environmental context can significantly alter the way a gene expresses itself. This theory, often referred to as gene-by-environment interaction, or G × E, would require sociology and genetics to work together to understand where behaviors come from. In the future, this should give all of us a great deal more insight into the nature vs. nurture debate.

Nature vs. Nurture What parts of your life are affected by your genes? by your society?

some other countries, show men with a greater variability in mathematical ability, studies in Lithuania, Germany, the Netherlands, Slovenia, and Denmark failed to produce the same results (Feingold 1992). For sociologists, this suggested that something much more complicated was going on. Despite these challenges, Steven Pinker seemed to feed a popular desire to find genes that "controlled" behaviors. From the

are real cases of children being raised by wolves, as well as works of fiction such as *Tarzan of the Apes* and *The Jungle Book*. Such stories present images of primitive humans who have survived outside society and who are both heathen and uncivilized yet pure and uncorrupt, who lack in social graces but possess the keenest of instincts. Legend has it that as far back as the thirteenth century, experiments were conducted by German emperor Frederick II to see whether humans could return to their natural and perfect state as depicted in the biblical Garden of Eden. Without human contact, the children who were used in these cruel experiments did not reveal any divine truths to the experimenters — they simply perished (Van Cleve 1972).

Although scientific ethics would never allow such experiments today, there are unfortunately real-life cases involving children who have lived in extreme social isolation. Sociologist Kingsley Davis (1940) studied several of these cases to better understand the relationship between human development and socialization.

One case from the 1930s involves a child named Isabelle, who was sequestered with her unmarried mother in a dark room of the family's Ohio home (Davis 1940; Davis and Moore 1947). The mother, a deaf-mute, communicated with her using only gestures. Isabelle consequently did not learn to speak at all and communicated by making low, croaking sounds. When Isabelle was finally discovered by authorities,

Mowgli, the "Man Cub" Fictional accounts of feral children, like Mowgli, the hero of the animated Disney film *The Jungle Book*, are quite different from real socially isolated children who struggle to learn language and interact with others.

Theories of the Self

Having a sense of one's self is perhaps the most fundamental of all human experiences. When seventeenth-century philosopher René Descartes exclaimed, "I think, therefore I am," he was expressing this basic fact — that we possess a consciousness about ourselves. More recently, some have examined whether higher mammals or primates might also have this same self-consciousness; while that has yet to be determined, we do know that consciousness is at the core of humanness.

The **self** is our experience of a distinct, real, personal identity that is separate and different from all other people. We can be "proud of ourselves," "lose control of ourselves," or want to "change ourselves," suggesting that we have the ability to think about ourselves as if we were more than one being and to see ourselves from the vantage point of an observer. Our thoughts and feelings emanate both *from* and *toward* ourselves; this is, in effect, how we come to "know" ourselves.

But just where does this sense of a self come from? How do we arrive at self-knowledge? When sociologists address these questions, they look at both the individual and society to find the answer. They believe that the self is created and modified through social interaction over the course of a lifetime. But while sociologists agree that the self is largely a social product, there are still a number of different theories about how the self develops, as we will see.

Psychoanalytic Theory: Sigmund Freud

The psychoanalytic perspective on the self, which is usually associated with Sigmund Freud, emphasizes childhood and sexual development as indelible influences on an individual's identity. While Freud's ideas have generated a great deal of controversy, they remain compelling for sociologists.

Perhaps his greatest contribution to understanding the self is his idea of the unconscious mind, as featured in *The Interpretation of Dreams* (1900/1955). Freud believed that the conscious level of awareness was but the tip of the iceberg and that just below the surface was a far greater area of the mind, the subconscious and the unconscious. He proposed that this unconscious energy was the source of our conscious thoughts and behavior. For example, the unconscious urge to slay our rivals may manifest itself in a conscious decision to work harder at the office in order to outshine a competitive co-worker.

According to Freud, the mind consists of three interrelated systems: the id, the ego, and the superego. The **id**, which is composed of biological drives, is the source of instinctive, psychic energy. Its main goal is to achieve pleasure and to avoid pain in all situations, which makes the id a selfish and unrealistic part of the mind. For example,

it was found that, in almost all ways, she had failed to develop like a normal child. Her behavior could only be described as primitive and bizarre, although there was never evidence of any congenital physical or mental disability. Isabelle did have a remarkable capacity for learning once she was exposed to regular human contact. But language skills were only part of what she later had to acquire in order to take her place as a member of society. Although she eventually overcame many of the effects of her social isolation, it was only through intensive training with medical and psychological specialists. It took two years after her rescue for her to acquire language and learn to interact with others, demonstrating that without socialization we are almost totally devoid of the qualities we normally associate with being human. Isabelle was able, with intensive remedial socialization, to "catch up" to her peers and become a normal child, something she was denied by her upbringing.

The socialization process begins in infancy and is especially productive once a child begins to understand and use language (Ochs 1986). But socialization is not complete at that point. It is a lifelong process that continues to shape us through experiences such as school, work, marriage, and parenthood, as we will see in the next few sections.

SELF the individual's conscious, reflexive experience of a personal identity separate and distinct from other individuals

ID, EGO, and SUPEREGO according to Freud, the three interrelated parts that make up the mind: the id consists of basic inborn drives that are the source of instinctive psychic energy; the ego is the realistic aspect of the mind that balances the forces of the id and the superego; the superego has two components (the conscience and the ego-ideal) and represents the internalized demands of society

Dreams and the Subconscious In his book *The Interpretation of Dreams*, psychoanalyst Sigmund Freud outlined three psychological systems—the id, the ego, and the superego—that regulate subconscious drives and help keep an individual mentally balanced.

despite all your hard work, sometimes that competitive co-worker is the one who gets the raise—not exactly what the pleasure-seeking id desired. The **ego**, by contrast, is the part that deals with the real world. It operates on the basis of reason and helps to mediate and integrate the demands of both the id and the superego. So the ego is the part of the self that says, "Okay, this time the other guy won, but if I keep trying, I'm bound to get that raise eventually."

The **superego** is composed of two components: the conscience and the ego-ideal. The conscience serves to keep us from engaging in socially undesirable behavior, and the ego-ideal upholds our vision of who we believe we should ideally be. The superego develops as a result of parental guidance, particularly in the form of the rewards and punishments we receive as children. It inhibits the urges of the id and encourages the ego to find morally acceptable forms of behavior. So the superego helps suppress the urge to kill your competitor and keeps you working toward getting that

raise in socially acceptable ways. Each of these systems serves a different mental or emotional function, yet they all work together to keep the individual in a more or less healthy state of balance.

Freud also proposed that between infancy and adulthood, the personality passes through four distinct **psychosexual stages of development** (1905). Each stage is associated with a different erogenous zone. Freud's theory emerged from his therapy work with adult patients who were asked to try to recall earlier periods from their lives. According to the theory, a child passes through the first three stages of development between the ages of one and five. Most people have little or no memory whatsoever of this period. Yet, according to psychoanalytic theory, it is supposed to set the stage for the rest of one's adult life. The last stage of development begins around the age of twelve, but few people successfully complete this final transition to maturity. In some cases, the transitions through the first three stages are not completely successful either, so that people may find themselves stuck, or "fixated," at an earlier stage. Perhaps you've known someone who is considered to have an "oral fixation"—this person, thought to be partially stuck in the first stage of development, might smoke, overeat, or be verbally aggressive. Someone who is "anal retentive"—a neatnik, tightwad, or control freak—is thought to be partially stuck in the second stage. These kinds of personality traits, rooted in early childhood (according to Freud), appear as "hang-ups" in the adult.

PSYCHOSEXUAL STAGES OF DEVELOPMENT four distinct stages of the development of the self between birth and adulthood, according to Freud; personality quirks are a result of being fixated, or stuck, at any stage

Other sociologists have extended Freud's work in this area, focusing especially on gender identity—our selves as feminine or masculine. Nancy Chodorow, a feminist and psychoanalytic sociologist, has written widely on human behavior and internal psychic structures, and how patterns of gendered parenting and early childhood development can lead to the reproduction of traditional sex roles in society (1978, 1994).

The Looking-Glass Self: Charles Cooley

Around the same time Freud was developing his theories (early 1900s), other social theorists interested in the self were working on the other side of the Atlantic. Charles Cooley, an early member of the Chicago School of sociology, devised a simple but elegant way to conceptualize how individuals gain a sense of self. His idea is captured in the following short poem, which summarizes a profound and complex process.

Each to each a looking-glass,
Reflects the other that doth pass.

Cooley referred to this concept as the **looking-glass self** (1909). He believed that we all act like mirrors to each other, reflecting back to one another an image of ourselves. We do this in three steps.

1. *We imagine how we look to others* — not just in a physical sense, but in how we present ourselves. For example, we may imagine that others find us friendly, funny, or hardworking. The idea we have of ourselves is particularly important in regard to significant others. Whether they are parents, bosses, friends, or partners, we care about how we look to these people.

2. *We imagine other people's judgment of us.* We try to picture others' reactions and to interpret what they must be feeling. What is their opinion of me? Do they think I am smart enough? Lazy? Boring? Too tall? Not talkative enough?

3. *We experience some kind of feeling about ourselves based on our perception of other people's judgments.* If we imagine, for instance, that they think of us as competent, we may feel pride; conversely, if we think they consider us inadequate, then we may feel shame or embarrassment. The important point here is that we respond to the judgments that we *believe* others make about us, without really knowing for sure what they think. And we're not always right. We may draw wildly unrealistic conclusions. But according to Cooley, it is these perceptions, not reality, that determine the feelings we ultimately have about ourselves.

The social looking-glass, the way we see ourselves reflected back from others, together with the feelings we develop as a result of what we imagine they see in us, forms our concept of self. For Cooley, there could be no sense of self without society, for there is no individual self without a corresponding "other" to provide us with our looking-glass self-image.

The suggestion that we are dependent on what others think of us — or rather what we think they think — for our own self-concept might seem appalling: are we really that hung up on what other people think? But while some of us may be influenced to a greater or lesser degree, *all* of us come to know ourselves through relationships, either real or imagined, with others.

Mind, Self, and Society: George Herbert Mead

Another member of the Chicago School, George Herbert Mead, expanded upon Cooley's ideas about the development of the self and laid the essential groundwork that became the theory of symbolic interactionism. Mead also believed that the self was created through social interaction. He believed that this process started in childhood — that children began to develop a sense of self at about the same time that they began to learn language. The acquisition of language skills coincides with the growth of mental capacities, including the ability to think of ourselves as separate and distinct and to see ourselves in relationship to others (Mead 1934).

According to Mead, the development of the self unfolds in several stages as we move through childhood. First is the **preparatory stage**. Children under the age of three lack a completely developed sense of self, and so they have difficulty distinguishing themselves from others. Such children begin the development process by simply imitating or mimicking others around them (making faces, playing patty-cake) without fully understanding the meaning of their behavior. After age three, children enter the **play stage** of development when they start to pretend or play at being "mommy," "firefighter," "princess," or "doctor." This is referred to as taking the role of the **particular or significant other**. As children learn the behavior associated with being a mother or doctor, they internalize the expectations of those particular others and begin to gain new perspectives in addition to their own. Such play also serves the purpose of anticipatory socialization for the real-life roles a child might play in the future.

In the final or **game stage** of development, children's self-awareness increases through a process Mead described using the example of games. By the early school years, children begin to take part in organized games. Each child must follow the rules of the game, which means that he or she must simultaneously take into account the roles of all the other players. Mead calls this overview the perspective of the **generalized other**. Thus children begin to understand the set of standards common to a social group — their playmates — and to see themselves from others' viewpoints. By taking the perspective of the generalized other, children are able to see themselves as objects. They gradually learn to internalize the expectations of the generalized other for themselves and to evaluate their own behavior. This is the beginning of understanding the attitudes and expectations of society as a whole.

LOOKING-GLASS SELF the notion that the self develops through our perception of others' evaluations and appraisals of us

PREPARATORY STAGE the first stage in Mead's theory of the development of self wherein children mimic or imitate others

PLAY STAGE the second stage in Mead's theory of the development of self wherein children pretend to play the role of the particular or significant other

PARTICULAR OR SIGNIFICANT OTHER the perspectives and expectations of a particular role that a child learns and internalizes

GAME STAGE the third stage in Mead's theory of the development of self wherein children play organized games and take on the perspective of the generalized other

GENERALIZED OTHER the perspectives and expectations of a network of others (or of society in general) that a child learns and then takes into account when shaping his or her own behavior

DUAL NATURE OF THE SELF the idea that we experience the self as both subject and object, the "I" and the "me"

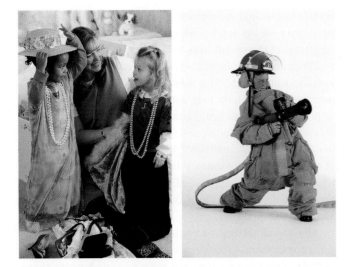

The Particular Other According to Mead, children begin to develop a sense of self through imitating others and playing roles.

Mead also recognized the dialectical or **dual nature of the self**; that is, the self as both subject and object. What we refer to as "I" is the subject component—the experience of a spontaneous, active, and creative part of ourselves, somewhat less socialized. What we refer to as "me" is the object component—the experience of a norm-abiding, conforming part of ourselves, more socialized and therefore reliant on others. The two components are inseparable and are united to form a single self in each of us. It is this process of recognizing the dual nature of the self, taking the role of the particular other, and seeing the perspective of the generalized other that Mead suggests leads to the development of the self.

Dramaturgy: Erving Goffman

Erving Goffman is another among the group of symbolic interactionists who see micro-level, face-to-face interaction as the building block of every other aspect of society. Goffman believes that all meaning, as well as our individual selves, is constructed through interaction. Many of his key ideas are expressed in *The Presentation of Self in Everyday Life* (1956).

To understand Goffman's work, we first need to briefly consider another of the early Chicago School sociologists, W. I. Thomas. What is now called the **Thomas theorem** states that "if people define situations as real, they are real in their consequences" (Thomas and Thomas 1928, p. 572). In other words, because we encounter ambiguous situations every day, many meanings are possible. The way we define each situation, then, becomes its reality.

For example, suppose you're walking down the street and you witness a woman slapping a man in public. What are the possible meanings of that situation? It could be a fight or spousal abuse; it could be a joke or a friendly greeting, depending on how hard the slap is; it could be that he has just passed out and she is hoping to revive him; or the participants could be actors shooting a scene from a film. Each of these definitions leads to a different set of potential consequences—you might intervene, call the police, stand by and laugh, ignore them, summon paramedics, or ask for an autograph, depending on which meaning you act upon. Each **definition of the situation** lends itself to a different approach, and the consequences are real.

Goffman looks at how we define situations interactionally—not just cognitively within our own heads, but in interaction with others. Think about it: how do you get your definition of the situation across to others? If you think a classroom lecture is boring, you may look over at your best friend and roll your eyes . . . she nods, indicating that she knows what you mean. The eye roll and the nod are **expressions of behavior**, tools we use to project our definitions of the situation to others.

What Goffman calls **expressions given** are typically verbal and intended—most of our speech falls into this category. Almost all of what we say, we *mean* to say, at least at that moment. Only in situations of extreme emotional response—such as fear, pain, or ecstasy—might we make unintended utterances. **Expressions given off**, like the eye roll and the nod, are typically nonverbal but observable in various ways and may be intended or unintended. Things like facial expressions, mannerisms, body language, or styles of dress are important indicators to others about the definition of the situation.

IMPRESSION MANAGEMENT Reading meaning in others' expressions of behavior requires a bit of caution. We know that people may deliberately say things to hide what they really feel, so we tend to think we get more real insight from expressions given off because we believe them to be unintended. But expressions given off can be manipulated as well. In a sense, Goffman is saying that it's not just what you say but how you say it that creates meaning. And he is a cynic, although he believes that everyday actors can be sincere. Goffman sees social life as a sort of

THOMAS THEOREM classic formulation of the way individuals define situations, whereby "if people define situations as real, they are real in their consequences"

DEFINITION OF THE SITUATION an agreement with others about "what is going on" in a given circumstance; this consensus allows us to coordinate our actions with those of others and realize goals

EXPRESSIONS OF BEHAVIOR small actions such as an eye roll or head nod that serve as an interactional tool to help project our definition of the situation to others

EXPRESSIONS GIVEN expressions that are intentional and usually verbal, such as utterances

EXPRESSIONS GIVEN OFF observable expressions that can be either intended or unintended and are usually nonverbal

IMPRESSION MANAGEMENT the effort to control the impressions we make on others so that they form a desired view of us and the situation; the use of self-presentation and performance tactics

DRAMATURGY an approach pioneered by Erving Goffman in which social life is analyzed in terms of its similarities to theatrical performance

FRONT in the dramaturgical perspective, the setting or scene of performances that helps establish the definition of the situation

PERSONAL FRONT the expressive equipment we consciously or unconsciously use as we present ourselves to others, including appearance and manner, to help establish the definition of the situation

REGION in the dramaturgical perspective, the context or setting in which the performance takes place

con game, in which we work at controlling the impressions others have of us. He calls this process **impression management**. Like actors on a stage, we play our parts and use all of our communicative resources (verbal and nonverbal) to present a particular impression to others. We say and do what we think is necessary to communicate who we are and what we think, and we refrain from saying and doing things that might damage the impression we want others to have of us.

It is this focus on the performance strategies of impression management that has led scholars to refer to Goffman's central ideas as **dramaturgy**—and the theatrical allusion is entirely intended. As in the theater, we use certain tools to aid in our impression management. The **front**, for example, is the setting that helps establish a particular meaning (like a classroom for teaching or a bar for drinking). Our **personal front**—appearance, manner, and style of dress (or "costume"), as well as gender, race, and age—helps establish the definition of the situation as well.

For example, Dr. Ferris is told quite often that she "doesn't look like a professor." This illustrates how we use elements of personal front to make judgments about people: if our images of professors involve gruff, grizzled, older men in unfashionable clothes, then someone who is younger, friendlier, and female and who wears edgy, hipper styles must work harder at convincing others that she is in fact a professor. Similarly, when a student happens to see Dr. Ferris at a restaurant, movie theater, or department store, the student's response is almost always the same: "what are you doing here?"

The social setting, or **region** (which includes the location, scenery, and props), makes a big difference in how we perceive and interact with the people we encounter there. Students and professors recognize one another and know how to interact when on campus or in the classroom. But in other venues, we are out of context, and this can confuse us. We seldom think of our professors as people who have off-campus lives—it's hard to see them as people who dine out, see movies, or buy underwear (for that matter, professors rarely think of their students this way either!). So when we encounter one another in unfamiliar regions, we often don't know how to behave because the old classroom scripts don't work.

In addition, there are places known as back regions, or **backstage**, where we prepare for our performances—which take place in front regions, or **frontstage**. We behave

Table 4.1 Theory in Everyday Life

Perspective	Approach to the Self and Interaction	Case Study: Identity in Childhood
Psychoanalysis	Freud's theory of the unconscious mind as composed of an interrelated system (id, ego, superego) that underlies human behavior; personality develops through psychosexual stages.	Parents instill a conscience (superego) in children through rules that govern their instinctual behavior (id) until children mature and are self-governing (ego).
Looking-Glass Self	Cooley's theory of the self concept as derived from how we imagine others see us, and the feelings about ourselves based on the perceived judgments of others.	Parents and significant others serve as a reflection to children, who develop a sense of self based on their appraisals, real or imagined.
Mind, Self, and Society	Mead's theory of the self that develops through three stages (preparatory, play, and game); in role taking the particular or generalized other, we learn to see ourselves as others do.	Children gain a sense of self through imitation, play, and games, in which they learn various roles and take on the perspectives of others.
Dramaturgy	Goffman's theory of the presentation of self; we are like actors on a stage whose performance strategies aid in impression management.	Children learn the arts of impression management and may present a different self to their parents than to other children or teachers.

Front and Back Regions Most of us maintain multiple selves and show a different face to different people. However, when the boundaries between front and back regions break down, as they did when news leaked about Arnold Schwarzenegger fathering a child with a member of his household staff, the results can be scandalous.

differently—and present different selves—frontstage than we do backstage; your professor behaved differently this morning while he showered, shaved, dressed, and made breakfast for his kids than he is behaving now, lecturing and answering questions in his sociology classroom. For Goffman, the key to understanding these nuances in impression management is to recognize that we present different selves in different situations, and the responses of others to those selves continually shape and mold our definitions of situation *and* self. Thus we can say that the self is a **social construction** (Berger and Luckmann 1966). The self is something that is created or invented in interaction with others who also participate in agreeing to the reality or meaning of that self as it is being presented in the situation.

We also make claims about who we are in our interactions. These claims can be either accepted or contradicted by others, which can make things either easier or harder for our self-image. Most of the time, others support the selves we project. For example, when your professor starts lecturing and you begin to take notes, you are supporting the version of self that he is presenting: he is "doing professor," and in response, you are "doing student." Another way that we support the selves that people present is to allow them to save face—to prevent them from realizing that they've done something embarrassing. Goffman calls this **cooling the mark out**, a phrase borrowed from con games, but it can be used as a tool of civility and tact as well. When the professor mixes up two related concepts in a lecture, for example, you let it pass because you know what she really meant to say. Or, even worse, you overlook the spinach between your professor's teeth until it can be called to his attention privately!

There are also situations in which the selves we project are contested or even destroyed. For example, if you raised your hand in a 200-person lecture hall and told the professor that he had spinach between his teeth, you would be undermining the self he is trying to present. His identity as an expert, an authority figure, and a senior mentor would be publicly damaged once you called attention to his dental gaffe (unless he was able to deflect the situation gracefully). In Goffman's view, then, the presentation of self and impression management are about power as well as about self. If you embarrass your professor in front of an auditorium full of students, he no longer possesses quite as much power as he did a few moments before.

Goffman's view of our interactions can be disturbing to some people, for it suggests that we are always acting, that we are never being honest about who we really are. But Goffman would challenge this interpretation of his work. Yes, some people deliberately deceive others in their presentation of self, but we must all present *some* type of self in social situations. Why wouldn't those selves be presented sincerely? As Goffman-inspired sociologist Josh Meyrowitz says, "While a dishonest judge may pretend to be an honest judge, even an honest judge must play the role of 'honest judge' " (1985, p. 30).

BACKSTAGE in the dramaturgical perspective, places in which we rehearse and prepare for our performances

FRONTSTAGE in the dramaturgical perspective, the region in which we deliver our public performances

SOCIAL CONSTRUCTION the process by which a concept or practice is created and maintained by participants who collectively agree that it exists

COOLING THE MARK OUT behaviors that help others to save face or avoid embarrassment, often referred to as civility or tact

DATA WORKSHOP
Analyzing Everyday Life

Impression Management in Action

This exercise in ethnography is designed to help make your own impression management visible—and to help you see how integral it is to your everyday life. You will observe yourself acting and interacting in two different social situations and will then do a comparative analysis of your presentation of self in each setting. Observing one's own behavior is a variant of the ethnographic method you learned about in Chapter 2 known as **autoethnography**.

AUTOETHNOGRAPHY
ethnographic description that focuses on the feelings and reactions of the ethnographer

AGENTS OF SOCIALIZATION
social groups, institutions, and individuals (especially the family, schools, peers, and the mass media) that provide structured situations in which socialization takes place

Step 1: Observation
Choose two different situations that you will encounter this week in everyday life, and commit to observing yourself for thirty minutes as you participate in each. For example, you may observe yourself at work, at a family birthday celebration, at lunch with friends, in your math class, riding on the bus or train, or watching an athletic match. The two situations you choose don't need to be extraordinary in any way; in fact, the more mundane, the better. But they should be markedly different from one another.

Step 2: Analysis
After observing yourself in the two situations, consider the following questions.

* What type of "front" do you encounter when you enter each situation?

* How does the "region" or setting (location, scenery, and props) affect your presentation of self there?

* Can you identify "backstage" and "frontstage" regions for each situation? Which of your activities are preparation and which are performance?

* What type of "personal front" (appearance, manner, dress) do you bring to each situation?

* How are your facial expressions, body language, and so forth ("expressions given off") different in each situation?

* What kinds of things do you say ("expressions given") in each situation?

* How do you modify what you do and say in each situation? Are there things you say or do in one that would be inappropriate, strange, or even absurd in the other?

* Who are you in each situation? Do you present a slightly different version of yourself in each? Why?

As you observe the most minute aspects of your interactions, you will probably discover that you perform somewhat different versions of yourself in the two situations. "Doing student," for instance, might be very different from "doing boyfriend."

A final Goffman-inspired question to ask is this: does engaging in impression management mean that we have no basic, unchanging self? If we bring different selves to different situations, what does that say about the idea of a "true self"? This issue is an important one, and we hope you use your Data Workshop findings to pursue it in greater depth.

There are two options for completing the Data Workshop.

Option 1 (informal): Take some informal notes about your observations in step 1, and jot down some of your responses to the questions asked in step 2. Compare your notes and experiences with other students in small-group discussions. Use this as a way to learn more about yourself and others in the group.

Option 2 (formal): For step 1, use ethnographic methods of data gathering. Create written fieldnotes to record your actions, interactions, and thoughts during each thirty-minute observation period. Be as detailed as possible. Then write a three- to four-page essay analyzing your experiences by addressing the questions in step 2. Refer to your fieldnotes in the essay, and include them as an attachment to your paper.

Agents of Socialization

Since our sense of self is shaped by social interaction, we should now turn our attention to the socializing forces that have the most significant impact on our lives. These forces, called **agents of socialization**, provide structured situations in which socialization takes place. While there are a variety of such influences in American society, notably religion, as well as our political and economic systems, we will focus here on what may be the four most predominant agents of socialization: the family, schools, peers, and the mass media.

The Family

The family is the single most significant agent of socialization in all societies. It's easy to see why. The family is the original group to which we belong. It is where early emotional and social bonds are created, where language is learned, and where we first begin to internalize the norms and values of our society. Most of our primary socialization, which teaches us to become mature, responsible members of society, takes place within the family. It is not surprising, then, that the family has perhaps the longest-lasting influence on the individual.

Much research has focused on the role of mothers in child-rearing practices (Goode 1982), although attention has also turned to the significance of fathers, as well as siblings and other relatives. For example, Scott Coltrane's book

Family Man (1997) looks at historical changes in the roles of men as active parents and how men feel about their involvement in their children's lives. The family has such a powerful impact on us partly because as young children we have limited outside contact (until we start day care or school) and therefore few if any other influences. The family is our world.

The family is also *in* the world. Where a family is located, both geographically and socially—its ethnic, class, religious, educational, and political background—will affect family members (Lareau 2003). For example, one of the most important lessons we learn in families is about gender roles: we see what moms and dads, sisters and brothers are expected to do (like mow the lawn or fold the laundry) and convert these observations into general rules about gender in society (Chodorow 1978).

Socialization differs from family to family because each family has its own particular set of values and beliefs. A single family can also change over time. As years pass, children may not be raised in the same way as their older siblings, for the simple reason that parents have no experience with babies when their first child is born but plenty of experience by the time the youngest comes along. Nor are all aspects of socialization deliberate; some in fact are quite unintentional (as when a father's violent temper or a mother's depression is passed down to the next generation).

Schools

Many people remember their school years with fondness, dread, or perhaps relief that they're over! No wonder school makes such a great subject for bad dreams and movie scripts. Public elementary and secondary schools were first established in the United States in the 1800s. While attendance was uneven at first, education advocates believed that schooling played a critical role in maintaining a democracy (though blacks and women still lacked the right to vote) and in shaping future generations of citizens. Over the years, schools have gradually taken on greater responsibilities than merely teaching a prescribed curriculum. Schools now provide physical education, meals, discipline, and child care, all formerly the provinces of other social institutions.

When children begin attending school (including preschool and day care), it may be their first significant experience away from home. School helps them to become less dependent on the family, providing a bridge to other social groups. In school, children learn that they will be judged on their behavior and on academic performance. They learn not only formal subjects but also a **hidden curriculum** (Jackson 1968), a set of behavioral traits such as punctuality, neatness, discipline, hard work, competition, and obedience (to be discussed in greater detail in Chapter 10). The socialization children receive from teachers, staff members, and other students occurs simultaneously and overlaps with what they learn in the family.

HIDDEN CURRICULUM values or behaviors that students learn indirectly over the course of their schooling because of the structure of the educational system and the teaching methods used

Recently, there has been increasing scrutiny regarding the role of teachers, especially in public schools. Because teachers are such potent role models for students, parents are concerned about the moral standing of those who are in charge of teaching their children, as well as their training and competence. There is increasing pressure for schools to take on even more responsibilities, including dealing with issues

Family Has the Longest-Lasting Influence The family is the original group to which each person belongs, and it is the most important of socialization.

Agents of Socialization **111**

that used to be taught at home or in church — such as sex, violence, drugs and alcohol, and general morality and citizenship.

Peers

Peer groups are groups of people who are about the same age and have similar social characteristics. Peers may be friends at school or from the neighborhood, members of a sports team, or cabin mates at summer camp. As children get older, peers often become more important than parents as agents of socialization. As the influence of peers increases, the influence of parents decreases. While the family still has the most long-lasting influence on an individual, it is peers who have the most intense and immediate effect on each other.

By adolescence, young people spend more time with their peers than with their parents or anyone else (Larson and Richards 1991). Membership in a peer group provides young people with a way of exercising independence from, and possibly reacting against, adult control. Young people tend to form peer subcultures that are almost entirely centered on their own interests, such as video gaming or disc golf or garage bands, with distinct values and norms related to those interests.

The need to "fit in" with a peer group may seem overwhelming to some young people. Some will do almost anything to belong, even betray their own values: Bradley and Wildman (2002) found that peer pressure was a predictor of adolescent participation in risky behaviors such as dangerous driving, unsafe sex, and drug and alcohol use. Peer groups, while providing important and enjoyable social bonds, can also be the source of painful self-doubt, ridicule, or rejection for many young people.

The Mass Media

The mass media's role as one of the most significant sources of socialization is a somewhat recent phenomenon. Television began infiltrating American homes in the 1950s, and usage of the internet has become widespread only in the past two decades. Yet, for many of us, it would be almost impossible to imagine life without the mass media — whether print, broadcast, or digital. This huge explosion, the dawning of the Information Age, is something we already take for granted, but we don't always see the ways in which it is changing our lives.

Many sociologists question whether the media may have even usurped some of the functions of the family in teaching us basic norms and values and giving advice on common problems. As an example, take the people of Fiji, a South Pacific island that lacked widespread access to television until 1995. A group of Harvard Medical School researchers took this unique opportunity to study the effects of television on the native population. Specifically, they were interested in the ways in which Western programs influenced eating habits and body image among adolescent girls in a

Fashion for Whom? Most women do not look like this model. Yet her body type is held up as the ideal in magazines and other forms of mass media.

culture that "traditionally supported robust appetites and body shapes" (A. Becker et al. 2002).

Through surveys and interviews with the young women (the mean age was around seventeen) in 1995, just months after television was introduced, and again in 1998, the researchers ascertained that Western television was in fact affecting body image and corresponding behaviors among the girls. In those three years, the percentage of subjects whose survey responses indicated an eating disorder jumped from 12 to 29, and the percentage who reported self-induced vomiting as a form of weight control rose from none to 11. Dieting and dissatisfaction with weight were prevalent — and 83 percent of the girls who were interviewed reported that they felt television "had specifically influenced their friends and/or themselves to feel differently about or change their body shape or weight" (A. Becker et al. 2002).

The women of Fiji only recently encountered mass media. How do we measure the cumulative effect of the ubiquitous exposure to the mass media that pervade American society, day in and day out? Whose messages are we listening to, and what are we being told about ourselves and each other? On average, Americans watch between two and seven hours of television per day and spend more hours listening to the radio or iPods, reading, watching movies, playing video games, surfing the web, or sending text messages and e-mail. By the time young people graduate from high school, they will have spent far more time with mass media than in the classroom. While some worry that this means kids are lost in a fantasy world, Hodge and Tripp (1986) have argued that watching TV actually helps kids learn to distinguish between reality and fantasy, an important developmental milestone. In addition to their ability to entertain, the media also have great potential to inform and educate. It is clear that we internalize many of the values, beliefs, and norms presented in the media and that their powerful influence in our lives only stands to increase as we proceed deeper into the Information Age.

DATA WORKSHOP
Analyzing Mass Media and Popular Culture

Television as an Agent of Socialization

Television is a powerful and surreptitious agent of socialization. It is everywhere, and we devour it—so it seems important to ask what kinds of messages we are getting about our society from our viewing. How does TV socialize us? This Data Workshop will use content analysis (see the discussion of using existing sources in Chapter 2) to help you answer this question.

Choose one of the most popular TV series currently on the air — at the time of this writing, your choices might include *NCIS*, *Bones*, *The Big Bang Theory*, or *How I Met Your Mother*. Choose a regular drama or comedy series rather than a newsmagazine, talk show, game show, or reality show.

Now choose some aspect of social status and individual identity that you want to focus on; for example, gender (how women or men are portrayed), race/ethnicity (how a particular ethnic group, such as African Americans or Latinos, is portrayed), sexuality (heterosexuals, gay men, or lesbians), or class (poor people, wealthy people, or the middle class). For instance, you might look at the depiction of women in *New Girl* or men in *Two and a Half Men*, the role of Latinos in *CSI: Miami* or African Americans in *Grey's Anatomy*, or the portrayal of gays in *Modern Family* or the wealthy in *Revenge*.

Watch an episode of your chosen program in its entirety (you might want to record the program or look for an epi-

sode on DVD or online so that you can review it if you need to). Take notes as you watch; note the program's content with reference to your particular topic choice. To give you an example of how to do this workshop, we use depictions of women (in brackets below) as our topic and the program *Brothers and Sisters* (which ended in 2011 after five seasons). You should substitute your own current program and choice of topic for each of the following questions:

1. In the program, how many [female] characters are there? How does the number of [female] characters compare with the number of other characters? Are the [female] roles major characters or minor characters? How can you tell?

2. What types of roles do the [female] characters have? What are their activities, attitudes, and interactions like on the show? What kinds of things do they do and say that tell you who they are and what they are like?

3. Are the portrayals of [females] positive or negative? Humorous or serious? One-dimensional or multidimensional? How can you tell?

4. What image(s) of [women] does this program portray? In other words, what messages do the words, pictures, plot lines, and characters convey to viewers about [women] in general?

In the case of *Brothers and Sisters*, there were some interesting portrayals of women to analyze. For example, the central character is a woman: we first meet Nora Walker at a family party where her husband suffers a heart attack and dies. As a new widow, Nora must step up to head her large family, as well as their struggling family business. These leadership roles are new to her and uncomfortable for the family. In addition, she must face such family secrets as her late husband's long-term infidelity. Other female characters include Nora's daughters, Kitty and Sarah, both career women and mothers with messy love lives, and Holly, the former mistress of Nora's husband. These women relate to each other, as well as the men in their lives, in ways that provided powerful messages about gender roles and femininity to both female and male viewers.

Now come the really important questions:

5. How does the content of this program contribute to our socialization process? What do we learn about [women] in society from watching the program? After finishing your analysis, what do you think about TV's powers of socialization?

There are two options for completing the work.

Option 1 (informal): Prepare written notes that you can refer to during in-class discussions. Discuss your

IN RELATIONSHIPS

Sister Pauline Quinn and Training Dogs in Prison

Can adopting a puppy change your fundamental sense of self for the better? According to Sister Pauline Quinn, a Dominican nun, it can when the puppies are adopted by prison inmates who train them to become service or therapy dogs. Sister Pauline knew something firsthand about life in a total institution, and not just the convent. Born Kathy Quinn, she was once a chronic runaway because of a dysfunctional family life and was eventually institutionalized for lack of another place for her to go. For several years afterward, she was homeless, staying in abandoned buildings and trying to avoid getting picked up by the police as a vagrant. Kathy Quinn could well have died on the streets of Los Angeles, but instead her life was turned around when she found Joni, a German Shepherd.

Quinn felt that the dog was the beginning of the process of resocialization that helped return her to being a functioning member of society. It was the first time she had a true friend, one whose unconditional love was restoring her badly damaged self-esteem. Her time in institutions had left her "depersonalized," stripped of any positive identity with which to tackle the demands of life on the "outside." The understanding and affection she received from Joni began to heal Quinn of the traumas she had sustained in her youth. The bond that forms between a human and a dog provides positive feedback and a loving relationship that can influence one's sense of self. The work that Quinn did in training Joni transformed not only the dog but the person as well, eventually leading her to a happier and more productive life devoted to helping others.

Quinn was particularly drawn to the plight of women prisoners and believed that they too could find similar benefits through contact with dogs. She knew that life in prison could be extremely depersonalizing, especially for women, and that rehabilitation, if it was offered at all, was too often unsuccessful, returning convicts to the streets without having rebuilt their identities and their lives. In 1981, with the assistance of Dr. Leo Bustad, a professor of veterinary science at the University of Washington, she approached the Washington State Correctional Center for Women and proposed that inmates volunteer to train puppies adopted from local shelters and rescue organizations to become service and therapy dogs. The result was the Prison Pet Partnership Program.

The women selected to participate in the program get more than just dogs to train; they get the opportunity for substantial resocialization, which helps them to develop new, positive identities and learn valuable social skills that can translate to the outside world. The labor-intensive process of training a dog is perfectly suited to the needs and abilities of inmates, who have a great surplus of time and a desperate need to find constructive ways to occupy it. The rigors of dog training, which place an emphasis on achieving discipline and obedience through repetition and positive reinforcement, is a lesson not lost on the trainers. During the months of training, the animals even sleep with the inmates, providing added psychological benefits. Prisons report significant improvements in morale and behavior once dog-training programs are in place. Allowing prisoners access to the dogs' unconditional love and giving the prisoners a chance to contribute to

reactions and conclusions with other students in small groups. Listen for any differences or variations in each other's insights.

Option 2 (formal): Write a three- to four-page essay answering the Data Workshop questions. Make sure to refer to specific segments of the TV show that support your analysis.

Adult Socialization

Being an "adult" somehow signifies that we've learned well enough how to conduct ourselves as autonomous members of society. But adults are by no means completely socialized. Life is continually presenting us with new situations and new roles with unfamiliar norms and values. We are constantly learning and adjusting to new conditions over the life course and thereby participating in secondary socialization.

For example, your college training will teach you a great deal about the behaviors that will be expected of you in your chosen profession, such as responsibility and punctuality.

Sister Pauline Quinn, pictured on the left, has started dog training programs in prisons in nineteen states. Participants include the inmates pictured on the right.

society in a meaningful way increase the likelihood that the prisoners will reenter mainstream society successfully.

While the program was originally motivated by Sister Quinn's desire to change the lives of prisoners, it has become "part of a chain reaction of good" that begins with the rescue of a dog, gives emotional support and job training to prisoners, and finally provides handicapped and disabled people service animals that improve their lives.

The original program, in the Washington penal system, has placed more than 700 dogs as service or therapy dogs. Prisons in at least nineteen states have established similar dog-training programs, and military prisons have begun comparable programs to train service dogs for disabled veterans. A service animal can cost as much as $10,000 to train, so these prison programs make a difference in placing more dogs with the people who need them. Just as importantly here, each relationship with a dog transforms the life of the inmate who gets another chance at developing a more positive sense of self in the process. In 2001, the story of Sister Pauline Quinn and the prison dog-training program was made into the original Lifetime TV movie *Within These Walls*.

But after graduating and obtaining a job, you will likely find further, unanticipated expectations. At the very least, you will be socialized to the local culture of a specific workplace, where new rules and customs (like "Always be closing!" in a real estate office) are observed. As your career unfolds, such episodes of socialization will recur as you take on different responsibilities or switch jobs.

Other examples of altered life circumstances include marrying, being divorced or widowed, raising a family, moving to a new community, losing a job, or retiring — all of which require modifying attitudes and behaviors. For example, being divorced or widowed after many years of marriage means jumping into a dating pool that may look quite different from the last time you were in it — "safe sex," "splitting the check," and other new norms may be hard for older daters to assimilate. Adult socialization often requires the replacement of previously learned norms and values with different ones, what is known as **resocialization**. Facing a serious illness or growing old also often involves intensive resocialization. In order to cope with a new view of what their aging body will permit them to do, people must

> **RESOCIALIZATION** the process of replacing previously learned norms and values with new ones as a part of a transition in life

Resocialization Joining the military and getting married are major life changes that require people to learn new norms and values.

discard previous behaviors in favor of others (not working out every day, for example).

Another dramatic example of resocialization is found in **total institutions** (Goffman 1961), such as prisons, cults, and mental hospitals, and, in some cases, even boarding schools, nursing homes, monasteries, and the military.

In total institutions, residents are severed from their previous relations with society, and their former identities are systematically stripped away and reformed. There may be different ends toward which total institutions are geared, such as creating good soldiers, punishing criminals, or managing mental illness, but the process of resocialization is similar: all previous identities are suppressed, and an entirely new, disciplined self is created.

Relatively few adults experience resocialization to the degree of the total institution. All, however, continue to learn and synthesize norms and values throughout their lives as they move into different roles and social settings that present

them once again with the challenges and opportunities of continued socialization.

Statuses and Roles

While agents of socialization play an important role in developing our individual identities, so does the larger scaffolding of society. This happens as we take on (or have imposed upon us) different statuses and roles.

A **status** is a position in a social hierarchy that comes with a set of expectations. Sometimes these positions are formalized: "professor," "president," or even "parent." Parental obligations, for example, are written into laws that prohibit the neglect and abuse of children. Other statuses are more informal: you may be the "class clown," for instance, or the "conscience" of your group of friends. The contours of these informal statuses are less explicit but still widely recognizable. We all occupy a number of statuses, as we hold positions in multiple social hierarchies at once. Some statuses change over the course of a lifetime (e.g., marital or parental status), while others usually do not (e.g., gender).

There are different kinds of statuses. An **ascribed status** is one we are born with that is unlikely to change (such as our gender or race). An **embodied status** is located in our physical selves (such as beauty or disability). Finally, an **achieved status** is one we have earned through our own efforts (such as an occupation, hobby, or skill) or that has been acquired in some other way (such as a criminal

TOTAL INSTITUTION an institution in which individuals are cut off from the rest of society so that their lives can be controlled and regulated for the purpose of systematically stripping away previous roles and identities in order to create new ones

STATUS a position in a social hierarchy that carries a particular set of expectations

ASCRIBED STATUS an inborn status; usually difficult or impossible to change

EMBODIED STATUS a status generated by physical characteristics

ACHIEVED STATUS a status earned through individual effort or imposed by others identity, mental illness, or drug addiction). All statuses influence how others see and respond to us. However, some ascribed, embodied, or achieved statuses take on the power of what sociologists call a **master status** — a status that seems to override all others in our identities.

Master statuses carry with them expectations that may blind people to other facets of our personalities. People quickly make assumptions about what women, Asians, doctors, or alcoholics are like and may judge us according to those expectations rather than our actual attributes. This kind of judgment, often referred to as **stereotyping**, is looked upon as negative or destructive. However, it is important to realize that we all use these expectations in our everyday lives; stereotyping, as problematic as it is, is all but unavoidable.

A **role** is the set of behaviors expected from a particular status position. Sociologists such as Erving Goffman (1956) and Ralph Turner (1978) deliberately use the theatrical analogy to describe how roles provide a kind of script, outlining what we are expected to say and do as a result of our position in the social structure. Professors, then, are expected to be responsible teachers and researchers. Employment contracts and faculty handbooks may specify the role even further: professors must hold a certain number of office hours per week, for example, and must obtain permission from the university in order to skip classes or take a leave of absence. Class clowns don't sign a contract, nor are they issued a handbook, but they have role expectations nonetheless: they are expected to turn a classroom event into a joke whenever possible and to sacrifice their own success in order to provide laughs for others.

Multiple Roles and Role Conflict

In setting out general expectations for behavior, roles help shape our actions in ways that may come to define us to ourselves and others. For example, we often describe ourselves according to personality traits: "I am a responsible person," "a nurturer," "competitive," or "always cheerful." These traits are often the same as the role expectations attached to our various statuses as professionals, parents, athletes, or friends. If a person can play a number of different roles well, it can enhance their sense of self, but it is not always easy to juggle the varying demands and expectations associated with multiple roles. Sometimes problems arise in our everyday lives because of our roles.

The story of ESPN sportscaster Chris Spielman illustrates some of these problems. In 1998, he was a linebacker with the Buffalo (New York) Bills, ready to return for another season. At the same time, his wife, Stefanie, was diagnosed with breast cancer. Chris faced a crisis of decision making: go to New York to play football, or stay home in Ohio to care for his wife and kids? He was experiencing what is known

as **role conflict**, a situation in which two or more roles have contradictory expectations. His occupational role as professional athlete required actions that were seemingly incompatible with his familial role as husband and father. Spielman's situation may have caused him to experience **role strain** as well, which occurs when there are contradictory expectations within one single role a person plays. It is easy to see how Chris fulfilled some of the traditional gender role expectations for men: a four-time Pro-Bowler, he was a big, tough guy nicknamed "Captain Crunch" who had a successful athletic career. But he was also a devoted family man, and he wanted to be home to provide hands-on care and nurturing for his sick wife and their children. Chris chose his family over football. As he said in an interview, "I wouldn't give my life for football, but I'd give my life for my family. There's no comparison. They're not even in the same stratosphere" (Cabot 1999). Sadly, Stefanie died in 2008, thrusting Chris into a process known as **role exit**, when a person leaves behind a role the person once occupied. He was no longer a "husband" and instead had become a "widower." Spielman continues to work at ESPN, care for his children, and raise funds for breast cancer research.

You may not become a professional athlete with a critically ill spouse, but it is certain that you will find yourself in situations where there are co_____ tween multiple roles or within a _____ resolve those tensi___

Status___ guid_____ own ___ to inte___ social se___

Emot___ Person___

As the Spielmans' experience demonstrates, role conflicts can be very emotional events. Our emotions are intensely personal responses to the unique situations of our lives. We react with happiness, anger, fear, or sorrow to our own experiences, as well as things that happen to others, even

MASTER STATUS a status that is always relevant and affects all other statuses we possess

STEREOTYPING judging others based on preconceived generalizations about groups or categories of people

ROLE the set of behaviors expected of someone because of his or her status

ROLE CONFLICT experienced when we occupy two or more roles with contradictory expectations

ROLE STRAIN the tension experienced when there are contradictory expectations within one role

ROLE EXIT the process of leaving a role that we will no longer occupy

Chris Spielman, his wife Stefanie, and their four children. Role conflict: football player or husband/father first?

fictionalized events in books, movies or video games. Individuals sometimes react very differently—what makes one person laugh may make another cry. It would seem, then, that our emotions are the one thing about our lives that aren't dictated by society, that can't be explained with reference to sociological concepts or theories.

Well, our emotions aren't fully determined by society, but they are indeed social. We respond individually, but there also are social patterns in our emotional responses. For example, some emotional responses differ according to the culture—even an emotion as personal as grief, as noted in the Global Perspective box on the next page.

ROLE-TAKING EMOTIONS emotions like sympathy, embarrassment, or shame that require that we assume the perspective of another person or many other people and respond from that person or group's point of view

FEELING RULES socially constructed norms regarding the expression and display of emotions; expectations about the acceptable or desirable feelings in a given situation

EMOTION WORK (EMOTIONAL LABOR) the process of evoking, suppressing, or otherwise managing feelings to create a publicly observable display of emotion

The Social Construction of Emotions

Sometimes our interaction with others affects our emotional responses: we may yell angrily at a political rally along with everyone else, realizing only later that we don't really feel that strongly about the issue at all; we may stifle our tears in front of the coach but shed them freely after the game. **Role-taking emotions**, such as sympathy, embarrassment, and shame, require that we be able to see things from someone else's point of view. When a friend is injured in an accident, you know she is feeling pain, so you feel sympathy for her. **Feeling rules** (A. Hochschild 1975) are socially constructed norms regarding the appropriate feelings and displays of emotion. We are aware of the pressure to conform to feeling rules even when they are unspoken or we don't agree with them (for example, "Boys don't cry," "No laughing at funerals"). Emotions are thus sociological phenomena, and our individual reactions are influenced (if not determined) by our social and cultural surroundings.

Finally, emotions can also be influenced by social institutions, such as workplaces or religious groups. Arlie Hochschild's (1983) study of flight attendants revealed that when airlines required their employees to be cheerful on the job, the employees' authentic emotions were displaced (they weren't necessarily always cheerful). Flight attendants were required to manage their own feelings as a requirement of their job—what Hochschild calls **emotion work**—maintaining a bright, perky, happy demeanor in-flight, no matter what they actually felt. Because of the structural pressures of emotion work, they became alienated from their own real feelings.

New Interactional Contexts

As we learned in earlier chapters, sociological theories and approaches can change over time—indeed, they must. As the society around them changes, sociologists can't always hold on to their tried-and-true ways of looking at the world. New and innovative approaches take the place of traditional paradigms.

GLOBAL PERSPECTIVE
Cross-Cultural Responses to Grief

When it comes to emotions, grief seems one of the strongest. No matter what we believe about the afterlife (or lack thereof), we mourn the passing of our loved ones. In many different societies, the cultural practices surrounding grief and mourning are directed toward giving the deceased a proper send-off and comforting those left behind. But you might be surprised at what other cultures consider comforting in times of grief!

For example, Maoris (the native people of New Zealand) believe that death is not final until all funeral rites are complete—which takes an entire year. Though the body is buried after three days, the relatives and friends of the deceased speak of and to her as if she were alive until the year of mourning is complete.

The Roma (often incorrectly referred to as "Gypsies") mourn in particularly intense and public ways: both men and women refuse to wash, shave, or comb their hair, neglect to eat for three days, and absorb themselves totally in the process of mourning, sometimes to the point of harming themselves. In addition to this passionate grieving, Roma mourners provide the dead with clothes, money, and other useful objects for their journey to the afterlife. In contrast to Western societies, where black is the prevailing color of grief, Roma mourners traditionally wear white clothes and the favored color for funeral decorations is red.

Red is also the color of grief for the Ashanti of Ghana, who wear red clothing, smear red clay on their arms and foreheads, and wear headbands festooned with red peppers. Proper Ashanti expressions of grief are distinguished by gender: women must wail, and men must fire guns into the air. In fact, the amount of gunpowder used in a funeral is considered a mark of the grieving family's status in the community.

When mourning their dead, many cultures, including the Irish, hold "wakes": long-lasting, heavily attended parties honoring and celebrating the lives of the dead. At a wake, while tears may fall, there is also likely to be singing, dancing, drinking, laughing, and all manner of seemingly celebratory emotional outbursts. So despite the fact that all cultures mourn and all individuals feel grief, we can express those emotions in different ways depending on the society of which we are a part.

How Different Cultures Grieve Maori warriors row a coffin to their burial ground (top), mourning Roma women weep over a coffin (center), and Ashanti women practice a traditional funeral dance (bottom).

ON THE JOB

The Wages of Emotion Work

According to executives at Nordstrom department stores, keeping the customer happy is what it's all about. Nordstrom, along with a host of other stores, takes a great interest in developing a corporate culture based on customer service (Zemke and Schaaf 1990; Spector and McCarthy 1996). After all, loyal, satisfied customers are the key to profit making. Nordstrom has become so successful at customer service that it ranks as the national standard. The secret to the company's success lies partly in what Hochschild (1983) calls "the commercialization of feeling," or emotion work.

Nordstrom became a leader in this area through a variety of training techniques. Through staff meetings and workshops, managers coached employees in customer service. Using videotapes and role-playing scenarios, workers learned how to act out various emotions convincingly. But their acting techniques went beyond such displays as smiling and showing friendliness. Salespeople were also supposed to take an in-depth interest in their customers by keeping a "client book" with detailed information about customers' likes and dislikes, favorite brands, style preferences, color choices, and anything else that might help salespeople to better anticipate their clients' needs. Some Nordstrom managers even required their salespeople to perform extra duties while off the clock, like writing thank-you notes to customers and delivering items to their homes.

While these practices were good for Nordstrom's bottom line, the consequences for the workers themselves were a different story. The work of producing emotions takes its toll. Though displays of feeling are actually "sold" to the customer as a kind of commodity, the worker is not necessarily compensated. What was once a private resource has now become a company asset, a new source of labor — emotional labor. But because it is impossible for anyone to be that upbeat all the time, workers must find ways to display or evoke the required emotions. They may do so through surface acting, displaying the emotion by wearing a smile, for example. In contrast, a very dedicated employee may do deep acting by trying to actually feel the emotion that he or she must display. There are consequences for faking or conjuring emotional responses: workers may experience "emotional exhaustion and burnout" (Grandey 2003) or become estranged from their real feelings (as did Hochschild's flight attendants) — a situation that Marx would refer to as alienation.

Despite a number of employee protests — and a 1991 class-action suit involving off-the-clock work — many of the problems relating to emotion work remain unresolved (Nogaki 1993). Employees at Nordstrom and elsewhere are still trying to figure out how to preserve some sense of authenticity while making the necessary emotional adjustments to perform their job. The risk remains that employees may become burned out, cynical, or numb from the demands of their occupational roles.

Many of you will be dealing with these same issues in your careers. How will you factor in the cost to yourself of emotional labor? Do you think employees should be compensated financially for emotion work, or do you consider it part of being a good employee? What other kind of compensation — extra days off, more frequent breaks — might be appropriate, especially for salespeople?

Emotion Work In many sales and service jobs, employees must engage in surface or deep acting to display the emotions that their jobs require.

Most sociological perspectives on interaction, for example, focus on interactions that occur in **copresence** — that is, when individuals are in one another's physical company. More and more, however, we find ourselves in situations outside physical copresence, aided by rapidly developing technologies.

Businesspeople can hold video conferences with colleagues in other cities. The lovelorn can seek relationship advice and learn the dos and don'ts of sex and dating through late-night radio. Students can text message their friends at faraway colleges and carry on real-time conversations using webcams. Doctors on the mainland can perform remote surgery on shipboard patients in the middle of the ocean. Do conventional theories have the explanatory power to encompass these new ways of interacting? And since interaction is vital to the development of the self, how do these new ways of interacting create new types of social identities?

Researchers like Josh Meyrowitz (1985), Marc Smith and Peter Kollock (1998), Steve Jones (1997), Philip Howard (Jones and Howard 2003), and Barry Wellman (2004) are among the pioneers in the sociology of technologically mediated interaction. They look at how we interact with each other in virtual space and via electronic media — and how we interact with the machines themselves. Sherry Turkle, for example, directs the Initiative on Technology and the Self at the Massachusetts Institute of Technology (MIT), where she and others study different ways that technology and identity intersect — through our use of computers, robots, technologically sophisticated toys, and so on (1997, 2005). danah boyd examines how the rapid adoption of social networking sites, such as Facebook, by teenagers is affecting their sense of self and their relationships with others (2007). These and other researchers seek answers to the following question: who will we become as we increasingly interact with and through digital technologies? Their work is helping sociology enter the age of interactive media and giving us new ways of looking at interactions and identities.

Postmodern theorists claim that the role of technology in interaction is one of the primary features of postmodern life. They believe that in the Information Age, social thinkers must arrive at new ways to explain the development of the self in light of the digital media that inundate our social world (Holstein and Gubrium 2000). We are now exposed to more sources and multiple points of view that may shape our sense of self and socialize us in different ways than ever before (Gottschalk 1993). Kenneth Gergen has coined the term the **saturated self** to refer to this phenomenon and further claims that the postmodern individual tends to have a "pastiche personality," one that "borrow[s] bits and pieces of identity from whatever sources are available" (Gergen 1991, p. 150). What this means is that the self is being constructed in new ways that were unforeseen by early symbolic interactionists, who could not have imagined that interaction would one day include so many possible influences from both the real world and the world of virtual reality.

CLOSING COMMENTS

By now you may be wondering, are we all just prisoners of socialization? How much freedom do we really have if we are all shaped and influenced to such an extent by others and by society? Are our ideas of ourselves as individuals — unique and independent — just a sorry illusion?

It is true that the process of socialization can be rather homogenizing. And it tends to be conservative, pushing people toward some sort of lowest common denominator, toward the mainstream. But still, not everybody ends up the same. In fact, no two people are ever really alike. Despite all the social forces at play in creating the individual, the process by which we gain a sense of self, or become socialized members of society, is never wholly finished.

We are not just passive recipients of all the influences around us. We are active participants. We possess what is called **agency**, meaning that we are spontaneous, intelligent, and creative. We exercise free will. Symbolic interactionism tells us that we are always doing the work of interpreting, defining, making sense of, and responding to our social environment. That gives us a great deal of personal power in every social situation. The process is not unilateral; rather it is reciprocal and multidirectional. Remember that you are shaping society as much as it is shaping you.

COPRESENCE face-to-face interaction or being in the presence of others

SATURATED SELF a postmodern idea that the self is now developed by multiple influences chosen from a wide range of media sources

AGENCY the ability of the individual to act freely and independently

Mediating Interaction Using new technologies like webcams, we can interact with each other outside of physical copresence. How will these new technologies affect our interactions and identities?

Everything You Need to Know about
Socialization

" Socialization is the process of learning and internalizing the values, beliefs, and norms of our social groups, by which we become functioning members of society. "

AGENTS OF SOCIALIZATION

* **Family:** the original group to which people belong, where early emotional and social bonds are created, language is learned, and where we first begin to internalize the norms and values of society

* **School:** helps people become less dependent on their family, and provides a bridge to other social groups

* **Peers:** provide young people with a way of exercising independence from, and possibly reacting against, adult control

* **Mass media:** entertains, informs, educates, and is responsible for the internalization of many values, beliefs, and norms of society

REVIEW

1. Think about a social issue that you hold a very different opinion from your grandparents or people their age, like drug legalization, sexual mores, or even fashion. How might this difference of opinion be the result of different socialization?

2. According to Erving Goffman, we all engage in impression management to control what others think of us. Choose one interaction, and list every aspect of the personal front you use to manage the impression you create.

3. Describe yourself in terms of your statuses and roles. Which are master statuses? Which roles are less important? Which statuses have changed over the course of your lifetime? Which roles do you anticipate occupying in the future?

Presentation of Self in the Age of Social Media

More privacy and reputation management on social networking sites

Unfriended Someone

63%

Deleted Comments

44%

Untagged Photos

37%

Posted Content Regret

11% of social media users have posted content they regret.

11%

Posted Content Regret

Males on social media sites such as Facebook or Twitter are almost twice as likely as females to express regret for posting content (15% vs. 8%).

15%

8%

% of Social Networking Site Users who Have Taken These Steps on Their Profiles

SOURCE: Pew Internet and American Life Project 2012, "Privacy management on social media sites."

EXPLORE

Harry's Law, Girls, **and the Media Marketplace**

Does popular entertainment provide an accurate representation of society? What does learning about society through television tell us? Visit the Everyday Sociology Blog to explore these questions through the lens of HBO's show *Girls.*

http://wwnPag.es/trw404

CHAPTER 5

Separate and Together: Life in Groups

We hope you're *not* familiar with these terms and their definitions: "hot seat" (being beaten with drum sticks, mallets, and straps while covered with a blanket in the back of the band bus) and "crossing over" (being kicked and hit by your bandmates as you run down the aisle of the bus). It might seem like being subjected to these brutal attacks would mean that it is time to quit the band. In reality, this ritual is how your bandmates might let you know that they want you to stay—and even advance in the band leadership hierarchy. But on November 19, 2011, this ritual went horribly wrong on the Florida A&M University (FAMU) band bus. Drum major Robert Champion suffered

severe injuries at the hands of his bandmates and died at a hospital later that night. His family, friends, fellow musicians, and university community were grief-stricken, of course. But his death also touched off a national controversy over "hazing" that has yet to subside.

The hazing process is meant to test newcomers and transform them into group members; if you can endure the abuse, you can be part of the group. Although hazing is usually associated with college fraternities, it has been known to occur in high school and college clubs, athletic teams, sororities, marching bands, and even police and fire departments and the military. In fact, according to a study in the medical journal *Contemporary Pediatrics* (2000), 24 percent of high school church group members reported being hazed. Although hazing is against the law in almost every state and is usually prohibited by group charters, it is still a popular—though risky—way of initiating new members. Every year, it results in at least one death and countless injuries, and alcohol plays a major role in most of these incidents (Nuwer 1999).

The FAMU hazing has left a tragic legacy. Twelve of Champion's bandmates were charged with manslaughter in his death, the band itself was suspended indefinitely, the band director was fired, and the FAMU president resigned in the wake of the incident. In addition, Champion's parents have filed a wrongful death lawsuit against the university. In response to all of these allegations, some of Champion's bandmates have protested that he and other students volunteered to be hazed that night because they wanted to be able to move into leadership roles in the band. This fact highlights a key question in all hazing cases: who is responsible when the consequences of hazing include illegality, injury, or even death—the host group or the individual who submits to hazing?

The relationship between the individual and the group is a complex one. We sometimes do things in groups, both good and bad, that we might never do as individuals. Exploring group dynamics from a sociological perspective can help us understand and even eliminate problems like hazing and maximize the benefits of group life as well.

HOW TO READ THIS CHAPTER

This chapter explores some of the different ways we organize our lives in groups. Here you will gain some of the analytic tools you can use to understand the specific groups we'll be investigating in later chapters. Concepts such as peer pressure, teamwork, bureaucratization, and anomie can be fruitfully applied to analyses of families, work and volunteer organizations, political groups, and religious communities. Consider this chapter an introduction to group dynamics in general—a springboard from which to begin our sociological analysis of particular types of groups. As you read, think about the groups you belong to and how they affect your values and behavior. What is your influence on such groups? Have you ever "gone along" with group rules but later wished you hadn't?

What Is a Group?

We often use the term "group" to refer to any collection of two or more people who have something in common, whether it's their appearance, culture, occupation, or just a physical proximity. When sociologists speak of a **group** or social group, however, they mean a collection of people who not only share some attribute but also identify with one another and have ongoing social relations—like a family, a *Star Trek* fan club, a soccer team, a sorority, or the guys you play poker with every month.

A **crowd**, such as the throngs of sightseers at a tourist attraction or people who gather to watch a fire, would not usually be considered a group in the sociological sense. While crowd members do interact (Goffman 1971), they don't necessarily have a sense of common identity, and they rarely assemble again once they disperse. Collections of people such as crowds, audiences, and queues are known as **aggregates**—people who happen to find themselves together in a particular physical location. People in aggregates don't form lasting social relations, but people in groups do. Similarly, people belonging in the same **category**—everyone eighteen years of age or all owners of Chevy trucks, for example—don't regularly interact with one another or have any common sense of connection other than their status in the category.

Primary and Secondary Groups

Groups in which we are intimately associated with the other members, such as families and close friends, are known as **primary groups**. Primary groups typically involve more face-to-face interaction, greater cooperation, and deeper feelings of belonging. Members often associate with each other for no other reason than to spend time together.

Charles Horton Cooley (1909) introduced the term *primary* for this type of group because such groups have the most profound effects on us as individuals. Primary groups provide most of our emotional satisfaction through interaction with other members, are responsible for much of our socialization, and remain central to our identities throughout our lives. We measure who we are, and perhaps how we've changed, by the way we interact with primary group members. To Cooley (as we saw in Chapter 4), primary groups represent the most important "looking glasses" in the formation of our social selves—they constitute our "significant others."

Larger, less intimate groups are known as **secondary groups**: these include co-workers, college classes, athletic organizations, labor unions, and political parties. Interaction here is more formal and impersonal. Secondary groups are usually organized around a specific activity or the accomplishment of a task. Membership is often temporary and usually does not carry the same potential for emotional satisfaction that primary group membership does. Nonetheless, a great deal of what we do involves secondary groups.

Because secondary groups can include larger numbers of people and be geographically diffuse, membership can be almost completely anonymous. At the same time, however, secondary group membership often generates primary group ties as well. Close personal relationships can begin with the more impersonal ties of secondary groups (the friends you make at work, for example) and are sometimes a direct outgrowth of our attempts to counteract the depersonalizing nature of secondary groups. For this reason, it is sometimes difficult to classify a particular group. Your soccer team may indeed be goal oriented, but you've probably also developed personal ties to at least some of your teammates. So is your team a primary or secondary group? It features elements of both, proving that real life can be even more complex than the models sociologists devise to explain it.

GROUP a collection of people who share some attribute, identify with one another, and interact with each other

CROWD a temporary gathering of people in a public place; members might interact but do not identify with each other and will not remain in contact

AGGREGATE a collection of people who share a physical location but do not have lasting social relations

CATEGORY people who share one or more attributes but who lack a sense of common identity or belonging

PRIMARY GROUPS the people who are most important to our sense of self; members' relationships are typically characterized by face-to-face interaction, high levels of cooperation, and intense feelings of belonging

SECONDARY GROUPS larger and less intimate than primary groups; members' relationships are usually organized around a specific goal and are often temporary

---

Primary Groups Are Typically Families or Close Friends
Deborah Daniels (front left, in pink) opened her home to four generations of her family after Hurricane Katrina destroyed their New Orleans homes in 2005.

There are other ways that seemingly insignificant relationships with near strangers can have a powerful and positive impact on our own lives. Many social researchers are interested in examining the ways in which people are making up for the loss of intimate contact that is commonly shared among those who belong to primary groups. Melinda Blau and Karen Fingerman (2009) have identified what they call "consequential strangers," people we might not think of as mattering much to our sense of happiness or well-being, but who nonetheless play an important role in our otherwise fragmented postmodern lives. These people are not total strangers, but are more likely to be acquaintances from the places we work, shop, play, or conduct business—from the local barista at the coffeehouse or our favorite manicurist to the checkout clerk at the grocery store or that guy at the gym—these are people who become familiar and essential parts of our everyday lives. These people serve as social anchors, just as our close friends or family members do. Blau and Fingerman suggest that we need a new framework or perspective with which to look at the people in our world and perhaps to expand the number and range, as well as the value we ascribe to them, when we include them in our larger social circle. It seems that we need both primary and secondary relationships, as well as those along the continuum between the two.

SOCIAL NETWORK the web of direct and indirect ties connecting an individual to other people who may also affect the individual

SOCIAL TIES connections between individuals

Social Networks

You and your family, your friends, peers, colleagues, teachers, and co-workers constitute a **social network**. Sociologists who study networks call the connections between individuals **social ties**. Social ties can be direct, such as the tie between you and your friend, or indirect, such as the tie between you and your friend's cousin whom you've never met.

To understand how a social network works, think of yourself at the center with lines connecting you to all your friends, family, peers, and so on. These lines represent direct ties. Now think about all the family, friends, and peers who belong to each of *these* people. The lines connecting you to this second group must pass through the people in your first network; this second set of lines represents indirect ties. Indirect ties can include business transactions—flows of goods, services, materials, or monies—between organizations or nations. They can even represent flows of ideas. For instance, when you read ancient Greek philosophy, you become part of a network that spans centuries of writing, thinking, and educating.

You've probably already heard about the principle of "six degrees of separation," which suggests that everyone in the world is connected to everyone else within six steps: "If you know 100 people, and each of them knows 100 more, then you have 10,000 friends of friends. Take that a step further to three degrees and you are connected to 1 million people. At six degrees, the number increases to nine billion" (Schofield 2004). This means, theoretically, that you're connected to every human on the planet. It might be the case that somebody you know knows someone who knows somebody else who knows the president of the United States or a yak herdsman in the Himalayas; in other words, you might be only separated from either of these others by just four degrees.

Sociologists who study networks are concerned not only with how networks are constructed but also how influence moves along a network, and thus which persons or organizations have more influence than others within the network. In his book *Six Degrees: The Science of a Connected Age* (2003), sociologist Duncan Watts examined not only the connections individuals have to one another but also how those connections shape our actions. He found, for example, that we may change our minds about whom to vote for if enough of our friends are voting for the other candidate. Social networks can help us understand everything from the spread of fads and fashions to the way people hear about job openings or how sexually transmitted diseases are spread among various segments of the population.

WINNERS, LOSERS, AND INFLUENCE How does the flow of influence work at the level of an international organization? We could take the World Trade Organization (WTO)

as an example. Comprising 148 member nations, the WTO monitors the trade rules between countries and resolves international disputes over trade. While all member nations are part of the network, they hold different positions of power within it. We might hypothesize that nations that win the most disputes have the most influence within the network. But Joseph Conti (2003, 2005) finds that while the United States, one of the most powerful members of the WTO, is involved in the vast majority of disputes, it usually loses. The question that remains for the network theorist is whether or not "winning" or "losing" is an effective way to measure influence. What Conti concludes is that America's centrality, a network analysis term that means an actor with the most ties in a given network, is what gives it powerful influence and not the actual outcomes of the disputes.

JOBS, GENDER, AND NETWORKS

How does the flow of influence work at the level of interactions between individuals? Sociologists look at how personal ties, both direct and indirect, can influence a person's life.

In the pathbreaking work "The Strength of Weak Ties" (1973), Mark Granovetter measures how a person's distant relatives and acquaintances, attached to different social networks, pass along information about job opportunities. An individual with high socioeconomic status, or SES (taking into account income, education, and occupation), for example, usually has relatives and acquaintances with similarly high SES. Because those relatives and acquaintances belong to different social networks, all with high SES, the job seeker now has indirect connections with a vast array of high-SES contacts who can provide job leads. In other words, if your father, mother, and sister are all actors, you would likely "inherit" a network of acting contacts. The implications of Granovetter's findings are that people tend to form homogeneous social networks — to have direct ties to those who are like themselves, whether through race, class background, national origin, or religion. Further, individuals with low SES are likely to form direct ties to others with low SES and thus indirect ties as well. Information about job opportunities is less likely to travel along those networks.

More recent findings about the strength of weak ties, from Matt Hoffman and Lisa Torres (2002), indicate that women who are part of networks that include more men than women are more likely to hear about good job leads. But if their networks include more women than men, then those same women are less likely to hear about quality jobs. The number of men or women within a man's network doesn't seem to matter; men are just as likely to get quality information about job opportunities from both men and women in their social networks. Hoffman and Torres offer two rationales to explain their findings. First, women are simply less likely than men to hear about job leads. Second, women who do hear about them are more likely to pass along that information to men; they may feel threatened by the idea of more

women in their places of employment and fear loss of their own jobs. So our networks work for us, but they may also work against us.

SEXUAL HEALTH AND NETWORKS

Nicholas Christakis and James Fowler (2009) provide another example of how transmission happens between individuals belonging to similar social networks. They explain two principles: first, all social networks have a *connection*, and second, there is *contagion*, which refers to what flows through social ties. While you may have complete control of whom you are connected to directly, we exert little control over our indirect connections. Contagion not only influences an individual's health but can spread everything from obesity to smoking and substance abuse. For example, sexually transmitted diseases are more likely among people who have had four or more partners in the past year. In particular, whites who have many partners tend to have sex with other whites who have many partners, and whites who have few partners tend to have sex with whites who have few partners. STDs, then, are kept in "core" groups of active white partners, and are found less often in less active groups. This spread of STDs can be seen as a literal consequence of the *contagion* principle of social networks.

When we think of someone as being "well connected," we imagine that they not only have lots of close friends but might have relationships and acquaintances in a large and diverse social circle. As the old adage goes, it's not *what* you know, it's *who* you know. And who they know, and who *they* know — and now you have a social network.

Separate from Groups: Anomie or Virtual Membership?

According to Durkheim, all the social groups with which we are connected (families, peers, co-workers, and so on) have this particular feature: the norms of the group place certain limits on our individual actions. For example, you may have wanted to backpack through Europe after you graduated from high school, but your parents demanded that you stay home, work, and save money for college. Durkheim argues that we need these limits — otherwise, we would want many things we could never have, and the lengths to which we would go in search of our unattainable desires would be boundless. Think about it: if you were always searching for but never getting the things you wanted, you would be very unhappy and over time might even become suicidal. Durkheim (1893 / 1964) called such a state of normlessness **anomie** and believed that group member-

ANOMIE "normlessness"; term used to describe the alienation and loss of purpose that result from weaker social bonds and an increased pace of change

IN THE FUTURE

A Lonely Future? Group Ties in a Digital World

You may know this person (in fact, you may be this person): the one who has 500, or 1,300, or 2,100, or even more Facebook friends. "How is this possible?" you wonder . . . can she really "know" all those people? Is he just a "friend collector" who seeks the status symbol of an astronomical number on his Wall? If one really does "know" that many thousands of people, what are the qualities of those connections? How many of those friends are known intimately and personally, "IRL" (In Real Life)? And what does this mean for the future of our social bonds?

The debate over the effects of social media on social life is intense. Some argue that internet technologies make us lonely, replacing our face-to-face bonds with a set of "broader but shallower" online connections that don't really do the trick (Marche 2012). This argument also includes the criticism that we are more disconnected from our communities as a result of our immersion in online worlds: we are not as committed to civic life, local politics, or public service as we should be or once were (this is an extension of Robert Putnam's [2000] view on the effects of television and other technologies). Even scholars who once saw promise in the rise of internet communication systems, like MIT's Sherry Turkle, now worry that we have come to prioritize technologies over relationships (2011).

There is another side to this issue, of course. The Pew Research Center study of the Internet and American Life (Hampton et al. 2011) produced a set of findings that contradict the anxieties of the authors cited above. According to the Pew study, users of social media may actually be more connected with others than non-users. Facebook users were found to have more close relationships and more social support, and were also more trusting of others and more politically engaged, than users of other social media and than non-users. In addition, sociologists Eric Klinenberg (2012) and Claude Fischer (2011) make the case that, despite a rise in social media use and an increase in single-person households, Americans are no more or less lonely or detached from one another than they have ever been.

So what will the future hold with regard to technology and our relationships with one another? In order to answer that, we might actually want to look to the past. Remember Émile Durkheim's concerns about anomie and modern life from Chapter 1? Sounds familiar, doesn't it? Durkheim was worried that the technological and cultural changes that accompanied the Industrial Revolution would cause people to become more disconnected from one another, and that this disconnection would be detrimental both to individuals (who might be more likely to commit suicide as a result) and for society (which would lack necessary cohesion and solidarity). Authors like Stephen Marche and Sherry Turkle express the same concerns, over 100 years later, about the changes associated with the Digital Revolution. It seems that rapid changes in technology and society, no matter what they look like or when they occur, arouse similar anxieties. When it comes to relationships and group ties, the future may not look as different as we think it will . . .

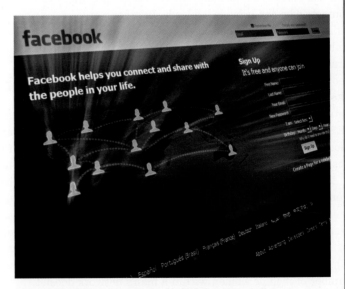

Social Networks Do web sites like Facebook facilitate relationships and civic engagement? Or do they undermine our "real world" connections?

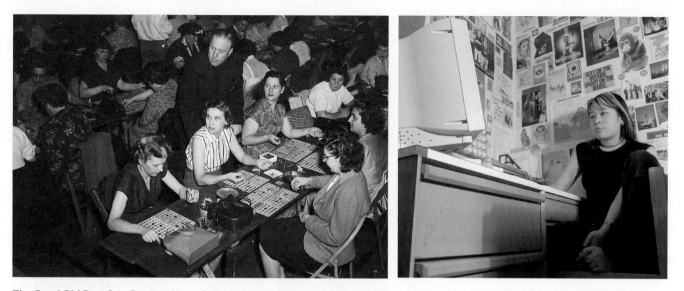

The Good Old Days? In *Bowling Alone*, Robert Putnam argues that the decline of group activities, like bingo nights or league bowling, represents a decline in civic engagement. However, technologies like the internet and social networking sites have allowed large numbers of people to gather, connect, and avoid anomie.

ship keeps us from feeling it. So group membership not only anchors us to the social world — it's what keeps us alive.

Durkheim was worried that in our increasingly fragmented modern society, anomie would become more and more common. Other scholars share Durkheim's position, noting that Americans today are less likely than ever to belong to the types of civic organizations and community groups that can combat anomie and keep us connected to one another. Harvard professor Robert Putnam, in his book *Bowling Alone: The Collapse and Revival of American Community* (2000), argues that we no longer practice the type of "civic engagement" that builds democratic community and keeps anomie at bay: fewer people bowl in leagues than ever before, and people are less likely to participate in organizations like the League of Women Voters, PTA, or Kiwanis or engage in regular activities like monthly bridge games or Sunday picnics. He even offers statistics on how many angry drivers "flip the bird" at other drivers every year — all part of his argument about our disintegrating collective bonds.

Putnam's critics argue that he longs for the "good old days" that will never be again (and perhaps never were). It may be true that we don't belong to bridge clubs anymore — but we have a new set of resources to help us connect with others and avoid anomie.

In the decade since Putnam's influential work first appeared, there has been an explosion of new communications technology. Some were concerned that the internet would only serve to exacerbate our condition of isolation and separation from one another, as individuals became further distanced from face-to-face contact and more immersed in living online. Yet, the internet has made it possible for people who might not otherwise have met to come together — albeit in cyberspace — and to belong to a variety of different online groups. From participants involved in Massively Multiperson Online Role-Playing Games (MMORPGs), such as World of Warcraft or Second Life, to support groups who "meet" regularly to deal with personal issues or medical conditions, or simply for fans of different authors, bands, artists, or filmmakers to swap comments, technology is offering us new opportunities to connect by making us members of **virtual communities**.

If both types of groups, the ones based on face-to-face contact and those that facilitate online interaction, can each serve as social anchors, then is one necessarily better for us (and for society) than the other?

VIRTUAL COMMUNITIES social groups whose interactions are mediated through information technologies, particularly the internet

DATA WORKSHOP
Analyzing Mass Media and Popular Culture

"Who's in your Feed?"

The idea of what constitutes a group has necessarily changed as modern society has evolved through the Industrial Revolution to the current Digital Age. Sociologists have had to

IN RELATIONSHIPS

Social Networking Sites: Pros and Cons or Think Before You Post

Who's reading about your life online? Perhaps more people than you might think.

In just a few short years, there has been astounding growth in the number of people participating in social networking sites. By the end of 2012, Facebook became the largest network, boasting more than one billion members. Facebook eclipsed Google, Yahoo, and YouTube (along with every other massively popular destination on the web) as the most-visited site on the internet, garnering almost 10 percent of all U.S. web-surfing minutes (Tsukayama 2010).

There were a number of social networking sites that preceded Facebook. In the 1990s, internet service providers like CompuServe and America Online (AOL) allowed registered users to form communities and interact with each other in chat rooms. As more and more people logged on to the internet in the 2000s, social networking sites flourished. Users flocked to such sites as Friendster, launched in 2002, and then MySpace, introduced in 2006. That same year brought Twitter, another service that allows users to interact through writing or following other people's "tweets," or short messages.

Facebook was created in 2004 when founder Mark Zuckerberg was a student at Harvard University, though its membership initially was limited to certain colleges. The site soon opened to all users and by 2008 had overtaken MySpace on its continued ascent to the top. Facebook became a publicly traded company in 2012, adding another dimension to its success and profitability.

The rise of social networking has been so rapid that social scientists can barely keep pace with studying what this new technology means, not just for our personal relationships and everyday lives but also for the nature of social interac-

tion in groups and for the kind of influence it is exerting in other spheres as a powerful new social institution. For everybody who participates in social networking, its rewards and benefits are easily appreciated. At the same time, we should be aware of some of the less positive and more threatening aspects of this ubiquitous presence.

In sociological terms, we can see how such sites as Facebook can help us make the most of our primary and secondary group connections. It is easier than ever to stay in touch with the important people in our lives (even if they are not in close physical proximity) and to reconnect with past acquaintances or to meet and interact with new people. Social networking has brought people together who might not have otherwise been able to find each other in the past when it was not possible to search for others based on their interests, backgrounds, and demographic details. On Facebook, "Every 60 seconds is packed with a lifetime's worth of social interactions" (Grossman 2010). That includes 79,364

broaden the definition of the term. Just what do you call a bunch of people who gather together to share interests, offer advice, provide support, or exchange ideas, but who may never meet in person? Such groups have come to be known as online or virtual communities. In the past, people wondering about their best friend in the third grade generally didn't have a way to contact that lost friend. Also, people with common interests had to use creative ways of locating each other such as wearing buttons or pins or posting flyers at community centers. The internet has allowed us the ability

to stay in touch with the important people in our lives (even if they live far away), and also to reconnect with lost or faded acquaintances, or to meet and interact with new people. It has brought together people who might not have otherwise been able to search for others based on their interest, backgrounds, and common friends. The social networking site Facebook is fairly comprehensive — allowing you to search for your sixth-grade teacher, to find other people who share an interest in henna, and to keep tabs on the people whom you see and text multiple times a day — all in one online location.

wall posts, 82,557 status updates, 98,604 friends approved, 135,849 photos added, 231,605 messages sent, 382,861 posts liked, and 510,404 comments made—every single minute!

All that, and we are still in the infancy of social networking and how it will become an increasingly important part of our everyday lives and the interactions that we have with the world beyond just our own family and friends. The web of connections that are being built on these sites promises to weave us ever more closely into contacts with a variety of social groups, products, and businesses and to seamlessly integrate into the rest of our online lives. Many people who are on social networking sites are frequent and enthusiastic users who may log on daily and perhaps throughout that day. Some 200 million people access Facebook on mobile devices like smart phones, which can keep them in touch on a regular if not constant basis. In many ways, we accept and embrace the emergence of this new way to live online. Yet of all the various interactions that are carried out through social networking (again with a total of 1,789,736 actions performed every minute on Facebook alone), we should not neglect the number of those that can have negative consequences for individuals and society.

In the past several years, the news has been full of stories detailing problems that have emerged in the context of such social networking sites as Facebook. Although these sites have privacy setting options that can scan posted information and protect certain personal content from general viewing, not all users know how to set such limits, and many are naive or unaware of the possible ramifications of what they write, upload, and respond to online. What happens online doesn't always stay online, and not everyone is using social networking with the best of intentions.

Social networking facilitates interactions between members, but participation in a virtual community can also leave you open to a variety of new types of interpersonal threats and challenges that sometimes result in real and detrimental consequences. There are numerous incidents when students have been suspended or expelled because of what they have posted in their profiles, including pictures of underage drinking or taking illegal drugs, and explicit threats of violence toward others. Social networking sites have also been at the center of some tragic cases of cyberbullying in recent years: in multiple cases, young people have committed suicide after being humiliated, harassed, or bullied (often about their sexuality). In addition to school officials, law enforcement agencies have used social networking sites to target illegal activity (everything from conspiracy to commit murder to sexual crimes, assault, and theft) to make arrests and prosecute suspects.

Many students have discovered that putting too much information, or the wrong kind, online might jeopardize their academic or professional futures. One commonly reported practice is the use of Facebook to screen prospective employees' lifestyles. Increasingly, individuals are being denied jobs because of the pictures and information that they have posted on their personal profiles. Usually cited are pictures of drinking, illegal drug use, and smoking as "red flags" about personal integrity and interpersonal skills and character (Tahmincioglu 2008). The same could potentially happen in academia, with students applying to a school being evaluated, in part, based on their online profiles.

This brings up some important issues about privacy and group affiliation with which we will continue to grapple as social media play an increasing part in our interactions. There will be new benefits and rewards, along with challenges, as the coming changes unfold in our lives around this rapidly changing new technology.

This Data Workshop asks you to examine how Facebook shapes group ties and social identity. You will conduct an interview about group experiences on Facebook or other social media. You can answer the interview questions yourself or interview a friend. See Chapter 2 for a review of these interview methods.

Consider asking the following questions:

✳ How do you decide to whom to send friend requests?

✳ How do you decide from whom to accept friend requests?

✳ Are there people in your life whom you refuse to friend on Facebook?

✳ What criteria do you use when deciding to ignore or block a person?

✳ Are most in your social networking circle people whom you know in real life? Why or why not?

✳ How many people do you feel comfortable having on your friends list? Why?

* When you look at the profile pictures on your friends list, is there racial, gender, class, age, sexuality, or subcultural diversity?

* What kind of groups have you joined online? Why?

* Does your friends list affect what you decide to post as a status?

* Are you set on public or friends only?

* Do you allow people to search for you on Facebook? Why or why not?

* How often do you post on Facebook?

* And finally, does your Facebook activity help you feel connected to others? If so, then how do you use Facebook as a medium for social ties? If not, then what function does Facebook play in your life?

There are two options for completing this Data Workshop.

Option 1 (informal): Prepare written notes that you can refer to in class. Share your observations and responses to the above questions with other students in small-group discussions. Listen for any differences in other's insights.

Option 2 (formal): Write a three- to four-page essay answering the Workshop questions. Make sure to refer to specifics to support your analysis.

By conducting this interview, you have begun to identify the way that group life is created, maintained, and changed online by group members who might share many things in common — especially other people.

Group Dynamics

Sociologists have always been interested in how groups form, change, disintegrate, achieve great goals, or commit horrendous wrongs — add all these phenomena together, and they constitute **group dynamics**. How do groups affect an individual's sense of self? What forces bind members to a group? How do groups influence their members? When do groups excel at the tasks they undertake? What are the qualities of group leaders? When are

GROUP DYNAMICS the patterns of interaction between groups and individuals

DYAD a two-person social group

TRIAD a three-person social group

groups destructive to the individual? How can relations between groups be improved? We will attempt to answer some of these questions in the next sections.

Dyads, Triads, and More

The size of a group affects how it operates and the types of individual relationships that can occur within it (Figure 5.1). A **dyad**, the smallest possible social group, consists of only two members — a romantic couple, two best friends, or two siblings, for example (Simmel 1950). Although relationships in a dyad are usually intense, dyads are also fundamentally unstable, because if one person wants out of the group, it's over. A **triad** is slightly more stable because the addition of a third person means that

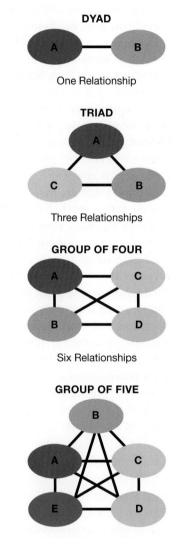

DYAD

One Relationship

TRIAD

Three Relationships

GROUP OF FOUR

Six Relationships

GROUP OF FIVE

Ten Relationships

Figure 5.1 **The Effects of Group Size on Relationships**

Smaller groups feature fewer and more intimate personal ties; larger groups feature more relationships, but they are also likely to be more impersonal.

conflicts between two members can be refereed by the third. As additional people are added to a group, it may no longer be possible for everyone to know or interact with everyone else personally (think of all the residents of a large apartment building), and so policies may have to be established to help with communication and resolve conflicts. The features of dyads and triads point out an important axiom of group dynamics in general: the smaller a group is, the more likely it is to be based on personal ties; larger groups are more likely to be based on rules and regulations (as we'll see later when we examine bureaucracies).

In-Groups and Out-Groups

An **in-group** is a group a member identifies with and feels loyalty toward. Members usually feel a certain distinctness from or even hostility toward other groups, known as **out-groups**. Most of us are associated with a number of in- and out-groups, stemming from our ethnic, familial, professional, athletic, and educational backgrounds, for example. Group loyalty and cohesion intensify when differences are strongly defined between the "us" of an in-group and the "them" of an out-group; we may also feel a sense of superiority toward those who are excluded from our in-group. School sports rivalries make clear in-group and out-group distinctions, as evident in this popular slogan seen on T-shirts and bumper stickers all over Los Angeles: "My favorite teams are UCLA and whoever's playing USC!"

As we might expect, in-group membership can be a source of prejudice and discrimination based on class, race, gender, sexual orientation, religion, or political opinion. The differences attributed to an out-group often become exaggerated, if not entirely fabricated to begin with — "All Irishmen are drunks," or "All Mexicans are lazy," for example. Robert Merton (1968) noted the phenomenon that the same qualities or behaviors are viewed positively when they are "ours" and negatively when they are "theirs": the out-group is "lazy," whereas the in-group is "laid-back"; they are "snobbish," we are "classy"; they are "zealots," we are "devout." At their worst, in-group / out-group dynamics create the backdrop for such social tragedies as slavery and genocide.

Reference Groups

Our perception of a group and what it takes to be a bona fide member can be crucial to our sense of self. When a group provides standards by which a person evaluates his own personal attributes, it is known as a **reference group**. A common reference group is one's family. We often try to "live up to" the standards of our parents, siblings, and extended family members. If we don't see ourselves as having the qualities of a "true" family member, we may adopt a negative self-image. A reference group may also be one to which we aspire to belong but of which we are not yet members; we saw one example at the beginning of this chapter, the musicians who wanted to belong to the marching band so much that they were willing to risk their own health, safety, and lives, as well as those of others.

DATA WORKSHOP
Analyzing Everyday Life

The Twenty Statements Test: Who Am I?

This Data Workshop, combining material from Chapters 4 and 5, asks you to look at how social affiliations with groups help shape our self-concept. You will be using a method that is similar to survey research to complete this Data Workshop (see Chapter 2 for a review). Start your work by completing Step 1 below, without reading any farther than the line of stars!

Step 1: The Twenty Statements Test (TST)
In the spaces provided below, write down twenty different responses to the question "Who am I?" Don't worry about evaluating the logic or importance of your responses — just write the answers in the order they occur to you. Give yourself five minutes to complete this task.

IN-GROUP a group that one identifies with and feels loyalty toward

OUT-GROUP any group an individual feels opposition, rivalry, or hostility toward

REFERENCE GROUP a group that provides a standard of comparison against which we evaluate ourselves

1. I am _____.
2. I am _____.
3. I am _____.
4. I am _____.
5. I am _____.
6. I am _____.
7. I am _____.
8. I am _____.
9. I am _____.
10. I am _____.
11. I am _____.
12. I am _____.
13. I am _____.
14. I am _____.
15. I am _____.

16. I am _____ .

17. I am _____ .

18. I am _____ .

19. I am _____ .

20. I am _____ .

Step 2: Analysis

Now it's time to analyze your responses. Rate each one according to the four categories listed below. Evaluate, to the best of your ability, which responses fall into the A-mode, B-mode, C-mode, and D-mode categories.

> *A-mode* responses are the type of physical characteristics found on your driver's license: "I am a blonde"; "I am short"; "I am a Wisconsin resident."

> *B-mode* responses describe socially defined statuses usually associated with group membership of some sort: "I am a college student"; "I am a Catholic"; "I am an African American"; "I am a quarterback."

> *C-mode* responses describe styles of behavior or emotional states: "I am a happy person"; "I am a country music fan"; "I am a fashionable dresser."

> *D-mode* responses are more general than individual: "I am part of the universe"; "I am a human being."

You may have some difficulty deciding how to categorize some of your responses — for example, where does "I am an American" go — in A, B, or D? Use your best judgment. Count the number of each type of response. Now compare the totals — which category got the most responses?

You may want to compare your findings with those of your classmates; where do your fellow students get their sense of self? We predict that, even if you yourself gave more B-mode responses, the predominant mode in your classroom is C. Those with more B-mode responses base their self-concept on group membership and institutional roles. Those with more C-mode responses see themselves as more independent and define themselves according to their individual actions and emotions rather than their connections to others. It is likely that there are few (if any) people whose responses fall predominantly in the A or D mode. Those with more A-mode responses may feel that they have a "skin deep" self-concept, based more on their appearance to others than on their internal qualities. Those with more D-mode responses are harder to categorize and may feel uncertain about the source of their sense of self.

The TST was developed by social psychologist Manfred Kuhn (Kuhn and McPartland 1954) as a way of determining the degree to which we base our self-concepts on our membership in different groups. The test was used later by Louis Zurcher (1977) to study the changing self-images of Americans. Zurcher found that in the 1960s individuals were more likely to give B-mode responses, but in the 1970s and 1980s people were more likely to give C-mode responses. While you might think it better to be an independent actor than to be defined by your group membership, Zurcher and his colleague Ralph Turner became concerned about this trend away from group identification and toward a more radically individualistic sense of self. Why were they so concerned?

The primary characteristics of the C-mode, or "impulsive," self (Turner 1976) are the pursuit of individual satisfaction, an orientation toward the present, and a sense that the individual should not be linked to others and that group obligations inhibit individual expression. The primary characteristics of the B-mode, or "institutional," self are a willingness to adhere to group standards and to accept group obligations as well as an orientation toward the future and a sense that the individual is linked to others. Zurcher and Turner worried that a society full of self-interested (and even selfish), impulsive individuals might no longer care about the common good and would only work to satisfy their own needs.

Do you do things for your own benefit or for the benefit of the group? What do you think are the consequences for a society overwhelmingly populated by one personality type or the other? Are these two orientations mutually exclusive, or can you combine the best parts of both? If the latter, what can you do in order to bring that about?

There are two options for completing this Data Workshop.

Option 1 (informal): Make some notes on your findings to share with other students in small-group discussions. How many "institutional" or "impulsive" selves are part of your discussion group? Do Zurcher and Turner's categories satisfactorily describe the way we consider our selves now, in the twenty-first century? Perhaps you can come up with a new category of self that better describes the individuals in your group.

Option 2 (formal): Find a small sample population of three to five other people and administer the TST to each of them. Collect, compare, and analyze your findings from the group. Answer the following questions in a three-page essay: If the majority of your fellow Americans fell into the same category, what would this mean for society? How would schools, families, workplaces, sports teams, governments, and charitable organizations operate if almost everyone fell into the same category? Make sure to refer to your TST data in the essay, and include the data as an attachment to your paper.

Group Cohesion

A basic concept in the study of group dynamics is **group cohesion**, the sense of solidarity or team spirit that members feel toward their group. Put another way, group cohe-

Group Cohesion Why might fraternity brothers feel more group cohesion than a large group of students attending a lecture?

sion is the force that binds them together. A group is said to be more cohesive when individuals feel strongly tied to membership, so it is likely that a group of fraternity brothers is more cohesive than a random group of classmates. The life of a group depends on at least a minimum level of cohesion. If members begin to lose their strong sense of commitment, the group will gradually disintegrate (Friedkin 2004).

Cohesion is enhanced in a number of ways. It tends to rely heavily on interpersonal factors such as shared values and shared demographic traits like race, age, gender, or class (Cota et al. 1995). We can see this kind of cohesion, for example, in a clique of junior high school girls or members of a church congregation. Cohesion also tends to rely on an attraction to the group as a whole or members' abilities to cooperate in achieving goals (Thye and Lawler 2002). This

might help explain cohesion among fans of the Green Bay Packers or members of a local Elks lodge.

GROUPTHINK Whereas a high degree of cohesion might seem desirable, it can also lead to the kind of poor decision making seen in hazing cases. In a process Irving Janus (1971, 1982) called **groupthink**, highly cohesive groups may demand absolute conformity and punish those who threaten to undermine the consensus. Although groupthink does help maintain solidarity, it can also short-circuit the decision-making process, letting a desire for unanimity prevail over critical reasoning. When this happens, groups may begin to feel invulnerable and morally superior (White 1989). Members who would otherwise wish to dissent may instead cave in to peer pressure (see the next section).

The problem of groupthink can reach the highest level of industry or government, sometimes with disastrous results. For instance, there are those who believe that the explosion of the space shuttle *Challenger* in 1986 may have been a result of NASA scientists' failing to take seriously those who suspected weaknesses in the shuttle's launch design (Vaughan 1996). More recently, groupthink may have been to blame for the failure of the CIA and the White House to accurately assess the state of Saddam Hussein's programs for weapons of mass destruction; the perceived existence of such weapons was a primary rationale for waging the Iraq War in 2003. A Senate Intelligence Committee report claims that a groupthink dynamic caused those involved to lose objectivity and to embellish or exaggerate findings that justified the U.S. invasion (Ehrenreich 2004; Isikoff 2004).

Social Influence (Peer Pressure)

While you may not have had any personal experience with groupthink, you are certain to find the next set of sociological concepts all too familiar. When individuals are part of groups, they are necessarily influenced by other members. Sociologists refer to this as social influence, or peer pressure. Knowing how **social influence** works can help you when you need to convince others to act in a certain way (like agreeing on a specific restaurant or movie). In turn, it can also help you to recognize when others are trying to influence you (to drink too much or drive too fast, for example).

The idea of social influence is not new: the ancient Greek philosopher Aristotle considered persuasion in his *Rhetoric*. But the more modern studies on social influence date back to

GROUP COHESION the sense of solidarity or loyalty that individuals feel toward a group to which they belong

GROUPTHINK in very cohesive groups, the tendency to enforce a high degree of conformity among members, creating a demand for unanimous agreement

SOCIAL INFLUENCE exerting group control over others' decisions

World War II, when social scientists were trying to help in the war effort by using motivational films to boost morale among servicemen. Since then, the study of social influence has become an expanding part of the field devoted to discovering the principles that determine our beliefs, create our attitudes, and move us to action (Friedkin and Cook 1990; Cialdini and Trost 1998; Friedkin and Granovetter 1998). Recent research on social influence has revealed that everything from our performance in school (Altermatt and Pomerantz 2005) to the likelihood that we will commit rape (Bohner et al. 2006) can be subject to the influence of others. We will focus here on how social influence functions in everyday situations.

Almost all members of society are susceptible to what is either real or imagined social pressure to conform. In general, we conform because we want to gain acceptance and approval (positive sanctions) and avoid rejection and disapproval (negative sanctions). We follow prescriptions, doing the things we're supposed to do, as well as proscriptions, avoiding the things we're not supposed to do.

Social psychologists have determined that social influence results in one of three kinds of conformity: compliance, identification, or internalization. Compliance, the mildest kind of conformity, means going along with something because you expect to gain rewards or avoid punishments (for example, shaking hands with your opponent after a tennis match even if you wish you didn't have to). When people comply, however, they don't actually change their own ideas or beliefs. Identification, a somewhat stronger kind of conformity, is induced by a person's desire to establish or maintain a relationship with a person or group (for example, emulating the sportsmanship of someone like Roger Federer in order to impress other tennis players). A person who identifies with a group conforms to their wishes and follows their behavior. Internalization, the strongest kind of conformity, occurs when an individual adopts the beliefs of a leader or group. An example of internalization would involve being a good sport, win or lose, because you believe it to be morally right. When internalization occurs, people believe in what they are doing.

Experiments in Conformity

Three rather famous social psychological studies were conducted in the 1950s, 60s, and 70s with the related goal of trying to understand more about the dynamics of social pressure and, in particular, about group conformity and obedience to authority.

THE ASCH EXPERIMENT The first of these experiments was a study on compliance conducted in 1951 by Solomon Asch (1958), who gathered groups of seven or eight students to participate in what he called an experiment on visual perception. In fact, only one of the students in each group was

Exhibit 1   **Exhibit 2**

Figure 5.2   Which Line in Exhibit 2 Matches Exhibit 1?

Solomon Asch's studies showed that some people will go against the evidence of their own senses if others around them seem to have different perceptions.

a real research subject; the others knew ahead of time how they were supposed to act. During the experiment, the participants were asked to look at a set of three straight lines and to match the length of a fourth line to one of the other three (see Figure 5.2). In each case, the real research subjects would be the last to give an answer. At first, all participants gave the same correct answer. After a few rounds, however, the confederates began to give the same consistently wrong answer. They were completely unanimous in perceiving the line lengths incorrectly. How would the real subjects react when it came to their turn?

Most subjects felt considerable pressure to comply with the rest of the group. A third (33 percent) were "yielders" who gave in at least half of the time to what they knew were the wrong answers. Another 40 percent yielded less frequently but still gave some wrong answers. Only 25 percent were "independents," refusing to give in to the majority. In a debriefing period after the experiment, some subjects reported that they had assumed the rest of the participants were right and they were wrong. Other subjects knew they were not wrong but did not want to appear different from the rest of the group. Almost all of them were greatly distressed by the discrepancy between their own perceptions and those of the other participants. Clearly, it can be difficult to resist peer pressure and to maintain independence in a group situation. What would you have done?

THE MILGRAM EXPERIMENT Stanley Milgram's experience as a graduate student of Solomon Asch's led him to further work on conformity. His first experiments were conducted in 1961, just after the trial of Nazi war criminal Adolf Eichmann had begun in Israel. Many of those who were prosecuted in the years after World War II offered the defense that they were "only following orders." But it was not just soldiers who sent millions of innocents to concentration camps—ordinary citizens turned in their neighbors.

GLOBAL PERSPECTIVE

Group vs. Individual Norms: Honor Killings

In American culture, when reports of family members murdering each other emerge, the reasons generally include abuse, crimes of passion, and monetary gain. The murder of Jose and Kitty Menendez by their sons, Lyle and Erik, is among the notorious cases of murder within a family. The Menendez brothers killed their parents with a shotgun in order to gain access to the family fortune, spending more than a million dollars in their first six months as orphans. Both brothers are now spending life in prison. Scott Peterson murdered his pregnant wife, Laci, in order to reduce their increasing debt and to date other women. Peterson is now living on death row in California's San Quentin State Prison. In these two cases, public opinion has painted the Menendez brothers and Peterson as dishonorable traitors to their families, men who were more concerned with their own personal gain than their loyalty to family.

What if the reason for a murder of a family member is to uphold the reputation of the family as a whole? **Honor killing** is the murder of a family member based on the belief that the victim is bringing dishonor to the family or the community. In an honor killing, which is primarily seen in Middle Eastern and South Asian cultures, the victim of the murder is usually a woman in the family who has not lived up to the moral codes set by the religion or community. Reasons for honor killings may include refusing to enter into an arranged marriage, being a rape victim, being immodest in dress or behavior, or having sex outside marriage.

HONOR KILLING the murder of a family member—usually female—who is believed to have brought dishonor to her family

The United Nations estimates that as many as 5,000 women a year are murdered in honor killings. The methods of killing range from being shot to being set on fire or stoned to death. In each case of honor killing, the person who commits the murder is seen as the norm enforcer and not the norm violator, as he is doing it in order to seek vindication and to right the wrong committed by the wife, daughter, or sister.

In this cultural context, the murdered woman is viewed as someone who deserved to die for betraying and dishonoring her family.

Honor killings are either sanctioned by law in countries like Jordan and Syria or not prosecuted in countries like Turkey, Pakistan, and Egypt. Richard Wilkinson maintains that in countries with less access to basic resources, health care, and human capital, there is a correlating lack of social power and equality for women (2005). Gender inequality is exacerbated in places where there are fewer social resources, making honor killings more likely. Clashes occur when the cultural practice of honor killing is brought to Western countries like France, Canada, and the United States, where a woman's sexual freedom may face informal sanctions but is widely accepted as the norm.

In October 2009, in a suburb of Phoenix, Arizona, twenty-year-old Noor Al-maleki was run over by a Jeep driven by her father, Faleh Al-maleki, formerly from Iraq, because he feared she was becoming too Westernized. Banned from wearing jeans, social networking on the internet, and interacting with boys, Noor had sought to live life as an American. Growing up in the United States since the age of four, Noor was immersed in American cultural norms. Defying her father's rules, Noor refused an arranged marriage at age seventeen, and eventually moved into her boyfriend's parents' home earlier in 2009 before being killed. Faleh Al-maleki faces up to fifty years in prison if convicted for his daughter's murder.

The cultural norm promoting strong family values that causes such disgust toward the Menendez brothers and Scott Peterson is the same norm behind honor killings. However, in honor killings, the family is seen as more important than each family member; therefore, an individual member should suffer severe punishment for bringing shame to the family. While Al-maleki's actions toward his daughter seem to most Americans' individualist notions of justice as a betrayal of the family, they are justified in his cultural understandings of family honor.

The Milgram Experiment How did Stanley Milgram test participants' obedience to authority? Do you think he would get the same results today?

Milgram wanted to know whether something particular about the German national psyche led so many to act as accomplices to the mass executions, why they complied with authority figures even when orders conflicted with their own consciences. While we usually think that following orders is a good thing, in the case of the Holocaust, it amounted to a "crime of obedience."

The Milgram experiment (1963, 1974) used a laboratory setting to test the lengths to which ordinary people would follow orders from a legitimate authority. The experiment included three roles: the "experimenter" (a scientist in a white lab coat), a "teacher," and a "learner." The teachers were the only real research subjects in the experiment: although the teachers were led to believe otherwise, the learners were actually confederates of the experimenters. When roles were assigned at the outset of the experiment, the research subjects were always picked to play the teacher, despite a seemingly random assignment of roles.

The stated goal of the experiment was to measure the effect of punishment on memory and learning. The teacher was instructed to read aloud a set of word pairs for the learner to memorize. The teacher would then repeat the first word in the pair, and for each incorrect answer, administer a shock of increasing voltage to the learner. The teacher watched while the experimenter strapped the learner to a chair and applied electrodes to his arms. The teacher was then directed to an adjoining room where he could communicate with, but not see, the learner. This room contained a machine with a series of levers indicating the increasing levels of voltage that would be administered for each successive incorrect answer. (In actuality, the machine was not connected to the learner, and he received no shocks.)

The experiment began. As the teacher amplified the voltage for each incorrect answer, the learner responded in increasingly vocal ways. In reality, the teacher was hearing a prerecorded tape that included exclamations, banging on the wall, complaints by the learner about a heart condition, and finally, silence. Many subjects grew uncomfortable at around 135 volts, often pausing and expressing a desire to check on the learner or discontinue the experiment. At that point, the experimenter would give a succession of orders, prodding the teacher to continue. After being assured that they would not be held responsible, most subjects continued, many reaching the maximum of 450 volts.

Milgram and his colleagues were stunned by the results. They had believed that only a few of the subjects would be willing to inflict the maximum voltage. In the first set of experiments, 65 percent of the participants administered the maximum voltage, though many were very uncomfortable doing so and all paused at some point. Only one participant outright refused to administer even low-voltage shocks. Milgram's results highlight the dynamics of conformity revealed in the Asch experiment. A subject will often rely on the expertise of an individual or group, in this case the experimenter, when faced with a difficult decision. We also see how thoroughly socialized most people are to obey authority and carry out orders, especially when they no longer consider themselves responsible for their actions. Clearly, few people have the personal resources to resist authority, even when it goes against their consciences.

THE STANFORD PRISON EXPERIMENT The Stanford Prison Experiment, conducted by Milgram's high school classmate Philip Zimbardo (1971), also examined the power of authority. Twenty-four undergraduates deemed psychologically healthy and stable were recruited to participate in a two-week mock prison simulation. Role assignment as prisoner or guard was based on a coin toss. Guards were given batons, khaki clothing, and mirrored sunglasses, and were told they could not physically harm the prisoners but could otherwise create feelings of boredom, fear, or powerlessness. Prisoners were "arrested" and taken to a mock "jail" set up in the basement of a university building, where they were strip-searched, dressed in smocks and stocking caps (to simulate shaven heads), and assigned identity numbers. A research assistant played the role of warden, while Zimbardo himself was the superintendent.

The students quickly inhabited their roles, but soon exceeded the experimenters' expectations, resulting in an abusive and potentially dangerous situation. Rioting began by the second day; the guards quelled it harshly, harassing the prisoners and depriving them of food, sleep, and basic sanitation. Several guards became increasingly sadistic as the experiment went on, degrading and punishing any prisoner who challenged their authority, and several prisoners

The Stanford Prison Experiment Why do you think the students in Zimbardo's experiment inhabited their roles so completely? What does it reveal about group behavior?

showed signs of psychological trauma. After only six days, Zimbardo was compelled to shut down the experiment after a graduate student researcher (whom he later married) became appalled by the conditions.

The Stanford Prison Experiment provided another example of the way situational dynamics, rather than individuals' personal attributes, can determine behavior.

MILGRAM REVISITED Some researchers have claimed that the Asch experiment was a "child of its time," that students in the 1950s were more obedient in their roles, and the culture placed greater emphasis on the value of conformity (Perrin and Spencer 1980, 1981). Researchers in recent decades who have replicated the Asch experiment have in fact seen significantly lower rates of compliance, suggesting that the historical and cultural context in which the experiment was conducted seemed to have an effect on how subjects performed (Bond and Sussex 1996). This conclusion echoes some of Ralph Turner's findings about the institu-

tional or impulsive self, discussed in an earlier Data Workshop: namely, he found that patterns of behavior can change over time and that separate generations may respond differently to social pressures.

The power of the group continues to interest sociologists, psychologists, and others who want to understand what drives our powerful impulse to comply (Cialdini 1998). Both the Milgram and the Stanford Prison experiments would be considered unethical by today's professional standards. Although each of the experiments revealed important truths about obedience to authority, some of the participants involved suffered real, and in some cases long-lasting, psychological pain beyond what is considered an acceptable threshold of minimal harm.

Yet the experiments remain relevant because real-life examples of crimes of obedience continue to occur — whether in the case of the prison guards at Abu Ghraib or in a serial telephone hoax perpetrated on fast-food workers in which a caller posing as a police officer instructed assistant managers to abuse fellow workers (Wolfson 2005).

Nearly half a century elapsed before researchers at Santa Clara University found a means of replicating the Milgram experiment that would pass the Institutional Review Board process for research on human subjects. After a careful screening process, Jerry Burger (2009) conducted a modified version of the famous experiment that protected the well-being of the participants while still providing a valid comparison to the original. Contrary to expectations, obedience rates were only slightly lower in Burger's replication than they had been in Milgram's lab more than forty-five years earlier.

Although we might like to imagine ourselves as being more able to resist the same forces of conformity that trip up research participants who consistently cave in to social pressure, it's likely that if we found ourselves in situations similar to those created in the laboratory, we might go along and obey authority too.

Teamwork

Are two heads better than one? Or do too many cooks spoil the broth? Early research on groups (Homans 1951) typically assumed that it was always more productive to work in a team rather than alone. However, researchers soon recognized that both the nature of the task and the characteristics of the group have a lot to do with the comparative advantage or disadvantage of working in a group (Goodacre 1953). When we measure productivity, groups almost always outperform single individuals. Things get a bit more complicated, however, when groups are compared with the same number of people working by themselves.

In one of the earliest attempts to systematically study group productivity, experimental social psychologist Ivan Steiner (1972) compared the potential productivity of a group (what they should be able to do) with their actual productivity (what they in fact got done). According to Steiner, actual group productivity can never equal potential productivity because there will always be losses in the team process. Two major sources of inefficiency in particular come with the group process, and both get worse as group size increases. One source is organization: coordinating activities and delegating tasks. For example, if four friends are going to help you move to a new apartment, some time will be lost while you figure out who should pack what, how the furniture will be arranged in the truck, where the boxes should go in the new apartment, and so forth.

Another source of inefficiency is the phenomenon known as **social loafing**, which means that as more individuals are added to a task, each one takes it a little easier (Karau and Williams 1993). Furthermore, as more people become involved, the harder it will be to discern individual effort. If it is impossible for any single person to receive credit or blame, motivation usually suffers. Have you ever asked too many people to help you move to a new apartment? If so, chances are a few did most of the work, some showed up late and helped out a bit, and others did very little but had a good time talking and eating pizza. Having too many "helpers" may contribute to social loafing.

Solutions to the problem of social loafing include recognizing individual effort and finding ways to make a task more interesting or personally rewarding, but such solutions are not always possible. It might be difficult, for instance, to make "moving day" more rewarding. Another solution, however, is suggested by **social identity theory**. Having a social identity, as opposed to a personal one, involves thinking and feeling like a representative of a group (Turner and Killian 1987); you have a real desire to belong to, not simply keep company with, the group. According to this model, the most efficient teams are characterized by the greatest social identity among their members; such social identity increases motivation and places the needs of the group above purely personal concerns.

SOCIAL LOAFING the phenomenon in which as more individuals are added to a task, each individual contributes a little less; a source of inefficiency when working in teams

SOCIAL IDENTITY THEORY a theory of group formation and maintenance that stresses the need of individual members to feel a sense of belonging

POWER the ability to control the actions of others

COERCIVE POWER power that is backed by the threat of force

INFLUENTIAL POWER power that is supported by persuasion

AUTHORITY the legitimate right to wield power

TRADITIONAL AUTHORITY authority based in custom, birthright, or divine right

LEGAL-RATIONAL AUTHORITY authority based in laws, rules, and procedures, not in the heredity or personality of any individual leader

CHARISMATIC AUTHORITY authority based in the perception of remarkable personal qualities in a leader

Qualities of Leadership: Power, Authority, and Style

Effective group leaders possess a variety of qualities, some of which are particular to the kind of group they lead. The leader of a therapeutic support group, for example, needs the proper credentials as well as experience and compassion for his patients. The captain of a sports team must display expertise at her game as well as the ability to inspire her teammates. An office manager must be well-organized and good at dealing with different kinds of people. A police commander must be in good physical shape, skilled in law enforcement tactics, and quick-thinking in a crisis.

One thing almost all leaders have in common, though, is **power**—the ability to control the actions of others. Whether it is **coercive power** (backed by the threat of force) or merely **influential power** (supported by persuasion), leadership involves getting people to do things they may or may not want to do. For example, a football coach might wield both coercive and influential power over his players. Although the athletes would definitely want to win games, they might not want to run their training drills every day. During a workout, team members might respond to either the threat of being kicked off the team or the encouragement they receive from the coach. Power, in whatever form it takes, is both a privilege and a requirement of leadership.

Since leadership requires the exercise of power, most formal organizations have institutionalized it in some officially recognized form of **authority**. Max Weber (1913 / 1962) identified three different types of authority that may be found in social organizations. **Traditional authority**, based in custom, birthright, or divine right, is usually associated with monarchies and dynasties. Kings and queens inherit the throne, not only through lineage but also by divine appointment, meaning by higher authority. Their personal qualities don't really matter, and they can't be replaced by legal proceedings. **Legal-rational authority**, on the other hand, is based in laws and rules, not in the lineage of any individual leader. Modern presidencies and parliaments are built on this kind of authority. The third type, **charismatic authority**, is based in the remarkable personal qualities of the leader her- or himself. Neither rules nor traditions are necessary for the establishment of a charismatic leader—indeed, the leader can be a revolutionary, breaking rules and defying traditions. This is perhaps the only place we will ever find Jesus Christ and Adolf Hitler in the same category: by all accounts both were extremely charismatic leaders.

The three types of authority are not necessarily mutually exclusive—they can coexist within the same leader. Bill Clinton and Ronald Reagan were appealing and charismatic leaders within the context of the legal-rational authority of the presidency; the Kennedy family is considered an American political dynasty of sorts, following a tradition of leadership within the structure of electoral politics. The late King Hussein of Jordan was revered for his extraordinary charisma and statesmanship despite his traumatic ascent to the throne: as a teenager, he witnessed his grandfather's assassination and, as his heir, was crowned less than a year later. For people like Bill Clinton (a legal-rational ruler) and King Hussein (a traditional ruler), their charisma was not necessarily the root of their authority, but it did play a part in their ability to rule.

In addition to different types of power and authority, group leaders may exhibit different personal leadership styles as well. Some are more **instrumental** — that is, they are task or goal oriented — while others are more **expressive**, or concerned with maintaining harmony within the group (Parsons and Bales 1955). An instrumental leader is less concerned with people's feelings than with getting the job done, whereas an expressive leader conveys interest in group members' emotions as well as their achievements. We often consider leadership styles through the lens of gender, expecting men to be more instrumental and women to be more expressive. In fact, we sometimes feel surprised or upset when these gendered expectations aren't met: a male leader with a more expressive style (like California governor Jerry Brown, once nicknamed "Moonbeam" for his emotive, touchy-feely style) is sometimes seen as weak, while a female leader with a more instrumental style (such as former U.S. secretary of state Hillary Rodham Clinton, whose ambition and drive earned her criticism both while her husband was in the White House and while she was campaigning herself in 2008) is sometimes seen as pushy.

Bureaucracy

Examples of **bureaucracies**, a specific type of secondary group, are everywhere in your life — your university, employer, internet service provider, fast-food restaurant, and even church are likely to be organized bureaucratically. Bureaucracies are designed to perform tasks efficiently, and they approach their tasks, whatever they are, with calculations designed deliberately to meet their goals.

Bureaucracies have certain organizational traits, which help them operate efficiently. Max Weber (1921/1968) identified these characteristics as follows:

1. Specialization: All members of a bureaucracy are assigned specialized roles and tasks.

2. Technical competence: Bureaucratic members are specially trained for their specific roles.

3. Hierarchy: Bureaucracies always feature the supervision of subordinates by higher-ranking managers and bosses.

Qualities of Leadership Nelson Mandela, pictured here with the South African rugby team, The Springboks, is an example of a leader with both legal-rational and charismatic authority. Mandela used his charismatic leadership to unite post-apartheid South Africa through rugby, culminating in a narrow victory in the 1995 Rugby World Cup final.

4. Rules and regulations: These are meant to make all operations as predictable as possible.

5. Impersonality: In a bureaucracy, rules come before people; no individual receives special treatment.

6. Formal written communication: Documents such as memos (or e-mails) are the heart of the organization and the most effective way to communicate.

You can see these traits in action at your own college or university. Take specialization and technical competence, for instance. Virtually none of your professors could teach another's classes: your sociology professor would likely be completely useless in a chemistry lab, a math classroom, or even an English seminar. The groundskeepers, campus police officers, soccer coaches, and librarians are all specially qualified to do their own jobs and no one else's. In addition, there are layers of hierarchy at a university, from the trustees and president to the vice chancellors, provosts, deans, and department chairs. Professors are, in some ways, at the bottom of the academic hierarchy

INSTRUMENTAL LEADERSHIP leadership that is task or goal oriented

EXPRESSIVE LEADERSHIP leadership concerned with maintaining emotional and relational harmony within the group

BUREAUCRACY a type of secondary group designed to perform tasks efficiently, characterized by specialization, technical competence, hierarchy, rules and regulations, impersonality, and formal written communication

ON THE JOB
Teamwork and the Tour de France

The Tour de France is the world's premiere competitive cycling event. It is a race that lasts more than three weeks, covers more than 2,000 miles, and traverses the European Alps. Each summer, it draws a television audience of millions worldwide, many of whom never ride their own bikes and do not pay attention to any other bicycle racing events at any other time of year. It has also seen more than its share of controversy: recently, seven-time Tour winner Lance Armstrong was stripped of his medals and banned from competitive cycling for life after admitting to "doping," or using banned substances to improve his athletic performance. Other recent winners, including American Floyd Landis and Spain's Alberto Contador, have also been stripped of their wins and been banned for doping; in fact, the 110 year history of the Tour de France has been fraught with doping scandals. Early riders used alcohol, ether, and strychnine to improve their stamina and speed.

Since 2010, the winners of the Tour have been verifiably drug-free. But they still cannot say that their victories were achieved without assistance. In fact, no one wins the Tour de France on their own. Winning riders are supported by teams of eight other premier athletes who must coordinate complex teamwork relations to prevail over the other twenty or so teams in competition. As in so many other areas of social life, individual success is buoyed by the work of many. No one can become President of the United States, win an Oscar, reach the summit of Mt. Everest, open a restaurant, meet their sales quota, or earn a bachelor's degree without relying on others — groups as well as individuals — to support their efforts. So, although the winner of the Tour is listed individually, he didn't do it alone.

Each team member has a particular specialty, and each stage of the race requires a different strategy. Sprinters may be needed to make a "breakaway" early in the race; "super-climbers" are necessary in the mountainous regions; and sometimes the entire team has to protect the team leader, "blocking" and "drafting" in order to save energy. Teamwork is required to organize bathroom and food breaks, as the race stops for no man. Extremely consistent riders (*rouleurs*) are prized, as are those who ride with aggressiveness and bravery (*combativité*). When the individual winner crosses the finish line on the Champs-Elysées in Paris, it is the sacrifices of his altruistic teammates that have made his win possible.

Which position will you find yourself in when you enter the workplace? Will you be the team leader, whose individual successes depend on the contributions of others? Or will you be the team member, whose special skills support the achievements of the group? It is likely that you will find yourself in both situations over the course of your working life. So remember, when you don the *maillot jaune* (the yellow jersey worn by the Tour de France leader), that in most cases it takes a team effort to get you to the winner's circle.

Group Effort Ukrainian cyclist Serhiy Honchar, in the yellow jersey, completes the ninth stage of the Tour de France with the support of his teammates.

Bureaucracies Are Everywhere Bureaucratic regulations are supposed to make organizations run smoothly; however, bureaucracy can also be impersonal, inflexible, and hyperrational.

(except for you, the students)! And every other campus unit (athletics, residence life, food service, facilities maintenance) has its own hierarchy as well.

Regulations keep a university running smoothly—or at least that's what they are meant to do. Undoubtedly, though, you have run up against a regulation that kept you from doing something you really wanted to do—add a class after a deadline, move into a campus apartment. This is where the feature of impersonality also comes into play: the rules of the bureaucracy trumped your individual needs, no matter how deserving you thought you were. This is especially true at larger universities; at small schools, special treatment is still sometimes possible. But big bureaucracies often treat you "like a number"—and in fact, you *are* a number to your college, as your student ID number is the first thing you are issued on arrival.

The McDonaldization of Society

Weber's model of bureaucracy seems cold and heartless, alienating and impersonal, rule-bound, inflexible, and undemocratic. Indeed, many bureaucracies *are* like this—they are highly efficient secondary groups that operate on the principle of **rationalization**, where the focus is on logical procedures, rules and regulations are paramount, and an individual's unique personal qualities are unimportant. Worse yet, some of the hyperrationalized features of successful bureaucracies are trickling down into other areas of our everyday lives.

Sociologist George Ritzer (1996) called this trickle-down rationalization process **McDonaldization**. We touch-tone our way through telephone calls at work, never speaking to a real person; at lunch, we construct our own salads at the salad bar and bus our own tables afterward; at the bank, we no longer interact with human tellers but rather drive through the ATM on the way home, where we microwave our dinners and watch increasingly predictable sitcoms or movie sequels on TV. Ritzer is critical of the dehumanizing aspects of McDonaldization and hopes that increased awareness of the process will help us avoid the "iron cage" of bureaucracy (a term coined by Weber to illustrate the way bureaucracies can trap individuals).

Sociologist Robin Leidner delves further into the McDonaldization phenomenon in her book *Fast Food, Fast Talk* (1993). Through fieldwork in actual McDonald's franchises, Leidner developed a model for understanding the increasing routinization of service industries, in this case the ubiquitous fast-food restaurant. In particular, she looks at how standardized "scripts" for interaction help to shape customers' experiences. The physical atmosphere of a McDonald's is not conducive to hanging out (unlike, say, a café); customers don't expect to sit down and be waited on. Rather, they respond to expectations that they will enter, order food from a predetermined menu and pay for it, eat quickly, deposit trash in the receptacles, and then leave. Leidner exposes these processes of routinization by looking at what happens when breakdowns occur in these expectations.

RATIONALIZATION the application of economic logic to human activity; the use of formal rules and regulations in order to maximize efficiency without consideration of subjective or individual concerns

MCDONALDIZATION George Ritzer's term describing the spread of bureaucratic rationalization and the accompanying increases in efficiency and dehumanization

McDonaldization In her ethnography *Fast Food, Fast Talk*, Robin Leidner studied how the routinization of services and physical atmosphere at McDonald's restaurants standardized the types of interactions occurring there.

For example, Leidner notes that McDonald's trains workers to refer to customers as "guests," reinforcing the obligation to serve them respectfully even if that respect is not reciprocated. Leidner observed that if customers were angry or uncooperative, workers tried even harder to serve them swiftly so that they would leave faster and have less time to make trouble in the restaurant. Workers developed a mindset that allowed them to handle problem customers in a way that minimized trouble and facilitated their routinized work.

Responding to Bureaucratic Constraints

Not everything about bureaucracies is bad. In fact, in contemporary, postindustrial society, just about everything you need or want is created, produced, distributed, and serviced by a bureaucracy. The water in the tap, the lights, the streets, the car and its insurance, the food on the table, the table itself, the clothes on your back, the movies, songs, and books you enjoy—all are the products of bureaucratic organizations. As problematic as they are, we can't live without them. So how can we benefit from our contact with bureaucracies without being controlled by them?

For one thing, even the most overrationalized, McDonaldized bureaucracy is populated by people who are capable of forming primary group relationships as well, who might celebrate birthdays, throw parties, and go out for drinks after work. Indeed, interpersonal interactions help humanize bureaucracies. Further, in forward-thinking organizations, new management strategies meant to address alienation and disenchantment are being implemented. Yes, bureaucracies

still seek to be as efficient and predictable as possible in their daily operations. But some, like Starbucks, UPS, and Apple, are trying to play up their human side as well—becoming "enlightened" bureaucracies by being inclusive, sharing responsibility, and providing opportunities for all to advance.

Businesses have also begun organizing corporate retreats to teach managers how to understand individual strengths and weaknesses, support individual skills and talents, and encourage teamwork, trust, and leadership. Some, like Fidelity Financial, Toyota, and Pella Windows, have adopted the Japanese management technique called *kaizen*, in which lower-level workers are encouraged to suggest new, innovative ways to improve the organization and upper-level managers are required to actually put these ideas into practice, rewarding individual creativity and benefiting the company at the same time (Pollack 1999; Hakim 2001). Make no mistake—corporations are not sacrificing the bottom line for the good of an individual. But often they are finding that the needs of the individual and those of the organization are not mutually exclusive.

BURNING MAN In the barren Black Rock Desert of Nevada, some people actively seek out an escape from their bureaucratically regimented life, at least for one week every

Burning Man Finale Each year thousands of "burners" gather in the Black Rock Desert to celebrate the rejection of values like conformity, bureaucracy, and capitalism.

summer, at a festival called Burning Man (Sonner 2002; Chen 2004). The festival, begun in 1990 on a beach near San Francisco with just 20 participants, drew more than 50,000 people in 2011. Burning Man is hard to describe for those who have never attended. It is a freewheeling experiment in temporary community, where there are no rules except to protect the well-being of participants ("burners") and where everyone gathers together to celebrate various forms of self-expression and self-reliance not normally encountered in everyday life.

Burning Man attracts a wide variety of individuals from different backgrounds (though it may be difficult to tell beneath the body paint, mud, or costumes that many wear). Unlike in many places in the real world, participants are encouraged to interact with each other; there are no strangers at "the Burn." Each year is characterized by a different theme—like "Hope and Fear" in 2006, "American Dream" in 2008, or "Rites of Passage" in 2011—and participants are invited to contribute in some meaningful way to its realization, most often artistically.

Much of what is appealing about Burning Man is that it challenges many of the norms and values of mainstream society, especially those that are associated with conformity, bureaucracy, and capitalism. Black Rock resembles a city when the thousands of participants converge there, but one composed of tents and RVs gathered into neighborhoods with names like "Tic Toc Town" and "Capitalist Pig Camp" (Doherty 2000, 2004). The city has its own informal economy as well. Once an admission fee is paid, money is no longer used. Participants must bring enough supplies to support themselves or use alternate forms of currency, such as barter, trade, gifts, or services. Corporate sponsorship is strictly avoided, and logos of any kind are banned. Despite its stated ideals, there is not total freedom at Burn-

ing Man. Over the years, various government and local law-enforcement agencies have imposed some restrictions on the event such as bans on fireworks, guns, and dogs.

On the last night of the festival, the giant wooden structure known as the Burning Man is lit on fire, and the celebrants discover their own personal epiphanies as they watch it burn. When the festival is over, participants are committed to leaving no trace behind. One burner called the festival "authentic life" with the other days of the year "a tasteless mirage, a pacific struggle against the backwardness of middle America—consumer culture, bad politics, *Fear Factor*, and fear thy neighbor" (Babiak 2004). So while Burning Man participants don't abandon permanently the web of contemporary bureaucracies that shapes their lives, they gain some relief by ditching it all once a year, just for a few days.

CLOSING COMMENTS

Groups make our lives possible by providing us with the necessities of our existence—food, clothes, cars, homes, and all the other things we use on a daily basis. Groups make our lives enjoyable by providing us with companionship and recreation—from our friends and families to the entertainment conglomerates that produce our favorite music and films. Groups also make our lives problematic—bureaucracies can squelch our individuality, major manufacturers can create social and environmental problems, and some organizations can engender conflict and prejudice between groups. We are at our best in groups, and our worst. We can do great things together, and horrible things. Sociology helps us understand group life at both extremes and everywhere in between.

Table 5.1 Theory in Everyday Life

Perspective	Approach to Groups	Case Study: Fraternities
Structural Functionalism	Life in groups helps to regulate and give meaning to individual experience, contributing to social cohesion and stability.	Affiliation groups like fraternities help create social cohesion in the context of a larger, possibly alienating, university system by bringing young men with shared values together.
Conflict Theory	Group membership is often the basis for the distribution of rewards, privileges, and opportunities in our society. An individual may be treated preferentially or prejudicially based on his or her group membership.	In-group and out-group dynamics can contribute to stereotyping and conflict as fraternity brothers develop an "us vs. them" perspective regarding other frats and non-Greeks.
Symbolic Interactionism	Group norms, values, and dynamics are generated situationally, in interaction with other members.	The pressure to conform to group culture (as in the cases of peer pressure and groupthink) can lead individuals to do things they might never do alone, and can have negative consequences, as in the case of fraternity hazing and binge drinking. It can also lead to positive actions, such as when fraternity members volunteer or raise money for charity.

Everything You Need to Know about Groups

TYPES OF GROUPS

* **Primary groups:** people who are most important to our sense of self; characterized by face-to-face interaction, high levels of cooperation, and intense feelings of belonging

* **Secondary groups:** larger and less intimate than primary groups; relationships are organized around a specific goal

* **Dyads:** the smallest possible group, consisting of only two members

* **Triads:** a slightly more stable small group consisting of three people; the third member can referee conflicts that arise between the other two

* **In-groups:** groups that members identify with and feel loyalty toward

* **Out-groups:** any group that an individual feels opposition, rivalry, or hostility toward

* **Reference group:** provides a standard of comparison against which we evaluate ourselves

REVIEW

1. Which groups serve as your reference groups? Are you a member of all your reference groups? How do these reference groups affect your self-image?

2. The text identifies three different types of conformity: compliance, identification, and internalization. Describe some moments when you've exhibited each type of conformity.

3. Theorist George Ritzer believes that McDonaldization, the spread of the organizational principles of bureaucracies to all areas of life, is a growing concern. Thinking about Weber's six characteristics of bureaucracies, can you identify areas of your life that have been McDonaldized?

Strong or Weak?

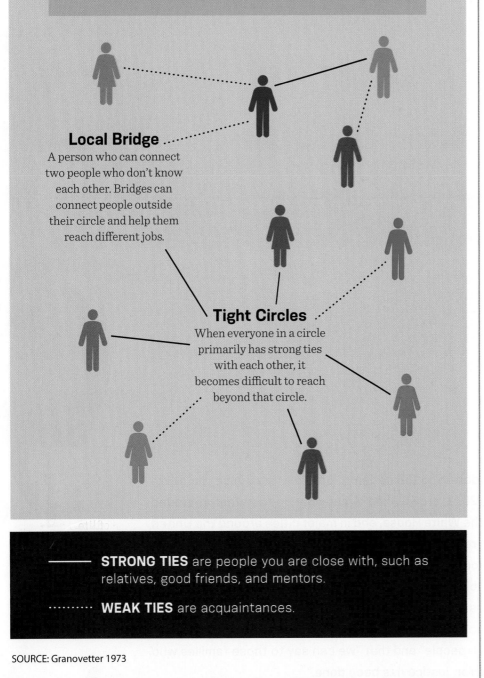

The kinds of people you know can determine your next job. "Ties" or contacts become a key method to network and reach a higher status.

Local Bridge
A person who can connect two people who don't know each other. Bridges can connect people outside their circle and help them reach different jobs.

Tight Circles
When everyone in a circle primarily has strong ties with each other, it becomes difficult to reach beyond that circle.

——— **STRONG TIES** are people you are close with, such as relatives, good friends, and mentors.

·········· **WEAK TIES** are acquaintances.

SOURCE: Granovetter 1973

EXPLORE

It Takes a Village . . . to Create Binge Drinkers.

What group of people do you think has the biggest influence over teens' drinking habits? The answer might not be what you think. Visit the Everyday Sociology Blog to discover how social groups can influence teen drinking.

http://wwnPag.es/trw405

CHAPTER 6

Deviance

Even before President Obama addressed the nation to officially announce the death of Osama bin Laden on May 1, 2011, crowds had already begun to gather at ground zero in New York City, outside the White House, and in major cities around the United States. Although many of the details remained unclear, the president's announcement set off spontaneous rallies all over the country. The news that a small team of American military had attacked a compound in Abbottabad, Pakistan, and after a firefight killed the most wanted terrorist in the world was seen as reason for celebration by many Americans. The president declared that the mission was "a testament to the greatness of our country and the determination of the American people" and that "we can say to those families who have lost loved ones to Al Qaeda's terror: justice has been done."

These sentiments were deeply and profoundly shared by people across the country. For some, especially young people, this led to boisterous public celebrations, with flag waving, fireworks, and loud music playing anything that sounded even vaguely patriotic (Weigel 2012). There was widespread news coverage of the party atmosphere among some of the crowds at ground zero and elsewhere. But not all were revelers. Some took it to be a more solemn occasion, and had come to the public gatherings to honor and remember lost loved ones or place objects at makeshift memorials (Parker 2011).

Around the world, many people shared these sentiments as well. In Nairobi, Kenya, similar crowds gathered, remembering the victims of the 1998 bombings of the American embassies in Kenya and Tanzania ordered by Osama bin Laden. Although more than 200 people were killed in the attacks, only 12 of them were Americans. At the site of the former embassy in Nairobi, a memorial was built for the many Kenyans who died; flowers were laid at the foot of a plaque commemorating the dead (Gettleman 2011). For all of these people, in the United States and abroad, it seemed obvious that Osama bin Laden and the Al Qaeda organization he had led were evil and that justice was served when he was killed.

However, there were some people who understood bin Laden's death in radically different ways. Although officially most governments publicly welcomed the terrorist leader's death, this official attitude did not always reflect the popular mood. Though the majority of people everywhere condemned the activities of Al Qaeda, there was a significant dissenting minority who still saw bin Laden as a heroic figure. Some refused to believe that he had actually been killed; others lashed out against the U.S. action. Pro–bin Laden demonstrations erupted in Pakistan, Sudan, and Egypt, among other places. The news media showed sympathetic crowds that had gathered to grieve and to pray for the slain leader who was described by them as a martyr.

How is it possible that there could be such differing reactions to the same person and event? It's not the first time we have seen such contrasting displays of emotion. There were also celebration and mourning in the wake of the terrorist attacks of September 11, 2001, as there were after bin Laden was killed in May 2011. It seems like we should be able to agree about the fundamental meaning of good and bad, right and wrong. But as we will see, there is no behavior that is inherently deviant (even murder); rather, it is the cultural context, the values and norms of a particular society, that makes it so.

HOW TO READ THIS CHAPTER

Have you ever driven faster than the posted speed limit? Have you ever gotten caught picking your nose in public? Did you have your first taste of beer, wine, or hard liquor before you reached the legal drinking age? Did you pierce something (your lip, eyebrow, or belly button) that your grandmother wouldn't have wanted you to pierce? If you work in an office, did you ever take home a pen, pencil, or packet of Post-it notes?

If you answered yes to any of these questions, you are the embodiment of what we seek to understand in this chapter: you are deviant. Remember this as you read the chapter.

Defining Deviance

Deviance is a behavior, trait, or belief that departs from a norm and generates a negative reaction in a particular group. The norms and the group reactions are necessary for a behavior or characteristic to be defined as deviant (Goode 1997). The importance of norms becomes clear when we remember that what is deviant in one culture might be normal in another (see Chapter 3); even within the same culture, what was deviant a century ago might be perfectly acceptable now (and vice versa). The importance of group reactions is clear when we look at the varied reactions that norm violations generate: some violations are seen as only mildly deviant (like chewing with your mouth open), but others are so strongly taboo that they are almost unthinkable (like cannibalism).

Deviant behavior must be sufficiently serious or unusual to spark a negative sanction or punishment. For example, if you were having dinner with friends and used the wrong fork for your salad, you would be violating a minor norm but your friends probably wouldn't react in a negative fashion; they might not even notice. On the other hand, if you ate an entire steak dinner—meat, mashed potatoes, and salad—with your hands, your friends probably *would* react. They might criticize your behavior strongly ("That's totally disgusting!") and even refuse to eat with you again. This latter example, then, would be considered deviant behavior among your group of friends—and among most groups in American society.

Because definitions of deviance are constructed from cultural, historical, and situational norms, sociologists are interested in a number of topics under the rubric of deviance. First, how are norms and rules created, and how do certain norms and rules become especially important? Second, who is subject to the rules, and how is rule breaking identified? Third, what types of sanctions (punishments or rewards) are dispensed to society's violators? Fourth, how do people who break the rules see themselves, and how do others see them? And finally, how have sociologists attempted to explain rule making, rule breaking, and responses to rule breaking?

Deviance across Cultures

It is important to remember that when sociologists use the term "deviant," they are making a social judgment, never a moral one. If a particular behavior is considered deviant, this means that it violates the values and norms of a *particular* group, not that it is inherently wrong or that other groups will make the same judgment.

Much of the literature on deviance focuses on crime, but not only do different cultures define strikingly different behaviors as criminal, they also differ in how those crimes are punished. Most serious crime in the United States today is punished by imprisonment. This method of punishment was rare until the nineteenth century, however, as maintaining a prison requires considerable resources. Buildings must

> **DEVIANCE** a behavior, trait, belief, or other characteristic that violates a norm and causes a negative reaction

be constructed and maintained, guards and other staff must be paid, and prisoners must be fed and clothed. For groups without these resources, incarceration is not a possibility, even assuming it would be a desirable option. Instead, there are a whole host of other techniques of punishment.

For example, the Amish, a religious community whose members do without modern devices like electricity, cars, and telephones, practice *meidung*, which means shunning those who violate the strict norms of the group (Kephart 2000). A biblical rule instructs them "not to associate with any one who bears the name of brother if he is guilty of immorality or greed, or is an idolater, reviler, drunkard, or robber—not even to eat with such a one" (1 Corinthians 5:11). In other words, the Amish believe they should not associate with rule breakers even when they come from within their own family. No one does business with, eats with, or even talks to the guilty party. The shunning is temporary, however: after a short period, the violator is expected to publicly apologize and make amends, and is then welcomed back into the community.

A much more permanent method of punishment is total banishment from the community. For many Native American people, the social group was so important that banishment was considered a fate worse than death (Champagne 1994). It was one of a variety of practices that were used to maintain social control (along with shaming songs, contests, and challenges of strength) and something of a rarity because it completely severed ties between the group and the individual. Banishment has a long history of use in all parts of the world, from the British prisoners who were "transported" to Australia to Russian dissidents exiled to Siberia,

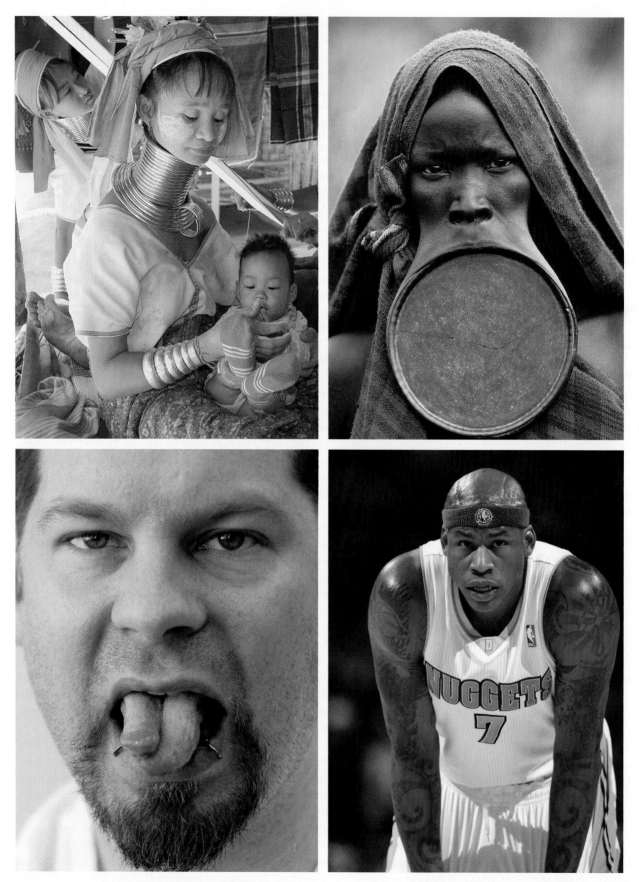

One Culture's Deviant Behavior Might Be Desirable or Normal in Another Padaung women use brass rings to stretch their necks, a Suri woman uses plates to modify her lip, an American man has split and pierced his tongue, and Al Harrington formerly of the Denver Nuggets sports extensive body tattoos.

and has been one of the most cost-effective methods of punishment ever discovered.

Just as methods of punishment vary between societies and groups, so they also change over time. In Colonial America, for example, corporal punishment was the rule for the majority of crimes (Walker 1997). These days, the phrase "corporal punishment" may conjure up images of elementary school teachers spanking students, probably because spanking was the last vestige of what was once a vast repertoire of techniques. Thieves, pickpockets, and others who would today be considered petty criminals were flogged, had their ears cropped, had their noses slit, had their fingers or hands cut off, or were branded. These punishments were designed not only to deliver pain but also to mark the offender. As such, the particular punishment was often designed to fit the crime. A pickpocket might have a hand cut off; a forger might have an "F" branded on his forehead. Brands were also used to mark African American slaves as property during the 1800s.

Body Modification

Branding has long since died out as a method of punishment, but in a perfect illustration of the mutability of deviance, it has made something of a comeback as a form of body decoration (Parker 1998). What used to be an involuntary mark of shame has been reclaimed as a voluntary mark of pride. Small branding irons of stainless steel are heated with a blowtorch until white hot and held on the skin for a second or two. Some

Branding Spencer Evans displays his fraternity Omega Psi Phi's brand on his chest. Branding of one's Greek letter organization by black men has a history dating back to the 1900s to symbolize unity and commitment among members.

who undergo the procedure burn incense to cover the smell of their own flesh burning. Many African American fraternities have a long tradition of branding, usually in the shape of one of the fraternity's Greek letters. The practice received a public boost as several popular athletes have prominently displayed their fraternity brands. Basketball star Michael Jordan sports such a brand, as does the Cleveland Browns' Christopher Owens. Branding is spreading to other subcultures, where it is just another extension of tattoos, Mohawks, and body piercings as an outward manifestation of youthful rebellion, or an expression of personal aesthetic or group identification.

When it comes to body modification, what Americans might label deviant might be identified as desirable or normal in other cultures and vice versa. Among the Suri of southwest Ethiopia, progressively larger plates are inserted into the lower lip so that it gradually becomes enlarged. The Padaung women of Burma stretch their necks with brass rings. Young girls begin by encircling their necks with just a few rings, then add more as they grow; by the time of maturity, their necks are considerably elongated. Breast augmentation surgery is commonplace in the United States, while butt augmentation is popular in Brazil.

Body modification does not always need to be dramatic. In reality, there are a great number of subtle methods of body modification practiced by most Americans that may not seem so obvious if we concentrate on nose rings and biker tattoos. First of all, there have always been body modifications for the middle and upper classes. Corsets, worn by women through the ages until the early twentieth century, are an obvious example. Stomachs were flattened with "stays," long strips of some rigid material like whalebone. A tightly laced corset could achieve a dramatically narrow waistline, but often at a serious cost to the wearer's health. Women sometimes even had ribs removed in order to accommodate them.

These days, we have a rich array of techniques to bring our bodies into line with contemporary standards. Injections of Botox, a strain of the deadly toxin botulism, work by freezing facial nerves, and thus reducing fine lines and wrinkles on the forehead that are otherwise caused by normal facial expressions. The hair salon is another great unacknowledged center for body modification. If you get a perm, you are breaking the disulfide bonds in your hair and reshaping them to straighten them or make them curly. Even a simple haircut is a type of body modification—luckily, for those of us who have gotten bad haircuts, they're temporary! Some body modifications seem so "normal" that we practice them as routines without considering how they may seem deviant elsewhere. Other cultures may view Americans' obsession with hair removal—shaving, plucking, tweezing, and waxing—as bizarre. As you can see, whether it's corsets, branding, or shaving your legs, the boundaries between beauty and deviance are fluid across time and place.

GLOBAL PERSPECTIVE

Delicious or Disgusting? Food, Culture, and Deviance

Although as Americans we enjoy a great number of ethnic foods, there are some food boundaries we will not cross. One is the ancient practice of *entomophagy*, the eating of insects. Even though the 1,462 known species of edible insects are very environmentally friendly to raise and have a better feed-to-meat ratio and better protein-to-fat ratio than any other animal, there are few taboos as indestructible in America as that against eating bugs.

People in Algeria traditionally eat desert locusts, aborigines in Australia snack on certain moths and grubs, some Africans sauté termites, and the Japanese sometimes eat fried grasshoppers. Probably the most notorious of culinary insects is the agave worm found in bottles of the Mexican liquor *mezcal*, usually eaten (if at all) in America as the result of a drunken dare rather than for its nutritional value.

One thing Americans *do* love is bacon cheeseburgers. For billions of people throughout the world, though, this is an abomination. It violates the dietary laws of three major world religions (Judaism, Hinduism, and Islam), and members of those groups may look on you with horror, disgust, or even pity as they watch you eat one. Jewish dietary laws called *kashrut* prohibit eating meat and dairy products at the same meal. The Hindu religion prohibits eating beef, the Islamic religion regards pork as *haraam*, or forbidden food, and Jewish laws also prohibit eating pork. Sociologists maintain that what is deviant is always socially learned, relative to a particular culture. Certainly with food, standards of deviance vary widely across cultures.

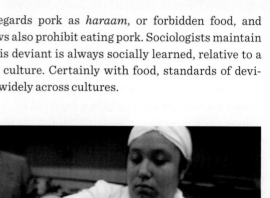

How to Eat Fried Worms A cook at the upscale restaurant Hostería Santo Domingo in Mexico City adds a dollop of guacamole to a plate of deep-fried worms.

Theories of Deviance

In this section, we will learn how three sociological paradigms we considered in Chapter 1—functionalism, conflict theory, and symbolic interactionism—can be applied to deviance. We will also learn about other, related theories that have been developed specifically to explain particular aspects of deviance.

Functionalism

As you may recall, adherents of functionalism argue that each element of social structure helps maintain the stability of society. What, then, is the function of deviance for society? Émile Durkheim came up with a couple of functions. First, deviance can help a society clarify its moral boundaries. We are reminded about our shared notions of what is right when we have to address wrongdoings of various sorts. In 2005, Terri Schiavo, a hospital patient from St. Petersburg, Florida, received national attention when a legal battle was fought over her life. Schiavo had been in a persistent vegetative state since 1990 and kept alive through a gastric feeding tube. Her husband, Michael, petitioned the courts in 1998 to end life support—he thought it was the right thing to do and was what Terri would have wanted. Her parents, Mary and Robert Schindler, took legal action against Michael's decision—they thought it was wrong. While most people might have had a vague idea of how they felt about artificially prolonging life, the Schiavo case forced them to think concretely about how such choices affect actual people. After a seven-year process, the courts sided with Michael Schiavo, and on March 18, 2005, his wife's feeding tube was removed. She died thirteen days later.

Another function of deviance is to promote social cohesion (one of functionalism's valued ideals); people can be brought together as a community in the face of crime or other violations. For example, while the country was divided over the decision in the Schiavo case, an opinion poll by ABC News on March 21, 2005, reported that 70 percent of Americans believed that Michael Schiavo had the authority to make decisions on behalf of his wife and that the case should not have been a federal matter. In the same poll, 63 percent maintained that the federal government was involved solely for political advantage. Whatever they believed about prolonging life, the majority of Americans thus agreed that the choice was best made by family and not the government.

STRUCTURAL STRAIN THEORY Sociologist Robert Merton (1938/1976) provides a bridge between functionalist and conflict theories of deviance. Like Durkheim, Merton acknowledges that some deviance is inevitable in society. But like conflict theorists, he argues that an individual's position in the social structure will affect his experience of deviance and conformity. Social inequality can create situations in which people experience tension (or strain) between the goals society says they should be working toward (like financial success) and the means they have available to meet those goals (not everyone is able to work hard at a legitimate job). The rewards of conformity, therefore, are available only to those who can pursue approved goals through approved means. Any other combination of means and goals is deviant in one way or another (see Figure 6.1). **Innovators**, for example, might seek financial success via unconventional means

(such as drug dealing or embezzlement). **Ritualists** go through the conventional motions while abandoning all hope of success, and (like dropouts or hermits) renounce the culture's goals and means entirely and live outside conventional norms altogether. At the far end of the continuum, **rebels** reject the cultural definitions of success and the normative means of achieving it and advocate radical alternatives to the existing social order.

For example, consider the characters in the 2008 film *The Dark Knight*, an action movie that documents Batman's clean-up of Gotham City. The goal is to combat the corruption that has overcome Gotham through multiple lucrative criminal mobs. In the movie, conformity is represented by Attorney General Harvey Dent, who is attempting to fight crime through the approved means of the law. Dent, along with Commissioner Gordon and Rachel Dawes, enact a tough campaign to convict all mob bosses through the testimony of their accountant. Batman is an innovator who fights crimes using cunning, high-tech weaponry and unconventional means that ignore legal process. As always, traditional bureaucrats like Commissioner Loeb and the Mayor are ritualists who operate within the parameters that they have been given with little hope of quelling the crime wave in Gotham. The corrupt officer Ramirez is a retreatist who actually helps out the mob rather than attempt to fight it. Finally, The Joker, whose famous portrayal by Heath Ledger won him a posthumous Academy Award, embodies the true spirit of the rebel. Rather than attempting to fight crime, The Joker causes mayhem for both law enforcers and the mob bosses with the ultimate goal of creating the downfall of all of Gotham. While the mob bosses stand to gain financially from their crime sprees, The Joker's sadistic goal is to see the entire city descend into chaos and anarchy.

INNOVATORS individuals who accept society's approved goals but not society's approved means to achieve them

RITUALISTS individuals who have given up hope of achieving society's approved goals but still operate according to society's approved means

REBELS individuals who reject society's approved goals and means and instead create and work toward their own (sometimes revolutionary) goals using new means

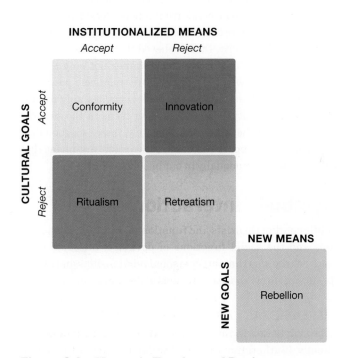

INSTITUTIONALIZED MEANS

Accept — *Reject*

CULTURAL GOALS — *Accept* / *Reject*

Conformity | Innovation
Ritualism | Retreatism

NEW MEANS

NEW GOALS

Rebellion

Figure 6.1 **Merton's Typology of Deviance**

Different orientations toward society's goals and differential access to the means to achieve those goals combine to create different categories of deviance.

Conflict Theory

Conflict theorists, who study inequalities of wealth and power, note that inequalities are present in our definitions of deviance as well. In other words, conflict theorists believe that rules are applied unequally and that punishments for rule violators are unequally distributed: those at the top are subject to different rules and sanctions than those nearer the bottom, and the behaviors of less powerful groups and individuals are more likely to be criminalized than the behaviors of the powerful. Norms, rules, and laws are used to regulate the behavior of individuals and groups. This

Rebel with a Cause In the 2008 film *The Dark Knight*, Batman is an innovator who fights crime unconventionally, Harvey Dent is a ritualist who conforms to established parameters, and the Joker is a rebel intent on bringing about the downfall of Gotham.

process is known as **social control**, and can be either informal, as in the exercise of control through customs, norms, and expectations, or formal, as in the exercise of control through laws or other official regulations. Both formal social control and informal social control can be exercised unequally in a hierarchical society, and this is what conflict theory is concerned with when it comes to the topic of deviance.

Sociologist William Chambliss looked at the history of vagrancy laws to demonstrate the relationship between power and deviance. According to Chambliss (1973), vagrancy laws have always been used to target different groups—the homeless, the unemployed, racial minorities—depending on who seemed most threatening to the elites at the time. When preparing for big events like political conventions or televised sports tournaments, for instance, local police officers may sweep "undesirables" from downtown areas so that a city appears to be free from panhandlers, drug users, hookers, or the homeless (at least until the cameras are turned off).

As recently as 2003, some U.S. states still imposed heterosexuality on their citizens through antisodomy laws, which prohibited any sexual acts that did not lead to procreation. While in theory antisodomy laws could include acts like masturbation and heterosexual oral sex, in practice these laws are generally imposed against same-sex partners. Before the Supreme Court repealed all state antisodomy laws in *Lawrence vs. Texas* (2003), sexual acts done in the privacy of your own home could be penalized with fines and jail time

in states like Virginia, Michigan, and Texas. From a conflict theorist perspective, antisodomy laws are a way for the heterosexual majority to control homosexuals.

As another example, in 2006, Rochester, New York, had the highest murder rate per capita in the entire state, including New York City. The mayor, Robert Duffy, proposed a new law that would require all young people age sixteen and under living within city limits to be off the streets from 11:00 PM to 6:00 AM during the summer break from school. Because statistics have shown that more crime occurs during the summer among youth living in the city, Duffy believed that the curfew would reduce violence. The curfew demonstrates not only ageism, in that control is wielded by adults over relatively powerless youth, but also classism, as the curfew applies only to kids who live in the city, leaving wealthier teens in the suburbs free to do what they like. Unfortunately, there is a good deal of evidence to support the conflict theorists' argument that rules are applied unequally in our hierarchical society.

Symbolic Interactionism

While conflict theorists and functionalists focus on inequalities and the social functions of deviance, interactionists consider the way that interpersonal relationships and everyday interactions shape definitions of deviance.

DIFFERENTIAL ASSOCIATION THEORY One such approach is Edwin Sutherland's **differential association theory** (Sutherland 1939; Sutherland et al. 1992), which asserts that we learn to be deviant through our interactions with others who break the rules. This is the theory of deviance that your parents subscribed to when you were a teenager: don't hang out with the bad kids! Simple peer pressure

SOCIAL CONTROL the formal and informal mechanisms used to increase conformity to values and norms and thus promote social cohesion

DIFFERENTIAL ASSOCIATION THEORY Edwin Sutherland's hypothesis that we learn to be deviant through our associations with deviant peers

Social Control The HBO series *The Wire* was set in Baltimore and focused on topics such as drug dealing, government corruption, and failed school systems. How might a conflict theorist analyze this scene?

by those you associate with can lead to deviant behavior. For instance, an athlete who uses steroids to help build strength might also influence his teammate to start "doping" although this practice is banned in most sports. Have you ever been influenced to do something deviant that you would have never tried on your own?

This theory of deviance seems at first glance to be pretty sensible—interacting often with those who break the rules would seem to socialize an individual into their rule-breaking culture. But, as it turns out, not all who hang out with deviants become deviant themselves, and plenty of people who engage in deviant acts have never consorted with other rulebreakers. Also, in cases where deviance is not the result of a willful act (mental illness, for example), a learning theory such as this one is not a useful explanation. While differential association theory seeks to explain "why they do it," it cannot fully explain every case of deviant behavior—nor can any theory of deviance.

LABELING THEORY Howard Becker's **labeling theory** (1963) proposes that deviance is not inherent in any act, belief, or condition; instead, it is determined by the social context. A man who kills an intruder who is attacking his child may be labeled a hero, while a man who kills a cashier in the process of robbing a store may be labeled a villain. Even though the act of homicide is the same, the way the person who did it is treated differs greatly depending on the label.

Labeling theory recognizes that labels will vary depending on the culture, time period, and situation. David Rosenhan's study "On Being Sane in Insane Places" (1973) provides a striking demonstration of the power of labeling and the importance of context. Rosenhan and seven other research-ers gained admission to psychiatric hospitals as patients. Other than falsifying their names and occupations, the eight subjects gave honest answers to all but one of the questions in the entrance examination; they all complained of hearing voices, a symptom often linked to schizophrenia. Nevertheless, the subjects felt certain that once they were hospitalized, they would be quickly exposed as "pseudo-patients," not really mentally ill.

LABELING THEORY Howard Becker's idea that deviance is a consequence of external judgments, or labels, that modify the individual's self-concept and change the way others respond to the labeled person

In fact, the opposite turned out to be true. Once admitted, the pseudo-patients turned immediately to the task of getting themselves discharged—and failed miserably. Although they behaved as normally and pleasantly as possible, doctors and nurses continued to treat them as mentally ill patients in need of treatment. No amount of explanation on the part of the pseudo-patients could convince the hospital staff of their sanity (though, in an interesting twist, it was usually obvious to the other patients). When they were finally discharged (after one to seven weeks!), it was not because the staff had finally seen through the deception; they were all released with their schizophrenia "in remission." As Rosenhan concludes, "Once labeled schizophrenic, the pseudo-patient was stuck with that label" (1973, p. 253). The effects of this "sticky" deviant label on actual patients can follow them through their lives, even after they leave the hospital.

Labeling theory is also concerned with how individuals think of themselves once a deviant label has been applied. Recall Cooley's concept of the "looking-glass self": how we

PRIMARY DEVIANCE
in labeling theory, the initial act or attitude that causes one to be labeled deviant

SECONDARY DEVIANCE
in labeling theory, the subsequent deviant identity or career that develops as a result of being labeled deviant

TERTIARY DEVIANCE
redefining the stigma associated with a deviant label as a positive phenomenon

SELF-FULFILLING PROPHECY an inaccurate statement or belief that, by altering the situation, becomes accurate; a prediction that causes itself to come true

perceive ourselves depends in part on how others see us, so if others react to us as deviant, we are likely to internalize that label (even if we object to it). Applying deviant labels can also lead to further deviance, as a person moves from **primary deviance** (the thing that gets her labeled in the first place) to **secondary deviance** (a deviant identity or career) (Lemert 1951). **Tertiary deviance** occurs when the person labeled deviant rejects the notion of deviance entirely and redefines her "deviant" attributes or behavior as normal.

If you watched VH1's *Celebrity Rehab with Dr. Drew*, you've seen examples of all three types of deviance. In the show, washed-up celebrities who suffered from addiction checked themselves into a fancy rehab center, and viewers followed the ups and downs of their treat-

ment over the course of each season. Their drug use, which is illegal, was an example of primary deviance, and their recognition that they were addicts was an example of secondary deviance.

Although deviant labels are sticky—they are hard to shake—it is sometimes possible for an individual to turn what could have been a negative identity into a positive one. John Kitsuse (1980) calls this tertiary deviance, and the *Celebrity Rehab* cast demonstrated this level of deviance as well. Every once in a while, one of the celebrities decided that he was no longer interested in undergoing rehab, often arguing that there was really nothing wrong with his drug use and that he should be able to indulge in it as he saw fit.

Some of the most exciting, but also disturbing, research on labeling theory has focused on **self-fulfilling prophecy**, a term coined by Robert Merton in his 1948 article of the same name. Merton's concept was derived from the so-called Thomas theorem, formulated by sociologist W. I. Thomas in 1928, which held that "if men define situations as real, they are real in their consequences." From this theorem, Merton developed his notion of the self-fulfilling prophecy, which is basically a prediction that causes itself to come true merely by being stated. He offers the example of a bank in

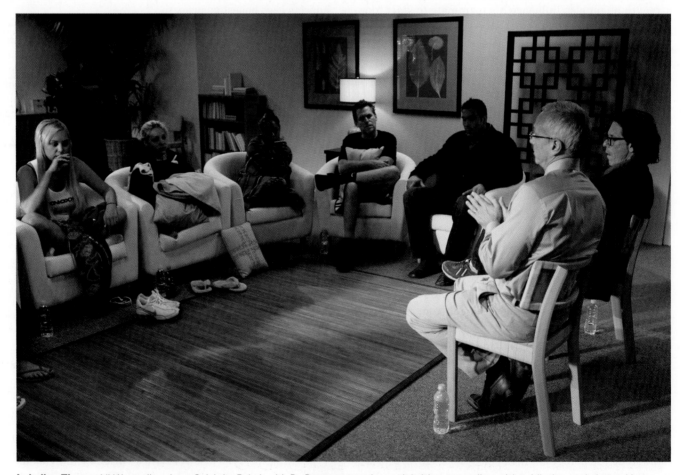

Labeling Theory VH1's reality show *Celebrity Rehab with Dr. Drew* centered on celebrities struggling with addiction and showed how their illness influenced their identity and how others perceived them.

the Depression-era 1930s that collapsed through "a rumor of insolvency," when enough investors became convinced that the bank was out of money (1948, p. 194).

Merton argues that the self-fulfilling prophecy can be used to explain racial and ethnic conflict in the United States, and subsequent research has borne him out. For example, Elijah Anderson's *Streetwise* (1990) details how the police and community perceive black male inner-city teenagers as a criminal element, with the result that they are more likely to be arrested than other teenagers, and citizens are also more likely to report black males for crimes. This cloud of suspicion that surrounds black urban teens requires them to defend their innocence in situations that other teens can negotiate with little or no difficulty. Young black males are also more likely to be incarcerated, which only feeds the public image of criminality. The racial discrimination and profiling by police and the community thus lead to a negative cycle that is difficult to break.

Labels alone are not 100 percent deterministic, and prophecies are not always self-fulfilling. But in our society, deviant labels can override other aspects of individual identity and exert powerful effects on self-image, treatment by others, and even social and institutional policies.

Stigma and Deviant Identity

In ancient Greece, criminals and slaves were branded with hot irons, making a mark called a **stigma**, from the Greek word for tattoo. The stigma was meant to serve as an outward indication that there was something shameful about the bearer, and to this day we continue to use the term to signify some disgrace or failing. Although we no longer live in a society where we are forced to wear our rule violations branded onto our bodies, stigmatized identities still carry serious social consequences.

Stigma, a central concept in the sociology of deviance, was analyzed and elaborated by Erving Goffman in his book of the same name (1962). Once an individual has been labeled as deviant, he is stigmatized and acquires what Goffman calls a "spoiled identity." There are three main types of stigma: physical (including physical or mental impairments), moral (signs of a flawed character), and

STIGMA Erving Goffman's term for any physical or social attribute that devalues a person or group's identity and that may exclude those who are devalued from normal social interaction

Table 6.1 Theory in Everyday Life

Perspective	Approach to Deviance	Case Study: Plagiarism
Structural Functionalism	Deviance clarifies moral boundaries and promotes social cohesion.	Punishing those who plagiarize separates those who should be in college from those who aren't responsible enough.
Structural Strain Theory	An individual's position in society determines whether she has the means to achieve goals or must otherwise turn to deviance.	A student's attitude about plagiarizing depends on whether she has the means to write the paper.
Conflict Theory	Definitions and rules of deviance are applied unequally based on power.	Students with fewer resources are punished more harshly and have fewer options afterward; students with more money or connections can either transfer to another school or rely on parents for help.
Symbolic Interactionism	The definition of deviance is relative and depends on the culture, time period, and situation.	Plagiarism may be labeled as deviant in U.S. courses but not in Russia or India courses.
Differential Association Theory	Deviance is learned through interactions with others who break the rules.	Students learn to cheat because they hang out with other students who plagiarize.
Labeling Theory	Deviance is determined by the reactions of others; applying deviant labels to an individual may lead them to further deviance.	A student who is caught plagiarizing may come to believe she is unable to write without cheating.

PASSING presenting yourself as a member of a different group than the stigmatized group you belong to

IN-GROUP ORIENTATION among stigmatized individuals, the rejection of prevailing judgments or prejudice and the development of new standards that value their group identity

tribal (membership in a discredited or oppressed group). Almost any departure from the norm can have a stigmatizing effect, including a physical disability, a past battle with alcohol or mental illness, time served in jail, or sexual transgressions. Goffman recognizes that what may once have been a stigmatized identity may change over time or may vary according to culture or social context. Being black or Jewish is a stigma only if one lives in a racist or anti-Semitic society. In a community entirely populated by African Americans, it is white people who may be stigmatized; an all-Jewish enclave may see non-Jews as outside the norm. Goffman is careful to note that not all stigmatized identities are just or deserved—only that they are specific to the norms and prejudices of a particular group, time period, or context.

Goffman was particularly interested in the effects of stigmatization on individual identity and interactions with others. At the macro level, society does not treat the stigmatized very well; if you suffer from depression, for example, you may find that your health insurance does not cover your treatment. At the micro level, you may also find that your friends don't fully understand your depression-related problems. In fact, you may find yourself working to keep others from finding out that you are depressed or receiving treatment for depression precisely in order to avoid such situations. Having a stigmatized identity—of any sort—makes navigating the social world difficult.

Passing

How can stigmatized individuals negotiate the perils of everyday interaction? One strategy analyzed by Goffman is called **passing**, or concealing stigmatizing information. The allusion to racial passing is entirely intended—Goffman means to call to mind the experiences of light-skinned African Americans who, for more than 300 years and particularly in the decades before the Civil Rights Movement of the 1960s, sought access to the privileges of whiteness (and relief from discrimination) by concealing their racial heritage and passing as white. The case of racial passing is instructive in developing an understanding of all types of passing—such as the passing a depressed person might engage in to hide his condition. There are reasons why members of other stigmatized groups might also use passing in order to conceal their deviant identities in certain social contexts.

In-Group Orientation

Not everyone can pass, though, because not all stigma is concealable. While it may be possible to conceal your status as an ex-convict or victim of rape, it is more difficult to conceal

Imitation of Life In this 1959 film, Juanita Moore (right) plays a widow whose daughter, played by Susan Kohner (left), tries to pass as white and shuns her mother.

extreme shortness or obesity. And while some people cannot pass, others refuse to do so as a matter of principle. These people don't believe that their identities should be seen as deviant, and they certainly don't believe that they should have to change or conceal those identities just to make "normals" feel more comfortable. They have what Goffman calls an **in-group orientation**—they reject the standards that mark them as deviant and may even actively propose new standards in which their special identities are well within the normal range. For example, such groups as PFLAG (Parents, Families, and Friends of Lesbians and Gays), NAD (National Association of the Deaf), and NAAFA (the National Association to Advance Fat Acceptance) have allowed members of stigmatized groups to feel greater self-esteem and to unite in fighting against prejudice and discrimination. Activism might also take a more individual form of merely being "out," open and unapologetic about one's identity. This in itself can be difficult and exhausting (as passing is); however, those with an in-group orientation see it as a more responsible, genuine, and powerful way to address society's changing definitions of deviance.

Deviance Avowal and Voluntary Outsiders

Under most circumstances, people reject the deviant label and what it seems to imply about their personal identity. However, there are some who *choose* to be called a deviant. Those who belong to a particular subculture, for example—whether outlaw biker, rock musician, or eco-warrior—may celebrate their membership in a deviant group. Howard Becker (1963) refers to such individuals as **outsiders**, people living in one way or another outside mainstream society. They may pass among "normals," continuing to work and participate in everyday life. Or their deviant identity may have become a master status, thus preventing them from interacting along conventional lines; when this happens, a person's deviance may be thought to reveal his underlying nature. For instance, members of the punk subculture, easily identified by their distinctive look, are generally assumed to be loud trouble-makers, whatever their individual personality traits may be.

Some potential deviants may actually initiate the labeling process against themselves or provoke others to do so, a condition Ralph Turner (1972) calls **deviance avowal**. Turner suggests that it may be useful to conceive of deviance as a role rather than as an isolated behavior that violates a single norm. And in some cases, it may be beneficial for an individual to identify with the deviant role. In the Alcoholics Anonymous program, for example, the first step in recovery is for a member to admit that she is an alcoholic. Since total abstinence from drinking is the goal, only those who believe they have a drinking problem and willingly accept the label of alcoholic can take the suggested steps toward recovery.

Deviance avowal can also help a person avoid the pressures of having to adopt certain conventional norms, or what Turner calls the "neutralization of commitment." For instance, a recovering alcoholic might resist taking a typical nine-to-five job, claiming that the stress of corporate work had always made him drink before. Another recovering alcoholic who refuses to attend family gatherings might offer as an excuse that she can't be around family because they drink at every occasion. In such ways, people become voluntary outsiders, finding it preferable to be a deviant in spite of the prevailing norms of mainstream society.

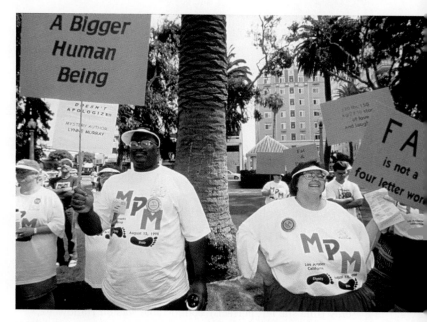

United Against Prejudice Through events like the Million Pound March, groups like the National Association to Advance Fat Acceptance embrace an in-group orientation and reject the standards that mark them as deviant.

Pollner and Jill Stein has focused on the role of narrative storytelling as a key feature of reconstructing the alcoholic's sense of self and turning a stigmatized identity into a valued asset in the process of recovery (Pollner and Stein 1996, 2001). You will be doing a content analysis of an existing source (see Chapter 2 for a review of this research method). The stories appear in *Alcoholics Anonymous* (1939/2001), often referred to by members as the "Big Book," which features accounts of thousands of recovered alcoholics as well as AA's basic twelve-step program. The first 164 pages have remained virtually the same since the first printing in 1939, but in each subsequent edition, the personal stories of additional members have been added. These stories are intended to help newcomers to the program to identify with and relate to the lives of other recovering alcoholics.

For this workshop, you will focus on "Women Suffer Too," one of the first stories published in the Big Book. The title refers to the fact that years ago many people believed that only men were alcoholics. The story is told from the perspective of a sober alcoholic looking back on her life and understanding that through the process of deviance avowal (by accepting her alcoholism) she was able to transform a negative past into a positive life.

The text of the story can be found in the Big Book or accessed online at www.silkworth.net /aabiography/margaretmann.html.

DATA WORKSHOP
Analyzing Everyday Life

Personal Stories of AA Members

In this Data Workshop, you will examine the life history of selected members of Alcoholics Anonymous in order to analyze the process of deviance avowal. Research by Melvin

OUTSIDERS according to Howard Becker, those labeled deviant and subsequently segregated from "normal" society

DEVIANCE AVOWAL process by which an individual self-identifies as deviant and initiates her own labeling process

IN RELATIONSHIPS

Forming Friendships in the Face of Stigma

In her book *Autobiography of a Face* (1994), poet Lucy Grealy tells the story of her struggle with childhood cancer and the disfiguring surgery that resulted. Because of a series of operations that removed one-third of her jaw, she survived Ewing's sarcoma but grew to adulthood looking—and feeling—very different from her peers.

When other kids reacted negatively to her scars, Grealy tried to cover them with turtlenecks, scarves, and hats but couldn't completely conceal her disfigurement. Boys at school yelled at her to "take off that monster mask!" Ironically, the only time she felt perfectly comfortable was on Halloween, when she could wear a mask and feel just like part of the crowd. Her high school years were lonely—she had a hard time making friends and worried that she would never have a boyfriend or be in love. She felt as though she fit in only when she was with her family—or on the children's ward in a hospital.

At Sarah Lawrence College, a private school just outside New York City, Grealy finally found a group of friends with whom she felt comfortable, who were themselves outsiders:

> To be on the fringe at a school as fringy as Sarah Law-rence was itself an accomplishment, but it was this very quality that I loved most about my friends. They wore their mantles as "outsiders" with pride, whether because of their politics, their sexuality, or anything else that makes a person feel outside of the norm. Their self-definition was the very thing that put me at ease with them. I didn't feel judged. (p. 196)

Grealy finally experienced real friendship when she was able to feel accepted by others, and she felt this only with those who were similarly stigmatized. While they didn't share her specific facial disfigurement, they each felt marginalized or abnormal in some way. They were, in Goffman's terms, "the own"—those who share the experience of being stigmatized and thus find comfort and safety in each other's presence.

Lucy Grealy

Grealy suffered through several more grueling recon-structive surgeries on her face, which left her in chronic pain. After college, she enrolled in the Iowa Writer's Work-shop, where her roommate was another student she had known from Sarah Lawrence, Ann Patchett. The two women became best friends and, as they moved from the Midwest to New York in pursuit of their careers, embarked on a rela-tionship that helped define their lives and work over the next twenty years. Grealy went on to win awards for her poetry and essays and wrote her critically acclaimed and hugely successful memoir. Patchett, too, became successful as an award-winning novelist (Patchett 2001).

Unfortunately, Lucy Grealy's story does not have a happy ending. Ultimately, fame, fortune, and friendship were not enough to save her from her own demons. Ann Patchett's book *Truth & Beauty: A Friendship* (2004) details Grealy's decline into depression, drug addiction, and repeated attempts to commit suicide. Grealy died in December 2002 from what was ruled an "accidental" overdose of heroin.

It would be too simplistic to conclude that Grealy killed herself because of the years of suffering she had endured as a result of her stigmatized identity. There are too many factors involved in her complex life story to assign blame with any assurance. Perhaps she would have become depressed or addicted even if she hadn't been disfigured. Perhaps it was the physical pain rather than the psychic pain that became too much for her. Whatever the reasons, these two books about Lucy Grealy's life and death reveal in gritty and compel-ling details the desperate desire to fit in and the lengths to which she went in order to pass as "normal" in society.

Read it in its entirety, keeping in mind how the study of life histories or oral histories can reveal important features of societal norms and everyday life. Pay close attention to how the story describes both deviant behavior and the process of deviance avowal, and consider the following questions.

* Identify the instances of deviance described in the writer's story. Why do we consider these behaviors deviant?

* In what ways was she in denial, or actively trying to dis-avow the deviant behavior?

* At what point did she engage in deviance avowal?

* How did deviance avowal affect her self-concept?

* In what ways did deviance avowal allow her to consider her past in a different light?

* How has her deviant identity become a positive part of her life?

There are two options for completing this Data Workshop.

Option 1 (informal): Prepare some written notes based on your answers to the questions above that you can refer to during in-class discussions. Share your reactions and conclusions with other students in small groups. Listen for any differences in each other's insights.

Option 2 (formal): Write a three- to four-page essay answering the questions above. Include your own reactions to the story. Make sure to refer to specific passages that support your analysis.

Studying Deviance

When studying deviance, sociologists have often focused on the most obvious forms of deviant behavior—crime, mental illness, and sexual deviance. This "nuts and sluts" approach (Liazos 1972) tends to focus on the deviance of the poor and powerless, while accepting the values and norms of the powerful in an unacknowledged way. Social scientists tended to apply definitions of deviance uncritically in their research and failed to question the ways in which the definitions themselves may have perpetuated inequalities and untruths.

One sociologist at University of California, Berkeley, David Matza (1969), set out to remedy this situation. Matza urged social scientists to set aside their preconceived notions in order to understand deviant phenomena on their own terms—a perspective he called "naturalism." Leila Rupp and Verta Taylor, for example, spent three years with a dozen drag queens in order to gain perspective for their research in *Drag Queens at the 801 Cabaret* (2003)—at one point, they even performed onstage (see Part II's introduction to read more). Matza's fundamental admonition to those studying deviance is that they must appreciate the diversity and complexity of a particular social world—the world of street gangs, drug addicts, strippers, fight clubs, outlaw bikers, homeless people, or the transgendered. If such a world is approached as a simple social pathology that needs correcting, the researcher will never fully under-

stand it. A sociological perspective requires that we seek insight without applying judgment—a difficult task indeed.

The Foreground of Deviance: The Emotional Attraction of Doing Bad Deeds

Most sociological perspectives on deviance focus on aspects of a person's background that would influence him to act in deviant ways. This is the case with both functionalist and conflict perspectives: for example, many sociological studies of crime make the case that youth with limited access to education may be more likely to turn to dealing drugs or theft. Labeling theory also suggests that a person's social location is a crucial determinant: it shapes how others see the person, as well as his or her own self-view, and these perceptions can lead a person from primary to secondary deviance and into a deviant career. One of the main problems with such theories, however, is that they can't explain why some people with backgrounds that should incline them to deviance never actually violate any rules, while others with no defining background factors do become deviant.

Approaches that focus exclusively on background factors neglect one very important element—the deviant's own in-the-moment experience of committing a deviant act, what sociologist Jack Katz refers to as the "foreground" of deviance. In *The Seductions of Crime* (1988), Katz looks at how emotionally seductive crime can be, how shoplifting or even committing murder might produce a particular kind of rush that becomes the very reason for carrying out the act. For example, what shoplifters often seek is not the DVD or perfume as much as the "sneaky thrill" of stealing it. Initially drawn to stealing by the thought of just how easy it might be, the shoplifter tests her ability to be secretly deviant—in public—while appearing to be perfectly normal. This perspective explains why the vast majority of shoplifters are not from underprivileged backgrounds but are people who could easily afford the stolen items. How else might we explain why a wealthy and famous actress such as Lindsay Lohan would try to steal a necklace from a jewelry store?

Similarly, muggers' and robbers' actions reveal that they get more satisfaction from their crimes than from the things they steal. They are excited by the sense of superiority they gain by setting up and playing tricks on their victims. In fact, they can come to feel morally superior, thinking that their victims deserve their fate because they are less observant and savvy. Even murderous rages can be seen as seductive ways to overcome an overwhelming sense of humiliation. A victim of adultery, for example, may kill instead of simply ending the relationship because murder, or "righteous slaughter," feels like the most appropriate response. In effect, he is seduced by the possibility of becoming a powerful avenger rather than remaining a wounded and impotent victim.

Katz's foreground model of deviance deepens our appreciation for the complexity of deviant behavior and reminds us that social actors are not mere products of their environment but active participants in creating meaningful experiences for themselves even if harmful to others.

Deviance in a New Interactional Context: Cyberbullying

Although parents and schools have been worried about cyberbullying ever since children and teenagers started using the internet, the phenomenon moved to the forefront of national consciousness after the suicide of thirteen-year-old Megan Meier in October of 2006. Megan had received a MySpace message from a boy named Josh, who said that he lived nearby but that his family didn't have a phone. During the next several weeks, they sent messages back and forth and seemed to have become close very quickly. Then, without warning, Josh started taunting and abusing her. Megan was devastated and hung herself in her closet. Several weeks later, the Meiers learned that "Josh" was not a real person and that the MySpace account had been created by their neighbor, Lori Drew, in order to get back at Megan for snubbing her daughter. But regardless of who was sending the messages, Megan was a victim of **cyberbullying**, the use of electronic media (web pages, social networking sites, e-mail, instant messengers, and cell phones) to tease, harass, threaten, or humiliate someone. Unfortunately, reports of other teen suicides linked to cyberbullying have continued to make headlines.

The one thing that seems beyond doubt is that cyberbullying is on the rise, with girls and older teens more likely to be at risk. A report from the Centers for Disease Control found 50 percent more teens reported being the victims of electronic harassment in 2005 compared to 2000. In 2009, somewhere between 9 and 35 percent of all young people said they had been the victim of cyberbullying (Hertz and David-Ferdon 2009). As more schools require laptops, and computers and cell phones become a more important part of the daily life of children and teenagers, this trend will surely continue.

Although cyberbullying is still less common than its off-line equivalent, in several ways it's more frightening. Like every phenomenon created by the Information Revolution,

CYBERBULLYING the use of electronic media (web pages, social networking sites, e-mail, instant messengers, and cell phones) to tease, harass, threaten, or humiliate someone

cyberbullying (sometimes called "electronic aggression") is faster and connects more people than off-line activity. Traditional bullying usually happens at school, while cyberbullying can happen anytime and in the privacy of your own home. Likewise, the effects are longer lasting. One of the most common forms of cyberbullying involves spreading rumors about someone. Traditional bullying relied on word of mouth or the proverbial graffiti on the bathroom wall to do this. But word of mouth is limited, and only so many people can read nasty comments scrawled on the stall in the bathroom before the janitor washes it off. Online, there is almost no limit to how many people might see a nasty comment, even if it is later taken down.

So far, most research has focused on cyberbullying that is perpetrated by someone who knows the victim in real life, but there have always been internet bullies (or "trolls") who seek to abuse people they've never met or only have encountered online. For example, after Megan Meier's suicide, a blog was created called "Megan Had It Coming" and contained posts from a cast of characters who purported to know Megan, all expressing a distinct lack of remorse. Later it was established that the entire blog was really the work of

Cyberbullying Tina Meier holds two pictures of her daughter Megan, who committed suicide after receiving cruel messages on MySpace.

IN THE FUTURE

Porn Studies and Changing Definitions of Deviance

Meet Dr. Chauntelle Tibbals.

She holds a Ph.D. in sociology from the University of Texas at Austin, and she has published her research in some of the highest-ranking academic journals in her field. Over the course of her career, she has earned a visiting scholar position at the University of Southern California, provided authoritative commentary in major media outlets like CNN, and spoken in prestigious venues such as the Stanford University School of Law. She maintains a popular blog and produces regular podcasts on issues related to her research. So, what is the area of expertise of this distinguished scholar?

Porn.

That's right. Dr. Chauntelle (as she's often called on the internet) is a sociologist who specializes in the study of pornography and the adult entertainment industry. Only a few years ago, a career like hers would have been unimaginable. The topics she addresses range widely and include condom use in adult content (Tibbals 2012), the increase and decline in breast augmentation among women adult performers (Tibbals 2010), and an ethnographic perspective on women's work behind the scenes in the porn industry (Tibbals 2011). While she is a feminist who takes a social justice perspective in her work, her research does not assume a negative perspective on the adult film industry.

Past studies have tended to concentrate on whether and how pornography is harmful to individuals (women, men, and children) and society (Attwood 2011), and the larger culture still seems committed to this view of pornographic media as dangerous and corrupting. Policy perspectives on sexuality tend to reflect this outlook. Indeed, in 2012, a tenured sociology professor was disciplined by Appalachian State University for showing a documentary about the pornography industry in her classroom (she had borrowed it from the school's own library!). But new research reflects a "paradigm shift" in social and cultural studies' view of pornography (Attwood 2011).

Porn itself is more available than ever before due to technological advances such as the internet and mobile phones— no longer does one have to hide one's stash of magazines under the proverbial mattress! Porn is also more influential in the wider media world, with mainstream media borrowing the "styles, gestures and aesthetics" of the genre (Attwood 2011, p. 15). Our culture itself is becoming more sexualized (Attwood 2009), and pornographic metaphors have crept into other areas of social life—people throw around terms like "food porn," "travel porn," or "car porn" to talk about media representations of alluring but out-of-reach victuals, vacations, and vehicles. Phrases like "money shot" and "fluffing" (which Dr. Chauntelle says is actually a myth) are moving into common parlance, and almost all of us have heard someone laughingly imitate 70s porn soundtracks: "bow-chicka-wow-wow." What used to be "obscene" is now "on-scene"—meaning that it is increasingly present in ordinary public discourse (Williams 2004).

As public responses to pornography change, so do those of social science researchers. For example, whereas scholars were once almost universally critical of porn as a media genre that objectifies women and contributes to sexual violence, people like Dr. Chauntelle are now addressing previously overlooked and under-researched topics and issues such as cybersex (Waskul 2004; Valkyrie 2011), women's porn consumption (McCleary and Tewksbury 2010), and the "pornification" of other media (Paasonen et al. 2007). This paradigm-shifting pornography research will likely make its way into public debates in the future, which means that society will have to expand its sense of what is "normal" to include things that had in the past been framed as dangerous and deviant . . . and legislate accordingly. Are we ready for that?

Chauntelle Tibbals is shedding light on the pornography industry through studies of condom use and breast augmentation.

a thirty-two-year-old computer programmer from Seattle with no connection to anyone involved in the case. As more and more of people's lives play out online, this sort of cyberbullying will only become more common.

DATA WORKSHOP
Analyzing Mass Media and Popular Culture

Norm Breaking on Television

It's clear that deviance is a fascinating subject not only for sociologists but for television viewers as well. In recent years, shows have begun to feature people breaking every kind of social norm from folkways to taboos. Some obvious examples might include MTV's reality series *16 and Pregnant*, which shows what happens when high schoolers deal with pregnancy and parenthood, or the VH1 reality series *Mafia Wives*, which portrays women whose husbands may be criminals with mob connections. But it's not just documentaries and reality shows that feature deviance. Various other types of programs like crime dramas such as *NCIS* or *Criminal Minds*, newsmagazine programs such as *Dateline NBC* or *48 Hours*, and even comedies such as *Glee* or *Family Guy* regularly deal with the pathological or dysfunctional.

Why is there so much deviance on television? Are these shows merely entertainment, or is something more going on here? When we watch them, do we feel morally superior or get some kind of vicarious thrill? Does the experience reinforce our social norms or serve to break them down?

This Data Workshop asks you to do a content analysis of an existing source, in this case a particular TV show (see Chapter 2 for a review of the research method). You will be documenting the ways in which deviant behavior is portrayed in the show you choose. Choose a show that is available on DVD or online, or simply record an episode off TV so that whatever format the show is in, you can watch it multiple times.

Consider the following:

✳ Who is the intended audience for this program? Why did you choose it?

✳ What kind of deviance is featured? Give specific examples of situations, scenes, dialogue, or characters, and explain why they are examples of deviance.

Married to the Mafia Deviance is a common thread in popular TV shows like *Mob Wives*, which follows the lives of a group of women who are connected to the Mafia through their husbands and fathers.

✳ Is the deviance celebrated or condemned?

✳ How does it make you feel to watch the program?

✳ What effect do you think the show has on other viewers?

✳ Do you think the program serves to reinforce or challenge prevailing social norms?

There are two options for completing this Data Workshop.

Option 1 (informal): Prepare some written notes that you can refer to in small-group discussions. Compare and contrast the analyses of the different programs in your group. What are the similarities and differences between programs?

Option 2 (formal): Write a three- to four-page essay answering the Workshop questions and reflecting on your own experience in conducting this content analysis. What do you think these shows tell us about contemporary American society and our attitudes toward deviance?

ON THE JOB

Is "Cash Register Honesty" Good Enough?

While we might like to think that most employees wouldn't take money from the cash register or merchandise from the showroom floor, wouldn't walk away with a laptop computer, drive away with the company car, or filter sales receipts to their own bank account, employee theft is still a major problem. According to a 2010 survey by the Association of Certified Fraud Examiners, the typical business is estimated to lose about 5 percent of its annual revenues to employee fraud. This translates to a median loss of $140,000 per organization (ACFE 2012). Others estimate that employee theft is involved in up to one-third of all U.S. corporate bankruptcies (Russakoff and Goodman 2011). The U.S. Chamber of Commerce reports that 75 percent of all employees steal once, and that half of those individuals will steal repeatedly (Jones 2012). Michael Cunningham, a professor of psychology at the University of Louisville and a consultant to the security industry, warns that only one in every three potential employees will be completely trustworthy. Of the other two, one may be tempted to steal given the opportunity, while the other will be more or less constantly looking for a chance to get away with taking company property.

Although we may consider ourselves the trustworthy ones, we may not recognize that our own behavior could still be contributing to the tens of billions of dollars lost each year. How? Well, have you ever taken home paper clips, Post-it notes, a pen, or a pad of paper from the office? Made personal copies on the Xerox machine? Used the company computer to surf the net, download MP3s, play solitaire, or send e-mail to a friend? Eaten or drunk company products? How about taking a little more time than you're supposed to on your lunch break or leaving work a little early?

It's called **pilfering**, and it happens on the job tens of thousands of times a day. And it all adds up. Most companies consider these kinds of losses as just another factor in the cost of doing business. But how is it that so many people think nothing of these small infractions in spite of prevailing social norms that discourage stealing and while otherwise being upstanding or even exemplary employees?

You could say that these people are practicing "cash register honesty." That is, they draw the line at actually stealing money (or its equivalent) out of the till but don't hesitate to make off with other odds and ends that might have a less easily calculable value. They might be appalled at the suggestion that they are less than honest, especially since everyone else seems to take something (if only internet or texting time) now and then. But is this kind of honesty really enough? Perhaps more employees should strive to adhere to a higher standard. Not because they are necessarily going to be caught by the boss or that they individually are costing the company a lot, but because of the inherent satisfaction of knowing that they are doing the right thing.

What kind of honesty do you practice in the workplace?

> **PILFERING** stealing minor items in small amounts, often again and again

Crime and Punishment

Crime is a particular type of deviance: it is the violation of a norm that has been codified into law for which you could be arrested and imprisoned. Official, state-backed sanctions, such as laws, exert more power over the individual than do nonlegal norms. For example, if you risked arrest for gossiping about your roommate, you might think twice about doing it. "Might," however, is the key word here, for the risk of arrest and jail time does not always deter people from breaking laws. In fact, ordinary people break laws every day without really thinking about it (driving faster than the speed limit, drinking while underage, taking pens or pencils home from work). As we saw earlier, being bad can feel good, and even murder can feel righteous at the time, depending on the circumstances (Katz 1988).

In the United States, crime is officially measured by the **Uniform Crime Report (UCR)**, the FBI's tabulation of every crime reported by more than 18,000 law enforcement agencies around the country. In particular, the UCR is used to track the "crime index," or

> **CRIME** a violation of a norm that has been codified into law
>
> **UNIFORM CRIME REPORT (UCR)** an official measure of crime in the United States, produced by the FBI's official tabulation of every crime reported by more than 18,000 law enforcement agencies

the eight offenses considered especially reprehensible in our society (see Figure 6.2). Murder, rape, aggravated assault, and robbery are categorized as **violent crime**. Burglary (theft inside the home), larceny-theft (of personal property), motor vehicle theft, and arson are considered **property crime**. Even though the UCR has been shown to be a flawed system, it is useful in helping to track trends in overall crime as well as particular patterns; it also records the number of arrests made compared with the number of crimes committed, which is the most traditional measure of police effectiveness.

VIOLENT CRIME crimes in which violence is either the objective or the means to an end, including murder, rape, aggravated assault, and robbery

PROPERTY CRIME crimes that did not involve violence, including burglary, larceny-theft, motor vehicle theft, and arson

WHITE COLLAR CRIME crime committed by a high-status individual in the course of his occupation

Through the UCR, criminologists are able to make comparisons in crime rates using such variables as year and region. One notable finding is that rates of violent crime declined significantly in the last decade of the twentieth century. The year 1991 saw the highest homicide rates in U.S. history, at 9.8 percent per 100,000 persons or 24,700 murders. Between 1991 and 2000, there was a dramatic drop in homicide rates, and the number continued to decline to 4.8 percent or 14,748 murders in 2010 (Federal Bureau of Investigation 2010b). Other findings include the observation that murder rates peak in the months of July and August. Perhaps related to the influence of heat, they are also higher in the southern states. Financial hardship may influence murder rates, as southern states also have the lowest median family incomes. It may also explain what appears to be a spike in the overall U.S. crime rate during 2010 and 2011, after several years of recession-related job loss and underemployment. Murder is committed most frequently by a friend or relative of the victim, seldom by a stranger. Robbery occurs most frequently in urban areas among youth.

Other trends are visible in the UCR as well. Property crimes occur more frequently than violent crime. The most common crime is larceny-theft, with burglary and motor vehicle theft trailing far behind. Although there has also been a decline in rates of property crime in the last decade, it is not as extreme as the drop in violent crime.

Crime and Demographics

When criminologists look at quantitative crime data, which provide information on who is more likely to commit or be a victim of crime, they may learn more about the cause of crime. We should, however, question the assumptions and biases of the data. For example, Robert Merton's theory of the self-fulfilling prophecy prompts us to ask, if society has a tendency to cast certain categories of people as criminal types, will this assumption ensure that they will indeed be labeled and treated like criminals? And, as David Matza warns, will our preconceived notions about a category of people influence our interpretations of numerical data? In this section, we will look at the relationship between crime and demographics like class, age, gender, and race and examine alternate explanations for what may seem like clear numerical fact.

CLASS Statistics consistently tell us that crime rates are higher in poor urban areas than in wealthier suburbs, but these higher crime rates may not actually be the result of increased criminal behavior. Rather, police tend to concentrate their efforts in urban areas, which they assume are more prone to crime, and thus make more arrests there. It appears that social class is more directly related to how citizens are officially treated by the police, courts, and prisons than to which individuals are likely to commit crime. And even if we do accept these statistics as an accurate representation of crime rates, such theorists as Robert Sampson and William Julius Wilson (2005) argue that the same factors that cause an area to become economically and socially disadvantaged also encourage criminal activity. Lack of jobs, lack of after-school child care, and lack of good schools, for example, are all factors that can lead to economic strain and criminal activity.

On the other end of the social class spectrum, **white collar crime** has been defined by sociologist Edwin Sutherland as "a crime committed by a person of respectability and high social status in the course of his occupation." White collar crime can include fraud, embezzlement, or insider trading, and most white collar criminals come from a relatively privileged background (Shover and Wright 2001).

AGE The younger the population, the more likely its members are to commit crimes. Criminologists have shown that this relationship between age and crime has remained stable since 1935, with the peak age for arrests being nineteen. In the United States, fifteen- to nineteen-year-olds make up about 7 percent of the population yet account for 19 percent of criminal arrests. On the other end of the spectrum, people sixty-five and older make up more than 13 percent of the population and account for fewer than 1 percent of arrests (U.S. Census Bureau 2010d, Federal Bureau of Investigation 2010a). We call this trend aging out of crime. Here too, however, we must be careful about what we read into official statistics. Since our stereotypical image of a criminal is youthful, it may be that the public and police are more likely to accuse and arrest young people and less likely to target seniors. In addition, youth may commit more visible crimes (like robbery or assault), while older people may commit crimes that are more difficult to detect, like embezzlement or fraud.

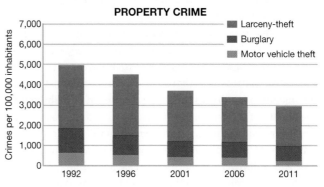

VIOLENT CRIME

Legend:
- Aggravated assault
- Robbery
- Rape
- Murder and nonnegligent manslaughter

y-axis: Crimes per 100,000 inhabitants (0–1000)
x-axis: 1992, 1996, 2001, 2006, 2011

PROPERTY CRIME

Legend:
- Larceny-theft
- Burglary
- Motor vehicle theft

y-axis: Crimes per 100,000 inhabitants (0–7,000)
x-axis: 1992, 1996, 2001, 2006, 2011

Figure 6.2 Crime in the United States, 1992–2011

SOURCE: Federal Bureau of Investigation, 2011a.

GENDER Males are more likely to commit crime. In fact, males constitute 78 percent of all violent crime arrests. Earlier researchers hypothesized that the gender difference in crime rates was based on physical, emotional, and psychological differences between men and women. The logic was that women were too weak, passive, or unintelligent to commit crime. This argument has been replaced by a focus on the social and economic roles of women. Starting in the 1970s, criminologists found that lower crime rates among women could be explained by their lower status in the power hierarchy. Conflict theorists such as James Messerschmidt (1993) argued that once women start gaining power in the labor market through education and income, crime rates among women will rise to more closely match those among men. This hypothesis has been largely supported by recent trends. Between 2001 and 2010, male arrest rates decreased by almost 7 percent, while female arrest rates increased by almost 11 percent. So while at first glance it may seem logical to argue that women's crime rates are lower because of biology, on closer examination, we see that social structure plays an important role.

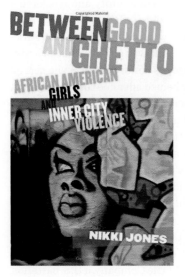

RACE The relationship between race and crime is a controversial one. According to the UCR, African Americans make up 12 percent of the U.S. population but account for 38 percent of violent crimes and 29 percent of property crimes. Once again, sociologists caution against making a link between biology and criminal activity. Instead, they maintain that the relationship can be explained by Merton's self-fulfilling prophecy and by class variables. For example, we could hypothesize that African Americans are exposed to higher rates of crime because more of them live in lower-class neighborhoods—and that here, it is class that matters more than race.

Finally, it is important to recognize that none of these variables—class, age, gender, race—affect crime rates in isolation; they work together to shape the experiences of individuals as well as the larger society. Nikki Jones's ethnographic study of inner-city African American girls in Philadelphia shows how all of these variables contribute to young women's experiences with violence in their everyday lives. For example, the girls Jones studied find themselves caught in a bind as they attempt to navigate community standards of both respectability and practicality. In order to be perceived as "respectable," they must adhere to expectations, be "good girls," and avoid violence, while also meeting feminine and race-based appearance norms (such as slender bodies and light complexions). On the other hand, the practical realities of life in what are often risky neighborhoods mean these girls must be ready at any time to look and act tough and be willing to fight to defend themselves and others. Thus, their race, class, gender, and age put them in a situation where they must navigate the competing demands of respectability and toughness, balancing their good girl image while always being prepared for the realities of crime and violence.

DETERRENCE an approach to punishment that relies on the threat of harsh penalties to discourage people from committing crimes

Deterrence and Punishment

The question of **deterrence** is part of an ongoing debate about our criminal laws. Theorists who maintain that offenders carefully calculate the cost and benefits of each crime argue that punishment has a deterrent effect—that if the punishment seems too severe, people won't commit the crime. That's the logic behind California's controversial "three strikes" law: the punishment for three felonies is an automatic life sentence. While deterrence theory seems practical enough, it is important to note that in matters of sociology, seldom is there such a direct and causal link between two factors; in this case, the cost of punishment vs. the benefit of the crime.

Other justifications for punishment include **retribution**—the notion that society has the right to "get even"—and **incapacitation**, the notion that criminals should be confined or even executed to protect society from further injury. Some argue, though, that society should focus not on punishment but on **rehabilitation**: the prison system should try to reform the criminal so that once released, he will not return to committing crimes again. Each approach to punishment invokes different ideas about who the criminal is and what his relationship is to the larger society: Is he someone who can plan ahead and curb his illegal behavior so as not to face a possible negative outcome? Is she someone who can work toward personal transformation? Is he someone who must be punished quid pro quo? Or should she just be removed from society permanently?

In the United States, the local, state, and federal government bureaucracies responsible for making laws together with the police, courts, and prison systems make up the **criminal justice system**—a system that, like any other social institution, reflects the society in which it operates. This means that while the American criminal justice system provides important benefits, such as social control and even employment for its workers, it also replicates some of the inequalities of power in our society. The research of Victor Rios focuses on this issue. Rios, a professor of sociology at University of California, Santa Barbara, went from gang member to Ph.D. partly because a teacher intervened and put him in touch with a mentoring program at a local university. Otherwise, Rios believes, he would have become another victim of the "youth control complex," his term for the way a variety of institutions, including law enforcement, the judicial system, and public schools, work together to "criminalize, stigmatize, and punish" working-class youth. Rios believes that the educational system has embraced a self-defeating strategy by adopting the attitudes and tactics of law enforcement, even as law enforcement and the judicial system have turned to increasingly draconian measures. Increasingly, our society attempts to control gang violence and drug use with brute force, but this sort of indiscriminate policing often creates the very crime it is designed to eliminate as "enhanced policing, surveillance, and punitive treatment of youth of color" help to create a "school-to-prison pipeline" (Rios 2009, p. 151).

In another example of the dysfunctions of the criminal justice system, in 2003, seventeen inmates on Illinois's death row were found to be innocent of the crimes for which they had been sentenced to die; some cases involved errors made by overworked or underqualified defense attorneys. Further, more than two-thirds of the inmates were African American, many of them convicted by all-white juries (Ryan 2003). As a result, then-governor George Ryan became convinced that **capital punishment** was unfairly and even wrongly applied in some cases, and he suspended the death penalty altogether. When inequities and errors such as these exist in the criminal justice system, we must question the true meaning of the word "justice" in our society.

"Positive" Deviance?

Are there instances in which a rule violation is actually a principled act that should generate a positive rather than negative reaction? The next two examples are cases of what we might call **positive deviance**. Both individuals broke laws; in hindsight, they are now considered heroes.

The first example is the simple act of civil disobedience by Rosa Parks on December 1, 1955, in Montgomery, Alabama, an act often considered pivotal in launching the Civil Rights Movement. In those days, a Montgomery city ordinance required buses to be segregated: whites sat in front and blacks in the back. Rosa Parks defied the law by refusing to give up her front seat to a white man and move to the back. Her arrest galvanized the black community and triggered a bus boycott and subsequent protests that eventually ended segregation in the South. It is worth recognizing that Parks was not an accidental symbol; she was an experienced activist. In her one small, courageous act of defiance, she served as a catalyst that eventually helped advance the fight against racial discrimination all across America. More than forty years after the day she had taken her seat on the bus, Parks was awarded the Presidential Medal of Freedom in 1996. When she died in 2005, it was front-page news. Her funeral was attended by luminaries of all types and races: mayors, members of Congress, presidents, CEOs, clergy, celebrities, and as many others as could fit into the packed church and spill outside its doors.

The second example is the story of three soldiers who put a stop to a massacre during the Vietnam War. On March 16, 1968, the men of Charlie Company, a U.S. battalion

RETRIBUTION an approach to punishment that emphasizes retaliation or revenge for the crime as the appropriate goal

INCAPACITATION an approach to punishment that seeks to protect society from criminals by imprisoning or executing them

REHABILITATION an approach to punishment that attempts to reform criminals as part of their penalty

CRIMINAL JUSTICE SYSTEM a collection of social institutions, such as legislatures, police, courts, and prisons, that create and enforce laws

CAPITAL PUNISHMENT the death penalty

POSITIVE DEVIANCE actions considered deviant within a given context but are later reinterpreted as appropriate or even heroic under the command of Lieutenant William Calley, stormed into the village of My Lai in South Vietnam on a "search and destroy" mission and opened fire on its civilian inhabitants. The boys and men of the village had gone to tend the fields, leaving only unarmed women, children, and the elderly. Hundreds were killed on that terrible day, in direct violation of military law. Although the soldiers should have ceased fire when they saw that the enemy (members of the Viet Cong) was not present, they obeyed the commands of their leaders and continued ravaging the village. Calley was later convicted in a court-martial; his men, claiming that they were only "following orders," were not held responsible.

The massacre would have continued unchecked had it not been for three other American soldiers—Hugh Thompson, Lawrence Colburn, and Glenn Andreotta—who flew their helicopter into the middle of the carnage at My Lai, against the orders of their superiors, and called for back-up help to airlift dozens of survivors to safety. They then turned their guns on their fellow Americans, threatening to shoot if they tried to harm any more villagers. For years, the army tried to cover up the three men's heroism in order to keep the whole ugly truth of My Lai a secret. But finally, in 1998, the men were recognized for their bravery and heroism with medals and citations—for having had the courage and skill to perform a perilous rescue and the moral conviction necessary to defy authority as well.

CLOSING COMMENTS

The sociological study of crime and deviance raises complicated issues of morality and ethics. When we study sensitive topics like rape and alcoholism or vulnerable populations like juvenile delinquents and the mentally ill, we have a responsibility as scholars to recognize the effects our attention may have on the people we study. As David Matza noted, we must try to eschew moral judgments in our work, no matter how difficult that may be. And as our professional code of ethics demonstrates, we must protect the people we study from any negative outcomes. Groups lodged under the rubric of deviance can be disempowered by this label, and policy decisions made on the basis of social science research may further injure an already marginal group. On the other hand, a sociological perspective on deviance and crime provides for the possibility that groups previously labeled and marginalized may someday receive assistance and legitimacy from the larger society as well. The sociological perspective is a powerful tool.

Everything You Need to Know about
Deviance

" Deviance is a behavior, trait, or belief that departs from the norm and generates a negative reaction in a particular group. "

THEORIES OF DEVIANCE

* **Functionalism:** deviance reminds us of our shared notions of wrong and right and promotes social cohesion

* **Structural strain:** social inequality creates tension between society's goals and the means an individual has to achieve those goals

* **Conflict:** both society's rules and the punishments for breaking those rules are applied unequally

* **Differential association:** we learn to be deviant through interactions with people who break rules

* **Labeling:** deviance is determined by the social context

REVIEW

1. There are many ways to be mildly deviant without breaking any laws. How do we sanction minor deviant acts?

2. Have you ever known someone to reject the "deviant" label and turn his or her negative identity into a positive one? What was the deviant identity? What term describes this sort of deviance? Do you know anyone who has embraced a stigmatized role through deviance avowal? How might these strategies be useful to individuals?

3. The United States has the dubious distinction of leading every other nation in both the largest total number and largest percentage of incarcerated citizens. Why do you think America has more prisoners than any other country?

Who Goes to Prison in the USA?

Prison Population (by Race and Hispanic Origin), 2010

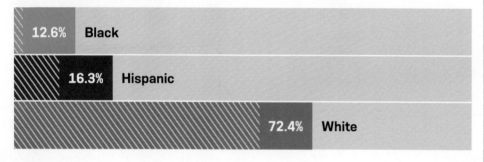

- 37.9% Black
- 22.3% Hispanic
- 32.2% White

Total U.S. Population (by Race and Hispanic Origin), 2010

- 12.6% Black
- 16.3% Hispanic
- 72.4% White

Prison Population (by Gender), 2010

- 7% Female
- 93% Male

Total U.S. Population (by Gender), 2010

- 50.8% Female
- 49.2% Male

SOURCES: Guerino et al. 2012; U.S. Census Bureau 2010, "Age and Sex Composition: 2010"; U.S. Census Bureau 2010, "Overview of Race and Hispanic Origin: 2010"

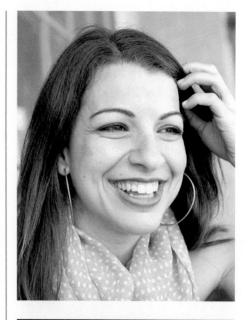

EXPLORE

Women, Gaming, and Violence

Women in the online gaming community are subject to intense scrutiny, and women in the games themselves are portrayed in stereotypical ways. Visit the Everyday Sociology Blog to find out what happens when a woman wants to study images of women in the gaming world.

http://wwnPag.es/trw406

PART III
Understanding Inequality

All societies have systems for grouping, ranking, and categorizing people, and within any social structure, some people occupy superior positions and others hold inferior positions. While such distinctions may appear to be natural, emanating from real differences between people, they are actually social constructions. Society has created and given meaning to such concepts as class, race, and gender, and consequently, those concepts have taken on great social significance. The social analyst's job is to understand how these categories are established in the first place, how they are maintained or changed, and ways they affect society and the lives of individuals.

For instance, sociologist Mitchell Duneier's book *Sidewalk* (Duneier and Carter 1999) includes the story of a marginalized group of New York City street vendors whose lives and social identities are much more complex than the casual passerby might imagine. The story considers the convergence of class (Chapter 7), race (Chapter 8), and gender (Chapter 9) in the social structure of the city and its inhabitants' everyday interactions. In many ways, *Sidewalk* brings together the themes of these next three chapters.

Duneier studied men and women who live on the streets of New York's Greenwich Village, selling used goods—mostly books and magazines—to passersby. Duneier befriended the vendors and became part of their curbside culture for five years, during which he conducted his ethnographic research. By examining the intersecting lives of people who frequent the Village, Duneier shows what social inequality looks like and feels like and what it means to those who live with it every day. On Sixth Avenue, the class differences between the vendors and their customers are obvious. The vendors live from day to day in a cash-based, informal economy; they are poor and often "unhoused"; most are African American males; some are educated, others are not; and all have stories of how they became part of the sidewalk culture. The passersby, on the other hand, are of all ages, races, and occupations, and they are likely to be both employed and housed. They are often well educated; some are wealthy. Interactions between these vendors and customers cut across boundaries of both class and race, and sometimes gender—all interrelated forms of social inequality.

A key insight in Duneier's work is that the street vendors are not necessarily what they seem at first glance. It would be easy to characterize these people as lacking any social aspirations, given that so many are homeless and don't fit into conventional social roles. Though they might offend some by their appearance, few are drug addicts, alcoholics, or criminals—and they are pursuing the same kinds of goals as many of the passersby. In this liberal neighborhood, sales of written material are allowed on the streets without permits or fees, thus providing these marginalized citizens an opportunity for entrepreneurial activity and a chance to earn an honest living. Most vendors say they are trying "to live 'better' lives within the framework of their own and society's weaknesses". Most work hard to construct a sense of decency and reputability in their dealings with customers. Although some of them violate social norms, in most ways the vendors adhere to a code of conduct that minimizes any negative impact they might have on the surrounding community.

Many vendors develop friendly, ongoing relations with regular buyers despite their different positions in social status hierarchies. Sometimes, however, the chasm between the vendors and their customers is difficult to bridge. For example, the male vendors in Duneier's study regularly engaged in flirtatious banter with female passersby. Their efforts at engaging the women in interactions brought a fleeting sense of entitlement and power to men who otherwise have few resources. Typically, the vendors were ignored or rebuffed by the women. When asked why this was the case, one of the vendors said, "She wants room and board, clothing, makeup, hairdos, fabulous dinners, and rent" (Duneier and Carter 1999, p. 196). In other words, because he is poor, he cannot provide these upper-middle-class amenities. The women, however, may perceive this behavior as sexual harassment, and accordingly may use standard streetwise avoidance techniques. Here, social class becomes the great divide in everyday gender relations.

Some people oppose the street vendors' presence in the neighborhood, and the vendors are frequently the target of anti-peddling campaigns by the mayor's office, police, and local businesses. Yet Duneier believes that expelling these

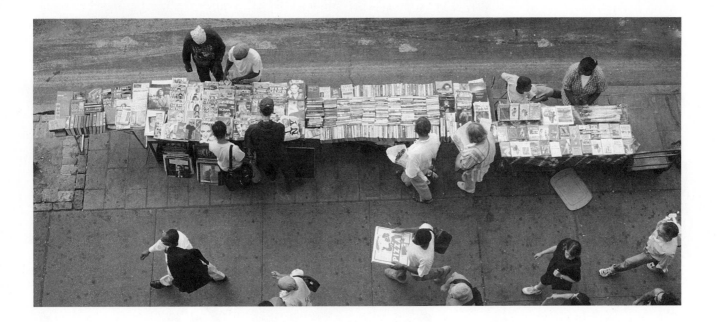

street vendors in an effort to "improve" the neighborhood would actually be counterproductive. Without the unconventional form of employment that street vending provides to these otherwise destitute people, there would likely be more crime, panhandling, and deviance. Moreover, as law-abiding citizens with a strong desire to conform to social norms, the vendors often serve as mentors to other homeless people, easing them back into mainstream society. Duneier contends that street vendors are an asset to the area and that they contribute to the vibrancy and health of the Village.

While the study is particularly focused on New York's Sixth Avenue vendors, it provides insights into the structure of difference and social inequality in the United States, showing that interactionist perspectives can also be relevant to the study of class, race, and gender, which are more often examined through macrosociological theories. What we come to learn is that the world of sidewalk vending is highly complex and organized, with its own rules and social order.

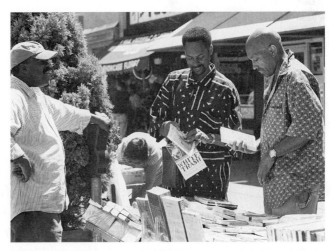

CHAPTER 7

Social Class: The Structure of Inequality

The photographs on page 183 show average families from six different countries—the United States, Iceland, Mali, Bhutan, Thailand, and Kuwait. They are each pictured outside the family home, with all their worldly goods displayed around them. These pictures, from Peter Menzel's book *Material World: A Global Family Portrait*, clearly illustrate some of the inequalities of wealth and power between societies worldwide.

Compare, for example, the U.S. and Thai families, the Skeens and the Kuenkaews. What are the differences between these families as evidenced by their possessions? The two Skeen children have their own bedrooms; the two Kuenkaew children sleep on one bed

covered in mosquito netting. The Kuenkaews own two water buffaloes, several chickens, and a family dog; their home is surrounded by banana, coconut, mango, and other fruit trees. In contrast, the Skeens have a pet dog and several stuffed deer heads hanging on the wall, trophies of Mr. Skeen's favorite pastime, hunting. The Skeens have three radios, three stereos, five telephones, two televisions, a VCR, a computer, and three different vehicles; the Kuenkaews own one radio, one black-and-white television, a recently-purchased handheld video game that the children and parents enjoy playing, and their most valued possession, a motorscooter.

Similar comparisons may be made between the Natoma family in Mali, the Namgay family in Bhutan, the Thoroddsen family in Iceland, and the Abdulla family in Kuwait. The younger Mrs. Natoma carries water from the village well in a bucket balanced on her head; the Abdullas have a private indoor swimming pool. The Thoroddsens enjoy weekend trips to the hot springs in their town; the Namgays own little and live near a Buddhist monastery where monks chant daily for peace. These photographs reveal stark contrasts between the world's wealthiest citizens in places like the United States and Kuwait and its poorest people in countries like Mali and Bhutan. What are the real meanings of terms like "rich" and "poor," and how do sociologists define them?

Family Portraits From the top left: the Skeens (Pearland, Texas), the Thoroddsens (Hafnarfjordur, Iceland), the Namgays (Shingkhey, Bhutan), the Abdullas (Kuwait City, Kuwait), the Kuenkaews (Ban Muang Wa, Thailand), and the Natomas (Kouakourou, Mali).

HOW TO READ THIS CHAPTER

In this chapter, we will examine, from a sociological perspective, the stratification that occurs in all human societies. Despite rhetorical claims about equality of opportunity for all, America is a profoundly hierarchical society, with the benefits and opportunities of living here unequally distributed among its citizens. A sociological perspective on stratification will increase your understanding in several important ways. First, it will help you to see inequities in places you may have overlooked, such as your own town, neighborhood, and school. Second, it will help you consider how positions in social hierarchies tend to shape the lives of individuals: access to health care, the justice system, employment, and housing are all governed by structures of inequality. Third, it should enable you to identify your own place in these social arrangements and to see how some of your own life chances have been shaped by your position (or your family's position) in certain hierarchies. Finally, a knowledge of stratification may help you play a role in changing systems of inequality. Look for ways that you can alleviate some of the problems that social inequality causes—if you can have an impact, even a small one, then this chapter will not have been in vain!

Social Stratification and Social Inequality

Social stratification in one form or another is present in all societies. This means that members of a given society are categorized and divided into groups, which are then placed in a social hierarchy. Members may be grouped according to their gender, race, class, age, or other characteristics, depending on whatever criteria are important to that society. Some groups will be ranked higher in the social strata (levels), while others will fall into the lower ranks. The higher-level groups enjoy more access to the rewards and resources within that society, leaving lower-level groups with less.

This unequal distribution of wealth, power, and prestige results in what is called **social inequality**. We find several different systems of stratification operating in the United States, where it is not hard to demonstrate that being wealthy, white, or male typically confers a higher status (and all that goes along with it) on a person than does being poor, nonwhite, or

SOCIAL STRATIFICATION the division of society into groups arranged in a social hierarchy

SOCIAL INEQUALITY the unequal distribution of wealth, power, or prestige among members of a society

SLAVERY the most extreme form of social stratification, based on the legal ownership of people

female. Because social inequality affects a person's life experience so profoundly, it is worthwhile to examine how stratification works.

There are four basic principles of social stratification. First, it is a characteristic of a society, rather than a reflection of individual differences. For instance, if we say that in Japan men rank higher in the social hierarchy than women, this doesn't mean that a particular woman, such as actress Ryoko Hirosue, couldn't attain a higher status than a particular man; it means only that in Japan as a whole, men rank higher. Second, social stratification persists over generations. In Great Britain, a child inherits not only physical characteristics such as race but also other indicators of class standing such as regional accent. It is because of this principle of stratification that wealthy families remain so through many generations.

Third, while all societies stratify their members, different societies use different criteria for ranking them. For instance, the criterion in industrialized nations is material wealth (social class), but in hunter-gatherer societies, such as the Khoisan Bushmen of southern Africa, it is gender. Fourth, social stratification is maintained through beliefs that are widely shared by members of society. In the United States, it is still common to think that people are poor not only because of the existing class structure but also because they have somehow failed to "pull themselves up by their bootstraps."

Systems of Stratification

In order to better understand social stratification, it is useful to examine different historical periods and to make global comparisons across cultures. So here we look at three major systems of stratification: slavery, caste, and social class.

Slavery

Slavery, the most extreme system of social stratification, relegates people to the status of property, mainly for the purpose of providing labor for the slave owner. Slaves can thus be bought and sold like any other commodity. They aren't paid for their labor and in fact are forced to work under mental or physical threat. Occupying the lowest rank in the social hierarchy, slaves have none of the rights common to free members of the same societies in which they live.

Slavery has been practiced since the earliest times (the Bible features stories of the Israelites as slaves) and has continued for millennia in South America, Europe, and the United States. Sometimes the race, nationality, or religion of the slave owners was the same as the slaves', as was the case in ancient Greece and Rome. Historically, a person could become enslaved in one of several ways. One way was through debt; a person who couldn't repay what he owed might be taken into slavery by his creditor. Another way was through warfare: groups of vanquished soldiers might become slaves to the victors, and the women and children of the losing side could also be taken into slavery. A person who was caught committing a crime could become a slave as a kind of punishment and as a means of compensating the victim. And some slaves were captured and kidnapped, as was the case of the transatlantic slave trade from Africa to the Americas.

Slavery as an economic system was profitable for the slave owner. In most systems of slavery, people were slaves for life, doing work in agriculture, construction, mining, or domestic service, and sometimes in the military, industry, or commerce. Their children would become slaves too, thus making the owner a greater profit. In some systems, however, slavery was temporary, and some slaves could buy their own freedom.

Slavery is now prohibited by every nation in the world, as declared in the Universal Declaration of Human Rights. Not only is it illegal, it is considered immoral as well. Nevertheless, the shocking fact is that it continues to exist today in such places as India, South Asia, and West Africa in the form of child slavery, serfdom, forced and bonded laborers, human trafficking, and sex slaves.

America is not exempt from these same shocking practices either, where people are held as agricultural, domestic, and sex slaves as well. And Americans may also play an indirect role in supporting slavery elsewhere in the world, by means of our material appetites and the type of labor utilized in certain countries to satisfy our varied consumer demands (Bales and Soodalter 2009). Using a somewhat broader definition of slavery that includes all of the above plus other conditions such as forced marriage or child soldiers, researchers believe there may be approximately 25 million people in slavery, more in terms of total numbers (not proportion) than at any other time in human history (Bales 2000). By that same definition, that number would have reached almost 30 million in 2010 (Kara 2008).

Caste

Caste represents another type of social stratification found in various parts of the world. The traditional **caste system** is based on heredity, whereby whole groups of people are born into a certain stratum. Castes may be differentiated along religious, economic, or political lines, as well as by skin color or other physical characteristics. The caste system creates a highly stratified society where there is little or no chance of a person changing her position within the hierarchy, no matter what she may achieve individually. Members must marry within their own group, and their caste ranking is passed on to their children. In general, members of higher-ranking castes tend to be more prosperous, whereas members of lower-ranking castes tend to have fewer material resources, live in abject poverty, and suffer discrimination.

India is the country most closely associated with the caste system, based there in the Hindu (majority) religion. The caste system ranks individuals into one of five categories: *Brahman* (scholars and priests), *ksatriya* or *chhetri* (rulers and warriors), *vaisya* (merchants and traders), *sudra* (farmers, artisans, and laborers), and *the untouchables* (social outcasts). The caste system is a reflection of what Hindus call *karma*, the complex moral law of cause and effect that governs the universe (Cohen 2001). According to this belief, membership in a particular caste is seen as a well-deserved reward or punishment for virtuous or sinful behavior in a past life. Caste is thus considered a spiritual rather than material status, but it still results in real world inequalities. Caste-related segregation and discrimination were prohibited in 1949 by India's constitution, but they are still prevalent. Resistance to social change remains, and thus far the social ramifications of the caste system have not been completely dismantled.

THE CASE OF SOUTH AFRICA An interesting example of the caste system was the **apartheid** system, a legal separation of racial and ethnic groups that was enforced between 1948 and 1991 in South Africa. The term itself literally means "apartness" in Afrikaans and Dutch. The consequence of apartheid was to create great disparity among those in the different strata of society.

South Africans were legally classified into four main racial groups: white (English and Dutch heritage), Indian (from India), "colored" (mixed race), and black. Blacks formed a

CASTE SYSTEM a form of social stratification in which status is determined by one's family history and background and cannot be changed

APARTHEID the system of segregation of racial and ethnic groups that was legal in South Africa between 1948 and 1991

Slavery Actress Demi Moore and Anuradha Koirala, chairperson of the organization Maiti Nepal that works to protect girls and women in Nepal from human trafficking and violence, stand with children at a rehabilitation center in Kathmandu.

large majority, at 60 percent of the population. These groups were geographically and socially separated from one another. Blacks were forcibly removed from almost 80 percent of the country, which was reserved for the three minority groups, and relocated to independent "homelands" similar to the Indian reservations in the United States. They could not enter other parts of the country without a pass—usually in order to work as "guest laborers" in white areas. Ironically, African Americans visiting South Africa were given "honorary white" status and could move freely within white and nonwhite areas. Social services for whites and nonwhites were separate as well: schools, hospitals, buses, trains, parks, beaches, libraries, theaters, public restrooms, and even graveyards were segregated. Indians and "coloreds" were also discriminated against, though they usually led slightly more privileged lives than blacks. Despite claims of "separate but equal," the standard of living among whites far exceeded that of any other group.

In South Africa under the apartheid system, whites held all the political, economic, and social power, despite being a numerical minority. It was not long before civil unrest and resistance to the system began developing within South Africa and among the international community. Blacks and even some whites began to organize to wage strikes and demonstrations, and sanctions were imposed by Western nations. The plights of high-profile anti-apartheid leaders such as Steve Biko and Nelson Mandela became known worldwide. Pressure on the white government continued to grow, until the country was in an almost constant state of emergency. In 1991, apartheid as a legal institution was finally abolished.

Its legacy, however, has been much more difficult to dismantle. Although nonwhites now share the same rights and privileges as whites, social inequality and discrimination between the races have decreased little (Nattras and Seekings 2001; Seekings and Nattras 2005). South Africa remains a country with one of the most unequal distributions of income in the world. The effects were evident in 2004, when 60 percent earned less than US$7,000 a year, whereas just over 2 percent earned more than US$50,000 per year. Blacks made up 90 percent of the poor. The income gap in South Africa has continued to grow, with the rich, and especially the already rich whites, getting richer (Boyle 2009). The restoration of land seized during apartheid is only slowly being accomplished and at a price to those making claims. In some ways, new patterns of class stratification are replacing rather than erasing old patterns of racial stratification.

SOCIAL CLASS a system of stratification based on access to such resources as wealth, property, power, and prestige

SOCIOECONOMIC STATUS (SES) a measure of an individual's place within a social class system; often used interchangeably with "class"

INTERSECTIONALITY a concept that identifies how different categories of inequality (race, class, gender, etc.) intersect to shape the lives of individuals and groups

Social Class

Social class, a system of stratification practiced primarily in capitalist societies, ranks groups of people according to their wealth, property, power, and prestige. It is also referred to by sociologists as **socioeconomic status (SES)** to keep in mind the social as well as economic basis of ranking. The social class system is much less rigid than the caste system. Although children tend to "inherit" the social class of their parents, during the course of a lifetime they can move up or down levels in the strata. Strictly speaking, social class is not based on race, ethnicity, gender, or age, although, as we will see, there is often an overlap between class and other variables.

It is important to recognize that while social statistics often address issues of inequality one variable at a time, social actors don't. In other words, we experience our lives not just as "middle-class" or "working-class" or "upper-class" people, but as women and men; blacks, whites, Latinos and Asians; college or high school graduates; Christians, Jews, or Muslims; spouses or singles; and so on. Our lived experience is one of **intersectionality**, a concept that acknowledges that multiple dimensions of status and inequality intersect to shape who we are and how we live. Our life chances are influenced by our class *and* our race *and* our gender *and* our religion *and* our age (*and* multiple other categories) all together, not one at a time.

An example of this can be seen in the ethnographic research of sociologist Karyn R. Lacy (2007), who studied black middle-class suburbanites in the Washington, D.C. region. As Lacy's findings show, social status is more complex than just a "middle-class" salary might indicate: her respondents' identities are shaped by their income, occupation (in mostly white-dominated professions), residential status (as suburban homeowners), and race. In fact, many reported being frustrated as they tried to convince others (such as store employees, realtors, and bankers) that they were among the middle class in the first place—their race obscured their class in the eyes of whites, and made it difficult for whites to see them as "belonging" in certain neighborhoods or business establishments at all. This is an example of how, in the reality of everyday life, race and class are experienced as inseparable; their effects on our experiences are intertwined, even as we attempt to unravel them in different chapters in sociology textbooks. Keep this concept of intersectionality in mind as you read on about class and then again in subsequent chapters when we address other forms of social inequality.

Sociologists are not always in agreement about what determines class standing or where the boundaries are between different social classes. We will consider some of these disagreements after first taking a look at the United States and its system.

Social Classes in the United States

It is difficult to draw exact lines between the social classes in the United States; in fact, it may be useful to imagine them along a continuum rather than strictly divided. The most commonly identified categories are upper class, middle class, and lower class. If we want to make even finer distinctions, the middle class can be divided into upper, middle, and lower (Wright et al. 1982). You probably have some idea of which class you belong to even if you don't know the exact definition for each category. Interestingly, most Americans claim that they belong somewhere in the middle class even when their life experiences and backgrounds would suggest otherwise. While keeping in mind that the borders between the classes can be blurry, let's examine a typical model of the different social classes (Figure 7.1).

The Upper Class

The **upper class** makes up just 1 percent of the U.S. population, and its total net worth is greater than that of the entire other 99 percent (Beeghley 2008). The upper class consists of elites who have gained membership in various ways. Some, like the Rockefellers and Carnegies, come into "old money" through family fortunes; others, like Mark Zuckerberg or Lady Gaga, generate "new money" through individual achievements. Members of this class earn in excess of $250,000 per year (sometimes far above that number) and are often highly educated, cultured, and influential. They tend to attend private schools and prestigious universities and display a distinctive lifestyle; some seek positions of power in government or philanthropy. The

UPPER CLASS an elite and largely self-sustaining group who posses most of the country's wealth; they constitute about 1 percent of the U.S. population

	Percentage of Population	Typical Household Incomes	Typical Occupations	Typical Education
	1%	More than $250,000	Investors, heirs, executives, media/sports personalities	Some prestigious university degrees
	14%	$89,000 to more than $150,000	Professionals and managers	College and university degrees, some graduate degrees
	30%	$55,000 to $88,000	Semi-professionals, lower-level managers, white collar and highly skilled blue collar jobs	two- and four-year college degrees
	30%	$23,000 to $54,000	Semi-skilled labor, service, manual and clerical jobs	High school degrees
	20%	Less than $10,500 to $22,000	Low and unskilled workers, lower-paid manual and service jobs, seasonal work	Some high school
	5%	Less than $7,500	Seldom or unemployed, part-time labor, many rely on public or private assistance	Some high school

Figure 7.1 The U.S. Social Class Ladder

upper class is largely self-sustaining, with most members remaining stable and few new ones able to gain its ranks.

The Upper-Middle Class

The **upper-middle class** comprises about 14 percent of the population. This group tends to be well educated (with college or postgraduate degrees) and highly skilled. Members work primarily in executive, managerial, and professional jobs. They may enjoy modest support from investments but generally depend on income from salaried work, making upward of $89,000 to $150,000 per year. As a result, the upper-middle class is most likely to feel some financial stability. They usually own their homes and may own a second one as well.

The Middle Class

The **middle class** makes up about 30 percent of the population, though some social analysts believe that the middle class is shrinking as a result of a variety of phenomena, including economic recession and the housing market crash, along with high unemployment, corporate downsizing, and outsourcing of work to foreign countries. Many people who would have once been considered middle class may have moved down to the lower-middle class, while some others have moved up to the upper-middle class. The middle class comprises primarily **white collar** workers, skilled laborers in technical and lower-management jobs, small entrepreneurs and others earning a range from $55,000 to $88,000. Most members have a high school education and a two- or four-year college degree. While members of the middle class have traditionally been homeowners (a sign of having achieved the American Dream), this trend changed during the recent recession and the associated banking and mortgage crises. Along with issues like the cost of housing, and

given other debts carried by many Americans, not all middle-class people can afford their own homes anymore.

The Working (Lower-Middle) Class

The **working class**, or **lower-middle class**, makes up about 30 percent of the population. Members typically have a high school education and generally work in manual labor, or **blue collar**, jobs, as well as in the service industry (retail, restaurant, tourism, etc.)—jobs that are often more routine, where employees have little control in the workplace. Members of the working class typically earn between $23,000 and $54,000 per year. A small portion, especially those who belong to a union, may earn above-average incomes for this class. Working-class people typically have a low net worth and live in rental housing or in a modest home they have inherited or long saved for.

The Working Poor and Underclass

The **working poor** constitute approximately 20 percent of the population. Members are generally not well educated; most have not completed high school and experience lower levels of literacy than the other classes. They may also lack other work skills valuable in the job market. Typical occupations include unskilled, temporary, and seasonal jobs—including minimum-wage jobs, housekeeping, day labor, and migrant agricultural work. The average income ranges from less than $10,500 to $22,000. This group suffers from higher rates of unemployment and underemployment, with some members receiving welfare subsidies.

In addition, another 5 percent of the population, the **underclass**, could be categorized as truly disadvantaged. These very poorest of Americans typically earn less than $7,500 per year and may have chronic difficulty getting enough money to support their basic needs. They may hold few steady jobs and depend on public benefits or charity to survive. They are most often found in inner cities, where they live in substandard housing or are homeless; their numbers are increasing in the suburbs as well. They are part of a group that is considered officially impoverished by federal government standards. A separate section later in this chapter will be devoted to discussing poverty and the poor.

Problematic Categories

Because SES is based on a collection of complex variables (including income, wealth, and education, as well as power or prestige), it is difficult to say exactly where, for example, middle class ends and upper class begins. In addition, individuals may embody a variety of characteristics that make precise SES classification difficult. Someone may be highly

---

UPPER-MIDDLE CLASS mostly highly-educated professionals and managers who have considerable financial stability; they constitute about 14 percent of the U.S. population

MIDDLE CLASS composed primarily of "white collar" workers with a broad range of education and incomes; they constitute about 30 percent of the U.S. population

WHITE COLLAR a description characterizing lower-level professional and management workers and some highly skilled laborers in technical jobs

WORKING CLASS or **LOWER-MIDDLE CLASS** mostly "blue collar" or service industry workers who are less likely to have a college degree; they constitute about 30 percent of the U.S. population

BLUE COLLAR a description characterizing skilled and semi-skilled workers who perform manual labor or work in service or clerical jobs

WORKING POOR poorly educated manual and service workers who may work full-time but remain near or below the poverty line; they constitute about 20 percent of the U.S. population

UNDERCLASS the poorest group includes the homeless and chronically unemployed who may depend on public or private assistance; they constitute about 5 percent of the U.S. population educated, for example, but make very little money while working on her novel. Also, as we learned during the financial crisis that began in 2008, people of all social classes, including the very wealthy, can find themselves unable to pay their mortgages when real estate "bubbles" burst.

So how would we categorize a person such as the late Sam Walton, founder of Wal-Mart? He was the product of a struggling "Okie" family, a farm boy and state college graduate who became a billionaire businessman. Walton did not come from a background of privilege; he neither attended an elite university nor worked in a prestigious occupation. He was called "America's shopkeeper," and despite amassing a huge fortune, Walton remained close to his midwestern roots. What sociologists would say is that Walton is an example of **status inconsistency**, or stark contrasts between the levels of the various statuses he occupied. Another example is Mother Teresa, a Catholic nun who ministered to the poor, sick, and dying in Calcutta, India. As a member of the clergy, she held some occupational prestige, but her religious order took vows of poverty, and she had virtually no personal wealth. Yet Mother Teresa was regularly ranked as among the most admired people of the twentieth century. She garnered numerous honors including the Nobel Peace Prize, but was most concerned about how to parlay whatever power she gained into helping the world's most needy.

Of course, not all examples are quite this dramatic, but status inconsistencies are especially prevalent in the United States because of our "open" class system. Class mobility (which will be discussed in more detail later) is more easily attainable here than in many other countries, so we are more likely to see people with a mixture of different statuses. While we seem to be able to recognize class distinctions implicitly, there are no systematic ways of delineating each category. Still, sociologists have made an effort to understand and define class, and we turn now to the theories that result from those efforts.

Theories of Social Class

In this section, we will look at social stratification from the perspectives of each of the major schools of thought within sociology. We start with classical conflict and Weberian theories and structural functionalism, and will also consider postmodern and symbolic interactionist theories. Each perspective offers different ideas about what determines social class, with the macro theorists focusing on larger-scale social structures and the postmodern and micro theorists focusing more on meaning and interpretation and interactions in everyday life.

Conflict Theory

Karl Marx formed his social theories at a time when monumental changes were occurring in the stratification systems that characterized nineteenth-century Europe. The **feudal system**, which consisted of a hierarchy of privileged nobles who were responsible for and served by a

STATUS INCONSISTENCY a situation in which an individual has differing levels of status in terms of the individual's wealth, power, prestige, or other elements of socioeconomic status

FEUDAL SYSTEM a system of social stratification based on a hereditary nobility who were responsible for and served by a lower stratum of forced laborers called serfs

Status Inconsistencies Sam Walton, the "Okie" billionaire, and Mother Teresa, the Catholic nun who was revered around the world but had no personal wealth, are two examples that complicate SES classifications.

Although stratification systems in other countries may appear different from those in the United States, they share many features. For one thing, most such systems result in patterns of inequality.

Brazil

Race is a powerful influence on social stratification in Brazil, where the situation is even more complex than in the United States. By any standards, Brazil is a remarkably diverse nation. The early settlers to the area were mainly European, and with their arrival the number of native inhabitants declined sharply as a result of violence and disease, although they remained a factor in the local population. Through the mid-1800s, slaves from Africa were imported, and in the twentieth century, a new wave of immigrants arrived from Asia and the Middle East.

For much of Brazilian history, the European whites enjoyed a privileged status. However, as people from different races married and raised children, new racial categories emerged. Sociologist Gilberto Freyre claimed in 1970 that this new mixture of races and cultures was a unique strength that led to something like a "racial democracy." Although the idea was appealing, it was subsequently chal-

Polite Racism As different ethnic groups in Brazil intermarried and had children, new racial categories emerged. Many have argued that this has led to a new "racial democracy"; however, critics say stratification still exists. They refer to it as "polite racism."

lower stratum of serfs (forced laborers), was breaking down. Cities were growing larger as more people moved from rural areas to take part in the new forms of industry that were emerging there. With these changes, what had traditionally determined a person's social standing (whether they were born a noble or a serf) was no longer as relevant. Marx was concerned about a new kind of social inequality that he saw emerging—between the capitalists (bourgeoisie), who owned the means of production, and the workers (proletariat), who owned only their own labor.

Marx argued that economic relationships were quickly becoming the only social relationships that mattered: the impersonal forces of the market were creating a new, rigid system of social stratification in which capitalists had every economic advantage and workers had none. He believed that the classes would remain divided and social inequality would grow;

WEALTH a measure of net worth that includes income, property, and other assets

---

that wealth and privilege would be concentrated among a small group of capitalists and workers would continue to be exploited. Contemporary conflict theorists continue to understand social class in a similar way. Erik Olin Wright (1997), for example, describes an animated film he made as a student in which the pawns on a chessboard attempt to overthrow the aristocracy (kings, queens, knights, and bishops) but realize that the "rules of the game" doom them to relive the same unequal roles—a metaphor for the way social structure shapes and sustains inequality.

Weberian Theory

Max Weber noted that owning the means of production was not the only way of achieving upper-class status; a person could also accumulate **wealth** consisting of income and property. As a contemporary example, Microsoft is a publicly traded lenged by other social scientists who argued that Brazil was still highly stratified by race, if only in a less obvious way (Telles 2004). Intermarriage may have eliminated clearly defined racial groups, but skin color still largely defines an individual's place in society, with light-skinned Brazilians enjoying privileges of wealth and power that their dark-skinned counter-parts. Contemporary critics have referred to this inequality as *racismo cordial,* or "polite racism."

Iran

The basis for social stratification in Iran has undergone radical changes since the Islamic Revolution in 1979, which transformed the country from a constitutional monarchy to a theocracy. Before the revolution, political and economic power was concentrated in the upper class, made up of land-owners, industrialists, and business executives; the middle class consisted of entrepreneurs, small-business owners, merchants, and members of the civil service. Economic mobility was an option largely for those with secular values and a Western education, that is, those who had gone to college in the United States or Europe and who believed in the separation of church and state. After the revolution, however, religion became a primary influence on stratification. Many

members of the civil service with Western university degrees were forced into exile; those who remained were required to attend special classes on Islamic law in order to keep their positions. Strict observance of Islamic law and custom has become a prerequisite for maintaining one's social position, and many of the new political elites are religious leaders.

Sweden

Sweden has deliberately attempted to craft a system that lessens social inequality, a policy made somewhat easier, perhaps, by the country's relative homogeneity of race, ethnicity, and religion. Sweden has provided its citizens with a far greater number of social services than the United States has: the government guarantees its citizens a high level of access to health care, education, child and elderly care, unemployment benefits, and public facilities like librar-ies and parks. In order to furnish such programs, taxes are high, with a top taxation rate of 60 percent for the wealthi-est Swedes. Although the Swedish system certainly has its problems (high taxation rates among them), there are dem-onstrated benefits, including increased life expectancy and literacy, and decreased infant mortality, homelessness, pov-erty, and crime.

company (which means that thousands of shareholders own it), but its CEO Steve Ballmer is one of America's top twenty richest individuals—and its chairman, Bill Gates, is the richest in the world. Weber suggests that power (the ability to impose one's will on others) should be considered as part of the equa-tion when measuring a person's class standing. Although they may not own their corporations, executives can exert influence over the marketplace, consumers, and the work lives of their employees.

Weber believed that another important element in social class has to do with **prestige**, the social honor granted to people because of their membership in certain groups. A person's occu-pation is a common source of prestige: in a typical ranking, you might find physicians near the top and janitors near the bottom (and note that athletes rank higher than sociologists on Table 7.1). People's relative prestige can affect not only their wealth or power but also how they are perceived in social situations. Wealth by itself can also be a source of prestige, though not always. In some

social circles, especially those that are more traditional or have a history of aristocracy, a distinction is made between "old money" and "new money." In the United States it is more prestigious to come from a family heritage of wealth than to have recently made a fortune.

For Weber, wealth, power, and prestige are interrelated because they often come together, but it is also possible to con-vert one to the other. Paris Hilton, for example, a socialite from a wealthy, hotel-owning family, turned that aspect of her sta-tus into a certain type of contemporary prestige—celebrity. Still, it is impor-tant to distinguish these three elements: property and wealth can be inher-ited or earned, power usually comes from occupying certain roles within organizations, and prestige is based on a person's social identity and bestowed by others.

> **PRESTIGE** the social honor people are given because of their membership in well-regarded social groups

Table 7.1 The Relative Social Prestige of Selected Occupations in the United States

White Collar Occupations	Prestige Score	Blue Collar Occupations	White Collar Occupations	Prestige Score	Blue Collar Occupations
Physician	86		Realtor	49	
Lawyer	75		Bookkeeper	47	
Professor	74			47	Mail Carrier
Architect	73		Musician/Composer	47	
Chemist	73			46	Secretary
Dentist	72		Bank Teller	43	
Member of the Clergy	69			42	Welder
Pharmacist	68			40	Farmer
Registered Nurse	66			39	Carpenter
Teacher	65			36	Child-Care Worker
Accountant	65			36	Hairdresser
Electrical Engineer	64			31	Auto Body Repairperson
Veterinarian	62		Salesperson	30	
Airplane Pilot	61			30	Truck Driver
Computer Programmer	61		Cashier	29	
Editor/Reporter	60			28	Garbage Collector
	60	Police Officer		28	Taxi Driver
Actor	58			28	Waiter/Waitress
Librarian	54			25	Bartender
	53	Firefighter		23	Farm Laborer
Social Worker	52			23	Household Laborer
	51	Electrician		22	Janitor
				9	Shoe Shiner

SOURCE: Data from National Opinion Research Center 2013.

Structural Functionalism

Functionalism emphasizes social order and solidarity based on commonly shared values about what is good and worthwhile. The system of stratification that has emerged over time, though not egalitarian, is still functional for society in a number of ways. Because there are a variety of roles to perform for the maintenance and good of the whole, there must be incentives to ensure that individuals will occupy those roles that are most necessary or important. Kingsley Davis and Wilbert Moore (1945) discuss some of the principles of stratification that result in a system of rewards that is unequally distributed among various roles. The assumption is that some roles are more desirable than others and may require greater talent or training. In addition, certain roles may be more critical than others to the functioning of society, as well as difficult to fill, so there must be a mechanism for attracting and securing the best individuals to those positions. This would mean that there is widespread consensus about which positions are most important—either in terms of their special qualifications or the potential scarcity of qualified individuals to occupy those positions—and that society accepts the need to bestow rewards upon people who are considered of greater importance.

Take, for instance, the role of a physician, which has the highest ranking of occupational prestige in American society. Doctors play an important role in providing highly prized services to other members of society. Think of the steps it takes to become a doctor. A person must have an extensive education and graduate training, and complete a long and intensive internship before being certified to practice medicine. This individual also devotes a great deal of her personal resources of time and money to this process. It is further

Postmodernism

Sociologist Pierre Bourdieu studied French schools to examine a phenomenon referred to as **social reproduction**, which means that social class is passed down from one generation to the next and thus remains relatively stable (1973, 1984). According to Bourdieu, this happens as a result of each generation's acquisition of what he called **cultural capital**: children inherit tastes, habits, and expectations from their parents, and this cultural capital either helps or hinders them as they become adults. For example, having highly educated parents who can help with homework and enforce useful study habits makes it more likely a child will succeed in school. Just the parents' expectation that their children will earn similar credentials can be a powerful incentive. Since better-educated parents tend to come from the middle and upper classes, their children will also have better chances to attain that same status.

> **SOCIAL REPRODUCTION** the tendency of social classes to remain relatively stable as class status is passed down from one generation to the next
>
> **CULTURAL CAPITAL** the tastes, habits, expectations, skills, knowledge, and other cultural assets that help us gain advantages in society

According to Bourdieu, cultural capital also shapes the perceptions that others form about a person. For instance, in job interviews, the candidates who can best impress a potential employer with their social skills may be chosen over other workers who may be equally qualified but less adept socially. Since cultural capital has such profound effects, people often try to acquire it—to "better" themselves. They may take adult education classes, attend lectures and concerts, join a tennis club, or travel to Europe—all in an attempt to improve their cultural capital. Often, however, the effects of early childhood are too powerful to overcome. It can be difficult for someone who grew up in a less privileged environment to project a different class background; their accent, for example, may give them away ("He talks like a hillbilly," "She just sounds too 'street'"). There is evidence that around half of all children will wind up with the same SES as their parents, despite any efforts to climb the social class ladder (Krueger 2002).

Symbolic Interactionism

If macrosociologists believe that there is little an individual can do to change systems of structured inequality, interactionists believe that all social structures—including systems of inequality—are constructed from the building blocks of everyday interaction. For instance, sociologist David Sudnow (1972) argues that we make split-second judgments about who people are and which social status they occupy based on appearance. We take action based on what we observe "at a glance." Along the same lines, Aaron Cicourel (1972) suggests that we make inferences about the status of

Social Reproduction Paris Hilton is heiress to the Hilton Hotel & Resort chain. How did Hilton's family influence her career path?

assumed that there are only so many people who might have the talent and determination to become doctors, and so it follows that there must be incentives or rewards for them to enter the field of medicine.

The functionalist perspective helps to explain the existing system of social stratification and its persistence, but it still leaves us with questions about the structured inequalities that it continues to reproduce. Is it really functional for social rewards (such as wealth, power, and prestige) to be so unequally divided among members of society? And while we might agree that doctors are very important to society, are they more so than teachers and carpenters? Our heroes of popular culture (famous actors, athletes, musicians) can rise to the highest ranks while our everyday heroes (day-care providers, firefighters, mechanics) may struggle to make a living. Whose values are structuring the system and, after closer scrutiny, is it clear that compensating stockbrokers more than bricklayers is really functional to society as a whole? Despite these questions, Americans largely agree with functionalist principles on social class. We will revisit some of these questions in later sections of the chapter.

EVERYDAY CLASS CONSCIOUSNESS awareness of one's own social status and that of others

others when we encounter them in different social situations. For example, you may assume that the passengers sitting in the first-class section of an airplane are wealthier than those in coach, whether or not this is true. Maybe one of those first-class passengers is a "starving student" whose seat was upgraded because coach was overbooked—by thrifty millionaires. "Wealthy," "poor," and "middle class" are statuses that, rather than existing in and of themselves, are continuously being negotiated in interaction.

Erving Goffman (1956) noted that we "read" different aspects of identity by interpreting the behavior of others and that we become accustomed to others "reading" our behavior in the same way. This means that our clothing, our speech, our gestures, the cars we drive, the homes we live in, the people we hang out with, and the things we do on vacation are all part of our presentation of self and provide information that others use to make judgments about our SES. In turn, we look for these same clues in the behavior of others. This type of **everyday class consciousness**, or awareness of our own and others' social status, is important for us to understand but difficult to identify empirically.

As a humorous answer to this dilemma, University of Pennsylvania English professor Paul Fussell (1983) created the "living room scale," which lists items that we may find in someone's living room and attaches point values to them. For example, if you have a copy of the *New York Review of Books* on your coffee table, add five points. A copy of *Popular Mechanics*? Subtract five. A working fireplace? Add four. A wall unit with built-in television and stereo? Subtract four. Add three points for each black-and-white family photograph in a sterling silver frame; subtract three points for any work of art depicting cowboys. When we total the final score, higher numbers indicate higher SES, and vice versa.

While Fussell's living room scale may seem like a joke, we really do make snap judgments about the status of others based on just this sort of information. (Here it should be noted that in Dr. Stein's living room, the fireplace and TV wall unit are side by side, while Dr. Ferris's living room features a silver-framed black-and-white photograph of her father as a child—dressed like a cowboy, on horseback! As we've said before, real life sometimes defies easy categorization.) The Data Workshop on the next page will help you see how swiftly and automatically you employ class categories in your interactions with others.

While we have considered the theories of macrosociologists and symbolic interactionists separately here, there are actually some intersections between interaction and structure. Our identities as "working-class" or "privileged" individuals may be structured by preexisting categories, yet those identities are also performed every day in our interactions with others. The structural perspective and the inter-

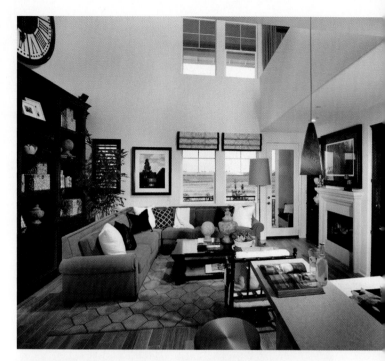

Everyday Class Consciousness Clothes, cars, homes, and vacation plans are all indicators of socioeconomic status. What impression does this living room give of who might live here?

actionist perspective are not mutually exclusive when it comes to a discussion of class: they are complementary. Status inequality is structured, categorical, and external; it is also interactionally created and sustained. Structure shapes interaction, and interaction generates structure.

Contemporary sociologists have conducted studies that make this connection clear. For example, Geoffrey Hunt and Saundra Satterlee, who studied drinking habits in village pubs (1986), found that pub interactions tended to reinforce class divisions in the larger society: the village men chose drinking and billiards companions based on the class divisions already in place outside the pub.

DATA WORKSHOP
Analyzing Everyday Life

Everyday Class Consciousness

How do you determine the class status of others? How do you deal with the fact that others will be assessing *your* class status? How do these assessments influence your thoughts and actions?

Table 7.2 Theory in Everyday Life

Perspective	Approach to Social Inequality	Case Study: Poverty
Structural Functionalism	Social inequality is a necessary part of society. Different reward structures are necessary as an incentive for the best qualified people to occupy the most important positions. Even poverty has functions that help maintain social order.	The functions of poverty for society include the facts that the poor take otherwise undesirable jobs and housing, purchase discount and secondhand goods, and provide work for thousands, including social service caseworkers and others who work with the poor.
Conflict Theory	Social inequality creates intergroup conflict—poor and rich groups have different interests and may find themselves at odds as they attempt to secure and protect these interests.	Social welfare programs that assist the poor are funded by tax dollars, which some wealthy citizens may be reluctant to provide because taxes reduce their net income. This can create conflict between rich and poor groups in society.
Symbolic Interactionism	Social inequality is part of our presentation of self. We develop everyday class consciousness as a way to distinguish the status of others.	Poor and wealthy persons have differential access to the "props" used to project particular versions of self. In particular, professional clothing such as business suits can be too expensive for poor individuals to purchase, which can put them at a disadvantage in job interviews, where a professional image is necessary. Organizations like Dress for Success provide professional clothing for those who can't afford it, leveling the playing field a bit in terms of impression management.

This Data Workshop asks you to do some participant observation research (see Chapter 2 for a refresher on ethnographic methods, if needed) to understand more about how we size up others in terms of their SES. Choose a site to conduct your study. Locate yourself in a busy public place. For example, you could be waiting for someone at the airport, sitting in the food court at the mall, or standing in line at the post office. Select the seventh person to walk by you, and spend several long moments looking closely at him or her. Ask yourself quickly: what class status do you think this person holds? Don't think too long; just register your guess. Then consider the following.

What did you look at to make the evaluation—height, weight, race, gender, hairstyle, tattoos, piercings, watch, makeup? Perhaps dress style, colors, fabrics, logos on a T-shirt, hat, purse, shoes, jewelry? Did you notice anything else, such as posture, voice, or mannerisms? If you observed someone outdoors, did you see the car he or she was driving? What was its make, age, or condition? Did you notice other status clues—a laptop or smart phone, a baby stroller or shopping bags? How did the setting itself (mall, post office, airport) influence your guess?

There are two options for completing this Data Workshop.

Option 1 (informal): Prepare written notes that you can refer to in class. Share your evaluations with other students in small-group discussions. Note similarities and differences in the criteria used by group members.

Option 2 (formal): Select two to three people in a public setting to evaluate. Write a three- to four-page essay describing your observations and answering the questions in the preceding paragraphs. Your field notes will serve as data for your analysis.

All the information that we gather at a glance is used to make evaluations of others' wealth, income, occupation, education, and other categories that indicate status and prestige. In some ways, it doesn't matter whether we're right or not—especially in anonymous public places like airports. You should be aware, however, that you do use these cues to evaluate the status of others in split seconds and that you act on those evaluations every day. Maybe you chose to stand on the bus or subway rather than sit next to someone who didn't look quite "right"—whatever that means to you. Often, we end up falling back on stereotypes that may lead us to false conclusions about a person's status or character. When it comes to everyday class consciousness, appearances are sometimes deceiving, but they are always consequential.

Socioeconomic Status and Life Chances

Belonging to a certain social class brings such profound consequences that it's possible to make general predictions about a person's life chances in regard to education, work, crime, family, and health just by knowing his SES. The following discussion may help you appreciate the respective privileges and hardships associated with different levels of the social hierarchy.

Family

Sociologists know that people are likely to marry or have long-term relationships with persons whose social and cultural backgrounds are similar to their own—not because they are looking for such similarities, but simply because they have more access to people like themselves. When you develop ties to classmates, fellow workers, neighbors, and members of clubs, these people may share your cultural background as well as your social class. It is from such groups that marriage and domestic partners most often come.

Social class also plays a role in the age at which people marry: the average age of first marriage for women with high school diplomas is twenty-five, while for women with graduate degrees it is thirty. The age at which people start a family and the number of children they have are also related to social class. The age at which people start a family and the number of children they have are also related to educational attainment. In 2011, more than 66 percent of new mothers had at least some college education, while 34 percent had a high school diploma or less. While 48 percent of new mothers without a high school diploma were younger than 25, only 3 percent of new mothers with a bachelor's degree were younger than 25. Less educated women have a higher average number of births throughout their lifetime than more educated women. On average, women without a high school diploma have 2.5 children, whereas women with a bachelor's degree have about 1.7 children (Livingston and Cohn 2013).

Health

Those at the bottom of the social class ladder are the least likely to obtain adequate nutrition, shelter, clothing, and health care and are thus more prone to illness. Often they cannot afford to see a doctor, fill a prescription, or go to a hospital. Instead of preventing an illness from becoming worse, they must wait until a health crisis occurs, and then they have no option but expensive emergency room care. Health-care reforms might help change that pattern.

Sociologists have found that people who occupy a higher SES are more likely to simply *feel* healthier. In one study of Americans older than twenty-five, researchers found that regardless of age, race, or gender, people with more education were more likely to report being in excellent health: fewer than 40 percent of those with less than a high school education reported being in good health, compared with nearly 80 percent of those with a college degree (Baum and Payea 2004). Another study found that not only do people of higher SES feel healthier, they in fact live longer—almost five years longer than people of low SES (Singh and Siahpush 2006).

One factor that contributes to disparities in health is exercise. As education and income increase, so does the likelihood of a person engaging in some exercise, as reported in 2011 by the CDC's National Center for Health Statistics (2012b). For instance, nearly 64 percent of respondents living below the poverty level did not meet guidelines for physical activity (aerobic or strength training exercise), compared with only 36 percent of those living at four times above the poverty level. Only 12 percent of individuals living below the poverty level reported exercising regularly, compared with almost 27 percent of those at the higher income level. Education may have something to do with these contrasts, as more knowledge about the health benefits of exercise may lead to more active participation. But we can also see exercise as rather a luxury for those in higher social classes, who are not struggling with the day-to-day efforts to survive that characterize the lives of the poor.

Education

How children perform in school usually determines whether and where they go to college, what professions they enter, and how much they are paid. And generally, those with more education make more money. According to a 2010 Census Bureau report, the average annual income for those with advanced (master's and doctorate) or professional (medical and law) degrees was $83,144, followed by $58,613 for those with bachelor's degrees, and $31,283 for those with high school diplomas (U.S. Census Bureau 2010b). On the surface, these earnings may seem fair; after all, shouldn't people with more education make more money? However, as sociologists, we must probe further and ask some fundamental questions; for example, who has access to education, and how good is that education?

One of the main goals of education is to make sure students get a chance to succeed both in school and in life. But to meet this goal, schools would have to serve all students equally, and they aren't always able to do so. Schools with low-income students often receive fewer resources, have greater difficulty in attracting qualified teachers, and experience less support from parents (Fischer and

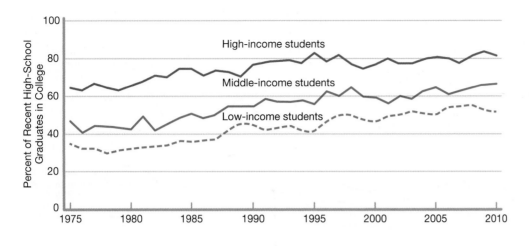

Figure 7.2

Students Enrolled in College the October Immediately after High-School Completion, by Family Income: 1975–2010

Although high-school graduation rates have been increasing overall, students with higher SES are still more likely to graduate.

SOURCE: National Center for Education Statistics 2012.

Kmec 2004). A student's social class background will also influence her attitude toward education. The higher the family's SES, the higher the student's expectations for educational achievement (see Figure 7.2). Students from higher social classes are expected to complete more years of school and are more likely to attend college than those from lower social classes (Berends 1995; Goyette and Xie 1999; Bozick et al. 2010).

According to a U.S. Census Bureau report (2011h), approximately 31 percent of adults aged twenty-five and over had a high school education, 17 percent had some college, 19 percent had a bachelor's degree, and 11 percent had advanced degrees. But although educational attainment is at an all-time high in the United States, a high school education doesn't mean what it once did. College and advanced degrees are becoming more important. If the trends continue, fewer and fewer jobs will be available to those without college degrees, and of those jobs, fewer will support middle-class lifestyles. Yet, not all students are equally prepared for or able to afford a college education, and this creates a risk that children from lower socioeconomic backgrounds will slip farther down the social class ladder.

Work and Income

In the past couple of decades, we have seen a widening income gap between those at the top, middle, and bottom of the scale (Bernstein et al. 2000; Wolff 2002; Figure 7.3). The 2011 census reported the largest income gap ever between the richest and poorest Americans (U.S. Census Bureau 2012f). Income is the product of work, and members of different social classes, with unequal educational opportunities, tend to work in different types of jobs.

At the bottom of the scale, members of the lower class generally experience difficulties in the job market and may endure periods of unemployment or underemployment (work-

ing in a job that doesn't pay enough to support a person's needs, or that doesn't make full use of his skills). Among the lower class are people receiving such government aid as Temporary Assistance for Needy Families (4.1 million in 2009; U.S. Census Bureau 2012m) or food stamps (40.3 million in 2010; U.S. Census Bureau 2012l) and the 3 million migrant farm workers who earn low wages picking strawberries, tomatoes, and other produce in places like California, Texas, and Kansas (González 2007).

Members of the working, or lower-middle, class work for wages in a variety of blue collar jobs. They can generally earn a dependable income through skilled or semiskilled occupations, but they may also experience periods of unemployment tied to fluctuations in the economy, layoffs, and plant closings. For example, in 2008 alone, the United States lost more than 600,000 jobs as a result of factory shutdowns and other problems associated with the economic downturn (Garr 2008).

While factory work and other types of skilled labor were once enough to support a middle-class lifestyle, most middle-class jobs today are found in the service, information, and technology sectors. Most households here require two incomes to maintain a comfortable lifestyle, and many middle-class jobs require some sort of college degree.

The upper-middle class tends to work in executive and professional fields. Some members are business owners; a small portion own large farms or ranches. Others, known as the "creative class" (Florida 2002)—architects, writers, scientists, artists, professors, and engineers—tend to cluster in "creative" cities, such as Austin, San Francisco, and Seattle.

Through exceptional success in any profession or art, or sometimes through inheritance, one can join the upper class. In the United States, the upper class is influential in politics, business, and culture, largely because of its economic

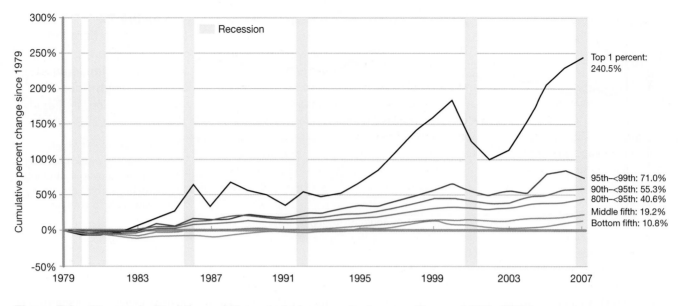

Figure 7.3 Change in Real Annual Household Income, by Income Group, 1979–2007

SOURCE: Economic Policy Institute 2012.

privilege: in our highly stratified society, the top 1 percent consistently controls more than 33 percent of the national wealth (Wolff 2004; Kennickell 2009). That trend has accelerated, and by 2011 the top 1 percent had gained control of 40 percent of the wealth (Stiglitz 2011).

As a result of the recent recession, more workers are at risk of layoffs because of outsourcing. Corporations seeking to cut costs have been relocating their operations overseas, in countries where labor costs are lower. Both manufacturing and service jobs are subject to outsourcing, meaning that blue collar and white collar workers—and even some higher-ranking executives—are now vulnerable.

Criminal Justice

In general, people of lower SES are more likely to encounter the criminal justice system, whether as a perpetrator or victim of a crime, than those of higher SES. But the statistics are not as straightforward as they might seem. One influential study (Blau and Blau 1982) showed that while poverty is associated with higher rates of violent crime, variables such as dense population and anomie (a sense of alienation or lack of social connections) have an even greater impact on crime rates.

People in lower classes are often more visible, less powerful, and thus more likely to be apprehended and labeled as criminals than those from higher social classes. There are also differences in how crimes are prosecuted. White collar criminals are less likely to be arrested, prosecuted, or convicted than ordinary "street" criminals (Schwellenbach 2008). White collar criminals (such as Enron heads Jeffrey

Skilling and the late Kenneth Lay, or Bernie Madoff whose Ponzi scheme bilked wealthy clients of billions of dollars) can also afford the best legal representation and hence enjoy distinct advantages in the courtroom. If white collar criminals are convicted, their sentences are likely to be lighter. Still, while Enron's Ken Lay avoided prison time by dying of a massive heart attack several months before his October 2006 sentencing date, Jeffrey Skilling was sentenced to 24 years in prison, and Madoff received 150 years for his crimes. Perhaps their punishments will serve as a deterrent for other high-status criminals.

Studies have claimed that 90 percent of inmates on death row could not afford to hire a lawyer when they were tried (Lane and Tabak 1991) and that the quality of representation, rather than the actual facts presented in a trial, determines whether someone is sentenced to death (ACLU 2003). Studies have also shown that race and SES influence whether the death penalty is sought. Prosecutors are more likely to seek the death penalty if the killer is black, or if the victim was white. SES influences the likelihood of a death sentence, as those who are able to hire legal counsel are less likely to be sentenced to death. Therefore, the intersection of race and SES can dramatically affect the outcome of criminal sentencing (Phillips 2009).

Lower-class people are also more likely to be the victims of violent crime. Statistics consistently show that poor people are more than one and a half times more likely to be victims of violent crime than those in higher social class brackets (Levinson 2002). At the same time, people with lower SES are also more likely to feel at risk of harassment by police. As both education and income decreased, respondents reported feeling more threatened by police; as education and income increased, they felt less threatened (Levinson 2002).

Social class affects more than just our financial or material state—it is intricately woven into the fabric of our lives. You may once have concluded that differences in people's education, work, family, or health were simply a matter of individual preference or effort, or that each individual is responsible for her own circumstances. While this may be true to some extent, research shows that social class background has a profound impact on one's life chances, leading those with different statuses into very different life courses. This means that we can't take for granted whatever advantages or disadvantages we might experience but should acknowledge how hierarchies of inequality have helped to create our particular social realities.

Social Mobility

How do people move from one social class to another? In other words, how do they achieve social mobility? Sociologists use the concept of **social mobility** to measure movement within the stratification system of a particular society, whether it's a small town, a state or nation. In some societies, social mobility is highly restricted by formal or informal rules. India's caste system is an example of what sociologists refer to as a **closed system**: there is very little opportunity for social mobility between classes. The United States, where social mobility is possible, is perceived to be an **open system**. It was not always so, however: in the period of history preceding the Civil War, slavery was widespread, keeping African Americans from climbing the social class ladder.

The movement of people between social classes can happen in three different ways: through intergenerational mobility, intragenerational mobility, or structural mobility. **Intergenerational mobility** refers to the movement that occurs from one generation to the next, when a child eventually moves into a different social class from that of her parents. Research shows that baby boomers (children born immediately after World War II) have, for the most part, achieved upward intergenerational mobility: they have generally amassed more wealth during the course of their lives

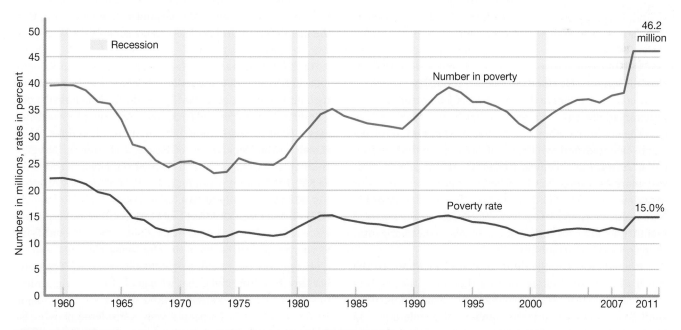

Figure 7.4 **Number in Poverty and Poverty Rate, 1959–2011**

Although poverty rates declined sharply during the "war on poverty" of the early 1960s, they have remained relatively stable in the decades since.

SOURCE: U.S. Census Bureau 2012f.

and consequently moved up the social class ladder. Some social scientists, however, claim that the distribution of income across generations has grown more static and that there are fewer opportunities for advancement than before (Krueger 2002). While the majority of Americans exceed their parents' income and wealth, the amount of their upward movement may not lift them to a higher position on the social class ladder (Mazumder 2012; PEW Charitable Trusts 2012). Conversely, there are many mechanisms in place, such as tax laws and social policies, that allow the wealthy to protect their assets and to pass them down to the next generation, making it more difficult for the middle and lower classes to improve their positions.

Intragenerational mobility refers to the movement that occurs during the course of an individual's lifetime. In other words, it is the measure between a person's ascribed status, the social class she is born into, and the social class status she achieves during her lifetime. Intragenerational mobility can be measured in two directions. **Horizontal social mobility**, which is fairly common, refers to the changing of jobs within a class: a therapist who shifts careers so that he can teach college experiences horizontal mobility. **Vertical social mobility** is movement up or down the social ladder, and thus is often called upward or downward mobility. If this same therapist marries a president of a large corporation, he might experience upward mobility. On the other hand, if he or his wife becomes unemployed, he might experience downward mobility. People are far more likely to experience horizontal than vertical social mobility.

Although we usually think of social mobility as the result of individual effort (or lack thereof), other factors can contribute to a change in one's social class. **Structural mobility** occurs when large numbers of people move up or down the social ladder because of structural changes in society as a whole, particularly when the economy is affected by large-scale events. For instance, during the Great Depression of the early 1930s, precipitated by the stock market crash of 1929, huge numbers of upper- and

middle-class people suddenly found themselves among the poor. Conversely, during the dot-com boom of the late 1990s, developing and investing in new technologies made many people into overnight millionaires. Both of these extreme periods eventually leveled out. Still, many people in the Depression era remained in their new class, never able to climb up the social ladder again.

Defining Poverty

Social mobility is most difficult—and most essential—for those who live at the bottom of the socioeconomic ladder. In this section, we look at what it means to be poor in America.

Poverty can be defined in relative or absolute terms. **Relative deprivation** is a comparative measure, whereby people are considered poor if their standard of living is less than that of other members of society—for example, a Wal-Mart clerk who works part-time for minimum wage is poor compared with a neurosurgeon whose salary is $500,000. **Absolute deprivation**, on the other hand, is a measure whereby people are unable to meet minimal standards for food, shelter, clothing, and health care. In Burundi, for example, 53 percent of children under the age of five experience chronic malnutrition, and in some poor provinces the number jumps to over 90 percent (UNICEF 2010). In Swaziland, more than 25 percent of adults are living with HIV. Poverty has resulted in a lack of access to health care, exacerbating the HIV epidemic and making this country among the lowest in terms of life expectancy, averaging less than fifty years (Central Intelligence Agency 2012). Hunger, malnutrition, and/or the inability to afford medications are some of the basic indicators of absolute poverty.

In the United States, the federal poverty line—an absolute measure, calculated annually—indicates the total annual income below which a family would be considered poor. These figures are derived from either the poverty thresholds established by the Census Bureau or the guidelines determined by the Department of Health and Human Services. In 2011, the Census Bureau defined the poverty threshold as $22,491 for a family of four, $17,057 for a family of three, $14,602 for a family of two, and $11,344 for an individual (U.S. Census Bureau 2012f). In fact, families making much more than these amounts, although not officially qualifying as poor, might still be unable to afford some basic necessities.

How many people fall below the poverty line? The numbers are startling, given that we usually think of the United States as a wealthy nation. In 2011, 15 percent of the population, or 46.2 million people, were considered poor, a rise in both numbers and percentage over the 2008 rate (U.S. Census Bureau 2012f). During the past forty years, the percentage of poor people has fluctuated in the low teens, but it has never dipped below 10 percent. In fact, the number has occasionally risen to more than 15 percent, as it did in 2009

INTRAGENERATIONAL MOBILITY the movement between social classes that occurs during the course of an individual's lifetime

HORIZONTAL SOCIAL MOBILITY the movement of individuals or groups within a particular social class, most often a result of changing occupations

VERTICAL SOCIAL MOBILITY the movement between different class statuses, often called either upward mobility or downward mobility

STRUCTURAL MOBILITY changes in the social status of large numbers of people as a result of structural changes in society

RELATIVE DEPRIVATION a relative measure of poverty based on the standard of living in a particular society

ABSOLUTE DEPRIVATION an objective measure of poverty, defined by the inability to meet minimal standards for food, shelter, clothing, or health care and 2011, while in the late 1950s it rose as high as 22 percent (see Figure 7.4).

Contrary to popular myth, most poor people are not unemployed; they are known as the working poor. The annual earnings of a full-time worker making $7.25 an hour (the prevailing federal minimum wage since 2009) still put him below the poverty line if he is trying to support a family. According to researchers, more than 80 percent of low-income minimum-wage workers, even if they are working full-time, are not earning enough to guarantee a decent standard of living, and many cannot afford some of the basic necessities (Wicks-Lim and Thompson 2010).

The poverty line has often been criticized because of the way it is uniformly applied without regard to regional or other differences. For instance, a family living in Washington, D.C., might need twice or three times as much income as a family in Des Moines, Iowa, for expenses like rent, transportation, health insurance, and child care (exceptions are made for Alaska and Hawaii, both states with extremely high costs of living). In addition, some families may be eligible for some form of government assistance, such as Food Stamps (SNAP) or the Earned Income Tax Credit (EITC), which makes a difference in the total amount of their household money. Many working families thus live close to the edge and struggle to make ends meet but are not included as part of the official poverty statistics (Waldron et al. 2004; Sherman 2012).

Poverty is also more prominent among certain population groups (Figure 7.5). For instance, poverty rates are higher among blacks and Hispanics than Asians or whites

(U.S. Census Bureau 2012f). They are higher for the elderly, disabled, and those who are foreign born, as well as for women, children, and single-parent households. And they are higher in the South, inner cities, and rural areas. In a disturbing new trend, poverty is increasing most rapidly in the suburbs (Plumer 2013).

Social Welfare and Welfare Reform

Some of the most heated debates about the nature of poverty involve how or even whether society should help the poor. Some argue that government assistance helps poor people become self-supporting; others say that it just fosters a dependence on aid and causes further problems.

The idea behind the current American welfare state, which consists of such programs as Social Security, unemployment insurance, and Temporary Assistance for Needy Families (TANF), was first proposed by President Franklin D. Roosevelt during the Great Depression of the 1930s. These programs, collectively called the New Deal, were a response to a national crisis and were meant to serve as a safety net for citizens, helping them in times of adversity or old age, poverty, or joblessness. The 1960s ushered in a new "war on poverty." A second wave of programs, such as Medicaid and Head Start, intended to solve a variety of social and economic problems, was proposed by President John F. Kennedy and instituted by President Lyndon B. Johnson as part of his Great Society program in 1964.

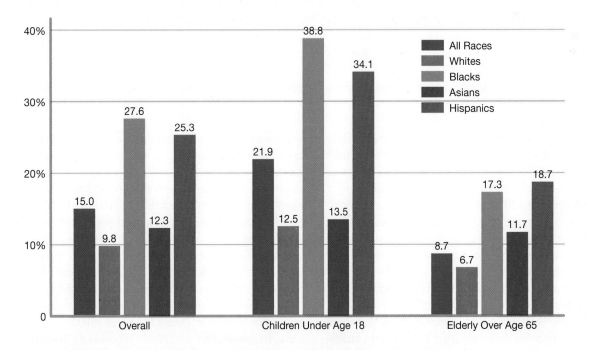

Figure 7.5 **Poverty in the United States by Selected Characteristics, 2011**

SOURCE: U.S. Census Bureau 2012f.

You say you don't judge a book by its cover? You say it's the person who matters, and not the social categories he or she belongs to? We may believe these things, but sociological studies strongly suggest that we don't act on them. When it comes to dating, courtship, and marriage ("mate selection" activities, as defined by social scientists), we tend to make homogamous choices. **Homogamy** ("like marries like") means that we choose romantic partners based on our similarities in background and group membership. Despite the old adage that "opposites attract," decades of sociological research show that we make choices based on similarities in race, ethnicity, religion, class, education, age—even height and levels of physical attractiveness (Kalmijn 1998). Homogamy based on socioeconomic status is especially clear: we tend to marry those who share the same economic and educational backgrounds as we do. This holds true even if we practice **heterogamy** (marrying someone who is different from us) in other areas, such as race or religion. Why is class-based homogamy so prevalent?

As it turns out, we have relatively few opportunities to meet people of different socioeconomic backgrounds during the course of our everyday lives. At home, at school, on the job, at the coffee shop or gym, we are likely to be surrounded by those who are like us, classwise. Homogamy is more strictly enforced in upper-class families than in other social classes. Those who enjoy the privileges of wealth often want to make sure those privileges continue into the next generation and may monitor their children's activities by sending them to prestigious schools and posh summer camps so that they don't get the opportunity to meet anyone but other privileged kids. This helps ensure that wealth and power remain consolidated within a relatively small community. If you spend all your free time at the country club pool instead of getting a summer job working at Starbucks or McDonald's, your opportunities to meet the *hoi polloi* are limited.

If we focus only on those in the public eye, it is easy to see how limits on opportunity result in marriages between affluent and powerful families. This happens in political families. For example, Julie Nixon, daughter of the former president, married David Eisenhower, grandson of another former president. Kerry Kennedy, daughter of former attorney general Robert Kennedy, married (and later divorced) Andrew Cuomo, son of former New York governor Mario Cuomo. And it happens among celebrities, whether movie stars Brad Pitt and Angelina Jolie, singers Beyoncé Knowles and Jay-Z, or NFL quarterback Tom Brady and supermodel Gisele Bündchen. All practiced a form of status homogamy

HOMOGAMY choosing romantic partners who are similar to us in terms of class, race, education, religion, and other social group membership

HETEROGAMY choosing romantic partners who are dissimilar to us in terms of class, race, education, religion, and other social group membership

---

The welfare system attempted to be fair by providing uniform, standard benefits to all the nation's needy without regard to their personal circumstances and with no time limit. Social Security and Medicaid lifted seniors out of poverty, and programs like Head Start and Upward Bound offered educational support for poor children. Food stamps improved nutrition for those with limited incomes, and job-training programs helped the poor gain marketable skills. By 1970, the poverty rate had declined from 22.2 percent to 12.6 percent (Califano 1999), the fastest it has ever dropped.

In the 1980s, political opinion turned against social welfare programs despite their successes. Critics claimed that these programs were responsible for creating a permanent underclass of people living off government checks—some receiving benefits they didn't deserve—and essentially discouraging them from seeking work. Much of the rhetoric surrounding welfare programs stems from concerns about federal spending. People commonly assume that welfare constitutes a large portion of the federal budget, when in fact welfare and unemployment together represented just over 13 percent of government spending in 2011, or $324 billion (Figure 7.6). Compare that with Social Security (about 21 percent of spending, or $608 billion) or defense and the war on terror (about 20 percent of spending, or $626 billion). But given these misconceptions, it makes sense that welfare abuse and reform have received so much press, both in past decades and now.

In response to criticism of welfare programs, reforms arrived in the 1990s. Under President Bill Clinton, the Personal Responsibility and Work Opportunity Reconciliation Act was passed into law in 1996. Often referred to as the Welfare Reform Act, it ended the concept of "entitlements" by requiring recipients to find work within two years of receivby partnering with people from the same social circles—other famous and wealthy celebrities. Whether they met on the set, at the yacht club, or at an awards show, they met in a status-restricted setting to which not everyone is eligible for entry.

Questions have arisen recently about how internet technologies may facilitate—or impede—our tendency toward homogamy. Dating sites such as eHarmony, Match.com, and others allow people who occupy vastly different social circles to meet online—and perhaps fall in love. In this way, it would seem that internet dating has the potential to inhibit our off-line predilection for people who belong to the same social groups as we do. On the other hand, internet dating can also assist us in choosing people who are like us, in that certain sites cater to particular social groups. J Date (for Jewish singles), The Right Stuff (for Ivy Leaguers), and other specialty sites select for social group membership and may actually strengthen homogamous effects in our online mate selection processes.

Vast differences in class standing between marital partners are usually the stuff of fairy tales and fantasy. The "Cinderella story," in which a low-status woman is romantically "rescued" by a high-status man, is familiar to us all—yet we likely have seen it happen only in storybooks and movie theaters. *Pretty Woman*, in which Julia Roberts plays a prostitute who is romanced by Richard Gere's wealthy businessman, is a perfect example of this type of heterogamous fantasy, as is *Maid in Manhattan*, in which Jennifer

Jay-Z and Beyoncé Knowles "Like marries like."

Lopez plays a hotel housekeeper who is wooed by Ralph Fiennes's character, a rich political candidate. The only touch of sociological reality in these tales is the portrayal of women's **hypergamy** and men's **hypogamy**; that is, when class boundaries are crossed, women usually marry up while men marry down. Take a look at the role of SES in your own mate selection activities: are you homogamous or heterogamous?

HYPERGAMY marrying "up" in the social class hierarchy

HYPOGAMY marrying "down" in the social class hierarchy

ing assistance and imposing a limit of five years as the total amount of time in which families could receive assistance. The act also decentralized the federal system of public assistance, allowing individual states to design their own programs, some of which would deny or reduce certain benefits, and impose their own criteria for eligibility. The rationale was to encourage people on welfare to take responsibility for working themselves out of poverty. In 2003, Congress approved changes to the act, requiring an even larger percentage of recipients to take jobs and work longer hours.

While welfare reform has been an economic success in terms of reducing the number of people on welfare, there is still a great deal to be learned about its success or failure in transforming the lives of the poor. Evidence suggests that moving from welfare to work does not increase income levels—in other words, federal assistance is merely replaced

with an equally low-paying job, which has the effect of keeping families beneath the poverty line once they're off welfare. The reasons for this—the increased costs of child care, health insurance, and transportation—make it difficult for former welfare recipients to succeed outside the system (Hays 2003).

Studies have sought to evaluate the consequences of welfare policy changes. One of the largest, "Welfare, Children, and Families: A Three-City Study," is a longitudinal study (one that follows the children of welfare over time) done in Boston, Chicago, and San Antonio. A team of researchers from three different universities, including sociologists, anthropologists, psychologists, and economists, using methods as diverse as survey research, interviews, and in-depth ethnographies, sought to discover whether welfare reform was really helping to eradicate poverty and what kind of an impact welfare reform had on the lives of struggling families. They

ON THE JOB

Digital Divide

In a postindustrial economy, most of us will have to demonstrate a certain level of computer proficiency in order to secure a job. One way or another, the majority of jobs in contemporary society involve computers, so you'll have to know how to use certain programs to do your work, whatever it may be—editing and publishing, say, or accounting or graphic design, fine woodworking or auto repair, teaching or engineering or nursing. Because you are attending college, you'll probably be lucky enough to acquire some of these skills in the course of your education. But not everyone has the opportunities you have, and many in the United States and around the world lack the basic computer skills, experience, and access necessary to secure a decent job. This inequality in access to and use of digital technology is known as the **digital divide**.

Actually, in the words of PBS media and technology reporter Mark Glaser, "there are many digital divides." The hierarchies of inequality in the larger society—such as race, class, and educational attainment—all shape one's access to technology (Glaser 2007). For example, while 78 percent of all adults in the United States use the internet regularly, only 68 percent of Hispanics, 62 percent of those with a household income under $30,000, 54 percent of adults with disabilities, 43 percent of those with less than a high school education, and 41 percent of seniors do so (Pew Internet and American Life Project 2012a).

> **DIGITAL DIVIDE** the unequal access to computer and internet technology, both globally and within the United States

These disparities mirror the contours of other sorts of social inequality, especially because computer and internet technology access requires resources—funds to purchase computers and subscribe to internet providers. The wealthy and privileged tend to have more of these resources than do the poor or underprivileged.

The digital divide is really about the benefits of technology access rather than merely the access itself. This is because access to computers and the internet offers additional related opportunities and privileges, especially in education and the job market. Sure, everyone deserves the opportunity to play video games, but think of the other things you do with your digital access: you take online classes, utilize job search and résumé-posting services, and develop skills that facilitate recruitment into your chosen career. Without these benefits, certain educational and employment opportunities would be closed to you, no matter how smart or ambitious you might be.

Just as there are digitally disadvantaged groups and individuals domestically, there are digitally disadvantaged countries—the digital divide is global. In underdeveloped and developing nations, real poverty leads to "information poverty" as well (Norris 2001) and creates further obstacles to development—a kind of self-sealing loop. The organization One Laptop Per Child (OLPC) has developed a small, sturdy, low-power portable computer with the goal of distributing the green and yellow machines to children in developing countries such as Uruguay, Cambodia, Peru, and Rwanda. As of early 2011, OLPC had distributed nearly 2 million units to children in more than a dozen nations. OLPC corporate sponsors such as Intel, Google, and eBay recognize the benefits of trying to help the organization bridge the digital divide; indeed, they may be helping to put computers in the hands of kids who will someday grow up to work for them!

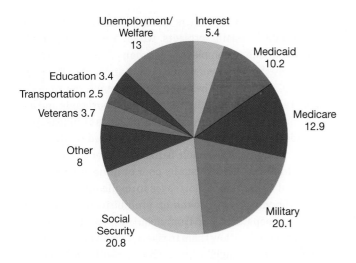

Figure 7.6 Federal Spending, 2011

Spending on welfare and unemployment combined represented just over 13 percent of the 2011 federal budget.

SOURCE: U.S. Government Printing Office 2011.

found that for families leaving welfare, their income rose only incrementally (less than 20 percent), and the impact on the lives of children (school achievement, mental health, etc.) was also only mildly positive (Hao and Cherlin 2004; Slack et al. 2006). So getting off welfare does bring positive results, but often those results aren't strong enough to serve as much of an incentive. It is likely that new policy recommendations will emerge in the future as a result of such research.

Support for a government social safety net to help the poor has waned in the last decade. In 2012, a majority of 59 percent still said that it is the government's responsibility to care for those who cannot care for themselves; this has declined from 63 percent in 2009 and 69 percent in 2007. Just 43 percent of Americans agree that the government should help more needy people, even if it means going deeper in debt, down from 48 percent in 2009 and 54 percent in 2007 (Pew Research Center 2012c). Americans remain conflicted in their opinions about the poor. Overall, 46 percent say that circumstances beyond one's control are more often to blame if a person is poor, while 38 percent say that an individual's lack of effort is more often to blame; 11 percent blame both (Pew Research Center for the People and the Press 2012b). A sizable majority contends that poor people work but are unable to earn enough money; far fewer believe that they do not work.

The "Culture of Poverty" Theory and Its Critics

Some argue that what keeps people poor is not public policy but rather the result of entrenched cultural attitudes. Oscar Lewis (1959) first promoted the idea of a **culture of poverty** after he studied poor Hispanics in Mexico and the United States. Lewis suggested that the poor, because they were excluded from the mainstream, developed a way of life that was qualitatively different from that of middle-class groups and allowed them to cope with the dire circumstance of poverty. This way of life includes attitudes of resignation and fatalism, which lead the poor to accept their fate rather than trying to improve their lot. It also emphasizes immediate gratification, making it difficult for the poor to plan or save for the future or to join trade unions or community groups that might help them improve their situation. Once such a culture is formed, Lewis argued, it takes on a life of its own and is passed on from parents to children, leaving them ill-equipped to change.

The culture of poverty theory was later adopted by other social scientists (Banfield 1970) and applied to the American poor, particularly those in inner cities. Not surprisingly, though, the theory has been met with considerable controversy, in part because it suggests that there is little point in trying to eradicate poverty because it's more a problem of culture (attitudes, lifestyle, and behavior) than of economics. By focusing on individual character and personality, the theory tends to blame the victims of poverty for their own misfortunes while overlooking the force of their social conditions.

CULTURE OF POVERTY
entrenched attitudes that can develop among poor communities and lead the poor to accept their fate rather than attempt to improve their lot

JUST-WORLD HYPOTHESIS
argues that people have a deep need to see the world as orderly, predictable, and fair, which creates a tendency to view victims of social injustice as deserving of their fates

The tendency to see victims of social injustice as deserving of their fates is explained by what social psychologists call the **just-world hypothesis**. According to this argument, we have a strong need to believe that the world is orderly, predictable, and fair in order to achieve our goals in life. When we encounter situations that contradict this belief, we either act quickly to restore justice and order or persuade ourselves that no injustice has occurred. This can result in assuming that the victim has "asked for it" or deserves whatever has befallen her. This attitude is continually reinforced through the morality tales that are a ubiquitous part of our news and entertainment, which tell us that good is rewarded and evil punished (say, in a news story about a homeless man who returns a lost wallet full of cash to its owner, who then shares the money with him).

The just-world hypothesis, developed by Melvin Lerner (1965, 1980), was tested through a series of experiments that documented how people can convince themselves that others deserve what they get. In these experiments, cash prizes were randomly distributed to students completing the exact same tasks in the exact same way. Observers, however, judged the cash recipients as the more deserving, harder workers. Other researchers (Rubin and Peplau 1975) have found that people with strong beliefs in a just world tend to "feel less of a need to engage in activities to change society or to alleviate the plight of social victims." In the face of poverty, many simply become apathetic. It is important to be aware of our own tendencies to follow such thinking, so that we might avoid becoming blind to others' misfortunes.

Another problem with the culture of poverty theory is that it lacks a certain sociological imagination. It fails to take into account the structural factors that shape culture and are part of the preexisting problem in which poor individuals find themselves. Dalton Conley argues that to solve the problem of poverty, we must examine wealth as well (2002). A social system that allows extremes of both wealth and poverty (as ours does) reveals structural reasons why poverty persists, such as laws that protect the inheritances of the wealthy but provide few breaks for working families. Research like Conley's helps us understand that there are alternative explanations for why people are poor and even suggests that extreme wealth ought to be conceptualized as a social problem similar to that of extreme poverty. This idea resonates with the Occupy Movement that emerged during the great recession. Activists question the health of an economic system where just 1 percent of the population has amassed so much of the nation's wealth and power.

RESIDENTIAL SEGREGATION
the geographical separation of the poor from the rest of an area's population

DISENFRANCHISEMENT
the removal of the rights of citizenship through economic, political, or legal means

The Invisibility of Poverty

Although we are used to seeing televised images of abject poverty from overseas—crying children with bloated bellies and spindly limbs in Asia, Africa, or Latin America—we rarely see similar images from the United States. While it may be true that few Americans are as poor as the starving Somalis or Bangladeshis, some 46.2 million Americans lived below the poverty line in 2011 (U.S. Census Bureau 2012f). That's more than 15 percent of the population of the wealthiest nation in the world. How can such large numbers of people remain hidden to their fellow Americans? What makes poverty invisible?

RESIDENTIAL SEGREGATION One factor is **residential segregation**—the geographical isolation of the poor from the rest of the city (or in the case of the rural poor, from any neighbors at all). Such segregation often occurs along racial as well as socioeconomic lines, further exacerbating class divisions (Massey and Denton 1993). In the phrase "wrong side of the tracks," used to describe poverty-stricken neighborhoods, there is usually a racial connotation as well, since railroad tracks traditionally served as boundaries that kept black neighborhoods separated from white ones in the nineteenth century (Ananat 2005).

Residential segregation is accomplished most notably through public housing projects, which are typically high-density apartment complexes in urban areas, funded and managed by the Department of Housing and Urban Development (HUD). Living in these apartment complexes, many of which are in low-income, high-crime neighborhoods and are poorly maintained, can be dangerous as well as unpleasant.

Residential segregation is also exacerbated by the practice of "redlining," in which banks and mortgage lenders identify high-risk areas (usually poor or minority neighborhoods) and either refuse mortgages to applicants from those neighborhoods or offer loans at prohibitively high rates. Redlining keeps the poor from acquiring assets (like real estate) that might allow them to rise out of poverty and move to a more affluent neighborhood. Though redlining is technically illegal, the practice is still in evidence today in banking, insurance, and other industries, disproportionately affecting the poor and minorities (Wilson 2009). In one instance, a major mortgage company, MidAmerica Bank, settled a redlining case in Chicago by agreeing to open more branches in poor and minority neighborhoods and to include poor and minority consumers in their advertising campaigns, which had previously targeted only buyers at higher income levels.

POLITICAL DISENFRANCHISEMENT The poor may remain invisible to the larger society because of their lack of political power as well. **Disenfranchisement** is a correlate of poverty: the poor are less likely to vote or otherwise participate in political life (Kerbo and Gonzalez 2003). When everyday life is a struggle to make ends meet, it is difficult to muster the extra energy necessary to work for political change. The poor may also feel that the system has not served them; if the government ignores their interests, why bother to become involved? Because of their lack of involvement, the poor lack political clout and the resources to make their plight a high-profile political priority. Politicians at the local and national levels have little motivation to address their needs, because as a constituency the poor wield less power than such groups as senior citizens, "soccer moms," and small-business owners. When the poor do organize politically, even their successes may not be well known. One group, Mothers of East Los Angeles (whose motto includes the phrase "not economically rich, but culturally wealthy"), has been successfully protecting its neighborhood from environmental degradation and exploitation for decades. The group has rebuffed plans to build a prison, toxic waste plants, and an oil pipeline near homes and schools in its community. But have you ever heard of it?

High-profile occasions, such as political conventions and major sporting events, put a media spotlight on city streets. In the summer of 2000, for example, on the eve of the Republican National Convention, the city of Philadelphia denied a permit to a group of welfare rights protesters who wanted to demonstrate against government poverty policies. The hope

Residential Segregation
High-density housing projects frequently isolate the poor from the rest of the city.

was that in denying the permit, the group would not make an appearance on streets already crawling with politicians, demonstrators, journalists, and photographers. But the protesters marched anyway—with a police escort—and were able to make their voice heard despite the lack of official permission to do so.

HOMELESSNESS In certain situations, the very poor are deliberately removed from public view. Police are sometimes ordered to scour the streets, rousting the homeless and herding them out of sight, as they did in 1988 in New York City's Tompkins Square Park (an infamous riot ensued).

Mostly, though, the poor and homeless remain invisible. We don't know exactly how many homeless live in the United States. The Census Bureau focuses its population counts on households, so the homeless living in long-term shelters may get counted, but not those on the streets. One recent estimate is that more than 3.5 million people (approximately 1 percent of the U.S. population) will experience homelessness at least once during a given year (National Law Center on Homelessness and Poverty 2010). The recession that started in 2008 and has continued during the past several years has left many people unemployed and their finances drained, creating a surge in homelessness that includes many who were formerly among the middle classes. "Nationally, homelessness has now reached crisis proportions not seen since the Great Depression," says Maria Foscarinis, executive director of the National Law Center on Homelessness and Poverty (Goodman 2010).

Each year, the city of New York attempts to measure the number of homeless men and women. Volunteers comb the streets in the overnight hours, making note of all those they find sleeping on park benches or in building stairwells. They do not, however, enter abandoned buildings or subway tunnels, where many of New York's homeless seek shelter. The 2010 count of homeless found a 34 percent increase in people living on the city's streets versus the previous year (3,111 in 2009 compared with 2,328 in 2008), along with another 38,000 living in shelters (Bosman 2010). Although this is sometimes a difficult population to locate and there may be questions about the accuracy of reports, such counts help the city estimate its needs for homeless services in the coming year.

The homeless also remain invisible to most of us because of our own feelings of discomfort and guilt. John Coleman, a former college president and business executive, discovered this when he lived in poverty, if only temporarily, on the streets of Manhattan. Coleman went "undercover" as a homeless man for ten days and found that the minute he shed his privileged identity, people looked at him differently—or not at all. During his days on the streets, Coleman passed by and made eye contact with his accountant, his landlord, and a co-worker—each looked right through him, without recognition. But he was not invisible to everyone. Police officers often shook him awake to get him moving from whatever meager shelter he had found for the night. A waiter at a diner took one look at him and forced him to pay up front for his 99-cent breakfast special. Other homeless men, though, showed him kindness and generosity (Coleman 1983).

To whom are the poor visible? Those who work with them: caseworkers, social service providers, government bureaucrats, volunteers and charity workers, clergy, cops, business owners (including those who may not want to deal with the poor, as well as those who may exploit them). And now, you.

With a sociological perspective, you can now see the effects of social stratification everywhere you turn. And when you recognize the multiple, complex causes of poverty—such as limited educational and job opportunities, stagnating wages, economic downturns, racism, mental illness, and substance

Counting the Homeless Two volunteers speak with a homeless man on a subway for the all-night Homeless Outreach Population Estimate (HOPE), run by the Department of Homeless Services in New York City. The goal is to obtain a city-wide estimate of individuals living on the street in order to help the government provide better services and resources for the homeless population.

abuse—it will no longer be as simple to consider each individual responsible for his or her own plight. Finally, the sociological perspective will give you the ability to imagine possible solutions to the problems associated with poverty—solutions that focus on large-scale social changes as well as individual actions, including your own. Don't let poverty remain invisible.

Inequality and the Ideology of the American Dream

Ask almost anyone about the American Dream and they are likely to mention some of the following: owning your own home; having a good marriage and great kids; finding a good job that you enjoy; being able to afford nice vacations; having a big-screen TV, nice clothes, or season tickets to your team's home games. For most Americans, the dream also means that all people, no matter how humble their beginnings, can succeed in whatever they set out to do if they work hard enough. In other words, a poor boy or girl could grow up to become president of the United States, an astronaut, a professional basketball player, a captain of industry, or a movie star.

MERITOCRACY a system in which rewards are distributed based on merit

One problem with the American Dream, however, is that it doesn't always match reality. It's more of an ideology: a belief system that explains and justifies some sort of social arrangement, in this case America's social class hierarchy. The ideology of the American Dream legitimizes stratification by reinforcing the idea that everyone has the same chance to get ahead and that success or failure depends on the person (Hochschild 1996). Inequality is presented as a system of incentives and rewards for achievement. If we can credit anyone who does succeed, then logically we must also blame anyone who fails. The well-socialized American buys into this belief system, without recognizing its structural flaws. We are caught in what Marx would call "false consciousness," the inability to see the ways in which we may be oppressed.

Nevertheless, it's not easy to dismiss the idea of the American Dream, especially when there are so many high-profile examples. Take, for instance, Oprah Winfrey. Born in Mississippi in 1954, Winfrey endured a childhood of abject poverty. In 2011, *Forbes* magazine listed her as number 139 of the 400 richest Americans, a ranking she has climbed to over a period of years, with a likewise impressive personal wealth of $2.7 billion. Not only is Winfrey the highest-paid black female, but she is also one of the highest-paid entertainers of all time. In 2010, *Forbes* honored her as the world's most powerful celebrity (of 100), based on a composite that included earnings ($165 million that year) and dominance across various media. In that same year, Oprah Winfrey launched her own independent cable network—the Oprah Winfrey Network or OWN. The accolades and awards span many categories. Not only is she extremely successful as a media mogul and personality, but Winfrey is also widely praised for her philanthropic efforts and is admired as a symbol of what can be achieved in pursuit of the American Dream. The problem is, we tend to think of her as representing the rule rather than the exception. For most Americans, the rags-to-riches upward mobility she has achieved is very unrealistic.

Though popular opinion and rhetoric espouse the American Dream ideology or that the United States is a **meritocracy** (a system in which rewards are distributed based on merit), sociologists find contrary evidence. In fact, no matter how hard they work or if they seek a good education, most people will make little movement at all. And the degree of

The American Dream Oprah Winfrey's meteoric rise from a childhood of poverty to her position as one of the most powerful celebrities in America is often cited as a prime example of the American Dream. How does Oprah's success represent the exception rather than the rule?

mobility they do achieve can depend on a person's ethnicity, class status, or gender rather than merit. For example, whites are more likely to experience upward mobility than persons of color (Davis 1995; Mazumder 2012), and married women are more likely to experience upward mobility than nonmarried women (Li and Singelmann 1998). Immigrant persons of color are the most likely to experience downward social mobility (McCall 2001). It is also harder for those who start at the bottom of the class ladder to rise up the ranks (DeParle 2012).

A poll of the Millennial generation (Americans ages eighteen to twenty-four) conducted in 2012 defined the American Dream as "If you work hard, you will get ahead." Survey results were split; 40 percent of young Millennials believe the American Dream still exists, while 45 percent believe it "once held true, but not anymore"; and another 10 percent said it has never existed (Jones, Cox, & Banchoff 2012). The numbers shift when broken down by such background factors as income, education, and race of the respondent (Bailey 2010). People with annual household incomes above $75,000 were more likely to believe in the dream (57 percent) than those making less than $25,000 per year (46 percent). More college graduates (58 percent) believe in the American Dream than those with just a high school education (48 percent). More nonwhites believe in it (57 percent) than whites (48 percent).

Although the American Dream tends to promote consumerism as a way to achieve "the good life," the fact is that chasing after it has left us feeling less secure and satisfied—not to mention less wealthy—than previous generations (De Graaf et al. 2002). Some pundits suggest that we have lost focus on the original meaning of the American Dream, that our increasing obsession with the idea of "more (or newer or bigger) is better" is leading to more debt, less free time, and greater discontent. Americans now carry twice as much credit card debt than they did in 1990 (Walker 2004). In 2009, the average credit card debt hit a high of $5,719; by 2012, credit card holders had lowered their average balance owed to $4,971 (Veiga 2012). An Ohio State University study reported that Americans have less free time and feel more rushed than they did thirty years ago (Sayer and Mattingly 2006).

A countervailing trend in American life, however, sometimes referred to as the **simplicity movement**, rejects rampant consumerism and seeks to reverse some of its consequences for the individual, for society, and for the planet. This movement, a backlash against the traditional American Dream, encourages people to "downshift" by working less, earning less, and spending less in order to put their lifestyles in sync with their (nonmaterialistic) values (Schor 1999). What does this mean in practice? Growing your own vegetables, perhaps, or riding your bike to work, wearing secondhand clothes, and spending more time with friends and family and less time commuting, shopping, or watching TV.

SIMPLICITY MOVEMENT a loosely knit movement that opposes consumerism and encourages people to work less, earn less, and spend less, in accordance with nonmaterialistic values

One of the most radical extensions of this philosophy is embraced by "freegans"—a term that merges "free" with "vegan" (a person who eats no animal products). Freegans are people who avoid consumerism and who engage in strategies to support themselves without participating in a conventional economic system. This can mean scavenging for usable food, clothing, and other goods, sometimes called "urban foraging" or "dumpster diving," along with sharing housing and transportation with others in order to work less and minimize their impact on the planet.

DATA WORKSHOP
Analyzing Mass Media and Popular Culture

Advertising and the American Dream

We are surrounded by advertising, which aims not only to give us information about products but also to create and stimulate a buying public with demands for an ever-increasing array of goods and services. Advertising shapes

IN THE FUTURE

Young Americans: Generation Screwed?

Nikita and Parissah, both eighteen, and Jack, nineteen, are college students. They anticipate being in debt by the time they graduate, though they do not foresee getting the kinds of good paying jobs their education should secure. Twenty-two-year-old Kate is a teacher, and twenty-nine-year-old Chayanne a university employee; they are both college students as well, trying to work and at the same time finish up their degrees. For Chayanne, things are tough; each day is a battle. Kate accepts that she will never do better than her parents. Elena, twenty-five, studied sociology, something she says was great for her brain but which has not so far led to a full-time job. Blanca, a lawyer, and Peter, a medical sales rep, are both thirty years old and refer to themselves as over-educated. Yet it took years before either could find gainful employment in their fields. Saeed, twenty-nine, quit high school and went to work at a grocery store while his college-bound friends ended up with what he calls lousy jobs anyway.

What do all these young people have in common? They are members of what's often called the Millennial generation, or alternately Generation Y—Americans under thirty-five years old, born roughly between the early 1980s and 2000. Lately they've been called other things as well, the least heartening of which might be "Generation Screwed." They are unlike other contemporary generations before them. The Millennials are entering the world of work and finance at a particularly challenging time that looks much less favorable to their generation. Their predominantly Boomer (and some Gen-X) parents started out as adults under much different, and much better, economic conditions. The current economic conditions were not created by the Millennials themselves, but it is what they are inheriting. To what extent the American economy may be recovering is still being determined, but the hurt from a prolonged downturn has inflicted significant, long-term wounds. The economy has undergone profound and lasting changes that are threatening the future prospects of this large group of approximately 80 million. They are at risk of losing in pursuit of an American Dream that their parents and grandparents before them could reasonably believe in, if not outright presume, for themselves.

So in just what ways are the Millennials screwed compared to previous generations? The widest wealth gap in history divides the young from the old. The net worth of households headed by sixty-five-year-olds rose more than 40 percent in the last twenty-five years; conversely, the net worth of younger households fell almost 70 percent. The Millennials suffered disproportionately during the recent recession and beyond. In 2012, the unemployment rate for people under thirty years of age was 50 percent higher than the national average (Kotkin 2012). And many older people who would have been retiring could not afford to leave the work force either, compounding problems of a tight job market. While a higher level of educational attainment usually translates to a higher income, the Millennials have seen their income drop by 11 percent in the past decade. Does a college education that continues to rise in cost actually pay off when more than 40 percent of recent graduates are working at jobs that don't require a college degree? And what about the debt that Millennials are carrying, from student loans as well as credit cards?

All this leaves many young people wondering and worrying about their prospects for the future. Will they be the first generation that ends up being downwardly mobile from their parents? A majority of Millennials already say that they do not expect to do as well as their parents financially. And it's affecting some major life decisions and delaying their entry into adulthood. One quarter of people between eighteen and thirty-four have moved back in with their parents, and almost one third have put off marriage or starting a family. The idea of homeownership, so central to the American Dream, may also be out of reach. The Millennials are growing up at a time that does not favor their collective success. When the aspirations of an entire generation are thwarted, it hurts not just them, but the whole country. What will be the larger repercussions of a "Generation Screwed?"

our consciousness and tells us what to dream and how to pursue those dreams. It provides us with a concept of the good life and tells us that it's available to everyone. Advertising equates shopping and acquisition with emotional fulfillment, freedom, fun, happiness, security, and self-satisfaction.

And the sales pitch seems to be working. Like no other generation, today's eighteen- to thirty-four-year-olds have grown up in a consumer culture with all its varied enticements, but they are having a harder time reaching financial stability in adulthood than did their parents. Tamara Draut (2006) describes their predicament in her book *Strapped: Why America's 20- and 30-Somethings Can't Get Ahead.* Many young people are finding themselves caught in a difficult job market where wages have declined at the same time they are carrying larger college loans and mounting credit card debt. Draut is critical of the credit card industry, which she claims is designed to keep people in debt. Many young people have embraced easy credit only to discover that late payment fees and high interest rates can keep them from paying down their balances. While some may be spending on luxuries like fancy clothes or restaurant meals, high-tech toys, and new cars that they really can't afford, many young people are using credit cards for basic household needs and expenses, such as prescription medications and car repairs. Almost two-thirds of young people are in debt: on average, their college loan debt is $26,600 (The Institute for College Access & Success 2012), revolving (credit card) debt is $3,173, and installment (car loans) debt is $17,208 (Fetterman and Hansen 2006; Credit.com 2011). Some are slipping into a troubling downward financial spiral. About 15 to 20 percent of all young adults are in debt hardship, where monthly debt payments reach 40 percent or more of household income, and they have the second-highest rates of bankruptcy of any age group (Draut and Silva 2004). So let's examine where some of this pressure to spend comes from—advertising.

In this Data Workshop, you will evaluate some advertisements in terms of the ideology of the American Dream. You will use existing sources to do a content analysis of the ads (see Chapter 2 for a review of the research method). To start your research, find three or more ads from magazines, newspapers, web sites, or other sources. Look for ads that are of interest to your particular age group or that are selling the idea of the "good life."

Consider the following questions for each ad.

* For whom is the message intended?

* What product or service is being advertised?

* In addition to a product or service, what else are the advertisers trying to sell?

* How does the message make you feel? Does it play on your emotions or sense of self-worth? If so, in what ways?

* Does the ad "work"? Would you like to buy the product? Why or why not?

More generally:

* How does advertising affect your life and buying habits?

* What ads have a strong effect on you? Why?

* What is the lure of shopping and material possessions?

* What kinds of pressures do you feel to keep up with the material possessions of your friends, neighbors, or co-workers?

There are two options for completing this Data Workshop.

Option 1 (informal): Bring your ads to class, and discuss your answers to the questions with other students in small groups. Compare and contrast each other's contributions.

Option 2 (formal): Write a three- to four-page essay discussing your general thoughts on consumption and the American Dream. Apply these thoughts to your analysis of about the specific ads you chose.

CLOSING COMMENTS

Social stratification is all about power. Stratification systems, like SES, allocate different types of social power, such as wealth, political influence, and occupational prestige, and do so in fundamentally unequal ways. These inequalities are part of both the larger social structure and our everyday interactions. In the following chapters, we will examine other systems of stratification, namely, race and ethnicity, and sex, gender, and sexual orientation. While we separate these topics for organizational purposes, they are not experienced as separate in our everyday lives. We are women or men, working class or upper class, black or white, gay or straight simultaneously. Our experiences of these social categories are intertwined.

Everything You Need to Know about
Social Stratification

> " Social stratification is present in all societies. People are categorized and divided into groups, including gender, race, class, and age, which are then placed in a social hierarchy. "

THEORIES OF SOCIAL CLASS

* **Conflict:** social classes are highly stratified and continue to grow further apart

* **Weberian:** wealth, power, and prestige are interrelated, but one can also be converted into another

* **Structural functionalism:** stratification is necessary for society to function

* **Postmodernism:** social class is passed down from one generation to the next through cultural capital

* **Symbolic interactionism:** we judge people's social class constantly during everyday interactions

REVIEW

1. Think about your own class status. Is it consistent across the criteria that make up socioeconomic status (income, wealth, education, occupation, and power)? Or are you an example of status inconsistency?

2. According to Pierre Bourdieu, the cultural tools we inherit from our parents can be very important in trying to gain economic assets. What sort of cultural capital did you inherit? Has it ever helped you materially? Have you ever done something to acquire more cultural capital?

3. Erving Goffman says we "read" other people through social interaction to get a sense of their class status. What sort of clues can tell you about a person's social class within thirty seconds of meeting that person?

How Rich Are You?

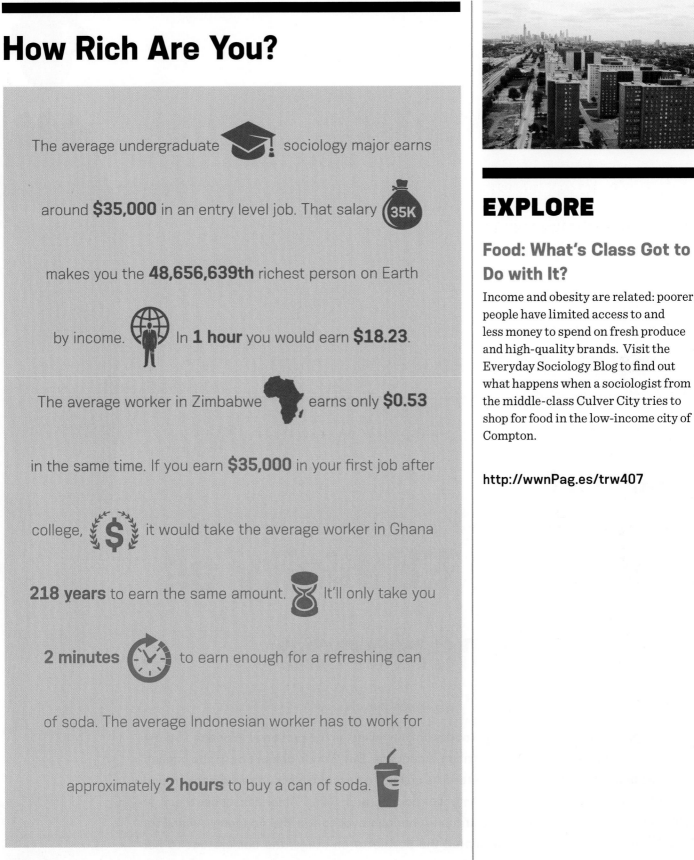

The average undergraduate sociology major earns around **$35,000** in an entry level job. That salary makes you the **48,656,639th** richest person on Earth by income. In **1 hour** you would earn **$18.23**.

The average worker in Zimbabwe earns only **$0.53** in the same time. If you earn **$35,000** in your first job after college, it would take the average worker in Ghana **218 years** to earn the same amount. It'll only take you **2 minutes** to earn enough for a refreshing can of soda. The average Indonesian worker has to work for approximately **2 hours** to buy a can of soda.

SOURCE: Poke 2013

EXPLORE

Food: What's Class Got to Do with It?

Income and obesity are related: poorer people have limited access to and less money to spend on fresh produce and high-quality brands. Visit the Everyday Sociology Blog to find out what happens when a sociologist from the middle-class Culver City tries to shop for food in the low-income city of Compton.

http://wwnPag.es/trw407

CHAPTER 8

Race and Ethnicity as Lived Experience

Despite recent scandal, Tiger Woods is often hailed as the person who opened up the field of professional golf to African Americans. But Woods doesn't describe himself as black: he's "Cablinasian," a term he coined to describe his multiracial background (which includes Caucasian, black, American Indian, and Asian American ancestries). In 2002, Halle Berry became the first African American ever to win the Academy Award for Best Actress. As she tearfully accepted the statuette on stage, the camera cut to her mother sitting in the audience, beaming with pride at her daughter's accomplishment—and unmistakably white. Former *American Idol* and *X-Factor* judge Paula Abdul, commonly

thought to be African American, is actually of Syrian, Jewish, Brazilian, and French-Canadian descent. And *Parks and Recreation*'s light-skinned, straight-haired Rashida Jones is black, Russian-Jewish, Irish, Portugese and Cherokee. "In the next 50 years," Jones says, "people will start looking more and more like me" (Melnick 2011).

She's right. Despite America's record of racial discrimination and segregation, there have always been multiracial people in its history, beginning with the European settlers who mixed with Native Americans and black slaves alike (Clinton and Gillespie 1997; Brooks 2002). More and more, we are recognizing and celebrating our multiracial heritage. In 2000, the Census Bureau gave Americans the opportunity for the first time to check multiple boxes to identify their race, thus creating sixty-three different racial categories. Approximately 7 million, or 2.4 percent of the population, took advantage of the new option. Ten years later, the 2010 Census reported that approximately 9 million Americans, or 2.9 percent of the population, identified themselves as belonging to more than one racial category, a 32 percent increase from 2000. The number identifying themselves as multiracial will only continue to grow, according to the bureau: by 2050, the population of multiracial identities will double to about 16 million. As the United States is a nation of immigrants (some involuntary), it is only logical that the separate lineages of the American population would eventually meld. We might, therefore, wonder: will race continue to be as important in the future as it has been in the past? In this chapter, we will examine the sociological understandings of race, which will provide us with the insights we need to answer this question.

HOW TO READ THIS CHAPTER

Our goal in this chapter is for you to acquire a fundamental understanding of race and ethnicity as socially constructed categories. While each is based on traits we may see as biological, such as skin color or facial features, the meanings attached to race and ethnicity are created, maintained, and modified over time through social processes in which we all take part.

When a society categorizes people based on their race and ethnicity (and all societies do), it creates a system of stratification that leads to inequality. Society's resources—wealth, power, privilege, opportunity—are distributed according to these categories, and this perpetuates inequalities that are all too familiar here in the United States. We also hope you will come to understand the importance of race and ethnicity in forming individual identity. Our racial and ethnic identities have profound effects on our sense of self, and our bonds to other people may be based on shared identities—or may transcend those categories entirely.

Defining Race and Ethnicity

"Race" and "ethnicity" are words we use so often in everyday speech that we might not think we need a definition of either. But people tend to use the words interchangeably, as if they mean essentially the same thing. There is, however, a significant difference between commonsense notions of race and ethnicity and what social scientists have to say about them.

The idea of different races as belonging to distinguishable categories has existed for hundreds of years. In the nineteenth century, biologists came up with a schema that grouped humans into three races: Negroid, Mongoloid, and Caucasoid (corresponding roughly to black, Asian, and white). It was believed that each race was characterized by its own biological makeup, separate and distinct from the others. Modern scientists, however, possess advanced tools for examining race in a much more sophisticated way. What they have found, ironically, is that there are no "pure" races, that the lines between races are blurry rather than fixed. A person who looks white will inevitably have biological material from other races, as will someone who looks black.

There is also no such thing as a "superior" race, as race itself is not the reason that different groups might display positive or negative characteristics (such as intelligence, athleticism, or artistic ability). Furthermore, there is greater genetic diversity *within* racial populations than between them. So within the Asian population, members differ more from each other (Koreans from Chinese, for example) than they do from whites. From a biological standpoint, the differ-

Can You Tell a Person's Race by Looking? Actress Rashida Jones, daughter of (black) producer Quincy Jones.

ence between someone with type O blood and someone with type A blood is much more significant than the differences between a dark-skinned and a light-skinned person. And yet blood types have no correlation to race at all.

New genetic testing technologies seem to hold out the prospect of accurately identifying biological differences between racial groups—some "ancestry testing" services purport to be able to identify clients' genetic and geographic origins down to the region, village, or tribe. However precise or imprecise such conclusions may be, they overlook the fact that all humans, whatever racial categories they seem to inhabit, are 99.9 percent genetically identical. And of that remaining 0.1 percent of our genetic material, only 15 percent of its variation occurs between geographically distinct groups. In other words, there's not enough "wiggle room" in the human genome for race to be a genetic trait (*Harvard Magazine* 2008).

Sociologists, then, have come to understand **race** as a social category, based on real or perceived biological differences between groups of people. Race is more meaningful to us on a social level than it is on a biological level (Montagu 1998). Actress Rashida Jones may "look white" to many, but in some Southern states in 1925, she could just as easily have been considered black or Native American. Does knowing

> **RACE** a socially defined category based on real or perceived biological differences between groups of people

ETHNICITY a socially defined category based on common language, religion, nationality, history, or another cultural factor

SYMBOLIC ETHNICITY an ethnic identity that is only relevant on specific occasions and does not significantly impact everyday life

SITUATIONAL ETHNICITY an ethnic identity that can be either displayed or concealed depending on its usefulness in a given situation

Jones's racial background now make you think of her in a different way?

Ethnicity is another social category that is applied to a group with a shared ancestry or cultural heritage. The Amish, for instance, are a distinct ethnic group in American society, linked by a common heritage that includes language, religion, and history; the Amish people, with few exceptions, are also white. The Jewish people, on the other hand, contrary to what the Nazis and other white supremacists may believe, are an ethnic group but not a race. The stereotypical image is challenged when we see a blond, blue-eyed Jew from Scandinavia or a black Ethiopian Jew.

As an example of the social construction of race and ethnicity, let's look at the evidence documenting the historical changes in the boundaries of the category "white." In the early 1900s, native-born Americans, who were frequently Protestant, did not consider recent Irish, Italian, or Jewish immigrants to be white and restricted where these groups could live and work (Ignatiev 1996; Brodkin 1999). Such housing discrimination forced new immigrants to cluster in urban neighborhoods or "ghettos." After World War II, however, as the second generation of Irish, Italian, and Jewish immigrants reached adulthood, the importance of ethnic

identity declined and skin color became the main way to differentiate between who was white and who was not. Today, the question is whether people of Middle Eastern descent are white. In the post–September 11 climate, Arabs and Muslims have been identified as racially and ethnically distinct in significant and even harmful ways. While these groups possess a range of skin colors and facial features, it may be their symbolic labeling in these difficult times that makes them "nonwhite."

"Ethnic Options": Symbolic and Situational Ethnicity

How do we display our racial and ethnic group membership? We may do so in a number of ways: through dress, language, food, religious practices, preferences in music, art, or literature, even the projects we find interesting and the topics we pursue at school. Sometimes, these practices make our group membership obvious to others; sometimes, they don't. White ethnics like Irish Americans and Italian Americans, for example, can actually choose when and how they display their ethnic group membership.

One way group membership is displayed is through **symbolic ethnicity**, enactments of ethnic identity that occur only on special occasions. For example, most Irish Americans have been so fully assimilated for multiple generations that their Irish ancestry may not matter much to them on a daily basis. But on St. Patrick's Day (especially in cities like Boston and New York), displays of Irish identity can be pretty overwhelming! Parades, hats, "Kiss me, I'm Irish" buttons,

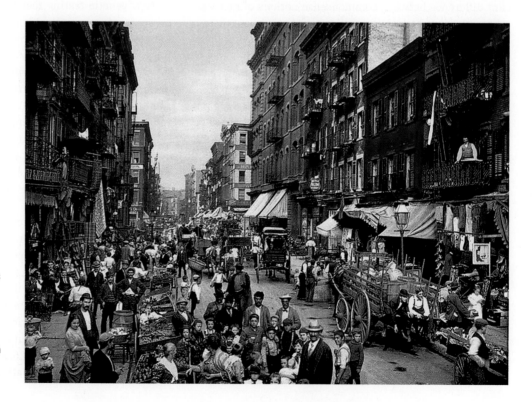

Mulberry Street at the Turn of the Century In the early 1900s, Irish, Italian, and Jewish immigrants were not considered "whites." Because of residential segregation, new immigrants poured into densely populated neighborhoods like this one on New York's Lower East Side, where they had little choice but to live in squalid tenements and work in sweatshops.

Ethnic Options We can display group membership by embracing ethnic identity on special occasions like St. Patrick's Day or Cinco de Mayo.

green clothing, green beer (and in Chicago, a green river!), corned beef and cabbage—all are elements of symbolic ethnicity. Similar ethnic displays occur on such holidays as Passover, Cinco de Mayo, and Nouruz.

Another way we can show group membership is through **situational ethnicity**, when we deliberately assert our ethnicity in some situations while downplaying it in others. Situational ethnicity involves a kind of cost-benefit analysis that symbolic ethnicity does not: we need to appraise each situation to determine whether or not it favors our ethnicity. For example, Dr. Ferris's Lebanese ancestry never mattered much, outside her own family, when she lived in Southern California. In fact, it was often something she felt she should downplay, given a political climate in which people of Arabic background were sometimes viewed with suspicion. But when she moved to Peoria, Illinois, she discovered that this small city had a relatively large population of Lebanese descent and that the mayor, a city councilman, the state senator, the congressman, local business, arts, and religious leaders, and prominent families were all Lebanese. This suddenly made Dr. Ferris's ethnicity a valuable asset in a way that it had never been before. She received a good deal of social support and made new friends based on shared revelations of ethnic group membership. In the case of situational ethnicity, we see how larger social forces can govern the identities we choose—if we have a choice.

Neither situational nor symbolic ethnicity is available to those who are visibly nonmainstream, whatever that may look like in a given society. In the United States, this generally means that nonwhites find themselves in fewer situa-

tions where they have a choice about whether to display their group membership (although this may eventually change as we become a "majority minority" nation). As sociologist Mary Waters says, "The social and political consequences of being Asian or Hispanic or black are not, for the most part, symbolic, nor are they voluntary. They are real, unavoidable, and sometimes hurtful" (1990, p. 156).

DATA WORKSHOP
Analyzing Everyday Life

Doing Symbolic Ethnicity

Choose a setting where you can watch people "doing" ethnicity. For instance, you can go to a St. Patrick's Day parade, if your city hosts one, or attend an ethnic festival of some sort (such as St. Anthony's Feast Day in Boston's Italian North End or Los Angeles's annual African Marketplace). Or just visit one of your city's ethnic neighborhoods: stroll through an Italian market in South Philadelphia, or shop the streets

GLOBAL PERSPECTIVE

Heritage Tourism: Getting in Touch with Our Roots

As global travel becomes easier, faster, and more affordable, a phenomenon called "heritage tourism" has been on the rise. Heritage tourism is related to the idea of the pilgrimage—a journey to a geographical location of significance to one's religion. Examples of traditional pilgrimages include the *hajj*, an excursion to Mecca in Saudi Arabia, which is required of all Muslims once in their lifetime. Catholics may travel to the Vatican or to other important sites, such as the grotto and sanctuary at Lourdes in France or the Cathedral of Santiago de Compostela in Spain. But heritage tourism is less about religion and more about the cultural legacies of different racial and ethnic groups. Members of racial and ethnic groups who now live outside the countries of their ancestors (such as African Americans or Irish Americans) are sometimes attracted by the possibility of traveling to the "old country," and tourism ministries worldwide market their countries and cultures as must-see places for members of the diaspora—displaced peoples who may have emigrated generations ago. Here are a few examples of heritage tourism campaigns from around the world:

Ireland

The U.S. Census reports that approximately 11 percent of the American population—or almost 35 million people—claimed Irish heritage in 2010 (U. S. Census Bureau 2012g). That's a lot of potential tourists from America (over seven times the population of Ireland itself), and the official Irish tourist bureau caters specifically to those who wish to investigate their Irish ancestry. The tourism industry in Ireland encourages people of Irish descent to take tours that trace their family's heritage. The tourism office, in association with the Irish Genealogical Project, entices travelers to visit Irish Family History Foundation Centres around the country and promises "a personal and emotional journey . . . of discovery" as travelers discover the roots of their family trees.

Israel

For many contemporary Jews, their Jewish identity is as much ethnic as it is religious, and the existence of a Jewish state may have an impact on their travel plans. For example, Israel's Ministry of Tourism encourages American Jewish families to consider traveling to Israel for their children's Bar or Bat Mitzvah celebrations. Ceremonies can be held at any of a number of well-known historical locations, such as the Western Wall or the Masada, and Bar or Bat Mitzvah visitors may also tour the important religious, cultural, and political sites of Jerusalem as part of their holiday. Parents and politicians alike hope that vacations such as these will strengthen the children's connection to their Jewish heritage and begin a process of attachment to Israel itself that may ultimately lead to "making *aliyah*," or moving there permanently.

Ghana

Because of the historical brutalities of slavery, it is often difficult for African Americans to pinpoint their cities or countries of ancestral origin—but since most African slaves were taken from West Africa, some countries in that region have begun exploring the touristic implications of slavery's tragic legacy. Ghanaian tourism officials, for example, want the far-flung "diasporan" descendants of American, European, and Caribbean slaves to think of Africa as home and to consider making a pilgrimage to the land of their ancestors. They offer tours that focus on slave-trade sites, like the forts in which newly enslaved Africans were imprisoned before being shipped to the New World (which most visitors find both deeply moving and disturbing). But they also entertain visitors and educate them about Ghanaian culture and customs with colorful festivals, dancing, and feasting. Ghanaian officials hope that some visitors will choose to make Ghana their permanent home, offering special visas for diasporans to make it easy to travel to and from the homeland.

of Chicago's Ukrainian Village, Greektown, or Pilsen (a Mexican American neighborhood). If you think your town is too tiny to have any ethnic diversity, think again: even minuscule Postville, Iowa (population 2,200), includes a large Hasidic Jewish population, with significant clusters of Mexican, Guatemalan, Ukrainian, Nigerian, Bosnian, and Czech immigrants. You may even find an appropriate setting on your college campus or at one of your own family gatherings.

For this Data Workshop you will be using ethnographic methods and doing participant observation (see Chapter 2 for a review). Once you have chosen a setting, join in the activities around you while at the same time carefully observing how the other participants display their ethnic membership. As part of your observation, consider the following.

* What are participants wearing: traditional ethnic costumes, contemporary T-shirts, other symbols displaying their ethnic identity?

* What kind of music is being played, and what types of foods or crafts are available?

* Are different languages being spoken? If so, by whom and in what situations?

* What are the differences in the activities of adults and children, men and women, members and visitors?

* Listen for snatches of conversation in which members explain such traditions as buying a goldfish on the first day of spring (Iranian), wrapping and tying a tamale (Mexican), or wearing the claddagh ring (Irish).

Finally, ask yourself the same questions about your own ethnic identity as you did about the people you observed. Do you have the option to display your ethnicity in some situations and withhold it in others? Why or why not? How do you decide whether/when/how to do this? What kind of cost-benefit analysis do you use? What role do ethnic and racial stereotypes play in this process? And how are these displays received by others? There are two options for completing this Data Workshop.

Option 1 (informal): Prepare written notes about your field work that you can refer to in class. Discuss your experience with other students in a small group. Consider all the questions and points above.

Option 2 (formal): Write a three- to four-page essay describing your observations and answering the questions in this workshop.

What Is a Minority?

A minority is commonly thought of as a group that's smaller in numbers than the dominant group. Thus, most Americans would say that in the United States, whites are a majority while African Americans, Asians, Hispanics/Latinos, and Native Americans are minorities, because whites outnumber each of these other groups. Figure 8.1 shows the breakdown of various racial and ethnic groups, and their percentage of the U.S. population. But numbers don't tell the whole story. In South

Africa, for instance, blacks dramatically outnumber whites by a ratio of seven to one, yet before the 1994 election of President Nelson Mandela, whites controlled the country while blacks occupied the lowest status in that society. California provides us with a different kind of example. In 2005, the Census Bureau reported that whites made up less than 45 percent of the state's population, whereas other ethnic groups (Hispanics, African Americans, Asian Americans, Native Americans) when added together constituted a majority of 56 percent (Longley 2005). California, then, is technically a "majority minority" state: whites are less than half the population but still remain the dominant group in terms of power, resources, and representation in social institutions (Hawaii, Texas, and New Mexico are also "majority minority" states, as well as the District of Columbia). Hispanics/Latinos continue to be underrepresented in the University of California system (as both students and faculty) as well as in the state government and as business owners, but overrepresented in prisons, in poverty counts, and as victims of violent crimes.

As sociologists, then, we must recognize that minority status is not just about numbers—it's about social inequalities. Sociologists define a **minority group** as people who are recognized as belonging to a social category (here either a racial or an ethnic group) and who suffer from unequal

MINORITY GROUP social group that is systematically denied the same access to power and resources available to society's dominant groups though they are not necessarily fewer in number than the dominant groups

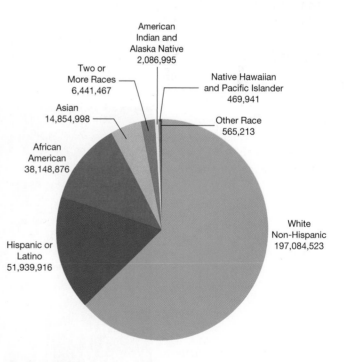

American Indian and Alaska Native
2,086,995

Two or More Races
6,441,467

Native Hawaiian and Pacific Islander
469,941

Asian
14,854,998

Other Race
565,213

African American
38,148,876

Hispanic or Latino
51,939,916

White Non-Hispanic
197,084,523

Figure 8.1 Racial and Ethnic Populations in America

Although a majority of the U.S. population is white, the percentage is declining rapidly.

SOURCE: U.S. Census Bureau 2011a.

RACISM a set of beliefs about the superiority of one racial or ethnic group; used to justify inequality and often rooted in the assumption that differences between groups are genetic

PREJUDICE an idea about the characteristics of a group that is applied to all members of that group and is unlikely to change regardless of the evidence against it

DISCRIMINATION unequal treatment of individuals based on their membership in a social group; usually motivated by prejudice

treatment as a result of that status. A minority group is denied the access to power and resources generally accorded to others in the dominant groups. Members of a minority group are likely to perceive themselves as targets of collective discrimination (Wirth 1945).

Membership in a minority group may serve as a kind of "master status," overriding any other status, such as gender or age. Members may be subjected to racist beliefs about the group as a whole and thus suffer from a range of social disadvantages. Unequal and unfair treatment, as well as lack of access to power and resources, typically generates a strong sense of common identity and solidarity among members of minority groups. Perhaps because of this sense of identification, minorities also tend to practice high rates of in-group marriage (endogamy), although the percentage of mixed-race couples in America continues to grow.

Racism, Prejudice, and Discrimination

In order for social inequality to persist, the unequal treatment that minority groups suffer must be supported by the dominant groups. **Racism**, an ideology or set of beliefs

about the superiority of one racial or ethnic group over another, provides this support; it is used to justify social arrangements between the dominant and minority groups. Racist beliefs are often rooted in the assumption that differences between groups are innate, or biologically based. They can also arise from a negative view of a group's cultural characteristics. In both cases, racism presumes that one group is better than another.

Prejudice and discrimination are closely related to racism, and though the terms are often used interchangeably, there are important distinctions between them. **Prejudice**, literally a "prejudgment," is an inflexible attitude (usually negative, although it can work in the reverse) about a particular group of people and is rooted in generalizations or stereotypes. Examples of prejudice include opinions like "All Irish are drunks" or "All Mexicans are lazy." Prejudice often, though not always, leads to **discrimination**: an action or behavior that results in the unequal treatment of individuals because of their membership in a certain racial or ethnic group. A person might be said to suffer discrimination if she is turned down for a job promotion or a home loan because she's black or Hispanic.

It is possible, though unlikely, that a person can be prejudiced and still not discriminate against others. For example, a teacher can believe that Asian American students are better at math and science, yet deliberately not let this belief influence his grading of Asian American students. Conversely, a person may not be prejudiced at all but still unknowingly participate in discrimination. For instance, a small child can innocently use the racist terminology she learns from her parents even though she herself holds no racist views. And prejudice and discrimination don't always flow from the dominant group toward minorities. The 2008

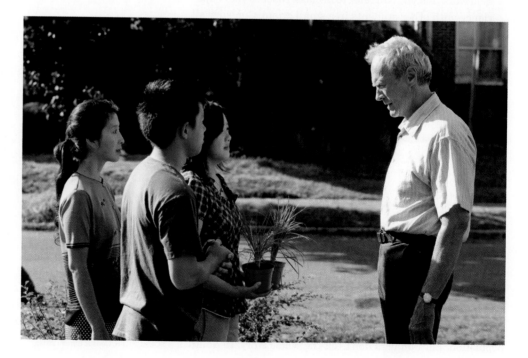

In the Film *Gran Torino,* both Clint Eastwood's white character and his Hmong neighbors draw conclusions about each other based on race.

film *Gran Torino* features Clint Eastwood as a crotchety old man with prejudices against his Italian barber, Irish construction workers, black street kids, and Asian neighbors. But in an interesting turn of storytelling, the prejudice goes both ways: for example, while Eastwood's character complains about the Hmong families moving into his neighborhood, his Hmong neighbors wish that he would move out of the neighborhood like all the other white people. And even given this mutual dislike based on ethnic backgrounds, Eastwood's character comes to know and love his Hmong neighbors, protecting them with a tremendous act of self-sacrifice.

Discrimination can also take different forms. **Individual discrimination** occurs when one person treats others unfairly because of their race or ethnicity. A racist teacher might discriminate against a Hispanic student by assigning him a lower grade than he deserves. **Institutional discrimination**, in contrast, is usually more systematic and widespread, and occurs when institutions (such as governments, schools, or banks) practice discriminatory policies that affect whole groups of individuals.

A rather startling example of institutional discrimination comes from Ira Katznelson (2005) in his book *When Affirmative Action Was White: An Untold History of Racial Inequality in Twentieth Century America*. We usually associate affirmative action with the advances of the Civil Rights Movement of the 1960s and with benefiting blacks and other minorities. Katznelson, however, examines one instance of special government policies benefiting whites. In 1944, Congress passed the G.I. Bill of Rights, which provided funding for college or vocational education and home loans to returning World War II veterans. While this should have supported black and white veterans alike, in practice blacks were largely impeded from taking advantage of the new benefits, while whites more easily climbed into the rapidly expanding American middle class. Typically, loans were granted only to those buying homes in all-white neighborhoods. And blacks were effectively barred from buying homes in those neighborhoods, either through legal restrictions or from hostile actions on the part of loan officers, realtors, and homeowners who were prejudiced against having blacks live next door. To make matters worse, loans were even denied to blacks who wished to buy homes in black neighborhoods; these were seen as risky investments. Later affirmative action programs were actually modeled after those of the postwar era that ironically benefited whites and created an even greater economic disparity between racial groups.

Another example comes from Lawrence Otis Graham, a Princeton- and Harvard-trained African American lawyer who investigated firsthand institutionalized racism in the upper-crust world of the East Coast elite. He found that, for example, he was not able to join a particular Connecticut country club as a member; however, he was welcome to serve in the capacity of busboy to the club's all-white membership and wait staff (1996). This shocked Graham; he believed his Ivy League credentials would have opened any door but discovered that in a racially stratified society, a black man with privileged socioeconomic status is still a black man in the end.

Some students have difficulty in recognizing just how persistent and pervasive racism is in contemporary American society, while others experience it on a daily basis. We hear claims that it has been erased. But although there have been tremendous strides, especially in the wake of the Civil Rights Movement, racism is not yet a thing of the past. There is still deep skepticism among minorities that negative racial attitudes are changing in America (Bobo, Kluegel, and Smith 1997; Bobo and Smith 1998). A survey conducted by Gallup in 2011 (Saad 2011) found that 35 percent of Americans believed race relations had gotten better since the 2008 election of President Barack Obama, while 23 percent said they had gotten worse. This included 48 percent of blacks and 31 percent of whites who agreed that race relations had improved. Those saying that race relations had remained unchanged included 27 percent of blacks and 45 percent of whites, while 24 percent of blacks and 22 percent of whites believed that race relations had gotten worse. Another striking result of the survey revealed that 44 percent of whites and 55 percent of blacks believed that relations between the two would always be a problem in the United States.

Racism today is neither as blatant as it once was—blacks and whites don't use separate bathrooms or drinking fountains—nor is it only a black-and-white issue. But it has taken other, more subtle forms (such as the high concentration of liquor stores in predominantly black urban areas or the concentration of Latino immigrants in low-wage jobs). If we are to have a truly egalitarian society, it will take much more education and change in the social conditions that perpetuate inequality.

> **INDIVIDUAL DISCRIMINATION** discrimination carried out by one person against another
>
> **INSTITUTIONAL DISCRIMINATION** discrimination carried out systematically by institutions (political, economic, educational, and others) that affect all members of a group who come into contact with it

Theoretical Approaches to Understanding Race

Sociologists reject the notion that race has an objective or scientific meaning, and instead seek to understand why race continues to play such a critical role in society. They have produced a number of different theories about the connections between race, discrimination, and social inequality.

For example, functionalist theory has provided a useful lens for analyzing how certain ethnic groups, mainly European immigrants (like the Irish and Italians) arriving in the early 1900s, eventually became assimilated into the larger society. Functionalism, however, has proven less successful in explaining the persistence of racial divisions and why other races and ethnicities, such as African Americans and Hispanics, have continued to maintain their distinct identities alongside the white majority culture today.

Perhaps what functionalism can best offer is an explanation of how prejudice and discrimination develop, by focusing on social solidarity and group cohesion. Groups have a tendency toward ethnocentrism, or the belief that one's own culture and way of life are right and normal. Functionalists contend that positive feelings about one's group are strong ties that bind people together. At the same time, however, this cohesiveness can lead members to see others, especially those of other races or ethnicities, in an unfavorable light. According to functionalists, these cultural differences and the lack of integration into the larger society on the part of minorities tend to feed fear and hostility.

Conflict theory focuses on the struggle for power and control. Classic Marxist analyses of race, developed by sociologists in the 1960s, looked for the source of racism in capitalist hierarchies. Edna Bonacich, for instance, argues that racism is partly driven by economic competition and the struggle over scarce resources. A "split labor market," in which one group of workers (usually defined by race, ethnicity, or gender) is routinely paid less than other groups, keeps wages low for racial and ethnic minorities, compounding the effects of racism with those of poverty (1980). William Julius Wilson believes that openly racist government policies and individual racist attitudes were the driving forces behind the creation of a black underclass, but that the underclass is now perpetuated by economic factors, not racial ones (1980). While this link between race and class is useful and important, it doesn't provide a satisfactory explanation for all forms of racial and ethnic stratification.

In recent years, conflict theorists have developed new approaches to understanding race. In his book *Racial Fault Lines: The Historical Origins of White Supremacy in California* (2008), for example, Tomas Almaguer looks at the history of race relations in California during the late nineteenth century. He describes a racial hierarchy that placed whites at the top, followed by Mexicans, blacks, Asians, and Native Americans at the bottom. Rather than focusing exclusively on class, he examines how white supremacist ideology became institutionalized. Racist beliefs became a part of political and economic life during that period. Ideas like "manifest destiny" (the belief that the United States had a mission to expand its territories) helped justify the taking of lands, and the notion that Native Americans were "uncivilized heathens" helped justify killing them. Sociologists also argue that race isn't just a secondary phenomenon that results from the class system: it permeates both lived experience and larger-scale activity, such as the economy and the government (Omi and Winant 1994).

Still others have sought to understand the meaning of race from the individual's point of view and have begun to analyze the ways that race, class, and gender inequalities intersect. For instance, writers like Patricia Hill Collins (2006), bell hooks (1990), and Gloria Anzaldúa (1987) argue

Table 8.1 Theory in Everyday Life

Perspective	Approach to Race and Ethnicity	Case Study: Racial Inequality
Structural Functionalism	Racial and ethnic differences are a necessary part of society. Even racial inequality has functions that help maintain social order.	The functions of racial inequality and conflict for society could include the creation of social cohesion within both the dominant and minority groups.
Conflict Theory	Racial and ethnic differences create intergroup conflict—minority and majority groups have different interests and may find themselves at odds as they attempt to secure and protect their interests.	Some members of majority groups (whites and men in particular) object to affirmative action programs that assist underrepresented groups. This can create conflict between racial groups in society.
Symbolic Interactionism	Race and ethnicity are part of our identity as displayed through our presentation of self.	Some individuals (white ethnics and light-skinned nonwhites in particular) have the option to conceal their race or ethnicity in situations where it might be advantageous to do so. This may allow them as individuals to escape the effects of racial inequality but does not erase it from society at large.

that race must be explained in the terms in which it is experienced, not as overarching general theories. Though some of these writers have been sharply critical of the symbolic interactionist tradition, which they believe does not take into account macro social forces that shape the realities of stratification, they share with interactionism a conviction that race, like all other aspects of social life, is created symbolically in everyday interactions. It is this idea to which we now turn.

The Social Construction of Race

Sociologists understand race as a social rather than a biological category. Students often find this confusing, because the everyday understanding of race in the United States is that it is based on skin color, which is an inherited physical trait. Sociologists who study race, however, point out that there is no physical trait that will always accurately identify what race someone belongs to. As Michael Omi and Howard Winant point out in *Racial Formation in the United States* (1994), "although the concept of race invokes biologically based human characteristics," which particular features are chosen to make racial distinctions "is always and necessarily a social and historical process" (55). Indeed, although Americans talk about skin color as the principal physical marker of racial identity, some scholars argue that hair is a more important factor (Banks 2000). Even though they are expressed in terms of physical traits, the definitions of different racial groups are "at best imprecise and at worst completely arbitrary" (Omi and Winant 1994, p. 55). The definition of race is not stable, but changes over time as racial categories are contested and developed.

This is not to say that race is unimportant. Omi and Winant show how racial groups are created socially and historically, by arguing that "race can be understood as a fundamental dimension of social organization and cultural meaning in the U.S." (viii). Real, physical bodies still matter to this process, but it is the meaning that is attributed to these bodies that determines what racial categories will exist, who will belong in them, and what they will mean.

For example, sociologist Stuart Hall was born in Jamaica, but immigrated to England as a young man, where he became one of the founding figures in the development of cultural studies. He explained the social construction of race by recounting a conversation he had with his young son, who was the product of a mixed marriage. Hall describes a moment when his "son, who was two and a half, was learning the colors," when his father explained to him, "'You're Black.' And he said, 'No. I'm brown'" (2006, p. 222). Hall's son was thinking in purely physical terms. If race really were biological, he would have been correct, but as Hall explains, he has the "wrong referent," because he was not "talking about your

Skin Deep Stuart Hall explains that race is not based on skin color alone—it's a social category framed in terms of biological features.

paintbox" (222). Hall understands that it is not skin color that created racial categories. If that were true, his son would belong to a different race than he. Race is not a pre-existing biological category; it is a social one that is framed in terms of biological features.

Another aspect of the social construction of race is that we "read" others through a myriad of cues, and we in turn make ourselves readable to others by our own self-presentations. Our identity is constructed in the negotiation between what we project and what others recognize. Even master statuses like race, gender, and age are negotiated in this way. So how *do* we project our racial or ethnic identities and read the racial or ethnic identities of others? We might think immediately of stereotypes like hip-hoppers with baggy pants, skateboard dudes, sorority girls, "welfare moms," and so on. But in fact there are more subtle ways in which we project and receive our racial and ethnic identities. The interactional accomplishment of race is often easiest to see in the most unusual situations.

Passing

Racial **passing**, or living as if one is a member of a different racial category, has a long history in the United States. Both during and after slavery, some light-skinned African Americans would attempt to live as whites in order to avoid the dire consequences of being black in a racist society. And people of different racial and ethnic backgrounds still pass, intentionally or unintentionally, every day in the United States. Passing involves manufacturing or maintaining a new identity that is more beneficial than one's real identity. A pioneer in the study of race, W.E.B. DuBois's concept of **double-consciousness**

PASSING presenting yourself as a member of a different racial or ethnic group than the one you were born into

DOUBLE-CONSCIOUSNESS W.E.B. DuBois's term for the divided identity experienced by blacks in America seems relevant to a discussion of passing. DuBois asked whether one could be black and at the same time claim one's rights as an American. Given the history of oppression and enslavement of African Americans, DuBois was not the only person to wonder if this is possible. There are many social forces that disenfranchise and exclude minorities, and the phenomenon of passing suggests that in some places and times, it has been more advantageous to appear white if at all possible.

Shirlee Taylor Haizlip, a Los Angeles journalist, chronicled the passing stories of one half of her family in her book *The Sweeter the Juice* (1994). Haizlip grew up the daughter of a prominent black Baptist minister, attended Wellesley College, and lived a life of privilege and comfort as a member of a small East Coast African American elite in the 1950s. She always knew that she had white relatives (75 percent of all African Americans do) and that these relatives had something to do with her mother's story of being abandoned as a child by her own father. Haizlip decided to use her journalistic skills to find out who these relatives were and how they had disappeared into the white world. She tracked down an aunt (her mother's sister) and learned that her grandfather, who was very light skinned, had apparently not been able to resist the desire to escape the constraints of blackness for the privileges of whiteness. So he fled with his lightest-skinned child (Haizlip's aunt), leaving his other, darker children behind—and lived the rest of his life as a white man, cut off from his black ancestry.

> **EMBODIED IDENTITY** those elements of identity that are generated through others' perceptions of our physical traits

In this story of passing, situational context is important: merely by surrounding himself with white people, Haizlip's grandfather accomplished whiteness rather effectively. In a segregated world, whom you hang out with goes a long way toward defining who you are, whether you are passing or not. But there are other requirements as well. Haizlip's aunt, for example, made sure her face was always well powdered, married a white man, and had no children, lest genes give her secret away. Indeed, while some of the white relatives

The Sweeter the Juice
Shirlee Taylor Haizlip's grandfather, who abandoned his family to live as a white man, is a dramatic example of racial passing.

Haizlip contacted knew about the black-white schism in the family, others did not—some were so surprised when Haizlip revealed that they had a former slave as a common great-grandfather, they blurted out, "Do you mean a *black* slave?" Their pasts had been so successfully erased through passing that after only one generation they were completely unaware of their black heritage.

What does passing tell us about the interactional accomplishment of race in general? Race is often as much in our interactional performances as it is in our bodies. We're all engaged in the same performances; it's just that those who pass have something to hide.

Embodied and Disembodied Identities

When we interact with others online, we're usually not able to see what they look like. This has been touted as one of the democratizing traits of the internet—that aspects of **embodied identity** (the way we are perceived in the physical world), historically used as the basis for discrimination, are not available to those interacting online. But in online communities that are *based* on racial identity, race must still be "done" interactionally (in this case, textually), as sociologist Byron Burkhalter found in his study of an internet community based on African American culture (1999). To sound authentically African American online, for instance, you have to include what Burkhalter calls "racially relevant" content and language—for example, "sister" to refer to other African American women. Responses also help establish racial identity: it's not just what you say, but how others receive it.

In some discussions, the African American identity of participants is accepted, but in other cases, that status is contested, in what Burkhalter calls "identity challenges." Identity challenges are usually accusations that one is not "really" black or not black enough, or that one is a "Tom" (a derogatory reference to a servile slave from the 1852 novel *Uncle Tom's Cabin*) or a racist. These challenges are usually made when postings reveal opinions that don't fit into a certain set of socially approved boundaries, such as opinions about the use of "proper" English versus slang.

Burkhalter argues that race is not irrefutably identifiable even in face-to-face interactions (as evidenced by the familiar, if irritating, question "What are you?") and that we must establish it interactionally both on- and off-line. Stereotypes come into play in both arenas but in different directions: in face-to-face interaction, seeing racial characteristics leads to stereotyping; online, applying stereotypical templates leads to assumptions about race. The internet is thus not a place where all the problematic distinctions disappear—they just manifest themselves in different ways.

DATA WORKSHOP
Analyzing Mass Media and Popular Culture

The Politics and Poetics of Racial Identity

I am the son of a black man from Kenya and a white woman from Kansas. I was raised with the help of a white grandfather who survived a Depression to serve in Patton's Army during World War II and a white grandmother who worked on a bomber assembly line at Fort Leavenworth while he was overseas. I've gone to some of the best schools in America and lived in one of the world's poorest nations. I am married to a black American who carries within her the blood of slaves and slaveowners—an inheritance we pass on to our two precious daughters. I have brothers, sisters, nieces, nephews, uncles and cousins, of every race and every hue, scattered across three continents, and for as long as I live, I will never forget that in no other country on Earth is my story even possible.

It's a story that hasn't made me the most conventional candidate. But it is a story that has seared into my genetic makeup the idea that this nation is more than the sum of its parts—that out of many, we are truly one.

—FROM BARACK OBAMA'S SPEECH TO THE NATION, MARCH 18, 2008, PHILADELPHIA, PENNSYLVANIA

Barack Obama, the forty-fourth president of the United States, is the first black man to be elected to the office (twice). Issues of race featured prominently in his first presidential bid in 2008, and during a campaign stop in Philadelphia, Obama gave one particularly famous speech on race that was discussed, analyzed, scrutinized, and evaluated by pundits and ordinary citizens alike for months afterward. In the speech, Obama ostensibly addressed some controversial comments about race delivered by the pastor of the church his family attended in Chicago. But he also spoke to bigger issues that everyone, regardless of race, has had to grapple with simply as part of being an American. Indeed, he presented the issue of racial prejudice as one of America's defining social problems and challenged all Americans to work toward solving it.

This Data Workshop asks you to do a content analysis of an existing source such as a speech, song, poem, or performance that deals with racial and ethnic identity (see Chapter 2 for a review of this research method). You can also look up other important political speeches at the Library of Congress's "American Memory" web site, dedicated to providing written and spoken words, sound recordings, still and moving images, prints, maps and sheet music that document the American experience.

You may also choose a poem from your favorite writer and consider how racial and ethnic identity is socially constructed in poetry. Or you might view an episode of the HBO series *Def Poetry Jam*, which features artists such as Mos Def, Jay-Z, Caroline Kennedy, Rakim, Erykah Badu, Mutaburuka, and Jill Scott. Or analyze the lyrics from your favorite musical artist. Consider other kinds of sources as well, such as the stand-up routines of Korean American comic Margaret Cho, the Chicano comedy troupe Culture Clash, the Middle Eastern comics in "Axis of Evil," or African Americans Key & Peele and the Queens of Comedy.

Racial Identity: "More than the Sum of Our Parts" President Barack Obama, left, listens to the inauguration ceremony at the U.S. Capitol on January 20, 2009. Behind Obama is his family, including wife Michelle, daughters Malia and Sasha, his sister Maya Soetoro-Ng and her husband Konrad Ng, and Obama's mother-in-law Marian Robinson.

IN RELATIONSHIPS

"Jungle Fever": Interracial Romance, Dating, and Marriage

Forty-one out of the fifty American states prohibited **miscegenation**—romantic, sexual, or marital relationships between people of different races—at some point in history. In 1958, for example, Mildred and Richard Loving, an African American woman and a white man, married and settled in their native state of Virginia. In July of that year, they were arrested for violating the state's "Act to Preserve Racial Purity" and convicted. The judge sentenced them to a year in prison but suspended the sentence on the condition that the couple leave the state. The Lovings moved to Washington, D.C., where in 1967 the Supreme Court overturned all such laws, ruling that the state of Virginia had denied the Lovings their constitutional rights. While the Loving decision technically cleared the way for interracial marriages nationwide, states were slow to change their laws; Alabama finally overturned its antimiscegenation statute in 2000.

Society at large does seem more accepting of interracial relationships now than it was in 1967. By 2002, almost 20 percent of eighteen- and nineteen-year-olds reported being in an interracial relationship (Kao and Joyner 2005). At the same time, though, about 27 percent of Americans still expressed disapproval. Despite all the steps we have taken toward racial equality and integration, American society is not ideally structured to promote interracial contact, let alone romance. Cultural stereotypes and media

MISCEGENATION
romantic, sexual, or marital relationships between people of different races

Mildred and Richard Loving Their interracial marriage was illegal in 1958.

images, for example, provide serious obstacles to interracial relationships. Several researchers point out that minorities tend to be exoticized or stereotyped by the general population. Thus, Asian women are seen as subservient, mysterious,

---

Finally, you could also write an original speech or poem about your own racial or ethnic identity experience, then discuss it using the principles of content analysis. Whichever option you choose, remember to focus on how the text expresses ideas about race, ethnicity, identity, inequality, and solidarity.

There are two options for completing this Data Workshop.

Option 1 (informal): Prepare written notes on your chosen text that you can refer to in class. Compare your notes and experiences with other students in small-group discussions.

Option 2 (formal): Write a three- to four-page essay analyzing your chosen text. Attach your excerpt of the source material.

Race, Ethnicity, and Life Chances

A law professor decides that it is time to buy a house. After careful research into neighborhoods and land values, she picks one. With her excellent credit history and prestigious job, she easily obtains a mortgage over the phone. When the mortgage forms arrive in the mail, she sees to her surprise that the phone representative has identified her race as "white." Smiling, she checks another box, "African American," and mails back the form. Suddenly, everything changes. The lending bank wants a bigger down payment and higher interest rates. When she threatens to sue, the bank backs down. She learns that the bank's motivation is falling property values in the proposed neighborhood. She doesn't under-seductive, and/or sex objects; conversely, Asian men are portrayed as nonsexual geeks or martial arts pros (Le 2001). Black men are mythologized as having especially strong sex drives, and black women are assumed to be unable to control their sexual urges (Foeman and Nance 1999); white women are thought to be accommodating in bed (Shipler 1997). These stereotypes, though they are not borne out in reality, still have the power to influence our attitudes and behavior.

Movies sometimes provide a warning. In both Spike Lee's 1991 movie *Jungle Fever* and the 2001 Julia Stiles movie *Save the Last Dance*, white women in interracial relationships are criticized by people in the African American community for taking available black men away from black women, a problem that is exacerbated by the higher levels of incarceration and death among young black men. A young African American woman is quoted in an *Ebony* magazine article as saying, "Every time I turn around and I see a fine Brother dating outside his race, I just feel disgusted. I feel like, what's wrong with us? Why do you choose her over me?" (Hughes 2003).

People who date interracially must deal with in-group pressures to date—and especially marry—someone of their own race. This phenomenon is most commented on in the African American community (though by no means exclusive to it). In fact, although blacks are as likely to date interracially as members of any other group, they are less likely to outmarry than any other nonwhite group. Anita Allen, a professor of law and philosophy at the University of Pennsylvania,

The Complexities of Interracial Dating The TV drama *Parenthood* features several storylines on interracial relationships, such as the romance of Hattie and Alex.

has observed that many African Americans view marrying a nonblack as being disloyal to the community (NPR 2003). Commentary on this subject can be found in scores of magazine articles, movies, and even comic strips (see Aaron McGruder's "Boondocks" or Darrin Bell's "Candorville").

How do you feel about interracial relationships? This topic is not just a hot-button issue for you to discuss with friends and family; it provides an opportunity for you to apply your sociological perspective to understand an important area of debate in everyday social life.

stand this because those property values were completely stable when she was researching the area. Then she realizes that *she* is the reason for the plummeting values.

As Patricia Williams's (1997) experience illustrates, membership in socially constructed categories of race and ethnicity can often carry a high price. We now look at other ways this price might be paid, in the areas of health, education, work, family, and criminal justice.

Family

Race, ethnicity, and their correlates (like SES) shape family life in a variety of ways. Data from the U.S. Census Bureau (2011e) showed that of the white population over eighteen years of age, 57.6 percent were married, 11.2 percent divorced, 6.7 percent widowed, and 22.8 percent never married. Of the African American population over age eighteen, 33.5 percent were married, 11.9 percent divorced, 6.1 percent widowed, and 43.8 percent never married. The Hispanic population fell between the white and African American populations with 48.9 percent over age eighteen married, 7.9 percent divorced, 3.8 percent widowed, and 35.3 percent never married. Thus, African Americans are more likely than whites and Hispanics to never marry or to be divorced.

Kathryn Edin (2000) argues that low-income women of all ethnicities see marriage as having few benefits. They feel that the men they are likely to encounter as possible husbands will not offer the advantages (financial stability, respectability, trust) that make the rewards of marriage worth the risks. This doesn't mean, of course, that most low-income women don't love their male companions; it only means that they believe a legal bond would not substantially improve their lot in life.

In 2010, the birth rates for American teenage mothers (ages fifteen to nineteen) varied significantly by race. The birth rate for white teenage moms was twenty-three per 1,000 births, while the birth rate for African Americans was fifty-one per 1,000; for Hispanics it was fifty-five per 1,000 (Hamilton et al. 2011). Social thinkers such as Angela Y. Davis argue that African American teenage girls in particular see fewer opportunities for education and work, and choose motherhood instead (2001). Davis believes that social policies aimed at punishing teenage mothers of color will be ineffective; only by attacking the racism inherent in the educational system and the workforce will these teens be at less risk of becoming mothers.

Health

Health is an area in which we find widespread disparity between racial and ethnic groups. Health-care consumers must rely on insurance benefits provided through their employer or buy individual policies in order to meet their medical needs. This has meant that many Americans cannot afford basic health-care coverage. In 2011, some 11.1 percent of whites were without health insurance, along with 16.8 percent of Asian Americans, 19.5 percent of blacks, and 30.1 percent of Hispanics (Figure 8.2). The Affordable Health Care Act of 2010 was designed to address such inequities by providing something like universal health-care coverage, but the law has remained an area of contention.

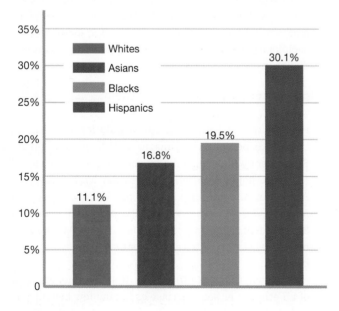

Figure 8.2

Americans without Health Insurance by Race, 2011

SOURCE: U.S. Census Bureau 2012f.

Disparities in access to health care can adversely affect members of a racial group. This may help explain the life expectancy rates for men and women of different races. White male children born in 2010 can expect to live to be 76.5 years old, while white females can expect to live to age 81.3. However, African American males' life expectancy is only 71.8 years, and African American females' is 78. Hispanic males' life expectancy, on the other hand, is 78.8 years, and Hispanic females' is 83.8 (Murphy et al. 2012). Minorities are also often disproportionately exposed to other factors that impact lifespan, such as dangers in the workplace, toxins in the environment, or personal behaviors like drinking and poor diet. While life expectancy statistics are only crude indicators of general health, they do reveal continuing race-based discrepancies, including the ongoing mystery of why Hispanics live longer, a question researchers are still trying to answer.

Education

One of America's cultural myths is that everyone has equal access to education, the key to a secure, well-paying job. However, by looking at those who actually receive degrees, we can see that the playing field is not that level. According to the U.S. Census Bureau (2011g), in 2011, 91.5 percent of white students age 18 and over earned a high school diploma, while 83.1 percent of African American students and 65.5 percent of Hispanic students did so. The reasons for dropping out are complex, but the highest rates are associated with those from economically disadvantaged and non–English-speaking backgrounds.

In higher education, the numbers are similar. In 2011, 46.4 percent of Asian Americans, 31.5 percent of whites, 17.5 percent of blacks, and 12.3 percent of Hispanics earned a bachelor's degree (Figure 8.3). Further, 17.5 percent of Asian Americans, 11 percent of whites, 5.7 percent of African Americans, and 3.4 percent of Hispanics age 18 and over earned advanced degrees (master's, professional degrees, and doctorates). Thus, Asian Americans and whites enjoy more success overall in the U.S. educational system than African Americans and Hispanics. The reasons for the disparity are again complex, involving both economic and cultural factors. Earning an education is extremely important in American society. Not only does it translate to greater success in the workforce, it also confers social status and cultural capital that can prove valuable in other arenas.

Work and Income

African Americans make up 10.8 percent and Hispanics 14.5 percent of the total workforce. If jobs were truly given to people regardless of racial or ethnic identity, we would expect to see these same distributions across occupations. However, that is not the case. For example, in 2011, African

ON THE JOB

Race in College Admissions

Affirmative action policies were first put in place in the 1960s to make sure that racial and ethnic minorities and women had equal access to opportunities that had historically been available only to whites and men. While in principle these policies were lauded as a way to create a "level playing field" for all Americans, problems began to surface in practice. In 1978, a white student named Alan Bakke sued the University of California for "reverse discrimination": Bakke claimed that his application to UC Davis's medical school had been rejected in favor of lesser-qualified minority applicants because the school had set aside 16 percent of its medical school slots for minority applicants. The case went to the Supreme Court, and while the Court upheld the idea of affirmative action in general, it outlawed the quota system that had contributed to Bakke's rejection.

Since then, colleges and universities, private employers, and governments at all levels have struggled with the principles of affirmative action. Influential state university systems in California, Washington, Texas, and Michigan have faced additional legal challenges to their admissions criteria and have attempted to craft race-blind policies that produce the same effects as affirmative action. While seeking to avoid quotas and "preferential treatment," these schools also wish to increase diversity and create opportunities for historically underrepresented groups. How can these goals be accomplished simultaneously? Not without difficulty, it seems. California's public university system saw a substantial decrease in the number of minority applicants immediately following the policy changes made in 1996 that prohibited using race, sex, or ethnicity as a basis for admission or financial aid (Weiss 2001). Although the admission rates in the University of California system for non-Asian minority students rose in Fall 1999 (almost to the levels of 1997, the last year of race-based admissions), they have not kept pace with the percentages of minority high school graduates in the years since (Perez 2012).

College admissions staff grapple with questions about race every day when they arrive at work. Rachel Toor, a former admissions officer at Duke University, maintains that "Duke was firmly committed to affirmative action," but evidently there was much confusion over what its affirmative action policies actually were. In her position on the admissions committee, Toor says, "I tried to discuss larger social and cultural issues relating to race. . . . I rolled my eyes when [colleagues]

Medical Student Alan Bakke succcessfully challenged the University of California's quota system.

made racist comments." But decisions taking race into account remained difficult and contentious. Toor herself supports affirmative action policies because, she says, "if left in the hands of admissions officers, the way Duke's rating system is set up, there would be very few students of color" (Toor 2001).

The problems facing Toor and her committee are not unique to Duke. Until 2003, the University of Michigan had affirmative action programs for both its undergraduate and law school students. The undergraduate admissions procedure was based on a rigid point system, which led white students who had been denied admission to complain that additional points given to minority students solely on the basis of race gave them an unfair advantage. The law school admissions procedure used race as one of several factors to be considered. In 2003, the Supreme Court upheld the law school policy and revised the undergraduate policy. Supporters at the University of Michigan argued that the Court had firmly endorsed the principle of diversity articulated by Justice Powell in the *Bakke* decision. Outgoing Dean Jeffrey Lehman said, "By upholding the University of Michigan Law School's admissions policy, the court has approved a model for how to enroll a student body that is both academically excellent and racially integrated." Further, "the question is no longer whether affirmative action is legal; it is how to hasten the day when affirmative action is no longer needed" (J. Peterson 2003).

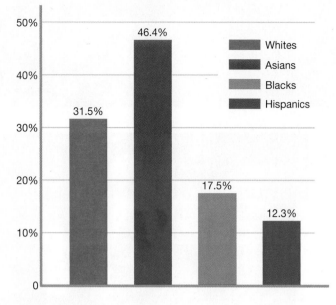

Figure 8.3
U.S. Bachelor's Degree Holders by Race, 2011

SOURCE: U.S. Census Bureau 2011g.

Americans constituted 8.4 percent and Hispanics 7.5 percent of all executive and managerial professions. That means that these positions, usually requiring advanced degrees, are primarily held by whites.

In contrast, persons of color carry the burden of some of society's most difficult jobs. In 2011, 33.1 percent of all nurses and home health aides and 26.4 percent of all postal clerks were black, while Hispanics were more likely to be employed in farming (43 percent of total) (U.S. Bureau of Labor Statistics 2011a). and as private household cleaners (39.9 percent of total). Except for nursing, these jobs are more likely to be semiskilled or unskilled. Thus, people of color, who are less likely to achieve high levels of education, are more likely to swell the bottom rungs of the job market. Interestingly enough, some lower-level jobs have shifted from African Americans to Hispanics over time. For instance, in 1983, African Americans accounted for 42.4 percent and Hispanics for 11.8 percent of all private household cleaners; by 2011, blacks accounted for only 16.5 percent. A similar shift may be seen with other low-wage jobs. This means that persons of color increasingly compete with each other for such jobs.

In 2011, the median income for whites was $55,412, for Hispanics $38,624, and for African Americans $32,229. Asian Americans had the highest median income at $65,129 (U.S. Census Bureau 2012f). The median incomes of Asian Americans and whites thus place them in the middle class, while those of blacks and Hispanics place them in the lower-middle (working) class. African Americans and Hispanics are more disproportionately represented than whites in the income brackets between $0 and $49,999, while whites are more disproportionately represented in income brackets above $50,000. In 2011, 9.8 percent of whites lived below the poverty line, compared with 27.6 percent of African Americans and 25.3 percent of Hispanics (U.S. Census Bureau 2012f). These numbers make it easy to see how race and class intersect to influence life outcomes.

Criminal Justice

Although the majority of the U.S. population is white—about 64 percent, as opposed to about 12 percent black and 11 percent Hispanic—we don't find these same proportions in the prison population. Of all state and federal male prisoners in 2009, 40 percent were African American, while 33 percent were white and 21 percent Hispanic (West 2010). Why are larger proportions of African American and Hispanic men in prison?

Some laws that don't seem race based still create racially differentiated outcomes (Table 8.2). For example, federal law until 2007 handed out tougher sentences to crack users (who are more likely to be black) than to users of powdered cocaine (who are more likely to be white): if you possessed a small amount of crack (for personal use), you'd get the same stringent sentence that you would if you possessed a huge amount of cocaine (enough for hundreds of uses). While this discrepancy was remedied in 2007, it left more than 17,000 people convicted of crack possession awaiting official reductions in their sentences—more than 15,000 of whom are black (U.S. Sentencing Commission 2010). Unemployment rates are higher among minority groups, as are dropout rates, and these may affect incarceration rates. There is also some evidence that there are connections to declining marriage rates and incarceration (Pettit and Western 2004).

Table 8.2 **Federal Cocaine Offenders by Race/Ethnicity, 2010**

Race/Ethnicity	POWDER		CRACK	
	Number	Percent	Number	Percent
White	930	16.7	347	7.3
Black	1486	26.7	3728	78.6
Hispanic	3054	54.9	617	13.0
Other	89	106	52	1.1
Total	5571	100.0	4751	100.0

SOURCE: U.S. Sentencing Commission 2011.

It is also clear that African Americans are far more likely than whites to be murdered: in 2010, while both whites and blacks, respectively, accounted for approximately 46 and 49 percent of murder victims nationwide, these percentages don't reflect the racial distribution of the U.S. population as a whole (Federal Bureau of Investigation 2011b). Finally, nearly half of the reported hate crimes in 2010 were attributed to racial discrimination (47.3 percent), with 69.8 percent targeting blacks (Federal Bureau of Investigation 2010d).

Intersectionality

As you might have already concluded, race and ethnicity do not shape our life chances in isolation from other social statuses and aspects of identity. Sociologist France Winddance Twine (2011b) demonstrates this in her ethnographic study of white women who have families with black men. As the intimate partners of black men, these women effectively lose some of their whiteness—especially in the eyes of their white working-class friends and family—and become "honorary blacks." This loss of whiteness is a form of punishment exacted by their ethnicity- and class-based communities, but which is not meted out equally to white men who marry black women. Twine's work identifies the intersection of class, race, and gender by showing the ways in which "interracial intimacy and the racism that accompanies it is a gendered experience" (p. 30).

An additional social status, motherhood, is also part of the intersectionality in Twine's study. White mothers of interracial children may or may not possess the racial literacy to raise those children in a world that will almost certainly see and treat them as black. From cooking and hair care to preparation for experiencing racism, these mothers—because they are women and because they are white—must calibrate their parenting practices in order to address race and racism in ways that their own mothers did not. In Twine's work, race, class, gender, and parenthood combine to shape the lived experiences of individuals and families.

Intergroup Relations: Conflict or Cooperation

The relationships between racial and ethnic groups in a society can take different forms. In some instances, groups may be tolerant and respectful of one another, while in other cases there is unending hostility. In this section, we will examine five basic patterns of intergroup relationships, from the most violent to the most tolerant. Keep in mind that some ethnic groups, such as Native Americans, may suffer several different patterns of hardship over a period of time.

France Winddance Twine studies the intersections of race, class, and gender in interracial families.

Genocide

The first pattern represents the worst possible outcome between a dominant and a subordinate group. Not only has **genocide**, the deliberate and systematic extermination of a racial, ethnic, national, or cultural group, taken place in the past, it continues today in certain parts of the globe.

The twentieth century witnessed numerous incidents of genocide. From 1915 to 1923, during and after World War I, the Turkish government massacred 1.5 million Armenians in what is often referred to as the "forgotten genocide." Nazi Germany under Adolf Hitler's rule killed two-thirds of the Jews of Europe. Few paid attention to the Armenian tragedy, and many refused to believe the initial reports of Hitler's death camps as well (Hitler himself recognized this, and is alleged to have asked, "Who remembers the Armenians?" when he embarked on his own genocidal project). In the latter half of the century, such events became all too common. From the atrocities of Darfur to Slobodan Milošević's ethnic cleansing in the Balkans and the Hutu slaughter of Tutsis in Rwanda, genocide has become a familiar feature of the modern landscape.

> **GENOCIDE** the deliberate and systematic extermination of a racial, ethnic, national, or cultural group
>
> **POPULATION TRANSFER** the forcible removal of a group of people from the territory they have occupied

It is also possible to consider the violence perpetuated by the early Americans against the Native American tribes who occupied North America as a form of genocide. While Native Americans died from diseases introduced by the settlers, they were also systematically killed by the European colonists. In the few hundred years that it took for the United States to be settled from coast to coast, the Native American population was almost completely wiped out. Estimates for the total number killed range anywhere from 15 million up to 100 million (Stannard 1993; Cook 1998).

Population Transfer

The treatment of Native Americans leads us to the next pattern of group relations—**population transfer**, or the forcible removal of a group of people from the territory they have occupied. In the early nineteenth century, Native Americans

Survivors of Genocide Holocaust survivor Ehud Valter displays the card documenting his transfer between the Auschwitz and Buchenwald concentration camps. Annie Karakaian, 101, survived the mass killings of Armenians in 1915 in what was then the Ottoman Empire.

who had not perished in battles with U.S. soldiers were forced by the U.S. government to move onto Indian reservations (also referred to as tribal lands or American Indian nations) west of the Mississippi River. They were often moved far away from the lands where they had lived for generations (mostly Southern states), as these were desirable territories that the whites wished to acquire for themselves. Between 1838 and 1839, in one of the most well-known examples, the state of Georgia and the federal government forcibly marched 17,000 Cherokees westward over 800 miles, a grueling journey known as the Trail of Tears. Along the way, more than 4,000 people died of hunger, exposure, or disease.

The separate territories established for the Native Americans are an example of a kind of partitioning that we can see happening today in Israel between the Israelis and Palestinians in the West Bank and Gaza Strip. There, the Israeli government restricts the movement of Palestinians and has even built miles of barriers designed to wall them in and keep them separate from the Israeli population. Sometimes, population transfer takes a more indirect form. For instance, it is possible to make life so miserable in a region that a group of people will choose to leave "voluntarily." This was the case with early Mormons, whose religious persecution in the East and Midwest between 1846 and 1869 drove 70,000 to cross the country (taking what is called the Mormon Pioneer Trail) and settle in the Great Salt Lake Valley region of Utah.

Internal Colonialism and Segregation

The term "colonialism" refers to a policy whereby a stronger nation takes control of a weaker foreign nation (the "colony") in order to extend the stronger nation's territory or to exploit the colony's resources for the stronger nation's own enrichment. The British Empire, which once included such distant countries as India, Burma (now Myanmar), the West Indies, South Africa, and Australia, as well as America before its independence, is an example of colonialism. **Internal colonialism** describes the exploitation of a minority group within the dominant group's own borders.

Internal colonialism often takes the form of economic exploitation and includes some sort of physical **segregation** of groups by race or ethnicity. For example, in the U.S. South up to the 1960s, not only did blacks live in separate neighborhoods, but they also were restricted to "coloreds"-only sections of buses, parks, restaurants, and even drinking fountains. If members of the minority group live close by yet in their own part of town (for instance, on the "other side of the tracks"), they are separate, and hence unequal, but still

INTERNAL COLONIALISM the economic and political subjugation of the minority group by the dominant group within a nation

SEGREGATION the physical and legal separation of groups by race or ethnicity

IN THE FUTURE

The Majority-Minority Generation

What is race going to look like in the future? In fictional and film renditions of the future, there are various depictions of race. In the very first *Star Trek* series in 1966, all races were equally represented in the future. This is a trend that remained through all the *Star Trek* franchises, with racially diverse casts staffing the U.S.S. *Enterprise* in the future. However, it is interesting to note that most of the central characters in the *Star Trek* franchise seem to be white. In Joss Whedon's *Firefly*, even though China and the United States have fused together to inhabit different planets in 2510, the cast is primarily white. *Blade Runner*'s dystopic future Los Angeles appears otherwise ethnically diverse, but almost devoid of blacks. In J. D. Robb's *In Death* series, which takes place in New York City in the late 2050s, whites are in the minority and most of the city is mixed race.

But we don't need science fiction to tell us what the racial future of the United States will be. In 2012, the U.S. Census reported that Latino, African American, Asian, and mixed race births made up the majority of births for the first time. In the twelve-month period ending in July 2011, Latino, African American, Asian American, and mixed race babies made up 50.4 percent of all live births (U.S. Census Bureau 2012i). This historical moment made for some odd headlines, as anyone who is in those racial categories is defined as a "minority." How can minorities be the majority? How will the rising number of nonwhites in America impact the future of our society? What will a future "majority-minority" nation be like?

The Census defines "majority" members as non-Hispanic, single-race whites, and projects that by 2042 we will become a country where that demographic is outnumbered by nonwhites. However, it doesn't mean that whites will become a minority group. As mentioned already in this chapter, a minority group consists of people who are recognized as belonging to a social category and who suffer from unequal treatment as a result of that status. Therefore, it is possible to be in the numerical majority and still have minority status with regard to power and oppor-tunity, as well as to be in the numerical minority and still hold majority status with regard to power and opportunity. For example, Texas and California are already "majority-minority" states, and although there are fewer whites than nonwhites, whites are still dominant.

But the change is visible in other areas of our social life: already, more and more advertising features nonwhite actors, as a way of reading out to a growing nonwhite customer base. Being multiracial is becoming more common and more accepted, and college-aged Americans, in particular, are used to seeing racially ambiguous faces. Indeed, the forty-fourth president of the United States, Barack Obama, had one white parent and one black parent. So, even though we have not reached a state of racial equality in the United States, the pos-sibility for social change as our demographics change seems hopeful.

Should we change the language of racial relations? Are the words "majority" and "minority" too confusing now that racial demographics have changed? At this moment in history, race is still a difficult and controversial topic for many people. But perhaps, as the babies born in 2012 grow up, racial difference will cease to be the basis of discrimina-tion and conflict, and race relations will become easier in a majority-minority nation.

Multiracial Families An increasing number of families are mixed-race, like the Greenwoods of Toms River, New Jersey.

Jackie Robinson is most often cited as the first athlete to break the "color barrier" in professional sports when he made his debut in major league baseball in 1947.

near enough to serve as workers for the dominant group. Segregation was not just confined to the South; it permeated other areas of society. Separation by races could be found in divisions serving in the U.S. military and among teams playing in professional sports like baseball, football, and basketball. Efforts to desegregate American society accelerated through the Civil Rights movement.

Assimilation

With **assimilation**, a minority group is absorbed into the dominant group: this process is the central idea behind America's "melting pot." On the surface, assimilation seems like a reasonable solution to the potential

conflicts between different groups. If everyone belongs to the same group, if the society is largely homogenous, then conflict will decrease.

During much of the twentieth century, immigrants to the United States were eager to adopt an American way of life, become citizens, learn English, and lose any trace of their "foreign-ness." The Irish, Italians, and Eastern Europeans were all once considered "ethnics" but eventually assimilated into the larger category of white Americans. Today, they are practically unrecognizable as distinct ethnic groups, unless they choose to emphasize characteristics that would so distinguish them. It is likely that this process will continue with the newer wave of immigrants; for instance, some census-type forms no longer distinguish Hispanic or Middle Eastern as separate categories from white.

But although there is something to be gained by assimilation, namely, membership in the dominant population, there is also something to be sacrificed. Minority group members may lose their previous ethnic or racial identity, either through **racial assimilation**, having children with the dominant group until the different races are completely mixed, or through **cultural assimilation**, in which members learn the cultural practices of the dominant group. In some cases, both types of assimilation take place at the same time.

In addition, the process of assimilation is not always entered into voluntarily. Sometimes, members of a minority group may be forced to acquire new behaviors and forbidden to practice their own religion or speak their own language, until these are all but forgotten. For some, assimilation results in the tragic loss of a distinctive racial or ethnic identity. This is true for many Native Americans, for instance, who in just a few generations have lost the ability to speak their tribal languages or have forgotten cultural practices of their not-so-distant ancestors.

Pluralism

Pluralism not only permits racial and ethnic variation within one society, it actually encourages people to embrace diversity as a positive feature of a society. The traditional image of the melting pot is exchanged with a "salad bowl" in which all of the different ingredients maintain their distinct qualities, even as they are tossed together. In the last few decades, the United States has seen more and more groups celebrating their racial or ethnic roots, developing a strong common consciousness, and expressing pride in their unique identity.

At the core of multiculturalism is tolerance of racial and ethnic differences. An example of successful multiculturalism is Canada. This country's population is diverse, composed of not only two official linguistic groups (English and French) but also ethnic and racial minorities that include

European, Chinese, and Indian immigrants as well as members of "First Nations," or Canadian native peoples. The Canadian government is committed to the ideals of multiculturalism, with a great deal of funding directed to programs aimed at improving race relations and encouraging multicultural harmony. As a sign of that commitment, the 1988 Canadian Multiculturalism Act declares that the role of government is to bring about "equal access for all Canadians in the economic, social, cultural, and political realms" (Mitchell 1993).

The United States is still moving toward becoming a more multicultural and egalitarian society, although in recent years there has been a backlash against the idea of pluralism. Some critics blame the educational system for allowing what they consider marginal academic areas, such as ethnic studies, women's studies, gay and lesbian studies, and the like, to be featured alongside the classic curriculum. Others question the need for bilingual education and English as a Second Language (ESL) programs, despite research showing benefits to nonnative speakers (Krashen 1996). And groups such as U.S. English and English First advocate for legislation making English the national language and setting limits on the use of other languages. Nevertheless, since the future seems sure to bring an ever-greater racial and ethnic mix to the country, Americans may yet be able to incorporate multiculturalism into our sense of national identity.

CLOSING COMMENTS

Constructing categories of race and ethnicity seems inevitably to lead to stratification and inequality and such destructive social processes as stereotyping, segregation, prejudice, and discrimination. Are there any positive consequences, either for society or for individuals? As it turns out, there are.

Racial and ethnic categories help create a sense of identity for members of these groups, which can lead to feelings of unity and solidarity—a sense of belonging to something that is larger than oneself, of cultural connection, and of shared history. We see this in action during ethnic festivals and holidays. When we share our own group unity with others in this way, we contribute to the diversity of our community and society. The more we understand and appreciate the diverse population of our nation, the less likely we may be to contribute to the destructive consequences of racial and ethnic categorization.

The important sociological insight here is that since categories of race and ethnicity are socially constructed, their meanings are socially constructed as well. Historically, we have constructed meanings that favor some and exploit and oppress others. Is it possible to construct meanings for racial and ethnic categories that value and celebrate them all? Over time, and with your newly acquired sociological insights, we hope you will be part of that transformation.

Everything You Need to Know about
Race and Ethnicity

"Race is a social category based on real or perceived biological differences among groups of people. Ethnicity is a social category based on a group's shared ancestry or cultural heritage."

THEORIES OF RACE AND ETHNICITY

* **Structural functionalism:** groups have a tendency toward ethnocentrism, which binds people together but also makes them act unfavorably toward those outside the group

* **Conflict theory:** majority groups use racism and ethnocentrism to protect their interests

* **Symbolic interactionism:** race and ethnicity are created symbolically in everyday interactions

REVIEW

1. How do you identify yourself in terms of race or ethnicity? Are there special occasions or situations in which you are more likely to display your ethnicity or race? Do you identify with more than one racial or ethnic group or know anyone who does? What does this tell you about the origin of these categories?

2. Affirmative action in college admissions is one of the most controversial topics in America today. Why would a college want to consider race or ethnicity when making admissions decisions? What factors do you think admissions boards should consider?

3. Although the Supreme Court ruled against antimiscegenation laws in 1967, homogamy, or assortive mating, is reinforced by social conventions. Would you date someone of a different race? Does your answer change depending on which racial or ethnic group you're thinking about?

U.S. Population by Race in 2060

Percent of total population | ■ 2012 ■ 2060

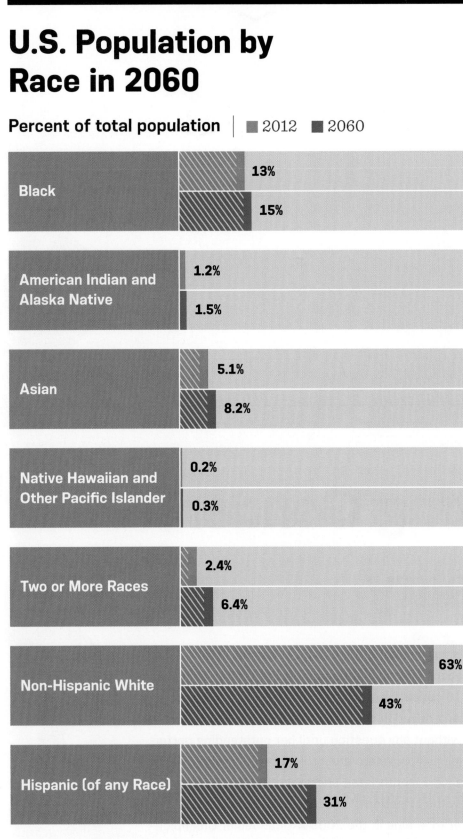

Black	
13%	
15%	

American Indian and Alaska Native
1.2%
1.5%

Asian
5.1%
8.2%

Native Hawaiian and Other Pacific Islander
0.2%
0.3%

Two or More Races
2.4%
6.4%

Non-Hispanic White
63%
43%

Hispanic (of any Race)
17%
31%

SOURCE: U.S. Census Bureau 2012, "U.S. Census Bureau Projections Show a Slower Growing, Older, More Diverse Nation a Half Century from Now"

EXPLORE

What's Funny about Racism?

Have you seen a comedic skit in which people pretend to be someone of another race? Such skits can be found on popular TV shows like *Saturday Night Live* but also in everyday life, like high schools. Visit the Everyday Sociology Blog to read about the problematic idea that racism is a viable form of entertainment.

http://wwnPag.es/trw408

CHAPTER 9

Constructing Gender and Sexuality

Eight seconds is an infinitesimally small amount of time to most people. In fact, there are very few tasks that you can accomplish in eight seconds. For Caster Semenya, eight seconds was enough time to cause the world to question her gender for an entire year. Semenya was born in 1991 and raised in the small village of Ga-Masehlong in South Africa. She lived her life as a girl without any question until her outstanding performance at the 2009 African Junior Championships, where she broke previous records with a time of 1:56.72 in the 800-meter race. One month later, she broke the world record at the 2009 World Championships. She drew the attention of the International Association of Athletics Federations (IAAF) because her race time in the 2009 African Junior Championships beat her performance in the 2008 competition by eight seconds. Eight seconds was all it took for Semenya to be cast into the world spotlight by the fall of 2009.

Female athletes frequently have to face the stigma of not being seen as feminine because of the physicality required to be a superior athlete. The low body-fat percentages and accentuated muscles that occur through sports training may even cause women to stop having menstrual periods. As our notions of gender are strongly linked to the body, female athletes often find themselves in the difficult position of defending themselves against the sanctions associated with being perceived as masculine or even lesbian. In fact, sex-determination testing has been a recurring theme for female athletes since the 1968 Olympics, when many Soviet female athletes were accused of being male. Sex-determination testing is generally performed by a team of physicians, including gynecologists and endocrinologists. Critics claim that these tests are humiliating, inaccurate, and insensitive.

In 2009, the IAAF required Semenya to undergo sex-determination testing to confirm eligibility to compete as a woman after her eight-second improvement in the 800-meter race. The public announcement of her testing coincided with her win at the World Championships. In the media storm that followed, the public at large speculated that Semenya may be intersexed and possess undescended testicles that produced extra testosterone that enhanced her performance. Bloggers, tabloids, and talk shows all made Semenya a household name around the world. It seemed like everyone had a diagnosis for Caster Semenya, and few of them involved her being female. In the eleven months that it took the IAAF to complete the testing, Semenya was banned from competing. If the testing revealed that she was not biologically female, her gold medals would be taken from her and she would relinquish her title as World Champion in the 800-meter.

On July 6, 2010, the IAAF publicly announced that Semenya could keep her title and medal, and that she was eligible to compete in future races as a woman. The results of the sex-determination test were never released to the public. She won the first 800-meter race that she was allowed to compete in after the IAAF made its decision, and won silver in the 800-meter race at the 2012 London Olympics. Unfortunately for Semenya, the stigma of having her sex questioned has already done its damage, as some still view her with suspicion and question her legitimacy on the racetrack.

Sports will continue to have to address the issue of gender as the awareness of intersexed, transgendered, and transsexual individuals increases. How will eligibility be determined for athletes in these categories? Does gender identity even still matter in athletic competition? Should having higher levels of testosterone disqualify an individual from competing as a woman? Should any female athlete have to face the public humiliation that Semenya did? It will be fascinating to see how future cases of sex-determination testing will be handled after the trauma that Semenya had to endure for almost an entire year. For Semenya, eight seconds changed her life as she knew it, and raised everyone's awareness of how important and complicated issues of gender are for society.

HOW TO READ THIS CHAPTER

We often think of gender and sexuality as part of our biological inheritance, unchanging and unchangeable. We hope that after reading this chapter you will understand the ways in which our gender and sexual identities are about *what we do* in addition to being about *who we are*. Gender and sexuality may be based in physiology, but their meanings are constructed in social contexts. As you read, pay attention to the processes involved in how the meaning of gender is constructed, as well as to the real consequences of gender inequality. As you become aware of these problems, perhaps you'll begin to think about solutions as well.

What Is Sex? What Is Gender?

Although people often use the terms "sex" and "gender" interchangeably, sociologists differentiate between the two: most view "sex" as biological but "gender" as social or cultural. Even though a person is usually the same sex and gender, this is not always the case, as we will see.

Sex

Sex refers to an individual's membership in one of two categories—male or female. The distinctions between male and female are based on such biological factors as chromosomes, hormones, and reproductive organs, all of which make up the primary sex characteristics. Males and females also possess different secondary sex characteristics, such as facial and body hair and musculature (Table 9.1).

Most people assume that everyone is either male or female. However, about seventeen babies in 1,000 are born **intersexed** (what used to be called "hermaphroditic"), having a variant chromosomal makeup and mixed or indeterminate male and female sex characteristics (Fausto-Sterling 2000). For these infants, since nature hasn't clearly indicated their sex, parents and doctors choose one and take the appropriate medical steps (in most cases, female is the most viable and expedient choice). In modern Western society, the prospect of an ambiguously sexed person seems so threatening and unacceptable that surgical and other procedures are quickly sought to remedy the situation.

Gender

Gender refers to the physical, behavioral, and personality traits that a group considers to be normal, natural, right, and good for its male and female members. In other words, gender reflects our notions about what is appropriately "masculine" or "feminine." Some societies, for example, expect men to be more aggressive and competitive and women to be more emotional and nurturing. We often think of such characteristics as biologically determined or "natural," but no society leaves it completely up to nature

SEX an individual's membership in one of two biologically distinct categories—male or female

INTERSEXED term to describe a person whose chromosomes or sex characteristics are neither exclusively male nor exclusively female

GENDER the physical, behavioral, and personality traits that a group considers normal for its male and female members

Table 9.1 Human Sex Characteristics

	Females	Males
Chromosomes	XX	XY
Dominant Hormone	Estrogen	Testosterone
Primary Sex Characteristics	Reproductive organs: vagina, cervix, uterus, ovaries, fallopian tubes, other glands	Reproductive organs: penis, testicles, scrotum, prostate, other glands
Secondary Sex Characteristics	Shorter than males; larger breasts; wider hips than shoulders; less facial hair; more subcutaneous fat; fat deposits around buttocks, thighs, and hips; smoother skin texture	Abdominal, chest, body, and facial hair; larger hands and feet; broader shoulders and chest; heavier skull and bone structure; greater muscle mass and strength; Adam's apple and deeper voice; fat deposits around abdominals and waist; coarser skin texture

GLOBAL PERSPECTIVE

Different Societies, Different Genders

In modern Western societies, we don't have a voice in what our gender will be. Someone looks us over at birth or even before and declares, "It's a boy!" or "It's a girl!" Even though some infants are born with indeterminate genitals, they are always assigned to one gender or the other as soon as possible, even if surgery is required. We have no words for someone who identifies as neither male nor female, nor do we find such an identity acceptable. Even those who undergo sex-reassignment surgery do so to move from one category to the other—very few individuals remain in gender limbo. But consider two societies that acknowledge a "third gender."

Berdaches or "Two-Spirit" People

When nineteenth-century explorers and missionaries wrote about the native tribes they encountered in America, they also described individuals within those tribes who were neither male nor female, but somehow both. These people—called berdaches by nonnatives and two-spirit by natives—were usually biological males who dressed as women and took on types of work we think of as feminine, such as cooking and domestic labor. They could also be biological females who took on traditionally male pursuits, such as hunting, trapping, and warfare. Male two-spirits have been documented in nearly 150 Native American cultures, and female two-spirits in almost half that number. Some researchers believe that people who became two-spirits were assigned to such a role from a very young age, if not from birth, for reasons of "demographic necessity" (Trexler 2002). In the northern reaches of Canada,

for example, couples who had given birth to all girls may have decided that their next child would be raised as a boy (and therefore a hunter who could provide food for the family)—no matter what. In more southern regions, a family who needed a female child may have deliberately raised a boy as a girl; male two-spirits were valued for their height and strength.

Research on two-spirits seems contradictory. Some believe that, based on the records of the early Europeans, they were looked down on by their own tribes. Others point out that some two-spirits were respected and played important roles in the religious life of their communities. What we do know is that two-spirits were acknowledged as a third gender. Indian creation myths include such references as "When the spirit people made men and women, they also made berdaches" (Roscoe 2000, p. 4)—allowing these people a recognized place in the order of things.

Hijras

The hijras of South Asia are a modern example of third-gender individuals. Like the berdaches, the hijras are recognized by their society as an acceptable variation on gender—neither male nor female, but something else entirely. They are usually biological males who have all or part of their genitals removed, and most become hijras voluntarily in their teens or twenties. They dress and live as females and are referred to as daughter, sister, grandmother, or aunt.

Like the berdache, hijras take part in the religious life of their people; they are specifically mentioned (and thus

to dictate the behavior of its male and female members. Gender, then, is something that is culturally transmitted or learned.

HUMAN SEXUAL DIMORPHISM the extent, much debated in recent years, to which inherent physical differences define the distinctions between the two sexes

Nature and Nurture

Despite the social scientific evidence to the contrary, some people argue that gender differences between

men and women are innate. To some extent, it is true that men and women really are built differently. We have different brain structures and different types of chemicals running through our bodies, which lead to somewhat different experiences and perceptions. But biology alone can't tell us everything about how sex and gender work. **Human sexual dimorphism**, the belief that anatomy defines men and women, is now highly contested owing to the media's attention to cross-dressers, transsexuals, and the transgendered, who broaden our definitions of sex and gender (Eller 2003). Biology may be neither the sole nor the primary factor in determining masculinity and femininity.

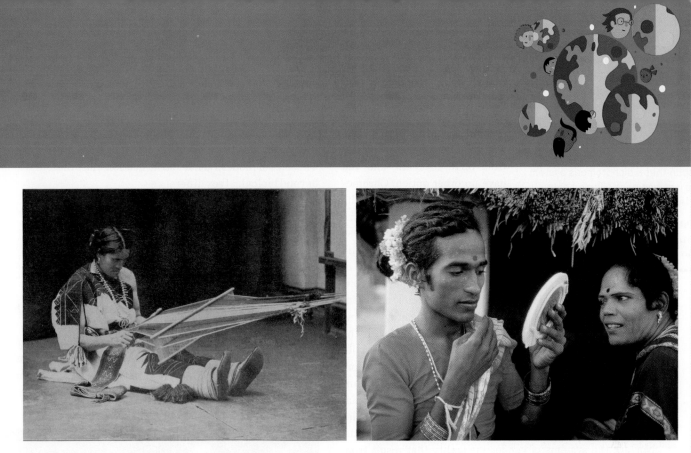

"Two-Spirit" People Berdaches (left), a term used by anthropologists and sociologists but considered insulting by many Native Americans, provide an example of a third gender that is neither male nor female. Hijras (right) occupy a similar place in the society of India. It is considered good luck to have a hijra at a wedding or at the birth of a male child.

validated) in the epic Indian Hindu texts as having been recognized by the deity Rama. Today, the presence of hijras at weddings and at the births of male children is thought to be auspicious. In 2012, the third gender option was added to Pakistan's national identity cards (Frayer 2012).

The two-spirit and hijra may sound similar to cross-dressers and transsexuals in Western society, but the analogy isn't entirely appropriate. For one thing, because of our two-gender system, we would still refer to someone who appeared to be a male but who felt like a female as "he"; if that same person decided to undergo sex-reassignment surgery, afterward we would call that individual "she." There is no room in our language for anything else. A two-spirit or hijra, on the other hand, is always referred to by that term, not "he" or "she." Keep in mind, then, that characteristics we think of as definitive, such as sexuality, dress, and biological gender, may be viewed differently in other cultures and time periods.

Here, it bears revisiting the "nature vs. nurture" debate we considered in Chapter 4. Too often, scientists fail to consider the interrelationship between these two forces. While nature may play some role in determining male or female traits, we must also consider the role of nurture—the social, cultural, and environmental context. In fact, Lepowsky (1993) suggests that in some cases, biological differences may be the result of culturally prescribed masculine and feminine behavior rather than the cause of it. For example, for both men and women, engaging in aggressive behavior increases the production of testosterone, a male hormone; it is thus possible that behavior influences biology, just as biology influences behavior (Sapolsky 1997).

Essentialist and Constructionist Approaches to Gender Identity

Depending on their field of study, sociologists look at gender from different perspectives. **Essentialists** see gender as immutable

ESSENTIALISTS those who believe gender roles have a genetic or biological origin and therefore cannot be changed and biological, and **gender identity**—an individual's self-definition or sense of gender—as an unambiguous, two-category system. According to this view, you're either male or female from birth to death, and you have no other option. Chromosomes, hormones, and genitalia determine your identity—the way you see yourself, the way you interact with others, and the activities you engage in every day. Culture plays no role.

Because it is a dispreferred perspective in sociology, essentialism is generally found outside the discipline in such fields as medicine, theology, and biology, and within sociology in the subfield of sociobiology. Some sociobiologists reduce male-female relationships to the biological function of procreation.

Most mainstream sociologists, however, use a **constructionist** approach to gender: they see gender as a social construction and acknowledge the possibility that the male-female categories aren't the only way to classify individuals. Nor are the systems of gender inequality that result from these labels necessary or natural. Constructionists believe that the meaning of masculinity and femininity may differ drastically in different societies and historical periods. We'll use a variety of sociological perspectives in this inquiry but will find ourselves returning again and again to constructionism as a helpful way to comprehend both the phenomenon of gender inequality and the theories that attempt to explain it.

Gender Inequality

Gender inequality can be found in all past and present societies. It invariably takes the form of **patriarchy**, or male domination. There is little evidence that a matriarchal (female-dominated) society has ever existed, although some societies have been more pro-feminine than others. The Vanatinai, for example, are a small society in New Guinea in which women share equal access to positions of prestige, power, and control over the means of production (Lepowsky 1993).

From the patriarchal point of view, gender inequality can be traced back to biological differences in early societies, when activities like hunting and warfare were more essential to the livelihood of human groups. Women could not participate as effectively as men in these activities because of their lesser physical strength and because of the demands of bearing and nursing children. Therefore, a division of labor arose, with women handling activities within the secured, "home" territory. Men delivered the scarcest and most prized resources to the group, such as game from hunting or territory from warfare, and thus became powerful by controlling the distribution of these resources.

But this account of the origins of gender inequality does not explain its persistence in contemporary societies. Physical strength is no longer required in the vast majority of jobs. Nor are large numbers of children required for the continuation of society, and women are not necessarily restricted in their activities because of the demands of caring for them. Theories of modern gender stratification must therefore look beyond biological sex differences.

Macro Theoretical Perspectives

There are two major macrosociological theories of gender inequality. Functionalists generally believe that there are still social roles better suited to one gender than the other, and societies are more stable when norms are fulfilled by the appropriate sex. In particular, functionalists emphasize how a particular "female" role may work in tandem with a particular "male" role within the family. Talcott Parsons, for example,

The Function of Gender Inequality In the 1950s, Talcott Parsons argued that gendered role expectations upheld the traditional family. Male "breadwinners" fulfilled an instrumental role by being task oriented and authoritative, while female "homemakers" embodied an expressive role by providing support and nurturing. *The Adventures of Ozzie and Harriet* featured the prototypical family of that era.

identified two complementary roles (Parsons and Bales 1955). One is an **instrumental role**: being task oriented, a "breadwinner," and an authority figure. The other is an **expressive role**: providing emotional support and nurturing. The expressive role is crucial not only to the care of children but also for stabilizing the personality of the instrumental partner against the stresses of the competitive world. In this view, since women are considered better suited to the expressive role and men to the instrumental role, gender segregation serves to uphold the traditional family and its social functions.

Expressive and instrumental roles may be complementary, but the social rewards for filling them are far from equal. The functionalist view does not explain very well why gender relations are characterized by such inequality. While the work of raising children and maintaining a household is intensive and difficult, there is a tendency to dismiss it as being unskilled and instinctive, which results in the devaluation of traditionally feminine work. Those who support a patriarchal society argue that this is again because resources provided by men in their instrumental roles are ultimately more valuable. This value, however, is being questioned in light of evidence indicating that juvenile delinquency and crime rates are higher when there is no adult supervision in the home and that expressive roles are thus important. The functionalist view also fails to acknowledge that families are often sources of social instability, with violence within families all too common.

Conflict theorists take a different approach. According to this perspective, men have historically had access to most of society's material resources and privileges, and consequently they generally seek to maintain their dominant status. Thus, conflict theorists see gender inequality in much the same way as they see race and class inequality—as manifestations of exploitation.

Some conflict theorists argue that gender inequality is just a derivative of class inequality and that it therefore originates with private property. This theory was introduced by Friedrich Engels in 1884. Engels noted that capitalists (the owners of property) benefited from maintaining patriarchal families, with women in the private sphere and men in the public workplace, in at least two ways. Women do the work of reproducing the labor force (on which the capitalists depend) without receiving any direct compensation, and they serve as an inexpensive "reserve army" of labor when the need arises. Engels suggested that if private property were abolished, the material inequalities producing social classes would disappear, and there would no longer be powerful interests forcing women into domestic roles.

Conflict theorists point out that whether or not gender inequality is a product of class conflict, all men benefit from it in the short term. Zillah Eisenstein (1979) notes that men stand to lose a good deal if gender segregation disappears: they would have to do more unpaid work, or pay to have their homes kept up and children cared for; they would have to find jobs in a larger and more competitive market; and they would lose some power and prestige if they were no longer the most viable breadwinners.

INSTRUMENTAL ROLE the position of the family member who provides the family's material support and is often an authority figure

EXPRESSIVE ROLE the position of the family member who provides emotional support and nurturing

Table 9.2 Theory in Everyday Life

Perspective	Approach to Gender Inequality	Case Study: Male- and Female-Dominated Occupations
Functionalism	Sex determines which roles men and women are best suited to; it is more appropriate for men to play instrumental roles and for women to play expressive roles.	Women are naturally more nurturing and thus make better nurses and teachers of young children; men are naturally more logical and thus make better lawyers and computer programmers.
Conflict Theory	Because of the traditional division of labor in families, males have had more access to resources and privileges and have sought to maintain their dominance.	Male-dominated occupations generally hold more prestige and are better paid; women may encounter difficulties entering male-dominated occupations, whereas men may more easily succeed in female-dominated occupations.
Symbolic Interactionism	Gender is learned through the process of socialization; gender inequalities are reproduced through interactions with family, peers, schools, and the media.	Girls and boys are socialized differently and may be encouraged to seek out gender-appropriate training, college majors, and career goals, leading them to enter male- and female-dominated occupations.

Interactionist Perspectives

While conflict theorists and functionalists focus on gender from a macrosociological perspective, interactionists emphasize how gender is socially constructed and maintained in our everyday lives. According to interactionists, gender identity is so important to our social selves that we can barely interact with anyone without first determining that person's gender. We need to categorize, and we need to be categorizable as well. For some people, this is no easy matter.

For example, **transgendered** (or TG) individuals' sense of self and gender identity may differ from their physical sex. A TG person may have female genitalia, for instance, but identify as a man. The TG category may also include others who transgress binary gender categories, such as cross-dressers, bi-gendered, ungendered, and intersexed people. The challenge for TG people is to present a social gender identity that differs from the expectations others may have of them.

In the 1960s, Harold Garfinkel (1967/1984), in one of the first studies to show how gender is based on interaction, conducted intensive interviews with "Agnes," a **transsexual** person born with male genitalia and raised as a boy, who was undergoing sex-reassignment treatment (including surgery and counseling) at the UCLA medical center. While Agnes had always known that she was a "120 percent natural normal woman," it was only when she was seventeen that she began to learn how to "do being female"—to look, behave, and talk like a woman. Agnes got a job and a roommate—even a boyfriend—and set about learning what would be expected of her as a woman. She carefully adopted her roommate's style of dress, makeup, and body language; she listened to what her friends said and how they spoke. She learned how to maintain proper deference to her male boss at work, and she listened to her boyfriend and his female family members as they expressed their expectations for her as a future wife and mother. Unlike other women, though, Agnes had to take extra precautions, such as avoiding sexual intercourse with her boyfriend (not too unusual in the early 1960s), wearing skirts and other clothing that would disguise her male anatomy, and avoiding activities (such as swimming at the beach) that would make her differences obvious until after she had gotten surgery. "Passing" as a female was a good deal of work for Agnes, and she constantly dealt with the fear that her secret would be discovered. But even Garfinkel, who knew her secret already, found her enactment of femininity quite convincing. Indeed, he was utterly charmed by her.

Even though you may think you have nothing in common with Agnes or other TG people, you actually enact gender in much the same way Agnes did. It is this process of observing and learning the feminine and masculine behaviors of others to which we now turn.

Gender Role Socialization

Gender role socialization—the subtle, pervasive process of becoming masculine or feminine—begins early and continues throughout our lives. It is accomplished primarily by the four major agents of socialization: families, schools, peers, and the media, though other social institutions, such as religion, may also play a part in the process.

Family

Families are usually the primary source of socialization. Indeed, Kara Smith (2005) argues that gender role socialization begins even before birth. Because the sex of the fetus now can be determined in utero, families may begin relating to the new baby as either a girl or a boy far in advance of the baby's arrival. Smith's research demonstrates how knowing the baby's sex affects how the mother talks to her fetus—the choice of words as well as tone of voice. Once babies are born, female and male clothes, rooms, and toys will differ, as will the stories the children are told.

Most telling, however, is the way in which significant others—parents, siblings, extended family, and caregivers—interact with the baby. Through **social learning**, the process of learning behavior and meanings through social interaction, babies respond to and internalize the expectations of others around them. For example, a baby girl who is treated gently may observe the roughhousing of baby boys with alarm. Sometimes there is a conscious effort to instill certain behaviors in children—by reprimanding a young boy, for example, for crying. At other times, social learning happens in a more subtle way, as the baby learns through observation, imitation, and play. Children rather quickly begin to exhibit gender-stereotyped behaviors. By the age of two, they are aware of their own and others' gender, and by age three, they begin to identify specific traits associated with each gender.

Gender pervades every aspect of family life. It may be implicit in the chores or privileges girls and boys are given (washing the dishes vs. mowing the lawn), the way they are disciplined or punished, where they go or don't go, or what they are encouraged or forbidden to do. Lessons such as "that's not very ladylike" and "big boys don't cry" are echoed in children's literature, in toys made specifically for girls or boys, and in the games they play. And as we grow up, we are always watching our other family members, using them as

---

TRANSGENDERED term describing an individual whose sense of gender identity transgresses expected gender categories

TRANSSEXUALS individuals who identify with the other sex and have surgery to alter their own sex so it fits their self-image

GENDER ROLE SOCIALIZATION the lifelong process of learning to be masculine or feminine, primarily through four agents of socialization: families, schools, peers, and the media

SOCIAL LEARNING the process of learning behaviors and meanings through social interaction

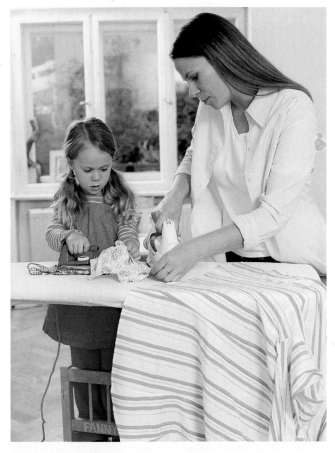

Gender Role Socialization Our families are among the primary agents of gender socialization. From a very young age, we learn and internalize gendered behaviors from our parents and siblings.

role models for our own beliefs and behaviors. In adulthood, our families may still influence what kind of career or mate we choose, how we run our household, and how we raise our own children.

Schools

Differences in the educational experiences of girls and boys also begin to appear early, both in the classroom and on the playground. By the fifth grade, gender norms are firmly established, as can be seen in the segregation that takes place even in co-ed schools. Girls and boys are frequently put in same-sex groups and assigned gender-stereotyped tasks, such as playing with dolls or playing with trucks. Same-sex groups also form on the playground, with girls and boys engaging in different kinds of social and athletic activities (Thorne 1993).

One of the key areas of difference is in the way that teachers, both women and men, typically interact with students. Whether or not they realize it, teachers tend to favor boys in several ways. Boys receive more attention and instructional time and are more likely to be called on in class. And boys are posed with more challenging questions or tasks, and are given more praise for the quality of their work. Boys are also, however, more likely to make teachers angry by misbehaving and therefore to receive some form of punishment more often (Smith 1999).

Despite boys' favorable treatment, girls in elementary school tend to earn higher grades. But their academic achievements are often discounted. In fact, the media often paint this gender discrepancy as a crisis for boys. When they do perform well, girls are typically credited for hard work rather than intellectual ability. They are encouraged to focus on social skills or appearance rather than brain power. By the time they reach middle or junior high school, girls begin to slip behind and to lose their sense of academic self-esteem. These troubles are compounded in adolescent girls, who begin to feel uneasy about competing with boys, embarrassed by their own success, or uncomfortable engaging in male-dominated subjects like math or science.

Gender role socialization in schools can take other forms as well. Textbooks often still contain sexist language and gender stereotypes. Women and minorities are underrepresented, both as subjects and as authors (Robson 2001). In the social structure of the school itself, women tend to be concentrated at the lower levels, as teachers and aides, while men tend to occupy upper management and administrative positions. In such ways, schooling as a whole reinforces gender stereotypes.

Peers

In Western societies, peer groups are an increasingly important agent of socialization. By the age of three, children develop a preference for same-sex playmates, a tendency that increases markedly as childhood progresses. Children in preschool are three times more likely to play with same-sex playmates—eleven times more likely in kindergarten—and it is not until well after puberty that this pattern changes even a little (Maccoby and Jacklin 1987). While some have argued that such gender segregation is the *result* of inherent differences between men and women, there is evidence to support the notion that same-sex peer groups can help *create* gendered behavior. Researchers have found, for example, that when children play with same-sex peers, their activities are more likely to be gender typed (girls have pretend tea parties, for example) than when boys and girls play together (Fabes, Martin, and Hanish 2003). In addition, children (especially boys) are punished (mocked) by their peers for crossing over these gendered borders (Thorne 1993).

C. J. Pascoe's ethnography of high school boys, *Dude, You're a Fag*, shows just how powerful peer groups can be in enforcing gender roles and the assumptions about sexuality that underlie them. Not only do boys police each others' performance of masculinity by criticizing non-normative (and, in their minds, effeminate) behavior, dress, and other practices, they "lay claim to masculine identities by lobbing homophobic epithets at one another" (Pascoe 2007, p. 5). Calling someone a "fag" inflates the offender's own sense of masculinity, while demonstrating to others the consequences of deviating from masculine norms.

The need to impress others and to feel popular with peers increases in the teenage years. Boys tend to gain prestige through athletic ability, a well-developed sense of humor, or taking risks and defying norms. Girls tend to gain prestige through social position and physical attractiveness. It's easy to imagine what kind of behaviors result from such peer pressure and the consequences of falling short in any way. In the extreme, it can lead to bullying and rebellious behavior on the part of boys and to eating disorders with girls. Similar pressures in regard to dating and mating continue through the early adult years as well.

The Media

From a variety of media sources, such as movies, comic books, or popular music, we learn "how to behave, how to be accepted, what to value, and what is normal" as well as "how gender fits into society" (Barner 1999). When it comes to television, there is no question that "sex-role behavior is portrayed in highly stereotypic fashion in virtually every aspect" of the programming (McGhee and Frueh 1980). Boys and girls learn that certain activities and attitudes are more appropriate for one gender than for the other. Girls should be beautiful, caring, sensitive, and reserved, while boys should be assertive, strong, and analytic. This starts at a particularly young age; chillingly, "by the time a child reaches kindergarten, she will 'know' more television characters than real people" (Barner 1999). In addition to TV, magazines like *Seventeen* and *Teen Vogue* are aimed mostly at adolescents. Some have even speculated that increases in anorexia and bulimia among teenage girls can be linked to the images of women they see in the media (Kilbourne 1999). Teenage girls may consider actresses and models the standard of beauty to aspire to, even though such women "often are far below the normal weight recommendations" (Schiller et al. 1998).

The case of video games presents some contradictions regarding media and gender role socialization. What was once thought of as a male bastion is becoming increasingly more gender balanced. It used to be that the stereotype of a video game enthusiast was a male player who preferred first-person shooter-style video games, with such popular series as *Call of Duty*, *Halo*, and *Bioshock*. While males still make up some 60 percent of video game players, some interesting changes are happening to the market. Females are beginning to represent a greater portion of game players, particularly when it comes to online games played on computers (as opposed to video games played on consoles). And the games that they are interested in most are such multiplayer games as *World of Warcraft* and the top-selling *The Sims* series, both of which focus on building relationships. An even

The Changing Culture of Gaming How are young women challenging stereotypes about video game fans?

greater number of females play arcade-style, or what are referred to as casual, games, where they represent 74 percent of all players. Gaming is no longer dominated by males, but the games that boys and girls choose to play may still be guided by gender differences.

For many centuries of human history, children have learned how to act appropriately from family, peers, and school. As the influence of the media becomes more pervasive in our society, we can see how it may compete with or even contradict that of other agents of socialization. At the same time, the media also serve to socialize families, peers, and educators, giving them an even more overarching power in society.

DATA WORKSHOP
Analyzing Mass Media and Popular Culture

The Fashion Police: Gender and the Rules of Beauty

This workshop will help you identify the messages about gender that permeate our lives through the media. You will be using existing sources as a research method and engaging in a content analysis (please see Chapter 2 for a review). Look through *two* magazines from *each* of the following lists of women's and men's magazines (there may be other comparable titles that you might also include). Keep in mind that you will need to photocopy or cut pages from these magazines at a later point.

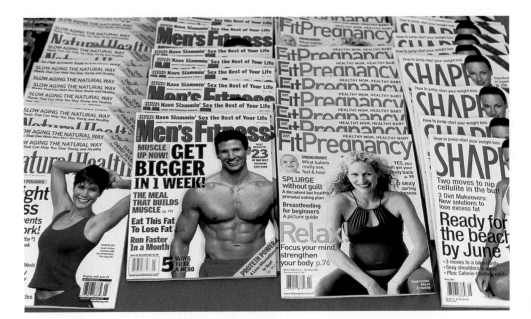

Rules of Beauty What do magazines like these tell us about the "rules" governing male and female appearance in our society?

* List A: *Cosmopolitan, Elle, Essence, InStyle, Glamour, Latina, Seventeen*

* List B: *Details, Esquire, GQ, Maxim, Men's Health, Men's Journal, Krave*

Immerse yourself in the *visual images* and the accompanying text in these magazines—in both articles and advertisements. As you look at the photos, cartoons, drawings, headlines, captions, and other features, ask yourself what they say about what is attractive for both males and females. Choose some pages from each magazine that stand out to you, and jot down answers to the following questions:

* What types of bodies are displayed? What shapes, sizes, colors?

* What kinds of activities are shown?

* What does the text say about the images?

* How do these images reflect the "rules" about male and female beauty in our society?

Next, compare and contrast the "rules of beauty" in the magazines from list A with those from list B. What are the similarities and differences, and how do you explain them? Besides gender, how do other factors—race, class, age, sexual orientation—seem to affect the rules of beauty in these magazines?

Finally, and just for fun, use some of the images and text you've found in the magazines to construct the "perfect" man or woman. Take "officially beautiful" parts from selected images and put them together to form a whole person. What does this person look like? Something more like Frankenstein's monster than a supermodel? What kinds of words are used to describe the feminine or masculine ideal?

What does that say about expectations for women and men? Perhaps when such words and images are broken down into their component parts, they are not so attractive after all.

There are two options for completing this Data Workshop.

Option 1 (informal): From your answers to the questions above, prepare some written notes that you can refer to in class. Make sure to bring examples you've chosen from the magazines. Compare your notes and experiences with those of other students in small-group discussions.

Option 2 (formal): Write a three- to four-page essay analyzing your data and addressing the specific standards of beauty presented in the magazines. Attach pages from the magazine you refer to in your essay.

Sex, Gender, and Life Chances

If two infants, one girl and one boy, are born at the same time in the same location from parents of similar racial and socioeconomic background, sociologists can predict answers to questions like the following: Who is more likely to live longer, go to college, or go to prison? Who might make a good living or live in poverty? Who is more likely to be married, divorced, or widowed, be a single parent or the victim of a violent crime, or join the military?

In this section, we will analyze how gender affects our lives. We will look specifically at how gender expectations shape our experiences with family, health, education, work and income, and criminal justice. For instance, women traditionally are caretakers of their families and more likely than men to go to college. Men make more money than women and are more likely to head religious institutions. These conditions are the result of values and norms that encourage certain behaviors in women and men.

It is important to remember, however, that gender is intertwined with other factors, such as race and class. Therefore, it is difficult to separate out the effects of gender on categories like marriage, education, and work. Single women with children are probably more likely to live in poverty, less likely to have a college education, and more likely to work in service-sector jobs. However, a person is not automatically poor or destined to be divorced because she is female. The categories all work together to construct the complexity of a person's life.

Family

When it comes to family, men are more likely than women to report never having been married, perhaps reflecting the stronger societal pressure for women to marry at some point in their lives. Men are also slightly more likely than women to report being married. About 9 percent of women are widowed (only 2.5 percent of men are), and 11 percent of women (9 percent of men) are currently divorced (U.S. Census Bureau 2011g). Some of these differences may be accounted for by the longer lifespans of women.

Divorce seems to be much more difficult for women with children than for men. Women are more likely to retain the primary caregiving role after divorce and to suffer financially because of it. In 2009, about five of every six custodial parents were mothers (or 82.2 percent). Fewer than half of all custodial partents received the full amount of child support due, and nearly 30 percent received none. In 2009, about 28 percent of all custodial parents and their children had incomes below the poverty level, a rate twice as high as the total population. The poverty rate of custodial mothers (30.4 percent) was significantly more than the poverty rate of custodial fathers (18.8 percent) (U.S. Census Bureau 2011f).

The legacy of a woman's traditional role as caretaker of her family can be seen in a variety of statistical data. First, women are more likely than men to be single parents. Women headed 67 percent of households of those who never married, 77 percent of those who were separated, and 75 percent of those who were divorced (U.S. Census Bureau 2011g).

And while women are contributing to household income by working outside the home, they are finding that they are still responsible for being the family's primary caretaker. In the workplace, this creates problems. Time taken out of work in order to care for sick children is seen as nonproductive time, and women who do take such time off may face discrimination (Wharton and Blair-Loy 2002). And most women, when they leave work, still face household chores at home—the "second shift."

Health

Of the almost 315 million Americans, more than half are female. Why are there more women? One reason is that women live longer; females born in 2010 are expected to live for an average of 80.8 years, whereas males are expected to live 75.7 years (U.S. Census Bureau 2012c). Research by Thomas Perls and Ruth Fretts at Harvard Medical School suggests that the sex hormones estrogen and testosterone may be a possible cause. For example, young men aged fifteen to twenty-four are four or five times likelier than young women to die from car accidents, homicides, and drownings. After age twenty-four, the gap narrows again until middle age. Then, starting at age fifty-five, death rates for men increase again, this time from heart disease, stroke, suicide, car accidents, and illness related to smoking and alcohol consumption. Perls and Fretts note that testosterone is linked to aggressive and violent behavior, as well as heart disease and harmful cholesterol in the blood. On the other hand, estrogen lowers harmful cholesterol and reduces the likelihood of heart disease and stroke. These days, however, more women are engaged in stress-related behavior—such as working outside the home, smoking, and drinking—so the gap may be closing. For example, female deaths from lung cancer have tripled in the past twenty years, leading Perls and Fretts to label smoking as "the great equalizer" (Perls and Fretts 1998).

While both women and men suffer from heart disease and cancer in fairly equal numbers, other health disorders are gender related. One example is depression, which women are twice as likely to suffer from as men (Kessler 2003). Historically, the medical profession has diagnosed women far more than men with depression, "hysteria," and other mental conditions. Thus, women have been denied equal rights and equitable working conditions and pay because they were thought, as a category, to be mentally unfit. This issue, however, is controversial. Some maintain that the larger percentage of depressed women may be a result of reporting rather than the actual numbers of cases. In other words, women may be more likely to report such symptoms, whereas men may ignore them or may feel a greater sense of stigma in reporting them (Byrne 1981).

Education

Women are more likely than men to finish high school and attend college. Of the estimated 16.6 million students in college in 2007, approximately 9.5 million were women and 7.1 million were men (*Christian Science Monitor* 2007). In fact, since 1980, women have increasingly outnumbered men in college, especially in the traditional eighteen-to-twenty-two age group (U.S. Bureau of Labor Statistics 2011b). However, men have been more likely to attain four-year and advanced degrees. In 2010, 30.3 percent of men twenty-five years and over had a bachelor's degree or higher compared with 29.6 percent of women (U.S. Census Bureau 2012b). (Even though women numerically earn more bachelor's and master's degrees, men proportionately earn more.) Men are also more likely to earn more money per degree granted.

In fact, men out-earn women at every level of education, from incomplete high school to advanced degrees. These wage discrepancies make gender inequality very difficult to ignore. Women with four-year and professional degrees earn significantly less than their male counterparts, as shown in Table 9.3.

Work and Income

In whatever aspect of work we analyze—the rates of participation in the labor force, the kinds of jobs, the levels of pay, the balance between work and family—gender inequality is highly visible. For example, in 2010, 71.2 percent of men were in the labor force, but only 58.6 percent of women (though women's participation rates have been increasing over time). Interestingly, while men and women have historically had relatively similar rates of unemployment, in 2010 significantly more men (10.5 percent) were unemployed than women (8.6 percent). But because traditional family dynamics still endure, women are more likely than men to be found outside the labor force altogether (U.S. Census Bureau 2012h).

Marriage seems to have opposite effects on women and men's participation rates. Single women are more likely to work than married women, while married men are more likely to work than single men. In 2010, 63.3 percent of single women (as opposed to 61 percent of married women) worked, while 75.8 percent of married men (compared with nearly 67.3 percent of single men) did. This discrepancy could possibly be explained by the assumption that men are head of the household, and single women are considered responsible for their own finances.

Since 1970, the number of mothers in the labor force has been on the rise. Only 53 percent of single mothers and 40.8 percent of married mothers in 1970 participated in the labor force. In 2009, this rose to 63.7 percent for single mothers and 61.7 percent for married mothers. These numbers are slightly less than the peak of 68.6 percent for single mothers and 62 percent for married mothers in 2000 (U.S. Census Bureau 2011j).

Many jobs are gendered; they traditionally have been and continue to be performed by women or men. As Table 9.4 shows, nurses, kindergarten teachers, dental hygienists, secretaries, paralegals, and housekeepers are female-dominated professions, whereas airplane pilots, auto mechanics, firefighters, carpenters, mechanical engineers, and the clergy are male-dominated professions. In 2010, 97.7 percent of all teachers of young children and 95.9 percent of secretaries were women. Only 1.4 percent of all automotive mechanics and 4.5 percent of all firefighters were women. Gendered jobs have far-reaching consequences. For example, physicians often earn four or more times as much as nurses. So when women constitute 91.1 percent of all nurses but only 33.8 percent of all physicians, the monetary stakes are striking.

Why are some jobs considered best performed by women and others by men? Why are women vastly underrepresented as pilots and auto mechanics and men nearly absent as nurses, secretaries, and child-care workers? Socially constructed categories of occupations are extremely resilient. Despite advances in workplace technologies that would enable both women and men to perform similarly in jobs, men still vastly outnumber women in certain professions,

Table 9.3 Hourly Earnings for Men and Women by Education Level, 1973–2007 (2007 Dollars)

Educational Attainment	Hourly Earnings, 1973		Hourly Earnings, 2007		Percent Change in Real Earnings, 1973–2007	
	Men	Women	Men	Women	Men	Women
Less than high school	$15.72	$9.48	$12.32	$9.72	−22.0%	2.5%
High school diploma	$18.64	$11.73	$16.68	$13.00	−10.5%	10.8%
Some college	$19.05	$12.68	$18.95	$15.09	−0.5%	19.0%
College graduate	$25.71	$17.56	$30.36	$22.72	18.0%	29.4%
Advanced degree	$28.56	$23.26	$38.10	$28.93	33.4%	24.4%

SOURCE: Mishel, Bernstein, and Shierholz 2009.

Table 9.4   Selected Occupations by Gender, 2010

Occupation	Percent Men	Percent Women
Preschool and kindergarten teachers	2.3	97.7
Secretaries and administrative assistants	4.1	95.9
Dental hygienists	2.5	97.5
Registered nurses	8.9	91.1
Maids and housekeepers	11.4	88.6
Paralegals and legal assistants	15.7	84.3
Librarians	13.8	86.2
Travel agents	20.6	79.4
Waiters and waitresses	30.5	69.5
Psychologists	28.8	71.2
Customer service representatives	33.5	66.5
Medical scientists	45.6	54.4
Retail salespersons	48.8	51.2
News reporters and correspondents	65.9	34.1
Lawyers	68.1	31.9
Physicians and surgeons	66.2	33.8
Chief executives	75.8	24.2
Computer programmers	79.2	20.8
Clergy	82.3	17.7
Firefighters	95.5	4.5
Aircraft pilots and flight engineers	95.7	4.3
Carpenters	97.7	1.9
Automotive service technicians and mechanics	98.6	1.4

SOURCE: U.S. Bureau of Labor Statistics 2011a.

especially those with high salaries and prestige. It is also interesting to note that jobs that are traditionally female are consistently undervalued and underpaid. "Pink-collar" jobs—nurses, secretaries, librarians—are considered less desirable in a patriarchal society (England 1992).

Income levels and poverty rates also show inequality between women and men. In 2009, men earned an average of $47,715, while the average for women was $36,931. The earnings ratio (sometimes called the earnings gap) has improved since the 1960s and 70s; however, the 2010 earnings ratio of 77:100 still translates to 77 cents earned by women for each dollar earned by men (Figure 9.1).

In 2010, the median income for married-couple households was $72,751. For male-headed households with no female

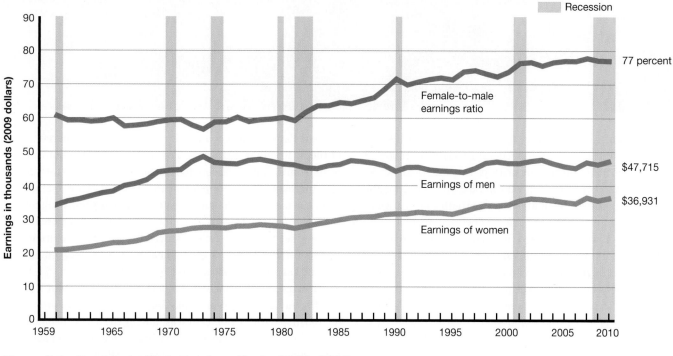

Figure 9.1 Female-to-Male Earnings Ratio, 1960–2010

The earnings gap between men and women has narrowed somewhat, but it has yet to close.

SOURCE: U.S. Census Bureau 2011i.

present, the median income was $49,718—dramatically higher than the $32,031 for female-headed households with no male present. The median household income for women living alone was $25,456, while for single men it was $35,627. Finally, women are more likely to live in poverty than men. This situation, often referred to as the **feminization of poverty**, results from a combination of social forces, including the gendered gap in wages, the higher proportion of single women taking on the financial responsibility of children, and increasing costs of child care. Of the 46.2 million Americans living below the poverty line in 2010, females constituted the largest group, whether living alone or in female-headed households (U.S. Census Bureau 2011i).

The Military

The military provides a particular case study when it comes to issues of work and gender. The huge institution that is the military is composed mostly of men. Until recently, women were restricted to non-combat units (though the reality of war meant they often found themselves in the midst of combat situations). In 2006, only 14.6 percent of enlisted personnel were female. Of the reserves, only 17 percent were women. At the end of 2006, 85.4 percent of the five branches of the military, including the Coast Guard, were male. In 2008, Lieutenant General Ann E. Dunwoody became the first woman promoted to the rank of four-star general in the

U.S. armed forces. Beginning in 2012, U.S. armed forces began implementing plans to include women in all units, including those previoulsy closed to them.

Slightly more women than men in the military report being the object of unwanted sexual attention. However, women are far more likely than men to report gender harassment. Laura Miller (1997) makes the distinction that gender harassment, rather than being sexual in nature, instead is used to enforce traditional gender norms, such as aggression in males and nurturing in females, as well as to punish violations of these norms. Interestingly, men in Miller's study were more likely to report being harassed by their drill sergeants, while women were more likely to be harassed by their fellow trainees. Rape is a growing problem in the military as well. A 2009 Pentagon report states that nearly 3,000 women were sexually assaulted in 2008—up almost 10 percent from the prior year—but that same report also acknowledges that 80 to 90 percent of military rapes go unreported as a result of fears of ostracism, retaliation, and lack of institutional response. Indeed, 80 percent of male service members convicted in sexual assault cases still receive honorable discharges (Gibbs 2010). Despite the progress made

FEMINIZATION OF POVERTY the economic trend showing that women are more likely than men to live in poverty, caused in part by the gendered gap in wages, the higher proportion of single mothers compared to single fathers, and the increasing costs of child care

ON THE JOB

The Mancession

February of 2009 saw a milestone in U.S. economic history. For the first time ever, the federal government reported that women made up the majority of the American workforce. The number of women who worked climbed dramatically through the second half of the twentieth century, while the number of men in the workforce declined. In 1950, only 34 percent of women worked, compared to 86 percent of men. By the 1990s, the proportion of men in the workforce had declined to 76 percent, while women's labor force participation had skyrocketed to 58 percent. These changes were largely seen as positive developments. The men who left the workforce were mostly those who wanted to, while new career paths were opened up for women (Toossi 2006, p. 25). These trends, however, took on a different meaning in the most recent economic downturn. The recession that hit the United States from 2007 to 2009 was called the "mancession" or "hecession" by some because of the way it hurt male workers.

Economic recessions have long affected men and women differently, but until the recession of 1981–82, it was usually women whose unemployment rate rose higher. Starting in the 1980s, this changed. While "unemployment rates by gender were approximately equal during economic expansions," they were "significantly higher for men than women during recessions" (Perry 2010, p. 5). The first "male-based recession" of 1981–1982 was "followed by subsequent male-based recessions in 1990–1991 and 2001" (Perry 2010, p. 5). However, while the recession of 2007–2009 followed the pattern of these previous economic crises, it did so on an unprecedented scale. During this recession, 7.5 million jobs vanished and "men accounted for 5.4 million, or 71 percent" of them (Kochhar 2011, p. 1). The male unemployment rate went from around 5 percent to 10.5 percent, while the female rate increased from 4.8 percent to 8 percent. This change, from the male unemployment rate being marginally higher than the female rate to the male rate being 2.5 percent higher, "set a new all-time historical record for the greatest male-female jobless gap" since the Labor Department started keeping such statistics (Perry 2010, p. 2).

Although a difference of 2.5 percent may not seem like much, this difference represents "huge, historically unprecedented disparities in jobless rates" during the period because "never before in American history has a recession had such a disproportionate effect on one gender" (Perry 2010, p. 5). What remains unclear is the effect that this will have in the long run. Since the economy began its recovery in mid-2009, this trend has sharply reversed, leading some to call the recovery a "he-covery," as the male unemployment rate fell sharply, while the female rate increased slightly. However, the implications of the "mancession" are profound. Men lost jobs so much more quickly because the industries hit hardest by the recession were male dominated, especially construction and manufacturing, while the industries least affected, like health care and education, have long been female preserves. These changes are almost certainly permanent. Manufacturing jobs have been declining for years, and "of the thirty professions projected to add the most jobs over the next decade, women dominate twenty, including nursing, accounting, home health assistance, child care and food

---

by women in ascending the ranks, the military can still be an inhospitable place for women.

Criminal Justice

The experience of men and women differs with regard to almost every social institution, and the criminal justice system is no exception. The social construction of masculinity as aggressive, dominant, and physical translates directly into statistics regarding gender and crime. Men are more likely to die violent deaths and to be victims of assault. Women are slightly more likely to be victims of personal theft and much more likely to be victims of rape. Also, women are far more likely to be victimized by their intimate partners (spouses or current or former boyfriends). Between 1998 and 2002, almost 85 percent of spousal abuse victims were female and a little more than 85 percent of dating partner abuse victims were female (U.S. Department of Justice 2005).

In analyzing arrest rates for 2009, we find that men are overwhelmingly represented in nearly all categories, including murder, rape, sex offenses, theft, assault, and drug charges. In only two categories do women and girls outnumber men and boys: prostitution and runaways (a juvenile offense). In 2009, there were 27,709 arrests of women for prostitution and 13,105 arrests of men for the same charge;

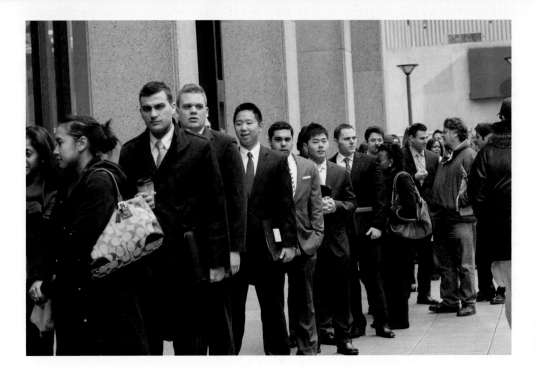

A He-covery? Job-seekers attended the Big East Career Fair in 2013.

preparation" (Rosin 2012, p. 124). Some speculate that this will lead to a dramatic shift in gender roles, as the work-home dichotomy that long structured masculinity and femininity is deconstructed. Others, like Hannah Rosin in her provocatively titled book *The End of Men: And the Rise of Women*, see this as the beginning of a female renaissance. Still others think that it will simply lead to a shift in the jobs that are primarily female, as men move into professions that used to be dominated by women. Regardless of what the future holds, the "mancession" has shown not only that the very nature of the U.S. economy changing but that as it changes, all of society will shift with it.

35,653 girls were arrested as runaways compared with 29,503 boys. It is important for us as sociologists to recognize this discrepancy as an example of how crime is influenced by the social construction of gender. Because of the tendency to think of girls as weak and needing protection, female runaways are more likely to be reported as missing by parents as well as intercepted by the police. On the other hand, because males are perceived as being more likely to be involved in violent and property crime, they are generally kept under more scrutiny by the police than are females. Of the nearly 2 million people in correctional institutions, the vast majority (around 90 percent) are men (Federal Bureau of Investigation 2010c).

By analyzing such visible indicators as labor participation rates, income levels, arrest rates, and experiences related to the family, work, education, and the military, we can easily see the real consequences of gender inequality: women and men experience life differently. So what can we say about the life outcomes of our two infants? The female is more likely to live longer. Though they are both likely to marry, she is more likely to be divorced or widowed. She is more likely to graduate from high school and to attend college. However, if the male also attends college, he is more likely to graduate. If they earn the same degree, he will probably earn more money. Each has a good chance of ending up in certain professions over others (the military for him, nursing for her). He is more likely to die a violent death, while she is more likely to experience rape or some other crime perpetrated by someone with whom she's intimate. While their gender categories surely do not guarantee these experiences, we as sociologists can safely make such predictions in the aggregate.

INTERSECTIONALITY Once again, the issue of intersectionality is important to keep in mind when we discuss gender and life chances: gender almost never shapes individual experience in isolation, but is instead linked to other social statuses in the effects it has on our lives. The intersection of gender with class, race, ethnicity, and immigration status is visible in Miliann Kang's study of the work of Asian immigrant women (mostly from Korea) in nail salons. Kang argues that the femininity that is central to the beauty rituals performed in salons is also racialized. For example, the expectations our society has for Asian women are different from the expectations for their non-Asian female clientele. Because the quality of "subservience," for instance, is often seen as "natural" in Asian women, customers may feel that they can make more demands upon their manicurists than they would with other service providers. Indeed, Kang observed manicurists providing "massage, elder-care, counseling for teens, community outreach [and] therapy for stressed-out clients" (Kang 2010, p. 240) in addition to the salon services for which they were ostensibly being paid. When customers and workers meet over the manicure table, they are not just coming together as women who share gendered experiences. Indeed, they may not share experiences at all, given their different class, race, and ethnic

SECOND SHIFT the unpaid housework and child care often expected of women after they complete their day's paid labor

identities. For example, you might think of manicures as a kind of girly indulgence—an activity that, while not strictly a necessity, is an important part of a woman's beauty regimen. But not all participants see their manicures the same way. One of Kang's respondents, an African American customer, talks about the meaning of her manicure by referencing race rather than gender: "Black people on a whole have not been the ones who get pampered. There was a time when only white people could do this" (Kang 2010, p. 165). For her, manicures are a symbol of progress (for black people, at least) in the arena of racial justice. Kang's work shows us how race and gender, along with other social statuses, intersect at the nail salon (and in other settings as well).

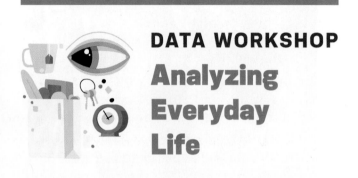

DATA WORKSHOP
Analyzing Everyday Life

The Second Shift: Gendered Norms and Household Labor

The **second shift**, a term coined by sociologist Arlie Hochschild, refers to the unpaid work—cooking, cleaning, laundry, child care, home repair, yard work—that must be done at home after the day's paid labor is complete. For this Data

Salons and Status Class, race, and gender intersect at the manicure table. For some women, manicures represent a hard-won indulgence; for the women who work at salons, their immigrant status is often linked to an expectation of subservience.

Workshop, you will investigate second shift work by using interviews as a research method (see Chapter 2 for further discussion) and asking a working parent about how he or she juggles family and work. Here are some guidelines to follow:

* Ask a working parent to be candid and to answer your questions as fully as possible. Prepare to take detailed notes, and ask if you can record the interview for later transcription.

* Come up with a list of questions before you start the interview. Include some open-ended as well as closed-ended questions.

* For starters, ask the person to describe *everything* he or she does in a typical day, perhaps using the previous day as an example. Be sure nothing is overlooked. For example, if the description starts with the parent's arrival at the office, remind him or her of earlier morning activities, such as making breakfast or getting children ready for school.

* Try to identify all the types of work that your respondent does in a typical day, including paid work, unpaid work, interaction work, emotion work, and so on.

* Find out how tasks are divided between members of the household (spouse/partner, children, others). Also try to determine how completing all these tasks (or not completing them) affects the respondent's relationships with other members of the household.

As you conduct the interview, you'll notice that some tasks must be done every day, or even several times each day—cooking meals, for example. Other tasks (such as laundry) are done less often but on a regular basis. Still others are irregular or seasonal: raking leaves or taking the car in for a tune-up. You'll also find that some tasks are focused on people (like planning birthday parties), whereas others (cleaning out the gutters) are focused on objects. And some tasks are paid labor, while some are not.

After completing the interview, look at all the tasks your respondents have mentioned. Then ask *yourself* these questions:

* Does there appear to be a gendered division of labor at home?

* How are the tasks divided?

* Who does most of the daily tasks?

Chances are, you'll find that there are gendered patterns in terms of who does what at home. Studies show that men tend to participate in more instrumental tasks, such as car repair and yard work, jobs that are more irregular and seasonal, while women tend to the daily needs of their family by doing the endless tasks of cooking and cleaning and by engaging in expressive work, such as mediating arguments and calming upset children. This is how women rack up an extra month of housework a year (that's a month of twenty-four-hour days)! What effects might these inequities have on marriages and live-in relationships? Does one person always seem to be doing more work than the other person? What are some possible solutions to this problem?

There are two options for completing this Data Workshop.

Option 1 (informal): Prepare some written notes, and compare your notes and experiences with those of other students in small-group discussions. Take this opportunity to learn more about how families do the everyday work required to keep a household running and about the different hierarchies of inequalities that shape this work.

Option 2 (formal): Write a three- to four-page essay analyzing your interview data. Make sure to use specific quotations from your respondent, and include a transcript of the interview (or your notes) as an attachment.

Gender and Language

* What is the difference between a stud and a slut?

* What do the following have in common: bitch, cow, heifer, angel, baby, doll, sweetie pie, cupcake, sugar?

* What do the following have in common: man-made, mankind, manpower, manslaughter?

To answer these questions, we need to think about how language reflects culture. Some sociologists argue that language shapes culture, while others say the opposite. In any case, by looking at our language, we can see how certain words reflect cultural values and norms, particularly sexism.

For instance, positions of power and authority often directly emphasize the male gender in their very names. Examples are "congressman," "chairman," "policeman," "fireman," and "mailman." Such words imply that one gender is more suited for a particular job than the other. Other words, like "nurse/doctor," "flight attendant/pilot," and "secretary/executive," have been gendered without the use of explicit male or female markers. In this case, markers are usually attached if the job holder is of "the other" gender: "woman doctor," "woman pilot," "woman astronaut," "male nurse," and "male secretary." Again, these examples reinforce stereotypes of gendered jobs.

The English language also seems to assume that the default category for all human experience is male. We have traditionally referred to the human race as "mankind" and noted that "all men are created equal." The root of words like "man-made," "manslaughter," and "manpower," "man," means "human." If something is man-made, it is made by humans. But clearly, not everyone experiences the world from a male perspective.

IN THE FUTURE

Human Trafficking

In 1995, law enforcement raided a factory in El Monte, a suburb on the eastern side of Los Angeles, because the people working in the factory were, effectively, slaves. It is not a word that is often used in a contemporary context, but seventy-two men and women were living there, prevented from leaving by armed guards and razor-wire fences. The "workers" were recruited under false pretenses in Thailand, then smuggled into the United States and told that if they tried to leave the factory they would be abused and deported. The vast majority of them were women, who were seen as more vulnerable and easier to control than men. "Some of the women were cowed by their captors' earlier descriptions of U.S. police, so much so that they refused to unlock the door when the factory was finally raided by law enforcement (Watanabe 2008). Some of the victims had been there more than four years at that point.

The incident was widely considered the first case of slavery in the United States since the Civil War, but since then others have come to light. This has led to a dramatic increase in the awareness of human trafficking around the world. In 2000, the United Nations organized a convention to fight transnational organized crime, and drafted the *Protocol to Prevent, Suppress and Punish Trafficking in Persons, Especially Women and Children*. This was the first time that there was an internationally recognized definition of human trafficking: "the recruitment, transportation, transfer, harbouring or receipt of persons, by means of the threat or use of force or other forms of coercion, of abduction, of fraud, of deception, of the abuse of power or of a position of vulnerability . . . for the purpose of exploitation." In other words, modern-day slavery not only exists but is perhaps a problem of greater proportion than we might expect.

Human trafficking takes many forms, and while labor trafficking is a significant problem, victims who are trafficked into the sex industry often garner more attention, because this crime seems even more heinous. Like all illegal activities, it is difficult to get accurate numbers on sex trafficking, with estimates ranging from 600,000 to more than 2.5 million people being trafficked worldwide each year. High or low, the numbers are shocking. Michelle Bachelet, former president of Chile and head of a new U.N. agency on women's rights and gender equality, called sex trafficking "one of the fastest growing" and most lucrative crimes in the world (Lederer 2012).

Because it is characterized by secrecy, it is hard to say with certainty how many people are trafficked each year. In the 1990s, some organizations were claiming "that there were 4 million sex workers in Thailand," which "would have meant that 24 percent of the female population . . . between

---

Our language is also a good site for analyzing double standards, which have long been researched by sociologists (Carns 1973; Sprecher, McKinney, and Orbuch 1987). For instance, in the workplace, aggressive men are called "go-getters," while aggressive women may be called "bitches." Men who frequently have sex are called "players," while women are called "sluts." To be called a player is a different experience than to be called a slut. The behaviors are similar, but the labels have very different connotations. A 2001 study of sex education films that were aimed at adolescents found the player/slut double standard embedded in the actual film scripts (Hartley and Drew 2001). These films legitimized male sexual desire while minimizing female desire, implying that males should engage in sexual pursuit while females should wait to be pursued. Women are often referred to as "cows," "heifers," "babies," or "cupcakes." Boyfriends aren't usually called "baby dolls," and males don't call their male friends "heifers." Food must be consumed, babies must be coddled, animals must be controlled. Sociologists under-stand that these nicknames for women function as mechanisms of social control.

Along with words, speech patterns also reflect our sexist culture (Tannen 2001). Conversation analysts, sociologists who study verbal and nonverbal language patterns, find that men dominate women in conversation. They are more likely to interrupt women than they are to interrupt men (Smith-Lovin and Brody 1989) and more likely to control the subject matter of conversations. Women tend to be more concerned with keeping a conversation going rather than with controlling its direction. However, some research suggests that authority rather than gender dictates conversation patterns (Kollock, Blumstein, and Schwartz 1985; C. Johnson 1994). Thus, women may control the conversation when they are in positions of legitimate authority, as a manager is when talking with her employee. Since men are more likely to occupy authoritative positions, however, they are still more likely to dominate in conversation.

It is worth noting that language can also reflect social change. It is now fairly common to see and hear "Will every-

Modern-day Slavery Victims of human trafficking line up at a Houston, Texas massage parlor.

the age of ten and thirty-nine was engaged in commercial sex work" (Feingold 2010, p. 51). One of the more rigorous studies that used sampling methods to survey sex workers in Cambodia arrived at an estimate of 20,829 total sex workers in the country, with about 2,488 of those being trafficked, a considerably lower number than usually mentioned by the media (Steinfatt et al. 2002).

In 1999, the State Department estimated that "50,000 slaves were pouring into the United States every year" and that many of them were forced into prostitution (Markon 2007). That estimate was later reduced to a lower number of cases, closer to 15,000. Between the years 2000 and 2007, there were only 1,362 victims of trafficking who were actually identified by the federal government. And in 2012, the United Nations estimated that there were 2.4 million victims of human trafficking across the globe, and that some 80 percent of them were being exploited as sexual slaves. But according to the United Nations, only 1 in 100 victims is ever rescued (Lederer 2012).

The trafficking of girls and women as sex slaves remains an emotional issue, regardless of the arguments about the accuracy of the numbers. It is still something that is hard to imagine can exist in modern-day form, in the United States or elsewhere in the world. Because it is a crime that is so difficult to combat, future efforts to stop trafficking must involve raising awareness of the issue, identifying and resolving the problems that make people vulnerable to trafficking (such as extreme poverty and gender bias), and coordinating international law enforcement efforts. Sociological insight is necessary for all of these things to occur.

one please open his or her book" or "their book" in place of "his book." Also, increasingly, we hear such gender-neutral references as "mail carriers," "firefighters," "servers," "chairpersons," and "humankind." These efforts at gender neutrality are efforts to reform sexist language. For if language shapes culture, then using gender-neutral language should facilitate social change. On the other hand, if language is shaped by culture, then the use of nonsexist words is a signal of positive social change.

The Women's Movement

Feminism is the belief in the social, political, and economic equality of the sexes *and* the social movements organized around that belief. Thus, feminism is both a theoretical perspective and a social movement. It is important to keep in mind that feminist concepts and goals are not static but are always focused on bringing about greater gender equality in

a particular time and place. Rebecca West, an early-twentieth-century feminist, put it this way in 1913: "I myself have never been able to find out precisely what feminism is. I only know that people call me a feminist whenever I express sentiments that differentiate me from a doormat or a prostitute" (Shiach 1999).

FEMINISM belief in the social, political, and economic equality of the sexes; also the social movements organized around that belief

FIRST WAVE the earliest period of feminist activism in the United States, including the period from the mid-nineteenth century until American women won the right to vote in 1920

First Wave

In the United States, the history of the women's movement can be divided into three historical waves. The **first wave** began with a convention held in Seneca Falls, New York, in 1848, organized by Elizabeth Cady Stanton and Lucretia

Mott. The convention, numbering about 300 people, issued a Declaration of Sentiments stating generally that "all men and women are created equal" and demanded specifically that women be given the right to vote. Stanton believed that in a democracy the right to vote was the fundamental right on which all others depended. Not surprisingly, then, the campaign to win the vote (known as the **suffrage movement**) became the cause most identified with the first wave of the women's movement, even though that goal would not be achieved until 1920. Neither Stanton nor Mott nor the well-known suffragist Susan B. Anthony would live to see victory. Of the 100 women and men who signed the Declaration of Sentiments, only one, a young worker named Charlotte Woodward, lived to cast a ballot.

Second Wave

Just as the first wave of feminism is most closely associated with the right to vote, the **second wave**, which took place during the 1960s and 70s, is associated with equal access to education and employment. The publication of Betty Friedan's *The Feminine Mystique* in 1963, the establishment of the National Organization for Women (NOW) in 1966, and the emergence of women's consciousness-raising groups were

key events in second-wave feminism. In those decades, young activists felt that the women's movement had lost its momentum after the vote was won and that other issues needed to be addressed. In the opening pages of *The Feminine Mystique*, Friedan spoke of "the problem that had no name," a problem that "lay buried, unspoken, for many years in the minds of American women" (1963/2001, p. 55): the sense of limitation and dissatisfaction that many women felt with their lives.

During one of the most prosperous periods in American history, Friedan was discovering that countless women were unhappy with the traditional roles they had been assigned, that the "mystique of feminine fulfillment" was no longer so fulfilling (1963/2001, p. 18). Women were restricted from pursuing activities outside these traditional roles, whether by cultural norms or by actual laws that barred them from schools, workplaces, and professional organizations. Women who tried to breach these barriers were seen as "unfeminine." Some were even told, as former North Carolina senator Elizabeth Dole was when she entered Harvard Law School in 1962, that they were taking an opportunity away from a more deserving man.

So the second wave of the women's movement pushed for and achieved such reforms as equal opportunity laws, legislation against sexual harassment and marital rape, and a general increase in public awareness about gender discrimination in our society. Some of the public, however, reacted with hostility to women's demands for legal and cultural "liberation," and there continues to be a certain amount of backlash against feminist causes as a result.

The Suffrage Movement Of the 100 women and men who signed the Declaration of Sentiments in Seneca Falls in 1848, only one, a young worker named Charlotte Woodward, lived to cast a ballot in 1920.

Third Wave

Beginning in the 1980s and 90s, the **third wave** of feminism focused primarily on diversity. These feminists criticize the first two waves for concentrating on "women" as one category (mainly white and middle class) and marginalizing the concerns of women of color, lesbians, and working-class women. Third-wave feminism is also concerned with the rights of women in all countries and with environmental and animal rights. The movement includes many if not most college students—even if you don't call yourself a feminist, you likely believe in feminist values, such as equality, diversity, and global interconnectedness. You are the third wave, and you will help make a difference.

The Men's Movement

The men's movement emerged from the same cultural climate in the late twentieth century that had ushered in the second and third waves of feminism. The women's movement had asked us to rethink gender roles and the place of women in society, and men have responded in a variety of ways. Some have countered feminists' arguments, some have agreed with and supported feminism, and some have taken positions somewhere in between. And just as feminism called womanhood into question, so too did men begin reexamining what it means to be man.

In the mid-1970s, the notion of **male liberationism** (or the need to free men from oppressive gender roles) became more widespread. Influential studies pointed to evidence that men suffer from greater stress, poorer health, and a shorter life expectancy, and argued that these resulted from pressures to achieve success combined with an inability to express themselves (Farrell 1975; Goldberg 1976). American men had become confused about what it means to be a "real man" (Kimmel 1987). They were facing new discomfort and anxiety about their masculinity. These ideas became fairly popular, largely among middle-class heterosexual men, and some sought counseling or formed discussion groups about "the male role" (Segal 1990). Men were coming together and organizing in an attempt to address their own concerns, and what was called a "crisis of masculinity" (Bly 1990; Connell 1995; Faludi 1999).

As the men's movement grew, it also splintered into two primary factions. The **men's rights movement** (which also includes the father's rights movement) argues that because of feminism, men are actually discriminated against and even oppressed both in the legal arena and in everyday life. These men (and some women too) suggest that feminism has created a new kind of sexism by privileging women,

THIRD WAVE the most recent period of feminist activity, focusing on issues of diversity and the variety of identities women can possess

MALE LIBERATIONISM a movement that originated in the 1970s to discuss the challenges of masculinity

MEN'S RIGHTS MOVEMENT an offshoot of male liberationism whose members believe that feminism promotes discrimination against men

The Problem That Had No Name In *The Feminine Mystique,* Betty Friedan (center) articulated a sense of limitation and dissatisfaction that many women felt with their lives.

or by attempting to erase differences altogether. The **pro-feminist men's movement**, on the other hand, is based in the belief that men should support feminism in the interest of fairness to women and because men's lives are also constrained by gender and sexism—and are enriched by feminist social change. Pro-feminists suggest that the idea that men are superior is a burden and that, in the long term, men will be happier if society becomes less sexist. They argue that men need to share more of the responsibilities of child care, contest economic disparities and violence against women, and generally respect women's lives. However much society has changed because of these movements, serious questions remain about men's and women's roles and the future of their relations with each other.

Sexuality and Sexual Orientation

What is **sexuality**? And what is it doing in a sociology textbook? The term "sexuality" is used in a variety of ways; for example, it is used to describe sexual behavior, desires, and fantasies (the things people actually do as well as the things we think or dream about doing). It is also used to describe **sexual orientation** or **sexual identity**, which is the inclination to feel sexual desire toward and engage in sexual behavior with persons of a particular gender.

Our society recognizes a number of different sexual identities or orientations, and they are each related to our two-category gender system. **Heterosexuality**, or sexual desire for the other gender, is the normative and dominant category, which may be why the slang term for it is "straight." Most people identify themselves as heterosexual, and there are privileges attached to membership in this category. **Homosexuality**, or sexual desire for the same gender, is a minority category—the National Survey of Sexual Health and Behavior found that about 4 percent of adults self-identify as gay or lesbian (Reece et al. 2010), and as with other minority statuses, there are a variety of difficulties and disadvantages attached to membership in this

category. **Bisexuality**—sexual attraction to both genders—is also a minority category, with about 3 percent of men and 4 percent of women identifying as bisexual (Reece et al. 2010). **Asexuality** involves the lack of sexual attraction of any kind. Asexual people are basically nonsexual and are a very small minority group, with only about 1 percent of adults identifying as asexual (Bogaert 2004).

Where does our sexual orientation originate? Is it genetic, or is it a result of cultural or environmental factors? This question has long been debated. In the late 1800s, Karl Heinrich Ulrichs, a German lawyer who was perhaps the first gay activist, contended that sexual orientation was linked to gender and that gender was a product of hereditary factors, probably related to hormones (Ulrichs 1994). This line of thinking has persisted, but it was only with the arrival of genetic research in the 1990s that it gained added awareness. Is there in fact a "gay gene," or is homosexuality the product of socialization? Or might it be a combination of both?

One of the first studies to gain widespread attention was conducted in the early 1990s by J. M. Bailey and R. C. Pillard, researchers who hypothesized that sexual orientation was at least in part congenital, or present at birth (1991). They tested this hypothesis by examining the sexual orientation of different sets of twins, and their results suggested that they were right. Bailey and Pillard found that 52 percent of the identical twins of gay men were also gay and that 48 percent of the identical twins of lesbian women were also lesbian. Another study, conducted in 1992 by Laura Allen and Roger Gorski, found that a segment of the fibers connecting the hemispheres of the brain was up to one-third larger in gay men, again suggesting a possible biological basis. Other studies by Simon LeVay (1991, 1993) and Dean Hamer (Hamer et al. 1993) also support the possibility of biological or genetic bases for homosexuality (and, by logical inference, heterosexuality).

Despite the evidence pointing to a genetic origin of homosexuality, some believe that scientists, the media, and gay activists have overestimated its significance. One problem with the studies is that they may neglect the fact that genes interact in complicated ways—the same gene, or combination of genes, may produce different results in different environments. In other words, possessing a particular gene doesn't guarantee that a person will have a particular sexual orientation. Along these same lines, sociologists have criticized the idea of a "gay gene" for its narrow understanding of sexual orientation. For instance, it doesn't explain bisexuality or how biology and social environments interact to produce various sexual behaviors.

It may be some time before science can resolve these issues, but it's easy to see what's at stake in favoring one side over the other. The genetic model is seen as a weapon in the fight for gay rights: after all, if sexual orientation is something a person is born with, then discrimination based on sexual orientation is as unacceptable as discrimination

PRO-FEMINIST MEN'S MOVEMENT an offshoot of male liberationism whose members support feminism and believe that sexism harms both men and women

SEXUALITY the character or quality of being sexual

SEXUAL ORIENTATION or **SEXUAL IDENTITY** the inclination to feel sexual desire toward people of a particular gender or toward both genders

HETEROSEXUALITY sexual desire for the other gender

HOMOSEXUALITY the tendency to feel sexual desire toward members of one's own gender

BISEXUALITY sexual attraction to both genders; bisexuals are sexually attracted to both males and females

ASEXUALITY involves the lack of sexual attraction of any kind; asexual people have no interest in or desire for sex

Civil Unions Legal recognition of same-sex couples' committed relationships grants them many of the benefits that are given to married heterosexual couples, such as insurance benefits and the right to make medical decisions for one's partner.

based on gender, race, or disability. The biological view also offers a way to bypass some of the moral and religious debates about homosexuality. In addition, straight Americans often become more tolerant when they assume that sexual orientation is something people are born with rather than a "lifestyle choice."

Heterosexuality, Homosexuality, and "Queer" Sexuality

As early as the late 1940s, the pioneering sex researcher Alfred Kinsey was suggesting that human sexuality was far more diverse than was commonly assumed. His own studies led him to believe that people were not exclusively heterosexual or homosexual but could fall along a wide spectrum (Kinsey et al. 1948/1998; Kinsey and Gebhard 1953/1998). Kinsey and his associates developed a scale to measure this spectrum based on the degree of sexual responsiveness people had to members

of the same and opposite sex. They took into account not only measurements but also an individual's fantasies, dreams, and feelings and the frequency of particular sexual activities. Kinsey and others who have followed him have suggested that we can best understand sexual orientation not through simplistic categories (gay vs. straight; biology vs. environment) but rather as a fluid continuum that can change over the course of a person's lifetime.

For most of the twentieth century, "queer" was a pejorative term for homosexuals, mainly gay men. But in the 1990s, with the emergence of "queer theory," the term underwent a remarkable transformation as both activists and academics began using it. Why did this change occur? For one thing, the term includes many different sexualities and is thus more manageable. **Queer theory** rejects the idea of a single gay, lesbian, bisexual, heterosexual, or transgender identity, emphasizing instead the importance of difference (Butler 1993). It asserts that being queer is about "possibilities, gaps, overlaps, dissonances and resonances" (Sedgwick 1993, p. 8). Thus, queer theory goes against the arguments made by mainstream gay rights advocates who focus on the biological basis of homosexuality and the equal treatment of gays and lesbians; it holds that innate, inborn sexual identity is too limiting. In this spirit, "queers" are sometimes called a "third sex," emphasizing the claim that people don't have to be restricted to either heterosexuality or homosexuality.

QUEER THEORY social theory about gender identity and sexuality that emphasizes the importance of difference and rejects as restrictive the idea of innate sexual identity

LGBTQ lesbian, gay, bisexual, transgender, and queer; sometimes "A" is added to include "allies"

Sexual Orientation and Social Issues

In a society in which heterosexuality is the dominant category of sexual orientation, those with other types of sexual identities, often referred to as the **LGBTQ** community, are

0	1	2	3	4	5	6
Exclusively heterosexual	Predominately heterosexual; only incidentally homosexual	Predominately heterosexual, but more than incidentally homosexual	Equally heterosexual and homosexual	Predominately homosexual, but more than incidentally heterosexual	Predominately homosexual; only incidentally heterosexual	Excusively homosexual

Figure 9.2 The Kinsey Scale of Sexuality

The Kinsey Scale shows the spectrum of human sexuality.

IN RELATIONSHIPS

"Hooking Up"

Something happened to dating in 2001, when the longtime practice among college students of "hooking up" gained national attention. The American Values Institute (AVI) released its report to the great dismay of parents, educators, cultural critics, and policy makers. The study, by a team of sociologists at the University of Texas, titled "Hooking Up, Hanging Out and Hoping for Mr. Right: College Women on Mating and Dating," looked at how young people meet and examined their experiences with sexuality, courtship, and marriage. The findings shocked the nation and generated a firestorm of media coverage. While knowledge of this practice worried many, to students themselves, the notion of hooking up was commonplace and largely accepted, hardly a matter for such alarm.

Much of the concern centered on the meaning of "hooking up" and what exactly young people were up to. The public perception was that hooking up meant casual sex without commitment, typically between people who were but brief acquaintances beforehand. Other terms were also used to refer to the behavior, including "booty call" and "friends with benefits." Some suggested that hooking up was connected to a variety of other social problems, such as binge drinking, drug abuse, and sexually transmitted diseases. The media featured numerous stories told in moralistic terms about how the culture of the hook up was leading young women, especially, to their own demise with respect to any hope of having decent relationships and the possibility of marriage. At the same time, others were celebrating the phenomenon, and books with such titles as *The Happy Hook-Up: A Single Girl's Guide to Casual Sex* and *Hooking Up: A Girl's All-Out Guide to Sex and Sexuality* appeared on the scene.

When asked to define hooking up themselves, the majority of college students responded that it was "when a girl and a guy get together for a physical encounter and don't necessarily expect anything further." The physical encounter, however, could mean anything from kissing to oral sex

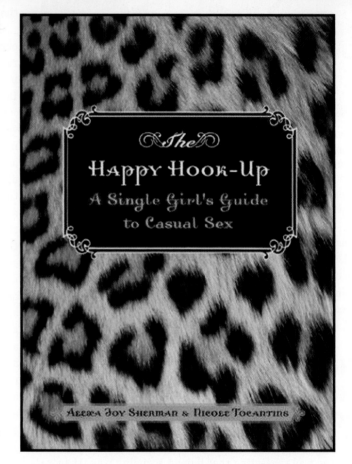

or intercourse. The ambiguity of the term might, in part, account for its popularity—it allows young people to remain vague about the nature or extent of an interaction when they say they hooked up with someone.

Paula England has done wide-scale research on the sexual behaviors of college students. Her Online College Social Life Survey (OCSLS) asked more than 14,000 students from nineteen different colleges and universities to report their participation in hook ups using "whatever definition of a hook up you and your friends use." Seventy-two percent of both men and women participating in the OCSLS reported at least one hook up by their senior year in college. Of these, roughly 40 percent engaged in three or fewer hook ups, 40 percent between four and nine hook ups, and 20 percent ten or more hook ups. Only about one-third engaged in intercourse in their most recent hook ups. Among the 80 percent of students who had intercourse by the end of college, however, 67 percent had done so outside of a relationship.

The AVI report warned that parents and other older adults were woefully unaware of how extraordinarily different today's behavior was from the "dating" of previous generations. Women reported that it was rare for men to ask them out on a date, that they would more often just "hang out," a loosely organized and undefined term for spending time together. Furthermore, after hanging out or hooking up, the women still did not know whether that constituted them as a couple. There was widespread confusion among women about how to navigate these encounters, and about the rules and expectations for hook ups as well as relationships. The report concluded that although women aspire to be married and believe that college is a good place to meet a husband, the current practices of hooking up and hanging out were not leading to that goal.

Laura Hamilton and Elizabeth Armstrong did an in-depth longitudinal ethnographic and interview study of a group of women who started college in 2004 at a university in the Midwest to uncover female college students' attitudes about hooking up. Although the sample was homogeneous—all the females were white, eighteen to twenty years of age, heterosexual except for two subjects, and overwhelmingly wealthy—Hamilton and Armstrong were able to present an alternative to the AVI's assumption that hooking up was problematic behavior for women. For many of the privileged females, college was seen as a time that they were allowed to be independent, as they expected to marry and have children shortly after they graduated. The ability to hook up rather than have relationships allowed them to be sexual without demanding the time, energy, and emotional labor that a relationship requires. Rather than simply being framed as women accommodating men's desires, the women in Hamilton and Armstrong's study expressed genuine interest in hooking up, with many claiming that the ability to experiment with sexual behavior was empowering to them. For at least some proportion of young women, hooking up is seen as a way to express sexual freedom.

Kathleen Bogle presents yet another alternative based on extensive interviews with college students. Bogle proposed that hooking up was not synonymous with the "one night stand" but rather, like dating, was a system of socializing with the opposite sex for the purpose of finding romantic partners. The big difference, however, was that in dating, people would get to know one another en route to sexual intimacy, while in hooking up, the sex comes first. Bogle claims that for the students involved, hooking up is about more than sex; it is a way for students to find a relationship. Although there are no strings attached in hooking up, and more often than not it does not evolve into anything else, it can still lead some couples to become exclusive.

So how worried should we be about the phenomenon of hooking up on college campuses? Have the social and sexual mores of students become too lax? Are young people doomed to superficial and fleeting encounters that leave them empty and confused? Or are they simply celebrating sexual freedom and finding new ways of relating to one another? Whatever your opinion on the matter, it is clear that the dating and mating game has changed and will continue to change in the future. And with the dominance of hooking up within the culture of the college social scene, young people may believe that they have few alternatives on the route to romance and marriage.

likely to experience certain disadvantages and be the objects of particular types of prejudices. Sexual orientation becomes a form of social stratification based on individual traits and identities, just like stratification systems based on race, class, or gender. Unfortunately, in our society, this means that there is a hierarchy of sexual orientations in which privileges, opportunities, prejudices, and discrimination are distributed based on category membership. Many believe that sexual minorities should not be granted the same rights as heterosexuals. The debates over same-sex marriage and the Don't Ask, Don't Tell laws help illustrate this problem.

While thirteen of the fifty states, plus the District of Columbia, perform or will begin to perform same-sex marriages in 2013, legal debates continue in each, and victories for gay rights can be short-lived and tenuous. In May 2008, the California Supreme Court overturned the state's previous ban, holding that statutes limiting marriage to heterosexual couples violated the state constitution, creating the opportunity for same-sex couples to begin marrying. Opponents to same-sex marriage immediately placed Proposition 8 on the November 2008 ballot to define marriage as solely "between a man and a woman." The ballot initiative passed, creating two legally distinct categories of California same-sex couples: those who no longer had the right to marry, and those who had married between May and November.

> **CIVIL UNIONS** proposed as an alternative to gay marriage; a form of legally recognized commitment that provides gay couples some of the benefits and protections of marriage

The issue of same-sex marriage in California went to the U.S. Supreme Court in June 2013, when the court decided that the plaintiffs had no "standing" or legal right to appeal the district court's decision to overturn Proposition 8. Although *Hollingsworth v. Perry* was decided on procedural details, the result was that same-sex marriage became legal again in California (Barnes 2013, Dolan et al. 2013).

While similar debates over same-sex marriage have been occurring in other states, both sides were energized by the Supreme Court decision *United States v. Windsor*, in which the court ruled that the section of the Defense of Marriage Act (DOMA) defining marriage as between one man and one woman was unconstitutional. However, the country is still a patchwork of laws regarding same-sex marriage, because the court left intact the section of DOMA that allows states to refuse to recognize same-sex marriages from other states (Jacobs 2013). The importance of marriage in society can be seen in the cultural, legislative, and judicial battles still to come: 30 percent of Americans now lives in a place that allows same-sex marriage, but 35 states specifically limit marriage to heterosexual couples (Eckholm 2013, NCSL 2013).

Opponents of same-sex marriage have used the rhetoric of "protecting marriage" or "protecting family," implying that gay marriage would harm or destroy those institutions. This largely ignores prolific research that shows that the psychological and physical well-being of children benefit from being raised by two parents whose union is legally recognized by social institutions. While polls of public opinion have shown an increase in favor of recognizing same-sex marriage, many believe that same-sex couples should only be granted **civil unions** and not "marriages." The term "marriage," for many, has religious meaning, which raises concern for many religions that do not support or condone same-sex relations: should gay marriage be legalized, they worry that clergy would be required to perform such unions.

It is worth noting that while civil unions afford many of the same rights as marriages, they do not confer the right to federal benefits and do not offer "portability," since civil unions performed in one state are not recognized by all states. This has financial ramifications for these families, as many couples who depend on social security, veteran's, or disability benefits cannot inherit those benefits upon their partner's passing. Even if a same-sex couple marries and then is eligible for federal benefits because of *United States v. Windsor*, their state of residence would have a significant impact on what benefits they would receive. A couple that gets married in a state that allows same-sex marriage, but actually lives in or moves to a state that does not, will have trouble receiving benefits from the state and even the federal government. Many federal agencies, such as the IRS and the Social Security Administration, base eligibility on state of residence (Halloran 2013).

As we can see, there is much at stake in the gay marriage debate. It is a political, social, civil rights, moral, and religious issue. If same-sex marriage is legally recognized, gay families will be afforded the same legal standing as heterosexual families.

Love and Marriage Supporters of same-sex marriage celebrate after the Supreme Court announces decisions in two significant cases, *United States v. Windsor* and *Hollingsworth v. Perry*.

While not often discussed, gay marriage is also an economic issue. A study conducted at UCLA (Sears and Badgett 2008) estimated that if same-sex marriage were legalized in California, it would provide $63.8 million in state and local government revenue over three years, a factor largely ignored but worth considering given California's ongoing budget crisis. Other states, as well as the federal government, might also consider these benefits.

Finally, it is important to note that amid these debates, generalizations run rampant. Opponents to gay marriage are largely portrayed as members of religious institutions and the conservative right, but there are many institutions and members within those groups that support same-sex marriage. Conversely, there are many within the LGBTQ community who do not support same-sex marriage, as it is viewed as assimilationist and accepts heteronormative structures, such as binary gender roles and monogamy, rather than critiquing them. Lisa Duggan (2003) and Cathy Cohen (2005) contend that arguing for same-sex marriage creates "hierarchies of worthiness," in that benefits are afforded to the most "socially acceptable" within the LGBTQ community—those who most closely mimic heterosexual unions.

Despite the erratic progress in same-sex marriage laws, the gay rights movement won a large victory in 2010 with the repeal of Don't Ask, Don't Tell (DADT). Signed into law in 1993, DADT arose amidst existing military policies that required the discharge of gay military service members, built on a rhetoric of difference, undesirability, and incompatibility with military practice. DADT was an attempt to curb those discharges by requiring that military administration not "ask" about a service member's sexual activity or orientation, and that service members not "tell" about it either. Initially offering promise that gay service members would be allowed to serve, DADT brought about an environment of secrecy in which gay military personnel had to keep silent or lie about their orientation and lives, as well as accept or engage in anti-gay activities and discourse or face discharge. This environment spurred witch hunts that brought the involuntary discharge of more than 14,000 service members. Its repeal, as with most social change, did not come easily or quickly. With his 2008 election, President Barack Obama promised to repeal DADT, but it took nearly two years, several filibusters in the U.S. Senate led by Obama's presidential competitor Senator John McCain, and a revised bill before that promise became a reality. With the repeal of Don't Ask, Don't Tell, gay service members are now legally permitted to serve openly without recrimination and cannot be discharged because of their sexual identity.

While the military was one of the last federal employers actively supported by law to discriminate based on sexuality, there are countless businesses that are still allowed to do so in states that do not have laws that prohibit such discrimination. A study conducted by William Rubenstein (2001), a law professor at UCLA, found that reports of discrimination based on sexual orientation are roughly equal in number to those based on race or gender. Considered in the context of the number of gay people in the workforce, this is a concerning statistic given that at the lowest estimate of gay people in the workforce, the rate of discrimination filings is several times higher than those based upon gender. The Employment Non-Discrimination Act (ENDA), a bill placed before Congress in 2010, would seek to correct this by placing sexual orientation within a protected class with race and gender, so that employers could not legally discriminate based upon the sexual orientation of their employees. But while legal discrimination against gay and lesbians may slowly be ending, other forms of prejudice can be harder to overcome.

Homophobia

In 1968, police raided a gay bar in New York City called the Stonewall Inn. At the time, patrons of gay bars were frequently singled out for harassment from the police. The pent-up resentment and frustration this caused erupted into violence during the raid. The Stonewall riots began a new era of campaigning for civil rights for gays, lesbians, bisexuals, and transgendered individuals. Although many gays and lesbians still remain "in the closet," not revealing their sexual orientation even to friends or family members, others are open and vocal: "We're here, we're queer, get used to it!" goes one motto. Sociologist Dana Rosenfeld, who studies gay and lesbian identity, asserts that there are at least two distinct cohorts, those who lived before the gay liberation movement of the 1960s and 1970s and those who lived during and after it. The earlier generation would have felt discredited if their sexual orientation had become public knowledge, whereas the later generation believed that making their orientation public was celebrating an essential aspect of the self that should not be denied (Rosenfeld 2003).

One reason gays and lesbians hide their identity is the extent of **homophobia**, "the dread of being in close quarters with homosexuals," in society (Weinberg 1972). Some have pointed out that homophobia is not a true "phobia," like agoraphobia or claustrophobia, which are psychological phenomena. Rather, it is a prejudice, like racism or anti-Semitism, which are cultural norms that are learned and transmitted socially. Homophobia as a concept is problematic because it suggests that the problems faced by gays and lesbians are the result of a few maladjusted individuals rather than the product of deeply institutionalized cultural values and norms (Kitzinger 1987). Indeed, some have suggested that "heterosexism" would be a more useful term in that it is analogous to sexism and racism and describes an ideological

HOMOPHOBIA fear of or discrimination toward homosexuals or toward individuals who display purportedly gender-inappropriate behavior system that stigmatizes any nonheterosexual behavior (Herek 1990; Rothblum 1996).

Queer Youth

For many queer youth, the most difficult period in dealing with their sexual and gender identities in a homophobic culture occurs during their adolescent years. Research shows that LGBTQ youth are up to four times more likely to attempt suicide and up to 8.4 times more likely among adolescents to be rejected by their families for being LGBTQ (Ryan et al. 2009). The middle school and high school years are challenging for any young person, but this is especially true for those with an LGBTQ identity. The 2009 National School Climate Survey (Kosciw et al. 2010) showed that nearly nine out of ten LGBTQ students experience harassment in school. Nearly 85 percent of LGBTQ students reported being verbally harassed, while 40.1 percent reported being physically harassed, and 18.8 reported physical assault in the past year because of their sexual orientation.

School administration and faculty can have a positive impact on these developmental years, as schools with supportive staff reported fewer incidents of their LGBTQ students being absent and/or feeling unsafe, and contributed to the greater academic achievement and higher educational aspirations of LGBTQ youth. Bullying has recently come to public attention as a problem for youth of all sexual orientations. Those schools that enact anti-bullying policies have not only lower instances of harassment but also higher rates of staff intervention in such instances—an important factor specifically for transgender youth who face even higher rates of harassment and abuse in school than their lesbian, gay, and bisexual peers. A supportive peer environment can also help LGBTQ students to be open about their sexual orientation and/or gender identity. School programs can heighten all students' awareness of stigma and its consequences (Rabow, Stein, and Conley 1999), and clubs such as Gay-Straight Alliances can enhance feelings of belonging, healthy development, and positive well-being.

The Mass Media and Sexual Stereotypes

As with other prejudices, there are both institutional and individual forms of homophobia. Individual homophobia is expressed through derogatory comments, discriminatory actions, and physical attacks. It is sometimes legitimized by institutional homophobia, which occurs when a government, business, church, or other organization discriminates against people on the basis of sexual orientation. One social institution that has played a particularly interesting role in creating and sometimes challenging sexual stereotypes is the mass media. While homosexuality is more visible now than it has ever been, many people still have no firsthand knowledge of homosexuality and turn to the media as their exclusive source for understanding it.

Before the 1960s, homosexuality was altogether absent from television. When it did appear, it was usually treated in a negative manner: in the 1967 CBS documentary *The Homosexuals*, one psychiatrist claims that "the fact that somebody's homosexual . . . automatically rules out the possibility that he will remain happy for long." In recent years, however, increasing levels of tolerance toward homosexual-

"Acting Out" In 2000, the comedy *Will & Grace* featured the first gay kiss on network television.

ity have been reflected in increasingly positive representations of gays and lesbians on television, although these gains have not been without controversy. In 1997, the ABC sitcom *Ellen* introduced the first lesbian lead character in a prime-time series; two years later, the NBC sitcom *Will & Grace* featured two gay male characters. Other shows followed, with a variety of minor gay and lesbian characters: *Dawson's Creek, Party of Five, NYPD Blue, Spin City, Friends*, and *Buffy the Vampire Slayer*, and later *Grey's Anatomy, Brothers & Sisters, Ugly Betty, Modern Family, Glee*, and *The New Normal*. Cable networks also developed gay- and lesbian-themed shows, such as *Queer as Folk, Queer Eye for the Straight Guy*, and *The L Word*.

Just because gay and lesbian characters are included on television, however, doesn't mean that they have achieved equal status. Clearly, there is not the same kind of acceptance of same-sex relations as of heterosexual relations, as evidenced by how romantic couples are treated on TV. Until 2000, there had never been a gay male kiss on a network program (although there had been two lesbian kisses). This issue was brought up in an episode of *Will & Grace* called "Acting Out," which featured a clever show-within-a-show format. Will and his best friend, Jack, both gay, are watching their favorite TV show, also about gay characters, which is supposed to feature the first prime-time gay kiss ever. However, right before the much-anticipated kiss, the cameras cut away and instead focus on the fireplace, a mere metaphor. Jack is upset but has trouble convincing Will that the incident really matters:

> Jack: I am outraged by this. Why aren't you?
> Will: Because I'm realistic. Clearly, nobody wants to see two men kissing on television, not the network, not the viewers, not the advertisers . . .
> Jack: That's right, Will. They wanna pretend we're invisible.

Later, a group of gays, including Will and Jack, gather outside the NBC studios to protest. There, the *Today Show* meteorologist, Al Roker, is giving the weather report in front of the usual early-morning crowd of fans. Jack calls out to him, and as the camera focuses on Jack, he grabs Will and kisses him, on live TV. And there it is, finally, the first-ever gay kiss on network television. However, the fact that this is done in a humorous and backhanded way may actually undermine to some extent the political message the writers of the show were trying to convey.

Some social scientists argue that the more personal contact between members of different social groups, the less prejudice and discrimination may occur between them (Pettigrew and Tropp 2011). If the mass media provide some people's only exposure to gays and lesbians, then it is all the more important that their portrayals represent those communities in realistic ways.

CLOSING COMMENTS

Sex, gender, and sexual orientation are status categories that structure social inequality and shape individual identities. They are different but interrelated, and we all experience their overlap in our everyday lives: we categorize ourselves and others and make assumptions about one another based on these perceived categories. A sociological perspective allows us to see the cultural and environmental influences on what may be considered biologically based identities, and lets us identify and critique the stratification systems that have resulted from these influences. Most important, a sociological perspective allows us to see how destructive sexism is for men and women and how crippling homophobia can be for the straight majority as well as the gay minority. Stereotypes are socially constructed; therefore, they can be socially deconstructed and socially reconstructed as well.

Everything You Need to Know about
Gender and Sexuality

"Sociologists differentiate *sex* as biological and *gender* as social. *Sex* refers to two biologically distinct categories: male or female. *Gender* refers to physical and behavioral traits that society considers "normal" for men and women."

THEORIES OF GENDER AND SEXUALITY

* **Functionalism:** men and women should remain in traditional social roles to keep society stable

* **Conflict theory:** men have control over most of society's resources and privileges, and will continue to maintain their dominant status through the exploitation of women

* **Symbolic interactionism:** gender is socially constructed and maintained in our everyday lives

REVIEW

1. Consider the ways you were socialized by your family. In what ways was your socialization gendered? What toys did you play with as a child? What extracurricular activities were you encouraged to pursue? What household chores did you perform?

2. Our society upholds expectations about which gender more appropriately fills the instrumental and the expressive roles. In your family, were the nurturing and emotional support primarily provided by women? How do these gendered expectations reinforce the traditional family structure? How do they perpetuate gender inequality?

3. The second shift refers to the housework that must be done after the day's paid labor is complete; women do a disproportionate amount of this work. Why do you think this is? What types of tasks does our society expect women to do? How do the tasks expected of men differ?

Number of Women on Corporate Boards of Directors

By Country

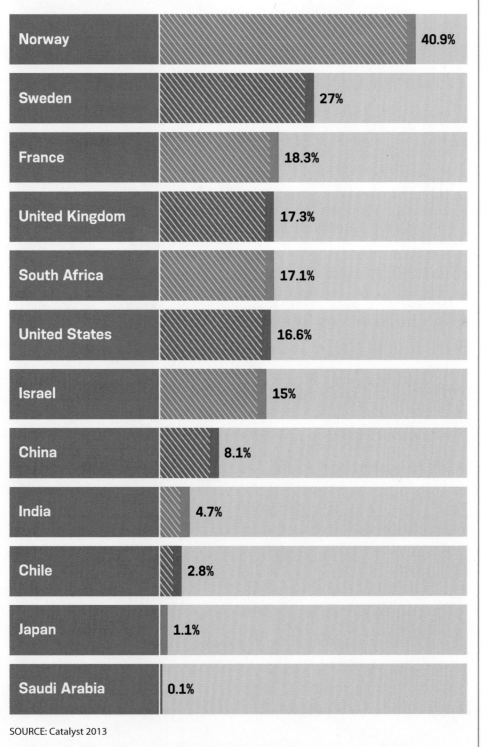

Country	Percentage
Norway	40.9%
Sweden	27%
France	18.3%
United Kingdom	17.3%
South Africa	17.1%
United States	16.6%
Israel	15%
China	8.1%
India	4.7%
Chile	2.8%
Japan	1.1%
Saudi Arabia	0.1%

SOURCE: Catalyst 2013

EXPLORE

Gender and Sports: Forty Years of Title IX

Title IX, passed in 1972, is an amendment to the Civil Rights Act banning gender discrimination in school sports. Even though it is now over forty years old and many female athletes have benefited from it, there are still significant challenges in getting equal funding, facilities, and support. Visit the Everyday Sociology Blog to read more about a sociologist's analysis of the effects of Title IX.

http://wwnPag.es/trw409

PART IV

Examining Social Institutions as Sites of Everyday Life

Our everyday lives take place within the contexts of many overlapping and interdependent social institutions. A social institution is a collection of patterned social practices that are repeated continuously and regularly over time and supported by social norms. Politics, the economy, family, religion, health care, and education are all social institutions, and you have contact with many of these (and others) on a daily basis. The patterns and structures of social institutions shape your individual experiences; at the same time, it's important to remember that social institutions are created, maintained, and changed by individual actions.

In the next four chapters, we will look at specific social institutions, such as politics, education, and religion (Chapter 10), the economy (Chapter 11), the family (Chapter 12), media and leisure (Chapter 13), and the health-care system (Chapter 14), and their role in structuring your everyday life. You will be introduced to a variety of sociological research that focuses on how these social institutions and others work; here, we highlight a sociological researcher whose work integrates many of them. In his book *Heat Wave: A Social Autopsy of Disaster in Chicago* (2002), Eric Klinenberg examines the circumstances surrounding Chicago's catastrophic heat wave in 1995, which killed more than 700 people. Klinenberg analyzes the week-long heat wave as more than a meteorological phenomenon. People died, he argues, because of a combination of disturbing demographic trends and dangerous institutional policies present at all times in all major urban areas.

For one week in mid-July of 1995, the city of Chicago suffered the worst heat wave in its history: temperatures exceeded 100 degrees for four days in a row, and heat indices (the "real feel" air temperature) hit a high of 126 degrees. Historic buildings baked like ovens, but fear of crime left many people feeling trapped inside their apart-

ments. Children passed out in overheated school buses. City residents blasted their air conditioning (if they had it), mobbed the tiny beaches on Lake Michigan, and broke open fire hydrants to stay cool. As a result, power outages peppered the area and water pressure dropped dangerously. Roads buckled, train tracks warped, and people suffered from heat-related illnesses in large numbers. The city's 911 emergency system overloaded, and some callers waited two hours for ambulances to arrive; more than twenty hospitals closed their emergency rooms, overwhelmed with patients. The death toll mounted, with the elderly and the poor especially vulnerable. In this single week, 739 Chicagoans died as a result of the heat. According to Klinenberg, the individual "isolation, deprivation, and vulnerability" that led to these deaths resulted from a variety of institutional structures, including poverty, racial segregation, family dislocation, and city politics. These institutional arrangements must be examined and changed in order to avoid future tragedies.

Many of those who died during the heat wave were elderly people who lived alone: sick or fragile, their mobility compromised, their neighborhoods changing around them, their families far away or neglectful, and their social networks dissolving. In many cases, the elderly victims of the heat wave were so isolated that no one ever claimed their bodies (Klinenberg 2002, p. 15). The story of Pauline Jankowitz, eighty-five, who survived the heat wave, illustrates these demographic trends (Klinenberg 2002, pp. 50–54). Pauline lived alone on the third floor of an apartment building with no elevator. She suffered from incontinence and walked with a crutch. She recognized her vulnerability and left her apartment only once every two months. Her two children lived in other states and rarely visited, so a volunteer from a charitable organization did Pauline's weekly grocery shopping. However, Pauline no longer had any connections with her immigrant neighbors and spent most of her time in her apartment listening to radio talk shows. Pauline's isolation is hardly unique. Her circumstances illustrate the ways that the geographic mobility of the contemporary family, the changing populations of urban neighborhoods, the financial limitations of retirement incomes, and the lack of supportive social services all contribute to situations in which elderly individuals may live, face crises, and die alone.

Klinenberg argues that race and class inequality also contributed to the death toll in the Chicago heat wave. He shows that the death tolls were highest in the city's "black belt," a group of predominantly African American neighborhoods on the south and west sides of the city. (These neighborhoods also have relatively high levels of poverty and crime and relatively large populations of elderly residents.) Social ties in these neighborhoods are hard to maintain: poverty contributes to residential transiency, so neighbors may not get to know one another before they must move to different housing elsewhere. Gang activity and crime make residents afraid to walk down the street or sit on their own front porches. And although some of the neighborhoods in question have powerful religious organizations in their midst, even the most proactive church needs significant financial resources to reach out to its members—and such resources may be hard to come by in poor neighborhoods. So a person's risk of heat-related death during July of 1995 was partly place-based. In Chicago, as in most major cities, place, race, and class are closely connected.

In July 1995, Chicago's government services also failed in a number of ways when the city's residents needed them most. However, Klinenberg argues that the city's bureaucracies were no more ill-prepared to deal with catastrophe during that week than during any other. Long-term, macro-level changes in city politics mean that both the political will and the material resources to provide assistance to the poor were fatally absent. For example, overextended paramedics and firefighters had no centralized office with which to register their observations or complaints. As a result, many problems went unheeded by the city until emergency services were too swamped to provide timely assistance. There was little coordination between the local, state, and federal agencies that dealt with social welfare and emergency services. Finally, Klinenberg indicts city officials for "governing by public relations" (p. 143); that is, for using the mass media to deflect attention from the city's problems, including minimizing both the scope of the heat wave and the city's accountability.

Klinenberg's "social autopsy" reveals the failure of social institutions on a massive scale—and the disturbing prospect that this disaster could happen again, anywhere, if we do not take steps to change flawed social systems. Structural and institutional arrangements—including city government, health-care providers, families, schools, religious organizations, and the media—must change in order to avoid individual tragedies. But individual actions help bring about institutional change, and *Heat Wave* reveals important ways in which all our fates intertwine, as they are shaped by the social institutions we encounter every day. How can we better manage this interdependence, for the good of all?

CHAPTER 10

The Macro-Micro Link in Social Institutions:

Politics, Education, and Religion

Y ou probably know the Pledge of Allegiance by heart and have said it countless times in elementary and high school, but you may not have thought much about its words or why you were required to say them.

I pledge allegiance to the Flag
of the United States of America,
and to the Republic for which it stands:
one Nation, under God, indivisible,
with Liberty and Justice for all.

Reciting the pledge was just a routine part of being a student in the United States. Could it possibly be controversial? A lot of people think so. As you will see, the Pledge of Allegiance brings together questions about three important social institutions in American life: politics, education, and religion.

The Pledge of Allegiance was originally written in 1892 and did not contain the phrase "under God"; that was added in 1954, when President Eisenhower signed a bill making the change official. The added words generated no controversy at the time. The president declared that their addition would affirm "the dedication of our nation and our people to the Almighty," and Senator Joseph McCarthy said "it was a clear indication that the United States was committed to ending the threat of 'godless' Communism" (Brinkley-Rogers 2002).

Since as early as 1943, the Supreme Court has ruled that children cannot be forced to recite the pledge. In 1943, the issue addressed was the patriotic nature of the pledge. However, a 2002 ruling by Judge Alfred Goodwin states that reciting the pledge in public schools "places students in the untenable position of choosing between participating in an exercise with religious content or protesting," an especially damaging scenario because "the coercive effect of the policy here is particularly pronounced in the school setting, given the age and impressionability of schoolchildren" (Weinstein 2003). After all, how many second graders will be willing to stand out from their peers in so dramatic a fashion?

Dr. Michael Newdow, an emergency room physician, attorney, and self-described atheist in California, is committed to preserving the separation of church and state. When his daughter's second-grade class began reciting the Pledge of Allegiance, Newdow became disturbed because it contained the phrase "one Nation, *under God*." Acting as his own attorney, Newdow filed a lawsuit, and in February 2003 the Ninth Circuit Court held the pledge to be in violation of the Constitution because the reference to God violated the separation of church and state.

Many civic and political leaders—liberals as well as conservatives—denounced the decision. The Senate passed a resolution condemning it, and the attorney general announced that the Justice Department would "spare no effort to preserve the rights of all our citizens to pledge allegiance to the American flag" (Weinstein 2003). Almost universally, lawmakers came out in defense of the pledge, agreeing with Judge Ferdinand Fernandez, who in his dissenting opinion argued that the phrase "under God" had "no tendency to establish a religion in this country or to suppress anyone's exercise, or non-exercise, of religion, except in the fevered eye of persons who most fervently would like to drive all tincture of religion out of the public life of our polity" (Egelko 2002). Ultimately, the case went all the way to the Supreme Court, which overturned the lower court's ruling on a technicality but did not address whether the language in the pledge violates the First Amendment.

Although there is a great deal of disagreement over what should be done in this case, all the participants agree, even if only implicitly, that social institutions play an important role in the lives of Americans. Social institutions (systems and structures that organize our group life, such as school, religion, and the government) shape and constrain our everyday lives. For example, if school starts at 8:00 am and ends at 3:00 pm, this structures the life of an entire household—it dictates what time children should go to bed and get up in the morning; when breakfast and dinner are prepared, served, and eaten; and what types of arrangements must be made for transportation, after-school activities, and child care. In turn, these same institutions are created and sustained through our everyday interactions. For example, a school exists only because of the actions of the teachers, students, parents, and administrators who are part of the surrounding community.

Social institutions represent a bit of a sociological paradox. They function at the macro level to shape our everyday interactions, but at the micro level those same everyday interactions construct social institutions. Because they are at the center of both micro- and macrosociology, social institutions give us the opportunity to examine the connection between interaction and structure, between the individual and society. In this chapter, we will focus on the social institutions of politics, education, and religion as places where the micro and the macro come together, and we will show how the intersections between social institutions shape everyday life.

HOW TO READ THIS CHAPTER

We have devoted entire chapters to other **social institutions** such as health care, work, and family, but here we have grouped politics, education, and religion together for a reason. These institutions intersect in distinctive and often unexamined ways in our everyday lives—the daily recitation of the Pledge of Allegiance is just one example. Local and national controversies over school vouchers or sex education are other examples of the ways in which political, educational, and religious concerns overlap. Every day we make decisions or engage in debates that address moral values, political practicalities, and educational expectations all bundled together.

When you read this chapter, we want you to be able to see the relationships among these three social institutions as well as to make the connection between micro- and macrosociology. This is a key opportunity to use the sociological theories and methods you have learned in previous chapters to find the intersections between individual experience and social structure, and the overlaps between various social institutions in everyday life. After reading this chapter, you should have a deeper understanding of how social institutions shape your individual experience and how you as an individual contribute to shaping those institutions.

What Is Politics?

Politics has concerned social thinkers since at least the time of the philosophers in ancient Greece. The word "politics" comes from the Greek *politikos*, meaning of or relating to citizens. As a sociological term, **politics** pertains especially to the methods and tactics of managing a political entity, such as a nation or state, as well as the administration and control of its internal and external affairs. But it can also mean the attitudes and activities of groups and individuals. To understand the relationship between citizens and their particular political environment, we must first look at the variety of different political systems and study the American system of democracy. Then we will examine elections and voting, lobbies and special interest groups, and the role of the media in the political process.

Political Systems: Government

Government is the formal, organized agency that exercises power and control in modern society. Governments are vested with the power and authority to make laws and enforce them. As you probably remember from Chapter 1, Max Weber defined **power** as the ability to get others to do one's bidding. When sociologists talk about **authority**, they refer to the legitimate, noncoercive exercise of power. Throughout the world and throughout history, governments have taken a variety of forms. When evaluating types of governance as sociologists, we ask certain questions about the relationship between leaders and followers: who has power and who does not, what kind of power is exerted, and how far does that power extend?

SOCIAL INSTITUTIONS systems and structures within society that shape the activities of groups and individuals

POLITICS methods and tactics intended to influence government policy, policy-related attitudes, and activities

GOVERNMENT the formal, organized agency that exercises power and control in modern society, especially through the creation and enforcement of laws

POWER the ability to impose one's will on others

AUTHORITY the legitimate, noncoercive exercise of power

AUTHORITARIANISM system of government by and for a small number of elites that does not include representation of ordinary citizens

TOTAL POWER AND AUTHORITY Authoritarianism is a political system that denies ordinary citizens representation by and control over their own government. Thus, citizens have no say in who rules them, what laws are made, or

Dictators Try to Control All Aspects of Citizens' Lives Leaders such as Kim Jong Un of North Korea, Augusto Pinochet of Chile, and Charles Taylor of Liberia are among the world's most notorious dictators.

how those laws are enforced. Generally, political power is concentrated in the hands of a few elites who control military and economic resources. A *dictatorship* is one form of authoritarian system. In most instances, a dictator does not gain power by being elected or through succession but seizes power and becomes an absolute ruler. Dictators may gain control through a military coup, as occurred when General Augusto Pinochet came to power in Chile in 1973. In other cases, leaders may be legally elected or appointed (often with coercion) but then become dictators once in power, abolishing any constitutional limits on their authority—such as President Charles Taylor of Liberia. In 2012, Taylor was sentenced by the war crimes tribunal in The Hague to fifty years in prison for crimes against humanity. Dictators are most often individuals but can also be associated with political parties or groups, such as the Taliban in Afghanistan.

Totalitarianism is the most extreme and modern version of authoritarianism. The government seeks to control every aspect, public and private, of citizens' lives. Unlike older forms of authoritarianism, a totalitarian government can utilize all the contrivances of surveillance technology, systems of mass communication, and modern weapons to control its citizens (Arendt 1958). Totalitarian governments are usually headed by a dictator, whether a ruler or a single political party. Through propaganda, totalitarian regimes can further control the population by disseminating ideology aimed at shaping their thoughts, values, and attitudes. An example of a modern totalitarian ruler is Kim Jong Un of North Korea, who succeeded his father, the notorious Kim Jong Il, in 2011. Under the Kims, North Korea has maintained one of the worst human rights records in the world, restricts the basic freedoms of its people, and has a stagnant, internationally isolated economy.

MONARCHY a government ruled by a king or queen, with succession of rulers kept within the family

DEMOCRACY a political system in which all citizens have the right to participate

MONARCHIES AND THE STATE Monarchies are governments ruled by a king or queen. In a **monarchy**, sovereignty is vested in a successive line of rulers, usually within a family, such as the Tudors of England, the Ming Dynasty of China, and the Romanovs of Russia. Nobility is handed down through family lines and can include numerous family members who hold royal titles. Monarchs are not popularly elected and not usually accountable to the general citizenry, and some may rule by "divine right," the claim that they are leaders chosen by God.

Monarchies can be divided into two categories: absolute and constitutional. Absolute monarchs typically have complete authority over their subjects, much like a dictator. Constitutional monarchs are royal figures whose powers are defined by a political charter and limited by a parliament or other governing body. Most monarchies were weakened, overthrown, or otherwise made obsolete during the many social revolutions of the eighteenth, nineteenth, and twentieth centuries, such as the French Revolution (1789) and the Russian Revolution (1917). In contemporary times, some Asian and European nations, such as Japan, Thailand, Great Britain, and Sweden, still enjoy their royal families as national figureheads and celebrities, though their kings, queens, princes, and princesses don't have any real power in these constitutional monarchies. There are, however, a few remaining modern examples of more absolute monarchies in the world, among them Saudi Arabia and Brunei.

CITIZENS AND DEMOCRACY Democracy originated in ancient Greece and represented a radical new political system. In a **democracy**, citizens share in directing the activities of their government rather than being ruled by an autocratic individual or authoritarian group. The idea is that educated citizens should participate in the election of officials who then represent their interests in law making, law enforcement, resource allocation, and international affairs. Democracy is not only a political system but also a

Table 10.1 Theory in Everyday Life

Perspective	Approach to Social Institutions	Case Study: Understanding Political Power in America
Structural Functionalism	Social institutions such as politics, education, and religion provide critical functions for the needs of society and help to maintain order and unity.	The theory of pluralism suggests that in a democracy, power is held in a variety of hands; each group is assumed to have equal access to power and can thus serve as a system of checks and balances.
Conflict Theory	Social institutions such as politics, education, and religion represent the interests of those in power and thus create and maintain inequalities in society.	The theory of the power elite suggests that power in the United States is concentrated in the hands of a small group of decision makers and that the masses have little power in the democratic process.
Symbolic Interactionism	Social institutions such as politics, education, and religion are created through individual participation; they give meaning to and are part of the everyday experience of members.	The theory of the social construction of presidential candidates suggests that the messages we receive from the media help to shape our perceptions and influence public opinion and voting behavior.

philosophy that emphasizes the right and capacity of individuals, acting either directly or through representatives, to control through majority rule the institutions that govern them. Democracy is associated with the values of basic human rights, civil liberties, freedom, and equality.

Democracy may seem like the ideal system of government, but remember that not all citizens are equally represented even by a democratic government. In many democratic nations, women, ethnic or racial minorities, members of certain religions, and immigrants have been excluded from citizenship or from equal participation in the political process. In the United States, women did not have the right to vote until 1920. And while the Fifteenth Amendment to the U.S. Constitution technically gave adult males of all races voting rights in 1870, barriers such as poll taxes, literacy tests, and "grandfather clauses" kept African Americans from exercising those rights for almost 100 years, until the 1965 Voting Rights Act was passed. Native Americans were legally excluded from voting in federal elections until 1924, and residents of the District of Columbia were not allowed to vote in presidential elections until 1961. As you can see, even the world's leading democracy has not always seen all citizens as equal.

The American Political System

When American colonists rebelled against British authority in 1776, they created the first modern democracy. American democracy, however, is much more complicated than "rule by the people." In the following sections, we focus on voting, theories about who governs, the power of interest groups, and the influence of the mass media on the political system.

VOTING IN THE UNITED STATES The American political system prides itself on being a democracy, a government that confers power to the people. In this form of government, power is formally exercised through the election process, which provides each person with a vote. Sociologists have long been interested in the social factors—such as age, education, religion, or ethnic background—that influence whether and how individuals vote.

By the end of the twentieth century, many had become concerned about a steady, decades-long decline in American voter turnout. For example, in the 1960 presidential election, 63 percent of the electorate cast ballots, but by 1996, that number fell to below 50 percent for the first time since 1924.

Voter turnout began improving in the 2004 presidential election, but it is important to consider how voter turnout has been measured. Prior to the 2004 election, the voter turnout rate was typically calculated by dividing the total number of votes by the "voting-age population"—*everyone* aged eighteen and older residing in the United States. This figure included people who were ineligible to vote—mainly noncitizens and felons—and excluded eligible overseas voters. Since the 2004 election, voting rates have been based on the "voting-eligible population," which changes the overall voting picture and challenges the notion of decline in voter turnout. In 2004, voter turnout was 55 percent for the "voting-age population" and 60 percent for the "voting-eligible population." And among eligible voters under age twenty-five, turnout rose by almost 6 percent over the 2000 election, with some 10.5 million of them going to the polls.

Voter turnout improved again in the presidential election of 2008 in which Barack Obama, the first African American president, was elected. An estimated 61.4 percent of the voting-eligible population, or 130.9 million Americans, cast their ballots. That represents an increase of 1.3 percentage points over 2004 but falls short of the record turnout of 62.5 percent in 1968. Among young voters aged eighteen to twenty-nine, the 2008 election represented the second highest turnout in history, with approximately 22 million to 24 million, or 49 percent to 54 percent of eligible voters, casting their ballots. The record youth voter turnout belongs to the election in 1972, the first year that eighteen-year-olds had the right to vote. Obama's reelection in 2012 featured a turnout rate of 58.2 percent of all eligible voters (McDonald 2013).

Even with these fluctuations, voter participation rates are much lower in the United States than in some comparable democratic nations. Why? A number of social factors affect the likelihood that someone will or will not vote. Age, race, gender, sexual orientation, religion, geographic location, social class, and education are all demographic variables that influence voter participation as well as how people vote. For example, Minnesota had the highest voter turnout of any state in the 2012 presidential election—almost 75 percent of its citizens voted, whereas only 44 percent of the eligible voters from Hawaii turned out (McDonald 2013). What explains this difference? Turnout may be affected by factors ranging from the number of other races on the ballot to the weather. Senior citizens are much more likely to vote than young adults—compare a 70 percent reported turnout for those over age fifty-five with a 41 percent reported turnout among eighteen- to twenty-four-year-olds (U.S. Census Bureau 2012p). But the top reason people give for not voting, according to surveys, is that they are simply too busy (Holder 2006).

DISENFRANCHISED stripped of voting rights, either temporarily or permanently

In some instances, however, people do not vote because they are **disenfranchised**—barred from voting. All states except Maine and Vermont disenfranchise convicted felons while they are incarcerated. Thirty-five states disenfranchise felons on parole, thirty-one do so for felons on probation, and seven others permanently disenfranchise them (Weedon 2004). Human rights groups have long protested this policy, arguing that it is not a legitimate function of the penal system. In addition, individuals may be mistakenly identified as former felons and improperly stricken from the rolls, which occurred in Florida in the 2000 presidential election (Hull 2002; Uggen and Manza 2002). Consequently, many eligible voters were turned away from the polls.

Another obstacle to potential voters lies with registration, which must be done well in advance of an election. In the United States, even individuals with the legal right to vote cannot do so unless they are registered. Recent legislation, such as the 2000 Motor-Voter Act, allows voters to register when renewing a driver's license and has made registration easier. Another problem for many working Americans is that elections are held on a Tuesday rather than a weekend or a national holiday (something done in other democratic countries). Finally, some states require voters to show photo identification in order to vote, even though studies show a decline in turnout when IDs are required (de Alth 2009).

Even when voters do appear at the polls, there may be other troubles. During the 2000 presidential election, irregularities in ballots and vote counts in Florida delayed the state's ability to declare a winner for several weeks. In some of Florida's poor and minority districts, faulty voting equipment, poorly trained poll workers, and scarce resources kept almost 200,000 votes from being counted—votes that were

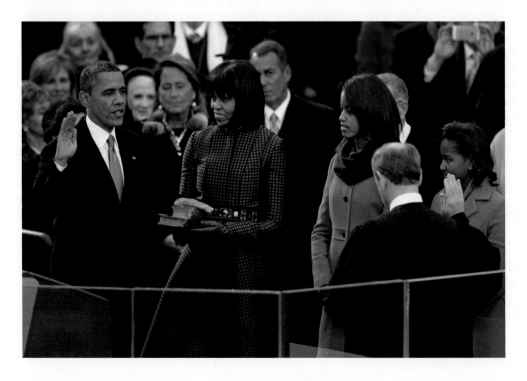

Barack Obama Joined by his wife Michelle, Obama takes the oath of office to inaugurate his second term as the president of the United States. He placed his hand on two Bibles—one owned by Martin Luther King Jr. and one by Abraham Lincoln.

likely predominantly Democratic. The National Association for the Advancement of Colored People (NAACP) brought a voting discrimination suit against the state of Florida that was settled with a donation to the organization's efforts toward voter education and mobilization. Much media attention has focused on the invisible disenfranchisement of poor and minority voters, and some states have enacted more progressive laws to deal with these problems by providing greater access to the disabled, making absentee balloting easier, or keeping the polls open longer. This election controversy is an example of how structural issues (unequal state voting resources) can affect individual experience (the ability to make one's vote count) and how those individual experiences in turn affect the larger society (electing Bush rather than Gore).

Who Rules America?

Ideally, in a democracy, elected officials represent the interests of the people in doing the business of government. But how much do we really know about what legislators do or how government business is conducted? What about the interests of other groups besides "the people"? To what extent do other groups influence how government is run? Who has the most power in directing the course of the nation? The president and Congress? Judges? Big business and the military? What happens behind the scenes? Who really rules America?

PLURALISM Sociologists have devised two answers to the question of who rules America—the *pluralist* theory of power and the idea of a *power elite*. According to the **pluralist model**, power is held by a variety of organizations and institutions (such as corporations, political parties, professional organizations, and ethnic and religious groups),

each with its own resources and interests. Each organization is assumed to have equal access to the power structure, and a system of checks and balances in the form of laws, policies, and the courts keeps any one group from having too much power over the others (Dahl 1961). Conflict theorists, however, argue that power is held by a small but extremely influential group of individuals who form an elite social class.

THE POWER ELITE C. Wright Mills was one of the first to propose a theory of the **power elite**, a relatively small number of influential individuals who occupy the top positions within the major economic, political, and military institutions of the country (1956, 1970). This insular and self-perpetuating group controls much of the key decision-making processes in the United States. Members of the power elite have the full power and weight of their respective institutions at their disposal. Their close association allows them to collaborate in ways that best serve their particular interests, which may not coincide with those of the people. Thus, their actions have tremendous implications for the rest of the population. For instance, military leaders may persuade the president to declare war, senators may pass legislation that cuts billions of dollars from social welfare programs, and corporate executives may post record gains for stockholders or downsize companies and lay off thousands of workers.

G. William Domhoff has studied the power elite extensively, looking at how the economic, political, and military institutions overlap and form a network of influence (1983,

> **PLURALIST MODEL** a system of political power in which a wide variety of individuals and groups have equal access to resources and the mechanisms of power
>
> **POWER ELITE** a relatively small group of people in the top ranks of economic, political, and military institutions who make many of the important decisions in American society

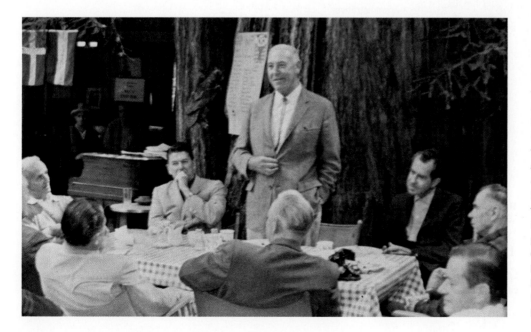

Power Elites Many of the most powerful men in the United States spend two weeks of every summer in a campground north of San Francisco called Bohemian Grove. Founded as a place for the nation's leaders to gather and escape from outside concerns like business, politics, and power, the men's club's members include every Republican president since 1923, many CEOs, and other prominent businessmen. In this photo, Ronald Reagan and Richard Nixon sit on either side of Harvey Hancock (standing).

1987, 1990, 2002). The power elite not only know each other personally and professionally, but they also recognize their status as part of the ultimate "members only" club. Many of them were born into powerful families who still control huge U.S. corporations. Many of the power elite attended the same prep schools and Ivy League colleges. They may live in the same neighborhoods or belong to the same country clubs. They may go to the same churches or give to the same charities. More important, they often serve on each other's boards of directors and do business directly with other members. A recent related study identified only 5,778 individuals in these elite positions, meaning that fewer than 0.0026 percent of the entire U.S. population are among the power elite. These individuals also tend to be white males, although a few powerful women and ethnic or racial minorities also hold elite positions (Dye 2002).

What are the implications of this class dominance theory of power? For one, it debunks the original American rags-to-riches mythology that says anyone who works hard can get to the top. If power is concentrated in such a small fraction of a percentage of the population, chances are that the average person will never wield any real power, regardless of his or her work ethic or life choices. Furthermore, the United States continues to be controlled by white, upper-class men. Finally, those who have the power to create social change by economic, political, or military reforms may choose to do so

SPECIAL INTEREST GROUPS organizations that raise and spend money to influence elected officials and/or public opinion

only when it is to their own advantage. So who runs America after all?

INTEREST GROUPS The American political system is organized so that individuals, groups, and organizations can contribute to candidates' campaigns. **Special interest groups** (sometimes called pressure groups) play an important role in the political process. These are organizations formed expressly to raise and spend money in order to influence elected officials and public opinion. Special interest groups can include corporate organizations, lobbies, political action committees (PACs), and, more recently, 527 committees. Despite strict regulations and recent reforms on campaign finance spending, these groups' contributions to candidates can reach into the hundreds of millions of dollars.

The average citizen may have little idea of the influence of wealthy donor organizations in the political process. There is almost always a positive correlation between a candidate's campaign spending and his success: money wins elections. During the 2008 election, for instance, in 93 percent of House of Representatives races and 94 percent of Senate races, the candidate who spent the most money won. And in the 2012 presidential race, Barack Obama, the victor, raised more than $715 million to Mitt Romney's $446 million (Figure 10.1). As in the presidential race, incumbents (those already occupying the electoral seat) are usually in the best position to raise money because of their high-profile position, and incumbency, therefore, is the most important advantage a candidate can have because it tends to lead to fund-raising success and victory at the polls.

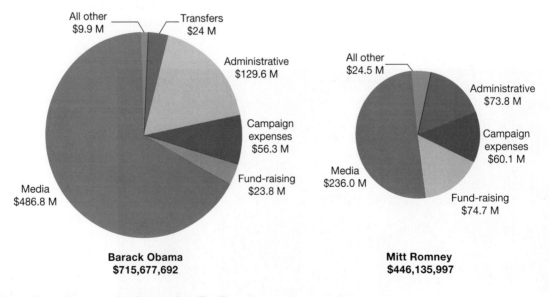

Figure 10.1 **Spending on the Campaign Trail**

Compare the proportion of each presidential candidate's 2012 campaign budget spent on media to the proportions devoted to all other campaign expenses. The size of each pie chart reflects the total expenditures of each candidate.

SOURCE: Center for Responsive Politics 2012a, 2012b, 2012c, 2012d.

Political action committees (PACs) are organizations designed to raise money to support the interests of a select group or organization. For instance, BAMPAC, or Black America Political Action Committee, represents the special interests of African Americans, while AAPAC, the Arab American PAC, lobbies for political interests of Arab Americans. NOW PAC, the National Organization for Women PAC, advocates feminist issues. The National Football League is represented by the "Gridiron PAC," and Major League Baseball has its own PAC as well. Even the interests of extraterrestrials are represented through X-PPAC, the Extraterrestrial Phenomena PAC.

As a result of a 2010 Supreme Court ruling, corporate funding of independent, campaign-related expenditures is no longer prohibited. In fact, the *Citizens United v. Federal Election Committee* decision allowed unlimited spending by corporations, unions, and other noncampaign entities, calling it a First Amendment right. This opened the door to a new kind of PAC—the "Super PAC," which can accept these unlimited contributions and use the monies to do things like produce and air issue-based ads, as long as they do not coordinate with the candidate or the candidate's political party. What this has meant in practice is that political candidates can benefit from the unlimited spending of a Super PAC without being in violation of the campaign finance laws that still apply to their own party organizations. In the 2012 presidential election cycle, the top two Super PACs spent almost $250 million in support of Republican candidate Mitt Romney and against President Barack Obama and other Democratic candidates and issues, while the third biggest Super PAC spent more than $60 million to oppose Romney's candidacy (Center for Responsive Politics 2013). These amounts are astronomically higher than they might have been had not *Citizens United* removed the limits on corporate donations by calling them "free speech."

Though it has been difficult to make definitive conclusions about the relationships between special interest groups and legislators, the staggering amounts of money these groups generate cannot be ignored. As sociologists, we seek to uncover the mechanisms of influence in our political system. Monitoring the actions of top donors, PACs, Super PACs, and other special interest groups brings insight into how our political system works.

> **POLITICAL ACTION COMMITTEES (PACs)** organizations that raise money to support the interests of a select group or organization

Patriotism and Protest

Even though freedom of speech is a legal right in the United States, when we criticize some policy or some action of the government, we may, ironically, be called unpatriotic by those who support it. This is especially true in times of war or national crisis, when many citizens believe we should pull together as a country and present a united front to the world. During the 1960s, for example, at the height of U.S. involvement in Vietnam, many Americans considered antiwar protesters

Corporate Speak Mitt Romney famously stated that "corporations are people, my friend," while the Citizens United decision allowed unlimited corporate donations by designating them as acts of "free speech."

"un-American" because of their vocal criticism of American intervention in Southeast Asia. After September 11, 2001, those who questioned the competence of U.S. intelligence agencies (such as journalists, elected representatives, and survivors of those killed in the attacks) were effectively silenced until more than a year later, when Congress impaneled a commission to investigate intelligence agencies' preparation for and response to the attacks. The commission's report confirmed problems within the intelligence community that contributed to the inability to foresee and forestall the attacks—corroborating the criticisms of "unpatriotic" protesters.

Numerous protests have occurred during the course of the Iraq War, attracting both proponents and critics. The protests at the 2004 Democratic and Republican national conventions in Boston and New York City were notable for their size, their creativity, and the intense response they provoked from law enforcement. Both protesters and police used the internet and mobile phones to coordinate their actions, and in one demonstration, 5,000 bicyclists clogged the streets of Manhattan for a protest ride. Using a different strategy, peace activist Cindy Sheehan, whose son was killed in Iraq, set up camp outside George W. Bush's Texas ranch in August 2005, vowing to stay there until the president came outside and spoke with her. He never did, and in July 2006 Sheehan purchased several acres of land near the Bush ranch to create a more permanent memorial to her son. In 2010, the Museum of Contemporary Art (MOCA) commissioned noted street artist Blu to paint a mural on the outside wall of their Geffen building in downtown Los Angeles. Before the painting could be viewed by the public, MOCA's director ordered it to be whitewashed. The museum had been unaware that Blu's mural would feature powerful antiwar symbolism in the form of coffins draped in dollar bills. While some, including the artist, called MOCA's action censorship, others were equally upset about the insensitivity of displaying the art so close to the Veteran's Administration Building and a nearby Japanese American war memorial (Vankin 2010). And beginning in 2011, the Occupy Movement spread from New York City's Zuccotti Park all over the country and the world, protesting social, economic and political inequality. Carrying signs saying "We Are the 99%," Occupy protesters expressed their opposition to a system that allows a small minority (the "1%") to hold a majority of the wealth and power while ordinary middle-class citizens suffered unemployment, foreclosure, and disempowerment in the great recession.

Is it unpatriotic to criticize your government or to call for change in times of national crisis? Those who do so argue that such criticism is the most patriotic act of all: that uncritical acceptance of government is not the same as patriotism and that citizens should make every effort to correct its flaws. Those on the opposite side may say, "My country, right or wrong" and believe that the decisions of our elected leaders, once made, are beyond criticism. Regardless of your views, keep in mind that those who criticize government policies are doing exactly what our democratic system calls for and protects. Dissent and its tolerance are crucial elements of an open society, and you have a constitutionally protected right to oppose, criticize, and protest.

The Media and the Political Process

THE MEDIA AS THE FOURTH ESTATE In addition to the executive, legislative, and judicial branches of government, the media play a key role in the political process. This has been true since the founding of the country and has taken on even

Blu's mural on the
Geffen Building

more significant proportions in the Information Age. Often referred to as the **Fourth Estate** of government, the media render checks and balances on power much like the three government branches. Although the media can also serve to entertain, they were originally intended to inform and educate the populace and to serve as a watchdog on government. In fact, the framers of the U.S. Constitution probably envisioned the watchdog role as the media's primary function. After all, they believed that a free press was essential to the health of the new democracy. Thus, the First Amendment guarantees freedom of expression and freedom of the press (along with other rights).

Still, it's hard to imagine that our founding fathers could have envisioned what "the press" would become. To them, it literally meant printing presses. There were no broadcast media or digital media back then—no mass media as we know them. So contemporary lawmakers have had to interpret the Constitution in light of modern concerns and developments. They must try to balance the rights of a free press while protecting the country from abuses of power by the media or by the individuals who own the media. And we must all consider the media's tremendous potential to sway and manipulate our thoughts and feelings and to impact the political process.

The media have always played a role in American politics, informing the public about the important issues of the day. But their role has increased dramatically during the past fifty years, coinciding with the spread of television in the 1950s and 60s and the internet in the 1990s and 2000s. Many of the social movements and landmark political events of the past several decades have unfolded before us on the TV or computer screen. It's unlikely that the Civil Rights Movement, the Vietnam War, Watergate, the impeachment of President Clinton, the attacks of 9/11, or the tragedy of Hurricane Katrina would have emerged, developed, and resolved the way they did without the media to bring those issues and images into our living rooms. And for a little while, Americans talked about those issues. The media can make momentous events a part of the national dialogue and involve voters, citizens, and even global attention, influencing public opinion and promoting political activism and change.

MEDIA INFLUENCE ON POLITICS

Some of the most significant changes in the political process have occurred in the realm of campaigns and elections. Political actors have adapted to a media-saturated society, and their strategies for success must include great media savvy (Skarzynska 2004). Any group or individual wishing to influence the voters must court the media, either through attempting to gain coverage of a particular issue or candidate or by directly buying space or time through advertisements. Fund-raising, gathering money to spend on media exposure, has become the first order of political business (Ulbrich 2004).

At one time, the voting public was informed of the issues through local political party representatives, town hall meetings, church groups, speeches made by politicians or activists out on the stump, or exhaustive coverage in newspapers or on radio. Nowadays, media coverage of politics is more likely to emphasize human interest stories, personalities, high-profile spectacles, and planned events—and less likely to explain the background and implications of issues and policy debates (Kellner 2005). And not all news programs offer strictly objective reporting. We hear a lot about politics through pundits, those who offer political media commentary.

FOURTH ESTATE the media, which are considered like a fourth branch of government (after the executive, legislative, and judiciary) and thus serve as another of the checks and balances on power

OPINION LEADERS high-profile individuals whose interpretation of events influences the public

The public is also influenced by **opinion leaders**, high-profile people who interpret political information for us (Katz and Lazarsfeld 1955). Instead of getting information about the issues directly, we allow our views to be shaped by these opinion leaders whom we trust to tell us what to believe. Someone like Oprah Winfrey, for instance, can influence not only what we read but also our political values. Even within your group of friends, there may be someone who, while not as famous as Oprah, is more politically savvy than the rest of the group and can communicate information to you in ways that may influence your opinions.

One of the first and most dramatic examples of the media's impact on politics occurred during the presidential campaign of 1960. The debates between John F. Kennedy, the Democrat, and Richard Nixon, the Republican, were the first to be broadcast live on television. Kennedy, the younger candidate, recognized the power of television and understood the importance of presenting a "telegenic" image. He allowed media handlers to advise him on makeup, hairstyle, clothes, and the appropriate demeanor for the TV cameras. Conversely, Nixon refused to make any special preparation for the event. As a seasoned politician, he planned to rely on his command of the issues and his considerable debating skills.

Those who watched the debates on television saw dramatic differences between the two candidates. Kennedy looked fresh, young, and energetic; Nixon looked sweaty, old, and tired. Those who listened to the debates on the radio, as previous generations had for years, judged the two candidates not by looks or mannerisms but by the content of their speech. When polled after the debates, audiences who watched on TV thought that Kennedy won the debate; audiences who listened on radio thought Nixon was the winner. As history shows, Kennedy won the election and helped to change the relationship between the media and political campaigns. Although Kennedy's performance during the debate was only one factor in the election, it was significant. Other presidential candidates

The Media's Role in the Political Process The power of television to bring political news from around the world has transformed the political process. For example, the Civil Rights Movement, the attacks on September 11, 2001, or the disaster surrounding Hurricane Katrina would not have had such widespread impact without mass media.

became so nervous about the effects of televised debates that none agreed to participate in them until 1976.

STYLE OVER SUBSTANCE? Another feature of modern politics is "sound bytes"—those short audio or visual snippets taken from press releases, press conferences, photo opportuni-

ties, or sometimes protests. In our postmodern era, the news has been condensed into just a few seconds' worth of information. What politicians say to the press is often scripted by "spin doctors" who manipulate rhetoric to give it a positive appearance designed to be catchy and compelling while not necessarily delivering much substance; many people form their views

Celebrity Politics How do politicians, such as Sarah Palin, carefully craft their image to make them relate more to the public?

of candidates from these processed bits of information. It is no wonder that celebrity politicians are becoming more common and popular. After all, who knows better how to use the media, how to stand before the cameras and speak in interviews, than those who have been professionally trained as actors? President Ronald Reagan, formerly a Hollywood actor and commercial spokesperson, is perhaps the greatest example of this. He knew how to hit his marks and deliver his lines. He was even called "The Great Communicator" despite his inability to speak extemporaneously.

Any form of celebrity seems to make an individual more visible and popular. Others have followed in Reagan's path, from basketball star Bill Bradley, astronaut John Glenn, and comedian Al Franken, who became senators, to wrestler Jesse Ventura and actor Arnold Schwarzenegger, who both became governors, singer Sonny Bono, who became a congressman, and actor Clint Eastwood, who became a mayor.

Sarah Palin is another kind of celebrity politician. The Republican vice presidential candidate in the 2008 election and former Alaska governor became a high-profile political figure and is an example of what some call "style over substance." Her image as a Washington outsider and folksy hockey mom was carefully promoted; she was coached and groomed for public appearances. Critics cited her lack of knowledge and experience, but it was her personal life, or at least the part of it that was portrayed in the media, that people were relating to. She continued to be popular among supporters, even after losing the election. She authored two best-selling books, starred in the reality-TV series *Sarah Palin's Alaska*, and was a regular contributor to Fox News. The media allowed Sarah Palin to become a galvanizing and controversial political figure.

Does the increased focus on a politician's style and personality, rather than on the politician's platform and policies, mean that we are getting less of real substance in what we consume? This Data Workshop may help you answer this question.

DATA WORKSHOP
Analyzing Mass Media and Popular Culture

Real and Fake News

Postmodern sociologist Jean Baudrillard claimed that "the image has come to replace the real" (1981/1994). By this, he meant that we have lost the ability to distinguish between what is real and what is fake, especially where media representations are involved, and that we also have come to accept the fake as sufficient—thereby no longer needing the real. He called this new artificially constructed "reality" the **simulacrum**, or a simulation that becomes as good as the original. Some would warn that we need to be more aware of how this plays out in the political arena, even beyond its role in style over substance.

> **SIMULACRUM** an image or media representation that does not reflect reality in any meaningful way but is treated as real

A key example of Baudrillard's simulacrum can be found in the growing popularity of "fake news" programs. These include such comedy TV shows as *The Daily Show, The Colbert Report, Saturday Night Live*'s Weekend Update segment, and the Onion News Network. Although these shows get their humor from parodying or satirizing real news, there are many instances where they generate and deliver real news, thus blurring the line between fake and real, and making it harder to tell the difference. Some young people may have little other regular exposure to news. More than

Real and Fake News *The Colbert Report* and *The Daily Show* blur the lines between real and fake news. At left, Stephen Colbert takes a more journalistic approach to interviewing Ray Odinero, commanding general of U.S. forces in Iraq. At right, Colbert and Jon Stewart poke fun at the divisive partisanship dominating major news organizations in their Rally to Restore Sanity and/or Fear.

40 percent of young people between eighteen and twenty-nine years of age cited Comedy Central's Jon Stewart and *The Daily Show* and Stephen Colbert of *The Colbert Report* as primary sources of political news (Pew Research Center for the People and the Press 2008). Jon Stewart has only half-jokingly been called "the most trusted name in fake news." These shows are consistently ranked among the most popular of any kind for the age group (Gross 2010). Although the primary intent of these programs is to be funny and entertaining, it doesn't prevent them from also taking on serious subjects and disseminating messages with a viewpoint and the potential to influence their audiences. Fake news has become an important voice in humor and in American political culture.

Stewart and Colbert play news anchors who cover the latest current events, talk with reporters in the field, and conduct live in-studio interviews with newsmakers. Although Stewart and Colbert play the role of journalist, their performances blur the distinction between real and fake, and they often exhibit the same qualities and characteristics of "real" journalists. Guests on their shows have ranged from celebrities and journalists to newsmakers and politicians, including an appearance on *The Daily Show* by President Obama in October 2010 in which Jon Stewart asked him hard questions about such issues as health-care reform and unemployment. Stewart and Colbert have each won numerous awards and have both written best-selling books about American politics that have as much substantive social commentary as they do funny lines. They make guest appearances on real news shows on other networks, further blurring their roles as mere comedians.

Stewart and Colbert are also ideally placed to make meta criticism about the state of journalism and news in this postmodern era. In late October 2010, just a week preceding the midterm elections, Stewart and Colbert organized a huge rally on the Mall in Washington, a place usually reserved for serious political activity, to protest against the increasingly caustic tone and divisive partisanship that are dominant among the major news organizations. The event was billed as the "Rally to Restore Sanity and/or Fear" (to represent their two respective viewpoints) and featured the two hosts and a variety of speakers and musical acts, including Kid Rock, Sheryl Crow, and Jeff Tweedy. A crowd of more than 200,000 was estimated to be in attendance (Montopoli 2010).

This Data Workshop asks you to analyze the new phenomenon of fake news, its real popularity, and its possible influence on young people and politics. Choose a recent episode of either *The Daily Show* or *The Colbert Report* that you can watch and refer to. You will be gathering data from an existing source (recorded or online) and making a content analysis of the program. (See Chapter 2 for more on these research methods.) Consider the following questions after viewing, or add your own commentary.

＊ In what ways does the show resemble a traditional network news program? Examine the format of the show, the cast and correspondents, the regular program segments (news reporting, interviews), the structure of the stage set, the design of the graphics, and other aspects of the production.

＊ Make a list of the topics that are covered on the show. Compare the stories presented on the fake news show with stories presented in the real news during the same time period. How much of the news is completely fake, and how much is actually about real world events?

＊ A fake news show, even when it covers real issues, is not held to the same journalistic standards as traditional news outlets. How does an audience member know what to believe about the truth of any particular statement or story?

* Despite being satirical, fake news shows also make serious commentary about important issues in American life. What are some of the underlying messages of the humorous material on the show?

* Are you among the audience members who get political news from fake news shows? To what extent do you believe these shows might influence people's political ideas? Do you think that they increase young people's awareness of issues, or are they a confounding distraction?

* If we consider what postmodernists say about the increasing power of the image or simulacrum in our everyday lives, how can we tell the difference between what is real and what is fake?

There are two options for completing this Data Workshop.

Option 1 (informal): Choose a recent episode of *The Daily Show* or *The Colbert Report* and take notes while watching. Keep in mind the Data Workshop questions and prepare to discuss your thoughts with other students in small groups.

Option 2 (formal): Choose a recent episode of *The Daily Show* or *The Colbert Report* and take notes while watching. Write a two- to three-page paper answering the Workshop questions and making your own reflections about the role of journalism—real and fake—in the American political process.

NEW MEDIA AND POLITICS As much as the mass media changed the political process in the twentieth century, it seems likely that the so-called new media will transform it all the more. Social media move beyond simply providing information, and stress interaction, networking, and user-generated content.

The internet has now become a leading source of campaign news for young people, and social networking sites play an important part in the story. 54% of 18–29 year olds and 43% of 30–49 year olds have the internet as a top source for campaign news, compared to only 28% of 50–64 year olds and 14% for 65 year olds and older (see Table 10.2).

But the power and potential of the new media in the political process cut both ways. It used to be that politicians only had to watch what they said when reporters were around, and even then they could go off the record if they needed to. But today, all it takes is one person with a camera phone or her own blog to turn an offhand comment into big news.

That is exactly what happened to Republican senator George Allen of Virginia in 2006 during a very tight race against Democrat Jim Webb. The Webb campaign had begun sending a video "tracker" to cover Allen's public appearances, a practice that has become common. For many of these events, the videographer was Shekar Ramanuja Sidarth, a campaign volunteer whose parents had immigrated to the United States from India before he was born. Although Sidarth reported that the campaign staff had been quite courteous to him up to that point, on August 11, Allen was giving a speech at a state park when he noticed Sidarth filming him. Ironically, Allen began by saying he was going to "run this campaign on positive, constructive ideas" but then

Table 10.2 For Young People, Internet Rivals TV as Campaign News Source

Top Sources for Campaign News	18–29	30–49	50–64	65+
	%	%	%	%
Television	64	68	83	86
Internet	54	43	28	14
Newspaper	14	17	27	41
Radio	17	20	18	12
Magazines	1	4	2	5
Other	7	2	2	2
Don't Know	6	5	2	1

SOURCE: Pew Research Center for the People & the Press 2012a.

proceeded to point out Sidarth, referring to him as "macaca, or whatever his name is," and asking the crowd to welcome him to America.

When asked about the incident later, Sidarth said, "I could feel his hostility. I just did my best to keep filming. As soon as I was finished I called the Webb campaign. They were shocked and they posted it on YouTube pretty quickly" (Baldwin 2007). The video swiftly went "viral," garnering hundreds of thousands of hits and showing up in blogs to underscore allegations of racism against Allen. The story, of course, was also picked up by the mainstream media. Allen tried to defend himself by claiming that "macaca" was just a made-up word, while his critics argued that it was a racist slur and that he had used it as such. Allen was defeated as much by his opponent Webb as by a shameful moment captured and disseminated through the new media.

Clearly, the media play an important role in informing and educating the voting public. Despite our "free press," however, we must also be aware of how the media can be used to achieve the purposes of powerful interest groups and individuals. The democratic system stands to suffer if only those with the most money or celebrity can influence public opinion by buying their way into the hearts and minds of Americans.

Politics: Linking Micro- and Macrosociology

Political institutions and their products (such as laws or bureaucratic systems) shape our everyday lives. A law such as Title VII of the Civil Rights Act of 1964 ensures your right to apply for and hold a job without being discriminated against because of race, gender, or religion. No matter who you are or what kind of work you do, you are protected by this law. And even if you have never experienced discrimination in the workplace, this law is probably one of the reasons why. Huge government bureaucracies like the Department of Education shape your everyday life as well. Even if you attend a private university, you had to fill out a FAFSA (Free Application for Federal Student Aid) in order to determine your eligibility for any type of financial aid—federal and state grants and loans and aid programs administered by your campus. All these student aid sources require the FAFSA, and your ability to attend the college of your choice may therefore depend on the decisions made by this government bureaucracy.

In addition to seeing how political institutions shape our everyday lives, it is important to remember that we have built these institutions ourselves, through our participation in the democratic process. When we vote, sign petitions, or partici-

> **EDUCATION** the process by which a society transmits its knowledge, values, and expectations to its members so they can function effectively

pate in demonstrations, we bring our individual influence to bear on the larger social structure—even if, ultimately, the cause or candidate we support doesn't prevail. So remember, micro-macro connections are made every day as you participate with others in political processes and live in a culture shaped by its political institutions.

Democratic processes require a free press and an educated polity; to make decisions and cast votes, you must have the tools to gather information and comprehend the issues your vote will influence. This is only one of the many links between political institutions and educational institutions in our society. As we move into the segment of this chapter that deals with education, try to think of all the ways that politics and education are connected—and remember to look for micro-macro connections as you learn about educational institutions as well.

What Is Education?

Most modern political systems recognize the importance of universal education. The framers of the U.S. Constitution realized that an informed public was essential to the survival of democracy. Education, therefore, was seen as critical to the founding of the new republic. In the United States, public education has traditionally been under state and local control, although the federal government began playing a larger role in the latter half of the twentieth century. However, private schools and religious schools are also involved in education. About 10 percent of K–12 students attend private schools (either religious or secular), 88 percent attend public schools, and 2 percent are homeschooled (U.S. Department of Education 2009).

Education is the central means by which a society transmits its knowledge, values, and expectations to its members. The general goal of education is to give students the necessary understanding for effective social functioning. Education often includes the transmission of information, principles and values, the regulation of personal character, and discipline of the mind. Education can be either formal or informal and can occur in a variety of settings, although we commonly think of it as tied to school systems.

A Brief History of Modern Education

Formal, institutionalized, secular education in Western civilization began in ancient Greece around the eighth century B.C.E., when students studied philosophy, mathematics, music, and gymnastics. Higher education was carried out by philosophers before the rise of schools as an institution. In the Middle Ages, the church was the main educator, with schools in monasteries and cathedrals, and until about 1200 C.E., the schools focused mainly on training students to be priests. During the thirteenth century, lay education emerged. It consisted of apprentice training for a small group of the common people or education in chivalry for the more privileged. During the Middle Ages, universities offered courses in three subjects—law, theology, and medicine—and these courses were available only to the most privileged members of the society: royals, aristocrats, and those from families with ties to the monarchy and the church.

While systems of education have evolved a great deal since the Middle Ages, the roots of what we would recognize as modern mass education can be traced back to the idealism of the European Enlightenment of the eighteenth and nineteenth centuries. During this period, the value of education greatly increased. The leading thinkers of the day, such as Voltaire, Locke, and Franklin, emphasized knowledge—reason, logic, and science—over religious tradition. They were convinced that the well-being and future of modern society depended upon enlightened self-knowledge, which could be achieved only through learning.

Education in the United States grew rapidly during this same period. The founders' belief that the government has the responsibility to provide basic education to all its citizens—and that fulfilling this obligation is beneficial for both society and the individual—helped to create the U.S. public education system. Schooling came to be seen as a necessity rather than a luxury and became legally mandatory for all children age sixteen and younger; Massachusetts was the first state to enact such a law in 1852. As larger proportions of the population began attending schools, curricula became more varied and included both academic and vocational education to prepare students for a diversifying set of future occupations (not just farming or housewifery). Elementary, junior high, and high schools had spread to every state and territory in the nation, including Alaska, by 1929, and opportunities for higher education also expanded, especially in the land-grant colleges of the western United States.

Higher education is now available to everyone in the United States. Before 1900, fewer than 2 percent of Americans finished high school, and even fewer went on to college. The current high school graduation rate has been hovering around 75 percent nationwide, up from 72 percent in 2001 but lower than the record high of 77 percent in 1969 (Dillon 2010; Khadaroo 2010). If you count adults up to twenty-five years of age, then 87.5 percent of Americans hold a high school degree or equivalency (U.S. Census Bureau 2011f). There are variations according to state and school district: Nevada had the lowest high school graduation rate of 56.3 percent and Wisconsin had the highest, at 90.7 percent (Balfanz et al. 2012). Different racial and ethnic groups have varying rates: blacks with 83.1 percent, Hispanics 65.5, whites 91.5, and Asian/Pacific Islanders at 88.3 percent (U.S. Census Bureau 2011g).

Education and the Reproduction of Society

Schooling serves a number of important functions in our society. The transmission of knowledge is a clear function of education, but in addition, we learn to follow society's rules and to respect authority, and we are socialized to develop other qualities that will eventually make us efficient and obedient workers. In school, we also learn our places in the larger

The Rise of Mass Education Beginning in the nineteenth century, schooling began to be considered a necessity for preparing children to enter modern industrial occupations.

society—practices such as **tracking**, in which students are identified as gifted or placed into remedial education, teach us about success and achievement and our chances for both. When placed in a lower ability or remedial track, for instance, students lose access to courses such as calculus and advanced placement classes (Useem 1990), which effectively locks them out of certain colleges, certain majors, and even certain future careers, all by the time they're sixteen.

EDUCATION AND INEQUALITY While we firmly believe, as a society, that education is the key to achievement and success, it is also true that educational institutions can replicate systems of inequality. Educational achievements do improve our life chances—U.S. Census data consistently indicate that those with higher educational attainment also have higher median incomes. In 2010, the average lifetime earnings for someone with an advanced degree totaled around $3 million, compared with $2.3 million for those with a bachelor's degree, or $1.3 million for those with only a high school diploma (Carnevale, Rose, and Cheah 2011). Women with the same educational achievement, however, made considerably less than their male counterparts (U.S. Census Bureau 2009). It is also worth noting some of the complexity of gender inequality in higher education, as we find that among young adults ages twenty-five to twenty-nine, there is a growing gap between the percent of women (35 percent) to men (27 percent) with a bachelor's degree or more (U.S. Census Bureau 2009). Thus, the data indicate that the benefit of a higher education does not operate in equal measure for all Americans. Stratification within schools often mirrors stratification systems in the larger society, wherein women and girls, minority group students, poor or working-class students, or students with disabilities are discriminated against both by individuals and by institutional systems (Oakes 1985; Orfield 2001). So education benefits everyone, but it does not benefit everyone equally, and inequality in educational benefits mirrors inequality in the larger society.

How do these patterns manifest themselves? What do these educational inequalities look and feel like for students in the classroom? Female students may notice, for instance, that their teachers pay more attention to male students, and they may learn to think that boys are smarter than girls. Caucasian or Asian students may notice that there are fewer African American and Hispanic students in the gifted classroom than in the remedial classroom, and they may learn to think that whites and Asians are smarter than blacks and Hispanics. Children without disabilities may see disabled kids left out of activities or sent to the special education center and learn to think that these students are less worthy than nondisabled kids. These micro-inequities are common in American classrooms. They are experienced by individuals but are the result of structural forces external to those individuals—in other words, micro-inequities result from macro-level inequalities in the larger educational and social systems. And these micro-inequities teach us as much as our more explicit lessons in math, literature, or history. Acquiring a sociological perspective on educational institutions and processes will help us "unlearn" these lessons and understand that educational attainment is often as much about social stratification as it is about individual ability.

THE HIDDEN CURRICULUM Sociologists have long been interested in the **hidden curriculum**, the lessons that students learn indirectly but that are an implicit part of their socialization in the school environment (Jackson 1968). Many sociologists have analyzed the hidden curriculum to explain the nonacademic roles filled by mass education.

One such role is the training of future workers, which was examined by Bowles and Gintis (1977) in their study *Schooling in Capitalist America*. They argue that schools train a labor force with the appropriate skills, personalities, and attitudes for a corporate economy. Although the official curriculum is supposed to promote personal improvement and social mobility, the hidden curriculum of "rules, routines, and regulations" actually produces a submissive and obedient workforce that is prepared to take orders and perform repetitive tasks. According to this analysis, schools look a lot like factories. Students have no control over their curriculum, must obey instructions, and gain little intrinsic satisfaction from their schoolwork. Because students learn these norms and values in school, they are willing to accept similar conditions when they become workers.

A similar analysis can explain how the hidden curriculum reinforces and reproduces conditions of social inequality by presenting and reinforcing an image of what is considered "normal," "right," or "good." While the official curriculum has come a long way toward recognizing the racial, ethnic, and gender diversity of the nation, there are still major gaps and exclusions (FitzGerald 1980; Thornton 2003). Schools cannot always rectify these oversights because the hidden curriculum can work through much more subtle mechanisms as well. How the curriculum is presented and the way the school is organized can be powerful messengers of the hidden curriculum. For instance, even schools that attempt to implement multicultural education may undermine their own efforts if the staff and administration do not mirror the lessons they teach. If teachers and administrators are mostly white, mostly heterosexual, or mostly male (or mostly female, as is the case in lower grades), they may belie the

TRACKING the placement of students in educational "tracks," or programs of study (e.g., college prep, remedial), that determine the types of classes students take

HIDDEN CURRICULUM values or behaviors that students learn indirectly over the course of their schooling because of the structure of the educational system and the teaching methods used

Hidden Curriculum Bowles and Gintis argue that schools train students to be ideal workers by promoting a curriculum of "rules, routines, and regulations." These honor students at Philadelphia High School for Girls (left) and soldiers at the U.S. Central Command's "Deployable Headquarters" (right) apply their training.

very lessons they try to teach—what students hear and what they see just don't add up. When schools attempt to alter only what is taught and not the way it is taught, they may change the curriculum, but they won't affect what students are learning (Falconer and Byrnes 2003; Christakis 1995).

Classic Studies of Education

Sociologists and other researchers have studied education from a variety of perspectives. In this section, we review three classic studies of education, each offering a different approach and distinctive insights into its significance, both as a social institution and in the lives of individuals.

A SYMBOLIC INTERACTIONIST STUDY The first study looks at education from the symbolic-interactionist perspective, which maintains that the social world is constructed through the interactions of individuals. Robert Rosenthal, a Harvard psychologist, and Leonore Jacobson, an elementary school principal, worked together on *Pygmalion in the Classroom: Teacher Expectation and Pupils' Intellectual Development* (1968). The researchers began the experiment by administering a basic IQ test to students in the first through sixth grades, although they told teachers the test was designed to predict which students would "bloom" academically in the next year. They then randomly selected an experimental group of students and falsely told their teachers that these students were predicted to develop rapidly in the coming school year. At the end of the year, the researchers administered the same IQ test and found that students in the experimental group had increased their IQ scores by a significantly greater margin than their peers in the control group. They concluded that the teachers' attitudes about

their students unintentionally influenced the students' academic performance. In other words, when teachers expected students to succeed, the students indeed tended to improve (and it was assumed that the opposite would be true as well).

The results of *Pygmalion in the Classroom* have been critiqued by other researchers, on both theoretical and methodological grounds, especially because the researchers used standardized IQ tests and small subject samples (Baker and Crist 1971). Nonetheless, this study and others support the proposition that teacher expectations affect students' behavior and achievement in measurable ways. Some studies indicate that student labeling is often arbitrary and biased, with the result that teachers—whether consciously or unconsciously—may be reinforcing existing class, ethnic, ability, and gender inequalities (Fairbanks 1992; Sadker and Sadker 1995). This also means that changes in classroom interaction could lead to an improvement in academic performance among students from underprivileged backgrounds.

A CONFLICT STUDY The next study, which also looks at inequalities in schools, is consistent with a conflict perspective, which sees society as a system characterized by inequality and competition. Former teacher Jonathan Kozol wrote *Savage Inequalities* (1991), which describes his ethnographic study of public schools in Chicago and its suburbs. Kozol contends that because schools are funded by local property taxes, children in poor neighborhoods are trapped in poor schools, which reinforces inequality. He documents the significant differences among America's schools: "the highest spending districts have twice as many art, music, and foreign language teachers . . . 75 percent more physical education teachers . . . 50 percent more nurses, school librarians, guidance counselors, and psychologists . . . and 60 percent more personnel in school administration than the low-spending districts" (Kozol 1991, p. 167).

When Kozol interviewed the parents and students in wealthy school districts, he discovered that many of them believe educational inequalities are a thing of the past, "something dating maybe back to slavery or maybe to the era of official segregation" but not to anything "recent or contemporary or ongoing" (Kozol 1991, p. 179). In stark contrast to this view, Kozol describes underfunded schools he visited—the hundreds of classrooms without teachers in Chicago, the thousands of children without classrooms in schools throughout New Jersey. His overall impression was that these urban schools were, by and large, extraordinarily unhappy places. How, he asks, could the children in these schools have an equal chance at success? A structural functionalist might respond that schools are not intended to provide equal chances.

A STRUCTURAL FUNCTIONALIST STUDY According to the structural functionalist perspective, educational inequality is merely preparation for occupational inequalities later in life. (Remember, functionalists believe that every social phenomenon has a role to play in keeping society at equilibrium.) In the third study, *The Credential Society*, sociologist Randall Collins (1979) argues that class inequalities are reproduced in educational settings and that there is very little schools can do to increase learning. Although many people assume that better teachers, better facilities, and better funding could increase test scores, he points out that when class background factors are held constant, none of these other factors seem to have any effect. Collins believes that reproducing the existing class structure is the true function of education. Schools, for example, provide the credentials to assure that the children of the middle class will continue to receive middle-class jobs. To protect their own job security, members of lucrative occupations, such as accountants, lawyers, and financial analysts, have set up a complicated credential system (education) to keep the number of job applicants down and to ensure that there is a large population forced to work at unpleasant jobs for low wages. Collins makes the radical recommendation that we consider "abolishing compulsory school requirements and making formal credential requirements for employment illegal" (Collins 1979, p. 198). This would make it illegal for employers to ask how much education a job applicant has, much as it is currently illegal to ask about race or gender.

The Crisis in Education

During the past several decades, many educators, parents, and legislators have come to believe that America's educational system is in crisis, that public schools are failing to provide adequate training for students. Critics list a variety of problems, including low rates of literacy and poor standardized test scores, lack of sufficient funding and crumbling infrastructure, low pay for teachers, overcrowded classrooms, and high rates of crime on campus.

A number of studies point to the problems. In 1983, the National Commission on Excellence in Education released a report on the state of American public schools. *A Nation at Risk* concluded, in apocalyptic terms, that the American educational system was in a crisis so serious that "if an unfriendly foreign power" had created it, "we might well have viewed it as an act of war." Largely on the basis of declining standardized test scores, the report argued that the United States was "committing an act of unthinking, unilateral educational disarmament." Since then, the conclusions of the commission have been affirmed. A 1999 study showed that although 40 percent of white students passed a history exam required for public high school graduation in Virginia, only 23 percent of Hispanic students and 13 percent of black students scored passing grades (Fairfax County Public Schools 1999). This type of "achievement gap" was visible in other states' educational data as well. And in 2010, data showed that 1.2 million students drop out of high school each year, and that 44 percent of dropouts under age twenty-four are jobless (Broad Foundation 2010). Data like these seemed to point to a decline in American educational standards and competitiveness, and politicians began to respond.

NO CHILD LEFT BEHIND To address some of these crises, Congress passed the "No Child Left Behind" (NCLB) act in 2002. According to this policy, each state is responsible for testing every student in its public education system at specific grade intervals to determine levels of success. Low-performing schools are identified with "school report cards" and are required to improve both student and teacher performance. Parents also have the option of removing their children from consistently low-performing schools and placing them in other schools within the district.

In theory, No Child Left Behind seems to promote equal education, but in practice it has had mixed results. NCLB relies on standardized test scores (in reading comprehension, writing, and math) even though researchers have long known that standardized test scores are ambiguous predictors of success for women and students of color (Epps 2001) and do not directly measure teacher or school performance at all. For many of these reasons, in 2010, President Obama proposed dismantling the law and replacing it with a new blueprint for change. The new mandate focuses on preparing students for either college or a career. Another feature would be a swifter and more aggressive response to the worst performing 5 percent of schools, which would include takeovers, firings, and possible closures. The new law would go by another name, as "No Child Left Behind" has become synonymous with the failings and frustrations of that law.

The Present and Future of Education

What will American education look like in the future? A number of educational trends are already in place and may play an important role in the years ahead: charter schools, early college high schools, homeschooling, school vouchers, community colleges, and distance learning.

CHARTER SCHOOLS **Charter schools** are public schools, but they are run by private entities, such as a parents' group or an educational corporation. Also, they operate with relative freedom from many of the bureaucratic regulations that apply to traditional public schools. Charter schools represent a compromise position between public and private schools and provide a way for parents to exercise control over their students' educational experiences without completely abandoning the public school system. By 2010, forty-one states and the District of Columbia had established charter school programs, and more than 5,400 charter schools were serving a total of more than 1.7 million students (Center for Education Reform 2010). State laws regarding charter schools governed sponsorship, number of schools, regulatory waivers, degree of fiscal or legal autonomy, and performance expectations.

The "charter" establishing such schools is a contract detailing the school's mission, program, goals, students served, methods of assessment, and ways to measure success. Charter schools are designed to support educational innovation; some have special emphases like arts or science; others offer special services like health clinics or community-based internships for students. A high school in St. Louis called the Construction Careers Center instructs students in the skills needed to work in the building trades while also teaching the traditional high school curriculum. In Madison, Wisconsin, educators started Nuestro Mundo Community School, a Spanish immersion program. By fifth grade, all the students are equally fluent in Spanish and English. The Madison school district created the school to help close the gap between the test scores of Hispanic students and their non-Hispanic peers. Ideally, charter schools can make changes and implement decisions faster than ordinary public schools because of their freedom from district governance. They can monitor their successes (and failures) more closely and are more responsive to the needs of students, parents, and communities.

In reality, charter schools face many challenges. They are difficult and sometimes expensive to launch and run. Many struggle to raise funds and meet endless lists of state and local regulations. There are also questions about whether charter schools are any better than ordinary public schools. They have met with only mixed success. A report on charter school students in California found great variation in how well the schools and their students performed (RAND Education 2003). Although achievement varies by school and by subject matter, charter school students generally have comparable or slightly lower test scores than those in conventional schools. These schools did not necessarily serve more minority students. Nonetheless, charter schools continue to be popular and more will probably open in the coming years, looking to benefit from both the experience of earlier charter schools and the findings of social scientific research.

EARLY COLLEGE HIGH SCHOOLS **Early college high schools** are new institutions that blend high school and college into a coherent educational program in which students earn both a high school diploma and two years of college credit toward a bachelor's degree. In addition to local efforts to create these schools, the Bill & Melinda Gates Foundation, in partnership with the Carnegie Corporation of New York, the Ford Foundation, and the W. K. Kellogg Foundation, has contributed over $120 million to launch early college high schools. In 2010, more than 208 schools in twenty-four states were serving over 47,000 students; through continued efforts, some 250 schools are planned that would serve more than 100,000 students. Each early college high school is a collaborative endeavor between a public school district and an accredited higher education partner. In Phoenix, Arizona, high school students can join the Gateway High School program and simultaneously get a high school diploma and an associate's degree from Gateway Community College. Antioch University in Seattle, Washington, offers a similar program for Native American youth, who have the highest college dropout rate and the lowest graduation rate of any ethnic group in the United States. The goal for these programs is to develop new high schools that engage low-income and underrepresented students by offering them challenging academic work while simultaneously providing the necessary guidance and support structures. Early college high schools are small (with no more than 75–100 students per grade) and thus can provide the benefits of a close community, an intimate learning environment, and personalized academic attention.

For many students, the path to postsecondary education is difficult. Large, impersonal middle and high school programs, limited financial resources, and the daunting processes of applying to and entering higher education may hinder academic achievement. By changing the structure of the high school and compressing the number of years required for an undergraduate degree, early college high schools are designed to reduce obstacles to student success.

> **CHARTER SCHOOLS** public schools run by private entities to give parents greater control over their children's education
>
> **EARLY COLLEGE HIGH SCHOOLS** institutions in which students earn a high school diploma and two years of credit toward a bachelor's degree

These schools are already having a significant impact on underserved youth, who are demonstrating high levels of attendance, improved promotion rates, and success in college-level courses.

HOMESCHOOLING **Homeschooling** or home-based education is the education of school-aged children under their parents' supervision outside a regular school campus. Many parents homeschool their children not only to control their academic education but also to limit their exposure to the socializing effects of peer culture in public schools. Some homeschooled children enroll in regular schools part time or share instruction with other families, but most of their education takes place at home. Many families homeschool their children for their entire K–12 years, but many others try it for only a short time.

Homeschooling in the United States has been growing steadily since the 1980s, with current growth rates of 5 percent to 12 percent a year. There were estimated to be more than 2 million homeschooled students in the United States in 2007–2008. This represents approximately 35 percent of the over 6 million privately schooled student population. Clearly, homeschooling is a significant phenomenon in education, but how is it working? One of the largest studies of homeschooling arrived at rather startling results. The academic achievement of homeschooled students, on average, was sig-nificantly above that of public school students (Ray 1997, 2008). In addition, homeschooled students did well even if their parents were not certified teachers and the state did not highly regulate homeschooling. One advantage of home-schooling seems to be the flexibility in customizing curriculum and pedagogy to the needs of each child. Yet, questions remain about the possible academic and social disadvantages to students removed from typical school environments.

SCHOOL VOUCHERS First proposed in the 1990s, **school vouchers** allow parents in neighborhoods where the public schools are inadequate to send their children to the private school of their choice. In other words, taxpayers receive a voucher for some of the money that a public school would have received to educate their child, and they apply that money to private school tuition. Most school-voucher programs fund 75 percent to 90 percent of the cost of a private school, with parents making up the rest. Proponents of school vouchers—most notably Bush administration Secretary of Education Margaret Spellings (2006)—argue that they give parents more choice and control over their children's education and pressure public schools to improve or risk the loss of their voucher-eligible student body. Opponents—such as President Barack Obama and Congresswoman Eleanor Holmes Norton (2006)—argue that vouchers do not improve public education but do the opposite: they drain funds from vulnerable public schools and cause them to deteriorate further. Opponents also say that if parents use vouchers for parochial schools, public monies are funding religious education, thus threatening the separation of church and state. While the Supreme Court has ruled the voucher system to be con-

HOMESCHOOLING the education of children by their parents, at home

SCHOOL VOUCHERS payments from the government to parents whose children attend failing public schools; the money helps parents pay private school tuition

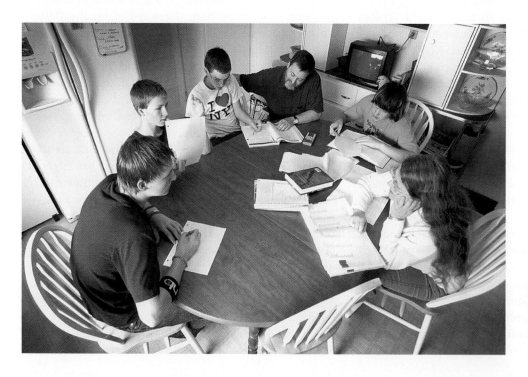

Homeschooling The Wilson family in Myrtle Point, Oregon, study together at the kitchen table as part of their homeschooling program.

stitutional and numerous experimental voucher programs are already in place, the privatization of public education remains controversial in any form.

COMMUNITY COLLEGES You know what a community college is—you may even attend one right now. A **community college** is a two-year school that provides general education classes for students who want to save money while preparing to transfer to a four-year university, right? While this definition of a community college is technically true, community colleges have become much more than just a springboard to a four-year degree. They provide vocational and technical training for people planning practical careers, retrain "downsized" workers seeking new career paths, offer enrichment classes for retirees, and currently provide opportunities of all sorts. In 1901, six students enrolled at the first "junior college" in Joliet, Illinois; just over 100 years later, there are 1,202 community colleges across the country (Merrow 2007). Community colleges account for almost half of all higher education enrollments, with almost 7 million students taking degree, certificate, or transferable courses in 2010–11. Another 5 million or more community college students take various noncredit courses, such as English as a Second Language or job force training. The contemporary community college typically offers more than just basic general education and college preparatory courses. Honors programs, study abroad options, intercollegiate sports, music programs, on-campus residence halls, and internships may now be part of the two-year experience. Community colleges help students prepare for careers that give back to the community—the two "hottest" community college programs of study are law enforcement and nursing, with 80 percent of firefighters, police officers, and EMTs and more than half of all new nurses and health-care workers trained at community colleges (American Association of Community Colleges 2011). Community colleges also struggle with such issues as declining public funding sources and the changing needs of a growing, diverse student body. Despite these hurdles, though, community colleges continue to provide a wealth of opportunities.

DISTANCE LEARNING **Online education** is not really a new concept—"correspondence courses" have been available for hundreds of years and served as a way for people in remote locations (like farmers and their families) or people who were homebound or physically disabled to benefit from the same educational opportunities available to others. In previous years, distance learning courses relied on the postal service and more recently on audiotapes and videos to help students learn independently. With the advent of the internet and real-time electronic communication, distance learning was transformed forever. Universities and private businesses use these technologies to offer courses to anyone with an internet connection. Certificates and degrees of all kinds are within the reach of students who, because of time, geography, or other constraints, cannot come to campus.

According to a frequently cited report by the Sloan Consortium (2010) on the state of online learning, in fall 2008, more than 4.6 million, or 25 percent of all college students, were taking at least one class online, a nearly 17 percent increase over the previous year. The growth rate in online enrollments far exceeds the 1.5 percent overall growth of the college student population. Furthermore, the growth rate is especially concentrated at two-year institutions, which account for more than one-half of all online enrollments for the past five years (Sloan Consortium 2010).

In addition, organizations like Coursera have begun to offer free online courses from some of the world's top universities—though if students want to actually receive credit for their work, they will have to pay a fee. As with any application of technology to education, there may be both pros and cons. Like the old-fashioned correspondence courses, online technologies provide educational access for those who might otherwise not be able to pursue a degree. However, distance learning sometimes lacks the personal touch and dynamic interaction of standard classroom instruction. For this reason, students may feel that there is something important (if intangible) missing from their educational experience. Since you will probably experience both traditional and online learning in your college career, ultimately you'll be the judge.

> **COMMUNITY COLLEGE** two-year institution that provides students with general education and facilitates transfer to a four-year university
>
> **ONLINE EDUCATION** any educational course or program in which the teacher and the student meet via the internet, rather than meeting physically in a classroom

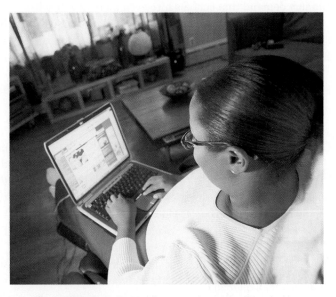

The Rise of Online Colleges Suzanne Lee, who lives in New Jersey, takes an online class in economic crime investigation at New York's Syracuse University.

A decade after the passage of No Child Left Behind, there is still widespread belief that the public school system in the United States continues to fail in its mission to educate generations of children. One of the problems of the law is that it didn't propose any new methods or techniques for improving schools beyond harsh sanctions for those that couldn't bring their scores up. At the same time, an increasing amount of evidence seemed to suggest that "excellence in teaching is the single most powerful influence" on student achievement (Hattie 2003). Even in poor schools with relatively overcrowded classrooms, students with excellent teachers learn more, test better, and achieve more academically.

Doug Lemov has held almost every position possible in a school, starting as a teacher, then working as dean of students and principal at a charter school he helped found, and finally working as a consultant for other schools. It was in this last capacity that he was confronted by a simple fact: he didn't know how to solve the most important and intractable problems facing schools. If the most important factor in a school's success is good teaching, the obvious answer is to hire better teachers. Unfortunately, none of the criteria schools use to hire teachers, like test scores, educational credentials, or teaching certificates, seem to help predict who will be a good teacher. Another solution would be to fire the bad teachers, but aside from the practical problems with this solution, it would just demand that schools hire even more new teachers. So Lemov took the last available option—figure out what the best teachers are doing right, and find ways to teach it to everyone else.

Unlike other educational reformers, Lemov is an advocate of standardized tests, but he sees them as a tool to evaluate the effectiveness of individual teachers rather than schools. This approach, sometimes called "value added" education reform, assumes that the change in students' test scores from the beginning of the year to the end of it is one measure (but not the only measure) of how good a job their teacher has done, or how much "value" the teacher has added to the students. In this way, Lemov is following a growing group of researchers who use the data generated by standardized testing to investigate the effectiveness of teachers and schools regardless of the powerful effects of such non-educational factors like poverty and family background.

Frustrated by the "dispiriting exercise in good people failing" that he saw in so many schools, Lemov decided to try to find out what the good teachers were doing differently (Green 2010). A self-described "data geek," he started with reams of information about student performance and began visiting the classrooms of the teachers who were getting above-average test scores out of schools in low-income neighborhoods (Green 2010). While Lemov is quick to emphasize that test scores are only one way to evaluate a teacher's effectiveness, those scores provided him with an effective map of high-performing teachers, whom he could then visit. Videotaping their classrooms helped him figure out how they taught and then later provided the raw materials for developing a book designed to demystify the teaching process and to teach other teachers. Lemov worried that too many people assume that great teachers are born, rather than made. Since America's schools employ millions

Education: Linking Micro- and Macrosociology

As societies change, so do educational institutions, and so does the individual's experience of education. For example, you likely enroll in your courses online, but before the advent of the internet, you might have had to enroll by phone or even stand in line at the registrar's office and sign up for classes in person. This is one of the many ways that macro-level change (in this case, the development of internet technology) affects your everyday life through your participation in the social institution of education. What you learn about the world in school on an everyday basis—as well as how you learn it—is shaped by larger social forces, such as politics and religion.

Education is not the only social institution concerned with teaching members of society important information, values, and norms. Religion is another social institution from which we learn a great deal about being members of society. Even if we rebel against our religious upbringing or have no religious affiliation, our lives are touched in important ways

RELIGION any institutionalized system of shared beliefs and rituals that identify a relationship between the sacred and the profane of teachers, this attitude amounts to giving up on the notion of improving education. Instead, Lemov looked at good teaching as a matter of deliberate technique, just like riding a bicycle—complicated at first, but easily learnable if properly taught. His book, *Teach Like a Champion: 49 Techniques That Put Students on the Path to College* (2010), was eagerly circulated among teachers as "Lemov's Taxonomy" long before it was published, for simple instructions like these:

The cold call: "To make engaged participation the expectation, call on students regardless of whether they have raised their hands."

Strong voice: Use words economically, don't talk over students who aren't listening, don't engage in conversation outside the topic, stand upright and still, and use silence. "Drop your voice, and make students strain to listen. Exude poise and calm."

Vegas: "The Vegas is the sparkle, the moment during class when you might observe some production values: music, lights, rhythm, dancing."

Everybody writes: "Set your students up for rigorous engagement by giving them the opportunity to reflect first in writing before discussing. As author Joan Didion says, 'I write to know what I think.' "

None of these, or the other forty-five techniques detailed and illustrated in his book, are original; Lemov simply collected them as a way to fill a void in the way teachers are trained. As he points out, education departments spend a lot of time teaching theory, and even teaching workshops designed to be more practical tend to focus on "inspiring messages, such as 'have high expectations' and 'teach kids not content' " which leave new teachers "excited and in touch with all the reasons" they want "to be a teacher" (Tucker 2010). But when they go to actually run a classroom, slogans aren't much help, and what they need are simple, practical steps. Only time will tell how much value-added reforms can change teaching, but Doug Lemov is convinced that one way or another, by paying close attention, carefully gathering data, and trying to see the world from the student's point of view, teaching—and learning—can change for the better.

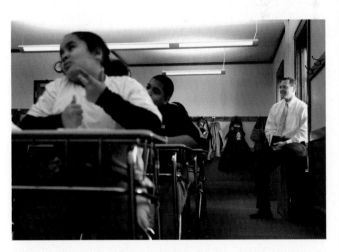

Teach Like a Champion Doug Lemov observes a teacher to evaluate her teaching strategy and effectiveness.

by religion because it is a dominant social institution. As you read the following section, think about the intersection of the micro and the macro in the study of religion and about the intersection of religion with other social institutions, including politics and education.

What Is Religion?

No doubt we each have our own definition of religion based on personal experience. But a sociological definition must be broad enough to encompass all kinds of religious experiences. For sociologists, **religion** includes any institutionalized system of shared **beliefs** (propositions and ideas held on the basis of faith) and **rituals** (practices based on those beliefs) that identify a relationship between the **sacred** (holy, divine, or supernatural) and the **profane** (ordinary, mundane, or everyday). Those who

BELIEF a proposition or idea held on the basis of faith

RITUAL a practice based on religious beliefs

SACRED the holy, divine, or supernatural

PROFANE the ordinary, mundane, or everyday

IN THE FUTURE

Educational Institutions and Individual Needs: "Flipping the Classroom"

One of the enduring complaints about public educational institutions in the United States is that such systems of mass education cannot always meet the unique needs of individual students. For example, students with physical or learning disabilities, students with less preparation or less help at home, older and returning students, students whose learning pace or style is different—these and other types of students are not always well served by the one-size-fits-all curricula of traditional educational institutions. As schools feel more pressure to standardize education, they may fail to meet even more individual needs. And this is where innovative private organizations like the not-for-profit Khan Academy, in Northern California, come into the picture.

Salman Khan, a Harvard MBA and former hedge-fund analyst, started by tutoring his cousins who were having problems with their math homework. As word spread to family members around the world who couldn't make it to in-person sessions, he started videotaping his lessons and posting them on YouTube. Once online, the tutoring sessions went viral, and were soon being used by students and educators across the globe. Originally funded by small donations from family and friends, word began to spread, and the Khan Academy is now funded by the Bill & Melinda Gates Foundation, Google, and other major foundations. Now it's Sal Khan's full-time job to create lesson plans and produce, star in (as the voice of the teacher), and post videos on his Khan Academy web site. He has a skilled and growing staff helping him do these things.

The academy provides free, open-access online education to any student, anytime, anywhere in the world, in about sixty languages. Khan breaks down tough lessons into smaller bits, and teaches them in a clear, concise, and easy-to-understand way. One concept, idea, or equation in about ten minutes—that's it. Graphing derivatives, say, or the Cuban Missile Crisis, or photosynthesis. His videos cover a variety of disciplines—math and sciences, art history, American government, economics, history, and even test prep for exams such as the SAT. The lessons range from elementary school to college-level material, and include a system for mapping students' progress toward mastery in different areas.

Students can watch the videos as often as they like in order to competently grasp a concept. This is different from an ordinary classroom, where a teacher doesn't have time to go over the concept repeatedly. The Khan approach is different, allowing students to master concepts before moving forward (rather than being swept along in grade-level groups whether they get it or not).

Khan's approach is called "flipping the classroom," a kind of inversion of traditional teaching methods. Instead of starting with an in-class lecture and then sending students home to work on questions, readings, and exercises on their own, Khan advocates doing problem-solving activities together, in class, with the "lectures" delivered via the internet, DVD, or other device, for students to watch as their "homework." This approach is being adopted by some schools but is still relatively uncommon. However, some wonder if most or all schooling will someday be accomplished in this way—outside of traditional, publicly funded, brick-and-mortar schools and in a more as-needed, self-paced way, with content provided by private organizations.

Is this a beneficial way to deal with the problems of institutional inertia and over-standardization in education? If public institutions are faltering, should we rely on private contractors to fill the voids? Is this the best way to reach society's educational goals while meeting individual needs? What will the future of education look like in the United States? The Khan Academy provides a preview.

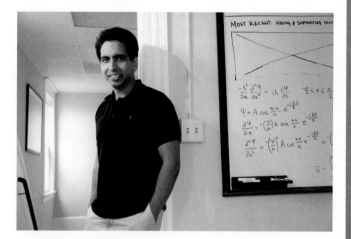

Khan Academy Salman Khan's educational approach involves "flipping the classroom," so that students work on problem-solving activities during class and watch lectures for homework.

study religion recognize that there are different types of religious groups: denominations (major subgroups of larger religions, such as Protestantism within Christianity or Shia within Islam), sects (smaller subgroups, such as the Amish or Mennonites), and cults (usually very small, intense, close-knit groups focused on individual leaders—like David Koresh and the Branch Davidians—or specific issues like the UFO cult Heaven's Gate). Sociologists do not evaluate the truth of any system of beliefs; they study the ways that religions shape and are shaped by cultural institutions and processes, as well as the ways that religions influence and are influenced by the behavior of individuals.

Theoretical Approaches to Religion

STRUCTURAL FUNCTIONALISM For members of any religion, beliefs and rituals serve a number of functions. First, religion shapes everyday behavior by providing morals, values, rules, and norms for its participants. From the Judeo-Christian commandment "Thou shalt not kill" to the Buddhist commitment to reconcile strife to the Qur'anic requirement to eschew alcohol and impure foods, religious rules govern both the largest and smallest events and actions of followers' daily lives. Religious practices usually include some type of penance or rehabilitation for those who break the rules: Catholics can confess their sins to a priest and be assigned prayer or good works to redeem themselves; Muslims spend the month of Ramadan fasting during daylight hours to purify their bodies and souls; Yom Kippur is the Jewish Day of Atonement and also involves fasting, as well as appeals for wrongs to be forgiven.

Another function of religion is to give meaning to our lives. Religious beliefs can help us understand just about everything we encounter because every religion has a system of beliefs that explains the fundamental questions like: How did we get here? What is our purpose in life? Why do bad things happen to good people? All religious traditions address these questions, helping their followers explain the inexplicable, making the terrible more tolerable, and assuring believers that there is a larger plan. Finally, religion provides the opportunity to come together with others—to share in group activity and identity, to form cohesive social organizations, and to be part of a congregation of like-minded others.

CONFLICT THEORY These are the (mostly unifying) functions of religion for individuals and for society, but there are also ways in which religion can promote inequality, conflict, and change. From a conflict perspective, the doctrines of the three major **monotheistic** religions—religions that worship one divine figure (Judaism, Christianity, and Islam)—are quite sexist. Orthodox Judaism mandates the separation of men and women in worship and in everyday life; Catholicism and many Protestant sects prohibit women from becoming priests or pastors; traditional, observant Muslim women must keep their bodies completely covered at all times. There are very few nonsexist religions, and those with strongly nonsexist values and practices (such as Wicca) are usually marginalized. Some religions have antihomosexual or racist doctrines as well: some Protestant sects refuse to ordain gay clergy, and until 1978 the Church of Jesus

> **MONOTHEISTIC** a term describing religions that worship a single divine figure

Religion and Social Justice Óscar Romero, archbishop of El Salvador (left), and Lech Walesa (right, speaking into a bullhorn) of Poland both led movements against repressive political regimes.

GLOBAL PERSPECTIVE

Thou Shalt Not Kill: Religion, Violence, and Terrorism

The history of religious conflict is extensive and convoluted, having been around for as long as humans have worshipped gods. No faith is exempt, and religion has played a significant role in conflicts from the ancient Israelites and Canaanites around 1200 B.C.E. to Al Qaeda's destruction of New York City's World Trade Center in 2001 to Sri Lanka's civil war between the Hindu Tamil Tigers and the Buddhist Sinhalese in which more than 50,000 lives were lost.

Mark Juergensmeyer's book *Terror in the Mind of God* (2003) analyzes the history and meaning of religious violence in general and terrorism in particular. He notes that groups using terror have historically had diverse agendas and motivations, but only within the past thirty years has religion come to play a prominent role in terrorist violence. A Pew Foundation study concurs, showing an increase in "social hostilities involving religion" in half the countries of the world in 2010 (Pew Forum on Religion and Public Life 2012c).

Juergensmeyer's work uses many examples to illustrate the cross-cultural similarities of religious violence. Within the Christian tradition, Juergensmeyer discusses a wide range of examples, from the Irish Republican Army (IRA) in Northern Ireland to the killing of doctors who perform abortions in the United States. Within Judaism, he examined the case of Baruch Goldstein, who killed twenty-eight Muslims in 1994 when he opened fire in the Ibrahim Mosque in the Cave of the Patriarchs, a shrine holy to both Jews and Muslims. Juergensmeyer also investigated Islamic terrorism, such as the first attempt to bomb the World Trade Center in 1993, and the activities of the Palestinian group Hamas, which pioneered the use of suicide bombings in the Middle East. Sikh terrorists were responsible for the assassinations of Indira Gandhi and Beant Singh, and a Buddhist Japanese cult, Aum Shinrikyo, launched the notorious sarin nerve gas attack on the Tokyo subway. But the list is long—we feel certain that you can name some incidents of even more recent religious violence.

Juergensmeyer argues that the common thread linking religious violence in such disparate traditions and far-flung corners of the world is a reliance on a particular kind of religious perspective. "The social tensions of this moment of history . . . cry out for absolute solutions," he says, and in a world that seems increasingly beyond individual control, religious violence offers a way to reassert some kind of power.

The list of wars, conflicts, and terrorist acts inspired or justified by religion is tragically long, extending throughout history and reaching across continents. Religious conflict is not a thing of the past, nor is your country (or your religion, whatever it may be) untouched by it.

Terror in the Mind of God Shoko Asahara (left) was the leader of a Japanese Buddhist cult, Aum Shinrikyo, whose 1995 nerve gas attack on the Tokyo subway killed twenty-seven people and injured thousands. The Provisional IRA (right), which emerged in 1969, sees itself as a continuation of the Irish Republican Army, which fought in the Irish War of Independence. Through bombings and other attacks, the IRA has tried to unite Northern Ireland with the Republic of Ireland.

Christ of Latter Day Saints (LDS, or Mormons) believed that people with dark skin were cursed by God and forbade African Americans from marrying in the temple.

Religious organizations have also been agents of social justice and political change. For example, religion has been closely linked to movements for African American rights.

The movement for the abolition of slavery was entwined with Christian reformers like the Methodists and Baptists. The Civil Rights Movement in the twentieth century began in southern Protestant churches and was led by a team of Christian ministers, including the Reverend Martin Luther King Jr. In Africa and Latin America, **liberation theology** has been instrumental in fighting exploitation, oppression, and poverty—Archbishop Óscar Romero of El Salvador used this distinctive combination of Marxism and Christianity to argue against the country's repressive military dictatorship. Though Romero was assassinated while saying mass in 1980, his legacy lives on in human rights movements all over the world. The Polish labor movement Solidarność, led by Catholic shipyard workers in Gdańsk and supported by the late Pope John Paul II, was the crucible for democratic change in the Eastern bloc in the 1980s. Communist regimes throughout Eastern Europe had restricted religious freedom and labor union organizing for decades—Solidarność helped break down both of those barriers.

From a conflict perspective, then, religion is complex: it can subjugate and oppress at the same time it can liberate. This may help explain Americans' seemingly contradictory approach to religion. While quasi-religious principles are at the core of many of our closely held national ideologies, many Americans also believe that religion should be kept separate from our collective political life.

SYMBOLIC INTERACTIONISM Symbolic interactionist approaches to religion focus on how religious meaning is constructed in interaction, and how religion is incorporated into the everyday life of individuals and groups. With its focus on interaction and interpretation, symbolic interactionism is appropriate for examining religious symbolism, religious communication, and religious practices. For example, one might think that being female in a conservative religion would be oppressive and difficult to tolerate (see section above on sexism in religion). But interactionist studies show that it is possible to refashion the meaning of religious proclamations

about gender in ways that benefit religious women's sense of value and personal power. Orit Avishai's 2008 study of Orthodox Jewish women, for example, shows that they are anything but "doormats"—rather, they are able to construct meaningful ways of "doing religion" that preserve their sense of personal agency and self-determination within the value system of their faith. Similar studies of religious women (Mahmood 2004; Bartkowski and Read 2003; Gallagher 2004) have identified related trends among Muslims and Christians: despite religious doctrines that appear to prescribe docility, woman are able to construct agency, empowerment, and resistance in their everyday interactions.

Religion in America

How religious is the American public? That depends on the measures used (Hill and Wood 1999). Sociologists usually define **religiosity** as the consistent and regular practice of religious beliefs, and gauge religiosity in terms of frequency of attendance at worship services and the importance of religious beliefs to an individual (see the next Data Workshop for more detailed measures of religiosity). One study found that 56 percent of Americans say religion is very important to them and that on average, 39 percent of Americans say they go to religious services at

Fashion Conscious Orthodox Jewish women in Jerusalem express their personal agency by seeking out designer fashions—even as they adhere to a strict code of modesty that requires them to cover their heads once they marry.

least once a week (Pew Forum on Religion and Public Life 2008). These numbers are somewhat misleading, however, because there are big differences in religious affiliation and participation across demographic groups. Gender, age, race, geographic region, political party, and education are all variables that influence religiosity.

DATA WORKSHOP
Analyzing Everyday Life

Measures of Religiosity

From what the majority of Americans report in polls, we can conclude that they are significantly more religious than people of other industrialized nations. Some researchers suspect, however, that these results may be caused by the discrepancy between what people say and what they actually do (Vedantam 2010).

The term "religiosity" refers to the extent of a person's commitment to a religion. Researchers have identified two broad categories of religiosity: extrinsic and intrinsic (Allport and Ross 1967). **Extrinsic religiosity** refers to a person's public display of commitment, such as attendance at religious services or activities at other related functions. **Intrinsic religiosity** refers to a person's inner religious life or personal relationship to the divine.

This Data Workshop asks you to examine the role of religion in everyday life by measuring religiosity in a sample of research participants. The data can be collected using either interview or survey methods. (See Chapter 2 on these research methods.)

In each case, choose a population for the research, construct a good questionnaire or instrument, administer it to your sample respondents, and analyze the findings. In choosing a population, consider such variables as race and ethnicity, class, national background, gender, and/or age for your sample. Researchers have documented variations of religiosity across different social groups. There are many possibilities for comparing and contrasting within or across categories.

With an interview, decide whether the questions will be closed- or open-ended and how many questions you must

EXTRINSIC RELIGIOSITY a person's public display of commitment to a religious faith

INTRINSIC RELIGIOSITY a person's inner religious life or personal relationship to the divine

have to gather sufficient data. This will help you determine how many people you will need to interview (for the formal option, we suggest at least three to five respondents). With a survey, the number of respondents will also depend on the length of the questionnaire (for the formal option, we suggest at least six to eight respondents). Remember that your questions will need to be structured according to the principles of survey research, by providing a set of possible answers for the respondents.

Questions about religious affiliation, membership, and attendance at services can tell you something about an individual's level of commitment, but there are many other ways you can measure religiosity, both extrinsic and intrinsic. You can create questions that measure people's concrete practice of religion and their abstract sense of what religion means to them. Regardless of whether you do an interview or survey, you can choose from the following list of questions (adapted from Lewis et al. 2001). You will need to modify the wording of these questions or add questions for either an interview guide or a survey questionnaire.

* Are you affiliated with any religion?

* Are you affiliated with any particular sect or denomination?

* Do you belong to a church, synagogue, temple, or other place of worship?

* How often do you attend religious services?

* Do you participate in other church-related activities?

* How often do you read or study sacred texts or scripture?

* How often do you pray or meditate or engage in some other religious practice?

* How important is your relationship with God [or another religious figure]?

* To what extent is your religious faith important to you?

* To what extent do you consider your religious faith to be an important part of who you are as a person?

* Do you look to your faith as a source of comfort?

* Do you look to your faith as a source of inspiration?

* Do you look to your faith as providing meaning, direction, or purpose in your life?

* Does your faith impact your relationships with other people?

* Does your faith impact your decisions in regard to family, friends, work, school, or other aspects of your life?

* How has your commitment to your religion changed over time?

After gathering data through interviews or surveys, describe and analyze your findings. See what kinds of patterns you can find—similarities, differences, comparisons, and contradictions. How do your findings confirm or refute any hypotheses you might have had before beginning the study? What do you think these data reveal about the role of religion in your subjects' lives? About the role of religion in society?

There are two options for completing this Data Workshop.

Option 1 (informal): Conduct interviews or administer surveys with a small sample of your population. Prepare written notes that you can refer to in class. Discuss your findings with other students in small-group discussions. Note the similarities and differences in your findings and those of your group members. Write a statement that identifies and incorporates the patterns found in the data gathered by the entire group.

Option 2 (formal): Conduct interviews or administer surveys to your sample following the suggested questions above. Write a two- to three-page essay describing and analyzing your findings, attaching any notes or transcripts to your paper.

Religious Affiliation Trends

A slim majority of Americans maintain the same religious affiliation throughout their lifetimes (56 percent according to a survey by the Pew Forum on Religion and Public Life [2011]), but there have been shifts in religious preferences in the past few decades. One of those trends is toward fundamentalism, which is not a religion in itself but a traditionalist approach that can be applied to any religion. Another trend is away from organized churches, toward an "unchurched" spirituality that borrows elements from many traditions but is affiliated with none.

FUNDAMENTALISM Fundamentalist approaches to religious belief and practice are on the rise both worldwide and in the United States. **Fundamentalism** is a way of understanding and interpreting sacred texts that can be part of any denomination or sect. Fundamentalist Christianity, for example, centers on a strict, sometimes literal, interpretation of the Bible and advocates a return to the historic founding principles of Christianity, arguing that modern approaches to Christianity are corrupt and inauthentic. Other religions have fundamentalist strains as well. Orthodox Judaism, for example, promotes a literal reading of the Torah and other Jewish spiritual and legal tracts. Fundamentalist Islam parallels Jewish and Christian fundamentalisms in that it also requires strict, literal, and traditional interpretations of the Qur'an and other sacred texts. Fundamentalist approaches to all three of these major religions gained popularity in response to the complex social changes of the 1960s and 1970s in the United States and around the world (Patterson 2004) because fundamentalism provides a return to tradition and to simple, unambiguous values and ideologies. Declaring one's loyalty to a traditional religious group that

> **FUNDAMENTALISM** the practice of emphasizing literal interpretation of texts and a "return" to a time of greater religious purity; represented by the most conservative group within any religion

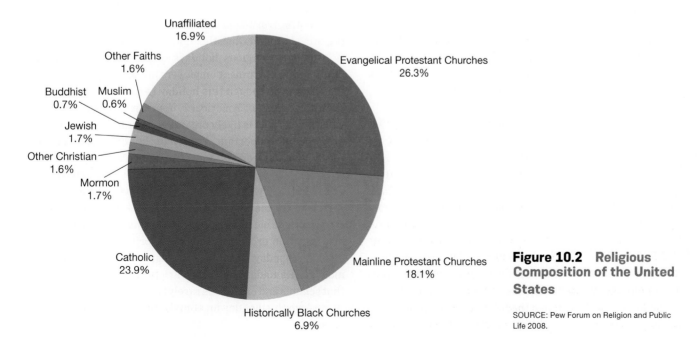

Figure 10.2 **Religious Composition of the United States**

Unaffiliated 16.9%
Other Faiths 1.6%
Buddhist 0.7%
Muslim 0.6%
Jewish 1.7%
Other Christian 1.6%
Mormon 1.7%
Catholic 23.9%
Historically Black Churches 6.9%
Mainline Protestant Churches 18.1%
Evangelical Protestant Churches 26.3%

SOURCE: Pew Forum on Religion and Public Life 2008.

Megachurches Rick Warren, the senior pastor of Saddleback Church and author of *The Purpose-Driven Life*, preaches to his congregation. Because his church attracts 20,000 parishioners on an average Sunday, Warren shows his sermons on video screens inside the church.

promises certainty in the face of change may be comforting to individuals—but it has broader social and political consequences as well.

Between 1990 and 2001, the number of Americans who described themselves as "Fundamentalist Christians" tripled, and the number describing themselves as "Evangelical Christians" (a variant of fundamentalist groups) more than quadrupled (Kosmin, Mayer, and Keysar 2001). With the rapidly increasing popularity of these groups, their beliefs have also spilled over into other areas of social life. Fundamentalists who take an **evangelical** approach attempt to convert individuals to their way of worshipping.

Evangelicals see their conversion work as a service to others—an attempt to save souls—and have adapted many modern technologies (including television and the internet) to their cause.

UNCHURCHED SPIRITUALITY About 20 percent of Americans claim no religious affiliation (Pew Forum on Religion and Public Life 2012a)—interestingly, this group is more likely to be younger and to live in western states, such as California, Colorado, Nevada, and New Mexico (Kosmin, Mayer, and Keysar 2001). Having no religious affiliation, however, does not necessarily mean they are "unbelievers." In fact, fewer than 2 percent describe themselves as atheists, and agnostics are another 2 percent. As yet

EVANGELICAL a term describing conservative Christians who emphasize converting others to their faith

UNCHURCHED a term describing those who consider themselves spiritual but not religious and who often adopt aspects of various religious traditions

SECULAR nonreligious; a secular society separates church and state and does not endorse any religion

another indicator of our paradoxical attitudes about religion, Americans are increasingly seeking guidance and fulfillment through nontraditional means, with many labeling themselves "spiritual but not religious." This trend involves new definitions of belief and practice, often expressed privately and individually rather than in organized group settings. As noted earlier, some organized religions still include elements of sexism, racial prejudice, homophobia, anti-Semitism, and conformity that turn people off, and so spiritual seekers may utilize a kind of "cafeteria" strategy, choosing elements from various traditions and weaving them together into something unique. This type of **unchurched** spirituality (Fuller 2002), frowned upon by some religious organizations, is becoming increasingly popular, as spiritual seekers mix bits of astrology, alternative healing, twelve-step programs, and even witchcraft with elements of more traditional doctrines.

A Secular Society?

The separation of church and state is a time-honored (and controversial) American principle, established by the founders to preserve freedom of religion—one of the main reasons Europeans came to North America. As important and central as this principle is to American politics, we haven't always been able to maintain it in practice. Consider the dollar bill with the motto "In God We Trust." Witness the 2003 controversy about displaying the Ten Commandments in public buildings in Alabama, or President George W. Bush's allocation of federal monies to "faith-based" charitable organizations. Even the school voucher debate centers on this issue: should public education funds be used to send children to private schools, many of which are religious? And, of course, specifically Christian values and practices shape the everyday life of all Americans—Christian or not. Whether we are a **secular** society, one that separates church and state, is a complicated issue.

In both government and private industry, schedules are organized around Christian holidays with little or no attention paid to religious holidays of other groups. Schools, banks, and government employers are all closed on Christmas Day, even though this holiday is not observed by more than 15 percent of Americans. Your university's system of vacation periods is likely organized around both Christmas and Easter—important Christian holidays. Universities rarely give days off for Yom Kippur or Passover, two very important Jewish holidays. This means that Jewish students and staff who observe these holidays must go through the hassle of making special arrangements to compensate for classes or meetings missed. They may have to use valuable vacation or sick time or even forfeit credit for exams given on that day. Eid al Fitr, the last day of the Muslim holy month of Ramadan, calls for a variety of special celebrations that schools and employers rarely recognize; those who wish to observe this holiday must make their own arrangements as well.

IN RELATIONSHIPS

Can We Have a Relationship with God?

Sociologists usually don't address questions like "Is there a God?" as these are not questions to which empirical, scientific methods can be applied. It is impossible to prove that God exists (at least by the rules of the scientific method)—and it is equally impossible to prove that God doesn't exist.

Social scientists don't have to answer the question of any god's existence to study the relationships people have with their particular deity. Those who believe in God may talk about that belief in terms usually used to describe interpersonal relationships. For instance, they may talk about speaking with God or having a conversation with God. Since sociology is, at one level, the study of various types of relationships, sociologists are interested in people's perceptions of their bonds with the divine.

John Caughey, a professor of American Studies, specializes in studying these relationships and argues that relationships with a god or gods (or, depending on the culture, spirits, saints, or dead ancestors) are necessary to participate in many cultures. In other words, in most cultures we are actually required to be able to carry on such relationships in order to seem normal (Caughey 1984, 1999).

Practices such as prayer, in which individuals speak directly to God, saints, or spirits, are ways of establishing relationships with these entities. Only in very unusual cases do individuals claim that a god or saint has spoken directly to them in anything resembling face-to-face interaction. Instead, we tend to look for the entity's response to our prayers in various sorts of signs. If we have appealed to God to intervene in a particular situation (to help us do well on an exam or to improve the health of a sick relative), we often see God's "reply" in seemingly unrelated places; for example, the parting of the clouds to reveal a sunny sky just as we set off to the lecture hall or hospital. Recent research by Shane Sharp shows that those who pray regularly use God as a source of social support in much the same way they turn to friends and family members: they "vent" to God when they are angry, look to God for positive feedback on their good behavior, and try to emulate God by forgiving others (Sharp 2010).

So can you have a relationship with God? Of course you can—if you believe. Sociologists will never be able to confirm or deny the existence of any deity; what we are interested in, ultimately, is the role that these faith-based relationships play in our everyday social lives.

Separation of Church and State? This portrait of Jesus has hung in the main hallway of Bridgeport High School, a public school in Bridgeport, West Virginia, for more than three decades. In 2006, the American Civil Liberties Union filed a lawsuit to have the portrait removed.

RELIGION IN THE WHITE HOUSE The only official eligibility requirements for the job of U.S. president are that the person be thirty-five years old, a natural-born U.S. citizen, and a resident in the United States for at least fourteen years. There is no requirement that the president be a man, though all of them have been, or a Christian, but all of them have been. It seems that an unspoken requirement for the presidency includes being a man of Christian faith, with Protestant Christianity being preferred. The only Catholic to hold the office, John F. Kennedy, endured a storm of controversy during his 1960 campaign, when critics feared that America would be ruled by the Pope if Kennedy was elected.

More recently, Republican Mitt Romney's Mormonism simmered beneath the surface of the 2012 presidential campaign. While many Americans are either ignorant about or uncomfortable with the LDS faith and its historic associations with things like polygamy and racism, Romney's advisors managed to minimize Mormonism as an issue while focusing on moral and social issues that appealed to his largely Christian Republican base. Meanwhile, 17 percent of Americans continued to believe that President Barack Obama was a Muslim, a rumor that may have derived from his middle name, Hussein, despite his clear affiliation as a Christian (Pew Forum on Religion and Public Life 2012b). About half of adults thought he was Christian, while more than 30 percent said they didn't know his religion. The view that Obama is Muslim is more widespread among his political opponents than it is among supporters (Pew Forum on Religion and Public Life 2012b).

Given America's explicit constitutional commitment to the separation of church and state, it seems we shouldn't be concerned about a president's religious affiliation (or lack thereof). But it matters.

The administration of George W. Bush was particularly notable for the controversy it stirred over the influence of religion on the leader of the free world. President Bush was famously quoted by former aide David Frum as saying that "I had a drinking problem . . . [and] there is only one reason I am in the Oval Office and not in a bar. I found faith. I found God" (Goodstein 2004). Bush managed, to some degree, to placate opponents concerned with the separation between church and state. His public comments on the subject were consistently conciliatory and inclusive. In his first press conference after winning reelection in 2004, Bush was asked by a reporter, "What do you say to those who are concerned about the role of a faith they do not share in public life and in your policies?" (Noah 2004). The president answered:

I will be your president regardless of your faith, and I don't expect you to agree with me necessarily on religion. As a matter of fact, no president should ever try to impose religion on our society. A great—the great—tradition of America is one where people can worship the way they want to worship. And if they choose not to worship, they're just as patriotic as your neighbor. That is an essential part of why we are a great nation. (Noah 2004)

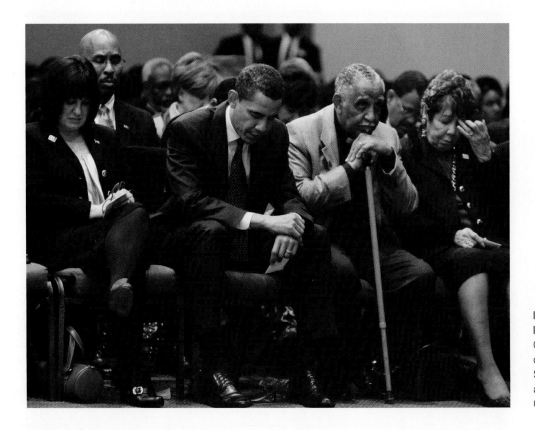

Religion and the White House President Barack Obama prays alongside churchgoers during a Sunday-morning service at the Harvest Cathedral Chapel in Macon, Georgia.

Bush is one of many presidents who were advised by the unofficial White House chaplain, the Reverend Billy Graham. Graham advised every president since Dwight D. Eisenhower up through George W. Bush on matters of state and personal spirituality. With a man of the cloth as such a high-profile presidential advisor, and with Christianity as an unstated requirement for holding presidential office, are we really a secular society? Are church and state truly separate? Is every person equally free to practice his or her faith in American society?

Religion: Linking Micro- and Macrosociology

Religion is a source of conflict and misunderstanding, but also a wellspring of comfort and meaning, for many. Whether you are Catholic or Methodist, Orthodox or Reform Jewish, Muslim or Buddhist, Mormon or Wiccan or Scientologist, you share common experiences with others in the practice of your religion, no matter how different your belief systems and rituals may be. A sense of meaning, a set of rules and guidelines by which to live your life, a way of explaining the world around you, a feeling of belonging and group identity—sociologists recognize these patterns across religious traditions.

Religion is yet another social institution that helps us see the link between macro-level social structure and micro-level everyday experience. Religious beliefs, practices, and prejudices can inflame global conflicts and resolve them, and can shape national political life in observable and unexamined ways. At the same time, religion is integral in the everyday lives of many Americans who find comfort and kinship in their religious beliefs and practices. "In God We Trust" is the motto for both our nation and many of its people, no matter what their faith.

CLOSING COMMENTS

All three of the social institutions examined in this chapter—politics, education, and religion—are part of the structure of our society, and they are linked in a variety of ways. For example, state and federal policy decisions about school vouchers affect individual students and neighborhood public schools, and they benefit parochial schools and the religious institutions that run them. Politics, education, religion, and other social institutions influence your everyday lives in ways you may not have realized. We hope you have gained greater awareness of how these social institutions shape your life as a member of society—and how you can influence them as well. Your vote changes the political landscape; your role as a student influences the culture of your college and university; your membership in a religious congregation affects the lives of fellow worshippers. Institutions impact individuals, but individuals can influence institutions as well—this is the essence of the sociological imagination and the macro-micro link.

Everything You Need to Know about
Social Institutions

"Social institutions such as school, religion, and government organize our group life and constrain our everyday lives. By studying them, we can examine connections between the individual and society."

THEORIES OF SOCIAL INSTITUTIONS

* **Structural functionalism:** social institutions provide critical functions and help to maintain order

* **Conflict theory:** social institutions represent the interests of those in power and thus create and maintain inequalities

* **Symbolic interactionism:** social institutions are created through individual participation

REVIEW

1. Were you eligible to vote in the last election? If so, did you? If you didn't vote, why not? The voting rates for voting-eligible U.S. citizens ages eighteen to twenty-four are much lower than those for senior citizens; why do you think that is?

2. Much of this chapter's discussion of education focuses on elementary and high schools. Do you think the same theories apply to college classrooms? Have you experienced a hidden curriculum since you left high school?

3. There is some debate over how to measure religiosity: Should it be based on how spiritual you feel or how often you attend religious services? Which way do you think is more valid? Why? Can you think of a better way than either of these?

Voter turnout in the 2012 Election by Educational Level

■ **Total Citizen Population**   ■ **Reported Voters**

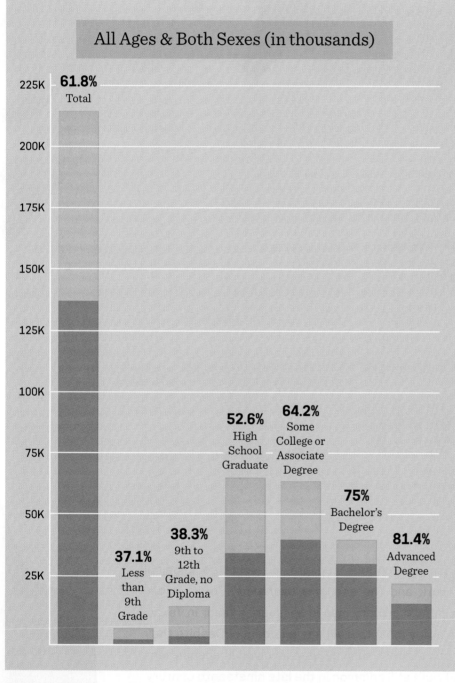

All Ages & Both Sexes (in thousands)

61.8%
Total

37.1%
Less than 9th Grade

38.3%
9th to 12th Grade, no Diploma

52.6%
High School Graduate

64.2%
Some College or Associate Degree

75%
Bachelor's Degree

81.4%
Advanced Degree

SOURCE: U.S. Census Bureau 2012, "Voting and Registration in the Election of November 2012 — Detailed Tables"

EXPLORE

Happy Interdependence Day!

The idea of interdependence is that everyone and everything is connected. Your personal successes and failures may also be the result of social systems like education and politics. Visit the Everyday Sociology Blog to read more on how interdependence can change society.

http://wwnPag.es/trw410

CHAPTER 11

The Economy and Work

The history of one family's jobs and occupations can provide some sociological insight into the development of work and the economy over time. For example, Dr. Ferris's great-grandfathers included a military man in Missouri, a tailor in Texas, and a stonemason and a butcher, both in a tiny mountain village in Lebanon. Despite their geographical and cultural distance from one another, they all were involved in occupations that have existed since ancient times and were still common in the late nineteenth century. Their various jobs represent much of the range of possible jobs in agricultural societies. Some people were skilled craftsmen, some were soldiers, and most others farmed. While

women sometimes helped with the farming or other types of work, their primary task was homemaking and child-rearing.

Moving up a generation in the family tree, you can see that in the first half of the twentieth century, Ferris's grandparents were involved in military and service work, with some industrial labor experience as well. One grandfather emigrated from Lebanon to Massachusetts, where he worked in the local brass foundry. This kind of hard physical labor in a stiflingly hot factory setting was the norm during the industrial era. While he worked at the foundry, his wife secretly worked at a local laundry, hiding her earnings from him. These secret earnings later helped them afford to take a step up in the occupational hierarchy: they bought a restaurant and ran it successfully. Ferris's other grandfather was an army doctor who was stationed all over the United States and the world. His wife followed, making a home with the children wherever they were stationed. She served as a hostess and provided crucial support for her husband's career, which was customary in the early twentieth century.

By the time Ferris's parents started working in the second half of the twentieth century, her mother was part of a new generation of women who were far more likely than their own mothers had been to pursue a college education and a career outside the home, even while raising children. Both of Ferris's parents earned advanced degrees (mom an MA and dad a JD); as a writer and an attorney, respectively, they both engage in service- and knowledge-based work. These areas experienced tremendous growth as the country moved into a postindustrial, Information Age economy. Dr. Ferris, as a professor with a Ph.D., is also a knowledge-worker—still just two generations away from great-grandparents without formal educations. Because of historical changes in gendered career expectations, she has enjoyed opportunities her grandmothers and great-grandmothers could never have imagined. And as we move further into the twenty-first century, developments in the economic and occupational landscape are likely to create a world in which Dr. Ferris's son, E. J., may hold a job that has not even been invented yet—perhaps in an entirely new, currently unimagined field.

Your own occupational family tree probably holds similar insights into the development of both world and U.S. economic systems over time. And this is no accident—as different as our families and their experiences may be, the patterns and trends in the kinds of work our relatives did can be a rich topic for sociological analysis. Our individual occupational choices are always made within the context of larger economic and social structures, both local and global. In this chapter, we will examine those structures and the experiences of individuals within them.

Kerry Ferris:
College professor

Father:
Lawyer

Mother:
Writer

Grandfather:
Restaurant owner

Grandmother:
Homemaker

Grandfather:
Military officer

Grandmother:
Homemaker

Great-
grandfather:
Stone mason

Great-
grandmother:
Homemaker

Great-
grandfather:
Butcher

Great-
grandmother:
Homemaker

Great-
grandfather:
Tailor

Great-
grandmother:
Homemaker

Great-
grandfather:
Military officer

Great-
grandmother:
Homemaker

HOW TO READ THIS CHAPTER

After reading this chapter, you should understand why work is a classic topic of sociological inquiry: it is a fulcrum point between the micro and the macro and a link between the individual and the social. You will see the connection between the everyday conditions of your life on the job and the larger structural changes related to history, technology, and the economic system in which you work. We want you to become familiar with the classic and more recent sociological studies in this area and how they have shaped our ways of thinking about the social world of economy and work. You will know something about the past and perhaps have more insight about the future and your place in it.

An economy deals not only with money but also with the production, distribution, and consumption of goods and services within a society. In this chapter, we look at issues regarding the economy, focusing specifically on work, because the economy shapes the types of work available as well as our patterns of working.

Historical and Economic Changes

We start with the history of U.S. economies, paying special attention to the agricultural, industrial, and postindustrial periods—and how new technologies have changed the nature of work in each of these periods.

Pre-Colonial United States: Hunting and Gathering and Horticultural Societies

Perhaps the earliest form of economy in the Americas was in pre-sixteenth-century Native American societies. An estimated 2 million to 10 million tribal people inhabited the continent prior to colonization by Europeans. Some were hunting and gathering societies, which had to be highly mobile, relocating for food and weather conditions. The division of labor revolved around survival, with the men hunting animals or foraging for plant sources of food. The women, children, and elderly cooked, sewed, and did other tasks at the campsite. Horticultural societies were different in that they were based on the domestication of animals, farming, and generating a surplus of resources. They had more permanent settlements and a greater diversification of labor because different types of workers, such as farmers, craftspeople, and traders, were all necessary to the economy.

The Agricultural Revolution

The **Agricultural Revolution** continued some of the social and economic changes that began with horticultural societies. Better farming and ranching techniques allowed larger groups to thrive and remain in one location for longer periods of time. The Agricultural Revolution lasted for many centuries, but in the eighteenth century, food production was greatly increased by new innovations in farming and animal husbandry: the invention of new types of plows and mechanized seed spreaders and new techniques of crop rotation, irrigation, and selective breeding.

The agricultural economy that flourished in the early United States encouraged a stratified labor force. For large plantation owners to accumulate wealth from cotton or sugarcane crops, they depended on cheap, plentiful labor. The division of labor fell largely along race, gender, and class lines (Amott and Matthaei 1996). In the pre–Civil War era, many of the plantations of the South that were owned by whites were farmed by black slaves brought from Africa (Davis 2001). Poor white people sometimes owned small farms or worked as tenant farmers or sharecroppers. White men were usually owners of land and small businesses, while white women were usually household managers.

AGRICULTURAL REVOLUTION the social and economic changes, including population increases, that followed from the domestication of plants and animals and the gradually increasing efficiency of food production

INDUSTRIAL REVOLUTION the rapid transformation of social life resulting from the technological and economic developments that began with the assembly line, steam power, and urbanization

The Industrial Revolution

The **Industrial Revolution** was a time of rapid technological, social, and economic change that almost completely transformed life in modern times—a radical break from the past, disrupting social patterns that had been relatively stable for centuries. When we discuss the Industrial Revolution in this section, we will look at the technological innovations of the era and how they changed American society and culture, the economy, and the lives of workers.

The Industrial Revolution began in England with the invention of the steam engine in 1769, which was first used to power machinery, starting with the manufacture of textiles.

Slaves at Work in the Field The southern agricultural economy depended on slave labor to grow cotton and tobacco.

By the end of the eighteenth century, Britain's steam-powered factories had spread to the United States and other nations (Hughes and Cain 1994). With more mechanized machinery such as the cotton gin, the American economy moved from manual labor to machine manufacturing. Even farming would change with the introduction of mechanical plows and reapers. The nineteenth century brought steam-powered ships and railways, the internal combustion engine, electrical power generation, and new tools and appliances. By the end of the 1800s, the modern corporation had emerged—a business that could manage a range of activities across geographic regions. A successful corporation not only manufactured products but also managed all aspects of marketing and distribution.

With the shift to a manufacturing economy, vast numbers of people migrated into cities from rural areas in search of work. There was a great influx of immigrants, primarily from Europe, who provided a steady source of cheap, easily exploitable labor. By 1910, more than 13 million people living in the United States were foreign born (Gibson and Lennon 2001). Densely populated neighborhoods sprang up to accommodate the masses, housing was often substandard, and many families lived in poverty. Employment in manufacturing meant that people no longer worked in or around their homes as artisans or craftsmen, as many had in the past, but that they went off into the industrial districts of large cities to work in factories. Wage labor replaced the household subsistence model of the agricultural society.

The industrial economy increased stratification of the workforce along class, race, and gender lines (Amott and Matthaei 1996). Wealthy white families owned the means of production, such as factories, energy sources, or land, and the financial institutions that supported the accumulation of wealth; the men were in the workplace, while the women ran the household. A middle class of educated, skilled workers

Women Working in a Shoe Factory Many factory jobs that were reserved for women paid meager wages and required working under dangerous conditions.

emerged, often in managerial professions. Working-class white men now earned a "family wage" at the factory, while women worked in the household. But for families that needed more than one income, women and even children joined the workforce. Poor women, immigrant women, and women of color increasingly performed domestic labor in white women's households (Amott and Matthaei 1996). But they also worked at factory jobs that were reserved for women, such as millwork and sewing in textile factories, for meager wages and under dangerous conditions.

The industrial economy revolved around the mass production of goods, aided by use of the assembly line in the manufacturing process, in which parts were added to a product in sequential order. The moving assembly line is attributed to Henry Ford, who in 1913 used it to manufacture automobiles in Detroit, Michigan. With assembly line production, the process of manufacturing became not only more mechanized but also more routine driven. In contrast to the artisan mode, in which one worker or a team of workers would produce an item in its entirety from start to finish, on an assembly line each worker would do one or two specific tasks over and over again. Many workers disliked the assembly line because they never had the satisfaction of seeing the finished product, and they were also frustrated with the unsafe, exhausting working conditions.

The Industrial Revolution changed not only working conditions but also the lives of workers. The United States and most other industrializing nations experienced great population booms not only because of immigration but also because of discoveries in science and medicine that led to increased life expectancy and decreased infant mortality. Also, many more people had access to dependable food and water sources and some form of health care. Laws giving some protections to workers, such as child labor reforms, also emerged as an important aspect of the overall health of working populations. Although many factory workers were

unskilled, the American workforce of the early twentieth century was becoming better trained and more educated than that of any previous generation.

The growing population of the United States became a market for the mass-produced goods it was manufacturing. Because industrial workers no longer worked on farms and in the home producing their own food and clothes, they had to purchase those items with the wages they earned for their labor. They also had to buy services, such as health care and child care, from other providers. Other changes in everyday life were also part of the Industrial Revolution: Americans were introduced to new forms of communication with the Morse telegraph in 1837 and the invention of the telephone in 1876, and they traveled more easily across the country with the completion of the transcontinental railroad in 1869.

The Information Revolution

The **Information Revolution** is the most recent of the historical and technological changes that have led to new economic and working conditions in the United States and around the world. Also referred to as the Digital Revolution, Digital Age, or Postindustrial Age, it is expected to bring about as dramatic a transformation of society as the revolutions that preceded it (Castells 2000). We may not recognize how truly radical this change is, partly because we are at the edge of a revolution that will continue to evolve over our lifetimes.

The Information Revolution began in the 1970s with the development of the microchip or microprocessor used in computers and other electronic devices. The performance of microprocessors in capacity and speed has continued to increase according to Moore's Law (doubling every eighteen months to two years). When computers were coupled with the introduction of the internet in the early 1990s and became more affordable, they were soon widely used. Other technologies associated with the Information Revolution include computer networking and all types of digital media, satellite and cable broadcasting, and telecommunications. These technologies have become a ubiquitous part of everyday life in the twenty-first century.

The Information Revolution brought a profound shift from an economy based on the production of goods to one based on the production of knowledge and services (Castells 2000). Of course, the United States is still involved in agriculture and manufacturing, but these are shrinking parts of our economy. As American companies compete on the global market, they may find it more profitable to move production overseas to exploit cheaper materials and labor in

INFORMATION REVOLUTION the recent social revolution made possible by the development of the microchip in the 1970s, which brought about vast improvements in the ability to manage information developing countries. According to the Department of Labor, the U.S. economy currently consists of some eleven "super-sectors," or areas in which people work. Fully two-thirds of these are in the knowledge or service sectors.

Supersectors of the U.S. Economy:

Construction

Education and Health Services

Financial Activities

Government

Information

Leisure and Hospitality

Manufacturing

Natural Resources and Mining

Professional and Business Services

Other Services

Trade, Transportation, and Utilities

A **knowledge worker** is anyone who works primarily with information or who develops and uses knowledge in the workplace (Drucker 1959, 2003). For these workers, information and knowledge are both the raw material and the product of their labor. Knowledge workers produce with their heads rather than with their hands. They create value in the economy through their ideas, judgments, analyses, designs, and innovations. Some examples of knowledge work include advertising, engineering, marketing, product development, research, science, urban planning, and web design. Microsoft, a major software development company, further broadens this category to include anyone who works with the flow of information within businesses.

The service sector, or service industry, also experienced tremendous growth in the postindustrial economy and employs a large number of American workers. **Service workers** provide a service to businesses or individual clients. Services may entail the distribution or sale of goods from producer to consumer (wholesaling and retailing) or transformation in the process of delivering goods (the restaurant business) or no goods at all (massage therapy). All service work has a focus on serving and interacting with people. Service work can be found in such industries as banking, consulting, education, entertainment, health care, insurance, investment, legal ser-

Knowledge Workers The Information Revolution has shifted the economy away from manufacturing toward jobs that produce knowledge and provide services. Knowledge workers, like these employees at Google, create value through their ideas, judgments, and analyses.

vices, leisure, news media, restaurants (including fast-food), retailing, tourism, and transportation.

Some service work pays well, particularly at the management and executive levels, and in certain fields, such as banking, entertainment, and law; but much service sector employment is unstable, part time or temporary, low paying, and often without such benefits as health care or retirement. Women, persons of color, and the poor are likely to be found in the service sector, thus perpetuating a lower-class status among those holding such positions (Amott and Matthaei 1996). Finally, unemployment rates for service sector workers remain higher than for knowledge workers (U.S. Bureau of Labor Statistics 2012b).

Since 2008, when the recent recession began, all sectors of the contemporary global economy have experienced slowdown, but some were hit harder than others. In the next few years, the United States saw some of its highest unemployment rates since the Great Depression—close to 10 percent overall, with much higher rates in certain regions and industries. States like California and Nevada, previously the sites of seemingly nonstop growth, topped the unemployment numbers along with more traditional "rust-belt" states like Michigan and Illinois, as well as in the south in places like Georgia and North Carolina (U.S. Bureau of Labor Statistics 2012c). This was the result of the crash in the real estate and finance sectors, in addition to the drop in the construction and manufacturing trades. The recession also affected groups of workers accustomed to seeing themselves as immune to layoffs—older workers, the college educated, men, and whites saw higher rates of unemployment compared with other groups (Anderson 2009).

The postindustrial economy presents a very different social reality from the economy in other periods in history. The Information Revolution has changed almost every

KNOWLEDGE WORKERS those who work primarily with information and who create value in the economy through their ideas, judgments, analyses, designs, or innovations

SERVICE WORKERS those whose work involves providing a service to businesses or individual clients, customers, or consumers rather than manufacturing goods aspect of our lives and has become a part of many of our social institutions, including the economy and work. And with those changes have come new vulnerabilities, as the recent recession has demonstrated. In the next sections, we look at current world economic systems and the features of work in industrial and postindustrial settings.

DATA WORKSHOP
Analyzing Mass Media and Popular Culture

The Work World of Prime-Time Television

FBI agent, salesperson, newscaster, football coach, presidential press secretary, firefighter, private investigator, district attorney, forensics expert, massage therapist, plastic surgeon, police officer, interior designer, school principal, military officer—these are just some of the jobs of characters in different prime-time network television shows. How do these jobs compare with those of your family, friends, or acquaintances? What kinds of work-related issues do characters on television experience compared to those of real people in those same job titles or industries?

Sociologists who are interested in the media often ask such questions when comparing media content to the real world. This Data Workshop asks you to look at how prime-time television portrays jobs and the realities of working life. Your instructor might want you to do all the exercises,

or she may ask you to choose just one or two. In all four exercises, you will be using existing sources, and in one, you will also be doing an interview. Refer to Chapter 2 for a refresher on these research methods.

Exercise One: What Are the Jobs in Prime Time?
Do a simple count of the jobs in prime-time television. Look at the lineup of current shows between 8:00 pm and 11:00 pm (depending on your time zone) on the major networks (CBS, NBC, ABC, FOX, and CW) and choose at least two shows over five nights for a total of ten or more shows to analyze. Review the key characters and see if you can determine what kinds of jobs they have. While some shows are based almost entirely in the workplace, others may rarely refer to work. There may be some characters whose job status is unclear or absent. Once you have compiled a list of jobs and the number of characters working in each job category, compare these to workers in the real world. What is the actual percentage of people who hold these types of positions? (Sources for this information include the U.S. Census Bureau [www.census.gov] and Bureau of Labor Statistics [www.bls.gov] among other web sites.) See if you can find out whether certain jobs are under- or overrepresented on television or whether there are other kinds of disparities between the statistics of the TV world and the real world. If you present your findings in essay form, use charts or graphs where necessary.

Exercise Two: Working Conditions and TV Jobs
Examine the workplace as depicted on prime-time television. You may choose one or more programs (depending on the context) to gather enough data to do a content analysis. Look at the way characters perform their jobs in television shows. Often workers are shown socializing or engaging in other kinds of personal activities while on the job. How much real work gets done? And when characters are actually working, what aspects of that work are featured during the program? Often we see only the most unusual or glamorous aspects of work

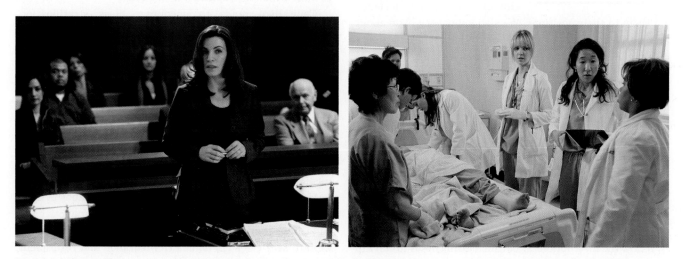

Working in Prime Time How do television shows like *The Good Wife* (left) and *Grey's Anatomy* (right) represent working life?

while the day-to-day routine or behind-the-scenes aspects rarely appear. Another dimension is how characters relate to their jobs and to their co-workers. Are they happy and fulfilled by the work they do? Do they complain about work, or experience other kinds of troubles with their jobs? How are power and resistance exercised in the workplace? Discuss your findings and assess the extent to which you believe the programs accurately reflect these professions in real life.

Exercise Three: Real Working Professionals and Representations on TV

For this exercise, you will need to identify a particular job or profession portrayed on a prime-time television program and find someone you know who works in that job or profession to interview. Find a relevant episode of the program that focuses on work life (you might also consider watching it with your interviewee). After you have viewed the program, discuss with the interviewee the similarities and differences between real work and the same work done by the characters on television. How closely does the show reflect the actual job or profession? In what ways does TV distort or otherwise misrepresent the job or profession? If your analysis of the interview is in essay form, include a transcript of your questions and answers.

Exercise Four: Making a Living on TV

As one of the most powerful sources of socialization in the lives of young people, television may contribute to our attitudes and ideas about the working world. What kinds of lessons do we learn about work and money from what we see on TV? How do television characters influence our career goals and aspirations? Some jobs are totally absent, some are shown as merely the butt of jokes, and others are made to seem hip, glamorous, or exciting. We rarely get much information about how characters have gotten their jobs or what kind of training or experience got them to their positions. We also know very little about how hard they work or what they get paid. TV characters often seem to live extravagant lifestyles with little relationship between actual salaries and what they can afford to buy. Take examples from one or more television shows and discuss the characters' standard of living. Could real people working comparable jobs afford the same lifestyle that the television characters seem to enjoy? Do a content analysis, viewing at least one episode of a chosen program and describing as many of the details of work and lifestyle of the characters as possible to answer these questions.

There are two options for completing this Data Workshop.

Option 1 (informal): Choose one of the exercises above and follow the instructions as outlined. Bring notes to class to discuss with others in small groups. Your instructor may organize groups so that all members have done the same exercise or all members have done a different exercise. In either case, compare your findings with those of other members of the group.

Option 2 (formal): Choose one of the exercises above (or your instructor may assign a specific exercise) and follow the instructions as outlined. Write a three- to four-page essay analyzing your findings.

Economic Systems: Comparing Capitalism and Socialism

Capitalism and socialism are political-economic systems found around the world, often in overlapping forms. Capitalism and socialism are ideal types, but most nations have a mix of both. For example, the United States, a capitalist nation, has some degree of socialism in government subsidies to businesses, regulation of markets, and support for public education and social welfare.

Capitalism

Capitalism is an economic system based on the laws of free market competition, privatization of the means of production, and production for profit. In its purest form, values for goods and services are derived solely by the market relationship between supply and demand. The resources necessary for production of goods and services are all privately owned. Owners, or capitalists, must employ workers to make products and perform services to generate a profit. Workers sell their labor to capitalists for a wage. The difference between the cost of production of a product or service and its price is profit to which the capitalist is entitled.

Capitalism tends to encourage class stratification. Because owners, or capitalists, make profits, they can accumulate wealth. Workers are not in a structural position to get ahead financially. The ideologies of the free market, private property, and profit-seeking motives that define capitalism also shape institutions other than the economy. In capitalist nations, we see increasing privatization of such basic human services as water and transportation systems or health care, housing, and education. Thus, hospitals, public schools, prisons, and even government health and welfare agencies are increasingly taken over by private for-profit firms.

Under capitalism, workers must sell their labor to capitalists for a wage. They are encouraged to be productive and efficient or they will suffer reduced wages, decreased social welfare services such as health insurance and retirement, downsizing, and layoffs. Until recently, under the capital-

CAPITALISM an economic system based on the laws of free market competition, privatization of the means of production, and production for profit ist system in the United States, disgruntled workers could withhold their labor by striking. Now, under a transnational capitalist system, firms experiencing strikes may decide to move their operations overseas to countries where few workers have the right to strike.

A capitalist economy encourages efficiency through technological innovation, expansion of markets, and reduction of production costs. Thus, owners or capitalists, in their efforts to seek efficiency, often seek to replace workers with new technologies, reduce social welfare spending, and cut labor costs. Therefore, workers are responsible for maintaining their own competitiveness. They must seek an education and/or skills to compete for jobs and maintain their competency over their working lifetimes. However, firms must also increase their competitiveness. They may move production operations to overseas sites where they can take advantage of deregulated environments and cheap labor costs.

Socialism

Socialism is an economic system based on collective ownership of the means of production, collective distribution of goods and services, and government regulation of the economy. Under socialism, there are no private for-profit transactions. In its purest form, socialism seeks to meet the basic needs of all citizens rather than encouraging profits for some individuals over others.

In a socialist system, the government rather than individuals owns or at least regulates the ownership of all businesses, farms, and factories, and profits are redistributed to the collective citizenry. This encourages a collectivist work ethic with workers theoretically working for the common good of all citizens. Citizens have access to such resources as health care, food, housing, and other social services to meet their basic needs. This is different from capitalism, as these services are an entitlement of all people, not just those who can afford them.

In socialism, a central and usually highly bureaucratic government regulates all aspects of the economy—ownership of resources and means of production, regulation of lending policies, interest rates, and currency values—as well as setting labor policies regarding such issues as parental leave, retirement, and the right to strike. Such intense regulation of the economy should effectively reduce class inequalities and extreme poverty. In **communism**, the most extreme form of socialism, the government owns everything and all citizens work for the government and are considered equal, with no class distinctions. Socialism and communism, like capitalism, are theoretical or ideal types. Thus, no nations are purely socialist or communist. Even communist countries like Cuba or China are increasingly incorporating capitalist ideologies into their regimes.

Under socialism, workers are not at risk of extreme poverty and class division as they might be within a capitalist society. They are not as vulnerable as capitalist workers

to being replaced by new technological innovations or the transnational movement of capital. However, they also do not enjoy the same consumption patterns that capitalist economies encourage. Socialism cannot provide capitalism's middle-class luxuries. Though class division is reduced, it is still present. Many socialist nations have political elites who enjoy a higher class of living than workers, and urban workers often benefit from having closer access to resources than rural workers. Further, reduction of class inequalities does not guarantee a reduction in other types of inequalities, such as racism, sexism, and ageism.

The United States: A Capitalist System with Some Socialist Attributes

To understand the political economy of various nations, think of capitalism and socialism as opposite ends of a continuum with nations placed along its span as being more capitalist or more socialist. The United States would undoubtedly lie closer to the capitalist side than would Sweden, but even U.S. capitalism is not a pure form.

While the United States is a capitalist nation, it also has socialist elements. Although capitalist businesses are privately owned, many benefit from government subsidies—grants, tax incentives, and special contracts. This is often referred to as "corporate welfare." In pure capitalism, such support would not exist. Government intervenes in the economy in other ways as well. Agencies such as the Federal Reserve Board often manipulate interest rates to stimulate the economy and control inflation. The Emergency Economic Stabilization Act of 2008 (also referred to as "the Bailout Bill") funneled more than $700 billion in government funds into banks, insurance companies, and other struggling private corporations in order to prop up the U.S. economy. Such government interventions constitute forms of socialism.

SOCIALISM an economic system based on the collective ownership of the means of production, collective distribution of goods and services, and government regulation of the economy

COMMUNISM a system of government that eliminates private property; the most extreme form of socialism, because all citizens work for the government and there are no class distinctions

If the United States were purely capitalist, such institutions as education and health care would all be privately owned. However, most schools and many universities are publicly owned and operated. Even private universities usually get government subsidies. Health care is a trickier example as much change is taking place in this arena. Medicare and Medicaid are long-standing federal programs that provide subsidized health care for the elderly and the poor. The Affordable Care Act of 2010 ushered in more federally mandated health care coverage for millions of Americans that rolled out in 2013–2014. But many individuals and their employers still buy health insurance from for-profit insurers, and hospitals are often run for profit as well.

The government also spends millions of dollars annually for other general assistance or public aid programs for low-income families, including the Supplemental Nutrition Assistance Program (or SNAP—previously known as Food Stamps) and Temporary Assistance to Needy Families, often referred to as "entitlements." Thus, the poor, elderly and disabled, current and former armed forces personnel, and expectant mothers, infants, and children have some public services to meet some of their basic needs. Even our Social Security system, though partially funded through payroll taxes, is a public system providing retirement, survivorship, and disability benefits to eligible Americans. Debates continue about whether these populations' needs are satisfactorily met and whether it's the government's responsibility to provide these services. Conservative politicians who periodically accuse their rivals of "socialist" tendencies may need to be reminded that things they enjoy every day—like streetlights and highway maintenance, police protection and fire fighters, libraries and public schools—are all part of a system of centrally funded and regulated services they likely would not want to do without.

In theory, capitalism and socialism are opposites. In reality, there is no pure form of either capitalism and socialism, rather nations typically have some features of both economic systems. Each system represents a different political ideology and economic reality for the people and workers in its economy. Economic systems evolve and change over time, and with them, the institution of work.

The Nature of Industrial and Postindustrial Work

Historical and technological changes leading to the Agricultural, Industrial, and Information Revolutions fundamentally changed societies across several centuries. Societies have also adopted economic systems—capitalist or socialist, or a combination of both—and these economic systems influence the types of work that are available as well as our patterns of working.

Industrial Work

The spread of industrialism in the eighteenth and nineteenth centuries created "work" in the modern sense. Before the Industrial Revolution, most of the population engaged in agriculture, and the production of goods was organized around the household or small craft shops. In the industrial world, progress meant making machines that could produce more goods, more efficiently.

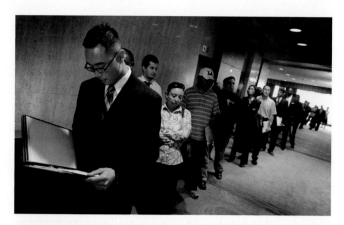

Social Welfare in the United States Hit hard by the recession, many unemployed Americans rely on government aid, such as the extension of unemployment benefits.

Industrialization changed how people worked. According to Karl Marx, the powerful had always exploited workers. As he asserted in *The Communist Manifesto*, "oppressor and oppressed stood in constant opposition to one another" in a perpetual struggle for economic resources, as all history "is the history of class struggles" (Marx 2001, p. 245). Though Marx studied ancient Rome and medieval Europe to help form his theories, they are most often associated with the Industrial Revolution, the capitalist economies that it produced, and the workers who toiled in its factories. However, much of what Marx asserted about class conflict and the circumstances of his time can apply with slight modification to capitalists and workers in the current industrial workplace.

Economic exploitation is still present in a modern industrial economy, which allows for the accumulation of what Marx called "surplus value." The proletariat, or workers, in an industrial economy possess only one thing of economic value, and that is their time, which they sell to capitalists who own the means of production. Workers are paid for their time and labor, but their wages do not represent the full profit from the sale of the goods they produce. The sale of the goods not only covers the workers' wages and the expenses of running the factory but also generates additional revenue or surplus value, which then belongs to the owner.

Marx believed that workers in capitalist societies experienced alienation as a result of this system of production, because they are paid for their labor but do not own the things they produce. He believed workers were alienated in four ways: from the product of their labor, from their own productive activity, from their fellow workers, and finally from human nature. First, the products of the worker's labor are the property of the capitalists to do with as they see fit. Unlike the farmers and craft workers of prior eras, the industrial worker is "robbed of . . . the objects of his work" and "the worker relates to the product of his labor as an alien object" (Marx 2001, p. 87). Workers feel no sense of personal satisfaction in producing goods that are owned and controlled by someone else.

Second, workers in a capitalist society are alienated from the process of work, their own productive activity. Marx argues that labor is "not the satisfaction of a need but only the means to satisfy needs" outside work (Marx 2001, p. 88), such as earning enough money to live on. In traditional, precapitalist societies, many found joy and fulfillment in the process of production. But the worker under capitalism cannot feel that kind of satisfaction.

Third, the worker is alienated from other people, "the alienation of man from man," as Marx calls it. Capitalism forces individuals into competition with each other, as "each man measures his relationship to other men by the relationship in which he finds himself placed as a worker" (Marx 2001, p. 91). Instead of cooperating, workers are forced to compete for scarce jobs and resources, making other workers an alien and hostile presence. Workers are also alienated from the owners, as they recognize work as "an activity that is under the domination, oppression, and yoke of another man" (Marx 2001, p. 92).

Fourth, workers are alienated from human nature, what Marx refers to as "human essence." He believes that work should not be an unhappy burden taken up only out of the need to preserve physical existence. Instead, he assumes that it is in our nature to seek out "work, vital activity, and productive life" (Marx 2001, p. 90). The essence of what it means to be human is to engage in free conscious activity, but capitalism degrades human labor to a mere means of survival. Marx acknowledges that all species must work to satisfy immediate physical needs, but only human beings "fashion things according to the laws of beauty" and find satisfaction in their work (Marx 2001, p. 90). However, in a capitalist economy, this capacity is largely lost, as workers are alienated from their own human qualities.

Twenty-First-Century Industrial Work Many workers still toil in the conditions that Marx criticized in the nineteenth century.

Marx was describing work in the industrial era of the nineteenth century, but his analyses can apply to today's industrial workers as well. Many workers are still toiling in the same conditions of exploitation, alienation, and class struggle that Marx thought needed to change.

Postindustrial Service Work

Social theorists of the Industrial Age, like Karl Marx and his contemporaries, were unable to predict how technological innovation would transform work and the economy in the twentieth century and beyond. They could not foresee the transition to a postindustrial, service-oriented economy. Nor could they foresee the advent of easily available consumer credit, which has meant that workers can now buy things they can't currently afford, materially improving their everyday lives without the hassle of starting a class revolution (even if it means they may never pay off their debts).

So are service workers exploited? Alienated? Ready to revolt? A look at the nature of service work in the Postindustrial Age and a case study seem to suggest that these old problems have taken on new forms in our current times.

Service work, as the dominant form of employment in the postindustrial economy, often involves direct contact with clients, customers, patients, or students by those rendering the service, whether they are waiters, cashiers, nurses, doctors, teachers, or receptionists. In service work, situations arise when the worker's concerns, standards, and expectations conflict with those of clients. For example, an emergency for a client may be routine for a worker, as when your TV cable service goes out during the Green Bay Packers' football game and the customer service representative just keeps telling you they're working on it! As another example, you have a toothache, but the dentist doesn't have an open appointment until tomorrow. It's not the dentist who has to give you the bad news but the receptionist who must try to convince you to wait until then.

At the same time, service workers are also subject to the scrutiny and critique of a manager or supervisor—so in addition to the potential clash between workers and clients, there are also issues of autonomy and control over their work. This can create distinctive tensions in service work interactions, and power relationships both subtle and more obvious are clearly present in this type of work.

Barbara Ehrenreich explored some of these power issues in her book *Nickel and Dimed: On (Not) Getting By in America* (2001). As research for the book, Ehrenreich took minimum-wage service jobs in three different cities—as a waitress in Florida, a hotel maid in Maine, and a Wal-Mart employee in Minnesota—and experienced the difficulties of trying to make ends meet and maintain her self-respect in low-wage service positions.

Ehrenreich found that service workers in these types of jobs are likely to be exploited in a number of ways. First, the low wages, lack of benefits, and grueling hours make it difficult to pay even the most basic bills. She discovered this herself when she couldn't scrape up enough money for a deposit on an apartment and ended up living in a sleazy hotel and getting her dinner from the local charity's food pantry. Her co-workers lived in flophouses, their cars, or small apartments crowded with family, friends, and strangers, and one ate nothing but a small bag of Doritos every day for lunch. They got fired for asserting their rights or for getting ill or injured, and they developed chronic health problems because of the stress and poor conditions under which they labored. And yet, they couldn't stop—they were all reliant on the next paycheck to get by (or not get by, as Ehrenreich argues), and so they had to endure abuse, exploitation, and all sorts of risks for the tenuous security of serving, scrubbing, and selling.

> **INFORMATION WORK** work that involves the production, analysis, and distribution of information or knowledge; workers primarily think for a living
>
> **TELECOMMUTING** working from home while staying connected to the office through communications technology

You encounter these people every day—when you eat at a restaurant, shop at a "big box" retailer, or stay at a hotel—and you may even be one yourself. Ehrenreich argues that there's no way to "make it" under these circumstances, and her experiences illustrate this argument with chilling clarity.

Inequalities of power in service work have many sources—gender, race, age, and immigration status—and those with greater power (clients, managers) may take advantage without even realizing it. Ehrenreich reminds us that even in "respectable" forms of service work, exploitation is common. What about jobs that are illegal—such as prostitution or the

Nickel and Dimed Barbara Ehrenreich found that many service workers barely scrape by working long hours for minimum wage and no benefits. Because many service workers live paycheck to paycheck, they often have trouble asserting their rights or taking time off for illnesses for fear of losing their jobs.

work of undocumented farm laborers? These workers lack the legal protections that even Wal-Mart workers or chain restaurant waitstaff have access to, and they may be subject to prosecution and punishment merely for doing their jobs.

Postindustrial Knowledge Work

In the twenty-first century, intellectual or **information work** is increasingly common while manual labor is increasingly rare (Tapscott 1997). The massive changes wrought by information technologies—sometimes referred to as the "new economy"—have transformed the nature of work again in ways that are not yet fully understood (Kellner 2001).

The majority of the workforce in the United States now hold jobs that involve working with information, and most new jobs created are primarily within this sector. While many of these technologies purport to increase productivity and save time, the average worker is also working more hours in a week than her predecessor in the pre–Information Age workplace.

Another important feature of the Information Age workplace is greatly diminished importance of place. This phenomenon has been called the "death of distance" (Caincross 1995). Work that can be done on a computer can be done from any location, as networking through computers, satellite, cell phones, and other technologies makes workers' location almost irrelevant to their ability to get the work done and to work with others (Poster 2002).

More and more workers are doing telework or **telecommuting**. They stay at home rather than commute to the office, and they are connected to their workplace through communications technology. About 10 percent of American workers (excluding the self-employed and volunteers) telecommute at least part-time (U.S. Census Bureau 2012d).

Supporters claim that telecommuting has many benefits for the worker, the business, and society at large. Employees get flexible work schedules. Traffic delays, parking problems, and time wasted commuting don't exist for the telecommuter. Businesses get increased productivity and fewer sick days when they allow employees to telecommute. Although many employers worry that allowing employees to work from home would reduce accountability, some believe that the opposite is true. In traditional office environments, the only measure of employee value is the number of hours present in the office, regardless of what gets done, whereas telecommuters must demonstrate their accomplishments more concretely. Telecommuting and similar uses of information technology have also made it easier for single parents, seniors, or workers with disabilities to stay employed full-time. Yet in a reverse trial, internet giant Yahoo restricted telecommuting in 2013 and asked many employees to return to the office.

There is much debate around the positive and negative aspects of telecommuting and other technologies that physi-

The Postindustrial Office?
To attract the best knowledge workers and to motivate them to work long hours, information and technology companies like Google and Microsoft go to great lengths to make the workplace appealing.

cally and geographically separate workers. Some suggest that new information technologies will actually increase the need for face-to-face contact and tightly knit workplaces. For example, workers who write codes for computer software can do it anywhere they have a computer and instantly send the results to those who will package and market the software, but software companies are still the most geographically concentrated of any industry. Microsoft, the world's largest software company, refers to its home office as "the campus" and has gone to great lengths to make it an appealing place for employees precisely because the company still needs them at the same location in order to work. In the Information Age, more and more work requires the creative manipulation of knowledge, and for this workers need to brainstorm and share ideas in more interactive ways than technology currently allows. The computer industry suggests that even when work can be done anywhere, there will still be a real need to bring people together, at least some of the time.

The rise of new technologies may roll back many of the original effects of the Industrial Revolution. Manufacturing made it necessary for many people to work at the same location, causing the growth of cities and the decline of rural and small-town populations. However, with new technologies that let people work from anywhere, perhaps telecommuting will cause cities to shrink again as more people will be able to live without reference to the company that employs them. Small towns are now offering an attractive alternative to outsourcing. High-tech jobs are beginning to relocate to rural areas, where companies are finding it cheaper to do business and more attractive for their employees (Pinto 2005). It's possible that information technology may one day reunite the worlds of work and home that the Industrial Revolution tore asunder.

Last, it's not just knowledge workers who rely on this new information technology. The Digital Age has also changed the way industrial and service work is conducted. Even jobs traditionally considered to be in manufacturing now have a knowledge component. For example, the big three automakers in the United States have in the past hired college graduates for the assembly line because they needed employees able to identify and suggest quality improvements (Brandon 1996). In the service sector, retail outlets and grocery stores use computer databases to predict exactly how much of a product they need to keep on hand and to order new merchandise in a timely fashion, a system called "just in time inventory," drastically reducing overhead and waste. Insurance companies use instant messaging (IM) to connect workers in different offices or in the field, "finding IM not only improves accuracy and provides timely customer response but adds dollars to their bottom line" (Chordas 2003).

> **RESISTANCE STRATEGIES**
> ways that workers express discontent with their working conditions and try to reclaim control of the conditions of their labor

Individual and Collective Resistance Strategies: How Workers Cope

Individuals and groups cope with their working conditions in a variety of ways called **resistance strategies**. These are tactics that let workers take back a degree of control over the conditions of their labor and feel that they have some

IN RELATIONSHIPS
With Virtual Colleagues

Ironically, all the communication technologies that increase connections among people may ultimately make them feel more alienated from other human beings. This is nowhere more true than among the millions of Americans who do knowledge or information work. In the postmodern workplace, face-to-face interactions between colleagues and co-workers are on the decline, while interactions at work are increasingly accomplished through electronic communications.

It is common for employees to actively work with co-workers and colleagues they rarely, if ever, see, or whom they have never met and probably never will. You may "know" these people only through disembodied relationships. How do we establish and maintain good working relationships in a virtual world we inhabit at work? Have new technologies improved our ability to connect and collaborate with one another, or have they created a work space that is increasingly impersonal and dehumanizing? What impact does this have on our work relationships and work lives?

These issues were already being defined and articulated at an earlier time, when this technology was first being introduced in work settlings. By the mid-1990s, there were debate and concern about whether this kind of change was positive or negative. The effects of this new technology on work relationships were becoming a little clearer. It was common to hear complaints about what was happening, particularly among workers in the information industries. Many workers were still dubious and viewed the phenomenon with ambivalence. Douglas Coupland, in his popular novel *Microserfs*, captured the dilemma of the wired workplace with his cynical character, a Microsoft employee. Here he describes one of the "advantages" of using e-mail for interpersonal communications at the office, being able to avoid real contact with your co-worker:

> I'm an e-mail addict. Everybody at Microsoft is an addict. The future of e-mail usage is being pioneered right here. The cool thing with e-mail is that when you send it, there's no possibility of connecting with the person on the other end. It's better than phone answering machines, because with them, the person on the other line might actually pick up the phone and you might have to talk. (Coupland 1995)

Of course Coupland's fiction is a farce, but the principle remains a familiar one. And since then, technology in the workplace has vastly proliferated. We use a variety of means to communicate: telephone, e-mail, text or instant messaging, videoconferencing, and more. If we consider the world that Coupland was describing, there is no doubt that the business practices first adopted by cutting-edge technology companies have influenced the way people work together in almost every other industry. New technology has become vastly more integrated into the flow and dynamics of communications in almost any current workplace.

Sometimes these technological changes can profoundly affect the way people experience their work. It can connect them in new ways, but just as easily cut them off from one another. In his article "Workers as Cyborgs: Labor and Networked Computers," Mark Poster detailed the increase in alienation that can come when a workplace switches to electronic communications. For instance, "a hospital in the Midwest that introduced a software program for ordering supplies from the Internet" saw increases in efficiency but also found that the technology "furthers the alienation of the worker" (Poster 2002). Using the new software may have gotten supplies ordered more quickly and with fewer errors, but it can get lonely when the only person you talk to is your computer.

As collegial relationships have taken on an increasingly virtual character, new challenges have appeared that require us to consider how to interact effectively. How can we establish a good rapport with others, or develop trust, respect, and maybe even friendship? These are considerations whether our virtual relationships are fleeting or persist over a long time. In contrast to face-to-face relationships, in a virtual work space, you may have to be more deliberate in how you communicate. It can be more difficult to convey the interactional cues that help to support and maintain a warm, cooperative, and mutually satisfying relationship.

All these situations indicate that if we want to avoid feeling further alienated in our postmodern workplaces, we must develop strategies to deal with new communications technologies, while seeking ways to maintain and nurture our virtual relationships with our disembodied colleagues.

sense of autonomy even in the face of dehumanizing, alienating constraints imposed by the terms and demands of their employment.

Individual resistance can range from the fairly benign, like using work time to surf the web, to the truly dangerous, like sabotaging the assembly line. More often, individual resistance may be simply personalizing the workspace with photos or daydreaming on the job as a type of escape (Roy 1960). Collective forms of resistance that seek solutions to shared workplace problems include union organizing and membership, strikes, walkouts, and work stoppages.

This discussion begins with an examination of individual resistance strategies within service work. We bring Max Weber's theory on bureaucracy into the present to see how workers today are coping with the constraints of those organizations. Last, we look at collective resistance strategies—union organization, both past and present.

Individual Resistance Strategies: Handling Bureaucratic Constraints

Bureaucratic organizations are found in almost every sector of the economy. In Weber's theory of bureaucracies, he highlighted the rational, impersonal, and coldly efficient nature of this form of social organization (refer to Chapter 5 for a review). Workers in highly bureaucratic organizations often feel the lack of autonomy in their everyday work lives. Autonomy is the ability to direct one's individual destiny—to have the power to control the conditions of one's labor—and this is generally lacking for people who work in highly structured, rule-bound, and depersonalized environments. Their daily tasks are structured by external forces; for example, the pace of the assembly line is decided for them and they cannot slow it down or speed it up if they need to take a break or want to finish work early.

In many corporate settings, employees at all levels are under various types of surveillance: electronic key cards monitor their comings and goings, cameras record their activities, computer transactions are screened, and phone calls are recorded. In retail sales, workers' interactions with customers are often scripted, so that even what they say to others is outside their control. Not only is there a lack of autonomy, but there is also a lack of individuality in the workplace. Workers are treated more like robots than people. Unlike a robot, however, human workers can resist and undermine the bureaucratic constraints that limit their autonomy in the workplace—and they do so in a wide variety of ways.

Robin Leidner's study *Fast Food, Fast Talk* provides an in-depth look at individual resistance strategies in the workplace (Leidner 1993). The study focuses on McDonald's employees and the routinized nature of their inter-

actions with customers. Under the golden arches, every contact between the counter staff and the hungry consumer is strictly scripted, seemingly with no room for improvisation or creativity. Or is there?

McDonald's workers are trained to interact with customers using "The Six Steps": greeting, taking orders, assembling food, presenting it, receiving payment, and thanking them for their business. As monotonous as these steps are, workers don't necessarily resent routinization—it helps them do their jobs effectively. And some workers, like this woman, improvise on the steps, personalizing them in tiny but still noticeable ways:

> Just do the Six Steps, but do it in your own way. It's not like you have to say "Hi, welcome to McDonald's." You can say, "Hi, how are you doing?" or "Good morning," "Good afternoon," "Good evening," things like that. (Leidner 1993, p. 138)

Leidner observed that there were limits within which workers could

> use the script as a starting point and inject [their] own personality into the interactions. Thus, some window workers joked or chatted with customers and tried to make the exchanges enjoyable for both parties. This stance implied an assertion of equality with customers and a refusal to suppress the self completely. (Leidner 1993, p. 190)

Leidner proposes that submitting to scripted interactions all day long suppresses the real self and that this sort of tightly controlled work environment can actually be damaging to the individual.

One of the functions of McDonald's service script is to regulate the power relationship between customer and

Fast Food, Fast Talk In her study of restaurant employees, Robin Leidner looks at the ways that workers subvert the scripts that McDonald's requires them to follow when interacting with customers.

IN THE FUTURE

How Much Is a College Degree Worth on the Job Market?

Young Americans are told a college degree is the best way to prepare for the job market. However, as far back as the 1970s, sociologists like Randall Collins wondered if college was always a sound investment. The usual argument in favor of higher education, even as it has become increasingly expensive, is that students are "investing in themselves." But this "investment" theory makes sense only if education is producing graduates who have skills and knowledge they can turn into higher wages. In *The Credential Society*, Collins argued that "job skills of all sorts are actually acquired in the work situation rather than in a formal training institution," while college only provides a credential (Collins 1979, p. 193). That credential can be enormously valuable, of course, but it's subject to inflation. As more and more people attend college, jobs that used to require high school diplomas start wanting bachelor's degrees, and so on. If Collins is correct, or even partially correct, then sooner or later school will become a bad investment.

Many experts stand by higher education as an investment. A 2011 report from Michael Greenstone and Adam Looney of the Brookings Institution told a familiar story, arguing that if an eighteen-year-old had $102,000 (the average cost of college today) to invest, far and away the best rate of return would come from investing in a bachelor's degree.

They calculate that "the average college graduate earns roughly $570,000 more than someone with only a high school diploma" and that "investment in a four-year college yields a rate of return of 15.2 percent per year"—more than double what the stock market traditionally yields (Greenstone and Looney 2011). Another study pointed out that "80% of individuals making less than $10,000 didn't finish college," while about "80% of those making more than $150,000 did" (Thompson 2012).

However, while supporters see these figures as zingers, there are some cracks in the consensus. The most obvious disclaimer when "investing" in a four-year college is the one attached to any investment: past returns are no guarantee of future returns. College was a terrific investment in the past, but will that still be true for those applying for admission today? In 2010, for the first time, Americans owed more in student loans than credit card debt, and "the amount of defaulted loans—$76 billion—is greater than the yearly tuition bill for all students at public two- and four-year colleges and universities" (Martin 2012). The fact that 80 percent of those making less than $10,000 a year didn't finish college is impressive, but it also means that 20 percent who do have a bachelor's degree are only making that same little amount. A *Newsweek* story titled "Is College a Lousy Invest-

---

worker: customers' demands can be delivered with all types of attitude, but workers must always serve customers with a smile. The script constrains workers' responses—if they have rude or even abusive customers, they must still stick to the script:

> You have to take their crap. [Laughs.] I'm not the type of person to say, "OK, have it your way." I mean, I have to admit, I'm tempted to backtalk a lot. That gets me in a lot of trouble. So I mean, when a customer's rude to me I just have to walk away and say, "Could you take this order please, before I say something I'm not supposed to say?" (Leidner 1993, p. 133)

If they do pervert the script or talk back to a rude customer, workers may be inviting a reprimand from their supervisor. But they are also engaging in resistance, asserting their own identities in the face of the depersonalizing routine. They are being active rather than passive, controlling the interaction

rather than being controlled by it. They are asserting their own autonomy on the job, and it is apparently worth the risk.

It is difficult to think of a form of employment that would allow us to avoid these bureaucratic constraints altogether. What types of resistance strategies have you used to regain a bit of independence and power in the workplace?

Collective Resistance Strategies: Unions

Although individual resistance strategies may provide a small measure of autonomy for some workers, they don't fundamentally change the working conditions or make permanent improvements to the terms of employment for all workers. That is why workers sometimes seek more lasting solutions to their problems by organizing to instigate collective resistance strategies—by forming unions.

New College Graduates Is the cost of a college degree still a smart investment?

ment" posed the question to Nobel Prize–winning economist James Heckman, who thinks that the answer depends on the student: "even with these high prices, you're still finding a high return for individuals who are bright and motivated," but for those who aren't "college ready, then the answer is no, it's not worth it" (McArdle 2012).

While much of this debate has been focused on the ability of indebted college graduates to find jobs that are good

enough to pay off their student loans, for other academics and critics there are more basic questions to be answered. Sociologist Juliet Schor has been writing about working and consuming in America for almost twenty years and is convinced we shouldn't just be asking if there will be any good jobs; we should be asking what a "good job" is. In *Plenitude: The New Economics of True Wealth* (2010), she argues that Americans are increasingly divided between the underemployed who are barely getting by and the overemployed who are well paid but poor in "true wealth." She reports that "thirty percent of U.S. male college graduates . . . are on schedules that usually exceed fifty hours" a week, even though during the recession of 2008–09 there were five job seekers for every job created (Schor 2010, p. 105).

She sees the focus on jobs that require more hours and more productivity for high wages as devastating to our lives and our environment. Her solution calls for jobs that support sustainable consumption, which she compares to the slow food movement. The answer is not to stop working or consuming, any more than the "answer" to fast food was to stop eating. Instead, she thinks we need jobs that allow for a life that is rich in time, ecologically light, small scale, and rich in satisfaction. But will such jobs be available to new college graduates?

A **union** benefits workers in various ways and serves to counterbalance the power of employers. A labor union is an association of workers who come together to improve their economic status and working conditions. The two main types of unions are craft unions, in which all the members are skilled in a certain craft (e.g., the International Brotherhood of Carpenters and Joiners), and industrial unions, in which all the members work in the same industry regardless of their particular skill (e.g., the Service Employees International Union). Some unions are local with small memberships; others are large, national organizations representing millions of workers. When disagreements arise between management and employees, unionized workers may threaten to or actually stage a temporary "walkout," "work stoppage," or "strike" to express their grievance and force corporate managers and owners to negotiate. Often the striking workers will try to discourage the public from patronizing the businesses implicated in the labor dispute

and try to prevent other, outside replacement workers (sometimes called "scab labor") from taking their jobs while they are out on strike. Union negotiations with employers about the terms of employment and working conditions are coordinated through collective bargaining in which contract decisions between management and union representatives must be mutually agreed upon rather than imposed unilaterally.

Unions have a long history in the United States. At various times, they have existed on the margins of society and been vigorously opposed by capitalists and other free-market supporters. Unions in the nineteenth and early twentieth centuries were brutally suppressed by capitalists, and union organizers were frequently arrested and jailed. Often they were charged with conspiracy because attempts to form unions were illegal for much of American history.

UNION an association of workers who bargain collectively for increased wages and benefits and better working conditions

Lawrence, Massachusetts, 1912 During the textile mill strike, workers demanded "bread and roses," eloquently capturing their desire for something more than just the wages needed to survive.

The Typographical Union (representing print typesetters), which formed in 1852, is usually considered the "first durable national organization of workers" in the United States. By 1881, a number of smaller labor groups banded together to form the American Federation of Labor (AFL), eventually becoming the AFL-CIO (by adding the groups in the Congress of Industrial Organizations), still recognized as a powerful union today.

Unions of this era fought for a variety of workplace reforms. During the 1912 textile mill strikes in Lawrence, Massachusetts, the workers' slogan was "bread and roses," emphasizing their desire for something more than wages sufficient to survive. Unions also led campaigns to end child labor, to establish an eight-hour workday and a five-day workweek, and to increase workplace safety. For this reason, unions are still sometimes referred to as "the people who brought you the weekend." We can now take for granted much of what the early unions won to improve the lives of American workers. It is not surprising that many were willing to fight for unionization even in the face of extreme opposition.

In 2011, approximately 14.8 million American workers belonged to a union organization (U.S. Bureau of Labor Statistics 2012d). However, union membership has been in steep decline since its peak in the 1950s. In 1955, approximately 35 percent of the labor force was unionized; by 2011, fewer than 12 percent of the workforce belonged to a union (U.S. Bureau of Labor Statistics 2012d). With a shift in the U.S. economy from manufacturing to the service sector, the only unions to grow since the early 1970s have been public sector employees' unions. At the same time that unions were growing in strength and numbers came challenges from industry and government. Beginning with the Taft-Hartley Act of 1947, laws have been established that limit the power of unions and the activities of members. Some twenty-four states have passed "right-to-work" laws that prohibit workplaces from making union membership a requirement of all employees. As long as the economy was growing rapidly, and wages and benefits continued to rise, the perceived need for unions waned. However, when the economy faltered in the 1970s, American corporations found it was cheaper to move production overseas to countries whose working conditions were practically unregulated. Industries that leave the United States, referred to as "runaway shops," have been especially prevalent in manufacturing, where firms take advantage of cheap labor and lax environmental laws in other countries. More recently, an increasing number of service sector jobs have been moved overseas. As a result, many unions have largely changed focus from fighting for better wages and working conditions to keeping jobs in this country.

The number of labor actions has also been on the decline. In the 1950s, an average of 352 major strikes occurred each year; by the 2000s, that number had fallen to fewer than 30 (Commission for Labor Cooperation 2003). Many strategies have been used by major U.S. corporations to successfully block union efforts across a variety of work disputes. Although strikes may occur less often now than in the past (and they are not always resolved in the workers' favor), there are still cases to show for their effectiveness in winning battles between unions and employers.

A strike at the ports of Los Angeles and Long Beach, California, is illustrative. In November 2012, a small number of striking clerical workers effectively shut down the nation's busiest shipping complex right as cargoes of holiday goods were headed for port. Unlike in other industries, union loyalty remains strong in shipping. At fewer than 800, the number of striking office and clerical workers was relatively small, but as a unit of the larger International Longshore and Warehouse Union (with close to 60,000 members), no dockworkers or truckers would cross the picket line, thereby crippling trade through the port terminals. At issue was not working conditions or wages; rather, the clerical workers' grievance

Millionaires versus Billionaires Labor disputes between the National Football League Player's Association union and NFL team owners threatened to disrupt the 2011 season. Players including Tom Brady, Drew Breese, Peyton Manning, and others entered into an anti-trust lawsuit against the owners after collective bargaining negotiations broke down.

was over job security, not just for current employees but for those in the future. The workers contended that their employers wanted to transfer higher-paying union jobs to other states or outsource them to other countries where lower-paid workers would be plentiful. The strike disrupted deliveries valued in the billions of dollars a day and brought to a standstill some 600,000 additional workers. The cost of the strike threatened not only the ports but also the fragile U.S. economy. It was settled after eight days with new contracts promising no outsourcing of union jobs (Lopez, White, and Pfiefer 2012). Whether such collective resistance strategies become more prevalent again in the future remains to be seen.

The Best (and Worst) of Corporate America

From a Weberian perspective, we can see that large bureaucracies laden with rules and procedures can deprive employees of a sense of autonomy, individuality, and control. From a Marxist perspective, we can see how large capitalist corporations sometimes exploit their workers and cause alienation and that their power hierarchies often exclude women and minorities. These criticisms are true in the aggregate—money, power, and influence converge in corporate America, and with these forms of power come opportunities for greed, exploitation and abuse. But not all corporations are evil, and sometimes we see major corporate players transcend self-interest and act with great altruism.

Compared to big Wall Street firms like Morgan Stanley or Goldman Sachs, Sandler O'Neill and Partners is a tiny investment banking and brokerage firm. It was located on the 104th floor of the World Trade Center in New York, and on September 11, 2001, it was devastated in the terrorist attacks. Sixty-six of its 171 employees died in the towers, all of their equipment and business information was destroyed, and only one of the senior partners survived. That partner, Jimmy Dunne, immediately began what seemed like an impossible task: address overwhelming grief, rebuild the company, and take care of the families of all sixty-six lost employees.

Within a matter of days, Dunne had set up shop in temporary offices (donated by Bank of America). Sandler O'Neill began trading again, but without the knowledge or experience of the employees it had lost. And in what constitutes a miracle in corporate America, its competitors began to help out. Stockbrokers from other companies started calling in market information to Sandler O'Neill's inexperienced traders. A retired vice president from Goldman Sachs just showed up one day and started volunteering at the equity desk. Major investment brokerages like Merrill Lynch and J. P. Morgan Chase cut Sandler O'Neill in on their deals, just so the crippled company could earn a portion of the commission. And Sandler O'Neill needed every penny it could get its hands on: Dunne had paid out the full year's salary and benefits to the families of all the dead employees and had guaranteed year-end bonuses as well.

These powerhouse investment brokerages—ordinarily in a position to squash a tiny firm like Sandler O'Neill—suspended their rivalries to get another corporation and its devastated employees back in the game. They shared office space, information, workers, deals, and commissions

Two Faces of Corporate America Jimmy Dunne helped rebuild his brokerage firm after devastating losses on September 11; Bernie Madoff committed the largest financial fraud scheme in U.S. history.

with a competitor. They subverted their own bureaucratic rules and the imperatives of capitalist competition to help a struggling company survive. And it did: Sandler O'Neill was profitable again before the end of 2001 and had the necessary funds to continue supporting the families of its lost staff members. Granted, September 11 created extraordinary circumstances, and many people and organizations rose to the challenge of this national tragedy. But the case of Sandler O'Neill shows that corporate competitors can become collaborators and provide support. Corporate America is, after all, populated by human beings.

Unfortunately, negative stories about corporate America are not scarce, whether it concerns oil and energy firms, pharmaceutical companies, health insurance providers, or again, the world of high finance. Cases of corporate malfeasance continue to occur as they have throughout the history of capitalism. Some involve illegal activities, while others are characterized by unethical, if not criminal, behaviors. There can be devastating and deadly consequences when corporations privilege profit making above any costs or damage done to individuals, society, or the planet. The financial crisis that hit the country in 2007–2008 was precipitated in part by financial scandals involving major Wall Street players such as Lehman Brothers, Merrill Lynch, Morgan Stanley, and Goldman Sachs (some of the same investment firms that had demonstrated such admirable behavior toward Sandler O'Neill after 9/11). After a slew of financial deceptions, security frauds, bankruptcies, bank failures, bailouts, and mortgage foreclosures, the U.S. economy suffered a deep and lengthy recession whose effects have continued to be far reaching. Despite the economic toll on the country and criminal actions on the part of some cor-

> **GLOBALIZATION** the cultural and economic changes resulting from dramatically increased international trade and exchange in the late twentieth and early twenty-first centuries

porate officers, many of those top executives still escaped legal prosecution or paying for the widespread losses they caused.

Globalization, Economics, and Work

Globalization describes the cultural and economic changes that have occurred as a result of dramatically increased international trade and exchange in the late twentieth and early twenty-first centuries. Although there has always been some global economic trade—East Asia's ancient spice and silk trade routes and the sixteenth-century English and Dutch shipping empires are early examples of this—the effects of globalization have become more highly visible since the 1970s. Globalization has been fostered through the development of international economic institutions; innovations in technology; the movement of money, information, and people; and infrastructure that supports such expansion. Today, it is possible to view the world as having one global economy, with huge corporations whose production processes span national borders, international regulatory bodies such as the World Trade Organization (WTO), financial bodies such as the International Monetary Fund (IMF), and transnational trade agreements such as the North American Free Trade Agreement (NAFTA) redefining economic relationships between and among nations.

Supporters of globalization believe that "free trade" can lead to more efficient allocation of resources, lower prices, more employment, and higher output, with all countries involved in the trade benefiting. Critics believe that free trade promotes a self-interested corporate agenda and that powerful and autonomous multinational corporations can exploit workers and increasingly shape the politics of nation-states. And the recent global recession, marked by financial crises in the United States, Europe, and China, shows us that all world economies are connected, for better or for worse.

International Trade: Shallow and Deep Integration

To explain economic globalization, social scientists have used the terms "shallow integration" and "deep integration" (Dicken 1998). Shallow integration refers to the flow of goods and services that characterized international trade until several decades ago. In a shallow integration model, a national company would arrange with a foreign company to either import or export products exclusively within that single nation's economy. For example, thirty years ago, a Japanese car would have been made almost entirely in Japan, and a pair of American jeans would have been made in the United States. Thus, Japan would export cars to the United States, which would import Japanese cars. And the United States would export jeans to Japan, which would import American jeans. To protect their interests, nations would impose taxes on imports, sometimes making those imports more expensive to buy than similar products made at home.

Deep integration refers to the global flow of goods and services in today's economy. While companies still make arrangements with other companies for imports and exports, their relationships are far more complex. Most significantly, companies are no longer national; they are multinational, with major decision-making, production, and/or distribution branches of a particular company spread all over the world. When we look at the labels on our clothing, the global nature of their origin is often concealed. The label may say "Made in . . . ," but the raw materials or other parts may have originated somewhere else.

When nations make laws to protect national economic interests, they must often do so with a host of other nations in mind. NAFTA is an excellent example of this complex web of global relationships. Many major apparel companies, such as Nike or the Gap, have marketing and design headquarters in the United States, but many of their garment factories are in Mexico, another country in NAFTA. Under NAFTA, American companies can avoid paying taxes when they export raw materials to Mexico and then import the finished products. These global trade agreements often benefit private industry much more than they do nations.

Transnational Corporations

Transnational corporations (TNCs) are another part of the global economy. These firms purposefully transcend national borders so that their products can be manufactured, distributed, marketed, and sold from many bases all over the world. We may think of companies like Coca-Cola or General Electric as quintessentially American, but they are more accurately understood as global or transnational corpora-

tions. What is distinctive about today's TNCs is the way they shape the global economy. In the past fifty years, they have experienced unprecedented growth in both numbers of firms and amount of economic impact.

The United Nations' 2011 list of "The World's Top 100 Non-Financial TNCs" assigns firms a "transnationality index" by assessing the ratios between foreign employment and total employment, foreign investments and total investments, and foreign sales and total sales (UNCTAD 2012). Among the top twenty "transnational" firms are four U.S. firms: General Electric (1), ExxonMobil (4), Chevron (11), and Anheuser-Busch (18). More than 50 percent of the workforce is foreign at General Electric, ExxonMobil, and Chevron, while almost 90 percent of Anheuser-Busch employees work outside the United States. All of these firms make products that are marketed strongly as "American" brands, yet they are clearly global institutions.

> **SWEATSHOP** a workplace where workers are subject to extreme exploitation, including below-standard wages, long hours, and poor working conditions that may pose health or safety hazards

Table 11.1 shows how much economic influence TNCs exert in the global economy. Among the top forty global economies, ranked by either Gross Domestic Product (GDP) or total sales, there are eight TNCs (noted in bold). Firms such as Wal-Mart and Royal Dutch Shell actually rank higher than the nations of Thailand, Denmark, and Colombia. As corporations grow new TNCs have been added to the list. When we consider that firms have the economic weight of nations, we can understand just how much political clout TNCs wield in terms of global governance. For instance, an American TNC can exercise powerful influence by donating huge amounts of money to lobbyists and political campaigns. Further, in international regulatory bodies, such as the WTO, TNCs are often able to influence trade law at a global level.

Another manifestation of the ever-increasing economic power of TNCs is competition in the global market. Because TNCs can take advantage of cheap pools of labor by either relocating their own factories or outsourcing the work, nations compete with each other for these contracts by undercutting their citizens' wages and offering incentives, such as tax-free zones. Scholars, politicians, activists, and commentators have called this the "race to the bottom." These kinds of policies hurt the local populations, often depriving workers of decent wages and the potential benefits, such as schools and hospitals, that would have been derived from taxes.

Global Sweatshop Labor

One way the race to the bottom hurts workers in their own countries is by creating an environment where sweatshop labor can exist. A **sweatshop** is a workplace where workers are subjected to extreme exploitation, including below-standard wages, long hours, and poor working conditions that may pose

Table 11.1 Ranking the World Economies

Rank 2011	Company/Country	GDP/Revenues (billions)	Rank 2011	Company/Country	GDP/Revenues (billions)
1	United States	14,991	21	Sweden	539
2	China	7,318	22	Poland	514
3	Japan	5,867	23	Belgium	513
4	Germany	3,600	24	Norway	485
5	France	2,773	25	Argentina	446
6	Brazil	2,476	**26**	**Wal-Mart Stores**	**421**
7	United Kingdom	2,445	27	Austria	417
8	Italy	2,193	28	South Africa	408
9	Russian Federation	1,857	**29**	**Royal Dutch Shell**	**378**
10	India	1,847	30	United Arab Emirates	360
11	Canada	1,736	**31**	**ExxonMobil**	**354**
12	Spain	1,476	32	Thailand	345
13	Australia	1,379	33	Denmark	333
14	Mexico	1,153	34	Colombia	333
15	Korea, Rep.	1,116	35	Venezula, RB	316
16	Indonesia	846	**36**	**BP**	308
17	Netherlands	836	**37**	**Sinopec Group**	273
18	Turkey	774	**38**	**China National Petroleum**	240
19	Switzerland	659	**39**	**State Grid**	226
20	Saudi Arabia	576	**40**	**Toyota Motor**	221

SOURCES: CNN Money 2011; World Bank 2011.

health or safety hazards. Sweatshop workers are often intimidated with threats of physical discipline and are prevented from forming unions or other workers' rights groups. Historically, sweatshops originated during the Industrial Revolution as a system where middlemen earned profits from the difference between what they received for delivering on a contract and the amount they paid to the workers who produced the contracted goods. The profit was said to be "sweated" from the workers, because they received minimal wages and worked excessive hours under unsanitary and dangerous conditions.

Sweatshops, however, are not a thing of the past. Unfortunately, there are many in the world today making large numbers of the goods that we unknowingly consume. Though perhaps more prevalent overseas, sweatshops exist in the United States as well. The General Accounting Office (GAO) defines a sweatshop as "an employer that violates more than one federal or state labor law governing minimum wage and overtime, child labor, industrial homework, occupational safety and health, workers compensation, or industrial regulation" (Ross 1997, p. 12). The Department of Labor estimated

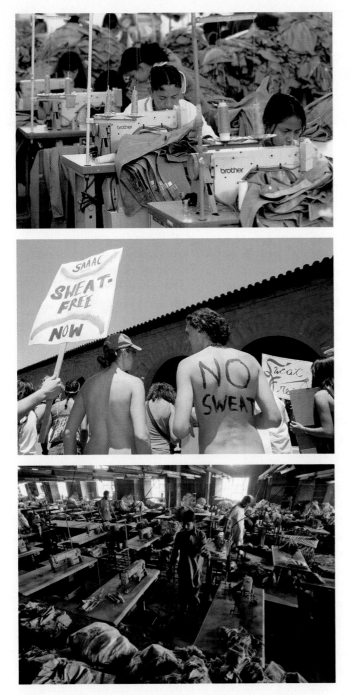

and clothing lines associated with Mary-Kate and Ashley Olsen and Sean "Diddy" Combs have all been charged with using sweatshop labor in Southeast Asia, Central America, and elsewhere and have been pressured to reform their practices. Factory fires in 2012 killed 289 garment workers in Pakistan and 117 in Bangladesh, and in April 2013, over 1,000 garment workers in Bangladesh were killed when their factory building collapsed. In the first two cases, workers were trapped in buildings without proper emergency exits, where clothing was made for American companies such as Wal-Mart, J. C. Penney, and Kohl's (Ahmed 2012). In the last case, the deadliest garment-industry accident in history, the building was made of shoddy materials and built on unstable ground, thus it could not withstand the vibrations of machinery within (Associated Press 2013).

Many universities have also been in the practice of purchasing their logo apparel from clothing manufacturers that use sweatshop labor. In 1999, students at the University of Michigan, University of North Carolina, University of Wisconsin, Madison, Duke University, and Georgetown University staged sit-ins to pressure their respective administrators into agreeing to fully disclose factory conditions and wages paid to workers who produce university apparel (Greenhouse 1999). Other similar campaigns were launched at Seattle Community College in 2004 and systemwide at the University of California in 2005 to change university purchasing policy to allow for preferences for union-made and verifiably sweatshop-free products. More than 170 colleges and universities have pledged to uphold the Fair Labor Association workplace code of conduct when it comes to choosing manufacturers for their apparel. We encourage you to do your own research on whether sweatshop products have reached the student store on your campus or wherever you shop for clothing—and whether such items are in your own closet already.

The Real Cost of Sweatshop Clothes At top, factory workers sew at *moquilos*, or sweatshops, such as this one in Guatemala City, Guatemala, while students at Stanford University wage protests to ensure that school apparel is made in factories where workers are paid a living wage. At bottom, a burnt-out sweatshop in Karachi, Pakistan, after a fire killed 289 garment workers in a building with no fire escapes.

DATA WORKSHOP
Analyzing Everyday Life

Are Your Clothes Part of the Global Commodity Chain?

You probably own and consume a large number of products that originated in faraway countries, including your car, clothing, or shoes. These items have traveled widely during

that in 2001 there were more than 7,000 sweatshops in U.S. cities such as New York, Los Angeles, New Orleans, Chicago, Philadelphia, and El Paso. It might be shocking to imagine that such abuse and exploitation of workers still occur in the United States. American companies may also manufacture goods overseas using foreign sweatshop labor. Nike, the Gap,

GLOBAL PERSPECTIVE

Sweatshop Labor and "Gold Farming" in China

Many people are familiar with the concept of sweatshops, where cheap labor is exploited to make clothing and goods for people in industrialized nations. While individuals are able to understand easily how labor can be exploited for the production of material goods, a more difficult concept to grasp is how labor can be exploited in the market for virtual goods. Rather than working long hours under inhuman conditions for little pay in order to produce luxury items such as Nikes and Levi's, "gold farmers" are exploited in order to create the ultimate luxury product—status in an online computer game.

Some of the most popular forms of video games are Massively Multiplayer Online Role Playing Games (MMORPGs) such as *World of Warcraft* (*WoW*), *Ultima Online*, and *Everquest*. *WoW* is the most popular of these games, with approximately 10 million subscribers as of 2012. As with many MMORPGs, players make an initial investment to purchase the software for the game, and they are also charged a monthly subscription fee in order to play. In *WoW*, players use a character avatar through which they explore the virtual world, complete quests, and interact with other players or nonplayer characters (NPCs). Quests are assignments given by an NPC (who is programmed into the game) that usually involve killing a monster, gathering resources, transporting an item from one location to another, or finding a difficult-to-locate object. Successful quests are rewarded with in-game money and experience points that a character can spend to buy new skills and equipment. As with most MMORPGs, there is an emphasis on character improvement. Because of the interactive nature of *WoW*, advancing in the game isn't just a matter of personal achievement but also a matter of reputation and status in the community.

"Gold farms" profit from the importance of advancement in an MMORPG. According to estimates, around 100,000 people in China are employed as "gold farmers," making $120 to $250 (U.S.) per month playing *WoW* for twelve- to eighteen-hour shifts (Vincent 2011). These Chinese gold farmers carry out in-game actions so that they can earn virtual money to buy equipment, skills, and status. These virtual assets are sold to real (recreational) players for real world money, creating a unique intersection of virtual and real world economies. Literally, a player can spend real world money to buy status and reputation in an online game. Since many of the beginning levels of *WoW* involve spending long hours doing repetitive and dull virtual tasks, the idea of being able to bypass this tedium to start at more advanced levels appeals to many players. Creating characters requires time and effort that players who use the services of gold farmers are unable or unwilling to devote to the game. So they buy the labor of gold farmers to advance their gaming strategies.

Many of the critiques of manufacturing sweatshops can be applied to the gold farming phenomenon. Gold farmers labor for the benefit of middle-class gamers in industrialized nations. Ge Jin, a Ph.D. student at the University of California—San Diego, has documented working conditions in the gold farming "sweatshops," where he filmed workers crowded into an airport hangar, bleary eyed, chain-smoking, and sleeping two to a single mat on the floor (Jin 2006). Are bad jobs better than no jobs? Certainly it is easier to live in most of modern society with money than without. Though most people in developed nations would view $3 a day as extremely low pay, in impoverished communities "$1 or $2 a day can be a life-transforming wage" (Kristof and WuDunn 2000). While there are those who argue that playing a computer game takes less of a physical toll than subsistence farming or factory work, it is evident that there is an imbalance between the amount of money that workers are paid to produce these virtual resources and the prices that gamers pay to buy them. The sum of $200 can buy 500 pieces of online gold in *WoW*, which would take an estimated 100 hours of playing to earn.

The gaming world is up in arms about the gold farming phenomenon. While some gamers find that the opportunity to buy gold augments their playing experience, other gamers hold that buying from gold farmers confers an unfair advantage to those with expendable income. Purists argue that MMORPGs should be free of the corruption of the real world and that escapism is not possible with people buying status and reputation in the virtual world. Players who use the services of gold farmers affect the virtual economy by driving up the prices of the rarest items. Traditional players then become resentful, as these price increases require them to work longer to acquire items that players with real world cash can purchase with little effort. On the other hand, does playing a game qualify as work? After all, it is "only a game."

Strategies for retaliation against players identified as gold farmers include verbal harassment inside the game. Rather than taking out their anger and frustrations on the gold farm brokers who benefit from the process, some traditional players will follow suspected gold farmers within the game and bombard them with racist comments. Gamers have put together racist videos to post on YouTube, venting their anger over the gold farming phenomenon. Gold farming then becomes a matter not just of class and economics, but also of race and racism.

Are gold farms good or bad? Are bad jobs better than no jobs at all? Should the virtual world be free of the corruption of the real world? Are gamers just too invested in their games? These are all questions to ask when pondering the intersections of the virtual world and real world that collide in the gold farming sweatshops.

Chinese Gold Farmers How has the popularity of online games such as *World of Warcraft* led to new types of sweatshops?

the process from production to consumption. Food, pharmaceuticals, and electronics are other examples of globally made products. Social scientists call such international movements of goods "global commodity chains" (Gereffi and Korzeniewicz 1994).

Global commodity chains are networks of corporations, product designers and engineers, manufacturing firms, distribution channels (such as ocean freightliners, railroads, and trucking firms), and consumer outlets (such as Wal-Mart). Global commodity chains start with a product design and brand name and end with the consumer making a purchase. But between start and finish is often a complex global process with many different people, in many different nations, all contributing to the final product.

The manufacturing of goods, from garments to electronics to automobiles, used to happen in the United States and other Western nations; today's manufacturing centers are primarily located in poorer nations, such as the Philippines, China, Indonesia, and many Latin American countries. American corporations such as Nike, the Gap, and Levi-Strauss have closed all their U.S. manufacturing plants and hired contractors and subcontractors from East Asia and Latin America to make their products at substantially lower prices. Now these companies focus large amounts of financial resources on "branding" their products (Klein 2000). Branding is the process, usually accomplished through advertising, by which companies gain consumers' attention and loyalty. Much of the money you pay for some products goes toward financing these branding campaigns, while a much smaller sum pays the workers who actually make the products.

OUTSOURCING "contracting out" or transferring to another country the labor that a company might otherwise have employed its own staff to perform; typically done for financial reasons

In this Data Workshop you will be using existing sources in your research and analysis (see Chapter 2 for a review of this method). The following three exercises will help you to understand where the things that you buy come from and the increasing disparity between product values and workers' wages.

Exercise One: The Global Closet

Pick out five to ten items of clothing from your closet. Now check the labels. Where were your clothes made? Make a list of the nations represented in your closet. How many nations are from East Asia or Latin America? Is there a difference between where an item is made and where it is assembled? Does the label indicate where the fabric originated?

Exercise Two: No Longer "Made in the U.S.A."

Ask your parents, aunts or uncles, or grandparents if you can look at the labels of their older clothes. Or go to a thrift store and look for older or vintage clothes there. Again pick out five to ten items of clothing. How many of those items were made

in the United States? Compare your answers in Exercise 1 and Exercise 2. What does this tell you about the globalization of the garment manufacturing industry over the past fifty years?

Exercise Three: Are Your Favorite Brands "Sweat Free"?

List your favorite brands of clothing, shoes, or other fashion accessories. What is your brand's stance on sweatshop labor? Do workers who make your favorite products earn a living wage? You can check many corporations' ethics regarding labor conditions by doing some research on the internet. See how your brands score at the following web sites:

* Institute for Global Labour and Human Rights: www.globallabourrights.org

* The Worker Rights Consortium: www.workersrights.org

* CorpWatch: www.corpwatch.org

* Global Exchange: www.globalexchange.org

* Interfaith Center on Corporate Responsibility: www.iccr.org

There are two options for completing this Data Workshop.

Option 1 (informal): Choose one of the exercises above and follow the instructions as outlined. Bring notes to class to discuss with others in small groups. Your instructor may organize groups so that all members have done the same exercise or all members have done a different exercise. In either case, compare your findings with those of other members of the group.

Option 2 (formal): Choose one or more of the exercises above (or your instructor may assign specific exercises) and follow the instructions as outlined. Write a three- to four-page essay analyzing your findings.

Outsourcing

The U.S. economy is increasingly affected by globalization, and as a result, American companies have sought out new business models to reduce costs and remain competitive. One increasingly popular approach is outsourcing or offshoring. **Outsourcing** involves "contracting out" or transferring to another country the labor that a company might otherwise have employed its own staff to perform. Typically, a company's decision to outsource is made for financial reasons and is usually achieved by transferring employment to locations where the cost of labor is much cheaper. In the 1990s, when this trend was just beginning, U.S. firms employed 7 million workers in other countries (O'Reilly

1992); but with technological advances, over the past couple of decades, more businesses have been able to increase their foreign employment pools significantly. Foreign employment by U.S. multinational companies grew to 11 million workers in 2010 (U.S. Department of Commerce 2012).

The economic benefits of outsourcing are gained by businesses, but the drawbacks are felt by the people who make up the American labor pool. Figures vary regarding the number of jobs that have been lost as the practice of outsourcing has continued to grow. While offshoring is practiced by numerous U.S. businesses, they are often reluctant to fully disclose details. Companies like General Electric, Caterpillar, Microsoft, and Wal-Mart employ close to one fifth of all American workers. Yet during the 2000s, companies like these shrank their domestic workforces by 2.9 million while increasing their rosters of foreign employees by 2.4 million (U.S. Department of Commerce 2012). There are a variety of different kinds of jobs that are suitable for outsourcing. Manufacturing jobs were some of the first to go, but an increasing number of service jobs have followed in the last couple of decades. Among these are office and clerical staff, purchasing, finance, and human resources workers.

Offshoring is also happening in other service areas requiring highly skilled workers. Jobs in information technology–producing industries, such as data entry, communication services, communication equipment, and computer hardware, software, and services, are some of the main jobs involved in outsourcing. In a recent five-year period, Oracle, a business hardware and software giant, hired twice as many workers abroad as in the United States (Wessel 2011). Over the last decade, Cisco Systems, another tech firm, increased its portion of foreign workers from 26 percent to 46 percent of all company employees. Although countries in Southeast Asia, such as the Philippines, and those in Eastern Europe are key sites for information technology offshoring, India has become the primary location for this practice because of the shared English language and cheap employment. It makes sense to employ workers abroad if, for instance, a company can hire a computer engineer in India for $10,000 a year compared with one who does the same work but costs $60,000 to $90,000 in the United States. By 2011, information technology export revenue from the United States to India had grown into a $59 billion business (Frauenheim 2012). More recently, China has become the second largest outsourcing provider to the United States, with service contracts totaling $23 billion in 2011 (Zheng 2012).

When we think about outsourcing, we may picture a foreign worker assembling an American model automobile, or we may remember the foreign accent of someone we spoke with at a help desk or call center who provided us with tech support or customer service. Although outsourcing is still most common in areas such as manufacturing and informa-

A Surrogate Baby Boom India has become a key site for outsourcing the womb. Young women serve as surrogates for infertile American couples who wish to have their own biological children at a fraction of the cost of an American surrogate.

tion services, it has spread into new and what might seem like far less likely types of employment.

Sociologist France Winddance Twine (2011a) has researched the growing trend in outsourcing the womb. For the past several decades, infertile couples who wish to have biological children have been hiring women to serve as surrogates who are impregnated in-vitro with the egg and sperm of a couple who are unable to conceive on their own. Although this practice is legal in the United States, it has been outlawed in other Western countries. In recent years, there has been a surrogate baby boom in places such as India. Outsourcing has occurred in this market for the same reasons as in other industries; there is an available workforce overseas where the costs are much cheaper than in the United States. There are a burgeoning number of agencies in India that specialize in surrogacy. Prospective American parents who use these services can more easily fulfill their desire for a biological baby and at a fifth of what it would cost at home. The arrangement also benefits the surrogate in India who might earn as much in nine months carrying a baby to term as she would for ten years of labor as a maid. While there are concerns about this practice and the exploitation of young, poor women in places like India, it is also an opportunity for them to afford a home for their families, something that would otherwise be out of reach. If we can now outsource pregnancy, what other jobs might be next?

Alternative Ways of Working

There are alternative ways of working, not all of which fit into typical categories of work. First we look at professional socialization, the process by which new members learn and internalize the norms and values of their group, examining case studies of workers in three unusual fields. Then we examine the contingent workforce—those who work in positions that are temporary or freelance or who work as independent contractors. Finally, there are the nonprofit corporations—private organizations whose missions go beyond the bottom line—and volunteerism, the work of people who seek no compensation for their investment of time and energy.

Professional Socialization in Unusual Fields

Every new job requires some sort of training for the prospective employee. Anyone in a new position confronts an unfamiliar set of expectations and workplace norms that must be learned so the new person can fit into the environment. This process, called professional socialization, involves learning not only the social role but also the various details about how to do the job. Several sociological studies have explored the process of professional socialization focusing on medical students (Fox 1957; Becker et al. 1961; Haas and Shaffir 1977, 1982), teachers (Lortie 1968), clergy (Kleinman 1984), nurses (Stimson 1967), social workers (Loseke and Cahill 1986), and lawyers (Granfield 1992).

Spencer Cahill's study of students preparing to become funeral directors focused on the practical skills developed by mortuary science students and the "emotional labor" (see Hochschild 1983) involved in this occupation. Most social interaction within the mortuary science program revolved around death; as a result, students learned how to engage in the practice of "normalizing talk." "Mortuary science education requires students to adopt an occupational rhetoric and esoteric language that communicate professional authority and a calm composure towards matters that most of the lay public finds emotionally upsetting" (Cahill 1999, p. 106). In addition, students were required to control their own emotional responses to the work. "Some students told me that they found 'cases' of young children emotionally disturbing.... Yet, these students reportedly did 'get used to it,' 'keep it down,' and deal with emotionally distressing 'cases'" (Cahill 1999, pp. 108–109). Cahill found that successful mortuary science students were those who could best deal with the emotional component of the work.

Loren Bourassa and Blake Ashforth studied how inexperienced newcomers are socialized into the work life onboard an Alaskan fishing boat. The occupation of a fisherman differs greatly from other occupations because it requires no previous experience or even a high school education, as physical strength and stamina are the primary prerequisites. Work on a fishing boat pays well for a relatively short amount of time, and this often lures a large number of workers. However, their romantic notions about life on a fishing boat are quickly dispelled. "New workers were indoctrinated collectively by their more experienced co-workers and underwent a process of divestiture.... Specifically, newcomers were called 'new guys,' rather than by name, were subjected to constant taunts and verbal abuse, were constantly made to perform the least desirable jobs and other odd tasks, were required to obey incessant and often arbitrary instructions, and were routinely denied the privileges given to more experienced members" (Bourassa and Ashforth 1998, p. 181). This intense socialization proved effective as newcomers worked hard and came to understand the culture of the fishing boat workplace. "It became a badge of honor to survive the initiation phase" (Bourassa and Ashforth 1998, p. 189). Yet, the fleeting moment of self-satisfaction and positive feelings gave way to the continuous physical demands. Even the promise of economic rewards failed to sustain them. "The money was generally held in bank accounts until the completion of a contract. Workers could not use their money or even hold their paycheck in their hands. Thus, onboard the ship, money remained an abstract and distant notion" (Bourassa and Ashforth 1998, p. 189).

Jacqueline Lewis examined the socialization of exotic dancers and what goes into learning their job. "For exotic dancers, achieving job competence involves getting accustomed to working in a sex-related occupation and the practice of taking their clothes off in public for money" (Lewis 1998, p. 1). On-the-job socialization was essential for the women who entered this line of work. "Similar to the socialization experiences of individuals in other occupations, novice dancers learn through interaction and observation while on the job.... Since there is no formal certification structure, peers play an important role in this transformation process" (Lewis 1998, p. 5). Lewis found that several women felt the socialization process "inadequately prepared them for some of the realities of the life of an exotic dancer" (Lewis 1998, p. 12)—mainly the negative impact it would have on their private lives and the difficulties of having long-term heterosexual relationships with men outside the industry.

The Contingent Workforce: Temps, Freelancers, and Independent Contractors

Traditionally, most Americans have hoped to find a job they would keep their whole lives, one that would provide forty-hour work weeks along with vacations and health and retirement benefits. Increasingly, this sort of job is becoming rare. A growing percentage of Americans have less steady work arrangements that could be defined as work that does not involve explicit or implicit contracts for long-term employment. These workers are referred to as the contingent workforce. It is made up of four categories: independent contractors, on-call workers, temporary help agency workers, and contract company workers—sometimes called "temps" or "freelancers." During the past couple of decades, contingent work has become an alternative to long-term, full-time employment and has grown three times faster than traditional jobs. If we count the self-employed in this group, the total contingent workforce in 2012 numbered almost 44 million or 31 percent of all workers. The U.S. Department of Labor projects that by 2020 there will be almost 65 million contingent workers constituting approximately 40 percent of the total workforce (U.S. Bureau of Labor Statistics 2012a).

Many see this situation as a potential disaster, as inferior jobs are created by corporations seeking to slash overhead, especially those costs associated with health benefits, which are almost never available to contingent workers. Employers have a number of financial and legal responsibilities to their regular workers—overtime pay, health insurance, Social Security, disability, and workers' compensation benefits—that don't apply to temps or independent contractors. Many fear businesses will increasingly turn to alternative employment arrangements solely to cut costs to the distinct disadvantage of their employees.

The case histories of two giant firms show the potential for the exploitation of contingent workers. Sometimes, businesses will classify workers as "independent contractors" even though they do the same work in the same place as regular workers. In an infamous example in the late 1990s, Microsoft was forced to pay $97 million to settle a lawsuit alleging it had wrongly classified a group of employees as independent contractors, making them ineligible for benefits. These workers had been hired as freelancers to work on specific projects, but "the workers were fully integrated into Microsoft's workforce, working under nearly identical circumstances as Microsoft's regular employees . . . the same core hours at the same location and the same supervisors as regular employees" (Muhl 2002).

A different, though equally exploitative, tactic was used by the contractors hired to clean Wal-Mart stores. In 2003, federal agents arrested 245 undocumented workers in sixty different Wal-Mart stores around the country. The workers came from eighteen nations, but very few of them actually worked for Wal-Mart. Instead, they were employed by independent contractors hired by Wal-Mart to do its nightly cleaning (Bartels 2003). Although companies are not responsible for the actions of subcontractors they hire, they can be held responsible if it is proven they knew something illegal was going on. This is especially important when the jobs offered to the illegal aliens are abusive. When contractors hire employees who work seven days a week and receive no overtime pay or benefits, then those contractors are in violation of overtime, Social Security, and workers' compensation laws. Furthermore, it is much harder for legitimate contractors to win bids for contracts when their competition can offer lower prices by illegally underpaying their workers.

It is not surprising to discover a lack of job satisfaction among temporary workers, mainly clerical and manufacturing workers, and on-call workers, like construction workers, nurses, substitute teachers, and truck drivers (Dickson and Lorenz 2009). Many temporary workers hope they will be able to use their temp job as a springboard to a permanent one, but often this does not happen. However, the flexibility and freedom of alternative work arrangements appeal to a substantial number of workers, such as students, parents with children at home, and retirees. Though the increase in nontraditional employment has many potential negative effects, there is a great deal of diversity in the characteristics of contingent workers, some of whom may experience more or less satisfaction with their work arrangements. While there is clearly a downside to being a temp or independent contractor, research indicates that there can also be great satisfaction among these freelance workers. Of the four categories tracked by the Bureau of Labor Statistics, independent contractors make up the largest group—almost two-thirds of the total. In contrast to the traditional worker, the occupational profile of the independent contractor is skewed toward several high-skilled fields, including writers and artists, insurance and real estate agents, construction trade employees, and other technical and computer-related professions. They tend to be better paid than the average worker and prefer their employment situation for the flexibility and freedom it offers (Cohany 1996). However, even in this category, a significant minority, especially women, make less money and are less satisfied with their situation. Some also suffer from alienation, disenchantment, and burnout.

The Third Sector and Volunteerism

Not all corporations seek a profit, nor do all workers get paid a wage for their labor. Numerous organizations engage in social welfare, social justice, and/or environmental services. Typically, these are churches, schools, hospitals, philanthropic foundations, art institutions, scientific research centers, and a multitude of other organizations, both permanent and temporary. They are private, rather than government, organizations and devoted to serving the general welfare, not their own financial interests. They are nonprofit organizations, designed to run as cost-effectively as possible and to direct any gains or earnings, above basic operating expenses, back into the causes they support. Together, these organizations and the workers who staff them constitute what social

ON THE JOB

Internships and Experiential Learning

Someone mentions an internship, and you think . . . what? Bored college students making coffee for the boss? Good-looking medical students on *Grey's Anatomy*? Monica Lewinsky? In fact, internships are an increasingly important part of the college experience. According to Ross Perlin (2011), author of *Intern Nation*, more than half of the graduating seniors of 2008 had participated in some sort of experiential learning program during their college careers. At worst, the hapless intern may get really good at adding toner to the copier and not much else; at best, an internship can benefit both the intern and the company and may be useful in the long run for everyone involved.

Although some internships come with some compensation, others are unpaid; in either case, you gain valuable work experience. You may arrange an academic internship through your college or university and receive academic credit, or you may set up a nonacademic internship that leaves out the school altogether. Firms of all kinds look for college students to fill some of their employment needs. Of course, there's always the possibility that the work you're assigned as an intern will be mind numbing or pointless, so why bother with an internship?

First and most important, an internship may help you decide what you want to be—or don't want to be—when you graduate. After interning in a state's attorney's office, you may decide that being a lawyer isn't everything you thought it would be but that you would like to work with crime victims in a social service capacity. Even if you are sure about your future career path, you may want to consider branching out in the internships you apply for. You'll gain diverse skills and experience and be exposed to careers you might like just as much. Most Americans don't remain in the same job for their entire working lives, so keeping your options open during college doesn't seem like such a bad idea.

An internship on your résumé is also likely to make you an attractive job candidate. Even if your experience doesn't deal directly with the job you're applying for, having completed an internship demonstrates to potential employers your ability to work hard and manage your time. According to the results from a 2012 survey by the National Association of Colleges and Employers, approximately 60 percent of students who worked in paid internships during college received at least one job offer (NACE 2012). In addition, many corporations turn first to their own interns when hiring. The entire internship can, in some respects, be viewed as an extended job interview.

There will always be competition for the most prestigious positions, though interning for a big name company doesn't necessarily guarantee a good experience. But even if you decide you'd prefer not to work for that corporation or in that field, the contacts you develop may help you find another position. These are people who are already established in the profession, and a good reference is always valuable when you're in the job market.

Internships work out well for employers too. At the very least, they're getting cheap (and often free) labor, but more than that, interns can be very beneficial for companies that need a highly educated or highly trained workforce. Taking on young workers can also help a company stay connected to younger consumers and may provide them with some new perspectives and ideas. Corporations also realize that providing internships can create goodwill—from the students who intern with them, from the universities through which the internships are organized, or from the general public.

INDEPENDENT (OR THIRD) SECTOR the part of the economy composed of nonprofit organizations; their workers are mission driven, rather than profit driven, and such organizations direct surplus funds to the causes they support

scientists call the **Independent (or Third) Sector** of the economy.

The Third Sector represents one of the most distinctive and commendable features of our society. In 2011, more than 1.6 million nonprofit organizations were registered with the U.S. Treasury Department and accorded tax privileges (Independent Sector 2012). The Third Sector helps society in a number of ways. First, these organizations play a significant part in the American system of pluralism, operating alongside the first two sectors of government and business while helping to strengthen and make them work better. Although we think of nonprofits, business, and government as separate, they are really interconnected through their impact on public policy. Second, nonprofit organizations deliver a wide range of vital services to millions of people in almost every social category. Last, they are a humanizing force in American society, allowing an important avenue of expression for altruism.

Table 11.2 Theory in Everyday Life

Perspective	Approach to Work and the Economy	Case Study: Outsourcing of Work
Functionalism	Different types of work (high prestige and pay to low prestige and pay) are necessary to the economy and have functions that help maintain social order.	Outsourcing is necessary to keep both national and global economies stable in the current market.
Conflict Theory	A stratified labor market creates intergroup conflict—wealthier capitalists may exploit less-powerful workers.	Outsourcing exploits poor and developing nations and laid-off local workers, all while enriching corporations.
Symbolic Interactionism	Work is central to our self-concept—we are intensely identified with our work, both by ourselves and by others.	Workers whose jobs are outsourced may come to see themselves as worthless and expendable because it seems that others see them that way too.

While most nonprofits have some paid employees, they also rely on volunteers to deliver their services to the public. Volunteerism reflects a profound and important American value, that citizens in a democracy have a personal responsibility to serve those in need. The U.S. Bureau of Labor Statistics (2012e) reported that in 2011, an estimated 64.3 million Americans, or more than 26 percent of the total population, engaged in some form of volunteer work. Volunteers each spent a median of fifty-one hours on volunteer activities during the given year. Women tend to volunteer in larger numbers, such that more than 29 percent of all U.S. women and 23 percent of men volunteered in 2011. Volunteers are represented fairly evenly from all age groups, though persons thirty-five to forty-four years old were the most likely to volunteer. Volunteer rates were lowest among those in their early twenties. Volunteers come from every socioeconomic level, but members of the middle and upper-middle classes are most likely to volunteer, as are those with a higher level of educational attainment. All races and ethnicities are represented as well. The estimated total value of donated hours in 2011 was more than $171 billion (Corporation for National & Community Service 2012).

People do volunteer work for many reasons—for social justice, social change, religious values, work experience, and participation in clubs and social groups, and even out of boredom. Not only does volunteering satisfy our most altruistic ideals; it can also be a way to enhance our careers, strengthen our relationships with others, and even let us live out fantasies or dreams that are not part of our normal, everyday lives. And in so doing, volunteers help create a different world for themselves and others. There are many ways of working—some conventional, some alternative. Not all workers have jobs in traditional fields; not all workers have permanent or full-time jobs; and not all workers do it for a paycheck.

CLOSING COMMENTS

You may never have imagined that work was such a big part of life. You might have had a job of some kind, but now you probably have a better idea of just how important work is on both a collective and an individual level. It is so important that sociologists have devoted much of their work to studying work. We can be fairly certain that work will remain a major reality in the human experience into the distant future. We hope that you have gained some insight into the structure and meaning of work in your own lives and the lives of others in society.

Everything You Need to Know about
the Economy and Work

> " Work is a fulcrum point between the micro and the macro and a link between the individual and the social."

THEORIES OF THE ECONOMY AND WORK

* **Structural functionalism:** different types of work, even ones with low prestige and pay, are necessary to the economy and help maintain social order

* **Conflict theory:** a stratified labor market creates intergroup conflict in which wealthier capitalists may exploit less-powerful workers

* **Symbolic interactionism:** we are intensely identified with our work, both by ourselves and others

REVIEW

1. Think about the jobs you would like to get after you finish college. Do any of them involve directly participating in the production of physical goods?

2. Thinking of the United States as a capitalist nation with some socialist elements, are there any ways you directly benefit from government intervention in the economy?

3. Marx described four ways that modern wage labor is alienating. Do you think these apply to you and to the job you have or would like to have? If you have a job, would you choose to keep it even if you became independently wealthy?

Who Works at Minimum Wage?

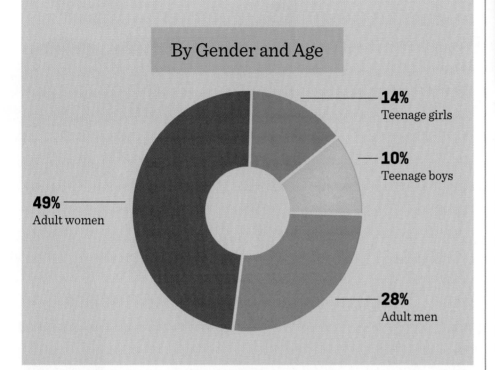

By Gender and Age

14%
Teenage girls

10%
Teenage boys

49%
Adult women

28%
Adult men

By Education

7%
Bachelors degree or higher

34%
Some college or associate degree

28%
Less than high school

31%
High school graduate

SOURCE: Kurtz 2013

EXPLORE

In Defense of Face Time

In the age of digital communication, why bother to meet with someone face-to-face? Meetings allow us to see expressions and hear tones—important social cues to someone's feelings and intent. Visit the Everyday Sociology Blog to read more about a sociology professor's thoughts on the benefits of meeting with students in person.

http://wwnPag.es/trw411

CHAPTER 12

Life at Home: Families and Relationships

Tom, a single doctor in his sixties, lived in the same home for thirty years with three much-loved dogs: two boxers named Blaze and Pepe, and a Boston terrier named Brownie. They were his devoted companions. When one of the dogs died, Tom would get a new dog of the same breed and keep the dog's name. Thus, if Blaze died, the new boxer would be named Blaze; if Brownie died, the new Boston terrier would also be Brownie. Tom's relationship with his dogs went on for thirty years. Are Tom and the dogs a family?

Stacie and Eric met in graduate school and married the year they received their degrees. Their job hunts, however, led them in different directions: Stacie took a job with an international policy agency in Washington, D.C., and Eric went to work for a major corporation in

Miami, Florida. Living in their respective cities, they spent lots of time Skyping and lots of money on weekend plane tickets. After about five years, Stacie became pregnant, and the baby is due in a few months. Are Stacie and Eric a family?

Jeannie and Elena also met in graduate school—almost twenty years ago. They are both professors in Minneapolis, Kansas, and together they bought and fixed up an old house. They would like to formalize their commitment to one another, but they cannot do so legally because Kansas does not allow same-sex partners to marry. Nevertheless, they've adopted a little boy named Conor and are looking forward to celebrating his first Christmas. Are Jeannie, Elena, and Conor a family?

For some of you, the answers may come easily, but others of you may find yourself wondering—are these groups really families? Tom loves Brownie, Blaze, and Pepe, but can you really be a family if most of your members aren't human? And is Tom's replacement policy similar to or different from the practice of remarrying when a spouse dies? What about Stacie and Eric—they're married and are having a biological child, which seems to make them easily definable as a family. Yet they don't live under the same roof or even in the same state. What does that make them? Even Tom and the dogs live together. And so do Jeannie and Elena; they can own property together and designate each other as heirs in their wills—though they can't legally marry. They're raising their son Conor together, even though Elena had to adopt Conor on her own first, and then Jeannie legally became his second parent later, since they could not adopt together like a married heterosexual couple can. Do these complications mean that they aren't a real family?

It all depends on how you define family. If emotional bonds and mutual support are the only criteria, then all of these groups are families. But if a marital bond is required, then only Stacie and Eric are a family. If other legal ties are included, then Elena, Jeannie, and Conor can be a family too. If you have to be heterosexual, then Jeannie and Elena are out, and we really don't know about Tom, do we? If the longevity of the relationships is the key, then Tom and the dogs win over both of these other potential families. But if you have to be human and irreplaceable, then all those Brownies, Blazes, and Pepes don't qualify. And if a shared residence must be part of the equation, then Tom and the dogs are in but Stacie and Eric are out. So how do you define family?

HOW TO READ THIS CHAPTER

In this chapter, we examine society's most basic social group—the family. Yet, what makes a family is subject to debate. Sociology doesn't define a family by who its members are but by what they do, how they relate to one another, and what their relationship is to the larger society. We'll look at the dynamic diversity of family forms in the contemporary United States, the functions of family for society, the hierarchies of inequality that shape family life, the work that gets done by and in families, the kinds of troubles families experience, and the political and cultural controversies that affect family life. You will learn that when it comes to family life, change is the only constant.

What Is the Family?

The U.S. Census Bureau defines family as two or more individuals related by blood, marriage, or adoption living in the same household. This definition is a good starting point, but it's too limited to encompass even the family arrangements described in the opening vignette. Contemporary sociologists use the word **family** to mean a social group whose members are bound by some type of tie—legal, biological, emotional, or a combination of all three. They may or may not share a household, but family members are interdependent and have a sense of mutual responsibility for one another's care. We don't define family by specific types of people (parents or children) or specific types of ties (marriage) because we believe the definition should be broad enough to encompass a variety of forms. However, this very variety is the source of controversy both within and outside academia. Regardless of the definition, most people recognize family as an integral social institution found in every society.

The family as an institution has always changed in response to its social, cultural, political, and economic milieu. Before the Industrial Revolution, "family" tended to mean **extended family**—a large group of **kin**, or relatives, which could include grandparents, uncles, aunts, and cousins living in one household. After the Industrial Revolution, this configuration was largely superseded by the **nuclear family**—a heterosexual couple in their own household raising children. Along the way, the family moved from a more public social institution to a private one, as many functions formerly associated with the family were transferred to other institutions. For example, work and production moved from the family to the factory, education moved from the family to the school, and government took over a variety of social welfare and services formerly taken care of by the extended family.

Subsequent waves of social change, such as the women's liberation movement and the move toward individual independence and self-fulfillment, have begun to erode the dominance of the married, heterosexual nuclear family, as increased divorce rates, working mothers, single parents, gay and lesbian families, and other alternative family arrangements become more common. Many sociologists speak of the sociology not of *the* family but rather of *families*. "Family situations in contemporary society are so varied and diverse that it simply makes no sociological sense to speak of a single ideal-type model of 'the family' at all" (Bernardes 1985, p. 209).

Even though a two-heterosexual-parent household with a stay-at-home mother is no longer the norm, this type of family remains the model by which new forms of family are judged. However, there are exceptions, as commonsense definitions of family reflect the changes occurring in the larger society at any given moment. Children seem to be important in our commonsense definitions, as one study found that unmarried couples, both gay and heterosexual, are more likely to be considered a family if children are present (Powell 2003). Unrelated roommates who are not romantically involved are significantly more likely to be considered family by those over the age of sixty-five:

> I call this the *Golden Girls* effect.... People at retirement, on one hand, tend to be very traditional about issues of sexuality, but in terms of what they count as family, they are more likely to accept housemates as a sort of family unit. Their views may be affected by major changes in life, such as a move to a retirement home or a loss of a spouse. (Powell 2003)

As you will see as you read this chapter, what constitutes the model or hypothetical family may be very different from how families define themselves "on the ground."

Diversity in Families

Artistic representations of the traditional family generally show a mother, a father, and their two children all with the same skin tone and hair color. These pictures reflect a practice called **endogamy** that refers to marrying someone from within the same social group. **Exogamy** refers to marrying someone from a different social group.

As an example of how family forms and definitions change over time, marriage between people of different racial, ethnic, or national backgrounds has

FAMILY a social group whose members are bound by legal, biological, or emotional ties, or a combination of all three

EXTENDED FAMILY a large group of relatives, usually including at least three generations living either in one household or in close proximity

KIN relatives or relations, usually those related by common descent

NUCLEAR FAMILY a heterosexual couple with one or more children living in a single household

ENDOGAMY marriage to someone within one's social group

EXOGAMY marriage to someone from a different social group

ANTIMISCEGENATION the prohibition of interracial marriage, cohabitation, or sexual interaction

MONOGAMY the practice of marrying (or being in a relationship with) one person at a time

POLYGAMY a system of marriage that allows people to have more than one spouse at a time

POLYGYNY a system of marriage that allows men to have multiple wives

POLYANDRY a system of marriage that allows women to have multiple husbands

POLYAMORY a system of multiple-person partnership

actually been prohibited for most of the history of the United States. From the time of slavery through the 1960s, mixed-race relationships were considered criminal and were also punished outside the law. Fears of interracial relationships led to the lynching of African American men and the creation of **antimiscegenation** laws in several U.S. states that prohibited the mixing of racial groups through marriage, cohabitation, or sexual interaction (Messerschmidt 1998). The most significant of these laws fell after the 1967 Supreme Court declared that Virginia's law banning marriage between persons of different races was unconstitutional under the Fourteenth Amendment (*Loving v. Virginia* 1967).

Though mixed-race unions are now legal, they are still uncommon but increasing. In 1960, only 0.4 percent of all couples were interracial, increasing to 2.2 percent by 1992 (U.S. Census Bureau 1994), 5.7 percent in 2000 (U.S. Census Bureau 2003), and 8.4 percent in 2010 (Pew Research Center for the People and the Press 2012d). Mixed-race couples still face discrimination; in their analysis of a white supremacist internet chat room, Glaser, Dixit, and Green (2002) found that respondents were far more threatened by interracial marriage than by persons of color moving into white neighborhoods or competing for jobs.

Monogamy, or marrying only one individual at a time, is still considered the only legal form of marriage in modern Western culture. **Polygamy**, or having multiple spouses, may be practiced among some subcultures around the world but is not widely acknowledged as a legitimate form of marriage. The more commonly known form of polygamy is **polygyny**, where a man is married to multiple wives. **Polyandry**, where a woman has multiple husbands, has been documented in Tibet but is the rarer form of polygamy. **Polyamory** is a type of multiple-person partnership in which each individual, regardless of gender or sexual orientation, is in a relationship with each other individual.

Sociological Perspectives on the Family

Among the sociological perspectives on the family, those with the structural functionalist view see it as a cultural universal and try to identify its functions for society. Conflict theorists argue that there are inherent inequalities both within and between families. Symbolic interactionists focus on the family as the product of interactional processes. Each of these theories offers useful insights into our understanding of the family unit.

Structural Functionalism

In *Suicide*, Émile Durkheim (1897/1951) argued that the Industrial Revolution and the division of labor had undermined the older social institutions that formerly regulated society, leaving some people suffering from anomie, or normlessness, that sometimes resulted in suicide. He found that marriage and family, at least for men, decreased their chances of suicide because these provide the structure and regulation that Durkheim believed people require to be happy.

The structural functionalists who followed Durkheim argued that society's survival requires institutions that can serve its essential functions: economic production, the socialization of children, instrumental and emotional support, and sexual control. Although the family is no longer directly involved in economic production, it performs the functions that allow production to happen. Talcott Parsons (1955) argued that "the modern nuclear family was especially complementary to the requirements of an industrial economy" because it freed individuals from onerous obligations to extended family members and made possible the geographic and social mobility demanded by the modern economy (Mann et al. 1997). In the most basic sense, the family is responsible for the reproduction of society as it produces and socializes children. This is what Parsons referred to as "pattern maintenance," whereby the values and norms of a society are passed on to the next generation. Family also, ideally, provides emotional support for its members and regulates sexuality by helping define with whom we can and cannot mate. These patterns, according to functionalists, help society run smoothly and maintain stability and order.

Conflict Theory

Conflict theorists recognize that the family produces and socializes children to function efficiently in a capitalist economy, but they see this function as problematic. The nuclear family, a relatively recent historical invention, acts as the primary economic unit in modern capitalist society, and since conflict theorists see capitalism as oppressive, they claim that this form of family contributes to that oppression—and is often understood as an oppressive institution in itself. Conflict theorists believe that society revolves around conflict over scarce resources and that conflict within the family is also about the competition for resources: time, energy, and the leisure to pursue more interesting recreational activities.

GLOBAL PERSPECTIVE

Talking about Kin

In P. D. Eastman's children's book *Are You My Mother?* a newly hatched bird wanders about asking everyone—and everything—she encounters, "Are you my mother?" Sadly for the newborn, neither the construction crane, nor the cow, nor the cat is the parent she is searching for. On the last page of the book, however, the tiny bird is serendipitously returned to her nest and reunited with a maternal-looking chickadee.

When reading something like *Are You My Mother?* most people in the Western world would assume that the word "mother" means "female parent." However, in the Hawaiian language, *makuahine* means both "mother" and "aunt" and refers to any female relative in the generation of that person's parents (*makuakane* is the equivalent term for men) (Stanton 1995; Schwimmer 2001). In Hawaiian, then, "Are you my mother?" could just as easily mean "Are you my father's brother's wife?" In China, though, kinship terms are very precise. There are particular terms for a "father's brother's wife" that vary depending on whether the wife is married to the older brother or a younger one (Levi-Strauss 1949/1969)!

One reason we name our kin is to delineate the relationships and obligations we share. In some cases, we use the term **fictive kin** to refer to people who are not related to us through blood or through marriage. Such kin are created through closely knit friendships to the family. You may have a family friend you call Auntie So-and-So. In other societies, fictive kin may be culturally prescribed. In Jordan, it is perfectly normal for adult strangers to address one another with the Arabic equivalents of brother/sister, maternal aunt/uncle, and paternal aunt/uncle. In addition, an older Jordanian woman may affectionately refer to a child (of either gender) as "mother" (Farghal and Shakir 1994).

In China, labeling an older individual as an uncle or an older brother is a required sign of respect (Baker 1979). Sometimes fictive kinship ties are formalized through ceremony, as when a female in India ties a sacred thread around the wrist of an unrelated close male friend to indicate that she considers him a brother. In Latin America, godparents (*compadrazgo*, a word that can be translated as "co-parent" rather than "godparent") are considered permanent members of their godchildren's family. Not surprisingly, the Spanish words for "daughter" and "son" are very close to the words for "goddaughter" and "godson" (Davila 1971; van den Berghe 1979).

Examining kinship terms is one way to understand the diversity of families and how kin fulfill their social roles. As you can see, aunts, elder brothers, godparents, and family friends can all be important family members.

FICTIVE KIN close relations with people we consider "like family" but who are not related to us by blood or marriage.

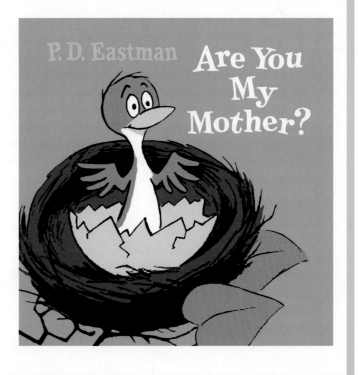

In this analysis, the family can allow exploitation through a sexual rather than a class-based division of labor. Conflict perspectives overlap with feminist perspectives on the family as feminists assume that the family is a gendered social institution and that men and women experience family differently. In patriarchal societies, men wield greater power than women, both within and outside the family, and women's contributions to family and society are devalued (Thorne 1992). In addition to gender, other systems of stratification (such as age and ability) may be the basis for inequality, conflict, and even violence within families, and will be discussed in more detail later in the chapter.

Symbolic Interactionism

As Jim Holstein and Jay Gubrium point out in their book *What Is Family* (1990), the *family* does not exist, only *families*. These symbolic interactionists consider it more effective to look at how family relations are created and maintained in interaction than how they are structured. Even though the legal bond of marriage has the same technical meaning for every couple, individual marriages may have very different expectations and rules for behavior. One couple may require sexual monogamy within their marriage, while their neighbors may not; one couple may pool their finances while another husband and wife may keep separate bank accounts. This approach conceives of family as a fluid, adaptable set of concepts and practices that people use "for constructing the meaning of social bonds" (Holstein and Gubrium 1995a), a set of vocabularies to describe particular relationships.

Consider the number of relatives, defined by blood or marriage, most people have who play no meaningful role in their lives, who "aren't really family." When we describe people in terms of family, we are making claims about the "rights, obligations, and sentiments" that exist within their relationships (Gubrium and Buckholdt 1982). Consequently, we are constantly evaluating and reevaluating the attitudes and behaviors of those around us, assigning family status to new people and dismissing others from our circle of meaningful family relations. In *All Our Kin*, an ethnography of kinship relations in an urban African American community, Carol Stack found this dynamic at work in the way people talked about family—including this woman, who says,

> Most people kin to me are in this neighborhood . . . but I got people in the South, in Chicago, and in Ohio too. I couldn't tell most of their names and most of them aren't really kinfolk to me. . . . Take my father, he's no father to me. I ain't got but one daddy and that's Jason. The one who raised me. My kids' daddies, that's something else, all their daddies' people really take to them—they always doing things and making a fuss about them. We help each other out and that's what kinfolks are all about. (Stack 1974)

A symbolic interactionist might say that "family members do not merely passively conform to others' expectations" but rather "actively and creatively construct and modify their roles through interactions" (Dupuis and Smale 2000)—that is, the people who help each other out, who care for each other, and who express that care are family, whether they are legally related or not.

Forming Relationships, Selecting Mates

You may think that you are attracted to certain people because of their unique individual characteristics or something intangible called "chemistry." In reality, however, Cupid's arrow is largely aimed by society. Two time-tested concepts in social science—homogamy and propinquity—tell us a lot about how the mate-selection process works. **Homogamy** literally means "like marries like": we tend to choose mates who are similar to us in class, race, ethnicity, age, religion, education, and even levels of attractiveness. You can certainly find examples of people whose romantic relationships cross these category lines—interracial or

HOMOGAMY the tendency to choose romantic partners who are similar to us in terms of class, race, religion, education, or other social group membership

---

Table 12.1 Theory in Everyday Life

Perspective	Approach to Family	Case Study: Marriage
Structural Functionalism	Family performs necessary functions, such as the socialization of children, that help society run smoothly and maintain social order.	Marriage regulates sexuality and forms the basis for family, with all its other functions.
Conflict Theory	Family is a site of various forms of stratification and can produce and reproduce inequalities based on these statuses.	Marriage as a civil right is extended only to heterosexual couples in most states and nations. This is both a cause and a consequence of homophobia in society.
Symbolic Interactionism	Family is a social construction; it is created, changed, and maintained in interaction.	Marriage is not made solely by completing a legal contract but is also constructed through the accretion of everyday interactions between partners over the years.

interreligious couples, or May/December romances—but these relationships are often viewed with disapproval by others in the couples' social circles. There are considerable social pressures to adhere to homogamy.

Propinquity refers to geographical proximity: we tend to choose people who live nearby. This is logical; we are likely to find possible mates among the people in our neighborhood, at work, or at school. The internet makes courtship and romance possible across much greater geographical areas, as we can now meet and converse with people in all parts of the world, so our pool of potential mates moves beyond local bounds. But even this technology may intensify homogamy by bringing together people with very specific interests and identities. Examples include internet services such as J-Date, for Jewish singles; Prime Singles, for people over age fifty; Athletic Passions, for people into fitness and sports; and Black Singles for African Americans.

Courtship, romance, and intimacy are all influenced by the larger culture—and are also historically specific. While we experience courtship at an individual, interactional level, it will always be shaped by macro-structural forces in the larger society, such as racial, ethnic, or religious prejudices, and gendered role expectations. But courtship changes as other aspects of the surrounding culture change. As our society becomes less racist, sexist, and heterosexist, romantic options will expand as well. The development of intimate romantic relationships is not something "natural"; it is socially constructed to *appear* natural.

Doing the Work of Family

When we think of work, we usually think of activities done for a paycheck. But paid labor is not the only type of work that sociologists are interested in—especially in the study of the family. Many types of work—both paid and unpaid—are necessary to keep a family operating: child care, housecleaning, car maintenance, cooking, bill-paying, vacation planning, and doing laundry—the list seems endless, especially when you are the one doing the work!

These tasks can be instrumental or expressive. **Instrumental tasks** generally achieve a tangible goal (washing the dishes, fixing the gutters), whereas **expressive tasks** generally achieve emotional or relational goals (remembering relatives' birthdays, playing Chutes and Ladders with the kids). In a real family, however, much of the work has both instrumental and expressive elements. The expressive work of remembering and celebrating birthdays, for example, includes all sorts of instrumental tasks, such as buying presents, writing cards, and baking cakes (Di Leonardo 1987; Pleck 2000).

As a social scientist committed to making the invisible labor of family visible, Marjorie DeVault (1991/1994) excavates all the knowledge, skills, and practices—both instrumental and expressive—we take for granted when, for example, we feed our families. Not only is the knowledge of cooking needed, but there must be appropriate shopping to keep a stocked kitchen; to make meals that account for family members' likes, dislikes, and allergies; and to create a varied and balanced menu. Producing meals that please, satisfy, and bring individuals together is just one of the ways that family is created and sustained through interactional work. We constitute family in and through meals and every other mundane activity of everyday life.

DATA WORKSHOP
Analyzing Everyday Life

Comparative Mealtime

Some of us carry a strong and positive image of our family gathered around the dining room table for dinner each evening. While we were growing up, dinner may have been the one time in the day when the whole family was together and shared food, stories, lessons, and news. For many of us, a great deal of socialization took place around the dinner table; we learned about manners ("Sit up straight," "Don't speak with your mouth full") as well as morality, politics, or anything else that seemed important to the adults raising us. Some of us, on the other hand, may have different memories of family mealtimes. Perhaps they were a time of tension and arguments, or perhaps the family rarely ate a meal together.

In this Data Workshop, you will be using participant observation as a research method (see Chapter 2 for a review) and doing ethnographic research on mealtime activity. You will compare two or more different mealtime settings and situations. You can choose from among a range of different possibilities, including the following:

* Which meal you study—breakfast, lunch, or dinner

* Where the meal takes place—in your family home; at a friend's or a relative's house; at your own apartment or dormitory dining hall; or at a workplace lunch room, picnic in the park, or restaurant

What's for Dinner? Compare these two family meals. What do our mealtime practices tell us about contemporary American families?

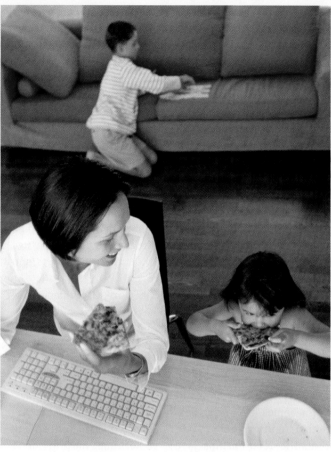

* Who is eating—family members, roommates, friends, co-workers, or strangers

After you participate in and observe two mealtimes, write down answers to the following questions:

* What are the prevailing rules, rituals, norms, and values associated with the setting and situation? For example, does everyone sit down to eat at the same time? Do people leave after they finish even if others are still eating?

* What kinds of complementary roles are the various participants engaged in? Who cooks the food, sets the table, clears the table, does the dishes, and so forth?

* What other types of activities (besides eating) are taking place at mealtime? Are people watching TV, listening to music or a ball game, reading the newspaper or texting?

* What social purposes does the setting or situation serve other than providing a mealtime environment for the participants? For example, what do the participants talk about? If children are involved, do they talk about school or their friends? Are family activities or problems discussed? What kinds of interactions do you see among co-workers or roommates?

In addition to taking detailed notes, you may also wish to interview some of the participants.

There are two options for completing the assigned work in the Data Workshop.

Option 1 (informal): Make the observations prescribed and conduct any formal or informal interviews you wish. Prepare some written notes that you can refer to during in-class discussions. Compare and contrast the analyses of the different family meals observed by participants in your group. What are the similarities and differences in your observations?

Option 2 (formal): Make the observations prescribed, and conduct any formal or informal interviews you wish. Write a three- to four-page essay answering the questions listed above and reflecting on your own experience in conducting this study. What do you think your observations tell us about contemporary American families and the practices of family mealtimes? Don't forget to attach your fieldnotes and interview transcripts.

Gender and Family Labor

Imagine working a labor-intensive forty to sixty hours waiting tables, making automobile parts, doing data entry, or teaching second graders. You arrive home feeling tired, hungry, and worn out, but you cannot sit down to relax. You still need to cook a meal, do some laundry and cleaning, and take care of your children or perhaps your elderly parents.

Who is more likely to come home to this scenario? Among heterosexual couples, women are more likely to have the dual workload of paid labor outside the home and unpaid labor inside the home. In this section, we will discuss the division of labor within the household.

Men and women have always performed different roles to ensure the survival of their families, but these roles were not considered unequal until after the Industrial Revolution. At that time, men began to leave their homes to earn wages working in factories. Women remained at home taking care of children and carrying out other domestic responsibilities. As men's earned wages replaced subsistence farming—in which women had always participated—these wages became the primary mechanism for providing food, clothing, and shelter for families, thus giving men economic power over women. Feminist sociologists contend that women's "second shift" is the legacy of this historic economic change.

Despite women's increasing participation in the paid workforce, they are still more likely to perform the bulk of household and caregiving labor. In a few cases, men share household chores (Coltrane 1997) but women bear the brunt of unpaid household labor. Arlie Hochschild and Anne Machung's 1989 study of working couples and parents found that women were indeed working two jobs: paid labor outside the home, or the first shift, and unpaid labor

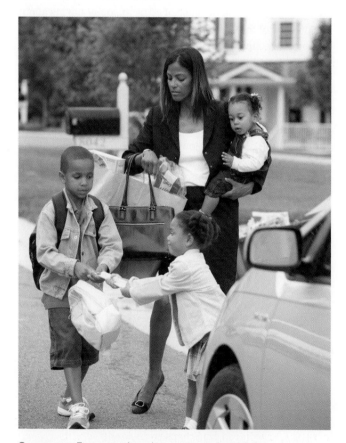

Supermom For many American women, "work" doesn't end when they leave the workplace. On returning home, many begin what Arlie Hochschild calls "the second shift," doing the unpaid work of running a household, including doing the laundry, feeding the children, and helping with homework.

inside the home, or the **second shift**. Hochschild and Machung found that these women tried numerous strategies to achieve balance between work and home: hiring other women to clean their houses and care for their children; relying on friends or family members for help; refusing to do certain chores, especially those considered to be generally "men's work"; lowering their expectations for cleanliness or quality of child care; or reducing the number of hours they worked outside the home. But some women accept their dual workloads without any help to avoid conflicts with spouses and children. Hochschild and Machung called these women "Supermoms" but also found that these "Supermoms" often felt unhappy or emotionally numb.

SECOND SHIFT the unpaid housework and childcare often expected of women after they return home from doing paid labor in the workforce

Although Hochschild and Machung's observations were groundbreaking in their analysis of post-feminist families, their concept of the "Supermom" has been applicable to working-class mothers all along. The stay-at-home parent is possible only when one salary can support the entire family. Before college-educated women were encouraged to work in the paid labor force, working-class women were there out of necessity. The strategies that middle-class women use to negotiate their second shift are available only to wealthier families. After all, a woman who cleans another family's house and takes care of their children rarely has the financial resources to hire someone to do the same for her.

Family and the Life Course

As an agent of socialization and the most basic of primary groups, the family molds everyone—young children, teenagers, adults, and senior citizens—and its influences continue throughout the life course.

When we are children, our families provide us with our first lessons in how to be members of society (see Chapter 4 on socialization). Children's experiences are shaped by family size, birth order, presence or absence of parents, socioeconomic status, and other sociological variables. Dalton Conley's 2004 work *The Pecking Order* maintains that inequality between siblings; things outside the family's control, such as the economy, war, illness, and death; and marital discord create effects that impact each child at different stages in his or her life, resulting in different experiences for each child. Conley argues that family proves not to be the consistent influence many people view it to be.

In addition, the presence of children shapes the lives of parents. Marital satisfaction tends to decline when there are small children in the house, and couples' gendered division of labor becomes more traditional when children are born, even if it has been nontraditional up to that point. As children get older, they may exert other types of influence on their parents—for example, children can pressure their parents into quitting smoking or eating healthier food. And of course, later in life, they may be called on to care for their elderly parents as well as their own offspring—a phenomenon known as "the sandwich generation" effect.

Aging in the Family

The American population is aging—the number of Americans sixty-five or older is growing twice as fast as the population as a whole (Werner 2011). This is because of the baby boom generation (the large number of Americans born in the post–World War II era) moving into middle age and beyond, concurrent with advances in medical technology. Current average life expectancy in the United States is approximately seventy-eight years (with women living an average of almost six years longer than men). More people are living longer, and that has an impact on families and society.

Planning for an aging population means taking into account both the basic and special needs of older individuals. Retirement income is an important part of this planning—Social Security benefits are the major source of income for about 65 percent of the elderly in the United States and the only source of income for 24 percent of America's retired population. Without other sources of income, retired citizens may find themselves with limited resources; currently, about 15 percent of the elderly live below the poverty line (U.S. Census Bureau 2012f). Some seniors solve the problems by living with their adult children or with nonfamily members; even so, about 50 percent of women and about 20 percent of men over age sixty-five live alone. Like other traditional functions of the family (such as educating children), the care of the elderly is no longer a primary duty of family and has been taken over by other institutions: more than 40 percent of senior citizens will spend time in a nursing home, being housed and cared for by people other than their family members (Baca Zinn and Eitzen 2002).

Coping with the transitions of retirement, widowhood, declining health, and death are central tasks for seniors. However, as the average life span extends, the elderly are also taking on new roles in society. Many live healthy, vibrant, active lives and are engaged with their families and communities in ways that are productive for both the individual and the person's groups.

Trouble in Families

While families are often a place of comfort, support, and unconditional love, some are not a "haven in a heartless world" (Lasch 1977). The family may be where we are at the greatest risk—emotionally, socially, and physically. "People are more likely to be killed, physically assaulted, sexually victimized . . . in their own homes by other family members than anywhere else, or by anyone else, in our society" (Gelles 1995, p. 450).

Because family is the site of unequal power relations and intense feelings, and because of current social norms about the privacy of family life, the circumstances for trouble and violence are ripe. The concept of private nuclear families did not occur in the United States until the early 1900s. In colonial times, child raising was a community activity in which community leaders and neighbors often overruled parental decisions about children. In the late 1800s, mothers looked to other mothers for advice about their children (Coontz 2000). Mothers' journals at the time show that the opinions of other women were often more important than the husband's in family decisions. Not until the 1900s did the isolated nuclear family become the ideal in the minds of Americans.

The New Senior Citizen Americans are living longer and leading vibrant, active lives. Marie Wilcox-Little and Donald Goo, both age 73, still enjoying swimming and surfing.

Domestic Violence and Abuse

Imagine that tomorrow's newspapers ran front-page headlines about a newly discovered disease epidemic that could potentially kill one-quarter of all American women. Between 1 million and 4 million women would be afflicted in the next year alone. What kind of public reaction would there be?

Let's reframe the scenario: in the United States, one out of every four women suffers physical violence at the hands of an intimate partner at some point in her adult life (National Coalition Against Domestic Violence 2007). In addition, millions of women suffer verbal, financial, and psychological abuse from those who are supposed to love them. Despite these statistics, such abuse is a silent epidemic, seldom reported.

Domestic violence is an umbrella term for the behaviors abusers use to gain and maintain control over their victims. These behaviors fall into five main categories: physical (slapping, punching, kicking, choking, shoving, restraining), verbal (insults, taunts, threats, degrading statements), financial (insisting on complete control of all household finances, including making decisions about who will work and when), sexual (rape, molestation), and psychological or emotional abuse (mind games, threats, stalking, intimidation). Although not all abusers are physically violent toward their partners, any one type of abuse increases the likelihood of the others. In an abusive relationship, it is extremely rare to find only one form of abuse.

Rates of domestic violence are about equal across racial and ethnic groups, sexual orientations, and religions (Bachman and Saltzman 1995). Women are certainly not the only demographic group to suffer from domestic abuse, but statistically, they are five to eight times more likely than men to be victimized by an intimate partner (Greenfeld et al. 1998; National Domestic Violence Hotline 2003). According to the U.S. Department of Justice, women between the ages of twenty and twenty-four are victims of abuse at the hands of an intimate partner more frequently than women in any other age group (National Coalition Against Domestic Violence 2007). Poor women are also more likely to be abused than women with higher incomes (Bachman and Saltzman 1995). Age and economic security, however, do not make someone immune to abuse.

Contrary to popular opinion, most abusive partners are not "out of control," nor do they have "anger management problems" in the traditional sense. They often seem charming and calm to co-workers, friends, and police officers; they deliberately decide to be violent with those least likely to report the crime and over whom they maintain the most control: their family members. Domestic violence results from the abuser's desire for power over the victim, and abusers often blame their victims: I wouldn't have beaten you if dinner had been on time, or if you hadn't been "flirting" with the sales associate at the mall. One abuser is reported to have said to police officers, "Yes, I hit her five or six times but it was only to calm her down" ("Even in the Best of Homes" 2003).

A four-stage **cycle of violence** seems to occur in almost every abusive relationship. In the first stage, the abusive partner is charming, attentive, and thoughtful; disagreements are glossed over and the relationship looks stable and healthy. However, tension is building to the second stage, often described as "walking on eggshells." Here, both parties sense that something will happen no matter what the victim may do to try to avoid it. During the third stage, acute battering and violence occur, lasting for seconds, hours, or even days. Whatever happens, the abuser will invariably blame the victim for the incident. The fourth stage, often referred to as "loving contrition," is the "honeymoon" phase and is one of the reasons victims remain in violent relationships. After the violence, the abuser will apologize profusely and promise that it will never happen again. The abuser may buy the victim gifts, beg forgiveness, and talk about getting help or making a change. Most abusers, however, have no interest in changing because they don't want to give up their control over their victims. Soon the cycle starts again, with flowers and gifts giving way to tension, uneasiness, and another battering.

Victims of domestic violence stay with their abusers for many reasons. After years of abuse, victims often believe what their abusers tell them: that they can't make it on their own and are somehow responsible for the abuse. If they have not been allowed to attend school or to work, they may not have employment skills. Often, children are involved, or abusers threaten to harm other family members. Many victims have been isolated from friends and family and are afraid to speak of the abuse to anyone, and they see no options but to remain where they are.

Child and Elder Abuse

Adult partners are not the only victims of domestic violence. Children and the elderly also suffer at the hands of abusive family members—and can suffer in distinctive ways that are linked to their special status in the family. Child abuse and elder abuse are likely to be underreported, partly because of the relative powerlessness of their victims and the private settings of the abuse. The estimates are that about 9 percent children in the United States are abused in some way (U.S. Department of Health & Human Services 2012) and

DOMESTIC VIOLENCE any physical, verbal, financial, sexual, or psychological behaviors abusers use to gain and maintain power over their victims

CYCLE OF VIOLENCE a common behavior pattern in abusive relationships; the cycle begins happily, then the relationship grows tense, and the tension explodes in abuse, followed by a period of contrition that allows the cycle to repeat

IN RELATIONSHIPS

Family Living Arrangements: From Boomerang Kids to the Sandwich Generation

When people talk about the disappearance of the nuclear family, they usually are referring to the divorce rate, but, especially for the baby boom generation, families are changing in other ways as well. Traditionally, becoming middle-aged was associated with the "mid-life crisis" but also with maturity, wisdom, and increased professional skills. While this might seem like a contradiction, changes in the nature of the family make these qualities seem more like a necessity! Increasing numbers of middle-aged people are becoming members of a "sandwich generation," adults who provide material and emotional support for both "young children and older living parents" (Lachman 2004, p. 322). This effect is magnified by the increasing number of so-called boomerang kids, who leave home at eighteen to attend college but often return home for at least a short period of time afterward.

Both of these dynamics are being driven less by choice than by demographic and economic necessity. In 1970, the average age at first marriage was less than twenty-one for women and a little over twenty-three for men. Today, the median age at first marriage for women is twenty-six and one-half, and for men it's almost twenty-nine. As a result, people are having children later, increasing the chances that child rearing and elder care will overlap. Advances in life expectancy also contribute to the sandwich effect, even as many of the medical advances that allow people to live longer also increase their need for material support. While there have always been adults caring for their elderly parents, never before have there been this many elderly. According to the U.S. Census Bureau, the number of the "oldest old," those eighty-five and older, increased 30 percent between 2000 and 2010, while the total U.S. population grew by only 10 percent during that time (Werner 2011). Meanwhile, between tuition increases, student loans, and the slow job market, students leaving college are more likely to need help from their parents than ever before. In 1980, fewer than 9 percent of all individuals between twenty-five and thirty-four lived with their parents. By 2011, this number had increased to almost 15 percent, still a small group, but one that has increased significantly during the past three decades.

Members of the sandwich generation have found themselves with more responsibilities than ever before. Not only are their parents living longer than before, but medical costs associated with old age are growing rapidly, and often they have children, of all ages, still dependent on them as well. Never before has there been a substantial cohort of Americans so directly burdened with such a wide range of family responsibilities. However, in some ways, the more the

---

NEGLECT a form of child abuse in which the caregiver fails to provide adequate nutrition, sufficient clothing or shelter, or hygienic and safe living conditions

INCEST sexual contact between family members; a form of child abuse when it occurs between a child and a caregiver

that about 5 percent of all seniors in this country have been subject to elder abuse in some form (Acierno et al. 2010).

In addition to physical violence and verbal, emotional, and sexual abuse, children may experience a distinctive type of abuse known as **neglect**— inadequate nutrition, insufficient clothing or shelter, and unhygienic or unsafe living conditions. Because children depend on adults for their care and well-being, they suffer when those adults abandon or pervert that responsibility. **Incest** is another form of child abuse that exploits the trust that children must place in their caregivers. Inappropriate sexual relationships between parents and children have devastating lifelong consequences for child victims, which may include self-destructive behavior (including eating disorders and substance abuse) and the inability to form trusting relationships later in life. In addition, those who were physically or sexually abused as children have a much higher likelihood of becoming abusers themselves.

Elder abuse can also take distinctive forms. As well as physical, verbal, emotional, and sexual abuse, there is financial exploitation or theft—relatives or other caregivers may steal or misuse the elder's property or financial resources. Another form is neglect and abandonment. Some elders are dependent on others to care for them. Refusal to provide food, shelter, health care, or protection can be as devastating to an elder as it is to a child. Both elder and child abuse exploit the special powerlessness of victims and are difficult to monitor and control.

Sandwich Generation Julie Winokur (far left) juggles taking care of her father, who is suffering from Parkinson's disease, and raising her daughter (on the far right). How typical is the Winokur family today?

between ages twenty-five and thirty-four are male. While men and women might be driven by the same financial troubles, moving back in with her parents has different consequences for a woman. She is likely to be asked to take on more domestic responsibilities, and typically she feels a greater loss of independence. Gender functions in similar ways for the sandwich generation, as it is still mostly women who are called on to provide the emotional and instrumental support for elderly parents, even when those women also work. In fact, "working women who do take on caregiving tasks may reduce their work hours" (Velkoff and Lawson 1998, p. 2), finding themselves having to prioritize family over career in ways men often don't.

Despite the many costs associated with being a member of the sandwich generation, there is good news as well. Although there are challenges associated with "dual responsibilities," these are mostly experienced as "a 'squeeze' but not stress," and these relationships are also a source of happiness and well-being (Lachman 2004, p. 322). And while there is still a certain stigma associated with moving back in with your parents, the fact that so many are willing to do so suggests that today's boomerang kids may enjoy closer relationships with their parents than kids of previous generations did.

sandwich generation adults and the boomerang kids change the family, the more they stay the same, especially in the way that gender roles manifest themselves. Even among eighteen- to twenty-four-year-olds, boys are more likely to live at home than girls, and 60 percent of the boomerang kids

DATA WORKSHOP
Analyzing Mass Media and Popular Culture

Family Troubles in Film

Family relations have long been the basis of good comedic, tragic, and dramatic films. This Data Workshop asks you to use existing sources as a research method (see Chapter 2 for a review) and to do a content analysis of a film concerning

family dynamics. Choose a film to watch and then analyze its relevance to some of the family issues discussed in this chapter. Although many films feature families, this assignment asks you to focus on one or more family problems.

The following films depict a variety of family troubles, such as marital problems, divorce, domestic abuse, parental neglect, disabilities and illnesses, sex and dating, pregnancy, death, delinquency, and financial difficulties. Other movies could certainly be added to this list, as long as your instructor approves the film you would like to choose. Whatever movie you choose must be available on DVD or online so that you can view it carefully. Please be aware of the MPAA ratings for these or other movies, and watch only those titles that are appropriate for your age group and that you would feel comfortable viewing.

The Kids Are Alright *The Ice Storm*
Amreeka *In America*

Family Troubles? What do films like *The Kids Are Alright* and *Amreeka* tell us about contemporary American families?

Affliction	*In the Bedroom*
American Beauty	*The Joy Luck Club*
Baby Boy	*Kramer vs. Kramer*
How to Deal	*Mi Familia (My Family)*
Mrs. Doubtfire	*Stepmom*
My Big Fat Greek Wedding	*Terms of Endearment*
Ordinary People	*Thirteen*
Pieces of April	*We Don't Live Here Anymore*
Rachel Getting Married	*What's Eating Gilbert Grape?*
The Royal Tennenbaums	*You Can Count on Me*
Saving Face	*About A Boy*

Select a movie that is primarily about contemporary family relations and problems. Once you have chosen a movie, read through the rest of the workshop points and guidelines. Then watch the film closely and pay attention to the plotlines, scenes, characters, and dialogues in which family troubles are depicted. Take notes as you watch the movie; you may have to review it several times before you can do a thorough content analysis. This assignment has several parts, and you may also wish to add your own questions or comments.

Consider the following points and answer these questions:

* Give some background information on the film and why you chose it.

* Using sociological terms, describe the family troubles that are the focus of the film. How are these problems manifested in the lives of the family members? How do the various characters deal with their problems? What solutions do they propose through their actions? How effective are these solutions in addressing the family's troubles?

* Put the family's problems in a broader sociological perspective. Do you believe the family's troubles are more psychological or sociological in nature? In what ways are the individual troubles of family members

linked to larger social patterns and problems? Compare the problems in the movie with their counterparts in the real world. Gather recent data relating to the family problems featured in the film, using sources such as the U.S. Census Bureau, other government or private agencies, or various news sources. How widespread are these problems? How are they being discussed and dealt with at a public level? How accurately do you think the family's troubles, and their possible solutions, were depicted in the film? What kind of a role, if any, do you think the media can play in helping to reduce family troubles or associated social problems?

There are two options for completing this Data Workshop.

Option 1 (informal): Do the research described above and answer the preceding questions. Then prepare some written notes that you can refer to during in-class discussions. Compare and contrast the analyses of the films observed by participants in your discussion group.

Option 2 (formal): Do the research described above and answer the preceding questions. Then write a three- to four-page essay talking about your answers and reflecting on your observations of the film. What do you think your observations tell us about contemporary American families and the ways in which family troubles are portrayed on film?

Divorce and Breakups

Although many people stay in bad relationships, many couples also break up every day. In this section, we consider the changing patterns of divorce and remarriage as they affect children and adults. We also look at the resulting social problems of custody, visitation, and child support.

Changing Patterns

For 2011, the U.S. Census Bureau reported that more than 126 million persons were married while about 27 million were divorced. Thus, in 2011, about 42 percent of the entire U.S. population were married while just fewer than 9 percent were divorced. Figure 12.1 shows the increase (and sometimes decrease) in divorce rates over time. The percentage of married people who have divorced has greatly increased since 1950, but it is not completely accurate to say that approximately 50 percent of all first marriages now end in divorce (Kreider and Fields 2001).

Most who divorce eventually marry other people. Among parents of young children, the remarriage rate is very high. According to Cherlin and Furstenberg (1994), 75 percent of divorced men and 67 percent of divorced women ultimately remarry, and between 75 percent and 80 percent of divorced parents remarry (Weissbourd 1994). But remarriage rates in the United States are actually lower now than they were before the 1960s, a fact attributable to the increase in **cohabitation**, or living together, among unmarried couples. Census data reveal that about 5 percent of all households are occupied by unmarried heterosexual couples, which may reflect a certain caution about marriage as a result of high rates of divorce.

In the early 1970s, the children of divorced parents were more than three times more likely to divorce than their peers from intact families. But by the mid-1990s, this figure had dropped to about one and a half times (Wolfinger 1999, 2000). According to Wolfinger (2003), the decline of intergenerational divorce and marriage rates probably has three sources. One is the growing acceptance of divorce. Children of divorced parents no longer suffer the social stigma that was once the by-product of divorce and are less likely to develop psychological problems as a result—which may have contributed to their divorces in the past. Second, the age of marriage has changed. Children of divorce are still more likely to marry as teenagers, but those not married by age twenty are more likely not to marry at all than their peers from intact families. Third, children of divorced parents are more likely to cohabit with their partners and are less likely to marry them than children of nondivorced parents. Therefore, the decline in marriage rates among children of divorced parents can be explained by both increased rates of cohabitation and an increased propensity not to marry at all.

Custody, Visitation, and Child Support

Reviewing the legal policies that address the consequences of divorce for children, sociologists are concerned with whether custody, visitation, and child support effectively replace the resources, both emotional and financial, of an intact household. Do they help children?

Custody is the physical and legal responsibility for the everyday life and routines of children. While mothers still disproportionately receive custody, there is a trend toward joint custody (Cancian and Meyer 1998). Parents who are well educated, have high socioeconomic status, live in cities, and are nonwhite are more likely than others to have joint custody of their children (Donnelly and Finkelhor 1993). A father is more likely to be awarded sole custody when his income is substantially more than the mother's (Cancian and Meyer 1998), when his children are older, or when the oldest child is male (Fox and Kelly 1995). A mother is more likely to receive sole custody when she has a high level of education, her children are younger, and the father is unemployed (Fox and Kelly 1995).

COHABITATION living together as a romantically involved, unmarried couple

CUSTODY the physical and legal responsibility of caring for children; assigned by a court for divorced or unmarried parents

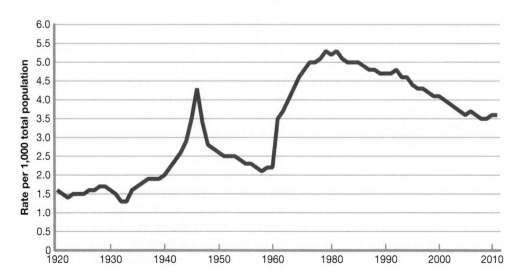

Figure 12.1

U.S. Divorce Rate, 1920–2011

SOURCES: U.S. Department of Health, Education, and Welfare 1964; U.S. Census Bureau 2012j; National Vital Statistics System 2013.

Courts award visitation to noncustodial parents to protect parent-child relationships. Generally, parents with regular visitation patterns are better able to meet the psychological and financial needs of their children. Fathers who visit regularly are more likely to maintain strong relationships with their children and to pay child support (Seltzer, Schaeffer, and Charng 1989). Despite increased vigilance of courts and lawmakers regarding mandated child support policies, noncustodial parents often fail to make regular payments to the custodial parent. Sociologists have found that many parents make informal arrangements, or decisions without the mediation of the legal system, about child support schedules soon after the divorce (Peters et al. 1993) and the stability of payments varies substantially, even among the most reliable payers (Meyer and Bartfeld 1998).

As children are more likely to live in poverty after their parents' divorce, child support policies are important. Women are more likely to suffer downward economic mobility after divorce, especially if they retain custody of their children. Furstenberg, Hoffman, and Shrestha (1995) found that women experience on average a 25 percent decline in their economic well-being after a divorce. Accompanying this post-divorce decline in financial resources are often scholastic failure, disruptive conduct, and troubled relationships in children of divorced families (Keith and Finlay 1988; Morrison and Cherlin 1995). Further, divorce seems to negatively affect male children more than female children, as boys are more likely to act out than girls.

Stepparents and Blended Families

Most divorced people will eventually marry someone else, which means that one in three Americans is a member of a stepfamily (Baca Zinn and Eitzen 2002). However, statistics about stepfamilies are inconsistent and often contradictory because quantifying and defining the intricate relationships involved in a stepfamily are difficult. The U.S. Census has not routinely accounted for them in its data gathering. There are historically no traditional norms or models for stepfamilies, and our firmly held notions of the "traditional" family lead many in stepfamilies to find the transition to a new family situation difficult. Stepfamilies face special challenges, for example, when there are children in different stages of the life cycle. The needs and concerns of teenagers may be vastly different from those of their infant half-sibling, and it may take more work to adjust to the new living situation. With the added challenges of blending in-laws, finances, and households, remarriages are even more likely to end in divorce than first marriages. However, in successful remarriages, partners are usually older and have learned important lessons about compatibility and relationship maintenance from the failure of their first marriages.

Trends in American Families

"There's this pervasive idea in America that puts marriage and family at the center of everyone's lives," says Bella M. DePaulo, visiting professor of psychology at the University of California, Santa Barbara, "when in fact it's becoming less and less so" (personal communication 2003). Many people live outside such arrangements. In fact, the average American now spends the majority of his or her life unmarried because people live longer, delay marriage, or choose a single lifestyle (Kreider and Fields 2002).

Being Single

The term "single" often implies a young adult who is actively seeking a partner for a relationship or marriage. But singles also include gays and lesbians who may not have the option to marry, people living alone who are in long-distance relationships, people living in communes, widows and widowers, minors in group homes, and some clergy members as well as those who are single as a result of divorce or deliberate choice.

Married couples were the dominant model through the 1950s, but their numbers have slipped from nearly 80 percent of households to just less than 50 percent now (U.S. Census Bureau 2011b). Married couples with children—the traditional model of family—total less than 20 percent of households, and that number is projected to drop. The remaining households are single parents, cohabiting partners, or others. A stunning 28 percent of all households consist of people who live alone, and in 2005, unmarrieds became the new majority (U.S. Census Bureau 2011c).

Among the growing movement of activists promoting the rights of unmarried people in the United States is the nonprofit Alternatives to Marriage Project and its associated advocacy group Unmarried America (Solot and Miller 2002). They engage in research, education, and advocacy for unmarried and single adults of all types and are concerned about discrimination that is built into the American social system, especially at an economic and political level but also in terms of culture and values. One of their efforts is to increase recognition of unmarrieds and singles as a constituency of voters, workers, taxpayers, and consumers worthy of equal rights and protection (Warner, Ihara, and Hertz 2001).

Cohabitation

Between 1960 and 2010, the number of unmarried cohabiting couples in the United States increased significantly. More than 7 million people are living with an unmarried partner, including both same-sex and different-sex couples (U.S. Census Bureau 2012e). In addition, marriage is no longer the prerequisite for childbearing. Forty percent of opposite-sex cohabiting couples have children, while about 14 percent of

IN THE FUTURE

The Future of Marriage—and Divorce

As of 2013, thirteen states (CA, CT, DE, IA, ME, MD, MA, MN, NH, NY, RI, VT, and WA) as well as the District of Columbia allow or will be implementing same-sex marriage (Freedom to Marry 2013). In June 2013, the Supreme Court ruled in *United States v. Windsor* that the section of the Defense of Marriage Act defining marriage between one man and one woman was unconstitutional. The decision opened the door for the federal government to recognize legally performed same-sex marriages and begin the process of extending over 1,000 benefits that heterosexual spouses already take for granted, such as joint income taxes, health insurance, Social Security, and inheritances (Shell 2013).

While it seems clear that the future is one where all gay and straight couples who want to marry will be able to do so, for now it goes state by state. And though no one goes into marriage thinking that they'll get a divorce, this has some unforeseen consequences for same-sex couples who may find themselves in need of one.

All fifty states, Washington DC, and Puerto Rico recognize heterosexual marriages performed in other states—in other words, if a hetero couple gets married in Massachusetts and moves to Texas (or any other state), they do not have to get married again in Texas. And if they decide to divorce, they do not have to return to Massachusetts to do so—they may legally divorce in Texas (or any other state)—as long as they are heterosexual.

But because of the state-by-state limits on same-sex marriage, a couple might wed in Massachusetts and move to Texas, a state which neither allows same-sex marriages nor recognizes same-sex marriages performed legally in other states. In the eyes of Texas, they are not a legally married couple. The couple also does not have the right to divorce in Texas. They could only obtain a divorce in Massachusetts, the state in which they were wed. And even in Massachusetts, a same-sex divorce is not the same legal event as a hetero divorce, since federal marriage and divorce laws do not apply to any same-sex unions.

For hetero couples, legal divorce is a way to officially dissolve a marriage, leaving each partner legally available to marry again. It also settles child custody, property, and financial issues. Gay spouses don't have access to these rights in most states, and so questions arise in the face of a breakup. If we don't get divorced, what happens if one of us wants to marry again—in another state? If we split up and I buy a house on my own, does she automatically own half of it anyway? Will he be the legal parent of any children I may have in the future, even though we're no longer together? Does she still get a piece of my retirement account or Social Security check? What are the tax ramifications? How do dilemmas like this get solved?

Right now at least, they get solved through complicated and expensive legal maneuverings. One solution is for the couple to move back to the state in which they were married, meet that state's residency requirements (anywhere from six months to two years), and then meet that state's divorce requirements (which may require additional residency time). Otherwise, a court in the state of residence must rule on the laws of the state of marriage in order to dissolve the union—something courts are not always willing to do. The costs, both financial and otherwise, are great. But these are the options that legally clear the exes to marry again, own property singly, divide retirement packages, and parent children on their own, without a legal link to their former spouse.

What does the future hold for the increasing number of same-sex couples who marry, and the increasing number of states in which such marriages can be legally performed (or at least recognized, even if performed in other states)? The future holds a new campaign for social and legal change: a movement for "divorce equality."

Divorce Equality After leading the fight to legalize same-sex marriage in Massachusetts, Julie and Hillary Goodridge filed for a divorce.

ON THE JOB

Constructing Families through Adoption

If you've read this far in this chapter, you've probably already gotten the sociological message: family doesn't "just happen." Family is the product of interactional work. And because family takes many different forms, some families are the products of different types of interactional work than others. Jennifer Mitchell, an adoption social worker in Rockford, Illinois, does some of that work herself, along with her colleagues at Children's Home and Aid Society, an adoption and family welfare agency based in Chicago.

Jennifer came to her career in a slightly roundabout way. She majored in psychology and worked as an office manager for the family business for several years, but after a series of life changes, she found herself thinking about a career in social services and returning to school for a Master's degree in counseling.

At Children's Home and Aid, Jennifer is one of several social workers who prepares prospective adoptive parents and helps them navigate the process of adding to their families through adoption (a different team of social workers at the agency counsels the birth parents, in order to avoid conflicts of interest). She screens prospective parents and takes them through the extensive state licensing procedures that will qualify them to adopt a child. Jennifer interviews people about their desire to be parents, their family life, and their hopes for the future. She visits their homes to make sure they provide a safe environment for a child. She collects all the information required by the state, including first aid and CPR certification, medical exams, letters of recommendation from friends and employers, and even veterinary clearances on the family pets! She leads training sessions where families learn about adoption and the important issues surrounding it—for example, how to talk about adoption with children and other family members, what to expect in cases of international or interracial adoption, or how to maintain an open relationship with an adopted child's birth family. And when a parent or parents bring their adopted child home for the first time, Jennifer monitors their first few months of family life, helping everyone adjust and making sure things are going well until all the legal procedures are completed.

Even after an adoption is legally finalized, Jennifer and her colleagues stay in the picture. The agency hosts parties for adoptive families, so that kids and parents can meet and connect with one another. Jennifer and her colleagues also offer post-adoption counseling as a way to help preserve adoptive families who are facing tough times. In some ways, this is what Jennifer likes most about her job—following the families she has helped construct, seeing how they develop, and keeping in touch with them as they make their futures together.

Jennifer has personal experiences that make her distinctively empathetic to the families she encounters in her line of work. She and her husband have been waiting for more than five years to adopt a baby from China. Because of changes in Chinese adoption laws and procedures, they do not know when—if ever—they will be matched with a Chinese child. In the meantime, they have become licensed foster parents and have welcomed two young brothers into their home. So Jennifer is now a foster mom—she gets the boys up in the morning, gets them fed and dressed and off to school, chauffeurs them to music lessons and sports practices, and makes sure they do their homework at night. She stays up with them when they're sick, takes them on fun vacations, and fills their stockings at Christmastime. She talks with them frankly about the situation they are in and what the chances are of returning to their family of origin. And if the court decides to make the boys available for adoption, Jennifer and her husband plan to become their legal parents.

same-sex male cohabiting couples and 26 percent of same-sex female cohabiting couples had children (Krivickas and Lofquist 2011, U.S. Census Bureau 2012a). One-quater of all first births are to cohabiting parents (National Center for Health Statistics 2012a). Most couples that choose to cohabit rather than marry are twenty-five to thirty-four years of age. A possible reason may be the growing economic independence of individuals today, resulting in less financial motivation for a marriage contract. Also, changing attitudes about religion have made sexual relationships outside marriage more socially acceptable.

Single Parenting

Although some people become single parents through divorce or death, others choose to have children without the support of a committed partner—through adoption, artificial insemination, or surrogacy. In the United States, only 15 percent of single parents are single fathers (Belkin 2011). Attitudes about single mothers vary greatly and are often dependent on the mother's age, education level, occupation, and income and the family's support network from friends and extended family members.

A prevailing middle-class assumption about poor single mothers is that young women in the inner city become mothers to access welfare benefits. Kathryn Edin and Maria Kefalas (2005) spent five years doing in-depth research with 162 low-income single mothers to understand their attitudes about parenthood and marriage. They dispelled the myth that these women become mothers to cash in on welfare benefits and instead found that for these young women, having a baby is a symbol of belonging and being valued. Being a good mother is an accessible role that can generate respect and admiration in the community.

Regardless of the circumstances of single parenting, raising children without the help of a partner is challenging and difficult. Financially, physically, and emotionally, single parents must perform a task that was traditionally shared by a community rather than an individual.

Intentional Communities

As an increasing number of people choose to remain or become single, cohabit with others, or choose something else altogether, they are creating alternative models to organize their lives. Some join an **intentional community**, an inclusive term for a variety of different groups who form communal living arrangements that include ecovillages, cohousing, residential land trusts, communes, monasteries and ashrams, farming collectives, student co-ops, and urban housing cooperatives. Though small in both size and number, intentional communities are attractive to people for a variety of reasons.

Members of an intentional community have chosen to live together with a common purpose, working cooperatively to create a lifestyle that reflects their shared core values. They may live on rural land, in a suburban home, or in an urban neighborhood, and they may share a single residence or live in a cluster of dwellings. Although quite diverse in philosophy and lifestyle, each of these groups places a high priority on fostering a sense of community—a feeling of belonging and mutual support that is increasingly hard to find in mainstream Western society (Kozeny 1995).

The Postmodern Family

Families adapting to the challenges of a postmodern society may create family structures that look very different from the "traditional" family. Sociologist Judith Stacey explored some of these adaptations for her book *Brave New Families* (1990). The families and households she studied expanded and contracted over time and included members who were never part of the traditional *Leave It to Beaver* model of the nuclear family. Ex-spouses and their new partners and children, adult children and other kin, and even nonkin—friends and co-workers—populated the working-class Silicon Valley households she studied. Multiple earners and a diversity of generations, genders, and relational connections were the rule rather than the exception in her study:

> No longer is there a single culturally dominant family pattern, like the modern one, to which a majority of Americans conform and most of the rest aspire. Instead, Americans today have crafted a multiplicity of family and household arrangements that we inhabit uneasily and reconstitute frequently in response to changing personal and occupational circumstances. (Stacey 1990, p. 19)

We have entered an era of improvisation or do-it-yourself family forms; household members respond to social-structural changes in ways that fit their family's needs. These improvisational forms are not new; they are merely new to mainstream working- and middle-class families. Minorities, the poor, and gays and lesbians have always had to improvise to fit into a society that ignored or devalued their needs and activities (Stack 1974; Weston 1991; Edin and Lein 1997; Stacey 1998). These improvisational, postmodern family forms will become more and more familiar to the rest of society as we all cope with the social and cultural changes of the twenty-first century.

CLOSING COMMENTS

When sociologists study the dynamics of family, they must define the subject of their interest. What exactly is family? This process sometimes leads to definitions that lie outside the traditional notions of biological or legal relations that have historically defined family. Certainly, this is true if one looks outside the United States at the astonishing variety of customs and practices that define family around the world. In the early-twenty-first century, the nature of the nuclear family is changing, as divorced and blended families are altering the structure and function of all families, with a tendency to decrease the amount of contact and assistance between generations. The emergence of these "brave new families" has led to a sea change in the study of families, with an increasing recognition of the diversity and plurality that characterize family arrangements.

INTENTIONAL COMMUNITY
any of a variety of groups who form communal living arrangements outside marriage

Everything You Need to Know about the Family

> " Sociology doesn't define a family by who its members are but by what they do, how they relate to one another, and what their relationship is to the larger society. "

THEORIES OF THE FAMILY

* **Structural functionalism:** the family is responsible for the reproduction of society as it produces and socializes children

* **Conflict theory:** conflict within the family is about the competition for scarce resources: time, energy, and leisure; exploitation occurs through a sexual rather than a class-based division of labor

* **Symbolic interactionism:** family is a social construction that is created, changed, and maintained through ongoing interaction

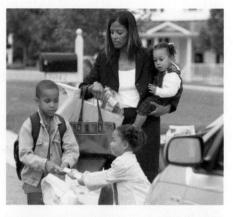

REVIEW

1. How does this chapter's definition of family differ from the one used by the U.S. Census Bureau? Make a list of everyone you consider a family member. Is there anyone on this list who wouldn't qualify according to the Census Bureau's definition?

2. Conflict theorists believe that strife within the family is fueled by competition for resources. What is the basis for inequality within the family? In families, who tends to receive fewer resources?

3. Arlie Hochschild and Anne Machung found that women who work outside the home often face a "second shift" of housework when they get home. How do men avoid doing their share of this work? Have you ever noticed someone—perhaps yourself—adopting these tactics?

Trends in American Families

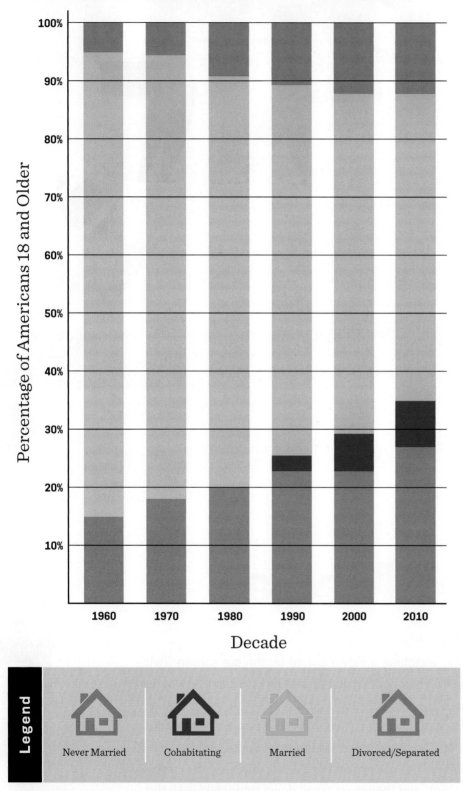

Percentage of Americans 18 and Older

y-axis: 100%, 90%, 80%, 70%, 60%, 50%, 40%, 30%, 20%, 10%

x-axis (Decade): 1960, 1970, 1980, 1990, 2000, 2010

Decade

Legend

| Never Married | Cohabitating | Married | Divorced/Separated |

SOURCE: Pew Research Social and Demographic Trends 2010, "Interactive: The Changing American Family"

EXPLORE

Family Rules:
What Is a Family?

When you think of a romantic couple, do you think of just two people involved? Yet other people are part of any romantic relationship, such as parents and friends but also society and the government, particularly if your relationship does not fall under the accepted norms. Visit the Everyday Sociology Blog to read a sociologist's explanation of different relationships.

http://wwnPag.es/trw412

CHAPTER 13

Leisure and Media

You're sitting in a darkened theater watching a movie unfold on the big screen. Two young lovers meet, woo, and marry. They honeymoon at a mountain resort—where, unfortunately, they are kidnapped by political rebels who break into song, swinging their rifles in unison as they dance in camouflage fatigues. After the ransom is paid, the couple return to the city, where they shop for housewares—at a store where clerks croon and shoppers dance in the aisles. But before they are allowed to live happily ever after, their baby is switched at birth with another infant, and they must track down their child with the help of a singing police detective/spiritual advisor. The film lasts more than three hours;

during that time, audience members (men in one section, women and children in another) come and go, fetching delicious snacks that extend far beyond prosaic popcorn and soda. They yell, groan, sing, talk back, and even throw things at the screen—but nobody shushes them. Where are you? You're in "Bollywood."

Unless you are South Asian, have traveled to India, or are a *very* dedicated film buff, you've probably never seen a Bollywood film. This term, an obvious takeoff on the American film capital, is used to describe a particular class of movies produced in Mumbai (or Bombay). The Indian film industry is the most prolific in the world, and the movies it produces are very different from those Americans are used to. A typical film usually includes romance, political intrigue, and dramatic events such as kidnappings, military battles, or natural disasters—and there is always lots of singing and dancing! In other words, Indian films are a mixture of what American audiences understand to be separate genres: romance, musical, action, thriller, and so on. As a result, Americans react to Indian films as strange, exhausting, and disorganized, while Indians find American movies boring, unemotional, and too short (Srinivas 1998).

Some American audiences got their first taste of Bollywood from British director Danny Boyle's *Slumdog Millionaire*, a film that borrowed some of the same stylistic elements and won the best picture Academy Award in 2009. The film was a "sleeper hit" that gradually grew in popularity by good word of mouth, much of it about how different the movie looked and felt. Still, it's unlikely that the theater-going experience for U.S. audiences was anything close to what is typical in India. In Indian theaters, silence is not the norm; audience members respond to what's on-screen in ways that seem startling or even wrong to Americans. The only American film experience that resembles the Bollywood model is the midnight showings of *The Rocky Horror Picture Show*, where enthusiastic fans dress up, sing along, talk back, throw toast, and shoot squirt guns at the screen. In Bollywood, though, this type of behavior is the rule.

HOW TO READ THIS CHAPTER

In this chapter, we will look at leisure and some of the many things we do for fun. This does not mean that the chapter is any less important than others that cover more traditional ground. In fact, we can and should treat the mass media, sports, entertainment, tourism, and hobbies with the same analytic approaches we use to examine other core aspects of culture and society. The production and consumption of leisure may seem lightweight or trivial at first glance, but they are worthy of serious sociological consideration. As social institutions, the leisure industries play a key role in contemporary life. We will look at the structure and meaning of leisure, its impact on society, and its ubiquitous place in our everyday experiences. Paying attention to your own leisure and media usage will add to your understanding of the chapter.

Studying Leisure

The term "leisure" is defined primarily in contrast to paid labor or other obligatory activities. **Leisure** is time that can be spent doing whatever you want, or just relaxing. This can include any activity that is satisfying or amusing, experienced as refreshing for body and mind. This means that just about any activity could fall under this heading, depending on individual preference, and that people can spend their leisure time engaged in all sorts of recreational activities (or not). The sociology of leisure is broad enough, then, to encompass all sorts of pastimes: playing volleyball, traveling to Italy, gardening, woodworking, doing needlepoint, listening to music, watching television, reading, shopping, writing poetry, hiking, baking cookies—the possibilities are endless. It's important to note that what makes something a leisure activity is not its appearance on this or any other list, but rather the experience of the activity itself. Does it feel enjoyable, liberating, even transformative? Then it's recreational. So what might be one person's job could be another person's recreational activity. If you bake cookies all day at work, for example, it's unlikely that you'll feel like doing so in your free time; those who do feel this way about their paid labor are extremely lucky!

Leisure activities have changed dramatically in recent history. In the premodern world, the line between work and play was not nearly as clearly defined as it is today—in part because there was an awful lot of work to be done and there were fewer recreational options. Activities we now engage in almost exclusively as **recreation** (like gardening, hunting and fishing, or knitting) were necessities in the past, and common pastimes like going to the movies and watching television didn't even exist. Even in the late nineteenth cen-

Rise of the Leisure Class Around the turn of the twentieth century, industrial productivity and new technologies created new opportunities for leisure among the middle and upper classes. Note this early travel magazine.

tury, low wages and long hours meant that only the wealthy had the time and resources to pursue recreational activities with any consistency. This situation began to change between 1890 and 1940, as the amount of time that the middle class could devote to leisure activities grew rapidly (Fischer 1994). The increase in leisure time was largely fueled by technological progress that increased work productivity and spurred time-saving inventions for the home such as the washing machine, dishwasher, and vacuum cleaner. Technological changes in the information age have also radically altered the nature

LEISURE a period of time that can be spent relaxing, engaging in recreation, or otherwise indulging in freely chosen activities

RECREATION any satisfying, amusing, and stimulating activity that is experienced as refreshing and renewing for body, mind, and spirit of leisure activities. We can now access digital media of all kinds, from video games to social networking, keeping us plugged in virtually 24/7.

Trends in Leisure

Most discussions of modern leisure-time activities emphasize three related trends that have changed the ways in which we engage in them. We now look at each of these developments in turn.

THE DECLINE OF PUBLIC LIFE Sociologist Richard Sennett argues that modernity has seen the "fall of public man," as people more and more seek refuge in "ties of family or intimate association" (Sennett 1977, p. 3). This decline in public life has affected leisure in far-reaching ways. After World War II, the mass migration to the suburbs and the introduction of television encouraged people to stay home and even usurped shared, public activities such as moviegoing (Fischer 1994). Television may have begun this process, but more recent developments have only intensified it. Video games, DVD players, personal computers, and the internet have all made the private home an even more attractive site for leisure. The internet in particular has begun to isolate individuals even within the home. While it can facilitate contact between people who live in different corners of the world, the internet can just as easily cut off individuals from family, friends, and spouses (Jackson 1999).

> **COMMODIFICATION** the process by which it becomes possible to buy and sell a particular good or service

One large-scale longitudinal study sponsored by the National Endowment for the Arts found that "Americans are increasingly less likely to go out for a dose of the arts, and more likely to stay home and enjoy performances in front of their home entertainment centers" (Yin 2003). The effect has been most obvious in music and theater, but even the visual arts are starting to see a change. People still visit museums and galleries, but a growing number are also looking at pictures online, or in books and magazines. Here again, technology is moving our recreation inside the home, away from public spaces.

COMMERCIALIZING LEISURE AND RECREATION The second development, and this one has made a greater mark on our leisure time than any other, is the massive increase in the **commodification** of recreational activities: where people formerly made their own fun, they now purchase it as goods and services. What Americans spend on entertainment per year hit $490 billion in 2012, and is expected to surpass $597 billion in 2016 (Snider 2012), most of it on media products (music, movies, TV, games, books, magazines, newspapers, and so on). Television in particular is referred to as "the 800-pound gorilla of leisure time" (Putnam 1995), but its tremendous popularity has begun to

dip as more online viewing options have become available. In 2011, more than 96 percent of American households still had television, down from a previous high of almost 99 percent (Stelter 2011). In fact, over one third of all households had four or more TVs in it (The Nielsen Company 2013). Television continues to be America's number one pastime, with the average viewer spending well over four and a half hours a day watching TV (Stelter 2012).

Simple, inexpensive outdoor activities like hiking are still popular, but they increasingly compete with "technologically innovative forms of play such as scuba diving, parasailing, skydiving, and hang-gliding, snowmobiling, and other kinds of off-road travel [that] have opened up new environments for the play experience" (Kraus 1995).

Even those activities that were once necessities, like hunting and fishing, now come with a dizzying array of commodities. Sport fishing relies on expensive boats, lures, rods, and sonar to help locate the fish. Hunting seems to demand special clothing, scent blockers, calls and decoys, infrared vision enhancement, and even special hearing aids that allow hunters to tune in to specific frequencies while stalking particular animals. Instead of visiting the local swimming hole, we pay to visit water parks. Instead of playing softball or soccer, many simply watch sports on TV, played by professionals. In almost every case, our recreation is mediated by goods and services that we seem to "require" in order to have fun.

The ultimate example of the commercialization of leisure, however, is shopping: where the purchase of commodities becomes an end in itself. Recreational shopping is a recent historical development. Until the mid-twentieth century, people shopped mainly to acquire food, clothing, fuel, and other essential goods. But now, in addition, we shop to live out daydreams, to experience a "sensual and emotional high" (Zukin 2004, p. 220). Shopping is no longer just about "bread"—it has also become its own "circus," with more than 100,000 malls and shopping centers nationwide to support our habit (U.S. Census Bureau 2012n).

Leisure, money, and business intersect in other ways as well. When you go to a professional baseball or basketball game, chances are that you're there to root for your favorite team, eat hot dogs and drink soda or beer, and generally have a good time with family or friends. Work is probably the last thing on your mind. But what about the people who help provide that experience for you—the parking attendants, ticket-takers, security officers, ushers, food and souvenir vendors, janitors, and maintenance workers? What about the team owners, talent scouts, agents, managers, coaches, trainers, and players themselves? If the game is covered by the media, then you can add announcers, reporters, sportscasters, photographers, camera crews, producers, editors, publishers, advertisers, and others.

Clearly, the business of recreation and leisure is a big business. To take baseball as an example, in 2008 the New York Yankees hit their all-time high record with more than

Commercialized Leisure Today, many of our forms of leisure and recreation are mediated by commodities, goods, and services that we seem to "require" in order to have fun. This boat show featuring the newest in bass fishing gear is an example.

4.3 million people attending eighty-one home games, an average of about 53,000 per game (ESPN 2008). Millions more tuned in to the games on radio and TV. Overall, the businesses that could be broadly classified as providing recreation or entertainment are easily worth trillions of dollars. As such, these industries account for a major part of the U.S. and global economies.

Like a baseball game, almost any kind of activity we enjoy must be supported in some way by others. From hiking in the local foothills (consider how the Parks and Recreation Department might be involved in maintaining trails) to eating an ice cream cone (consider the manufacturing, delivery, and service involved in getting the cone to your hand), many people work to make these activities possible. By some estimates, there are more than 25 million leisure and recreation jobs that are staffed in the United States alone.

FORMALIZING RECREATION: ORGANIZATION OVER SPONTANEITY In addition to moving from the public to the private sphere and becoming increasingly commodified, many forms of leisure and recreation seem to have shifted from spontaneous or informal activities to organized and formal. This "development of organization over spontaneity" is illustrated by the rise of Little League baseball as an organized alternative to after-school sand-lot games (Fischer 1994). There is a great deal of debate as to whether the rise of organization is good or bad. Technology has indirectly assisted this process: cell phones, e-mail, the internet, and radio and TV advertising all make it easier to organize people in different geographic locations. Even hiking, what used to be a casual walk in the woods, has become organized.

For instance, local chapters of the Sierra Club sponsor regular weekly group hikes, where members are advised about the proper gear to bring and encouraged to carpool.

Leisure: The Opposite of Work?

Work has typically been understood as serious and consequential, while leisure activities are seen as minor and unimportant. Leisure activities, though, absorb so much time, energy, and resources that they must represent "important developmental goals and meet other personal needs of both children and adults" (Kraus 1995). In many ways, it is leisure that provides the most "meaningful experiences" and allows people "opportunities to reveal their true selves" (Havitz and Dimanche 1999).

Many people think of their nonwork time as free time, or leisure time (using the terms interchangeably). Therefore, leisure must be the opposite of work, right? Consider the following scenario. With final exams looming around the corner, Amber, Zack, and Juan—all taking the same sociology class—plan an evening study session at a local café. Amber arrives late from her job as a sales clerk. Zack and Juan have already outlined a few chapters and drunk a few cups of coffee. The three chat for a while before continuing to study. The café is bustling with other students studying, too. At the end of the night, they plan to meet again the following day.

When does work end and leisure begin? In our scenario, it is difficult to decide which is which. Meeting at a café to study seems more like a leisure activity than doing retail sales at a store. However, studying at a café seems more like work than merely meeting friends to chat.

Rather than understanding leisure as the opposite of work, sociologists see the two as complementary activities within a capitalist economic system—two activities linked by **consumption** (Rojek 1985, 1995). Thus, we work for wages to consume a variety of goods and services, including leisure. As we consume more leisure, we must earn more wages to pay for it. As we have seen, leisure is itself a booming industry, with millions of workers servicing our leisure desires. We choose leisure time to supplement our working lives, and the connection between the two is more than merely oppositional.

So, what is free time? Sociologist Chris Rojek warns us not to equate free time (or nonworking time) with leisure time (1985, 1995, 2000). Consider the following example. When Cheryl finishes work for the day, picks up her children from school, cooks her family an evening meal, helps her children with their schoolwork, and then puts them to bed, has she had any free time? Is free time only the time not spent working for wages? What about an office worker who realizes that he is already prepared for a meeting and thus has a few minutes with nothing to do; are those few minutes free time? Is time spent driving to class or to work or volunteering at a local homeless shelter free time? Or is free time when we have "nothing" to do? If so, what constitutes "nothing"?

> **CONSUMPTION** the utilization of goods and services, either for personal use or in manufacturing

Free time is as ambiguous as it is difficult to measure. Arguably, Cheryl continues to work after she leaves her job at 5:00 PM and thus has no free time. She, however, may think of spending time with her family as her free time. Rojek argues that leisure, by its very definition, constitutes some kind of choice about how to spend one's time (1985). People make choices to *do* something with their time, whether it's honing their tennis skills or studying a new language. Therefore, free time is not necessarily leisure time.

Leisure and Inequality

Leisure activities can range from sleeping in to building houses for Habitat for Humanity. For some people, watching TV is a leisure activity. For others, leisure means such activities as skydiving or snowboarding. For many, it's both.

Sociologists have long associated types of leisure activities with social class. Thus, working-class people do different things with their leisure than wealthy elites do. Interestingly, the wealthy do not necessarily have more leisure time; rather, their work sometimes closely resembles play (Rojek 1997, 2000). Networking on the golf course, for example, is still a kind of work but vastly divergent from teaching school. Also, professional athletes' work would not be considered in the same way by people who play football with their neighbors on the weekends, nor would professional musicians' work by

people who play in a local amateur band. Successful actors and actresses work by managing what they eat, "working" out, attending lavish parties, and just looking beautiful for the cameras. In this way, many people strive for leisure activities that resemble the work of elites, celebrities, athletes, and musicians.

Spectatorship

As spectators, we have many choices of how to watch a sports or other event. We can attend a live soccer match in our own country or watch it beamed from another country on TV or the internet. We can also choose when to watch it, if we record the game. Via the internet, we can participate through social media or gambling rings and role-playing games associated with our favorite sport. In such ways, spectatorship has become a huge and complex leisure activity.

The Structure of Media Industries

As we have seen, people spend their leisure time engaged in a wide variety of activities. For many Americans, consuming media—reading the newspaper, watching TV, listening to the radio, or surfing the internet—accounts for a large portion of this time. Clearly, the media are a major social institution and one with increasing power and importance in the Information Age. At first glance, we might conclude that its purpose is simply to supply information, educate, or entertain. While this is not incorrect, it is a somewhat naïve view of a complex and sophisticated social institution.

The Media and Democracy

One of the first things to remember about the media is their intimate relationship to a democratic system of government. The media have always been seen as both an instrument of the state and a tool for social change. Some of the original struggles during the fight for American independence were waged around these very issues. Early American leaders recognized the importance of news in educating and mobilizing the new citizenry. They were opposed to European governments' control over the media (which consisted at that time of books and newspapers) and sought instead to free the press so that it could be used as a voice of the people. That is precisely why the framers of the U.S. Constitution included guarantees to freedom of expression and freedom of the press in the First Amendment:

> Congress shall make no law respecting an establishment of religion, or prohibiting the free exercise thereof; or abridging the freedom of speech, or of the press; or the right of the people peaceably to assemble, and to petition the Government for a redress of grievances.

ON THE JOB

Musicians "Playing" Music

Who wouldn't want to be a rock star? Lear-jetting from city to city, mobbed by adoring fans, staying in four-star hotel suites, partying backstage with models and celebrities. And getting paid tons of money to play, and the operative word is "play," music.

This stereotype of the rock and roll lifestyle is widespread, and one of the most underappreciated aspects of the work that professional musicians do is that it *is* work. Certainly no musician could deny the perks and privileges that come with success. But they would also say that there is no such thing as an overnight success, that practically everyone has had to pay his dues, and that few ever become rich and famous. Many professional musicians work in relative obscurity as band members, session players, songwriters, or producers. Their careers can be tenuous and short-lived.

Musicians recognize that their work is not manual labor, that they're not out sweating in the fields or laying bricks, nor are they stuck in an office from 9:00 to 5:00. But neither is what they do as fun and easy as it might appear.

In order to achieve and maintain success over the years, it is necessary for any musician, regardless of how talented, to work consistently and hard. Professionals typically devote endless hours to learning and practicing their craft. The work conditions can be difficult and the days long and grueling. Writing, recording, rehearsing, and touring require sustained concentration, teamwork, and stamina. The work is often characterized by drudgery and repetition rather than spontaneity and creativity. After years in the business, some musicians suffer from the same kind of disenchantment with their careers that workers in other fields experience, despite whatever notions of romance might have attracted them to music in the first place (Stein 1997).

The rewards of working in any glamorous profession, whether it's music, show business, or sports, probably seem worth any of these difficulties. As social observers, however, we need to consider what goes on behind the scenes and to remember that what looks like play to one person might feel a lot more like work to another.

Playing and Working The band Sonic Youth performing on stage and working in the recording studio since 1981. Longevity in the music business is the exception, and remaining successful requires a strong work ethic on the part of the musicians.

These are among our most precious and fiercely defended rights as Americans. Furthermore, the press was also to serve as a kind of "**Fourth Estate.**" The press could act like a separate branch of the government which could independently examine political leaders and give the people another means of checks and balances against the three branches (or "estates") of the government. It would ensure that no branch, whether the executive, legislative, or judicial, amassed too much power. Thus the media are a last defense of an open, democratic system. They play a critical role in uncovering and exposing all kinds of government malfeasance, corruption, and incompetence.

While the principle of a free press still stands today, it is worth considering just who is free to own what we currently refer to as "the press"; in other words, a media outlet. Who has access to the media, who controls media products, whose voice is reaching a mass audience, and what kind of message is being sent by these powerful instruments of "free speech"?

Concentration of Media Power

Media companies are among the many big businesses that drive the American economy, and their profits and losses are closely followed by investors in the stock market. Media products are among the country's biggest exports, and there are almost too many publishers, production companies, TV networks, film studios, radio stations, and record labels to name. What is not readily evident from this seeming proliferation is that the businesses are often owned by the same large parent companies. The trend toward **conglomeration** began growing in the 1990s (McChesney 2000). Huge corporations were acquiring media companies as part of their larger holdings. This is why a company like Seagram's, which manufactured alcoholic beverages, bought (and later sold) Universal (then MCA), which produces film, television, and music. Or how General Electric, which makes everything from washing machines to warheads, came to own the NBC television network. Buying successful media companies made sense as an economic investment, so it is not surprising that other corporations might want to share in the huge profits generated in the entertainment industry.

A typical media conglomerate might comprise many divisions: book and magazine publishing, radio and TV broadcasting, a cable network, a movie studio and theaters, record labels, videogame distribution, web sites, a theme park, even a sports franchise. Also referred to as horizontal integration, this allows the company to take advantage of its own organizational structure and market its products across a wide range of different media formats and outlets. Media companies favor products they can "cross-promote" along their various divisions, thus creating what is called **synergy**. For example, a company might produce a movie that is adapted from a book it published, distribute the film to theaters it owns, advertise and review it in company newspapers and magazines, put the soundtrack on its record label, create recognizable characters that appear in commercials or at its theme park, release the movie on its DVD label, and later broadcast it on the company's cable channel and television network.

The cornucopia of media choices is thus somewhat deceiving. Many different brands and labels are all really just different company identities within its larger structure. There are actually very few "independent" media producers that can remain viable in such a marketplace. Often, once an independent becomes successful, it is quickly bought out by a larger conglomerate, which is searching for ways to increase revenues. Another trend consists of a **merger** between two or more companies to create an even bigger media giant. The model for this trend, and at the time the largest media company ever, took place in 2000 with the merger between a new media company, AOL (America Online), and an older one, Time Warner (Disney has since surpassed it in size).

DATA WORKSHOP
Analyzing Mass Media And Popular Culture

Mega-Hits (and Flops) and the Movie Business

When the Walt Disney Co. bought Lucasfilm (home of "Star Wars") for over $4 billion in 2012, the acquisition made big headlines across the business news. Just a few years earlier in 2009, Disney had pulled off another aggressive buyout of Marvel, the comic book and movie studio, for the same amount of $4 billion (Barnes 2009). Taken together, these two deals presented some of the most lucrative possibilities

FOURTH ESTATE the media is considered like a fourth branch of government (after the executive, legislative, and judiciary) and thus serves as another of the checks and balances on power

CONGLOMERATION the process by which a single corporation acquires ownership of a variety of otherwise unrelated businesses

SYNERGY a mutually beneficial interaction between parts of an organization that allows it to create something greater than the sum of its individual outputs

MERGER the legal combination of two companies, usually in order to maximize efficiency and profits by eliminating redundant infrastructure and personnel

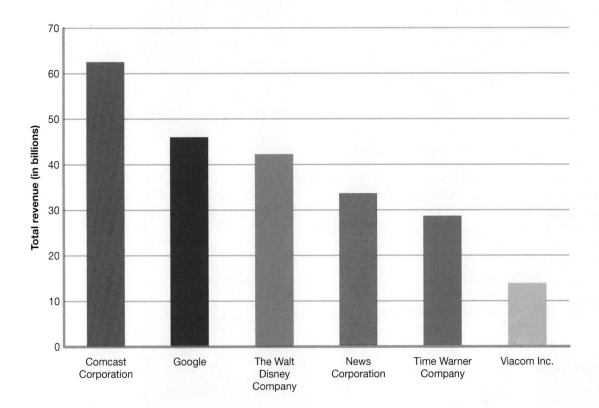

Figure 13.1 **The Concentration of Media Outlets**

Media conglomerates and their subsidiaries are often household names. Comcast owns NBC Universal and Universal Films. Google owns the mobile operating system Android and YouTube. The Walt Disney Company owns Marvel Entertainment, Lucasfilm, and ESPN. News Corporation owns FOX and the Wall Street Journal. Time Warner owns HBO and Warner Brothers Entertainment. Viacom Inc. owns MTV, Comedy Central, and Paramount Pictures.

SOURCES: CJR 2010, Comcast Corporation 2012, Google Inc. 2012, News Corp. 2012, Time Warner Inc. 2012, Viacom Inc. 2012, The Walt Disney Company 2012.

ever in terms of Disney's added ability for synergy, marketing, and future growth (Gabler 2012). Disney now owned some of the most recognizable and bankable brands in entertainment and was poised to translate them into greater successes and profits, a situation to which any media company would aspire. Disney had already been a media giant before these buyouts, but the new acquisitions positioned the company to become even more powerful and dominate more of the market among the "Big 6" media conglomerates.

Most people think of movies as primarily a form of entertainment. But in this Data Workshop we want you to consider them as a business. And the movie business is big business, especially when it comes to those mega, blockbuster hits. Making movies for a mass audience is expensive (and risky), but it can also be highly profitable. The major studios that make these kinds of movies must necessarily come up with strategies to help maximize the potential for profits and minimize the potential risks of financing a costly "flop." How can media companies ensure that their biggest movies become their biggest hits? This is where their corporate practices and structures can benefit the bottom line.

Media companies are increasingly structured around horizontal integration, a type of organization where the company can control almost every aspect of the production and distribution process and use their various corporate divisions to market movies across many different platforms. In other words, they can benefit from cross-promotion. The greater the variety and reach of a company's divisions, the more opportunities there are to create synergy. The most attractive properties are those that might start as a comic book but can then be turned into a movie and a video game, where the stars of the movie can be featured on TV talk shows or magazine covers and where fans will be able to follow additional story lines and converse with other fans on web sites. Think of all the avenues for promotion that a media giant might own and exploit.

One common practice in filmmaking follows the adage that "nothing succeeds like success." Studio execs favor movie "franchises" from which many hits can be spawned. Think *James Bond, Mission Impossible, X-Men, Iron Man, Spider-Man, Transformers, Star Wars*, and such. These films were the basis for producing many other, sometimes even more successful, films in the form of prequels, sequels, and spin-offs.

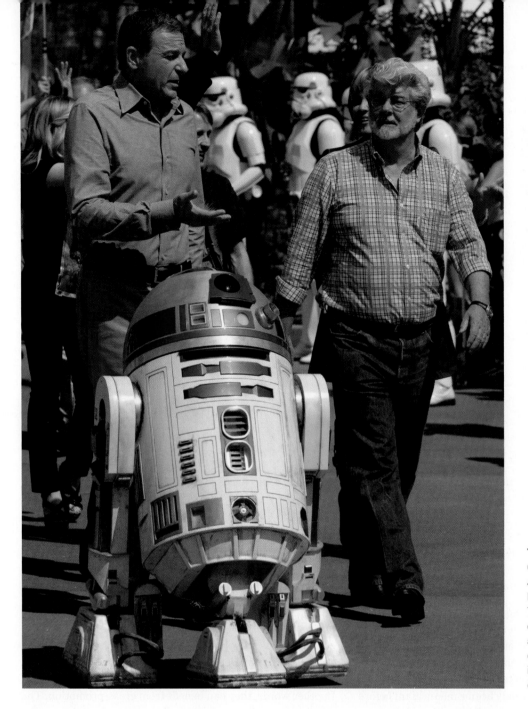

The Disney Empire Disney CEO Robert Iger, left, and *Star Wars* creator George Lucas in Walt Disney World. Through acquisitions of major companies like Lucasfilm and Marvel, Disney now occupies a more horizontally integrated position in the entertainment industry.

A related approach is to do re-makes by producing an updated version of an older film that was successful, for instance, *Footloose.*

Another strategy for increasing the odds of a hit, or at least diminishing the losses that might incur from a flop, is to partner with an outside company and engage in what is referred to as "co-promotion." In these relationships, the partner company invests in the film for some kind of consideration, primarily rights to promote its products in conjunction with the film. This takes several shapes. The partner can provide product placement within the film to more covertly "advertise" their particular brand (whether it's an automobile, cell phone, or soda) to audiences. Or the partner might be involved in merchandising tie-ins with the film (for example, toy action figures, collector's cups, t-shirts, or backpacks). See Morgan Spurlock's 2011 documentary *POM Wonderful Presents: The Greatest Movie Ever Sold* for some insight (and humor) about the role of advertising in contemporary filmmaking. Not quite ironically, the film was financed entirely by corporate partners.

For this Data Workshop you will be asked to use existing sources as a research method (see Chapter 2 for a review). Investigate the marketing and promotion for a recent blockbuster movie hit. How many elements from the strategies described above can you find to help account for its success? Did the movie studio take advantage of all possible avenues to reap the greatest profits, or can you suggest other ways the studio could have improved or expanded its sales campaigns?

There are two options for completing the assigned work.

Option 1 (informal): Choose a blockbuster film to examine. Look at how the movie was marketed. Make notes about what you find to bring to class. Discuss with others in small groups, comparing the different films and their promotional campaigns.

Option 2 (formal): Write a three- to four-page essay addressing the questions above and the various ways that movie studios attempt to produce hits. Make reference to the data you collect about the marketing campaigns.

Mergers and acquisitions associated with conglomeration result in yet another major trend: **concentration**. The ownership of media companies of all kinds is now concentrated in the hands of fewer and fewer large conglomerates. Communication researchers who follow media ownership saw a consistent trend through the 1980s and 1990s characterized by mergers and buyouts and resulting in fewer but larger media companies in the 2000s (McChesney 1997, 2004; Bagdikian 2004). Researchers often refer to the "Big 6" global media conglomerates, down from more than twenty-five such companies just a decade or two ago, that now dominate the media industries (Klinenberg 2007; Shah 2007; FreePress.net 2011). While few in number, these media giants keep getting bigger. That leaves only a small percentage of media companies truly independent from this corporate reality.

Two government agencies, the Federal Communications Commission (FCC) and the Securities and Exchange Commission (SEC), are charged with regulating the large conglomerates. The FCC has established some restrictions on media-outlet ownership by any single company in order to avoid a **monopoly** in any one market. Otherwise, one media giant might be able to own all the newspapers and TV and radio stations in a region, effectively stifling any competition and potentially providing a single voice for information where several voices serve a democracy better. And the SEC is involved in **antitrust legislation**, governing mergers between companies and further discouraging monopolies from forming. However, in recent years, increasing **deregulation**, the reduction or removal of government restrictions on the media industry, has allowed companies to gain control of ever-larger chunks of the media market. These decisions are often fiercely debated by the U.S. Congress, media companies, and media watchdog groups. Social critics are concerned about increasing concentration and its possible consequences for a democratic society that values freedom of the press and a plurality of voices. If the largest companies are allowed to control the dissemination of information, does that undermine the constitutional rights of average citizens to have their voices heard?

CONCENTRATION the process by which the number of companies producing and distributing a particular commodity decreases, often through mergers and conglomeration

MONOPOLY a situation in which there is only one individual or organization, without competitors, providing a particular good or service

ANTITRUST LEGISLATION laws designed to maintain competition in the marketplace by prohibiting monopolies, price fixing, or other forms of collusion among businesses

DEREGULATION reduction or removal of government controls from an industry to allow for a free and efficient marketplace

POWER SHIFTS IN THE MEDIA INDUSTRY—APPLE EDITION So how will the structure of the media industry change in the future? One answer is being provided by Apple and the iPods, iPads, and iPhones that Apple has made

Media Mergers and Buyouts Cable television company Comcast purchased a majority stake in NBC Universal from General Electric in 2011, allowing the company to control both the content and delivery of television shows like *Low & Order* to audiences.

The Structure of Media Industries **383**

IN THE FUTURE

Change in the Media Industry

What will the media industry look like in the future, and what will be our experience using new communication technologies? Quantitatively, media industries are changing faster and more extensively than ever before. Qualitatively, media industries are rapidly shifting from a broadcast-based model to a networked one. Much will be new in the near future, and much will repeat patterns that characterize the past and present realities.

In simple quantitative terms, the twenty-first century has seen enormous volatility in the technology we consume our media with. Amazon first introduced its e-book reader, the Kindle, in 2007, and it sold out within hours. It wasn't the first commercially available e-book reader, but it was the start of a dramatic change in the way books are produced, sold, and consumed. Other e-readers quickly followed, and in 2010 Apple released the iPad, a tablet computer that was, along with many other functions, marketed as an e-reader, and it came with a built-in digital bookstore to sell e-books. The effect has been dramatic. In 2007, e-books barely existed. In 2013, 27 percent of Americans own either an e-reader or a tablet computer that is designed to display e-books, and 43 percent of adults report having "either read an e-book in the past year or hav[ing] read other long-form content such as magazines, journals, and news articles" on one of these devices (Rainie et al. 2012, p. 3). Meanwhile, the Borders chain of bookstores declared bankruptcy, and the Barnes and Noble chain has aggressively marketed its own e-reader, the Nook.

Along with the increasing volatility of media industries, there was also a fundamental shift in the nature of media industries, from those based on broadcast to those based on networks. Traditional media companies were based on broadcasting information. A small number of people at a central location would produce and disseminate information to a mass audience. The twenty-first century saw this model become increasingly less important compared to "new media," which are based on the internet and digital technology, which allows for media that are instantaneous and interactive. Even when traditional media companies, like major television networks, remain important, they almost always have added elements of "new media" to the mix. For example, MSNBC's *The Rachel Maddow Show* is a classic example of traditional media, but the show's host also has a Twitter account. On Friday, December 21, 2012, those watching Wayne LaPierre, the head of the National Rifle Association (NRA), when he gave a speech addressing the school shooting in Newton, Connecticut, could also follow Maddow's Twitter feed. There she argued that "the NRA has rickrolled the whole country into watching just another standard Wayne LaPierre stump speech saying we need more guns" (Maddow 2012). The metaphor was itself a product of internet culture. "Rickrolling" is a kind of practical joke in which someone is fooled into clicking on a link that surreptitiously leads them to a video of Rick Astley's 1987 hit "Never Gonna Give You Up." The reference became part of the broadcast show that night, but as a tweet it also allowed thousands of people to retweet it, whether they agreed or not, and so have an interactive conversation about the issue, rather than simply watching a television.

However, as much as things have changed, in some ways the new media landscape resembles the old. Perhaps the biggest shift in media in the twenty-first century was the rise of social networking exemplified by Facebook. Certainly

ubiquitous. Apple represents a fundamental shift in the way that media industries work, with power transferring from the companies that produce products to companies that distribute them. In this way, Apple is part of a postmodern economy, as David Harvey described it, where the need to sell more products faster will lead to "a shift from the consumption of goods and into the consumption of services," including "entertainments, spectacles, happenings, and distractions" (1990 p. 285). Harvey predicted this shift back in the 1990s when he noticed that there are "limits to the accumulation and turnover of physical goods," making more "ephemeral" products like an mp3 or a downloaded movie ideal for an economy that needs to sell more this year than it did last year.

This business model has served Apple well. Even the physical products it sells, the iMac computer, the iPod, iPad, and iPhone, are all designed to allow customers to buy other things—software, music, movies, apps, and games. In fact, it's even possible to buy a song from iTunes without involving anyone but the record company that owns the song and Apple, which owns "the Web browser software (Safari), the computer media player (iTunes), the portable digital music player (iPod), the streaming technology to play music videos (Quicktime), the software that creates the service (Web-Objects), the computer itself (Macintosh), and the operating system (MacOS)" (Strauss 2003). What is becoming clear is that in a digital age, the companies that provide access to enter-social media have been a volatile area as well, as MySpace was replaced as the most popular social network by Facebook. However, even as online social networks reshape how people interact and spend their leisure time, they also replicate many social dynamics that preceded the internet. Sociologist danah boyd has researched the online activity of teenagers and come up with some surprising explanations for their behavior. Most famously, she argued that MySpace had not generally lost teen users to Facebook, but that there had been a "white flight" as a subset of users who were much more likely to be white and affluent switched social networks. boyd argued that "new media" like online social networks "reflected a reproduction of social categories that exist in schools throughout the United States" and so "the choice between MySpace and Facebook became racialized" (boyd 2011, p. 2). In this way, changes in media that are radical in some ways can also simply repeat old, and in this case very unfortunate, social patterns.

Books of the Future Readers consume e-books on an iPad and a Kindle. How has media consumption changed in the twenty-first century, and how has it remained the same?

tainment and media will be at least as important as the companies that actually make the entertainment. We look at more changes in the media industry in this chapter's In the Future box.

New Voices in Media

Even in today's heavily concentrated media market, there are still opportunities for alternative voices to be heard. These voices, though, are often confined to small, marginal outlets. Bloggers and podcasters are able to circumvent the constraints of commercial radio and print journalism to transmit their opinions and musical sensibilities to an (admittedly small) audience. Web sites like YouTube allow individuals to upload their homemade videos. Someone may garner thousands of followers on Twitter. Online and print "zines" (underground self-publications) are created by individuals who feel that a topic close to their hearts (such as a favorite band or comic book or an important political issue) is not getting proper treatment from the mainstream press. Punk rock bands like the 1970s' Sex Pistols and New York Dolls, as well as their more contemporary descendants like Fugazi, Bikini Kill, and Sleater-Kinney, produced and promoted their music outside the major record-label system, as part of a "D.I.Y." (do-it-yourself) movement (Shippers 2002). With the rapid development of faster and cheaper digital media, more people now have more access to technologies that allow them to produce and distribute their own work in the global marketplace. It's worth asking, though: whose voices get heard in a saturated media landscape?

Self-Regulation and Censorship

Another area of intense debate about media industries revolves around the content they produce and government censorship. The FCC imposes regulations on what the media may produce, once again qualifying the notion of absolute freedom of expression. As you may be aware, certain types of speech are not protected under the Constitution. Material considered to be obscene, for example, is illegal. The criteria used to define obscenity are based on a momentous 1959 Supreme Court decision, *Roth vs. United States*. According to the ruling, child pornography and other "material which deals with sex in a manner appealing to prurient interest" are considered obscene. However, the line between "indecent" material, which is restricted but not forbidden, and obscene material is sometimes hard to draw.

Over the past several decades, various media industries have turned to self-regulation of the materials they produce, often in the face of threats of censorship and in an effort to avoid outside regulation by government agencies. These efforts first began in 1968 when the Motion Picture Association of America established the movie ratings with which you are likely familiar. Those ratings are G, PG, R, and more recently PG-13 and NC-17, the latter to distinguish material unfit for anyone under seventeen from adult or pornographic material carrying an X rating. Next was the music business in 1985, when the Recording Industry Association of America agreed to place warning stickers on certain albums containing songs about drugs, sex, violence, and other potentially objectionable subjects. These labels ("Parental Advisory: Explicit Lyrics") were the recording industry's response to pressure from U.S. Senate hearings and lobbying from the Parents' Music Resource Center, headed by Tipper Gore (former wife of then senator and future vice president Al Gore).

The 1990s ushered in self-regulation for other media industries. The Entertainment Software Rating Board established a rating system for video games in 1993 based on age-appropriateness. In 1997, television programs began featuring a ratings system that not only suggests the appropriate age for viewers but also warns of violence (real-life or cartoon), sex (including dialogue with sexual innuendo), and offensive language. The "V-chip" in TVs allows parents to block reception of violent programs altogether.

These voluntary measures at regulating content, self-imposed by media industries, acknowledge the concern that some material is unsuitable, especially for children. Some studies of the effectiveness of these measures indicate that children are still being exposed to objectionable material and that parents may be misled if they believe ratings systems are preventing their children from having access to those materials (Garry and Spurlin 2007). The internet has further facilitated widespread access to all forms of media. With the massive proliferation of adult material that is available online, it is increasingly difficult to police content and the possibility of exposure.

Debates about the content and power of the media rage on. Some claim that media content, especially when it is violent or sexual in nature, has a negative effect on society and should therefore be restricted; others support a media free-market or believe that the right to free speech or artistic freedom should in no way be infringed. These issues are frequently in the spotlight, often in the wake of some high-profile or controversial event that exposes large audiences to something inappropriate and that should be prohibited viewing. The Super Bowl halftime show provides a couple of examples such as singer Janet Jackson's "wardrobe malfunction" in 2004 and rapper M.I.A.'s flipping of the middle finger in 2011. These types of controversies highlight some of the conflicts between different types of culture, media, and audiences.

High, Low, and Popular Culture

"Culture wars" about audiences and the appropriateness of material can be fought just about anywhere. In the summer of 1998, an exhibit opened at the Guggenheim Museum in New York City that was uniformly panned by the critics. The *New Republic* called the exhibit "a pop nostalgia orgy masquerading as a major artistic statement," and *Salon's* art critic accused the Guggenheim of "wear[ing] its cultural pants around its ankles" and "sucking down to our lowest impulses." What were they so upset about?

Are Video Game Ratings Effective? The Entertainment Software Rating Board created ratings such as "T" for teen and "M" for mature for video games in the 1990s.

The exhibit was entitled "The Art of the Motorcycle," and the critics were upset because motorcycles weren't, in their opinion, art. The public, on the other hand, loved it—the exhibit broke all previous museum attendance records. People who might never otherwise have set foot in the museum came to view this colorful collection of motorcycles dating back to 1868.

The motorcycles at the Guggenheim stirred up a long-standing debate that questioned the very definitions of art and culture. The critics' objections were based on their perception that **popular culture**, or mass culture (motorcycles), had invaded a **high culture** venue (the Guggenheim Museum). In this case, popular culture was seen as unsavory and even dangerous—the implication being that pop culture is a mass phenomenon that somehow threatens the position of the elites by challenging their preferences. As with so many sociological concepts, these terms come originally from the German; in this case, *kultur* (the culture of the elite classes) and *massenkultur* (the culture of the masses). But are these two categories really that separate?

First, there are multiple high cultures and multiple pop cultures, based on differences in taste and aesthetics. Also, each category has its own set of hierarchies. For example, rap and hip-hop music are definitely pop culture phenomena. Produced by mostly minority artists for whom "street credibility" is one of the most important qualifications, these musical forms have widespread popular appeal, especially among teenagers and young adults. But rap and hip-hop have their own elites, artists who are at the top of the charts and who have a great deal of influence within and outside their pop culture domain. Examples such as Kanye West, Dr. Dre, Queen Latifah, Beyoncé, and Jay-Z, the elites of the rap and hip-hop worlds, show that the distinction between mass and elite is a fuzzy one.

There is another way in which this distinction is problematic. In the real world, most cultural products contain elements of both mass and high culture. Why do you think we call certain TV programs soap "operas"? The storylines and intense emotions of *The Young and the Restless* parallel and sometimes rival those of Giacomo Puccini's *Madama Butterfly* and Wolfgang Amadeus Mozart's *Don Giovanni*. Led Zeppelin and Van Halen songs, when written out in standard musical notation, show a recognizable symphonic structure. Rap and hip-hop overtly draw on other types of music in the practice of sampling, and Ludwig von Beethoven, Georges Bizet, and Béla Bartók have all been sampled by R&B artists. These examples, and many others, indicate that high and pop culture are not mutually exclusive and can coexist within the same product.

The distinctions between high and popular culture are based on the characteristics of their audiences. Differences of class, education, race, and even religion help create these categories. Sociologist Herbert Gans (1999) calls the groups of people who share similar artistic, recreational, and intellectual interests **taste publics**. Taste publics aren't necessarily organized groups, but they do inhabit the same aesthetic worlds, which Gans calls **taste cultures**; that is, people who share the same tastes will also usually move in the same cultural circles. For example, sociologist David Halle (1993) found that members of the upper class are more likely to have abstract paintings hanging in their homes, while members of the working class are more likely to display family photographs in their homes.

The music, movies, clothes, foods, art, books, magazines, cars, sports, and television programs you enjoy are influenced at least in part by your position in society. Unknowingly, you belong to a number of taste publics and inhabit a number of taste cultures, in that you share your interests with others who are similar to you sociologically. What you think of as your own unique individual preferences are in some ways predetermined by your age, race, class and education levels, and regional location.

Polysemy, Audiences, and Fans

The saga of the motorcycles at the Guggenheim should help us understand an important concept in the study of media and culture: polysemy. Sociologists use the term **polysemy** to describe how any cultural product is subject to multiple

Is This Art? The 1998 show "The Art of the Motorcycle" at the Guggenheim Museum in New York broke attendance records but attracted negative reviews from art critics for "sucking down to our lowest impulses."

POPULAR CULTURE usually contrasted with the high culture of elite groups; forms of cultural expression usually associated with the masses, consumer goods, and commercial products

HIGH CULTURE those forms of cultural expression usually associated with the elite or dominant classes

TASTE PUBLICS groups of people who share similar artistic, literary, media, recreational, and intellectual interests

TASTE CULTURES areas of culture that share similar aesthetics and standards of taste

POLYSEMY having many possible meanings or interpretations

High Art and Pop Art Are Not Mutually Exclusive Even though Andy Warhol's work is now exhibited in high culture venues like esteemed modern art museums, he was perceived as a threat to the "real" art world when he began his work in the 1960s. At the bottom is Warhol's subversion of a high art masterpiece, Leonardo da Vinci's *The Last Supper* (above).

interpretations and hence has many possible meanings (Hall 1980; Fiske 1989). For instance, a cartoon like *The Simpsons* can be enjoyed on a variety of levels, by children and adults, for its humor alone, and for its social commentary. Polysemy helps us understand how one person can absolutely love the same movie (or song, painting, cartoon, necklace, car, meal, or tattoo) that another person absolutely hates. Meaning is not a given, nor is it entirely open—we make meaning individually and together, as audiences and consumers of culture.

Media researchers have sought to understand whether popular culture can influence certain types of behavior (Gerbner and Gross 1976; Gerbner et al. 1980; Malamuth and Donnerstein 1984; Weinstein 1991, 2000). Do TV crime shows increase our propensity to violence? Do pornographic magazines lead to the abuse of women? Does heavy metal

music make teenagers suicidal? Such questions suggest that cultural products impose their intrinsic meanings on their audiences in a simplistic, stimulus-and-response fashion. But while it is true that mass media products are potentially powerful transmitters of cultural values and norms, the process is neither immediate nor uncomplicated. As we know, audiences come from different backgrounds, which help define experiences and interpret the cultural products they consume. This makes it more likely, then, that polysemy will come into play: that audience members will interpret the same texts in different ways.

We may acknowledge that things like watching soap operas, reading comic books, and playing video games are trivial in the larger scheme of things, but if these forms of pop culture give us pleasure and connect us with others, they may not be so trivial after all. Serious sociological insights can be gained from studying what appear to be superficial pursuits (Postman 1987; Schudson 2003). Recreation, leisure, culture, and media are actually serious business and are empirically analyzable from a sociological perspective.

Mass Media Consumption: Passive vs. Active Audiences

Sometimes dramatic current events like the 2012 mass shooting of audience members during a midnight showing of *The Dark Knight Rises* raise concerns about the relationship between media content and real life. The influence or effects of the media on society have been studied for many decades by scholars in a range of disciplines including psychology, communications, and sociology. The theories they have generated run along a spectrum, from the media having great power and influence over audiences, to their having little or none, to audiences themselves being central in the creation of meaning. It is worth examining what each of these theories has to say about the effects of media on society and the individual and to consider the applicability of any theory to the postmodern, digital world in which we now live.

The Hypodermic Needle (or Magic Bullet) Theory

In the early years of mass media, it was thought that audience members of all sorts (including readers) were passive recipients of content and that whatever meaning was in the "texts" they consumed was transmitted, unaltered, and absorbed straight into their consciousness. (The term "text" is a general one that can include sound and image as well as print.) This notion was contained in the model known as the **hypodermic needle theory** (or **magic bullet theory**). The assumption was that, like an injection, media content was shot directly into the audience members, who responded instantaneously to its stimulus (Lazarsfeld and Katz 1955). One of the key examples often cited to support this theory was the 1938 radio broadcast of H. G. Wells's short story "War of the Worlds" narrated by Orson Welles. The radio show used a mock news-bulletin format and was played uninterrupted by commercial breaks. Listeners who tuned in after the beginning of the show did not realize it was merely a dramatization of a Martian invasion. It was reported that audience members numbering in the millions actually believed the "news" was true and were so frightened as to have sparked widespread panic. Though this might seem rather exaggerated now, the theory still points to an important principle about the media's potential to directly influence behavior.

Minimal Effects Theories

Media scholars quickly realized that the hypodermic needle theory was not accurate or applicable for the most part—that audience members were not as passive or easily persuaded as first believed and that the various forms of media themselves were not as all-powerful in their influence over individuals. A number of related theories were developed during the 1960s and 70s that proposed the media had limited or minimal effects.

The focus of research shifted. Instead of asking, "What do media do to people?" scholars began to ask, "What do people do with media?" (Severin and Tankard 1997). The **uses and gratifications paradigm** contains several theories that emphasize a more actively engaged audience member (Katz 1959). Blumler and Katz (1974) highlighted five areas in which audiences sought gratification and fulfilled needs through their use of the media. First, audiences could achieve some sense of escape from reality; second, audiences could use media for social interaction, forming relationships to characters, or conversing with others about products and programs; third, they could gain some aspect of personal identity by incorporating elements found in the media into their everyday lives; fourth, the media could serve to inform and educate audiences; and fifth, audience members could consume media purely for the sake of entertainment.

Many media scholars have been interested in the persuasive powers of the media, whether they were used in advertising to get consumers to buy products or used in the political arena to sway public opinion or to garner votes. Two related theories suggest that the influence of the media is more limited than marketing executives or campaign managers might otherwise wish. **Reinforcement theory** argues that individuals tend to seek out and listen to only those messages that are in alignment with their existing attitudes and beliefs. Thus audience members typically tune out anything that might seem too challenging and instead prefer only those messages that support what they already believe (Atkin 1973, 1985; Klapper 1960). The **agenda-setting theory** focuses on how the mass media can influence the public by the way stories are presented in the news

HYPODERMIC NEEDLE THEORY (MAGIC BULLET THEORY) a theory that explains the effects of media as if their contents simply entered directly into the consumer, who is powerless to resist their influence

USES AND GRATIFICATIONS PARADIGM approaches to understanding media effects that focus on individuals' psychological or social needs that consumption of various media fulfills

REINFORCEMENT THEORY theory that suggests that audiences seek messages in the media that reinforce their existing attitudes and beliefs and are thus not influenced by challenging or contradictory information

AGENDA-SETTING THEORY theory that the mass media can set the public agenda by selecting certain news stories and excluding others, thus influencing what audiences think about

(McCombs and Shaw 1972, 1977). Depending upon which stories are chosen as newsworthy and how much time and space are devoted to their coverage, the public then gets a sense of the value or importance of any given event. The media may not be able to tell audiences what to think, but they do set the agenda for what (stories) to think about. Finally, the **two-step flow model** of communication suggests that audiences get much of the information from "opinion leaders" who can convey and explain important news rather than from more direct or firsthand sources (Lazarsfeld and Katz 1955). Certainly someone like Oprah Winfrey exemplifies this; she is known for her widespread ability to influence and can introduce millions of her audience members to whatever is her latest concern.

Active Audiences and Cultural Studies

Media research since the 1980s and 90s has focused largely on **active audiences**, suggesting that media consumers bring to the experience different **interpretive strategies**. This approach argues that different individuals, because of their different experiences, perspectives, and personalities, may respond to media content in unique and idiosyncratic ways. This means that whatever meanings may be inherent in texts, consumers may read them in the intended ways but can also modify and even invert the meanings of texts depending upon their own backgrounds and purposes.

Working within the cultural studies perspective, Stuart Hall's **encoding/decoding model** (1980) combines elements of the hypodermic needle/magic bullet and active audience theories. This model assumes on the one hand that specific ideological messages are loaded, or encoded, into cultural products and that they therefore have the potential to influence individuals, especially with regard to promoting the interests of capitalist elites. On the other hand, individuals may respond to messages embedded in the media in a variety of ways.

Textual Poaching *Star Trek* fans manipulate old footage in order to create new stories that suggest a very different interpretation of Kirk and Spock's relationship than the one portrayed on the show.

In fact, when faced with ideologically encoded cultural products like movies or music, for example, we may decode them in novel ways. Further, we can engage in "cultural resistance" or choose "oppositional" or "against the grain" readings of products, subverting their original or dominant meaning. For example, Madonna's classic video "Like a Virgin" can be read in a number of ways. It was widely seen by cultural critics as sexually exploitative and demeaning, while teen fans brought interpretive resistance to their understanding, subverting the meaning and embracing the video as empowering to them as young women.

Henry Jenkins extends the model to something he calls **textual poaching** (1992), wherein audience members take the original product and manipulate it themselves—often to tell stories or express ideologies very different from the original. For example, fans of the TV show *Star Trek* have used videotaped programs and home-editing equipment to create stories (called "K/S," or "Slash") in which Captain Kirk and Mr. Spock are not just best friends and co-workers, but passionate gay lovers. This oppositional restructuring indicates that viewers can read different meanings into the text than were intended by the producers—indeed, can reproduce the text in order to make those meanings central.

Interpretive Communities and Shared Meanings

Responding to cultural texts is thus an exercise in the distribution of power. The more active the audience is in interpreting the text, the less control the producers have over the messages that are communicated. While you may not go so far as one of Jenkins's "textual poachers," neither are you a passive recipient of predigested pop-culture pabulum. Your consumption of media (film, television, music, books) and live performance (concerts, theater, sports) is active in the sense that you contribute your own interpretive resources—context, experience, and perspective. And to the extent that

TWO-STEP FLOW MODEL theory on media effects that suggests audiences get information through opinion leaders who influence their attitudes and beliefs, rather than through direct firsthand sources

ACTIVE AUDIENCES a term used to characterize audience members as active participants in "reading" or constructing the meaning of the media they consume

INTERPRETIVE STRATEGIES the ideas and frameworks that audience members bring to bear on a particular media text to understand its meaning

ENCODING/DECODING MODEL a theory on media that combines models that privilege the media producer and models that view the audience as the primary source of meaning; this theory recognizes that media texts are created to deliver specific messages and that individuals actively interpret them

TEXTUAL POACHING Henry Jenkins's term describing the ways that audience members manipulate an original cultural product to create a new one; a common way for fans to exert some control over the media they consume you share these experiences with others, you may find that you are part of an **interpretive community**—a group of like-minded people who enjoy cultural products in the same way.

The concept of the interpretive community is usually attributed to literary theorist Stanley Fish (1980), who believed that although an author might have intended a certain meaning in a text, it is individual readers who inevitably interpret the text in their own ways, thus creating the potential for an almost infinite number of meanings of the same text. The fact that we usually end up interpreting the same books in the same ways has to do with shared culture and frameworks that members of the same interpretive communities have in common. Janice Radway (1991), in her ethnography of romance-novel readers, argued that cultural context is the reason that readers share similar sets of reading strategies and interpretive codes. Whether visiting a museum exhibit, going to a concert, or watching a TV show, members of interpretive communities bring with them shared sensibilities about understanding cultural products through their own particular lenses.

Recreation, Leisure, and Relationships

Our recreational choices can lead us to form unique bonds with others. Some of those bonds take the form of **role model** relationships, in which more prominent members of a leisure subculture serve as examples for us to strive toward. It is a widely accepted practice to look up to, admire, and mold ourselves after exceptional people and celebrities of all types.

Let's look at sports figures. In the 1990s, for instance, kids chanted "I wanna be like Mike" to communicate their admiration for Chicago Bulls player Michael Jordan. Tiger Woods, who in 1997 became the youngest golfer and first person of color ever to win the Masters Tournament, generated the same type of hero worship among youngsters, who intoned "I am Tiger Woods" as they stepped up to the tee in record numbers. Role models like Woods and Jordan may inspire us to excel in sports and in other areas as well, since both of them have excelled in business and in charity. But their personal failures (both men admitted to marital infidelity) make us wonder what kinds of role models they really are. Some would argue that sports figures are not appropriate role models: even though they must work hard in order to excel, they still possess unique skills and talents that the rest of us don't. In fact, another basketball player, Charles Barkley, who played with the Phoenix Suns at the time, famously asserted "I am not a role model," arguing that parents and teachers were more appropriate examples for children to follow. And interestingly, each of the above quotes ("I wanna be like Mike," "I am Tiger Woods," *and* "I am not a role model") was eventually used in Nike commercials—all to inspire consumers to buy expensive sporting goods. In a more recent Nike commercial, Miami

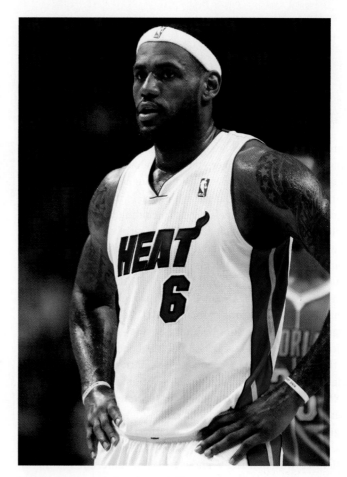

LeBron James Is he a role model?

Heat star LeBron James riffs on the "I am not a role model" theme by asking "What should I do?" of his audience. "Should I be who you want me to be?" or should he just be himself and not worry about what fans think of him? Can any celebrity afford to be that cavalier?

Aside from celebrity role models, we also build relationships with people who share our interests—our soccer teammates, fellow collectors of *Star Wars* memorabilia, bluegrass aficionados, or backgammon players. These are important members of our social world.

Leisure and Community

Your friendship with the people you play pick-up basketball with every Thursday evening, the members of your gardening club, or the folks you watch *Survivor* with is unlikely to be confined solely to a love of basketball, gardening, or television; your bonds probably extend into other areas of your lives as well. But it is your shared interests that have brought you

INTERPRETIVE COMMUNITY a group of people dedicated to the consumption and interpretation of a particular cultural product and who create a collective, social meaning for the product

ROLE MODEL an individual who serves as an example for others to strive toward and emulate

IN RELATIONSHIPS

Fan-Celebrity Relations

Interacting with a god or gods, spirits, or ancestors is compulsory in many cultures—but what about our own? In his book *Imaginary Social Worlds*, John Caughey (1984) argues that the contemporary American equivalents are relationships between fans and celebrities (including politicians and athletes). These are people with whom few of us have actual, face-to-face interaction but whom many of us feel we know—sometimes intimately. "It is simply taken for granted," Caughey observes, "that an American will know about a huge swarming throng of unmet figures through his [sic] consumption of the various media" (p. 32). Celebrities can be important in the lives of ordinary people—as role models, objects of desire, or just friendly figures encountered daily on the TV screen. Just because these relationships are one-sided doesn't mean that they aren't relationships.

If there was ever an athlete, actor, musician, or politician whom you admired but never met, then you have engaged in some version of the asymmetrical relationships Caughey outlines in his book. Maybe you read a magazine article or watched a TV show to learn more about this person; maybe you bought a ticket to a performance with the hopes of seeing him or her after the show. Most of us put very little energy into developing these relationships—frankly, we don't have to, as we are bombarded with information about celebrities all the time. We can't help but acquire information about their professional and personal lives (Ehrenreich 1990).

In addition to reading *People* and *Us Weekly* magazines or watching *Entertainment Tonight* and *Access Hollywood*, some fans attend organized activities such as book signings or store openings in which face-to-face contact with a celebrity is available and highly regulated (Ferris 2001). At these prestaged events, buying a ticket and standing in line will yield a brief, formulaic encounter with the celebrity in which a few words are exchanged, an autograph is signed, and the line moves on. Unstaged encounters ("celebrity sightings")—at the supermarket, say, or in line at the post office—are exciting, but by definition uncertain (Ferris 2004a).

Fan-staged encounters help solve this problem: here the fan seeks out and uses information about the celebrity in ways that put the fan in control. For example, one avid fan

A Prestaged Event Fans meet actor Johnny Depp on the red carpet at a movie premiere.

sneaked onto a television studio lot and came away with a celebrity address list: "We couldn't get onto the set, but I took a bunch of stuff, papers, from the bike messenger's basket when it was parked. I figure that's not stealing, they can just make more Xeroxes. Anyway, the addresses were on it. . . . They live in the Hills, mostly, and I can go by their houses" (Ferris 2001, p. 39). Fan-staged encounters avoid the restrictions of prestaged events and the unpredictability of celebrity sightings. They partially solve the problem of asymmetry that characterizes fan-celebrity relations—fans can ensure that they will be able to see and maybe speak with their favorite celebrity, as though the relationship were an ordinary personal one. It should be noted, however, that fan-staged encounters usually occur without the consent of the celebrity herself, which means that the fan can feel unwelcome and even dangerous to the celebrity, even if the fan may mean no harm.

Recently the internet has opened up new means for fans wishing to encounter celebrities and improved the odds of having an actual celebrity sighting. Gawker, TMZ, Popsugar, and PerezHilton are a few of a proliferation of web sites that are making big business out of celebrity watching. They all carry the latest gossip and prized candid photos of the stars that generate millions of web traffic visitors every month. Gawker, which is based in New York City, distinguished itself by introducing Gawker Stalker, a feature that tries to visually pinpoint celebrities as soon as they are spotted. In order to help readers in their "celebrity-hunting adventures," Gawker encourages fans to send the whereabouts of any celebrity they might see, whether at a restaurant, dry cleaners, or market, and Gawker will immediately post the exact location using Google Maps. With more and more people accessing the internet via handheld devices like the iPhone and BlackBerry, news about celebrities travels fast, as do those wishing to chase them.

Which brings us to the phenomenon of real celebrity stalking. Stalking is usually defined as any unwanted pursuit or threat and can be practiced by ex-spouses, business rivals, or total strangers. But the most familiar type is celebrity stalking. Security experts usually try to keep the details under wraps, but it is safe to say that most public figures have a number of potentially dangerous fans whose activities are monitored by both public law enforcement and private security firms. Several celebrities have been killed (ex-Beatle John Lennon, actress Rebecca Shaeffer, Tejano star Selena) or seriously wounded (actress Theresa Saldana) by obsessed fans. Others have endured repeated home break-ins (singer Madonna, director Steven Spielberg, talk-show host David Letterman, actor Brad Pitt), and many are plagued by "pop-up" visits from fans who have followed them surreptitiously and then revealed themselves in airports, restaurants, or public restrooms. Threatening letters are sometimes sent to the stars' management offices and even delivered to their home addresses—a danger signal, say stalking experts. In order to protect Hollywood celebrities and other public figures from dangerous fans, the Los Angeles Police Department has created a division called the Threat Management Unit, and California further led the nation in passing anti-stalking laws in 1990 that have served as models for those in other states. Unfortunately, legislation doesn't deter all stalkers.

For some people, celebrity stalking is a professional obligation. These people include members of the press, and especially the paparazzi, freelance photographers who pursue celebrities in order to get candid shots. Paparazzi may charter helicopters, hack through forests, or scale castle walls in such daring stunts as the two photographers dressed in camouflage who attempted to photograph the new twin babies of actors Brad Pitt and Angelina Jolie. Their intrusiveness can even provoke violence from a celebrity, as witnessed in singer Britney Spears beating the car of a member of the paparazzi with the wooden handle of an umbrella, or rapper Kanye West smashing the expensive camera equipment belonging to another. In some instances, it is actually the photographer who is assaulted, as in the case of one who took a punch in the jaw from actor Alec Baldwin.

While paparazzi can be annoying to celebrities, we consume their products every day. When we read supermarket tabloids, watch TV entertainment shows, or surf the web for photos of our favorite actors, we support the paparazzi's activities—because they support ours. They feed our imaginations, provide us with information about celebrities, and help us envision the worlds of those who are part of our everyday lives yet not personally known to us.

Celebrity Sightings What role do gossip magazines play in fan-celebrity relations?

together, and these activities speak to the heart of Émile Durkheim's pioneering sociological questions about community and social cohesion, first asked more than 100 years ago and still central today.

Some scholars argue that a critical problem has emerged in contemporary society that undermines social cohesion. They contend that group values in important social groups such as the family, the church, or a labor union have been eclipsed by a rhetoric that espouses radical individual rights first and foremost. For instance, dinner with the family might be passed up in favor of a mother's Pilates lesson or a brother's going to a friend's house to watch the fight on TV. Or the Catholic requirement to attend mass each week might be fulfilled only on Christmas and Easter. Sociologist Amitai Etzioni is the leading proponent of a movement that seeks to remedy this problem: **communitarianism** argues that individual rights do not cancel out collective responsibility. The movement is an attempt to rebuild a sense of group values that benefit all rather than merely the individual. Etzioni's version of communitarianism (1996) is specific in its proposals about how to balance individual rights with social responsibilities. But the question for us here is this: Are bonds based on shared leisure interests enough to constitute a sense of group responsibility compatible with communitarian aims? Or are basketball, gardening, television, and the like just too flimsy a basis for real group identity?

COMMUNITARIANISM a political and moral philosophy focused on strengthening civil society and communal bonds

LIFESTYLE ENCLAVES groups of people drawn together by shared interests, especially those relating to hobbies, sports, and media

THIRD PLACE any informal public place where people come together regularly for conversation and camaraderie when not at work or at home

Robert Bellah, whose work has examined group values in America, supplies another critique, but also hints at a potential answer for us. He argues that bonds based on shared interests like those mentioned above don't create real community. Rather, such groups constitute **lifestyle enclaves**, which are different from real communities in that they are likely to remain private and segmented, focused on their own shared interests rather than involved in the larger group life (Bellah, Sullivan, and Tipton 1985). So you and your fellow ball players, gardeners, or TV fans may find your connections to each other to be personally rewarding, but you aren't necessarily contributing to the common good. Or are you?

In Dr. Ferris's research on *Star Trek* and soap opera fan clubs, she found that while people in these clubs did initially bond solely because of their dedication to particular TV shows, these bonds developed over time in ways that Bellah might not have predicted. Eventually, the groups branched out from their narrow focus and began to pursue things like charitable fund-raising and community service projects that expanded the boundaries of their lifestyle enclave. One *Star Trek* fan club, for example, raised money to help an animal welfare organization that was sponsored by *Trek* actor William Shatner; while their contributions were guided by their specific interests (how many other people even know what Shatner's favorite charity is?), their community spirit was obvious. So perhaps a sense of shared mission within a small group of TV viewers or tulip enthusiasts is not incompatible with a larger sense of social responsibility after all. You can indulge your individual sense of play and work for the common good as well.

Collectors and Hobbyists

Sports are not the only recreational pursuits that draw people together. Many collectors' groups organize annual conventions so that members with shared interests can hobnob with one another for one intensive weekend. Collectors of Dolly Parton memorabilia, for example, meet once a year in Pigeon Forge, Tennessee, to buy, sell, and trade Dolly-related items and share their love of the country music diva. Fans of a different kind of dolly, Barbie, also meet annually to connect with others who collect Barbie, her friends, and all their accessories (in 2001, this convention was hijacked by fans of the Ken doll, with the goal of making Barbie's long-suffering boyfriend the star of the show!). And at yet another weekend convention, collectors gather together to "keep history alive" and honor real military heroes both past and present, by buying, selling, and trading twelve-inch action figures die cast in the image of notable members of the armed forces.

But collectors and hobbyists are no longer limited to meeting face-to-face at an annual convention or weekend workshop. The internet has helped spawn a myriad of virtual communities where enthusiasts can interact online.

Do-it-yourselfers and garage woodworkers who might normally work alone have found compatriot crafters with whom they can converse. Connecting with others who share the same interests is facilitated by blogs, wikis, Facebook, YouTube, and auction sites like eBay where collectors and hobbyists can meet, organize activities, swap tips, and search for the perfect purchases (Rubel and Rosman 2001).

Hangouts: The Third Place

Away from work or school, where else do you spend your time? Researcher Robert Putnam (2000) laments that, in the United States at least, you will probably be watching television at home rather than gathering in a public place to talk with others. But if you lived in France, you might head to the corner café; in Germany, the neighborhood Bierstube; in Greece, the local taverna. Establishments such as these bear the label **third place** (after home and work, which are first and second). They are informal public places where people come together regularly for conversation and camaraderie. Roy Oldenburg (1999) worries that there are few such places left in the United States—and that we might be suffering as a society because of it.

You know the place—the local diner with a counter that's always full of old men, talking about fishing for bluegill, complaining about the cost of prescription medications, or bemoaning the irresponsibility of youth. You might have thought such talk trivial or silly, but the interactions and relationships that develop in third places are important far beyond any specific conversational content.

Coffeehouse, bar, or barbershop—third places are more than just hangouts. Oldenburg argues that they are core settings for informal but essential aspects of public and community life. They provide opportunities to connect with others in ways that relieve alienation and anomie, problems Durkheim attributed to modern society. And there are more generalized benefits to society as well—the feeling of

public spirit generated in third places can strengthen **civil society**, increase political awareness and participation, and sustain democracy from the ground up. So that local diner—or barbershop or bar—is more important than it appears to be. It helps maintain social cohesion and links the individual to the community. Where's your third place?

DATA WORKSHOP
Analyzing Everyday Life

Observing a Hangout

This Data Workshop asks you to investigate the phenomenon of the local hangout using participant observation (see Chapter 2 for a review of ethnographic methods). It doesn't matter which kind of hangout you choose; it could be a bar, restaurant, gym, park, student union, or bookstore. What's important is to make sure that it's a real hangout, someplace where people linger, that they return to regularly to socialize. Part of your work will be to determine just what constitutes a good hangout. So think a bit about your own habits and those of your friends, and choose what you think is a good hangout to study where you'll be both a participant and an observer.

CIVIL SOCIETY those organizations, institutions, and interactions outside government, family, and work that promote social bonds and the smooth functioning of society

IDIOCULTURE the customs, practices, and values expressed in a particular place by the people who interact there

Once you've chosen one, make some ethnographic fieldnotes describing both the physical and social setting. What makes this place a good hangout for the people there? You'll also need to distinguish who are the "regulars" and who are not. How do you tell a one-time visitor from a regular? How do people establish themselves as regulars? What kinds of interactions take place at the hangout? Interview a few people you think are regulars. What does the hangout mean to them? How does it function in their everyday life? In what respect is being a regular a part of their identity? In writing up your analysis, include some examples of the particular **idioculture** you find—the customs and values expressed in the place and in the interactions of the people who hang out there.

Where's Your Third Place? Whether it's a coffeehouse, a barbershop, or a neighborhood pub, third places are informal public places where people come together regularly for conversation and camaraderie.

GLOBAL PERSPECTIVE

The Other Football

Do you know the rules for cricket? What's up with the Canadians and curling? And why can't anyone get Americans to care about football? No, not *that* football—the other one. What Americans call soccer but everyone else calls football is wildly popular internationally, but it has not yet taken off in the United States, especially at the professional level.

In the United States, soccer is primarily a youth sport; of the country's 18 million soccer players, only about 5 million are adults, and many of these are part of a recent influx of foreign-born players. American interest in soccer spikes every four years when the World Cup games roll around; otherwise, major league soccer is not even as popular as ice hockey and lags well behind the professional sports behemoths of football, baseball, and basketball. The rest of the world, however, thinks Americans are crazy. In almost every other country, football (soccer) is a major sport—there are local and national competitions between teams and international competition between national teams. Salaries for top players often surpass deals made with top American athletes, with tens of millions of dollars going to players like Didier Drogba, Lionel Messi, and Iker Casillas. When the former England captain and soccer superstar David Beckham signed a very lucrative five-year deal in 2007 to play with the Los Angeles Galaxy team, his celebrity status drew more attention to soccer in the United States.

It's not just the money and the competition that make international soccer unique, it's the fans—more specifically, the rowdy and violent fans often referred to as "hooligans." Violence in American sports is certainly not unheard of (ever been to an Oakland Raiders game?), but the scale of soccer hooliganism overseas is in another league entirely. The British, especially, are infamous for the mobs of "yobs" (slang for hooligans) who cause damage both in Great Britain and elsewhere in the soccer-playing world. Soccer actually has a violent history: in the medieval period, entire towns would participate in soccer matches to resolve disputes,

and kings and queens at times had the game banned because of violence. In those days, it was the players who had to be concerned for their safety; since the rise of contemporary hooliganism, spectators must also be wary.

Since the 1960s, there have been hundreds of deaths caused by upheaval at soccer matches. Although most soccer-playing countries endure some form of hooliganism, the English yobs are infamous and were, until recently, the only fans who traveled abroad with their teams and brought their violence with them (Taylor 2000). One of the most notorious riots took place in Brussels, in 1985, at a match between the English team from Liverpool and the Italian team Juventus. The Liverpool yobs, later revealed by videotape to have come to the match with ski masks and weapons, instigated attacks on the rival fans, which resulted in a crush of people trying to flee. In the end, thirty-nine Italian spectators were killed, and British teams were banned from European competition for five years (Haley and Johnston 1998).

Some theorists speculate that the fanaticism of hooligans is only an excuse to be violent. Skinheads and other racists, for example, sometimes use soccer matches to broadcast their beliefs. Others speculate that fandom can develop into a nationalistic fervor that increases the likelihood of violence. For example, for British fans who feel united against a foreign team while in a foreign country, it may be easy to feel both isolated and compelled to defend the honor of their team and country—especially when emotions are already heightened with the fury of athletic competition (King 1995).

Why is true mob violence rare in the United States? Is it because U.S. teams are seldom involved in truly international competition? Or because there are so many professional sports and teams to follow? Or is it simply because hooliganism is endemic to a sport with a long history of violence—the real football—which is not yet widely popular in this country?

Yobs English football fans are particularly famous for their fanaticism. Here, English hooligans (rear) chase a French supporter (front) in Charleroi, Belgium. At the Euro 2000 championships, English fans attacked celebrating French supporters who drove in a convoy through the city center.

Table 13.1 Theory in Everyday Life

Perspective	Approach to Recreation and Leisure	Case Study: Spectator Sports in America
Structural Functionalism	Social institutions such as recreation and leisure provide for the needs of society and its members and help to maintain social cohesion and unity.	Participation in spectator sports helps to reaffirm social bonds; rooting for a team underscores the value of performance and competition.
Conflict Theory	Social institutions such as recreation and leisure reflect the existing power structures in society and thus create and maintain social inequalities.	Participation in spectator sports legitimizes conflict between groups in society and the belief in winners and losers.
Symbolic Interactionism	Social institutions such as recreation and leisure are produced when people act together; they play a meaningful role in the everyday lives of members.	Participation in spectator sports provides members with a sense of group affiliation and personal identification.

There are two options for completing the assigned work.

Option 1 (informal): Prepare written fieldnotes that you can refer to during in-class discussions. Share your reactions and conclusions with other students in small groups. Listen for any differences or variations in each other's insights.

Option 2 (formal): Write a three- to four-page essay answering the questions posed above. Use specific excerpts from your fieldnotes to support your analysis and attach them to your paper.

Travel and Tourism

While some people find respite in hangouts close to home, others relax and rejuvenate by seeing the world. The travel and tourism industries (which include airlines, hotels, car-rental agencies, restaurants, theme parks, resorts, and other attractions) are multibillion-dollar businesses and play an important part in the U.S. economy. And it's a sector that keeps growing. In 2012, the travel and tourism industries in the United States employed 5.6 million workers directly and helped support another 2.2 million jobs in related industries. Travel and tourism sales generated a total of $1.46 trillion. The United States was the second-most popular destination (after France) for world travelers: more than 67 million or 6.5 percent traveled to the United States and spent over $165 billion on travel- and tourism-related goods and services. These dollar figures are important to the overall economy: travel and tourism contribute 25 percent of America's exports (U.S. Department of Commerce 2013).

The impact of tourism on a place is more than just economic. Tourism can have a profound effect on a culture as well. Ideally we may travel in order to learn to appreciate different cultures, but we may also exoticize or even mistreat other groups as we fit them into our own recreational needs, rather than learning about them on their own terms (Urry 1990, 1992, 2002). Travel and tourism shape not just our individual relations with others but also political relations between nations on a global scale. One area of contention concerns the impact of travel and tourism on an environmental level.

Ecotourism is characterized by the efforts of tourists and the travel industry to lessen the negative consequences of tourism on the environment as well as local cultures. Ecotourism promotes a consciousness about environmentally and culturally sensitive travel options. Ecotourists are often from highly industrialized nations and are usually visiting less developed nations. But if they are truly aware of their potential to cause harm, shouldn't they avoid environmentally sensitive locations such as rain forests or the habitats of endangered species?

Sociologists who study ecotourism have mixed views about its effectiveness. Some argue that it is merely consumerism with a "green" wrapping, that the "eco" part of the label is a marketing technique to make tourists

ECOTOURISM foreign travel with the goal of minimizing the environmental consequences of tourism as well as its possible negative effects on local cultures and economies, typically involves people from highly industrialized nations traveling to less developed countries

Finca Esperanza Verde Ecolodge in Nicaragua is part organic coffee farm, part eco-friendly tourist lodge.

feel less guilty about traveling to places where they can't help but make a negative impact. Other sociologists argue that ecotourism, if effectively managed, *can* make positive contributions to both the environment and local communities (Bandy 1996; Wearing and Wearing 1999; Scheyvens 2000; Weinberg, Bellows, and Ekster 2002; Wood 2002). Tourists and travel companies must actively attempt to counterbalance their impact with sensitivity to the environment as well as to the values of local communities. The question remains whether ecotourism can live up to its claims and place environmental and cultural concerns before profits.

CLOSING COMMENTS

Who would have thought that the things you do for fun might actually be important? The many activities considered part of leisure—travel, entertainment, sports, hobbies—while prevalent features of our everyday lives, play an increasingly significant role in the shape of society. We hope we haven't spoiled their pleasure by asking you to examine their various structures and meanings—you can still enjoy your lesiure activities even after you've learned to take a critical, sociological perspective on them!

Everything You Need to Know about
Leisure and the Media

" **Leisure is time that can be spent doing whatever you want. A large portion of Americans' leisure time is spent consuming mass media.** "

THEORIES OF LEISURE AND THE MEDIA

* **Structural functionalism:** leisure activities and the media help maintain social cohesion through taste publics

* **Conflict theory:** leisure activities and the media reflect existing power inequalities, particularly in the commodification of leisure; the types of leisure and media we consume differ based on our social class

* **Symbolic interactionism:** people's everyday lives are greatly affected by shared leisure activities or the consumption of the same media

REVIEW

1. What does "commercialization of leisure" mean? Think of one of your favorite leisure activities and make a list of every aspect of this activity that costs money, either directly or indirectly.

2. Sociologists have long associated types of leisure activities with different social classes. Which leisure activities are associated with wealthy elites or with the working class? Which leisure activities, if any, have no class-associations?

3. How powerful are the media in persuading us to buy certain products or hold particular beliefs? Discuss reinforcement theory, agenda setting, and/or the two-step flow model. Which of these theories best explains the influence of the media?

Leisure Time on an Average Day

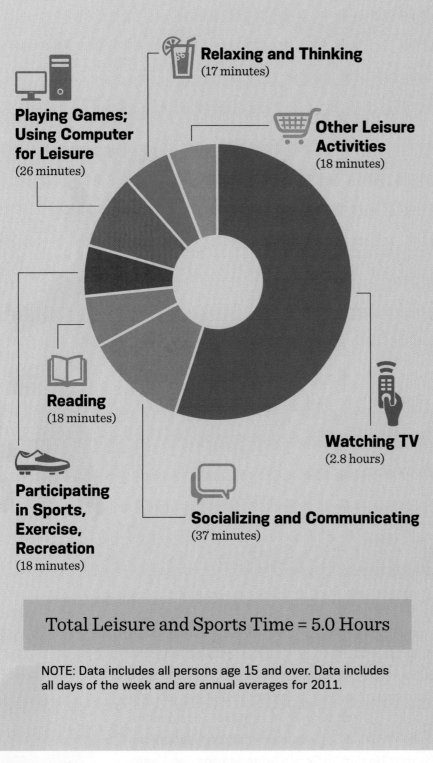

Playing Games; Using Computer for Leisure
(26 minutes)

Relaxing and Thinking
(17 minutes)

Other Leisure Activities
(18 minutes)

Reading
(18 minutes)

Participating in Sports, Exercise, Recreation
(18 minutes)

Socializing and Communicating
(37 minutes)

Watching TV
(2.8 hours)

Total Leisure and Sports Time = 5.0 Hours

NOTE: Data includes all persons age 15 and over. Data includes all days of the week and are annual averages for 2011.

SOURCE: Bureau of Labor Statistics 2011, American Time Use Survey

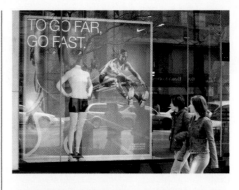

EXPLORE

Consuming Elite Athleticism

Eugene, Oregon is a major location for running and track and field, in part because of Bill Bowerman, the late coach for the University of Oregon and the co-founder of Nike. A running culture is prevalent in Eugene: the city celebrates its identity as TrackTown USA, formal activities like the Olympic trials are often held there, and many people wear Nike clothes and shoes. Nike had a significant presence at the 2012 Olympic trials, including shuttle buses with the Nike logo and a "Shoe Lab" showcasing the latest technology in running shoes. Visit the Everyday Sociology Blog to read more about a sociologist's analysis of how Nike successfully markets elite athleticism to consumers.

http:wwnPag.es/trw413

CHAPTER 14

Health and Illness

In the 1995 film *Leaving Las Vegas*, Nicolas Cage plays Ben, a down-and-out screenwriter who heads to Vegas intending to drink himself to death. His plan is delayed when he meets and befriends a local sex worker, Sera (played by Elisabeth Shue). Ben and Sera connect for a short while and come to an agreement: he won't ask her to quit her job, and she won't ask him to quit drinking. They provide each other with acceptance, companionship, and a temporary respite from their isolated lives. But not even their connection can stop Ben from fulfilling his self-destructive goal. He dies in Sera's arms, leaving Las Vegas the way he always planned. Cage won a Best Actor Oscar and Golden Globe Award for his

performance (while Shue received corresponding Best Actress nominations), and the film has taken its place among top Hollywood portrayals of the desperation and destruction of alcoholism.

But there's more to this story than the suicide of a fictional alcoholic in a seedy hotel. Las Vegas itself can be seen as another main character—a real American city with an unfortunate connection to self-destruction. According to sociologist Matt Wray and his colleagues (2008), merely being in Las Vegas, as either a resident or a tourist, increases one's suicide risk. Vegas residents' odds of suicide are 50 percent greater than those of people who live elsewhere, and visitors' risk of suicide doubles while there, compared with those who stay home or travel elsewhere. Indeed, if you are a resident of the city, getting out of town is good for you—leaving Las Vegas results in a reduction in suicide risk of more than 20 percent. Should Las Vegas, which consistently has the highest urban suicide rate in the nation, also be referred to as "Suicide City" in addition to its nickname of "Sin City"? What explains these disturbing statistics?

Wray and his colleagues (2008) offer three possible explanations: ecological, selection, and contagion theories of suicide. The ecological argument is place-based: there must be something about the city itself that makes people suicidal. For example, Vegas has long been one of the fastest-growing cities in the nation, although growth has slowed dramatically since the recession. This kind of rapid social change can lead to social isolation and dislocation and a weakening of community bonds (Trudeau 2008), all factors classically correlated with suicide by Émile Durkheim (1897/1951). Additionally, some research suggests that gambling or the large number of hotel rooms (where chances of rescuing someone midattempt are slim) make Vegas conducive to suicide (Phillips, Welty, and Smith 1997; Gemar, Zarkowski, and Avery 2008). The selection argument is somewhat more psychological: Vegas residents and tourists might be disproportionately prone to impulsiveness or other risky behaviors (Wray et al. 2008), and indeed may be choosing Vegas as a site for making a new start or having a "last hurrah," a gamble that more frequently ends in their suicide because the city beckons people with these and other relevant personality traits, such as depression. The contagion argument combines ecological and selection concerns: the high suicide rate may inspire a kind of "copycat" effect (Cosgrove-Mather 2004), and through processes of social imitation the rate remains high.

So is it the place, the people, or a combination of the two that makes Las Vegas the suicide capital of the country? Wray and his colleagues cannot provide us with a definitive answer just yet. But their research recognizes what we will be exploring in this chapter: that although health, illness, and mortality are physiological phenomena, they are also unquestionably shaped by social factors.

HOW TO READ THIS CHAPTER

Health and illness are constants of human existence, a natural part of having a physical body that is subject to injury, disease, aging, and death. Health and illness are not just physical states—they also include aspects of our mental well-being and are influenced by shifting cultural beliefs about what is ideal and desirable. As a society, we have established the social institution of medicine to address the challenges of our physical existence. Sociologists ask you to consider how larger social forces help to shape this institution and your own experience of health or illness.

The Sociology of Medicine, Health, and Illness

Why is sociology interested in topics that might seem more at home in a medical school textbook? Well, for one thing, our bodies (where health and illness are ostensibly located) are social objects. Our physical selves have socially constructed meanings and are affected by social forces. This means that the very definition of health is social; it also means that our individual health is subject not just to cross-cultural or historically specific interpretive differences, but to different influences depending on where and when we live, as well as what statuses we hold in our society.

Let's look at a couple of examples where the nature of health is defined by its social rather than biological context. Think about what having a healthy body means in a developed country like the United States. We value slim, athletic bodies and consider people with these body types

to be healthier than people with fleshy builds. But in Dakar, Senegal, people tend to value body types that in the United States would be considered clinically overweight. Senegalese women in particular associate these body types with health (and by extension with wealth enough to eat well): slimmer women actually want to gain weight in order to attain the "desirable," "healthy" build (Holdsworth et al. 2004). Another example: in the United States, "healthy" teeth are not just free of cavities, but also straight and white. So in addition to brushing teeth daily and visiting the dentist regularly, Americans spend big money on orthodontic and whitening procedures. Meanwhile, in many other parts of the world, irregularly shaped or unevenly colored teeth are not necessarily seen as "bad" or "unhealthy," and cosmetic dentistry is far less common. These examples indicate that our definitions of health (and beauty as a sign of health) are determined at least in part by our cultural context, and not always by a biological bottom line.

Another important aspect of health as a social phenomenon involves the spread of disease. Think about it: you've caught a good number of illnesses from other people. Someone behind you in the movie theater coughed, and you got a cold (if you were lucky) or tuberculosis (if you were unlucky). Someone flipping burgers at the fast-food restaurant forgot to wash her hands, and you got an upset stomach (if you were lucky) or hepatitis A (if you were unlucky). If you have young children in school or day care, you know that kids are like family disease vectors—they catch bugs from other kids, bring them home, and spread them around to family members.

As an example of how social milieu affects risk of disease, take the recent whooping cough epidemic in California. The disease, which can easily be fatal in small children, is highly contagious but has an effective vaccine. In 2010, California saw an unprecedented increase in whooping cough cases, with five infants dead by the end of July (McKinley 2010). The areas with the most cases included Fresno County, a largely agricultural

Health in a Cultural Context The Senegalese women live in a society that values fuller body types that might be classified as overweight in other cultures. The United States puts such a strong emphasis on straight, white teeth that many people spend thousands of dollars on cosmetic dental procedures.

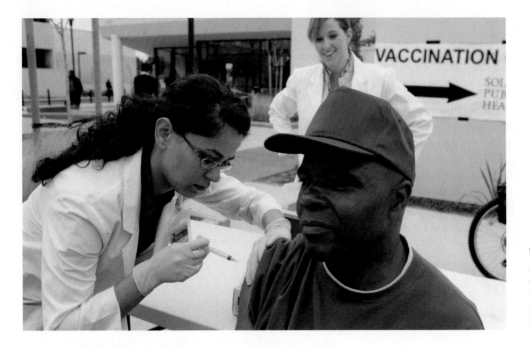

Whooping Cough Epidemic
A doctor administers a Tdap vaccination to a man in Vallejo, California, to protect him against the outbreak of whooping cough.

area with a high population of vaccination-averse immigrants, and Marin County, a wealthy suburb of San Francisco that has the highest rate of voluntary vaccine refusal in the state (DeNoon 2010). So some parents (like those in Fresno) may not have access to vaccines, may come from countries that don't vaccinate, or may fear contact with the medical establishment because of their immigration status. Other parents (like those in Marin) believe, despite lack of empirical support, that vaccines increase their child's risk of such conditions as autism, and opt out. Either way, failing to vaccinate puts everyone in their communities at risk of contracting disease.

Our bodies are social objects, and our social experiences and social location shape our prospects for health and risks of disease. These are only some of the reasons that health and illness are social phenomena. As you read this chapter, you'll find that there are social, cultural, and subcultural factors affecting just about everything having to do with health and illness. How we categorize illnesses, how we treat them, and who gets to treat them are all sociological questions.

Definitions of Health and Illness

Terms such as "healthy" or "sick" may seem straightforward, but their meanings are not absolute or universal. The World Health Organization (a division of the United Nations

charged with overseeing global health issues) defines health as "a state of complete physical, mental, and social well-being and not merely the absence of disease or infirmity" (WHO 1946). Let's look further at how illnesses are defined and treated in the United States.

Types of Illnesses

Diseases and illnesses are commonly categorized as either acute or chronic. **Acute diseases** have a sudden onset, may be briefly incapacitating, and are either curable or fatal. These illnesses are often caused by an organism such as a germ, virus, or parasite that infects the body and disrupts the normal functioning of one or more areas. Many acute illnesses are contagious and can spread from one person to many people. The common cold, pneumonia, and measles could all be considered acute illnesses. **Chronic diseases** develop over a longer period of time and may not be detected until later in their progression. They can sometimes be related to environment, lifestyle, and personal choices. Many chronic diseases are manageable, but others progress and eventually become fatal. Cancer, cerebrovascular disease, and some forms of diabetes can all be considered chronic diseases.

The kinds of diseases that affect us can vary over time and by place. For most of history, humans worried about becoming afflicted with acute diseases. Indeed, prior to 1900, the leading causes of death in the United States were influenza, pneumonia, tuberculosis, and gastroenteritis. Over the past century, there have been drastic changes in medicine and public health that have all but wiped out certain acute diseases (such as polio), while chronic ones (such as diabetes) have grown vastly in proportion (CDC 1998). Chronic dis-

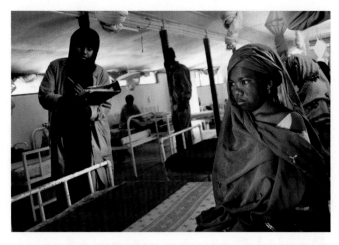

Acute Diseases Patients in Sudan wait for treatment in the TB ward of a hospital. Diseases such as tuberculosis, diarrheal diseases, and malaria are the top causes of death in the developing world.

eases have become among the most important factors governing health and illness today. The top three causes of death in the United States are currently heart disease, cancer, and chronic respiratory illnesses like asthma and emphysema (Hoyert and Xu 2012). However, acute diseases continue to pose significant threats to people living in the developing world, where the top killers still include respiratory infections, diarrheal diseases, tuberculosis, and malaria (WHO 2008).

Approaches to Medical Treatment

The health-care system in the United States is characterized by three approaches: curative or crisis, preventive, and palliative. **Curative** or **crisis medicine** treats the disease once it has become apparent. Sometimes this works well, especially in the case of acute illnesses, like food poisoning, or sports injuries, like a torn ligament, that have no early treatment option. But in the case of chronic illnesses, a delay in recognizing causes or symptoms before the disease advances may mean the difference between recovery and death. **Preventive medicine** aims to avoid or forestall the onset of disease by making lifestyle changes: regular exercise, proper diet and nutrition, smoking cessation, stress reduction, and other measures to maintain or improve one's health. Lifestyle changes are often the most effective and least costly ways to prevent a range of chronic conditions (McKinlay 1997). **Palliative care** focuses on symptom and pain relief and on providing a nurturing and supportive environment to those suffering from a serious illness or at the end of life, either in addition to or in place of fighting the illness or disease.

DATA WORKSHOP
Analyzing Everyday Life

Student Health Issues Survey

For many young people, moving away from home and going to college mark the beginning of their independent lives as adults. While there is much to celebrate at this milestone, it can also be a time full of new demands and challenges. Perhaps you or someone you know is dealing with homesickness, an abusive relationship, or stress and anxiety. As a college student, you can learn to become more responsible and disciplined, and more conscientious about taking care of yourself. But you can also be threatened by alcohol or substance abuse, eating disorders, or depression. The college years are an important phase of development and one in which many young people struggle to some degree with their newfound adult lives.

The American College Health Association (ACHA) is an organization that partners with colleges and universities to conduct large-scale surveys on the habits, behaviors, and perceptions affecting the health and well-being of their student populations. In 2012, the ACHA surveyed over 90,000 students; the results are helping colleges and universities offer education and support services regarding a variety of issues (2012).

This Data Workshop asks you to conduct your own small-scale study on health and wellness issues. There are a number of ways that you can structure your survey questionnaire (see Chapter 2 for a review of survey research methods). You might want to ask a handful of students about a wide range of issues, or you might want to ask a greater number of students more in-depth questions about one or two specific areas.

The following are possible topics that you might want to consider using in your study. Feel free to add your own topics.

CURATIVE or **CRISIS MEDICINE** type of health care that treats the disease or condition once it has manifested

PREVENTIVE MEDICINE type of health care that aims to avoid or forestall the onset of disease by taking preventive measures, often including lifestyle changes

PALLIATIVE CARE type of health care that focuses on symptom and pain relief and providing a supportive environment for critically ill or dying patients, rather than fighting the illness or disease

College Health A student at the University of Northern Iowa visits the school's student health clinic.

anger
depression
drugs and alcohol
eating disorders
exercise
gambling
grief and loss
homesickness

pregnancy
relationships
sexual assault
sexually transmitted diseases
sleep difficulties
stress and anxiety
suicide
tobacco

You might ask students about their lifestyles—what they eat, how much they sleep, whether they exercise, drink or smoke, or practice safe sex. Do they play a musical instrument, are they on a sports team, or do they belong to any campus clubs? You might ask about their physical health—how often they get sick, or what they do to stay healthy. Or you might ask about their mental health—whether they experience stress, depression, and/or anxiety, what causes them to feel it, and what they do to alleviate it. Typically, survey questions are closed-ended and provide quantitative results, but you may also include open-ended questions or write-in answers. There's no right way to structure the survey, but do keep the questionnaires as clear and simple as possible.

You might also ask your respondents about their demographic backgrounds, such as age or gender. Remember that you're dealing with human subjects and you'll need to get informed consent from anyone who participates. Because of ethical concerns, it may not be possible to ask about certain personal or sensitive issues. However interesting the data, you will need to respect the privacy and confidentiality of your respondents.

There are two options for completing this Data Workshop:

Option 1 (informal): Prepare a set of questions in survey format to administer to students. Conduct your survey with a small pilot group (three to five students). Discuss your findings with other students in small-group discussions.

Option 2 (formal): Conduct your survey on a small pilot group (five to eight students). Write a three- to four-page essay describing your preliminary findings. Be sure to attach your survey questionnaire to the paper.

MEDICALIZATION the process by which some behaviors or conditions that were once seen as personal problems are redefined as medical issues

Medicalization and the Social Construction of Health and Illness

Since what constitutes illness can be socially constructed, it's interesting to look at how some problems that were once not considered medical conditions have been transformed into illnesses over time. This process is known as **medicalization**, and it has affected our perspective on a variety of forms of deviance. A century ago, we thought of alcoholism and addiction as the result of weak will or bad character, but we now see them as hereditary diseases that respond to medical and therapeutic treatment. Kids who might have been written off as "unruly" or "incorrigible" in the 1950s are now diagnosed with attention-deficit/hyperactivity disorder, or ADHD, and given drugs to keep them calm and focused (Conrad 2006). Obesity, once seen as a failure of willpower, can now be treated with surgery and drugs.

Even birth and death have been medicalized. In the early years of the twentieth century, more than half of American women gave birth at home, attended only by family, friends, or midwives, without drugs or surgeries (Cassidy 2006). By 1955, that number had declined steeply, to about 1 percent of American women, and it continues at about that rate to this day (Cassidy 2006). We now see pregnancy as a "medical condition" for which a hospital birth—and, often, a doctor's intervention in the form of an episiotomy or caesarean section—is the "treatment." Death has undergone the same transformation: once a natural (though sad) part of family life, it is now something that we will go to great medical lengths to delay (though we can never stave it off forever). Death also used to occur at home, but today at least 75 percent of patients die in hospitals or nursing homes (Cassel and Demel 2001), despite the fact that studies show it is less stressful for terminally ill patients to die at home (Searing 2010). For many people living great distances away from relatives, dying at home is no longer even an option.

Medicalization changes both the meaning of a condition and the meaning of the individual who suffers from it. In the

IN THE FUTURE

Solving the Mystery of Autism

Autism Spectrum Disorders, as defined by the American Psychiatric Association (APA 2012), are a "range of complex developmental disorders that can cause problems with thinking, feeling, language and the ability to relate to others." These challenges can range from severe to very mild, and thus are categorized as a "spectrum."

ASD symptoms generally become evident before the age of three and last throughout a person's life, though symptoms may improve over time with social skills training and behavioral therapy (Handleman and Harris 2000).

What causes ASD remains unclear, as no definite genetic link has been found, though a widely accepted hypothesis is that ASD is multifactoral, in that both genetics and environment influence its prevalence (Hultman, Sparén, and Cnattingius 2002). There are a number of studies that indicate that advanced maternal age (King et al. 2009), closely spaced pregnancies, birth weight, prematurity, and birth order (Cheslack-Postava, Liu, and Bearman 2011) as well as exposure to toxins, viruses, or hormones (London and Etzel 2000) may be etiological factors in ASD.

While the causes for ASD are unclear, how we understand disabilities is socially constructed and thus has important ramifications for how a group of people are medically and socially treated. For example, Asperger's syndrome, one disorder in the ASD family, first appeared in the *Diagnostic and Statistical Manual of Mental Disorders* (DSM) in 1994, and was later removed in the fifth edition in 2013, to be folded back into ASD (*New York Times* 2012). These epidemiological changes are not simply a matter of categorization; diagnosis, treatment of disorders, and access to services often rest on the ability to identify and differentiate the disorders. Thus, how ASD and other disorders are understood can have far-reaching impacts. King and Bearman (2009) indicate that in years when diagnostic criteria changed, the odds of a patient being diagnosed with ASD increased. Thus 26.4 percent of the increased California caseload of ASD diagnoses between 1992 and 2005 are a result of diagnostic changes.

Interactional as well as structural changes can further impact the diagnosis of disorder. For example, Liu, King, and Bearman (2010) show that independent of other factors, children living near another child diagnosed with autism are more likely to also be diagnosed with ASD. Evidence indicates that parents learn how to manage ASD primarily through interaction with other parents who have children with ASD. Thus, awareness of the characteristics and criteria of ASD may lead parents to seek diagnosis for their own child.

Children with ASD often have difficulty navigating social situations, as their language skills may be less developed, and behavior may be disruptive and occasionally violent. This behavior can be challenging for parents of children with ASD. They may experience stigma via hostile staring, avoidance, and rude comments from others (Gray 2002) and thus must engage in strategies to cope with stress. The most common and most effective, as reported by Gray (1994), are the use of service agencies and family support.

On the Spectrum These twin boys function on opposite ends of the autism spectrum. How is our understanding of ASD socially constructed?

case of birth and death, it turns a natural part of the human life cycle into something unfamiliar that we fear we can't handle on our own. We therefore turn to medical experts who may or may not intervene in ways that actually help and may in fact further traumatize patients and their families.

In other cases, such as with forms of deviance like addiction, obesity, or mental or emotional problems, medicalization takes the pressure off the person. The fact that they drink too much, eat too much, can't concentrate, or are sad all the time is no longer their fault as individuals—it is the fault of

Table 14.1 Theory in Everyday Life: Explanations of Addiction

	Approach to Medicine and Health	Case Study: Explaining Drug and Alcohol Addiction
Structural Functionalism	Disease is a threat to social order, and sick people cannot fulfill their roles and contribute to society; the health-care system should return patients to health and normal functioning as members of society.	People who become addicted to drugs or alcohol may be responding to strains in the social system and their own lives; they may adapt by retreating or escaping through drugs or alcohol.
Conflict Theory	Health and the health-care system are seen as valuable resources that are unequally shared in society; conflict may arise between different groups seeking access to and control over these resources.	Those in power can define social policy and create laws regarding medicine and health care; people of lower social status are more likely to be scrutinized as problem drinkers or drug addicts, and may be unduly punished.
Symbolic Interactionism	The meaning of health and illness are dependent upon historical, cultural, and situational contexts. Stigma may be attached to certain disease states and those who suffer from them.	People learn to use alcohol and drugs in social interaction and are influenced by peers and other groups; they may attach different meanings and values to substances and behaviors.

the disease. We would never advise someone to "just get over" pneumonia or a broken leg—and as the process of medicalization continues, we are less likely to think of addiction, obesity, and depression as conditions people should "just get over" on their own.

The Changing Meaning of Mental Illness

Understanding that disease can be socially constructed allows us to see how its meanings can change over time. For example, take the social meaning of mental illness. Over the course of history and in different societies, theories of the causes of mental illness have varied widely. Each new theory led to a different type of treatment (and justification for that treatment), some of which seem shockingly inhuman to us now. For example, in fourteenth-century London, Bethlem Royal Hospital (which is still in operation today) became a kind of prison for those suffering from mental illnesses. Based on the theory that mental illness was a moral failing caused by demon possession or individual weakness, the "treatment" for those who suffered was their removal from society. Bethlem, or Bedlam as it came to be known, warehoused the mentally ill under the most horrifying of conditions, which included overcrowding, lack of food, water, and sanitation, whippings, and "exorcisms."

In Colonial America, the prevailing theory was that mental illness was caused by the astrological position of the moon at the time of the individual's birth; hence the term "lunatic." According to this theory, mental illness was located inside a lunatic's body, and the only possible cures involved treatments meant to release the illness, such as bleeding (which often killed the patients) and long-term induced vomiting (also potentially fatal). In the 1930s, the cause of mental illness was believed to be located in a particular portion of the brain, whose removal would thus provide the cure. The lobotomy, in which a bit of the brain (or lobe) was surgically removed, often without anesthesia, seemed to work nicely; patients became calm enough to leave the hospital and return home. We now know that lobotomies merely disconnected two critical parts of the brain from one another, leaving patients unable to feel emotions or act on the information provided to them by their senses.

These approaches to mental illness now seem ridiculous and cruel. We know that mental illness is not caused by demon possession, a weak will, or astrological accidents, and we know that beatings, exorcisms, and lobotomies cannot restore mental health. We are certain (aren't we?) that mental illness is caused by problems of brain chemistry and that proper treatment involves medicines that restore that chemistry to its healthy balance. But given the history of changing meanings and treatments, we have to ask: What makes this theory any better than the others? How can we be sure that this time we've gotten it right? Isn't it possible that, a hundred years from now, we'll discover the "real" cause of mental illness and that drug treatments will seem as useless and inhuman as surgeries and bleedings do now?

A Misguided Treatment
Dr. Walter Freeman revolutionized the lobotomy procedure, which he performed with an ice pick–like instrument that severed nerve connections in the front part of the brain.

Disease Patterns as Social Epidemiology

As we have noted, sociologists are interested in the social aspect of disease patterns. The study of these patterns is known as **epidemiology**. Epidemiologists collect and analyze data in order to understand the causes of a particular illness, how it is communicated, the factors affecting its development and distribution in a population, where it is likely to spread, and what the most effective interventions might be. Over many centuries of human history, major illnesses such as cholera, typhus, yellow fever, and smallpox swept across vast stretches of the globe and decimated populations from practically every continent. More recently, such illnesses as tuberculosis, malaria, and measles continue to kill millions around the world. What future illnesses might threaten humanity next, and can we identify them before widespread devastation occurs? Epidemiologists combine data and methods from the biological and social sciences with a public health orientation to answer important questions about the origins and spread of disease.

Epidemiologists swing into action whenever a new disease emerges or an unexpected outbreak of a previously eradicated disease resurfaces. For example, in the H1N1 influenza (or "swine flu") **epidemic** of 2009, epidemiological researchers established the connection between hundreds of seemingly unrelated patients, analyzed the genetic makeup of the virus that infected them, and confirmed that they were suffering from a strain of influenza virus that had not previously infected humans—all in a matter of weeks (Novel Swine-Origin Influenza A [H1N1] Virus Investigation Team 2009). As a result of this research, a vaccine was developed and a widespread public health awareness campaign was put in place to educate people about the transmission, prevention, and treatment of the disease.

The H1N1 outbreak of 2009 began as an epidemic, but eventually became what is known as a **pandemic**. What are the differences between those two terms? An epidemic occurs when a significantly higher number of cases of a particular disease occur during a particular time period than might otherwise be expected, while the term "pandemic" is used when those cases also cover an especially large geographical region (say, a continent or the entire globe). What constitutes an epidemic is usually determined by national public health organizations—in the United States, that would be the

EPIDEMIOLOGY the study of disease patterns to understand the cause of illnesses, how they are spread, and what interventions to take

EPIDEMIC occurs when a significantly higher number of cases of a particular disease occur during a particular time period than might otherwise be expected

PANDEMIC occurs when a significantly higher number of cases of a disease also spreads through an especially large geographical region spanning many countries or even continents

GLOBAL PERSPECTIVE

HIV and AIDS around the World

For a long time, the story of the human immunodeficiency virus (HIV) and the disease it causes, acquired immunodeficiency syndrome (AIDS), had a single narrative. Genetic analysis has led researchers to believe that the simian immunodeficiency virus (SIV) was present in primates in Africa for at least 32,000 years (Worobey et al. 2010). Researchers still disagree as to why, but at some point in the late nineteenth or early twentieth century, a strain of this virus mutated into a form that infected humans. Analysis of blood samples taken at different points in time suggests that HIV moved from the Congo to Haiti, and then migrated to the United States through Haitian immigrants. The disease continued its spread throughout the world.

At least 25 million people have died since AIDS was identified in the early 1980s, and approximately 33 million people are currently infected with HIV (UNAIDS 2009, 2010). AIDS is now a pandemic—a global event made possible by the increasing connections that come with a global economy—but it has also become a series of epidemics. AIDS is always the same disease, but it is a very different epidemic depending on where it is.

One of the most important ways in which medical researchers study AIDS is by determining the different ways in which it is transmitted and which parts of the population are most affected. In many places, AIDS is a concentrated epidemic, with the majority of cases transmitted by a particular method and concentrated in a particular subpopulation within a given country. In Central Europe and Central Asia, intravenous drug use is responsible for the majority of cases (O'Neill 2007). In Latin America, the routes by which HIV is transmitted are much more diverse, but same-sex male intercourse is a more common route to infection. In Southeast Asia, commercial sex workers make up a much larger percentage of the HIV-positive population. In sub-Saharan Africa, AIDS is a generalized epidemic,

spread through the entire population, such that in some countries more than 30 percent of adults are infected.

Understanding the ways in which HIV spreads is vital for those who seek to treat those who are infected and prevent future infections, but these differences are not the most important ways in which AIDS is experienced differently around the world. For one thing, AIDS is distributed disproportionately: only about 4 percent of all cases are in the developed world, places like the United States, Western Europe, Japan, and other wealthy, industrialized nations. This is important because in the developed world the vast majority of AIDS sufferers have access to antiretroviral drugs, which transform the disease into something much closer to a chronic condition and significantly improve the physical, emotional, and mental life of those who receive them. In the developing world, however, these drugs are prohibitively expensive for the vast majority of AIDS patients (Beard, Feeley, and Rosen 2009).

The expense of antiretroviral drugs has led to important discussions about how the international community should respond to AIDS in the developing world. Some advocate a pragmatic approach, focusing on education and other preventive strategies rather than treating the disease. Those who hold this position assume that antiretroviral drugs are both too expensive to supply and too complicated to administer. For example, new treatment regimens for both mother and baby can entirely eliminate the transmission of AIDS from mother to child. However, this care has not been comprehensively extended to pregnant women with AIDS in the less-developed world. Not only are the drugs very expensive, but the regimen requires pregnant women to undergo a lengthy course of oral and injected treatments and to refrain from breastfeeding. The baby also undergoes six weeks of drug treatments, and both mother and infant must be carefully monitored for side effects (Varmus and

Centers for Disease Control (CDC) in Atlanta (Koerner 2003). The World Health Organization (WHO), in Geneva, Switzerland, monitors and defines pandemics.

Epidemiologists are now identifying the role of global climate change in spreading some of the most important diseases afflicting the world, and they are tracking how this process occurs (Associated Press 2006). Because climate affects things like the availability of fresh water and "arable" (or farmable) land, it also affects where people live and

their patterns of migration. As people leave places where climate change has made food, water, and other resources scarce, they crowd into other areas that may then experience overpopulation. When people live in very close quarters, the risks rise for malnutrition, water-borne illnesses such as cholera, and other infectious diseases to spread (Khasnis and Nettleman 2005).

Global climate change can also affect animal populations that spread diseases among humans. Even small increases

Satcher 1997). Following the pragmatic approach means that millions of people are being condemned to suffering and an early death even though proven medical treatments exist.

This approach has also led to intense controversy in the research world. In 1997, the Public Citizen Health Research Group wrote an editorial for the *New England Journal of Medicine* (Lurie and Wolfe 1997) condemning a number of clinical trials for new AIDS treatments, many of which were funded by the U.S. government. The trials in question compared the performance of new AIDS treatments and drugs against a placebo group that received no treatment, rather than comparing the new therapies to antiretrovirals, which were recognized as the most effective treatment. The

editorial compared the research to the infamous Tuskegee Syphilis Experiment (see the Global Perspective box in Chapter 2), and pointed out that the World Medical Association's (WMA's) ethical guidelines would prohibit this research: the WMA's Helsinki Declaration says that medical research must always ensure that "every patient—including those of a control group, if any—should be assured of the best proven diagnostic and therapeutic methods" (1964). When researchers test only newer, cheaper treatments and compare them against each other rather than against the best available treatment, they are accepting that the treatment afforded AIDS patients in the developed world cannot be extended to the many millions of people suffering in the developing world.

Seeking Treatment Patients wait at the HIV/AIDS clinic in Arua Regional Hospital in northern Uganda, where Doctors Without Borders provides medical care and access to antiretroviral drugs.

in temperature can multiply the numbers of **vector organisms** that carry and spread pathogens (germs or other infectious agents) in a given area. Mosquitoes carrying malaria, for example, used to be limited to sub-Saharan Africa and other hot or tropical regions. But in Kenya, malaria has recently penetrated mountainous regions that were once too chilly for mosquitoes to survive, and similar reports have come from parts of Europe and as far north as Moscow, Russia (Associated Press 2006). Other illnesses such as Lyme disease (car-

ried by ticks), yellow and dengue fevers and West Nile virus (carried by mosquitoes), avian influenza (carried by birds), and even plague (carried by fleas on rodents) may skyrocket as climate change drives these vector animals out of their customary territories and into new ecosystems (Dell'Amore 2008).

VECTOR ORGANISMS animals like mosquitoes, ticks, and birds that carry and spread pathogens (germs or other infectious agents) in a given area

Climate Change and Health A woman hands out hand sanitizer in Times Square to help prevent the spread of H1N1. As the climate changes, vector organisms carry and spread pathogens outside their normal habitat to contribute to the spread of such illnesses.

Foreseeing this serious threat to human health and the possibility of its resulting in greater epidemics in the future, networks of scientists have called for action by all nations to mandate caps on greenhouse gas emissions, as well as to begin preparing for what appear to be the unavoidable public health consequences of the global climate change that has already occurred.

Social Inequality, Health, and Illness

As we have seen in previous chapters, a person's socioeconomic status, race, and gender also shapes their experiences of health and illness. Answers to such questions as "Who gets sick?" "What kinds of diseases do they get?" "Who gets treatment?" and "What kind of treatment do they get?" are all influenced by social hierarchies and structures of inequality. Since we gave you a fairly comprehensive picture of the relationships between different forms of inequality and different health outcomes in the prior chapters, we'll just summarize some of the main findings first, and then go into more depth here about a specific problem that is linked to a variety of illnesses and is caused largely by social inequalities.

Health and Intersections of Class, Race, and Gender

It's easy to see how one's social class might have an effect on one's health. People of higher socioeconomic status (SES) not only can afford more and better health-care services (insurance plans, doctor visits, diagnostic tests and treat-ments, prescription medications) but also may have greater access to other resources (better nutrition, cleaner neighborhoods, more preventive practices like exercise) that positively impact their health. People of higher SES can expect to live longer lives, and they generally enjoy feeling more physical well-being than those in lower groups. Being on the lower end of the social class ladder brings many problems that are the inverse of the advantages above. People with lower SES have substantially higher rates of various diseases along with higher death rates and shorter life expectancy (Lynch et al. 1998). They may have little regular access to health-care providers and may lack the ability to participate in preventive practices or have trouble affording prescription medications and other recommended procedures (Lynch et al. 1997). The effects of poverty consistently correlate with higher incidences of depression and other mental health problems (Groh 2007).

Inequalities of race and gender are often connected to lower socioeconomic status. When we add race or gender to the health equation, we find significant differences between groups who are higher or lower in the social hierarchy. Many problems that affect people of lower SES are further exacerbated in minority groups. African Americans have long been discriminated against and still suffer disproportionately from the stresses of poverty. They have higher rates of death and disease, and shorter life expectancy than whites. African Americans and Hispanics are less likely to be able to afford health insurance and, consequently, to engage in regular health practices (Centers for Disease Control 2011). Researchers have shown that minorities are more often exposed to unhealthful surroundings, whether in the workplace or in residential neighborhoods. For example, Emily Rosenbaum (2008) found that Hispanics and blacks in New York City tended to live in poorer quality housing

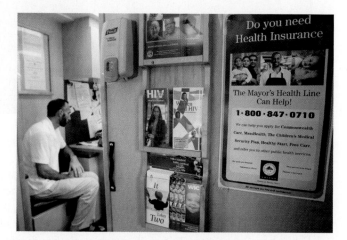

Socioeconomic Status and Health A man visits the Family Van in Boston, Massachusetts, to get his blood pressure checked. Many residents from low-income neighborhoods visit the Family Van, a nonprofit clinic, to get free health screenings they wouldn't normally have access to.

in lower-income neighborhoods, and to suffer much higher incidents of asthma than their Asian, white, and higher-SES counterparts.

Gender is another source of inequality that complicates the health picture for men and women. Health is one place where gender inequality tends to benefit women over men, as women are generally healthier and enjoy a longer life expectancy in spite of having a lower SES than men. Traditional male gender role expectations may result in men who work in more dangerous occupations and engage in more risky lifestyle behaviors (like smoking, drinking, drugging, and driving fast). The more strongly men identify with the "macho" aspects of masculinity, the more likely they are to avoid preventive health care, regardless of their level of SES (Springer and Mouzon 2011). Men and women suffer some diseases, such as cancer and diabetes, in about equal numbers. However, men still have a higher incidence of heart disease and strokes, while women more often report that they suffer mental health disorders like anxiety or depression (WomensHealth.gov 2010).

Health and the Problem of Food Deserts

A **food desert** is a community in which the residents have little or no access to fresh, affordable, healthy foods. Most food deserts are located in densely populated, urban areas that may have convenience stores and fast-food restaurants, but no grocery stores or other outlet for fresh fruits, vegetables, meats, and other healthy foods. (Sparsely populated rural areas, where stores are far away and hard to access,

can also be considered food deserts.) For example, more than 20 percent of Chicago's 3 million residents live in neighborhoods without supermarkets (Gray 2009), which means that they may have to shop at drug stores, liquor stores, or corner mini-marts for food items, or subsist on the chicken nuggets, burritos, or burgers and fries from the takeout chain on the corner. People who live in food deserts may have few meal choices that aren't highly processed and loaded with fat, sugar, and chemicals.

Food deserts are often in neighborhoods that are predominantly low-income or nonwhite in population. This means that the effects of food deserts are experienced disproportionately by the poor, African Americans, Hispanics, and other minority groups. The health effects of living in a food desert are significant: the risk of obesity, diabetes, and heart disease for African Americans increases by half, and for Hispanics by two-thirds (Whitacre et al. 2009; Powell et al. 2007). So, while any given individual may be at risk for obesity, diabetes, or heart disease, living in a food desert increases those risks.

Why do food deserts exist? They are not a new phenomenon. Grocery chains began leaving urban areas for the suburbs in the 1960s and 1970s as a result of perceived problems with security, profitability, real estate costs, and parking (Ferguson and Abell 1998). In their place, bodegas, liquor stores, and fast-food chains popped up, leaving central urban populations with far fewer healthy food options. Some city and state governments are trying to entice supermarkets back to these neighborhoods with programs like tax incentives,

> **FOOD DESERT** a community in which the residents have little or no access to fresh, affordable, healthy foods, usually located in densely populated, urban areas

Food Deserts The absence of grocery stores contributes to the lack of healthy food options available in urban and poor neighborhoods.

IN RELATIONSHIPS

Concierge Medicine: Paying for Your Own Private Doctor?

You break out in an itchy rash on your leg . . . or you pull a muscle in your back . . . or you've got another splitting sinus headache and it's not getting any better. You should probably go see the doctor. But that process may end up being a bigger pain than the physical hurt in your leg, back, or head. Why? First of all, it may be weeks (or even months for certain specialties) before you can get into the doctor's office in the first place: nationally, it takes an average of about three weeks to get an appointment (Merritt Hawkins & Associates 2009). Once you arrive, you may sit for quite a long time in the waiting room—an average of more than twenty minutes, according to the AMA (Arnst 2010). Once you get into the exam room, you may wait some more (this time in a flimsy paper gown). And when the doctor finally arrives, it may not be the same doctor you saw last time, so you may have to spend extra time bringing her up to speed. That time is precious—studies indicate that you will only have ten minutes with your doctor once she arrives in the exam room (Ohtaki, Ohtaki, and Fetters 2003)—ten minutes to give your history, describe your symptoms, receive your diagnosis, and discuss your treatment. And let's not even talk about the process of paying for this visit: insurance company paperwork and bureaucracy may be the biggest pain of all.

Is there a solution to this tedious, impersonal approach to health care? Maybe. You could have a very different relationship with your doctor—no waiting, no insurance forms, and maybe even house calls—if you've got enough cash. We're talking about a phenomenon known as concierge medicine, where doctors provide direct care to patients who have paid an annual fee ($1,500 or more in addition to the costs of their actual care) so that they can retain the services of a personal physician who is always available to address their health-care needs. It's a growing niche—the American Academy of Private Physicians estimates that there are now 5,000 doctors practicing this type of medicine, only fifteen years after such "boutique" medical practices began to appear (Wahlgren 2010). And in 2009, concierge medicine even broke into the world of popular culture, with USA Network's television series *Royal Pains*, about a doctor-for-hire in the Hamptons and his wealthy, demanding patients.

There are obvious advantages for both the patients who get twenty-four-hour care with no waiting and for the doctors who get to avoid many of the bureaucratic nightmares of belonging to health management organizations (HMOs). Concierge doctors tend to have far fewer patients and can spend far more time with each patient as a result—one doctor predicted that his daily consultations would drop from twenty-five to six if he made the switch from conventional to concierge care (Sonn 2004). Concierge medicine allows doctors to forge more substantial relationships with their patients, which is what may have inspired them to practice medicine in the first place. James Benoit, an M.D. from Colorado, started a concierge practice and says that "it's changed my life . . . [and] given me my profession back" (Sonn 2004). Patients feel similarly: "I'm so grateful to know that truly he's at my beck and call," says Marilyn Morris about her concierge physician (Archer 2010). And Joan Holzman says of her concierge doctor's practice: "I adore it. . . . Before, wherever you went, you felt like cattle. But everyone here is top-notch—the doctors, the secretaries, the nurses. They're warm, like family. It's a wonderful feeling of security" (Zuger 2005).

But the fact that patients must pay a steep price for this kind of personal connection with their health-care providers means that questions of inequality arise. Because of the additional fees, concierge services will be obtainable only

---

grants, or loans for big food retailers and subsidies for farmers' markets. Similar programs are being proposed at the federal level (Haber 2010).

As we have seen, our individual health is shaped by our neighborhood context, which is itself shaped by race and class inequality, the actions of big corporations, and the responses of governmental bodies at all levels. This phenomenon is known as **deprivation amplification**, meaning that our individual disease risks (based on our heredity and physiology) may be amplified by social factors (Macintyre, Macdonald, and Ellaway 2008). The solutions to these health problems are not going to be found merely at the individual level—they must incorporate social action as well. Yes, you need to eat more healthily in order to control your diabetes . . . but you must be able to find healthy foods close by and at affordable prices in order to do so, and you are more likely to do that in

DEPRIVATION AMPLIFICATION
when our individual disease risks (based on our heredity and physiology) are amplified by social factors

by those in higher income brackets. What about the patients who can't come up with the required fees? Where will they go for medical care if their doctor decides to switch to a smaller practice with fewer, more affluent patients? Does concierge medicine stratify the health-care system even more than it already is? Harvard Medical School professor John Goodson uses the term "country club medicine" to describe concierge practices (Williams 2006), and worries that those not in the "club" will no longer be able to find the health care they deserve. While all patients may want a more personal, more

committed connection with their doctor, is it fair if only those with the deepest pockets can get it? Medical ethicists caution doctors that this type of practice may violate their professional obligations and be at odds with their philosophical codes (Zuger 2005).

Should our relationships with those who hold our health—and even our lives—in their hands depend on the size of our bank accounts? Use your sociological perspective to consider this issue, and then decide: what do you think about "concierge medicine"?

Royal Pains The TV series features private doctors for hire in the wealthy enclaves of the Hamptons.

some neighborhoods than in others, which you may be more likely to live in depending on your gender, race, and SES.

Medicine as a Social Institution

For proof that medicine is a social institution, take a look at the American Medical Association (AMA). The AMA is usually thought of as an organization that makes health recom-

mendations on such topics as childhood obesity and cancer prevention to benefit the general public. But physicians and other medical professionals know the AMA as a trade union that creates the rules and regulations governing medical licensure (AMA 2010). Almost all issues concerning medicine in both public health and professional regulation are governed by the AMA.

Milton Friedman, the winner of the 1976 Nobel Prize in Economics, was a vocal critic of the AMA. Friedman argued that the AMA limits admissions to medical schools

Medicine as a Social Institution Medical students shadow a doctor in an emergency room. The path to becoming a doctor is often regimented, and only more rules and regulations apply once one becomes a doctor.

and restricts medical licensing to advance the interests of physicians. He viewed the AMA as a monopolizing organization that reduced the quantity and quality of medical care by forcing the public to pay more for medical services because of the lack of qualified physicians (Friedman 1994).

For example, the AMA does not allow physicians who are trained in foreign countries to practice in the United States without passing the United States Medical Licensing Exam (USMLE). For many of these physicians, fulfilling the requirements of the USMLE is a lengthy and arduous process that often necessitates repeating medical residency before they are allowed to practice medicine—even though they were fully licensed and practicing physicians in their country of origin. The AMA and the American College of Obstetricians and Gynecologists also restrict such practices as home births. Even though trained midwives and doulas (who provide emotional support) can safely assist at home births, pregnant women have their options limited by the pressure that the AMA places on women to have labor and delivery at a hospital attended by physicians. As a result, these professionals are forced to operate on the margins of the industry, while physicians and hospitals are able to make more profit from hospital births.

The AMA serves a number of purposes: it establishes and transmits the norms and values of medicine and medical knowledge; it regulates, licenses, and legitimizes the practitioners of medicine; and it polices various forms of encroachment on its own powers. In these ways, medicine itself can be seen as a social institution, with the AMA playing a primary role in creating and maintaining social order, legitimacy, and control.

The Power of the Institution to Define the Situation

The institutional context can have a powerful effect on the interactions that occur within it. You might remember David Rosenhan's study "On Being Sane in Insane Places" (1973) from Chapter 6, in which "pseudo-patients" who were admitted to a mental hospital were unable to convince hospital staffers of their sanity. In this case, the place itself overrode the individuals' claims to normalcy: once they were defined by and situated within the institution, they could no longer exert any power over their own status, and every interaction they had served as "proof" of their presumed mental illness. Erving Goffman found something very similar in his study of hospitalized mental patients, *Asylums* (1961): psychiatric patients frequently offered explanations for being there that highlighted their normalcy and attempted to reframe their selves as sane and healthy. They inevitably failed to change anyone's mind, however, since the power of their institutionally inflicted diagnoses was indisputable.

Sociologist Elaine Feder-Alford's ethnomethodological analysis of her own hospitalization (for streptococcal pneumonia) shows that these social processes are still at work in medical institutions. She describes being treated like a "piece of meat," an object, or an "incompetent child" by hospital staff during her illness (2006). She felt dehumanized and powerless, as if they saw her as a diagnosis, rather than as a human being. Medical professionals plunged long syringes into her stomach without explaining why and accused her of being an alcoholic because she contracted a liver infection. The institution she inhabited as a patient defined her very differently than she defined herself, creating conflict at just the point in time when she was most ill, and hence least able to defend her definition of herself and the situation. As her condition improved, so did her ability to assert her humanity and negotiate for better treatment within the institutional setting. But her experience left her dismayed at the power of the hospital to reduce the patient to an object, and led her to promote "proposals that acknowledge patients in a hospital setting as human beings with individual needs and feelings" (p. 618).

Doctor-Patient Relations

The institutional context of medicine shapes the interactions between individuals within it. But those interactions also contribute to the shape of the institution itself. Since the 1970s, ethnographers, conversation analysts, and other observational sociologists have studied interactions in health-care settings. Studies of doctor-patient interactions have shown that while we may think that doctors automatically have more status (and hence more power) than patients, this actually has to be established in the interaction—it is not an inevitable feature of medical settings (Pilnick, Hindmarsh, and Teas Gill 2009). Other findings are equally counterintuitive: while you might think that what constitutes good or bad medical news is pretty obvious (say, a benign tumor versus a malignant one), doctors and patients do not always agree on whether a particular diagnosis is pleasant or unpleasant, trivial or serious (Heritage and Stivers 1999; Maynard and Frankel 2006). So the institutional setting does not always exert the type of power we might think it does over the interactions that occur within it. Instead, the people involved in interactions must establish who has power or status, as they must also distinguish good news from bad. It is through such subtle interactional processes that social institutions are constituted, maintained, or changed.

Additional research on medical interaction has moved beyond focusing merely on doctor-patient interaction, acknowledging that there are other important dyads (and triads and groups) in medical institutions that are worth examining. Interactions between patients and speech therapists, pharmacists, or dentists are structured differently and address different issues than those between patients and physicians. And interactions between health-care practitioners (such as doctor-nurse, surgeon-anesthetist, or trainee-teacher), either within or outside of patients' presence, are equally important. So are interactions facilitated by medical technologies, such as ultrasound or x-ray screenings (Pilnick, Hindmarsh, and Teas Gill 2009). One powerful analysis of an emergency services call shows what happens "when words fail," as the dispatcher becomes irritated with the panic-stricken caller, and their clash about what constitutes an appropriate call for help results in the victim's

death (Whalen, Zimmerman, and Whalen 1988). Studies such as this one indicate that rules, roles, and other elements of institutional order are emergent and situational. They are not necessarily written down somewhere for the rest of us to follow, but instead are created and maintained (and sometimes distorted) in interaction.

The Sick Role

Of course, in addition to being shaped in interaction, rules and roles in medical institutions are influenced by external social structures as well. One example of this is the **sick role**. This concept, advanced by functionalist Talcott Parsons, was a way of encapsulating the actions and attitudes that society expects from someone who is ill, as well as the actions and attitudes that a person might expect from other members of society (1951).

> **SICK ROLE** the actions and attitudes that society expects from someone who is ill

Being ill is, from a functionalist perspective, a form of deviance. So, as part of the sick role, a patient is exempted from his or her regular responsibilities (such as work, child care, or other, less tangible obligations), and is not held responsible for his or her illness. However, the patient also has a new set of duties as well, which include seeking medical help as part of an earnest effort to recuperate and get back to normal. If the sick person abides by these requirements, he or she will not be treated as deviant by society; but if the sick

Sick Role and Genetic Risk How might people who have a genetic risk of certain diseases but who show no symptoms exist in a space between the healthy and the sick?

ON THE JOB

Cultural Competence in Health Professions

Lia Lee was a baby when her epileptic seizures began. In 1985, when she was three years old, she had an especially serious attack, and her parents, Hmong immigrants living in California's Central Valley, brought her to the Merced County Medical Center for treatment. What happened to Lia, her family, and her doctors during the next two years is the subject of journalist Anne Fadiman's 1998 book *The Spirit Catches You and You Fall Down*.

The book's title refers to the way the Hmong, a Southeast Asian ethnic group, see Lia's affliction. Indeed, their understanding of all health problems involves malevolent attempts by evil spirits, known as *dabs*, to meddle with human souls. The differences between Hmong understandings of epilepsy and its treatment and those of the Western medical establishment created the conflict in which Lia Lee was trapped.

CULTURAL COMPETENCE
the concept of acknowledging and incorporating a patient's cultural background as part of the treatment process; the recognition that patients' beliefs shape their approach to health care

---

The details of Lia's case are heart-wrenching: both her parents and her doctors tried their best to heal her. But because of cultural and language differences, they were unable to understand each other's perspective. They became suspicious and mistrustful of each other, which made collaboration even harder. The doctors firmly believed in Western biomedical approaches to epilepsy—they thought that if the Lees gave Lia the right medicines at the right times, she would be fine. Meanwhile, the Lees firmly believed that the *dab* had Lia's soul in its grip, and that traditional Hmong procedures (such as shamanic healing ceremonies) should be part of her treatment.

Both parties saw the other side's actions as counterproductive; they resisted cooperating because they each believed the other's approach would make Lia's condition worse. Caught in this standoff between Western medicine and Hmong tradition, Lia did get worse, eventually suffering "The Big One," a seizure that left her with severe and permanent brain damage. Today, Lia lingers in a vegetative state, tended lovingly by her family but representing failure to the team of medical professionals who treated her.

Lia Lee's case has been the touchstone for a number of recent attempts to increase the cultural awareness of health-care professionals, with the hopes of avoiding future cases like hers. This movement has coined the term **cultural competence** to describe the concept of acknowledging and incorporating a patient's cultural background as part of the treatment process. The recognition that patients' beliefs shape their approach to health care may not seem like news to sociology majors, but the cultural competence movement for health professionals (including doctors, nurses, medical social workers, pharmacists, and physical therapists) is less than fifteen years old.

For example, the Association of American Medical Colleges (AAMC) is among the many organizations that have instituted cultural competence initiatives. The AAMC has produced a set of curriculum recommendations for medical schools, and provides evaluation tools for assessing the

---

person languishes for too long, doesn't do much to improve his or her condition, or seems too interested in staying sick, that person is likely to experience negative sanctions from society. In this case, it is society's definition of deviance that shapes patients' experiences and their contact with medical institutions.

As you might imagine, the concept of the sick role has changed over the many decades since Parsons first proposed it, in part because of advances in diagnostic technology. For example, with genetic testing, we can now identify people who are at risk of certain diseases before they ever become ill (indeed, not everyone who is at risk becomes ill). What does this new diagnostic label—"at risk"—mean for the performance of the sick role? Those people with genetic risk factors but no symptoms of disease exist in a liminal space between the healthy and the sick. They inhabit a "potential sick role," with a different set of expectations than in Parson's traditional model. One particularly interesting finding is that those who are in the lowest risk category sometimes try to get themselves recategorized as high risk. This may be because it is easier to determine the expectations for a high-risk patient (regular screenings, warning family members that they might be at risk, etc.) than for a low-risk patient. Research such as this suggests a more dynamic, nuanced definition of the "sick role" and provides for the possibility that the experience of health and illness is not as straightforward as Parsons originally hypothesized.

impact of cultural competency initiatives once they are in place (2009). The goal is to train new physicians to recognize the importance of cultural knowledge and beliefs—their patients' and their own—in health-care encounters, and to provide them with strategies for effective diagnosis, treatment, and interaction in cross-cultural encounters.

As part of the AAMC's plan, students are encouraged to examine their own cultural backgrounds, assumptions, and biases, and to exercise nonjudgment when asking questions and listening to patients discuss their own health beliefs. They are trained to respect patients' diverse ideas about health and illness, to recognize when to use interpreters, and even to collaborate with traditional healers from their patients' cultures. They are also urged to appreciate the power imbalances between doctors and patients, and to work to eliminate racism and stereotyping from health-care practices.

Students often assume that they should major in a "hard" science if they want to go into a health profession, particularly a life science such as biology. But given the rising importance of cultural competence in health professions, this may not be the ideal foundation. A student with a social science major, like sociology, may be even better prepared for working in the medical field than a biologist. An understanding of such issues as ethnocentrism, inequality, and the importance of culture in the lives of individuals means that students of sociology are already ahead of bio majors when it comes to issues of cultural competence in the practice of medicine.

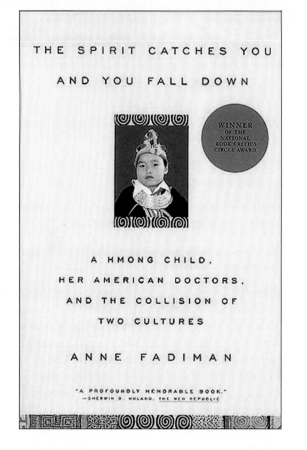

THE SPIRIT CATCHES YOU
AND YOU FALL DOWN

WINNER OF THE NATIONAL BOOK CRITICS CIRCLE AWARD

A HMONG CHILD,
HER AMERICAN DOCTORS,
AND THE COLLISION OF
TWO CULTURES

ANNE FADIMAN

"A PROFOUNDLY MEMORABLE BOOK."
—SHERWIN B. NULAND, THE NEW REPUBLIC

DATA WORKSHOP
Analyzing Mass Media and Popular Culture

Medicine on Television

From *M*A*S*H* to *St. Elsewhere*, from *Dr. Kildare* to *Doogie Howser* and *House*, Americans have long been captivated by television shows about hospitals. Medical dramas and comedies have been some of the most critically acclaimed and highest-rated primetime television shows over the years. Many medical shows have multiple fan sites for discussing every detail of every episode. And because these dramas are so prevalent and popular, they impact America's perception of different diseases and treatments, the roles of patients and medical staff, and the nature and function of the medical institution.

In conventional American television, the medical problems faced by the protagonists are easily solved. There is generally a patient or multiple patients with medical conditions that are triaged, diagnosed, treated, and healed within a single episode. Anyone who has dealt with a serious illness or accident knows that the reality of health care in America is a prolonged process that involves long waits, multiple visits to

Medicine on Television *Nurse Jackie* and *House* are both medical dramas that portray hospitals in ways that don't often resonate with real life.

multiple doctors and different facilities for testing, and complicated interactions with insurance providers. The anger, sadness, and frustration of the patient's experience are generally glossed over in favor of the viewpoint of the medical professionals involved in the process.

For this Data Workshop, you will be using existing sources to do a content analysis comparing the world of TV with the real world (refer to Chapter 2 for a reminder about this research method). Select a scripted medical drama or comedy (not a reality or documentary show), using the examples above or the following list as inspiration. You may choose a show that is currently being broadcast or one that is available online or on DVD, for example:

Chicago Hope	*Nurse Jackie*
ER	*Private Practice*
Grey's Anatomy	*Royal Pains*
HawthoRNe	*Scrubs*
House, M.D.	*St. Elsewhere*

Select an episode or scene that deals with a specific disease or condition. Next, look up the epidemiology of that disease or condition. You may start with the internet, but make sure that you are consulting a medical journal site or an organization such as the Mayo Clinic or Centers for Disease Control rather than Wikipedia or WebMD. For example, articles from the *New England Journal of Medicine*, the American Medical Association, or American Association of Family Physicians will yield more thorough and accurate data for the purposes of this exercise.

You may want to consider the following questions when looking at the disease's epidemiology:

* How common is the disease or condition?

* What are the causes of and contributing factors to the disease or condition?

* Does it affect different groups (for example, men and women, or patients of different races or ethnicities) in different ways?

* Which groups are more likely to contract the disease or condition? Why?

* Who is involved in the diagnosis and treatment of the disease or condition?

* How expensive, rare, dangerous, and/or available are the treatments, and are there any side effects?

* How rich, lucky, or well-insured would a patient have to be to undergo treatments?

Compare and contrast the show's treatment of the disease or condition to the statistics your research has revealed. How accurate was the portrayal? How does the television show's treatment of illness reflect the average experience of an American patient with the same illness? And most importantly, what kind of effects would any discrepancies have on audiences', patients', or even physicians' perceptions of the disease or condition and its treatment? How does this affect America's understanding of the health-care system?

There are two options for completing this Data Workshop:

Option 1 (informal): Prepare written notes for in-class discussions. Go over your response to the above questions with other students in small-group discussions. Compare and contrast your findings.

Option 2 (formal): Write a three- to four-page essay detailing your content analysis and comparative work.

Issues in Medicine and Health Care

The fields of medicine and health care have continued to evolve and advance, often affecting individual lives in profound ways and addressing some of the most pressing problems facing humanity. While much of the progress over the last decades has been tremendously positive, there are still unfulfilled promises and new questions to resolve. In this last section, we examine some of the current trends and future challenges in medicine and health care.

Health-Care Reform in the United States

In 1974, when Richard Nixon gave his final State of the Union address before a joint session of Congress, he called for "a new system that makes high-quality health care available to every American in a dignified manner and at a price he can afford" (1974). Nixon, a Republican, had previously described comprehensive health-care reform as the highest priority on his unfinished agenda for America (1972). It would remain a national priority that eluded many other politicians for many more decades until March 2010, when the Patient Protection and Affordable Care Act was signed into law. This legislation, commonly known as health-care reform (and also somewhat derisively as "ObamaCare"), finally brought something like universal health-care coverage to all U.S. citizens. Yet the act was not met with universal approval. The bill simultaneously frustrated many longtime advocates of health-care reform by not going far enough, while infuriating others by going too far.

Almost as soon as the legislation was passed, opponents began organizing to repeal the law. Some believe that it will cost too much, raise taxes, hurt businesses, and lead to a government takeover of health care, among other complaints. The midterm elections in November 2010 brought many new members into the U.S. House of Representatives, effectively changing it to a Republican majority that vowed to dismantle the new reforms. A vote in February 2011 to defund the law was largely symbolic, but it reflected some of the controversy and dissension over how to provide health care to Americans (Condon 2011). Opponents have also challenged the constitutionality of the new law, taking their cause to state and federal courts. Health-care reform is likely to remain a battleground, and new legislation may alter some aspects of the recent reforms. In the meantime, the legislation will

be phased in slowly over ten years, with many important changes coming into effect in 2014.

Two major elements of the bill took effect shortly after it was signed into law in 2010. The first focused on increasing coverage for children and young adults: insurance companies must now allow children to remain on their parents' insurance plan through age twenty-six, rather than the previous limits of age twenty-one or after college graduation. Also, insurance companies are no longer allowed to deny coverage to children with preexisting conditions (starting in 2014, no one will be denied coverage for this reason). The second element of the bill closed loopholes that allowed insurance companies to deny or limit coverage to people who became ill. Insurers are no longer allowed to impose lifetime spending caps—allotting a certain amount of money for a given patient over that patient's lifetime—a limit surpassed by many who have serious illnesses. Additionally, the new law bans **rescission**—canceling coverage only after a person gets sick. The new law allows an insurance company to act in the case of fraud, but not simply to look for technicalities that would allow them to cancel a policyholder's coverage when that policyholder needs it most.

In the long term, the bill is designed to cover 32 million currently uninsured people. Part of this extended coverage will be achieved through insurance reforms (like the ones described above), but one of the most important new provisions will be the creation of state-run insurance exchange systems to cover the unemployed, self-employed, and anyone else without insurance. Other mandates will require more people to buy into coverage plans. There will be some exceptions for the poor, and subsidies for other low-income individuals and families to help in purchasing insurance. Companies that employ more than fifty people will also have to provide health insurance or suffer fines, but new small-business exchanges will be created to help companies comply. The bill will also provide changes in Medicare for seniors (closing the "donut-hole" for prescription drug coverage) and expand Medicaid by opening it up to all adults of working age, not just the disabled or pregnant (The White House 2011).

> **RESCISSION** the practice by insurance companies of canceling coverage only after a person gets sick

Until "ObamaCare," the United States was the last wealthy, industrialized nation in the world without some form of universal health coverage for its citizens. Although there may be challenges in the future that change some aspects of the new law, it undeniably constitutes a major change to America's health-care system.

Complementary and Alternative Medicine

In all likelihood, you or someone you know has participated in some form of alternative medicine. If you've ever tried

Health-Care Reform What will be the impact of the health-care legislation passed in 2010?

deep-breathing for relaxation or a nutritional supplement to gain or lose weight, or an herbal remedy for a cold, if you've gone to a chiropractor, had a massage, or taken a yoga class, then you've made use of alternative medicine. Complementary or alternative medicine (CAM) is a group of medical treatments, practices, and products that includes acupuncture, homeopathy, hypnosis, and meditation, as well as traditional healers like shamans and movement therapies like Pilates. **Complementary medicine** can be used in conjunction with conventional Western medicine, whereas **alternative medicine** is used instead of it. Some of these practices or products are ancient (like acupuncture or herbs), while others are only new to the Western world—or arose in the past few decades (like biofeedback and "super food" formulas).

Complementary and alternative medicine has generated both enthusiasts and critics. Some skeptics call this type of medicine "quackery," nothing more than modern-day "snake oil" that promotes false hopes to a vulnerable public. Others who may have found few satisfactory answers within the medical establishment become staunch believers in the benefits of various CAM treatments. Indeed, some CAM practices and practitioners are slowly gaining legitimacy (and popularity), and **integrative medicine** is a burgeoning part of the field that combines conventional medicine with particular CAM practices that have proven most safe and effective. Scientific studies of CAM practices lag behind those done on conventional medicine, and more evidence is needed about whether and how the great variety of CAM practices work and on which patients with what conditions. It's possible that some forms of alternative medicine may one day prove better at treating some conditions than conventional medicine. But it is still rare for insurers to cover alternative medicine, so patients currently seeking those treatments typically have to pay out of pocket.

The increasing number of people who have turned to CAM practices is remarkable. In the United States, more than 38 percent of adults and nearly 12 percent of children used one or more forms of CAM within the past year (Barnes, Bloom, and Nahin 2008). Celebrities and professional athletes often attribute successful recoveries from illnesses or injuries to CAM therapies. Both the New York Yankees and the San Francisco Giants employ a "staff acupuncturist" (Healthcmi .com 2010), and former NBA star Grant Hill said in a recent

Alternative Medicine A man receives acupuncture treatment, an ancient medical practice that is sometimes used instead of conventional Western medicine.

interview, "Chiropractors, massage therapists, acupuncture, if it makes me feel good and it's legal, then I'm gonna do it. All of that stuff aids and helps with recovery, so I've been willing to incorporate it into my preparation" (Blinebury 2010).

The largest category of CAM users is women with higher levels of education and income. Natural supplements (non-vitamin products such as fish oil/omega 3, glucosamine, echinacea, flaxseed, and ginseng), deep breathing, meditation, chiropractic, yoga, and massage are some of the most frequently used forms of CAM. Americans are most likely to seek these treatments for neck, back, joint, and headache pain, but may also use them for anxiety, high cholesterol, head and chest colds, and insomnia. In 2007, American adults spent close to $34 billion on CAM treatments: two-thirds on self-care CAM products, classes, and materials; and one-third on visits to CAM practitioners. That amounts to just more than 11 percent of the total out-of-pocket U.S. spending on all forms of health care (Nahin et al. 2009).

Medical Technology and Bioethics

Medical science continues to progress at a rapid pace, bringing new discoveries and producing innovations that are bound to change human health in the future. We tend to think of these advancements as having a uniformly positive impact on society, but this is not always true. In many cases, new advancements bring new and sometimes troubling issues to the fore. **Bioethics** is the study of controversial moral or ethical issues related to scientific and medical advancements. Among hot topics are questions about extending life through artificial means, stem cell research, the use of animals in medical experiments, or even the idea of human cloning.

COMPLEMENTARY MEDICINE a group of medical treatments, practices, and products that can be used in conjunction with conventional Western medicine

ALTERNATIVE MEDICINE a group of medical treatments, practices, and products that are used instead of conventional Western medicine

INTEGRATIVE MEDICINE the combination of conventional medicine with complementary practices and treatments that have proven to be safe and effective

BIOETHICS the study of controversial moral or ethical issues related to scientific and medical advancements

The Human Genome Project (HGP) is a scientific endeavor that seeks to identify and map the 20,000 to 25,000 genes that make up human DNA from both a physical and functional perspective. The project began in 1990, and the first version of the genome was completed in 2003, although research based on the project continues. Scientists hope that decoding DNA will help uncover how the human body works. One of the results of the HGP is the ability to identify predisposition to hereditary diseases such as certain types of cancer, cystic fibrosis, and liver disease through genetic testing. Results from the HGP may also provide the key to the management of such diseases as Alzheimer's.

The rapid advancement of medical technologies like the HGP also brings numerous ethical issues to the table. One of the more controversial aspects of these advances is genetic testing in utero and at birth. For example, pre-implantation genetic diagnosis allows doctors to test DNA samples from embryos that are grown in vitro. These tests can tell whether or not a baby will be born with certain disorders and allow for the selection of only certain embryos for implantation. Genetic testing in utero can inform parents of possible genetic mutations in the embryo, potentially allowing parents to choose whether or not to have a disabled child. There are ethical concerns about genetic testing becoming a modern-day form of **eugenics**, in which the human gene pool is "improved" through science.

In cases where genetic testing reveals future susceptibility to disease for otherwise healthy individuals, there are ethical issues about the use of the genetic profiles. Can a person be stigmatized because of his or her genetic profile? Will insurance companies be able to deny coverage or even treatment of illnesses that can now be revealed through in-utero genetic testing? Will parents be encouraged to end pregnancies if the fetus's genetic profile reveals a torturous, expensive, or stigmatizing condition? Certainly, medical technology is advancing rapidly enough to cause a cultural lag in the legal, ethical, and social issues surrounding its use.

End-of-Life Care

Another area in which this lag is apparent is end-of-life care. On the one hand, we now possess the technologies and treatments to prolong the lives of patients who in prior eras would have died much more rapidly than they now do from diseases such as ALS (Lou Gehrig's disease), Alzheimer's disease, cystic fibrosis, and certain cancers and from traumatic injuries. In addition, hospice and palliative care can now make terminally ill patients more comfortable and give

them more time to prepare for the inevitable. On the other hand, this ability to prolong life can sometimes make it more difficult to distinguish between "living" and "dying" (such as cases of patients in persistent vegetative states), and hence to respond appropriately to those who are close to death (Kaufman 2005). The ability to rescue patients from the brink of death and to keep on life support those who would otherwise pass away raises the question, just because we can keep someone alive, does that mean that we always should do so?

Organizations such as the Hemlock Society and Final Exit promote the right of terminally ill patients to invoke medically assisted suicide (which is legally allowed only in Oregon) and the ability to "die with dignity." But critics worry that this approach will encourage ending life for the "wrong" reasons, such as treatable depression or disability. This often leaves critically ill patients and their families wondering what to do and when to do it. How to approach death and dying has always challenged us as members of society; there is every indication that, even in our age of advanced medical technology, it will continue to do so.

EUGENICS an attempt to selectively manipulate the gene pool in order to produce and "improve" human beings through medical science

CLOSING COMMENTS

Concerns about health and illness are a constant part of human existence. As individuals, we will each face the pleasures and difficulties of living in a physical body that is further affected by our lifestyles and life chances. A sociological approach is especially helpful in allowing us to understand the links between social structures and processes and health outcomes. We recognize that health is not merely a biological state, but another important area of human life affected by social institutions and social inequalities. Medicine and health care are rapidly advancing, and as a result, we may someday live longer and healthier lives, but we will always be shaped by the social contexts in which our lives take place. Science may soon discover new treatments for old diseases, but it is just as likely that we will have to continue dealing with current and as-yet-unknown challenges to our health in the future. It is certain that there will be cultural changes in our values and beliefs that bring about new understandings and practices regarding the relationship between society and the health of people and the planet.

Everything You Need to Know about
Health and Illness

> " Health, illness, and mortality are physiological phenomena; they are also unquestionably shaped by social factors. "

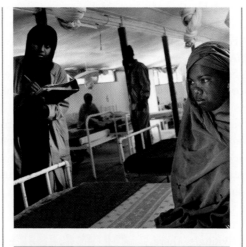

THEORIES OF HEALTH AND ILLNESS

* **Structural functionalism:** disease is a threat to social order; therefore, the health-care system should return patients to health and normal functioning as members of society

* **Conflict theory:** health and the health-care system are valuable resources that are unequally shared in society

* **Symbolic interactionism:** the meaning of health and illness are dependent upon historical, cultural, and situational contexts

REVIEW

1. What do you think about the process by which such things as hyperactivity or obesity are now seen as medical conditions as opposed to behavioral problems? Can you think of other behaviors or conditions that are becoming "medicalized"? Should we consider video game or internet addiction as a medical condition?

2. Do you believe that the U.S. health-care reforms of 2010 will be successful in bringing comprehensive medical coverage to more Americans? Do you believe that health care is a basic right that should be provided to all citizens, or is it a privilege that individuals must earn? What are some of the benefits included in universal health-care systems in such countries as France, Canada, and Britain?

Female Life Expectancies in the Washington DC Area

National Average (2010): 80.8 Years

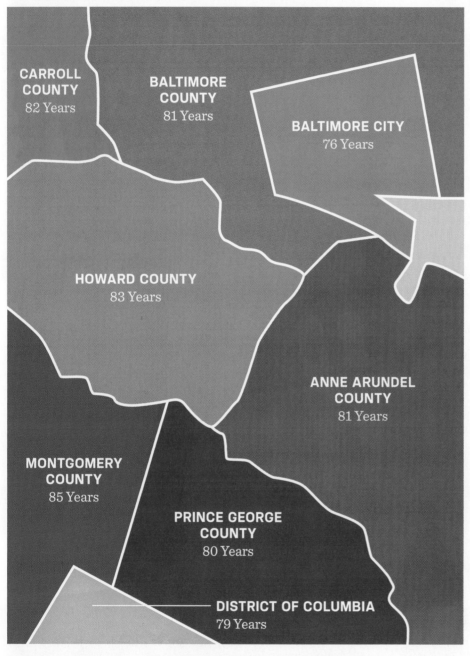

CARROLL COUNTY
82 Years

BALTIMORE COUNTY
81 Years

BALTIMORE CITY
76 Years

HOWARD COUNTY
83 Years

ANNE ARUNDEL COUNTY
81 Years

MONTGOMERY COUNTY
85 Years

PRINCE GEORGE COUNTY
80 Years

DISTRICT OF COLUMBIA
79 Years

Learn more about the health of your community at
www.countyhealthrankings.org

SOURCE: Institute for Health Metrics and Evaluation 2013

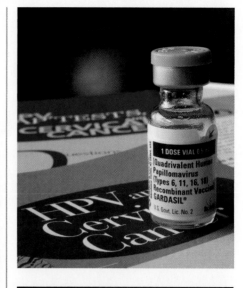

EXPLORE

Marketing Health

The HPV vaccine Gardasil has been highly controversial since it was first approved in 2006. It was originally approved for females, and marketed particularly toward eleven- and twelve-year-old girls. Later, Gardasil was approved for males, and now it is approved for females and males ages 9–26. The marketing message for Gardasil has changed throughout the years, from an anti-STD vaccine to an anti-cancer vaccine to an anti-STD vaccine again. Visit the Everyday Sociology Blog to read more about a sociologist's analysis of how social gender norms affected the marketing of this vaccine.

http://wwnPag.es/trw414

PART V
Envisioning the Future and Creating Social Change

Las Vegas—Sin City, Entertainment Capital of the World, home of glitz, glitter, and gambling; fantasy mecca, international tourist destination where fortunes and marriages are made and broken; populated by showgirls, gangsters, high-rollers, and Elvis impersonators. This is the "Hollywood Vegas" according to Mark Gottdiener, Claudia C. Collins, and David R. Dickens. Their book, *Las Vegas: The Social Production of an All-American City* (1999), chronicles the development of Las Vegas from its days as a pit stop for Spanish explorers in the early 1800s to the neon marvel it has become.

Gottdiener, Collins, and Dickens analyze the Hollywood Vegas, but they argue that there is another Las Vegas as well, where regular people live, work, and go to school, the supermarket, and the movies. What is the real Las Vegas like? It's big, it's growing fast, and its demographic, economic, and cultural trends represent the social changes taking place in many cities across the country—even those without pulsating neon or posh casinos.

The 2000 Census confirmed that Las Vegas was the fastest growing metropolitan area in the United States—its population increased 83 percent during the 1990s and continued to grow into the twenty-first century, with the Clark County Metro Area (of which Las Vegas is a part) hitting the 2 million mark in 2007. Las Vegas's population boom started to taper off in 2008, the county population having reached about 2 million (Access Clark County 2009). The 2010 census showed a continued population decline in this once-burgeoning locale (El Nasser 2010).

People flocked to Las Vegas because of its booming employment and housing market, and they came from all over the country and the world. A large proportion of newcomers to Las Vegas were former residents of California, seeking refuge from skyrocketing housing prices and a tight job market. Another major segment of the Las Vegas population boom was senior citizens, who now make up 25 percent of the populace. Retirees are valued consumers who spend money on new homes and other items when they arrive in the city; however, as they age, they may create a strain on local health-care resources. Another major population segment is Hispanic Americans, who make up almost 25 percent of Las Vegas's population. They are the fastest growing ethnic group in southern Nevada, and they, too, are valued consumers, courted by advertisers in both English- and Spanish-language media. In addition, the area has a growing population of undocumented Hispanic immigrants, who work at casinos, hotels, and resorts and whose labor supports the region's biggest industry, tourism.

In addition to these demographic trends, Las Vegas is also an economic trendsetter, for better or worse. Its employment rates were consistently high because of the large number of service jobs in the casino, resort, and tourist industries, but these jobs generally offer low pay and few benefits. There is also other work to do in Las Vegas. Major industries include construction and real estate sales (though these industries have been hit hard by the recent recession), banking, and other financial services, often related to the casino industry (Gottdeiner et al. 1999, p. 112). As the economy diversifies, the population grows—and as the population grows, more services and other work become necessary. Cards must be dealt, meals must be cooked, hotel rooms must be cleaned, children must be taught, cars must be repaired, and houses must be built, sold, and financed. However, if a population begins to decline, the market for all those goods and services diminishes, and jobs of all sorts become harder to find.

Las Vegas's housing boom began in the 1970s with the advent of master-planned communities. These residential developments, often built around golf courses, were move-in-ready when the economy began growing and diversifying in the 1980s, and more middle-class families began moving into the city. Master-planned suburbs continue to sprout in and around Las Vegas, filling Clark County with people and all the things they use, like houses, schools, stores, roads, and cars. During the recent recession, this boom went bust. In 2008, Las Vegas held one of the highest real estate foreclosure rates in the country (*International Business Times* 2008). Whatever takes place in the larger U.S. real estate market happens even more spectacularly in Las Vegas.

Environmental issues are important to life in the real Las Vegas, which is located in a desert ecosystem where water is scarce and rainfall is infrequent. Hundreds of thousands of people live in this ecosystem, in sprawling suburban housing developments. Lawns, pools, and golf courses require billions of gallons of water that the immediate environment does not provide, yet growth continues. Las Vegas competes with several other arid states, including California, for water resources. Water from the Colorado River is pumped in at great expense from Lake Mead to fill pools and water lawns, as well as for household use. Lake Mead is also the destination for all of Las Vegas's outgoing effluent—treated sewage and runoff full of lawn chemicals. These environmental toxins cycle back into the drinking water consumed by the area's residents.

Water isn't the only environmental issue that Las Vegas faces. Atomic test sites from the 1950s and 60s, located in the Mojave Desert, were once in the middle of nowhere—but suburban sprawl continues to draw closer to these areas. The same is true of a number of desert chemical plants in areas that are also being encroached upon by residential development. Recently, environmental activists have successfully prohibited nuclear waste transport and dumping in the Las Vegas area.

A fluctuating population; an economy dominated by service industry work; a natural environment strained to its limits by desert sprawl—this is the real Las Vegas. Add the glittery, neon-lit Hollywood fantasy town, and you have a vanguard city for the twenty-first century. Economic, environmental, and demographic trends that already appear in Las Vegas—including the booms and busts of the larger economy—will become increasingly visible in other U.S. cities.

Cultural and social changes occurring in Las Vegas may also be visible where you live—including the legalization of gambling. While Las Vegas was once the center of a gambling industry dominated by organized crime, legal casinos are now operated all over the country by groups of all sorts, including state governments and Native American tribes.

Gambling boats float on many midwestern lakes and rivers, and resort casinos continue to spring up on Indian reservations in almost half the U.S. states.

Las Vegas is also the site of unusually powerful labor unions, which represent many of the service employees—cooks, waiters, musicians, hotel employees—whose work keeps the city running. At a time when union membership is down in the rest of the country, Las Vegas is a strong union city—ironically located in Nevada, a right-to-work state. Union laborers tend to have higher wages and more benefits than nonunion workers because of the power of collective bargaining. The resurgence of union membership in Las Vegas's service industries may inspire workers in other cities with service- and tourism-dominated economies.

Gottdiener and his coauthors argue that "in many ways Las Vegas represents, though often in exaggerated form, several important trends in contemporary American society as a whole" (Gottdiener et. al 1999, p. xi). In Part V, we will examine many of those trends from a sociological perspective as part of our focus on social change. In Chapter 15, we will examine a variety of demographic, economic, and environmental trends, such as suburbanization, migration, and aging. And we will consider processes of cultural and social change, such as activism by labor unions and environmentalists, in Chapter 16. As you read these chapters, think about your own city or town and the trends you have observed close to home. Also, think about the changes you would like to see in your surroundings; a sociological perspective can help you strategize to make those changes happen. In any case, keep an eye on Las Vegas for changes yet to come—because, as Gottdiener, Collins, and Dickens demonstrate, what happens in Vegas doesn't necessarily stay in Vegas!

CHAPTER 15

Populations, Cities, and Environments

Chris McCandless was the picture of success. The son of upper-middle-class professionals in Washington, D.C., he had just graduated from Emory University in Atlanta and was headed for law school. Nonetheless, he felt constrained and even betrayed by a society that perpetuated poverty and inequality and often seemed to care so little for its individual members. He wanted to experience the personal freedom of being untethered from obligations to family, school, and work—even though that meant letting go of the emotional and material security they provide.

In the summer of 1990, Chris headed for the wilderness, which he saw as pure and untainted while he saw society as corrupt and damaged. Chris moved in and out of the social world during the next two years; he lived in the wilderness successfully for long stretches of time but always came back to civilization for supplies, to earn a little money, and to make some human connections. After spending months alone in the deserts of the Southwest, he arrived in Bullhead City, Arizona, and took a job at McDonald's. He was leather-skinned and malnourished, had no money or belongings, and had lost his car in a flash flood—but he was still alive, and after a brief stint in what he considered the most sinister of all social institutions (the fast-food industry), he disappeared back into nature again, this time headed to the great unspoiled expanses of Alaska.

Chris did a lot of reading in preparation for his journey, and he seemed able to endure the physical and emotional hardships of being alone in the wilderness for months at a time. His journal entries reveal that he often felt exhilarated and truly believed that his was the superior way of life. But Chris's story did not end happily. Two years after he left Atlanta, his body was found on the Alaskan tundra many miles outside Fairbanks by a group of moose hunters. In his book *Into the Wild*, Jon Krakauer reconstructed Chris's journey through diaries and interviews. Krakauer determined that while living on the tundra for four months alone, Chris had inadvertently eaten something that may have poisoned him. Realizing how sick he was, he began to yearn for the saving presence of other humans—for both assistance and companionship. At the very end, Chris's journal entries reveal a desire to return to the social world and a recognition of the protection society offers from the rigors of nature. Chris did not get to reenter society with his newfound insight, but perhaps we can learn more about our own relationship to both the natural and the social worlds from his story.

HOW TO READ THIS CHAPTER

This chapter covers three big and deeply connected topics in sociology: population, urbanization, and the environment. To this point, we have focused mostly on society, on people and their effect on each other. But humans live in a natural as well as a social world, and their environment is another key factor in their lives. They are affected by and have a profound effect on the planet Earth. The number of humans who live on the planet has more than tripled in just the past fifty years, from 2 billion to more than 7 billion now. Population studies show that an ever-greater number of people are settling into large, sprawling cities—a trend called urbanization. Growing populations and increased urbanization create new demands and pressures on the global environment as more natural resources are consumed and more pollution and waste are produced, and this has a profound effect on the Earth and its inhabitants. Remember that these huge global shifts are the result of the cumulative actions of many individuals over time.

Population

If we want to understand the relationship between the social world and the natural world, we must examine human population. The next sections look at how sociologists study population and its related issues. To paraphrase sociologist Samuel Preston, the study of population has something for everyone: the confrontations of nature and civilization; the dramas of sex and death, politics and war; and the tensions between self-interest and altruism.

Demography

Demography is the study of the size, composition, distribution, and changes in human population. Sociologists and others who study population are called demographers. Demography is essentially a macro-level, quantitative approach to society, but it is more than just simply counting heads. Population dynamics are influenced not only by biological factors such as births and deaths but also by sociological factors such as cultural values, religious beliefs, and political and economic systems. People are not just animals who reproduce by instinct, but are subject to structural constraints as well as individual agency, all of which affect their behavior and ultimately the world in which they live.

The U.S. government has long been interested in keeping track of those residing within its geographic boundaries. The U.S. Census Bureau, a part of the Department of Commerce, conducts regular studies of the population, going back to the first such attempt in 1790. Each new decade, census takers try to contact every person living in the country. Surveys, either short or long form, are sent to every household to gather a range of demographic information from the size and age of family members to their gender, education level, income, and ethnic background. Other countries are less systematic at gathering data, so many statistics that refer to global population are necessarily based on scientific estimates.

Three basic demographic variables are crucial to understanding population dynamics. The first is **fertility rate**—the average number of births per 1,000 people in the total population. The total fertility rate is the average number of children a woman would be expected to have during her childbearing years. The estimated total fertility rate for 2013 in the United States is approximately 2.1. Fertility rates vary across the globe, with some of the highest rates in sub-Saharan Africa, with Niger at 7.0, and some of the lowest in Southeast Asia, with Singapore at 0.8 (Central Intelligence Agency 2013f).

The next demographic variable is **mortality rate** (or death rate)—the number of deaths that can be expected per 1,000 people per year. This statistic is usually modified by other factors, so the mortality rate within a particular country varies within different age, sex, ethnic, and regional groups. A related concept is **infant mortality** rate, or the average number of deaths per 1,000 live births. The estimated death rate for 2013 in the United States was approximately 8.4 and the infant mortality rate was 5.9. Mortality and infant mortality rates vary across the globe, some of the highest being in African countries, with a death rate of 14.8 in Chad, for example, and an infant mortality rate of 91.9. Some of the lowest mortality rates are found in wealthier Middle Eastern countries such as Qatar with 1.5, and some of the lowest infant mortality rates are found in Asian countries such as Japan with 2.2 (Central Intelligence Agency 2013a).

Another related concept is **life expectancy**, or the average age to which a person can expect to live. Here, too, other factors are involved, so life expectancy of people within a particular country varies by sex, ethnicity, and social class. In general, life expectancy rose dramatically in the twentieth century. The estimated life expectancy for 2013 in the United States on average was approximately 78.6 years of age; the average for men was 76.2, while for women it was 81.2

DEMOGRAPHY study of the size, composition, distribution, and changes in human population

FERTILITY RATE a measure of population growth through reproduction; often expressed as the average number of births per 1,000 people in the total population or the average number of children a woman would be expected to have

MORTALITY RATE a measure of the decrease in population due to deaths; often expressed as the number of deaths expected per 1,000 people per year in a particular population

INFANT MORTALITY average number of infant deaths per 1,000 live births in a particular population

LIFE EXPECTANCY average age to which people in a particular population live

IN THE FUTURE

Living to 150

Author Sonia Arrison predicts that her own son, born in 2010, may very well live to be 150 years old (Arrison 2011). This preschooler and his generational cohort are poised to reap the benefits of health and technological advances that promise to extend their lifetimes far, far beyond those of their ancestors.

You are probably already familiar with some of the developments contributing to our increased life spans. Medical advances have conquered (or at least controlled) many of the diseases that once kept us from growing old, such as smallpox, measles, diphtheria, polio, and tuberculosis. Injuries that were once guaranteed to be fatal are now treatable and survivable through advanced surgical techniques. Public health measures have improved things like sanitation, food safety, water purity, and community education. New concerns with environmental degradation, pollution, pesticides, and chemicals are leading to less toxic exposure. Of course, all of these things are more likely to be true in wealthier, developed regions such as the United States and Europe—life spans are still much shorter in areas where these advances are not widely available.

Even so, centenarians—people who live to be over 100 years of age—are getting more common worldwide. The United Nations estimated about 317,000 in 2012, with the United States, Japan, and China in the top three positions with approximately 50,000 centenarians each. Most current centenarians are women. And most current centenarians got old the old-fashioned way: clean living, healthy food, exercise, stress-management, and good genes. Arrison's son and his friends may have the assistance of technological advances that sound like science fiction, but are or will soon be reality.

Drugs to treat chronic illnesses such as diabetes, heart disease, and even inflammation may have the side-effect of extending lifespans (Duncan 2012). Stem cell research may allow the regeneration of damaged cells, organs, and other body parts. Gene therapy may eradicate killers such as sickle cell disease, cystic fibrosis, various cancers, and other hereditary diseases (Glor 2012). Technology that replaces human body parts with machines and connects those machines directly to our brains may expand the number of "cyborgs" or partially bionic humans, in addition to expanding our definition of what constitutes "natural" life (Duncan 2012).

These possibilities sound fascinating, don't they? But they all focus solely on keeping individuals healthy and alive. What happens to society if people start living much longer, healthier lives? Arrison addresses some of these questions in her book.

For one thing, longer lives mean that we must reconsider the whole notion of retirement. Retiring at sixty-five seems ridiculous (not to mention boring!) if you'll be living another eighty years or so. The prospect arises, then, of people pursuing multiple careers (including the multiple educations necessary to prepare for them) in one lifetime. So, an individual may find himself retiring two, three, or more times in his one hundred plus years.

Our current notion of marriage as a "'til death do us part" contract also may deserve some revision if we're going to live to 150. Will we just marry later? Or will multiple marriages over the course of a lifetime become more common and acceptable? Will marriage contracts have to include "sunset clauses" or expiration dates, at which time we may renew them if we choose? Don't laugh—this has already been proposed by lawmakers in Mexico! And what about family planning? Will we push the boundaries of fertility as we push the boundaries of longevity? If so, will nuclear families be larger? Will extended family living become more common?

Finally, what will happen to our values, morals, and beliefs? So many of the social rules about things like marriage, family, and life in general are rooted in religion—how will religion itself respond if and when we find ourselves living longer and hence calling some of these rules into question? We already worry that attempts to extend life and stave off death amount to "playing God." If we live longer, will religions be forced to pay more attention to this life, and less to the afterlife?

All we can say in answer to these questions is, stick around and see for yourselves . . .

(Central Intelligence Agency 2013g). Life expectancy also varies greatly across the globe, with some of the highest averages in wealthier nations like Monaco at almost ninety, and some of the lowest in African countries like Chad at approximately forty-nine years—in large part because of the AIDS epidemic (Central Intelligence Agency 2013b). **Life span**, or **longevity**, has also increased dramatically—again, depending on where you live. More people around the globe are living past 100 years of age. The current record for oldest living person, at 122 years, has already been reached several times and may soon be surpassed.

The last demographic variable that we will consider is **migration**—the movement of people from one geographic area to another for the purposes of resettling. Migrations have occurred throughout human history and have played an important part in populating the planet. As a demographic variable, migration neither adds to nor subtracts from the total number of people on the planet; it simply refers to their relocation from place to place. Related concepts are **immigration** and **emigration**. Immigrants are those people coming into a country or region to which they are not native. Emigrants are those departing from a country or region with the intention of settling permanently elsewhere. **Internal migration** refers to patterns within a country, where the movement is generally from rural to urban areas. The **net migration** for any country is the difference between the number of persons entering and leaving a country during the year per 1,000 persons. The estimated net migration for 2013 in the United States was 3.6, which means that after adjusting for the people who emigrated, there was a total of 3.6 persons per 1,000 who immigrated. In general, worldwide migration patterns show that people are moving from least industrialized to most industrialized countries. There are often other economic or political reasons for migration, with refugees pouring in and out of some countries. Countries with the highest net migration rates include Syria and Jordan, while those with the lowest rates include Qatar and Zimbabwe (Central Intelligence Agency 2013c).

The study of population dynamics involves the interplay among the three sources of population change: fertility, mortality, and migration. These variables are used to construct current population models and future projections. We can apply demographic variables to the global population or to a population within a particular region or country.

If we focus on the United States, we could track several interesting population trends. The United States is currently the third most populous nation after China and India, with more than 313 million people (Central Intelligence Agency 2013d). It is also the fastest growing industrialized nation. According to the Census Bureau, between 2000 and 2030 the net population change will be most evident in three states—California, Texas, and Florida. They will account for nearly 46 percent of the nation's population growth. Projected immigration during that period will be highest in California (8.7 million), New York (3.8 million), and Florida (1.8 million). The fastest growing states will be Nevada with a 114.3 percent increase in population, followed by Arizona at 108.8 percent and Florida with 79.5 percent. A few states will even see shrinking populations; the District of Columbia will decrease by 24.2 percent, North Dakota by 5.5 percent, and West Virginia by 4.9 percent. Some of this change will be internal migration among the states, with people moving to the "sunbelt" states in the South and West from "rustbelt" states in the North and East (U.S. Census Bureau 2005). See Figure 15.1 for reference on these trends.

Theories on Population Growth

Concerns about population growth first emerged in the eighteenth century during the Industrial Revolution. Many demographic variables at that time contributed to rapid growth in the newly burgeoning urban areas of Europe. Mechanization, which increased agricultural production, and the introduction of a hearty new staple from South America—the potato—made available enough food for people to sustain themselves and support larger families. Other technological and scientific advances helped decrease infant mortality rates while increasing fertility and extending life expectancy. As a result, the first real population boom in human history occurred.

Thomas Malthus, a British clergy member turned political economist, was one of the first scholars to sound the alarm on overpopulation. Although he lived at a time when people believed in technology and progress, the promise of prosperity and abundance, and the perfectibility of human society, he himself was less than optimistic about the future. Based on his observation of the world around him, Malthus wrote a book in 1798 called *An Essay on the Principle of Population*, in which his basic premise, the **Malthusian theorem**, stated that the population would expand at a much faster rate than agriculture; inevitably at some future point, people would far outnumber the available land and food sources. If population increases surpass the ability of Earth to

LIFE SPAN or **LONGEVITY** the uppermost age to which a person can potentially live

MIGRATION movement of people from one geographic area to another for the purpose of resettling

IMMIGRATION entering one country from another to take up permanent residence

EMIGRATION leaving one country to live permanently in another

INTERNAL MIGRATION movement of a population within a country

NET MIGRATION net effect of immigration and emigration on an area's population in a given time period; expressed as an increase or decrease

MALTHUSIAN THEOREM the theory that exponential population growth will outpace arithmetic growth in food production and other resources

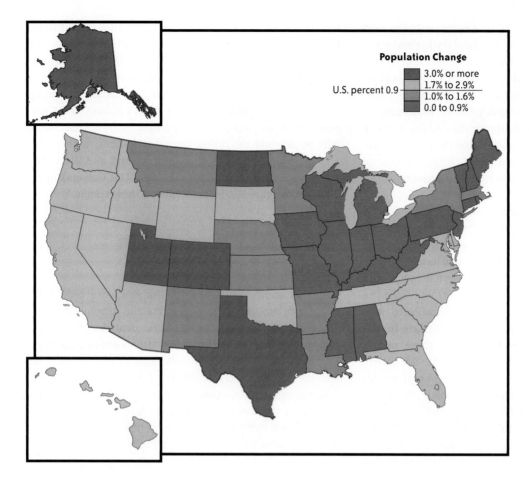

Figure 15.1 Population Change in the United States, 2010–2012

Population Change

U.S. percent 0.9

■	3.0% or more
■	1.7% to 2.9%
■	1.0% to 1.6%
■	0.0 to 0.9%

The populations of Midwest and East Coast states are holding steady or decreasing, while the populations of many inter-Mountain West, Pacific Northwest, and Southern states are growing.

SOURCE: U.S. Census Bureau 2013b.

provide a basic level of subsistence, then massive suffering will follow. His theory has two simple principles: that population growth is exponential or geometric (1, 2, 4, 8, 16, 32 . . .) and that production is additive or arithmetic (1, 2, 3, 4, 5, 6 . . .).

According to his calculations, society was headed for disaster, or what is called the **Malthusian trap**. To avoid such a catastrophe, Malthus made several rather radical policy recommendations. He may have been the first to propose that humans should collectively limit their propagation to save themselves and preserve their environments. He urged "moral restraint" in sexual reproduction to curtail overpopulation. If human beings were unable to restrain themselves (by postponing marriage or practicing abstinence), nature would exert "positive checks" on population growth through famine, war, and disease (Malthus 1798/1997). Malthus also advocated state assistance to the lower classes so they could more readily achieve a middle-class lifestyle supported by decent wages and benefits and adopt the values associated with later marriage and smaller families (New School 2004).

Malthus's ideas were not always popular, though they were influential and widely read. Charles Darwin noted that Malthusian theory was an important influence on his own theory of evolution and natural selection. Malthus also influenced whole new generations of social thinkers, not just demographers but others as well, and their respective ideas on population growth.

More than 200 years later, some people, the **Neo-Malthusians**, or New Malthusians, essentially still agree with him. Among the notable modern voices looking at the problem of overpopulation are William Catton (1980), Paul and Ann Ehrlich (1990), and Garrett Hardin (1993). They worry about the rapid pace of population growth and believe that Malthus's basic prediction could be true. In some respects, they claim, the problem has even gotten worse. There are a lot more people on the planet in the twenty-first century, so their continued reproduction expands even more quickly than in Malthus's time. And with continued technological advancements—such as wars that use "surgical

MALTHUSIAN TRAP Malthus's prediction that a rapidly increasing population will overuse natural resources, leading inevitably to a major public health disaster

NEO-MALTHUSIANS contemporary researchers who worry about the rapid pace of population growth and believe that Malthus's basic prediction could be true

Figure 15.2 **World Population Growth over 2,000 Years**

The world's population grew slowly for most of human history, then began to increase rapidly in the nineteenth century. With the world population continuing to grow, it could reach 10–11 billion by 2100.

SOURCE: Population Reference Bureau 2010.

strikes," modern standards of sanitation, and the eradication of many diseases—people are living much longer than before. When Malthus was alive, there were approximately 1 billion people on the planet; it was the first time in recorded history that the population reached that number. The time required for that number to double and for each additional billion to be added has continued to shorten (Figure 15.2). Today there are more than 7 billion people on the planet—and counting. The United Nations predicts that world population will surpass 9 billion by 2050 and continue to grow to more than 10 billion before it stabilizes and plateaus at the end of the century (United Nations News Centre 2011).

The New Malthusians also point to several sociological factors that influence the reproductive lives of many and promote large families. Religion still plays a role in many societies, with the Old Testament commanding, "Go forth and multiply." The Catholic Church still forbids members to practice any birth control besides the rhythm method, even though 78 percent of American Catholics said the church should allow them to use some form of artificial contraception (CNN 2005). In many poorer nations, more children mean more financial support for the family. They work various jobs in their youth to help sustain the household, and for parents, children may be the only source of support they have in old age. Some governments encourage the expansion of their population base and promote the addition of new citizens who can become taxpayers or soldiers. They may even provide incentives to parents, such as tax deductions for each child. Last, cultural influences, from "family values" to "machismo," sometimes confer more prestige on those with

children; women gain status in the valued role of mother, while men gain status for their perceived virility.

At the same time, contrary arguments are proposed by the **Anti-Malthusians**. Economists such as Julian Simon (1996, 2000) and demographers such as William Peterson (2003) believe that Malthus reached faulty conclusions and that he couldn't have envisioned the many modern developments that would impact population dynamics. In fact, the Anti-Malthusians worry more about the population shrinking and the possibility of a **demographic free fall** than they do about it growing indefinitely. Some countries, such as Japan, are already dealing with new problems caused by a rapidly shrinking population. They don't see that happening immediately, but they forecast a very different future when the pattern of **demographic transition**, now occurring in many industrialized nations, spreads to the rest of the developing world.

The Anti-Malthusians believe that when people have a better standard of living, they also prefer smaller families, as children become more of an economic liability than an asset.

ANTI-MALTHUSIANS
contemporary researchers who believe the population boom Malthus witnessed was a temporary, historically specific phenomenon and worry instead that the worldwide population may shrink in the future

DEMOGRAPHIC FREE FALL
decrease in fertility rates among populations that have industrialized their economies as children become an economic liability rather than an asset

DEMOGRAPHIC TRANSITION
a theory suggesting the possible transition over time from high birth and death rates to low birth and death rates, resulting in a stabilized population

Better education and easier access to health care bring more reproductive choices such as methods of **family planning**. Governments in some countries are adopting policies that discourage large families. Further, the Anti-Malthusians claim that technological advancements have enabled humans to produce much larger quantities of food than ever before, thus providing for the nutritional needs of more of the world's population.

So who is right? Will the world population eventually stabilize, or will it continue to spiral out of control? We may not know the answer to those questions for many years, so in the meantime we continue to speculate. The populations of some countries continue to grow rapidly, while others remain stable or begin to decline. The **growth rate** is the number of births minus deaths plus net migration of a population, expressed as a percentage change from the beginning of the time period measured, often resulting in what is referred to as a **natural increase**. The estimated growth rate for 2013 in the United States was 0.9 percent. It was highest in countries such as Qatar at 4.2 percent and Zimbabwe at 4.4 percent and lowest in Pacific Islands such as Micronesia at –0.4 percent and Cook Islands at –3.1 percent (Central Intelligence Agency 2013e).

What about the other elements in Malthus's theorem? Food production has grown remarkably since Malthus's time. In particular, the "Green Revolution" that began in Mexico in 1948 and spread to India and other less developed nations in the 1960s caused an explosion in food production. This was partly because of better agricultural mechanization as well as newly engineered seeds, pesticides, and artificial fertilizers. Was this a unique increase, or can it be expected again in the future? The United Nations Food and Agriculture Organization estimates that world agriculture will grow at a slower pace, from an annual 2.1 percent over the past two decades to 1.6 percent from 2005 to 2015 and 1.3 percent from 2015 to 2030. Growth in agriculture will continue to surpass world population growth, estimated to be 1.2 percent from 2005 to 2015 and 0.8 percent from 2015 to 2030 (UN Food and Agriculture Organization 2012).

Nonetheless, hunger remains widespread, not only in foreign countries but also in the United States. Worldwide, an estimated 1 billion people suffer from chronic hunger and malnutrition—a lack of adequate food plus other factors such as insufficient protein and nutrients, poor feeding habits, and unsafe water and sanitation. Some 10 million people die every year from hunger or hunger-related causes; three-fourths of them are children under the age of five (United Nations World Food Programme 2007). In the United States, every day 15 percent of households—over 50 million people—experienced hunger or food insecurity in 2011, that is, the limited or uncertain ability to acquire adequate and safe foods (U.S. Department of Agriculture 2012).

Other factors must also be considered in projecting the future of population impacts. Science constantly brings technological advancements that enhance health and prolong life, but new and deadly diseases such as AIDS claim an ever-greater death toll in nations too poor to afford the medicines to treat these diseases. As the world's current occupants, we have to live now with the consequences of our choices. Many policy and advocacy groups concerned with population matters have been established in the past few decades, including Zero Population Growth, World Overpopulation Awareness, the Population Institute, and the Population Reference Bureau. To find out more, visit their web sites.

Urbanization

The dynamics of population growth (and sometimes shrinkage) throughout human history have been accompanied by the development of larger cities in which more people are now living. Cities, however, are not a modern development. They have been in existence for thousands of years. We find evidence of ancient cities in the Middle East, Africa, Asia, and South America. By comparison to today's standards, these early cities would be considered quite small. They generally had just several thousand residents and were typically agricultural centers along major trade routes. Some much larger cities, however, had hundreds of thousands of residents, such as the Mediterranean cities of Athens and Rome. One reason cities were able to thrive was the advances in agriculture that allowed surpluses of food to be readily available to support a population that was not directly involved in its production. People were thus freed to engage in other activities necessary for the functioning of the city and its residents.

Cities were not the prevalent residential areas until well into the nineteenth and twentieth centuries. Until then, the vast majority of people worldwide lived in **rural** or country areas. The wide-scale development of cities, or **urban** areas, was made possible by the significant social, economic, and political changes accompanying the Industrial Revolution, when masses of people were drawn into cities to find housing and the manufacturing jobs they needed to earn

FAMILY PLANNING contraception, or any method of controlling family size and the birth of children

GROWTH RATE expression of changes in population size over time figured by subtracting the number of deaths from the number of births, then adding the net migration

NATURAL INCREASE change in population size that results from births and deaths; linked to a country's progress toward demographic transition

RURAL relating to sparsely settled areas; in the United States, any county with a population density between 10 and 59.9 people per square mile

URBAN relating to cities; typically describes densely populated areas a living. Fewer families were involved in farming, as large companies, or agribusiness, began to emerge. Cities were populated not only by migrants from rural areas but also by immigrants from other countries, seeking opportunity and a better way of life. Industrialization provided the jobs and the means of communication and transportation to build the burgeoning city infrastructure that could support growing numbers of residents. This process in which growing numbers of people move from rural to urban areas is called **urbanization**.

In the early 1800s, only about 3 percent of the world's population lived in urban areas and only one city had a population greater than 1 million people: Peking, China (now called Beijing). In the early 1900s, almost 14 percent of the world's population lived in urban areas, and another dozen or so cities around the world (including New York City, London, Paris, Moscow, and Tokyo) had 1 million or more residents. In the early 2000s, more than 50 percent of the world's population were living in urban areas, and we now have to count as large cities those with 5 million people or more; there are more than sixty of these in the world (United Nations 2006).

A similar pattern can be seen in the United States. In the early 1800s, just 6 percent of the population lived in urban areas, whereas 94 percent lived in rural areas. In the early 1900s, the split was 40 percent urban and 60 percent rural. In the early 2000s, 79 percent of the population was urban and 21 percent was rural (see Figure 15.3). As of 2010, nine American cities had populations over 1 million; the largest among them, New York City, has over 8 million (U.S. Census Bureau 2011k).

Features of Urbanization

The term "city" is currently used to refer to an urban settlement with a large population, usually at least 50,000 to 100,000 people. Although a few states, including North Dakota, West Virginia, and Vermont, have no cities with populations of 100,000 people or more, California has sixty-one cities with more than 100,000 people, followed by Texas with twenty-five and Florida with seventeen. Urban demographers use the word **metropolis** to refer to an urban area with an even larger population—usually at least 500,000 people—that typically serves as the economic, political, and cultural center for a region. The U.S. Census Bureau defines the term **Metropolitan Statistical Area (MSA)**, also called an **agglomeration**, as a metropolitan area that includes a major city of at least 50,000 inhabitants that is surrounded by an adjacent area that is socially and economically integrated with the city. In 2009, the United States (including Puerto Rico) contained 374 MSAs; more than fifty of these had populations of 1 million or more (U.S. Census Bureau 2012k). Many of the largest American cities, such as New York City, Los Angeles, Chicago, Houston, Philadel-

phia, Phoenix, and San Diego, have continued to grow rapidly in the past decade.

Largest of all is a **megalopolis**, also sometimes called a **megacity**—a group of densely populated metropolises (or agglomerations) that grow contiguous to each other and eventually combine to form a huge urban complex (Gottman 1961). One American megalopolis is referred to as "ChiPitts," or the Great Lakes Megalopolis, a group of metropolitan areas in the Midwest, extending from Pittsburgh to Chicago (and including Detroit, Cleveland, Columbus, Cincinnati, and Indianapolis), with a total population of almost 60 million. The ChiPitts metro areas are linked not only by geographic proximity but also by economics, transportation, and communications systems (Gottman and Harper 1990). Another megalopolis is "BosWash" or the Northeast Megalopolis, extending from Boston to Washington, D.C., and including twenty-two other metropolises such as New York City and Philadelphia. BosWash has a total population of almost 50 million, or approximately 17 percent of the entire population of the country. Megalopolises are found worldwide, in countries including Brazil, Mexico, Indonesia, India, China, and Japan (Castells and Susser 2002). These are sometimes called megaregions or **global cities** to emphasize their position in an increasingly globalized world as centers of economic, political, and social power (Sassen 1991).

Cities are often characterized by **urban density**, measured by the total number of people per square mile. Some of the most densely populated cities in the United States include Union City, New Jersey, with 52,972 residents per square mile; New York City with 26,401; San Francisco with 16,633; and Chicago with 12,749 (U.S. Census Bureau 2005). By contrast, rural areas are characterized by low density. Rural counties are those with populations of 10 to 59.9 people per square mile; frontier counties are those with 0.5 to 9.9 people; and remote counties are those with 0.04 people per square mile or fewer. Alaska is the most rural state in the United States, followed by Wyoming, Nevada, Utah, New Mexico, and North Dakota.

URBANIZATION movement of increasing numbers of people from rural areas to cities

METROPOLIS an urban area with a large population, usually 500,000 to 1 million people

METROPOLITAN STATISTICAL AREA (MSA) or **AGGLOMERATION** one or more adjacent counties with at least one major city of 50,000 or more inhabitants that is surrounded by an adjacent area that is socially and economically integrated with the city

MEGALOPOLIS or **MEGACITY** a group of densely populated metropolises that grow dependent on each other and eventually combine to form a huge urban complex

GLOBAL CITIES a term for megacities that emphasizes their global impact as centers of economic, political, and social power

URBAN DENSITY concentration of people in a city, measured by the total number of people per square mile

Trends in Urbanization

Along with urbanization, an important countertrend surfaced in the years immediately following World War II. **Suburbanization** is the shift of large segments of population away from the urban core and toward the edges of cities, where larger expanses of land were available for housing developments that provided families with a chance to buy a home of their own and avoid the overcrowding of central urban life. One of the first significant suburbs in the late 1940s was called Levittown (based on the name of the builders), a community of 17,450 tract houses for 75,000 people in Hempstead, New York. The simply designed homes were mass-produced and sold at prices affordable to returning veterans and the new growing middle class (Wattel 1958). In the 1950s, the second Levittown was built near Philadelphia, and in the 1960s a third in New Jersey. Herbert Gans's study *The Levittowners* (1967) found that homeownership gave suburbanites a sense of pride and more privacy and space, which they valued greatly.

Suburbanization also reflected a retreat from some of the problems associated with city living—close quarters, noise, and crime. As more families were able to afford single-family homes, large yards with the proverbial white picket fence and a two-car garage became the literal image of the "American Dream" (Fava 1956; Kelly 1993). But suburban life has its own problems: long commutes, little contact between neighbors, and de facto racial segregation in housing and schools. Some observers have also criticized the monotonous uniformity of the new suburbs, claiming that they promote listless personalities, conformity, and escapism (Riesman 1957; Whyte 1956; Jackson 1985). The decades-long shift of populations to the suburbs has accelerated and expanded throughout the nation, with more families moving farther and farther away into what's been called the "exurbs" (Frey 2003).

A problem related to suburbanization is **urban sprawl** (sometimes also called suburban sprawl). This phenomenon has to do with how cities and suburbs grow. It is often a derogatory term applied to the peripheral expansion of urban boundaries and is associated with irresponsible or poorly planned development. Critics say these areas are often unsightly, characterized by a homogenous landscape of housing subdivisions, office parks, and corner strip-malls lacking character or green space (Kunstler 1993; Duany, Plater-Zyberk, and Speck 2001; Gutfreund 2004) and bringing problems of traffic, pollution, crowded schools, and high taxes.

While most suburbs remain "bedroom communities" or primarily residential, others have become **edge cities** with their own centers of employment and commerce (Garreau 1992). Edge cities are usually in close proximity to intersecting highways and urban areas. "Silicon Valley" is a prime example: the once-sleepy suburb of San Jose became a center of high-tech industry during the dot-com boom of the 1990s. Edge cities are one answer to the problems associated with suburbanization. **Smart growth** advocates are also promoting alternatives to suburban growth, emphasizing redevelopment of inner cities or older suburbs to create better communities. Elements of smart growth include town centers; transit- and pedestrian-friendly streets; a greater mix

SUBURBANIZATION beginning after World War II, the shift of large segments of population away from the urban core and toward the edges of cities

URBAN SPRAWL a derogatory term applied to the expansion of urban or suburban boundaries, associated with irresponsible or poorly planned development

EDGE CITIES centers of employment and commerce that began as suburban commuter communities

SMART GROWTH term for economic and urban planning policies that emphasize responsible development and renewal

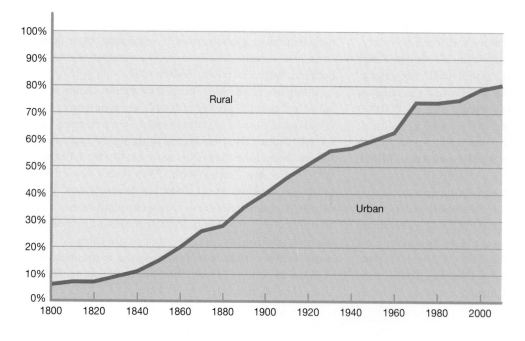

Figure 15.3 Rural/ Urban Makeup of U.S. Population, 1800–2010

As the U.S. population grew, so did the proportion of urban dwellers compared to rural inhabitants.

SOURCE: U.S. Census Bureau 1993, 2013a.

of housing, commercial, and retail properties; and the preservation of open space and other environmental amenities.

Many long-established cities suffered when populations began moving to the suburbs—such as Detroit, Chicago, and Philadelphia in the North and East (the rustbelt) as well as New Orleans, St. Louis, and San Francisco in the South, Midwest, and West (U.S. Census Bureau 2005). Since the 1950s and 60s, people have left cities not only to find more space and bigger homes in the nearby suburbs but also because they were fleeing other problems endemic to the city. Largely, those escaping the cities were upper- and middle-class whites who could afford to leave—a trend often referred to as **white flight** (or sometimes suburban flight). Those remaining in cities were predominantly minorities, seniors, immigrants, working class, or poor. White flight left urban areas abandoned by businesses and financial institutions, leading to broken-down and boarded-up shops and streets and creating ghettos that further exacerbated the problems associated with inner cities (Wilson 1996).

In the 1960s and 70s, to address the problem of decaying inner cities, local city governments and private investors took advantage of **urban renewal** efforts that included renovation, selective demolition, commercial development, and tax incentives aimed at revitalizing business districts and residential neighborhoods (Frieden and Sagalyn 1992). Urban renewal has been a limited success. While it did revitalize many areas, it often came at a high cost to existing communities. In many cases, it resulted in the destruction of vibrant, if rundown, neighborhoods (Mollenkopf 1983).

Urban renewal is linked to another trend that has also changed many formerly blighted cities: **gentrification**. This is the transformation of the physical, social, economic, and cultural life of formerly working-class or poor inner-city neighborhoods into more affluent middle-class communities as wealthier people return to the cities (Glass 1964). This trend, which took off in the 1990s, is evident in some of the nation's largest cities, such as Boston, New York, Philadelphia, Chicago, and San Francisco (Mele 2000). Various higher-income individuals, whether they were young professionals ("yuppies"), artists, or retirees, recognized the potential for rehabilitating downtown buildings (Castells 1984). They valued the variety and excitement of urban living more than the mini-malls of sleepy suburbia (Florida 2004). The term "gentrification" carries a distinct class connotation; while converting, renovating, remodeling, and constructing new buildings beautifies old city neighborhoods, it also increases property values and tends to displace poorer residents (Zukin 1987, 1989). Gentrification, then, does not eradicate the problems of poverty; it forces the poor to move elsewhere.

Although urbanization (or suburbanization) is still the predominant demographic trend in the United States, an interesting reversal emerged in the 1990s, called the **rural rebound** (Johnson and Beale 1994, 1995, 1998). An increase

WHITE FLIGHT movement of upper- and middle-class whites who could afford to leave the cities for the suburbs, especially in the 1950s and 60s

URBAN RENEWAL efforts to rejuvenate decaying inner cities, including renovation, selective demolition, commercial development, and tax incentives

GENTRIFICATION transformation of the physical, social, economic, and cultural life of formerly working-class or poor inner-city neighborhoods into more affluent middle-class communities

RURAL REBOUND population increase in rural counties that adjoin urban centers or possess rich scenic or amenity values

Table 15.1   Theory in Everyday Life

Perspective	Approach to the Natural Environment	Case Study: Urban Sprawl
Structural Functionalism	The natural world exists in order to keep the social world running smoothly. The environment provides raw materials and space for development in order to meet society's needs.	As populations increase, cities must grow in order to accommodate the growing population, so urban sprawl is functional for society.
Conflict Theory	Not all groups or individuals benefit equally from society's use of the natural environment.	Urban sprawl creates largely white, upper- and middle-class suburbs around cities whose residents are minorities, seniors, immigrants, working class, and/or poor. This means that suburban residents may have access to resources, like well-funded schools, which urban dwellers may not.
Symbolic Interactionism	The meanings assigned to the natural environment will determine how society sees and uses it.	Redefining open land as a scarce resource, and redefining urban areas as valuable spaces, may lead to the reduction of urban sprawl: open land could be conserved, while urban spaces could be rehabilitated and revitalized.

Real or Fake? People mingle outside Pastis restaurant in New York City's meatpacking district. Contrast this urban scene with Universal CityWalk in Los Angeles, which was designed to feel like an urban street.

in rural populations has resulted from a combination of fewer people leaving such areas and the in-migration of urban and suburban dwellers (Long and Nucci 1998). While most rural counties continue to decline, those near urban centers or with rich scenic or amenity values are generally experiencing an upsurge in population. Gains have been greatest in the Mountain West, Upper Great Lakes, the Ozarks, parts of the South, and rural areas of the Northeast. Rural migrants include families with young children, small-scale farmers, retirees, blue-collar workers, single professionals, and disenchanted city dwellers all seeking a better way of life. They are willing to forsake the amenities of the city in exchange for a simpler, slower, more traditional rural lifestyle (Johnson 1999).

Another example of our contemporary ambivalence about city life is simulated cities—social spaces engineered to maximize the benefits of city life without the risks. A prime example is Universal CityWalk, a collection of shops, restaurants, and movie theaters in a suburb of Los Angeles. CityWalk mimics an urban shopping street, with sidewalk café seating and strolling street performers. However, it has no connection to a real urban street—CityWalk is bordered on one side by a theme park (Universal Studios) and on the other by a vast expanse of parking lots and freeway traffic. The parking fees to visit this street range from $10 to $30, which makes CityWalk a semiprivate attraction—distinctly unlike a real city street, which anyone can walk on without paying high fees for parking. The parking fees were instituted to minimize certain kinds of visitors found on real city streets, including homeless people and hustlers of various sorts.

The urban experience provided by CityWalk is sanitized, soothing, and a model of social control through architectural planning. As one critic noted, "They omitted . . . the handbill-passers, bag ladies, streetcorner salesmen, and three-card-monte—because part of CityWalk's

attraction rests on the certainty that distractions will remain pleasing, never truly surprising, let alone shocking" (McNamara 1999). CityWalk doesn't reject the grit of urban life entirely: when laying the sidewalks, developers embedded fake trash in the concrete. CityWalk and other artificial urban environments such as Celebration and Seaside, Florida, reveal our desire to experience the positive aspects of urban life without having to endure the problems. But this kind of engineering tends to turn cities into theme parks, erasing what is authentically urban—for better and for worse.

DATA WORKSHOP
Analyzing Mass Media and Popular Culture

Imagining the Cities of Tomorrow

People have always been interested in the future. Storytellers, inventors, scientists, politicians, and daydreamers have tried to imagine and, in some instances, create a vision of what will come.

Imagining the city of tomorrow is an almost constant theme in contemporary popular culture—books and comics, radio and TV, movies, and video games. Some of these represent a brighter vision of tomorrow, a **utopia** where humankind is finally freed from drudgery and disease, strife, and suffering. Some represent a darker vision of tomorrow, a **dystopia** where humankind is trapped in a ruthless, apocalyptic world of machines and nature gone mad.

Although examples of the city of the future appear in many different media, this Data Workshop asks that you focus on film. See Chapter 2 for more on how to do research using existing sources. You may have a favorite movie depicting the future, whether it's in the genre of science fiction, action adventure, thriller, horror, drama, or comedy. In deciding which movie to choose for your content analysis, consider whether the movie proposes a serious or realistic possibility of the future and avoid anything too far out in terms of monsters, aliens, or fantasy worlds.

The following is a partial list of movies that could satisfy the assignment. This list is not exhaustive, and you may prefer to use a film not in the list. (Please be aware of MPAA ratings for movies and select appropriate material for your age group.)

12 Monkeys	*Independence Day*
1984	*Left Behind*
A.I. (Artificial Intelligence)	*Mad Max*
Back to the Future	*The Matrix*
District 9	*Metropolis*
V for Vendetta	*Minority Report*
Blade Runner	*Road Warrior*
Brazil	*Slaughterhouse Five*
Children of Men	*Solaris*
The Day after Tomorrow	*Strange Days*
Demolition Man	*The Terminator*
eXistenZ	*Terminator 2: Judgment Day*
Fahrenheit 451	*Total Recall*
The Fifth Element	*Tron*
Gattaca	*The Truman Show*
Idiocracy	*Videodrome*

Watch the movie while keeping in mind the concepts you have learned from this chapter, especially with regard to urbanization. Note the settings and environments in the movie. Capture key scenes or dialogue that can serve as examples of your argument. In conducting your content analysis, consider some of the following questions.

UTOPIA literally "no place"; an ideal society in which all social ills have been overcome

DYSTOPIA opposite of a utopia; a world where social problems are magnified and the quality of life is extremely low

* At what point in the future does the movie take place?

* What is the major theme of the movie? What is its overall message?

* Does the movie represent a utopian or dystopian vision of the future? Does it represent positive or negative changes to society?

* What sorts of futuristic elements are included in the movie, such as time travel, virtual reality, mind control, wars between humans and machines, apocalyptic destruction?

* How is the modern city or landscape of the future depicted? What are its structural features in both public and private realms?

* Compare the future with the present. How is the future the same or different? How is it better or worse?

* What are people like in the future? How are they affected by their environment? How does their environment impact their lives?

* Could this version of the future realistically occur? Would you like to live in such a future?

There are two options for completing this Data Workshop.

Option 1 (informal): Follow the instructions for viewing the movie and reflect on the Workshop questions. You may wish to take notes to prepare for a discussion with other students in small groups. Compare and contrast the

City of the Future In the film *The Fifth Element*, flying cars buzz between ultra-tall skyscrapers. Could this version of the future realistically occur? Would you like to live in such a future?

ON THE JOB

Agriculture: From the Country to the City

John Peterson is not your average midwestern farmer. First of all, he's an organic farmer: no pesticides or chemical fertilizers are allowed at Angelic Organics (angelicorganics .com), a one hundred-acre biodynamic farm located almost two hours west of Chicago. Angelic Organics is also one of the largest **community supported agriculture (CSA)** farms in the nation: the farm is supported in part by local shareholders, who buy a share of the farm and then receive a portion of its harvest, meaning that no supermarkets or cross-country truck travel stands between the shareholders and their weekly boxes of onions, kale, squash, tomatoes, peppers, basil, and rutabagas. John's unique and colorful story of saving his family's failing conventional farm by transforming it into a thriving organic CSA was featured in the critically acclaimed documentary, *The Real Dirt on Farmer John*. Farmer John is an eccentric, biodynamic, community-supported vegetable and herb farmer in Caledonia, Illinois. And he's a man on a mission.

COMMUNITY SUPPORTED AGRICULTURE (CSA) a model of food production and distribution in which small farms recruit subscribers to purchase shares of the farm's harvest; subscribers or shareholders pay at the beginning of the year, and then receive regular deliveries of the farm's produce throughout the growing and harvest seasons

Understanding the need for education and outreach, Farmer John teamed up with Tom Spaulding and other Chicago-area shareholders to create a Learning Center at Angelic Organics. Angelic Organics Learning Center (AOLC) is dedicated to spreading the word about organic food production throughout the greater Chicago area. AOLC recognizes that while not everyone is destined to become a real rural famer, even city dwellers can incorporate some of Farmer John's practices into their own backyard gardening endeavors and everyday household practices. Classes in soap making, chicken care, beekeeping, cheesemaking, and composting teach urban gardeners skills that help them save money, care for their families' health, and become more responsible stewards of their little patches of earth.

Angelic Organics Learning Center also sponsors an "urban initiative" that brings community gardening to the inner city. For example, their Roots and Wings program in Rockford, Illinois, involves local youth in growing organic produce in city plots. The kids also learn to cook, serve, and eat the fresh food they have produced themselves, and they sell their surplus at local farmers' markets so that their neighbors can enjoy the bounty as well. The youth participants don't just reap the benefits of learning about food and urban agriculture—they also become skilled at business, leadership, and problem solving. AOLC runs similar

movies you watched with others in the group. What similarities or differences are there between movies?

Option 2 (formal): Follow the instructions for viewing the movie, and write a three- to four-page essay answering the Workshop questions.

Living in the City

Who lives in cities? What about city life continues to attract droves of people? Big cities offer residents bright lights, a fast pace, excitement, and opportunity. They differ from small rural towns and suburban neighborhoods, so a certain type of person is more likely to be found living there.

Louis Wirth, a member of the Chicago School of sociology, proposed "urbanism as a way of life" that affected the outlook, mentality, and lifestyle of those who lived in the city. He believed that cities provided personal freedom, relaxed moral restraints, relative anonymity, variety, and diversity. At the same time, there was a certain social cost involved. People tend to belong to more formal organizations with more narrow goals and to engage less frequently in intimate interaction with one another. His analysis was in line with the belief that cities cause **social atomization**, that they are filled with free-floating individuals rather than members of a community (Wirth 1938).

Another sociologist, Claude Fischer, found that people create a sense of community by dividing the city into little worlds within which they feel familiar and involved. These groups allow for informal and close relationships, giving city programs with city partners in the Chicago neighborhoods of Englewood and Little Village.

Urban farming like the type that Farmer John and the Angelic Organics Learning Center advocates and teaches is becoming more popular in the United States. Gardeners lay sod on top of skyscrapers in New York City, Washington, D.C., Chicago, Detroit, and San Francisco, to grow vegetables and herbs for local chefs (Burros 2009). These rooftop gardens also provide insulation and drainage for the buildings and contribute to cooler cities (temperature-wise, that is). At ground level, community gardens provide space for apartment dwellers to grow their own healthy fruits and vegetables, as well as saving money and making connections with others by doing so. More chickens are becoming urban-dwellers, too, as backyard coops spring up to provide city families with fresh eggs and early morning wake-up calls (Mann 2012).

There is probably an urban farm in your city or town. There may even be an urban farmer in your neighborhood. And anyone who recognizes the benefits—for individuals, society, and the environment—can try their hand at urban farming. All it takes is a little dirt.

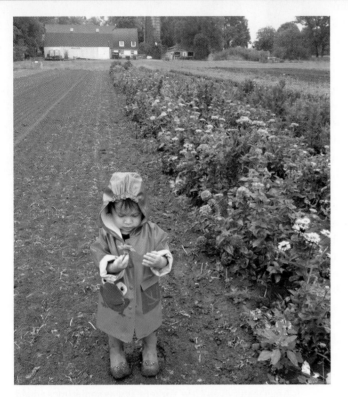

Community Supported Agriculture Toddler picking flowers during a visit to Angelic Organics, a community-supported farm in Caledonia, Illinois.

dwellers more intimacy and a feeling of belonging (Fischer 1976).

In 1962, Herbert Gans published a major ethnographic study, *The Urban Villagers*, in which he identified distinct categories of **urbanites**, or people who live in urban areas. The first are called "cosmopolites"—students, intellectuals, artists, entertainers, and other professionals who are drawn to the city because of its cultural benefits and convenience to their lifestyles. The next group are the "singles," unmarried people seeking jobs, entertainment, and partners with whom to settle down. Singles may include cosmopolites as well. When singles do find a marriage partner or mate, they tend to move to the suburbs, often in preparation to start a family.

Another group of city dwellers are the "ethnic villagers," often recent immigrants to the area. They tend to settle near others with whom they share a common racial, ethnic, national, religious, or language background; these are often distant relatives or others with whom they have a connection. This is why many major cities still have Chinatowns, Little Italys, and other ethnic neighborhoods. Once here, immigrants form tightly knit ethnic enclaves that resemble the villages of their home countries. The last group of urban dwellers is the "deprived" and the "trapped." These are the people at the bottom of the social hierarchy—the poor, homeless, disabled, elderly, and mentally ill. Without resources and means of support, they cannot afford to leave the city, even if they could find jobs, services, or housing elsewhere; they are inescapably stuck where they are. This perpetuates a cycle of poverty and despair.

SOCIAL ATOMIZATION a social situation that emphasizes individualism over collective or group identities

URBANITES people who live in cities

Alienation and Altruism: The Case of New York City

As products of the Industrial Revolution, cities are celebrated for providing unprecedented degrees of freedom for individuals. Life in rural agricultural communities was much more restrictive, with family and neighbors placing tight constraints on behavior. However, sociology has been suspicious of cities, seeing this very freedom as a source of **alienation**. Early sociologist Georg Simmel argued that while urban environments "allowed a much greater degree of individual liberty," they did so only "at the expense of treating others in objective and instrumental terms" relating to others only through a "cold and heartless calculus" (Harvey 1990). In short, except for their chosen subcultures, city dwellers fail to develop community, feel little connection with neighbors, have relationships that are largely shallow and impersonal, and fail to care about each other (Simmel 1950).

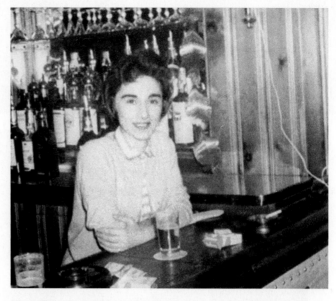

Kitty Genovese Her murder case shocked the nation. How could so many bystanders have failed to intervene? What did this say about the harsh realities of modern big-city life?

ALIENATION decreasing importance of social ties and community and the corresponding increase in impersonal associations and instrumental logic

ALTRUISM unselfish concern for the well-being of others and helping behaviors performed without self-interested motivation

BYSTANDER EFFECT or **DIFFUSION OF RESPONSIBILITY** the social dynamic wherein the more people who are present in a moment of crisis, the less likely any one of them is to take action

The murder of Catherine "Kitty" Genovese in New York City has come to represent all such fears about modern urban life. Late on March 13, 1964, she was returning home from her job as a bar manager when she was attacked by a man named Winston Moseley. He first attacked Genovese after she parked her car outside the Kew Gardens apartment building where she lived. She was stabbed several times before her attacker was frightened off when lights went on in nearby apartments. Badly wounded and bleeding, Genovese was later reported to have shouted, "Oh, my God, he stabbed me! Please help me! Please help me!" (Gansberg 1964). Somehow, she then made her way to the back of the building, apparently trying to get to the staircase that led to her apartment. However, her assailant returned and stabbed and beat her to death, before sexually assaulting her. The entire attack, although intermittent, was reported to have lasted nearly thirty minutes.

As horrible as this was, it wouldn't be remembered today if it were just a tragic murder. What has made this case memorable was the number of bystanders who must have heard the crime taking place but failed to take action. According to National Public Radio in 2004, some forty years after the crime took place:

> The police later established that thirty-eight people either saw Kitty Genovese stabbed and raped or heard her scream for her life, but no one called the police; no one rushed down to the street to try to scare off her attacker. Her death was a small story in the next day's newspapers, but two weeks later, the *New York Times* ran a story on how shocked the Queens police had been that so many people heard Kitty Genovese being murdered and didn't lift a finger to help her. The story set off a national soul-searching. How could so many Americans, even New Yorkers, it was sometimes added, have turned away from cries for help? The murder of Kitty Genovese became a kind of modern morality tale. Her death seemed to symbolize an age in which people counseled, "Don't get involved" and "Mind your own business." (Simon 2004)

A. M. Rosenthal, who was the editor of the *New York Times* in 1964, later wrote a book about the incident, which focused attention on the most disturbing aspect of the case: why didn't somebody help her? For many, this seemed to be the ultimate indictment of big cities in general, and New York City in particular, and much of the press coverage seemed to demonize the individuals involved. Regardless of individual responsibility, it's important to also look at the social factors that made the situation possible.

Especially useful in understanding the social origins of this unfortunate incident has been the work of social psychologists John Darley and Bibb Latane (1968), who conducted several experiments on **altruism** and helping behaviors. These experiments were designed to test what came to be called the **bystander effect**, or the **diffusion of responsibility**. In one experiment, different-sized groups of test subjects heard what sounded like a woman having an accident in the next room. Darley and Latane found that

IN RELATIONSHIPS
Encounters with Strangers

Cities are places where strangers come together. Before there were cities, there were also no strangers; those who were unknown were driven off, killed, or quickly assimilated into the clan, tribe, or group (Lofland 1973). With the advent of cities came the prospect of living life in close proximity to hundreds, thousands, or even millions of people we will never know and from whom we cannot be completely segregated. City life would seem to bring the prospect for all sorts of chaos and conflict—and yet every day, in contemporary cities, millions of people go about their business in relative harmony, brushing elbows with each other on the sidewalk or subway in encounters that are neither friendly nor unfriendly but merely orderly.

What are the interactional structures that order urban life? Public interactions with strangers can be treacherous, as we encounter people we do not know and whose reactions we cannot predict. For the most part, we are not talking about the danger of physical attack. More common than getting mugged is being "looked at funny," getting "goosed," or being the target of "wolf whistles." These are threats to self more than anything else—being treated as a nonperson, or as a piece of meat. How do we guard against these minor molestations when we walk down the street every day?

A specific way we deal with strangers in public is by doing what Erving Goffman calls **civil inattention**. This is a taken-for-granted rule of public place interaction, a basic public courtesy we extend to one another that helps guard against unpleasant interactions with strangers (Goffman 1971). About eight or ten feet away from one another, we tend to look at and then look away from the person we are approaching—all in one sweep of our gaze. We have looked, but not too intently or for too long. This allows us to navigate through urban spaces without bumping into strangers and to avoid the kinds of interactions that might lead to trouble. The practice of civil inattention is so commonplace that you may not realize you do it every day. Now, walk down the street and notice your own gazework and that of others—with full comprehension of how this simple act helps avoid conflict, enables smooth

CIVIL INATTENTION an unspoken rule governing interactions in public places, whereby individuals briefly notice others before ignoring them

interactions between strangers, and basically makes city life possible.

What might move us to violate civil inattention—to interact with strangers in ways that might otherwise be forbidden? Anything, Goffman suggests, that makes us more "open." Open persons are those whose identities expose them to the overtures of others. Examples of open persons are police officers (and others in uniform), pregnant women, small children, the disabled, those with unusual physical characteristics such as height or hair color, same-sex couples . . . the list goes on and on. One type of open person you have probably encountered is a person walking a dog. Dogs serve as what Goffman calls "bridging devices"—excuses for strangers to begin conversations that the rules of civil inattention would otherwise prevent. Dogs facilitate interactions in public places—indeed, dogs serve as (perhaps unwitting) team members in their masters' performances (Robins, Sanders, and Cahill 1991). They can be referred to by others as a kind of icebreaker as well (Wood et al. 2007)—we've all found ourselves exclaiming, "Cute puppy!" or "Wow, that's a big dog" as we pass dogwalkers on the street, and sometimes those utterances develop into longer conversations.

And of course, there's the classic notion of the dog as "chick magnet" or "dude magnet," helping its owner attract, converse with, and pick up women or men for romantic purposes. So perhaps we should give our pooches more credit for helping connect us with each other and make city life more humane. But if you have a dog, you probably already do that.

the higher the number of bystanders present, the lower the chances that any of them would attempt to help. Basically, they theorized that the responsibility "diffused" throughout the crowd so that no one person felt responsible enough to do anything, most assuming that someone else would help. However, when groups were small, the chances that someone would do something increased greatly.

In a similar experiment, they placed different-sized groups of subjects in a room, under the pretense of taking a test, and gradually filled the room with smoke. Again, they found that the greater the number of subjects in a room, the lower the chances that anyone would mention the smoke. Here, along with the diffusion of responsibility, they argued that **pluralistic ignorance** was at work. When large groups of people encounter an ambiguous or unusual situation, they tend to look to each other for help in defining the situation. If no member of the group decides that it is an emergency, and therefore worthy of reacting, it is likely that all members will continue to ignore the situation.

On the twentieth anniversary of the Genovese murder, Fordham University held the "Catherine Genovese Memorial Conference on Bad Samaritanism," which attempted to shed some light on what sorts of situations would produce bystanders who would help. Although no single character trait correlated with being a Good Samaritan, researchers largely confirmed earlier findings—that bystanders in groups were tentative about helping, especially when they were unsure of the nature of the problem.

These conclusions can also help explain a time when New Yorkers did come to each other's aid out of a sense of belonging and **community**: in the September 11, 2001 attacks on the World Trade Center. In the hours and days after the attacks, Americans rushed to help however they could. "Tens of thousands of patriotic Americans rolled up their sleeves and gave blood," monetary donations poured in, and ordinary New Yorkers rushed to pitch in (Stapleton 2002). Some of the most heroic rescue efforts at the World Trade Center were made by ordinary people who rushed to help as soon as they heard. Two Port Authority police officers, Will Jimeno and John McLoughlin, were the last people to be found alive in the collapsed remains of the World Trade Center towers. They were discovered by Charles Sereika, a former paramedic, and David Karnes, an accountant from Connecticut who "had changed into his Marine camouflage outfit" and driven down to Manhattan as soon as he heard the news (Dwyer 2001). The movie *World Trade Center* (2006) by Oliver Stone depicts their story. And even if things have somewhat returned to normal (meaning people are less friendly now),

almost everyone agrees that New Yorkers "were wonderful during the crisis, and we were tender to each other. . . . Volunteers streamed to the site" and "after only a few days there were so many, they were turned away by the hundreds. . . . Strangers spoke to each other in the street, in stores, and on the subway" (Hustvedt 2002).

So what made the difference in the two events? Many of those who heard Kitty Genovese being murdered believed that it was a bar fight or a lover's quarrel. Not knowing what was happening, they were unsure how to respond. With September 11, there was no ambiguity and many people understood where to go and what to do to help. In 1964, the "911" emergency system didn't exist, and many people were reluctant to get personally involved with the police. This largely supports the conclusions of sociologists like Lee Clarke (2001), who has studied how people respond to various kinds of disasters. His work shows that altruism, rather than panic, tends to prevail in disasters. Clarke posits that the rules for behavior in extreme situations are essentially the same as the rules of ordinary life—that when faced with danger, people help those next to them before helping themselves. This was the case in the destruction of the World Trade Center. People survived the disaster because they did not become hysterical but instead helped to facilitate a successful evacuation of the buildings (Clarke 2001). There are many obvious reasons why the September 11 attacks would bring people together in ways that the attack on Kitty Genovese did not. September 11 was clearly and obviously a disaster; it was also an attack on the entire country, so loyalties were further cemented. Formal institutions were set up so people could easily volunteer and receive positive social sanctions in return. Kitty Genovese was just one young woman living in a building full of immigrants and elderly pensioners. However, whenever bystanders do jump in to help, it is in part because of the outrage her murder provoked. In the aftermath of the Kitty Genovese murder, the "911" emergency system was created, neighborhood watch groups were formed, Good Samaritan laws were passed to protect bystanders from liability in emergencies, and people started to get more involved. So, while alienation is part of life in cities, so is altruism. Both are part of our shared social worlds.

The Environment

The final section of this chapter once again considers the connection between the social and the natural worlds. Human populations have grown tremendously, as have the cities in which most of them live. Now how do those people interact with the natural environment and what impact does the environment have on how they live? Whether we go camping, surfing, or just take a walk through Central Park, we all go to nature to escape, to recreate, to relax. It is ironic that we now seek out nature as a retreat from the demands of society, because society itself originated and evolved at least in part to protect us against the demands of nature.

The cooperation and interdependence that characterize most social groups allow individuals to withstand the risks of the natural environment. The products of culture—clothing, architecture, automobiles, and many others—contribute to our ability to live in what would otherwise be inhospitable surroundings. Without her insulated house and its furnace, her layers of clothing topped with a Gore-Tex parka, and her car with a remote starter and all-weather tires, Dr. Ferris would have a hard time surviving the harsh winters in northern Illinois. And all these survival tools are supplied because she is part of a society whose other members have created what she needs to be safe and warm in the elements. Society provides all of us with a buffer against nature; without it, we wouldn't last very long in the ocean, the snowdrifts, or the desert.

Social Ecology

While society buffers individuals against the rigors of nature, it also allows them to impact the natural world. Trees are cut down to build homes; furnaces and automobiles burn fuels and create air pollution; and manufacturing artificial fibers creates chemical waste—just a few of the ways the collective actions of a society impact the natural world. The study of human populations and their impact on the natural world is called **social ecology**. Under this heading, you might study how cities are organized, how populations migrate, or how technological developments influence the social order, to see how these social developments occur within a physical environment that shapes and responds to social trends.

Sociologists are interested in both the social and the natural worlds because those worlds interact with each other. Even the most remote corner of the Amazon rain forest is not immune from the effects of society, even if no human has ever set foot there. Global climate change is slowly impacting that forest's environment; jets fly above the trees, creating noise and pollution; and animals that have been squeezed out of their natural habitats elsewhere (by trends like urban sprawl) may begin moving into new territories, upsetting the balance of native creatures and plants. Society impacts nature relentlessly—and vice versa—as the rhythms, rigors, and risks of the natural world shape how society is organized.

Studying the Environment

The environment is a recent area of interest among sociologists, coinciding with the general public's concern about environmental issues (Guber 2003). When sociologists use the term **environment**, it encompasses aspects of both the natural and the human-made environment and includes everything from the most micro level of organisms to the entire **biosphere**. Sociologists study the ways that societies are dependent on the natural world; how cultural values and beliefs shape views about and influence usage of the environment; the politics and economics of natural resources; and the social construction of conflicts, problems, and solutions that are a result of our relationship to the natural world.

SOCIAL ECOLOGY the study of human populations and their impact on the natural world

ENVIRONMENT in sociology, the natural world, the human-made environment, and the interaction between the two

BIOSPHERE the parts of Earth that can support life

Social Ecology Society affects nature even in the remotest places— including on the highest mountaintops and in outer space! Hikers leave garbage on Mount McKinley and NASA illustrates the objects orbiting Earth.

Environmental sociology is a growing subfield within the larger discipline that has continued to gain scholarly interest and to impact other academics, policy makers, and society as a whole. Its emergence paralleled the modern environmental movement in the late 1970s. The contours of the subfield are still being established.

First, we will look at the environment as a social problem. This encompasses two big areas: problems of consumption and problems of waste. Sociologists, however, must look beyond descriptions of problems and attempt to apply analytic frameworks for understanding the social complexities underlying them.

The Environment as a Social Problem

Many students first become acquainted with the subject of the environment as a social problem. Learning the "three R's" in schools has now come to mean Reduce, Reuse, Recycle. We need to help "save" the environment because it is under threat from consumption and waste.

PROBLEMS OF CONSUMPTION: RESOURCE DEPLETION The planet Earth provides an abundance of natural resources, including air, water, land, wildlife, plants, and minerals. We have learned to exploit these resources not only for basic survival but also to build everything in material culture that is part of the modern world. Humans have long been presented with the challenge of managing their use of natural resources, but those challenges have changed in the postindustrial era.

Renewable resources are natural resources that can be regenerated; for instance, oxygen is replenished by plants and trees, water by evaporation and rain clouds, trees and plants by pollens and seeds, and animals by mating and reproduction. The wind blows and the sun shines in ample abundance. **Nonrenewable resources** are those that cannot be replaced (except through tens of thousands of years of geological processes); for instance, fossil fuels like oil, or minerals like coal, copper, or iron. All natural resources are susceptible to overuse or overconsumption and eventually to depletion or even exhaustion. As a result of rising demands, we have already seen rising costs or outright shortages for such commodities as seafood, timber, and gasoline.

ENVIRONMENTAL SOCIOLOGY the study of the interaction between society and the natural environment, including the social causes and consequences of environmental problems

RENEWABLE RESOURCES resources that replenish at a rate comparable to the rate at which they are consumed

NONRENEWABLE RESOURCES finite resources that can become exhausted; includes those that take so long to replenish as to be effectively finite

It may be hard to imagine that we'll ever run out of some things, like air and water, but even these are threatened. We may not be aware of the connection between the things we consume in our everyday life and their sources. We're removed from the fields and the mines, the oceans, and the mountains that are the origin of our goods. But we are already confronting real problems of resource depletion, and the course of such depletion may now be irreversible.

One of the world's most pressing problems is how to meet enormous and growing demands for energy. We need energy—gas, electric, or nuclear—to help us power everything from our cars and televisions to factories and airplanes. But these forms of energy are not inexhaustible. We have relied primarily on nonrenewable sources, such as coal and fossil fuels to meet our needs. The current mix of fuel sources comes from 36 percent petroleum, 25 percent natural gas, 20 percent coal, 8 percent nuclear, and only 9 percent renewable energy sources (U.S. Energy Information Administration 2012). Some renewable sources besides wood and hydroelectric (water-generated) power, such as wind or solar power, are being developed, but they are not sufficient yet to provide us with the substantial quantities of energy we will need in the future.

Industrialized nations are the largest consumers of energy, using approximately 70 percent of the total energy produced in the world; of those nations, America uses nearly 20 percent, Russia uses more than 6 percent, and Germany 4.5 percent. Developing nations that now use the remaining 30 percent are becoming more industrialized, and their energy needs will also increase, thus closing the energy usage gap among nations during the next twenty-five years. In that same time, total worldwide energy consumption is projected to grow between 50 percent and 60 percent (U.S. Energy Information Administration 2004). Oil is a finite resource, and at some point the supply will be exhausted. We may have already hit a peak of production and be in decline though there is high demand for more domestic oil exploration and production. Hydraulic fracturing or "fraking" involves drilling thousands of feet underground to extract natural gas stores from shale. The practice is not without dangers and controversy. We know that limited amounts and rising costs of energy are likely to spur development of substitutes for oil.

Another critical area of consumption is the rain forests in South America, Central America, Australia, Africa, and Southeast Asia. Rain forests are ecosystems located in tropical and temperate regions that are home to diverse plant and animal life (as well as indigenous peoples). Although rain forests cover only about 6 percent of the Earth's landmass, they contain close to 50 percent of all microorganisms and plant and animal species in the world (Mittermeier, Myers, and Mittermeier 2000). Previously unknown life forms are being discovered there every year, while at the same time thousands are being driven to extinction. Products derived from the rain forest include not only foods and woods, but importantly, pharmaceuticals; more than 7,000 medical compounds are derived from native plants. Rain forests also play a key role in global climate control, evaporation and rainfall, and clearing the air of carbon dioxide (Myers and Kent 2005).

In 1950, rain forests covered twice as much area as they do today, and they are disappearing at an alarming rate. Currently, there are approximately 3.5 billion acres of rain forest worldwide, down from more than 7 billion. More than 78 million acres of rain forest are lost every year—215,000 acres every day, or about 150 acres every minute! Destruction of the rain forests is of sociological import because it results from collective human behavior. The immediate cause of this destruction is to accommodate the logging, mining, and ranching industries. Although these industries may benefit the peoples of those regions, they are primarily providing for the consumption demands of the more developed nations of the world (Myers and Kent 2004).

In addition to rain forests, worldwide **biodiversity** is in dangerous decline. According to a 2005 United Nations report (U.N. Millennium Ecosystem Assessment 2005) prepared by 1,360 scientists from ninety-five countries, humans pose a distinct threat to thousands of other species on the planet. The report asserts that the natural rate of extinction has multiplied by as much as a thousand times within the past century. Perhaps hardest hit has been marine life, with a 90 percent decrease in the number of fish in the world's oceans. In addition, roughly 12 percent of birds, 23 percent of mammals, 32 percent of amphibians, and 25 percent of conifers are threatened with extinction. These mass die-offs are being driven by human activities, including the destruction of habitats, pollution, the introduction of nonnative species, and overuse. "We will need to make sure that we don't disrupt the biological web to the point where collapse of the whole system becomes

irreversible," says Anantha Duraiappah of Canada, who co-chaired the study (Couvrette 2005).

PROBLEMS OF WASTE: POLLUTION Problems of consumption are linked to problems of waste, often two sides of the same coin. Consider water and air. Water is another natural resource that can be overused—we understand what happens during a drought, or when lakes, rivers, or underground aquifers are drained and then go dry. But water can also be damaged by what we put into it. And while we don't normally think of consuming air, it is an essential natural resource, and we can damage its quality and change for the worse the very atmosphere of the planet. Let's look at these examples of **pollution**.

Water is indispensable for life. Some 70 percent of the Earth's surface is covered with water. Almost 97 percent of this is in oceans of saltwater, home to a vast array of sea creatures and plants. Only 1 percent of the total accounts for freshwater, found in lakes, rivers, and underground aquifers; the other 2 percent is in polar ice caps and glaciers. This is a small percentage to meet human needs—from drinking water to water for agricultural and ranching purposes. The world's water supply, both in oceans and freshwater, has been under increased threat from pollution by industrial development and population growth—mostly by allowing contaminants to enter the oceans, lakes, and rivers or to seep into underground water supplies. The sources of this pollution are many: factories dumping chemical and solid wastes, agricultural run-off of manure, pesticides, and fertilizers, human sewage and urban run-off, and toxic chemicals falling from the skies in rain.

Access to freshwater is not equal throughout the world. Most Americans can take ample

BIODIVERSITY the variety of species of plants and animals existing at any given time

POLLUTION any environmental contaminant that harms living beings

Threats to Biodiversity and the Climate Rain forests, which play a key role in regulating the global climate and are home to almost 50 percent of the world's plant and animal species, are being destroyed at a rate of millions of acres each year.

and safe drinking water for granted. Although the **Environmental Protection Agency (EPA)** claims that the United States has one of the safest supplies of drinking water, even here more than 10 percent of water systems in the nation don't meet EPA standards (U.S. EPA 2008). In developing nations, water-borne diseases are a significant cause of disease and death. There is a definite link between water scarcity and poverty; in some African countries, up to 50 percent of the population are without access to adequate water (Gleick 1998).

The atmosphere is made up of thin layers of gases surrounding the planet and making life possible. It interacts with the land, oceans, and sun to produce the Earth's climate and weather. The air that we breathe is ubiquitous, so that we might not even think of it as a natural resource. But our Earth's atmosphere and its ability to sustain life are at risk from pollution. Not all threats came from humans; for instance, volcanoes or forest fires started by lightning can emit massive clouds of smoke, ash, and debris into the atmosphere. Human activity, however, accounts for a tremendous amount of air pollution, especially emissions from factories, power plants, and automobiles. The most common

pollutants (carbon monoxide, lead, nitrogen dioxide, ozone, sulfur dioxide, and particulates such as soot, smoke, and dust) together are often referred to as **greenhouse gases**. These not only create ugly smog and haze but also are hazardous to the health of humans and other species.

The U.S. Congress passed the first Clean Air Act in 1963, which has been followed over the decades by numerous amendments and other legislation to help regulate industries involved in emissions. Regulations and technological advancements have helped reduce air pollution in the United States. Still, we have the highest per capita rate of any nation, emitting some 6.6 tons of greenhouse gases per person per year. It is estimated that more than 100 million people, or about 40 percent of the U.S. population, live in areas reporting higher levels of ozone than are safe by national standards (U.S. EPA 2003). Pollution problems may be even greater in developing nations that are rapidly becoming industrialized.

Greenhouse gases are also contributing to a change in the makeup of the Earth's atmosphere. Scientists call this the **greenhouse effect**. The Earth's climate is regulated through a process in which some of the sun's heat and energy is retained within the atmosphere. Naturally occurring gases (such as water vapor or carbon dioxide) help trap some of the Earth's outgoing heat, which in turn maintains a stable, livable climate. An increase in greenhouse gases from air pollution results in greater retention of heat within the Earth's atmosphere, leading to **global warming**, an increase in the world's average temperature.

Scientists believe that in the past 50 to 100 years, the average temperature of the Earth has risen one degree Fahrenheit. They predict that greenhouse gases will continue to increase the Earth's temperature another one to five degrees over the next fifty years, and two to ten degrees in the next

Climate Change Maldivian Minister of Fisheries and Agriculture Ibrahim Didi calls attention to the threat of global warming to low-lying countries by holding an underwater meeting to sign a document calling on all nations to cut down their carbon dioxide emissions.

100 years (U.S. EPA 2000). A climate change of a few degrees can cause catastrophic consequences for the world and its inhabitants. Even slightly higher temperatures could melt polar ice caps and increase the sea level, shrink the land-masses of islands and continents, change global weather patterns, and alter ecosystems that support life on Earth.

In addition to the greenhouse effect, pollutants in the air have caused **global dimming** (or **solar dimming**). This newly discovered phenomenon means that the Earth is becoming darker than it used to be. Because of all the particles in the atmosphere, some natural and some from human activity, less light from the sun's rays reaches Earth. Climate researchers estimate that the Earth's surface is receiving 15 percent less sunlight than it did just fifty years ago (Boyd 2004). The sun has remained as bright as always, but the amount of energy or solar radiation that hits the Earth has been shrinking by about 3 percent per decade. In some respects, global dimming is counteracting global warming, but that only means that global warming would be worse were it not for the pollutants that are blocking the sun.

Another pollution problem is garbage. U.S. waste production is twice that of any other nation. The average American generates over four pounds of trash per day—1,617 pounds per year. The country dumps about 250 million tons of garbage a year, and about 34.7 percent of it is recycled, leaving the rest for landfills and incinerators (U.S. Environmental Protection Agency 2011). Some of our trash even gets blasted into outer space (such as satellites and other objects that have become obsolete), where nearly 30,000 pieces of litter are orbiting the planet (BBC 2013)! And have you ever thought about light pollution or noise pollution? Depending on your sensitivity to these, you may be dismayed not to see stars in the night sky because of so many street lights and neon signs, or be annoyed by the almost constant sound of traffic and other noise, both of which are part of life in big cities.

DATA WORKSHOP
Analyzing Everyday Life

Measuring Student Attitudes on Environmentalism

"Sustainability," "environmentalism," and "being green" are all terms that refer to reducing human impact on the environment. Even though environmentally based social movements have become so mainstream that there is now an entire television channel, Planet Green, devoted to the topic, there are those who believe that environmentalists are alarmists who have invented issues like global warming, resource depletion, and growing landfills.

This Data Workshop asks you to examine the attitudes of your fellow college students in order to determine the extent of their environmental beliefs and behaviors. Do they believe that climate change has human causes? Do they recycle or conserve various resources, and, if so, how? Do they worry about things like their "carbon footprint"?

For this assignment, construct a survey about environmental attitudes and actions, administer it to your fellow students, and analyze the findings. Refer to Chapter 2 for further information on survey research design. Make sure to collect some demographic data such as age, gender, class, race/ethnicity, GPA, major, so that you can determine whether there is any relationship between backgrounds and attitudes.

In constructing the survey, consider using a Likert scale in order to collect data on attitudes, as this will help streamline your analysis. Survey respondents can select the degree to which they agree or disagree with statements. You can use the following statements as a starting place, and modify or add new ones when you construct your own survey questionnaire.

* Eating facilities on campus should use environmentally friendly products.

* I use environmentally friendly products at home as much as I can.

* I feel motivated to recycle.

* I use the recycling bins on campus.

* There are enough recycling bins on campus.

* If I see a piece of trash on the ground when I am outside, I will pick it up and dispose of it properly.

* Global warming is a threat to our planet.

* Humans and industry have contributed to global warming.

* I make attempts to reduce my carbon footprint by driving less and conserving energy in my daily life.

* Sustainability is an important issue for the entire world.

* If we don't reduce, reuse, and recycle, our world will face serious consequences.

* Environmentalism is a worthwhile cause.

GLOBAL PERSPECTIVE

The Asian Brown Cloud: Pollution in China and India

China and India are the two most populated countries in the world, with more than 1 billion residents in each. In comparison, the United States, the third most populated country, has just 313 million residents. According to calculations from the United Nations, no other country besides China and India will reach a population size of 1 billion. Despite the fact that the United States is the third most populated country, making up only 5 percent of the world's total population, it also consumes approximately 25 percent of its resources—in other words, we're currently the pigs of the planet. Unfortunately, though, as China and India develop into completely industrialized countries, they are following in the resource-hogging footsteps of the United States.

The "Asian Brown Cloud" is a name given to the layer of pollution that hangs over China, India, and parts of Southwest Asia. In satellite photos, the Asian Brown Cloud appears as a giant brown stain over this part of the world during the months of January through March. To the residents of China and India, the Asian Brown Cloud appears as a haze of air pollution hovering over their countries. Environmen-

The Asian Brown Cloud This photo from a NASA satellite shows the layer of pollution that hangs over China, India, and parts of Southwest Asia.

Administer the survey to your fellow students. For the purposes of this exercise, you should start with a small pilot group and collect between ten to twenty surveys. After gathering data, describe and analyze your findings. See what kinds of patterns you can find. Are college students concerned about the environment? Does this concern translate into action? How do your findings confirm or refute any hypotheses that you might have had before beginning this study? What do you think your data reveal overall?

There are two options for completing this Data Workshop.

Option 1 (informal): Bring your survey questionnaires to share with the rest of your class. Discuss the findings in small groups. Note the similarities and differences in your findings and those of your group members. Write a statetal scientists maintain that the Asian Brown Cloud consists of airborne pollutants from car and factory combustion and biomass burning that collect when there are no rains to wash it away. This atmospheric pollution has both immediate and long-term impacts on the citizens of Asia. Mumbai and Beijing report high rates of chronic respiratory problems, including cancer. Air quality in large cities such as Beijing is so poor—and even dangerous—that Chinese officials have spent more than $17 billion in the past few years on attempts to reduce the air pollution. Despite these efforts, some Olympians refused to participate in the 2008 Summer Olympics in Beijing because of the fear that the air quality would affect their health and performance. Projected long-term effects of this cloud of pollution include reduced crop growth leading to famine, melting glaciers creating devastating floods, and global warming affecting rainfall average, potentially leading to drought.

Much of the pollution in India and China has been a result of factory emissions, coal-burning, and garbage-burning. Now that there are stricter regulations governing the emissions produced by factories and garbage dumps, a new culprit is emerging. In recent years, both China and India have registered record-breaking economic growth rates. Personal incomes have increased, and because of the constant barrage of images from the Western media, more and more Asian citizens are buying private cars rather than relying on public transportation or more traditional forms of commuting like bicycles. In Beijing alone, 1,300 new cars are registered every day. In 2008, India's Tata motors introduced the Nano, a $2,500 car that will make car ownership accessible for millions of Indians. Environmentalists fear that the Nano will flood already gridlocked roads and release millions of tons of carbon dioxide into the already polluted air.

America is still the most disproportionate consumer of fossil fuels in the world. Not only do Americans drive more cars than citizens from almost any other country, but also use many times more gas than anyone else. At 446 gallons per capita annually, we're gallons ahead of the Canadians (311 gallons), boatloads ahead of countries like Germany and Italy (130 gallons and 114 gallons, respectively), and veritable oceans ahead of almost everyone else (United Nations Development Programme 2000). At the same time, developing countries like India and China are putting more and more cars on the roads. India consumed nearly 120 million tons of petroleum products in 2007, according to the Petroleum Ministry, up from 113 million tons the previous year. China also saw a record high in terms of petroleum consumption in 2008, with a rise of 16.5 percent from the previous year. While the cars sold in China and India are not as gas-guzzling as American cars, the collective impact of the sheer number of cars owned in these densely populated countries is potentially devastating.

Rajendra Pachauri, head of the 2007 Nobel Prize–winning Intergovernmental Panel on Climate Change (IPCC), said that investing in improving urban public transportation and enforcing restrictions on industrial waste are ways that countries such as China and India could balance the need for fighting climate change with that for economic growth. However, the burden of the problem does not lie in the hands of the Chinese and Indian governments. Ultimately, the images transmitted from the United States are inspiring the world to aspire to the same excessive lifestyle and standard of living as those of Americans. People in developing countries want to achieve our level of economic development, and our own trade policy benefits from their consumption rates when they buy our products. Can America lead by example? If we become more environmentally conscious, will the world follow suit? These are pressing questions that we will have to address in the very near future.

ment that identifies and incorporates the general patterns found in the data gathered by the entire group.

Option 2 (formal): Write a three- to four-page essay describing your research project and analyzing your findings. Attach your completed surveys and any notes to your paper.

Environmental Sociology

To analyze problems of the environment, sociologists have developed "environmental sociology," a distinct subfield of sociology that describes environmental issues and examines the reciprocal interactions between the physical environment, social structure, and human behavior. Although this subfield is still developing, four major analytic frameworks within environmental sociology have emerged during the past thirty years. These concern the political economy of the environment, attitudes about the environment, environmental movements (including environmental justice), and sustainable development.

THE POLITICAL ECONOMY OF THE ENVIRONMENT

The political economy of the environment is a core area of study within environmental sociology that takes a classical or neo-Marxist and Weberian approach to understanding the environment (Schnaiberg 1975). Its focus is on how economic factors influence the way organizations (typically corporations) use the environment and how this use is often supported by political systems and policies.

Contemporary industrial societies have been built on the premise of progress—on conquering nature and using natural resources to fuel production and expand profits (Schnaiberg and Gould 1994). Government policies and economic systems have frequently supported this belief. While progress has usually meant great wealth for some and goods and services for many, it has come at a price: environmental degradation and the accompanying social problems.

Environmental sociologists refer to this process as the **treadmill of production**. They assert that the drive for economic growth in capitalist societies persists, even at the expense of the environment and despite opposition from activists and other groups, because corporate expansion provides critical taxable wealth and the jobs essential to the economic life of a society. Although such development creates a multitude of problems, there are also serious consequences for attempts at regulating or limiting the production practices of these corporations (Schnaiberg 1975). Large corporations can typically defend themselves against calls for accountability for damages and exercise considerable influence through political lobbying and campaign contributions as well as appeals to change public opinion. Attacking the practices of these corporations can also be detrimental to the workers who need their jobs and to governments that may depend on these industries for products critical to the nation's well-being and security (Schnaiberg and Gould 1994). Even though the treadmill of production is not an environ-mentally friendly process, numerous societies are invested in its continued existence, and we will likely see enduring conflict between the economy and the environment at the international, national, regional, and local levels.

ENVIRONMENTAL ATTITUDES Understanding societal attitudes about the environment is an essential part of environmental sociology. Early work in this area began with a group of Chicago School sociologists including Robert Park (1961) and Amos Hawley (1950), who helped to establish the field of human ecology. Extending on this in the 1970s, William Catton and Riley Dunlap developed the **new ecological paradigm** (Catton and Dunlap 1978, 1980).

Historically, Westerners have had a particularly **anthropocentric**, or human-centered, relationship with the environment, perceiving nature as something to master. Nature is believed to be inexhaustible and hence can be used with impunity to serve humankind. Consumption is equated with success. This is consistent with the Judeo-Christian belief in man's dominion over the Earth. Western culture thus perpetuates **human exceptionalism**, an attitude that humans are exempt from natural ecological limits (Dunlap and Catton 1994). Much of our progress through industrialization supports this notion that technology will allow us to overcome any environmental challenge. In contrast, the new ecological paradigm poses humans as part of the ecosystem or biosphere, one of many species that interact with the natural environment. Nature has limits that we must respect, and this may constrain economic development. The new ecological paradigm recognizes that human activity can have both intended and unintended consequences that shape social life and life on the planet.

Scientists as well as environmental advocates and policy makers are in disagreement about the future consequences of global climate change. Some argue that global warming is part of the natural progression of the Earth. Others say it has been brought about primarily by human activity and that we are headed toward catastrophe. Still others argue that though global warming exists, it is not a cause for concern. How such problems as global warming are defined and understood depends on underlying values and beliefs. You might not consider global climate change so bad if you also thought that extinction of some plant and animal life was an acceptable part of the evolutionary process of natural selection. Or you might not be so concerned by such issues if you thought that clean air, fossil fuels, or other natural resources were commodities in a free market and that nations must compete for their availability and take responsibility for their consequences. Our definitions and interpretations of evidence regarding environmental problems are also filtered through our own cultural beliefs and values.

Research on environmental attitudes has had a marked influence on studies of environmental movements (Dunlap and Catton 1979; Buttel 1987). Environmental sociologists

TREADMILL OF PRODUCTION term describing the operation of modern economic systems that require constant growth, which causes increased exploitation of resources and environmental degradation

NEW ECOLOGICAL PARADIGM a way of understanding human life as just one part of an ecosystem that includes many species' interactions with the environment; suggests that there should be ecological limits on human activity

ANTHROPOCENTRIC literally "human centered"; the idea that needs and desires of human beings should take priority over concerns about other species or the natural environment

HUMAN EXCEPTIONALISM the attitude that humans are exempt from natural ecological limits are interested in the processes that create attitude change and the relationship between attitudes and behavior. They want to understand why certain groups have become more "biocentric" (as opposed to anthropocentric), or more environmentally sensitive, and what inspires great numbers of people to participate in environmental movements.

THE ENVIRONMENTAL MOVEMENT People have long been concerned about the relationship between humans and nature and about the impact of society on the environment. When people organize around these concerns, their collective efforts can have profound impacts. When sociologists study the **environmental movement**, topics of interest include the origins of the groups involved, their internal organization and social network formation, their political role, and their presence at local, regional, national, and international levels. In this section, we will trace the four major eras in the history of the environmental movement in the United States while discussing major flashpoints in its development.

Most social scientists and historians date the beginning of the American environmental movement to the writings of Henry David Thoreau in the mid-1800s, especially *Walden; or, Life in the Woods*, which concerns the rejection of urban materialism and the virtues of simple living. Thoreau has inspired many generations, and his central argument, about how humans impact the natural environment and thus must actively choose to preserve it, continues to be the backbone of environmental activism in the United States. While preservation or conservation remains a key focus, the environmental movement has become increasingly interested in how to respond to or prevent ecological disasters.

The late nineteenth and early twentieth centuries are often referred to as the **conservation era**; environmentalism in that time tended to reflect Thoreau's preservation argument. In this time, state and national parks, such as Yosemite (1864), Yellowstone (1872), and the Grand Canyon

John Muir An early conservationist, Muir led the movement to establish national parks like Yosemite.

(1906), were established through legislative protection and funding. Congress approved the creation of the National Park Service in 1916 and continued to pass environmental laws to protect the wilderness and to regulate industries that impinged on it, such as mining and logging. Early environmental groups such as the Audubon Society (1886) and the Sierra Club (1892) that emphasized the conservation of wildlife and nature were also established around that time and are still in existence today.

From the mid-twentieth century on, environmentalism changed in response to several ecological disasters. For example, in 1948, in the town of Donora, Pennsylvania, twenty people died and more than 7,000 others were hospitalized when industrial waste that formed concentrated smog was released into the atmosphere and settled over the town, severely compromising the air quality for its residents. Congress responded to that ecological disaster (albeit late) by passing some of the first environmental legislation of the modern era, the Air Pollution Control Act of 1955.

The second era, the **modern environmental movement**, began in the 1960s in part as a response to Rachel Carson's landmark book *Silent Spring* (1962). Her book was an impassioned critique of the effects of pesticide use, specifically dichloro-diphenyl-trichloroethane, commonly known as DDT. The 1950s had witnessed an explosion of development in new chemicals such as fertilizers and pesticides, often hailed as revolutionary and miraculous in the practice of agriculture. But these same chemicals harmed or killed beneficial organisms and wildlife such as songbirds (hence the title of the book). There was even speculation that they could work their way up the food chain, becoming carcinogens in humans. Although the companies manufacturing DDT and other chemicals vigorously fought such allegations, public outcry eventually led to government hearings and an EPA ban on DDT in the United States and other countries (Bailey 2002).

While there has been considerable debate about the validity of the science behind the DDT scare, it drew unprecedented public attention to environmental issues that had never been addressed before. As former vice president Al Gore explained in the foreword to the twenty-fifth anniversary edition of the book, *Silent Spring* "brought environmental issues to the attention not just of industry and government; it brought them to the public, and put our democracy itself on the side of saving the Earth." As awareness about environmental issues grew, so

ENVIRONMENTAL MOVEMENT a social movement organized around concerns about the relationship between humans and the environment

CONSERVATION ERA earliest stage of the environmental movement, which focused on the preservation of "wilderness" areas

MODERN ENVIRONMENTAL MOVEMENT beginning in the 1960s, the second major stage of the environmental movement; focused on the environmental consequences of new technologies, oil exploration, chemical production, and nuclear power plants did the amount of environmental legislation. As a result, environmentalism was able to find credibility in American society, and its practice has become an enduring force in public policy.

Unfortunately, many other ecological disasters occurred in the decades that followed. Some of the most notable were the oil spill in Santa Barbara in 1969 (Molotch 1970) and the *Exxon Valdez* spill off the coast of Alaska in 1989; the discovery of toxic waste in the Love Canal in 1978; the nuclear accident at Three Mile Island in 1979 and the catastrophic nuclear meltdown at Fukushima, Japan, in the wake of the 2011 Sendai earthquake and tsunami; the discovery of a thirty-year oil spill at the Guadalupe Dunes in California in 1994 (Beamish 2002); and an even larger oil spill in the Gulf of Mexico in 2010. Each of these events elicited public outrage. Through a series of amendments and executive orders, the EPA was given broader powers that included the means to investigate ecological crises, organize cleanups, punish offenders, establish further regulations, and research environmentally friendly technologies.

The third era of the environmental movement, referred to as **mainstream environmentalism**, began in the 1980s. It emerged, in part, as a response to the Reagan administration's antienvironmental deregulation policies. National and international environmental organizations, such as the Sierra Club and Greenpeace as well as other watchdog groups, were becoming increasingly institutionalized. They began using well-crafted promotional campaigns and sophisticated political tactics to gain the attention of legislators and secure victories in their ongoing battles. Mainstream environmentalism evolved into a cluster of public interest groups, many of which had their own political action committees, or PACs, to lobby for positive legislative change. In addition to legal expertise, they developed economic and scientific expertise to support research, generate grants, and acquire land for preservation.

A link between the modern era and the mainstream era of environmentalism is **Earth Day**. The original event was conceived of by environmental activist and then senator Gaylord Nelson as both a "teach-in" and a protest gathering to express concerns about environmental issues. In the first Earth Day, celebrated on March 22, 1970, 20 million people participated. Earth Day is still celebrated nationally and internationally. Typically, it includes a variety of groups—environmentally friendly businesses, nonprofit organizations, local government agencies, and others—teaching people about ways to help the environment while celebrating their relationship to it.

A fourth era of the environmental movement, representing grassroots efforts, emerged after criticism that although mainstream environmental organizations were serving important functions in the overall effort, they were too accommodating to industry and government.

Nuclear Disaster Evacuees from Fukushima, Japan receive radiation scans. This nuclear plant suffered severe damage from an earthquake-generated tsunami in 2011.

Grassroots environmentalism is distinguished from mainstream environmentalism by its belief in citizen participation in environmental decision making. Its focus is often regional or local, and it can include both urban and rural areas. Grassroots groups are often less formally organized than their mainstream counterparts, and, in some instances, this frees members from ineffective bureaucratic structures as they fight for issues of great importance to them. Grassroots environmentalism draws on a variety of ideologies, including feminist, native, and spiritual ecologies, and cuts across ethnic, racial, and class lines.

NIMBY, which stands for "Not In My Back Yard," was originally a derogatory term applied to those who complained about any kind of undesirable activity in their neighborhoods that would threaten their own health or local environment but were not concerned if it happened to people somewhere else. Now the term "NIMBY" has been appropriated by the environmental movement for the people "somewhere else" who are fighting against environmental degradation on their home turf, often without significant resources, to protect their families and surrounding communities. Sometimes it makes sense to wage battles at the local level where the problems are readily apparent and the approaches to solving them more tangible. And, of course, if people everywhere were willing to fight in this way, then anti-environmental corporations would have to change their practices or be forced out of all possible locations.

Another expression of grassroots environmentalism is the **Green Party**. Established in 1984, the basic Green Party platform of ten principles includes a commitment to environmentalism, social justice, decentralization, community-based economics, feminism, and diversity. The environmental goal is a sustainable world in which nature and human society coexist in harmony. The Green Party seeks to be an alternative voice in political and policy debates that often challenges the mainstream Republican and Democratic parties and rejects corporate backing. Members would like to see the political process returned to the people. Candidates from the Green Party have been elected to various political seats at the local and state levels, and Ralph Nader, a long-time consumer protection advocate, was its candidate in the presidential election of 2000, garnering enough votes to have perhaps changed the outcome of that election.

Ecoterrorism is an example of radical grassroots environmentalism. Ecoterrorists (or ecoextremists) use violent and often criminal methods to achieve their goals of protecting the environment. These groups operate underground, without centralized organization or known membership. Law enforcement officials call ecoterrorist tactics—including arson, explosives, vandalism, theft, sabotage, and harassment—"direct action" campaigns to disrupt or destroy businesses and organizations the groups believe are a threat to the environment. They have so far avoided targeting people, though there may be victims in the course of ecoterrorist operations. FBI counter-terrorism agents recently told a Senate committee that radical environmental and animal rights activists represented the nation's top domestic terrorist threat (Heilprin 2005).

It is unclear how many ecoterrorist groups currently exist in the United States, Canada, England, and elsewhere. One visible group calls itself the Earth Liberation Front, or ELF, and claims to have originated in 1977 near Santa Cruz, California. Although it disavows any connection to illegal activity, the ELF acknowledges that some individuals have used its name to claim responsibility for their actions. The ELF says that those individuals have acted on their own without ELF's direction or endorsement.

NIMBY short for "Not In My Back Yard"; originally referred to protests that aimed at shifting undesirable activities onto those with less power; now sometimes used without negative connotations to describe local environmental activists

GREEN PARTY a U.S. political party established in 1984 to bring political attention to environmentalism, social justice, diversity, and related principles

ECOTERRORISM use of violence or criminal methods to protect the environment, often in high-profile, publicity-generating ways

Ecoterrorism To protest logging, wild horse roundups, genetic engineering of plants, SUV sales, and the expansion of the Rocky Mountain resort town of Vail, Colorado, ecoterrorists firebombed this mountain lodge restaurant and other buildings in the Northwest.

Targets are often chosen for their symbolic nature and have included logging operations, sport utility vehicle dealerships, recreational resorts, and new home and condominium developments.

The **environmental justice** (or "ecojustice") movement represents a significant branch of the environmental movement and is also an example of grassroots organization. It emerged as a response to environmental inequities, threats to public health, and the differential enforcement and treatment of certain communities with regard to ecological concerns. Despite significant improvements in environmental protections, millions of people in the United States live in communities threatened by ecological hazards. The poor and minorities are disproportionately at risk and bear a greater portion of the nation's environmental problems. The term **environmental racism** is applied when an environmental policy or practice negatively affects individuals, groups, or communities based on race or color (Bullard 1993). Access to environmental equality, or living in a healthy environment, has been framed as a basic human right.

Research on environmental justice is one of the fastest growing areas of scholarship within environmental sociology. Sociologist Robert Bullard is among the leading researchers in this area, linking social justice to environmental movements. His book *Dumping in Dixie: Race, Class, and Environmental Quality* (Bullard 1990) examined the economic, social, and psychological impacts associated with locating noxious facilities (such as landfills, hazardous-waste dumps, and lead smelters) within lower-income African American communities where they have been less likely to meet with significant opposition.

Blacks have historically been underrepresented in the environmental movement. Often, they were already engaged in other civil rights causes that seemed more pressing. They also lacked the experience and money to fight large corporations, and many had little hope of change, even though they strongly opposed environmental destruction, especially the kinds found in their communities. However, some groups have been moved to action.

Bullard looked at five black communities in the South that challenged public policies and industrial practices threatening their neighborhoods. After years of environmental prob-lems, these activists began to demand environmental justice and equal protection. They grew increasingly incensed at the industries and the government regulatory agencies that allowed those industries to violate codes and continue polluting. The industries, though heavy polluters, had often gained favor in the communities by promising a better tax base and much-needed jobs. Real environmental justice, however, would mean that communities could enjoy jobs and economic development but not at the expense of their health and the environment. That is just what they achieved.

Work by Bullard and others in the field of environmental justice has had profound impacts not only on academia but also on public policy, industry practices, and community organizations. Environmental justice groups are beginning to sway administrative decisions and have won several important court victories (Bullard and Wright 1990; Kaczor 1996; Bullard, Johnson, and Wright 1997). The EPA was even convinced to create an Office on Environmental Equity. There is still much work to be done in this area. Some of the most important battles in the environmental justice movement will be fought beyond the U.S. borders, in other countries suffering from similar and even worse environmental problems.

SUSTAINABLE DEVELOPMENT The study of **sustainable development** is among the most recent areas of environmental sociology, having emerged in the 1990s, and it continues to generate some controversy (McMichael 1996). The idea of sustainable development was popularized in a United Nations World Commission on Environment and Development report entitled "Our Common Future," often referred to as the Brundtland Report (1987). Sustainable development is a broad concept that tries to reconcile global economic development with environmental protection; it is based on the premise that the development aspirations of all countries cannot be met by following the path already taken by industrialized nations because the world's ecosystems cannot support it. Yet, since improving the conditions of the world's poor is an international goal, we must find ways to promote economic growth that both respect social justice and protect the environment, not only in the present but for future generations (Humphrey, Lewis, and Buttel 2002; Agyeman, Bullard, and Evans 2003).

One way to grasp the magnitude of supporting humans on the planet is the **ecological footprint**, an estimation of how much land and water area is required to produce all the goods we consume and to assimilate all the wastes we generate. The current ecological footprint of the average American, approximately thirty acres, represents about three times her fair share of the Earth's resources (Wackernagel and Rees 1996). Compare that to someone from the United Kingdom, whose ecological footprint is approximately fifteen acres, or someone from Burundi with a little over one acre (People and the Planet 2002). Modern industrialized countries are appropriating the carrying capacity of "land vastly larger

ENVIRONMENTAL JUSTICE
a movement that aims to remedy environmental inequities such as threats to public health and the unequal treatment of certain communities with regard to ecological concerns

ENVIRONMENTAL RACISM
any environmental policy or practice that negatively affects individuals, groups, or communities because of their race or ethnicity

SUSTAINABLE DEVELOPMENT economic development that aims to reconcile global economic growth with environmental protection

ECOLOGICAL FOOTPRINT an estimation of the land and water area required to produce all the goods an individual consumes and to assimilate all the wastes she generates than the areas they physically occupy" (Rees and Wackernagel 1994). Projections are that we would need four additional planet Earths to support the world's population if everyone else were to adopt the consumption habits of Americans. (You can measure your own ecological footprint by going to the Earth Day web site.)

Working toward sustainable development is a challenge. We have to find ways to meet the needs of a growing world population—for food, shelter, health care, education, and employment—while ensuring that we sustain nature and the environment, whether that is fresh water, clean air, natural resources, nontoxic communities, or the protection of wildlife. Often, these goals are posed as adversaries. It is even more important to work toward sustainable development as we become increasingly globalized and have to think about the rest of the world and far into the future (Holdren, Daily, and Ehrlich 1995).

Some solutions toward sustainable development are already being implemented. These include lifestyle modifications—engaging in voluntary simplicity, recycling, vegetarianism and veganism, buying organic foods, and using goods or services from environmentally friendly and fair trade companies. Others are modifications to our infrastructure, such as green building, ecological design, xeriscape (water-conserving) gardening, and land conservation. Technological changes can be made in the way we use energy—from hybrid or biodiesel cars to solar power. Some state and local governments are enforcing higher environmental standards and regulations than those imposed at the federal level. In 2005, more than 160 U.S. mayors signed on to an urban anti-global warming agreement that some call the "municipal Kyoto" in reference to the Kyoto Protocol, an international treaty on global climate change that the United States has declined to ratify (Caplan 2005). All these efforts help move us toward sustainable development, but much more must be done if we are to create that vision for the future.

CLOSING COMMENTS

In this chapter, we have crossed a huge terrain—from population through urbanization to the environment. We hope that you can now see the connection among these three seemingly disparate areas of study. Human population has grown throughout history, particularly in the past 200 years. The rate at which the population increases is influenced by both biological and social factors. Where all these people live has also changed over time. As more of them locate in cities, cities play a key role in how we inhabit the world and what kind of world that becomes. The billions of people inhabiting the planet are part of an ecosystem, and they continue to have an impact on it. The natural environment both affects and is affected by human activity. So population, urbanization, and the environment are intimately related. There is a mutual effect and interdependence between them, where trends and changes in one reverberate through the others. As residents of planet Earth, we all take part in the dynamic, both enjoying or suffering current realities and creating future ones.

Everything You Need to Know about
Populations, Cities, and Environments

"Environment is a key factor in people's lives. Environment is influenced by several sociological factors, including demographics."

THEORIES OF POPULATIONS, CITIES, AND ENVIRONMENTS

* **Structural functionalism:** the natural world exists in order to keep the social world running smoothly

* **Conflict theory:** not all groups or individuals benefit equally from society's use of the natural environment

* **Symbolic interactionism:** the meanings assigned to the natural environment will determine how society uses it

REVIEW

1. How many children would you like to have? The demographic predictions of the Neo-Malthusians and the Anti-Malthusians disagree sharply. According to the Anti-Malthusians, what changes in social structure might make people less interested in having lots of children?

2. This chapter described Americans as "pigs of the planet," in reference to the way we consume resources. Make a list of all the ways you use water other than for drinking. Do you believe that the planet can continue to support the kind of consumption in the American standard of living? What do you think will happen when growing populations in developing nations want to live like Americans?

3. Do you prefer to live in a dense urban area or a more lightly populated suburban one? What are the advantages and disadvantages of each? What sorts of social and/or environmental problems are created by the situation you prefer?

Estimated World Population

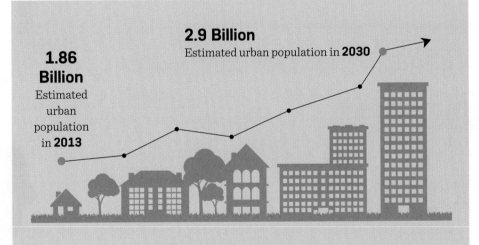

7.1 Billion
Estimated world population in **2013**

8.3 Billion
Estimated world population in **2030**

1.86 Billion
Estimated urban population in **2013**

2.9 Billion
Estimated urban population in **2030**

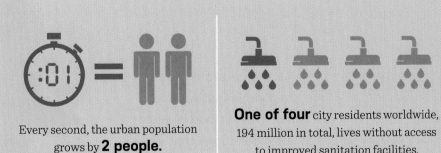

Every second, the urban population grows by **2 people.**

One of four city residents worldwide, 194 million in total, lives without access to improved sanitation facilities.

SOURCE: UN-Water 2013

EXPLORE

Social Movements and the Environment

Today it seems like environmental concerns are finally coming to a head: debates are roiling over climate change, overpopulation, the growing energy demands of China and India, and hydraulic fracturing. However, another big energy crisis occurred in 1973: OPEC embargoed oil to the United States. Individuals and businesses started practicing conservation . . . at least until the 1980s, when environmentalism seemed bad for business. Visit the Everyday Sociology blog to read more about environmentalism in the late twentieth century, and what issues are relevant for today.

http://wwnPag.es/trw415

CHAPTER 16

Social Change: Looking Toward Tomorrow

If you haven't seen one already, ask your parents (or maybe one of your professors) to show you the scar from their smallpox vaccination. It's a dime-sized circle that was made with multiple pricks of a tiny fork-like needle that held one drop of vaccine, and it would now be almost invisible as it sits at the top of their left arm. This little scar shows that your parents and professors were protected from a disease that has killed billions of people and left billions more blind and disfigured, for which there is no effective treatment. Yet, if you check your own arm, you will see that you do *not* have a similar scar; you are not protected from smallpox. Why not?

Smallpox is one of the diseases that have been effectively eliminated by the advances of medical technology. Scientific discoveries during the eighteenth and nineteenth centuries meant that by the middle of the twentieth century, a global campaign to stamp out the disease was well under way. The last natural case of smallpox in the world occurred in Somalia in 1977, and a lab accident killed a British researcher in 1978. But since then, no one has contracted the disease. The World Health Organization (WHO) declared smallpox officially eradicated in 1979, and vaccinations were discontinued worldwide by 1986.

Does the WHO declaration mean that the smallpox virus no longer exists? No. Two high-security research labs, one in the United States and one in Russia, hold samples of the virus, and another lab in the Netherlands houses the seed virus used to produce the vaccine. Why keep samples of a vanquished virus? If it ever reappears, if even the smallest amount somehow escapes laboratory quarantine, an epidemic is almost certain: smallpox is transmitted through face-to-face contact before individuals even know they are infected, and it can also be spread through building ventilation systems. It will thus be critical for us to have stores of the virus ready so that more vaccines can be made. The fact that large portions of the world's population—including you—are unprotected makes us vulnerable to the use of smallpox as a biological weapon. In the wake of the terrorist attacks of 9/11, U.S. health officials began considering reinstituting mass vaccination programs, although at this date, they have not yet done so.

The story of smallpox is a story of social change—change in the incidence, experience, and meaning of smallpox over time. The disease was a ubiquitous killer for thousands of years, up to the 1940s; in some cultures, families waited to name babies until after the babies had contracted and survived smallpox. It killed peasants and royalty alike, but through deliberate human effort a defense against the disease was eventually developed. Medicine, politics, culture, demography, individual and collective actions—smallpox was conquered through the synergy of all these elements. In the late 1700s, for example, English physician Edward Jenner observed a pattern of smallpox immunity in milkmaids who had previously contracted the less virulent cowpox, and he developed the first vaccine. Beginning in the 1950s, the WHO sought political and financial support for a worldwide vaccination campaign. Your grandparents obeyed the law and took your parents to be vaccinated when they were children. All of these processes contributed to change in the meaning and incidence of smallpox. And the meaning may change yet again as a result of the actions of another group: international terrorists. So perhaps no disease can ever truly be eradicated—ironically, it is our lingering fear of smallpox that means we must keep it with us in some form.

HOW TO READ THIS CHAPTER

There are a couple of reasons why we are ending this book with a chapter on social change. The first is that, to paraphrase an old cliché, change is the only constant. It is happening everywhere, all the time, in myriad variations. One of your challenges after reading this chapter will be to identify some of these social changes and to understand their patterns, causes, and consequences.

The other reason is more personal: we hope that reading this chapter will motivate you to work for social change yourself. The study of sociology can sometimes be a bit disheartening, as we learn the many ways in which our lives are constrained by social forces and institutional structures. But this chapter helps us remember that C. Wright Mills's "intersection of biography and history" is a two-way street: while society shapes the individual, the individual can shape society. You have the power to bring about social change, especially when you work together with others who share your views, values, and visions for a better world. So we want you to read this chapter with optimism; by understanding the processes of social change, you will be better qualified to make it happen yourself.

What Is Social Change?

No doubt you've heard your parents, grandparents, or other older family members reflect on "the way things were" when they were children. Hard-to-imagine times such as those before indoor plumbing or television, or during the Great Depression or World War II, undeniably made their lives very different from your own. People born even one generation apart can have different overall life experiences as a result of ongoing processes of social change. Consider how different life might be for American children growing up in the immediate aftermath of the tragedies of September 11, 2001, or for those who have never known a time without cell phones and the internet. Our culture evolves over time, as do our social institutions—the family, work, religion, education, and political systems. Sociologists define the transformation of culture over time as **social change**.

It's easy to identify particular historical periods where major social transformation was unmistakable: the Renaissance, the French Revolution, the Civil War, the women's rights movement. But it's important to realize that social change is occurring at all times, not just at moments of obvious cultural or political upheaval. The rate at which it happens, however, varies over time, with some historical periods experiencing rapid social change and others experiencing more gradual change. For example, social scientists recognize several major "social revolutions"—periods of time during which large-scale social change took place so rapidly that the whole of human society was dramatically redefined. The Agricultural Revolution made it possible for previously nomadic peoples to settle in one place, store surplus food for future use, and sustain larger populations with the products of their farms, herds, and flocks. The Industrial Revolution altered the way people worked, produced, and consumed goods and lived together in cities. And the Information Revolution (which is ongoing) has launched us into cyberspace thanks to digital technology and the internet, and again society is being transformed because of it (Castells 2000).

In addition to the pace, other elements of social change vary as well. Some changes are deliberate or intended, while others are unplanned or unintentional. For example, the invention of the automobile brought about intended changes—like the ability to travel greater distances more efficiently—yet it also brought about unforeseen events, such as the pollution of the atmosphere and the deaths of more than 30,000 people every year in car accidents. Some social changes are more controversial than others—the racial integration of public schools, for example, versus salsa's overtaking ketchup as America's top condiment—and some are more important than others. Most fashion trends have little lasting impact—remember the fingerless lace gloves of the 1980s? We thought not. But some—like pants for women, miniskirts, and the bikini—are extremely influential in their impact on gender roles in society.

So society is always changing, and the rates, intentionality, controversy, and importance of individual changes vary. But how does social change occur? One way is through a major physical event: tornadoes, hurricanes, earthquakes, tsunamis, and volcanic eruptions can radically alter the structures and cultures of the communities they strike. Demographic factors also come into play; for instance, as the baby boomers have aged, American society has had to build schools and colleges (in the 1950s and 60s), suburbs (in the 1960s, 70s, and 80s), and retirement facilities (in the 2000s) to accommodate this huge population bulge. Another source of social change lies in discoveries and innovations, such as fire or the wheel. Try to imagine what your life would be like if humans had not figured out how to generate light and heat by striking sparks into kindling.

Social change is often the result of such human action. Jonas Salk, for example, developed a cure for polio, and Helen Keller overcame her own handicaps to advocate for the rights of the disabled. But our most important contributions to social change are made through collective action: the Civil Rights Movement led by Martin Luther King Jr., for example, fundamentally reshaped American society. For this reason, we will spend a good portion of this chapter examining collective behavior in its many variations.

SOCIAL CHANGE the transformation of a culture over time

What Are the Sources of Social Change? Disasters such as the wildfires that swept across Australia in 2009 can radically change the structures and cultures of the communities they destroy.

Collective Behavior

When we join a group, we don't disappear as individuals. But we do tend to act differently in groups than we might alone. **Collective behavior** occurs when individuals converge, thus creating a group or crowd, who join in some sort of shared action. Crowds may form for different reasons, and people may gather for different purposes, but there is a common pattern to their behavior. While crowds may seem disorderly from the outside, collective behavior theories suggest that such occurrences are often organized and do maintain a certain amount of order.

One of the earliest theories to focus on collective behavior was **contagion theory** (Le Bon 1896). Contagion theory suggested that when people come together, they get swept up in a crowd which develops a "mob mentality." Contagion theorists likened such groups to herds of animals, where individuality and rational thought disappear and the external stimulus of the collective action takes over. So, in the case of rampaging soccer hooligans, contagion theory would argue that these fans have given their rational thought over to a mob impulse and can no longer make independent decisions about their actions. But while the theory may seem useful when looking at cases like hooliganism, it doesn't fully explain the wide range of collective behavior beyond the mindless mob.

A more recent idea gives us a better understanding. **Emergent norm theory** (Turner and Killian 1987) argues that collective behavior is not as uniform as Le Bon suggests, and that there are any number of factors that motivate people to participate in crowd activities. The underlying assumption here is that a group is guided by norms (shared cultural expectations for behavior) that emerge in response to a situation, and, as a result, the behavior of those in the crowd is structured to fit within the collective action. So while it may appear that a crowd is one large, indistinguishable mass, the individuals who make it up can have varying understandings of what their roles are within the crowd as well as the meaning of their actions.

Collective behavior generally takes three different forms: crowd behavior, mass behavior, and social movements. While these three types are discussed separately here, they are not mutually exclusive. In the real world, they may overlap whenever collective behavior actually occurs.

Crowd Behavior

A **crowd** is formed when a large number of people come together, either on purpose or randomly. If you have ever strolled around a large city, you may have noticed a street performer (such as a mime or break dancer) trying to entertain people as they walk by. In time, a crowd starts to develop. So despite the fact that those who are stopping to watch had different reasons to be walking down that street at that particular time, they have now become part of a crowd whose purpose is to be an audience for a street performer. As a crowd, they must adjust their behavior somewhat: perhaps they put away their cell phones so as not to disturb the performer or those around them, and they clap at the end of the performance. Even with this conformity of behavior, however, the fact

COLLECTIVE BEHAVIOR behavior that follows from the formation of a group or crowd of people who take action together toward a shared goal

CONTAGION THEORY one of the earliest theories of collective action; suggested that individuals who joined a crowd could become "infected" by a mob mentality and lose the ability to reason

EMERGENT NORM THEORY a theory of collective behavior that assumes individual members of a crowd make their own decisions about behavior and that norms are created through others' acceptance or rejection of these behaviors remains that the individual motivation for joining the onlookers may vary. One person may have stopped because he was struck by the performer's talent, another because her feet hurt from walking. At a certain point, others may pause simply because they see the existing crowd and are curious.

While the street performer type of crowd comes about in a somewhat random way and doesn't yield any demonstrative action, other types of crowds form in a more deliberate manner and lead to highly expressive action. Two examples took place in 1999: a concert in Woodstock, New York, and protests at the World Trade Organization (WTO) meeting in Seattle.

"Woodstock 1999" was the second rock concert (a previous one occurred in 1994) that attempted to emulate the success of the original Woodstock concert of 1969. Around 200,000 attended the three-day event. Like its 1969 predecessor, Woodstock 1999 was supposed to be both a culture-shaping event and financial success; however, it failed on both counts because of poor security, high prices ($150 for a ticket and $4 for a bottle of water), and lack of sanitation. With such tenuous conditions, the crowd began to vent their frustration on the evening of the last day by tearing down and burning fences, breaking into ATM machines, and looting vendor booths and setting them afire. Such action was characterized as a **riot**: a group of people engaged in disorderly behavior directed toward other people and/or property that results in disturbing the peace.

The Seattle protests led to riots on a larger scale. While protests against the WTO are part of an ongoing and larger social movement against current forms of globalization, much attention has been paid to the 1999 meeting in Seattle, where crowds numbering 50,000 to 100,000 gathered to protest. Protesters came from all over the world and included human rights groups, students, environmental groups, religious leaders, and labor rights activists, all seeking fairer trade with less exploitation. While the majority were peaceful, a small group became violent and began looting, leading the Seattle police and National Guard to declare a state of emergency. This was followed by the issuing of curfews, arresting, tear-gassing, pepper spraying, and even shooting rubber bullets at nonviolent protesters. The riots that ensued were an incredibly significant moment in the history of popular protests. People from diverse constituencies that represented a wide range of interests had succeeded in coming together and disrupting the meetings of the world's most influential trade-governing bodies.

CROWD a temporary gathering of individuals, whether spontaneous or planned, who share a common focus

RIOT continuous disorderly behavior by a group of people that disturbs the peace and is directed toward other people and/or property

MASS BEHAVIOR large groups of people engaging in similar behaviors without necessarily being in the same place

Both Woodstock 1999 and the Seattle WTO protests demonstrate how collective behavior can develop into riots. Furthermore, we can see in these two events how collective behavior can be both organized and chaotic, depending on the shared norms that emerge (McPhail 1991).

Mass Behavior

Mass behavior occurs when large groups of people not necessarily in the same geographical location engage in similar behavior. Mass behavior can range from buying a certain type of jeans or getting a tattoo to playing FarmVille 2 on Facebook. Sociologists have focused on three areas of mass behavior in particular. Two areas, fads and fashions, should be familiar to you. The third too often goes unrecognized by those involved: social dilemmas.

"I Predict a Riot" While the majority of the people at the WTO protest in Seattle were peaceful, a small group started some violence and looting that led the Seattle police and National Guard to declare a state of emergency. They issued curfews and even shot rubber bullets and tear gas at innocent, nonviolent protesters.

FADS interests or practices followed enthusiastically for a relatively short period of time

FASHION the widespread custom or style of behavior and appearance at a particular time or in a particular place

SOCIAL DILEMMA a situation in which behavior that is rational for the individual can, when practiced by many people, lead to collective disaster

FADS AND FASHIONS Fads are interests that are followed with great enthusiasm for a period of time. They can include products (such as Razor scooters or iPods), words or phrases ("random" or "don't go there"), clothing styles (head bands or Ugg boots), activities (Wii Fit or text messaging), or even pets (purse-sized toy dogs or anything mixed with a poodle, e.g., a Labradoodle). For fads to continue for any length of time, social networks are necessary to spread the enthusiasm (Aguirre, Quarantelli, and Mendoza 1988; Jones 2009). While fads tend not to result in lasting social change, they do follow certain social norms and can create a unified identity for those who practice them (Best 2006). Dieting is a good example. Many Americans have followed such fad diets of the past as the all-grapefruit or all-white-food diet, and in recent years many joined the low-carbohydrate fad of the Atkins and South Beach diets. During their heyday in the mid-2000s, the low-carbohydrate diets in particular had an impact on food industries, with grocery stores and fast-food chains trying to cater to the needs of their customers. Now, those same low-carb products take up less shelf space, and it may be harder to find a "bunless" burger on the menu. Gluten-free products seem to be the current rage, with millions of consumers making these specialty products more and more popular. Whatever comes next, it is likely that in wealthy countries like the United States, diet fads are sure to continue.

Another type of mass behavior is **fashion**: a widespread style of behavior and appearance. Fashion can mark you as belonging to a certain group: military fatigues and school uniforms are two examples. Like fads, certain fashions (such as extremely baggy clothes for boys and miniskirts for girls) can enjoy huge popularity for a time. Celebrities can also drive fashion. The hit TV show *Mad Men* became popular not only for its interesting content and great writing and acting but also for its celebration of 1960s fashion. The men's dapper suits and the women's full skirts and cinched waists brought retro glamour back to the world of fashion. Similarly, *Gossip Girl* was as closely watched for the New York designer label clothing worn by its high school stars as for its shifting romantic relationships. The real-life stars of both shows are also closely followed in the tabloids and fashion magazines, where fans like to critique or emulate their styles, both onscreen and off.

SOCIAL DILEMMAS In the third category of mass behavior, called a **social dilemma**, behavior that is rational for an individual can lead to collective disaster. Let's take an example that's familiar to everyone: getting stuck in a traffic jam. You creep along slowly for what seems like forever and finally arrive at the source of the holdup. It's an accident, with two cars, a police car, and an ambulance pulled over to the shoulder. But the accident isn't even on your side of the freeway; it's on the other side, and there's nothing blocking your lanes of traffic. The holdup on your side is a result of everybody slowing down to get a good look. If they had just kept on driving at their normal speed, you wouldn't have had a traffic jam. So what do you do when you finally get up to the scene of the accident? You slow down and take a look too.

When many people make that same (seemingly) rational decision (to slow down for only a few seconds), the cumulative effect causes a kind of collective disaster (a traffic jam). As social beings, we deal with such situations almost daily,

Fashion The clothing styles of the 1960s, as shown here on the TV show *Mad Men*, have become popular fashion choices today.

yet rarely do we see how best to handle them. According to many social thinkers, going all the way back to philosopher Thomas Hobbes (1588–1679), we live in a world governed by self-interest. How is our self-interest balanced with the interests of the collective? Social dilemmas help us understand this calculation.

There are two classes of social dilemmas. The first is known as a **tragedy of the commons**. In 1968, Garrett Hardin wrote an essay describing why this kind of dilemma emerges in society. He begins with the classic example of the "commons," which in the past served as a pasture shared by the whole community and on which anyone could graze their livestock. Because access to the commons was free and without restriction, each individual had an incentive to put as many head of livestock on the commons as possible, thereby increasing his own personal gain. But as everyone made that same decision, the commons inevitably became overgrazed. When a common resource is used beyond its carrying capacity, it eventually collapses, becoming totally incapable of supporting any life at all. In a tragedy of the commons, therefore, the benefit is to the individual but the cost is shared by all.

The example of the commons applies to recent history as well. Our natural resources, such as water, air, fossil fuels, forests, plants, and animals, might all be considered similar to a commons. In the case of the U.S. fishing trade, especially, we have seen how, as Hardin put it, "freedom in a commons brings ruin to all" (1968). For example, Dr. Stein remembers living in Santa Barbara in the late 1970s, when local abalones were plentiful. Divers off the California coast and around the Channel Islands could make a good living harvesting these mollusks along rocky shorelines. Any good seafood restaurant regularly offered abalone steaks on its menu, and a casual beachgoer might find abalone shells strewn along the sand. By the 1990s, however, abalones had all but disappeared. As each diver reached the same conclusion—that catching as many abalones as possible would increase his own profits—and more divers moved into the same fishing territory, the abalones were no longer able to regenerate their stocks and were eventually depleted to near extinction.

In a variety of similar cases, like the lobster trappers off the New England coast, regulatory agencies have had to step in and place restrictions on the amount of yields allowed. Otherwise, a tragedy of the commons is likely to ensue. We might also consider social, as well as natural, resources as similar to a commons. For example, when too many people crowd the freeways at rush hour or throw litter out the window of their cars, the result is the commons in ruin.

So what can we do to solve these problems? If we could somehow increase the number of abalones in the sea or the number of lanes on the freeway, then that would help solve two of them, but only temporarily. At some point, use overwhelms supply. To Hardin, social dilemmas are a "class of human problems which can be classified as having 'no technical solution'"

Tragedy of the Commons Abalone divers rest after making a climb up a cliff. Since the 1990s, abalones have all but disappeared from the coast of California. As the population of the mollusks dwindled, their price increased (they can sell for $100 apiece on the black market), which led more divers to move into the same fishing areas and deplete the population to near extinction.

(1968). What he means is that science or technology alone cannot solve the problems. The solutions must come from the members of society: people will have to change their behavior.

The other class of social dilemmas is called a **public goods dilemma**, in which individuals must contribute to a collective resource they may or may not ever benefit from. Blood banks are a good example. Because human blood can't be stored for much longer than a month at a time, many people must volunteer to donate blood regularly in order to keep supplies steady. Blood donors can be viewed as helping to create what is referred to as a "public good," in this case a blood bank. What motivates these people, on average some 9.5 million a year, to contribute something vital to themselves for which they may never receive anything in return? Everyone is equally entitled to draw from the blood bank regardless of whether or not they have ever given blood. People who take advantage of a public good without having contributed to its creation are called "free riders." In a public goods dilemma, unlike a tragedy of the commons, the cost is to the individual but the benefit is shared by all.

So how do we get people to contribute to a public good if they are not required to? There are numerous examples of this social dilemma in everyday life, as you know if you've ever witnessed a membership drive on public radio or public television. These noncommercial networks must appeal to individuals to contribute money so that they can continue to produce and broadcast programs. But whether or not

TRAGEDY OF THE COMMONS
a type of social dilemma in which many individuals' overexploitation of a public resource depletes or degrades that common resource

PUBLIC GOODS DILEMMA
a type of social dilemma in which individuals incur the cost to contribute to a collective resource, though they may never benefit from that resource

anyone responds to the pledge drive, as free riders they can still tune in anytime for nothing. Public goods dilemmas are also a class of human problems for which there are no technical solutions. This is why the government requires us to make certain contributions, in the form of taxes, in order to create such public goods as roads, schools, and fire departments. But there are many other types of public goods, like blood banks, that only individuals can create through their own voluntary contributions.

By examining social dilemmas, we are presented with a dramatic example of mass behavior. We begin to see how seemingly small individual acts add up and cumulatively shape society. So the next time you are faced with a problem like where to throw your litter or whether to give blood, ask yourself what kind of collective outcome you would like your behavior to contribute to.

Social Movements

If you're like most Americans, the term **social movement** is inextricably linked in your mind to thoughts of long-haired hippies, Volkswagen buses, and the antiwar protests of the 1960s. You may not think of the Nineteenth Amendment to the U.S. Constitution, birth control, the AFL-CIO, Protestantism, the Revolutionary War, or Nazism—and yet all of these were, at the time of their inceptions, rightly termed "social movements."

SOCIAL MOVEMENT any social groups with leadership, organization, and an ideological commitment to promote or resist social change

So what precisely is a social movement? Does the term as accurately describe the efforts of liberals to elect a Democrat to Congress as it does the efforts of peace activists to end war? The answer is no. According to Perry and Pugh, "Social movements are collectives with a degree of leadership, organization, and ideological commitment to promote or resist change" (1978, p. 221); Meyer adds that social movements "challenge cultural codes and transform the lives of their participants" (2000, p. 39). A political campaign cannot usually be described as a social movement, because although it may be considered an organized collective with leadership and (sometimes) ideological commitment, and although it may indeed transform the lives of its participants, its purpose is not to fundamentally alter the status quo. Antiwar protesters, on the other hand, are usually trying not only to stop a specific violent conflict but also to change cultural support of war as an accepted means of solving disputes.

We can safely say that most of the institutions with which we are familiar began as social movements. How did they arise? Why do people join them? And how do today's radicals become tomorrow's establishment?

Several theories attempt to address these questions, but the assumptions behind them have evolved over time. For example, scholars working in the 1940s, 50s, and early 60s generally viewed social movements with suspicion—as "dysfunctional, irrational, and exceptionally dangerous" (Meyer 2000, p. 37). People who joined a movement were thought to be attracted not by its ideals but by the refuge it offered "from the anxieties, barrenness, and meaninglessness of an individual existence" (Eric Hoffer, quoted in Zirakzadeh 1997,

Table 16.1 Theory in Everyday Life

Perspective	Approach to Social Change	Case Study: The Environmental Movement
Structural Functionalism	Sometimes social change is necessary to maintain equilibrium and order in society.	Natural resources are necessary for the survival of society, so the growth of a social movement dedicated to the wise use and conservation of natural resources is functional for society.
Conflict Theory	Social change is the inevitable result of social inequality and conflict between groups over power and resources.	Environmental privileges (such as scenic natural vistas, clean water, and unpolluted air) are unequally distributed among different groups in society. The environmental movement works to secure the rights of all citizens, rich and poor, to a clean, healthy, beautiful, and sustainable world.
Symbolic Interactionism	Social change involves changes in the meanings of things as well as changes in laws, culture, and social behavior.	The environmental movement works to safeguard animal species by having them declared "endangered" or "threatened." Redefining groups of animals in this way allows for their protection through endangered species laws rather than their decimation through hunting or habitat reduction.

p. 9). This explanation, labeled by sociologists as **mass society theory**, was not so remarkable when you consider that researchers in those decades had witnessed the impacts of Nazism, Fascism, Stalinism, and McCarthyism, all of which originated as social movements that eventually devastated millions of lives (Zirakzadeh 1997).

By the 1960s, however, a sea change had occurred, and a new generation of scholars researching the hows and whys of social movements were inclined to be more sympathetic. After all, the 1960s had seen the rise and relative success of the Civil Rights Movement. While people of color may have been alienated from the larger white society, they were certainly not isolated "joiners" who took up with social movements simply to "satisfy some kind of psychological need" (Meyer 2000, p. 37). The Civil Rights Movement and others were practical political responses to inequality and oppression and provided opportunities for the oppressed to "redistribute political and economic power democratically and fairly" (Zirakzadeh 1997, p. 15). This explanation is called **relative deprivation theory** because it focuses on the actions of deprived or oppressed groups who seek rights already enjoyed by others in society—they are deprived relative to other groups.

VOTING RIGHTS A look at the history of voting rights in America shows the power of relative deprivation theory in explaining certain types of social movements. For more than a hundred years, women and persons of color lobbied hard for the right to vote. (We could also turn this claim on its head by saying that for more than a hundred years, many white men fought hard to exclude women and persons of color from voting.) Officially, African American males were granted the right to vote with the Fifteenth Amendment in 1870, but individual states effectively nullified this right by passing regulations requiring literacy tests, prohibitive poll taxes, and grandfather clauses (if your grandfather had voted, you could too) that specifically excluded them from voting. It wasn't until the 1965 Voting Rights Act was passed that African Americans (men *and* women) gained the ability to exercise their constitutionally protected freedom to vote.

The Voting Rights Act has achieved significant inroads in protecting African Americans' right to vote, in part by requiring certain states (AL, AK, AZ, GA, LA, MS, SC, TX, and VA) to seek federal approval to change voting laws. In fact, it has been so successful that the Supreme Court decided in June 2013 to strike down that requirement, even though supporters of the VRA argue that policies like redistricting, voter ID, proof of citizenship, and limited early voting discriminate against minority voters (Liptak 2013, Hurley 2013).

Women, meanwhile, had won the right to vote in 1919 with passage of the Nineteenth Amendment. To reach this point, suffragists had spent decades protesting male-only voting through parades, written propaganda, debates, sit-ins, and hunger strikes. The suffrage movement, however, was primarily a white women's battle. At a rally in 1851, Sojourner Truth gave a famous speech ("Ain't I a Woman") highlighting the exclusion of women of color from the movement. These women would have to wait until the Voting Rights Act of 1965 before they could legally vote.

But neither the Voting Rights Act nor the Nineteenth Amendment secures voting rights for all Americans. To become a registered voter, you must be a U.S. citizen (either native born or naturalized), legally reside in the state in which you vote, and have an address of some kind. Most states do not allow ex-convicts, prisoners, or those designated mentally ill to vote. There are presently social movements under way to secure this right for some of these disenfranchised Americans, such as certain categories of prisoners and people with no stable addresses.

MOBILIZING RESOURCES The kind of society we live in has a lot to do with whether or not we are likely to join social movements, the tactics those movements will use, and whether or not the movements will succeed. For example, in a country like the United States, with strong free-speech protections, anyone wanting to support same-sex marriage can publish books and articles, march in the streets (with some restrictions), promote their views through social media, or start a letter-writing campaign to pressure lawmakers. On the other hand, under a restrictive regime like that of the Taliban in Afghanistan, peaceful protest is not an option, and merely teaching a female to read has been met with suspicion and

MASS SOCIETY THEORY a theory of social movements that assumes people join not because of the movements' ideals, but to satisfy a psychological need to belong to something larger than themselves

RELATIVE DEPRIVATION THEORY a theory of social movements that focuses on the actions of oppressed groups who seek rights or opportunities already enjoyed by others in the society

Malala Yousafzai is a Pakistani student who was shot by Taliban gunmen for promoting education for girls.

hostility. In 2012, the Pakistani Taliban shot fourteen-year-old Malala Yousafzai in the head because she spoke out in favor of educating girls. She survived the attack, and was transferred to a British hospital for treatment. She has become an international symbol for women's rights and continues her activism, but from afar; it is too dangerous for her to return to her home country, where she is still wanted by the Taliban (Walsh 2013).

In addition to a tolerant society, social movements need a long list of practical and human resources without which it would be impossible to accomplish their goals. This includes volunteers, funding, office space, telephone banks, computers, internet access, copy machines, and pens and pencils—as well as the know-how to put these into action. Recruitment and fundraising will be critical to the success of a group. Funding may go to support staff or pay for overhead, but much of what is raised will be spent on producing and soliciting media coverage to get their message out. Theorists who focus on how these practical constraints help or hinder social movements operate under the assumptions of **resource mobilization theory**. However interesting or important a type of social change may be, no progress will be made unless certain practical resources are available. So if we consider the plight of women in Taliban-ruled parts of Pakistan or Afghanistan, for instance, we realize that some of the most basic human activities, such as reading and meeting together freely, are actually social movement resources that not everyone can take for granted.

have broken out in the lines and the aisles. In 2008, a woman who was eight months pregnant miscarried after being crushed by people stampeding to buy merchandise. Every year seems to bring another extreme case where someone is trampled to death by crowds rushing through the doors.

Protesting the rampant consumerism of Black Friday, a group of social activists has started promoting "Buy Nothing Day." *Adbusters*, an anticonsumerist group founded in Vancouver in 1989 by Kalle Lasn and Bill Schmalz, promotes Buy Nothing Day "as a day for society to examine the issue of overconsumption." The basic goal of Buy Nothing Day is to actually spend no money purchasing items on Black Friday in order to raise awareness of the dangers of consumerism and overconsumption. However, *Adbusters* also encourages other forms of awareness. Groups have staged protests by holding credit card cut-ups in shopping malls where protesters hold up scissors and encourage customers to liberate themselves from debt. Other protesters go on Buy Nothing Hikes to connect with nature instead of shopping. The messages about Buy Nothing Day are largely spread using posters, the internet, and e-mail.

For some, the idea of Buy Nothing Day has grown into a Buy Nothing Year. The Compact is an anticonsumerist group whose members pledge to go a year without buying anything new. Members are only allowed to purchase new underwear, food, and health and safety items, such as brake fluid and toilet paper. Otherwise, they have to make do with the items that they already have in their homes (come on: how many bottles of lotion or sunscreen are lurking in your bathroom cabinet

DATA WORKSHOP
Analyzing Everyday Life

Activist Groups and Social Change

The day after Thanksgiving is also known as "Black Friday," the biggest shopping day of the year. On that day, which is thought of by many as the kickoff day to the Christmas shopping season, retailers give incentives to customers by offering extended hours, tremendous discounts, and free gifts. Customers sleep in parking lots waiting for the stores to open, and are so eager to buy merchandise at discounted prices that injuries and even deaths have resulted. Numerous people have been knocked over and stepped on, and fights

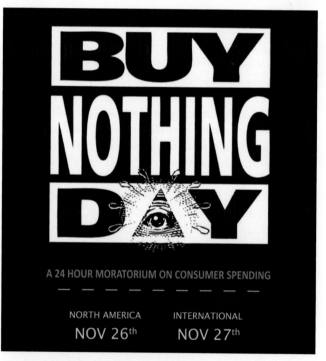

Anticonsumerism How do activist groups protest the excesses of consumerism?

right now?), buy from secondhand stores, or make their own items. Members take The Compact pledge in order to counteract the negative global environmental and socioeconomic effects of U.S. consumerist culture and to simplify their lives. Many of The Compact members blog about their experience participating in a Buy Nothing Year. While it might seem extreme to most Americans to go for an entire year without buying new items, many of the members of The Compact find multiple benefits to taking the pledge and, through their example, are able to raise other people's consciousness about consumption, waste, and carbon footprints.

This Data Workshop asks you to analyze any activist group that is working for social or political change (for more on activism and political interest groups, refer to Chapter 10). You will be using existing sources to do a content analysis of various materials developed by the organization (see Chapter 2 for a review of this research method). In particular, you will be looking at how the group uses media technology to advance its agenda. Examine the group's use of various forms of media—the so-called new media (web sites, e-mail, and texting) as well as more traditional kinds (radio, television, newspapers, magazines, and brochures).

1. Choose an activist or interest group. Identify the group's commitment to a larger social movement or cause, and discuss its larger goals.

2. Discuss the ways in which the group is attempting each of the three aspects of resource mobilization listed below. What specifically would your group like to accomplish in each category?

   a. recruiting members and organizing supporters
   b. raising funds
   c. transforming public opinion or achieving change

3. How does your group attempt to achieve each of these goals? Is it through old or new media, or some combination? Do you think they would be more successful if they found ways to use new media more often? Why or why not?

4. In addition to the use of media, does the group employ any other strategies to achieve its goals? For instance, does the group organize rallies or protests, or participate in community events? (These activities may be connected to larger media strategies; for example, a film screening or protest march might be advertised to attract greater support, or be covered by news agencies.)

You can complete this Workshop in one of two ways.

Option 1 (informal): Jot down your observations and the answers to the Workshop questions in informal notes. Use these notes as points of reference for discussion with classmates in small groups. Compare your analyses and insights with others in your group.

Option 2 (formal): Write a three- to four-page essay in which you answer the Workshop questions.

STAGES IN A SOCIAL MOVEMENT Social movements begin with a few ideas and some people who believe in them. How do they reach the point of marching in the streets (or recruiting members online)? They develop in stages, and those stages were identified by Armand Mauss (1975), who described the first one as the "incipient" stage, when the public takes notice of a situation and defines it as a problem (Perry and Pugh 1978). People do not start organizing because they are content; rather, they "see a discrepancy, either real or perceived, between what they are getting and what they believe they should be getting" and decide to take action (Perry and Pugh 1978, p. 237).

For example, in the late nineteenth and early twentieth centuries, many laborers were frustrated over their long working hours, low wages, lack of free weekends, and unsafe working conditions. In response, they began to organize—or, in Mauss's words, to "coalesce," which is the second stage—and their movement gained momentum. Laborers, long an exploited segment of the workforce, drew on both traditionally accepted means of dissent, such as pushing for legislation that would improve working conditions, and tactics that were (at the time) "at the edges of political legitimacy," such as striking (Meyer 2000, p. 40).

Today, working conditions have greatly improved for many (though by no means all) blue collar workers, and unions, once considered marginal or radical, are now seen as part of the establishment. Mauss and others would argue that all successful social movements are eventually incorporated into institutions—that they become "bureaucratized" (stage three). Perry and Pugh assert that "in order to survive, social movements must adapt to their host society or succeed in changing it. When they are successful, they become social institutions in their own right" (1978, p. 265). To take another example, early American colonists rebelling against British rule were part of a social movement, but by the late 1700s, they had ceased to be radicals and had become part of the new nation's government themselves.

A social movement's development can sometimes look a lot like failure; that is, one way or another, the movement will eventually "decline" (stage four). If it succeeds, it is incorporated into the dominant culture; if it fails, it ceases to exist as an active movement—but may have left an indelible mark on its host society nevertheless. Prohibitionists are an excellent case in point. Although those who wished to outlaw alcohol in the United States eventually failed, after the Eighteenth Amendment (Prohibition) was repealed in 1933,

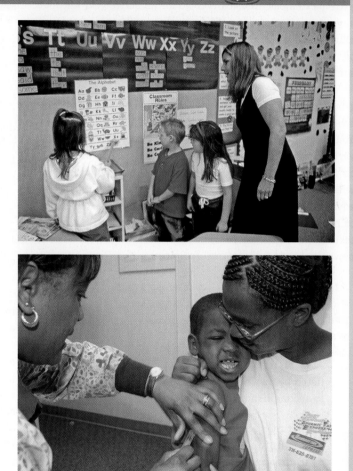

Does it sometimes seem as though there's no possible way you could ever make a contribution to changing the world? You're just one person, after all, and you may not be rich, famous, or all that influential. Right now, your primary concerns probably include graduating and perhaps getting your teaching credential (or social work certification or nursing license) so you can get a job! Also on the "to do" list: find a life partner, start a family, maybe buy a house. But don't think that focusing on your personal goals means that you're totally out of the social change loop. The way you live your life can make a difference all by itself.

Many sociology majors enter what are termed helping professions—these include nursing, counseling, and teaching, and can also include careers in the social service, nonprofit, and law enforcement sectors. If you do go into this type of profession, you will find that every individual encounter you have with a client, student, patient, or offender will be an opportunity to make a tiny step toward social change.

As a first-grade teacher, for example, you will be able to introduce students to the joys of reading—a contribution to overcoming illiteracy, even if it involves only twenty kids. As a public health nurse, you urge patients with tuberculosis to finish their courses of antibiotics or you vaccinate children against polio, diphtheria, and measles—and in doing so, you protect the community's health as well as your patients'. When, as a social worker or psychologist, you lead a therapy group for husbands who batter their wives, you have the opportunity to help change the behavior of these men—and to protect their children from continuing a generational cycle of violence. When, as a police officer, you help run your neighborhood's antigang program, you give teenagers alternatives to violent crime, and their choices affect the entire community. When, as a lawyer, you donate your services to a legal clinic that helps undocumented workers gain residency, work permits, and citizenship, you contribute to solving the problems associated with illegal immigration and help change the demographic makeup of your city, state, and country. And even when you volunteer at the adult education center, teaching a computer-training class just once a week, you give your students the opportunity to add a new set of

Teaching and Nursing Are among the Helping Professions

skills to their résumés, find new jobs, and reduce your county's unemployment figures, even if minutely.

Your contributions to social change don't stop here—whom you marry, where you choose to live, and what you teach your children all contribute to the ever-present, ongoing processes of social change. So you don't have to sail away on Greenpeace's *Rainbow Warrior* to make a difference in the world—you can do so in your everyday life as a member of a helping profession, as a community volunteer, and as a parent.

their efforts had a huge impact on American culture. There are still "dry" municipalities (where alcohol is not sold) in the country, for example, and a number of infamous gangsters like Al Capone got their start smuggling booze during Prohibition.

WHO TAKES PART What kind of individual is most likely to respond to the recruitment efforts of a particular group? Certainly, more people are asked to join a social movement than ever actually end up participating. Studies done on student protesters in the 1960s showed that they "were more likely than their less active colleagues to be politically oriented, socially engaged, and psychologically well adapted" and that "participation in non-conventional politics tend[ed] to be an addition rather than an alternative to conventional means of participation" (Meyer 2000, pp. 37, 42). In other words, despite the assumptions of theorists working in the mid-twentieth century, activists are not disaffected loners but are instead highly engaged individuals seeking to address perceived injustices on several fronts.

Interestingly, the poorest and most oppressed people tend not to participate in social movements. For these individuals, the consequences of participation may be too high, and they may not have the resources necessary to join in (Perry and Pugh 1978; Zirakzadeh 1997). After all, if someone is working three jobs to support her family, it is unlikely that she would have the time or energy to carry a sign in a street protest. There have been notable exceptions to this trend. In the American West during the 1960s and 70s, migrant farm workers organized successfully under the leadership of Cesar Chavez. In the 1980s and 90s, thousands of low-income janitors across the United States gained fairer wages and benefits by organizing unions as part of a Justice for Janitors campaign. And more recently, low-wage workers in New York City (in industries such as retail, fast-food, airport, and car washing) have continued to demand fair wages and the right to unionize (Lewis 2013).

It is perhaps impossible to overstate the importance of social movements in any given society; life as we know it has been shaped by the rise and fall of all sorts of such movements. Imagine what the religious makeup of the world would be like if Martin Luther and his Protestants had not rebelled against the Catholic Church in the early sixteenth century, or what American culture would be like if Martin Luther King Jr. and the Civil Rights Movement hadn't successfully organized. What would world politics have been like if the Nazis hadn't come to power in the 1930s or the Soviet Union hadn't broken up in 1991? The list is endless. Take a moment to consider a few ideas and movements that in today's culture seem radical. Whether or not those movements succeed in the traditional sense of the word, it is a pretty safe bet that they will help shape the world for generations to come. And while the progress made by any social movement tends to happen slowly, the possibility for change and a better society for those future generations is the driving force for those who participate.

Emergent Social Movements: Promoting and Resisting Change

Because society is constantly changing, new social movements are always on the horizon, and even long-standing ones change their goals, strategies, and organizational forms over time. For example, American feminism has taken multiple forms during the past 150 years. Contrast the focus in the early twentieth century on voting rights for women with the 1960s' broader concerns with equal opportunity and "liberation" from the constraints of sexism, and then with the 1990s' crusade to include previously excluded groups like minority women (see Chapter 9 for a review of the different "waves" of feminist activism). Feminism's self-definition, public profile, objectives, and tactics have changed in response to the movement's own successes and failures.

You may be involved yourself in social movements that didn't even exist in your grandparents' or parents' generation (or even ten years ago). Movements like Critical Mass (cyclists who ride through city streets in large groups each month to protest an automobile-centric society), Straight Edge (nonviolent, drug-free, politically aware, and sometimes even vegan punk rockers who reject promiscuous youth cultures), and PETA (People for the Ethical Treatment of Animals, which campaigns against meat, leather and furs, animal experimentation, and other forms of cruelty) have taken shape since you were born. You have different

Arab Spring In 2011, Egyptians gathered to overthrow the regime of President Hosni Mubarak. Protests and demonstrations continued throughout the Arab world, often coordinated through social media sites like Facebook, Twitter, and YouTube.

ACTIVISM any activity intended to bring about social change

REGRESSIVE term describing resistance to particular social changes, efforts to maintain the status quo, or attempts to reestablish an earlier form of social order

PROGRESSIVE term describing efforts to promote forward-thinking social change

TECHNOLOGICAL DETERMINISM a theory of social change that assumes changes in technology drive changes in society, rather than vice versa

opportunities for **activism** because you live in a different world than your parents did—even if you're still in the same town.

Some emerging social movements are actually **regressive**, or reactionary; that is, they explicitly resist certain social changes, working to make sure things stay the same or even move backward to earlier forms of social order. For example, reactionary hate movements like Matt Hale's World Church of the Creator, a white supremacist group in Illinois, want to stop the ethnic and religious integration of American society and live in a homogeneous, all-white society. Other regressive movements aren't necessarily motivated by prejudice or hatred of diversity. The voluntary simplicity movement urges members to downsize in all areas of their lives—consumption, time at work, hours in front of the TV or computer screen, impact on the environment—in the belief that returning to a simpler approach to life will allow them more personal freedom and will benefit society in the long run by conserving resources and reducing stress. Similarly, the Slow Food movement, founded in 1989 as a radical response to the "McDonaldization" of world cuisines, focuses on fresh, local, traditional foods, prepared with care and served in an atmosphere of calm and hospitality—the polar opposite of overprocessed, reheated burgers and fries served in a paper bag and eaten in the car.

The "rural rebound" that started in the 1990s, in which urban residents moved to nonmetropolitan areas in unprecedented numbers, is a type of demographic change that seems, on its face, to represent a regressive, back-to-basics movement as well (Johnson 1999). But a rural rebound doesn't necessarily mean that people have returned to declining rural industries, such as farming or mining. The rebound occurred at least in part because of **progressive**, or forward-thinking, social changes—new technologies that made rural living less isolating and facilitated new ways of working. The internet facilitates telecommuting from anywhere in the world, which means that high-powered stock brokers needn't live in Manhattan and work in a "pit" on Wall Street. They can move to Eagle County, Colorado, or Walworth County, Wisconsin, and enjoy cheaper real estate, less crime, and more natural beauty while still performing their jobs.

Emerging social movements, whether progressive, regressive, or some combination of both, will undoubtedly change the social landscape over time. If your activism is successful—and even if it isn't—then the social world will be a different place by the time your children are your age. What kinds of activism will they be able to engage in?

Technology and Social Change

As we have already seen, revolutionary social change is often the result of a technological development, whether that technological development is the plow, the assembly line, or the microchip. Social movements can arise as a result of technological advancements as well: labor unions multiplied in the factories of the Industrial Revolution, and today the internet can bring more people together to work for social change than ever before. As you might imagine, then, sociologists have generated theories that seek to explain the role of technology in social change (Kurzweil 1990; Pool 1997). One common characteristic of these theories is an emphasis on **technological determinism**—the idea that technology plays a defining role in shaping society. As one of the earliest proponents of this approach, William Ogburn (1964) described the process of social change as beginning with invention or discovery and proceeding when the invention is spread from one group or society to another. In the remainder of the chapter, we look at the relationship between technology and social change.

Faith in Technology: Can It Solve Social Problems?

At the beginning of this chapter, we saw how the same medical breakthrough that vanquished smallpox has now made us vulnerable to an epidemic of this virus. It seems that no social change is without its unforeseen, unintentional outcomes, some of which are positive and some of which are not.

This is often especially noticeable in the case of technological advances. We may welcome the invention of a new vaccine, the World Wide Web, in-vitro fertilization, or sport utility vehicles (SUVs) and notice only later that they bring unanticipated problems. For example, the web speeds up communication and gives us access to information, goods, services, and people we would never have been able to find otherwise. However, it has also created the opportunity for new kinds of problems: advertisers can now learn about your spending habits by infiltrating your PC with spyware; hackers use similar strategies to shut down entire networks with worms, bots, and viruses; states lose revenues to untaxed internet purchases; and travel agencies struggle to stay in business as individuals use the internet to make their own plane and hotel reservations. Similarly, in-vitro fertilization has opened up a Pandora's Box of ethical and moral questions about intervening in the natural process of conception. And SUVs, besides guzzling gasoline (a nonrenewable resource), are more likely than other cars to kill or injure people when involved in an accident.

As a society, how do we respond to technological developments that seem to solve one set of problems (such as disease, infertility, communication, and transportation) while creating new ones? Often we must play "catch-up," scrambling to fix a problem once it manifests itself, rather than being able to plan ahead and prevent it in the first place. **Cultural lag** is the term sociologists use to describe this disconnect between a changing social condition and cultural adjustment to that change. Material culture (such as the technologies discussed above) often changes faster than nonmaterial culture (like beliefs and laws), and we struggle to create new values and norms that correspond with new technologies.

DATA WORKSHOP
Analyzing Mass Media and Popular Culture

The "Unplug" Experiment

Zen sociologist Bernard McGrane (McGrane 1994; McGrane and Gunderson 2010) is noted for having designed a series of experiments that are widely used in teaching sociology students (this includes the "Doing Nothing" Data Workshop from Chapter 1). While the experiments may appear simple at first, the ideas they highlight are very sophisticated. Students are required to use "Beginner's Mind" (setting aside all their prior judgments, opinions, and even experiences) to achieve an unusual level of consciousness about a particular aspect of their everyday lives.

One of the most popular experiments is the "Un-TV Experiment." In it, students are instructed to watch TV, but not in the normal way. As McGrane explains, "I want you to watch *TV*—not a show, or a program, *just* TV" (McGrane 1994, p. 61). That's right, he asks students to watch TV while it's turned off. The point of the experiment is to get students to take a step back and become more aware of the role of technology in their lives, and how that technology affects them.

What were some of the insights and patterns that emerged when students conducted the experiment on themselves? First, McGrane's students all had a strong emotional reaction to the assignment itself; they felt anger about and resistance to "wasting" time in front of a blank TV screen, despite the fact that most of us can readily admit to vol-

untarily "wasting" at least some time on TV and a myriad of other distractions. But those who stuck with it discovered more. They began to see the various effects of this particular technology on both a personal and societal level. Many found themselves wrestling with profound issues of meaning vs. meaninglessness; passivity vs. activity; isolation vs. socialization; entertainment vs. hypnosis; and reality vs. fantasy. TV, they concluded, makes real life seem dull, isolates people from social interaction, and deadens feeling as effectively as any addictive substance.

CULTURAL LAG the time between changes in material culture or technology and the resulting changes in the broader culture's relevant norms, values, meanings, and laws

The "Un-TV" experiment is not as easy as it looks, and we would like to ask you to do something similar in this Data Workshop. Here we ask you to choose some form of media technology that you will stop using, one that regularly takes up some of your time and attention and that might be hard for you to put down. For most people, the most ubiquitous device in their world is a cell phone, but you could also choose a computer or a tablet that connects you to the internet and your favorite web sites, or some other media format you use a lot, like cable TV, radio, or video gaming. Think about how long you can go without using this technology or device on a typical day (or longer). If you're like many people, even a few hours away from your cell phone or computer screen might seem like a very long time. How are you going to feel when you can't text message, watch videos on YouTube, or check the news feed on Facebook?

We take these technologies for granted and cannot imagine our lives without them—but maybe life would be better! A great part of the difficulty of this experiment is actually getting yourself to do it. But even more so, it can be a challenge to confront your own habits and dependencies on a deep level. The "Unplug" experiment asks you to do just that.

In this Data Workshop, you will be doing participant observation research while also preparing to write an autoethnography of your experience (see Chapter 2 for a review of ethnographic methods). You will be writing detailed fieldnotes of what you observe during the experiment. Remember that you are attempting to use Beginner's Mind. Don't try to figure out what will happen before you begin. Just "see what you can see." The idea is for you to notice the way the technology permeates your everyday life and what happens when you try to resist using it. Follow the numbered prompts below.

1. Choose a media technology for the experiment. This should be something you use regularly, but that you can safely turn off for a period of time. Why did you choose this technology, and how does it represent an interesting experiment?

IN RELATIONSHIPS
Social Media and #OccupyWallStreet

How does an Estonian-Canadian filmmaker who runs a magazine in Vancouver, Canada, become inspired by social activism in Egypt to organize a protest in midtown Manhattan? It sounds like a riddle, but the answer is simple. He did it on Twitter. Kalle Lasn is the founder and editor of the magazine *Adbusters*. Along with Micah White, a senior editor at the magazine, he had watched the Egyptian protests in Tahrir Square with interest, and concluded that "America needs its own Tahrir" (Schwartz 2011). After some brainstorming, the team at *Adbusters* sent out an email to their mailing list calling for a protest in New York City. They created a poster, showing a ballerina atop the famous statue of a charging bull in Bowling Green Park near Wall Street, with a line of protesters wearing gas masks emerging behind it. In order to publicize the upcoming event, they started using the hashtag #occupywallstreet on Twitter. No one from the *Adbusters* team ever traveled to New York, or played any significant role in organizing the protest. Instead, people on the *Adbusters* mailing list used Twitter and Reddit (another social news site) to spread the word and raise awareness of the demonstration. On September 17, 2011, protesters marched on Wall Street, eventually gathering in Zuccotti Park after other places were blocked by police. At the end of the day, when most of the crowd dispersed, 300 people remained behind to camp in the park, "occupying" Wall Street.

Unlike traditional protest marches, this one didn't end. Many protesters returned, every day, and many continued to sleep in the park every night. On November 15, 2011, New York City police closed the park and arrested those who refused to leave, but by that time, other "Occupy" protests had sprung up all around the world and in hundreds of communities in the United States. Clearly this could not

have happened had the message of Occupy Wall Street not struck a chord with people around the country, as many were deeply concerned with economic inequality, corporate corruption, and the role that money played in contemporary politics. Shared concerns alone, however, cannot explain the incredibly rapid spread of the protests. What allowed the single protest to turn into a movement so quickly were social media: listservs, Twitter, Facebook, and YouTube. These new media made it possible not just to organize the original protest but also for activists around the country to bring together grassroots communities and coordinate protests far beyond the confines of Zuccotti Park. Not only did social media help people connect and organize, but the steady stream of pictures, status updates, and videos of the protests helped "shape the narrative about the movement" and generate "online conversations" about the issues at hand (Lubin 2012, p. 187).

At the height of the Occupy Movement, there were hundreds of Facebook pages devoted to the protests, almost 2 million YouTube videos were tagged "occupy" or "ows," and the official Twitter feed (@OccupyWallStNYC) had more than 137,000 followers (Preston 2011). Some observers see the protests as a failure, since they achieved no tangible political goals, but their supporters argue the movement had intentionally eschewed organizing around any one particular goal. *Adbusters* founder Kalle Lasn had initially hoped the protests would pick a single demand, hoping that protesters would refuse to leave until it was met. However, only days after the protests began, the protesters released a "Declaration of Occupation" that laid out a general critique rather than any particular demand: "We write so that all people who feel wronged by the corporate forces of the world can know that we are your allies. . . . No true democracy is

2. Determine how long you will go without this technology; it could be for an afternoon hour or three days, depending upon how often you use it. What's important is to create an impact by turning it off. Why is the designated time period adequate in length to create some results in conducting the experiment?

3. Go about your daily business while you refrain from using your chosen technology during the designated time period. Don't become distracted. Keep a part of

your focus on what's happening with the experiment and check in on yourself frequently. Take field notes at points during the research process or immediately upon completing.

4. What happens as the experiment unfolds? Are you having any difficulties going without? When and why? What are your thoughts, feelings, and sensations? How attentive are you to the details of your reactions?

attainable when the process is determined by economic power" (Schwartz 2011).

In many ways, this declaration reflected the organization and methods of the occupiers. They organized horizontally, without leaders or hierarchy, and attempted to work through consensus or supermajority rule. This organizational style reflected a movement that was resolutely grassroots. Social media helped bring together an unprecedented range of people from a wide variety of backgrounds and political orientations. One of the most celebrated moments in the occupation of Zuccotti Park came when union members affiliated with the AFL-CIO joined the protesters to help prevent police from clearing the park. As one commentator put it, "hard hats and hippies—together at last" (Wiener 2011). The OWS protests didn't achieve any specific political goal, but they did change the conversation about politics and economics in America, something that happened because the protests lived as much on Twitter as they did in the park.

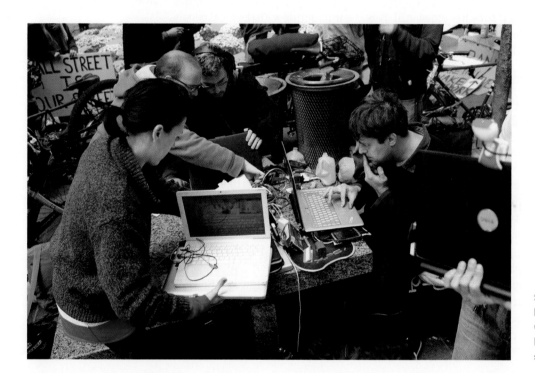

Social Media and Social Protest How different would Occupy Wall Street have been without social media sites like Twitter?

5. What happens as time progresses? How is it different the further or closer you are to the end of the allotted time for the experiment? Are you relieved to turn on your device again? Or were there some unexpected benefits of turning it off? What do you see now about using the technology that you did not notice before? Does it feel any different to start using the technology again after having conducted the experiment?

There are two options for completing this Data Workshop.

Option 1 (informal): Complete your observations, and prepare some written notes that you can refer to during in-class discussions. Compare your notes and experiences with other students in small groups.

Option 2 (formal): Complete your observations, and write a three- to four-page essay analyzing your experience. Make sure to attach your fieldnotes.

GLOBAL PERSPECTIVE

Bhutan and Gross National Happiness

While change may be inevitable, perhaps we may be able to determine the direction, elements, and pace of that change. That is exactly what the current leaders of Bhutan are attempting to do. They provide an example of how to hold on to tradition, maintain a unique cultural identity, and exercise control over the pace of social change.

Bhutan is a tiny country of fewer than one million people, precariously perched at the "roof of the world" in the Himalayan Mountains. Despite its remote location between two of the world's most powerful and populous nations—China to the north and India to the south—Bhutan has remained a sovereign, independent nation throughout its history. In this ancient land, it seems almost as if time has stood still. It is only in the past few decades that Bhutan has emerged from its almost total isolation and taken some cautious steps into the postmodern era.

Bhutan is a predominantly Buddhist country that until recently had been ruled by a king who had four wives (who were all sisters!) along with a cadre of mostly Western-educated officials. In 2008, at the behest of its enlightened monarch, Bhutan held its first democratic elections. Despite that political change, it may still be the only country in the world where the government's number-one concern is something it calls "Gross National Happiness": a blend of economic development and cultural richness; food, clothing, and shelter; health care and education; spiritual values; and individual contentment.

The government hopes to achieve Gross National Happiness by carefully identifying and adopting what the West is doing right while also rejecting its cynicism and consumerism. For example, the Bhutanese do not allow exploitation of their natural resources. There is no lumber industry in their millions of acres of lush forests, which instead have been designated national parks. Although Mt. Everest is nearby in Nepal, mountain climbers are forbidden to ascend the peaks of Bhutan's mountains. The Bhutanese have, however, taken advantage of one natural resource originating in the snow-cap—immense, fast-flowing rivers that generate hydroelectric power, which is then exported to neighboring countries. Tourism to Bhutan could also have become a lucrative trade. But here, too, the government has limited the number of visitors who can enter the country each year, and this small group is reminded to practice cultural sensitivity when interacting with the local people.

For the most part, Bhutan has managed to avoid being overwhelmed by the forces of globalization and cultural leveling. While some Bhutanese enjoy basic modern conveniences like cell phone service and wireless internet, in the capital city of Thimphu there are still no chain stores—no Starbucks, no Gap, no Wal-Mart or Burger King. Especially remarkable is that the Bhutanese have so far been able to defend themselves against what might be the most powerful global intruder of all—television.

While networks like MTV and CNN do sneak in via satellite, the government has created its own national television network, the Bhutan Broadcasting Service (BBS), to balance Western networks. Yet a homegrown production can barely compete with *CSI*; the Bhutanese are already sophisticated enough to be critical when comparing a local show with those from Hollywood. So far, the BBS has produced only limited programming, including a daily half-hour newscast in both English and the native language of Dzongkha.

Technology in the Global Village

Over the years, social thinkers have expressed concerns about the effects of new technology. Some believed that electronic media would prove to be a dangerous, divisive, and degrading force in modern culture. Marshall McLuhan (1964), a Canadian communications researcher who also subscribed to the notion of technological determinism, expressed a degree of optimism that amounted to a utopian vision of what the various media could do for human society. McLuhan was particularly interested in television, which in the early 1960s was just then infiltrating practically every household in America. He imagined that television could re-create a sense of intimate community by linking people in disparate locations around the world through its broadcasts. Just as tribe members had once gathered to share stories around the light of a campfire, people would now sit in the glow of their TV

VIRTUAL COMMUNITY a community of people linked by their consumption of the same digital media

GLOBAL VILLAGE Marshall McLuhan's term describing the way that new communication technologies override barriers of space and time, joining together people all over the globe

Still, would-be TV producers have been pitching new ideas that are responsive to audiences' taste for soap operas but include a particularly Bhutanese touch, and they still align themselves with the guiding principle of their country. They see audience members not as primarily consumers, but as citizens in need of knowledge that can help them in their pursuit of Gross National Happiness (Schell 2002).

It is important not to romanticize life in Bhutan or even the pursuit of Gross National Happiness. Although the country is now a democracy, it still endures high rates of infant mortality, poverty, and illiteracy. Life expectancies are low, and women's opportunities are limited. Certain types of social change would seem to be necessary and inevitable. However, as they prepare for change, Bhutanese leaders remain idealistic about the ability of their traditional culture to resist Western values and to avoid the social problems that are so commonplace in the other parts of the world.

Gross National Happiness
Global networks like MTV and CNN that cross borders via satellite concern Bhutanese leaders who see their children emulating foreign television programs. To counterbalance Western influence, the government created a national television network, the Bhutan Broadcasting Service (BBS).

screens, making television a kind of "virtual campfire" and those watching together members of a **virtual community**. McLuhan coined the term **global village** to capture that notion. He did not live to see the advent of the internet a few decades later, but he certainly understood the potential for media to extend the human senses and join us to one another in unprecedented ways.

CULTURAL DIFFUSION The intervening years have not totally confirmed McLuhan's utopian vision. New technologies have in fact had a profound impact on society, but in what ways and whether this has been positive or negative are still to be determined. What we do know is that media technology, through the process of **cultural diffusion**, has become a global reality. Social scientists use the term **globalization** to refer to social structures and institutions, like politics or commerce, that must now be conceived on a global rather than national scale. We can no longer remain isolated from social and political forces

CULTURAL DIFFUSION the dissemination of beliefs and practices from one group to another

GLOBALIZATION the increasing connections between economic, social, and political systems all over the globe that reverberate around the world. There are now billions of people who have access to television and the internet. More than 1 billion were estimated to have watched the first walk on the moon in 1969. Since then, other events such as the funeral of Princess Diana in 1997 and the Live 8 concert in 2005, as well as footage of catastrophic events like the 9/11 attacks or the tsunamis in Indonesia and Japan, have attracted even larger audiences. These are among the most significant images burned into our collective minds.

Most of these global TV events are produced by media conglomerates in the United States and other industrialized nations. For example, the largest television networks belong to MTV and CNN, which broadcast to 164 and 212 countries, respectively. In 2011, the most popular dramatic television series in the world was *CSI: Crime Scene Investigation*, which ranked highest on viewing surveys of sixty-five countries. *Desperate Housewives* was the number-one comedy in the world, and *The Bold and the Beautiful* topped the list of global soap operas (Harnick 2012). Programs like these potentially attract billions of viewers each week. Very few other countries have the infrastructure or budgets to produce similar shows with the same technical quality.

CULTURAL IMPERIALISM With this proliferation of Western media, we also find that the contents tend to reflect Western values. Communication researchers often talk about the "politics of information flow," and we can see that the message, or ideology, embedded in TV shows or films tends to disseminate from industrialized countries like the United States to the rest of the world (Schiller 1976, 1992, 1996; Tomlinson 1991). Americans brought up on the principle of a free press and living in a media-saturated society are not typically alarmed by the proliferation of our popular culture to other parts of the globe. In fact, we might assume that ours is the voice of freedom and democracy, a force for positive change in places where there have been censorship and disinformation (Rothkop 1997). But others question this flood of ideas, especially ideas about individualism and consumerism, coming from the West.

And Western ideas can cross cultural boundaries all too easily: it is almost impossible to block the reception of satellite and internet communications to audiences anywhere in the world. This sets up a new kind of tension in the struggle for power and influence. It is now possible for a country to be "occupied" by an invisible invader that arrives through the airwaves or by satellite and wireless networks. A country can be conquered by ideas rather than by force, a phenomenon known as **cultural imperialism**. Some consider the Western media's powerful influence as a kind of cultural domination. The result of this domination is often **cultural leveling**, a homogenizing process whereby societies lose their particular uniqueness as they all start to resemble one another.

As media technology makes possible a multiplicity of voices, Westerners have also been influenced by Eastern ideas (witness the popularity of yoga). Yet Western values

Cultural Diffusion *CSI*, one of the most popular TV shows in the world, acts as a medium for spreading American culture and ideas to other countries.

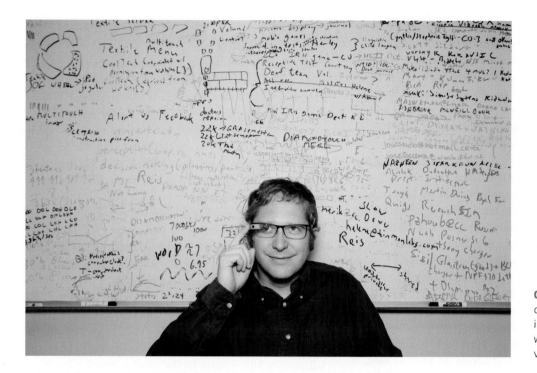

Google Glass is a wearable computer that displays information and connects with the internet—mostly by voice commands.

continue to dominate and to shape the "village" that is the global village. They sometimes conflict with the values of other nations, some of which have tried to resist the Western media stranglehold and maintain their own distinctive cultural identity (see the case of Bhutan in this chapter's Global Perspective box). Challenges persist as to whether meaningful and egalitarian communication on a global level can really take place (Gozzi 1996; Fortner and Fackler 2011). Perhaps as technology advances, cultural distinctions can be maintained while divisions continue to fade, thus approaching McLuhan's vision of a world united.

Implications for a Postmodern World

Today, the Digital Age is but a few decades old, and already most of you probably cannot remember a time when you did not have a remote control, game controller, mouse, or cell phone in hand. And you cannot imagine living without them. It is safe to assume that we will see many more scientific and technological advancements in the near future. In particular, media technologies are likely to become cheaper, lighter and easier to use, faster, more flexible, interactive, and capable of carrying more information. Despite what some call the "digital divide" (the uneven distribution of technology among different groups of people), technologies will play an increasingly important role in almost every aspect of our lives, and technological literacy will be a necessary skill for anyone participating in contemporary society.

Is all progress good? Is every technological advance beneficial? These questions arise because our society is in the midst of a major transformation: we are moving from a modern society to a postmodern society. **Modernity** refers to the social conditions and attitudes characteristic of industrialized societies, which include the decline of traditional community, an increase in individual autonomy and diversity of beliefs, and a strong belief in the ability of science and technology to improve our quality of life (Berger 1977). In many ways, this last promise of modernity has in fact been fulfilled. Since the Industrial Revolution, rates of infant mortality have declined, life expectancies have increased, and a number of common diseases have been cured or controlled. However, along with these advances have come increases in income inequality, violent crime, and child poverty (Miringoff and Miringoff 1999). So while modern society has its benefits, there are also problems, which is where the postmodern critique begins.

Postmodernity refers to the social conditions and attitudes characteristic of postindustrialized societies, which include a focus on ideas and cultural debates rather than material things and a questioning of the achievements of

MODERNITY a term that characterizes industrialized societies, including the decline of tradition, an increase in individualism, and a belief in progress, technology, and science

POSTMODERNITY a term that characterizes postindustrial societies, including a focus on the production and management of information and skepticism of science and technology science and technology. According to postmodern thought, the progress promised by modernity has failed to solve important social problems (such as income inequality), and modern institutions (families, schools, workplaces, governments) are implicated in this failure. Although change is forecast in all these areas, there is no agreed-upon blueprint for what that change might look like. The Industrial Revolution transformed Western society from traditional to modern. The Information Revolution is transforming Western society from modern to postmodern. While we are not yet certain what this particular transformation will mean in our everyday lives, we can be sure that it will not be the final transformation our society will undergo. Society will continue to be shaped by technology, not only at the macro level of culture and social institutions but also at the micro level of groups and individuals. Technology will change what the world looks like as well as how we perceive it. It will greatly extend our abilities to obtain information and will influence the way we use it. We will become more comfortable with multitasking; navigating through nonlinear hyperspace, dealing with symbols, image, and sound as well as text; moving at a rapid pace; coping with a fractured sense of self; socializing online; experimenting with game strategies; and accepting the unpredictable.

Should we call such developments progress? What will we gain, and what do we stand to lose? Your parents and grandparents will not understand the postmodern, digital era in the same way that you do. So it is you who will be engineering the terms of the future. Perhaps now would be a good time to ask yourself what you can do as part of this new social revolution. Can you risk just sitting back to watch what will happen? Or are you willing to take what you have learned and go out and make a difference? We hope this chapter has given you the insight and tools you will need to take an active role in creating whatever positive social change you envision.

CLOSING COMMENTS

Throughout this text, we have focused on the sociological features of everyday life, including the role of mass media and popular culture in society. The media are often the place where new developments, trends, or social changes first become visible. And our everyday lives are the places where we experience both social constraints and social change at the most fundamental level. You now have the tools necessary to understand these phenomena, because you now possess the sociological perspective.

The sociological perspective sometimes highlights distressing facts—the persistence of poverty and prejudice, for example, or the realities of crime. But it allows for optimism as well. This is because the intersection of biography and history goes both ways: society shapes individual lives, but individuals impact their society as well. Any disconcerting realizations you may have had during the course of this semester should be tempered by your knowledge that change is possible, and that *you* are its primary source.

Ultimately, this should be the most relevant element of your education in sociology. Years from now, no one will care whether you remember the details of labeling theory or the difference between organic and mechanical solidarity. What will continue to matter is your sense of investment in your society—your commitment to your family, your workplace, your community, and your world. Your mindful involvement in all of these areas can make each of them better places—to raise children, to live, to work, to collaborate with others. Armed with the sociological perspective, you now have a new set of responsibilities: to investigate and participate in your social world, both locally and globally. We hope you do so with optimism and persistence, and in partnership with others.

IN THE FUTURE

So what's next? It's an exciting question to ask. Perhaps one that evokes equal parts curiosity and fear about the future. What's going to happen in the world around us? How will things change? And what kind of a world will that be to live in? If you've been practicing to be a sociologist, then you've acquired some tools that might be useful when the answers come. We know already that change is constant. Hold on to the sociological perspective and you'll have a better chance of actually seeing the revolution while you're living it. Because it's happening right now. By the time you arrive here, you'll have something to tell us about.

So What's Next? Honda Motor Company president Takanobu Ito with Honda's humanoid robot Asimo (short for "Advanced Step in Innovative Mobility").

Everything You Need to Know about
Social Change

THEORIES OF SOCIAL CHANGE

* **Structural functionalism:** sometimes social change is necessary to maintain equilibrium and order in society

* **Conflict theory:** social change is the inevitable result of social inequality and conflict between groups over power and resources

* **Symbolic interactionism:** social change involves changes in the meanings of things as well as changes in laws, culture, and social behavior

REVIEW

1. People born even one generation apart can have quite different life experiences because of ongoing social and technological changes. List at least three technologies that did not exist when your parents were your age. What social changes have these technologies generated?

2. "Cultural lag" is the term sociologists use for the period of time when norms, values, and laws are not yet up to date with new technology because material culture changes faster than nonmaterial culture. Describe at least one change in material culture for which there is still some degree of cultural lag. What evidence suggests that we haven't developed adequate norms yet?

Changing Social Attitudes in the United States

Same-Sex Marriage (Percentage who Favor)

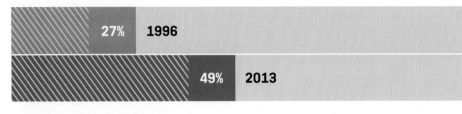

27% 1996

49% 2013

Legalized Marijuana (Percentage who Support)

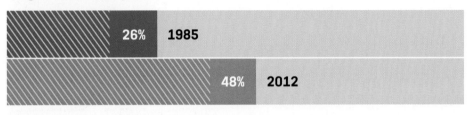

26% 1985

48% 2012

Black President (Percentage who Would Vote for)

76% 1978

96% 2012

Interracial Marriage (Percentage who Approve)

4% 1958

86% 2011

Female President (Percentage who Would Vote for)

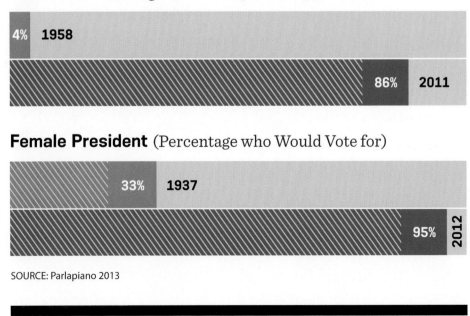

33% 1937

95% 2012

SOURCE: Parlapiano 2013

EXPLORE

Life after Your Sociology Class

What happens when your sociology class ends? Visit the Everyday Sociology Blog for a sociology professor's suggestions on how to continue exploring the sociological imagination.

http://wwnPag.es/trw416

Glossary

absolute deprivation an objective measure of poverty, defined by the inability to meet minimal standards for food, shelter, clothing, or health care

access the process by which an ethnographer gains entry to a field setting

achieved status a status earned through individual effort or imposed by others

action research the presentation of detailed data on interactions and meaning within a cultural context, from the perspective of its members

active audiences a term used to characterize audience members as active participants in "reading" or constructing the meaning of the media they consume

activism any activity intended to bring about social change

acute diseases diseases that have a sudden onset, may be briefly incapacitating, and are either curable or fatal

agency the ability of the individual to act freely and independently

agenda-setting theory theory that the mass media can set the public agenda by selecting certain news stories and excluding others, thus influencing what audiences think about

agents of socialization social groups, institutions, and individuals (especially the family, schools, peers, and the mass media) that provide structured situations in which socialization takes place

aggregate a collection of people who share a physical location but do not have lasting social relations

Agricultural Revolution the social and economic changes, including population increases, that followed from the domestication of plants and animals and the gradually increasing efficiency of food production

alienation decreasing importance of social ties and community and the corresponding increase in impersonal associations and instrumental logic; also, according to Marx, the sense of dissatisfaction the modern worker feels as a result of producing goods that are owned and controlled by someone else

alternative medicine a group of medical treatments, practices, and products that are used instead of conventional Western medicine

altruism unselfish concern for the well-being of others and helping behaviors performed without self-interested motivation

anomie "normlessness"; term used to describe the alienation and loss of purpose that result from weaker social bonds and an increased pace of change

anthropocentric literally "human centered"; the idea that needs and desires of human beings should take priority over concerns about other species or the natural environment

Anti-Malthusians contemporary researchers who believe the population boom Malthus witnessed was a temporary, historically specific phenomenon and worry instead that the worldwide population may shrink in the future

antimiscegenation the prohibition of interracial marriage, cohabitation, or sexual interaction

antithesis the opposition to the existing arrangements in a dialectical model

antitrust legislation laws designed to maintain competition in the marketplace by prohibiting monopolies, price fixing, or other forms of collusion among businesses

apartheid the system of segregation of racial and ethnic groups that was legal in South Africa between 1948 and 1991

applied research research designed to gather knowledge that can be used to create some sort of change

ascribed status an inborn status; usually difficult or impossible to change

asexuality involves the lack of sexual attraction of any kind; asexual people have no interest in or desire for sex

assimilation a pattern of relations between ethnic or racial groups in which the minority group is absorbed into the mainstream or dominant group, making society more homogenous

authoritarianism system of government by and for a small number of elites that does not include representation of ordinary citizens

authority the legitimate right to wield power

autoethnography ethnographic description that focuses on the feelings and reactions of the ethnographer

backstage in the dramaturgical perspective, places in which we rehearse and prepare for our performances

basic research the search for knowledge without any agenda or desire to use that knowledge to effect change

beginner's mind approaching the world without preconceptions in order to see things in a new way

belief a proposition or idea held on the basis of faith

bias an opinion held by the researcher that might affect the research or analysis

biodiversity the variety of species of plants and animals existing at any given time

bioethics the study of controversial moral or ethical issues related to scientific and medical advancements

biosphere the parts of the earth that can support life

bisexuality sexual attraction to both genders; bisexuals are sexually attracted to both males and females

blue collar a description characterizing skilled and semi-skilled workers who perform manual labor or work in service or clerical jobs

bourgeoisie owners; the class of modern capitalists who own the means of production and employ wage laborers

bureaucracy a type of secondary group designed to perform tasks efficiently, characterized by specialization, technical competence, hierarchy, rules and regulations, impersonality, and formal written communication

bystander effect or **diffusion of responsibility** the social dynamic wherein the more people who are present in a moment of crisis, the less likely any one of them is to take action

capital punishment the death penalty

capitalism an economic system based on the laws of free market competition, privatization of the means of production, and production for profit

caste system a form of social stratification in which status is determined by one's family history and background and cannot be changed

category people who share one or more attributes but who lack a sense of common identity or belonging

causation a relationship between variables in which a change in one directly produces a change in the other

charismatic authority authority based in the perception of remarkable personal qualities in a leader

charter schools public schools run by private entities to give parents greater control over their children's education

chronic diseases diseases that develop over a longer period of time and may not be detected until symptoms occur later in their progression

civil inattention an unspoken rule governing interactions in public places, whereby individuals briefly notice others before ignoring them

civil society those organizations, institutions, and interactions outside government, family, and work that promote social bonds and the smooth functioning of society

civil unions proposed as an alternative to gay marriage; a form of legally recognized commitment that provides gay couples some of the benefits and protections of marriage

class consciousness the recognition of social inequality on the part of the oppressed, leading to revolutionary action

closed system a social system with very little opportunity to move from one class to another

closed-ended question a question asked of a respondent that imposes a limit on the possible responses

code of ethics ethical guidelines for researchers to consult as they design a project

coercive power power that is backed by the threat of force

cohabitation living together as a romantically involved, unmarried couple

collective behavior behavior that follows from the formation of a group or crowd of people who take action together toward a shared goal

collective conscience the shared morals and beliefs that are common to a group and which foster social solidarity

collective effervescence an intense energy in shared events where people feel swept up in something larger than themselves

commodification the process by which it becomes possible to buy and sell a particular good or service

communism a system of government that eliminates private property; the most extreme form of socialism, because all citizens work for the government and there are no class distinctions

communitarianism a political and moral philosophy focused on strengthening civil society and communal bonds

community a group of people living in the same local area who share a sense of participation, belonging, and fellowship

community college two-year institution that provides students with general education and facilitates transfer to a four-year university

community supported agriculture (CSA) a model of food production and distribution in which small farmers recruit subscribers to purchase shares of the farm's harvest; subscribers or shareholders pay at the beginning of the year, and then receive regular deliveries of the farm's produce throughout the growing and harvest seasons

comparative and historical methods methods that use existing sources to study relationships among elements of society in various regions and time periods

complementary medicine a group of medical treatments, practices, and products that can be used in conjunction with conventional Western medicine

concentration the process by which the number of companies producing and distributing a particular commodity decreases, often through mergers and conglomeration

confidentiality the assurance that no one other than the researcher will know the identity of a respondent

conflict generated by the competition between different class groups for scarce resources and the source of all social change, according to Karl Marx

conflict theory a paradigm that sees social conflict as the basis of society and social change, and emphasizes a materialist view of society, a critical view of the status quo, and a dynamic model of historical change

conglomeration the process by which a single corporation acquires ownership of a variety of otherwise unrelated businesses

conservation era earliest stage of the environmental movement, which focused on the preservation of "wilderness" areas

constructionists those who believe that notions of gender are socially determined, such that a dichotomous system is just one possibility among many

consumption the utilization of goods and services, either for personal use or in manufacturing

contagion theory one of the earliest theories of collective action; suggested that individuals who joined a crowd could become "infected" by a mob mentality and lose the ability to reason

content analysis a method in which researchers identify and study specific variables—such as words—in a text, image, or media message

control group the part of a test group that is allowed to continue without intervention so that it can be compared with the experimental group

control in an experiment, the process of regulating all factors except for the independent variable

conversation analysis a sociological approach that looks at how we create meaning in naturally occurring conversation, often by taping conversations and examining them

cooling the mark out behaviors that help others to save face or avoid embarrassment, often referred to as civility or tact

copresence face-to-face interaction or being in the presence of others

correlation a relationship between variables in which they change together, and may or may not be causal

counterculture a group within society that openly rejects and/or actively opposes society's values and norms

crime a violation of a norm that has been codified into law

criminal justice system a collection of social institutions, such as legislatures, police, courts, and prisons, that create and enforce laws

critical theory a contemporary form of conflict theory that criticizes many different systems and ideologies of domination and oppression

crowd a temporary gathering of individuals, whether spontaneous or planned, who share a common focus

cultural assimilation the process by which racial or ethnic groups are absorbed into the dominant group by adopting the dominant group's culture

cultural capital the tastes, habits, expectations, skills, knowledge, and other cultural assets that help us gain advantages in society

cultural diffusion the dissemination of beliefs and practices from one group to another

cultural imperialism cultural influence caused by adopting another culture's products

cultural lag the time between changes in material culture or technology and the resulting changes in the broader culture's relevant norms, values, meanings, and laws

cultural leveling the process by which societies lose their uniqueness, becoming increasingly similar

cultural relativism the principle of understanding other cultures on their own terms, rather than judging or evaluating according to one's own culture

culture of poverty entrenched attitudes that can develop among poor communities and lead the poor to accept their fate rather than attempt to improve their lot

culture shock a sense of disorientation that occurs when you enter a radically new social or cultural environment

culture the entire way of life of a group of people (including both material and symbolic elements) that acts as a lens through which one views the world and is passed from one generation to the next

culture wars clashes within mainstream society over the values and norms that should be upheld

curative or crisis medicine type of health care that treats the disease or condition once it has manifested

custody the physical and legal responsibility of caring for children; assigned by a court for divorced or unmarried parents

cyberbullying the use of electronic media (web pages, social networking sites, e-mail, instant messengers, and cell phones) to tease, harass, threaten, or humiliate someone

cycle of violence a common behavior pattern in abusive relationships; the cycle begins happily, then the relationship grows tense, and the tension explodes in abuse, followed by a period of contrition that allows the cycle to repeat

deception the extent to which the participants in a research project are unaware of the project or its goals

deconstruction a type of critical postmodern analysis that involves taking apart or disassembling old ways of thinking

definition of the situation an agreement with others about "what is going on" in a given circumstance; this consensus allows us to coordinate our actions with those of others and realize goals.

democracy a political system in which all citizens have the right to participate

demographic free fall decrease in fertility rates among populations that have industrialized their economies as children become an economic liability rather than an asset

demographic transition a theory suggesting the possible transition over time from high birth and death rates to low birth and death rates, resulting in a stabilized population

demography study of the size, composition, distribution, and changes in human population

dependent variable factor that is changed (or not) by the independent variable

deprivation amplification when our individual disease risks (based on our heredity and physiology) are amplified by social factors

deregulation reduction or removal of government controls from an industry to allow for a free and efficient marketplace

deterrence an approach to punishment that relies on the threat of harsh penalties to discourage people from committing crimes

deviance a behavior, trait, belief, or other characteristic that violates a norm and causes a negative reaction

deviance avowal process by which an individual self-identifies as deviant and initiates her own labeling process

dialectical model Marx's model of historical change, whereby two extreme positions come into conflict and create some new third thing between them

differential association theory Edwin Sutherland's hypothesis that we learn to be deviant through our associations with deviant peers

digital divide the unequal access to computer and internet technology, both globally and within the United States

discrimination unequal treatment of individuals based on their membership in a social group; usually motivated by prejudice

disenchantment the rationalization of modern society

disenfranchised stripped of voting rights, either temporarily or permanently

disenfranchisement the removal of the rights of citizenship through economic, political, or legal means

domestic violence any physical, verbal, financial, sexual, or psychological behaviors abusers use to gain and maintain power over their victims

dominant culture the values, norms, and practices of the group within society that is most powerful (in terms of wealth, prestige, status, influence, etc.)

double-barreled questions questions that attempt to get at multiple issues at once, and so tend to receive incomplete or confusing answers

double-consciousness W.E.B. DuBois's term for the divided identity experienced by blacks in America

dramaturgy an approach pioneered by Erving Goffman in which social life is analyzed in terms of its similarities to theatrical performance

dual nature of the self the idea that we experience the self as both subject and object, the "I" and the "me"

dyad a two-person social group

dysfunction a disturbance to or undesirable consequence of some aspect of the social system

dystopia opposite of a utopia; a world where social problems are magnified and the quality of life is extremely low

early college high schools institutions in which students earn a high school diploma and two years of credit toward a bachelor's degree

Earth Day an annual event conceived of by environmental activist and former senator Gaylord Nelson to encourage support for and increase awareness of environmental concerns; first celebrated on March 22, 1970

ecological footprint an estimation of the land and water area required to produce all the goods an individual consumes and to assimilate all the wastes she generates

ecoterrorism use of violence or criminal methods to protect the environment, often in high-profile, publicity-generating ways

ecotourism foreign travel with the goal of minimizing the environmental consequences of tourism as well as its possible negative effects on local cultures and economies, typically involves people from highly industrialized nations traveling to less developed countries

edge cities centers of employment and commerce that began as suburban commuter communities

education the process by which a society transmits its knowledge, values, and expectations to its members so they can function effectively

embodied identity those elements of identity that are generated through others' perceptions of our physical traits

embodied status a status generated by physical characteristics

emergent norm theory a theory of collective behavior that assumes individual members of a crowd make their own decisions about behavior and that norms are created through others' acceptance or rejection of these behaviors

emigration leaving one country to live permanently in another

emotion work (emotional labor) the process of evoking, suppressing, or otherwise managing feelings to create a publicly observable display of emotion

empirical based on scientific experimentation or observation

encoding/decoding model a theory on media that combines models that privilege the media producer and models that view the audience as the primary source of meaning; this theory recognizes that media texts are created to deliver specific messages and that individuals actively interpret them

endogamy marriage to someone within one's social group

environment in sociology, the natural world, the human-made environment, and the interaction between the two

environmental justice a movement that aims to remedy environmental inequities such as threats to public health and the unequal treatment of certain communities with regard to ecological concerns

environmental movement a social movement organized around concerns about the relationship between humans and the environment

Environmental Protection Agency (EPA) a government agency organized in 1969 to protect public health and the environment through policies and enforcement

environmental racism any environmental policy or practice that negatively affects individuals, groups, or communities because of their race or ethnicity

environmental sociology the study of the interaction between society and the natural environment, including the social causes and consequences of environmental problems

epidemic occurs when a significantly higher number of cases of a particular disease occur during a particular time period than might otherwise be expected

epidemiology the study of disease patterns to understand the cause of illnesses, how they are spread, and what interventions to take

essentialists those who believe gender roles have a genetic or biological origin and therefore cannot be changed

ethnicity a socially defined category based on common language, religion, nationality, history, or another cultural factor

ethnocentrism the principle of using one's own culture as a means or standard by which to evaluate another group or individual, leading to the view that cultures other than one's own are abnormal or inferior

ethnography a naturalistic method based on studying people in their own environment in order to understand the meanings they attribute to their activities; also the written work that results from the study

ethnomethodology the study of "folk methods" and background knowledge that sustains a shared sense of reality in everyday interactions

eugenics an attempt to selectively manipulate the gene pool in order to produce and "improve" human beings through medical science

Eurocentric the tendency to favor European or Western histories, cultures, and values over other non-Western societies

evangelical a term describing conservative Christians who emphasize converting others to their faith

everyday class consciousness awareness of one's own social status and that of others

existing sources materials that have been produced for some other reason, but that can be used as data for social research

exogamy marriage to someone from a different social group

experimental group the part of a test group that receives the experimental treatment

experiments formal tests of specific variables and effects, performed in a controlled setting where all aspects of the situation can be controlled

expressions given expressions that are intentional and usually verbal, such as utterances

expressions given off observable expressions that can be either intended or unintended and are usually nonverbal

expressions of behavior small actions such as an eye roll or head nod that serve as an interactional tool to help project our definition of the situation to others

expressive leadership leadership concerned with maintaining emotional and relational harmony within the group

expressive role the position of the family member who provides emotional support and nurturing

expressive tasks the emotional work necessary to support family members

extended family a large group of relatives, usually including at least three generations living either in one household or in close proximity

extrinsic religiosity a person's public display of commitment to a religious faith

fads interests or practices followed enthusiastically for a relatively short period of time

false consciousness a denial of the truth on the part of the oppressed when they fail to recognize the interests of the ruling class in their ideology

family a social group whose members are bound by legal, biological, or emotional ties, or a combination of all three

family planning contraception, or any method of controlling family size and the birth of children

fashion the widespread custom or style of behavior and appearance at a particular time or in a particular place

feeling rules socially constructed norms regarding the expression and display of emotions; expectations about the acceptable or desirable feelings in a given situation

feminism belief in the social, political, and economic equality of the sexes; also the social movements organized around that belief

feminist theory a theoretical approach that looks at gender inequities in society and the way that gender structures the social world

feminization of poverty the economic trend showing that women are more likely than men to live in poverty, caused in part by the gendered gap in wages, the higher proportion of single mothers compared to single fathers, and the increasing costs of child care

feral children in myths and rare real-world cases, children who have had little human contact and may have lived in social isolation from a young age

fertility rate a measure of population growth through reproduction; often expressed as the average number of births per 1,000 people in the total population or the average number of children a woman would be expected to have

feudal system a system of social stratification based on a hereditary nobility who were responsible for and served by a lower stratum of forced laborers called serfs

fictive kin close relations with people we consider "like family" but who are not related to us by blood or marriage

fieldnotes detailed notes taken by an ethnographer describing her activities and interactions, which later become the basis of the ethnographic analysis

first wave the earliest period of feminist activism in the United States, including the period from the mid-nineteenth century until American women won the right to vote in 1920

527 committees organizations that have no official connection to a candidate but that raise and spend funds like a campaign does; named after the section of the tax code that authorizes their existence

folkway a loosely enforced norm involving common customs, practices, or procedures that ensure smooth social interaction and acceptance

food desert a community in which the residents have little or no access to fresh, affordable, healthy foods, usually located in densely populated, urban areas

Fourth Estate the media is considered like a fourth branch of government (after the executive, legislative, and judiciary) and thus serves as another of the checks and balances on power

front in the dramaturgical perspective, the setting or scene of performances that helps establish the definition of the situation

frontstage in the dramaturgical perspective, the region in which we deliver our public performances

fundamentalism the practice of emphasizing literal interpretation of texts and a "return" to a time of greater religious purity; represented by the most conservative group within any religion

game stage the third stage in Mead's theory of the development of self wherein children play organized games and take on the perspective of the generalized other

gender identity an individual's self-definition or sense of gender

gender role socialization the lifelong process of learning to be masculine or feminine, primarily through four agents of socialization: families, schools, peers, and the media

gender the physical, behavioral, and personality traits that a group considers normal for its male and female members

generalized other the perspectives and expectations of a network of others (or of society in general) that a child learns and then takes into account when shaping his or her own behavior

genocide the deliberate and systematic extermination of a racial, ethnic, national, or cultural group

gentrification transformation of the physical, social, economic, and cultural life of formerly working-class or poor inner-city neighborhoods into more affluent middle-class communities

gestures the ways in which people use their bodies to communicate without words; actions that have symbolic meaning

global (or **solar**) **dimming** a decline in the amount of light reaching the earth's surface because of increased air pollution, which reflects more light back into space

global cities a term for megacities that emphasizes their global impact as centers of economic, political, and social power

global village Marshall McLuhan's term describing the way that new communication technologies override barriers of space and time, joining together people all over the globe

global warming gradual increase in Earth's temperature, driven recently by an increase in greenhouse gases and other human activity

globalization the increasing connections between economic, social, and political systems all over the globe

government the formal, organized agency that exercises power and control in modern society, especially through the creation and enforcement of laws

grassroots environmentalism fourth major stage of the environmental movement; distinguished by the diversity of its members and belief in citizen participation in environmental decision making

Green Party a U.S. political party established in 1984 to bring political attention to environmentalism, social justice, diversity, and related principles

greenhouse effect the process in which increased production of greenhouse gases, especially those arising from human activity (e.g., carbon dioxide, nitrous oxide, and methane) cause the Earth's temperature to rise

greenhouse gases any gases in the Earth's atmosphere that allow sunlight to pass through but trap heat, thus affecting temperature

grounded theory an inductive method of generating theory from data by creating categories in which to place data and then looking for relationships among categories

group a collection of people who share some attribute, identify with one another, and interact with each other

group cohesion the sense of solidarity or loyalty that individuals feel toward a group to which they belong

group dynamics the patterns of interaction between groups and individuals

groupthink in very cohesive groups, the tendency to enforce a high degree of conformity among members, creating a demand for unanimous agreement

growth rate expression of changes in population size over time figured by subtracting the number of deaths from the number of births, then adding the net migration

Hawthorne effect a specific example of reactivity, in which the desired effect is the result not of the independent variable but of the research itself

hegemony term developed by Antonio Gramsci to describe the cultural aspects of social control, whereby the ideas of the dominant social group are accepted by all of society

heterogamy choosing romantic partners who are dissimilar to us in terms of class, race, education, religion, and other social group membership

heterosexuality sexual desire for the other gender

hidden curriculum values or behaviors that students learn indirectly over the course of their schooling because of the structure of the educational system and the teaching methods used

high culture those forms of cultural expression usually associated with the elite or dominant classes

homeschooling the education of children by their parents, at home

homogamy the tendency to choose romantic partners who are similar to us in terms of class, race, religion, education, or other social group membership

homophobia fear of or discrimination toward homosexuals or toward individuals who display purportedly gender-inappropriate behavior

homosexuality the tendency to feel sexual desire toward members of one's own gender

honor killing the murder of a family member—usually female—who is believed to have brought dishonor to her family

horizontal social mobility the movement of individuals or groups within a particular social class, most often a result of changing occupations

human exceptionalism the attitude that humans are exempt from natural ecological limits

human sexual dimorphism the extent, much debated in recent years, to which inherent physical differences define the distinctions between the two sexes

hypergamy marrying "up" in the social class hierarchy

hypodermic needle theory (magic bullet theory) a theory that explains the effects of media as if their contents simply entered directly into the consumer, who is powerless to resist their influence

hypogamy marrying "down" in the social class hierarchy

hypothesis a theoretical statement explaining the relationship between two or more phenomena

id, **ego**, and **superego** according to Freud, the three interrelated parts that make up the mind: the id consists of basic inborn drives that are the source of instinctive psychic energy; the ego is the realistic aspect of the mind that balances the forces of the id and the superego; the superego has two components (the conscience and the ego-ideal) and represents the internalized demands of society

ideal culture the norms, values, and patterns of behavior that members of a society believe should be observed in principle

ideology a system of beliefs, attitudes, and values that directs a society and reproduces the status quo of the bourgeoisie

idioculture the customs, practices, and values expressed in a particular place by the people who interact there

immigration entering one country from another to take up permanent residence

impression management the effort to control the impressions we make on others so that they form a desired view of us and the situation; the use of self-presentation and performance tactics

incapacitation an approach to punishment that seeks to protect society from criminals by imprisoning or executing them

incest sexual contact between family members; a form of child abuse when it occurs between a child and a caregiver

Independent (or Third) Sector the part of the economy composed of nonprofit organizations; their workers are mission driven, rather than profit driven, and such organizations direct surplus funds to the causes they support

independent variable factor that is predicted to cause change

individual discrimination discrimination carried out by one person against another

Industrial Revolution the rapid transformation of social life resulting from the technological and economic developments that began with the assembly line, steam power, and urbanization

infant mortality average number of infant deaths per 1,000 live births in a particular population

influential power power that is supported by persuasion

Information Revolution the recent social revolution made possible by the development of the microchip in the 1970s, which brought about vast improvements in the ability to manage information

information work work that involves the production, analysis, and distribution of information or knowledge; workers primarily think for a living

informed consent a safeguard through which the researcher makes sure that respondents are freely participating and understand the nature of the research

in-group a group that one identifies with and feels loyalty toward

in-group orientation among stigmatized individuals, the rejection of prevailing judgments or prejudice and the development of new standards that value their group identity

innovators individuals who accept society's approved goals but not society's approved means to achieve them

institutional discrimination discrimination carried out systematically by institutions (political, economic, educational, and others) that affect all members of a group who come into contact with it

institutional review board a group of scholars within a university who meet regularly to review and approve the research proposals of their colleagues and make recommendations for how to protect human subjects

instrumental leadership leadership that is task or goal oriented

instrumental role the position of the family member who provides the family's material support and is often an authority figure

instrumental tasks the practical physical tasks necessary to maintain family life

integrative medicine the combination of conventional medicine with complementary practices and treatments that have proven to be safe and effective

intentional community any of a variety of groups who form communal living arrangements outside marriage

intergenerational mobility movement between social classes that occurs from one generation to the next

internal colonialism the economic and political domination and subjugation of the minority group by the dominant group within a nation

internal migration movement of a population within a country

interpretive community a group of people dedicated to the consumption and interpretation of a particular cultural product and who create a collective, social meaning for the product

interpretive strategies the ideas and frameworks that audience members bring to bear on a particular media text to understand its meaning

intersectionality a concept that identifies how different categories of inequality (race, class, gender, etc.) intersect to shape the lives of individuals and groups

intersexed term to describe a person whose chromosomes or sex characteristics are neither exclusively male nor exclusively female

intervening variable? a third variable, sometimes overlooked, that explains the relationship between two other variables

interviews face-to-face, information-seeking conversations, sometimes defined as a conversation with a purpose

intragenerational mobility the movement between social classes that occurs during the course of an individual's lifetime

intrinsic religiosity a person's inner religious life or personal relationship to the divine

iron cage Max Weber's pessimistic description of modern life, in which we are caught in bureaucratic structures that control our lives through rigid rules and rationalization

just-world hypothesis argues that people have a deep need to see the world as orderly, predictable, and fair, which creates a tendency to view victims of social injustice as deserving of their fates

kin relatives or relations, usually those related by common descent

knowledge workers those who work primarily with information and who create value in the economy through their ideas, judgments, analyses, designs, or innovations

labeling theory Howard Becker's idea that deviance is a consequence of external judgments, or labels, that modify the individual's self-concept and change the way others respond to the labeled person

language a system of communication using vocal sounds, gestures, or written symbols; the basis of symbolic culture and the primary means through which we communicate with one another and perpetuate our culture

latent functions the less obvious, perhaps unintended functions of a social structure

law a common type of formally defined norm providing an explicit statement about what is permissible and what is illegal in a given society

leading questions questions that predispose a respondent to answer in a certain way

legal-rational authority authority based in laws, rules, and procedures, not in the heredity or personality of any individual leader

leisure a period of time that can be spent relaxing, engaging in recreation, or otherwise indulging in freely chosen activities

LGBTQ lesbian, gay, bisexual, transgender, and queer; sometimes "A" is added to include "allies"

liberation theology a movement within the Catholic Church to understand Christianity from the perspective of the poor and oppressed, with a focus on fighting injustice

life expectancy average age to which people in a particular population live

life span or **longevity** the uppermost age to which a person can potentially live

lifestyle enclaves groups of people drawn together by shared interests, especially those relating to hobbies, sports, and media

Likert scale a way of organizing categories on a survey question so that the respondent can choose an answer along a continuum

literature review? a thorough search through previously published studies relevant to a particular topic

looking-glass self the notion that the self develops through our perception of others' evaluations and appraisals of us

macrosociology the level of analysis that studies large-scale social structures in order to determine how they affect the lives of groups and individuals

mainstream environmentalism beginning in the 1980s, the third major stage of the environmental movement; characterized by enhanced organization, improved promotional campaigns and political tactics, and an increased reliance on economic and scientific expertise

male liberationism a movement that originated in the 1970s to discuss the challenges of masculinity

Malthusian theorem the theory that exponential population growth will outpace arithmetic growth in food production and other resources

Malthusian trap Malthus's prediction that a rapidly increasing population will overuse natural resources, leading inevitably to a major public health disaster

manifest functions the obvious, intended functions of a social structure for the social system

mass behavior large groups of people engaging in similar behaviors without necessarily being in the same place

mass society theory a theory of social movements that assumes people join not because of the movements' ideals, but to satisfy a psychological need to belong to something larger than themselves

master status a status that is always relevant and affects all other statuses we possess

material culture the objects associated with a cultural group, such as tools, machines, utensils, buildings, and artwork; any physical object to which we give social meaning

McDonaldization George Ritzer's term describing the spread of bureaucratic rationalization and the accompanying increases in efficiency and dehumanization

means of production anything that can create wealth: money, property, factories, and other types of businesses, and the infrastructure necessary to run them

mechanical solidarity term developed by Emile Durkheim to describe the type of social bonds present in premodern, agrarian societies, in which shared traditions and beliefs created a sense of social cohesion

medicalization the process by which some behaviors or conditions that were once seen as personal problems are redefined as medical issues

megalopolis or **megacity** a group of densely populated metropolises that grow dependent on each other and eventually combine to form a huge urban complex

men's rights movement an offshoot of male liberationism whose members believe that feminism promotes discrimination against men

merger the legal combination of two companies, usually in order to maximize efficiency and profits by eliminating redundant infrastructure and personnel

meritocracy a system in which rewards are distributed based on merit

metropolis an urban area with a large population, usually 500,000 to 1 million people

Metropolitan Statistical Area (MSA) or **agglomeration** one or more adjacent counties with at least one major city of 50,000 or more inhabitants that is surrounded by an adjacent area that is socially and economically integrated with the city

microsociology the level of analysis that studies face-to-face and small-group interactions in order to understand how they affect the larger patterns and institutions of society

middle class composed primarily of "white collar" workers with a broad range of education and incomes; they constitute about 30 percent of the U.S. population

midrange theory an approach that integrates empiricism and grand theory

migration movement of people from one geographic area to another for the purpose of resettling

minority group social group that is systematically denied the same access to power and resources available to society's dominant groups though they are not necessarily fewer in number than the dominant groups

miscegenation romantic, sexual, or marital relationships between people of different races

modern environmental movement beginning in the 1960s, the second major stage of the environmental movement; focused on the environmental consequences of new technologies, oil exploration, chemical production, and nuclear power plants

modernism a paradigm that places trust in the power of science and technology to create progress, solve problems, and improve life

modernity a term that characterizes industrialized societies, including the decline of tradition, an increase in individualism, and a belief in progress, technology, and science

monarchy a government ruled by a king or queen, with succession of rulers kept within the family

monogamy the practice of marrying (or being in a relationship with) one person at a time

monopoly a situation in which there is only one individual or organization, without competitors, providing a particular good or service

monotheistic a term describing religions that worship a single divine figure

more a norm that carries great moral significance, is closely related to the core values of a cultural group, and often involves severe repercussions for violators

mortality rate a measure of the decrease in population due to deaths; often expressed as the number of deaths expected per 1,000 people per year in a particular population

multiculturalism a policy that values diverse racial, ethnic, national, and linguistic backgrounds and so encourages the retention of cultural differences within society rather than assimilation

natural increase change in population size that results from births and deaths; linked to a country's progress toward demographic transition

nature vs. nurture debate the ongoing discussion of the respective roles of genetics and socialization in determining individual behaviors and traits

negative questions survey questions that ask respondents what they don't think instead of what they do

neglect a form of child abuse in which the caregiver fails to provide adequate nutrition, sufficient clothing or shelter, or hygienic and safe living conditions

Neo-Malthusians contemporary researchers who worry about the rapid pace of population growth and believe that Malthus's basic prediction could be true

net migration net effect of immigration and emigration on an area's population in a given time period; expressed as an increase or decrease

new ecological paradigm a way of understanding human life as just one part of an ecosystem that includes many species' interactions with the environment; suggests that there should be ecological limits on human activity

NIMBY short for "Not In My Back Yard"; originally referred to protests that aimed at shifting undesirable activities onto those with less power; now sometimes used without negative connotations to describe local environmental activists

nonrenewable resources finite resources that can become exhausted; includes those that take so long to replenish as to be effectively finite

norm a rule or guideline regarding what kinds of behavior are acceptable and appropriate within a culture

nuclear family a heterosexual couple with one or more children living in a single household

objectivity impartiality, the ability to allow the facts to speak for themselves

online education any educational course or program in which the teacher and the student meet via the internet, rather than meeting physically in a classroom

open system a social system with ample opportunities to move from one class to another

open-ended question a question asked of a respondent that allows the answer to take whatever form the respondent chooses

operational definition a clear and precise definition of a variable that facilitates its measurement

opinion leaders high-profile individuals whose interpretation of events influences the public

organic solidarity term developed by Emile Durkheim to describe the type of social bonds present in modern societies, based on difference, interdependence, and individual rights

out-group any group an individual feels opposition, rivalry, or hostility toward

outsiders according to Howard Becker, those labeled deviant and subsequently segregated from "normal" society

outsourcing "contracting out" or transferring to another country the labor that a company might otherwise have employed its own staff to perform; typically done for financial reasons

palliative care type of health care that focuses on symptom and pain relief and providing a supportive environment for critically ill or dying patients, rather than fighting the illness or disease

pandemic occurs when a significantly higher number of cases of a disease also spreads through an especially large geographical region spanning many countries or even continents

paradigm shift the term used to describe a change in basic assumptions of a particular scientific discipline

paradigm a set of assumptions, theories, and perspectives that make up a way of understanding social reality

participant observation a methodology associated with ethnography whereby the researcher both observes and becomes a member in a social setting

particular or significant other the perspectives and expectations of a particular role that a child learns and internalizes

passing presenting yourself as a member of a different group than the stigmatized group you belong to

patriarchy literally meaning "rule of the father"; a male-dominated society

personal front the expressive equipment we consciously or unconsciously use as we present ourselves to others, including appearance and manner, to help establish the definition of the situation

pilfering stealing minor items in small amounts, often again and again

pilot study a small study carried out to test the feasibility of a larger one

play stage the second stage in Mead's theory of the development of self wherein children pretend to play the role of the particular or significant other

pluralism a cultural pattern of intergroup relations that encourages racial and ethnic variation and acceptance within a society

pluralist model a system of political power in which a wide variety of individuals and groups have equal access to resources and the mechanisms of power

pluralistic ignorance a process in which members of a group individually conclude that there is no need to take action because of the observation that other group members have not done so

political action committees (PACs) organizations that raise money to support the interests of a select group or organization

politics methods and tactics intended to influence government policy, policy-related attitudes, and activities

pollution any environmental contaminant that harms living beings

polyamory a system of multiple-person partnership

polyandry a system of marriage that allows women to have multiple husbands

polygamy a system of marriage that allows people to have more than one spouse at a time

polygyny a system of marriage that allows men to have multiple wives

polysemy having many possible meanings or interpretations

popular culture usually contrasted with the high culture of elite groups; forms of cultural expression usually associated with the masses, consumer goods, and commercial products

population transfer the forcible removal of a group of people from the territory they have occupied

positive deviance actions considered deviant within a given context but are later reinterpreted as appropriate or even heroic

positivism the theory, developed by Auguste Comte, that sense perceptions are the only valid source of knowledge

postmodernism a paradigm that suggests that social reality is diverse, pluralistic, and constantly in flux

postmodernity a term that characterizes postindustrial societies, including a focus on the production and management of information and skepticism of science and technology

power elite a relatively small group of people in the top ranks of economic, political, and military institutions who make many of the important decisions in American society

power the ability to impose one's will on others

pragmatism a theoretical perspective that assumes organisms (including humans) make practical adaptations to their environments; humans do this through cognition, interpretation, and interaction

praxis practical action that is taken on the basis of intellectual or theoretical understanding

prejudice an idea about the characteristics of a group that is applied to all members of that group and is unlikely to change regardless of the evidence against it

preparatory stage the first stage in Mead's theory of the development of self wherein children mimic or imitate others

prestige the social honor people are given because of their membership in well-regarded social groups

preventive medicine type of health care that aims to avoid or forestall the onset of disease by taking preventive measures, often including lifestyle changes

primary deviance in labeling theory, the initial act or attitude that causes one to be labeled deviant

primary groups the people who are most important to our sense of self; members' relationships are typically characterized by face-to-face interaction, high levels of cooperation, and intense feelings of belonging

probability sampling any sampling scheme in which any given unit has the same probability of being chosen

profane the ordinary, mundane, or everyday

pro-feminist men's movement an offshoot of male liberationism whose members support feminism and believe that sexism harms both men and women

progressive term describing efforts to promote forward-thinking social change

proletariat workers; those who have no means of production of their own and so are reduced to selling their labor power in order to live

property crime crimes that did not involve violence, including burglary, larceny-theft, motor vehicle theft, and arson

propinquity the tendency to marry or have relationships with people in close geographic proximity

psychosexual stages of development four distinct stages of the development of the self between birth and adulthood, according to Freud. Personality quirks are a result of being fixated, or stuck, at any stage

public goods dilemma a type of social dilemma in which individuals incur the cost to contribute to a collective resource, though they may never benefit from that resource

qualitative research research that works with nonnumerical data such as texts, fieldnotes, interview transcripts, photographs, and tape recordings; this type of research more often tries to understand how people make sense of their world

quantitative research research that translates the social world into numbers that can be treated mathematically; this type of research often tries to find cause-and-effect relationships

queer theory a paradigm that proposes that categories of sexual identity are social constructs and that no sexual category is fundamentally either deviant or normal

queer theory social theory about gender identity and sexuality that emphasizes the importance of difference and rejects as restrictive the idea of innate sexual identity

race a socially defined category based on real or perceived biological differences between groups of people

racial assimilation the process by which racial minority groups are absorbed into the dominant group through intermarriage

racism a set of beliefs about the superiority of one racial or ethnic group; used to justify inequality and often rooted in the assumption that differences between groups are genetic

rapport a positive relationship often characterized by mutual trust or sympathy

rationalization the application of economic logic to human activity; the use of formal rules and regulations in order to maximize efficiency without consideration of subjective or individual concerns

reactivity the tendency of people and events to react to the process of being studied

real culture the norms, values, and patterns of behavior that actually exist within a society (which may or may not correspond to the society's ideals)

rebels individuals who reject society's approved goals and means and instead create and work toward their own (sometimes revolutionary) goals using new means

recreation any satisfying, amusing, and stimulating activity that is experienced as refreshing and renewing for body, mind, and spirit

reference group a group that provides a standard of comparison against which we evaluate ourselves

reflexivity how the identity and activities of the researcher influence what is going on in the field setting

region in the dramaturgical perspective, the context or setting in which the performance takes place

regressive term describing resistance to particular social changes, efforts to maintain the status quo, or attempts to reestablish an earlier form of social order

rehabilitation an approach to punishment that attempts to reform criminals as part of their penalty

reinforcement theory theory that suggests that audiences seek messages in the media that reinforce their existing attitudes and beliefs and are thus not influenced by challenging or contradictory information

relative deprivation a relative measure of poverty based on the standard of living in a particular society

relative deprivation theory a theory of social movements that focuses on the actions of oppressed groups who seek rights or opportunities already enjoyed by others in the society

reliability the consistency of a question or measurement tool; the degree to which the same questions will produce similar answers

religion any institutionalized system of shared beliefs and rituals that identify a relationship between the sacred and the profane

religiosity the regular practice of religious beliefs, often measured in terms of frequency of attendance at worship services and the importance of religious beliefs to an individual

renewable resources resources that replenish at a rate comparable to the rate at which they are consumed

replicability research that can be repeated, and thus verified, by other researchers later

representative sample a sample taken so that findings from members of the sample group can be generalized to the whole population

representativeness the degree to which a particular studied group is similar to, or represents, any part of the larger society

rescission the practice by insurance companies of canceling coverage only after a person gets sick

residential segregation the geographical separation of the poor from the rest of an area's population

resistance strategies ways that workers express discontent with their working conditions and try to reclaim control of the conditions of their labor

resocialization the process of replacing previously learned norms and values with new ones as a part of a transition in life

resource mobilization theory a theory of social movements that focuses on the practical constraints that help or hinder social movements' action

respondent someone from whom a researcher solicits information

response rate the number or percentage of surveys completed by respondents and returned to researchers

retribution an approach to punishment that emphasizes retaliation or revenge for the crime as the appropriate goal

riot continuous disorderly behavior by a group of people that disturbs the peace and is directed toward other people and/or property

ritual a practice based on religious beliefs

ritualists individuals who have given up hope of achieving society's approved goals but still operate according to society's approved means

role the set of behaviors expected of someone because of his or her status

role conflict experienced when we occupy two or more roles with contradictory expectations

role exit the process of leaving a role that we will no longer occupy

role model an individual who serves as an example for others to strive toward and emulate

role strain the tension experienced when there are contradictory expectations within one role

role-taking emotions emotions like sympathy, embarrassment, or shame that require that we assume the perspective of another person or many other people and respond from that person or group's point of view

rural rebound population increase in rural counties that adjoin urban centers or possess rich scenic or amenity values

rural relating to sparsely settled areas; in the United States, any county with a population density between 10 and 59.9 people per square mile

sacred the holy, divine, or supernatural

sample the part of the population that will actually be studied

sanction positive or negative reactions to the ways that people follow or disobey norms, including rewards for conformity and punishments for violations

Sapir-Whorf hypothesis the idea that language structures thought and that ways of looking at the world are embedded in language

saturated self a postmodern idea that the self is now developed by multiple influences chosen from a wide range of media sources

school vouchers payments from the government to parents whose children attend failing public schools; the money helps parents pay private school tuition

scientific method a procedure for acquiring knowledge that emphasizes collecting concrete data through observation and experiment

second shift the unpaid housework and child care often expected of women after they complete their day's paid labor

second wave the period of feminist activity during the 1960s and 1970s often associated with the issues of women's equal access to employment and education

secondary deviance in labeling theory, the subsequent deviant identity or career that develops as a result of being labeled deviant

secondary groups larger and less intimate than primary groups; members' relationships are usually organized around a specific goal and are often temporary

secular nonreligious; a secular society separates church and state and does not endorse any religion

segregation the physical and legal separation of groups by race or ethnicity

self the individual's conscious, reflexive experience of a personal identity separate and distinct from other individuals

self-fulfilling prophecy an inaccurate statement or belief that, by altering the situation, becomes accurate; a prediction that causes itself to come true

service workers those whose work involves providing a service to businesses or individual clients, customers, or consumers rather than manufacturing goods

sex an individual's membership in one of two biologically distinct categories—male or female

sexual orientation or **sexual identity** the inclination to feel sexual desire toward people of a particular gender or toward both genders

sexuality the character or quality of being sexual

sick role the actions and attitudes that society expects from someone who is ill

sign a symbol that stands for or conveys an idea

simple random sample a particular type of probability sample in which every member of the population has an equal chance of being selected

simplicity movement a loosely knit movement that opposes consumerism and encourages people to work less, earn less, and spend less, in accordance with nonmaterialistic values

simulacrum an image or media representation that does not reflect reality in any meaningful way but is treated as real

situational ethnicity an ethnic identity that can be either displayed or concealed depending on its usefulness in a given situation

slavery the most extreme form of social stratification, based on the legal ownership of people

smart growth term for economic and urban planning policies that emphasize responsible development and renewal

social atomization a social situation that emphasizes individualism over collective or group identities

social change the transformation of a culture over time

social class a system of stratification based on access to such resources as wealth, property, power, and prestige

social construction the process by which a concept or practice is created and maintained by participants who collectively agree that it exists

social control the formal and informal mechanisms used to increase conformity to values and norms and thus promote social cohesion

social Darwinism the application of the theory of evolution and the notion of "survival of the fittest" to the study of society

social dilemma a situation in which behavior that is rational for the individual can, when practiced by many people, lead to collective disaster

social ecology the study of human populations and their impact on the natural world

social identity theory a theory of group formation and maintenance that stresses the need of individual members to feel a sense of belonging

social inequality the unequal distribution of wealth, power, or prestige among members of a society

social influence exerting group control over others' decisions

social institutions systems and structures within society that shape the activities of groups and individuals

social learning the process of learning behaviors and meanings through social interaction

social loafing the phenomenon in which as more individuals are added to a task, each individual contributes a little less; a source of inefficiency when working in teams

social mobility the movement of individuals or groups within the hierarchical system of social classes

social movement any social groups with leadership, organization, and an ideological commitment to promote or resist social change

social network the web of direct and indirect ties connecting an individual to other people who may also affect the individual

social reproduction the tendency of social classes to remain relatively stable as class status is passed down from one generation to the next

social sciences the disciplines that use the scientific method to examine the social world, in contrast to the natural sciences, which examine the physical world

social stratification the division of society into groups arranged in a social hierarchy

social ties connections between individuals

socialism an economic system based on the collective ownership of the means of production, collective distribution of goods and services, and government regulation of the economy

socialization the process of learning and internalizing the values, beliefs, and norms of our social group, by which we become functioning members of society

society a group of people who shape their lives in aggregated and patterned ways that distinguish their group from other groups

sociobiology a branch of science that uses biological and evolutionary explanations for social behavior

socioeconomic status (SES) a measure of an individual's place within a social class system; often used interchangeably with "class"

sociological imagination a quality of the mind that allows us to understand the relationship between our individual circumstances and larger social forces

sociological perspective a way of looking at the world through a sociological lens

sociology the systematic or scientific study of human society and social behavior, from large-scale institutions and mass culture to small groups and individual interactions

solidarity the degree of integration or unity within a particular society; the extent to which individuals feel connected to other members of their group

special interest groups organizations that raise and spend money to influence elected officials and/or public opinion

spurious correlation the appearance of causation produced by an intervening variable

status a position in a social hierarchy that carries a particular set of expectations

status inconsistency a situation in which an individual has differing levels of status in terms of the individual's wealth, power, prestige, or other elements of socioeconomic status

stereotyping judging others based on preconceived generalizations about groups or categories of people

stigma Erving Goffman's term for any physical or social attribute that devalues a person or group's identity and that may exclude those who are devalued from normal social interaction

structural functionalism a paradigm based on the assumption that society is a unified whole that functions because of the contributions of its separate structures

structural mobility changes in the social status of large numbers of people as a result of structural changes in society

structure a social institution that is relatively stable over time and that meets the needs of society by performing functions necessary to maintain social order and stability

subculture a group within society that is differentiated by its distinctive values, norms, and lifestyle

suburbanization beginning after World War II, the shift of large segments of population away from the urban core and toward the edges of cities

suffrage movement the movement organized around gaining voting rights for women

survey a research method based on questionnaires that are administered to a sample of respondents selected from a target population

sustainable development economic development that aims to reconcile global economic growth with environmental protection

sweatshop a workplace where workers are subject to extreme exploitation, including below-standard wages, long hours, and poor working conditions that may pose health or safety hazards

symbolic culture the ideas associated with a cultural group, including ways of thinking (beliefs, values, and assumptions) and ways of behaving (norms, interactions, and communication)

symbolic ethnicity an ethnic identity that is only relevant on specific occasions and does not significantly impact everyday life

symbolic interactionism a paradigm that sees interaction and meaning as central to society and assumes that meanings are not inherent but are created through interaction

synergy a mutually beneficial interaction between parts of an organization that allows it to create something greater than the sum of its individual outputs

synthesis the new social system created out of the conflict between thesis and antithesis in a dialectical model

taboo a norm ingrained so deeply that even thinking about violating it evokes strong feelings of disgust, horror, or revulsion

target population the entire group about which a researcher would like to be able to generalize

taste cultures areas of culture that share similar aesthetics and standards of taste

taste publics groups of people who share similar artistic, literary, media, recreational, and intellectual interests

technological determinism a theory of social change that assumes changes in technology drive changes in society, rather than vice versa

technology material artifacts and the knowledge and techniques required to use them

telecommuting working from home while staying connected to the office through communications technology

tertiary deviance redefining the stigma associated with a deviant label as a positive phenomenon

textual poaching Henry Jenkins's term describing the ways that audience members manipulate an original cultural product to create a new one; a common way for fans to exert some control over the media they consume

the Chicago School a type of sociology practiced by researchers at the University of Chicago in the 1920s and 30s that centered on urban sociology and field research methods

theories in sociology, abstract propositions that explain the social world and make predictions about the future

thesis the existing social arrangements in a dialectical model

thick description the presentation of detailed data on interactions and meaning within a cultural context, from the perspective of its members

third place any informal public place where people come together regularly for conversation and camaraderie when not at work or at home

third wave the most recent period of feminist activity, focusing on issues of diversity and the variety of identities women can possess

Thomas theorem classic formulation of the way individuals define situations, whereby "if people define situations as real, they are real in their consequences"

total institution an institution in which individuals are cut off from the rest of society so that their lives can be controlled and regulated for the purpose of systematically stripping away previous roles and identities in order to create new ones

tracking the placement of students in educational "tracks," or programs of study (e.g., college prep, remedial), that determine the types of classes students take

traditional authority authority based in custom, birthright, or divine right

tragedy of the commons a type of social dilemma in which many individuals' overexploitation of a public resource depletes or degrades that common resource

transgendered term describing an individual whose sense of gender identity transgresses expected gender categories

transsexuals individuals who identify with the other sex and have surgery to alter their own sex so it fits their self-image

treadmill of production term describing the operation of modern economic systems that require constant growth, which causes increased exploitation of resources and environmental degradation

triad a three-person social group

two-step flow model theory on media effects that suggests audiences get information through opinion leaders who influence their attitudes and beliefs, rather than through direct firsthand sources

unchurched a term describing those who consider themselves spiritual but not religious and who often adopt aspects of various religious traditions

underclass the poorest group includes the homeless and chronically unemployed who may depend on public or private assistance; they constitute about 5 percent of the U.S. population

Uniform Crime Report (UCR) an official measure of crime in the United States, produced by the FBI's official tabulation of every crime reported by more than 18,000 law enforcement agencies

union an association of workers who bargain collectively for increased wages and benefits and better working conditions

upper class an elite and largely self-sustaining group who possess most of the country's wealth; they constitute about 1 percent of the U.S. population

upper-middle class mostly highly-educated professionals and managers who have considerable financial stability; they constitute about 14 percent of the U.S. population

urban density concentration of people in a city, measured by the total number of people per square mile

urban relating to cities; typically describes densely populated areas

urban renewal efforts to rejuvenate decaying inner cities, including renovation, selective demolition, commercial development, and tax incentives

urban sprawl a derogatory term applied to the expansion of urban or suburban boundaries, associated with irresponsible or poorly planned development

urbanites people who live in cities

urbanization movement of increasing numbers of people from rural areas to cities

uses and gratifications paradigm approaches to understanding media effects that focus on individuals' psychological or social needs that consumption of various media fulfills

utopia literally "no place"; an ideal society in which all social ills have been overcome

validity the accuracy of a question or measurement tool; the degree to which a researcher is measuring what he thinks he is measuring

value-free sociology an ideal whereby researchers identify facts without allowing their own personal beliefs or biases to interfere

values ideas about what is desirable or contemptible and right or wrong in a particular group; they articulate the essence of everything that a cultural group cherishes and honors.

variables one of two or more phenomena that a researcher believes are related and hopes to prove are related through research

vector organisms animals like mosquitoes, ticks, and birds that carry and spread pathogens (germs or other infectious agents) in a given area

verstehen "empathic understanding"; Weber's term to describe good social research, which tries to understand the meanings that individual social actors attach to various actions and events

vertical social mobility the movement between different class statuses, often called either upward mobility or downward mobility

violent crime crimes in which violence is either the objective or the means to an end, including murder, rape, aggravated assault, and robbery

virtual communities social groups whose interactions are mediated through information technologies, particularly the internet

virtual community a community of people linked by their consumption of the same digital media

wealth a measure of net worth that includes income, property, and other assets

weighting techniques for manipulating the sampling procedure so that the sample more closely resembles the larger population

white collar a description characterizing lower-level professional and management workers and some highly skilled laborers in technical jobs

white collar crime crime committed by a high-status individual in the course of his occupation

white flight movement of upper- and middle-class whites who could afford to leave the cities for the suburbs, especially in the 1950s and 60s

working class or **lower-middle class** mostly "blue collar" or service industry workers who are less likely to have a college degree; they constitute about 30 percent of the U.S. population

working poor poorly educated manual and service workers who may work full-time but remain near or below the poverty line; they constitute about 20 percent of the U.S. population

References

Access Clark County. 2009. "Clark County/Las Vegas Valley average population and growth rates, 1990–2008." www.accessclark county.com

Acierno R., Hernandez M. A., Amstadter A. B., Resnick H. S., Steve K., Muzzy W., et al. (2010). Prevalence and correlates of emotional, physical, sexual, and financial abuse and potential neglect in the United States: The national elder mistreatment study. American Journal of Public, 100(2), 292–297.

ACLU. 2003. "Inadequate representation." American Civil Liberties Union online publication, October 8. www.aclu.org/capital /unequal/10390pub20031008.html

Adler, Patricia A.; and Adler, Peter. 1991. *Backboards and Blackboards: College Athletes and Role Engulfment.* New York: Columbia University Press.

———. 2000. *Constructions of Deviance: Social Power, Context and Interaction.* Belmont, CA: Wadsworth.

Adorno, T.; and Horkheimer, M. 1979. "The culture industry: Enlightenment as mass deception." In T. Adorno and M. Horkheimer, eds., *Dialectic of Enlightenment.* London: Verso.

Aguirre, Benigno; Quarantelli, Enrico; and Mendoza, Jorge L. 1988. "The collective behavior of fads: The characteristics, effects and career of streaking." *American Sociological Review,* vol. 53: 569–589.

Agyeman, Julian; Bullard, Robert D.; and Evans, Bob; eds. 2003. *Just Sustainabilities: Development in an Unequal World.* Cambridge, MA: MIT Press.

Ahmed, Farid. 2012. "At least 117 killed in fire at Bangladeshi clothing factory." CNN, November 25. www.cnn.com/2012/11/25/world /asia/bangladesh-factory-fire/index.html

Alatas, Syed Farid; and Sinha, Vineeta. 2001. "Teaching classical sociological theory in Singapore: The context of Eurocentrism." *Teaching Sociology,* vol. 29, no. 3: 316–331.

Alcoholics Anonymous. 2001 (orig. 1939). *Alcoholics Anonymous: The Story of How Many Thousands of Men and Women Have Recovered from Alcoholism.* 4th ed. New York: Alcoholics Anonymous World Service.

Alexander, Jeffrey. 1988. "Parsons' 'structure' in American sociology." *Sociological Theory,* vol. 6, no. 1: 96–102.

Alexander, Jeffrey; and Smelser, Neil. 1998. *Diversity and Its Discontents: Cultural Conflict and Common Ground in Contemporary American Society.* Princeton, NJ: Princeton University Press.

Allen, Laura S., and Roger A. Gorski. 1992. "Sexual orientation and the size of the anterior commissure in the human brain." Proceedings of the National Academy of Sciences of the United States of America 89(15): 7199–7202.

Allport, G.; and Ross, M. 1967. "Personal religious orientation and prejudice." *Journal of Personality and Social Psychology,* vol. 5, no. 4: 432–443.

Almaguer, Tomas. 2008. *Racial Fault Lines: The Historical Origins of White Supremacy in California.* Berkeley, CA: University of California Press.

Altermatt, Ellen Rydell; and Pomerantz, Eva M. 2005. "The implications of having high-achieving versus low-achieving friends: A longitudinal analysis." *Social Development,* vol. 14, no. 1: 61–81.

American Association of Community Colleges. 2011. http://aacc .nche.edu/pages/default.aspx

American College Health Association. "American College Health Association-National College Health Aessment II: Reference Group Executive Summary Spring 2012." Hanover, MD: American College Health Association; 2012. www.acha-ncha.org/docs

American Psychiatric Association (APA). 2012. "Autism spectrum disorders." www.psychiatry.org/mental-health/key-topics/autism

American Sociological Association (ASA). 2012. Sociology Degrees Awarded by Degree Level. www.asanet.org

Amott, Teresa; and Matthaei, Julie. 1996. *Race, Class, Gender, and Work: A Multicultural Ethnic History of Women in the United States.* 2nd ed. Boston: South End Press.

Ananat, Elizabeth Oltmans. 2005. "The wrong side of the tracks: Estimating the causal effects of racial segregation on city outcomes." Unpublished working paper. MIT Department of Economics.

Anderson, Doug. 2009. "The Changing Face of Unemployment." Nielsenwire. March 1. blog.nielsen.com/nielsenwire/consumer /the-changing-face-of-unemployment

Anderson, Elijah. 1990. *Streetwise: Race, Class and Change in an Urban Community.* Chicago: University of Chicago Press.

Anderson, Steven W.; Bechara, Antoine; Damasio, Hann; Tranel, Daniel; and Damasio, Antonio R. 1999. "Impairment of social and moral behavior related to early damage in human prefrontal cortex." *Nature Neuroscience,* vol. 2, no. 11 (November): 1032–1037.

"Angelic Organics Farm." Angelicorganics.com

Anzaldúa, Gloria. 1987. *Borderlands/La Frontera: The New Mestiza.* San Francisco: Aunt Lute Books.

Archer, Kim. 2010. " 'Concierge medicine': Patients pay extra to keep doctor." *Tulsa World,* July 6. www.tulsaworld.com/news/article .aspx?subjectid=17&articleid=20100706_17_A1_DrJohn537025

Arendt, Hannah. 1958. *The Origins of Totalitarianism.* London: Allen and Unwin Press.

Armitage, Angus. 1951. *The World of Copernicus.* New York: Mentor Books.

Arnst, Catherine. 2010. "Tired of waiting for the doctor? Try one that gives same-day appointments." *Kaiser Health News–Boston Globe,* July 14. www.kaiserhealthnews.org/stories/2010/july/14 /waiting-for-the-doctor.aspx?referrer=search

Arrison, Sonia. 2011. *One Hundred Plus: How the Coming Age of Longevity Will Change Everything, from Careers and Relationships to Family and Faith.* Boston: Basic Books.

Asch, S. 1958. "Effects of group pressure upon the modification and distortion of judgments." In E. E. Maccoby, T. M. Newcomb, and E. L. Hartley, eds., *Readings in Social Psychology.* New York: Holt, Rinehart, & Winston.

Associated Press. 2006. "Global warming causing disease to rise: Malaria, dengue fever increasing as temperature heats up, experts warn." MSNBC, November 14. www.msnbc.msn.com /id/15717706

———. 2013. "Bangladesh factory collapse blamed on swampy ground and heavy machinery." www.guardian.co.uk/world/2013 /may/23/bangladesh-factory-collapse-rana-plaza

Association of American Medical Colleges. AAMC-HHMI. 2009. "Scientific Foundations for Future Physicians." http://www.hhmi .org/grants/pdf/08-209_AAMC-HHMI_report.pdf

Association of Certified Fraud Examiners. 2012. *2012 Report to the Nations: Key Findings and Highlights.* www.acfe.com/rttn-high lights.aspx

Atkin, C. 1973. "Instrumental utilities and information seeking." In P. Clark, ed., *New Models for Mass Communication Research.* Beverly Hills, CA: Sage.

———. 1985. "Informational utility and selective exposure." In D. Zillmann and J. Bryant, eds., *Selective Exposure to Communication.* Hillsdale, NJ: Erlbaum.

Attwood, F.; ed. 2009. *Mainstreaming Sex: The Sexualization of Western Culture.* London and New York: I. B. Tauris.

———. 2011. "The paradigm shift: Pornography research, sexualization and extreme images." *Sociology Compass,* vol. 5, no. 1: 13–22.

Avishai, Orit.. 2008. "Doing religion in a secular world: Women in conservative religions and the question of agency." *Gender and Society,* vol. 22, no. 4: 409–433.

Babbie, Earl. 2002. *The Basics of Social Research.* Belmont, CA: Wadsworth.

Babiak, T. 2004. "Everything goes at Burning Man: Counterculture fest is everything that North America isn't." *National Post,* September 6, p. B10.

Baca Zinn, Maxine; and Eitzen, D. Stanley. 2002. *Diversity in Families.* Boston: Allyn and Bacon.

Bachman, R.; and Saltzman, L. 1995. "Violence against women: Estimates from the redesigned survey." Bureau of Justice Statistics Special Report. www.ojp.usdoj.gov/bjs/pub/pdf/femvied.pdf.

Bagdikian, Ben H. 2004. *The New Media Monopoly.* Boston: Beacon Press.

Bailey, Holly. 2010. "ABC News/Yahoo! News Poll: People are losing faith in the American Dream," *Yahoo! News.* September 21. www .news.yahoo.com

Bailey, J. M.; and Pillard, R. C. 1991. "A genetic study of male sexual orientation." *Archives of General Psychiatry,* vol. 48: 1089–1096.

Bailey, Ronald. 2002. "*Silent Spring* at 40: Rachel Carson's classic is not aging well." *Reason Online Magazine,* June 12. http://reason .com/rb/rb061202.shtml

Baker, H. D. R. 1979. *Chinese Family and Kinship.* London: Macmillan Press.

Baker, J. P.; and Crist, J. L. 1971. "Teacher expectancies: A review of the literature." In J. D. Elashoff and R. E. Snow, eds., *Pygmalion Reconsidered: A Case Study in Statistical Inference: Reconsideration of the Rosenthal-Jacobson Data on Teacher Expectancy.* Worthington, OH: Charles A. Jones.

Baldwin, Tom. 2007. "Fear and blogging on the campaign trail." *London Times,* December 29. Times Magazine: 36.

Bales, Kevin. 2000. *Disposable People: New Slavery in the Global Economy.* Berkeley, CA: University of California Press.

———; and Soodalter, Ron. 2009. *The Slave Next Door: Human Trafficking and Slavery in America Today.* Berkeley, CA: University of California Press.

Balfanz, R.; Bridgeland, J. M.; Bruce, M.; and Fox, J. H. 2012. "Building a grad nation." www.americaspromise.org

Bandura, A. 1965. "Influence of models' reinforcement contingencies on the acquisition of imitative response." *Journal of Personality and Social Psychology,* vol. 1: 589–595.

Bandy, Joe. 1996. "Managing the other of nature: Sustainability, spectacle, and global regimes of capital in ecotourism." *Public Culture,* vol. 8, no. 3: 539–566.

Banks, Ingrid. 2000. *Hair Matters: Beauty, Power, and Black Women's Consciousness.* New York: New York University Press.

Barner, Mark R. 1999. "Sex-role stereotyping in FCC-mandated children's educational television." *Journal of Broadcasting & Electronic Media,* vol. 43, no. 4 (fall): 551.

Barnes, Brooke. 2009. "Disney swoops into action buying Marvel for $4 billion." *New York Times,* August 31. www.nytimes.com

Barnes, P. M.; Bloom, B.; and Nahin, R. 2008. "Complementary and alternative medicine use among adults and children: United States, 2007." *National Health Statistics Reports,* no. 12 (December 10): 1–23.

Barnes, Robert. 2013. "At Supreme Court, victories for gay marriage." Washington Post. June 26. www.washingtonpost.com

Bartels, Chuck. 2003. "Wal-Mart starting to look at all its 1.1 million U.S. workers.*" Times-Picayune* (New Orleans, LA), October 25, "Money," p. 1.

Barry, Dave. 1987. *Dave Barry's Bad Habits: A 100% Fact-Free Book.* New York, NY: Henry Holt and Co., p. 203.

Bartkowski, John P.; and Read, Jen'nan Ghazal. 2003. "Veiled submission: Gender, power, and identity among evangelical and Muslim women in the United States." *Qualitative Sociology,* vol. 26: 71–92.

Batan, Clarence M. 2004. "Of strengths and tensions: A dialogue of ideas between the classics and Philippine sociology." *UNITAS,* vol. 77, no. 2: 163–186.

Baudrillard, Jean. 1994 (orig. 1981). *Simulacra and Simulation.* Trans. Sheila Glaser. Ann Arbor, MI: University of Michigan Press.

Bauer, Martin W.; and Gaskell, George; eds. 2000. *Qualitative Researching with Text, Image and Sound.* London: Thousand Oaks; New Delhi: Sage.

Baum, S.; and Payea, K. 2004. "Education pays: The benefits of higher education for individuals and society." New York: The College Board. http://eprints.ecs.org/html/Document .asp?chouseid=5664

BBC News. 2013, April 25. "'Urgent need' to remove space debris." www.bbc.co.uk

Beamish, Thomas. 2002. *Silent Spill: The Organization of an Industrial Crisis.* Boston: MIT Press.

Beard, Jennifer; Feeley, Frank; and Rosen, Sydney. 2009. "Economic and quality of life outcomes of antiretroviral therapy for HIV/AIDS in developing countries: A systematic literature review." *AIDS Care,* vol. 21, no. 11: 1343–1356.

Becker, A.; Burwell, R.; Herzog, D.; Hamburg, P.; and Gilman, S. 2002. "Eating behaviours and attitudes following prolonged exposure to television among ethnic Fijian adolescent girls." *The British Journal of Psychiatry.* 180: 509–514.

Becker, Howard S. 1963. *Outsiders: Studies in the Sociology of Deviance.* Chicago: University of Chicago Press.

———. 1986. *Doing Things Together: Selected Papers.* Evanston, IL: Northwestern University Press.

———; Greer, Blanche; Hughes, Everett C.; and Strauss, Anselm L. 1961. *Boys in White: Student Culture in Medical School.* Chicago: University of Chicago Press.

Beeghley, Leonard. 2008. *The Structure of Social Stratification in the United States*. Boston: Allyn and Bacon.

Bell, Daniel. 1976. *The Coming of Post-Industrial Society: A Venture in Social Forecasting*. New York: Basic Books.

Bellah, Robert; Sullivan, William; and Tipton, Steven. 1985. *Habits of the Heart: Individualism and Commitment in American Life*. Berkeley, CA: University of California Press.

Belkin, Lisa. 2011. "With more single fathers, a changing family picture." *New York Times*, June 2. http://parenting.blogs .nytimes.com/2011/06/02/with-more-single-fathers-a -changing-family-picture/

Berends, M. 1995. "Educational stratification and students' social bonding to school." *British Journal of Sociology of Education*, vol. 16, no. 3: 327–351.

Berger, Peter. 1963. *Invitation to Sociology*. New York: Bantam Doubleday.

———. 1977. *Facing Up to Modernity: Excursions in Society, Politics, and Religion*. New York: Basic Books.

———; and Luckmann, Thomas. 1966. *The Social Construction of Reality: A Treatise in the Sociology of Knowledge*. Garden City, NY: Doubleday.

Bernardes, Jon. 1985. "Do we really know what the family is?" In P. Close and R. Collins, eds., *Family and Economy in Modern Society*. New York: Macmillan.

Bernstein, Jared; McNichol, Elizabeth C.; Mishel, Lawrence; and Zahradnik, Robert. 2000. "Pulling apart: A state-by-state analysis of income trends." Economic Policy Institute Study. www.epi.org /content.cfm/studies_pullingapart

Best, Joel. 2006. *Flavor of the Month: Why Smart People Fall for Fads*. Berkeley, CA: University of California Press.

Best, Samuel J., and Brian S. Krueger. 2004. *Internet Data Collection*. Sage University Paper Series no. 141. Thousand Oaks, CA: Sage.

Blau, Judith R.; and Blau, Peter M. 1982. "The cost of inequality: Metropolitan structure and violent crime." *American Sociological Review*, vol. 47, no. 1 (February): 114–129.

Blau, Melinda; and Fingerman, Karen. 2009. *Consequential Strangers: The Power of People Who Don't Seem To Matter . . . But Really Do*. New York: Norton.

Blaunstein, Albert; and Zangrando, Robert; eds. 1970. *Civil Rights and the Black American*. New York: Washington Square Press.

Blinebury, Fran. 2010. "Hurting? If a few needles can help Hill, they can help me." *NBA.com*. May 24. www.nba.com/2010/news /features/fran_blinebury/05/23/healing.hill/index.html

Bloom, Allan. 1987. *The Closing of the American Mind*. New York: Simon & Schuster.

Blumer, Herbert. 1969. *Symbolic Interactionism: Perspective and Method*. Berkeley, CA: University of California Press.

Blumler, J. G.; and Katz, Elihu. 1974. *The Uses of Mass Communication: Current Perspectives on Gratifications Research*. Beverly Hills, CA: Sage.

Bly, Robert. 1990. *Iron John: A Book About Men*. Upper Saddle River, NJ: Addison-Wesley.

Bobo, Lawrence; Kluegel, James R.; and Smith, Ryan A. 1997. "Laissez-faire racism: The crystallization of a 'kindler, gentler' anti-black ideology." In Jack Martin, ed., *Racial Attitudes in the 1990s: Continuity and Change*. Westport, CT: Praeger.

Bobo, Lawrence; and Smith, Ryan A. 1998. "From Jim Crow racism to laissez-faire racism: The transformation of racial attitudes in America." In Wendy Katkin, Ned Landsman, and Andrea Tyree, eds., *Beyond Pluralism: Essays on the Conception of Groups and Group Identities in America*. Urbana, IL: University of Illinois Press.

Bogaert, Anthony F. 2004. "Asexuality: Prevalence and Associated Factors in a National Probability Sample." *Journal of Sex*, vol. 41, no. 3: 279–287.

Bohner, Gerd; Siebler, Frank; and Schmelcher, Jurgen. 2006. "Social norms and the likelihood of raping: Perceived rape myth acceptance of others affects men's rape proclivity." *Personality and Social Psychology Bulletin*, vol. 32, no. 3: 286–297.

Bonacich, Edna. 1980. *The Economic Basis of Ethnic Solidarity: Small Business in the Japanese American Community*. Berkeley, CA: University of California Press.

Bond, Rod; and Sussex, Peter B. 1996. "Culture and conformity: A meta-analysis of studies using Asch's (1952b, 1956) line judgment task." *Psychological Bulletin*, vol. 119, no. 1: 111–137.

Booth, A.; Shelley, G.; Mazur, A.; Tharp, G.; and Kittock, R. 1989. "Testosterone and winning and losing in human competition." *Hormones and Behavior*, vol. 23: 556–571.

Bordo, Susan. *Unbearable Weight: Feminism, Western Culture, and the Body*. Berkeley: University of California Press, 1995.

Bosman, Julie. 2010. "Number of People Living on New York Streets Soars." *New York Times*. March 19. www.nytimes.com /2010/03/20/nyregion/20homeless.html

Boudon, Raymond. 1991. "What Middle-Range Theories Are." *Contemporary Sociology*, vol. 20, no. 4: 519–22.

Bourassa, Loren; and Ashforth, Blake E. 1998. "You are about to party *Defiant* style: Socialization and identity aboard an Alaskan fishing boat." *Journal of Contemporary Ethnography*, vol. 27 (July): 171–196.

Bourdieu, Pierre. 1973. "Cultural reproduction and social reproduction." In Richard Brown, ed., *Knowledge, Education, and Social Change: Papers in the Sociology of Education*. London: Tavistock.

———. 1984. *Distinction: A Social Critique of the Judgement of Taste*. Cambridge, MA: Harvard University Press.

Bowles, Samuel; and Gintis, Herbert. 1977. *Schooling in Capitalist America: Educational Reform and the Contradictions of Economic Life*. New York: Basic Books.

boyd, danah. 2007. "Why youth (heart) social network sites: The role of networked publics in teenage social life." In *MacArthur Foundation Series on Digital Learning—Youth, Identity and Digital Media Volume*, ed. David Buckingham. Cambridge, MA: MIT Press.

———. 2011. "White flight in networked publics? How race and class shaped American teen engagement with MySpace and Facebook." In Lisa Nakamura and Peter A. Chow-White, eds., *Race After the Internet*. New York: Routledge.

Boyd, Robert. 2004. "World may be darkening as clouds, air pollution dim the sun's rays." Knight Ridder News Service, *Santa Barbara News-Press*, May 9.

Boyle, Brendan. 2009. "Income gap is growing: The rich are getting richer—and rich whites quicker than rich blacks." *South African Times*, October 8. www.timeslive.co.za/business/article143706 .ece

Bozick, Robert; Alexander, Karl; and Entwisel, Doris, et al. 2010. "Framing the Future: Revisiting the Place of Educational Expectations in Status Attainment." *Social Forces*, vol. 88, no. 5: 2027–2052.

Bradley, Graham; and Wildman, Karen. 2002. "Psychosocial predictors of emerging adults' risk and reckless behaviors." *Journal of Youth and Adolescence*, vol. 31, no. 4: 253–265.

Brandon, Michael C. 1996. "From need to know to need to know." *Communication World*, vol. 13, no. 8 (October–November): 18.

Brief, Arthur P.; Buttram, Robert T.; Elliott, Jodi D.; Reizenstein, Robin M.; and McCline, Richard L. 1995. "Releasing the beast: A study of compliance with orders to use race as a selection criterion." *Journal of Social Issues*, vol. 51, no. 3 (fall): 177–193.

Brinkley-Rogers, Paul. 2002. "Pledge of allegiance reflects timeline of nation's history." *Columbus Dispatch*, June 28, p. 2A.

The Broad Foundation. 2010. "Statistics on American K–12 education." www.broadeducation.org

Brodkin, Karen. 1999. *How Jews Became White Folks and What That Says about Race in America*. New Brunswick, NJ: Rutgers University Press.

Brooks, James F. 2002. *Confounding the Color Line: The Indian-Black Experience in North America*. Lincoln, NE: University of Nebraska Press.

Bullard, Robert. 1990. *Dumping in Dixie: Race, Class and Environmental Quality*. Boulder, CO: Westview Press.

———. 1993. *Confronting Environmental Racism: Voices from the Grassroots*. Boston: South End Press.

———; Johnson, Glenn S.; and Wright, Beverly H. 1997. "Confronting environmental injustice: It's the right thing to do." *Race, Gender & Class*, vol. 5, no. 1: 63–79.

Bullard, Robert; and Wright, Beverly H. 1990. "The quest for environmental equity: Mobilizing the African-American community for social change." *Society and Natural Resources*, vol. 3: 301–311.

Burger, Jerry M. 2009. "Replicating Milgram: Would People Still Obey Today?" *American Psychologist*, vol. 64, no. 1: xxxx.

Burkhalter, Byron. 1999. "Reading race online." In Marc Smith and Peter Kollock, eds., *Communities in Cyberspace*. London: Routledge

Burros, Marian. 2009. "Urban farming, a bit closer to the sun." *New York Times*, June 16.

Butler, Judith. 1993. *Bodies That Matter: On the Discursive Limits of "Sex."* New York: Routledge.

———. 1999. *Gender Trouble*. New York: Routledge.

Buttel, Frederick H. 1987. "New directions in environmental sociology." *Annual Review of Sociology*, iss. 13: 465–488.

Byrne, D. G. 1981. "Sex differences in the reporting of symptoms of depression in the general population." *British Journal of Clinical Psychology*, vol. 20: 83–92.

Cabot, Mary Kay. 1999. "Against opponents or cancer, Stefanie and Chris Spielman prove what devotion can do." *Cleveland Plain Dealer*, May 9.

Cahill, Spencer. 1999. "Emotional capital and professional socialization: The case of mortuary science students (and me)." *Social Psychology Quarterly*, vol. 62 (June): 101–116.

Caincross, Francis. 1995. "The death of distance." Survey Telecommunications, *The Economist*, 30 (September): 5.

Califano, Joseph A., Jr. 1999. "What was really great about the Great Society." *Washington Monthly*, October.

Cancian, Maria; and Meyer, Daniel R. 1998. "Who gets custody?" *Demography*, vol. 35, no. 2: 147–157.

Caplan, Jeremy. 2005. "How green is my town." U.S. Snapshot, *Time*, July 18.

Carnevale, A.; Rose, S. J.; and Cheah, B. 2011. "The college payoff: Education, occupations, lifetime earnings." Georgetown University Center on Education and the Workforce, August 5. www.cew .georgetown.edu/collegepayoff.com

Carns, Donald. 1973. "Talking about sex: Notes on first coitus and the double standard." *Journal of Marriage and the Family*, vol. 35, no. 4 (November): 677–688.

Carroll, Andrew, ed. 2006. *Operation Homecoming: Iraq, Afghanistan, and the Home Front, in the Words of U.S. Troops and Their Families*. New York: Random House.

Carson, Rachel. 1962. *Silent Spring*. New York: Houghton Mifflin.

Cassel, Christine K.; and Demel, Beth. 2001. "Remembering death: Public policy in the USA." *Journal of the Royal Society of Medicine*, vol. 94, no. 9: 433–436.

Cassidy, Tina. 2006. *Birth*. New York: Atlantic Monthly Press.

Castells, Manuel. 1984. "Cultural identity, sexual liberation and urban structure: The gay community in San Francisco." In *The City and the Grassroots: A Cross-Cultural Theory of Urban Social Movements*. Berkeley, CA: University of California Press.

———. 2000. *The Rise of the Network Society*, vol. 1. 2nd ed. Malden, MA: Blackwell.

———; and Susser, Ida. 2002. *The Castells Reader on Cities and Social Theory*. Malden, MA: Blackwell.

Catalyst. 2013. Women on Boards. May 31. http://catalyst.org /knowledge/women-boards

Catton, William R., Jr. 1980. *Overshoot: The Ecological Basis of Revolutionary Change*. Urbana, IL: University of Illinois Press.

———; and Dunlap, Riley E. 1978. "Environmental sociology: A new paradigm." *American Sociologist*, vol. 13: 41–49.

———. 1980. "A new ecological paradigm for post-exuberant society." *American Behavioral Scientist*, vol. 24, no. 1: 15–47.

Caughey, John L. 1984. *Imaginary Social Worlds: A Cultural Approach*. Lincoln, NE: University of Nebraska Press.

———. 1999. "Imaginary social relationships." In Joseph Harris and Jay Rosen, eds., *Media Journal: Reading and Writing about Popular Culture*. Boston: Allyn and Bacon.

Center for Education Reform. 2010. "Charter School Laws Across the States 2010–2011." December 1. www.edreform.com/download /CER-Charter-Laws-2011.pdf

Center for Responsive Politics. 2012a. Barack Obama: Expenditures Breakdown. www.opensecrets.org/pres12/expend.php?id =N00009638

———. 2012b. Barack Obama: Summary. www.opensecrets.org /pres12/candidate.php?id=N00009638

———. 2012c. Mitt Romney: Expenditures Breakdown. www.open secrets.org/pres12/expend.php?id=N00000286

———. 2012d. Mitt Romney: Summary. www.opensecrets.org /pres12/candidate.php?id=N00000286

———. 2013. "2012 Outside Spending, by Super PAC." www .opensecrets.org/outsidespending/summ.php?cycle=2012&chrt =V&type=S&ql3

Centers for Disease Control and Prevention. 1998. "Leading Cause of Death, 1900–1998." www.cdc.gov/nchs/data/dvs/lead1900_98 .pdf

———. 2011. "Health Disparities and Inequalities Report—United States, 2011." January 2011. www.cdc.gov/minorityhealth /reports/CHDIR11/ExecutiveSummary.pdf

———. 2012. Prevalence of Obesity in the United States, 2009-2010. By Cynthia L. Ogden, Margaret D. Carroll, Brian K. Kit, and Katherine M. Flegal. NCHS Data Brief no. 82. www.cdc.gov/nchs/data /databriefs/db82.pdf

Central Intelligence Agency. 2012. *CIA World Factbook*. Swaziland. June 25. www.cia.gov/library/publications/the-world-factbook /geos/wz.html

———. 2013a. "Country Comparison: Infant Mortality Rate." The World Factbook. www.cia.gov/library/publications/the-world -factbook/rankorder/2091rank.html

———. 2013b. "Country Comparison: Life Expectancy at Birth." The World Factbook. www.cia.gov/library/publications/the-world -factbook/rankorder/2102rank.html

———. 2013c. "Country Comparison: Net Migration Rate." The World Factbook. www.cia.gov/library/publications/the-world -factbook/rankorder/2112rank.html

————.2013d. "Country Comparison: Population." The World Factbook. www.cia.gov/library/publications/the-world-factbook/rankorder/2119rank.html

————. 2013e. "Country Comparison: Population Growth Rate." The World Factbook. www.cia.gov/library/publications/the-world-factbook/rankorder/2002rank.html

————. 2013f. "Country Comparison: Total Fertility Rate." The World Factbook. www.cia.gov/library/publications/the-world-factbook/rankorder/2127rank.html

————. 2013g. "North America: United States." The World Factbook. www.cia.gov/library/publications/the-world-factbook/geos/us.html

Chambliss, William J. 1973. "The saints and the roughnecks." *Society.* (November): 24–31.

Champagne, Duane. 1994. *Native America: Portrait of the People.* Canton, MI: Visible Ink Press.

Charles, Camille Zubrinsky. 2001. "Processes of racial residential segregation." In Alice O'Connor, Chris Tilly, and Lawrence Bobo, eds., *Urban Inequality: Evidence from Four Cities.* New York: Russell Sage.

Chen, Katherine K. 2004. "The Burning Man organization grows up: Blending bureaucratic and alternative structures." Doctoral Dissertation. Harvard University.

Cherlin, Andrew J., and Furstenberg, Frank F., Jr. 1994. "Stepfamilies in the United States: A reconsideration." *Annual Review of Sociology,* vol. 20: 359–381.

Cheslack-Postava, Keely; Liu, Kayuet; and Bearman, Peter S. 2011. "Closely spaced pregnancies are associated with increased odds of autism in California sibling births." *Pediatrics,* vol. 127, no. 2: 246–253.

Chodorow, Nancy. 1978. *The Reproduction of Mothering: Psychoanalysis and the Sociology of Gender.* Berkeley, CA: University of California Press.

————. 1994. *Femininities, Masculinities, Sexualities: Freud and Beyond.* Lexington, KY: University Press of Kentucky.

Chordas, Lori. 2003. "Instant connection: Instant messaging is taking the business world by storm, and some insurers already are finding it improves productivity and reduces costs." *Best's Review,* vol. 104, no. 3 (July): 100.

Christakis, N. A. 1995. "The similarity and frequency of proposals to reform U.S. medical education: Constant concerns." *Journal of the American Medical Association,* vol. 274: 706.

————; and Fowler, James. 2009. *Connected: The Surprising Power of Our Social Networks and How They Shape Our Lives.* New York: Little, Brown and Company.

Christian Science Monitor. 2007. "Gender bias in college admissions." July 24. www.csmonitor.com/2007/0724/p08s01-comv.html

Cialdini, Robert B. 1998. *Influence: The Psychology of Persuasion,* rev. ed. Foxboro, Canada: Perennial Currents.

————; and Trost, M. R. 1998. "Social influence: Social norms, conformity, and compliance." In D. T. Gilbert, S. E. Fiske, and G. Lindzey, eds., *Handbook of Social Psychology,* vol. 2. 4th ed. Boston: McGraw-Hill.

Cicourel, Aaron V. 1972. "Basic and normative rules in the negotiation of status and role." In D. Sudnow, ed., *Studies in Social Interaction.* New York: Free Press.

Clarke, Lee. 2001. *Mission Improbable: Using Fantasy Documents to Tame Disaster.* Chicago: University of Chicago Press.

Clayman, Steven E. 2002. "Sequence and Solidarity." *Advances in Group Processes,* vol. 19: 229–253.

Clinton, Catherine; and Gillespie, Michelle; eds. 1997. *The Devil's Lane: Sex and Race in the Early South.* New York: Oxford University Press.

CNN. 2005. "Poll: U.S. Catholics would support changes." April 3. www.edition.cnn.com/2005/US/04/03/pope.poll/

CNNMoney. 2011. "Global 500." www.money.cnn.com/magazines/fortune/global500/2011/full_list/

Cohany, Sharon. 1996. "Workers in alternative employment arrangements." *Monthly Labor Review,* vol. 119, no. 10 (October): 31.

Cohen, Cathy J. 2005. "Punks, Bulldaggers, and Welfare Queens: The Radical Potential of Queer Politics?" in *Black Queer Studies.* Edited by E. Patrick Johnson and Mae G. Henderson. Durham, N.C.: Duke University Press: 24.

Cohen, S. P. 2001. *India: Emerging Power.* Washington, DC: Brookings Institution Press.

Coleman, John R. 1983. "Diary of a homeless man." *New York Magazine,* February.

Collins, Patricia Hill. 2006. *From Black Power to Hip Hop: Racism, Nationalism, and Feminism.* Philadelphia: Temple University Press.

Collins, Randall. 1979. *The Credential Society: An Historical Sociology of Education and Stratification.* New York: Worthington Press.

Coltrane, Scott. 1997. *Family Man: Fatherhood, Housework and Gender Equity.* New York: Oxford University Press.

Columbia Journalism Review (CJR). 2010. "Who Owns What?" www.cjr.org/resources.com

Comcast Corporation (CMCSA). 2012. Income Statement. December 30. Yahoo! Finance. www.finance.yahoo.com/q/is?s=CMCSA&annual.com

Commission for Labor Cooperation. 2003. "Work stoppages in North America." Briefing Note, October. www.naalc.org/english/pdf/work_stoppage_eng.pdf

Community Organizing and Family Issues (COFI). 2009. "Why isn't Johnny in preschool?" www.cofionline.org/files/earlylearningreport.pdf

Comte, Auguste. 1988 (orig. 1842). *Introduction to Positive Philosophy.* Edited, with introduction and revised translation, by Frederick Ferré. Indianapolis, IN: Hackett.

Condon, Stephanie. 2011. "GOP rep. calls health reforms "worst bill" ever, House votes to defund laws." *CBS News Political Hotsheet.* February 18. www.cbsnews.com/8301-503544_162-20033441-503544.html

Conley, Dalton. 2000. *Honky.* Berkeley and Los Angeles: University of California Press.

————. 2002. *Wealth and Poverty in America: A Reader.* Malden, MA: Blackwell.

————. 2004. *The Pecking Order: Which Siblings Succeed and Why.* New York: Pantheon.

————. 2009. *Elsewhere, U.S.A.: How We Got from the Company Man, Family Dinners and the Affluent Society to the Home Office, Black-Berry Moms and Economic Anxiety.* New York: Pantheon Books.

Connell, R. W. 1995. *Masculinities.* Berkeley, CA: University of California Press. *Contemporary Pediatrics.* 2000, vol. 17, no. 10 (October): 12.

Conrad, Peter. 2006. *Identifying Hyperactive Children: The Medicalization of Deviant Behavior.* Burlington, VT: Ashgate.

Conti, Joseph. 2003. "Trade, power, and law: Dispute settlement in the World Trade Organization, 1995–2002." Unpublished Master's Thesis. University of California, Santa Barbara.

————. 2005. "Power through process: Determinants of dispute resolution outcomes in the World Trade Organization." Unpublished Dissertation. University of California, Santa Barbara, Department of Sociology.

Cook, Noble David. 1998. *Born to Die: Disease and New World Conquest, 1492–1650.* Cambridge, UK: Cambridge University Press.

Cooley, Charles Horton. 1909. *Social Organization: A Study of the Large Mind.* New York: Scribner.

Coontz, Stephanie. 2000. *The Way We Never Were: American Families and the Nostalgia Trap.* New York: Basic Books.

Corporation for National & Community Service. 2012. "Volunteering and civic life in America 2012." December. www.volunteeringinamerica.gov/assets/resources/FactSheetFinal.pdf

Cosgrove-Mather, Bootie. 2004. "The suicide capital of America: They come to Las Vegas not to gamble but to kill themselves." Associated Press, *CBS News Healthwatch,* February 9. www.cbsnews.com/stories/2004/02/09/health/main599070.shtml

Cota, A. A.; Evans, C. R.; Dion, K. L.; Kilik, L. L.; and Longman, R. S. 1995. "The structure of group cohesion." *Personality and Social Psychology Bulletin,* vol. 21: 572–580.

Council for Research Excellence. 2009. "Video consumer mapping study." March 26. www.researchexcellence.com/documents/research/15.pdf

Coupland, Douglas. 1995. *Microserfs.* New York: HarperCollins.

Couvrette, Phil. 2005. "World's Biodiversity Declining at an Alarming Rate." Associated Press. May 20. www.enn.com/top_stories/article/1604

Credit.com. 2011. "Student Credit & Debt Statistics." www.credit.com/press/statistics/student-credit-and-debt-statistics.html

Crenshaw, Kimberle; Gotanda, Neil; Peller, Garry; and Thomas, Kendall; eds. 1996. *Critical Race Theory: The Key Writings That Formed the Movement.* New York: New Press.

Dahl, Robert A. 1961. *Who Governs?* New Haven, CT: Yale University Press.

Darley, John; and Latane, Bibb. 1968. "Bystander intervention in emergencies: Diffusion of responsibility." *Journal of Personality and Social Psychology,* vol. 8.

Davila, M. 1971. "Compadrazgo: Fictive kinship in Latin America." In N. Graburn, ed., *Readings in Kinship and Social Structure.* New York: Harper and Row.

Davis, Angela Y. 2001. "Outcast mothers and surrogates: Racism and reproductive politics." In Laurel Richardson, Verta Taylor, and Nancy Whittier, eds., *Feminist Frontiers IV.* Boston: McGraw-Hill.

Davis, Kingsley. 1940. "Extreme social isolation of a child." *American Journal of Sociology,* vol. 45 (January): 554–565.

———.; and Moore, Wilbert. 1945. "Some Principles of Stratification." *American Sociological Review,* vol. 10, no. 2. 1944 Annual Meeting Papers (April): 242–249.

———. 1947. "Final note on a case of extreme isolation." *American Journal of Sociology,* vol. 52, no. 5: 432–437.

Davis, T. 1995. "The occupational mobility of Black males revisited—Does race matter?" *Social Science Journal,* vol. 32, no. 2: 121–135.

De Alth, Shelley. 2009. "ID at the polls: Assessing the impact of recent state voter ID laws on voter turnout." *Harvard Law and Policy Review,* vol. 3: 185–202.

De Graaf, John; Waan, David; and Naylor, Thomas. 2002. *Affluenza: The All-Consuming Epidemic.* San Francisco: Berrett-Koehler.

Dell'Amore, Christine. 2008. " 'Deadly dozen' diseases could stem from global warming." *National Geographic News,* October 7. www.news.nationalgeographic.com/news/2008/10/081007-climate-diseases.html

DeNoon, Daniel. 2010. "Whooping cough epidemic hits California." *WebMD Health News,* July 21. http://children.webmd.com/vaccines/news/20100721/whooping-cough-epidemic-hits-california

DeParle, Jason. 2012. "Harder for Americans to Rise From Lower Rungs." *New York Times.* January 4. http://www.nytimes.com/2012/01/05/us/harder-for-americans-to-rise-from-lower-rungs.html?pagewanted=all

DeVault, Marjorie. 1994 (orig. 1991). *Feeding the Family: The Social Organization of Caring as Gendered Work.* Chicago: University of Chicago Press.

Di Leonardo, Micaela. 1987. "The female world of cards and holidays: Women, families, and the work of kinship." *Signs,* vol. 12, no. 3: 340–350.

Diamond, Sara. 1995. *Roads to Dominion: Right Wing Movements and Political Power in the United States.* New York: Guilford Press.

Dicken, Peter. 1998. *The Global Shift: Transforming the World Economy,* 3rd ed. New York: Guilford Press.

Dickson, Kevin; and Lorenz, Alicia. 2009. "Psychological empowerment and job satisfaction of temporary and part-time nonstandard workers." *Institute of Behavioral and Applied Management* www.ibam.com/pubs/jbam/articles/vol10/no2/JBAM_10_2_2.pdf

Dillon, Sam. 2010. "U.S. School Graduation Rate Is Rising." *New York Times,* November 30. www.nytimes.com/2010/11/30/education/30graduation.html

Doherty, Brian. 2000. "Burning Man grows up." *Reason,* vol. 31: 24–33. www.reason.com/0002/fe.bd.burning.shtml

———. 2004. *This Is Burning Man.* New York: Little, Brown and Company.

Dolan, Maura, Anthony York, and Maria L. La Ganga. 2013. "Gay weddings resume in California." LA Times. June 28. www.latimes.com

Domhoff, G. William. 1983. *Who Rules America Now? A View from the Eighties.* Englewood Cliffs, NJ: Prentice Hall.

———. 1987. *Power Elites and Organizations.* Newbury Park, CA: Sage.

———. 1990. *The Power Elite and the State: How Policy Is Made in America.* New York: de Gruyter.

———. 2002. *Who Rules America Now? Power and Politics in the Year 2000.* 3rd ed. Mountain View, CA: Mayfield.

Donnelly, Denise; and Finkelhor, David. 1993. "Who has joint custody? Class differences in the determination of custody arrangements." *Family Relations,* vol. 42, no. 1: 57–60.

Draut, Tamara; and Silva, Javier. 2004. "Generation broke: The growth of debt among young Americans." A Demos Group Report, October 13.

Draut, Tamara. 2006. *Strapped: Why America's 20- and 30-Somethings Can't Get Ahead.* New York: Doubleday.

Drucker, Peter. 1959. *Landmarks of Tomorrow: A Report on the New "Post-Modern" World.* New York: Harper.

———. 2003. *The Essential Drucker: The Best of Sixty Years of Peter Drucker's Writings on Management.* New York: Collins.

Duany, Andres; Plater-Zyberk, Elizabeth; and Speck, Jeff. 2001. *Suburban Nation: The Rise of Sprawl and the Decline of the American Dream.* New York: North Point Press.

Duggan, Lisa. 2003. *The Twilight of Equality?: Neoliberalisam, Cultural Politics, and the Attack on Democracy.* Boston: Beacon Press.

Duncan, David Ewing. 2012. "How long do you want to live?" *New York Times Sunday Review,* August 25.

Duneier, Mitchell; and Carter, Ovie. 1999. *Sidewalk.* New York: Farrar, Straus and Giroux.

Dunlap, Riley, E.; and Catton, William, Jr. 1979. "Environmental sociology." *Annual Review of Sociology,* iss. 5: 243–273.

———. 1994. "Struggling with human exemptionalism: The rise, decline, and revitalization of environmental sociology." *American Sociologist,* vol. 25, no. 1: 5–30.

Dupuis, Sherry L.; and Smale, Bryan J. A. 2000. "Bittersweet journeys: Meanings of leisure in the institution-based caregiving context." *Journal of Leisure Research,* vol. 32, no. 3 (June): 303.

Durkheim, Emile. 1951 (orig. 1897). *Suicide: A Study in Sociology.* Trans. John A. Spaulding and George Simpson. Glencoe, IL: Free Press of Glencoe.

———. 1964 (orig. 1893). *Suicide.* New York: Free Press.

———. 1984 (orig. 1893). *The Division of Labor in Society.* Trans. W. D. Halls. New York: Free Press.

———. 1995 (orig. 1912). *The Elementary Forms of Religious Life.* Trans. Karen E. Fields. New York: Free Press.

Dwyer, Jim. 2001. "A nation challenged." *New York Times*, November 6, p. A1.

Dye, Thomas R. 2002. *Who's Running America? The Bush Restoration.* 7th ed. Upper Saddle River, NJ: Prentice Hall.

Eckholm, Erik. 2013. "Both Sides on Same-Sex Marriage Issue Focus on the Next State Battlegrounds." *New York Times*, June 27.

Economic Policy Institute. 2012. The State of Working America. 12th edition. www.stateofworkingamerica.org

Edgerton, Robert B. 1992. *Sick Societies: Challenging the Myth of Primitive Harmony.* New York: Free Press.

Edin, Kathryn. 2000. "Few good men." *American Prospect*, vol. 11, no. 4 (January 3).

———; and Kefalas, Maria. 2005. *Promises I Can Keep: Why Poor Women Put Motherhood Before Marriage.* Berkeley, CA: University of California Press.

———; and Lein, Laura. 1997. *Making Ends Meet.* New York: Russell Sage Foundation.

Egelko, Bob. 2002. "Pledge of allegiance ruled unconstitutional; many say ruling by S. F. court hasn't a prayer after appeals." *San Francisco Chronicle*, June 27, p. A1.

Ehrenreich, Barbara. 1990. *The Worst Years of our Lives: Irreverent Notes from a Decade of Greed.* New York: Pantheon.

———. 2001. *Nickel and Dimed: On (Not) Getting by in America.* New York: Metropolitan Books.

———. 2004. "All together now." *New York Times*, July 15.

Ehrlich, Paul R.; and Ehrlich, Anne H. 1990. *The Population Explosion.* New York: Simon & Schuster.

Eisenstein, Zillah. 1979. "Capitalist patriarchy and the case for socialist feminism." *Monthly Review*, February.

El Nasser, Haye. 2010. "Downturn Douses Nevada's population Growth Streak. *USA Today*, November 8.

Eller, Cynthia. 2003. *Am I a Woman? A Skeptic's Guide to Gender.* Boston: Beacon Press.

Ellis, Carolyn. 1995. "Emotional and ethical quagmires in returning to the field." *Journal of Contemporary Ethnography*, vol. 24: 68–96.

———. 1997. "Evocative autoethnography: Writing emotionally about our lives." In W. G. Tierney and Y. S. Lincoln, eds., *Representation and the Text: Re-framing the Narrative Voice.* Albany, NY: SUNY Press.

Emerson, Robert. 2002. *Contemporary Field Research: Perspectives and Formulations* (2nd ed.) Long Grove, IL: Waveland Press.

England, Paula. 1992. *Comparable Worth: Theories and Evidence.* Edison, NJ: Aldine Transaction.

Epps, Edgar. 2001. "Race, class, and educational opportunity: Trends in the sociology of education." In Bruce R. Hare, ed., *Race Odyssey: African Americans and Sociology: A Critical Analysis.* Syracuse, NY: Syracuse University Press.

ESPN. 2008. "Major league baseball attendance report 2008." www.sports.espn.go.com/mlb/attendance

Etzioni, Amitai. 1996. "The responsive community: A communitarian perspective." *American Sociological Review*, vol. 61, no. 1: 1–11.

Fabes, Richard A.; Martin, Carol Lynn; and Hanish, Laura D. 2003. "Young children's play qualities in same-, other-, and mixed-sex peer groups." *Child Development*, vol. 74, no. 3 (May–June): 921.

Fadiman, Anne. 1998. *The Spirit Catches You and You Fall Down.* New York: Farrar, Straus and Giroux

Fairbanks, C. 1992. "Labels, literacy and enabled learning: Glenn's story." *Harvard Educational Review*, vol. 62, no. 4: 475–493.

Fairfax County Public Schools, Office of Testing and Evaluation. 1999. "Assessments: State & Fairfax County public schools passing rates." Data: Virginia Standards of Learning, 11/4/99, as cited in Bracey, Gerald. 2000. "High Stakes Testing." Center for Education Research, Analysis, and Innovation, School of Education, University of Wisconsin-Milwaukee. www.asu.edu/educ/epsl/EPRU/documents/cerai-00-32.htm#_ednref22

Falconer, Renee C.; and Byrnes, Deborah A. 2003. "When good intentions are not enough: A response to increasing diversity in an early childhood setting." *Journal of Research in Childhood Education*, vol. 17, no. 2 (spring–summer): 188.

Faludi, Susan. 1999. *Stiffed: The Betrayal of the American Man.* New York: William & Morrow.

Farghal, M.; and Shakir, A. 1994. "Kin terms and titles of address as relational social honorifics in Jordanian Arabic." *Anthropological Linguistics*, iss. 36: 240–253.

Farrell, Warren. 1975. *The Liberated Man.* New York: Bantam.

Fausto-Sterling, Anne. 2000. *Sexing the Body: Gender Politics and the Construction of Sexuality.* New York: Basic Books.

Fava, S. F. 1956. "Suburbanism as a way of life." *American Sociological Review*, vol. 21: 34–37.

Federal Bureau of Investigation. 2010a. Arrests by Age, 2010. www.fbi.gov/about-us/cjis/ucr/crime-in-the-u.s/2010/crime-in-the-u.s.-2010/tables/10tbl38.xls#overview

———. 2010b. *Crime in the United States, by Volume and Rate per 100,000 Inhabitants, 1991–2010.* www.fbi.gov/about-us/cjis/ucr/crime-in-the-u.s/2010/crime-in-the-u.s.-2010/tables/10tbl01.xls

———. 2010c. "Five-year arrest trends by sex, 2005–2009." www2.fbi.gov/ucr/cius2009/data/table_35.html,

———. 2010d. "Hate Crime Statistics, 2010." www.fbi.gov/about-us/cjis/ucr/hate-crime/2010/narratives/hate-crime-2010-incidents-and-offenses

———. 2011a. "Crime in the United States: by Volume and Rate per 100,000 Inhabitants, 1992–2011." www.fbi.gov/about-us/cjis/ucr/crime-in-the-u.s/2011/crime-in-the-u.s.-2011/tables/table-1

———. 2011b. "Murder Victims by Race and Sex, 2010." www.fbi.gov/about-us/cjis/ucr/crime-in-the-u.s/2010/crime-in-the-u.s.-2010/tables/10shrtbl01.xls

Feder-Alford, Elaine. 2006. "Only a piece of meat: One patient's reflections on her eight-day hospital experience." *Qualitative Inquiry*, vol. 12, no. 3: 596–620.

Ferguson, Bruce; and Abell, Barbara. 1998. "The urban grocery store gap." *Commentary* (Winter): 6–14.

Feingold, Alan. 1992. "Sex differences in variability in intellectual abilities: A new look at an old controversy." *Review of Educational Research*, vol. 62: 61–84.

Feingold, David. 2010. "Trafficking in numbers." In Peter Andreas and Kelly Greenhill, eds., *Sex, Drugs, and Body Counts.* Ithaca, NY: Cornell University Press.

Ferris, Kerry. 2001. "Through a glass, darkly: The dynamics of fan-celebrity encounters." *Symbolic Interaction*, vol. 24, no. 1 (February).

———. 2004. "Seeing and being seen: The moral order of celebrity sightings." *Journal of Contemporary Ethnography*, vol. 33, no. 3 (June): 236–264.

Fetterman, Mindy; and Hansen, Barbara. 2006. "Young People struggle to deal with kiss of debt." *USA Today*, November 22. www.usatoday.com/money/perfi/credit/2006-11-19-young-and -in-debt-cover_x.htm

Fine, Gary Alan. 1993. "The sad demise, mysterious disappearance, and glorious triumph of symbolic interactionism." *Annual Review of Sociology*, vol. 19: 61–87.

———. 1996. *Kitchens: The Culture of Restaurant Work.* Berkeley, CA: University of California Press.

———. 1998. *Morel Tales: The Culture of Mushrooming.* Cambridge, MA: Harvard University Press.

———. 2001. *Gifted Tongues: High School Debate and Adolescent Culture.* Princeton, NJ: Princeton University Press.

Fischer, Claude S. 1976. *The Urban Experience.* New York: Harcourt Brace Jovanovich.

———. 1994. "Changes in leisure activities, 1890–1940." *Journal of Social History*, vol. 27, no. 3 (spring): 453.

———. 2011. *Still Connected.* New York: Russell Sage Foundation.

Fischer, Mary J.; and Kmec, Julie A. 2004. "Neighborhood socioeconomic conditions as moderators of family resource transmission: High school completion among at-risk youth." *Sociological Perspectives*, vol. 47, no. 4 (winter): 507–527.

Fish, Stanley. 1980. *Is There a Text in This Class? The Authority of Interpretive Communities.* Cambridge, MA: Harvard University Press.

Fishman, Pamela. 1978. "Interaction: The work women do." *Social Problems*, vol. 25: 433.

Fiske, Jonathan. 1989. *Understanding Popular Culture.* London: Unwin Hyman.

FitzGerald, Frances. 1980. *America Revised: History Schoolbooks in the Twentieth Century.* New York: Vintage Books.

Florida, Richard. 2002. *The Rise of the Creative Class: And How It Is Transforming Work, Leisure, Community and Everyday Life.* New York: Basic Books.

———. 2004. *Cities and the Creative Class.* New York: Routledge.

Foeman, A. K.; and Nance, T. 1999. "From miscegenation to multiculturalism: Perceptions and stages of interracial relationship development." *Journal of Black Studies*, vol. 29: 540–557.

Forbes Four Hundred Richest People. 2011. *Forbes*, September 21. www.forbes.com/forbes-400

Fortner, Robert S.; and Fackler, Mark P. 2011. *The Handbook of Global Communication and Media Ethics.* Hoboken: Wiley-Blackwell.

Fox, Greer Litton; and Kelly, Robert F. 1995. "Determinants of child custody arrangements at divorce." *Journal of Marriage and the Family*, vol. 57, no. 3: 693–708.

Fox, John. 1997. *Applied Regression Analysis, Linear Models, and Related Methods.* Thousand Oaks, CA: Sage.

Fox, Renee. 1957. "Training for uncertainty." In Robert Merton, ed., *The Student Physician.* Cambridge, MA: Harvard University Press.

Frauenheim, Ed. 2012. "Outsourcing and the new global economy." *Workforce Management*, June 5. www.workforce.com /article/20120605/WORKFORCE90/120609985/vineet-nayar -interview-offshore-outsourcing-and-the-new-global-economy

Frayer, Lauren. 2012. "Pakistan's transgenders in a category of their own." National Public Radio, September 3. www.npr .org/2012/09/03/160496712/pakistans-transgenders-in-a-cate gory-of-their-own?sc=17&f=1001

Freedom to Marry. 2013. "States." www.freedomtomarry.org/states

FreePress.net. 2011. "Ownership Chart: The Big Six." www.freepress .net/ownership/chart/main

Freud, Sigmund. 1955 (orig. 1900). *The Interpretation of Dreams.* London: Hogarth.

———. 1905. *Three Essays on the Theory of Sexuality.* New York: Avon Books.

Frey, William H. 2003. "The new migration equation." *Orlando Sentinel*, November 9.

Friedan, Betty. 2001 (orig. 1963). *The Feminine Mystique.* New York: Norton.

Frieden, Bernard; and Sagalyn, Lynne B. 1992. *Downtown, Inc.: How America Rebuilds Cities.* Cambridge, MA: MIT Press.

Friedkin, Noah E. 2004. "Social cohesion." *Annual Review of Sociology*, vol. 30 (August): 409–425.

———; and Cook, Karen S. 1990. "Peer group influence." *Sociological Methods and Research*, vol. 19, no. 1: 122–143.

———; and Granovetter, Mark, eds. 1998. *A Structural Theory of Social Influence.* Structural Analysis in the Social Sciences. Cambridge, UK: Cambridge University Press.

Friedman, Milton. 1994. "Medical licensure." *Freedom Daily*, January. www.fff.org/freedom/0194e.asp

Fuller, Robert C. 2002. *Spiritual but Not Religious: Understanding Unchurched America.* New York: Oxford University Press.

Furstenberg, Frank; Hoffman, Saul; and Shrestha, Laura. 1995. "The effect of divorce on intergenerational transfers: New evidence." *Demography*, vol. 32, no. 3: 319–333.

Fussell, Paul. 1983. *Class: A Guide Through the American Status System.* New York: Touchstone.

Gabler, Neil. 2012. "It's a brand-news day in Hollywood." *Los Angeles Times*, November 10. www.latimes.com/entertainment/movies /moviesnow/la-et-mn-ca-disney-lucasfilm-marvel -20121111,0,7695955.story

Galbraith, Patrick W. 2012. *Otaku Spaces.* Seattle, WA: Chin Music Press.

Gallagher, Sally K. 2004. "The marginalization of evangelical feminism." *Sociology of Religion*, vol. 65, no. 3: 215–237.

Gans, Herbert J. 1967. *The Levittowners: Ways of Life and Politics in a New Suburban Community.* New York: Columbia University Press.

———. 1971. "The uses of poverty: The poor pay all." *Social Policy*, July–August: 20–24.

———. 1999. *Popular Culture and High Culture: An Analysis and Evaluation of Taste.* New York: Basic Books.

Gansberg, Martin. 1964. "37 who saw murder didn't call the police: Apathy at stabbing of Queens woman shocks inspector." *New York Times*, March 27.

Garber, Marjorie. 1997. *Vested Interests: Cross Dressing and Cultural Anxiety.* London: Routledge.

———. 1998. *The Symptoms of Culture.* New York: Routledge.

Garr, Emily. 2008. "The unemployment trend by state." Economic Policy Institute Economic Snapshots. www.epi.org/content.cfm /webfeatures_snapshots_20080924

Garreau, Joel. 1992. *Edge City: Life on the New Frontier.* New York: Anchor Books.

Garry, Patrick M.; and Spurlin, Candice J. 2007. "The effectiveness of media rating systems in preventing children's exposure to violent and sexually explicit media content: An empirical study." *Oklahoma City University Law Review*, vol. 32, no. 2. http://ssrn.com /abstract=1139167

Garvin, Glenn. 2008. "Too Pretty? That's When It Got Ugly." *The Miami Herald*, March 23.

Geertz, Clifford. 1973. "Deep play: Notes on the Balinese cockfight." *The Interpretation of Cultures.* New York: Basic Books.

Gelles, Richard J. 1995. *Contemporary Families: A Sociological View.* Thousand Oaks, CA: Sage.

Gemar K, Zarkowski P, Avery D. "Hotel room suicide: Las Vegas and Clark County." *Social Psychiatry and Psychiatric Epidemiology*, 2008, 43: 25–27.

Gerbner, George; and Gross, L. 1976. "Living with television: The Violence Profile." *Journal of Communication* (spring).

———; Morgan, M.; and Signorielli, N. 1980. "The mainstreaming of America: Violence Profile No. 11." *Journal of Communication*, vol. 30: 10–29.

Gereffi, Gary; and Korzeniewicz, Miguel; eds. 1994. *Commodity Chains and Global Capitalism*. Westport, CT: Praeger.

Gergen, Kenneth. 1991. *The Saturated Self*. New York: Basic Books.

Gettleman, Jeffrey. 2011. "Africans greet news with relief and hope." *New York Times*, May 3, F10.

Gibbs, Nancy. 2010. "Sexual Assaults on Female Soldiers: Don't Ask, Don't Tell." *Time.com*, March 8. www.time.com/time/magazine/article0,9171,1968110,00.html

Gibson, Campbell; and Lennon, Emily. 2001. "Historical census statistics on the foreign-born population of the United States: 1850–1990." U.S. Bureau of the Census, Population Division. www.census.gov/population/www/ documentation/twps0029.html

Gibson, William. 2001. "Modern boys and mobile girls." *The Observer*. www.guardian.co.uk/books/2001/apr/01/science fictionfantasyandhorror.features

Glaser, Jack; Dixit, Jay; and Green, Donald P. 2002. "Studying hate crime with the Internet: What makes racists advocate racial violence?" *Journal of Social Issues*, vol. 58, no. 1: 177–193.

Glaser, Mark. 2007. MediaShift. PBS. "Your guide to the digital divide." January 17. www.pbs.org/mediashift/2007/01/digging_deeperyour_guide_to_th.html

Glass, Ruth. 1964. "Aspects of change." In Centre for Urban Studies, ed., *London: Aspects of Change*. London: MacGibbon and Kee.

Gleick, P. H. 1998. "The world's water 1998–1999." Washington, DC: Island Press. Companion web site: www.worldwater.org/table7.html

Glor, Jeff. 2012. "Could babies born today live to 150?" CBS News, February 9. www.cbsnews.com/8301-505269_162-57373788/could-babies-born-today-live-to-150

Goffman, Erving. 1956. *Presentation of Self in Everyday Life*. Garden City, NY: Anchor Books.

———. 1961. *Asylums: Essays on the Social Situation of Mental Patients and Other Inmates*. Garden City, NY: Anchor Books.

———. 1962. *Stigma: Notes on the Management of Spoiled Identity*. Upper Saddle River, NJ: Prentice Hall.

———. 1971. *Relations in Public: Microstudies of the Public Order*. New York: Basic Books.

Goldberg, Herb. 1976. *The Hazards of Being Male*. New York: Nash.

González, Eduardo. 2007. "Migrant farm workers: Our nation's invisible population." National Extension Diversity Center. www.ediversitycenter.net/migrantfarmers.php

Goodacre, Daniel M. 1953. "Group characteristics of good and poor performing combat units." *Sociometry*, vol. 16, no. 2 (May): 168–179.

Goode, Erich. 1997. *Deviant Behavior*. 5th ed. Upper Saddle River, NJ: Prentice Hall.

Goode, William J. 1982. *The Family*. Englewood Cliffs, NJ: Prentice Hall.

Goodman, Peter. 2010. "U.S. Offers a Hand to Those on Eviction's Edge." *New York Times*, April 21. www.nytimes.com/2010/04/22/business/economy/22prevent.html

Goodstein, Laurie. 2004. "Personal and political, Bush's faith blurs lines." *New York Times*, October 26, p. A21.

Google Inc. (GOOG). 2012. Income Statement. Yahoo! Finance. December 31. www.finance.yahoo.com/q/is?s=GOOG+Income+Statement&annual

Gottdiener, Mark; Collins, Claudia C.; and Dickens, David R. 1999. *Las Vegas: The Social Production of an All-American City*. Malden, MA: Blackwell.

Gottman, Jean. 1961. *Megalopolis: The Urbanized Northeastern Seaboard of the United States*. New York: Twentieth Century Fund.

———; and Robert Harper. 1990. *Since Megalopolis: The Urban Writings of Jean Gottman*. Baltimore, MD: Johns Hopkins University Press.

Gottschalk, Simon. 1993. "Uncomfortably numb: Countercultural impulses in the postmodern era." *Symbolic Interaction*, vol. 16, no. 4: 357–378.

Goyette, Kimberly; and Xie, Yu. 1999. "Educational expectations of Asian-American youth: Determinants and ethnic differences." *Sociology of Education*, vol. 71: 24–38.

Gozzi, Raymond, Jr. 1996. "Will the media create a global village?" *ETC: A Review of General Semantics*, vol. 53: 65–68.

Graham, Lawrence Otis. 1996. *A Member of the Club: Reflections on Life in a Racially Polarized World*. New York: Harper Perennial.

Gramsci, Antonio. 1985. *Selections from Cultural Writings*. Cambridge, MA: Harvard University Press.

———. 1988. *An Antonio Gramsci Reader*. Ed. David Forgacs. Boston: Schocken.

Grandey, A. 2003. "When 'the show must go on': Surface and deep acting as determinants of emotional exhaustion and peer-rated service delivery." *Academy of Management Journal*, vol. 46, no. 1: 86–96.

Granfield, Robert. 1992. *Making Elite Lawyers*. New York: Routledge.

Granovetter, Mark. 1973. "The strength of weak ties." *American Journal of Sociology*, vol. 78, no. 6: 1360–1380.

Gray, David E. 2002. "'Everybody just freezes. Everybody is just embarrassed': Felt and enacted stigma among parents of children with high functioning autism." *Sociology of Health & Illness*, vol. 24, no. 6: 734–749.

———. 1994. "Coping with autism: Stresses and strategies." *Sociology of Health & Illness*, vol. 16, no. 3: 275–300.

Gray, Steven. 2009. "Can America's urban food deserts bloom?" *Time*, May 26. www.time.com/time/nation/article/0,8599,1900947,00.html

Grealy, Lucy. 1994. *Autobiography of a Face*. Boston: Houghton Mifflin.

Green, Elizabeth. 2010. "Building a Better Teacher." *New York Time Magazine*, March 2. www.nytimes.com/2010/03/07/magazine/07Teachers-t.html

Greenfeld, L., et al. 1998. "Violence by intimates: Analysis of data on crimes by current or former spouses, boyfriends, and girlfriends." *Bureau of Justice Statistics Factbook*. www.ojp.usdoj.gov/bjs/pub/pdf/vi.pdf

Greenhouse, Steven. 1999. "Activism surges at campuses nationwide, and labor is at issue." *New York Times*, March 29. www.sweatshopwatch.org/swatch/headlines/1999/nyt_mar.html

Greenstone, Michael; and Looney, Adam. 2011. "Where is the best place to invest $102,000: In stocks, bonds, or a college degree?" The Hamilton Project, Washington, DC. June. www.brookings.edu/papers/2011/0625_education_greenstone_looney.aspx

Groh, Carla J. 2007. "Poverty, Mental Health, and Women: Implications for Psychiatric Nurses in Primary Care Settings." *Journal of the American Psychiatric Nurses Association*, vol. 13, no. 5: 267–274.

Gross, Terry. 2010. "Jon Stewart: The Most Trusted Name in Fake News." National Public Radio. Oct. 4. www.npr.org/templates/story/story.php?storyId=130321994

Grossman, Lev. 2010. "Person of the Year: Mark Zuckerberg." *Time Magazine*, December 27.

Guber, Deborah Lynn. 2003. *The Grassroots of a Green Revolution: Polling America on the Environment.* Cambridge, MA: MIT Press.

Gubrium, Jaber; and Buckholdt, D. R. 1982. "Fictive family: Everyday usage, analytic, and human service considerations." *American Anthropologist*, vol. 84, no. 4: 878.

Guerino, Paul, Paige M. Harrison, and William J. Sabol. 2012. Prisoners in 2010. Bureau of Justice Statistics. www.bjs.gov/content/pub/pdf/p10.pdf

Gutfreund, Owen. 2004. *Twentieth Century Sprawl: Highways and the Reshaping of the American Landscape.* New York: Oxford University Press.

Haas, Jack; and Shaffir, William. 1977. "The professionalization of medical students: Development competence and a cloak of competence." *Symbolic Interaction*, vol. 1: 71–88.

———. 1982. "Taking on the role of doctor: A dramaturgical analysis of professionalization." *Symbolic Interaction*, vol. 5: 187–203.

Haber, Gary. 2010. "Bill tries to lure grocers to Maryland's poor areas." *Baltimore Business Journal*, March 26. http://baltimore.bizjournals.com/baltimore/stories/2010/03/29/story4.html

Habermas, Jürgen. 1984. *The Theory of Communicative Action, Vol. 1: Reason and the Rationalization of Society.* Trans. Thomas McCarthy. Boston: Beacon Press.

———. 1987. *The Theory of Communicative Action, Vol. 2: Lifeworld and System: A Critique of Functionalist Reason.* Trans. Thomas McCarthy. Boston: Beacon Press.

Hagberg, Richard; and Heifetz, Julie. 2002. "How to tell the CEO his baby is ugly." http://w3.hcgnet.com/research_uglybaby.html

Haimoff, Michelle. 2012. "Not so modern family: Top sitcoms make for sexist, inaccurate television." *Christian Science Monitor*, January 27. www.csmonitor.com/Commentary/Opinion/2012/0127/Not-so-Modern-Family-Top-sitcoms-make-for-sexist-inaccurate-television

Haizlip, Shirlee Taylor. 1994. *The Sweeter the Juice: A Family Memoir in Black and White.* New York: Simon & Schuster.

Hakim, Danny. 2001. "Fidelity picks a president of funds unit." *New York Times*, May 22, p. C1.

Haley, A. J.; and Johnston, B. S. 1998. "Menaces to management: A developmental view of British soccer hooligans, 1961–1986." *Sport Journal*, vol. 1. www.thesportjournal.org/1998journal/vol1-no1/menaces.asp

Hall, Stuart. 1980. "Encoding/decoding." In S. Hall, D. Hobson, A. Lowe, and P. Willis, eds., *Culture, Media, Language.* London: Hutchinson.

———. 2006. "Constructing difference: Creating 'other' identities." In Paula Rothenberg, ed., *Beyond Borders: Thinking Critically About Global Issues.* New York: Worth Publishers.

Halle, David. 1993. *Inside Culture: Art and Class in the American Home.* Chicago, IL: University of Chicago Press.

Halloran, Liz. 2013. "After DOMA: What's Next for Gay Married Couples." NPR. June 26. www.npr.org/blogs/thetwo-way/2013/06/26/195881288/after-doma-whats-next-for-gay-married-couples

Hamer D. H.; Hu, S.; Magnuson, V. L.; Hu, N.; and Pattatucci, A. M. 1993. "A linkage between DNA markers on the X chromosome and male sexual orientation." *Science*, vol. 261, no. 5119: 321–327.

Hamilton, Brady E.; Martin, Joyce A.; and Ventura, Stephanie J. 2011. National Vital Statistics Reports. Births: Preliminary Data for 2010. www.cdc.gov/nchs/data/nvsr/nvsr60/nvsr60_02.pdf

Hampton, Keith N.; Goulet, Lauren Sessions; Rainie, Lee; and Purcell, Kristen. 2011. "Social networking sites and our lives." Washington, D.C.: Pew Research Center's Internet and American Life Project, June 16. http://pewinternet.org/~/media//Files/Reports/2011/PIP%20-%20Social%20networking%20sites%20and%20our%20lives.pdf

Handleman, J. S.; and Harris, S., eds. 2000. *Preschool Education Programs for Children with Autism* (2nd ed). Austin, TX: Pro-Ed.

Hao, Lingxin; and Cherlin, Andrew J. 2004. "Welfare reform and teenage pregnancy, childbirth, and school dropout." *Journal of Marriage and Family*, vol. 66: 179–194.

Hardin, Garrett. 1968. "The tragedy of the commons." *Science*, vol. 162: 1243–1248.

———. 1993. *Living within Limits.* New York: Oxford University Press.

Harnick, Chris. 2012. "Most-watched TV show in the world is 'CSI: Crime Scene Investigation.'" *Huffington Post*, June 6. www.huffingtonpost.com/2012/06/14/most-watched-tv-show-in-the-world-csi_n_1597968.html

Hartley, Heather; and Drew, Tricia. 2001. "Gendered messages in sex ed films: Trends and implications for female sexual problems." *Women & Therapy*, vol. 24, nos. 1–2: 133–146.

Harvard Magazine. 2008. "Race in a genetic world." May–June: 62–65.

Harvey, David. 1990. *The Condition of Postmodernity: An Enquiry into the Origins of Cultural Change.* Cambridge, MA: Wiley-Blackwell.

Hattie, J. A. 2003. "Teachers make a difference: What is the research evidence?" Paper presented at the 2003 ACER Research Conference at the Carlton Crest Hotel in Melbourne, Australia. Oct. 19–21.

Havitz, Mark E.; and Dimanche, Frederic. 1999. "Leisure involvement revisited: Drive properties and paradoxes." *Journal of Leisure Research*, vol. 31, no. 2 (spring): 122.

Hawley, Amos H. 1950. *Human Ecology: A Theory of Community Structure.* New York: Ronald Press.

Hayase, Nozomi. 2010. "Otaku: A silent cultural revolution." Cultureunplugged.com. http://truthseekers.cultureunplugged.com/truth_seekers/2010/07/otaku-a-silent-cultural-revolution.html

Hays, Sharon. 1996. *The Cultural Contradictions of Motherhood.* New Haven, CT: Yale University Press.

———. 2003. *Flat Broke with Children: Women in the Age of Welfare Reform.* New York: Oxford University Press.

Healthcare Medicine Institute. Acupuncture Continuing Education. "San Francisco Giants and New York Yankees Acupuncture." May 25, 2010. www.healthcmi.com/acupuncturist-news-online/260-sanfranciscogiantsnewyorkyankeesacupuncture

Heilprin, John. 2005. "FBI: Radical-activist groups are major threat." *Seattle Times*, May 19. http://seattletimes.nwsource.com/html/nationworld/2002280292_ecoterror19.html

Herek, G. M. 1990. "The context of anti-gay violence: Notes on cultural and psychological heterosexism." *Journal of Interpersonal Violence*, vol. 5: 316–333.

Heritage, J.; and Stivers, T. 1999. "Online commentary in acute medical visits: A method of shaping patient expectations." *Social Science and Medicine*, vol. 49, no. 11: 1501–1517.

Herrnstein, R.; and Murry, C. 1994. *The Bell Curve: Intelligence and Class Structure in American Life.* New York, NY: Free Press.

Hertz, Marci Feldman, and David-Ferdon, Corrine. 2009. "Electronic media and youth violence: A CDC issue brief for educators and caregivers." Atlanta, GA: Centers for Disease Control.

Hewitt, John. P. 2000. *Self and Society: A Symbolic Interactionist Social Pyschology.* Boston: Allyn and Bacon.

Hill, Peter; and Wood, Ralph. 1999. *Measures of Religiosity.* Birmingham, AL: Religious Education Press.

Hochschild, Arlie Russel. 1975. "The sociology of feeling and emotion." In Marcia Millman and Rosabeth Moss Kanter, eds., *Another Voice.* Garden City, NJ: Doubleday.

———. 1983. *The Managed Heart: The Commercialization of Human Feeling.* Berkeley, CA: University of California Press.

———; and Machung, Anne. 1989. *The Second Shift: Working Parents and the Revolution at Home.* New York: Viking.

Hochschild, Jennifer L. 1996. *Facing Up to the American Dream: Race, Class, and the Soul of the Nation.* Princeton, NJ: Princeton University Press.

Hodge, Robert; and Tripp, David. 1986. *Children and Television: A Semiotic Approach.* Cambridge, UK: Polity Press.

Hoffman, Matt; and Torres, Lisa. 2002. "It's not only 'who you know' that matters: Gender, personal contacts, and job lead quality." *Gender and Society,* vol. 16, no. 6: 793–813.

Holder, Kelly. 2006. "Voting and registration in the election of November 2004." U.S. Census Bureau Report, March.

Holdren, John P.; Daily, Gretchen; and Ehrlich, Paul R. 1995. "The meaning of sustainability: Biogeophysical aspects." In M. Munasinghe and W. Shearer, eds., *Defining and Measuring Sustainability: The Biogeophysical Foundations.* Washington, DC: World Bank.

Holdsworth, M.; Gartner, A.; Landais, E.; Maire, B.; and Delpeuch, F. 2004. "Perceptions of healthy and desirable body size in urban Senegalese women." *International Journal of Obesity and Related Metabolic Disorders,* vol. 28, no. 12: 1561–1568.

Holstein, James; and Gubrium, Jaber. 1995. "Deprivatization and the construction of domestic life." *Journal of Marriage and the Family,* vol. 57, no. 4 (November): 894.

———. 2000. *The Self We Live By: Narrative Identity in a Postmodern World.* New York: Oxford University Press.

Homans, George. 1951. *The Human Group.* New York: Harcourt Brace Jovanovich.

hooks, bell. 1990. *Yearning: Race, Gender and Cultural Politics.* Boston: South End Press.

———. 2003. *We Real Cool: Black Men and Masculinity.* London: Routledge.

Howard, Philip, et al. 2011. "Opening closed regimes: What was the role of social media during the Arab Spring?" Working paper no. 2011.1. *Project on Information Technology and Political Islam.* http://pitpi.org/wp-content/uploads/2013/02/2011_Howard-Duffy-Freelon-Hussain-Mari-Mazaid_pITPI.pdf

Hoyert, Donna, and Xu, Jiaquan. 2012. "Deaths: Preliminary data for 2011." *National Vital Statistics Reports,* vol. 61, no. 6. www.cdc.gov/nchs/data/nvsr/nvsr61/nvsr61_06.pdf

Hughes, Jonathon; and Cain, Louis. 1994. *American Economic History.* 4th ed. New York: HarperCollins College Publishers.

Hughes, Z. 2003. "Why some brothers only date whites and 'others.'" *Ebony,* vol. 58: 70–74.

Hull, Elizabeth. 2002. "Florida's former felons: You can't vote here." *Commonwealth,* vol. 129, no. 12 (June 14): 16.

Hultman, Christina M.; Sparén, Pär; and Cnattingius, Sven. 2002. "Perinatal risk factors for infantile autism." *Epidemiology,* vol. 13, no. 4: 417–423.

Humphrey, Craig R.; Lewis, Tammy L.; and Buttel, Frederick H. 2002. *Environment, Energy, and Society: A New Synthesis.* Belmont, CA: Wadsworth.

Hunt, G.; and Satterlee, S. 1986. "Cohesion and division: Drinking in an English village." *Man* (New Series), vol. 21, no. 3: 521–537.

Hurley, Lawrence. 2013. "Supreme Court guts key part of landmark Voting Rights Act. *Reuters.* www.reuters.com/article/2013/06/25/us-usa-court-voting-idUSBRE95OOTU20130625

Hustvedt, Siri. 2002. "9/11 six months on." *The Observer,* March 10, Special Supplement, p. 6.

Ignatiev, Noel. 1996. *How the Irish Became White.* London: Routledge.

Independent Sector. 2012. "Scope of the nonprofit sector." www.independentsector.org/scope_of_the_sector

The Institute for College Access & Success. The Project on Student Debt. "Student Debt and the Class of 2011." October 2012. http://projectonstudentdebt.org/files/pub/classof2011.pdf

Institute for Health Metrics and Evaluation. 2013. U.S. Health Map. http://www.healthmetricsandevaluation.org/tools/data-visualization/us-health-map accessed 7/23/13

Insurance Institute for Highway Safety. "Fatality Facts, 2010." www.iihs.org/research/fatality.aspx?topicName=Alcohol&year=2010

International Business Times. 2008. "Which U.S. cities rank highest in foreclosure rates?" October 23. www.ibtimes.com/articles/20081023/which-cities-rank-highest-foreclosure-rates.htm

Isikoff, Michael. 2004. "The dots never existed." *Newsweek,* July 19.

Ito, Mitzuko; Okabe, Diasube; and Tsuji, Izumi. 2012. *Fandom Unbound: Otaku Culture in a Connected World.* New Haven, CT: Yale University Press.

Jackson, Edgar L. 1999. "Leisure and the Internet." *Journal of Physical Education, Recreation & Dance,* vol. 70, no. 9 (November): 18.

Jackson, K. T. 1985. *Crabgrass Frontier: The Suburbanization of the United States.* New York: Oxford University Press.

Jackson, Phillip. 1968. *Life in Classrooms.* New York: Holt, Rinehart, and Winston.

Jackson-Jacobs, Curtis. 2004. "Taking a beating: The narrative gratifications of fighting as an underdog." In Hayward et al., eds., *Cultural Criminology Unleashed.* London: Glasshouse.

Jacobs, Deborah L. 2013. "After the DOMA Ruling, FAQs about the Rights of Same-Sex Couples." *Forbes.* June 27. www.forbes.com/sites/deborahljacobs/2013/06/27/after-the-doma-ruling-faqs-about-the-rights-of-same-sex-couples/

Janus, Irving L. 1971. "Groupthink." *Psychology Today,* November.

———. 1982. *Groupthink.* 2nd ed. Boston: Houghton-Mifflin.

Jenkins, Henry. 1992. *Textual Poachers: Television Fans and Participatory Culture.* London. Routledge.

Jin, Ge. 2006. "Chinese gold farmers." www.we-make-money-not-art.com/archives/2006/03/ge-jin-a-phd-st.php

Johnson, Cathryn. 1994. "Gender, legitimate authority, and leader-subordinate conversations." *American Sociological Review,* vol. 59, no. 1 (February): 122–135.

Johnson, Kenneth M. 1999. "The rural rebound." *Population Reference Bureau Reports on America,* vol. 1, no. 3 (August).

———. 1995. "The rural rebound revisited." *American Demographics,* July.

———. 1998. "The revival of rural America." *Wilson Quarterly,* vol. 22, no. 2: 16–27.

Johnson, Kenneth M.; and Beale, Calvin L. 1994. "The recent revival of widespread population growth in nonmetropolitan America." *Rural Sociology,* vol. 59, no. 4: 655–667.

Jones, Andrew R. 2009. *Fads, Fetishes, and Fun: A Sociological Analysis of Pop Culture.* San Diego: Cognella

Jones, Greg. 2012. "Good workers gone bad: How to spot employee theft." *CNBC,* February 12. www.cnbc.com/id/46556452/Good_Workers_Gone_Bad_How_to_Spot_Employee_Theft

Jones, Robert P.; Cox, Daniel; and Banchoff, Thomas. 2012. *A Generation in Transition: Religion, Values, and Politics among College-Age Millennials.* Washington, DC: Public Religion Research Institute, Georgetown University, 2012.

Jones, Steve. 1997. *Virtual Culture: Identity and Communication in Cybersociety.* Thousand Oaks, CA: Sage.

———; and Philip Howard, eds. 2003. *Society Online: The Internet in Context.* Thousand Oaks, CA: Sage.

Juergensmeyer, Mark. 2003. *Terror in the Mind of God: The Global Rise of Religious Violence.* Berkeley, CA: University of California Press.

Kaczor, Bill. 1996. " Neighborhood blames years of woe on 'Mount Dioxin.'" *Charleston Gazette*, March 11.

Kalmijn M. 1998. "Intermarriages and homogamy—Causes, patterns, trends." *Annual Review of Sociology*, vol. 24: 395–421.

Kang, Miliann. 2010. *The Managed Hand: Race, Gender, and the Body in Beauty Service Work.* Berkeley, CA: University of California Press.

Kao, Grace; and Joyner, Kara. 2005. "Interracial relationships and the transition to adulthood." *American Sociological Review*, vol. 70, no. 4: 563–582.

Kara, Siddharth. 2008. *Sex Trafficking—Inside the Business of Modern Slavery.* New York: Columbia University Press.

Karau, S. J.; and Williams, K. D. 1993. "Social loafing: A meta-analytic review and theoretical integration." *Journal of Personality and Social Psychology*, vol. 65: 681–706.

Katz, Elihu. 1959. "Mass communication research and the study of popular culture." *Studies in Public Communication*, 2.

———; and Lazarsfeld, Paul F. 1955. *Personal Influence: The Part Played by People in the Flow of Mass Communications.* New York: Macmillan Free Press.

Katz, Jack. 1988. *Seductions of Crime: Moral and Sensual Attractions of Doing Evil.* New York: Basic Books.

———. 1997. "Ethnography's warrants." *Sociological Methods & Research*, vol. 25, no. 4: 391–423.

Katznelson, Ira. 2005. *When Affirmative Action Was White: An Untold History of Racial Inequality in Twentieth Century America.* New York: Norton.

Kaufman, Jason. 2008. Harvard University, Department of Sociology home page. www.wjh.harvard.edu/soc/faculty/kaufman/

Kaufman, Sharon. 2005. *. . . And a Time to Die: How American Hospitals Shape the End of Life.* New York: Scribner.

Keith, Verna M.; and Finlay, Barbara. 1988. "The impact of parental divorce on children's educational attainment, marital timing, and likelihood of divorce." *Journal of Marriage and the Family*, vol. 50, no. 3: 797–809.

Kellner, Douglas. 2001. "Globalization, technopolitics and revolution." *Theoria*, iss. 98: 14–34.

———. 2005. *Media Spectacle and the Crisis of Democracy: Terrorism, War and Election Battles.* Boulder, CO: Paradigm.

Kelly, Barbara. 1993. *Expanding the American Dream: Building and Rebuilding Levittown.* Albany, NY: State University of New York Press.

Kennickell, Arthur B. 2009. "Ponds and Streams: Wealth and Income in the U.S., 1989 to 2007." Federal Reserve Board Working Paper, January 7. Figure A3a: 63.

Kephart, William. 2000. *Extraordinary Groups: An Examination of Unconventional Lifestyles.* New York: W. H. Freeman.

Kerbo, Harold R.; and Gonzalez, Juan J. 2003. "Class and non-voting in comparative perspective: Possible causes and consequences in the United States." *Research in Political Sociology*, vol. 12: 175–196.

Kessler, R. C. 2003. "Epidemiology of women and depression." *Journal of Affective Disorders*, vol. 74, no. 1: 5–13.

Khadaroo, Stacy Teicher. 2010. "Graduation rate for US high-schoolers falls for second straight year." *Christian Science Monitor*, June 10. www.csmonitor.com/USA/Education/2010/0610/Graduation-rate-for-US-high-schoolers-falls-for-second-straight-year

Khasnis, Atul A.; and Nettleman, Mary D. 2005. "Global warming and infectious disease." *Archives of Medical Research*, vol. 36, no. 6: 689–696.

Kilbourne, Jean. 1999. *Killing Us Softly 3.* Dir. Sut Jhally. Center for Media Literacy.

Kimmel, Michael. 1987. *Changing Men: New Directions in Research on Men and Masculinity.* Thousand Oaks, CA: Sage.

King, A. 1995. Outline of a practical theory of football violence." *Sociology*, vol. 24: 635–652.

King, Marissa D.; Fountain, Christine; Dakhlallah, Diana; and Bearman, Peter S. 2009. "Estimated autism risk and older reproductive age." *American Journal of Public Health*, vol. 99, no. 9: 1673–1679.

King, Marissa; and Bearman, Peter. "Diagnostic change and the increased prevalence of autism." *International Journal of Epidemiology*, vol. 38, no. 5: 1224–1234.

Kinsey, Alfred C.; Pomeroy, Wardell B.; and Martin, Clyde E. 1998 (orig. 1948). *Sexual Behavior in the Human Male.* Bloomington, IN: Indiana University Press.

———; and Gebhard, Paul H. 1998 (orig. 1953). *Sexual Behavior in the Human Female.* Bloomington, IN: Indiana University Press.

Kitsuse, John I. 1980. "Coming out all over: Deviants and the politics of social problems." *Social Problems*, vol. 28: 1–13.

Kitzinger, C. 1987. *The Social Construction of Lesbianism.* London: Sage.

Klapper, J. 1960. *The Effects of Mass Communication.* New York: Free Press.

Klein, Naomi. 2000. *No Logo: Taking Aim at the Brand Bullies.* New York: Picador.

Klinenberg, Eric. 2002. *Heat Wave: A Social Autopsy of a Disaster in Chicago.* Chicago: University of Chicago Press.

———. 2007. "Breaking the news." *Mother Jones*, March/April. www.motherjones.com/news/feature/2007/03/breaking_the_news.html

———. 2012. "Facebook isn't making us lonely." *Slate*, April 19. www.slate.com/articles/life/culturebox/2012/04/is_facebook_making_us_lonely_no_the_atlantic_cover_story_is_wrong_.single.html

Kleinman, Sherryl. 1984. *Equals Before God: Seminarians as Humanistic Professionals.* Chicago: University of Chicago Press.

Kochhar, Rakesh. 2011. "Two years of economic recovery: Women lose jobs, men find them." Pew Social & Demographic Trends Report. Washington, DC: Pew Research Center.

Koerner, Brendan I. 2003. "Outbreaks vs. epidemics: Whether it's time to freak about the flu." *Slate*, December 19. www.slate.com/id/2092969

Kolbe, Richard H.; Langefeld, Carl D. 1993. "Appraising gender role portrayals in TV commercials." *Sex Roles*, vol. 28, no. 7: 393–417.

Kollock, Peter; Blumstein, Phillip; and Schwartz, Pepper. 1985. "Sex and power in interaction: conversational privileges and duties." *American Sociological Review*, vol. 50, no. 1. (February): 34–46.

Kosciw, Joseph G.; Greytak, Emily A.; Diaz, Elizabeth M.; and Bartkiewicz, Mark J. 2010. "The 2009 National School Climate Survey." www.glsen.org/cgibin/iowa/all/library/record/2624.html?state=research&type=research

Kosmin, Barry A.; Mayer, Egon; and Keysar, Ariela. 2001. "American Religious Identification Survey." The Graduate Center of the City University of New York. www.gc.cuny.edu/faculty/research_briefs/aris/aris_index.htm

Kotkin, Joel. 2012. "Generation Screwed." *Newsweek*, July 23 and 30. www.thedailybeast.com/newsweek/2012/07/15/are-millennials-the-screwed-generation.html

Kozeny, Geoff. 1995. "Intentional communities: Lifestyle based on ideals." www.ic.org/pnp/cdir/1995/01kozeny.html

Kozol, J. 1991. *Savage Inequalities: Children in America's Schools.* New York: Crown Publishing.

Krakauer, Jon. 1997. *Into the Wild.* New York: Anchor Books.

Krashen, S. D. 1996. *Under Attack: The Case against Bilingual Education*. Culver City, CA: Language Education Associates.

Kraus, Richard G. 1995. "Play's new identity: Big business." *Journal of Physical Education, Recreation & Dance*, vol. 66, no. 8 (October): 36.

Kreider, Rose M.; and Fields, Jason M. 2001. "Number, timing, and duration of marriages and divorces: Fall 1996." In U.S. Bureau of the Census, *Current Population Reports*, P70-80. Washington, DC: U.S. Government Printing Office.

———. 2002. "Number, timing, and duration of marriages and divorces: 1996," in U.S. Bureau of the Census, *Current Population Reports*. Washington, DC: U.S. Government Printing Office.

Kristof, N.; and WuDunn, S. 2000. "Two cheers for sweatshops." *New York Times Magazine*, September 24. www.nytimes.com/library/magazine/home/20000924mag-sweatshops.html

Krivickas, Kristy, and Daphne Lofquist. 2011. U.S. Census Bureau: Fertility & Family Statistics Branch. "Demographics of Same-Sex Couple Households with Children." www.census.gov/hhes/samesex/files/Krivickas-Lofquist%20PAA%202011.pdf

Krueger, Alan B. 2002. "The apple falls close to the tree, even in the land of opportunity." *New York Times*, November 14, p. C2.

Kuhn, Manfred; and McPartland, T. S. 1954. "An empirical investigation of self-attitude." *American Sociological Review*, vol. 19: 68–79.

Kuhn, Thomas S. 1970 (orig. 1962). *The Structure of Scientific Revolutions*. Chicago, IL: University of Chicago Press.

Kunstler, J. H. 1993. *The Geography of Nowhere: The Rise and Decline of America's Man-Made Landscape*. New York: Simon & Schuster.

Kurtz, Annalyn. 2013. Who makes minimum wage? February 13. http://economy.money.cnn.com/2013/02/13/who-makes-minimum-wage/?iid=EL

Kurzweil, Ray. 1990. *The Age of Intelligent Machines*. Cambridge, MA: MIT Press.

Lachman, Margie. 2004. "Development in midlife." *Annual Review of Psychology*, vol. 55: 305–31.

Lacy, Karyn R. 2007. *Blue Chip Black: Race, Class, and Status in the New Black Middle Class*. Berkeley, CA: University of California Press.

LaMarre, Thomas. 2004. "An introduction to the otaku movement." *EnterText*, vol. 4, no. 1: 151–87.

Lane, J. Mark; and Tabak, Ronald J. 1991. "Judicial activism and legislative 'reform' of federal habeas corpus: A critical analysis of recent developments and current proposals." *Albany Law Review*, vol. 55, no. 1: 1–95.

Lareau, Annette. 2003. *Unequal Childhoods: Class, Race and Family Life*. Berkeley, CA: University of California Press.

Larson, R. W.; and Richards, M. H. 1991. "Daily companionship in late childhood and early adolescence: Changing developmental contexts." *Child Development*, vol. 62: 284–300.

Lasch, Christopher. 1977. *Haven in a Heartless World: The Family Besieged*. New York: Basic Books.

Lawrence v. Texas, 539 U.S. 558 (2003).

Lazarsfeld, Paul; and Katz, Elihu. 1955. *Personal Influence*. New York: Free Press.

Le, C. N. 2001. "Interracial dating and marriage." *Asian-Nation: The Landscape of Asian America*. www.asian-nation.org/issues3.html

Le Bon, Gustave. 1896. *The Crowd: A Study of the Popular Mind*. New York: Viking Press.

Leaper, Campbell; and Ayers, Melanie M. 2007. "A Meta-Analytic Review of Gender Variations in Adults' Language Use: Talkativeness, Affiliative Speech, and Assertive Speech." *Personality and Social Psychology Review*. November.

Lederer, Edith. 2012. "U.N.: 4 million human trafficking victims." Associated Press, April 3. www.news.yahoo.com/un-2-4-million-human-trafficking-victims-004512192.html

Leidner, Robin. 1993. *Fast Food, Fast Talk*. Berkeley, CA: University of California Press.

Lemert, Edwin M. 1951. *Social Pathology: A Systematic Approach to the Theory of Sociopathic Behavior*. New York: McGraw-Hill.

Lemov, Doug. 2010. *Teach Like a Champion: 49 Techniques That Put Students on the Path to College*. San Francisco: Jossey-Bass.

Lepowsky, Maria Alexandra. 1993. *Gender and Power from Fruit of the Motherland*. New York: Columbia University Press.

Lerner, Melvin. 1965. "Evaluation of performance as a function of performer's reward and attractiveness." *Journal of Personality and Social Psychology*, vol. 1, no. 4.

———. 1980. *The Belief in a Just World: A Fundamental Delusion*. New York: Plenum Press.

LeVay, Simon. 1991. "A difference in hypothalamic structure between heterosexual and homosexual men." *Science*, vol. 253: 1034–1037.

———. 1993. *The Sexual Brain*. Cambridge, MA: MIT Press.

Levinson, David. 2002. *Encyclopedia of Crime and Punishment*. Thousand Oaks, CA: Sage.

Levi-Strauss, C. 1969 (orig. 1949). *The Elementary Structures of Kinship*. Rev. ed. Ed. R. Needham. Trans. J. Bell and J. von Sturmer. Boston: Beacon Press.

Lewis, Christopher Alan; Shelvin, Mark; McGuckin, Conor; and Navratil, Marek. 2001. "The Santa Clara Strength of Religious Faith Questionnaire: Confirmatory factor analysis." *Pastoral Psychology*, vol. 49, no. 5. www.infm.ulst.ac.uk/~chris/64.pdf

Lewis, Jacqueline. 1998. "Learning to strip: The socialization experiences of exotic dancers." *Canadian Journal of Human Sexuality*, vol. 7: 1–16.

Lewis, Jason. 2013. "New report details plans for low-wage worker justice." *The Village Voice*, February 14. http://blogs.villagevoice.com/runninscared/2013/02/new_report_deta.php

Lewis, Oscar. 1959. *Five Families: Mexican Case Studies in the Culture of Poverty*. New York: Basic Books.

Li, J.; and Singelmann, J. 1998. "Gender differences in class mobility: A comparative study of the United States, Sweden, and West Germany." *Acta Sociologica*, vol. 41, no. 4: 315–333.

Liazos, Alexander. 1972. "The poverty of the sociology of deviance: Nuts, sluts and perverts." *Social Problems*, vol. 20: 103–120.

Liptak, Adam. 2013, June 25. "Supreme Court Invalidates Key Part of Voting Rights Act." *New York Times*.

Liu, Ka-Yuet; King, Marissa; and Bearman, Peter S. 2010. "Social influence and the autism epidemic." *American Journal of Sociology*, vol. 115, no. 5: 1387–1434.

Livingston, Gretchen, and D'Vera Cohn. 2013. "Record Share of New Mothers are College Educated." Pew Research Social and Demographic Trends. ay 10. www.pewsocialtrends.org/2013/05/10/record-share-of-new-mothers-are-college-educated/

Lofland, Lyn. 1973. *A World of Strangers: Order and Action in Urban Public Space*. New York: Basic Books.

London, Eric; and Etzel, Ruth A. 2000. "The environment as an etiologic factor in autism: A new direction for research." *Environmental Health*, vol. 108, no. 3: 401–404.

Long, L.; and Nucci, A. 1998. "Accounting for two population turnarounds in nonmetropolitan America." *Research in Rural Sociology and Development*, iss. 7: 47–70.

Longley, Robert. 2005. "Number of 'majority-minority' states grows: Texas' minority population hits 50.2 percent." About.com. http://usgovinfo.about.com/od/censusandstatistics/a/minmajpop.htm

Lopez, Ricardo; White, Ronald D.; and Pfeifer, Stuart. 2012. "Deal brings end to L.A., Long Beach ports strike." *Los Angeles Times*,

December 5. www.latimes.com/business/la-fi-1205-ports-talks
-20121205,0,7425017.story

Lortie, Dan. 1968. "Shared ordeal and induction to work." In Howard Becker, Blancher Greer, David Reisman, and Robert Weiss, eds., *Institutions and the Person.* Chicago: Aldine.

Loseke, Donileen; and Cahill, Spencer. 1986. "Actors in search of a character: Student social workers' quest for professional identity." *Symbolic Interaction,* vol. 9: 245–258.

Loving v. Virginia. 1967. 388, U.S. 1. June 12.

Lubin, Judy. 2012. "The 'Occupy' Movement: Emerging protest forms and contested urban spaces." *Berkeley Planning Journal,* vol. 25, no. 1, p. 184-197.

Lurie, P and S. Wolfe. 1997. "Unethical Trials of Interventions to Reduce Perinatal Transmission of the Human Immunodeficincy Virus in Developing Countries." *The New England Journal of Medicine.* September 18; 337(12).

Lynch, J.W.; Kaplan, G.A.; and Shema, S.J. 1997. "Cumulative impact of sustained economic hardship on physical, cognitive, psychological, and social functioning." *New England Journal of Medicine.* December 25; 337(26):1889–1895.

———. 1998. "Income inequality and mortality in metropolitan areas of the United States." *American Journal of Public Health.* July; 88(7): 1074–1080.

Lynd, Robert S.; and Lynd, Helen Merrell. 1937. *Middletown in Transition: A Study in Cultural Conflicts.* New York: Harcourt Brace.

———. 1959 (orig. 1929). *Middletown: A Study in Modern American Culture.* San Diego, CA: Harvest Books/Harcourt Brace.

Maccoby, E. E.; and Jacklin, C. N. 1987. "Sex segregation in childhood." In H. W. Reese, ed., *Advances in Child Development and Behavior.* Orlando, FL: Academic Press.

Macintyre, S.; MacDonald, L.; and Ellaway, A. 2008. "Do poorer people have poorer access to local resources and facilities? The distribution of local resources by area deprivation in Glasgow, Scotland." *Social Sciences & Medicine,* vol. 67, no. 6: 900–914.

MacKinnon, Catharine A. 2005. *Women's Lives, Men's Laws.* Cambridge, MA: Belknap Press.

Maddow, Rachel (@maddow). 2012. "The NRA has rickrolled the whole country into watching just another standard Wayne LaPierre stump speech saying we need more guns." *Twitter,* December 21. https://twitter.com/maddow/status/282156104589377536

Mahmood, Saba. 2004. *Politics of Piety: The Islamic Revival and the Feminist Subject.* Princeton, NJ: Princeton University Press.

Malamuth, Neil; and Donnerstein, Edward; eds. 1984. *Pornography and Sexual Aggression.* New York: Academic Press.

Malthus, Thomas. 1997 (orig. 1798). *An Essay on the Principle of Population: An Essay on the Principle of Population, as it Affects the Future Improvement of Society with Remarks on the Speculations of Mr. Godwin, M. Condorcet, and Other Writers.* London: printed for J. Johnson, St. Paul's Churchyard. Rendered into HTML format by Ed Stephan, 8/10/97. www.ac.wwu.edu/~stephan/malthus/malthus.0.html

Mann, Leslie. 2012. "Tips for raising backyard chickens to avoid getting egg on your face." *Chicago Tribune,* August 29. http://articles.chicagotribune.com/2012-08-29/health/ct-x-0829-backyard-chickens-salmonella-20120829_1_backyard-chickens-chicken-owners-raw-chicken

Mann, Susan A.; Grimes, Michael D.; Kemp, Alice Abel; and Jenkins, Pamela J. 1997. "Paradigm shifts in family sociology? Evidence from three decades of family textbooks." *Journal of Family Issues,* vol. 18, no. 3 (May): 315.

Marche, Stephen. 2012. "Is Facebook making us lonely?" *The Atlantic,* May 2012. www.theatlantic.com/magazine/archive/2012/05/is-facebook-making-us-lonely/8930

Marcuse, Herbert. 1991 (orig. 1964). *One-Dimensional Man: Studies in the Ideology of Advanced Industrial Society.* Boston: Beacon Press.

Markon, Jerry. 2007. "Human trafficking evokes outrage, little evidence: U.S. estimates thousands of victims, but efforts to find them fall short." *Washington Post,* September 23.

Martin, Andrew. 2012. "Debt collectors cashing in on student loan roundup." *New York Times,* September 9, p. A1.

Martin, Laura. 1986. "Eskimo words for snow: A case study in the genesis and decay of an anthropological example." *American Anthropologist,* vol. 88, no. 2: 418–423.

Martineau, Harriet. 1837. *Society in America.* London: Saunders and Otley.

———. 1838. *Retrospect of Western Travel.* London: Saunders and Otley.

———. 1853. *The Positive Philosophy of Auguste Comte.* London: Chapman

Marullo, Sam. 1999. "Sociology's essential role: Promoting critical analysis in service learning." In J. Ostrow, G. Hesser, and S. Enos, eds., *Cultivating the Sociological Imagination: Concepts and Models for Service Learning in Sociology.* Washington, DC: American Association for Higher Education.

Marx, Karl. 1982 (orig. 1848). *The Communist Manifesto.* New York: International.

———. 2001. *Selected Writings.* Ed. David McLellan. Oxford: Oxford University Press.

———. 2006 (orig. 1890). *Das Kapital.* Miami, FL: Synergy International of the Americas, Ltd.

Maslin Nir, Sarah. 2010. "Embracing A Life of Solitude." *New York Times,* April 14.

Massey, D. S.; and Denton N. A. 1993. *American Apartheid: Segregation and the Making of the Underclass.* Cambridge, MA: Harvard University Press.

Matsuda, Mari J.: Lawrence, C. R.; Delgado, Richard; and Crenshaw, Kimberle. 1993. *Words That Wound: Critical Race Theory, Assaultive Speech and the First Amendment.* Boulder, CO: Westview Press.

Matza, David. 1969. *Becoming Deviant.* Englewood Cliffs, NJ: Prentice Hall.

Mauss, Armand L. 1975. *Social Problems as Social Movements.* Philadelphia, PA: J. B. Lippincott.

Maynard, D.W.; and Frankel, R.M. 2006. "On diagnostic rationality: bad news, good news, and the symptom residue." In J. Heritage and D. Maynard, eds., *Communication in Medical Care: Interaction between Primary Care Physicians and Patients.* Cambridge: Cambridge University Press.

Mayo, Elton. 1949. Hawthorne and the Western Electric Company, The Social Problems of an Industrial Civilisation, New York, NY: Routledge.

Mazumder, Bhashkar. 2012. "Upward intergenerational economic mobility in the United States." PEW Charitable Trusts.

McArdle, Megan. 2012. "Is college a lousy investment?" *Newsweek,* September 9.

McCaa, Robert. 1994. "Child marriage and complex families among the Nahuas of ancient Mexico." *Latin American Population History Bulletin,* 26: 2–11.

McCall, L. 2001. "Sources of racial wage inequality in metropolitan labor markets: Racial, ethnic, and gender differences." *American Sociological Review,* vol. 66, no. 4 (August): 520–541.

McCandless, Douglas, Pearl Doughty-White, and Alexia Wdowski. 2009. "Colours in Culture." Information is Beautiful. April. http://www.informationisbeautiful.net/visualizations/colours-in-cultures/

McChesney, Robert. 1997. *Corporate Media and the Threat to Democracy.* Open Media Pamphlet Series. New York: Seven Stories Press.

———. 2000. *Rich Media, Poor Democracy: Communication Politics in Dubious Times.* New York: New Press.

———. 2004. *The Problem of the Media: U.S. Communication Politics in the Twenty-First Century.* New York: Monthly Review Press.

McCleary, Richard; and Tewksbury, Richard. 2010. "Female patrons of porn." *Deviant Behavior*, vol. 31, no. 2 (February): 208–223.

McCombs, Maxwell; and Shaw, Donald. 1972. "The agenda-setting function of mass media." *Public Opinion Quarterly*, vol. 36, no. 2 (summer): 176–187.

———. 1977. "The agenda-setting function of the press." In D. Shaw and M. McCombs, eds., *The Emergence of American Political Issues: The Agenda-Setting Function of the Press* (89–105). St. Paul, MN: West Publishing.

McDonald, Michael P. 2013. "2012 General Election Turnout Rates." United States Election Project. http://elections.gmu.edu/Turnout_2012G.html

McGhee, Paul E.; and Frueh, Terry. 1980. "Television viewing and the learning of sex-role stereotypes." *Sex Roles*, vol. 6, no. 2: 179.

McGinn, Daniel. 2006. "Marriage by the numbers." *Newsweek*, June 5.

McGrane, Bernard. 1994. *The Un-TV and the 10 MPH Car: Experiments in Personal Freedom and Everyday Life.* New York: Small Press.

———; and Gunderson, John. 2010. *Watching TV Is Not Required: Thinking About Media and Thinking About Thinking.* New York: Routledge.

McIntyre, Shelby; Moberg, Dennis J.; and Posner, Barry Z. 1980. "Preferential treatment in preselection decisions according to sex and race." *Academy of Management Journal*, vol. 23, no. 4 (December): 738–749.

McKinlay, J.B. 1997. "A case for refocusing upstream: the political economy of health and illness." In P. Conrad, ed., *The Sociology of Health and Illness: Critical Perspectives.* New York: St. Martin's Press.

McKinley, Jesse. 2010. "Whooping cough kills 5 in California; State declares an epidemic." *New York Times*, July 23.

McLuhan, Marshall. 1964. *Understanding Media: The Extensions of Man.* New York: McGraw Hill.

McMichael, Philip. 1996. *Development and Social Change: A Global Perspective.* Thousand Oaks, CA: Pine Forge Press.

McNamara, Kevin. 1999. "CityWalk: Los(t) Angeles in the shape of a mall." In Ghent Urban Studies Team, ed., *The Urban Condition.* Rotterdam: 010 pub.

McNicol, Tony. 2006. "Meet the geek elite." *Wired Magazine*, vol. 14, no. 7 (July). www.wired.com/wired/archive/14.07/posts.html?pg=5

McPhail, Clark. 1991. *The Myth of the Madding Crowd.* New York: de Gruyter.

Mead, George Herbert. 1934. *Mind, Self and Society.* Ed. Charles Morris. Chicago: University of Chicago Press.

Mele, Christopher. 2000. *Selling the Lower East Side: Culture, Real Estate, and Resistance in New York City.* Minneapolis, MN: University of Minnesota Press.

Melnick, Meredith. 2011. "Mixed race celebrities on race, in their own words." *Time Magazine*, February 15. www.healthland.time.com/2011/02/15/mixed-race-celebrities-in-their-own-words/

Merritt Hawkins & Associates. "2009 Survey of Physician Wait Times." www.merritthawkins.com/pdf/mha2009waittimesurvey.pdf

Merrow, John. 2007. "Dream catchers." *New York Times.* Education Life special section. April 27, sec. 4A, 18–22.

Merton, Robert K. 1948. "The self-fulfilling prophecy." *Antioch Review*, vol. 8, no. 2 (June): 193–210.

———. 1938. "Social Structure and Anomie." *American Sociological Review* 3 (5): 672–682.

———. 1968. *Social Theory and Social Structure.* 2nd rev. ed. New York: Free Press.

———. 1976. *Sociological Ambivalence and Other Essays.* New York: Simon & Schuster.

———. 1996. *On Social Structure and Science.* Chicago: University of Chicago.

Messerschmidt, James W. 1993. *Masculinities and Crime: Critique and Reconceptualization of Theory.* Totowa, NJ: Rowman and Littlefield.

———. 1998. "Men victimizing men: The case of lynching: 1865–1900." In Lee H. Bowker, ed., *Masculinities and Violence.* Thousand Oaks, CA: Sage.

Meyer, D. 2000. "Social movements: Creating communities of change." In R. Teske and M. Tetreault, eds., *Conscious Acts and the Politics of Social Change.* Columbia, SC: University of South Carolina Press.

Meyer, Daniel R.; and Bartfeld, Judi. 1998. "Patterns of child support compliance in Wisconsin." *Journal of Marriage and the Family*, vol. 60, no. 2: 309–318.

Meyrowitz, Joshua. 1985. *No Sense of Place: The Impact of Electronic Media on Social Behavior.* New York: Oxford University Press.

Milgram, Stanley. 1963. "Behavioral Study of Obedience." *Journal of Abnormal Social Psychology*, vol. 67: 371–378.

———. 1974. *Obedience to Authority: An Experimental View.* New York: Harper & Row.

Miller, Alice. 1990. *For Your Own Good: Hidden Cruelty in Child-Rearing and the Roots of Violence.* New York: Noonday Press.

Miller, Donald E.; and Miller, Lorna Touryan. 1999. *Survivors: An Oral History of the Armenian Genocide.* Berkeley, CA: University of California Press.

Miller, Laura. 1997. "Women in the military." *Social Psychology Quarterly*, vol. 60, no. 10 (March).

Mills, C. Wright. 1959. "The promise." *The Sociological Imagination.* New York: Oxford University Press.

———. 1970 (orig. 1956). *The Power Elite.* New York: Oxford University Press.

Miner, Horace. 1956. "Body ritual among the Nacirema." *American Anthropologist*, vol. 58, no. 3 (June).

Miringoff, Marc; and Miringoff, Marque-Luisa. 1999. *The Social Health of the Nation: How America Is Really Doing.* New York: Oxford University Press.

Mishel, Lawrence, Jared Bernstein, and Heidi Shierholz 2009. Table 3.16, page 166. *The State of Working America 2008–2009.* Ithaca, NY: Cornell University Press.

Mitchell, Katharyne. 1993. "Multiculturalism, or the united colors of capitalism?" *Antipode*, vol. 25, no. 4: 263–294.

Mitchell, Richard. 2001. *Dancing at Armageddon: Survivalism and Chaos in Modern Times.* Chicago: University of Chicago Press.

———; and Charmaz, Kathy. 1996. "The myth of silent authorship: Self, substance and style in ethnographic writing." *Symbolic Interaction*, vol. 19, no. 4 (winter): 285–302.

Mittermeier, Russell A.; Myers, Norman; and Mittermeier, Cristina Goettsch. 2000. *Hotspots: Earth's Biologically Richest and Most*

Endangered Terrestrial Ecoregions. Arlington, VA: Conservation International.

Mollenkopf, John. 1983. *The Contested City.* Princeton, NJ: Princeton University Press.

Molotch, Harvey. 1970. "Oil in Santa Barbara and power in America." *Sociological Inquiry*, vol. 40: 131–144.

Montagu, A. 1998. *Man's Most Dangerous Myth: The Fallacy of Race.* 6th ed. Thousand Oaks, CA: Altamira Press.

Montopoli, Brian. 2010. "Jon Stewart Rally Attracts Estimated 215,000." *CBS News,* Oct. 30. www.cbsnews.com/8301-503544_162 -20021284-503544.html

Morrison, Donna Ruane; and Cherlin, Andrew J. 1995. "The divorce process and young children's well-being: A prospective analysis." *Journal of Marriage and the Family*, vol. 57, no. 3: 800–812.

Muhl, Charles J. 2002. "What is an employee? The answer depends on the federal law; in a legal context, the classification of a worker as either an employee or an independent contractor can have significant consequences." *Monthly Labor Review*, vol. 125, no. 1 (January).

Mullins, N. 1973. *Theories and Theory Groups in Contemporary American Sociology.* New York: Harper and Row.

Murphy, Sherry L.; Xu, Jiaquan; and Kochanek, Kenneth D. 2012. Deaths: Preliminary Data for 2010. National Vital Statistics Reports. www.cdc.gov/nchs/data/nvsr/nvsr60/nvsr60_04.pdf

Musgrove, Mike. "Twitter is a Player in Iran's Drama" *Washington Post.* June 17, 2009. http://articles.washingtonpost.com/2009-06-17 /world/36805373_1_tweets-twitter-revolution-twitter-interface

Myers, Norman; and Kent, Jennifer. 2004. *The New Consumers: The Influence of Affluence on the Environment.* Washington, DC: Island Press.

———, eds. 2005. *The New Atlas of Planet Management.* Berkeley, CA: University of California Press.

Nahin, Richard, et al. 2009. "Costs of complementary and alternative medicine (CAM) and frequency of visits to CAM practitioners: United States, 2007." *National Health Statistics Reports*, July 30. www.cdc.gov/NCHS/data/nhsr/nhsr018.pdf

National Association of Colleges and Employers (NACE). May 9, 2012. *The College Class of 2012 Student Survey Report.* www.naceweb .org/uploadedFiles/NACEWeb/Research/Student/2012 -student-survey-executive-summary.pdf

National Center for Education Statistics. 2012. The Condition of Education. http://nces.ed.gov/pubsearch/pubsinfo.asp?pubid =2012045

National Center for Health Statistics. 2012a. "Fertility of Men and Women Aged 15-44 Years in the United States: National Survey of Family Growth, 2006–2010." National Health Statistics Reports No. 51. April 12. www.cdc.gov/nchs/data/nhsr/nhsr051.pdf

———. 2012b. "Health, United States, 2011: With Special Feature on Socioeconomic Status and Health." Hyattsville, MD. www.cdc .gov/nchs/data/hus/hus11.pdf

National Coalition Against Domestic Violence (NCADV). 2007. "Domestic Violence Facts." www.NCADV.org

National Conference of State Legislatures (NCSL). 2013. State Laws Limiting Marriage to Opposite-Sex Couples. June 26. www.ncsl .org/issues-research/human-services/state-doma-laws.aspx

National Domestic Violence Hotline. 2003. "What is domestic violence?" www.ndvh.org/dvInfo.html

National Law Center on Homelessness and Poverty. 2010. "Homelessness and Poverty in America." http://nlchp.org/hapia.cfm

National Opinion Research Center, University of Chicago. 1999. "The emerging 21st century American family." GSS Social Change Report No. 42.

———. 2013. *General Social Survey 1972-2012: Cumulative Codebook.* Storrs, CT: Roper Center for Public Opinion Research. http://publicdata.norc.org/GSS/DOCUMENTS/BOOK/GSS _Codebook.pdf

National Public Radio. 2003. "Interracial marriage." *Odyssey*. WBEZ, Chicago. February 28.

———, Kaiser Family Foundation, and Harvard University Kennedy School of Government. 2001. National Survey on Poverty in America: Summary of Findings. www.kff.org/kaiserpolls/3118 -index.cfm

National Vital Statistics System. 2013. National Marriage and Divorce Rate Trends: Provisional number of marriages and marriage rate: United States, 2000–2011. www.cdc.gov/nchs/nvss /marriage_divorce_tables.htm

Nattras, Nicoli; and Seekings, Jeremy. 2001. "Two nations? Race and economic inequality in South Africa today." *Daedalus*, vol. 139 (winter): 45–70.

New School. 2004. "Thomas Robert Malthus, 1766–1834." Economics Department, New School. The History of Economic Thought web site. http://cepa.newschool.edu/het/profiles/malthus.htm

Newman, David M. 2000. *Sociology: Exploring the Architecture of Everyday Life.* 3rd ed. Thousand Oaks, CA: Pine Forge Press.

Newton, Michael. 2004. *Savage Girls and Wild Boys: A History of Feral Children.* New York: Picador.

NewsCorp. (NWSA). Income Statement. June 29, 2012. Yahoo! Finance. http://finance.yahoo.com/q/is?s=NWSA+Income+Statement &annual

The Nielsen Company. 2013. "State of the media: U.S. Consumer usage report." January 7. www.nielsen.com/content/dam/corporate/us /en/reports-downloads/2013%20Reports/Nielsen-US-Consumer -Usage-Report-2012-FINAL.pdf

Nixon, Richard. 1974. "Address on the state of the union delivered before a joint session of the Congress," January 30. *The American Presidency Project* (J. T. Wooley and G. Peters, eds.). www .presidency.ucsb.edu/ws/index.php?pid=4327

Noah, Timothy. 2004. "Something nice about Bush." *Slate*, November 4. http://slate.msn.com/id/2109228/

Nogaki, Sylvia Weiland. 1993. "Judge oks Nordstrom lawsuit settlement." *Seattle Times*, April 13.

Norris, Pippa. 2001. *Digital Divide: Civic Engagement, Information Poverty, and the Internet Worldwide.* Cambridge: Cambridge University Press.

Norton, Eleanor Holmes. 2006. "Where's school voucher 'success' in Washington, D.C.?" *USA Today*, August 23.

Novel Swine-Origin Influenza A (H1N1) Virus Investigation Team. 2009. "Emergence of a novel swine-origin influenza A (H1N1) virus in humans." *New England Journal of Medicine*, vol. 360: 2605–2615.

Nuwer, Hank. 1999. Wrongs of Passage: Fraternities, Sororities, Hazing and Binge Drinking. Bloomington, IN. Indiana University Press.

Oakes, Jeannie. 1985. *Keeping Track: How Schools Structure Inequality.* New Haven, CT: Yale University Press.

O'Brien, Jodi; and Kollock, Peter. 1997. *The Production of Reality: Essays and Readings on Social Interaction.* Thousand Oaks, CA: Pine Forge Press.

Ochs, Elinor. 1986. "Introduction." In Bambi B. Schieffelin and Elinor Ochs, eds., *Language and Socialization Across Cultures.* New York: Cambridge University Press.

Ogburn, William. 1964. *On Cultural and Social Change: Selected Papers.* Chicago: University of Chicago Press.

Ohtaki, Sachiko; Ohtaki, Toshio; and Fetters, Michael D. 2003. " Doctor–patient communication: a comparison of the USA and Japan" *Family Practice*, vol. 20, no. 3: 276–282.

Oldenburg, Ray. 1999. *The Great Good Place.* New York: Marlowe and Company.

Omi, Michael; and Winant, Howard. 1994. *Racial Formation in the United States: From the 1960s to the 1990s.* 2nd ed. New York: Routledge.

O'Neill, J. 2007. "HIV/AIDS in the developing world: What can we do?" In R. Gallo, ed., *Retroviruses: Biology, Pathogenic Mechanisms and Treatment, The Biomedical & Life Sciences Collection.* London: Henry Stewart Talks.

O'Reilly, Brian. 1992. "Looking ahead: Jobs are fast moving abroad." *Fortune*, December 14, pp. 52–66.

Orfield, Gary. 2001. "Schools more separate: Consequences of a decade of resegregation." Civil Rights Project Report. Harvard University. www.civilrightsproject.harvard.edu/research/deseg/separate _schools01.php

Osborne, Lawrence. 2002. "Consuming rituals of the suburban tribe." *New York Times Magazine*, January 13.

Paasonen, S.; et al. 2007. "Pornification and the education of desire." In S. Paasonen et al., eds., *Pornification: Sex and Sexuality in Media Culture.* Oxford: Berg.

Park, Robert Ezra. 1961. "Human ecology." Reprinted in G. A. Theodorson, ed., *Studies in Human Ecology.* New York: Row, Peterson & Company.

Parker, Ashley. 2011. "Live blog: New York reacts to bin Laden's death." *New York Times*, May 2. http://cityroom.blogs.nytimes .com/2011/05/02/live-blog-new-york-reacts-to-bin-ladens -death

Parker, Lonnae O'Neal. 1998. "Brand identities." *Washington Post*, May 11.

Parlapiano, Alicia. 2013. "Movement on Social Issues." New York Times, March 25.

Parsons, Talcott. 1951. *The Social System.* Glencoe, IL: The Free Press.

———. 1955. "The American family: Its relation to personality and social structure." In Talcott Parsons and R. Bales, eds., *Family Socialization and Interaction Process.* New York: Free Press.

———; and Bales, R.; eds. 1955. *Family, Socialization and Interaction Process.* New York: Free Press.

Pascoe, C. J. 2007. "Dude, you're a fag: masculinity and sexuality in high school." University of California Press, 5.

Patchett, Ann. 2001. *Bel Canto.* New York: Harper Perennial.

———. 2004. *Truth & Beauty: A Friendship.* New York: HarperCollins.

Patterson, Margot. 2004. "The rise of global fundamentalism." *National Catholic Reporter*, May 7.

PBS. 2001. Frontline: Merchants of Cool. pbs.org/wgbh/pages /frontline/shows/cool/

Peavy, Linda; and Smith, Ursula. 1998. *Pioneer Women: The Lives of Women on the Frontier.* Norman, OK: University of Oklahoma Press.

People and the Planet. 2002. "Two more Earths needed by 2050." www.peopleandplanet.net/doc.php?id+1685&section=17

Perez, Erica. 2012. "Despite diversity efforts, UC minority enrollment down since Prop. 209." *California Watch.* http://californiawatch .org/dailyreport/despite-diversity-efforts-uc-minority-enroll ment-down-prop-209-15031

Perlin, Ross. 2011. *Intern Nation: How to Earn Nothing and Learn Little in the Brave New Economy.* New York: Verso.

Perls T. T.; and Fretts, R. 1998. "Why women live longer than men." *Scientific American Presents: Women's Health: A Lifelong Guide*, vol. 9, no. 4: 100–104.

Perrin, S.; and Spencer, C. P. 1980. "The Asch effect: A child of its time." *Bulletin of the British Psychological Society*, vol. 32: 405–406.

———. 1981. "Independence or conformity in the Asch experiment as a reflection of cultural and situational factors." *British Journal of Social Psychology*, vol. 20: 215–210.

Perry, J.; and Pugh, M. 1978. *Collective Behavior: Response to Social Stress.* St. Paul, MN: West Publishing Company.

Perry, Mark J. 2010. "The great mancession of 2008–2009." Paper presented at the Statement before the House Ways and Means Committee Subcommittee on Income Security and Family Support on Responsible Fatherhood Programs. American Enterprise Institute for Public Policy Research, June 17.

Peters, H. Elizabeth; Argys, Laura M.; Maccoby, Eleanor E.; and Mnookin, Robert H. 1993. "Enforcing divorce settlements: Evidence from child support compliance and award modifications." *Demography*, vol. 30, no. 4: 719–735.

Peterson, Julie. 2003. "U.S. Supreme Court rules on University of Michigan cases." www.umich.edu/news/Releases/2003/Jun03 /supremecourt.html

Peterson, William. 2003. *From Persons to People: Further Studies in the Politics of Population.* Edison, NJ: Transaction.

Pettigrew, Thomas F., and Linda R. Tropp. 2011. When Groups Meet: The Dynamics of Intergroup Contact. East Sussex, UK: Psychology Press.

Pettit, Becky; and Western, Bruce. 2004. "Mass imprisonment and the life course: Race and class inequality in U.S. incarceration." *American Sociological Review*, vol. 69: 151–169.

PEW Charitable Trusts. "Pursuing the American Dream: Economic mobility across generations." www.pewstates.org/uploadedFiles /PCS_Assets/2012/Pursuing_American_Dream.pdf

Pew Forum on Religion and Public Life. 2008. U.S. Religious Landscape Survey. http://religions.pewforum.org

———. 2011. "Changes in Religious Affiliation in the United States." February 2011. www.pewforum.org/files/2009/04/fullreport.pdf

———. 2012a. "Nones" on the Rise: One-in-Five Adults Have No Religious Affiliation. www.pewforum.org/uploadedFiles /Topics/Religious_Affiliation/Unaffiliated/NonesOnTheRise -full.pdf

———. 2012b. Little Voter Discomfort with Romney's Mormon Religion. www.pewforum.org/2012/07/26/2012-romney-mormonism -obamas-religion/

———. 2012c. Rising Tide of Restrictions on Religion. www .pewforum.org/Government/Rising-Tide-of-Restrictions -on-Religion-findings.aspx

Pew Internet and American Life Project. 2012a. Digital Differences, April 13. http://pewinternet.org/~/media//Files/Reports/2012 /PIP_Digital_differences_041312.pdf

———. 2012b. Privacy management on social media sites. February 24. http://pewinternet.org/~/media//Files/Reports/2012 /PIP_Privacy_management_on_social_media_sites_022412 .pdf

Pew Research Center for the People and the Press. 2008. "Growing doubts about McCain's judgment, age and campaign conduct." Section 2: Candidate Traits. Survey Report, October 21. http: //people-press.org/report/462/obamas-lead-widens

———. 2012a. "Cable Leads the Pack as Campaign News Source." February 7, 2012. www.people-press.org/2012/02/07 /cable-leads-the-pack-as-campaign-news-source/

———. 2012b. Partisan Polarization Surges in Bush, Obama Years. Trends in American Values: 1987–2012. Section 3: Values about Economic Inequality and Individual Opportunity. www .people-press.org/2012/06/04/section-3-values-about-economic -inequality-and-individual-opportunity

———. 2012c. Partisan Polarization Surges in Bush, Obama Years. Trends in American Values: 1987–2012. Section 4: Values About Government and The Social Safety Net. www.people-press.org /2012/06/04/section-4-values-about-government-and-the -social-safety-net

———. 2012d. "The rise of intermarriage." pewsocialtrends.org

Pew Research Social and Demographic Trends. 2010. Interactive: The Changing American Family. November 18. www.pewsocialtrends .org/2010/11/18/five-decades-of-marriage-trends/

Phillips DP, Welty WR, Smith MM. "Elevated suicide levels associated with legalized gambling." *Suicide Life Threat Behavior* 1997 Winter; 27(4): 373–378.

Phillips. S. 2009. "Criminology: Legal Disparities in the Capital of Capital Punishment." *Journal of Criminal Law & Criminology*, vol. 99, no. 3: 717. Retrieved from EBSCO*host*.

Pilnick, Alison; Hindmarsh, Jon; and Teas Gill, Virginia. 2009. "Beyond 'doctor and patient': developments in the study of healthcare interactions." *Sociology of Health & Illness*, vol. 31 no. 6: 787–802.

Pinker, Steven. 2005. "PSYCHOANALYSIS Q-and-A: Steven Pinker." *The Harvard Crimson*, January 19. www.thecrimson.com /article/2005/1/19/psychoanalysis-q-and-a-steven-pinker -in-an/

Pinto, Barbara. 2005. "Small town USA may offer solution to outsourcing: Company redeploys workers to rural towns instead of sending jobs overseas." *ABC World News Tonight*, television broadcast, August 25.

Pleck, Elizabeth H. 2000. *Celebrating the Family: Ethnicity, Consumer Culture, and Family Ritual.* Cambridge. MA: Harvard University Press.

Plumer, Brad. 2013. "Poverty is growing twice as fast in the suburbs as in cities." Washington Post. May 23. www.washingtonpost .com/blogs/wonkblog/wp/2013/05/23/poverty-is-now-growing -twice-as-fast-in-the-suburbs-as-in-the-city/

Poke. 2013. Global Rich List. www.globalrichlist.com

Pollack, Andres. 1999. "Aerospace gets Japan's message: Without military largess, industry takes the lean path." *New York Times*, March 9, p. C1.

Pollner, Melvin; and Stein, Jill. 1996. "Narrative mapping of social worlds: The voice of experience in Alcoholics Anonymous." *Journal of Symbolic Interaction*, vol. 19, no. 3: 203–223.

———. 2001. "Doubled-over in laughter: Humor and the construction of selves in Alcoholics Anonymous." In Jaber Gubrium and James Holstein, eds., *Institutional Selves: Personal Troubles in Organizational Context*. New York: Oxford University Press.

Pomerantz, Dorothy. 2012. "The world's most powerful celebrities." *Forbes*, May 16. www.forbes.com/celebrities

Pool, Robert. 1997. *Beyond Engineering: How Society Shapes Technology.* Oxford, UK: Oxford University Press.

Population Division of the Department of Economic and Social Affairs of the United Nations Secretariat, 2010. "World Population Prospects: The 2010 Revision", http://esa.un.org/unpd /wpp/Documentation/pdf/WPP2010_Volume-I_Comprehen sive-Tables.pdf

Population Reference Bureau. 2010. "World Population Data Sheet." www.prb.org/pdf10/10wpds_eng.pdf

Poster, Mark. 2002. "Workers as cyborgs: Labor and networked computers." *Journal of Labor Research*, vol. 23, no. 3 (summer): 339.

Postman, Neil. 1987. *Amusing Ourselves to Death: Public Discourse in the Age of Show Business.* New York: Methuen.

Powell, Brian. 2003. Unpublished survey results. Indiana University, Department of Sociology, Center for Survey Research, Bloomington.

Powell, L.M.; Slater, S.; Mirtcheva, D.; Bao, Y.; and Chaloupka, F.J. 2007. "Food store availability and neighborhood characteristics in the United States." *Preventive Medicine*, vol. 44, no. 3: 189–195.

Preston, Jennifer. 2011. "Protesters look for ways to feed the Web." *New York Times*, November 24.

Pullum, Geoffrey K. 1991. *The Great Eskimo Vocabulary Hoax and Other Irreverent Essays on the Study of Language.* Chicago: University of Chicago Press.

Putnam, Robert D. 1995. "Tuning in, tuning out: The strange disappearance of social capital in America." *Political Science & Politics*, vol. 28, no. 4 (December): 664.

———. 2000. *Bowling Alone: The Collapse and Revival of American Community.* New York: Simon & Schuster.

Rabin, Roni Caryn. 2008. "Severe Heart Attacks Deadlier for Women." *The New York Times*, December 8.

Rabow, Jerome; Stein, Jill; and Conley, Terri. 1999. "Teaching social justice and encountering society: The pink triangle experiment." *Youth and Society*, vol. 30, no. 4: 483–514.

Radway, A. Janice. 1991. *Reading the Romance: Women, Patriarchy, and Popular Literature.* Chapel Hill, NC: University of North Carolina Press.

Rajaram, Shireen S. 2007. "An action research project: Community lead poisoning prevention." *Teaching Sociology*, 35(2): 138–150.

Rainie, L.; Zickuhr, K.; Purcell, K.; Madden, M.; and Brenner, J. 2012. *The Rise of E-reading.* Online Pew Internet and American Life Project. http://libraries.pewinternet.org

RAND Education. 2003. *Charter School Operation and Performance: Evidence from California.* Santa Monica, CA: The Rand Corporation. www.rand.org/pubs/monograph_reports/MR1700

Ray, Brian. 1997. "Strengths of their own—home schoolers across America: Academic achievement, family characteristics, and longitudinal traits." Salem, OR: National Home Education Research Institute.

———. 2008. "Research facts on homeschooling." National Home Education Research Institute. www.nheri.org/Research-Facts-on -Homeschooling.html

Reece, M.; Herbenick, D.; Schick, V.; Sanders, S.; Dodge, B.; and Fortenberry, J. 2010. "Condom Use Rates in a National Probability Sample of Males and Females, Ages 14 to 94 in the United States." *Journal of Sexual Medicine* 7 (suppl. 5): 266–267.

Rees, W.; and Wackernagel, M. 1994. "Ecological footprints and appropriated carrying capacity: Measuring the natural capital requirements of the human economy." In A-M. Jansson, M. Hammer, C. Folke, and R. Costanza, eds., *Investing in Natural Capital: The Ecological Economics Approach to Sustainability.* Washington, DC: Island Press.

Rennison, Callie Marie. 2001. "Intimate partner violence and age of victim, 1993–1999." Bureau of Justice Statistics Special Report. Washington, DC: U.S. Department of Justice. NCJ #187635.

Reuters. 2008. "Visa study shows Canada and Mexico are top destinations for Americans traveling abroad." July 24. www.reuters.com /article/pressRelease/idUS135782+24-Jul-2008+BW20080724

Riel, M. 2010. Understanding Action Research, Center for Collaborative Action Research. Pepperdine University. http://cadres .pepperdine.edu/ccar/define.html

Riesman, D. 1957. "The suburban dislocation." *Annals of the American Academy of Political and Social Science*, vol. 314: 123.

Rios, Victor. 2009. "The Consequence of the Criminal Justice Pipeline on Black and Latino Masculinity." *The Annals of the American Academy of Political and Social Science.* May: 150–162.

Ritzer, George. 1996. *The McDonaldization of Society*. Thousand Oaks, CA: Pine Forge Press.

Robins, Douglas; Sanders, Clinton; and Cahill, Spencer. 1991. "Dogs and their people: Pet-facilitated interaction in a public setting." *Journal of Contemporary Ethnography*, vol. 20, no. 1: 3–25.

Robson, D. 2001. "Women and minorities in economics textbooks: Are they being adequately represented?" *Journal of Economic Education*, vol. 32, no. 2 (spring): 186–191.

Rojek, Chris. 1985. *Capitalism and Leisure Theory*. London: Tavistock.
———. 1995. *Decentering Leisure: Rethinking Leisure Theory*. London: Sage.
———. 1997. "Leisure theory: Retrospect and prospect." *Loisir et Société/Society and Leisure*, vol. 20, no. 2: 383–400.
———. 2000. "Leisure and the rich today: Veblen's thesis after a century." *Leisure Studies*, vol. 19, no. 1: 1–15.

Roscoe, W. 2000. "How to become a berdache: Toward a unified analysis of gender." In G. Herdt, ed., *Third Sex, Third Gender: Beyond Sexual Dimorphism in Culture and History*. New York: Zone Books.

Rosenbaum, Emily. 2008. "Racial/Ethnic Differences in Asthma Prevalence: The Role of Housing and Neighborhood Environments." *Journal of Health and Social Behavior*. June, vol. 49, no. 2: 131–145.

Rosenbloom, Stephanie. 2007. "On Facebook, scholars link up with data." *New York Times*, December 17. www.nytimes.com/2007/12/17/style/17facebook.html?ex=1355720400&en=33ca15953318a6f5&ei=5124&partner=permalink&exprod=permalink

Rosenfeld, Dana. 2003. *The Changing of the Guard: Lesbian and Gay Elders, Identity, and Social Change*. Philadelphia: Temple University Press.

Rosenhan, David. 1973. "On being sane in insane places." *Science*, vol. 179 (January): 250–258.

Rosenthal, A. M. 1964/2008. *Thirty-Eight Witnesses: The Kitty Genovese Case*. New York: Melville House.

Rosenthal, R.; and Jacobson, L. 1968. *Pygmalion in the Classroom: Teacher Expectation and Pupils' Intellectual Development*. New York: Rinehart and Winston.

Rosin, Hannah. 2012. *The End of Men: And the Rise of Women*. New York: Riverhead Books.

Ross, Andrew. 1997. "Introduction." In Andrew Ross, ed., *No Sweat: Fashion, Free Trade and the Rights of Garment Workers*. New York: Verso.

Rothblum, Esther. 1996. *Preventing Heterosexism and Homophobia*. Thousand Oaks, CA: Sage.

Rothkop, David. 1997. "In praise of cultural imperialism? Effects of globalization on culture." *Foreign Policy*, June 22.

Roy, Donald. 1960. "'Banana time': Job satisfaction and informal interaction." *Human Organization*, vol. 18: 158–168.

Rubel, Paula; and Rosman, Abraham. 2001. "The collecting passion in America." *Zeitschrift fur Ethnologie* (English), vol. 126, no. 2: 313–330.

Rubenstein, William B. 2001. "Do Gay Rights Laws Matter? An Empirical Assessment." *Southern California Law Review*, vol. 75, 65: 65–120. www.law.ucla.edu/williamsinstitute/programs/dogayrightslawsmatter.pdf

Rubin, Zick; and Peplau, Letitia Anne. 1975. "Who believes in a just world?" *Journal of Social Issues*, vol. 31, no. 3: 65–89.

Rupp, Leila; and Taylor, Verta. 2003. *Drag Queens of the 801 Cabaret*. Chicago: University of Chicago Press.

Russakoff, Rich; and Goodman, Mary. 2011. "Employee Theft: Are You Blind To It?" *CBS Money Watch*. July 14, 2011. www.cbsnews.com/8301-505143_162-48640192/employee-theft-are-you-blind-to-it/

Ryan, Caitlin; Huebner, David; Diaz, Rafael; and Sanchez, Jorge. 2009. "Family Rejection as a Predictor of Negative Health Outcomes in White and Latino Lesbian, Gay, Bisexual Young Adults." *Pediatrics*, vol. 123, no. 1. January: 346–352.

Ryan, George. 2003. "The death penalty: Arbitrary and capricious." www.salon.com

Saad, Lydia. 2011. "One-Third in United States See Improved Race Relations under Obama." *Gallup Politics*, August 24. www.gallup.com/poll/149141/one-third-improved-race-relations-obama.aspx

Sadker, Myra; and Sadker, David. 1995. *Failing at Fairness: How Our Schools Cheat Girls*. New York: Scribner.

Sampson, Robert J.; and Wilson, William Julius. 2005. "Toward a theory of race, crime and urban inequality." In Shaun L. Gabbidon and Helen Taylor Greene, eds., *Race, Crime and Justice: A Reader*. New York: Routledge.

Sanchez-Jankowski, Martin. 1991. *Islands in the Street: Gangs and American Urban Society*. Berkeley, CA: University of California Press.

Sapir, Edward. 1949. *Selected Writings in Language, Culture, and Personality*. Ed. David G. Mandelbaum. Berkeley, CA: University of California Press.

Sapolsky, Robert. 1997. *Trouble with Testosterone and Other Essays on the Biology of Human Nature*. New York: Scribner.

Sassen, Saskia. 1991. *The Global City: New York, London, Tokyo*. Princeton, NJ: Princeton University Press.

Sayer, Liana C.; and Mattingly, Maribeth. 2006. "Under pressure: Gender differences in the relationship between free time and feeling rushed." *Journal of Marriage and Family*, vol. 68, no. 1 (February): 205–221.

Schegloff, Emanuel. 1986. "The routine as achievement." *Human Studies*, vol. 9, nos. 2–3: 111–151.
———. 1999. "What next? Language and social interaction study at the century's turn." *Research on Language and Social Interaction*, vol. 32, nos. 1–2: 141–148.

Schein, Edgar H. 1997. *Organizational Culture and Leadership*. San Francisco: Jossey-Bass.
———. 2010. *Organizational Culture and Leadership* (4th ed.) Hoboken, NJ: Jossey-Bass.

Schell, Orville. 2002. "Gross national happiness." *Red Herring*, January 15. www.pbs.org/frontlineworld/stories/bhutan/gnh.html

Scheyvens, Regina. 2000. "Promoting women's empowerment through involvement in ecotourism: Experiences from the Third World." *Journal of Sustainable Tourism*, vol. 8, no. 3: 232–249.

Schiller, Herbert I. 1976. *Communication and Cultural Domination*. White Plains, NY: International Arts and Sciences Press.
———. 1992. *Mass Communications and American Empire*. 2nd ed. Boulder, CO: Westview Press.
———. 1995. "The global information highway: Project for an ungovernable world." In J. Brook and I. A. Boal, eds., *Resisting the Virtual Life: The Culture and Politics of Information*. San Francisco: City Lights Books.
———. 1996. *Information Inequality*. New York: Routledge.
———; Schlenker, Jennifer A.; Caron, Sandra L.; and Halteman, William A. 1998. "A feminist analysis of *Seventeen* magazine: Content analysis from 1945 to 1995." *Sex Roles: A Journal of Research*, vol. 38, no. 1–2: 135.

Schlosser, Eric. 2002. *Fast Food Nation: The Dark Side of the All-American Meal*. New York: Perennial.
———. 2003. *Reefer Madness: Sex, Drugs and Cheap Labor in the American Black Market*. Boston: Houghton Mifflin.

Schnaiberg, Allan. 1975. "Social synthesis of the societal-environmental dialectic: The role of distributional impacts." *Social Science Quarterly*, vol. 56: 5–20.

———; and Gould, Kenneth Alan. 1994. *Environment and Society: The Enduring Conflict*. New York: St. Martin's Press.

Schofield, Jack. 2004. "Social network software; software to help you network." *Computer Weekly*, March 16, p. 32.

Schor, Juliet B. 1999. *The Overspent American: Why We Want What We Don't Need*. New York: HarperCollins.

———. 2010. *Plenitude: The New Economics of True Wealth*. New York, Penguin Press.

Schudson, Michael. 2003. *The Sociology of News*. New York: Norton.

Schutz, Alfred P. 1962. "The stranger: An essay in social psychology." In A. Brodersen, ed, *Collected Papers II: Studies in Social Theory*. Dordrecht, The Netherlands: Martinus Nijhoff.

Schwartz, Mattathias. 2011. "Pre-occupied: The origins and future of Occupy Wall Street." *The New Yorker*, November 28. www.newyorker.com/reporting/2011/11/28/111128fa_fact_schwartz#ixzz2LdswEsh1

Schwellenbach, Nick. 2008. "Finance: A good time to be a white-collar criminal?" Center for Public Integrity, December 18. www.publicintegrity.org/blog/entry/1096

Schwimmer, B. 2001. "Figure 43. Hawaiian kin terms (actual usage)." www.umanitoba.ca/faculties/arts/anthropology/tutor/image_list/43.html

Searing, Linda. 2010. "Study: Dying at home may be less traumatic for patients as well as caregivers." *Washington Post*, September 27. www.washingtonpost.com/wp-dyn/content/article/2010/09/27/AR2010092705374.html

Sears, Brad; and Badgett, M.V. Lee. 2008. "The Impact of Extending Marriage to Same-Sex Couples on the California Budget." The Williams Institute. UCLA School of Law. www.law.ucla.edu/williamsinstitute/publications/EconImpactCAMarriage.pdf

Sedgwick, Eve Kosofsky. 1993. *Tendencies*. Durham, NC: Duke University Press.

Seekings, Jeremy; and Nattras, Nicoli. 2005. *Class, Race and Inequality in South Africa*. New Haven, CT: Yale University Press.

Segal, Lynne. 1990. *Slow Motion: Changing Masculinities, Changing Men*. New Brunswick, NJ: Rutgers University Press.

Seidman, Steven. 2003. *The Social Construction of Sexuality*. New York: Norton.

Seigel, Taggart. 2005. "The real dirt on Farmer John." CAVU Pictures, distributors. PBS Independent Lens documentaries.

Seltzer, Judith A.; Schaeffer, Nora Cate; and Charng, Hong-Wen. 1989. "Family ties after divorce: The relationship between visiting and paying child support." *Journal of Marriage and the Family*, vol. 51, no. 4: 1013–1031.

Sennett, Richard. 1977. *The Fall of Public Man*. New York: Norton.

Severin, W. J.; and Tankard, J. W. 1997. *Communication Theories: Origins, Methods, and Uses in the Mass Media*. 4th ed. New York: Longman.

Shah, Anup. 2007. "Media conglomerates, mergers, concentration of ownership." *Global Issues*, April 29. www.globalissues.org/article/159/media-conglomerates-mergers-concentration-of-ownership

Shanahan, M. J.; Bauldry, S.; and Freeman, J. 2010. "Beyond Mendel's ghost." *Contexts*, vol. 9: 34–39.

Sharp, Shane. 2010. "How does prayer help manage emotions?" *Social Psychology Quarterly*, vol. 73: 417–437.

Shell, Elizabeth. 2013. "15 Federal Benefits Same-Sex Couples Can Now Look Forward To." PBS NewsHour. June 26. www.pbs.org/newshour/rundown/2013/06/some-federal-benefits-same-sex-couples-can-now-look-forward-to.html

Sherman, Aloc. 2012. "SNAP (food stamps) and earned income tax credit had big antipoverty impact in 2011." Center on Budget and Policy Priorities. September 12. www.offthechartsblog.org/snap-food-stamps-and-earned-income-tax-credit-had-big-antipoverty-impact-in-2011

Shiach, Morag. 1999. *Feminism and Cultural Studies*. New York: Oxford University Press.

Shipler, D. K. 1997. *A Country of Strangers: Blacks and Whites in America*. New York: Alfred A. Knopf.

Shippers, Mimi. 2002. *Rockin' Out of the Box: Gender Maneuvering in Alternative Hard Rock*. New Brunswick, NJ: Rutgers University Press.

Shover, Neal; and Wright, John Paul. 2001. *Crimes of Privilege: Readings in White-collar Crime*. New York, NY: Oxford University Press.

Simmel, Georg. 1950. *The Sociology of George Simmel*. Ed. Kurt Wolff. New York: Free Press.

Simon, Julian. 1996. *The Ultimate Resource 2*. Princeton, NJ: Princeton University Press

———. 2000. *The Great Breakthrough and Its Cause*. Ann Arbor, MI: University of Michigan Press.

Simon, Scott. 2004. "Friend of Kitty Genovese discusses her memories of Kitty and her murder." *National Public Radio*, "Weekend Edition Saturday," March 13.

Singh, Gopal K.; and Siahpush, Mohammad. 2006. "Widening socioeconomic inequalities in U.S. life expectancy, 1980–2000." *International Journal of Epidemiology*, online journal, May 9. http://ije.oxfordjournals.org/cgi/reprint/dyl083v1.pdf

Skarzynska, Krystyna. 2004. "Politicians in television: The big five in impression formation." *Journal of Political Marketing*, vol. 3, no. 2: 31–45.

Slack, Kristin, et al. 2006. "Family economic well-being following the 1996 welfare reform: Trend data from five non-experimental panel studies." *Children and Youth Services Review*, vol. 29, no. 6: 698–720.

Sloan Consortium. 2010. "Learning on Demand: Online Education in the United States, 2009." http://sloanconsortium.org/publications/survey/pdf/learningondemand.pdf

Smelser, Neil. 1985. "Evaluating the model of structural differentiation in relation to educational change in the nineteenth century." In Jeffrey C. Alexander, ed., *Neofunctionalism*. Beverly Hills, CA: Sage Publications.

Smith, Dorothy. 1999. "Schooling for inequality." *Signs: Journal for Women in Culture and Society*, vol. 5, no. 4: 1147–1151.

Smith, Herbert L. 1990. "Specification problems in experimental and nonexperimental social research." *Sociological Methodology*, vol. 20: 59–91.

Smith, Kara. 2005. "Gender talk: A case study in prenatal socialization." *Women and Languages*, March 22.

Smith, Marc; and Kollock, Peter. 1998. *Communities in Cyberspace*. London: Routledge.

Smith-Lovin, Lynn; and Brody, Charles. 1989. " Interruptions in group discussions: The effects of gender and group composition." *American Sociological Review*, vol. 54, no. 3 (June): 424–435.

Snider, Mike. 2012. "Net connections, movies and music are worthy expenditures despite downturn." *USA Today*, June 11. http://usatoday30.usatoday.com/tech/news/story/2012-06-12/entertainment-spending/55530446/1

Sociological Initiatives Foundation. 2010. "Chicago mothers receive Chall Award." February 18. www.sifoundation.org/2010/02/chicago-mothers-recieve-chall-award/#more-35

Solot, Dorian; and Miller, Marshall. 2002. *Unmarried to Each Other: The Essential Guide to Living Together as an Unmarried Couple*. New York: Marlowe and Co.

Sonn, Bill. 2004. "Concierge medicine: Physicians weigh financial, ethical issues." *Physician's Practice*, vol.14, no. 3. www.physicianspractice.com/display/article/1462168/1590867

Sonner, Scott. 2002. "Burning Man gives fodder for questing sociologists." Associated Press, August 28. www.religionnewsblog.com/641-Scientists_find_Burning_Man_a_research_bonanza.html

Southern Poverty Law Center. 2013. "The Year in Hate and Extremism." Intelligence Report, issue 149. www.splcenter.org/home/2013/spring/the-year-in-hate-and-extremism#.UZz-uNLFVxw

Spector, Robert; and McCarthy, Patrick D. 1996. *The Nordstrom Way: The Inside Story of America's #1 Customer Service Company.* Hoboken, NJ: John Wiley & Sons.

Spellings, Margaret. 2006. "Opportunity for all children." *USA Today,* August 13.

Spencer, Herbert. 1862. *First Principles.* London: Williams and Norgate.

————. 1873. *The Study of Sociology.* London: King.

————. 1897. *The Principles of Sociology.* 3 vols. New York: Appleton.

Sprecher, Susan; McKinney, Kathleen; and Orbuch, Terri. 1987. "Has the double standard disappeared? An experimental test." *Social Psychology Quarterly,* vol. 50, no. 1 (March): 24–31.

Springer, Kristen W.; and Mouzon, Dawne. 2011. "Masculinity and Health Care Seeking among Older Men: Implications for Men in Different Social Classes." *Journal of Health and Social Behavior.*

Srinivas, Lakshmi. 1998. "Active viewing: An ethnography of the Indian film audience." *Visual Anthropology,* vol. 11, no. 4.

Stacey, Judith. 1990. *Brave New Families: Stories of Domestic Upheaval in Late Twentieth-Century America.* New York: Basic Books.

————. 1998. "Gay and lesbian families: Queer like us." In Mary Ann Mason, Arlene Skolnick, and Stephen D. Sugarman, eds., *All Our Families: New Policies for a New Century.* New York: Oxford University Press.

Stack, Carol. 1974. *All Our Kin.* New York: Harper & Row.

Stannard, David E. 1993. *American Holocaust: The Conquest of the New World.* New York: Oxford University Press.

Stanton, M. E. 1995. "Patterns of kinship and residence." In B. Ingoldsby and S. Smith, eds., *Families in Multicultural Perspective.* New York: Guilford Press.

Stapleton, Christine. 2002. "Donated blood sold off overseas after 9/11." *Atlanta Journal-Constitution,* September 8, p. 19A.

Stein, Jill. 1997. "Rock musician careers: The culture of the long-term professional." Unpublished doctoral dissertation. University of California, Los Angeles.

Steiner, I. D. 1972. *Group Process and Productivity.* New York: Academic Press.

Steinfatt, T. M.; Baker, S.; and Beesey, A. 2002. *Measuring the Number of Trafficked Women in Cambodia: 2002.* Part I of a series. Manoa, HI: University of Hawaii, Globalization Research Center.

Stelter, Brian. 2011. "Ownership of TV Sets Fall in United States." *New York Times,* May 3.

————. 2012. "Youths Are Watching, But Less Often on TV." *New York Times,* February 8.

Stiglitz, Joseph. 2011. "Of the 1%, by the 1%, for the 1%." *Vanity Fair,* May. www.vanityfair.com/society/features/2011/05/top-one-percent-201105

Stimson, Ida H. 1967. "Patterns of socialization into professions: The case of student nurses." *Sociological Inquiry,* vol. 37: 47–54.

Strauss, Neil. 2003. "The pop life: Apple finds a route for online music sales." *New York Times,* May 29, p. E5.

Sudnow, David. 1972. "Temporal parameters of interpersonal observation." In D. Sudnow, ed., *Studies in Social Interaction.* New York: Free Press.

Sue, Valerie M., and Lois A. Ritter. 2007. *Conducting Online Surveys.* Thousand Oaks, CA: Sage.

Sumner, William Graham. 1906. *Folkways: A Study of the Sociological Importance of Usages, Manners, Customs, Mores, and Morals.* Boston: Ginn and Co.

Sutherland, Edwin. 1939. *Principles of Criminology.* 3rd ed. Philadelphia: J. B. Lipincott.

————; Cressey, Donald R.; and Luckenbill, David F. 1992. *Principles of Criminology.* 11th ed. Dix Hills, NY: General Hall.

Sutton, Robert. 2001. *Weird Ideas That Work: 11Ω Practices for Promoting, Managing and Sustaining Innovation.* New York: Free Press.

Tahmincioglu, Eve. 2008. "Facebook friends as job references?" MSNBC, August 18. www.msnbc.msn.com/id/26223330/

Tannen, Deborah. 2001. *You Just Don't Understand: Men and Women in Conversation.* New York: Perennial Currents.

Tapscott, Don. 1997. *Growing Up Digital: The Rise of the Net Generation.* New York: McGraw-Hill.

Taylor, R. 2000. "The empire strikes back: Soccer violence continues to be England's ugliest export." *Time International,* vol. 155 (July 19): 36.

Telles, Edward. 2004. *Race in Another America: The Significance of Color in Brazil.* Princeton, NJ: Princeton University Press.

Thomas, W. I.; and Thomas, D. S. 1928. *The Child in America.* New York: Alfred A. Knopf.

Thompson, Derek. 2012. "The power of a college degree: 2 awesome clip-and-save graphs." *The Atlantic,* September 14. http://m.theatlantic.com/business/archive/2012/09/the-power-of-a-college-degree-2-awesome-clip-and-save-graphs/262423

Thorne, Barrie. 1992. "Feminism and the family: Two decades of thought." In Barrie Thorne and Marilyn Yalom, eds., *Rethinking the Family: Some Feminist Questions.* Boston: Northeastern University Press.

————. 1993. *Gender Play: Girls and Boys in School.* New Brunswick, NJ: Rutgers University Press.

Thornton, Stephen J. 2003. "Silence on gays and lesbians in social studies curriculum." *Social Education,* vol. 67, no. 4 (May–June): 226.

Thye, Shane R.; and Lawler, Edward J., eds. 2002. *Advances in Group Processes: Group Cohesion, Trust and Solidarity,* vol. 19. Oxford, UK: Elsevier Science.

Tibbals, Chauntelle Anne. 2010. "From The Devil in Miss Jones to DMJ6—Power, Inequality, and Consistency in the Content of US Adult Films." *Sexualities* 13(5): 625–644.

————. 2012. "'Anything that forces itself into my vagina is by definition raping me . . .'—Adult Performers and Occupational Safety and Health." *Stanford Law and Policy Review (SLPR)* 23(1): 231–251.

————. 2013 (early release 2011). "Sex Work, Office Work—Women Working Behind the Scenes in the U.S. Adult Film Industry" *Gender, Work & Organization* 20(1): 20–35.

Time Warner, Inc. 2012. "Income Statement." *Yahoo! Finance,* December 30. http://finance.yahoo.com/q/is?s=TWX+Income+Statement&annual

Tomlinson, John. 1991. *Cultural Imperialism.* Baltimore, MD: John Hopkins University Press.

Toor, Rachel. 2001. *Admissions Confidential: An Insider's Account of the Elite College Selections Process.* New York, NY: St. Martin's Press.

Toossi, Mitra. 2006. "A new look at long-term labor force projections to 2050." *Monthly Labor Review* (November): 19–39.

Trexler, R. C. 2002. "Making the American berdache: Choice or constraint." *Journal of Social History,* vol. 35: 613–636.

Trudeau, Michelle. 2008. "Las Vegas: The Suicide Capital Of America." *NPR*, December 10. www.npr.org/templates/story/story.php?storyId=98042717

Tsukayama, Hayley. 2010. "Facebook More Popular Than Google." *Washington Post*, December 30. http://voices.washingtonpost.com/posttech/2010/12/the_circuit_facebook_more_popu.html

Tucker, Ian. 2010. "A Different Class." *The Observer Magazine*, sec. 36.

Turkle, Sherry. 1997. *Life on the Screen: Identity in the Age of the Internet*. New York: Touchstone Books.

———. 2005. *The Second Self: Computers and the Human Spirit* Cambridge, MA: MIT Press.

———. 2011. *Alone Together*. New York: Basic Books.

Turner, Ralph. 1972. "Deviance avowal as neutralization of commitment." *Social Problems*, vol. 19, no. 3: 308–321.

———. 1976. "The real self: From institution to impulse." *American Journal of Sociology*, vol. 81: 989–1016.

———. 1978. "The role and the person." *American Journal of Sociology*, vol. 84, no. 1: 1–3.

———; and Killian, Lewis M. 1987. *Collective Behavior*. 3rd ed. Englewood Cliffs, NJ: Prentice Hall.

Twine, France Winddance. 2011a. *Outsourcing the Womb: Race, Class and Gestational Surrogacy in a Global Market*. Florence, KY: Routledge.

———. 2011b. *A White Side of Black Britain: Interracial Intimacy and Racial Literacy*. Durham, NC: Duke University Press.

Uggen, Christopher; and Manza, Jeff. 2002. "Democratic contraction? Political consequences of felon disenfranchisement in the United States." *American Sociological Review*, vol. 67, iss. 6: 777–803.

Ulbrich, Chris. 2004. "Blogs pump bucks into campaigns." *Wired*, February 18.

Ulrichs, Karl H. 1994. *The Riddle of Man-Manly Love: The Pioneering Work on Male Homosexuality*. Amherst, NY: Prometheus Books.

UNAIDS. 2009. *Towards Universal Access: Scaling Up Priority HIV/AIDS Interventions in the Health Sector*. www.who.int/hiv/pub/2009progressreport/en/

———. 2010. *Global Report: UNAIDS Report on the Global AIDS Epidemic, 2010*. www.unaids.org/GlobalReport/Global_report.htm

UNCTAD. 2012. "The world's top 100 non-financial TNCs, ranked by foreign assets, 2011." United Nations Conference on Trade and Development, *World Investment Report 2012*. http://unctad.org/Sections/dite_dir/docs/WIR12_webtab28.xls

United Nations. 2006. "World population prospects, 2006 revision." www.un.org/esa/population/publications/wpp2006/WPP2006_Highlights_rev.pdf

United Nations Development Programme. 2000. *World Resources 2000–2001*. Washington, DC: World Resources Institute.

United Nations Millennium Project. 2001. www.unmillenniumproject.org

United Nations World Commission on Environment and Development. 1987. *Our Common Future*. Oxford, UK: Oxford University Press.

United Nations World Food Programme. 2007. "World hunger series: 2007." www.wfp.org/policies/introduction/other/documents/pdf/WHS_leaflet_English_2007.pdf

UN Food and Agriculture Organization. 2012. "Part 3: Feeding the World." Statistical Yearbook 2012: World Food and Agriculture. www.fao.org/docrep/015/i2490e/i2490e03a.pdf

UNICEF. 2010. "Humanitarian Action Report 2010: Eastern and Southern Africa, Feature Story for Burundi." www.unicef.org/har2010/index_burundi_feature.html

United States v. Windsor, 570 U. S. ___ (2013).

U.N. Millennium Ecosystem Assessment. 2005. Ecosystems and Human Well-Being: the Biodiversity Synthesis Report. United Nations Environment Program.

UN News Centre. 2011. "Global population to pass 10 billion by 2100, UN projections indicate." May 3. www.un.org/apps/news/story.asp?NewsID=38253

UN-Water. 2013. Statistics: Graphs & Maps. www.unwater.org/statistics_urb.html

Urry, John. 1990. *The Tourist Gaze*. London: Sage.

———. 1992. "The tourist gaze and the 'environment.'" *Theory, Culture & Society*, vol. 9, no. 3: 1–26.

———. 2002. *The Tourist Gaze*. 2nd ed. London: Sage.

U.S. Bureau of Labor Statistics. 2011a. "Employed persons by detailed occupation, sex, race and Hispanic or Latino ethnicity." www.bls.gov/cps/aa2011/cpsaat11.pdf

———. 2011b. "Household data annual averages." www.bls.gov/cps/cpsaat18.pdf

———. 2011c. "Leisure time on an average day." www.bls.gov/tus/charts/chart9.pdf

———. 2012a. "Employment outlook: 2010–2020 industry employment and output projections to 2020." www.bls.gov/opub/mlr/2012/01/art4full.pdf

———. 2012b. "Unemployed persons by industry and class of worker, not seasonally adjusted." www.bls.gov/news.release/empsit.t14.htm

———. 2012c. "Unemployment rates for states." www.bls.gov/web/laus/laumstrk.htm

———. 2012d. "Union members summary." www.bls.gov/news.release/union2.nr0.htm

———. 2012e. "Volunteering in the U.S., 2011." www.bls.gov/news.release/volun.nr0.htm

———. 2013. "Employed persons detailed by occupation, sex, race and Hispanic or Latino ethnicity." www.bls.gov/cps/cpsaat11.pdf

U.S. Census Bureau. 1993. "Table 4. Population: 1790 to 1990." www.census.gov/population/censusdata/table-4.pdf

———. 1994. "Table 1. Race of wife by race of husband: 1960, 1970, 1980, 1991, and 1992." www.census.gov

———. 2003. "Married couple and unmarried partner households: 2000." Census 2000 Special Report. February. www.census.gov/prod/2003pubs/censr-5.pdf

———. 2005. "Interim projections: Ranking of census 2000 and projected 2030 state population and change: 2000 to 2030." April. www.census.gov/Press-Release/www/2005/stateproj7.xls

———. 2009. "Educational attainment in the United States: 2009." http://census.gov/hhes/socdemo/education/data/cps/2009/tables.html

———. 2010a. "Age and sex composition: 2010." www.census.gov/prod/cen2010/briefs/c2010br-03.pdf

———. 2010b. "Census Bureau Reports nearly 6 in 10 advanced degree holders age 25–29 are women." www.census.gov/newsroom/releases/archives/education/cb10-55.html

———. 2010c. "Overview of race and Hispanic origin: 2010." www.census.gov/prod/cen2010/briefs/c2010br-02.pdf

———. 2010d. "Profile of general population and housingcharacteristics: 2010." http://factfinder2.census.gov/faces/tableservices/jsf/pages/productview.xhtml?pid=DEC_10_SF2_SF2DP1&prodType=table

———. 2011a. "2011 American community survey 1-year estimates: Demographic and housing estimates." http://factfinder2.census.gov/bkmk/table/1.0/en/ACS/11_1YR/DP05/0100000US

———. 2011b. "2011 American community survey 1-tear estimates: Households and families." http://factfinder2.census.gov/faces/tableservices/jsf/pages/productview.xhtml?pid=ACS_11_1YR_S1101&prodType=table

———. 2011c. "2011 American community survey 1-year estimates: Marital status." http://factfinder2.census.gov/faces/tableservices/jsf/pages/productview.xhtml?pid=ACS_11_1YR_S1201&prodType=table

———. 2011d. "America's families and living arrangements: 2011." www.census.gov/hhes/families/data/cps2011.html

———. 2011e. "America's families and living arrangements: 2011." www.census.gov/population/www/socdemo/hh-fam/cps2011.html

———. 2011f. "Custodial mothers and fathers and their child support: 2009." www.census.gov/prod/2011pubs/p60-240.pdf

———. 2011g. "Educational attainment in the United States: 2011." www.census.gov/hhes/socdemo/education/data/cps/2011/tables.html

———. 2011h. "Educational attainment of the population 25 years and over, by selected characteristics: 2011." www.census.gov/hhes/socdemo/education/data/cps/2011/Table2-Both.xls

———. 2011i. "Income, poverty and health insurance coverage in the United States: 2010." www.census.gov/prod/2011pubs/p60-239.pdf

———. 2011j. "Labor, force, employment, and earnings." http://census.gov/prod/2011pubs/11statab/labor.pdf

———. 2011k. "Population distribution and change: 2000 to 2010." www.census.gov/prod/cen2010/briefs/c2010br-01.pdf

———. 2012a. "Table UC3. Opposite sex unmarried couples by presence of biological children under 18, and age, earnings, education, and race and Hispanic origin of both partners: 2012." www.census.gov/hhes/families/files/cps2012/tabUC3-all.xls

———. 2012b. "Educational Attainment by Race and Hispanic Origin: 1970–2010." www.census.gov/compendia/statab/2012/tables/12s0229.pdf

———. 2012c. "Expectation of life at birth, 1970 to 2008, and projections, 2010 to 2020." www.census.gov/compendia/statab/2012/tables/12s0104.pdf

———. 2012d. "Home-based workers in the United States: 2012." www.census.gov/hhes/commuting/files/2010/P70-132.pdf

———. 2012e. "Households and families: 2010." www.census.gov/prod/cen2010/briefs/c2010br-14.pdf

———. 2012f. "Income, poverty, and health insurance coverage in the United States: 2011." www.census.gov/prod/2012pubs/p60-243.pdf

———. 2012g. "Irish American heritage month (March) and St. Patrick's Day (March 17): 2012." www.census.gov/newsroom/releases/archives/facts_for_features_special_editions/cb12-ff03.html

———. 2012h. "Labor force, employment, and earnings." www.census.gov/prod/2011pubs/12statab/labor.pdf

———. 2012i. "Most children younger than age 1 are minorities." www.census.gov/newsroom/releases/archives/population/cb12-90.html

———. 2012j. "Births, Deaths, Marriages, and Divorces." www.census.gov/prod/2011pubs/12statab/vitstat.pdf

———. 2012k. "Annual estimates of the population of metropolitan and micropolitan statistical areas: April 1, 2010 to July 1, 2012." www.census.gov/popest/data/metro/totals/2012/tables/CBSA-EST2012-01.csv

———. 2012l. "Federal food programs: 1990 to 2010." www.census.gov/compendia/statab/2012/tables/12s0570.pdf

———. 2012m. "Temporary assistance for needy families (TANF)—Families and recipients: 1980 to 2009." www.census.gov/compendia/statab/2012/tables/12s0565.pdf

———. 2012n. "Shopping centers—number and gross leasable area: 1990–2010." www.census.gov/compendia/statab/2012/tables/12s1061.pdf

———. 2012o. "U.S. Census Bureau projections show a slower growing, older, more diverse nation a half century from now." www.census.gov/newsroom/releases/archives/population/cb12-243.html

———. 2012p. "Voting and registration in the election of November 2012." www.census.gov/hhes/www/socdemo/voting/publications/p20/2012/tables.html

———. 2013a. "Urban, urbanized area, urban cluster, and rural population, 2010 and 2000: United States." www.census.gov/geo/reference/ua/urban-rural-2010.html

———. 2013b. "Percent change in population for states and Puerto Rico: April 1, 2010 to July 1, 2012." www.census.gov/popest/data/maps/2012/perchg-2010-2012.html

U.S. Department of Agriculture. 2012. "Food Security in the U.S.: Key Statistics & Graphics." www.ers.usda.gov/topics/food-nutrition-assistance/food-security-in-the-us/key-statistics-graphics.aspx

U.S. Department of Commerce. Bureau of Economic Analysis. 2012. "Summary estimates for multinational companies: Employment, sales, and capital expenditures for 2010." www.bea.gov/newsreleases/international/mnc/mncnewsrelease.htm

U.S. Department of Commerce, International Trade Administration (ITA), Office of Travel and Tourism Industries (OTTI). 2011. "Fast facts: United States travel and tourism industry, 2011." www.tinet.ita.doc.gov/outreachpages/download_data_table/Fast_Facts.pdf

———. 2013. "Fast facts: United States travel and tourism industry, 2012." www.tinet.ita.doc.gov/outreachpages/download_data_table/Fast_Facts_2012.pdf

U.S. Department of Education, National Center for Education Statistics. 2009. "Numbers and types of public elementary and secondary schools from the common core of data: School year 2006–2007." http://nces.ed.gov/pubs2009/2009304.pdf

U.S. Department of Health & Human Services, Children's Bureau. November 2012. "Child maltreatment, 2011." www.acf.hhs.gov/sites/default/files/cb/cm11.pdf

U.S. Department of Health, Education, and Welfare. 1964. "Vital statistics of the United States 1960: Volume III—Marriage and divorce." www.cdc.gov/nchs/data/vsus/mgdv60_3.pdf

U.S. Department of Justice. 2005. "Bureau of Justice statistics, family violence statistics: Including statistics on strangers and acquaintances, at 31–32." www.ojp.usdoj.gov/bjs/pub/pdf/fvs.pdf

U.S. Energy Information Administration. 2004. "International energy outlook 2004: Highlights." www.eia.doe.gov/oiaf/ieo/highlights.html

———. 2012. "Monthly Energy Review." www.eia.gov/energy_in_brief/major_energy_sources_and_users.cfm

U.S. Environmental Protection Agency (EPA). 2000. "Climate—global warming." http://yosemite.epa.gov/oar/globalwarming.nsf/content/climate.html

———. 2003. "The Ozone Report: Measuring progress through 2003." Office of Air Quality Planning and Standards Emissions, Monitoring, and Analysis Division. Triangle Park, NC. EPA Publication No. EPA 454/K-04-001. www.epa.gov/air/airtrends/pdfs/2003ozonereport.pdf#page=8

———. 2008, November. "Factoids: Drinking water and ground water statistics for 2008." www.epa.gov/safewater/databases/pdfs/data_factoids_2008.pdf

———. 2011. "Municipal solid waste generation, recycling, and disposal in the United States: Facts and figures for 2010." www.epa.gov/osw/nonhaz/municipal/pubs/msw_2010_rev_factsheet.pdf

U.S. Government Printing Office. 2011. "Budget of the U.S. government." www.gpo.gov/fdsys/pkg/BUDGET-2011-BUD/pdf/BUDGET-2011-BUD.pdf

U.S. Sentencing Commission. 2010. "Preliminary Crack Cocaine Retroactivity Data Report." www.ussc.gov

———. 2011. "Report to Congress: Mandatory Minimum Penalties in the Federal Criminal Justice System." www.ussc.gov/Legislative_and_Public_Affairs/Congressional_Testimony_and_Reports/Mandatory_Minimum_Penalties/20111031_RtC_PDF/Chapter_08.pdf

Useem, E. L. 1990. "You're good but you're not good enough: Tracking students out of advanced mathematics." *American Educator,* vol. 14, no. 3, 24–27: 43–46.

Valkyrie, Zek Cypress. 2011. "Cybersexuality in MMORPGs: Virtual sexual revolution untapped." *Men and Masculinities,* vol. 14, no. 1 (April): 76–96.

Van Cleve, Thomas Curtis. 1972. *The Emperor Frederick of Hohenstaufen, Immutator Mundi.* Oxford, UK: Clarendon Press.

van den Berghe, P. L. 1979. *Human Family Systems: An Evolutionary View.* New York: Elsevier/North-Holland.

Van Goozen, S.; Frijda, N.; and Van DePoll, N. 1994. "Anger and aggression in women: Influence of sports choice and testosterone administration." *Aggressive Behavior,* vol. 20: 213–222.

Van Maanen, John. 1973. "Observations on the making of policemen." *Human Organizations,* vol. 32: 407–418.

———. 1983. *Qualitative Methodology.* Thousand Oaks, CA: Sage.

———. 1988. *Tales of the Field: On Writing Ethnography.* Chicago: University of Chicago Press.

Vankin, Deborah. 2010. "Blue says MOCA's remova of his mural amounts to censorship." *Los Angeles Times,* Dec. 15. www.latimes.com/entertainment/news/la-et-moca-mural-20101215,0,6698582.story

Varmus, Harold; and Satcher, David. 1997. "Ethical complexities of conducting research in developing countries." *New England Journal of Medicine,* vol. 337: 1003–1005.

Vaughan, Diane. 1996. *The Challenger Launch Decisions: Risky Technology, Culture and Deviance at NASA.* Chicago: University of Chicago Press.

Veblen, Thorstein. 2004 (orig. 1921). *Engineers and the Price System.* Whitefish, MT: Kessinger Publishing.

Vedantam, Shankar. 2010. "Why do Americans claim to be more religious than they are?" *Slate,* December 22. www.slate.com/id/2278923

Veiga, Alex. 2012. "Average credit card debt is almost $5,000." *Associated Press,* August 13. www.deseretnews.com/article/765596879/Average-credit-card-debt-is-almost-5000.html?pg=all

Velkoff, Victoria; and Lawson, Valerie. 1998. "Caregiving." *Gender and Aging,* December: 1–7.

Viacom Inc (VIA). Income Statement. *Yahoo! Finance,* September 29, 2012. www.finance.yahoo.com/q/is?s=VIA+Income+Statement&annual

Vincent, Danny. 2011. "China used prisoners in lucrative internet gaming work." *The Guardian,* May 25. www.guardian.co.uk/world/2011/may/25/china-prisoners-internet-gaming-scam

Wackernagel, Mathis; and Rees, William. 1996. *Our Ecological Footprint: Reducing Human Impact on the Earth.* Philadelphia: New Society.

Wahlgren, Eric. 2010. "Concierge Medicine: Patients Pay Up for a Doctor's Undivided Attention." *Daily Finance,* February 10. www.dailyfinance.com/story/concierge-medicine-patients-pay-up-for-a-doctors-undivided-att/19349963

Waldron, T.; Roberts, B.; and Reamer, A. 2004. "Working hard, falling short: America's working families and the pursuit of economic security." A national report by the Working Poor Families Project. Baltimore, MD: Annie E. Casey Foundation.

Walker, Samuel. 1997. *Popular Justice: A History of American Criminal Justice.* New York: Oxford University Press.

Walker, Susan C. 2004. "U.S. consumer credit card debt may crash economy." FoxNews.com, December 31.

Wallis, Claudia. 2012. "A powerful identity, a vanishing diagnosis." *New York Times.* www.nytimes.com/2009/11/03/health/03asperger.html

Walsh, Declan. 2013. "Girl shot by Pakistani Taliban is discharged from hospital." *New York Times,* January 4. www.nytimes.com/2013/01/05/world/asia/malala-yousafzai-shot-by-pakistani-taliban-is-discharged-from-hospital.html

The Walt Disney Company (DIS). 2012. Income Statement. *Yahoo! Finance,* September 28. www.finance.yahoo.com/q/is?s=DIS+Income+Statement&annual

Warner, Ralph; Ihara, Toni; and Frederick Hertz. 2001. *Living Together: A Legal Guide for Unmarried Couples.* Berkeley, CA: Nolo.

Waskul, D. D.; ed. 2004. *Net.SeXXX: Readings on Sex, Pornography, and the Internet.* New York: Peter Lang.

Watanabe, Teresa. 2008. "Home of the freed." *Los Angeles Times,* August 14. www.articles.latimes.com/2008/aug/14/local/me-thai14

Waters, Mary. 1990. *Ethnic Options: Choosing Identities in America.* Berkeley, CA: University of California Press.

Wattel, Harold. 1958. "Levittown: A suburban community." In William M. Dobriner, ed., *The Suburban Community.* New York: Putnam.

Watts, Duncan. 2003. *Six Degrees: The Science of a Connected Age.* New York: Norton.

Wearing, Stephen; and Wearing, Michael. 1999. "Decommodifying ecotourism: Rethinking global-local interactions with host communities." *Loisir et Société/Society and Leisure,* vol. 22, no. 1: 39–70.

Weber, Max. 1930 (orig. 1904). *The Protestant Ethic and the Spirit of Capitalism.* Trans. Talcott Parsons. New York: Scribner's.

———. 1962 (orig. 1913). *Basic Concepts of Sociology.* Westport, CT: Greenwood Publishing.

———. 1946 (orig. 1925). "Science as a vocation." In Hans Gerth and C. Wright Mills, ed. and trans., *From Max Weber: Essays in Sociology.* New York: Oxford University Press.

———. 1968 (orig. 1921). *Economy and Society.* Ed. and trans. Guenther Roth and Claus Wittich. New York: Bedminster Press.

Weedon, Joey R. 2004. "Voting rights restored." *Corrections Today,* vol. 66, iss. 6: 16.

Weigel, David. 2011. "Outside the White House on V-OBL Day." *Slate,* May 2. www.slate.com/content/slate/blogs/weigel/2011/05/02/outside_the_white_house_on_v_obl_day.html

Weinberg, Adam; Bellows, Story; and Ekster, Dara. 2002. "Sustaining ecotourism: Insights and implications from two successful case studies." *Society and Natural Resources,* vol. 15, no. 4: 371–380.

Weinberg, George. 1972. *Society and the Healthy Homosexual.* New York: St. Martin's Press.

Weinstein, Deena. 1991. *Heavy Metal: A Cultural Sociology.* New York: Macmillan/Lexington.

———. 2000. *Heavy Metal: The Music and Its Culture.* New York: DaCapo.

Weinstein, Harvey. 2003. "Controversial ruling on pledge reaffirmed." *Los Angeles Times,* Metro Desk, March 1, 1:1.

Weiss, Kenneth R. 2001. "Minority applications to UC rise." *Los Angeles Times,* January 31.

Weissbourd, Richard. 1994. "Divided families, whole children." *American Prospect,* vol. 18 (summer): 66–72.

Wellman, Barry. 2004. "Connecting community: On- and off-line." *Contexts* vol. 3, no. 4 (fall): 22–28.

Werner, Carrie A. 2011. "The older population: 2010." U.S. Census Briefs. www.census.gov

Wessel, David. 2011. "Big U.S. firms shift hiring abroad." *Wall Street Journal,* April 19.

West, Heather C. 2010. "Prison Inmates at Midyear 2009—Statistical Tables." Bureau of Justice Statistics. http://bjs.ojp.usdoj.gov /content/pub/pdf/pim09st.pdf

Weston, Kath. 1991. *Families We Choose.* New York: Columbia University Press.

Whalen, J.; Zimmerman, D.; and Whalen, M. 1988. "When words fail: a single case analysis." *Social Problems,* vol. 35, no. 4: 335–362.

Wharton, Amy S.; and Blair-Loy, Mary. 2002. "Employees' use of work–family policies and the workplace social context." *Social Forces,* vol. 80, no. 3: 813–845.

Whatley, Marianne H.; and Henken, Elissa R. 2000. *Did You Hear About the Girl Who . . . ? Contemporary Legends, Folklore, and Human Sexuality.* New York: New York University Press.

Whitacre, Paula Tarnapol; Tsai, Peggy, and Mulligan, Janet (Rapporteurs); National Research Council. 2009. *The Public Health Effects of Food Deserts: Workshop Summary.* Washington, D.C: The National Academies Press.

White, Glen. 1989. "Groupthink reconsidered." *Academy of Management Review,* vol. 14.

The White House. 2011. Health Care Reform. www.whitehouse.gov /healthreform

Whitehead, Jay. 2005. "Outsourcing pioneers another niche." *Human Resources Outsourcing Today Magazine,* June.

Whorf, Benjamin. 1956. *Language, Thought and Reality: Selected Writings of Benjamin Lee Whorf.* Ed. John B. Carroll. Cambridge, MA: MIT Press.

Whyte, W. H. 1956. *The Organization Man.* New York: Simon & Schuster.

Wicks-Lim, Jeannette; Thompson, Jeffrey. 2010. "Combining minimum wage and earned income tax credit policies to guarantee a decent living standard to all U.S. workers." Amherst, MA: Political Economy Research Institute. October 18. www.peri .umass.edu/236/hash/9b8a787cfa16226190e4f96e582348cd /publication/428

Wiener, Jon. 2011. "Hard hats and hippies, together at last: The action at Occupy Wall Street." *The Nation,* October 14. www.thenation .com/blog/163983/hard-hats-and-hippies-together-last-action -occupy-wall-street#sthash.bRyK8MEO

Wilkinson, Richard G. 2005. *The Impact of Inequality.* New York: The New Press.

Williams, Christine L. 1995. *Still a Man's World: Men Who Do Women's Work.* Berkeley, CA: University of California Press.

Williams, David E. 2006. "Boutique medicine: When wealth buys health." CNN, October 20. www.cnn.com/2006/US/10/19/bil .healthy.wealthy/index.html?iref=allsearch

Williams, Linda. 2004. "Porn studies: Proliferating pornographies on/scene: An introduction." In Linda Williams, ed., *Porn Studies.* Durham, NC: Duke University Press.

Williams, Patricia J. 1997. "Of race and risk." *The Nation,* December 29:10.

Williams, Robin. 1965. *American Society: A Sociological Interpretation.* 2nd ed. New York: Knopf.

Wilson, Edward O. 1975/2000. *Sociobiology: The New Synthesis.* Cambridge, MA: The Belknap Press of Harvard University Press.

———. 1978. *On Human Nature.* Cambridge, MA: Harvard University Press.

Wilson, William Julius. 1980. *The Declining Significance of Race.* Chicago: University of Chicago Press.

———. 1996. *When Work Disappears: The World of the New Urban Poor.* New York: Knopf.

———. 2009. *More Than Just Race: Being Black and Poor in the Inner City.* New York: Norton.

Wirth, Louis. 1938. "Urbanism as a way of life." *American Journal of Sociology,* vol. 44: 3–24.

———. 1945. "The problem of minority groups." In Ralph Litton, ed., *The Science of Man in the World Crisis.* New York: Columbia University Press.

Wiseman, Rosalind. 2002. *Queen Bees and Wannabes.* New York: Three Rivers Press.

Wolf, Rosalie S. 2000. "The nature and scope of elder abuse." *Generations,* vol. 24 (summer): 6–12.

Wolff, Edward. 2002. *Top Heavy: The Increasing Inequality of Wealth in America and What Can Be Done about It.* New York: New Press.

———. 2004. "Changes in household wealth in the 1980s and 1990s in the U.S." Working paper no. 407. Levy Economics Institute of Bard College.

Wolfinger, Nicholas H. 1999. "Trends in the intergenerational transmission of divorce." *Demography,* vol. 36, no. 3: 415–420.

———. 2000. "Beyond the intergenerational transmission of divorce: Do people replicate the patterns of marital instability they grew up with?" *Journal of Family Issues,* vol. 21: 1061–1086.

———. 2003. "Parental divorce and offspring marriage: Early or late?" *Social Forces,* vol. 82, no. 1: 337–353.

Wolfson, Andrew. 2005. "A hoax most cruel." *Courier-Journal.* Louisville, KY. October 9. www.courier-journal.com/apps/pbcs.dll /article?AID=/20051009/NEWS01/510090392

WomensHealth.gov. 2010. The National Women's Health Information Center. U.S. Department of Health and Human Services. www.womenshealth.gov/faq/alpha-index.cfm

Wood, Lisa J.; Giles-Corti, Billie; Bulsara, Max K.; and Bosch, Darcy. 2007. "More than a furry companion: The ripple effect of companion animals on neighborhood interactions and sense of community." *Society and Animals,* vol. 15, 43–56.

Wood, Megan Epler. 2002. *Ecotourism: Principles, Practices and Policies for Sustainability.* Burlington, VT: International Ecotourism Society.

The World Bank. 2011. "GDP (current US$)." http://data.worldbank .org/indicator/NY.GDP.MKTP.CD?order=wbapi_data_value _2011+wbapi_data_value+wbapi_data_value-last&sort=desc

World Health Organization (WHO). 1946. "Constitution of the World Health Organization." World Health Organization, July 26. www .who.int/governance/eb/constitution/en/

———. 2008. "The 10 leading causes of death by broad income group (2004)." Fact sheet no. 310, October. www.who.int/mediacentre /factsheets/fs310/en/index.html

World Medical Association. 1964. "Laws related to the protection of human subjects: World Medical Association declaration of Helsinki." Adopted by the 18th World Medical Assembly, Helsinki, Finland, June 1964 (latest amendment by 41st Assembly, Hong Kong, September 1989). Office of History, National Institutes of Health. http://history.nih.gov/about/timelines/helsinki.html

Worobey, Michael, et al. 2010. "Island biogeography reveals the deep history of SIV." *Science,* vol. 329, no. 5998: 1487.

Wray, M.; Miller, M.; Gurvey, J.; Carroll, J.; and Kawachi, I. 2008. "Leaving Las Vegas: Exposure to Las Vegas and risk of suicide." *Social Science and Medicine,* vol. 67, no. 11: 1882–1888.

Wright, Erik Olin. 1997. *Class Counts: Comparative Studies in Class Analysis.* Cambridge, UK: Cambridge University Press.

Wright, Erik Olin; Costello, Cynthia; Hachen, David; and Spragues, Joey. 1982. "The American class structure." *American Sociological Review*, vol. 47, no. 6: 709–726.

Yin, Sandra. 2003. "The art of staying at home." *American Demographics*, vol. 25, no. 9 (November 1).

Yuan, Jada. 2007. "The White-Castle Ceiling." *New York Magazine*, March 4.

Zellner, William W. 1995. *Countercultures: A Sociological Analysis.* New York: St. Martin's Press.

Zemke, Ron; and Schaaf, Dick. 1990. *The Service Edge: 101 Companies That Profit from Customer Care.* New York: Plume.

Zerubavel, Eviatar. 2003. *Time Maps: Collective Memory and the Social Shape of the Past.* Chicago: University of Chicago Press.

Zheng, Yangpeng. 2012. "Economic downturn benefits China's service outsourcing." *China Daily.* September 25. www.chinadaily .com.cn/china/2012-09/25/content_15782738.htm

Zimbardo, Philip G. 1971. "The power and pathology of imprisonment." *Congressional Record.* (Serial No. 15, October 25, 1971). Hearings before Subcommittee No. 3, of the Committee on the Judiciary, House of Representatives, 92nd Congress, *First Session on Corrections, Part II, Prisons, Prison Reform and Prisoner's Rights: California.* Washington, DC: U.S. Government Printing Office.

Zirakzadeh, C. 1997. *Social Movements in Politics: A Comparative Study.* London: Longman.

Zuger, Abigail. 2005. "For a retainer, lavish care by 'boutique doctors.'" *New York Times*, October 30. www.nytimes.com/2005/10/30 /health/30patient.html

Zukin, S. 1987. "Gentrification: Culture and capital in the urban core." *American Review of Sociology*, vol. 13: 139–147.

———. 1989. *Loft Living: Culture and Capital in Urban Change.* New Brunswick, NJ: Rutgers University Press.

———. 2004. *Point of Purchase: How Shopping Changed American Culture.* London: Routledge.

Zurcher, Louis. 1977. *The Mutable Self.* Beverly Hills, CA: Sage.

Credits

Text

Box 3.3: "Moore Thoughts and Girl Interrupted" by James Sosnicky, copyright © 2006 by James Sosnicky, "Introduction and Headnotes" by Andrew Carroll, copyright © 2006 by Andrew Carroll, "One Small Village" by Jared Jones, copyright © 2006 by Jared Jones, from *Operation Homecoming*, edited by Andrew Carroll. Used by permission of Random House, Inc.

Figure 7.3: Figure 2M from *The State of Working America, 12th* Edition, by Lawrence Mishel, Josh Bivens, Elise Gould, and Heidi Shierholz. An Economic Policy Institute Book, Ithaca: NY.: Cornell University Press, 2012. Used by permission of the publisher, Cornell University Press.

Table 10.2: From "Cable Leads the Pack as Campaign News Source". Pew Research Center for the People & the Press. February 7, 2012. Reprinted with permission from The Pew Research Center for People & the Press.

Photo

Part Opener 1: p. 4 center Courtesy Pepper Schwartz; **p. 4 left** AP Photos; **p. 4 right** August Jennewein/UMSL

Chapter 1: p. 11 James Leynse/Corbis; **p. 13 bottom** Time & Life Pictures/Getty Images; **p. 13 top** AP/Wide World Photos; **p. 14 center** Olivier Douliery/UPI /Landov; **p. 14 left** Bettmann/Corbis; **p. 14 right** © New Line/courtesy Everett Collection; **p. 16 left** © McPHOTOS; **p. 16 right** AP Photo/Demitrius Balevski; **p. 17** Joe Raedle/Getty Images; **p. 18** Mark Scheuern / Alamy; **p. 20 bottom** Bridgeman Art Library; **p. 20 left** Bettmann/Corbis; **p. 20 right** Hulton-Deutsch Collection/Corbis; **p. 22** Bettmann/Corbis; **p. 24 left** American Sociological Association; **p. 24 right** American Sociological Association; **p. 25** Bettmann/Corbis; **p. 27 bottom** Librado Romero/The New York Times/Redux; **p. 27 top** AP/Wide World Photos; **p. 28** Getty Images; **p. 29** Granger Collection, NY; **p. 30** Trip/Alamy; **p. 31 left** Courtesy of University Archives, University of Missouri at Columbia; **p. 31 right** Library of Congress; **p. 32 left** Library of Congress; **p. 32 right** University of Pennsylvania Archives; **p. 34** ontd.livejournal.com; **p. 35 center** STF/AFP/Getty Images; **p. 35 left** Steve Pyke/Getty Images; **p. 35 right** Steve Pyke/Getty Images; **p. 39** Jeff Greenberg / Alamy

Chapter 2: p. 43 © Ovie Carter; **p. 44** Bandura, Ross and Ross, from "Social Learning of Aggression through Imitation of Film-Mediated Aggressive Models," Journal of Abnormal and Social Psychology 66 (1963), **p. 3–11; 46** © Elliott Landy/Magnum Photos; **p. 47** © Kathryn Edin and Maria Kefalas. University of California Press; 2 edition (March 21, 2007).; **p. 49** AP Photos; **p. 51** Brooke Fasini/Corbis; **p. 53** Antonio Perez/Chicago Tribune/MCT/Newscom; **p. 57** Bettmann/Corbis; **p. 59** © Christin Gilbert; **p. 60** Michael Dunning/Getty Images; **p. 62** AP Photo; **p. 63** Bettmann/Corbis; **p. 65** Corbis; **p. 66** © Universal Images Group (Lake County Discovery Museum) / Alamy; **p. 68** © Christin Gilbert; **p. 68 left** © Elliott Landy/Magnum Photos; **p. 69** © Ovie Carter

Part Opener 2: p. 72 Courtesy Verta Taylor and Leila Rupp; **p. 72 top** Courtesy Verta Taylor and Leila Rupp; **p. 73 bottom** Courtesy Verta Taylor and Leila Rupp

Chapter 3: p. 78 Getty Images; **p. 80 center** AP Photo; **p. 80 left** Robert Nickelsberg/Getty Images; **p. 80 right** AP Photo; **p. 81** Carl & Ann Purcell/Corbis; **p. 82 top left** Alessandro Digaetano/Polaris; **p. 82 top center** Peter A. Smith / Boston Herald / Polaris; **p. 82 top right** Getty Images; **p. 82 bottom left** AP/Wide World Photos; **p. 82 bottom center** AP/Wide World Photos; **p. 82 bottom right** CARL DE SOUZA/AFP/Getty Images; **p. 83 left** Everett Collection; **p. 83 right** Mean Girls, 2004. Paramount Pictures; **p. 84 left** AP Photo/Alex Brandon; **p. 84 right** Eric Grigorian/Polaris; **p. 88** © Androniki Christodoulou; **p. 89 left** Tom Strickland /ABC / American Broadcasting Companies, Inc.; **p. 89 right** AP/Wide World Photos; **p. 90** © Jeff Greenberg; **p. 93** AP Photo/Hiroshi Otabe; **p. 94** John Moore/Getty Images; **p. 96 left** CARL DE SOUZA/AFP/Getty Images; **p. 96 right** © Jeff Greenberg; **p. 97** NBC/Photofest

Chapter 4: p. 103 Carol and Mike Werner/Photo Researchers; **p. 104** © Walt Disney Pictures/Courtesy: Everett Collection; **p. 105** Smithsonian American Art Museum, Washington, DC / Art Resource, NY. © 2009 The Jacob and Gwendolyn Lawrence Foundation, Seattle / Artists Rights Society (ARS), New York.; **p. 107 left** Jupiter Images; **p. 107 right** Getty Images; **p. 109** FRANCIS SPECKER/epa/Corbis; **p. 111** Photofest; **p. 112** LaModa / Alamy; **p. 115 left** Courtesy Sister Pauline Quinn; **p. 115 right** Courtesy Sister Pauline Quinn; **p. 116 left** AP Photos; **p. 116 right** AP Photos; **p. 118** Ohio State Athletics; **p. 119 bottom** AP Images; **p. 119 center** Alan Chin/Corbis Sygma; **p. 119 top** AP Images; **p. 120** Sven Hagolani/fStop/Getty Images; **p. 121** AP/Wide World Photos; **p. 122 left** Photofest; **p. 122 right** AP/Wide World Photos; **p. 123** Apatow Productions / The Kobal Collection / Art Resource

Chapter 5: p. 128 AP Photos; **p. 131 left** Bettmann/Corbis; **p. 131 right** Getty Images; **p. 132** Alamy; **p. 137 bottom** Alamy; **p. 137 top** Jan Greune/LOOK/Getty Images; **p. 140** Courtesy of Alexandra Milgram; **p. 141** PGZimbardo Inc.; **p. 143** PETER MCKENZIE/Maxppp /Landov; **p. 145** © 2006 Scott Adams, Inc. Dist. By UFS, Inc.; **p. 146 bottom** AP Images; **p. 146 top** Andy Rain/epa/Corbis; **p. 148** © 2006 Scott Adams, Inc. Dist. By UFS, Inc.; **p. 149** Jan Greune/LOOK/Getty Images; **p. 144** JAVIER SORIANO/AFP/Getty Images

Chapter 6: p. 154 bottom right AP Photos; **p. 154 bottom left** AP Images; **p. 154 top left** Gavriel Jecan/Corbis; **p. 154 top right** Remi Benali/Corbis; **p. 155** BEYOND THIS PLACE © JARRAD HENDERSON. ALL RIGHTS RESERVED, 2009-2012; **p. 156** AP Photos; **p. 158** WARNER BROS/DC COMICS / THE KOBAL COLLECTION/Art Resource, NY; **p. 159** HBO/Courtesy Everett Collection; **p. 160** VH1/Photofest; **p. 162** Everett Collection; **p. 163** Gilles Mingasson /Liaison/Getty Images; **p. 164** © Marion Ettlinger; **p. 166** AP Photos; **p. 167** Photo by Beau Holland; **p. 168** Electus/Justjenn Productions/Weinstein Company / The Kobal Collection; **p. 171** Rutgers University Press; **p. 174 left** Remi Benali/Corbis; **p. 174 right** AP Photos; **p. 175** Anita Sarkeesian /Wikimedia Commons; **p. 176** WARNER BROS/DC COMICS/THE KOBAL COLLECTION/Art Resource, NY

Part Opener 3: p. 179 left © Ovie Carter; **p. 179 right** © Ovie Carter; **p. 179 top** © Ovie Carter

Chapter 7: p. 183a–f ©1994 Peter Menzel www.menzelphoto.com Material World; **p. 185** PRAKASH MATHEMA/AFP/Getty Images; **p. 189 left** Reprinted through the courtesy of the Editors of TIME Magazine © 2009

Time Inc/PARS International Corp.; **p. 189 right** Tim Graham/Corbis; **p. 190** Wolfgang Kaehler/Corbis; **p. 193** Alejandro Godinez/Clasos.com/LatinContent/Getty Images; **p. 194** BUILT Images / AlamyWY001931; **p. 203** Kevin Mazur/WireImage/Getty Images; **204** Jeff Christensen /Reuters/Landov; **p. 207** Robert Maass/Corbis; **p. 208** Mario Tama/Getty Images; **p. 209** MARIO ANZUONI/Reuters /Landov; **p. 212 left** Wolfgang Kaehler/Corbis; **p. 212 right** BUILT Images / AlamyWY001931; **p. 213** Robert Maass/Corbis

Chapter 8: p. 217 Jon Kopaloff/FilmMagic; **p. 218** Library of Congress; **p. 219 left** AP Photo; **p. 219 right** Nik Wheeler/Corbis; **p. 222** Warner Bros. Pictures/Photofest; **p. 225** David LeveneDavid Levene/eyevine/Redux; **226** Photo by Roger Erickson. Courtesy Faith Childs; **p. 227** AP Photo; **p. 228** Time Life Pictures/Getty Images; **p. 229** Byron Cohen/NBC/NBCU Photo Bank. © NBC Universal, Inc.; **p. 231** Roger Ressmeyer/Corbis; **p. 233** Courtesy France Winddance Twine; **p. 234 left** Ziv Koren/Polaris; **p. 234 right** Getty Images; **p. 235** Wolfgang Kaehler/Corbis; **p. 235** Mylan Canon/The New York Times/Redux; **p. 236** MLB Photos via Getty Images; **p. 238** Wolfgang Kaehler/Corbis; **p. 238** Library of Congress; **p. 239** The Kobal Collection / NBC-TV / Edelson, Dana

Chapter 9: p. 245 left National Anthropological Archives/Smithsonian Institution; **p. 245 right** Karan Kapoor /Corbis; **p. 246** Courtesy Everett Collection; **p. 249** Mel Svenson/Getty Images; **p. 250** Jeff Greenberg/ The Image Works; **p. 251** Jeff Greenberg/Photo Edit; **p. 257** Frances M. Roberts/Newscom; **p. 258** Don Smith/MCT/Newscom; **p. 261** Van Ditthavong/Redux; **p. 262** Bettmann/Corbis; **p. 263** JP Laffont /Sygma/Corbis; **p. 265** AP Photo; **p. 266** © Joy Alexa Sherman and Nicole Tocantins. Ten Speed Press (October 1, 2004); **p. 268** The Washington Post/Getty Images; **p. 270** © NBC/Courtesy: Everett Collection; **p. 272 left** Karan Kapoor /Corbis; **p. 272 right** Mel Svenson/Getty Images; **p. 273** Jim Ketsdever / KRT / Newscom

Part Opener 4: p. 276 left Maury Tannen/Polaris Images; **p. 276 right** Getty Images

Chapter 10: p. 282 center AFP/Getty Images; **p. 282 right** AFP/Getty Images; **p. 284** AP Photo/Carolyn Kaster; **p. 285** Berkeley National Lab; **287** REUTERS/Jim Young/Newscom; **p. 288** © Blu; **p. 290 bottom** Vincent Laforet/epa/Corbis; **p. 290 left** Bettmann/Corbis; **p. 290 right** Sean Adair Reuters/Corbis; **p. 291 left** Discovery Communications/PhotofestN/A; **p. 291 right** AP Photo/Fox News Channel, Shealah Craighead; **p. 292 left** Scott Gries/PictureGroup via AP IMAGES; **p. 292 right** JIM BOURG/Reuters /Landov; **p. 295** Granger Collection, NY; **p. 297 left** AP Photo; **p. 297 right** Getty Images; **p. 300** AP Photo; **p. 301** Najlah Feanny/Corbis; **p. 303** Benjamin Norman for The New York Times; **p. 304** Jim Wilson/The New York Times/Redux; **p. 305 left** Leif Skoogfors/Corbis; **p. 305 right** J.L. Atlan/Corbis Sygma; **p. 306 left** AP Photo; **p. 306 right** Corbis Sygma; **p. 307** AP Photo/Maya Hasson; **p. 310** Jehad Nga/Corbis; **p. 311** AP Photo; **p. 312** Jason Reed / Reuters/ Landov; **p. 314** Jason Reed / Reuters/ Landov; **p. 314** Granger Collection, NY; **p. 315** Ocean/Corbis

Chapter 11: p. 319 Courtesy Kerry Ferris; **320** Schomburg Center in Black Culture, New York Public Library; **p. 321** Granger Collection, NY; **p. 322** Kimberly White/Corbis; **p. 323 left** CBS/Photofest; **p. 323 right** ABC/Photofest; **p. 326** MARK RALSTON/AFP/Getty Images; **p. 327** Jeff Greenberg/Photo Edit; **p. 328** David Bacon/ The Image Works; **p. 329** William Perlman / Star Ledger / Corbis; **p. 331** Bill Aron / Photo Edit; **p. 333** Mario Anzuoni/Reuters/Corbis; **p. 334** Granger Collection. NY; **p. 334** Shailesh Raval/The India Today Group/Getty Images; **p. 335** Dilip Vishwanat/Getty Images; **p. 336 left** Ruth Fremson/The New York Times/Redux; **p. 336 right** AP Photo/Stuart Ramson; **p. 339 bottom** AP Photo/Fareed Khan; **p. 339 center** AP Photo; **p. 339 top** AP Photo; **p. 341** Ge Jin, copyright 2008; **p. 348 left** Bill Aron / Photo Edit; **p. 348 right** Mario Anzuoni/Reuters/Corbis; **p. 349** Thomas Barwick / Getty Images

Chapter 12: p. 355 © P. D. Eastman. Random House Books for Young Readers; 1 edition (June 12, 1960); **p. 358 left** Charles Gullung/zefa/Corbis; **p. 358 right** Pixland/Corbis; **p. 359** Getty Images; **p. 360 left** Etta Clark Photography; **p. 360 right** Etta Clark Photography; **p. 363** Ed Kashi/Corbis; **p. 364 left** © Focus Features/courtesy Everett; **p. 364 right** © National Geographic/courtesy Everett Collection; **p. 367** AP Photo/Elise Amendola; **p. 370 left** Charles Gullung/zefa/Corbis; **p. 370 right** Getty Images; **p. 371** AP Photo/Elise Amendola

Chapter 13: p. 375 Advertising Archives; **p. 377** Alamy; **p. 379 left** Robb D. Cohen/ Retna Ltd.; **p. 379 right** J. Scott Wynn/Retna Ltd.; **p. 382** AP Photo/Phelan M. Ebenhack; **p. 383** AP Photo/Richard Drew; **p. 385** Richard B. Levine / Alamy; **p. 386** Eric Fowke / Photo Edit; **p. 387** AFP/Getty Images; **p. 388 left** Bridgeman Art Library; **p. 388 right** The Last Supper, 1986. Founding Collection, The Andy Warhol Museum, Pittsburgh. (c) Andy Warhol Foundation for the Visual Arts/ARS, New York; **p. 390** Everett Collection; **p. 391** AP Photo/Tom DiPace; **p. 392** Landov; **p. 393** RICHARD B.; LEVINE/Newscom; **p. 395 right** Robert Voets / Showtime / Courtesy Everett Collection; **p. 395 top** Monty Brinton / © CBS / Courtesy Everett Collection; **p. 396** Getty Images; **p. 397** Reuters / Corbis; **p. 399** Nik Wheeler / Corbis; **p. 400 left** Nik Wheeler / Corbis; **400 right** Alamy; **p. 401** Tim Boyle/Getty Images

Part Opener 5: p. 431 left Jon Hicks/Corbis; **p. 431 right** Lindsay Hebberd/Corbis

Chapter 14: p. 405 left Bartek Wrzesniowski / Alamy; **p. 405 right** Darcy Padilla/The New York Times/Redux; **p. 406** Justin Sullivan/Getty Images; **p. 407** Riccardo Venturi/Contrasto/Redux; **p. 408** Republished with permission © 2013 SourceMedia Group, Cedar Rapids, Iowa; **p. 409** Jodi Cobb/National Geographic Society/Corbis; **p. 411** Bettmann/CORBIS; **p. 413** Vanessa Vick/Redux; **p. 414 bottom** Brian Snyder/Reuters; **p. 414 top** TIMOTHY A. CLARY/AFP/Getty Images; **p. 415** Carlos Javier Ortiz/Redux; **p. 417** © USA Networks/Courtesy Everett Collection; **p. 418** Erik S. Lesser/The New York Times/Redux; **p. 419** AGStockUSA / Alamy; **p. 421** © Anne Fadiman. Farrar, Straus and Giroux; 1 edition (September 28, 1998); **p. 422 left** Phil Caruso/©Showtime Networks Inc./Courtesy Everett Collection; **p. 422 right** Fox Broadcasting Co./Photofest; **p. 423** AP Photo/J. Scott Applewhite; **p. 424** Tek Image/Photo Researchers, Inc.; **p. 426 left** Riccardo Venturi/Contrasto/Redux; **p. 426 right** Erik S. Lesser/The New York Times/Redux; **p. 427** HARRY CABLUCK/AP

Chapter 15: p. 436 The Yomiuri Shimbun via AP Images; **p. 444 left** Richard Levine / Alamy; **p. 444 right** Larry Brownstein / Ambient Images; **p. 445** © Columbia / Tristar Pictures / Courtesy Everett Collection; **p. 447** Courtesy of Kerry Ferris; **p. 448** New York Daily News; **p. 449** AP Photo/Springfield News-Leader, Christina Dicken; **p. 451 left** Galen Rowell / Corbis; **p. 451 right** NASA/Getty Images; **p. 453 left** Julio Etchart / Alamy; **p. 453 right** Rickey Rogers / Reuters/ Corbis; **p. 454** AP Photo/Mohammed Seeneen; **p. 456** NASA/Goddard Space Flight Center, The SeaWiFS Project and GeoEye, Scientific Visualization Studio; **p. 459** Library of Congress; **p. 460** GO TAKAYAMA/AFP/Getty Images; **p. 461** AP Photo; **p. 464 left** Julio Etchart / Alamy; **p. 464 right** Mark Peterson/Redux; **p. 465** NASA/Goddard Space Flight Center, The SeaWiFS Project and GeoEye, Scientific Visualization Studio

Chapter 16: p. 470 Ian Waldie/Getty Images; **p. 471** David Butow/Corbis Saba; **p. 472** © AMC/courtesy Everett Collection; **p. 473** AP Photos; **p. 475** AP Photo/Queen Elizabeth Hospital; **p. 476** Image courtesy of adbusters.org; **p. 478 bottom** Mario Villafuerte / Getty Images; **p. 478 top** Spencer Grant / Photo Edit; **p. 479** The Yomiuri Shimbun via AP Images; **p. 483** Andrew Lichtenstein/Corbis; **p. 485** Alamy; **p. 486** CBS/Photofest; **p. 487** David Walter Banks/The New York Times/Redux; **p. 489** AP Photo/Itsuo Inouye; **p. 490 left** The Yomiuri Shimbun via AP Images; **p. 490 right** © AMC/courtesy Everett Collection; **p. 491** Roel Burgler/Redux

Index

Note: Page numbers in **boldface** refer to definitions of key words.

Gorski, Roger, 264
Gossip Girl, 472
Gottdiener, Mark, 430
government, **281**–83
    criminal justice system, 172
    groupthink in, 137
Graham, Billy, 313
Graham, Lawrence Otis, 223
Granovetter, Mark, 129
Gran Torino, 222, 223
grassroots environmentalism, **460**–62
Gray Album (Danger Mouse), 36
Grealy, Lucy, 164
Great Britain, 184, 282, 396–97
Great Depression, 200, 201
Great Lakes Megalopolis (ChiPitts),
    441
great recession, 322
    and "mancession," 256–57
    personal vs. public issues in, 17
Great Society program, 201
Greeley, Andrew, 4–5
greenhouse effect, **454**
greenhouse gases, **454**–55
Green Party, **461**
Greenstone, Michael, 332
Greenwich Village, New York, 178–79
Greenwood family, 235
Grey's Anatomy, 93, 271
Gridiron PAC, 287
grief, cross-cultural responses to, 119
Gross National Happiness (Bhutan),
    484–85
grounded theory, **49**
group cohesion, 136–**37**
group dynamics, 134, **134**
group(s), 124–47, **127**
    and anomie, 129, 131
    bureaucracies, 143, 145–47
    conformity experiments, 138,
        140–41
    dyads, 134
    group cohesion, 136–37
    group dynamics, 134
    honor killings, 139
    in- and out-groups, 135
    intergroup conflict or cooperation,
        based on race/ethnicity,
        233–37
    leadership qualities, 142–43
    primary, 127–28
    reference, 135
    secondary, 127–28
    social influence in, 137–41
    social networks, 128–29
    teamwork, 141–42, 144

triads, 134
    virtual, 131–34
groupthink, **137**
growth rate, **440**
Guatemala, 339
Gubrium, Jay, 356
Guggenheim Museum, 386–87

H
Haizlip, Shirlee Taylor, 226
Hale, Matt, 79, 480
Hall, Stuart, 225
Halle, David, 387
Hamer, Dean, 264
Hamilton, Laura, 267
Hancock, Harvey, 284
hangouts, 394–95, 398
Hardin, Garrett, 438, 473
Harold and Kumar film series, 15
Harrington, Al, 154
Harry's Law, 123
Harvey, David, 384
hate crimes, 233
Hawaii, 201, 221, 284, 355
Hawley, Amos, 458
Hawthorne effect, **64**
Hays, Sharon, 36
hazing, 124, 126
Head Start, 53, 201, 202
health, 402–25
    definitions of, 406
    fad diets, 472
    and gender, 252
    and illness
        definitions of, 406
        epidemiology, 411–14
        medicalization of, 408–10
        medical treatment approaches,
          407
        mental illness, 410
        spread of disease, 405
        types of illnesses, 406–7
    inequalities in, 414–17
        food deserts, 415–17
        intersections of class, race, and
          gender, 414–15
    issues in, 422–25
    and race/ethnicity, 230
    smallpox, 466, 468
    and socioeconomic status, 196
    sociology of, 405
   health care (medicine)
    concierge medicine, 416–17
    cultural competence in, 420–21
    and extended life spans, 436
    issues in, 422–25

    medicalization of illness, 408–10
    as social institution, 417–22
    on television, 421–22
    treatment approaches, 407
    in the United States, 325–26, 423
Heat Wave (Klinenberg), 276–77
Heavy Metal in Baghdad, 76
heavy metal music, 74, 76
Heckman, James, 333
hegemony, **86**
Hell's Kitchen, 8
helping professions, 478
heritage tourism, 220
Herrnstein, Richard, 102
heterogamy, **202**
heterosexism, 269–70
heterosexuality, **264,** 265
hidden curriculum, **111, 296**–97
high culture, **387**
hijras, 244–45
Hill, Grant, 424
Hillbilly Hand Fishing, 8
Hilton, Paris, 191, 193
Hinduism, 156, 185
hip-hop, 36
Hirosue, Ryoko, 184
Hispanic/Latino Americans
    birth rates for, 230, 235
    and criminal justice, 232
    and "culture of poverty" theory, 205
    education level of, 230
    family status of, 229
    health inequalities for, 414–15
    health insurance for, 230
    high school graduation rate for, 295
    internet use by, 204
    in Las Vegas, 430
    life expectancy of, 230
    as minority group, 221
    poverty rate for, 201
    work and income for, 232
Hispanic Mexicans, 205
Hitler, Adolf, 57, 142, 233
Hmong, 420
Hobbes, Thomas, 473
hobbyists, 394
Hochschild, Arlie, 51, 53–54, 118, 258,
    359
Hoffman, Matt, 129
Hohl, August C., Jr., 92
Hollingsworth v. Perry, 268
Holstein, Jim, 356
Holzman, Joan, 416
homelessness, 207–8
Homeless Outreach Population
    Estimate (HOPE), 207, 208

social memory, 83
social mobility, **199**–200, 208–9
social movement(s), **474**–77
  emergent, 479–80
  Marxist ideas in, 27
  stages in, 477, 479
social networking, 384–85
social networking sites
  interaction via, 121
  pros and cons of posting on, 132–33
  relationship data for, 12–13
  ; see also *individual sites*
social networks, **128**–29
social reproduction, **193**
social revolutions, 469
social sciences, **10**
Social Security, 201, 202, 205, 326
social stratification, **184**
  by caste, 185–86
  and poverty, 207–8
  in schools, 296
social theories, 18, 20–22
social ties, **128**
social welfare
  organizations engaging in, 345–46
  programs for, 326
  and welfare reform, 201–3, 205
social work, 32
societal bonds, 22
society, **9**
  education's reproduction of,
    295–97
  secular, 310–13
Society in America (Martineau), 20
sociobiology, **102**–3
Sociobiology (Wilson), 102
socioeconomic status (SES), **186**; *see
    also* social class
sociological imagination, **12**–15, 17
sociological perspective, **10**–15
sociology, **9**–10
  Barry on, 42
  environmental, 457–63
  jobs in, 14–15
  macro-, 16–19
  micro-, 16–19
  personal vs. public issues in, 17
  roots of, 18, 20–22
  value-free, 61
solar dimming, **455**
solidarity, 22–**23**
Solidarność, 307
Sonic Youth, 379
Sosnicky, James R., 92
"sound bytes," 290–91
South Africa, 185–86, 221

South Asian cultures
  honor killings in, 139
  slavery in, 185
Southeast Asia
  fertility rate in, 435
  HIV/AIDS in, 412
Southwest Asia, pollution in, 456–57
"sovereign citizens," 87
So You Think You Can Dance, 8
spanking, 155
Spaulding, Tom, 446
Spears, Britney, 393
special interest groups, **286**–87
speech
  expressions given and expressions
    given off, 107
  sexist patterns of, 260
Spellings, Margaret, 300
Spencer, Herbert, 20, 22, 23
Spielberg, Steven, 393
Spielman, Chris, 117, 118
Spielman, Stefanie, 117, 118
Spin City, 271
*Spirit Catches You and You Fall Down,
    The* (Fadiman), 420, 421
spirituality, unchurched, 310
"spoiled identity," 161
sports
  commercialization of, 376–77
  fan-celebrity relations, 392–93
  gender discrimination in, 273
  role model relationships in, 391
  soccer, 396–98
  violence in, 396–97
  ; see also *individual teams*
spring break, 84, 85
spurious correlation, **45**
Spurlock, Morgan, 382
Stacey, Judith, 368, 369
Stack, Carol, 356
stalking, 393
Stanford Prison Experiment, 140–41
Stanton, Elizabeth Cady, 261–62
Starbucks, 146
Star Trek, 235, 390, 394
Star Wars, 382
status, **116**–17, 129
status inconsistency, **189**
Stein, Jill, 163
Steiner, Ivan, 141–42
Stephanopoulos, George, 89
stepparents, 366
stereotyping, **117**
  based on status, 117
  gender, 250
  in the media, 15, 270–71

  of racial/ethnic groups, 228–29
  sexual, 270–71
Stewart, Jon, 291
stigma, **161**
  and deviance, 161–64
  for female athletes, 242
Stiles, Julia, 229
Stone, Oliver, 450
Stonewall riots (New York City), 269
Straight Edge, 479
Strapped (Draut), 211
stratification, 355
  in capitalism, 324
  by sexual orientation, 268
  by slavery, 184–85
  by social class, 186
  and social mobility, 199–200
  of workforce, 320–21
Streetwise (Anderson), 161
strikes, 333–35
structural functionalism, **22**–24
  conflict theory vs., 27–28
  culture in, 95
  deviance in, 156–57, 161, 165
  in education study, 298
  family in, 354, 356
  gender inequality in, 247
  groups in, 147
  medicine and health in, 410
  natural environment in, 443
  race and ethnicity in, 224
  recreation and leisure in, 398
  religion in, 305
  on shared values, 84
  social change in, 474
  social class in, 192–93
  social inequality in, 195
  social institutions in, 283
  society in, 37
  structural strain theory, 157,
    161
  work and the economy in, 347
structural mobility, **200**
structural strain theory, 157, 161
structure(s), **23, 24**
student loan debt, 211
Study of Sociology, The (Spencer),
    22
subculture(s), **86**
  as deviant groups, 163
  heavy metal, 74, 76
  of Key West, 72
sub-Saharan Africa
  fertility rate in, 435
  HIV/AIDS in, 412
suburbanization, **442**

transnational corporations (TNCs), 337, 338
transportation, spending on, 205
transsexuals, **248**
travel and tourism, 398–99
treadmill of production, **458**
triad, **134**
tribal stigma, 162
Truth, Sojourner, 475
Truth & Beauty (Patchett), 164
Tunisia, 94
Turkey, 139, 233
Turkle, Sherry, 121, 130
Turner, Ralph, 117, 136, 141, 163
Tuskegee Syphilis Study, 65, 413
Twenty Statements Test (TST), 135–36
Twine, France Winddance, 233, 343
Twitter, 59, 94, 132, 384, 482, 483
two-step flow model, **390**

U

Ugly Betty, 271
Ulrichs, Karl Heinrich, 264
Unbearable Weight (Bordo), 17
unchurched, **310**
unchurched spirituality, 310
unconscious, 104
underclass, 187, **188**
Undercover Boss, 8
unemployment, during great recession, 256, 322
unemployment insurance, 201, 205
Uniform Crime Report (UCR), **169**–70
union(s), 332–35, **333**
United Kingdom, 462
United Nations, 260, 261
United States
    American culture, 85, 93, 95
    and the American Dream, 188, 208–11
    body modification practices in, 155
    body type values in, 405
    capitalism in, 325–26
    causes of death in, 406–7
    changing social attitudes in, 491
    contemporary slavery in, 185
    corporal punishment in, 155
    corporate America, 335–36
    corporate culture in, 89
    countercultures in, 87
    criminal justice system in, 172
    cultural variations in, 85
    demographics of crime in, 170–71
    dental procedures in, 405
    diffusion of media content from, 91, 93

    drinking water in, 454
    ecological footprint in, 462
    educational crisis in, 298
    education in, 295
    ethnicity in, *see* ethnicity
    gasoline use in, 457
    health-care reform in, 230
    HIV/AIDS in, 412
    and human trafficking, 260, 261
    immigrant assimilation in, 236
    internet use in, 204
    life expectancy in, 360, 435, 437
    Martineau on civil rights in, 20
    material possessions of families in, 180, 182–83
    measuring crime in, 169–70
    as a meritocracy, 208
    migration in, 437
    mob violence in, 397
    mortality rates in, 435
    multiculturalism in, 237
    multiracialism in, 216
    norms in, 84, 85
    other societies' influence on culture in, 91
    political system of, 283–85; *see also* politics
    population trends in, 437, 438, 440–42
    poverty in, 206–8
    poverty line in, 200–201
    pre-colonial, 319–20
    prestige of occupations in, 192–93
    public schools in, 111, 302–3
    race in, *see* race
    racial future of, 235
    religion in, 307–13
    representation in, 283
    rulers of, 285–87
    segregation in, 234, 236
    soccer in, 396
    social class in, 187–88
    social mobility in, 199
    social stratification in, 184
    subcultures in, 86
    supersectors of economy in, 322
    sweatshops in, 338–39
    travel and tourism in, 398
    unions in, 333–35
    values in, 84
    waste production in, 455
    in WTO disputes, 129
United States Medical Licensing Exam (USMLE), 418
United States v. Windsor, 268, 367

Universal CityWalk (Los Angeles), 443–44
Universal Declaration of Human Rights, 185, 380
University of California, 231, 339
University of Chicago, 29
University of Michigan, 231, 339
University of North Carolina, 339
University of Wisconsin, Madison, 339
Unmarried America, 366
unmarried people, rights of, 366
Un-T and the 10 MPH Car, The (McGrane), 11
upper class, **187**–88, 197–98
upper-middle class, 187, **188,** 197
UPS, 146
Upward Bound, 202
urban, **440**
urban density, **441**
urbanites, **447**
urbanization, 440–44, **441**
urban renewal, **443**
urban sprawl, **442**
Urban Villagers, The (Gans), 447
U.S. Census Bureau, 56, 61, 435
usernames, 98–99
uses and gratifications paradigm, **389**
utopia, **445**

V

validity, **55**
Valter, Ehud, 234
value-free sociology, **61**
values, 83–**84**
    in action research, 53
    Christian, 310
    in college life, 86
    group, 394
    maintaining, 354
    moral, 93
    political, 93, 95
    in research, 61, 63
    shared, 23
Van Halen, 387
Van Maanen, John, 67
variable, **44**
vector organisms, **413**
Ventura, Jesse, 291
verbal communication, 50, 107–10
verstehen, **29**
vertical social mobility, **200**
veterans, spending on, 205
Viacom Inc., 281
video games, 88, 250, 340–41, 386
Vietnam War, 172–73, 287–88